AMERICAN COMBAT PLANES

Fighter styles of four wars: the Spad biplane of World War I, the P-51 monoplane of World War II, the F-86 jet of the Korean War, and the supersonic F-100 used in Vietnam.   AF

RAY WAGNER

AMERICAN COMBAT PLANES

Third, Enlarged Edition

DOUBLEDAY & COMPANY, Inc

GARDEN CITY, NEW YORK

Library of Congress Cataloging in Publication Data

Wagner, Ray.
  American combat planes.

  Bibliography: p.
  Includes index.
  1. Airplanes, Military—History.   2. Aeronautics, Military—
United States—History.   I. Title.
UG1243.W33   1981   623.74′6′0973

ISBN: 0-385-13120-8

Library of Congress Catalog Card Number 77-16952

Printed in the United States of America

Third Edition   9 8 7 6 5 4 3 2

Preface

Purpose

Combat planes by the thousands have been built in the United States since 1917. Fighters, bombers, and attack types are the striking weapons of air power and have made world history. Yet, despite their importance, a complete and accurate history of these planes and their characteristics was not available.

The purpose of *American Combat Planes* is to offer this history, both as a reference and as an interesting story of aviation and war. All combat types built in the United States for the Air Force, Navy Air, or for foreign governments are included, together with foreign aircraft bought for American fighting outfits.

Plan

This book describes the planes designed to attack an enemy with guns, bombs, or rockets. It excludes the trainers, transports, and unarmed liaison or reconnaissance aircraft, which also contribute to air power but can be better decribed in separate studies. Armed reconnaissance aircraft and those derived from fighter designs have been added to this edition.

Attention is given both little-known experimentals and famous mass-production jobs with their major modifications. The description, armament, and history of each type are related to other designs and to their intended military missions.

Photographs enable identification of each type, and are accompanied by dimensions, weight, and performance. Most of these characteristics are drawn from flight tests and specifications given in official documents once classified but recently made available.

Why each combat plane was built—the most important question about each type—is best answered by placing each design in the historical period in which it was developed. Part One describes how observation, ground attack, and bombing missions emerged from World War I, along with parallel naval missions. The first chapter orients readers on historical and technical factors influencing aircraft design and gives a brief summary of information needed to follow warplane history, such as aircraft and engine designations.

Separate chapters describe the aircraft designed for each mission in the order of their appearance. This provides a more understandable review of progress than a mere alphabetical listing, or listing aircraft only by official designation, often a poor guide to chronology or even design antecedents.

Part Two shows how the technical revolution in design style, from biplane to monoplane, prepared the way for the aircraft fleets that were built for World War II. Again, an introductory chapter orients the reader, followed by separate chapters for each mission, and this form of organization is continued in Part Three, which covers the jet age from 1945 to contemporary aircraft.

Acknowledgments

The origins of this material are discussed in full in the Notes on Sources. When the author made his first research trip to the National Archives and the Smithsonian Institution in December 1956, he had the good fortune to be introduced to Navy Air historian Lee Pearson and Major James F. Sunderman of the Air Force Book Program, who encouraged this project in its early stage. Peter M. Bowers was the first of many members of the Aviation Historical Society to provide hundreds of photographs not otherwise available.

Doubleday published the first edition of this book in 1960, which has subsequently found wide acceptance as a basic reference work on combat plane development. Since then Senior Editor Harold Kuebler has encouraged the author to enlarge and improve earlier editions with the information available from new research and recently declassified documents. We have tried, in the concluding Notes on Sources, to mention many of those who helped in the research. All deserve the thanks of aviation history enthusiasts.

Photo credits are abbreviated in the right-hand corner of each picture, and a list of the sources follows.

AF: United States Air Force photograph

AMC: Prints made by Peter Bowers from the old Air Matériel Command files at Wright Field. (Original negatives later destroyed.)

ARC: National Archives, Washington, D.C.

ARNOLD: Henry W. Arnold, San Diego, Calif.

BESECKER: Roger F. Besecker, Allentown, Penn.

GANN: Harry Gann, Buena Park, Calif.

IWM: Imperial War Museum, London

LAWSON: Robert L. Lawson, Bonita, Calif.

LEVY: Howard Levy, Brooklyn, N.Y.

MA: Musée de l'Air, Paris

MFR: Manufacturer of aircraft supplied print

NACA: National Advisory Committee on Aeronautics (now NASA)

PMB: Peter M. Bowers, Seattle, Wash.

SDAM: San Diego Aerospace Museum

SI: Smithsonian Institution (National Air and Space Museum), Washington, D.C.

SHIPP: Warren D. Shipp, San Diego, Calif.

TITC: Title Insurance and Trust Co., Historical Collection print, San Diego, Calif.

USN: United States Navy official photograph

WILLIAMS: Gordon Sear Williams, Seattle, Wash.

WL: William T. Larkins, Concord, Calif.

Contents

List of Tables

PART ONE:

The Biplane Period, 1917–32

Chapter 1
The Role of the Combat Plane: A Historical Sketch

Since powered flight began in America, many different types of airplanes have been built. From the viewpoint of the long-range impact on world history, those designed for combat have been most important.

Each aircraft design has its own story. The original prototype is rolled, fresh and untried, out of the factory. Shining and new, it awaits the test flights that will show whether its performance equals the hopes of its designers.

Sometimes the roll-out is accompanied by a publicity flourish, like the 3,000 guests invited to the B-1A's debut. Sometimes the introduction is veiled behind military secrecy or is simply ignored by all but the aircraft's builders.

Many designs never live up to their designers' hopes, and drop from sight, unmentioned even by their builders. Luckier types go into production, and a long list of modifications gradually changes their original appearance. A few aircraft have made such an impact on history that names like Mustang and Thunderbolt and numbers like B-17 and B-29 have become a conspicuous part of life in the 20th century.

Each combat aircraft represents a response to a challenge, an invention mothered by some warlike necessity, an actor hoping to fill a role written by forces far removed from the engineer's drawing board.

The value of a design depends on its mission and how well the aircraft fulfills it. Defective concepts of mission may cripple an aircraft more than defects in engineering. The mission of a combat plane is decided by its place in the nation's preparations for war and the shape of the aircraft built at the time.

Three distinct periods can be distinguished in the history of American combat planes, based on both the shape of the aircraft and the world situation at the time. Beginning with America's entrance into World War I in 1917, the aircraft used were biplanes with open cockpits, constructed, for the most part, of a fabric-covered frame. Their missions were intended to fit into the kind of fighting that occurred during the battles on the Marne and at Jutland.

The second period began around 1931 when the all-metal monoplane appeared with such refinements as enclosed cockpits, retractable wheels, and more powerful engines with variable-pitch propellers. Such progress fulfilled the more ambitious strategic role aircraft were to play in World War II, which came to its climax in 1945.

A third period of American combat aircraft history began after 1946, when the piston engine was replaced by the gas turbine, and aircraft performance, together with aircraft costs, reached heights undreamed of 60 years earlier. The confrontation of two superpowers armed with nuclear weapons dominated aviation just as it dominated politics.

When the first military airplane was purchased by the American Government in the first decade of the century, no such future could be envisioned. The specification issued by the Army called for no weapons, just a two-place aircraft with a speed of 40 mph, a range of 125 miles, "and the ability to steer in all directions without difficulty." A contract was signed February 10, 1908, with the Wright brothers, who built and began testing the 30-hp aircraft that September. The first fatal airplane crash in aviation history delayed acceptance of the aircraft until August 2, 1909.

The $25,000 "flying machine" had no bloodthirsty intentions. Its use was only to train the first Army aviators to fly its kitelike successors. Only gradually were there tests of missions of communications, scouting, and spotting for coast artillery.

The Army gradually experimented with weapons aboard aircraft, firing a rifle from an aircraft on August 20, 1910, and dropping live bombs in January 1911. A prototype of the new Lewis machine gun was fired at a ground target from a Wright biplane on June 7, 1912, but the Army was not yet ready to purchase the Lewis gun. The inventor took his weapon to Europe, where it won rapid acceptance.

The First War in the Air

When World War I began in 1914, Europe's airplanes were as bare of weapons as America's, but existed in much larger numbers. The initial mission of these aircraft was reconnaissance, and however violent the ground fighting, the soldiers of the skies found their flights across the lines relatively peaceful. For such purposes unarmed, single-engine, two-place aircraft were adequate.

But the temptation to make use of the advantages of flight for purposes of attack was too strong. On August 14, 1914, a pair of French biplanes dropped artillery shells on hangars at Metz, and on November 21 three British Avros bombed Zeppelin sheds at Friedrichshafen. A German plane dropped the first bomb on English soil on December 19, 1914. Zeppelins began raids in January 1915, and warfare had truly entered a new dimension

Later chapters of this book will describe how the "military aeroplane" became *the* combat plane by developing a series of specialties. Single-engine, two-seat observation biplanes were fitted with bomb racks under the wings and became light bombers. Smaller single-seaters with a machine gun became *avions de chasse,* or pursuit ships, for attacking enemy aircraft, while larger multiengine machines were built for long-range bombing. Naval aviation developed its own specialties: Flying boats to patrol the sea and torpedo-carrying seaplanes to

The only American-built plane used in combat by the Army in World War I was a version of the De Havilland DH-4 powered by a Liberty engine.   AF

attack enemy shipping were joined by fighters carried by the fleet on vessels with flight decks.

The airplane as a scout had developed into the airplane as a bomber and as a destroyer of other aircraft, but this development was European, not American, and happened without any comparable activity on this side of the Atlantic.

The AEF's Air Arm

Although the United States had produced the world's first successful powered plane and had purchased the first plane for military purposes, it had not participated in the wartime development of the air weapon. Not even a prototype of up-to-date design was available when we entered the war.

Aircraft had been used by the U.S. Army in Mexico in 1916 when the 1st Aero Squadron's eight Curtiss JN-3 two-seaters had searched for Pancho Villa. While much more serviceable aircraft than the Wright B, and later developed into the famous JN-4 primary trainer, these biplanes had no combat capability.

America's weakness in military aviation was due not only to its reluctance to arm, but to the military posture of the day. The missions of the armed forces were specifically the defense of the continental United States, its overseas possessions, and its maritime commerce. For these purposes a strong Navy was needed, but mass armies of the European type were unnecessary since only Mexico's army presented any threat on land. The pride of American military technology were the giant cannons, the 14-inch rifles installed in coastal fortifications and battleship turrets that could fire a 1,560-pound projectile over 13 miles. Compared to such destructive power, little airplanes seemed properly limited to the Aviation Section of the Signal Corps.

When the United States declared war against Germany on April 6, 1917, there were no specific plans to use airpower on a massive basis, but it was realized how far the United States was behind Europe in developing the air weapon. There were no guns or bomb racks on any of the some 130 Army aircraft in commission at that time. Most of these were the famous Curtiss "Jenny" trainers. The 1st Aero Squadron at Columbus, New Mexico, and the 3rd, at San Antonio, Texas, faced the Mexican border with 11 Curtiss R-2 and six Curtiss R-4s between them. These were heavier two-seaters than the "Jenny," using 160 hp (R-2) and 200 hp (R-4) engines, but there is no evidence that guns or bombs were ever carried except perhaps for a test. The only other Aero Squadron was the 2nd, at Manila, with only three Martin floatplanes to spot for coast artillery.

When the French Prime Minister requested, on May 24, 1917, an American force of 4,500 planes in

Most of the Army's fliers in 1918 flew French-built fighters like the Nieuport 28, first AEF type to score air victories. AF

1918, a massive aviation program was launched, and in June 1917 the Bolling Mission sailed for France to gain information on aircraft types. Samples of several Allied warplanes were selected and shipped to the United States for production here. To fill the gap until American-built aircraft became available, the French contracted, on August 30, 1917, to supply 5,875 aircraft to the American Expeditionary Force (AEF).

United States production of training planes aided the dispatch of fliers to France, but of the combat types selected, only the DH-4 was produced in quantity. As the following chapters will tell, the American squadrons at the front depended principally on French equipment. The 36 squadrons at the front on November 1, 1918, included 15 with the Spad and one with the SE-5A single-seater, and 10 with the Salmson, eight with the U.S.-built DH-4, and two with the Breguet two-seaters. None had twin-engine equipment.

During the war the Army received a total of 16,-831 planes; 6,287 were delivered to the AEF before the Armistice, including 2,696 trainers and 3,591 service types. The origin of these AEF planes is shown in Table 1. On Armistice Day the AEF had 740 planes at the front. Table 2 shows how this number compared with the forces of other countries.

Two LePere two-seat fighters were the only combat planes designed in the U.S. to reach France. SDAM

Table 1

SOURCES OF AEF AIRCRAFT

From France	4,791	(incl. 2,186 service types)
From Britain	261	(incl. 189 service types)
From Italy	19	trainers
From U.S.		
DH-4	1,213	service types
LePere	2	experimental
DH-9	1	experimental
	6,287	(incl. 3,591 service types)

Table 2

COMPARISON OF AIRPLANE STRENGTHS OF ALLIED AND ENEMY AIR SERVICES, NOVEMBER 11, 1918

	Pursuit	Observation	Bombardment Day	Night	Total Airplanes
British	759	503	306	190	1,758
French	1,344	1,505	225	247	3,321
American	330	293	117	0	740
Italian	336	360	36	80	812
Belgian	45	100	0	8	153
German	1,020	1,442	0	268	2,730
Austrian	220	391	0	11	622
Combined Allies	2,814	2,761	684	525	6,784
Combined Enemy	1,240	1,833	0	279	3,352

Beginnings of Navy Air

The Navy's air arm at the opening of the war included 45 training seaplanes, six flying boats, and three landplanes, none of them armed or designed for combat. Experience had been obtained in operating aircraft at sea, and Britain supplied information on her use of planes over the North Sea.

U-boats were the war's chief naval threat, so when a British flying boat sank one for the first time on May 20, 1917, the immediate role for naval aircraft was written. Orders were placed for hundreds of flying boats for shore-based antisub patrol.

Because of the difficulty encountered getting enough planes, the government built its own Naval Aircraft Factory in Philadelphia. States a Navy text:

> The Army's requirements for an enormous quantity of planes created a decided lack of interest among aircraft manufacturers in the Navy's requirements for a comparatively small quantity of machines. The Navy Department therefore concluded that it was necessary to build and put into production an aircraft factory to be owned by the Navy, in order, first, to assure a part, at least, of its aircraft supply; second, to obtain cost data for the Department's guidance in its dealings with private manufacturers; and third, to have under its own control a factory capable of producing experimental work.

While the flying boats proved of great value in spotting submarines, it was seen that a more direct attack could be made by bombing the sub bases. For this purpose the Northern Bombing Group was organized, with DH-4, DH-9, and Caproni landplanes obtained from the Army and the Allies.

Unlike the AEF, the Navy obtained most of its planes at home. Only 142 of the Navy's 2,705 machines were procured abroad. U.S.-built were 1,444 service types, 1,084 training planes, and 36 experimentals, as well as 155 DH-4s and 144 trainers transferred from the Army.

American Air Power Between the Wars

The Armistice left the United States with a stockpile of aircraft, some limited experience in air warfare, and the rudiments of a theory of air power.

The major item in the Army's stock of airplanes was the thousands of DH-4s designed for day bombing and observation, together with several hundred pursuits of foreign origin, and a few night bombers. Just what should be done to replace this rapidly aging armada? Viewpoints on this issue depended, in part, on positions on the role of air power.

The existing organization of the Army Air Service reflected the conservative view that aviation existed primarily to assist the ground army, and that bombing and pursuit aircraft in themselves were unlikely to affect the course of war. (An example of this thinking is the lengthy World War I history that mentions only scouting as a wartime aviation activity.) The view once expressed that "the duty of the aviator is to see, not to fight" seemed to be reflected in the dispersal of air force strength into observation squadrons attached to various ground units.

Subordination of the Air Service to the Army had a bad effect on both morale and equipment. Of 517 Air Service crash deaths from January 1919 to June 1925, all but 12 were in aging aircraft built before

All U.S. Navy aircraft in World War I flew from shore bases, like this H-16 flying boat.   ARC

The most widely used Army planes of the 1920s were observation biplanes, like this Douglas O-2H.   AF

Marine pilots in Nicaragua still had DH-4Bs in 1927.   LAWSON

the end of the war. The lack of improved and safer replacements was criticized, and a long debate on the control of air power ensued. Since this argument centered around the use of the bomber, it will be discussed in the chapters devoted to that weapon.

The organizational impasse of the period was reflected in the relatively slow technical advance. Most of the aviation headlines were made by the skill of individual aviators rather than by a startling advance in performance. Compare the service aircraft of 1930, a dozen years after the Armistice, with those of the war period. Still we see the same open cockpit, fabric-covered biplanes dragging struts, and exposed undercarriages. Advances in top speed were modest. Fighters had gone from the 135 mph of the Spad to 166 mph for the P-12B; bombers from 94 mph for the Handley-Page to 114 mph for the B-3A; two-seaters from 124 mph for the DH-4 to 139 mph for the A-3B.

The Army Air Service, as it was constituted from 1920 to 1926, was viewed almost entirely as an organization to support the ground arms: infantry and cavalry, coast and field artillery. In case of war, plans called for the mobilization of six field armies, each of nine divisions in three corps. Each army would have an attack group, two pursuit groups, and an observation group, as well as observation squadrons for each division and corps, or a total force of four attack, eight pursuit and 16 observation squadrons per army. A General Headquarters element would have the only bomber group, along with attack, observation, and pursuit groups.

The actual peacetime Army Air Service was planned as the cadre for a rapid wartime expansion and in 1922 consisted of 14 observation, four attack, seven bombing and seven pursuit squadrons. They were deployed in the United States as the 1st Pursuit, 2nd Bombardment, 3rd Attack, and 9th Observation groups, as well as an observation squadron for each of the nine Army corps. Overseas possessions were protected by three composite groups with mixed squadrons; the 4th Composite Group in the Philippines, the 5th in Hawaii, and the 6th in the Panama Canal Zone.

In 1926 the Air Service became the Air Corps,

and began a five-year expansion of pursuit and bomber squadrons. By 1932 there were 15 groups of combat planes, including ten in the United States and five overseas, and the Air Corps kept this organizational framework until 1940.

Naval aviation in the 1920s made progress by beginning the organization of a carrier-based striking force. In 1918 most operational Navy service planes were shore-based flying boats plus some Marine DH-4s. A small postwar force, including fighting, observation, and torpedo planes, was established to operate on wheels or floats from shore bases. The next step was obviously to perfect means by which these aircraft could accompany the fleet to sea; the Bureau of Aeronautics (BuAer), established in 1921, devoted itself to this problem.

Early shipboard operations involved seaplanes catapulted from battleships and cruisers and lifted back by cranes after landing on the sea. There were disadvantages to this method: Only a few seaplanes could be carried without impairing the ship's fighting ability; it was difficult to recover the launched aircraft; and, most important, the seaplanes were inferior to landplanes in performance.

As early as July 1917 the British Royal Navy had commissioned HMS *Furious*, which answered the problem by adding to the fleet a specialized aircraft carrier that could launch and recover landplanes from a large flight deck. Congress authorized, in July 1919, conversion of the collier *Jupiter* to the first American aircraft carrier, the USS *Langley* (CV-1). The first takeoff from the *Langley* was made on October 17, 1922, by a Vought VE-7SF. Conventional landplanes were thus able to begin operations with the fleet, modified by strengthened landing gear and arresting hooks.

The *Langley* arrived in the Pacific in November 1924, and became the Flagship, Aircraft Squadrons, Battle Fleet. For a dozen years it operated out of San Diego, taking two squadrons at a time to sea to perfect carrier operations. However, the CV-1 lacked the speed and defenses to be fit for combat and would be converted to an aircraft tender in 1937.

Two battle cruisers, the *Lexington* and the *Saratoga*, canceled by the Washington Naval Treaty in 1922, were ordered completed as aircraft carriers. In March 1925 the Navy called upon designers for models to fit the fine new ships, and the industry responded with the Curtiss F6C fighter, the Vought O2U scout, and the Martin T3M torpedo plane.

In 1928 the two carriers began operations, each with two squadrons of fighters, one of scouts and one of torpedo bombers. The largest Navy ships yet, they soon proved themselves powerful weapons in Pacific Fleet maneuvers. On January 26, 1929, the *Saratoga* achieved the theoretical de-

The first American aircraft carrier, the *Langley*, taking aboard a Martin MO-1.   USN

The *Saratoga* (CV-3) which made surprise attacks on Hawaii during maneuvers, and her sister ship the *Lexington*, were the Navy's first really combat-ready carriers.   USN

struction of the Panama Canal with 83 aircraft launched in a surprise attack.

A surprise attack on Pearl Harbor one Sunday morning (February 7, 1932) was made by the two big carriers during maneuvers. Rear Admiral Harry Yarnell used the cover of night to bring his task force northeast of Oahu, launching 152 biplanes just before dawn. Boeing fighters, Martin dive bombers and torpedo planes caught the defenders unprepared and had to be credited, in the theoretical sense of war games, with knocking out the defender's ships and aircraft. The concept of a carrier strike had been demonstrated; instead of simply following the battleships, the carriers now operated as separate task forces.

Much of the Navy's success in developing the carrier-based strike force during the biplane period was due to the leadership of air-minded admirals such as the tall, white-bearded Joseph Reeves, Commander of Aircraft Squadrons, Battle Fleet; William Moffett, the first Chief of the Bureau of

Aeronautics; and William Sims, Naval War College President, who foresaw the carrier becoming the capital ship of the future.

Building The Warplane: The Designer's Task

Military leaders demand of plane builders not only a machine to do a certain job but a machine which can do that job better than foreign types. Since the physical laws of aerodynamics are true all over the world, and engineering textbooks everywhere have much the same formulas, the engineer can only hope that his model appears a little earlier than those of his competitors.

The first airplane designers had no computers and little relevant experience to guide them through their difficulties, and trial and error was the chief learning method. This section will provide the reader with a very simplified introduction to the characteristics of the early combat plane.

Essentially, the combat plane is an airborne weapons carrier whose value lies in its ability to get from point to point in the skies. The four physical forces which act on aircraft in flight are, on the negative side, *drag* and *gravity*, and, on the positive side, *thrust* and *lift*.

This age of streamlining has made us conscious of the problem of reducing drag, or air resistance. Counteracting drag is thrust, the energy converted into forward motion by the engine. The effect of air movement around the wings creates lift to counteract gravity. The designer's task is to balance these forces to produce the best possible performance.

Armament and Equipment

Armament is that part of a combat plane's weight that is the reason for its existence. The weapons carried must be sufficient for their task but yet not unduly hamper performance. In this respect, a lesson was taught by the first British effort to attack an enemy plane.

On August 22, 1914, a Farman pusher with a Lewis gun attached to the bow took off in pursuit of an Albatros patrolling at 5,000-foot altitude. The added weight of the gun had a deplorable effect on the Farman's climb, however, and the Allied plane found itself unable to pass the 3,500-foot level, while the Albatros returned home undisturbed.

Such incidents suggest why armament is always limited by the power of the aircraft. With improvements in design, the weight carried has steadily increased. During World War I, the bombs dropped were seldom as large as the shells from the heaviest artillery, but by the end of World War II, the bombs had grown as heavy as the 44,000-pound T-10.

To fight other aircraft, the rifle-caliber machine

Carrier operations required special gear, like the arresting hook on this Vought O2U-2.　　　USN

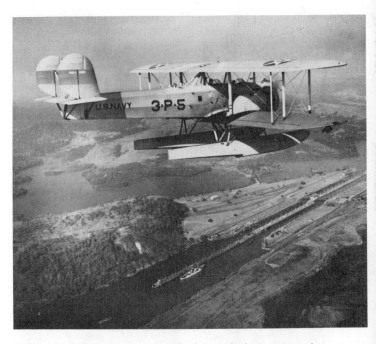

Defense of the Panama Canal, shown below a Douglas P2D-1 from Coco Solo, was a primary U.S. objective between the world wars.　　　ARC

Lewis guns on DH-4's Scarff ring had drum magazines.　　　AF

gun came into general use in 1915. The Lewis was the first Allied machine gun favored for aircraft work. Light in weight, it was used throughout the 1914–18 war, but its drum feeding required frequent reloading. The belt feeding of the heavier water-cooled Vickers gun was more suitable for a pilot-fired synchronized weapon.

Both of these weapons had been invented by Americans but were first put into mass production by Britain using caliber .303 ammunition, and aircraft delivered by the Allies to American forces standardized on the Vickers for fixed mountings and the Lewis gun for flexible mountings. By 1917 both were being produced in the United States for the Allies, so the American services were able to get all the Lewis guns needed, modified with 97-round drums of U.S. .30-caliber ammunition.

Output of the Vickers gun was already committed

to the ground forces, so the Marlin M1917, an air-cooled, gas-operated weapon, was provided as the fixed weapon on U.S. aircraft built during 1918. John Browning also developed an air-cooled, recoil-operated aircraft machine gun that was too late for combat use in the war, but its high rate of fire and reliability made it the standard weapon between the wars, first as a fixed gun and then as a movable gun.

The need for larger-caliber guns, especially against ground targets, resulted in the Browning .50-caliber guns developed at the war's end and successfully adopted by the U.S. Army for specialized tasks. A 37-mm aircraft gun firing explosive shells was developed by France in 1917, but its hand loading was slow and inconvenient. The Baldwin 37-mm gun tested in the United States in 1919 was little better.

Performance Goals

Once an aircraft has been provided with a crew, weapons, and equipment appropriate for its mission, the warplane's value is determined by its mobility, or performance. Speed, climb, ceiling, and range are the measurements of performance—how fast, high, and far the plane's weapons can be taken.

For the early designers the chief enemy of performance was weight, against which thrust and lift must be arrayed. The measurement of the burden of gravity against thrust is *power loading*—the gross weight divided by the power or thrust available. The measurement of the burden upon lift is *wing loading*—the gross weight divided by the area of the wing. These expressions must be kept in mind in describing the achievement of high performance.

Top speed is the measurement of the airplane's ability to catch or escape the enemy. Primarily, it is determined by an aircraft's power loading and its

Twin Vickers guns on Spad 13 were synchronized with
    propeller.   AMC

Browning .30-caliber M-2 flexible gun on YB-4 of 9th
    Bombardment Squadron.   AF

Table 3

AMERICAN AIRCRAFT GUNS

Type	Length (inches)	Weight of Gun (pounds)	Weight of Bullet (ounces)	Muzzle Velocity (ft/sec)	Rate of Fire (rds/min)	Range (yards)
.30-cal M-2	40	21	.34	2,600	1,350	1,800
.50-cal M-2	57	64	1.71	2,810	800	7,200
.50-cal M-3	57.25	63	3.92	2,840	1,200	7,400
20-mm M-2	94	102	4.82	2,850	650	5,500
20-mm M-3	78	112	4.82	2,750	800	—
20-mm M-39	72.3	179	8.96	3,330	1,500	4,270
20-mm M-61	72	260	8.96	3,300	6,000	4,270
37-mm M-4	89	213	21.44	2,000	150	4,000
37-mm M-9	104	365	21.44	2,900	125	8,875
75-mm M-4	141	1,297	—	2,090	—	12,000

Barling's six-engine triplane was an example of poor performance due to an excess of drag and weight.   AF

drag.[1] The lower the power loading, the faster the aircraft; thus, the lighter the weight and the greater the power, the higher the speed. The drag of any airframe is steadily reduced as the aircraft gains in altitude; this is due to the thinning density of the air. Therefore, the higher the altitude of a given power loading, the faster the plane. Unfortunately, the thinner density of the air also means poorer engine performance, a condition which may be corrected by supercharging the engine so that sea-level pressures are maintained up to a high altitude. Without supercharging an engine giving 1,000 hp at sea level may give only 700 hp at 10,000 feet, 470 hp at 20,000 feet, and 295 hp at 30,000 feet.

An airplane makes its highest speed at the altitude at which the advantage of the lower drag is greater than the disadvantage of the loss of power due to the thinning air. This is known as the critical altitude. In unsupercharged airplanes the critical altitude is at sea level, for the loss of power as the plane goes higher is not compensated by the reduction in drag. In the Curtiss P-6E, the last of our unsupercharged Army pursuits, top speed dropped from 198 mph at sea level to 196 at 5,000 feet, 189 at 10,000 feet, and 182 at 15,000 feet. On the other hand, the Boeing 281 had a single-stage supercharger which maintained power into higher altitudes. Top speed therefore went from 215 mph at sea level to 235 at 6,000 feet (its critical altitude) and to 232 at 11,000 feet.

This effect was gained by a built-in, or integral, supercharger run by the crankshaft of the engine. Later types used turbosuperchargers, run by the exhaust gases of the engine, which are heavier and can maintain power up to 35,000 feet. The disadvantage of superchargers is their increased weight, which handicaps the supercharged aircraft's performance at sea level.

As far as fighter aircraft are concerned, rate of climb and ceiling come second only to top speed as performance criteria. *Rate of climb* is simply the time taken to reach a given altitude, or the feet gained in one minute's climb. *Service ceiling* is the altitude at which rate of climb is 100 feet per minute, while *absolute ceiling* is the highest altitude an aircraft may achieve. Service ceiling is the criteria for tactical purposes.

The climbing ability of an aircraft is determined by both power loading and wing loading. The lower each is, the better the climb. Unfortunately, a low power loading and high speed are not always compatible with a low-wing loading and good climb. The larger the wing, the lower the wing loading, but the larger the wing, the more the drag. Therefore, it can be seen that a fast plane with a small wing may not match in climbing ability a slower plane with a more generous wing area. An example of this was the Japanese Zero, whose low-wing

---

[1] Propulsive efficiency is also a factor, but since propellers tended to be standardized, they are not considered in comparing aircraft designs in this book.

loading gave it a distinct advantage in climb and maneuverability over faster American types.

Maneuverability is the plane's ability to change direction. Wing loading and inertia are determining factors here. Maneuverability is adversely affected by aircraft inertia, or the natural resistance to any rotation about its center of gravity. Any heavy weights at a distance from the center of gravity will make maneuvers more difficult. The more compact and lighter the aircraft, the more maneuverable it will be, often forcing designers to choose between a fighter's ability to catch his enemy and his ability to maneuver into a good firing position.

Range, another vital characteristic, is determined by the number of hours an aircraft's fuel will allow it to stay in the air times the cruising speed. *Cruising speed* depends on altitude, gross weight, and power used, and thus is very variable. The range of an aircraft also has numerous possibilities, depending on the amount of fuel carried. Throughout this book range is usually given at the normal cruising condition with the usual fuel load. Maximum ranges suggest the possibilities of the plane with its largest possible fuel load and the most economical speed and altitude. *Endurance,* more easily measured in older aircraft than range, is given in hours and minutes and is most often quoted at top speed. *Radius of action* is about 40 percent of range.

Running engines at too high a speed may waste fuel, as in this example: With 2,290 gallons of fuel and a gross weight of 55,000 pounds the B-24D could achieve a range of about 2,950 miles at a cruising speed of 200 mph at 25,000 feet. Increasing the speed to 250 mph reduces the range to 2,400 miles. At an altitude of 5,000 feet, however, B-24D range is only 1,000 miles at 250 mph and 2,400 miles at 200 mph. The inefficiency of the supercharged engines at lower altitudes is evident. Any increase in the bomb load carried will reduce this range, while a substitution of fuel for bombs can increase the range.

Landing speed, while not tactically significant, is included in the specifications because it is a measure of relative safety and is one of the earliest limiting points selected in the design of an aircraft. The faster the necessary landing speed, the more difficult the landing. Landing speed depends on wing loading and the lifting efficiency of the wing.

A designer begins his task with a proposed specification which gives the armament and performance required. Design procedure starts with an estimate of weight, as this is the prime limiting factor of aircraft. A list of the essential parts of the *useful load* is totaled, including crew, armament, equipment, and probable fuel required. This is added to a rough estimate, from past experience, of the engine and airframe weight required to support such a load. Useful load and empty weight are added to get estimated gross weight.

An appropriate wing section and form is then selected: a hi-lift airfoil for a bomber or a low drag airfoil for a fighter. *Aspect ratio* (the ratio of the wingspan to the mean wing chord) is decided upon: a high aspect ratio for a long-range machine like the B-29 or a short, stubby wing for an interceptor.

The wing loading which would permit the desired landing speed is then determined. Dividing the gross weight by the wing loading gives the necessary *wing area.* Since 1930, lift-increasing devices such as landing flaps and wing slots have been added to reduce the wing area without raising the landing speed. The introduction of tricycle landing gear on combat planes in 1939 made feasible higher landing speeds, since the nose wheel permits more sudden stops. However, wing loading should not be increased to a point detrimental to climb and maneuverability.

Once the weight has been estimated, the wing chosen, and the general layout planned, the performance of aircraft depends on its power loading. This leads us to the next problem: the selection of a power plant.

Power Plants

To a designer, the important features of an airplane engine are its power, weight, size, arrangement and number of cylinders, and method of cooling. The reader should notice what the official designation tells about an engine. Allison's V-1710 has an in-line *Vee* cylinder arrangement and an approximate piston displacement of 1,710 cubic inches, while Wright's R-2600 is a *radial* of some 2,600-cubic-inch piston displacement.

A piston engine's power is rated in hp available for takeoff and at a rated altitude. Jet (gas turbine) engines are rated by pounds of static thrust.

Early aircraft engines had their cylinders lined up behind one another in two rows and were liquid-cooled (water until the 1930s; chemicals since then). The most widely used in-line engines were the Liberty 12 (V-1650) of 1918, the Curtiss D-12 (V-1150) of 1922, the Curtiss Conqueror (V-1570) of 1926, the Allison (V-1710) of 1935, and the Packard Merlin (V-1650) of 1941. All had 12 cylinders.

The radiator and cooling systems required by liquid-cooled engines added weight, drag, and maintenance problems. Air cooling offered the obvious advantage of low weight and simplified servicing, if only the engine could be kept from overheating. The rotary engines used on the World War I Nieuports, with their circle of whirling cylinders, represented an effort in this direction, but they could develop only limited power.

The radial engine first used on American combat

The end of the biplane era; a formation of 17th Pursuit Squadron P-6Es.   AF

planes was the 9-cylinder Lawrence J-1 of 1922, used in the Navy's Curtiss TS fighter. Air cooling became so popular in the Navy that after the more powerful 9-cylinder Pratt & Whitney Wasp (R-1340), Hornet (R-1690), and the early Wright Cyclone (R-1750) became available in 1927, radial engines were standard on Navy combat planes.

Although the period after World War I had not changed the basic shape of combat aircraft, and open-cockpit biplanes remained the common style, still the engineers and aviators had built a solid foundation of experience to prepare the way for the next generation of aircraft.

A Guide to Designations of Combat Aircraft

During World War I, aircraft were known by the rather random names and numbers given by their own manufacturers. Most companies continued their own numbering series, but from 1919 to 1924 the Air Service used an adaption of the French system. A more simplified classification with many modifications was then used until 1948. Table 4 lists older designations used by Army combat planes, with the dates in use.

We might mention the block designations used on World War II Army planes to denote minor modifications and factory of origin. Thus, the Douglas A-24A-DE was built at the El Segundo, California, plant; the A-20B-DL at the Long Beach, California, facility; the A-20C-DO at the main Santa Monica, California, shop; and the A-24-DT at the firm's Tulsa, Oklahoma, shop. The Boeing-designed B-17G-VE was built by Lockheed's subsidiary, Vega. Since there are only a few cases in which the block designation was important, they are not often used in this work.

Air Force combat types after June 11, 1948, only had two designations: "F" for fighter and "B" for bomber, as in the F-86 and B-50. Reconnaissance versions are prefixed by "R," as in the RF-80 and RB-45C. The basic mission symbol could also be preceded by status symbols such as "X" for experimental, "Y" for service test aircraft procured in limited quantities, or "J" for temporary special test configurations, or "N" for a permanent special test configuration.

Table 4

ARMY COMBAT TYPE DESIGNATIONS

A—Attack and light bombardment, 1926–48
B—Bombardment, 1926 to present
DB—Day bombardment, 1920–23
F—(Photographic reconnaissance, 1938–46)
    Fighter, 1948 to present
FM—Fighter-multiplace, 1937–40
GA—Ground attack, 1920–22
HB—Heavy bombardment, 1926–27
LB—Light bombardment, 1925–30
NBL—Night bombardment—long distance, 1923
NBS—Night bombardment—short distance, 1921–24
P—Pursuit, 1925–48
PA—Pursuit—air-cooled, 1922
PB—Pursuit—biplace, 1935
PG—Pursuit—ground attack, 1922
PN—Pursuit—night, 1921
PW—Pursuit—water-cooled, 1921–28

Navy combat aircraft were known as "A" for attack, "F" for fighter, and "P" for patrol from 1946 to 1962. These designations were simplified from the 1923 system, which included combinations of "TB" (torpedo bomber) and "PB" (patrol bomber). Naval aircraft were listed by a manufacturer's letter, with modification letters following. Thus, the P5M-2 is the fifth patrol design by Martin, second model, and the F6C-1 is the sixth fighter by Curtiss, first model. Designations prior to 1923 are a babel of privately assigned labels. Like the Army, the Navy used "X" as a prefix for experimental, as in the XF12C-1.

A new joint Department of Defense designation system was established in 1962. In the future, fighters of both services will be numbered in the same series. Although the system did not change most existing Air Force combat aircraft, all Navy types did change. The manufacturer's letter was dropped in favor of the block letter showing factory of origin. Thus the A3D-2 became the A-3B-DL. Other changes are described in the appropriate chapters. Table 5 shows the letters assigned to factories building Navy aircraft and is followed by a list of suffixes used by the Navy to denote modified missions.

Table 5

LETTERS ASSIGNED TO MANUFACTURERS OF NAVY COMBAT TYPES
(Dates indicate last deliveries of now defunct firms)

Navy 1923–62	Dept. of Defense Since 1962	Company	Location
A	—	Atlantic-Fokker (1930)	Teterboro, New Jersey
A	—	Brewster (1944)	Long Island City, New York
B	BH	Beech	Wichita, Kansas
B	BO	Boeing	Seattle, Washington
B	BN	Boeing	Renton, Washington
B	BW	Boeing	Wichita, Kansas
C	—	Curtiss (1947)	Buffalo, New York
D	DO	Douglas	Santa Monica, California
D	DL	Douglas	Long Beach, California
D	DT	Douglas	Tulsa, Oklahoma
E	—	Bellanca	New Castle, Delaware
F	GR	Grumman	Bethpage, New York
G	GO	Goodyear	Akron, Ohio
G	—	Great Lakes (1936)	Cleveland, Ohio
H	—	Hall (1940)	Bristol, Pennsylvania
H	MC	McDonnell	St. Louis, Missouri
J	—	Berliner-Joyce (1934)	Dundalk, Maryland
J	NA	North American	Inglewood, California
J	NH	North American	Columbus, Ohio
K	—	Kaiser (1946)	Bristol, Pennsylvania
K	—	Keystone (1930)	Bristol, Pennsylvania
L	BC	Bell	Buffalo, New York
L	—	Loening (1929)	New York, New York
M	MA	Martin	Baltimore, Maryland
M	—	Eastern (General Motors)	Trenton, New Jersey
N	—	Naval Aircraft Factory (1945)	Philadelphia, Pennsylvania
O	LO	Lockheed	Burbank, California
—	LM	Lockheed	Marietta, California
—	RE	Republic	Farmingdale, New York
R	RY	Ryan	San Diego, California
S	SI	Sikorsky	Stratford, Connecticut
T	NO	Northrop	Hawthorne, California
U	VO	Vought	Dallas, Texas
V	LO	Lockheed (ex-Vega)	Burbank, California
W	—	Canadian Car & Foundry (1945)	Fort William, Ontario, Canada
Y	CO	Consolidated (Convair)	San Diego, California
Y	CF	General Dynamics (Convair)	Fort Worth, Texas

To the above list should be added suffixes sometimes added since World War II to denote special modifications, such as the F4U-5N. On combat types they include:

A—Amphibious version
B—Special Armament version
C—Carrier version
D—Special Drop Tank version
E—Special Electronic Gear version

G—Search-Rescue version
K—Target Drone version
L—Searchlight version
M—Missile launcher
N—Night version

P—Photographic version
Q—Radar Countermeasure version
S—Antisubmarine version
W—Early Warning version

Chapter 2
Close Support for the Army, 1917–23

Two-seat Biplanes for the AEF, 1918

When America entered the war, the most common aircraft type at the front was the two-seat biplane used for observation and light bomber work. Germany had 1,557 two-seaters at the front on April 30, 1917, compared with 686 single-seat biplanes and 71 twin-engine bombers.

Missions for these two-seaters included observation of enemy activities behind the front lines, the direction of artillery fire, photographic reconnaissance, and light ("day") bombing. Such close-support aircraft had first priority for army leaders, and the Bolling Commission chose Britain's De Havilland 4 as the best type for production in America.

Since the first American two-seater squadrons arrived at the front before their DH-4s, French types were used. The 1st Aero Squadron made its first mission on April 11, 1918, with Spad 11A2s, and on May 8 this squadron was joined to the 12th (Dorand A.R.1) and 88th (French-built Sopwith 1 A2) Aero Squadrons to become the I Corps Observation Group.

These aircraft were considered obsolete and were replaced in June by the Salmson 2A2. Fortunately the Group sector was quiet and there was no air combat in the first weeks. At this time Corps observation missions were short-range, but Army observation squadrons were expected to make deep penetrations. The first American squadron to undertake a long-range mission was the 91st, whose Salmsons made their first sorties on June 7, 1918. These Salmsons had to do a lot of hard fighting to bring their information back home. During the Argonne drive, observation squadrons were credited with destroying 26 enemy planes, 17 of which were downed by the 91st Squadron's Salmsons.

Salmson armament consisted of a Vickers gun for the pilot and a pair of Lewis flexible guns for the

SALMSON 2A2
Salmson Z9, 250 hp
DIMENSIONS: Span 38′6″, Lg. 27′10″, Ht. 9′6″, Wing Area 401 sq. ft.
WEIGHT: Empty 1835 lb., Gross 3036 lb. Fuel 70 gal.
PERFORMANCE: Speed—Top 116 mph at s. 1., 109 mph at 6500′. Service Ceiling 20,500′, Climb 6560′/11 min. Range 319 miles.   AF

observer. The pilot sat ahead of the wings, behind a radial engine water-cooled by a circular radiator. Beginning in April 1918, the AEF received 705 Salmsons, which were used in combat by ten squadrons.

The first American bombing mission was flown by the 96th Aero Squadron against a railroad yard on June 14, 1918. They used the standard French light bomber, the Brequet 14B2 powered by the 300-hp Renault 12F with a prominent exhaust stack pointing upward. The lower wing had full-span trailing edge flaps for landing, and the racks for 32 16-pound bombs or their 520-pound equivalent in larger bombs. Defensive armament comprised one fixed Vickers and two flexible Lewis guns.

Forty-seven Brequet 14B2 bombers were given to the AEF, along with 229 14A2 observation and 100 14E2 trainer models. A second AEF Brequet squadron, the 9th, was assigned to the front on Au-

BREGUET 14B2
Renault 12F, 300 hp
DIMENSIONS: Span 47'1", Lg. 29'6", Ht. 10'10", Wing Area
    540 sq. ft.
WEIGHT: Empty 2283 lb., Gross 3892 lb. Fuel 70 gal.
PERFORMANCE: Speed—Top 110 mph at 6500'. Service
    Ceiling 19,000', Climb 10,000'/16.5 min. Range 300
    miles, Endurance 2¾ hrs.   MA

gust 26 for night observation work. The 96th was
the only American bomber outfit until it joined with
the 11th and 20th Squadrons, flying the new DH-4,
on September 10 to form the First Day Bombardment Group. Its mission would be bombing the
transportation system of the German armies during
the Saint-Mihiel offensive.

The DH-4

The long-heralded DH-4 was the only American-
built army plane to be flown in combat in World
War I, and became the most widely used American
warplane of its decade. Typical of the period, it had
two open cockpits, a big flat nose radiator for its
water-cooled engine, wood-frame construction, and

DAYTON-WRIGHT DH-4
Liberty 12, 400 hp
DIMENSIONS: Span 42'5½", Lg. 29'11", Ht. 9'8", Wing Area
    440 sq. ft.
WEIGHT: Empty 2391 lb., Gross 3582 lb. Fuel 66 gal.
PERFORMANCE: Speed—Top 124 mph at s. l., 120 mph at
    6500'. Service Ceiling 19,500', Climb 10,000'/14 min.
    Range 270 miles.   PMB

fabric-covered wings held together with four pairs
of struts and numerous bracing wires.

The DH-4 had first flown in Britain in August
1916; its performance was highly recommended to
the Americans. A sample, without engine or equipment, arrived in the United States on July 18, 1917,
and was sent to the Aviation Section's Technical
Staff at McCook Field, Dayton, Ohio, by August 15.
Fortunately, a successful 12-cylinder engine had
been designed in America, and a DH-4 was flown
with a "Liberty" engine on October 29.

On October 8, 1917, the DH-4 was ordered into
production by Dayton-Wright, a new company
formed by automobile executives who planned to
achieve rapid mass production in order to bypass
the small aircraft manufacturers and thereby win
the major share of government aviation spending.
Much publicity was given to their promises, but
production of wooden airplanes requiring thousands of engineering changes had little resemblance to automobile production.

Fisher Body (General Motors) at Cleveland,
Ohio, was added to the program on November 7,
and Standard Aircraft of Patterson, New Jersey,
which had been building trainers, got a DH order
on January 24, 1918. The first nine Dayton-Wright
DH-4s were completed in February 1918, while
Fisher's appeared in July and Standard's first appeared in August. By October 1918 deliveries exceeded 1,000 planes a month.

The "Liberty Plane" looked warlike enough,
armed with two fixed .30-caliber Marlin guns with
1,000 rounds, two flexible .30-caliber Lewis guns
with 970 rounds, and bomb racks under the wings
for four 112-pound bombs or their equivalent.
Flight tests demonstrated a top speed at full 400 hp
of 124.7 mph—as fast as many fighters. Endurance
was 1 hour 13 minutes at full power and three hours
at half power.

These flight tests also indicated that many mechanical problems, or "bugs," had to be worked out,
as was the case with most aircraft. The first squadron to use the DH-4 at the front was the 135th Aero,
which made its first sortie, with 15 planes and General Foulois as an observer, on August 9, 1917.[1]
America had already been in the war 16 months,
with only three months left to go, yet this was the
first sortie by American pilots in American aircraft!

During this period of fighting, 33 DH-4s were
lost in combat, and 249 others crashed at the front,
while some 45 enemy planes had been shot down
by DH-4 squadrons. At the war's end, on November
11, 1918, there were 196 DH-4s in France assigned

---

[1] This date and 15 a/c is as given in Lieutenant Larry Smart's
personal account; Hudson says August 7, with 18 a/c. See Bibliography, section III.

to five day bombing, one night bombing, five corps observation, and two Army observation squadrons. The AEF also had 332 DH-4s in depots and 270 in flying schools.

Heavy criticism was leveled at the DH-4's combat record. The wood construction was considered weak compared to the Duralumin tube framework of the Brequet, the pilot's view upwards was blocked by the wing, and the fuel tanks lacked the self-sealing covering of the Salmson and (after July) the Brequet. Worst of all, the main gas tank was between the crewmen, which prevented easy communication, was a danger in crashes, and vulnerable to enemy fire. The phrase "flaming coffin" was used, although not statistically justified.

In the meantime, production in the United States had reached a volume of 3,431 planes by Armistice Day, of which 1,213 had been received overseas. When production ended in 1919, 4,846 had been built. The U.S. Navy received 155 Dayton-built DH-4s during the war, of which 51 went to the Marines of the Northern Bomber Group in September 1918 for operations on the Channel Coast.

Table 6

U.S. PRODUCTION OF THE DE HAVILLAND-4

Company	No. Built	Canceled After Armistice
Dayton-Wright	3,106	1,900
Fisher Body	1,600	2,400
Standard	140	860

Improved De Havillands

In July 1917, the British developed a new De Havilland version, the DH-9, with greater endurance and a gas tank moved ahead of the pilot's cockpit. Two aircraft were purchased without engines by the United States, and 13,750 were ordered by the Army before full details were available. Using Liberty engines, they would be known as USD-9s and would replace the DH-4 on the production line as soon as possible.

The British, however, found the DH-9 unsuccessful and replaced it with the DH-9A, which had more fuel, wider wings, and American Liberty engines, with deliveries to the RAF beginning in June 1918. The U.S. version of this would be the USD-9A, and the Army's Engineering Division at McCook Field pushed prototype development. Army engineers built two USD-9 prototypes in August 1918, and the first of seven USD-9A models began flight tests September 24, 1918. Dayton-Wright also completed construction of four USD-9As.

With the crew's cockpits together and an enlarged fuel tank in front, the DH-4's worst fault had been overcome. Armament included a new .30-caliber

ENGINEERING DIVISION USD-9A
Liberty 12, 400 hp
DIMENSIONS: Span 45'11", Lg. 30'3", Ht. 11'2", Wing Area 490 sq. ft.
WEIGHT: Empty 2815 lb., Gross 4322 lb. as recon. (4872 lb. as bomber). Fuel 142 gal.
PERFORMANCE: Speed—Top 126 mph (121) at s. l., 117 mph (115) at 10,000'. Service Ceiling 18,700' (14,400'), Climb 6500'/7.5 (12) min. Range 400 miles as recon., 350 miles as bomber.   AMC

Browning gun under the right-hand side of the cowl, with 750 rounds and two Lewis guns with 970 rounds in the rear cockpit. The usual bomb load was 550 pounds carried in racks below the wings and fuselage; wireless and camera equipment could be installed in the reconnaissance version.

While the war's end closed the USD-9A program, its main improvements could be made on the DH-4. In July 1918, Dayton-Wright had delivered two improved DH-4s: The first was the DH-4A, with a modified 110-gallon fuel system; and the other was reworked by October as the DH-4B, with crew's cockpits together, an 88-gallon main tank placed ahead of the pilot, and the landing gear moved forward.

After the war, the Army's stockpile of DH-4s was so huge that it was cheaper to destroy most of those in Europe in the "Billion-Dollar Bonfire" than to repack and ship them home. But several American aircraft factories were kept going between 1919 and 1923 with "maintenance" contracts modifying some 1,538 DH-4s to DH-4B configuration. These planes equipped most of the postwar Air Service squadrons, the Marines, the Air Mail Service, and the Border Patrol.

A further development was the DH-4M (M standing for modernized), whose fuselage was of welded steel tubing covered by fabric, assembled with parts from old DH-4s. Boeing delivered 147 DH-4M-1s from January to September 1924, and 30 similar Marine Corps O2B-1s in March 1925; Atlantic Aircraft built 135 DH-4M-2s. These aircraft lingered on with the Army for nearly a decade. In April 1926, 623 of the 1,510 Air Service planes in inventory were De Havillands. Two DH-4Bs and 78 DH-4Ms remained in 1931, the last being retired in April 1932. It is interesting to note that De Havilland's

DAYTON-WRIGHT DH-4B
Liberty 12A, 416 hp
DIMENSIONS: Span 42'5", Lg. 29'11", Ht. 9'8", Wing Area
  439 sq. ft.
WEIGHT: Empty 2939 lb., Gross 4595 lb. Fuel 88 gal.
PERFORMANCE: Speed—Top 118 mph at s. 1., Cruising 94
  mph, Landing 64 mph. Service Ceiling 12,800', Absolute Ceiling 14,700', Climb 5000'/8.2 min. Range 305
  miles.   ARC

BOEING DH-4M-1   MFR

design played a similar role in Russia, where most
Red Air Force planes in 1929 were still R-1s, the
Soviet-built version of the Liberty-powered DH-
9A.

Experimental Two-Seaters

Other designers also produced two-seat prototypes
for missions similar to those of the DH-4. The
L. W. F. Engineering Company, a partnership formed

by Edmond Lowe, Jr., Charles Willard, and Charles
Fowler, had been building a series of trainers with
a unique laminated wood monocoque (single-shell)
fuselage. They received a contract for an advanced
reconnaissance trainer that would use the "U. S.
Standard Aircraft Engine," as the Liberty was
known. The L. W. F. Model G was flown in January
1918 but had a fatal crash on January 16, 1918.

It had been unarmed, like previous L. W. F. aircraft, but the second prototype, L. W. F. G-2, was
heavily armed with seven guns, 66 pounds of cockpit armor, and underwing racks for up to 592 pounds
of bombs. Four fixed guns were grouped around
the engine, two more guns were on the gunner's
ring, and another fired though a hole behind and
below the gunner. According to *Jane's* (see Bibliography, section IC), flight tests in the summer of
1918, at a gross weight of 4,023 pounds, including
90 gallons of fuel, showed a remarkable 138 mph
and four hours endurance. Equipped for bombing,
with full fuel, bombs, and armor, the G-2 weighed
4,880 pounds. Great hopes were held, but the war
ended and the two-seater crashed on November 18.

A French engineer, Captain Gene LePere, had
been loaned to the Army to design aircraft around
the Liberty engine, and McCook Field finished a
prototype LUSAGH-11 (LePere United States
Army ground harassment) in November 1918. With
a squarish appearance and 408 hp (Liberty engines
varied on flight-test output), the heavy LUSAGH-
11 had a .50-caliber fixed gun, two flexible .30-cal-
iber Lewis guns, 450 pounds of bombs and 390
pounds of armor for low-level work with infantry.
A second prototype, LUSAGH-21, with a new 420-
hp Bugatti, was completed in January 1919, but by
then the need for production had dissipated.

L.W.F. G-2
Liberty 12, 435 hp
DIMENSIONS: Span 41'7", Lg. 29'1", Ht. 9'4", Wing Area
516 sq. ft.
WEIGHT: Empty 2675 lb., Gross 4023 lb., Max. 4880 lb.
Fuel 90–120 gal.
PERFORMANCE: Speed—Top 138 mph at s. l., 130 mph at
10,000', Landing 50 mph. Absolute Ceiling 21,000',
Climb 10,000'/9.3 min. Range 520 miles at 130 mph
(360 miles as bomber).   PMB

ENGINEERING DIV. LUSAGH-11
Liberty 12, 408 hp
DIMENSIONS: Span 47'1", Lg. 24'4", Wing Area 601 sq. ft.
WEIGHT: Empty 3913 lb., Gross 5109 lb., Max. 5600 lb.
Fuel 67 gal.
PERFORMANCE: Speed—Top 114 mph at s. l., 107 mph at
10,000', Landing 61 mph. Service Ceiling 15,300', Ab-
solute Ceiling 17,000', Climb 6500'/9.4 min., 875'/1
min. Range 275 miles at 107 mph.   AF

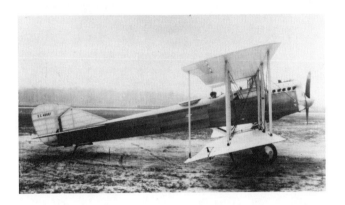

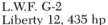

POMILIO BVL-12
Liberty 12, 400 hp
DIMENSIONS: Span 48'3", Lg. 31'7", Ht. 9'9", Wing Area
578 sq. ft.
WEIGHT: Empty 2824 lb., Gross 4552 lb. Fuel 115 gal.
PERFORMANCE: Speed—Top 111 mph at s. l., 106.5 mph
at 6500', Cruising 94 mph, Landing 61.5 mph. Service
Ceiling 13,700', Absolute Ceiling 15,900', Climb 6500'/
11.8 min., 710'/1 min. Range 485 miles/350 lbs.
bombs.   AMC

ENGINEERING DIVISION LUSAO-11
Two Liberty 12, 425 hp
DIMENSIONS: Span 54'6", Lg. 38'2", Ht. 13'6", Wing Area
870 sq. ft.
WEIGHT: Empty 5455 lb., Gross 8577 lb. Fuel 272 gal.
PERFORMANCE: Speed—Top 112 mph at s. l., 106 mph at
10,000', Service Ceiling 15,350', Climb 6500'/9.3 min.
Range 477 miles.   AF

An Italian engineer, Ottorino Pomilio, was also
loaned to the United States, and he designed the
BVL-12 day bomber, which also appeared in January 1919. A plywood fuselage was suspended between the wings, three pairs of struts connected the
wings, while one fixed Browning gun, two Lewis
flexible guns, and 350 pounds of bombs comprised
the armament.

Unique among American aircraft designed for observation missions was LePere's USAO-1, a triplane
with two Liberty engines, a pilot and two observers
with two pairs of Lewis guns, and a 4.5-hour endurance at 106 mph for "long-range" penetrations.

Only two prototypes were finished by the Engineering Division, the first in February 1919.

Ground Attack

During the war's last year, German fliers gave outstanding close support to their own troops by low-
level attacks on Allied infantry. Special squadrons
(*Schlachtstaffeln*) of light two-seaters were formed
in 1917 to strafe enemy trench and road systems
with machine-gun fire. In 1918 they were joined by
heavy two-seaters with added firepower and armor
protection.

After the war the Americans considered these methods, and in 1921 the First Surveillance Group at Kelly Field, Texas, which had been patrolling the Mexican border, was redesignated the Third Attack Group. Their equipment remained the DH-4B for many years while the Air Service made several unsuccessful attempts to develop a specialized attack plane. Such a type should have armor protection and heavier firepower, perhaps including the 37-mm Baldwin semiautomatic cannon experimentally mounted in a Martin GMB bomber in 1919.

The Air Service issued a circular proposal for an armored ground-attack design on October 15, 1919, but not a single private company responded—despite postwar hunger for contracts. This left the task to the Army's own prototype producer, the Engineering Division at McCook Field, Dayton, Ohio.

The GAX (Ground Attack Experimental) was designed by Isaac M. Laddon of the Engineering Division. Mr. Laddon, at age 25, had not yet reached the competence that his famous PBY and B-24 designs would later demonstrate and he faced a task that private aircraft companies had rejected.

ENGINEERING DIV. GAX
Liberty 12A, 421 hp
DIMENSIONS: Span 65'6", Lg. 33'7", Ht. 14'3", Wing Area 1016 sq. ft.
WEIGHT: Empty 7532 lb., Gross 9740 lb. Fuel 112 gal.
PERFORMANCE: Speed—Top 105 mph at s. l., 102 mph at 4000', Cruising 89 mph, Landing 64 mph. Service Ceiling 9600', Absolute Ceiling 11,500', Climb 600'/1 min., 2000'/3.7 min. Range 160 miles.   AF

Powered by two Liberty engines turning four-bladed pusher propellers, the GAX was a triplane. All that lift seemed necessary for the ton of 3/16-inch armor protecting the engines and three crewmen. Slow and awkward, the prototype had a 37-mm Baldwin cannon for the front gunner, and eight .30-caliber Lewis guns. Four of these pointed front and downward, another faced aft over the wings, and all were fired by the busy front gunner. The rear gunner handled two belly guns and one upper gun. Some of these guns had to be removed to permit carrying ten small fragmentation bombs.

The GAX was tested on May 26, 1920, but was severely criticized by the test pilot, who found it unmaneuverable and complained of the long take-off run, poor visibility, and especially of vibration and noise from the armored sides. Nevertheless, a contract for 20 planes to be designated GA-1 had been given to Boeing on June 7, 1920, but the quantity was reduced to ten before the first example was delivered in May 1921. Shipped to Kelly Field for the 3rd Attack Group, the GA-1s were seldom flown, and were scrapped in April 1926.

A smaller single-engine attack biplane designed around an experimental 700-hp Engineering Division W-1A-18 engine was planned by Army engineers. Two of these three-place GA-2s were built by Boeing in 1922. Mounted behind the engine, at the leading edge of the lower wing, was a 37-mm

BOEING GA-2
Engineering Div. W-1A-18, 700 hp
DIMENSIONS: Span 54', Lg. 37', Ht. 12', Wing Area 851 sq. ft.
WEIGHT: Empty 6784 lb., Gross 9085 lb., Max. 9150 lb.
PERFORMANCE: Speed—Top 110 mph, Cruising 100 mph. Service Ceiling 11,100', Absolute Ceiling 13,000', Climb 6500'/16.5 min. Range 165 miles.   AMC

GA-2 (close-up)   MFR

cannon and two .50-caliber guns movable 60° in the vertical plane and 15° in the horizontal. Another .50-caliber gun fired back and down through a tunnel, while two Lewis guns guarded the upper hemisphere. Protection was furnished by 1,600 pounds of ¼-inch armor and the duplication of all struts, bracing and control wires, and spars. The GA-2 is the sole example of this weighty and expensive safety device. Like the GA-1, this Boeing sacrificed performance for ferocity.

More conventional was the Orenco IL-1 (Ordinance Engineering infantry liaison), an armored two-seat biplane for low-altitude infantry support work. Closely resembling a DH-4B, but with double-bay triple struts, a fixed .50-caliber Browning, and two Lewis guns, two were delivered in 1921. A test report made in August 1921 indicated that the IL-1 was far too heavy for the performance needed.

A single-seat ground attack sesquiplane was designed by I. M. Laddon around the Wright K, a Hispano H with a 37-mm Baldwin cannon firing through the hollow engine crankshaft. The cockpit was protected by 165-pound armor and a .50-caliber gun was added so the PG-1 (pursuit ground) could be used both for ground strafing and attacking hostile armored aircraft. Vee struts connected the narrow lower wing to the upper wing atop the fuselage, with the pilot's head poking through the center section. A radiator positioned in front of him further blocked his visibility.

After the cannon engine was produced in July 1920, bids for the PG-1 were solicited from private firms. Four submitted bids, and Aeromarine, of Keyport, New Jersey, received the contract in May 1921, for three PG-1 prototypes. The first was delivered as a static test airframe and the second was flown in August 1922 with a Wright H, which failed on takeoff, destroying the aircraft. A 346-hp Packard 1237 was used on the third prototype, tested in 1923. Its top speed of 116 mph at a 3,342-pound gross weight was below that expected of the original configuration, as shown in the data accompanying the photo.

The most advanced aircraft style of that time was the all-metal, low-wing monoplane of Junkers. A New York dealer, John Larsen, imported from Germany several Junkers F 13 cabin planes built of corrugated dural. One was offered to the Army in December 1921 as the JL-12 attack with a Liberty engine, 30 Thompson M1921 submachine guns, 3,000 rounds of .45-caliber ammunition, and 400 pounds of ⅛-inch armor. Two "Tommy guns" fired out the cabin windows on each side, while the rest were fixed to fire downward.

The 28 belly guns were mounted in the floor; 12 pointed slightly forward, six directly down, and ten inclined to the rear. Half the guns could be fired at

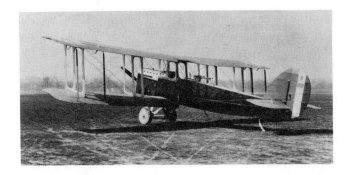

ORENCO IL-1
Liberty 12, 408 hp
DIMENSIONS: Span 46', Lg. 32', Ht. 11'5", Wing Area 602 sq. ft.
WEIGHT: Empty 4437 lb., Gross 5686 lb. Fuel 86 gal.
PERFORMANCE: Speed—Top 107 mph at s. 1., 103 mph at 6500', Cruising 98 mph, Landing 60 mph, Service Ceiling 11,500', Absolute Ceiling 13,100', Climb 685'/1 min., 6500'/13 min. Range 343 miles.   AF

AEROMARINE PG-1
Wright K-2, 330 hp
DIMENSIONS: Span 40', Lg. 24'6", Ht. 8', Wing Area 389 sq. ft.
WEIGHT: Empty 3030 lb., Gross 3918 lb. Fuel 45 gal.
PERFORMANCE: Speed—Top 130 mph, Landing 58 mph. Service Ceiling 17,000', Absolute Ceiling 19,000', Climb 6500'/9.5 min. Range 195 miles at top speed.   AMC

JUNKERS JL-12
Liberty 12, 420 hp
DIMENSIONS: Span 49', Lg. 33', Ht. 10'4", Wing Area 417 sq. ft.
WEIGHT: Empty 2900 lb., Gross 5000 lb. Fuel 140 gal.
PERFORMANCE: Speed—Top 125 mph at s. 1., Landing 60 mph. Climb 10,000'/18 min. Range 400 miles.   SDAM

once, or a single trigger could set off all 28, delivering a fire volume for once justifying the old cliché about a rain of bullets. The test pilot, however, opposed purchase of the plane, describing it as a bad flier, expensive, and with an armament array of doubtful efficiency.

The general failure of these armored ground strafers was due to engineering inadequacies at the time: not enough strength and power and too much weight and drag. Throughout the decade following the war, therefore, attack-squadron equipment, like that of the observation outfits, had to be drawn from the wartime stock of DH-4s.

One effort was made to develop a light bomber of really advanced layout. Stimulated by the success of the metal low-wing, internally braced monoplanes built by Junkers, the Army ordered the Gallaudet DB-1 on December 24, 1920. A low-wing two-seater minus outside wing bracing, it had a 700-hp Engineering Division W-1A water-cooled engine. Between the pilot and gunner's cockpit was

a bay for 600 pounds of bombs and fuel to last, they hoped, for eight hours. Top speed was expected to be 141 mph.

But when the DB-1 (Day Bomber One) was delivered in December 1921, it proved to be overweight: 9,207 pounds instead of the 7,050 pounds estimated. When the control system tended to buckle the Duralumin skin, it was decided not to fly the ship but use it for static tests only. A lighter second machine with a new wing was ordered in February 1922 as the DB-1B.

The DB-1B made the first of its few flights on August 1, 1923, showing eccentricities that discouraged many further tests. It was armed with 600 pounds of bombs and about 1,400 rounds for four guns: one in the nose, two Lewises in the rear cockpit, and a belly gun. Unlike other postwar attack planes, it was intended for daylight bombing raids instead of ground strafing, but the design was too advanced for the day's structural knowledge.

GALLAUDET DB-1
Engineering Div. W-1A-18, 700 hp
DIMENSIONS: Span 67', Lg. 44', Ht. 10'2", Wing Area 663 sq. ft.
WEIGHT: Empty 9207 lb., Gross 11,160 lb. Fuel 248 gal.
PERFORMANCE: (Estimated) Speed—Top 144 mph at s. l., 140 mph at 10,000', Cruising 128 mph. Service Ceiling 17,150', Absolute Ceiling 18,850', Climb 10,000'/12.4 min. Endurance 8 hrs.   AMC

GALLAUDET DB-1B
Engineering Div. W-1A-18, 700 hp
DIMENSIONS: Span 66'7", Lg. 42'6", Ht. 12'7", Wing Area 684 sq. ft.
WEIGHT: Empty 5348 lb., Gross 8600 lb. Fuel 248 gal.
PERFORMANCE: Speed—Top 127 mph at s. l. Service Ceiling 13,400', Absolute Ceiling 15,500', Climb 706'/1 min.   AMC

Chapter 3
Multiengine Bombers, 1917-32

The First Big Bombers

When land warfare settled down to a long deadlock in World War I, the airplane's appeal as an offensive weapon grew. Attacks against people on the ground became more serious, and aircraft specially designed for carrying bombs over great distances were demanded by the warring powers.

Respectable bomb loads, increased fuel supply, and a crew sufficient to operate the airplane and its armament required much larger machines than the frail scouting types then available. Builders began bomber designs by adding a second or more engines to their aircraft for the additional power needed.

Only Russia had such a plane at the war's beginning: Igor Sikorsky's Ilya Mourometz, an improvement on the world's first four-engine airplane, the Sikorsky Grand, flown May 13, 1913. The larger (113 foot span) Ilya Mourometz had four 100-hp engines on the lower wing and an enclosed cabin for the crew. It was ordered into production in 1914, and after the war began a "squadron of flying ships" was formed. On February 15, 1915, the Ilya Mourometz V carried 600 pounds of bombs over the German lines on its first combat mission.

Germany also formed bombing units in 1915, using the twin-engine G types by AEG and Gotha and the larger multiengine R types by Siemens and VGO. Italy began operations with the three-engine Caproni biplanes in 1915.

The general arrangement which became the classic pattern for the next dozen years of bombers was established by the first British Handley-Page bomber, flown on December 18, 1915. The upper wing spanned 100 feet, overhanging a smaller lower wing; between them were suspended two 250-hp Rolls-Royce engines. A squarish fuselage began with a gunner's cockpit in the bow, followed by side-by-side seats for the pilot and co-pilot. A rear gunner sitting behind the wings had his rearward view limited by a boxlike tail of two horizontal and two vertical surfaces. A pair of .30-caliber Lewis guns were mounted at the front and rear cockpits, and a fifth gun aimed downward through a trap door. Eight 250-pound bombs could be carried on eight-hour missions. The Handley-Page first went into action in March 1917 with a Royal Navy flight, but the improved 0/400 version was also ordered for the RAF's "Independent Force," which began strategic-bombing operations in 1918.

Although none of these big bombers made any real difference as far as the strategy or outcome of the war was concerned, they brought the reality of war to civilians behind the lines, who, in the past, had not feared for their lives. The most severe of these raids occurred on June 13, 1917, when 20 Gothas attacked London, killing 162 and injuring 432 persons. This was a modest bit of homicide, considering the statistics of World War II, but it was the best the earlier war could offer; it caused many to feel then that the likelihood of such horrors would cause nations to abstain from future wars.

Early Americans

After the United States entered the war, the Bolling Mission was sent to Europe to recommend types for an American aircraft program. Production of bombers here, however, was delayed by the inability to decide how many should be made and of what type.

The former decision should have been determined by current doctrines of airpower employment, but since no such doctrines had yet been formulated, the number of bombers programed was based on an inaccurate estimate of production capacity. After much wavering, the program of July 1918 finally projected a ratio of 3:5:2 for pursuit, observation, and bombardment-plane production, respectively. Although the Bolling Mission had recommended Caproni bombers in July 1917, consideration of the Handley-Page caused a rivalry that, along with fluctuating production targets, delayed the placing of contracts. Both were finally ordered, to be powered with U.S.-designed Liberty engines.

The first true multiengine bomber seen in the United States was the three-engine Caproni Ca 33, sent from Italy with Italian pilots and flown at Langley Field September 11, 1917. As the largest plane yet seen in America, it attracted much attention flying over Liberty Bond parades to drop patriotic leaflets and advertise the Italian Air Force.

Although Curtiss had received a contract on September 19 for 500 Capronis with Liberty engines, it was canceled on November 17, 1917, because there were neither aircraft plans on hand nor any firm decision as to whether the Caproni or Handley-Page bombers would be used.

While the Caproni project was stalled, the British proposed, in December 1917, that parts for Handley-Page bombers be manufactured in America and assembled in England, along with Liberty engines. An agreement was signed on January 26, 1918, by British and American officials, and several manufacturers were lined up to make the parts for 500 aircraft, as stipulated in contracts drawn up between March 12 and April 13, 1918. Standard Aircraft, in Elizabeth, New Jersey, contracted on April 1 to assemble 50 of the bombers for tests and training in the United States, while the other components were to be packed and shipped to England.

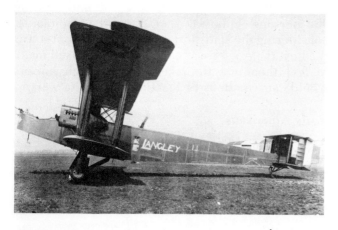

STANDARD HANDLEY-PAGE
Liberty 12-N, 350 hp
DIMENSIONS: Span 100', Lg. 62'11", Ht. 22', Wing Area 1655 sq. ft.
WEIGHT: Empty 8721 lb., Gross 14,425 lb. Fuel 390 gal.
PERFORMANCE: Speed—Top 94 mph at s. 1., 82 mph at 6500', Cruising 84 mph. Service Ceiling 7400', Absolute Ceiling 9600', Climb 400'/1 min., 6500'/27 min. Range 550 miles/2000 lbs. bombs.   SDAM

The first Standard Handley-Page, christened the Langley, was flown on July 1, 1918, and successfully passed its tests with the performance listed on our photo caption. Parts for 100 were shipped to England, and a second example was flown by Standard just before the war ended and production was curtailed. Standard completed three more by April 1919 and two were apparently assembled by the Air Service itself. The aircraft shipped abroad were not assembled, but were returned to America and soon forgotten.

In the meantime, work on the Caproni was revived by the arrival on January 17, 1918, of an Italian engineering mission to organize design, manufacture, and testing of a Liberty-powered bomber. Count Caproni had insisted that his engineer have absolute control, "even in the slightest detail" of the project. Standard Aircraft was chosen as the builder, although an order for the first prototype was not signed until April 9, and that was replaced by a contract for four on May 20.

The Standard Caproni, first flown on July 4, 1918, was powered by three Liberty engines, one being at the rear of the center nacelle and the others at the front of the twin booms leading back to the stabilizer and rudder. The engine used in both the Caproni and Handley-Page was the 350-hp, low-compression model thought more reliable for long-distance work. One or two Lewis guns could be mounted in the bow cockpit, and another pair was operated by a gunner standing on a platform over the rear engine. Performance was better than that of the Handley-Page, but armament accommodation was awkward.

As it turned out, that first Standard Caproni was the only one flown before the war's end. The reasons for this have been analyzed at length by John Casari (see Bibliography, section II). The main facts relating to the program's breakdown are as follows: Five hundred Capronis were ordered from Curtiss on June 7, 1918, and 500 more from Fisher the next day. But development at Standard had gone so slowly that prototype work was shifted to Fisher in Cleveland, which undertook to build three planes to entirely new drawings. The first Fisher airframe was forwarded to McCook Field for static tests on November 21, 1918. The production program was canceled on Armistice Day, but the second Fisher prototype was flown on January 16, 1919, and in June the Air Service accepted both the last Fisher-built prototype and the second Standard prototype, which had been completed by Fisher.

Besides the four American-built Capronis flown, Air Service pilots also flew Italian-built Capronis; the original Ca 33 import named after Julius Caesar and a Ca 5 of 1918, which was also tested by the Navy on a sea sled. The latter was a craft designed

STANDARD CAPRONI
Liberty 12-N, 350 hp
DIMENSIONS: Span 76'10", Lg. 41'2", Ht. 12'1", Wing Area
  1420 sq. ft.
WEIGHT: Empty 7700 lb., Gross 12,350 lb., Max. 12,900
  lb. Fuel 400 gal.
PERFORMANCE: Speed—Top 103 mph at s. 1., Landing
  61.5 mph. Service Ceiling 11,500', Absolute Ceiling
  13,500', Climb 670'/1 min., 6500'/14 min. Range 762
  miles/1330 lbs. bombs.   SDAM

to carry bombers across the North Sea until they were near enough to the target to launch. American pilots in Italy attached to the Italian Air Force flew Capronis on 65 bombing missions, beginning on June 20, 1918.

Navy pilots also trained in Italy on Capronis, which were chosen for the Night Wing, Northern Bomber Group, and were flown from Milan to fields in northern France. Nine Ca 5s were delivered in July and nine in August, but there were 16 crashes with nine pilot fatalities on the way to the Calais area from Italy. In those days flight delivery of aircraft was as dangerous as combat. Nevertheless, 13 arrived by the war's end. The first Navy raid by a single Caproni was made August 15, 1918.

Concentrating on foreign-designed planes, the U.S. Government was reluctant to purchase untried native designs, but on January 17, 1918, Glenn L. Martin received a contract for a twin-engine four-place *Corps d'Armée* reconnaissance plane, which was first flown on August 15, 1918, and could also be used for bombing. That the first American bomber was ordered as a scout for land armies is symbolic of the outlook that was to limit Army bomber development throughout so much of its history.

The Martin GMB (MB-1) was of similar layout to the Handley-Page but smaller. Two 400-hp Liberties were suspended between the wings, four wheels were aligned on a single axle, and the tail assembly of two rudders obstructed the rear gunner's view less than the older type's *empennage*. Five .30-caliber guns and 1,040 pounds of bombs comprised the armament. The original contract for six was increased to 50 on October 22, 1918, but then cut back in January 1919 to ten, the last being completed as a transport in February 1920.

An improved version of the Martin bomber, the MB-2, was ordered in June 1920. This model had new, larger wings to carry a heavier load, with the

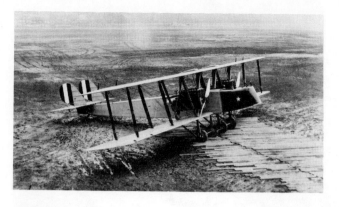

MARTIN GMB
Liberty 12A, 400 hp
DIMENSIONS: Span 71′5″, Lg. 46′10″, Ht. 14′7″, Wing Area
1070 sq. ft.
WEIGHT: Empty 6702 lb., Gross 10,225 lb. Fuel 214 gal.
PERFORMANCE: Speed—Top 105 mph at s. 1., 100 mph at
6500′, Cruising 92 mph, Landing 67.5 mph. Service
Ceiling 10,300′, Absolute Ceiling 12,250′, Climb 630′/
1 min., 6500′/14.6 min. Range 390 miles/1040 lbs.
bombs.   MFR

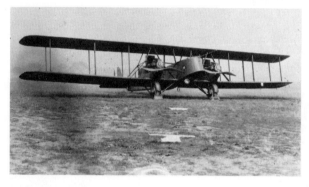

MARTIN MB-2
Liberty 12A, 410 hp (Photo shows supercharged version)
DIMENSIONS: Span 74′2″, Lg. 42′8″, Ht. 14′8″, Wing Area
1121 sq. ft.
WEIGHT: Empty 7069 lb., Gross 12,027 lb. Fuel 300 gal.
PERFORMANCE: Speed—Top 98 mph at s. 1., Cruising 91
mph, Landing 59 mph. Service Ceiling 7700′, Absolute
Ceiling 9900′, Climb 445′/1 min., 6500′/23.8 min.
Range 400 miles/2000 lbs. bombs.   MFR

Liberty engines lowered to the bottom wing and a
simplified landing gear with two wheels. Five Lewis
guns were mounted, paired in the front and rear
cockpits, with one aimed downwards and to the
rear through a trapdoor. Six 300-pound or three 625-
pound bombs could be carried inside the fuselage,
or external racks could hold two 1,130-pound or one
2,000-pound bomb. The latter had been developed
to give bombers a punch equal to that of the biggest
guns of battleships and coastal forts. More extravagant was a 4,300-pound, 172-inch-long bomb; too
big for Martins, it was first test dropped from a
Standard Handley-Page on September 28, 1921.

Twenty Martin MB-2s were built in Cleveland

and redesignated NBS-1 (Night Bomber, Short distance), the first tested September 3, 1920. This ship
was fitted the next year with General Electric turbosuperchargers that, on a December 8, 1921 test,
enabled the NBS-1 to climb past its normal 9,900-
foot ceiling to 25,341 feet. The plan to use superchargers in service was premature, however, for reliable and serviceable applications would not be
available on bombers until the B-17B of 1939.

Those 20 Martins were a modest force even for
1921, but with them the airmen were about to challenge the traditional champions of American defense, the battleship and the coastal fortification.

Bombers Against Battleships

After the war a return to normalcy was expected,
and the nation turned to domestic problems. However, any return to the conservative military habits
of the past was resisted by those who saw in new
weapons a need for a complete reorganization of
America's defense establishment.

Foremost in the campaign for greater emphasis
on aviation was Brigadier General William Mitchell, Assistant Chief of Air Service and wartime commander of the AEF's combat planes. Details concerning General Mitchell's life and opinions may
be found elsewhere (see Bibliography) but the
bomber history here presented demands a summary
of his position.

Mitchell said that air bombardment would become the most important instrument of warfare. Instead of a tedious wearing down of hostile land
forces, bombers would strike immediately at enemy
industrial centers, thereby destroying the enemy's
ability and will to wage war before its armies were
defeated. For a nation surrounded by the sea,
bombers would replace battleships and, with the
aid of submarines, cause surface fleets to "disappear" as a major military force. If air power were to
play this role, it would have to be freed from the
dominance of ground commanders and have its own
leadership, doctrine, and equipment. The organization most suitable for this purpose was a unified
department of defense, with a department of air
coequal with the Army and Navy.

The greatest resistance to these views came from
those who held naval historian Alfred T. Mahan's
theory of sea power as the basis of national strength,
and so Mitchell aimed his attack at 16 expensive
16-inch-gun capital ships then being built as part of
a naval race with Britain and Japan. His bombers
could sink any battleship afloat, he insisted, and
offered to prove it by actual test. Then he struck a
low blow at the big ships by proclaiming that "1,000
bombardment airplanes can be built and operated
for the price of one battleship." Irritated by Mitch-

ell's appeal to the economy-minded public, Secretary of the Navy Josephus Daniels had offered to stand bareheaded on a battleship deck while bombers tried to hit it. This offer was not accepted, but target ships were provided.

The tests were carried out in July 1921 on captured German ships. Attacking with Martins from Langley Field, Virginia, the airmen first sank a destroyer with 300-pound bombs, then a cruiser with 600-pound bombs, and finally climaxed the demonstration by sinking a battleship with six new 2,000-pound bombs, then the largest available.

There was no agreement on the experiment's significance; a joint Army and Navy board report signed by General Pershing concluded that the "battleship was still the backbone of the fleet and the bulwark of the nation's sea defense," while Mitchell's own report flatly contradicted this position, asserting that bombers alone could accomplish the defense of our coasts. In Congress, Senator William E. Borah questioned the necessity of the expensive battleship building program, while a bill was introduced providing for conversion of two forthcoming battle cruisers into aircraft carriers.

In the midst of this debate, the Washington Conference on the Limitation of Armaments was held. At the suggestion of the United States, an agreement was made to limit battleship construction; many ships on hand or on order were to be scrapped and the size of future ships limited. As a result, the United States halted work on eleven capital ships, converted two others to aircraft carriers, and scrapped some prewar battleships, including three sunk in more bombing tests in 1923.

But those who thought the end of the battleship race would result in more funds for bombers were disappointed. With Europe and Asia apparently pacified by diplomacy, there was little interest in armaments—not even in substituting economy-sized wood-frame airplanes for costly steel dreadnoughts. Air Service appropriations dropped from 35.1 million in fiscal 1921 to 12.6 million in fiscal 1924.

In order to spread limited funds to the furthest degree possible, the Army purchased its aircraft by inviting competitive bids from prospective contractors. Proprietary rights to military designs were then held by the government, which could assign production to the company offering the lowest bid.

In February 1922, when Martin offered to build more NBS-1s for $23,925 each, he discovered that he had been underbid by his competitors. Curtiss received a contract for 50 NBS-1s at a price of $17,490 each; 35 were ordered from the L. W. F. Engineering Company, and 25 more from Aeromarine. Tests on the first Curtiss ship began in September 1922 and showed characteristics like those of its predecessors. However, a loss of $300,000 on the

MARTIN-CURTISS NBS-1
Liberty 12A, 420 hp
DIMENSIONS: Span 74′2″, Lg. 42′8″, Ht. 14′8″, Wing Area 1121 sq. ft.
WEIGHT: Empty 7269 lb., Gross 12,064 lb., Max. 12,119 lb. Fuel 300 gal.
PERFORMANCE: Speed—Top 98.7 mph at s. l., 91 mph at 6500′, Cruising 91 mph, Landing 62 mph. Service Ceiling 8500′, Absolute Ceiling 10,000′, Climb 391′/1 min., 6500′/22.5 min. Range 429 miles/1797 lbs. bombs, 558 miles/1262 lbs. bombs.   AF

NBS-1 contract was admitted by Curtiss officials.

All eight Army bombing squadrons of this period used the NBS-1: the 11th, 20th, 49th, and 96th with the 2nd Bomb Group at Langley Field, Virginia (today the oldest USAF base in service); the 23rd and 72nd with the 5th Composite Group in Hawaii; the 25th with the 6th Composite Group in the Canal Zone; and the 28th with the 4th Composite Group in the Philippines. They remained in service until replaced by Keystone bombers in 1928–29.

Liberty engines from the wartime stockpile were used on these planes, as well as on the next four bomber projects of the Air Service. The first project was the three-engine L.W.F. H-1 Owl, designed by Raoul Hoffman for mail or bombing work. A Caproni-like layout included a center plywood nacelle for a crew of three and the center Liberty, with booms running back from outboard engines to triple rudders. The center nacelle was equipped only for carrying mail when the Army purchased the Owl on April 16, 1920, and began tests at Mitchel Field on May 22, 1920. After a crash in June 1921, the aircraft went back to the factory and reappeared at Mitchel Field in September 1922 with the nacelle equipped for bombing, a new nose radiator, the pilot's cockpit ahead of the wings, and a gunner's cockpit in the back, with twin Lewis guns on the ring and a third firing downward. Fuel was carried in the outer booms, and a 2,000-pound bomb between the wheels.

The flight data given was evidently an estimate and was not actually achieved in tests, for the Owl did not hold Army interest and was scrapped.

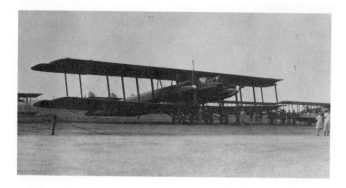

L.W.F. OWL
Liberty 12, 400 hp
DIMENSIONS: Span 106′8″, Lg. 53′9″, Ht. 17′6″, Wing Area
    2216 sq. ft.
WEIGHT: Empty 12,600 lb., Gross 20,200 lb., Max. 21,186
    lb.
PERFORMANCE: Speed—Top 110 mph, Landing 56 mph.
    Service Ceiling 17,500′, Climb 6000′/9 min. Range
    1100 miles/2000 lbs. bombs.   AMC

L.W.F. proposed a twin-engine metal bomber called
the NBS-2, but the company went out of business
in April 1923 before it could be built.

The largest bomber of that generation was designed for the Engineering Division by Walter Barling and built in sections by Witteman-Lewis in
Peterboro, New Jersey. Designated XNBL-1 (Night
Bombardment, Long distance), the Barling plans
were dated May 15, 1920, and the aircraft parts
were shipped in crates for assembly at Wilbur
Wright Field. The parts arrived by truck on July 22,
1922, but the XNBL-1 did not make its first flight
until August 22, 1923.

Three wings, four rudders, six engines, and ten
landing wheels gave this behemoth a configuration
more likely to antagonize the air than to pass
through it. Four 420-hp Liberty 12A engines were
arranged as tractors, with two as pushers. Seven
.30-caliber guns guarded a crew of eight. Up to

BARLING XNBL-1
Liberty 12A, 420 hp
DIMENSIONS: Span 120′, Lg. 65′, Ht. 27′, Wing Area 4200
    sq. ft.
WEIGHT: Empty 27,703 lb., Gross 32,203 lb., Max. 42,569
    lb. Fuel 2088 gal.
PERFORMANCE: Speed—Top 96 mph at s. l., 93 mph at
    5000′, Cruising 61 mph, Landing 55 mph. Service Ceil-
    ing 7725′, Absolute Ceiling 10,200′, Climb 352′/1 min.,
    5000′/19.7 min. Range 170 miles/5000 lbs. bombs, 335
    miles max.   AF

2,000 gallons of gasoline made a six-ton load, for two thirds of which bombs might be substituted. A record flight was made to 6,722 feet, with a 4,400-pound load, but this modest altitude capability prevented a flight over the mountains to either coast.

Although Mitchell said the Barling "was entirely successful from an experimental standpoint," it was elsewhere described as "Mitchell's Folly," and an Air Force history admits it had "disappointing speed, load, and endurance," with a range of 170 miles with load divided between fuel and bombs and 335 miles with fuel only. Considering the $350,000 cost, it was hardly a great achievement. Mitchell wanted to go ahead with the Martin XNBL-2, an advanced four-place monoplane with two 700-hp, 18-cylinder W-2779 Engineering Division engines in the 98-foot wing's leading edge, but the order for two prototypes was canceled. The Barling triplane itself made its last flight in 1925, was scrapped in June 1928, and nothing comparable in size was to be seen in U.S. bombers until 1937.

Traditional bomber patterns reappeared in the Elias XNBS-3 and the Curtiss XNBS-4, four-place biplanes with two Libertys, boxlike biplane tails, and five .30-caliber guns in the usual nose, rear, and tunnel positions. The XNBS-3 was tested in August 1924 and did 101 mph with a 1,692-pound bomb load. The Curtiss XNBS-4 was like the NBS-1 but had a welded steel-tube, instead of wood, fuselage structure, and carried a 1,907-pound bomb load. Two were delivered, the first in May 1924.

Neither of these ships was ordered, for they incorporated no real advance over service types. With little performance progress made since the war, Air Service bomber squadrons hardly seemed likely to replace the battleship as the first line of defense. In July 1925 the bomber force was limited to 90 NBS-1s, the same type used five years earlier.

Despite the modest size of his striking force, Mitchell continued attacking "battleship admirals" and ground generals and predicted enormous capabilities for future aircraft. President Calvin Coolidge demoted him to the rank of colonel, and he was sent into "exile" in Texas, but the disaster to the dirigible *Shenandoah* in September 1925 gave Mitchell an excuse to issue his most violent denunciation of "incompetency, criminal negligence, and almost treasonable administration."

This statement resulted in Mitchell's famous court martial in the fall of 1925. The accompanying publicity led to the presidential appointment that same year of a nine-member board to investigate aviation, under the chairmanship of banker-diplomat Dwight W. Morrrow. Scores of witnesses presented data and opinions of air power to the Aircraft Inquiry Board, most of them hostile to Mitchell.

It was against the limited range of the existing

ELIAS XNBS-3
Liberty 12A, 425 hp
DIMENSIONS: Span 77′6″, Lg. 48′5″, Ht. 16′10″, Wing Area 1542 sq. ft.
WEIGHT: Empty 8809 lb., Gross 14,343 lb. Fuel 340–56 gal.
PERFORMANCE: Speed—Top 101 mph at s. l., 96 mph at 6500′, Landing 65 mph. Service Ceiling 8680′, Absolute Ceiling 11,500′, Climb 405′/1 min., 5000′/16 min. Range 485 miles/1692 lbs. bombs.   AMC

CURTISS XNBS-4
Liberty 12A, 436 hp
DIMENSIONS: Span 90′2″, Lg. 46′5″, Ht. 15′9″, Wing Area 1524 sq. ft.
WEIGHT: Empty 7864 lb., Gross 13,795 lb. Fuel 334 gal.
PERFORMANCE: Speed—Top 100 mph at s. l., 95 mph at 5000′, Landing 53 mph. Service Ceiling 10,750′, Absolute Ceiling 13,000′, Climb 529′/1 min., 5000′/11.5 min. Range 505 miles/2000 lbs. bombs.   AMC

bombers that witnesses before the Morrow Board directed their main fire. The conservative position was expressed very strongly by the Assistant Director of the Navy's War Plans Division, Captain Claude S. Pye. In the first place, argued the Navy spokesman, since bombers were then very limited in striking radius, to abandon battleships for bombers would be to assume an "essentially defensive" military posture. "Without a fleet, our world trade would soon become a sacrifice to the air fetish." Do we wish to adopt a policy "like that of China and build a wall of air defense along our shores, outside of which the nations of the world can rob us of our commerce on which our national prosperity . . . depends?"

Even if one were to suppose, Captain Pye continued, that offensive operations by aircraft alone were possible, could Americans use such weapons? No, he said, quoting liberally from Mitchell's *Winged Defense* to show that air bombardment meant "ruthlessly" bombing "civil population and economic resources." But under existing international law this "means of coercing an enemy people is banned." But the Navy "does not subscribe to the theory of ruthlessness and believes that any organization based on . . . war according to such [a] theory is unsound. The Navy further believes that if the people of the United States will seriously consider this subject they will reject this theory of ruthlessness and with such rejection the principal excuse for an independent air service will disappear."

Thus testified a representative of the Navy on October 14, 1925. Not all Navy men deprecated bomber striking power, and later chapters in this book detail progress made in carrier aviation. Yet aviation was seen by the majority as an arm of surface elements, whether fighting ships or infantry divisions. An independent air force built around bombers would be unsound because it could not protect our overseas commerce and would commit the United States to a theory of ruthlessness. The Morrow Board must have been impressed, for the final report firmly rejected Mitchell's theories, and two weeks later he was found "guilty as charged" of insubordination and resigned from the Army effective February 1, 1926.

Bombers Under the General Staff

Aside from changing the Air Service name to Air Corps and promising enough funds to build a modern force of 1,800 planes, the Air Corps Act of 1926 embodied Morrow Board ideas and left the airmen still under the thumb of a General Staff of ground officers. Appropriations steadily increased from $13.5 million in 1925 to $38.9 million in fiscal 1931, but much was siphoned off for observation planes. On June 30, 1925, the Army had 90 bombers, compared with 249 observation planes and 28 fighters; on December 31, 1928, there were only 60 bombers to 506 observation planes, 190 fighters, and 69 attack planes.

Bomber strength was declining, and a replacement for the NBS-1 was required. More range was needed if bombers were to grow in importance, and this aim seemed to be advanced by the Huff-Daland XLB-1 (light bomber), which appeared in August 1925. Substituting a single 750-hp Packard 1A-2540 for the usual two Libertys, the XLB-1 was of fabric-

HUFF-DALAND XLB-1
Packard 2A-2540, rated 800 hp, actual 750 hp
DIMENSIONS: Span 66'6", Lg. 46'2", Ht. 14'11", Wing Area 1137 sq. ft.
WEIGHT: Empty 5740 lb., Gross 10,346 lb. Fuel 290 gal.
PERFORMANCE: Speed—Top 121 mph at s. l., 117 mph at 6500', Cruising 114 mph, Landing 55 mph. Service Ceiling 14,425', Absolute Ceiling 17,300', Climb 176'/ 1 min., 6500'/23.5 min. Range 940 miles.　　AMC

HUFF-DALAND LB-1
Packard 2A-2540, 787 hp
DIMENSIONS: Span 66'6", Lg. 46'2", Ht. 14'11", Wing Area 1137 sq. ft.
WEIGHT: Empty 6237 lb., Gross 12,415 lb. Fuel 295–350 gal.
PERFORMANCE: Speed—Top 120 mph at s. l., 114 mph at 5000', Cruising 105 mph, Landing 61 mph. Service Ceiling 11,150', Absolute Ceiling 13,700', Climb 530'/ 1 min., 6500'/14 min. Range 430 miles/2750 lbs. bombs.　　MFR

HUFF-DALAND XHB-1
Packard 2A-2540, 787 hp
DIMENSIONS: Span 84'7", Lg. 59'7", Ht. 17'2", Wing Area 1648.5 sq. ft.
WEIGHT: Empty 8070 lb., Gross 16,838 lb. Fuel 412 gal.
PERFORMANCE: Speed—Top 109 mph.　　MFR

covered steel-tube construction, with two men side by side behind the engine and a gunner near the single tail. Two Lewis guns were mounted at the gunner's pit, a third on the floor, and two .30-caliber Brownings were fixed on the lower wings' leading edge. About 1,500 pounds of bombs could be carried 8.25 hours over a range of 940 miles, the best yet for an American bomber.

Ten LB-1s, called Pegasus by the company, were ordered in November 1925 for service trials. In July 1927 tests began on the LB-1, which had provision for a fourth crewman and larger useful loads than the prototype.

An enlarged heavy bomber version of the LB-1 appeared in October 1926 as the Huff-Daland XHB-1. Since the 1,200-hp engine expected had failed to materialize, the same 787-hp Packard 2A-2540 had to be used. Christened Cyclops by the company, the only Army plane bearing "HB" letters carried four men; two in an open cockpit ahead of the wing, one near the tail with twin Lewis guns, and the other with a "retractable gun platform" which could be lowered below the fuselage. Two fixed Browning wing guns and over 4,000 pounds of bombs were also carried.

The Cyclops was the Army's last single-engine bomber, for as early as April 1926 an Army board declared single-engine aircraft unsatisfactory for bombardment missions. A twin-engine layout was safer and allowed a nose cockpit for gunnery and bomb-aiming.

The NBS-1s were aging on the flying fields, and the Army began shopping for better twin-engine replacements.

Huff-Daland, which in March 1927 became the Keystone Aircraft Corporation, offered the XLB-5

HUFF-DALAND XLB-5
Liberty V-1650-3, 400 hp
DIMENSIONS: Span 66'6", Lg. 45', Ht. 16'10", Wing Area 1137 sq. ft.
WEIGHT: Empty 6848 lb., Gross 11,992 lb. Fuel 200–340 gal.
PERFORMANCE: Speed—Top 108 mph, Cruising 87 mph, Landing 60 mph. Service Ceiling 7875', Absolute Ceiling 10,300', Climb 420'/1 min.   AMC

in November 1926. This ship, called the Pirate by the company, had war-surplus Libertys, gunners in the bow and rear, and the LB-1's tapered wing and single rudder.

Ten LB-5s and 25 LB-5As were ordered at a cost of $28,000 each. The former, with triple rudders, were delivered from July to December 1927, while the LB-5As, with twin rudders, appeared from January to July 1928. Armament included five .30-caliber Lewis guns and 2,121-pounds of bombs.

An air-cooled version of the Pirate was planned in the XLB-3, which was to be a twin to the XLB-5, using inverted air-cooled Libertys. When the XLB-3 appeared in December 1927, it had the LB-5 airframe and triple rudders. The original engines did not work out and were replaced by 410-hp R-1340 Wasp radials, and the designation became XLB-3A.

During that same December, Keystone completed the last LB-5, modified with a larger wing and two 525-hp R-1750-1 Wrights, but this XLB-6 prototype had twin tails and its engine nacelles were located between the wings, above the turbulent air flow over the lower wing. A stability problem persisted until positive dihedral and sweepback were added to the wings and the tail was modified.

Keystone also built a heavy bomber, the XB-1, which was a twin-engine development of the XHB-1. Originally 510-hp Packard 2A-1530s were used in September 1927, but since this engine proved unsatisfactory during LB-1 service trials, they were replaced by 600-hp Curtiss V-1570-5 Conquerors and the Keystone became the XB-1B.

Now that funds were available to reequip Army bomber squadrons, Keystone found itself in competition with a Curtiss design by George Page, a bomber version of the Fokker C-2 transport monoplane, and a Sikorsky design that Consolidated had agreed to finance in April 1927. The Curtiss XB-2 Condor was a large five-place biplane with twin rudders and Curtiss Conquerors. Both the XB-1B and the XB-2 shared the first improvement in defensive armament since the war; instead of a single rear gunner with the view blocked by the tail assembly, there were two gunners, one seated in each engine nacelle, with a clear fire to the rear. Two Lewis guns were provided for each, with a third pair in the nose. Bomb load, normally 2,508 pounds, could be increased to 4,000 on short flights. First tested in September 1927, the Curtiss Condor showed the best performance of any bomber of that decade.

Igor Sikorsky, now transplanted to America, offered a descendant of the Ilya Mourometz: the Sikorsky S-37B Guardian. Powered by two air-cooled Pratt & Whitney 525-hp Hornets, the S-37B had a

KEYSTONE LB-5
Liberty V-1650-3, 420 hp
DIMENSIONS: Span 67', Lg. 44'8", Ht. 16'10", Wing Area 1138.7 sq. ft.
WEIGHT: Empty 7024 lb., Gross 12,155 lb. Fuel 200 gal.
PERFORMANCE: Speed—Top 107 mph. Service Ceiling 8000', Absolute Ceiling 8800', Climb 5000'/20 min. Range 435 miles/2312 lbs. bombs. AF

KEYSTONE XLB-3A
Pratt & Whitney R-1340-1, 410 hp
DIMENSIONS: Span 67', Lg. 45', Ht. 16'10", Wing Area 1138.7 sq. ft.
WEIGHT: Empty 6065 lb., Gross 11,682 lb. Fuel 245–350 gal.
PERFORMANCE: Speed—Top 116 mph at s. l., 113 mph at 5000', Cruising 93 mph, Landing 59 mph. Service Ceiling 11,210', Absolute Ceiling 13,700', Climb 550'/1 min., 5000'/11.3 min. Range 544 miles at top speed. AMC

KEYSTONE LB-5A (As LB-5 with twin rudders) AMC

KEYSTONE XLB-3
As LB-5 inverted, air-cooled Liberty V-1410-1. AMC

KEYSTONE XLB-6
Wright R-1750, 525 hp
DIMENSIONS: Span 74'9", Lg. 43'6", Ht. 18'1", Wing Area 1148 sq. ft.
WEIGHT: Empty 6605 lb., Gross 13,018 lb. Fuel 350 gal.
PERFORMANCE: Speed—Top 116 mph at s. l., 114 mph at 5000', Cruising 93 mph, Landing 58 mph. Service Ceiling 14,770', Absolute Ceiling 17,050', Climb 746'/1 min., 5000'/7.9 min. Range 440 miles/2000 lbs. bombs. MFR

KEYSTONE XB-1B (Original version shown)
Curtiss V-1570-5, 600 hp
DIMENSIONS: Span 85', Lg. 62', Ht. 19'3", Wing Area 1604 sq. ft.
WEIGHT: Empty 9462 lb., Gross 16,500 lb., Max. 17,039 lb. Fuel 444 gal.
PERFORMANCE: Speed—Top 117 mph at s. l., Landing 56 mph. Service Ceiling 15,000'. Range 700 miles/2508 lbs. bombs.　　　　　MFR

CURTISS B-2 (Below)
Curtiss V-1570-7, 633 hp
DIMENSIONS: Span 90', Lg. 47'6", Ht. 16'3", Wing Area 1499 sq. ft.
WEIGHT: Empty 9039 lb., Gross 16,516 lb. Fuel 444 gal.
PERFORMANCE: Speed—Top 132 mph at s. l., 128 mph at 5000', Cruising 114 mph, Landing 53 mph. Service Ceiling 17,100', Absolute Ceiling 19,400', Climb 850'/1 min., 5000'/6.8 min. Range 780 miles/2508 lbs. bombs.　　　　　MFR

CURTISS XB-2 (Above)
Curtiss GV-1570, 600 hp
DIMENSIONS: Span 90', Lg. 47'6", Ht. 16'3", Wing Area 1499 sq. ft.
WEIGHT: Empty 8732 lb., Gross 16,344 lb. Fuel 444 gal.
PERFORMANCE: Speed—Top 130 mph at s. l., Cruising 104 mph, Landing 53 mph. Service Ceiling 16,140', Absolute Ceiling 18,435'.　　　　　MFR

SIKORSKY S-37B
Pratt & Whitney R-1690, 525 hp
DIMENSIONS: Span 100', Lg. 45', Ht. 16'2", Wing Area
    1074 sq. ft.
WEIGHT: Empty 8794 lb., Gross 15,109 lb. Fuel 350 gal.
PERFORMANCE: Speed—Top 108 mph, Landing 57 mph.
    Service Ceiling 12,800', Climb 546'/1 min. Range 575
    miles/1952 lbs. bombs.   MFR

100-foot-span upper wing overhanging a 58-foot-
span lower wing. Five men were accommodated in
the traditional manner in the fuselage; twin rudders
made up the tail. Armed with five .30-caliber guns
and 1,952 pounds of bombs, the Guardian did not
even garner an official Army designation.

The first twin-engine Air Corps bomber built as
a monoplane was the Atlantic-Fokker XLB-2. De-

ATLANTIC-FOKKER XLB-2
Pratt & Whitney R-1340, 410 hp (R-1690-1, 525 hp)
DIMENSIONS: Span 72'10", Lg. 51'5", Ht. 13'3", Wing Area
    748 sq. ft.
WEIGHT: Empty 5916 lb. (6236 lb.), Gross 12,039 lb.
    (12,655 lb.). Fuel 295 gal. (340 gal.).
PERFORMANCE: Speed—Top 116 mph (123 mph) at s. l.,
    112 mph at 5000', Cruising 93 mph, Landing 67 mph.
    Service Ceiling 10,925' (13,700'), Absolute Ceiling
    13,400', Climb 540'/1 min. (762'/1 min.), 5000'/
    11.5 min. Range 540 miles (650 miles) /2052 lbs.
    bombs.   MFR

veloped from the Fokker transport, the XLB-2 had
410-hp Pratt & Whitney R-1340 Wasps suspended
below the high cantilever wing. Top speed with
these engines was 116 mph, but speed was later
increased to 123 mph by using the 525-hp R-1690-
1. The crew of five was armed with five .30-caliber
guns and 2,052 pounds of bombs.

This firm had planned to build a larger monoplane in 1926, the XHB-2, with two Packard 2A-
2540s, 108-feet 4-inch span and 24,478 pounds
gross. It was never built, for, as in the case of Martin's XNBL-2 and a projected Huff-Daland XHB-3,
authorities were not ready to trust a big monoplane.
Reticence about all-metal aircraft also resulted in
the dropping of the XLB-4 project, a biplane with
R-1690 Hornets proposed by Martin.

When an Army board of seven officers met in
February 1928 to choose a bomber type for production, it dismissed the XB-1B, XLB-2, and S-37 but
disagreed on the merits of the Curtiss XB-2 and
Keystone XBL-6. Although the former had by far
the best performance, critics complained that it cost
too much and was "too big for existing hangars."
A 4-to-3 decision put the Keystone ship into production, but on June 23, 1928, Curtiss did get a
$1,050,473 contract for 12 B-2s and made deliveries
from May 1929 to January 1930. The B-2s remained
in service until 1934.

Although the Keystone bombers were conservative in design and performance, they were favored
because of their low cost, economical operation,
and stable flying qualities. Between 1927 and 1932,
210 Keystones, representing 19 different models,
were delivered to the Air Corps. All were twin-
engine, five-place biplanes constructed of steel tubing covered by fabric. Below the bow gunner were
windows for the bombardier, and behind and above
him sat the pilots. The rear gunner behind the
wings had, like the front gunner, two Lewis guns
on a ring (a single Browning was substituted later),
and another gun firing downward through the floor
opening.

With their open cockpits, struts, wires, and exposed wheels, they looked and performed much the
same as the NBS-1s they replaced—certainly not
enough to make national policy makers feel they
had advanced far beyond the planes that sank the
old target ships.

The first production series was the previously
mentioned Pirates. These planes could be recognized by their water-cooled Libertys and 67-foot
tapered wing; one became the XLB-6 with air-
cooled Cyclones and a 75-foot wing. On May 7,
1928, 35 Keystones were ordered at a cost of $24,-
750 each. Labeled Panther by the company, they
had a longer fuselage, 75-foot wings, and twin rudders. Sixteen LB-6s with Wright R-1750-1 Cyclones

KEYSTONE LB-6

Wright R-1750-1, rated 525 hp at s. l., actual 536 hp
DIMENSIONS: Span 75', Lg. 43'5", Ht. 18'1", Wing Area 1148 sq. ft.
WEIGHT: Empty 6836 lb., Gross 13,440 lb. Fuel 352 gal.
PERFORMANCE: Speed—Top 114 mph at s. l., 106 mph at 5000', Cruising 95 mph, Landing 58 mph. Service Ceiling 11,650', Absolute Ceiling 14,000', Climb 600'/1 min., 5000'/10.3 min. Range 632 miles/2003 lbs. bombs.   MFR

KEYSTONE LB-7

Pratt & Whitney R-1690-3, 525 hp at s. l.
DIMENSIONS: As LB-6
WEIGHT: Empty 6556 lb., Gross 12,903 lb. Fuel 350 gal.
PERFORMANCE: Speed—Top 114 mph at s. l., 110 mph at 5000', Cruising 95 mph, Landing 55 mph. Service Ceiling 13,325', Absolute Ceiling 15,700', Climb 660'/1 min., 5000'/9.1 min. Range 432 miles/2000 lbs. bombs.   AF

had exhaust collector rings *behind* their cylinders, while 16 LB-7s had Pratt & Whitney R-1690-3 Hornets distinguished by their exhaust collectors on the *front* of the cylinders. The LB-7s were delivered first, from February to June 1929, and the LB-6s arrived between August and September of that year. Armament included five Lewis guns and a ton of bombs in internal racks.

The seventeenth aircraft on this contract became the LB-8, delivered in November 1929 with the geared GR-1860-3 Cyclone, followed by an LB-9 with the GR-1750. A new single rudder with the R-1750-1 was introduced on the LB-10 as early as July 1929, while the LB-11 was the last LB-6 to be converted in 1930 to direct-drive R-1750-3 Cyclones. The first LB-7 became the XLB-12 when R-1860-1 Hornets were installed. The purpose of these modifications was to choose the best engines for the next bomber series.

On March 15, 1930, the Bristol, Pennsylvania, builder got an order for 73 ships originally labeled LB-10A, LB-13, and LB-14. But by the time delivery began the Army had dropped the LB designation and was listing all bombers in the B series beginning with XB-1B and B-2. All ships in this Keystone series had a 74-foot 9-inch span and were distinguished from their predecessors by a single balanced rudder. Three Browning flexible guns with 500 rounds per gun (rpg) and up to 2,500 pounds of bombs comprised the armament. First was the B-3A, which appeared in October 1930 with

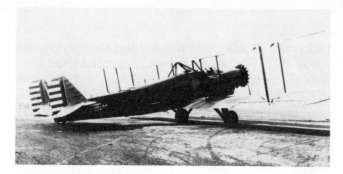

KEYSTONE LB-8
Pratt & Whitney GR-1860-3, 550 hp
DIMENSIONS: Span 75', Lg. 42'6", Ht. 18'1", Wing Area
  1148 sq. ft.
WEIGHT: Empty 7357 lb., Gross 13,745 lb. Fuel 363 gal.
PERFORMANCE: Speed—Top 126 mph at s. l., 121 mph at
  5000', Cruising 100 mph, Landing 59 mph. Service
  Ceiling 16,800', Absolute Ceiling 18,700', Climb 977'/
  1 min., 5000'/14.5 min.   MFR

KEYSTONE LB-10
Wright R-1750-1, 525 hp
DIMENSIONS: Span 75', Lg. 49'3", Ht. 15'6", Wing Area
  1148 sq. ft.
WEIGHT: Empty 6993 lb., Gross 13,285 lb. Fuel 340 gal.
PERFORMANCE: Speed—Top 116 mph at s. l., 113 mph at
  5000', Cruising 93 mph, Landing 58 mph. Service Ceiling 13,440', Absolute Ceiling 15,800', Climb 660'/1
  min., 5000'/9 min. Range 352 miles/2587 lbs.
  bombs.   MFR

KEYSTONE B-3A
Pratt & Whitney R-1690-3, 525 hp at s. l.
DIMENSIONS: Span 74'8", Lg. 48'10", Ht. 15'9", Wing Area
  1145 sq. ft.
WEIGHT: Empty 7705 lb., Gross 12,952 lb. Fuel 235–535
  gal.
PERFORMANCE: Speed—Top 114 mph at s. l., 109.5 mph
  at 5000', Cruising 98 mph, Landing 56 mph. Service
  Ceiling 12,700', Absolute Ceiling 15,000', Climb 650'/
  1 min., 5000'/9.4 min. Range 860 miles.   AF

KEYSTONE B-5A
Wright R-1750-3, 525 hp at s. l.
DIMENSIONS: As B-3A
WEIGHT: Empty 7705 lb., Gross 12,952 lb. Fuel 235–535
  gal.
PERFORMANCE: Speed—Top 111 mph at s. l., 106 mph at
  5000', Cruising 98 mph, Landing 57 mph. Service Ceiling 10,600', Absolute Ceiling 13,000', Climb 540'/1
  min., 5000'/11.7 min. Range 815 miles.   MFR

525-hp R-1690-3 Hornets, two-bladed propellers, and aft exhaust ring. Thirty-six B-3As delivered by March 1931 were followed by 27 B-5As with 525-hp R-1750-3 Cyclones and forward exhaust rings. In June 1931 Keystone also completed five Y1B-4s with 575-hp R-1860-7 Hornets and five Y1B-6s with 575-hp R-1820-1 Cyclones, the latter the first to use three-bladed propellers.

On April 28, 1931, the Army placed its last biplane bomber contract for 25 B-4A and 39 B-6A

Keystones. First came the B-6As delivered from August 1931 to January 1932 with Cyclones, while the Hornet-powered B-4As were accepted from January to April 1932. Both had three-bladed propellers, but they could be distinguished by the exhaust rings, which were positioned in front on the Cyclones and aft on the Hornets.

When biplane bomber production ended in 1932, the ten Air Corps bombardment squadrons included:

20th, 49th, and 96th Squadron, 2nd Bomb
Group, Langley Field, with B-6A
9th and 31st Squadron, 7th Bomb Group, March
Field, with B-4A
11th Squadron, 7th Bomb Group, March Field,
with B-2
23rd Squadron, 5th Composite Group, Luke
Field (Hawaii), with LB-6
72nd Squadron, 5th Composite Group, Luke
Field, with B-5A
25th Squadron, 6th Composite Group, France
Field (Canal Zone), with B-3A
28th Squadron, 4th Composite Group, Nichols
Field (Philippines), with B-3A

In addition, the 19th Bomb Group was activated
in June 1932 with only nine B-3As, and the training

squadron at Kelly Field had a few B-5As and
LB-7s.

Keystone biplanes formed almost the entire U.S.
bombardment strength during the international social crisis of 1931–33, which finally led to World
War II. If their striking power, range, and ability to

KEYSTONE B-4A
Pratt & Whitney R-1860-7, 575 hp at s. l.
DIMENSIONS: As B-3A
WEIGHT: Empty 7951 lb., Gross 13,209 lb. Fuel 235–535
gal.
PERFORMANCE: Speed—Top 121 mph at s. l., Cruising 103
mph, Landing 57 mph. Service Ceiling 14,000', Climb
690'/1 min., 5000'/8.6 min. Range 855 miles.   MFR

KEYSTONE B-6A
Wright R-1820-1, 575 hp
DIMENSIONS: As B-3A
WEIGHT: Empty 8057 lb., Gross 13,334 lb., Fuel 235–535
gal.
PERFORMANCE: Speed—Top 121 mph at s. l., 116 mph at
5000', Cruising 103 mph, Landing 57 mph. Service
Ceiling 14,100', Absolute Ceiling 16,500', Climb 690'/
1 min., 5000'/8.6 min. Range 363 miles/2500 lbs.
bombs, 825 miles maximum.   AF

defend themselves were no greater than that of their predecessors, if their top speed reflected only that improvement bestowed by more hp, then airmen might explain the limited technical advance by asking, "What would have happened to the au-tomobile if the railroads had controlled its development?" A better excuse was that fabric-covered biplanes could go just so fast and just so far, but no farther.

KEYSTONE (*close-up*)   AF

Chapter 4
The First Fighter Planes, 1915–20

The Gun and the Plane

The early history of aerial warfare was leisurely and unspectacular. A routine of trips across the lines for scouting and artillery spotting was only occasionally interrupted by picayune bombing raids. The first attack by one aircraft against another has not been definitely recorded, but there were awkward engagements between reconnaissance pilots who fired pistols, rifles, and crudely mounted machine guns. The French were the most aggressive, killing a German flier with pistol shots on August 26, 1914. On October 5 an Aviatik was downed by a machine gun mounted on a Voison two-seater pusher.

The tractor plane, with its propeller facing forward, was more efficient, but how could a machine gun be mounted to avoid hitting the propeller? Roland Garros fired his machine gun forward through his Morane single-seat monoplane's propeller. Metal deflector blades on the wooden propeller blades repelled those bullets that struck them.

When Garros and his Morane were captured by the Germans in April 1915, Anthony Fokker was asked to make a response. Fokker's answer was the E I, the single-seat monoplane armed with a 7.9-mm gun synchronized to fire through the propeller by a mechanical interrupter gear. These Fokkers were the first true fighter planes. They made their first kill on July 1, 1915, and in a few months they became known as the "Fokker Scourge" that destroyed many Allied planes that dared to cross the German lines.

The French answer to the Fokker was the Nieuport 11, a tiny biplane with a Lewis gun mounted on the top wing that fired over the propeller. This type became the principal Allied fighter in 1915 and was the fighter issued to the first American fighter pilots in the war, the volunteers of the Lafayette Escadrille. That famous squadron arrived at the front on April 20, 1916, and scored their first

victory on May 18, flying the Nieuport 11 *chasse*, or pursuit plane.

Since the Nieuport 11 was the mount of the first American fighter pilots and the first successful Allied fighter, its specifications are quoted here as a starting point for the measurement of fighter progress. It was called a sesquiplane since the narrow lower wing was about half the size of the upper one, with V struts between them. An 80-hp Gnome or Le Rhone rotary gave a top speed of 97 mph, and the Lewis gun had a drum with 47 rounds.

In 1916–17 the Nieuport fighter went through a rapid development when models 16, 17, 21, 23, 24, and 27 introduced increases in horsepower, larger and stronger structures, and replaced the Lewis gun with a synchronized, belt-fed Vickers. Most of these

NIEUPORT 11
Gnome "A," 80 hp
DIMENSIONS: Span 24'6", Lg. 19', Ht. 8', Wing Area 140 sq. ft.
WEIGHT: Empty 759 lb., Gross 1210 lb. Fuel 21 gal.
PERFORMANCE: Speed—Top 97 mph at s. l., landing 30 mph. Service Ceiling 15,000', Climb 3280'/5 min., 6500'/11 min. Endurance 2 hrs.   MA

models were used by the Lafayette Escadrille until the French Army selected the Spad as its standard fighter.

Fighters in the AEF

When the AEF arrived in France, it trained its future fighter pilots on a batch of 872 old-model Nieuports. The idea was that pilot proficiency would increase with the power of the planes tried. The first fighter used in combat by the AEF was the more advanced Nieuport 28, which had already been rejected by the French in favor of the Spad.

The first 36 Nieuport 28s were turned over to the Americans in March 1918, but the lack of guns delayed their entrance into combat until April 14, when two 94th Aero Squadron pilots scored the first American Army fighter victories of World War I. By the end of May, all four squadrons of the 1st Pursuit Group were at the front, and they continued to use Nieuports until Spads began arriving in July.

The Nieuport 28's Gnome had nine cylinders spinning around until the two-hour fuel supply ran out. Two Vickers guns were mounted on the left side of the cowl and the wing struts were straight instead of vee-shaped. The AEF had 297 of this type, but the Nieuport's reputation for wing failures led the Americans to quickly discard the type when Spads were available.

Spad fighters had a Hispano-Suiza water-cooled eight-cylinder inline engine behind a rounded radiator, with equal-span wings strengthened by a second pair of articulated struts between the fuselage and the outer struts. The first model used by the French was the Spad 7, which had a 180-hp direct-drive Hispano-Suiza 8A and a single Vickers gun. By August 1917 the heavier Spad 13, with two guns and a geared 220-hp Hispano-Suiza 8B, was at the front.

The Lafayette Escadrille was using Spad 13s when it became the Army's 103rd Aero Squadron in February 1918, and the first Spad 13 was ferried in to the 1st Pursuit Group on July 5 by Eddie Rickenbacker. During the last four months of the war, Rickenbacker, Frank Luke, and other AEF pilots made the robust French fighter part of the American military mystique. By the war's end 15 of the 16 AEF pursuit squadrons at the front used the Spad 13. Of 189 Spad 7s and 893 Spad 13s acquired by the Air Service, 58 Spad 7s and 435 Spad 13s were shipped to the United States for postwar work. Post-Armistice forces in Europe until April 1919 included two Spad 7 and six Spad 13 squadrons.

Two .303-caliber (7.7-mm) Vickers synchronized guns were mounted over the Spad 13's engine and provided with 800 rounds, but in the United States, Marlin guns were substituted for the Vickers. There were various models of the Hispano-Suiza, the 220-

NIEUPORT 28
Gnome 9N, 155 hp
DIMENSIONS: Span 26'9", Lg. 21', Ht. 8'1", Wing Area 172 sq. ft.
WEIGHT: Empty 961 lb., Gross 1539 lb. Fuel 33 gal.
PERFORMANCE: Speed—Top 128 mph at s. l., 123 mph at 6500'. Service Ceiling 19,685', Climb 6500'/5.3 min. Endurance 2 hrs.   AF

SPAD 13
Hispano-Suiza 8BEc, 235 hp (Wright-Hispano 8Ba, 220 hp on U.S.A. test)
DIMENSIONS: Span 26'4", Lg. 20'4", Ht. 7'6", Wing Area 227 sq. ft.
WEIGHT: Empty 1255 lb. (1464 lb.), Gross 1811 lb. (2036 lb.). Fuel 30 gal.
PERFORMANCE: Speed—Top 138.5 (131.5) mph at s. l., 135 (128) mph at 6500', Cruising (124.5 mph), Landing 59 mph. Service Ceiling 22,300' (18,400'), Climb 6500'/4.7 min. (6.5 min.). Endurance 2.5 hrs.   AF

hp or 235-hp geared versions being used in the AEF, while the 180-hp direct-drive model available in the United States was preferred for postwar flying because it was less troublesome. Numerous variations in detail appeared in the Spad series, which accounts for the variety of specifications given for this type. For example, wingtip modification reduced the wing area from 227 to 217 square feet, and wingspan was slightly reduced accordingly. The specifications given here are for a typical AEF version, compared with a lighter configuration tested at McCook Field in April 1921.

At the same time the French had introduced the Spad 13, they had tested, in small quantities, the similar Spad 12, incorporating the first cannon on a single-seat fighter. Armament consisted of one Vickers .303-caliber machine gun and a 37-mm cannon mounted to fire through the propeller shaft of a geared 220-hp Hispano 8C. Fourteen rounds of ammunition were carried for the single-shot, hand-loaded cannon. The French ace Captain René Fonck downed seven Germans with the experimental weapon, but felt handloading an inconvenient distraction. A single example of the Spad 12 went to the Americans in July 1918.

American fighter pilots trained by the British went into action on the British sector of the front using British fighters. Of these, by far the most famous was the Sopwith Camel, which had appeared at the front in July 1917 as the first Allied fighter with two synchronized guns. Most often powered by a 130-hp Clerget rotary engine and armed with two .303-caliber Vickers guns under the hump, and racks for four 20-pound bombs, the Camel was very maneuverable but was considered dangerous and tricky to fly. It has been credited with more victories than any other Allied fighter plane of that war, despite a relatively low top speed.

SOPWITH CAMEL F-1
Clerget 9-Bc, 130 hp
DIMENSIONS: Span 28′, Lg. 18′8″, Ht. 8′6″, Wing Area 231 sq. ft.
WEIGHT: Empty 929 lb., Gross 1453 lb. Fuel 31.5 gal.
PERFORMANCE: Speed—Top 115 mph at 6500′, 113 mph at 10,000′. Service Ceiling 19,000′, Climb 6500′/6 min. Range 300 miles. Endurance 2.5 hrs.   AF—PMB

The two AEF Camel Squadrons were the 17th and the 148th. Both squadrons were involved in hard fighting, the latter scoring the first kill on July 13, 1918, and George Vaughn became the leading American Camel ace by scoring 13 victories. During 1918 the AEF received 143 Camels. While the 17th and 148th Camel Squadrons turned theirs in for Spads on November 1, 1918, the 41st Aero Squadron used Camels for post-Armistice duties.

Another famous British fighter used by Americans was the Royal Aircraft Factory's S.E.5A which had a 200-hp geared Hispano-Suiza 8B, nose radiator, one synchronized Vickers over the engine, and one Lewis gun on the upper wing. Although the S.E.5A was used in large numbers by the British, only 38 were acquired by the AEF in October 1918. They were issued to the 25th Aero Squadron, whose arrival at the front on November 1 was too late for combat, but its leader, Reed Landis, had scored ten victories flying the S.E.5A with the RAF. Back in the United States, however, the S.E.5A played a small role in America's efforts to manufacture its own fighters.

Native Single-Seaters

No American-designed single-seat fighters were delivered during the 19 months of war. Although several low-powered single-seaters were produced—such as the Curtiss S-3, Standard E-1, Heinrich "Pursuit," Thomas-Morse S-4, and Orenco C—all were unarmed trainers. American-designed fighters were officially foregone in favor of tested foreign types.

The Spad had been selected for production in America by the Bolling Commission on July 30, 1917, but a sample aircraft did not arrive until September 18, and Curtiss received an order for 3,000 on October 8, 1917. This order was canceled because a suitable power plant could not be produced in time. The Hispano-Suiza had been licensed for production by the Wright-Martin Company on behalf of the French, but production deliveries beginning in November 1917 were of the 150-hp Model A, suitable only for trainers. By the time the 180-hp model appeared in August 1918, the geared 235-hp version was being used in Europe, and an American 300-hp unit was not available in quantity until 1919. As for the Liberty 12, that big engine could not be fitted into any existing single-seater. Cancellation of the U.S. Spad program meant the AEF would depend entirely upon its Allies for fighters.

After much rivalry among the Allied military missions on behalf of their own designs, Curtiss received a contract on June 8, 1918, for 1,000 S.E.5 trainers equipped with the 180-hp Wright-Hispano. Only one example was completed in August, using the first of these engines, but the Armistice canceled the rest. To fill the gap until U.S. production got under way, 56 S.E.5A airframes had been imported from Britain for assembly by Curtiss on an August 23, 1918, contract. Curtiss delivered one in September, three in October, 13 by the year's end, and the rest in 1919, all with the Wright-Hispano engines.

In 1922–23, 50 more planes, known as the S.E.5E

pursuit-trainers, were built with plywood fuselages by Eberhardt. The specification provided here gives the test results of the first Curtiss S.E.5A, along with a photograph of an Eberhardt version.

As far as American designs are concerned, the only single-seater available when the United States entered the war was the Curtiss Scout offered to the Army in 1916. After tentative tries with an S-1 and S-2 biplane, in October Curtiss tested an S-3 triplane with a 100-hp OX-2 and big spinner. Four were ordered November 20, 1916, and delivered, without spinner or guns, in June and July 1917. A later one, the S-6, was tested with a pair of forward-firing Lewis guns.

These scouts were not up to the standards for combat on the western front, and neither were several unarmed single-seat prototypes ordered with American-built 100-hp Gnome rotaries. They included the Victor Aircraft Corporation's "Pursuit," a neatly streamlined biplane design by Albert S. Heinrich, ordered April 11, 1917, and delivered in December; the obscure Pigeon Fraser monoplane, delivered in September 1917; and the Nieuport-like Schiefer-Robbins,[1] purchased from a San Diego furniture firm in January 1918. Despite the manufacturer's claims, these were essentially only trainers.

While none of these light single-seaters passed the prototype stage, the Thomas-Morse S-4, first tested in June 1917, was successful. The Air Sevice realized that for cadet pilots to jump from the "Jenny" to a high-powered pursuit was too much, and so 100 Thomas-Morse S-4Bs were ordered on October 3, 1917, as pursuit-trainers. Designed by a British immigrant, B. D. Thomas, and using the 100-hp Gnome, they were delivered from November 1917 to May 1918, and were followed by 50 S-4Cs with modified controls. The Gnome engine proved unsatisfactory, and the 80-hp Le Rhone was substituted in June 1918 for the remaining 447 S-4Cs completed when production ended in December 1918.

The "Tommy" became well known to would-be fighter pilots. Although sometimes fitted with a Marlin gun for target practice, it was a trainer, not a fighter, and is included here because of its close association with pursuit aviation. In the same vein was the Standard E-1, a double-bay biplane of which two prototypes delivered in January and April 1918 had Gnomes, while of 126 production E-1s between August and December 1918, 30 had Gnomes and the rest had 80-hp Le Rhones. Quite similar were six Le Rhone-powered Orenco Cs delivered from June to November 1918.

<hr>

[1] Schiefer, not Schaefer, is the correct spelling. Nova Robbins was the designer.

EBERHARDT S.E.5E
Wright-Hispano E, 180 hp
DIMENSIONS: Span 26′9″, Lg. 20′10″, Ht. 10′, Wing Area 247 sq. ft.
WEIGHT: Empty 1486 lb., Gross 2060 lb. Fuel 35 gal.
PERFORMANCE: Speed—Top 122 mph at s. l., 120 mph at 6500′. Service Ceiling 20,400′, Climb 6500′/8 min. Range 280 miles at top speed.   PMB

CURTISS S-3   PMB

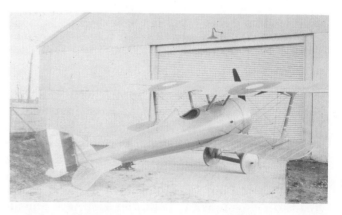

VICTOR PURSUIT   AF

SCHIEFER PURSUIT   SDAM

THOMAS-MORSE S-4C
Le Rhone, 80 hp
DIMENSIONS: Span 26′6″, Lg. 19′10″, Ht. 8′1″, Wing Area
   234 sq. ft.
WEIGHT: Empty 963 lb., Gross 1373 lb. Fuel 27 gal.
PERFORMANCE: Speed—Top 95 mph. Service Ceiling
   15,000′, Climb 7500′/10 min.   PMB

STANDARD E-1
Le Rhone, 80 hp
DIMENSIONS: Span 24′, Lg. 18′11″, Ht. 7′10″, Wing Area
   153 sq. ft.
WEIGHT: Empty 828 lb., Gross 1144 lb. Fuel 17 gal.
PERFORMANCE: Speed—Top 100 mph at s. l., 85 mph at
   10,000′, Absolute Ceiling 14,800′, Climb 6000′/10 min.
   Endurance 2 hrs.   PMB

ORENCO D PROTOTYPE
Hispano-Suiza H, 300 hp
DIMENSIONS: Span 30', Lg. 21'6", Ht. 7'9", Wing Area 261 sq. ft.
WEIGHT: Empty 1776 lb., Gross 2432 lb. Fuel 55 gal.
PERFORMANCE: Speed—Top 147 mph at s. l., 142 mph at 6500', Cruising 139 mph, Landing 56 mph. Service Ceiling 22,000', Absolute Ceiling 23,600', Climb 6500'/5.2 min. Endurance 2.5 hrs. at 139 mph.   AMC

CURTISS-ORENCO D
Wright H, 330 hp
DIMENSIONS: Span 33', Lg. 21'5½", Ht. 8'4", Wing Area 273 sq. ft.
WEIGHT: Empty 1908 lb., Gross 2820 lb. Fuel 53 gal.
PERFORMANCE: Speed—Top 139.5 mph at s. l., 136 mph at 6500', Cruising 133.5 mph, Landing 64.5 mph. Service Ceiling 18,450', Absolute Ceiling 20,250', Climb 1140'/1 min., 6500'/6.9 min. Endurance 2.5 hrs.   AMC

POMILIO FVL-8
Liberty 8, 290 hp
DIMENSIONS: Span 26'8", Lg. 21'8", Ht. 8'2", Wing Area 284 sq. ft.
WEIGHT: Empty 1726 lb., Gross 2284 lb. Fuel 40 gal.
PERFORMANCE: Speed—Top 133 mph at s. l.   AMC

VOUGHT VE-8
Wright-Hispano H, 338 hp
DIMENSIONS: Span 31', Lg. 21'4", Ht. 8'8", Wing Area 307 sq. ft.
WEIGHT: Empty 1764 lb., Gross 2657 lb. Fuel 68 gal.
PERFORMANCE: Speed—Top 127.5 mph at s. l., 121 mph at 10,000'. Service Ceiling 18,400', Absolute Ceiling 20,250', Climb 6500'/7.2 min. Endurance 3.8 hrs., Range 460 miles.   AMC

Not until after the Armistice did completed single-seat fighters of U.S. design appear. First was the Orenco D of January 1919. Four were built by the Ordnance Engineering Corporation from an Army Engineering Division design. Powered by a 300-hp Wright-Hispano H, this double-bay biplane had a plywood fuselage, one-piece elevator, and had "good flying qualities," according to the test pilot, handling better than the Spad and other rival fighters. Fifty production models with balanced ailerons were built by Curtiss, the first being flown on November 10, 1920.

Two other single-seat fighters of 1919 failed to win production contracts. The Pomilio FVL-8 was designed by an Italian engineer at McCook around the eight-cylinder version of the Liberty. A plywood fuselage hung above the lower wing and a four-bladed propeller were distinctive features. The first of six FVL-8s was delivered in February. More conventional was the Lewis & Vought VE-8, a double-bay biplane with a Wright-Hispano and the top wing close to the fuselage top. The first of four ordered was delivered in July 1919, but flight tests showed it to be too sluggish for a fighter.

The most successful single-seater of this period—and the one finally selected to equip all postwar Army pursuit squadrons—was the Thomas-Morse MB-3, designed by B. D. Thomas. Four prototypes were ordered from the Ithaca, New York, company in September 1918, and the first was flown on February 21, 1919, with the 300-hp Wright-Hispano. Performance was so superior to the S.E.5s and Spads then being used by the Air Service that 50 more MB-3s were ordered June 19, 1920. They were delivered in 1921, followed by 11 built for the Marine Corps in February 1922.

At that time all military designs became Army property and bidding on production contracts was open. Thomas-Morse was underbid by other firms,

with Boeing winning a contract for 200 MB-3As at $1,455,740 ($7,279 each) in April 1921. It would be the largest pursuit contract until 1937 and placed Boeing firmly into Army business.

Delivered between July and December 1922, the MB-3A differed from the original in many details. Its radiator, moved from the upper wing, was split and placed on either side of the fuselage. The vertical fin was redesigned. While the MB-3's two .30-caliber guns had been exposed, the MB-3A's Brownings were under a fairing. One of the .30s could be replaced by a .50-caliber gun when desired, an arrangement standard on Army fighters up to World War II. Although performance of the MB-3A was good, visibility was hampered by the upper wing. In March 1923 one was fitted with a 37-gallon belly fuel tank—the first in the United States—which extended the range to 400 miles.

All eight Army pursuit squadrons of this period used the MB-3A. Four squadrons made up the 1st Pursuit Group, which was to remain at Selfridge Field, Michigan, from July 1, 1922, to December 8, 1941. Two squadrons were stationed in Hawaii, one in the Philippines, and one in the Canal Zone, a deployment that reflects American defense posture at the time. After the Curtiss Hawk became the standard Army fighter in 1926, the MB-3As were gradually retired to Kelly Field, Texas, home of the tactical training school.

THOMAS-MORSE MB-3
Hispano H, 300 hp
DIMENSIONS: Span 26', Lg. 20', Ht. 8'6", Wing Area 250.5 sq. ft.
WEIGHT: Empty 1506 lb., Gross 2094 lb. Fuel 41 gal.
PERFORMANCE: Speed—Top 152 mph at s. l., 148 mph at 6500', Cruising 144 mph, Landing 58 mph. Service Ceiling 23,700', Absolute Ceiling 24,900', Climb 1930'/1 min., 6500'/3.9 min. Range 288 miles.   AMC

BOEING MB-3A
Wright H-3, 300 hp
DIMENSIONS: Span 26', Lg. 20', Ht. 8'7", Wing Area 229 sq. ft.
WEIGHT: Empty 1716 lb., Gross 2539 lb. Fuel 45 gal.
PERFORMANCE: Speed—Top 141 mph at s. l., 138 mph at 6500', Cruising 125 mph, Landing 55 mph. Service Ceiling 19,500', Absolute Ceiling 21,200', Climb 1235'/1 min., 6500'/6.7 min. Endurance 2 hrs. 15 min.   AF

Two-seat Fighters

The American aircraft industry actually had more luck during World War I with two-seat fighter designs than with single-seaters. Several prototypes were flown in 1918.

These designs found their main inspiration in England's Bristol Fighter, a double-bay biplane with a 275-hp Rolls-Royce engine, pilot and gunner back to back, and fuselage suspended between the wings. It entered the war in April 1917 with two fixed Vickers guns and two flexible Lewis guns. Its excellent maneuverability made the Bristol quite successful against enemy fighters. The combination of the front guns with the rear guns for tail protection helped Canadian ace Major Andrew E. McKeever win 30 victories and established the two-seater biplane as a standard fighter type.

A sample Bristol arrived in the United States on September 5, 1917. Immediately the Americans tried to redesign it for use with the "United States Standard Aircraft Engine," as the Liberty 12 was called. Curtiss received a contract on November 3 to produce 1,000 (later increased to 2,000) Liberty-powered Bristols. Armament was to be two Marlin fixed guns and two Lewis flexible guns. The first Curtiss-Bristol to use the Liberty engine began flight tests on March 5, 1918. While the British Bristol had done 119 mph with a weight of 2,779 pounds, the Curtiss version was supposed to do 138 mph at 2,937 pounds. The actual weight came to 3,600 pounds, making the engine too heavy for the airframe.

It was also unsafe, for the second example crashed on May 5, another on June 10, and a third on July 12. On July 20, 1918, the Curtiss-Bristol program was canceled—only 27 aircraft had been completed—and the factory then concentrated on the S.E.5 program.

An alternate program with lighter engines was initiated, beginning with the USB-1 (United States Bristol), actually the first imported Bristol airframe powered with the first 300-hp Wright-Hispano, test-flown on July 4, 1918. A second imported Bristol with the Liberty 8, the USB-2, was readied but crashed on September 6, 1918.

The Engineering Division developed a new plywood fuselage that was both stronger and lighter, and this was used on four XB-1A prototypes powered by the 360-hp Wright-Hispano and armed with two Browning and two Lewis guns. While the first flight on July 3, 1919, had missed the war, 40 XB-1As were ordered on June 28, 1920, from Dayton-Wright, with more fuel in leakproof tanks, and they were used in 1921–22 by the 12th Observation and 13th Attack squadrons in Texas.

Captain Gene LePere had been loaned to the

CURTISS-BRISTOL FIGHTER (LIBERTY 12)   MFR

ENGINEERING DIV. USB-1
Hispano H, 300 hp
DIMENSIONS: Span 39'4", Lg. 25'5", Ht. 8'3", Wing Area 403 sq. ft.
WEIGHT: Empty 1842 lb., Gross 2910 lb. Fuel 53 gal.
PERFORMANCE: Speed—Top 114.5 mph at s. l. "Theoretical Ceiling" 25,000', Climb 6500'/3.5 min.   MFR

Engineering Division by the French Government, and his first project was a two-seat fighter designed around the Liberty 12 and armed with two Marlin and two Lewis guns. The first LUSAC-11 prototype made its first flight on May 15, 1918, at McCook Field and the businesslike biplane looked promising enough to warrant ordering 25 LUSAC-11s from Packard on June 15, 1918.

Packard delivered two LePeres in September 1918 and five in October. By October 23, 3,500 had been ordered from Fisher, Packard, and Brewster, but these contracts ended with the war. Packard did produce 25 planes by 1919, along with three LUSAC-21s (similar, but with the experimental Bugatti engine) and apparently five prototypes from McCook. Two of the Packard planes went to France in time for a flight on November 4, 1918—the only U.S.-designed Army planes there for World War I. One still hangs in the Musée de l'Air, possibly the oldest American combat plane surviving in its original condition. One prototype at McCook Field became the first U.S. plane to test an exhaust-driven turbosupercharger, beginning in September 1919. Several altitude records were set, including a flight to 34,508 feet on September 28, 1921.

ENGINEERING DIVISION XB-1A
Wright-Hispano H, 300 hp
DIMENSIONS: Span 39'4", Lg. 25'6", Ht. 9'9", Wing Area
   406 sq. ft.
WEIGHT: Empty 2010 lb., Gross 2994 lb. Fuel 54 gal.
PERFORMANCE: Speed—Top 124 mph at s. l., 121 mph at
   6500', Cruising 118 mph, Landing 59 mph. Service
   Ceiling 20,900', Climb 6500'/7.8 min. Endurance 2.4
   hrs.   AF

DAYTON-WRIGHT XB-1A
Wright-Hispano H, 330 hp
DIMENSIONS: Span 39'4", Lg. 25'6", Ht. 9'10", Wing Area
   406 sq. ft.
WEIGHT: Empty 2155 lb., Gross 3791 lb. Fuel 100 gal.
PERFORMANCE: Speed—Top 130 mph, Cruising 101 mph.
   Service Ceiling 18,900', Absolute Ceiling 21,000',
   Climb 6500'/7.5 min. Range 495 miles at 125
   mph.   AMC

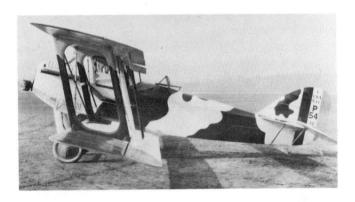

PACKARD-LEPERE LUSAC-11
Liberty 12, 425 hp
DIMENSIONS: Span 41'7", Lg. 25'3", Ht. 10'7", Wing Area
   415 sq. ft.
WEIGHT: Empty 2561 lb., Gross 3746 lb. Fuel 73 gal.
PERFORMANCE: Speed—Top 133 mph at s. l., 130 mph at
   6500', Cruising 118 mph, Landing 50 mph. Service
   Ceiling 20,200', Absolute Ceiling 21,500', Climb 6500'/
   6 min. Range 320 miles.   AMC

PACKARD-LEPERE LUSAC-11 (with first U.S. turbo-supercharger)   AF

A 300-hp Wright-Hispano H powered the remarkable Loening M-8, the first American monoplane fighter. The wings were joined to the top of
a narrow fuselage and braced by struts underneath,
leaving the upper field of fire clear for the observer's Lewis guns. Two Marlin guns were
mounted at the engine's sides, above a neat tunnel
radiator. Careful design reduced the time required
to produce the type. Ordered in March 1918, the
M-8 was first flown in August. Two went to the
Army before the Armistice ended plans to put the
Loening into production, but six were ordered as

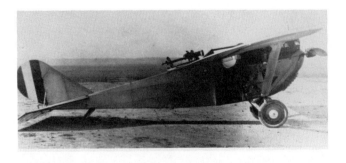

LOENING M-8
Wright-Hispano H, 300 hp
DIMENSIONS: Span 32'9", Lg. 24', Ht. 8'4", Wing Area 215
   sq. ft.
WEIGHT: Empty 1663 lb., Gross 2639 lb. Fuel 55 gal.
PERFORMANCE: Speed—Top 143.5 mph at s. l., 138 mph
   at 6500', Landing 58 mph. Service Ceiling 18,600',
   Absolute Ceiling 19,900', Climb 6500'/5.2 min., 10,-
   000'/9.2 min. Endurance 2 hrs. at top speed.   AMC

observation planes by the Navy in June 1919.

Three other two-seaters built in 1918 were powered by the 400-hp Liberty 12, but little is known about them. The Engineering Division's USAC-1 of October 1918 was a large, overweight biplane, while the Thomas-Morse MB-1 was a light, high-wing monoplane braced by a wide strut. Efforts to keep the MB-1 light were a bit extreme, for the machine collapsed while being taxied out for flight trials. The Ithaca, New York, firm tried again with the MB-2 biplane of November 1918, but there is no evidence that this ship completed flight tests either. It should be mentioned, however, that Thomas-Morse was more successful with its MB-3 single-seater.

In 1918 Curtiss designed its own two-seater fighter with the Liberty engine and biplane wings so close together that the top wing was level with the laminated wood-veneer fuselage top. This gave the observer a good fire field, but the pilot's view down was poor. Known as the CB ("Curtiss Battleplane"), the machine crashed during testing, and

no specifications have been located.

Far better flying qualities were obtained by the Curtiss two-seater, designed for the Navy with a 350-hp Curtiss Kirkham K-12. After borrowing a Navy prototype in August 1918, the Army ordered its own examples. The first appeared in February 1919 as the 18-T, a triplane, and in June 1919 the 18-B biplane version was completed; two of each were built. The triplane 18-T set a new U.S. altitude record of 32,450 feet in August 1919.

World War I had provided American fighter pilots with a pattern for future development. The well-liked Spad was superseded in the postwar period by the MB-3A, which followed the same general arrangement. The two-seater fighter, however, was not incorporated into the postwar air service in spite of the success of the wartime Bristol and the promising Loening monoplane. The dozen years following the war saw the production of a great variety of types—the fighter was cheaper and easier to build than the bomber—but only a small technical advance over the wartime tradition was evident.

THOMAS-MORSE MB-1
Liberty 12, 400 hp
DIMENSIONS: Span 37′, Lg. 22′.
WEIGHT: Gross 2375 lb.
PERFORMANCE: Never flown.   MFR

CURTISS 18-T
Kirkham K-12, 350 hp
DIMENSIONS: Span 31′11″, Lg. 23′4″, Ht. 9′10″, Wing Area 309 sq. ft.
WEIGHT: Empty 1724 lb., Gross 2901 lb.
PERFORMANCE: Speed—Top 151 mph at s. l., 145 mph at 10,000′, Landing 58 mph. Service Ceiling 22,000′, Climb 10,000′/6.9 min. Endurance 1¾ hrs.   MFR

CURTISS 18-B
Kirkham K-12, 350 hp
DIMENSIONS: Span 37′6″, Lg. 23′4″, Wing Area 306 sq. ft.
WEIGHT: Empty 1690 lb., Gross 2867 lb. Fuel 53 gal.
PERFORMANCE: Not Available.   MFR

THOMAS-MORSE MB-2
Liberty 12, 400 hp
DIMENSIONS: Span 31′, Lg. 24′, Ht. 8′, Wing Area 323 sq. ft.
WEIGHT: Empty 2047 lb., Gross 2773 lb. Fuel 50 gal.
PERFORMANCE: Not available.   AMC

Chapter 5
Army Pursuits: The Biplane Period, 1920–32

Postwar Experiments

Between 1921 and 1923 a great variety of single-seaters were tested by the Air Service to explore the directions future fighter design might take. None were ordered in quantity, but several supplied data of value for later machines.

The first single-seat fighter of the postwar generation was the VCP-1, designed by Alfred Verville and V. L. Clark of the Engineering Division. Powered by a 300-hp Wright-Hispano, it had a laminated wood-veneer fuselage and tapered wings, with I struts and balanced ailerons on the lower surfaces.

Two examples were ordered, the first for static tests and the second for flying; and this prototype system was followed on most of the subsequent fighter designs. The first VCP-1 was delivered for the sand-bag ordeal in August 1919, and the second began flight trials on June 11, 1920. Different nose radiators were tried.

Increased speed was the chief objective of pursuit development then, and a practical way of pushing development was for the air services themselves to participate in the air racing so prominent that decade. By August 1920 the new fighter had been refitted with a 660-hp Packard 1A-2025 V-12. Called the VCP-R, it won the first Pulitzer Prize Race in November, beating standard MB-3 and Orenco D entrants. The Verville was rebuilt as the R-1 for the 1922 Pulitzer, but it was eclipsed by the speeds attained by the Curtiss R-6.

A whole series of "R" ships were flown with greater or lesser success to gain experience with "hi-speed" flight. Most unique was a Dayton-Wright XPS-1, a high-wing parasol monoplane ordered on June 29, 1921, and first delivered in November 1922 with a 200-hp Lawrance J-1 radial and one of the first retractable wheel arrangements. The wheels folded up into the fuselage, as on the Grummans a decade later.

VERMILLE VCP-1
Wright-Hispano H, 300 hp
DIMENSIONS: Span 32′, Lg. 22′6″, Ht. 8′4″, Wing Area 269 sq. ft.
WEIGHT: Empty 2014 lb., Gross 2669 lb. Fuel 41 gal.
PERFORMANCE: Speed—Top 154 mph at s. l., 152 mph at 6500′, Cruising 149 mph, Landing 61.5 mph. Service Ceiling 25,400′, Absolute Ceiling 27,000′, Climb 1690′/1 min., 6500′/4.4 min. Range 298 miles.   AMC

VERVILLE VCP-R   AF

DAYTON-WRIGHT XPS-1   AMC

CURTISS PN-1
Liberty 6, L-825, 220 hp
DIMENSIONS: Span 30′10″, Lg. 23′6″, Ht. 10′3″, Wing Area
   300 sq. ft.
WEIGHT: Empty 1631 lb., Gross 2311 lb. Fuel 53 gal.
PERFORMANCE: Speed—Top 108 mph. Service Ceiling
   23,900′, Absolute Ceiling 25,600′, Climb 6500′/5.5 min.
   Range 255 miles at top speed.   AMC

LOENING PA-1
Wright R-1 (R-1454), 350 hp
DIMENSIONS: Span 28′, Lg. 19′9″, Ht. 8′8″, Wing Area 283
   sq. ft.
WEIGHT: Empty 1536 lb., Gross 2463 lb. Fuel 69 gal.
PERFORMANCE: Speed—Top 130 mph at s. l., 124 mph at
   10,000′. Service Ceiling 19,200′, Absolute Ceiling
   21,000′, Climb 6500′/7 min.   AMC

ENGINEERING DIV. PW-1
Packard 1A-1237, 350 hp
DIMENSIONS: Span 32′, Lg. 22′6″, Ht. 8′4″, Wing Area 269
   sq. ft.
WEIGHT: Empty 2069 lb., Gross 3005 lb. Fuel 61.5 gal.
PERFORMANCE: Speed—Top 146 mph at s. l., 144 mph at
   6500′, Cruising 131.5 mph, Landing 65 mph. Service
   Ceiling 19,300′, Absolute Ceiling 21,000′, Climb 10,-
   000′/11 min. Endurance 2.5 hrs. at 131.5 mph.   AMC

ENGINEERING DIV. PW-1A
Packard 1A-1237, 350 hp
DIMENSIONS: Span 31′2″, Lg. 22′6″, Ht. 8′10″, Wing Area
   288 sq. ft.
WEIGHT: Empty 2139 lb., Gross 3075 lb. Fuel 61.5 gal.
PERFORMANCE: Speed—Top 134 mph at s. l., 133 mph at
   6500′, Cruising 115.5 mph. Service Ceiling 17,200′,
   Absolute Ceiling 18,800′, Climb 10,000′/12.3 min. En-
   durance 2.5 hrs. at 115.5 mph.   AMC

In September 1920 the Army adopted a system of aircraft designation to replace the previous confusion of builders' letters and numbers. The new system provided for PW, PA, and PN types (pursuit, water-cooled; pursuit, air-cooled; and pursuit, night). The heavy PG-1 (pursuit ground) has already been discussed in connection with attack planes (see Chapter 2).

The only example of the specialized night fighter was the Curtiss PN-1 biplane, with a 220-hp Liberty L-825 (six cylinder) engine, long exhaust pipes, and an overhanging upper wing with balanced ailerons. The theory behind this design seems to have been to get a low-wing loading for easy operation out of small blacked-out wartime fields. Since the top speed was barely above that of the bombers it was supposed to stop, only two such planes were built. The static-test article of November 1920 had cantilever wings, but N struts were added to the second PN-1, delivered in August 1921.

The contract to build the Army's first fighter with an air-cooled radial attracted nine bidders on November 15, 1920. Loening won the right to build the PA-1 with a Wright R-1454, and delivered a single example in April 1922. The gas tank in the thick upper wing allowed a shorter fuselage for quick turns. The only other air-cooled fighter tested (in July 1921) was an imported British Aerial Transport F.K. 23 "Bantam," a very light design by Koolhoven, with a monocoque fuselage and a 184-hp A.B.C. Wasp A radial.

The first fighter under the "pursuit, water-cooled" designation was the biplane designed by Alfred Verville for the Engineering Division. Originally called the VCP-2, the PW-1 had a tunnel radiator below the Packard 1A-1237, a fuselage of fabric-covered, welded steel tubing, the tapered I strut wings of the VCP-1, droppable fuel tank beneath the cockpit, and two Browning guns. The flight article was tested in November 1921 and soon

LOENING PW-2
Wright H, 320 hp
DIMENSIONS: Span 39′8″, Lg. 24′2″, Ht. 9′, Wing Area 287 sq. ft.
WEIGHT: Empty 1876 lb., Gross 2788 lb. Fuel 59 gal.
PERFORMANCE: Speed—Top 132 mph at s. l., 131 mph at 6500′, 127.5 mph at 10,000′, Cruising 120.5 mph, Landing 61 mph. Service Ceiling 20,000′, Absolute Ceiling 21,800′, Climb 6500′/6.2 min., 10,000′/10.6 min. Range 301 miles.   AMC

LOENING PW-2A
Wright H, 322 hp
DIMENSIONS: Span 39′9″, Lg. 26′1/2″, Ht. 8′1″, Wing Area 299 sq. ft.
WEIGHT: Empty 1876 lb., Gross 2799 lb. Fuel 60 gal.
PERFORMANCE: Speed—Top 136 mph at s. l., 133.5 mph at 6500′, 131 mph at 10,000′, Cruising 125 mph, Landing 63 mph. Service Ceiling 21,400′, Absolute Ceiling 23,000′, Climb 1340′/1 min., 10,000′/9.8 min. Endurance 2.5 hrs.   AF

LOENING PW-2B
Packard 1A-1237, 352 hp
DIMENSIONS: Span 34′1″, Lg. 23′4″, Ht. 8′1″, Wing Area 225 sq. ft.
WEIGHT: Empty 2040 lb., Gross 2976 lb. Fuel 61 gal.
PERFORMANCE: Speed—Top 140 mph at s. l., 137 mph at 6500′, Cruising 134 mph, Landing 71 mph. Service Ceiling 17,150′, Absolute Ceiling 18,600′, Climb 6500′/6.1 min., 10,000′/11 min. Endurance 2¾ hrs.   AMC

ORENCO PW-3
Wright H, 320 hp
DIMENSIONS: Span 27′9″, Lg. 23′10″, Ht. 8′1″, Wing Area 240 sq. ft.
WEIGHT: Empty 1870 lb., Gross 2669 lb. Fuel 50 gal.
PERFORMANCE: Never Flown.   AMC

rebuilt as the PW-1A, with Fokker-style straight cantilever wings and N struts.

Wing flutter was hardly known when Loening built his first monoplanes, but as the designer wryly remarked after the first flights, "We knew all we wanted to know about it." Since early monoplanes tended to shed their wings, the government preferred biplanes, but in April 1921 the first Loening PW-2 high-wing monoplane, with a 300-hp Wright, was delivered. Three PW-2s (one with twin rudders) were to be followed by ten PW-2As with revised tails, but on October 20, 1922, a PW-2A lost its wings and gave Lieutenant Harold R. Harris the unwanted distinction of being the first American pilot to save himself by a parachute. The PW-2A contract was cut back to four, one becoming the PW-2B with a Packard 1A-1237.

The PW-3 biplane began as the Orenco D-2, with odd struts and a 320-hp Wright H. Three, the first delivered in April 1922, were condemned as unsafe because of unsatisfactory workmanship. Gallaudet's single PW-4 of 1922 was not flown either, but was used for static tests. The first American all-metal fighter ever built, the PW-4 had bullet lines, I struts, and a 350-hp Packard 1A-1237.

Anthony Fokker had built many successful fighters for the Kaiser's air force during World War I, the most famous being the D VII. After the Armistice, he moved his factory to the Netherlands and began selling planes to his erstwhile adversaries. The Air Service brought back 142 D VIIs captured from Germany, actually used them in service, and had great respect for Fokker's sturdy cantilever structures. Fokker sent to the United States a development of his wartime D VIII high-wing monoplane, the V-40, with a 334-hp Wright H. During a mock

GALLAUDET PW-4
Packard 1A-1237, 350 hp
DIMENSIONS: Span 29'10", Lg. 22'8", Ht. 8', Wing Area
    245 sq. ft.
WEIGHT: Empty 2203 lb., Gross 3040 lb. Fuel 60 gal.
PERFORMANCE: Speed—Top (Estimated 145 mph). Not
    Flown.   AMC

dogfight with a Loening PW-2 on March 13, 1922, the V-40's wings failed and the pilot was killed. Nevertheless, ten heavier examples designated PW-5 were purchased.

Fokker also sent a D IX biplane, the PW-6, for tests in September 1922. The fuselage had a nose radiator for the Wright H-2, and N struts between the wings became common on later American biplanes. In February 1924 the Army began tests on three Fokker D XI sesquiplanes. Known here as the PW-7, they had a 440-hp Curtiss D-12 engine and plywood upper wings much larger than the lower wings. It is noteworthy that the Fokker D XI was the standard Soviet Air Force fighter in 1922–25.

All-metal construction and cantilever monoplanes were audacious experiments in those days, but some German designers combined both in their

FOKKER V-40
Wright H, 334 hp
DIMENSIONS: Span 39'5", Lg. 26'1", Ht. 9', Wing Area 247
    sq. ft.
WEIGHT: Empty 1935 lb., Gross 2686 lb. Fuel 51 gal.
PERFORMANCE: Speed—Top 144.5 mph at s. l., 141 mph
    at 10,000', Landing 62 mph. Service Ceiling 23,750',
    Absolute Ceiling 25,400', Climb 1585'/1 min., 10,000'/
    8 min. Endurance 2 hrs. at top speed.   PMB

FOKKER PW-6 (D-IX)
Wright H-2, 315 hp
DIMENSIONS: Span 29'6", Lg. 23'3", Ht. 9', Wing Area 238
    sq. ft.
WEIGHT: Empty 1926 lb., Gross 2763 lb. Fuel 58 gal.
PERFORMANCE: Speed—Top 138.5 mph at s. l., 129 mph
    at 10,000', Cruising 117 mph, Landing 62 mph. Service
    Ceiling 16,750', Absolute Ceiling 18,200', Climb 6500'/
    6.3 min., 10,000'/11.4 min. Range 293 miles.   AMC

FOKKER PW-5
Wright H-2, 300 hp
DIMENSIONS: Span 39'5", Lg. 27'2", Ht. 9', Wing Area 246
    sq. ft.
WEIGHT: Empty 2170 lb., Gross 3015 lb. Fuel 61 gal.
PERFORMANCE: Speed—Top 138 mph at s. l.   AMC

FOKKER PW-7 (D-XI)
Curtiss D-12, 440 hp
DIMENSIONS: Span 38'4", Lg. 23'11", Ht. 9'4", Wing Area
    250 sq. ft.
WEIGHT: Empty 2271 lb., Gross 3176 lb. Fuel 65 gal.
PERFORMANCE: Speed—Top 151 mph at s. l., Cruising 145
    mph, Landing 63 mph. Service Ceiling 20,700', Abso-
    lute Ceiling 22,000', Climb 1690'/1 min. Range 338
    miles.   AMC

fighter designs. One was the all-metal "Falke" single-seater with a high wing built in Switzerland by Dornier. Inspected at McCook Field in April 1923, its high costs and the fear that the wing might come off prevented its production.

Curtiss Army Hawks Versus Boeing Biplanes

For several years the Curtiss Hawk was the dominant Army fighter type until vigorous competition from Boeing elbowed these single-seaters aside. Streamlining in the Curtiss racer series resulted in neater lines and the "Eversharp pencil" nose characteristic of the fighter design started on May 22, 1922. Other features were a 440-hp Curtiss D-12, brass radiators on the upper wing, thin, wood-covered wings, and a fuselage of fabric-covered steel tubing. Two .30-caliber guns with 600 rounds each could be accommodated, or the right-hand one could be replaced by a .50-caliber gun with 200 rounds.

The Curtiss PW-8 was first flown in January 1923 and was sold to the Army on April 27, 1923, along with two more prototypes. It became the XPW-8 when the Air Service adopted the X prefix on May 14, 1924, as the symbol for experimental planes. Twenty-five PW-8 production models were ordered September 14, 1923. The second prototype was tested in March 1924, with landing gear and wing refinements also used on the PW-8s delivered from June to August 1924. Made famous by Lieutenant Russell L. Maughan's transcontinental flight, the PW-8 was the last double-bay biplane fighter, with two pairs of N struts. The wing radiators were the least desirable feature, for a puncture in their wide area might subject the pilot to a stream of hot water.

Boeing's Model 15, first flown on June 2, 1923, to compete with the Curtiss ships, had single-bay tapered wings, a D-12 engine, a tunnel radiator, cross-axle landing gear, and an arc-welded, steel-tube fuselage structure that owed much to thorough study of the Fokker D VII. Delivered to McCook Field in June 1923, it soon showed an advantage in maneuverability over the Curtiss design, so the Army purchased the Boeing 15 as the XPW-9, along with two more prototypes, on September 29, 1923. These two modified XPW-9s were delivered May 6, 1924, and while performance varied on different tests with changes in propeller and weight,[1] comparative testing against the Curtiss design won Boeing a contract for 12 PW-9s on September 19; the order was increased to 30 on December 16, 1924.

Deliveries of the PW-9, which had split-axle landing gear, were made from October to December, followed by 25 similar PW-9As delivered from June 1926 to February 1927 with the D-12C engine. The last of these became the PW-9B when it was temporarily fitted with a D-12D, which also powered 40 strengthened PW-9Cs delivered from July to August 1927. Last came 16 PW-9Ds, ordered August 12, 1927, and delivered between April and May 1928. Additional weight, such as wheel brakes, reduced performance below that of earlier models and required a balanced rudder, but the Boeing fighters were still generally considered a bit more maneuverable than the Curtiss types. PW-9 production, after the three prototypes, totaled 111

[1] Eight different PW-9 and five different PW-8 Official Performance Tests were seen in Army files; those cited here seem typical.

CURTISS XPW-8 (1st prototype)
Curtiss D-12, 440 hp
DIMENSIONS: Span 32', Lg. 22'6", Ht. 8'8", Wing Area 265 sq. ft.
WEIGHT: Empty 1879 lb., Gross 2784 lb.
PERFORMANCE: Speed—Top 169 mph at s. l., 160 mph at 10,000', Landing 70 mph. Service Ceiling 27,150', Absolute Ceiling 28,600', Climb 2500'/1 min. Endurance 2 hrs. 48 min.   MFR

CURTISS PW-8 (2nd prototype)
Curtiss D-12 (Low-Compression), 438 hp
DIMENSIONS: Span 32', Lg. 22'6", Ht. 8'10", Wing Area 267 sq. ft.
WEIGHT: Empty 2191 lb., Gross 3151 lb. Fuel 75 gal.
PERFORMANCE: Speed—Top 168 mph at s. l., 163 mph at 6500', Cruising 159 mph, Landing 63 mph. Service Ceiling 20,350', Absolute Ceiling 21,500', Climb 1830'/ 1 min., 10,000'/7.4 min. Endurance 2.75 hrs. at 159 mph.   AMC

CURTISS PW-8 (First production model)
Curtiss D-12, 440 hp
DIMENSIONS: Span 32′, Lg. 22′6″, Ht. 8′10″, Wing Area
287 sq. ft.
WEIGHT: Empty 2191 lb., Gross 3151 lb. Fuel 75 gal.
PERFORMANCE: Speed—Top 165 mph at s. l., 162 mph at
6500′, Cruising 160 mph, Landing 61 mph. Service
Ceiling 21,700′, Absolute Ceiling 23,300′, Climb 10,-
000′/9 min. Range 440 miles.   AMC

BOEING XPW-9
Curtiss D-12, 440 hp
DIMENSIONS: Span 32′1″, Lg. 22′10″, Ht. 8′9″, Wing Area
248 sq. ft.
WEIGHT: Empty 2011 lb., Gross 2971 lb. Fuel 75 gal.
PERFORMANCE: Speed—Top 161 mph at s. l., 154 mph at
6500′, Cruising 150 mph, Landing 64 mph. Service
Ceiling 22,000′, Absolute Ceiling 22,850′, Climb 2055′/
1 min., 10,000′/6.7 min. Endurance 2.83 hrs. at 150
mph.   MFR

BOEING XPW-9 (2nd prototype)
Curtiss D-12, 448 hp
DIMENSIONS: As first XPW-9
WEIGHT: Empty 2052 lb., Gross 3015 lb. Fuel 75 gal.
PERFORMANCE: Speed—Top 163 mph at s. l., 159 mph at
6500′, Cruising 156 mph, Landing 64 mph. Service
Ceiling 21,000′, Absolute Ceiling 22,600′, Climb 10,-
000′/9.1 min. Endurance 2.6 hrs. at 156 mph.   AMC

BOEING PW-9 (First production model)
Curtiss D-12, 430 hp
DIMENSIONS: Span 32′1″, Lg. 22′10″, Ht. 8′8″, Wing Area
242 sq. ft.
WEIGHT: Empty 2166 lb., Gross 3020 lb. Fuel 63 gal.
PERFORMANCE: Speed—Top 165 mph at s. l., 160 mph at
10,000′, Landing 65 mph. Service Ceiling 20,175′, Absolute Ceiling 21,400′, Climb 1710′/1 min., 10,000′/7.9
min. Endurance 2 hrs. 35 min. at top speed.   AF

BOEING PW-9C   GSW

BOEING PW-9D
Curtiss D-12D, 435 hp
DIMENSIONS: Span 32′, Lg. 24′2″, Ht. 8′8″, Wing Area 241
sq. ft.
WEIGHT: Empty 2328 lb., Gross 3234 lb. Fuel 63 gal.
PERFORMANCE: Speed—Top 155 mph at s. l., 152 mph at
5000′, Cruising 124 mph, Landing 63 mph. Service
Ceiling 18,230′, Absolute Ceiling 19,600′, Climb 5000′/
4 min. Endurance 2.87 hrs.   AMC

planes, most of them put into service with the overseas squadrons.

Curtiss responded to Boeing's challenge by completing the third XP-8 prototype as the XPW-8A, which had shorter, single-bay wings like those of the PW-9. At first the radiator was put in the center section of the XPW-8A's wing, but then a tunnel radiator, again like the Boeing's, was fitted for competitive flight tests held in October 1924. Top speed was greatly improved, but the Boeing's maneuverability was still superior. In December 1924 the same prototype was ordered converted to the XPW-8B with new tapered wings. Designed by George Page, Jr., the new wings and tail became standard on future Curtiss Hawks from the P-1 to the P-23. The P-1s ordered into production in March 1925, parallel with the Boeing PW-9, were nearly identical to the XPW-8B prototype.

Although the Boeing and Curtiss fighters were single-seaters, the Army also tested two-seater pursuits. The last pursuit type built by the Army itself was the Engineering Division's TP-1 biplane, whose lower wing was larger than the upper. Tests were made in 1924 with two versions of the Liberty engine. When fitted with an experimental Type F turbosupercharger and a radiator in the upper wing, the top speed increased from 125 mph at sea level to 150 mph at 20,300 feet, and a ceiling of 29,462 feet was reached on March 27, 1924. When tested with a conventional Liberty and nose radiator in November 1924, only 129 mph at sea level and 123 mph at 6,500 feet was achieved. Two flexible Lewis Guns on the rear cockpit ring and another at a floor trapdoor were added to the usual two fixed guns. A second prototype was finished as the CO-5.

The only two-seat fighter offered by a private firm was the Thomas-Morse TM-12, tested February 1925 with a 440-hp Curtiss D-12. This biplane's upper wing was also smaller than the lower wing, and was supported by an ugly arrangement of V and N struts. Other unconventional features were the short, corrugated aluminum fuselage and radiators in the wing roots. No Army contract or designation was given, but the firm also tried the Thomas-Morse TM-23 single-seat biplane with the same Curtiss D-12 and small wings joined by I struts.

Rejected the first time, the TM-23 was rebuilt with a new strut system and the radiator under the fuselage, but official performance tests in March 1926 brought complaints that the TM-23 flew badly and had too high a landing speed.

As Boeing's PW-9 series made progress and Thomas-Morse tried unsuccessfully to get some fighter business, Curtiss went into production on the popular P-1 Hawks. Ten P-1s ordered March 7, 1925, began the fighter designation series that con-

CURTISS PW-8A
Curtiss D-12, 440 hp
DIMENSIONS: Span 30', Lg. 22'6", Ht. 8', Wing Area 255 sq. ft.
WEIGHT: Empty 2007 lb., Gross 2820 lb. Fuel 53 gal.
PERFORMANCE: Speed—Top 178 mph at s. l., 171.5 mph at 6500', Cruising 169 mph, Landing 68 mph. Service Ceiling 22,250', Absolute Ceiling 23,400', Climb 10,000'/6.91 min. Range 338 miles.   AMC

CURTISS XPW-8B
Curtiss D-12, 435 hp
DIMENSIONS: Span 31'6", Lg. 22'2", Ht. 8'6", Wing Area 250 sq. ft.
WEIGHT: Empty 2032 lb., Gross 2802 lb., Max. 2926 lb. Fuel 50–100 gal.
PERFORMANCE: Speed—Top 167 mph at s. l. (162 mph with drop tank), 163 mph at 5000', Landing 61 mph. Service Ceiling 21,400', Absolute Ceiling 22,600', Climb 1800'/1 min., 10,000'/7.3 min. Endurance 1 hr. 35 min.   AMC

ENGINEERING DIV. TP-1
(Photo shows supercharged version)
Liberty 12, 423 hp
DIMENSIONS: Span 36', Lg. 25'1", Ht. 10', Wing Area 375 sq. ft.
WEIGHT: Empty 2748 lb., Gross 4363 lb. Fuel 93 gal.
PERFORMANCE: Speed—Top 129 mph at s. l., 123 mph at 6500', Cruising 117 mph, Landing 63 mph. Service Ceiling 13,450', Absolute Ceiling 15,200', Climb 495'/1 min., 6500'/9.2 min. Endurance 3.6 hrs.   AMC

THOMAS-MORSE TM-24
Curtiss D-12, 440 hp
DIMENSIONS: Span 30′, Lg. 20′5″, Wing Area 237 sq. ft.
WEIGHT: Empty 1969 lb., Gross 3470 lb. Fuel 84 gal.
PERFORMANCE: Speed—Top 143 mph at s. l., 138 mph at 15,000′, Cruising 114 mph, Landing 63 mph. Service Ceiling 15,600′, Absolute Ceiling 17,050′, Climb 1178′/1 min., 5000′/5.1 min. Endurance 2¾ hrs. at 114 mph/15,000′.　　ARC

THOMAS-MORSE TM-23
Curtiss D-12, 440 hp
DIMENSIONS: Span 23′, Lg. 16′8″, Wing Area 200 sq. ft.
WEIGHT: Empty 1918.5 lb., Gross 2706.5 lb. Fuel 50–61 gal.
PERFORMANCE: Speed—Top 167 mph at s. l., 150.6 mph at 15,000′, Cruising 125 mph, Landing 80 mph. Service Ceiling 20,150′, Absolute Ceiling 21,275′, Climb 10,-000′/7.3 min. Endurance 2¼ hrs. at 125 mph.　　AMC

tinued to 1962. Essentially a refined PW-8B with a 435-hp V-1150-1 (the new Curtiss D-12 engine designation), the P-1, delivered from August to October 1925, had fabric covering over wooden wing spars and a steel-tubed fuselage and tail. A 50-gallon main tank could be supplemented by a 50-gallon auxiliary tank attached behind the tunnel radiator,

increasing endurance from two to four hours. Armament was one .30-caliber and one .50-caliber fixed gun.

Twenty-five similar P-1As ordered September 9, 1925, were delivered beginning April 1926, and 25 P-1Bs were purchased August 17, 1926. Tested in July 1927, the P-1B had a V-1150-3, larger wheels, and an improved radiator. A V-1150-5 and wheel brakes distinguished 33 P-1Cs ordered October 3, 1928, and delivered from January to April 1929. Tests indicated that continuous increments of weight had depressed the Hawk's performance. Cost of the P-1C, $9,862 each, was very low compared to today's fighters. Navy Hawks of this type were designated F6C-3s. One P-1A was sold to Japan, and Chile bought eight P-1As and eight P-1Bs. In addition, in 1929 52 of the 71 Hawks built as low-powered AT-4 and AT-5 advanced trainers were converted, using D-12 engines, to P-1D, P-1E, and P-1F fighter trainers to be used at Kelly Field for advanced students. Earlier P-1 pursuits equipped the four squadrons (17, 27, 94, and 95) of the First Pursuit Group.

While these Hawks went into service, the same basic airframe was used to test other engine arrangements. Five Curtiss P-2s bought on the first P-1 contract and flown in December 1925 had the 505-hp Curtiss V-1400. Like most previous types, this was a water-cooled inline engine, but the Curtiss XP-3 was the last P-1A fitted with a 400-hp air-cooled Curtiss R-1454 radial in October 1926. When this power plant failed, a 410-hp Pratt & Whitney R-1340-9 radial was substituted for April 1928 tests as the XP-3A (or XP-451). Five P-3As with the R-1340-3 had been ordered on December 27, 1927, and delivery began in October 1928. Early flights showed that the naked ring of cylinders handi-

CURTISS P-1
Curtiss V-1150-1, 435 hp
DIMENSIONS: Span 31'7", Lg. 22'10", Ht. 8'7", Wing Area 250 sq. ft.
WEIGHT: Empty 2058 lb., Gross 2846 lb., Max. 3238 lb. Fuel 50–100 gal.
PERFORMANCE: Speed—Top 163 mph at s. l., 159 mph at 5000', Cruising 136 mph, Landing 59 mph. Service Ceiling 22,500', Absolute Ceiling 23,800', Climb 1810'/ 1 min., 5000'/3.1 min. Range 325 miles at top speed.   MFR

CURTISS P-1A (Above)
Curtiss V-1150-1, 435 hp
DIMENSIONS: As P-1
WEIGHT: Empty 2041 lb., Gross 2866 lb. Fuel 50–100 gal.
PERFORMANCE: Speed—Top 160 mph at s. l., 155 mph at 10,000', Cruising 128 mph, Service Ceiling 20,200', Absolute Ceiling 21,350', Climb 2170'/1 min., 5000'/ 2.6 min.   AF

CURTISS P-1B (Below)
Curtiss V-1150-3, 435 hp
DIMENSIONS: Span 31'7", Lg. 22'8", Ht. 8'11", Wing Area 250 sq. ft.
WEIGHT: Empty 2105 lb., Gross 2932 lb., Max. 3562 lb. Fuel 50–100 gal.
PERFORMANCE: Speed—Top 159.6 mph at s. l., 157 mph at 5000', Cruising 127 mph, Landing 57 mph. Service Ceiling 21,400', Absolute Ceiling 22,900', Climb 1540'/ 1 min.   AF

CURTISS P-1C
Curtiss V-1150-5, 435 hp
DIMENSIONS: Span 31'6", Lg. 23'3", Ht. 8'6", Wing Area
252 sq. ft.
WEIGHT: Empty 2136 lb., Gross 2973 lb. Fuel 50–100 gal.
PERFORMANCE: Speed—Top 154 mph at s. l., 148 mph at
10,000', 153 mph at 5000', Cruising 124 mph, Landing
58 mph. Service Ceiling 20,800', Absolute Ceiling
22,300', Climb 1460'/1 min., 5000'/3.9 min., 10,000'/9.1
min. Range 554–650 miles.   AF

CURTISS P-2
(Photo shows supercharger added)
Curtiss V-1400, 505 hp
DIMENSIONS: Span 31'7", Lg. 22'10", Ht. 8'7", Wing Area
250 sq. ft.
WEIGHT: Empty 2081 lb., Gross 2869 lb., Max. 3255 lb.
Fuel 50–100 gal.
PERFORMANCE: Speed—Top 172 mph at s. l., 151 mph at
15,000', Cruising 138 mph, Landing 65 mph. Service
Ceiling 22,950', Absolute Ceiling 24,000', Climb 2170'/
1 min., 6500'/3.5 min. Range 400 miles at top
speed.   AMC

capped performance. In May 1929 Air Corps engineers at Wright Field[2] added a cowl with front shutters and prop spinner to the first P-3A, while Curtiss in Buffalo modified the XP-3A the same month with a deeper cowl of their own design. Both were known as XP-3A, but the Army version carried the XP-524 project number while the Curtiss conversion retained the XP-451 number. The former demonstrated an increase in speed from 153 mph to 171 mph on its May 22, 1929, trials and by June 1930, 190 mph had been achieved. Other P-3As were given simple Townsend ring cowls, and the two XP-3As became temporary test-beds for the 300-hp R-985-1 Wasp, Jr., in December 1930 and were labeled XP-21.

Another path of engine development was the turbosupercharger, developed by Dr. Sanford Moss of General Electric. After static tests conducted at Pikes Peak in September 1918, flight trials were made on a LePere fighter in February 1920, followed by further tests on an MB-2 bomber, TP-1, PW-8, and the first P-2. Boeing also delivered a turbosupercharged high-altitude fighter, the XP-4,

[2] Air Corps testing moved from McCook Field to nearby Wright Field in Dayton, Ohio, on October 12, 1927.

CURTISS P-3A (Below)
(Data applies to uncowled, standard version)
Pratt & Whitney R-1340-3, 410 hp
DIMENSIONS: Span 31'7", Lg. 22'5", Ht. 8'9", Wing Area
252 sq. ft.
WEIGHT: Empty 1956 lb., Gross 2788 lb. Fuel 50–100 gal.
PERFORMANCE: Speed—Top 153 mph at s. l., 151 mph at
5000', 148 mph at 10,000', Cruising 122 mph, Landing
58 mph. Service Ceiling 23,000', Absolute Ceiling
24,400', Climb 1742'/1 min., 5000'/3.2 min.   MFR

CURTISS XP-3A (XP-524)
Pratt & Whitney R-1340-3, 410 hp (440 hp actual)
DIMENSIONS: Span 31'6", Lg. 22'11", Ht. 8'9", Wing Area
  252 sq. ft.
WEIGHT: Empty 2107 lb., Gross 2788 lb., Fuel 37–100 gal.
PERFORMANCE: Speed—Top 171 mph at s. l., 168 mph at
  5000', 164 mph at 10,000', Cruising 136 mph, Landing
  58 mph. Service Ceiling 23,525', Absolute Ceiling
  24,900', Climb 1800'/1 min.   AF

BOEING XP-4
Packard 1A-1500, 510 hp
DIMENSIONS: Span 32', Lg. 23'11", Ht. 8'10", Wing Area
  308 sq. ft.
WEIGHT: Empty 2703 lb., Gross 3650 lb. Fuel 100 gal.
PERFORMANCE: Speed—Top 161 mph. Service Ceiling
  22,000', Absolute Ceiling 22,850', Climb 2055'/1 min.
  Range 375 miles.   AMC

CURTISS XP-3A (XP-451)   MFR

in July 1926. The overweight XP-4—actually the
last PW-9 reworked with a 510-hp Packard, four-
bladed propeller, and enlarged lower wing—was
grounded after only 4.5 flying hours. An unusual
feature was provision for two .30-caliber guns in
the lower wings.

A contract placed May 14, 1927, called for five
Curtiss P-5 Hawks to be built with turbosuperchargers on V-1150-3 engines. Delivery began in
January 1928. Except for cockpit heater, oxygen
supply, longer wheel struts, and enlarged propellers, the P-5 was similar to the P-1. The turbosupercharger's weight reduced sea-level speed to 146
mph, but at 25,000 feet 173 mph was attained. Since
these turbosuperchargers were driven by hot exhaust gases and compressed, frigid high-altitude air,

CURTISS P-3A (with ring cowl)   AF

CURTISS P-5
Curtiss V-1150-3, 435 hp
DIMENSIONS: Span 31'6", Lg. 23'8", Ht. 9'3", Wing Area
    252 sq. ft.
WEIGHT: Empty 2520 lb., Gross 3349 lb. Fuel 50–100 gal.
PERFORMANCE: Speed—Top 146 mph at s. l., 173.5 mph
    at 25,000', Cruising 117 mph, Landing 62 mph. Service
    Ceiling 31,900', Absolute Ceiling 32,500', Climb 1110'/
    1 min., 10,000'/8.4 min., 15,000'/12.4 min. Endurance
    1.31 hrs. at s. l./top speed.   MFR

CURTISS XP-6
Curtiss V-1570-1, 600 hp
DIMENSIONS: Span 31'7", Lg. 22'8", Ht. 8'11", Wing Area
    250 sq. ft.
WEIGHT: Empty 2204 lb., Gross 3037 lb. Fuel 50 gal.
PERFORMANCE: Speed—Top 176 mph at s. l., 168 mph at
    10,000', 143 mph at 20,000', Cruising 141 mph, Land-
    ing 61 mph. Service Ceiling 23,110', Absolute Ceiling
    24,200', Climb 2271'/1 min., 10,000'/5.7 min.   MFR

CURTISS XP-6A RACER   MFR

they required metals able to withstand great ex-
tremes of temperature. It would take another decade of work before turbosuperchargers would be
reliable enough for production and service.

When the 600-hp Curtiss V-1570-1 Conqueror
became available, two Hawks were rebuilt to try it
out at the September 1927 air races. The XP-6 was
a P-2 with a Conqueror installed, while the XP-6A
had a high-compression Conqueror, P-1A body,
XPW-8A wings, and wing radiators. At the races the
XP-6A came in first with a speed of 201 mph, leaving the XP-6 in second place, but it should be remembered that the XP-6A was strictly a racer whose
wing radiators had already been found unsuitable
for service. Another conversion was the XP-6B, a P-
1C rebuilt with the Conqueror and a 250-gallon fuel
capacity for a July 1929 flight to Alaska.

Eighteen P-6s were ordered with the P-1C on
October 19, 1928, and deliveries began a year later.
Like previous Hawks, the first ten P-6s had water-
cooling for their V-1570-17, but the last eight P-6As
had V-1570-23s cooled by ethylene glycol (com-
mercially sold as Prestone). Chemical cooling permitted smaller radiators, and had been tried on
modified P-1Bs and P-1Cs before the first P-6A was
flown in November 1930. Older P-6s were also
modified to P-6A standards and were used by the
27th Pursuit Squadron.

Eight more P-6s were built for the Dutch East
Indies from April to September 1930 and, together
with six more built in Holland by Aviolande, served
the first fighter squadron stationed there until 1937.
The export P-6 was called the Hawk I, and one was
purchased by Mitsubishi in 1930. Incidentally, the
Japanese firm's inspector at Curtiss then was Jiro
Horikoshi, who later became chief designer of the
Zero and earlier Japanese fighters. Cuba also received three P-6S Hawks in January 1930, but they
were powered by a 450-hp Pratt & Whitney air-
cooled radial.

No P-6C appeared, but the XP-6D was a P-6A
modified by an F-2 turbosupercharger on a V-1570-
23. This ship had a two-bladed propeller like most
biplanes, but a dozen P-6Ds converted from February to August 1932 from P-6 and P-6As had three-
bladed propellers whose bite would take better
advantage of the turbosupercharger's high-altitude
capabilities. They served with the 37th Pursuit
Squadron at Langley Field until 1935.

Boeing continued to give Curtiss stiff competition
for fighter contracts during this period. Like every
other firm, they had failures as well as successes.
The Army ordered that the last PW-9 be completed
with a V-1570-1 Conqueror, and the aircraft was
delivered as the XP-7 in September 1928. In July
1927, however, the Boeing Model 66 had been completed with an inverted 600-hp Packard 2A-1530

CURTISS P-6
Curtiss V-1570-17, 600 hp
DIMENSIONS: Span 31'6", Lg. 23'7", Wing Area 252 sq. ft.
WEIGHT: Gross 3150 lb., Max. 3310 lb. Fuel 50–100 gal.
PERFORMANCE: Speed—Top 178 mph at s. l., 171 mph at 10,000', 144 mph at 20,000'. Service Ceiling 22,700', Absolute Ceiling 24,000', Climb 2140'/1 min., 10,000'/6.6 min. Range 260 miles normal, 520 max.   AMC

CURTISS P-6A
Curtiss V-1570-23, 600 hp
DIMENSIONS: Span 31'6", Lg. 23'7", Ht. 8'7", Wing Area 252 sq. ft.
WEIGHT: Empty 2389 lb., Gross 3172 lb. Fuel 50 gal.
PERFORMANCE: Speed—Top 178 mph at s. l., 177 mph at 5000', 173.5 mph at 10,000', 160 mph at 20,000', Cruising 154 mph, Landing 60 mph. Service Ceiling 27,200', Absolute Ceiling 28,400', Climb 10,000'/5.8 min.   AMC

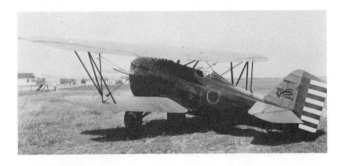

CURTISS XP-6B
Curtiss V-1570-1, 600 hp
DIMENSIONS: Span 31'6", Lg. 23'7", Ht. 8'9", Wing Area 252 sq. ft.
WEIGHT: Empty 2545 lb., Gross 3269 lb. Fuel 250 gal.
PERFORMANCE: Speed—Top 178 mph at s. l., 175 mph at 5000', Cruising 142 mph, Landing 62.4 mph. Service Ceiling 22,600', Absolute Ceiling 23,800', Climb 5000'/2.7 min. Endurance 1.9 hrs. normal, 3.8 hrs. max. MFR

CURTISS P-6D
Curtiss V-1570-23, 600 hp
DIMENSIONS: Span 31'6", Lg. 23'7", Ht. 8'7", Wing Area 252 sq. ft.
WEIGHT: Gross 3483 lb. Fuel 50–100 gal.
PERFORMANCE: Speed—Top 197 mph at 13,000', 190 mph at 10,000', 172 mph at s. l., Landing 63 mph. Service Ceiling 32,000', Climb 1720'/1 min., 15,000'/8.7 min.   PMB

CURTISS HAWK I (Export)
Curtiss V-1570, 630 hp
DIMENSIONS: Span 31'6", Lg. 22', Ht. 9'1", Wing Area 252 sq. ft.
WEIGHT: Empty 2542 lb., Gross 3376 lb. Fuel 50–98 gal.
PERFORMANCE: Speed—Top 187 mph at s. l., Cruising 144 mph, Stalling 61 mph. Service Ceiling 22,000', Climb 10,000'/5.7 min. Endurance 1 hr. 40 min. at s. l., 2.5 hr. at 15,000'.   MFR

cooled by a radiator built into the juncture of lower wing and fuselage. This prototype was purchased by the Air Corps on January 27, 1928, as the XP-8. The final report described the XP-8 design as good (it was similar to the Navy's F2B) but handicapped by an unsatisfactory engine.

Although biplanes dominated the aviation picture, the Army and Boeing signed a $60,000 contract on June 13, 1928, for an XP-9 monoplane with a V-1570-15 engine and strut-braced straight wings attached to the top of an all-metal stressed-skin fuselage, the first since 1922. When the XP-9 was, at last, flown on November 18, 1930, the pilot called it "a menace" due to its exceedingly poor vision and dangerous flying qualities.

CURTISS HAWK P-6S (Cuba)
Pratt & Whitney R-1340, 450 hp
DIMENSIONS: Span 31'6", Lg. 22'10", Ht. 8'6", Wing Area 252 sq. ft.
WEIGHT: Gross 2910 lb. Fuel 100 gal.
PERFORMANCE: Speed—Top 157 mph at s. l. Service Ceiling 21,800', Climb 1820'/1 min., 12,500'/10 min. Endurance 2.54 hr.   MFR

BOEING XP-8
Packard 2A-1530, 600 hp
DIMENSIONS: Span 30'1", Lg. 23'4", Ht. 8'4", Wing Area 237 sq. ft.
WEIGHT: Empty 2390 lb., Gross 3421 lb. Fuel 90 gal.
PERFORMANCE: Speed—Top 170 mph at s. l., 166 mph at 5000', Cruising 136 mph, Landing 64 mph. Service Ceiling 20,950', Absolute Ceiling 22,500', Climb 1800'/1 min., 5000'/3.1 min.   AMC

BOEING XP-7
Curtiss V-1570-1, 600 hp
DIMENSIONS: Span 32', Lg. 24', Ht. 9', Wing Area 241 sq. ft.
WEIGHT: Empty 2323 lb., Gross 3157 lb. Fuel 50 gal.
PERFORMANCE: Speed—Top 167.5 mph at s. l., 163.5 mph at 5000', Cruising 134 mph, Landing 62 mph. Service Ceiling 21,120', Absolute Ceiling 22,300', Climb 1867'/1 min., 10,000'/7.1 min. Endurance 92 hr. at s. l./top speed.   AMC

BOEING XP-9
Curtiss V-1570-15, 600 hp (583 hp actual)
DIMENSIONS: Span 36'7", Lg. 25'8", Ht. 7'9", Wing Area 214 sq.ft.
WEIGHT: Empty 2694 lb., Gross 3604 lb. Fuel 81–135 gal.
PERFORMANCE: Speed—Top 181 mph at s. l., 179.5 mph at 5000', Cruising 144 mph, Landing 70 mph. Service Ceiling 25,300', Absolute Ceiling 26,400', Climb 2430'/1 min., 5000'/2.3 min. Endurance 1.5 hrs. at top speed.   MFR

CURTISS XP-10
Curtiss V-1710-15, 600 hp
DIMENSIONS: Span 33', Lg. 24'6", Ht. 10'10"
WEIGHT: Gross 3700 lb.
PERFORMANCE: Speed—Top 173 mph.   MFR

On June 18, 1928, the Army ordered the Curtiss XP-10 biplane. Designed for good maneuverability, pilot visibility, and high speeds at 13,000 feet, the XP-10 had a V-1570-15 engine, plywood wings gulled into the fuselage, and wing-skin radiators; this cooling system was too vulnerable to bullet damage and was not used again. The XP-10 was completed in May 1930 but tests were stopped in October 1930 due to trouble with these coolers.

The next Curtiss design was a development of the familiar Hawk layout. The Curtiss XP-11 was to be a P-6 with the experimental 600-hp Curtiss H-1640-1. This engine, flight-tested on the Thomas-Morse XP-13, was a failure, and the XP-11 project, together with a more advanced Curtiss XP-14 designed around this engine, was abandoned. Two of three P-11 airframes ordered in January 1929 were completed as P-6s, while the third became the YP-20.

The most successful Boeing fighter family began in June 1928 with the Model 83 biplane, a private venture powered by a 400-hp Pratt & Whitney R-1340C Wasp. Together with the later Model 89, it was submitted to the Navy and became the XF4B-1. Impressed by Navy reports, the Army, on November 7, 1928, ordered nine P-12s and one XP-12A for service trials. First flown on April 11, 1929, the P-12 had a 450-hp R-1340-7 with cylinder fairings and the usual two guns in front of the pilot. The XP-12A displayed a deep NACA cowl, new Frise ailerons,

BOEING P-12
Pratt & Whitney R-1340-7 (SR-1340C), 450 hp at 5000'
DIMENSIONS: Span 30', Lg. 20'1", Ht. 9'7", Wing Area 227.5 sq. ft.
WEIGHT: Empty 1758 lb., Gross 2536 lb. Fuel 52–99 gal.
PERFORMANCE: Speed—Top 171 mph at 5000', 158 mph at s. l., Cruising 135 mph, Landing 60 mph. Service Ceiling 28,200', Absolute Ceiling 29,600', Climb 2080'/1 min., 10,000'/5.77 min.   MFR

BOEING XP-12A   MFR

BOEING P-12B
Pratt & Whitney R-1340-7 (SR-1340C), 450 hp at 5000'
DIMENSIONS: Span 30', Lg. 20'3", Ht. 8'10", Wing Area
227.5 sq. ft.
WEIGHT: Empty 1945 lb., Gross 2638 lb. Fuel 50–99 gal.
PERFORMANCE: Speed—Top 166.5 mph at 5000', 157 mph
at s. l., Cruising 135 mph, Landing 59 mph. Service
Ceiling 27,450', Absolute Ceiling 28,800', Climb 2040'/
1 min., 10,000'/5.9 min. Range 540 miles normal, 622
miles max.
AF

BOEING MODEL 100
Pratt & Whitney SR-1340D, 525 hp
DIMENSIONS: Span 30', Lg. 20'1", Ht. 9'3", Wing Area
227.5 sq. ft.
WEIGHT: Empty 1815 lb., Gross 2597 lb. Fuel 50 gal.
PERFORMANCE: Speed—Top 192 mph at 8000', 168 mph
at s. l., Cruising 155 mph, Landing 60 mph. Service
Ceiling 29,900', Absolute Ceiling 31,000', Climb 2010'/
1 min., 10,000'/5.9 min.
MFR

and shorter landing gear, but was destroyed in a collision with a P-12 in May 1929 after only four hours flying.

The first air-cooled pursuits widely used by the Army were 90 P-12Bs ordered June 10, 1929, delivered by rail from February to May 1930, and first flown May 30. They had the XP-12A's ailerons and elevators but lacked the cylinder fairings.

Meanwhile, Boeing turned out four Model 100s in 1929, civilian P-12s powered by 525-hp SR-1340Ds. One tested at Wright Field in March 1930 showed a top speed with ring cowl of 192 mph and 177.5 mph with cowl. Another was sold to Japan.

A monoplane development of the P-12 series was Boeing's 202, built with a 525-hp SR-1340D, metal fuselage, and high, strut-braced, metal-covered wing. The model 202 was completed in January 1930 and loaned to the Army for tests on March 10. Designated XP-15, it did 185 mph with a ring cowl on May 3, 1930, and 178 mph when flown with bare cylinders. An XF5B-1 Navy version had a curved rudder, later installed on the XP-15. The aircraft was returned to Boeing without purchase.

Although the XP-15's performance was good, on June 20, 1930, the Army ordered 96 P-12C and 35 P-12D biplanes. Delivered from August 1930 to February 1931, the P-12C had a 450-hp R-1340-9 under a ring cowl and a crossed-axle landing gear instead of the older split-axle style. The P-12Ds delivered from February to March 1931 were similar except for a 500-hp R-1340-17 and a different auxiliary tank.

BOEING P-12C
Pratt & Whitney R-1340-9, 450 hp at 8000'
DIMENSIONS: Span 30', Lg. 20'1", Ht. 8'8", Wing Area
    227.5 sq. ft.
WEIGHT: Empty 1938 lb., Gross 2630 lb. Fuel 50–110 gal.
PERFORMANCE: Speed—Top 178 mph at 8000', Cruising
    141 mph, Landing 58 mph. Service Ceiling 26,200',
    Absolute Ceiling 27,600', Climb 1410'/1 min., 10,000'/
    6.1 min. Range 580 miles normal, 668 miles max.   HA

BOEING XP-15
Pratt & Whitney SR-1340D, 525 hp at 8000'
DIMENSIONS: Span 30'6", Lg. 21', Ht. 9', Wing Area 157
    sq. ft.
WEIGHT: Empty 2050 lb., Gross 2790 lb. Fuel 50–128 gal.
PERFORMANCE: Speed—Top 185 mph at 8000', 163.5 mph
    at s. l., Cruising 150 mph, Landing 71 mph. Service
    Ceiling 26,550', Absolute Ceiling 27,650', Climb 1860'/
    1 min.   AMC

BOEING P-12D
Pratt & Whitney R-1340-17, 500 hp at 7000'
DIMENSIONS: As P-12C
WEIGHT: Empty 1956 lb., Gross 2648 lb.
PERFORMANCE: Speed—Top 188 mph at 7000', Cruising
    163 mph, Landing 58 mph. Service Ceiling 25,400',
    Climb 10,000'/5.8 min. Range 475 miles normal, 622
    miles max.   HA

The fabric-covered metal tube structure of early
P-12 fuselages was replaced by the all-metal semi-
monocoque body of the XP-15 on the Boeing Model
218, first flown September 29, 1930, and tested by
the Army in December as the XP-925. Sometimes
seen with wheel pants, it became the XP-925A in
August 1931 when the 450-hp SR-1340C was replaced by a 500-hp R-1340F. Sent to China for demonstration purposes, the XP-925A became the first
American fighter to combat Japanese planes, but was
destroyed near Soochow on February 22, 1932, in
the Japanese Navy's first air victory. Pilot Robert
Short had attacked three Type 13 three-place bombers from the *Kaga*, killing the commander and
wounding the gunner of one, but was killed when
three escorting Type 3 fighters joined the fight.

Best known of the Boeing biplanes is the P-12E,
which was ordered on March 20, 1931, with the
Model 281's metal fuselage. Powered by an R-1340-
17, it had a 55-gallon fuel tank behind the engine
and an auxiliary belly tank for 55-gallons could be
added. Like the others in the series, it was armed
with two .30-caliber guns, the right one replaceable
by a .50-caliber weapon when required. Bomb racks
handled five 30-pound or two 122-pound bombs.

Delivered by train (Boeing then had no airfield
for flyaway delivery) between September 15 and
October 15, 1931, the 110 P-12Es were popular with
Air Corps pilots for their maneuverability and flying
qualities. Twenty-five P-12F pursuits purchased
under the same contract, but with the R-1340-19,
were delivered from March 6 to May 17, 1932, the
last with a cockpit canopy. Boeing delivered 336
Army P-12 series aircraft, in addition to two 100E
(P-12E) fighters that were shipped to Siam in November 1931, the civilian and export models mentioned before, and, of course, the Navy's F4B series,
discussed in Chapter 10.

BOEING MODEL 202   AMC

BOEING 218 (later XP-925)
Pratt & Whitney SR-1340C, 450 hp
DIMENSIONS: Span 30′, Lg. 20′5″, Ht. 9′1″, Wing Area
   227.5 sq. ft.
WEIGHT: Empty 1976 lb., Gross 2667 lb. Fuel 50 gal.
PERFORMANCE: Speed—Top 190 mph at 5000′, Cruising
   157 mph, Landing 58 mph. Service Ceiling 29,000′,
   Absolute Ceiling 30,000′, Climb 10,000′/2.3 min. MFR

BOEING XP-925A (Modified 218)
Pratt & Whitney SR-1340F, 500 hp at 10,000′
DIMENSIONS: Span 30′, Lg. 23′, Ht. 8′10″, Wing Area 227.5
   sq. ft.
WEIGHT: Empty 1981 lb., Gross 2673 lb. Fuel 50 gal.
PERFORMANCE: Speed—Top 205 mph at 10,000′, 176 mph
   at s. l., Landing 58 mph. Service Ceiling 31,925′, Absolute Ceiling 33,000′, Climb 2310′/1 min., 10,000′/4.8
   min. USN

BOEING P-12E (Above)
Pratt & Whitney R-1340-17 (SR-1340E), 500 hp at 7000′
DIMENSIONS: Span 30′, Lg. 20′3″, Ht. 9′, Wing Area 227.5
   sq. ft.
WEIGHT: Empty 1999 lb., Gross 2690 lb. Fuel 55–110 gal.
PERFORMANCE: Speed—Top 189 mph at 7000′, Cruising
   160 mph, Landing 60 mph. Service Ceiling 26,300′,
   Absolute Ceiling 27,400′, Climb 10,000′/5.8 min.
   Range 475–570 miles. AF

BOEING P-12F (Below)
Pratt & Whitney R-1340-19, 600 hp takeoff, 500 hp at
   10,000′
DIMENSIONS: As P-12E
WEIGHT: Empty 2035 lb., Gross 2726 lb. Fuel 55–110 gal.
PERFORMANCE: Speed—Top 194.5 mph at 10,000′, Cruis-
   ing 166 mph, Landing 59 mph. Service Ceiling 31,400′,
   Absolute Ceiling 32,400′, Climb 2595′/1 min., 10,000′/
   4.2 min. AF

A number of P-12 models were converted by means of engine modifications. They include the XP-12G, the first P-12B with a turbosupercharger and a three-bladed propeller. The XP-12H was a D with a geared Wasp, and the P-12J was an E used for testing the H Wasp. In 1934, seven P-12Es testing fuel injection systems became the YP-12Ks, and one with an F-7 supercharger became the XP-12L.

Two smaller firms tried to win some pursuit business but met with little success. Thomas-Morse, luckless since the MB-3, built the XP-13, purchased in June 1929 during flight tests. An all-metal biplane with I struts and a corrugated metal fuselage, the Viper had an experimental air-cooled 600-hp Curtiss H-1640-1. A twin-row radial with the second row of six cylinders directly behind the first row of six, the engine had cooling difficulties that were not solved until later twin-row radials with a staggered arrangement were introduced.

When the XP-13 failed to win a contract, the Thomas-Morse firm was absorbed by Consolidated Aircraft in August 1929. A Pratt & Whitney Wasp

and a new tail were installed on the aircraft by the Army in September 1930, and the fighter redesignated XP-13A.

Ebb Tide for Biplanes

Boeing had been doing well in the fight for pursuit contracts, but Curtiss did not let its West Coast competitor capture the field entirely. New versions of the Hawk appeared, sporting the latest wrinkles in design.

The Curtiss XP-17 was actually the first P-1 airframe modified by Army engineers to test, in June 1930, the 480-hp air-cooled inverted inline Wright V-1460-3 Tornado. A pair of Curtiss designs, the XP-18 biplane and the XP-19 low-wing monoplane, were planned for the 600-hp Wright V-1560-1, but both were discarded on the drawing board.

The next Curtiss Hawk also had an air-cooled power plant, in this case the Wright R-1820-9 Cyclone. The YP-20 was actually a P-11 completed in October 1930 with this new radial, a ring cowl, and wheel pants. This was a very busy year in pursuit

BOEING P-12F (with canopy)   AF

THOMAS-MORSE XP-13
Curtiss H-1640-1, 600 hp
DIMENSIONS: Span 28′, Lg. 23′6″, Ht. 8′5″, Wing Area 189 sq. ft.
WEIGHT: Empty 2262 lb., Gross 3256 lb. Fuel 80 gal.
PERFORMANCE: Speed—Top 173 mph at s. l., 170 mph at 5000′, Cruising 138 mph, Landing 67 mph. Service Ceiling 20,775′, Absolute Ceiling 22,000′, Climb 5000′/3 min.   AMC

THOMAS-MORSE XP-13A
Pratt & Whitney SR-1340C, 450 hp
DIMENSIONS: As XP-13
WEIGHT: Empty 2224 lb., Gross 3194 lb. Fuel 74 gal.
PERFORMANCE: Speed—Top 188.5 mph at 5000′, Cruising 150 mph, Landing 67 mph. Service Ceiling 24,150′, Absolute Ceiling 25,600′, Climb 5000′/3.5 min.   AMC

CURTISS XP-17
Wright V-1460-3, 480 hp
DIMENSIONS: Span 31′7″, Lg. 22′10″, Ht. 8′7″, Wing Area 250 sq. ft.
WEIGHT: Empty 2204 lb., Gross 2994 lb. Fuel 43 gal.
PERFORMANCE: Speed—Top 165 mph at s. l., 161 mph at 5000′, Cruising 130 mph, Landing 62 mph. Service Ceiling 21,400′, Absolute Ceiling 22,800′, Climb 10,000′/8 min.   AMC

aviation at Wright Field, what with the P-6A, XP-9, XP-10, P-12B, P-12C, XP-13A, XP-15, XP-16, XP-17, Model 100, and the YP-20.

The Curtiss XP-22 appeared in May 1931 as a rebuilt P-6A with a V-1570-23 in a neatly streamlined nose, three-bladed propeller, and Prestone cooler between the legs of a single-strut panted landing gear. Flight tests in June demonstrated a 202-mph speed, the highest yet for an Army fighter.

In June 1931 an Army board met to consider the respective merits of the best fighters then available: the turbosupercharged P-6D, the air-cooled P-12D and YP-20, and the liquid-cooled XP-22. The supercharger still seemed unready for squadron service, and the YP-20, while slightly superior in speed and climb to 5,000 feet, was inferior to the P-12D in maneuverability and visibility. The XP-22 was the fastest up to 15,000 feet, but less maneuverable than the Boeing fighters. While the P-12 was the more acceptable pursuit, the board recommended purchase of 46 P-22s to further development of the liquid-cooled engine in pursuit airplanes and for "the desirability of giving the Curtiss Company business." Lieutenant Colonel Henry H. Arnold recommended a contract on July 10, 1931, for 46 Curtiss fighters at $12,211 each, but designated the aircraft P-6E.

The contract was approved July 24, and by November 4, 1931, Curtiss had assembled a prototype XP-6E by installing the XP-22's engine, nose, and landing gear on the YP-20's airframe. A more shallow fuselage, larger headrest, and tail wheel distinguished it from the XP-22. During January 1932 tests, this ship did 198 mph at sea level, but the 45 regular P-6E production ships delivered from De-

cember 1931 to March 1932 were less agile. Fifty gallons of fuel were contained behind the V-1570-23 engine, and a 50-gallon belly drop tank, or 244 pounds of bombs in wing racks, could be added.

The first P-6E went to Wright Field, as was customary, and 44 went to Selfridge Field for the 17th and 94th Pursuit squadrons. Famous at the time for their good-looking markings, the Curtiss Hawk was easy to fly but was usually outmaneuvered in mock dogfights with the lighter P-12Es of the other 1st Pursuit Group Squadron, the 27th. Seven P-6Es were lost between February 10 and June 2, 1932, by the 94th Squadron, but these accidents were due to collisions and weather and were not the fault of the aircraft.

In March 1933 the XP-6E became the XP-6F when it was modified with a turbosupercharged V-1570-55, a cockpit canopy, and open-sided wheel pants. Top speed of the XP-6F increased with altitude from 183 mph at sea level to 225 mph at 18,000 feet, but engine overheating prevented higher flights, and tests were discontinued on August 1, 1933.

A temporary installation of a V-1570-51 on a P-6E in August 1932 was represented by the XP-6G designation, but more significant was the XP-6H, the first Army multigun single-seater. Two .30-caliber synchronized guns, with 600 rpg, had been standard on pursuit ships since 1918, the only difference on the P-6E being that the guns were lowered from their usual position on the cowl to fire through troughs below the exhaust stacks. But the need for more firepower was felt, and a P-1B with another pair of .30-caliber guns in the upper wing had been tested in December 1931. Conversion of the first P-

CURTISS YP-20
Wright R-1820-9, 575 hp
DIMENSIONS: Span 31'6", Lg. 23'9", Ht. 9'2", Wing Area 252 sq. ft.
WEIGHT: Empty 2477 lb., Gross 3233 lb. Fuel 50–103 gal.
PERFORMANCE: Speed—Top 187 mph at s. l., 184 mph at 5000', Cruising 149 mph, Landing 61 mph. Service Ceiling 26,700', Absolute Ceiling 27,800', Climb 2400'/ 1 min., 5000'/2.3 min. Endurance 1.1 hrs. at top speed.   MFR

CURTISS XP-22
Curtiss V-1570-23, 600 hp
DIMENSIONS: Span 31'6", Lg. 23'7", Ht. 8'9", Wing Area 252 sq. ft.
WEIGHT: Empty 2597 lb., Gross 3354 lb. Fuel 50–100 gal.
PERFORMANCE: Speed—Top 202 mph at s. l., 200 mph at 5000', 195.5 mph at 10,000', Cruising 172 mph, Landing 61 mph. Service Ceiling 26,500', Absolute Ceiling 27,700', Climb 2400'/1 min., 5000'/2.3 min., 10,000'/5.2 min.   AMC

CURTISS XP-6E
Curtiss V-1570-23, 600 hp
DIMENSIONS: Span 31'6", Lg. 23'2", Ht. 8'10", Wing Area
    252 sq. ft.
WEIGHT: Empty 2699 lb., Gross 3392 lb. Fuel 50–100 gal.
PERFORMANCE: Speed—Top 198 mph at s. l., 194.5 mph
    at 5000', 189.5 mph at 10,000', Cruising 175 mph,
    Landing 61 mph. Service Ceiling 24,700', Absolute
    Ceiling 25,800', Climb 2400'/1 min., 5000'/2.3 min.,
    10,000'/5.3 min. Range 285 miles normal, 572 miles
    max.   AF

CURTISS P-6E
Curtiss V-1570-23, 600 hp
DIMENSIONS: As XP-6E
WEIGHT: Empty 2743 lb., Gross 3436 lb. Fuel 50–100 gal.
PERFORMANCE: Speed—Top 193 mph at s. l., 188 mph at
    10,000', Cruising 167 mph, Landing 61 mph. Service
    Ceiling 23,900', Absolute Ceiling 24,900', Climb 2460'/
    1 min.   MFR

CURTISS XP-6F
Curtiss V-1570-55, 600 hp at 15,000'
DIMENSIONS: As P-6E
WEIGHT: Empty 3149 lb., Gross 3842 lb. Fuel 50 gal.
PERFORMANCE: Speed—Top 225 mph at 18,000', 183 mph
    at s. l., 212 mph at 10,000'. Service Ceiling not deter-
    mined. Climb 1400'/1 min., 10,000'/6.1 min. Range 200
    miles at top speed.   PMB

CURTISS XP-6H
Curtiss V-1570-51, 600 hp
DIMENSIONS: As P-6E
WEIGHT: Gross 3854 lb.
PERFORMANCE: Speed—Top 190 mph at s. l. Service Ceil-
    ing 22,800', Absolute Ceiling 24,000', Climb 2000'/1
    min., 13,400'/10 min. Range 256 miles.   PMB

6E into a six-gun XP-6H—with an additional pair
of .30-caliber guns in the upper wing with 600
rounds each, and one with 450 rounds in each lower
wing—was approved on September 11, 1932, and
completed in April 1933. Wing guns added too
much weight for the airframe's safety and the project was discontinued.

The last and the finest of the Army's 247 Curtiss
Hawks was the final aircraft on the P-6E contract.
A metal monocoque fuselage and wing structure, a

600-hp V-1570-23 Conqueror with a turbosupercharger on the side, and a finely streamlined nose
pointed by a three-bladed prop characterized the
XP-23 delivered April 16, 1932. This good-looking
Curtiss resembled Britain's Hawker Fury, and it is
too bad that new monoplanes elbowed it out of the
way. A company report credited the XP-23 with 223
mph at 15,000 feet. In June 1932 the prototype was
refitted with the geared 600-hp V-1570-27 minus
the turbo and with a two-bladed prop. Redesignated

CURTISS XP-23
Curtiss V-1570-23, 600 hp
DIMENSIONS: Span 31'6", Lg. 23'10", Ht. 9'6", Wing Area
    252 sq. ft.
WEIGHT: Empty 3274 lb., Gross 4124 lb. Fuel 78–128 gal.
PERFORMANCE: Speed—Top 223 mph at 15,000', Cruising
    190 mph, Landing 70 mph. Service Ceiling 33,000',
    Climb 1370'/1 min. Range 435 miles normal, 703 miles
    max.   AMC

CURTISS YP-23   AMC

BERLINER-JOYCE XP-16
Curtiss V-1570A, 600 hp
DIMENSIONS: Span 34', Lg. 28'5", Ht. 8'11", Wing Area
    279 sq. ft.
WEIGHT: Empty 2756 lb., Gross 3927 lb. Fuel 78 gal.
PERFORMANCE: Speed—Top 186 mph at 5000', 176 mph
    at s. l., Cruising 148 mph, Landing 68 mph. Service
    Ceiling 26,200', Absolute Ceiling 28,000', Climb 2260'/
    1 min., 5000'/2.6 min.   AF

BERLINER-JOYCE Y1P-16
Curtiss V-1570-25, 600 hp
DIMENSIONS: Span 34', Lg. 28'2", Ht. 9', Wing Area 279
    sq. ft.
WEIGHT: Empty 2803 lb., Gross 3996 lb. Fuel 85–160 gal.
PERFORMANCE: Speed—Top 175 mph at s. l., 172 mph at
    5000', Cruising 151 mph, Landing 66 mph. Service
    Ceiling 21,600', Absolute Ceiling 22,800', Climb 1970'/
    1 min., 5000'/2.9 min. Range 650 miles.   AF

YP-23, this version had a more prosaic performance. Armament is reported to have consisted of two .30-caliber and one .50-caliber gun, plus four 122-pound bombs.

The last biplane fighter to enter service with an Army squadron was also the the only two-seat biplane pursuit in production for the Army since 1918. A design competition for two-seat fighters was held in April 1929, and Berliner-Joyce was chosen over Boeing and Curtiss proposals for a prototype contract in June. The first two-seat fighter since the TM-24, the Berliner-Joyce XP-16 arrived at Wright Field on September 1, 1930. A 600-hp Curtiss V-1570-25 Conqueror turned a two-bladed prop above

the tunnel radiator, and biplane wings were gulled into the fuselage. Armament included two .30-caliber nose guns, a flexible .30-caliber rear gun, and two 122-pound bombs.

A three-bladed propeller distinguished 25 YP-16s ordered March 31, 1931. The first arrived at Wright Field on March 1, 1932, and the others went to the 94th Pursuit Squadron, which passed its P-6Es on to the 33rd Squadron. Redesignated PB-1 (pursuit-biplace) in 1935, P-16s had better endurance than single-seaters in use at the time but were handicapped by low speed and bad visibility for landing. Without their prototypes' supercharger, performance at altitude was poor.

As the biplane period drew to an end, Army pursuit strength had increased from 12 squadrons in 1931 to 20 squadrons in 1933. These included one squadron each of P-6Es, P-12Es, and P-16s (the 17th, 27th, and 94th squadrons) with the 1st Pursuit Group at Selfridge, while the 8th Pursuit Group at Langley had the 33rd Squadron with the P-6E, the 37th with the P-6D, and the 35th and 36th with P-12s.

Boeings were also used by the 17th Pursuit Group (34th, 73rd, and 95th squadrons) at March Field, and the 20th Pursuit Group (55th, 77th, and 79th squadrons) at Barksdale Field. Older P-12s equipped the overseas units: the 3rd Squadron in the Philippines; the 16th Pursuit Group (24th, 29th, 74th, and 78th squadrons) in the Canal Zone; and the 18th Pursuit Group (6th and 19th squadrons) in Hawaii. Finally, there were the elderly pursuit-trainers at Kelly Field.

Chapter 6
Observation and Attack Aircraft, 1922-33

Experiments in Corps Observation, 1922–24

For the top Army leadership the most important role of aviation was still that of the observation squadrons. Improvements in speed or firepower were secondary to the ability to respond to the needs of ground units. A prototype development program consisting of two-seat Corps Observation (CO) aircraft, aimed at missions up to 12 miles behind enemy lines, explored the technical means of serving artillery and infantry forces.

All of these prototypes were Liberty-powered biplanes except the first, the CO-1. Designed by I. M. Laddon, of the Engineering Division, the CO-1 was the Army's first all-metal, high-wing monoplane. Two prototypes were built at McCook Field, one used for static tests, and the other first flown in August 1922. Two crewmen were carried along with 287 pounds of observation equipment and 300 pounds of defensive armament (two fixed Browning and two flexible Lewis guns).

Gallaudet received the contract to develop a production version because of its work on the low-wing, all-metal DB-1 bomber. Its CO-1 version, improved with balanced ailerons and strengthened landing gear, first flew June 20, 1923, but only one example was built. The wing arrangement was considered bad for the observer's vision, so a projected CO-3 that would have replaced the corrugated dural skin with a fabric covering was dropped.

In 1922 the Engineering Division also built a conventional biplane, the CO-2, designed by Jean A. Roche with the usual Liberty, four guns, and fabric covering, but the prototype crashed during tests.

A rival from the Netherlands was the imported Fokker C IV, tested early in 1922. Designated CO-4 by the Air Service, this two-seat biplane, in typical Fokker style, included a steel-tubed, fabric-covered fuselage, wooden cantilever wing structure with N

ENGINEERING DIVISION CO-1
Liberty 12, 390 hp
DIMENSIONS: Span 55'9", Lg. 33'7", Ht. 10'4", Wing Area 480 sq. ft.
WEIGHT: Empty 2977 lb., Gross 4751 lb. Fuel 119 gal.
PERFORMANCE: Speed—Top 118 mph at s. l., 114 mph at 6500', 111 mph at 10,000', Stalling 58 mph. Service Ceiling 16,600', Absolute Ceiling 18,400', Climb 775'/1 min., 10,000'/18.6 min. Range 510 miles, Endurance 4.6 hrs., at 111 mph.   AF

GALLAUDET CO-1
Liberty 12A, 420 hp
DIMENSIONS: Span 56'2", Lg. 33'8", Ht. 10'2", Wing Area 492 sq. ft.
WEIGHT: Empty 3042 lb., Gross 4751 lb. Fuel 117 gal.
PERFORMANCE: Speed—Top 121 mph at s. l.   AF

struts, and square nose radiator. The main gas tank was between the wheels, a feature intended to protect the crew in case of fire. However, it was a hazard in a crash landing and was not used on two more CO-4s delivered in 1923 with a rounded radiator.

Five CO-4A two-seaters were delivered in 1924 with a streamlined nose and side radiators that could be extended to suit temperature requirements. Three of these planes were service-tested at Langley Field.

The last Fokker observation biplane tested by the Army was the Atlantic AO-1, built by the New Jersey factory affiliated with Fokker. Essentially a CO-4 refinement with the circular radiator, it was tested in November 1924. AO then stood for Army Observation, a role calling for deeper penetrations of enemy territory than that expected of Corps observation planes. Actually a twin-engine three-seater like 1919's LePere triplane was envisioned, but the designation was allocated to this Atlantic two-seater—temporarily, as it turned out, for the Army didn't buy the aircraft.

Another foreign design tested in 1924 was the Cox-Klemin CO, a modified Heinkel HD 17 pow-

ENGINEERING DIVISION CO-2
Liberty 12, 390 hp
DIMENSIONS: Span 41'1", Lg. 30'9", Ht. 10'9", Wing Area 402 sq. ft.
WEIGHT: Empty 2669 lb., Gross 4084 lb.
PERFORMANCE: Speed—Top 115.5 mph at s. l., 124.5 mph at 10,000'. Service Ceiling 21,250', Absolute Ceiling 23,300', Climb 550'/1 min., 10,000'/17.1 min. Range 500 miles, Endurance 4 hrs.   AF

FOKKER CO-4A (Below)
Liberty 12A, 423 hp
DIMENSIONS: Span 39'6", Lg. 30'4", Ht. 10'7", Wing Area 407 sq. ft.
WEIGHT: Empty 3140 lb., Gross 4694 lb. Fuel 92 gal.
PERFORMANCE: Speed—Top 134 mph at s. l., 121 mph at 10,000', Landing 58 mph. Service Ceiling 14,950', Absolute Ceiling 17,060', Climb 820'/1 min., 10,000'/18.4 min. Endurance 3.7 hrs.   AF

FOKKER CO-4 (Above)
Liberty 12A, 420 hp
DIMENSIONS: Span 39'6", Lg. 29'8", Ht. 10'10", Wing Area 417 sq. ft.
WEIGHT: Empty 2911 lb., Gross 4494 lb. Fuel 90 gal.
PERFORMANCE: Speed—Top 131 mph at s. l., 122.6 mph at 10,000', Stalling 67 mph. Service Ceiling 16,100', Absolute Ceiling 17,900', Climb 990'/1 min., 10,000'/14.8 min. Range 367 miles, Endurance 3 hrs.   AF

ATLANTIC AO-1
Liberty 12, 435 hp
DIMENSIONS: Span 39'6", Lg. 30'4", Wing Area 397 sq. ft.
WEIGHT: Empty 2967 lb., Gross 4525 lb. Fuel 91 gal.
PERFORMANCE: Speed—Top 135 mph at s. l., 122 mph at 10,000', Landing 58 mph. Service Ceiling 15,300', Absolute Ceiling 16,850', Climb 1050'/1 min., 10,000'/14.25 min. Range 439 miles.   AF

COX-KLEMIN CK-CO2
Napier-Lion 450 hp
DIMENSIONS: Span 42'4", Lg. 30'6", Ht. 10'8", Wing Area 420 sq. ft.
WEIGHT: Empty 3021 lb., Gross 4741 lb. Fuel 89 gal.
PERFORMANCE: Speed—Top 90 mph at s. l., 96 mph at 6500', 102 mph at 15,000', Landing 55 mph. Service Ceiling 19,150', Absolute Ceiling 20,850', Climb 1230'/1 min., 10,000'/11 min. Range 408 miles.   AF

ENGINEERING DIVISION CO-5
Liberty 12A, 428 hp
DIMENSIONS: Span 43', Lg. 27'2", Ht. 10'2", Wing Area 438 sq. ft.
WEIGHT: Empty 2869 lb., Gross 4427 lb. Fuel 93 gal.
PERFORMANCE: Speed—Top 133 mph at s. l., 123 mph at 10,000', Stalling 58 mph. Service Ceiling 17,750', Absolute Ceiling 19,500', Climb 1090'/1 min., 10,000'/12.8 min. Range 450 miles.   AF

ENGINEERING DIVISION XCO-6
Liberty 12, 428 hp
DIMENSIONS: Span 48', Lg. 29'8", Ht. 9'8", Wing Area 481 sq. ft.
WEIGHT: Empty 3049 lb., Gross 4607 lb. Fuel 91 gal.
PERFORMANCE: Speed—Top 134 mph at s. l., 122 mph at 10,000', Stalling 64.5 mph. Service Ceiling 15,900', Absolute Ceiling 17,450', Climb 1125'/1 min., 10,000'/13 min. Range 440 miles.   AF

ered by a British 450-hp Napier Lion with internal supercharger. For some reason it was labeled the CK CO-2 during tests, and had no provisions for military equipment when tested.

The Engineering Division next offered the CO-5, which used the wings of the second TP-1 fighter, but reversed them, putting the larger one above the fuselage to improve visibility downward. The first version was tested in October 1923 with 375-square-foot, single-bay wings and frontal radiator, but in November 1924 it reappeared with wider 438-square-foot wings and a "chin" radiator. The data given here is for this version, but the photograph shows the aircraft after a turbosupercharger and wider two-bay wings were installed to enable

it, as the XCO-5A, to set an American altitude record of 38,704 feet on January 29, 1926.

The last Engineering Division prototype was the XCO-6 (by now all experimental aircraft had the X prefix). Designed by Roche, it was first fitted with an inverted Liberty but was tested in November 1924 with a standard engine and chin radiator (later called the XCO-6B); finally, as the XCO-6C it became a test-bed for an inverted air-cooled Liberty. Performance and flying qualities were said to be excellent, but the double-bay, wire-braced wing was bad for maintenance work. Three guns were provided.

The officer's board that met in December 1924 to evaluate observation planes considered the XCO-6

BOEING XCO-7B
Liberty 12 (V-1410) inverted, 420 hp
DIMENSIONS: Span 45′, Lg. 30′11″, Ht. 10′8″, Wing Area
　440 sq. ft.
WEIGHT: Empty 3107 lb., Gross 4665 lb. Fuel 93 gal.
PERFORMANCE: Speed—Top 122 mph at s. l., 110.5 mph
　at 10,000′, Stalling 55 mph. Service Ceiling 13,050′,
　Absolute Ceiling 14,850′, Climb 810′/1 min., 10,000′/
　20.5 min. Range 330 miles.　　　　　　　　　　AF

ATLANTIC XCO-8
Liberty 12A, 400 hp
DIMENSIONS: Span 45′, Lg. 30′, Wing Area 495 sq. ft.
WEIGHT: Empty 3065 lb., Gross 4680 lb. Fuel 93 gal.
PERFORMANCE: Speed—Top 130 mph at s. l., 117 mph at
　10,000′, Stalling 62 mph. Service Ceiling 16,350′, Ab-
　solute Ceiling 18,000′, Climb 1080′/1 min., 10,000′/13.5
　min. Range 440 miles.　　　　　　　　　　　AF

the best of the observation types discussed thus far, followed, in order of merit, by the AO-1, CO-5, CO-8, and the Cox-Klemin, but the board stated that the new Curtiss and Douglas types were "so far superior to all of the others that no consideration should be given to the rest." After this, the Army left all aircraft construction to private firms, and the McCook Field facility limited itself to testing. Since 1918 it had produced about 37 prototypes, some of which had made important advances in the "state of the art."

The observation board also agreed that the worst of the observation types tested was the "very poor" CO-7, which Boeing made by combining a standard DH-4M-1 fuselage with a tapered wing and new landing gear. Three airframes were made: one without an engine for static tests, the XCO-7A with a standard Liberty, and the XCO-7B flown with an inverted Liberty.

The last aircraft in the Corps Observation series was the Atlantic XCO-8. After that, all observation planes were numbered in a series from 0-1 to 0-63. The XCO-8 was simply a DH-4M-2 with the Loening wings used in the COA-1. Performance was better than on the standard DH-4 but inferior to the other types being considered. Twenty sets of Loening wings were ordered for use on DH-4s in airmail service.

Amphibians

Grover Loening had proposed to the Air Service on September 23, 1923, an amphibian aircraft that would use the same engine and layout as the DH-4B and have superior performance. Realizing the usefulness of such a type, especially to the three overseas observation squadrons in the "islands" and the Canal Zone, the Army ordered a prototype, the XCOA-1.

The prototype was ready on June 9, 1924, and although a pilot's error ended the first day's flights with a crash, ten COA-1 amphibians were ordered in July. The first was flight delivered January 17, 1925, and immediately lived up to its promise. The wheels folded up into the fuselage above the metal-covered hull, an inverted Liberty turned a four-bladed propeller, and while the wing had the DH-4 planform, the Loening had improved airfoil section, metal ribs, and N struts. A Scarff ring around the observer's cockpit could accommodate a Lewis gun for defense, and a fixed Browning was on the engine cowl.

Contracts for 15 OA-1A, 9 OA-1B, and 10 OA-1C amphibians followed. Similar to the OA-1 except for a three-bladed metal propeller and new vertical tail, they were delivered from October 1926 to February 1928 from the Manhattan factory and rapidly became famous for their usefulness in exploration, mapping, and patrol of overseas departments.

The XO-10, a new version of the Loening, was designed (and known at one point as the XOA-2). It had the experimental Wright Tornado inverted, air-cooled engine with two-bladed propeller and a single main wheel retracting into the hull's centerline. The XO-10 was flight delivered July 3, 1929, after eight more had been ordered as the OA-2. Performance tests were not completed until No-

LOENING COA-1
Liberty V-1650-1, 428 hp
DIMENSIONS: Span 45', Lg. 34'7", Ht. 12'1", Wing Area
    495 sq. ft.
WEIGHT: Empty 3440 lb., Gross 5010 lb. Fuel 91 gal.
PERFORMANCE: Speed—Top 119 mph at s. l., 107 mph at
    10,000', Stalling 65 mph. Service Ceiling 11,900', Ab-
    solute Ceiling 14,160', Climb 630'/1 min., 5100'/10
    min. Range 348 miles.   AF

vember and showed marked degradation of climb
at high altitude.

The eight OA-2s were built at Bristol, Pennsylvania, by Keystone, which had bought Loening's
amphibian company, and delivered with the regular
retractable twin-wheel gear from June to September 1930. The Tornado engine's output was so poor
that it took more than 59 minutes to climb to 10,000
feet, and this engine was never again used in an
Army plane. While Keystone then offered an O-37
design as a counterpart of the Navy's Wasp-powered
OL-9, none were actually built.

Although the Army continued buying amphibians
with OA designations, they were no longer combat
planes with gun mounts but were ordinary commercial types used for transport and utility service
until World War II.

Douglas O-2 Series

The most important event in observation aviation
was the work of the officer's board convened to
select a standard replacement for the DH-4B. By
December 1, 1924, seven officers, led by Captain

LOENING OA-1C
Liberty V-1650-1, 428 hp
DIMENSIONS: Span 44'11", Lg. 35'6", Ht. 11'11", Wing
    Area 504 sq. ft.
WEIGHT: Empty 3745 lb., Gross 5316 lb. Fuel 90–110 gal.
PERFORMANCE: Speed—Top 120 mph at s. l., 116 mph at
    10,000', Cruising 96 mph, Landing 58 mph. Service
    Ceiling 13,225', Absolute Ceiling 15,450', Climb 5000'/
    8.8 min. Range 363 miles at top speed.   AF

LOENING XO-10
Wright V-1460-1, 480 hp
DIMENSIONS: Span 46'1", Lg. 35', Wing Area 488 sq. ft.
WEIGHT: Empty 3565 lb., Gross 5134 lb. Fuel 145 gal.
PERFORMANCE: Speed—Top 116.5 mph at s. l., 104 mph
    at 10,000', Stalling 58 mph. Service Ceiling 11,090',
    Absolute Ceiling 13,650', Climb 533'/1 min., 10,000'/
    33.7 min.   AF

KEYSTONE OA-2
Wright V-1460-1, 480 hp
DIMENSIONS: Span 44'11", Lg. 34'11", Ht. 12', Wing Area
   504 sq. ft.
WEIGHT: Empty 3841 lb., Gross 5414 lb. Fuel 90 gal.
PERFORMANCE: Speed—Top 112 mph at s. l., 106.5 mph
   at 5000', 86 mph at 10,000', Landing 56 mph. Service
   Ceiling 8475', Absolute Ceiling 10,725', Climb 5000'/
   14.2 min.   MFR

Gerald Brower, had begun flight trials on eleven
two-seat biplane types.

What was wanted was a "good general utility
ship" for the observation squadrons, and speed was
not a major objective. The Liberty engine would be
the power plant, although the airframe should be
adaptable to more recent units like the Packard. As
stated in the board's report, the new type should
have the following characteristics:

- ability to get in and out of small, poor fields easily
  and safely with comparatively inexperienced pilots
- best possible safety features (flying characteristics,
  structure, tank location, etc.)
- tank capacity sufficient for long cruising range
- good vision for cross-country work in bad weather
- provision for carrying quantities of freight, baggage, etc., on airways, transport and similar
  work—including the ability to carry varying loads
  without changing the balance of the airplane
- best possible accommodations, arrangements, vision, gunfire, comfort, etc., in the rear cockpit for
  observation work, attack work, gunnery training,
  transformation flying, and passengers on cross-
  country

- rugged construction, ability to withstand rough
  handling by inexperienced mechanics, accessibil-
  ity of parts, ability to stand weathering in all cli-
  mates
- adaptability to being fitted with skis and pontoons

The board was unanimous in recommending that
the Douglas O-2 be adopted as the standard observation type, adding:

This airplane with Liberty engine proved to be
without doubt the logical successor to the DH-4B.
Its flying qualities appeared to be perfect, it was
very maneuverable and controlled beautifully. It
could not be made to spin from a stall, and when
attempts were made to force it in, it brought itself
out immediately. It appeared to have no tricks,
landed very easily and handled well on the ground.
An outstanding characteristic was that each one who
flew it felt perfectly at home in it from the first
momement. For observation work, the plane was
exceptionally good. The angles of vision and of flexible gunfire were excellent, and cockpit location
nearly ideal and the arrangement very well worked
out. The flexible guns were operated at high speed
in dives and zooms with very pleasing results, the
slipstream not affecting the accuracy of fire. The
pilot's angles of vision were very good for cross-
country. In construction, the plane is a very simple
and straightforward chrome molybdenum steel tube,
wire-braced fuselage, with single-bay wire-braced
wings and wide-tread axleless landing gear . . . .

Douglas had already won the Army's favor with
its successful "World Cruiser" planes of 1924, and

DOUGLAS XO-2
Liberty V-1650-1, 425 hp
DIMENSIONS: Span 39'8", Lg. 29'6", Wing Area 411 sq. ft.
WEIGHT: Empty 2812 lb., Gross 4427 lb. Fuel 92.5 gal.
PERFORMANCE: Speed—Top 137 mph at s. l., 127 mph at
10,000', Cruising 116 mph, Stalling 60 mph. Service
Ceiling 16,900', Absolute Ceiling 18,600', Climb 1075'/
1 min., 10,000'/13.4 min. Range 408 miles.   AF

DOUGLAS O-2
Liberty V-1650-1, 439 hp
DIMENSIONS: Span 39'8", Lg. 29'7", Ht. 10'10", Wing Area
411 sq. ft.
WEIGHT: Empty 3032 lb., Gross 4785 lb. Fuel 118–30 gal.
PERFORMANCE: Speed—Top 128 mph at s. l., 114 mph at
10,000', Cruising 103 mph, Landing 65 mph. Service
Ceiling 12,275', Absolute Ceiling 14,025', Climb 807'/
1 min., 6500'/10.9 min. Range 400 miles.   AF

the new XO-2's simple and neat proportions seemed to suit its role. Ordered in July 1924, the XO-2 was built by the Santa Monica firm in time for its McCook Field tests to be completed by December 11. A second airframe for static tests was supplied in May 1925.

The prototype had a Liberty with a smoothly shuttered chin radiator, but was also tested on January 12, 1925, with the 500-hp Packard 1A-1500 and shorter wings. Top speed rose from 137 to 150 mph and the service ceiling from 16,900 to 21,200 feet. This engine seemed unready for service adoption,

however, so Liberty engines were specified for 75 production aircraft ordered on February 16, 1925. It was the largest contract Douglas had received to date, and the largest Army two-seater contract since 1918.

Production deliveries on the first 45 Douglas O-2s began in January 1926. Normal armament was one .30-caliber Browning fixed gun over the engine and one or two Lewis guns on the observer's Scarff ring, but when the 3rd Attack Group became the first to receive the O-2s to replace its DH-4Bs, a pair of .30-caliber Brownings and bomb racks were added to the lower wings.

Aircraft specialized for ground attack were required, and in March 1926 the 46th O-2 was ordered converted to the XA-2 attack (the XA-1 designation had been used for a Cox-Klemin ambulance plane). Powered by an inverted air-cooled Liberty—thus dispensing with the vulnerable water radiator—the XA-2 was armed with six .30-caliber Brownings firing forward and two flexible Lewis guns for the gunner. Two of the fixed guns were in the nose,

DOUGLAS XA-2
Liberty V-1410, 433 hp
DIMENSIONS: Span 39'8", Lg. 29'7", Ht. 11', Wing Area
    414 sq. ft.
WEIGHT: Empty 3179 lb., Gross 4985 lb.
PERFORMANCE: Speed—Top 130 mph. Climb 800'/1
    min.   AF

THOMAS-MORSE O-6
Liberty V-1650-1, 435 hp
DIMENSIONS: Span 39'9", Lg. 28'8", Ht. 11', Wing Area
    418 sq. ft.
WEIGHT: Empty 2947 lb., Gross 4734 lb. Fuel 120 gal.
PERFORMANCE: Speed—Top 129 mph at s. l., 116 mph at
    10,000', Cruising 101 mph, Stalling 66 mph. Service
    Ceiling 13,175', Absolute Ceiling 14,825', Climb 892'/
    1 min., 10,000'/18.6 min. Range 424 miles.   AF

two were in the upper wing, two were in the lower
wing, and bombs were in internal racks.

Eighteen Douglases were delivered in 1926 as
O-2As with night-flying equipment and six unarmed O-2Bs had dual controls for use as senior
officers' personal transports. The remaining five aircraft covered by the contract were used for power
plant development. Douglas also delivered six O-5
seaplanes, an armed twin-float version of the famed
Liberty-powered World Cruiser used in the Philippines.

Thomas-Morse contracted April 21, 1926, to build
an all-metal version of the O-2 that was to be called
the O-6. The first of five O-6 biplanes was tested at
McCook Field May 18, 1926.

Three Douglas O-2s with Packard engines were
known as the O-7 and first tested April 26, 1926.
The O-8 was another O-2 tested in October with a
400-hp Wright R-1454 radial, while the last O-2
became the O-9 with a geared Packard and four-
bladed propeller. All five of these aircraft reverted
to the normal Liberty engine O-2 configuration after
these tests.

Douglas next received a contract for the O-2C,
which introduced a new nose radiator, and built 46
O-2Cs, two unarmed O-2D transports, and an O-2E
with modified tail fin. Two more O-2Cs went to a
San Diego Marine unit as the OD-1. There was no
O-2F or G model. Eight O-2Cs were sold to Mexico.

The most widely used model was the O-2H, with
a pronounced forward wing stagger and refined
landing gear, nose, and tail. Armament still included the standard fixed Browning gun, but a second Browning replaced the traditional drum-fed
Lewis guns in the rear cockpit. There were 141 O-
2Hs delivered between 1927 and 1929 to both Air
Corps and National Guard squadrons, along with
three O-2J transports and 59 O-2K dual-control

DOUGLAS O-7
Packard 1A-1500, 504 hp
DIMENSIONS: Span 39'8", Lg. 29'6", Wing Area 411 sq. ft.
WEIGHT: Empty 2914 lb., Gross 4708 lb. Fuel 120 gal.
PERFORMANCE: Speed—Top 137 mph at s. l., 131 mph at
    10,000', Cruising 110 mph, Stalling 67 mph. Service
    Ceiling 17,350', Absolute Ceiling 19,125', Climb 1065'/
    1 min., 10,000'/13.3 min.   MFR

DOUGLAS O-8   MFR

DOUGLAS O-2C (as OD-1)
Liberty V-1650, 439 hp
DIMENSIONS: Span 39'8", Lg. 29'6", Ht. 10'10", Wing Area
    411 sq. ft.
WEIGHT: Empty 2941 lb., Gross 4630 lb. Fuel 110 gal.
PERFORMANCE: Speed—Top 126 mph at s. l. Service Ceil-
    ing 12,275', Absolute Ceiling 14,025', Climb 10,000'/
    21.7 min. Range 606 miles.   AF

DOUGLAS O-2H
Liberty V-1650, 433 hp
DIMENSIONS: Span 40', Lg. 30', Ht. 10'6".
WEIGHT: Empty 2818 lb., Gross 4485 lb. Fuel 113 gal.
PERFORMANCE: Speed—Top 133 mph at s. l., 128 mph at
    10,000', Cruising 107 mph, Landing 58 mph. Service
    Ceiling 17,100', Absolute Ceiling 18,900', Climb 1050'/
    1 min., 10,000'/13.6 min. Range 512 miles.   AF

WRIGHT XO-3
Wright V-1950 (T-3), 645 hp
DIMENSIONS: Span 45', Lg. 31', Ht. 10'7", Wing Area N/A.
WEIGHT: Empty 4193 lb., Gross 5997 lb.
PERFORMANCE: Speed—Top 146 mph., Cruising 132 mph.
    Service Ceiling 18,450', Absolute Ceiling 20,200',
    Climb 6500'/6.9 min. Range 395 miles.   AF

basic trainers. The latter were redesignated BT-1
for school use and were the last Liberty-powered
Army planes to remain in service, not retiring until
September 1935.

Army observation aviation during this period consisted of a twelve-plane squadron for each of the
nine continental corps areas and three overseas departments. By January 1930, 19 National Guard
squadrons were active, and two school squadrons
at Kelly and Maxwell fields got the secondhand
aircraft. Douglas O-2 biplanes were used by nearly
all of these squadrons by the end of the 1920s.

Curtiss Falcons

While the Curtiss Falcon came in second in the
observation competition, it seemed to hold first
place in the public imagination, possibly both because of its sharp-looking engine cowl and swept-
back upper wing and the appropriate name assigned to it by company publicity.

Designed by Rex Beisel, the XO-1 prototype was
tested with a Liberty engine on December 8, 1924,
and showed "remarkably high performance," excellent flying qualities, and "handled exactly like
a pursuit plane." Doubts were raised by the observation board about its suitability for "average
pilots," as well as the maintenance of its riveted
duraluminum tube fuselage structure. The board
suggested a service-test purchase of the Curtiss
type.

In January 1925 the XO-1, like the XO-2, was
tested with the Packard 1A-1500, and although performance was best on the Curtiss competitor, no
order for this version was placed. Another type appearing at this time was the Wright XO-3, a double-
bay biplane with an experimental Wright V-1950
engine. It was not purchased by the Army, and the
Wright Company abandoned efforts at aircraft construction to concentrate quite successfully on engines. Another observation project of the period,
the Liberty-powered Martin XO-4, was canceled
before completion.

Ten Curtiss Falcons had been ordered for service
tests. The first appeared in February 1926 with the
small and neatly cowled Curtiss D-12 (V-1150), the
ninth was tested in October 1926 as the O-1A with
a 430-hp Liberty, and another became the XO-11.
It was the Liberty version that was first ordered in
1926 as the O-11 for observation squadrons. Sixty-
six O-11s went into service in 1927–28 armed with
the one .30-caliber fixed and two .30-caliber flexible
guns usual on observation planes. They served with
the 5th, 12th, and 99th squadrons, as well as with
the National Guard.

As for the Army's attack units, a board convened
on August 2, 1926, had agreed that the Curtiss was

CURTISS XO-1
Liberty V-1650-1, 431 hp
DIMENSIONS: Span 38′, Lg. 28′7″, Wing Area 350 sq. ft.
WEIGHT: Empty 2460 lb., Gross 4075 lb. Fuel 92–119 gal.
PERFORMANCE: Speed—Top 152 mph at s. l., 136 mph at 10,000′, Cruising 126 mph, Landing 63 mph. Service Ceiling 18,700′, Absolute Ceiling 20,300′, Climb 1235′/1 min., 10,000′/11.1 min. Range 440 miles.
(with Packard 1A-1500, 510 hp)
WEIGHT: Empty 2277 lb., Gross 3857 lb.
PERFORMANCE: Speed—Top 154 mph at s. l., 147 mph at 10,000′, Service Ceiling 23,400′, Absolute Ceiling 24,800′, Climb 1753′/1 min., 10,000′/7.4 min. Range 424 miles.   AF

CURTISS O-1
Curtiss V-1150, 448 hp
DIMENSIONS: Span 38′, Lg. 28′4″, Ht. 10′1″, Wing Area 350 sq. ft.
WEIGHT: Empty 2417 lb., Gross 4165 lb. Fuel 113 gal.
PERFORMANCE: Speed—Top 143 mph at s. l., 135.5 at 10,000′, Landing 64 mph. Service Ceiling 17,375′, Absolute Ceiling 19,100′, Climb 1070′/1 min., 10,000′/13.1 min. Range 560 miles at 112 mph.   AF

CURTISS O-11
Liberty V-1650-1, 433 hp
DIMENSIONS: Span 38′, Lg. 28′4″, Ht. 10′1″, Wing Area 353 sq. ft.
WEIGHT: Empty 2887 lb., Gross 4561 lb. Fuel 113–69 gal.
PERFORMANCE: Speed—Top 146 mph at s. l., 134 mph at 10,000′, Cruising 115 mph, Landing 64 mph. Service Ceiling 16,630′, Absolute Ceiling 18,350′, Climb 1066′/1 min., 10,000′/13.6 min. Range 689 miles.   MFR

CURTISS A-3
Curtiss V-1150-3, 435 hp
DIMENSIONS: Span 38′, Lg. 28′4″, Ht. 10′1″, Wing Area 353 sq. ft.
WEIGHT: Empty 2612 lb., Gross 4378 lb. Fuel 113–69 gal.
PERFORMANCE: Speed—Top 141 mph, Cruising 116 mph, Landing 61 mph. Service Ceiling 15,600′, Absolute Ceiling 17,300′, Climb 1046′/1 min., 5000′/5.8 min. Range 630 miles at top speed.   AF

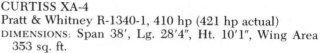

CURTISS XA-4
Pratt & Whitney R-1340-1, 410 hp (421 hp actual)
DIMENSIONS: Span 38', Lg. 28'4", Ht. 10'1", Wing Area
353 sq. ft.
WEIGHT: Empty 2348 lb., Gross 4114 lb. Fuel 114 gal.
PERFORMANCE: Speed—Top 139 mph at s. l., 136 mph at
5000', Cruising 112 mph, Landing 58 mph. Service
Ceiling 15,975', Absolute Ceiling 17,700', Climb 1040'/
1 min.   MFR

CURTISS O-1B
Curtiss V-1150-3, 435 hp
DIMENSIONS: Same as A-3 and O-11
WEIGHT: Empty 2577 lb., Gross 4240 lb. Fuel 113 gal.
PERFORMANCE: Speed—Top 140 mph at s. l., 132 mph at
10,000', Cruising 111 mph, Landing 60 mph. Service
Ceiling 16,325', Absolute Ceiling 18,350', Climb 1060'/
1 min., 10,000'/13.7 min. Range 612 miles.   AF

CURTISS A-3B
Curtiss V-1150-5, 435 hp
DIMENSIONS: Span 38', Lg. 27'2", Ht. 10'6", Wing Area
353 sq. ft.
WEIGHT: Empty 2875 lb., Gross 4458 lb., Max. 4476 lb.
Fuel 113–49 gal.
PERFORMANCE: Speed—Top 139 mph at s. l., 136 mph at
5000', Cruising 110 mph, Landing 60 mph. Service
Ceiling 14,400', Absolute Ceiling 16,100', Climb 948'/
1 min., 5000'/6.25 min. Range 628 miles.   AF

the most suitable plane until a more satisfactory
type could be developed. On February 2, 1927, 65
Falcons were ordered, and a September contract
added 36 more. They were delivered as 76 A-3, 21
O-1B, and four O-1C Falcons, the latter being unarmed official transports.

The first A-3 was ready by October 31, 1927. A
435-hp Curtiss D-12D engine was under the smooth
cowling, the radiator was underneath, and a neat
prop spinner gave the nose the characteristic "Eversharp pencil" appearance. The lower wing was
straight, while the upper wing was swept back from
a straight center section. There were two nose guns
and two wing guns firing forward, as well as two
flexible Lewis rear guns. All were .30-caliber, with
400 rounds provided for the wing guns and 600

rounds for the others. Wing racks for 200 pounds of
fragmentation bombs were attached, or a 56-gallon
auxiliary tank could be carried behind the tunnel
radiator.

Weapons were removed and dual controls installed on six A-3s, which became the A-3A trainers.
The second A-3 was fitted with the new air-cooled
Pratt & Whitney Wasp radial and tested in May
1928 as the XA-4. Twenty-one O-1B observation
versions were similar to the A-3 but had only one
Browning gun firing forward.

The next Falcon contract, dated June 19, 1929,
ordered the A-3B and O-1E versions using the V-
1150-5, balanced (Frise) ailerons and elevators, and
a .30-caliber Browning flexible gun in the rear instead of the drum-fed Lewis guns. Seventy-eight A-

CURTISS O-1E
Curtiss V-1150-5, 435 hp
DIMENSIONS: Same as A-3B
WEIGHT: Empty 2922 lb., Gross 4347 lb. Fuel 113 gal.
PERFORMANCE: Speed—Top 141 mph at s. l., 128 mph at
10,000', Cruising 122 mph, Landing 59 mph. Service
Ceiling 15,300', Climb 980'/1 min., 10,000'/14.4 min.
Range 550 miles.   AF

CURTISS XO-1G (Y10-1G)
Curtiss V-1150-5, 435 hp
DIMENSIONS: Same as A-4, O-1E
WEIGHT: Empty 3143 lb., Gross 4488 lb. Fuel 103 gal.
PERFORMANCE: Speed—Top 145 mph at s. l., 136 mph at
10,000', Cruising 116 mph, Landing 61 mph. Service
Ceiling 16,750', Climb 1060'/1 min., 10,000'/13.6 min.
Range 510 miles.   AF

3Bs were built under two contracts. The first was
tested in April 1930 and was armed with five
Browning guns and 2,700 rounds. Attack Falcons
equipped all four of the Air Corps ground attack
squadrons: the 8th, 13th, and 90th of the 3rd Attack
Group at Fort Crockett, Texas, and the 26th Attack
Squadron in Hawaii.

Similar to the A-3B but armed with just one fixed
and one flexible Browning with 500 rounds per gun,
was the O-1E, which appeared in December 1929.
Curtiss built 35 O-1Es, one unarmed O-1F transport, and, in October 1930, one XO-1G (later Y1O-
1G) that introduced such refinements as a new rear
gun mount allowing for more cockpit room and a
place to fold the gun away, added wheel pants, and
a tail wheel. The latter was adapted and retrofitted
to earlier Falcons, but the pants proved unsuitable
for service. Thirty O-1G Falcons were ordered January 17, 1931, and delivery began in May 1931.

Since each Army observation squadron worked
independently with ground forces, group organization had been limited to the 9th Observation
Group, formed with the three squadrons (1st, 5th,
and 99th) based at Mitchel Field, New York. The
group was equipped with Curtiss Falcons, which

CURTISS O-1G
Curtiss V-1150-5, 435 hp
DIMENSIONS: Span 38', Lg. 27'4", Ht. 9'11", Wing Area
360 sq. ft.
WEIGHT: Empty 3090 lb., Gross 4425 lb. Fuel 104 gal.
PERFORMANCE: Speed—Top 143.5 at s. l., 131 mph at 10,-
000', Cruising 123 mph, Landing 60 mph. Service Ceiling 14,275', Absolute Ceiling 16,075', Climb 910'/1
min., 10,000'/17.5 min.   ARNOLD

CURTISS XO-13
Curtiss V-1570-1, 600 hp
DIMENSIONS: Span 38', Lg. 28'4", Ht. 10'1", Wing Area
    353 sq. ft.
WEIGHT: Empty 2637 lb., Gross 4318 lb. Fuel 113 gal.
PERFORMANCE: Speed—Top 164 mph at s. l., 157 mph at
    10,000', Cruising 130 mph, Landing 60 mph. Service
    Ceiling 21,775', Absolute Ceiling 23,300', Climb 1540'/
    1 min., 10,000'/8.5 min. Range 346 miles. (Photo shows
    XO-13A)   ARNOLD

CURTISS YO-13C
Curtiss V-1570-1, 600 hp
DIMENSIONS: Span 38', Lg. 27'6", Wing Area 353 sq. ft.
WEIGHT: Empty 3144 lb., Gross 4542 lb. Fuel 108–64 gal.
PERFORMANCE: Speed—Top 156 mph at s. l., 146 mph at
    10,000', Cruising 125 mph, Landing 60 mph. Service
    Ceiling 19,750', Absolute Ceiling 21,400', Climb 1290'/
    1 min., 10,000'/10.46 min.   PMB

CURTISS XO-16
Curtiss V-1750-1, 600 hp
DIMENSIONS: Same as YO-13C
WEIGHT: Empty 3025 lb., Gross 4305 lb. Fuel 100 gal.
PERFORMANCE: Speed—Top 162 mph at s. l., 156 mph at
    10,000', Cruising 130 mph, Landing 59 mph. Service
    Ceiling 21,750', Absolute Ceiling 23,300', Climb 10,-
    000'/8.59 min.   MFR

also went to the 12th and 16th Observation squadrons. In October 1930 the 12th Observation Group was activated at Brooks Field to control the O-1, O-2, and O-19 squadrons in the western states.

The Falcon series also included several examples testing new engines. First was the air-cooled Pratt & Whitney R-1340-1, installed in the XO-12, which looked like the XA-4 and had originally been an O-11 airframe. The Curtiss V-1570-1 Conqueror was used in September 1927 by the XO-13 and XO-13A conversions of O-1 airframes, with the XO-13A having wing radiators good for racing but not for service use. There was also an O-13B transport converted from an O-1C, and three YO-13C Falcons with the usual tunnel radiators followed the O-1E off the Curtiss line in August 1930.

The Conqueror engine was adapted for Prestone cooling and used on the XO-16 ordered December 28, 1927, and completed in May 1930. The usual two Brownings were carried, but the rear gun was on the new foldaway mount.

An experimental air-cooled Curtiss H-1640-1 engine was tried on the XO-18. The XO-16 and XO-18 were to have attack counterparts as the XA-5 and XA-6, but these projects were canceled. The first XO-18 had been converted from the first O-1B, but tests were stopped on July 24, 1930, because the cooling failed. A second O-18 converted from an O-11 was tested in January 1931, but the engine never worked out. The last aircraft on the O-1E contract was completed with a geared, Preston-cooled Conqueror as the Y1O-26.

The last Air Corps Falcons were ten O-39s with V-1570-25 engines ordered May 12, 1931, and the first was officially tested in September 1931. They had a smooth engine cowl with small Preston radiator underneath and a smaller rudder, but the wheel pants and cockpit canopy on the first example were usually removed from the aircraft serving at Mitchel Field.

Curtiss also built Falcons for export. Columbia purchased one with a D-12 engine in 1928, and 30 with 712-hp Wright R-1820F-2 Cyclones in 1932, which were used on both twin floats and wheels during the 1933 war with Peru. Peru itself had bought ten D-12 Falcons, while a reported 18 were acquired in 1931 by Chile, who transferred at least seven to Brazil in September 1932. Bolivia received seven Cyclone-powered Falcons in 1933.

The last Falcon built was a prototype with a SR-1820F-53, streamlined single-strut landing gear, and a long cockpit enclosure later used on the SBC and SOC types. Known only as the Falcon II, or F-1-37, it was first flown on November 6, 1934, and was destroyed on its fifth flight when the wings ripped off in a dive.

CURTISS XO-18

Curtiss H-1640, 600 hp

DIMENSIONS: Span 38′, Lg. 27′4″, Ht. 10′3″, Wing Area 353 sq. ft.

WEIGHT: Empty 2814 lb., Gross 4296 lb. Fuel 113 gal.

PERFORMANCE: Speed—Top 148.5 mph at s. l., 142.5 mph at 10,000′, Cruising 127 mph, Landing 59 mph. Service Ceiling 17,650′, Absolute Ceiling 19,200′, Climb 1255′/ 1 min., 10,000′/11.6 min. MFR

CURTISS Y10-26

Curtiss V-1570-11, 600 hp

DIMENSIONS: Span 38′, Lg. 27′6″, Ht. 10′6″, Wing Area 353 sq. ft.

WEIGHT: Empty 3179 lb., Gross 4587 lb. Fuel 109 gal.

PERFORMANCE: Speed—Top 167.5 mph at s. l., 159.5 mph at 10,000′, Cruising 143 mph, Landing 60 mph. Service Ceiling 20,400′, Absolute Ceiling 21,800′, Climb 10,- 000′/9.4 min. MFR

CURTISS O-39

Curtiss-1570-25, 600 hp

DIMENSIONS: Span 38′, Lg. 27′, Ht. 10′11½″, Wing Area 349.6 sq. ft.

WEIGHT: Empty 3301 lb., Gross 4647 lb. Fuel 106–42 gal.

PERFORMANCE: Speed—Top 174 mph at s. l., 167 at 10,- 000′, Cruising 153 mph, Landing 57 mph. Service Ceiling 22,400′, Climb 1550′/1 min., 10,000′/7.7 min. Range 540–650 miles. ARNOLD

CURTISS FALCON II

Wright SR-1820F-3, 700 hp at 8000′

DIMENSIONS: Span 38′, Lg. 26′6″, Ht. 10′3″, Wing Area 348 sq. ft.

WEIGHT: Empty 3447 lb., Gross 4770 lb., Max. 5100 lb. Fuel 103–58 gal.

PERFORMANCE: Speed—Top 205 mph at 8000′, Cruising 183 mph, Stalling 60 mph. Service Ceiling 26,000′, Climb 1600′/1 min. Range 367–560 miles. MFR

CURTISS FALCON II Seaplane   MFR

Observation Biplanes, 1928–31

The next trio of prototypes were designed as lightweight, unarmed two-seaters for training National
Guard pilots. Ordered December 12, 1927 and completed around November 23, 1928, the Douglas XO-
14 had a Wright Whirlwind, as did the Keystone
XO-15 ordered the same week.

In May 1928 a Consolidated PT-3 trainer using
the same engine was tested with observation equipment as the XO-17, and it was decided that the most
economical way of meeting the requirement was to
use standard primary trainers. Twenty-nine O-17s
and one O-17A (R-790-3 engine) were purchased
for the National Guard.

Thomas-Morse received a contract for four all-
metal, air-cooled observation biplanes on June 16,
1928, with two more added on December 20. They
were constructed of riveted dural tubing, with corrugated dural covering the fuselage and control.

DOUGLAS XO-14
Wright R-790-5, 240 hp
DIMENSIONS: Span 30′1″, Lg. 23′10″, Ht. 8′8″, Wing Area
    237 sq. ft.
WEIGHT: Empty 1758 lb., Gross 2500 lb. Fuel 40 gal.
PERFORMANCE: Speed—Top 121 mph at s. l., 113 mph at
    10,000′, Cruising 100 mph, Landing 53 mph. Service
    Ceiling 15,250′, Absolute Ceiling 17,100′, Climb 925′/
    1 min., 10,000′/16.3 min. Range 250 miles.   MFR

KEYSTONE XO-15
Wright R-790-5, 236 hp
DIMENSIONS: Span 37′3″, Lg. 27′1″, Ht. 7′9″, Wing Area
    256 sq. ft.
WEIGHT: Empty 1784 lb., Gross 2518 lb.
PERFORMANCE: Speed—Top 119 mph at s. l., 112 mph at
    10,000′, Cruising 95 mph, Landing 52 mph. Service
    Ceiling 16,600′, Absolute Ceiling 18,625′, Climb 925′/
    1 min., 10,000′/15.5 min.   AF

CONSOLIDATED XO-17
Wright R-790-1, 237 hp
DIMENSIONS: Span 34'6", Lg. 28'1", Ht. 10'3", Wing Area
295 sq. ft.
WEIGHT: Empty 1880 lb., Gross 2770 lb. Fuel 60 gal.
PERFORMANCE: Speed—Top 103 mph at s. l., 91 mph at
10,000', Cruising 83 mph, Landing 52 mph. Service
Ceiling 11,880', Absolute Ceiling 14,100'.   AF

THOMAS-MORSE XO-19
Pratt & Whitney R-1340-3, 450 hp
DIMENSIONS: Span 39'9", Lg. 28'6", Ht. 9'10", Wing Area
348 sq. ft.
WEIGHT: Empty 2342 lb., Gross 3994 lb. Fuel 112 gal.
PERFORMANCE: Speed—Top 146 mph at s. l., 141 mph at
10,000', Landing 58 mph. Service Ceiling 21,425', Absolute Ceiling 23,000', Climb 1250'/1 min., 10,000'/9.7
min.   .AF

THOMAS-MORSE YO-20
Pratt & Whitney R-1690-1, 525 hp
DIMENSIONS: Same as XO-19
WEIGHT: Empty 2559 lb., Gross 3907 lb. Fuel 103 gal.
PERFORMANCE: Speed—Top 147 mph at s. l., 140 mph at
10,000', Service Ceiling 22,600', Absolute Ceiling
24,400', Climb 1350'/1 min., 10,000'/9.5 min.   MFR

THOMAS-MORSE XO-21
Curtiss H-1640-1, 600 hp
DIMENSIONS: Span 39'9", Lg. 29'2", Ht. 10'4", Wing Area
348 sq. ft.
WEIGHT: Empty 2659 lb., Gross 4280 lb., Fuel 106 gal.
PERFORMANCE: Test data unavailable.   MFR

THOMAS-MORSE YO-23
Curtiss V-1570, 600 hp
DIMENSIONS: Span 39′9″, Lg. 28′10″, Ht. N/A, Wing Area
   348 sq. ft.
WEIGHT: Empty 2842 lb., Gross 4190 lb. Fuel 105 gal.
PERFORMANCE: Speed—Top 156 mph at s. l., 151 mph at
   10,000′, Cruising 125 mph, Landing 59 mph. Service
   Ceiling 22,275′, Absolute Ceiling 23,750′, Climb 1596′/
   1 min., 10,000′/8.2 min.   AF

VOUGHT O-28
Pratt & Whitney R-1340-C, 625 hp
DIMENSIONS: Span 36′, Lg. 24′8″, Ht. 10′1″, Wing Area
   327 sq. ft.
WEIGHT: Empty 2404 lb., Gross 3865 lb. Fuel 110 gal.
PERFORMANCE: Speed—Top 156.6 mph at s. l., 152 mph
   at 10,000′, Cruising 125 mph, Landing 58 mph. Service
   Ceiling 22,100′, Absolute Ceiling 23,600′, Climb 1570′/
   1 min., 10,000′/8.3 min.   AF

THOMAS-MORSE O-19B
Pratt & Whitney R-1340-7, 450 hp
DIMENSIONS: Span 39′9″, Lg. 28′4″, Wing Area 348 sq. ft.
WEIGHT: Gross 3800 lb., Fuel 82 gal.
PERFORMANCE: Speed—Top 139 mph at s. l., 135 mph at
   10,000′, Cruising 121 mph, Landing 57 mph. Service
   Ceiling 20,500′, Climb 1200′/1 min., 10,000′/11 min.
   Range 397–462 miles.   AF

The first prototype was the XO-19 of April 1929,
with an R-1340-3 Wasp, fixed Browning gun, and a
Lewis gun on the observer's ring, while the R-1340-
9 was used on the O-19. Next was the YO-20, in
September 1929, with an R-1690-1 Hornet, and the
fourth prototype became the XO-21 with a Curtiss
H-1690-1, which later changed to the XO-21A with
a Wright R-1750. The second prototype contract
produced another Wasp-powered O-19 and an O-
19A with a smaller 88-gallon fuel tank.

Thomas-Morse also produced a prototype with a
water-cooled V-1570-1 Conqueror engine. The YO-
23, ordered November 3, 1928, and tested September 18, 1929, lost out to the Douglas O-25 as the
Army's Conqueror-powered two-seater.

Another company tried to compete with the O-19
as the Wasp-powered observation type. Chance
Vought's O-28 was an Army version of the Navy's
O2U-3. Purchased May 5, 1928, off the Vought production line, the O-28 had an R-1340 Wasp C rated
at 450 hp but actually yielding 625 hp. The Thomas-
Morse design was the Air Corps choice, however.

Seventy O-19B aircraft were ordered August 16,
1929, a few days after the Thomas-Morse Company
had been sold to Consolidated Aircraft. The first O-
19B appeared in March 1930, armed with one
Browning fixed gun and one Browning flexible gun

THOMAS-MORSE O-19C
Pratt & Whitney R-1340-7, 450 hp
DIMENSIONS: Span 39'9", Lg. 29', Ht. 10', Wing Area 348
  sq. ft.
WEIGHT: Empty 2769 lb., Gross 3921 lb. Fuel 76 gal.
PERFORMANCE: Speed—Top 143 mph at s. l., 137 mph at
  10,000', Cruising 124 mph, Landing 57 mph. Service
  Ceiling 20,000', Absolute Ceiling 21,800', Climb 1810'/
  1 min., 10,000'/11 min. Range 377–436 miles.   AF

with 900 .30-caliber rounds. Seventy-one O-19Cs ordered June 12, 1930, began appearing in November 1930 with ring cowl and tail wheel. The O-19D was a C converted to transport service, while a new R-1340-15, supercharged to 5,000 feet, powered 30 O-19Es ordered February 1931 and delivered beginning in September. They were to be the last aircraft built by Thomas-Morse, whose few assets merged with Consolidated.

The O-19 series totaled 177 aircraft and served with eight of the 13 Army observation squadrons in 1931. These included all four overseas units (the 2nd in the Philippines, 4th and 50th in Hawaii, and the 7th in the Canal Zone), as well as the 12th, 15th, 22nd, and 88th in the United States. They also served to demonstrate the suitability of all-metal construction for Army aircraft.

Thomas-Morse had been less successful in adapting its aircraft to the more powerful Curtiss Conqueror engine with Preston cooling. A geared V-1570-11 was installed in the first O-19B, which was rebuilt in August 1930 as the Y1O-33, but the Douglas O-25C and Curtiss O-39 got the Air Corps contracts for observation types with this engine.

The last prototype built by Thomas-Morse was a sesquiplane (small lower wing) known as the XO-932 when first tested at Wright Field in June 1931. A geared, Prestone-cooled Conqueror in a neat cowl, N struts, and wheel pants were featured. The type was rejected by an Army board because the basic structure seemed weak and the board now believed that "a monoplane is the most desirable type for observation purposes because of its superior qualities of vision." While not sold to the Army, the aircraft received the Y1O-41 designation and was used as a Consolidated Company hack until it was sold to Mexico. The end of the biplane was in sight.

The Last Douglas Biplanes

Despite vigorous competition from Curtiss and Thomas-Morse, Douglas kept winning most of the Air Corps observation business during the biplane period. Douglas two-seaters were the last combat biplanes bought by the Army. Part of its success was due to variety in development of the basic airframe, and when the Air Corps seemed uncertain as to whether to choose air-cooled or liquid-cooled power plants, Douglas could sell aircraft of both styles.

Five two-seat configurations of Douglas biplanes appeared in 1929. First were the three YO-22s ordered January 17, 1929, and first delivered to Wright Field in September 1929. They had a Pratt

THOMAS-MORSE Y1O-41 (XO-932)
Curtiss V-1570-29, 600 hp
DIMENSIONS: Span 40′8″, Lg. 29′3″, Ht. 10′, Wing Area 299 sq. ft.
WEIGHT: Empty 3254 lb., Gross 4394 lb. Fuel 79 gal.
PERFORMANCE: Speed—Top 188 mph at s. l., 181 mph at 10,000′, Cruising 164 mph, Landing 63 mph. Service Ceiling 24,250′, Absolute Ceiling 25,500′, Climb 1840′/ 1 min., 10,000′/6.9 min.   SDAM

THOMAS-MORSE Y1O-33 (Left)
Curtiss V-1570-11, 600 hp
DIMENSIONS: Span 39′9″, Lg. 29′2″, Ht. 10′2″, Wing Area 348 sq. ft.
WEIGHT: Empty 3130 lb., Gross 4291 lb. Fuel 77.5 gal.
PERFORMANCE: Speed—Top 165 mph at s. l., 158 mph at 10,000′, Cruising 143 mph, Landing 58 mph. Service Ceiling 22,600′, Absolute Ceiling 24,000′, Climb 1840′/ 1 min., 10,000′/6 min. Range 443 miles at 143 mph. AF

DOUGLAS YO-22 (Above)
Pratt & Whitney R-1340-1, 450 hp
DIMENSIONS: Span 38′1″, Lg. 28′4″, Ht. 9′8″, Wing Area 316 sq. ft.
WEIGHT: Empty 2389 lb., Gross 3841 lb. Fuel 88 gal.
PERFORMANCE: Speed—Top 146 mph at s. l., 137 mph at 10,000′, Cruising 115 mph, Landing 59 mph. Service Ceiling 20,750′, Absolute Ceiling 22,600′, Climb 1207′/ 1 min., 10,000′/10.9 min. Range 405 miles.   ARNOLD

DOUGLAS O-25A
Curtiss V-1570-7, 600 hp
DIMENSIONS: Span 40′, Lg. 30′8″, Ht. 10′7″, Wing Area 364 sq. ft.
WEIGHT: Empty 3260 lb., Gross 4657 lb. Fuel 109–46 gal.
PERFORMANCE: Speed—Top 153 mph at s. l., 151 mph at 10,000′, Cruising 136 mph, Landing 61 mph. Service Ceiling 21,100′, Climb 1560′/1 min., 10,000′/8.1 min. Range 553–612 miles.   AF

& Whitney R-1340-1 Wasp radial and swept-back upper wing, N struts, ring cowl, and auxiliary tank under the fuselage.

The other prototypes were standard airframes with the Liberty engines replaced by new power plants. A 600-hp Curtiss V-1570-5 Conqueror turned an O-2H into an O-25, which was tested in September 1929 with water-cooling and in November with a Prestone cooler. The O-29 was an O-2K flown in September with an air-cooled 525-hp Wright R-1750-1 Cyclone and later, as the O-29A, with a 575-hp R-1820-1 Cyclone.

A 450-hp R-1340-3 Wasp was used in September 1929 to make the O-32, which later became the BT-2 basic trainer series, while another O-2K tested with the 525-hp Pratt & Whitney Hornet was the predecessor of the O-38 series.

An Air Corps production contract on October 18, 1929, first called for 36 O-25A and 30 O-32A aircraft, but the latter were converted to BT-2A trainers after delivery in 1930. Future observation aircraft built with single-row Wasps would be trainers, while the standard observation type would have larger engines. The first O-25A appeared at Wright in June 1930 with a water-cooled 600-hp V-1570-7. As a result of a contract addition, Douglas built 50 O-25As armed with two .30-caliber Brownings and 1,000 rounds and three O-25B unarmed transports.

The Curtiss Conqueror was also used on the YO-34, converted from the third YO-22 in March 1930, but the Army preferred to develop the O2M series airframe with the air-cooled Pratt & Whitney Hornet radial. Deliveries of this type actually began in April 1929 with nine O2M biplanes built for Mexico. These had Hornet engines, enlarged fuel tanks, bomb racks, and twin Lewis guns on a rear cockpit ring. They were followed by three Mexican O2M2s and ten Hornet-powered O2MC two-seaters for China—among the first American warplanes for that country.

On June 13, 1930, the Army ordered the Hornet-powered Douglas as the O-38. The first four aircraft were delivered to the National Guard on October 30, 1930. While the first was an unarmed O-38A transport, 45 O-38s had the usual fixed and flexible guns, with 800 rounds, and their bumped ring cowls

DOUGLAS O-29
Wright Cyclone R-1750-1, 525 hp (R-1820-1, 575 hp on O-29A)
DIMENSIONS: Span 40', Lg. and Ht. N/A, Wing Area 364 sq. ft.
WEIGHT: Empty 2781 lb., Gross 4095 lb.
PERFORMANCE: Speed—Top 137 mph at s. l., 131 mph at 10,000'. Service Ceiling 20,600', Absolute Ceiling 22,300'.   MFR

DOUGLAS YO-34
Curtiss V-1570-11, 600 hp
DIMENSIONS: Span 38', Lg. 28', Ht. 10'5", Wing Area 316 sq. ft.
WEIGHT: Empty 2871 lb., Gross 4656 lb. Fuel 80 gal.
PERFORMANCE: Speed—Top 156 mph at s. l., 149 mph at 10,000', Cruising 125 mph, Landing 63 mph. Service Ceiling 21,500', Absolute Ceiling 23,075', Climb 10,000'/8.68 min.   MFR

DOUGLAS O-2M for Mexico
Pratt & Whitney "Hornet," 525 hp
DIMENSIONS: Span 40', Lg. 30', Ht. 10'10", Wing Area 361 sq. ft.
WEIGHT: Empty 2580 lb., Gross 4550 lb. Fuel 206 gal.
PERFORMANCE: Speed—Top 145 mph at s. l., Cruising 120 mph, Landing 56 mph. Service Ceiling 17,500', Absolute Ceiling 18,900', Climb 1350'/1 min. Range 800 miles.   ORTIZ

DOUGLAS O-38
Pratt & Whitney R-1690-3, 525 hp
DIMENSIONS: Span 40', Lg. 31'3", Ht. 10'10", Wing Area
    364 sq. ft.
WEIGHT: Empty 3046 lb., Gross 4421 lb. Fuel 110 gal.
PERFORMANCE: Speed—Top 143 mph at s. l., 139 mph at
    10,000', Cruising 121 mph, Landing 59 mph. Service
    Ceiling 19,750', Absolute Ceiling 21,600', Climb 1140'/
    1 min., 10,000'/11.7 min. Range 600 miles, 325 miles
    at top speed.   AF

DOUGLAS O-25C
Curtiss V-1570-7, 600 hp
DIMENSIONS: Span 40', Lg. 31'4", Ht. 10'10", Wing Area
    376 sq. ft.
WEIGHT: Empty 3428 lb., Gross 4816 lb. Fuel 110 gal.
PERFORMANCE: Speed—Top 161 mph at s. l., 153 mph at
    10,000', Cruising 139 mph, Landing 61 mph. Service
    Ceiling 21,000', Absolute Ceiling 22,600', Climb 1510'/
    1 min., 10,000'/8.8 min.   AF

were familiar sights on National Guard fields (none
went to Air Corps units) for many years.

Underwing bomb racks for four 100-pound or ten
30-pound bombs were added to the O-38B, first
ordered December 22, 1930, with deliveries beginning in April 1931. Forty-five were built to Air
Corps contracts, while 18 more for the National
Guard began appearing in December 1931 with a
new smooth cowl and exhaust system that was later
retrofitted to earlier O-38s. A single O-38C delivered to the Coast Guard in December 1931 had no
guns.

DOUGLAS O-38B
Pratt & Whitney R-1690-5, 525 hp
DIMENSIONS: Span 40', Lg. 32', Ht. 10'8", Wing Area 371
sq. ft.
WEIGHT: Empty 3072 lb., Gross 4458 lb. Fuel 110–46 gal.
PERFORMANCE: Speed—Top 149 mph at s. l., 143 mph at
10,000', Cruising 128 mph, Landing 59 mph. Service
Ceiling 20,700', Absolute Ceiling 22,500', Climb 1240'/
1 min., 10,000'/10.6 min. Range 600–706 miles.   AF

DOUGLAS O2MC-4 for China   RW

The Air Corps was not yet finished with inline
engines, however, and on May 12, 1931, ordered 30
O-25Cs with Prestone-cooled V-1570-27 Conquerors. Tested at Wright Field on October 23, 1931,
the O-25C was the fastest of the O-2 developments,
with a neatly streamlined nose and the same armament (two guns and 400 pounds of bombs) as its
O-38B contemporary. They served with the 16th
and 91st Observation squadrons at Fort Riley, Kansas, and Crissy Field, San Francisco.

Douglas continued with export versions of the O-
38B, building 72 O2MC-2s to O2MC-10s from 1932
to 1936 for China, where they played an active role
in civil warfare with Kuomintang attacks on rebels
at Fukien and on the "Long March." Hornet engines powered 25 of these Chinese models, with 24
using Wasps and the last 23 using Wright Cyclones.
Peru received six Wright-powered O-38P convertible land or seaplanes with enclosed cockpits beginning in November 1932.

DOUGLAS O-38E
Pratt & Whitney R-1690-9, 625 hp
DIMENSIONS: Span 40', Lg. 32', Ht. 10'5", Wing Area 371
sq. ft.
WEIGHT: Empty 3481 lb., Gross 4870 lb. Fuel 110–46 gal.
PERFORMANCE: Speed—Top 154 mph at s. l., 147 mph at
10,000', Cruising 133 mph, Landing 60 mph. Service
Ceiling 19,200', Climb 1230'/1 min., 10,000'/11.1 min.
Range 468 miles.   MFR

Air Corps observation contracts had reached a peak during the six months of 1931, with seven different types ordered: 115 O-1G, O-19E, O-25C, O-38B and O-39 biplanes and 18 YO-27 and YO-31 monoplanes for service tests. The day of the open-cockpit biplane was ending, and after 1932 monoplanes with enclosed cockpits would be the prevailing combat plane style.

Enclosed cockpits were used on the last batch of Army service biplanes. Such an enclosure had appeared on the single O-38D, a dual-control, unarmed transport with an R-1820-1 Cyclone bought for a National Guard general. The O-38E, first ordered December 7, 1932, had a canopy over the pilot and his observer, and obtained a rounded fuselage by addition of wooden stringers built over the steel-tube framework. Powered by a 625-hp Hornet, the O-38E had the usual two guns and bomb racks. Thirty-seven were delivered, beginning in May 1933, and scattered among the 19 National Guard squadrons. Five O-38B, the O-38D, and five O-38E biplanes still remained in service in November 1941, representing the last biplanes in squadron use.

Included among the last biplanes were seven O-38F dual-control unarmed transports with enclosed cockpits. They were used for high-ranking officers at locations like Bolling Field, and one was flown in Russia by the Army's military attaché in Moscow. Since the O-1C, some 30 officers' transports had been delivered under the "O" designation, which tended to cover the use of Army funds for this purpose.

Chapter 7
Flying Boats for Navy Patrols, 1917–32

Patrol planes were the first American aircraft in wartime service, and were the first to sink an enemy vessel, so they make an appropriate beginning for the story of Navy combat types. Certainly their heavy armament and long battle record qualify patrol planes as combat types, despite the monotonous nature of the average wartime patrol.

Flying Boats Versus U-Boats

Throughout its history, the naval patrol plane has been linked to the submarine. Originally envisioned as passive observers of fleet movements, patrol planes were called into combat action when German U-boats were inflicting heavy losses on Allied shipping during World War I. With land warfare stalemated, the only possible German answer to the British blockade had been a counterblockade by submarines. Unrestricted submarine warfare by the Germans shocked American public opinion (which never dreamed the United States would later use the same methods against Japan) into accepting war, but was calculated to starve England out before a single U.S. division arrived. In April 1917 the sinkings rose to so high a level that it seemed the Germans calculated rightly.

In this emergency, British flying boats patrolled the most dangerous areas, and in 1917 a Curtiss H-12 hit the first U-boat sunk by aircraft. Others were not usually so successful, but flying boats handicapped the subs by reporting their location and driving them below the surface, where their speed was reduced. Other devices played a larger part in beating the subs and saving England—the convoy system, mine barrage, and hydrophones—so aircraft shared the credit for only five of 140 U-boats sunk, but the flying boat had demonstrated its future possibilities.

The flying boats used then were developments of the Curtiss America, a 5,000-pound, 74-foot span biplane with a single-step boatlike hull, two Curtiss engines, and 300 gallons of fuel, built in 1914 at Hammondsport, New York, for a proposed first attempt to fly the Atlantic. The war prevented the America's flight, but a British officer saw its possibilities and the two experimental Curtiss America boats were shipped to Britain on September 30, 1914. Like four similar H-4s delivered in 1915, they had two 90-hp Curtiss OX-5 water-cooled engines, but when this power plant proved inadequate, 100-hp Anzanis were used on 50 H-4s ordered March 1915 and used for training and limited patrols by the Royal Naval Air Service.

These flying boats were called Small Americas by the British and were followed by larger Curtiss H-8 Large Americas. Two 160-hp Curtiss engines powered the first one delivered in July 1916, but again the biplane was underpowered and 275-hp Rolls-Royce Eagles were substituted. These aircraft became the Curtiss H-12, the first American plane used in combat.

Open cockpits were provided for a pilot, co-pilot, engineer, and "wireless operator," two 230-pound bombs were carried under the wings, a pair of .30-caliber Lewis guns were in the bow cockpit, and another Lewis gun was in the rear cockpit. These guns destroyed the first enemy aircraft downed by an American airplane. On May 14, 1917, a Curtiss H-12 swept down below and alongside a German Zeppelin. A short burst from the bow guns and the L-22 caught fire and fell into the North Sea. On May 20 another H-12 attacked a submarine, the UC-36, and UB-32 was sunk by an H-12 on September 28, 1917.[1]

---

[1] The official RAF history considers the UC-36 as having been sunk by the H-12, but a German historian blames the loss on mines. The UB-32 sinking is accepted by historians. Austrian aircraft sank two Allied submarines in 1916.

CURTISS H-12
Rolls-Royce Eagle, 250 hp, or Liberty 12, 350 hp
DIMENSIONS: Span 93', Lg. 46', Ht. 16'9", Wing Area 1108
  sq. ft.
WEIGHT: Empty 6351 lb., Gross 9092 lb. Fuel 218 gal.
PERFORMANCE: Speed—Top 93 mph at 2000', Landing 55
  mph. Service Ceiling 12,000', Climb 6000'/14.5 min.
                                                          USN

CURTISS HS-1L
Liberty 12, 360 hp
DIMENSIONS: Span 62'1", Lg. 38'6", Ht. 14'7", Wing Area
  653 sq. ft.
WEIGHT: Empty 4070 lb., Gross 5910 lb. Fuel 141 gal.
PERFORMANCE: Speed—Top 87 mph, Landing 57 mph.
  Service Ceiling 2500', Climb 1725'/10 min. Endurance
  3.7 hrs. at top speed, 5.7 hrs. cruising.   USN

Seventy-one Curtiss H-12s were built to British
orders without engines, but 20 were turned over to
the United States Navy. The first Navy H-12, in
March 1917, had the original Curtiss engines, while
the rest were delivered with Liberty 12 engines to
Hampton Roads beginning in January 1918.

When the United States entered the war, the
Navy looked for a single-engine flying boat that
could be put into production more quickly, take up
less shipping space, and use shallow water. Curtiss
offered the HS-1 (for Hydroplane, single-engine)
with an America-style single-step wooden hull and
a 200-hp Curtiss V-X-3 eight-cylinder engine between the wings from the R-type seaplane, with
three pairs of interplane struts on each side. When
the first 360-hp Liberty 12 became available, the
Curtiss prototype was flown as the HS-1L (for Liberty) on October 21, 1917, and all production aircraft received this engine.

Navy demands for the HS boats were too great
for Curtiss to build them in its Buffalo and Garden
City, New York, factories, so other firms became
involved in the work. The first HS-1s were delivered to Hampton Roads on January 14, 1918, began
service at Miami in March, and eight became the
first American aircraft shipped to France, arriving
on May 24. American Navy pilots in France had
been flying their first patrols in French Tellier and
Donnet-Denhaut flying boats until the HS boats
were ready to begin patrols on June 13, 1918.

The three-seat HS-1 was armed with a Lewis gun
in the front cockpit and two 180-pound bombs under the wings. To increase the lift so that 230-pound
bombs and heavier loads could be carried, the
wingspan was increased by 12 feet and another
pair of struts were added on each side. This version
became the HS-2, and it appears that most of the

CURTISS HS-2
Liberty 12, 350 hp
DIMENSIONS: Span 74', Lg. 38'6", Ht. 14'7", Wing Area
  803 sq. ft.
WEIGHT: Empty 4300 lb., Gross 6432 lb. Fuel 141 gal.
PERFORMANCE: Speed—Top 82.5 mph, Cruising 78 mph,
  Landing 50 mph. Service Ceiling 5200', Climb 2300'/
  10 min. Endurance 4.6 hrs. at top speed, 7.6 hrs.
  cruising.   TITC

HS boats in production were completed or converted to this standard.

The first recorded attack by an HS boat on a
submarine occurred on July 21, 1918, on the U-156,
off Cape Cod, but the bomb was a dud, and there
is no evidence that other incidents were much more
successful. Ten Navy stations in France got 182 HS
boats during the war, but most served on the American coastline. A wireless transmitter was sometimes carried, but carrier pigeons were more often
used for emergency dispatches. Over 1,000 HS
boats were built, including 675 by Curtiss, 250 by
L.W.F., 80 by Standard, 60 by Gallaudet, 25 by
Boeing, two by Loughead, and 25 erected after the

CURTISS H-16
Liberty 12, 400 hp
DIMENSIONS: Span 95'1", Lg. 46'2", Ht. 17'9", Wing Area
    1164 sq. ft.
WEIGHT: Empty 7400 lb., Gross 10,900 lb. Fuel 307–410
    gal.
PERFORMANCE: Speed—Top 95 mph at 2000', Landing
    56 mph. Service Ceiling 9950', Climb 5000'/10 min.
    Range 378 miles.   USN

The British had improved on the Curtiss hull design at their Felixstowe station with a series of twin-engine flying boats, F-1 to F-5. Plans for the F-5 were brought to the NAF in March 1918. The design was modified for quantity production as the F-5L with Liberty engines to distinguish it from British types powered by Rolls-Royce engines.

The first NAF F-5L was flown (by British test pilots) on July 15, 1918, with open pilots' cockpits,

N.A.F. H-16 (modified)   USN

war at naval air stations from spare parts. Many were sold to private operators after the war. Modified hulls were tried on four HS-3s built by Curtiss, and two HS-3s finished at the Naval Aircraft Factory had metal wing structures.

Curtiss also delivered the twin-engine H-16 on February 1, 1918, a larger H-12 development with a two-step hull and heavier armament. Britain ordered 125 and fitted the 75 that were actually delivered with 345-hp Rolls-Royce Eagles, but 124 Curtiss H-16s for the U.S. Navy had 400-hp Liberty engines. On November 20, 1917, an order for H-16s was given to the new Naval Aircraft Factory in Philadelphia and 150 were completed between March and October 1918. Armament of the H-16 included four 230-pound bombs and five or six Lewis guns: one or two in the bow, one or two in the rear cockpit, and one at an opening on each side of the hull. This type cost $37,850, compared to $16,900 for each HS-2.

Naval Aircraft Factory (NAF) H-16s, the first of which was flown March 27, 1918, and then forwarded to a Navy station in England, differed from the Curtiss model. Plans had been redrawn to expedite production: The enclosure over the pilots' cockpit was later deleted; a higher, balanced rudder was used; and horn-balanced ailerons like those of the F-5 were installed.

N.A.F. F-5L
Liberty 12A, 420 hp
DIMENSIONS: Span 103'9", Lg. 49'4", Ht. 18'9", Wing Area
    1397 sq. ft.
WEIGHT: Empty 8720 lb., Gross 13,256 lb., Max. 13,600
    lb. Fuel 495 gal.
PERFORMANCE: Speed—Top 90 mph at s. l., Landing 52
    mph. Service Ceiling 5500', Climb 2625'/10 min.
    Range 608 miles at top speed, 830 miles cruising. USN

straight-balanced ailerons, and a rounded rudder balanced below the horizontal surface. Later a taller rudder balanced at the top and tested on two F-6 prototypes delivered in January 1919 was fitted to all the F-5 and H-16 boats in service. The first F-5s arrived at Hampton Roads on September 3, 1918— too late for action, although production continued into 1919.

Thirty-three of 137 built by the NAF were completed by December 31, 1918, and 343 were canceled. Sixty more were built by Curtiss and 30 were produced in Canada. The F-5L carried four 230-pound bombs under the wings and six Lewis guns at the bow and rear cockpits and waist openings. The 37-mm Davis gun was also tested in the front cockpit. The twin-engine biplane pattern of the H-12, H-16, and F-5 established a tradition in Navy flying boats.

Curtiss also built for Britain a single triplane flying boat in 1916 that had four 250-hp engines and a 134-foot wingspan. Known as the Curtiss T, it was shipped to Britain for its first flight but was wrecked on its first test.

Four NC (Navy Curtiss) boats ordered in December 1917 were the largest American planes of 1918, designed to fly across the Atlantic to join in antisubmarine patrols. When first flown on October 4, 1918, the NC-1 had three 400-hp Libertys, but a fourth was added in 1919 behind the center engine to turn a pusher propeller. Biplane tail surfaces were mounted high on spruce outriggers from the hull and huge wings, an arrangement calculated to clear waves and "permit a machine gun to be fired straight aft . . . without interference," although the field of fire in almost every other direction was cluttered. A 45-foot hull contained a bow cockpit, side-by-side pilots' pits, rear compartment, radio, and fuel tanks. Top speed was 90 mph light and 81 mph loaded—not much of a margin over the landing speed. A gunner's position was installed on the NC-1's upper wing but not on the three other NCs built at the Garden City Curtiss Factory. The last, NC-4, first flew April 30, 1919, but six more were built as NC-5/-10s at the NAF.

In May 1919 the NC-4 became the first plane to fly across the Atlantic. Two sister ships that also attempted the Newfoundland-Azores-Lisbon-Plymouth flight landed at sea and were unable to take off again.

When the Navy entered World War I it had only six flying boats; by Armistice Day 1,172 were on hand, most of them single-engine HS types. After the German U-boats were gone, so was the reason, it seemed, to build any more patrol planes, although millions were invested in new battleships, with their tall basket masts and armored turrets. It was

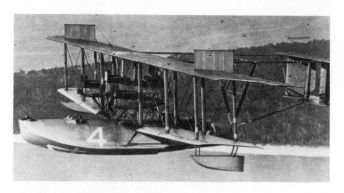

CURTISS-NAVY NC-4
Liberty 12, 420 hp
DIMENSIONS: Span 126', Lg. 68'3", Ht. 24'6", Wing Area 2380 sq. ft.
WEIGHT: Empty 15,874 lb., Gross 21,500 lb., Max. 28,000 lb. Fuel 1800 gal.
PERFORMANCE: Speed—Top 90 mph light, 81 mph fully loaded, Landing 62 mph. Service Ceiling 4500', Climb 1050'/5 min. Range 1470 miles.   USN

a decade before new flying boats were built in quantity.

There were 347 HS, 106 H-16, and 172 F-5L boats on hand July 1, 1921, and by June 30, 1925, the Navy's aging patrol force consisted of 44 F-5L and 33 H-16 twin-engine boats, 40 single-engine HS-2s, and 80 assorted unserviceable airframes of these types. Fortunately the NAF was developing experimentally a new class of flying boats to relieve the spruce framework of these antiques.

Navy Patrol Flying Boats, 1920–32

A smaller flying boat was designed by the Navy to provide a twin-engine, three-place escort fighter to support the larger patrol planes. Called the NAF TF (Tandem Fighter), it resembled a small-sized NC, with two Wright-Hispano engines back-to-back in a center nacelle and twin rudders. The first of

N.A.F. TF
Wright-Hispano H, 300 hp
DIMENSIONS: Span 60', Lg. 44'5", Ht. 17', Wing Area 930 sq. ft.
WEIGHT: Gross 8846 lb.
PERFORMANCE: Speed—Top 107 mph at s. l. Service Ceiling 8000'.   USN

four built was flown at Philadelphia in October 1920.

The largest flying-boat project designed at Philadelphia was a "Giant Boat" for use over the vast distances of the Pacific. It was to be a 63,000-pound, 164-foot span triplane with *nine* Liberty engines; something had to be done to use up that war surplus stockpile! Fortunately, they did not complete this monstrosity; at that stage of engineering it would probably have been even less successful than the Army's Barling bomber.

Two Engines and Two Wings

The traditional wartime approach to twin-engine flying boats was improved by a baker's dozen of trial aircraft built by the Naval Aircraft Factory. The first two were designated PN-7 (Patrol, Navy), the 7 following the wartime F-5 and F-6 designations. The first PN-7 was delivered in January 1924 and the second in June. Both had a modified F-5 hull with new 72-foot 10-inch span wings, only one pair of interplane struts on each side, and two 525-hp Wright T-2 inline engines mounted in streamlined nacelles, with the water radiators hanging from the upper wing. A crew of five, four 230-pound bombs, and Lewis guns fore and aft were carried.

Another pair of Navy boats were built with metal hulls, a new tail, and increased fuel capacity for a proposed flight to Hawaii. The first flew in March 1924 as the PN-8 with Wright T-3 engines, while the second was delivered in May 1925 as the PN-9 with 480-hp Packard 1A-1500 engines behind large water radiators. The PN-8 was soon converted to the PN-9 configuration, and on August 31, 1925, took off for the first attempt to fly from San Francisco to Hawaii. The fuel lasted 28½ hours—long enough to cover 1,841 miles against headwinds and set a world's-distance record—but after it ran out of fuel the PN-9 came down at sea some 360 miles short of Pearl Harbor. Then the hull demonstrated good flotation qualities, keeping the five-man crew safe for ten days, until they reached the islands using sails improvised from the wing's fabric covering.

The first flying boat built by a private company to a Navy design since 1919 was the Boeing PB-1 completed August 1925 for the same trans-Pacific flight as the PN-9. Powered by two big 800-hp Packard 2A-2540s placed back-to-back between the hull and upper wing, turning one tractor and one pusher propeller, the PB-1 had five cockpits and a new composite hull design with metal bottom and plywood deck. Three Lewis guns and 4,000 pounds of bombs could be carried, but engine difficulties prevented participation in the Hawaii flight.

The next pair of boats were the PN-10s, delivered

NAVY PN-7
Wright T-2, 525 hp
DIMENSIONS: Span 72'10", Lg. 49'1", Ht. 15'4", Wing Area 1217 sq. ft.
WEIGHT: Empty 9637 lb., Gross 14,203 lb. Fuel 489 gal.
PERFORMANCE: Speed—Top 104.5 mph at s. l., Landing 54.5 mph. Service Ceiling 9200', Climb 5000'/10.2 min. Range 655 miles.   ARC

NAVY PN-9
Packard 1A-1500, 480 hp
DIMENSIONS: Span 72'10", Lg. 49'2", Ht. 16'6", Wing Area 1217 sq. ft.
WEIGHT: Empty 9125 lb., Gross 19,610 lb. Fuel 1300 gal.
PERFORMANCE: Speed—Top 114.5 mph at s. l., Landing 68 mph. Service Ceiling 3080', Climb 1750'/10 min. Range 2550 miles.   USN

in November 1926 with metal wing structure, 525-hp Packard 2A-1500s, and three-bladed propellers. Distance records of 947 miles in 11 hours/7 minutes, with a 4,400-pound load and 1,569 miles in 20 hours/15 minutes with a 1,100-pound load were set

BOEING PB-1
Packard 2A-2540, 800 hp
DIMENSIONS: Span 87′6″, Lg. 59′5″, Ht. 22′2″, Wing Area
   1823 sq. ft.
WEIGHT: Empty 12,742 lb., Gross 24,000 lb., Max. 26,822
   lb. Fuel 1881 gal.
PERFORMANCE: Speed—Top 125 mph at s. l., Cruising 80
   mph, Landing 69 mph. Service Ceiling 3300′, Climb
   5000′/46 min. Range 2230 miles.   MFR

in the summer of 1927, and two more PN-10s were
ordered.

Up to this point water-cooled engines had been
used on Navy patrol planes, but in 1928 the Navy
changed to air-cooled radials on flying boats.
Boeing's ship was rebuilt at the NAF as the XPB-2,
with two Pratt & Whitney R-1690 Hornets instead
of the unsatisfactory Packards, and was test-flown
in April 1928. The second PN-10 became the XPN-
12 when fitted with 525-hp Wright R-1750 Cyclones
in December 1927, and the same engines powered
the boat ordered as the fourth PN-10 but delivered
in June 1928 as a PN-12. Pratt & Whitney R-1690

Hornets were mounted on the first and third PN-
10s which were also redesignated PN-12, and set
an altitude record in June 1928 of 15,426 feet with
a load of 4,400 pounds.

The first PN-12 version with Wright engines was
the prototype for the first production flying boats
ordered since the war. Twenty-five Douglas PD-1s
ordered December 29, 1927, entered service with
Patrol Squadron VP-7 in June 1929 in San Diego;
they were later all concentrated at Pearl Harbor
with VP-4 and VP-6. Armament comprised two flexible guns and four 230-pound bombs.

Meanwhile, the Naval Aircraft Factory built two
PN-11 boats with a new metal hull, lacking the
sponsons seen on Navy boats since the H-12, with
a new airfoil section for the wings, and twin rudders. The first was delivered in October 1928 with
Hornet engines and the second in June 1929 with
Cyclones.

On May 31, 1929, the Navy ordered 25 Martin
PM-1 and three NAF XP2N boats. Martin's contract
was increased to 30 PM-1s, delivered from July to
October 1930, with 575-hp Wright R-1750D Cyclones. The PM-1s were almost identical to the
Douglas PD-1s except for rounded engine nacelles;
they were later fitted for R-1820-64 Cyclones in ring
cowls.

NAVY PN-10
Packard 2A-1500, 525 hp
DIMENSIONS: Span 72′10″, Lg. 49′2″, Ht. 16′9″, Wing Area
   1217 sq. ft.
WEIGHT: Empty 10,060 lb., Gross 18,994 lb., Max. 19,029
   lb. Fuel 858 gal.
PERFORMANCE: Speed—Top 114 mph at s. l., Landing 66
   mph. Service Ceiling 4500′, Climb 5000′/29 min.
   Range 1508 miles.   USN

BOEING XPB-2
Pratt & Whitney GR-1690, 475 hp
DIMENSIONS: As PB-1, except height 20'10".
WEIGHT: Gross 24,374 lb. Fuel 1881 gal.
PERFORMANCE: Speed—Top 112 mph at s. l., Landing
64.4 mph. Service Ceiling 4470', Climb 2500'/10
min.   USN

NAVY XPN-12
Wright R-1750D, 525 hp
DIMENSIONS: Span 72'10", Lg. 49'2", Ht. 16'9", Wing Area
1217 sq. ft.
WEIGHT: Empty 7669 lb., Gross 14,122 lb. Fuel 858 gal.
PERFORMANCE: Speed—Top 114 mph, Landing 58 mph.
Service Ceiling 10,900', Climb 5000'/16 min. Range
1309 miles.   PMB

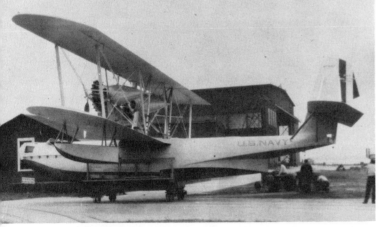

NAVY XPN-11
Pratt & Whitney R-1690, 525 hp
DIMENSIONS: Span 72'10", Lg. 53'6", Ht. 17'6", Wing Area
1154 sq. ft.
WEIGHT: Empty 7923 lb., Gross 16,870 lb.
PERFORMANCE: Speed—Top 120 mph, Landing 63 mph.
Service Ceiling 7700', Climb 5000'/16.1 min. Range
1948 miles.   PMB

DOUGLAS PD-1
Wright R-1750, 525 hp
DIMENSIONS: Span 72'10", Lg. 49'2", Ht. 16', Wing Area
1162 sq. ft.
WEIGHT: Empty 8319 lb., Gross 14,988 lb. Fuel 759 gal.
PERFORMANCE: Speed—Top 121 mph at s. l., Cruising 100
mph, Landing 59 mph. Service Ceiling 11,600', Climb
605'/1 min., 5000'/9.8 min. Range 1465 miles. USN
(ARC)

MARTIN PM-1
Wright R-1820-64, 575 hp
DIMENSIONS: Span 72'10", Lg. 49'2", Ht. 16'4", Wing Area
   1236 sq. ft.
WEIGHT: Empty 8970 lb., Gross 16,117 lb. Fuel 750 gal.
PERFORMANCE: Speed—Top 118.7 mph at s. l., Landing
   60.5 mph. Service Ceiling 8500', Climb 5000'/13.3 min.
   Range 1305 miles.   USN

N.A.F. XP4N-1
Wright R-1820-64, 575 hp
DIMENSIONS: Span 72'10", Lg. 54', Ht. 17'7", Wing Area
   1154 sq. ft.
WEIGHT: Empty 9770 lb., Gross 17,900 lb., Max. 20,340
   lb. Fuel 1270 gal.
PERFORMANCE: Speed—Top 115 mph, Landing 65 mph.
   Service Ceiling 9000', Climb 5000'/11.3 min. Range
   1510 miles normal, 1930 miles max.   ARC

MARTIN PM-1 (modernized)   USN

N.A.F. XP4N-2
Wright R-1820-64, 575 hp
DIMENSIONS: As XP4N-1
WEIGHT: Empty 9843 lb., Gross 17,595 lb., Max. 21,585
   lb. Fuel 1420 gal.
PERFORMANCE: Speed—Top 114 mph, Landing 64 mph.
   Service Ceiling 9300', Climb 5000'/11.7 min. Range
   1350 miles normal, 2050 miles max.   USN

The Navy XP2Ns were redesignated, the first
being delivered December 23, 1930, as the XP4N-
1 with the PN-11 hull, twin rudders, and 575-hp
Wright Cyclones. Two XP4N-2s, similar to the
XP4N-1 but with an increased fuel capacity, were
not delivered until March 1932, the last prototype
flying boats from Philadelphia.

Twin rudders were also used on 18 Keystone PK-
1s ordered November 30, 1929, and 25 Martin PM-
2s bought June 10, 1930, but ring cowls on their
575-hp Cyclones gave them a little more speed.
Keystone deliveries went to VP-1 at Pearl Harbor
from April to December 1931, while the Martin
boats were delivered from June to September 1931.
Cockpit enclosures were later fitted to both PM-1s
and PM-2s.

Charles Ward Hall, a specialist in aluminum aircraft structures, was given a contract on December

KEYSTONE PK-1
Wright R-1820-64, 575 hp
DIMENSIONS: Span 72', Lg. 48'11", Ht. 16'9", Wing Area
   1226 sq. ft.
WEIGHT: Empty 9387 lb., Gross 16,534 lb., Max. 17,074
   lb. Fuel 750–840 gal.
PERFORMANCE: Speed—Top 120 mph at s. l., Landing 62
   mph. Service Ceiling 9700', Climb 5000'/11 min.
   Range 1250 miles normal, 1355 miles max.   USN

MARTIN PM-2
Wright R-1820-64, 575 hp
DIMENSIONS: Span 72′, Lg. 49′, Ht. 16′9″, Wing Area 1236
    sq. ft.
WEIGHT: Empty 9919 lb., Gross 17,284 lb., Max. 19,062
    lb. Fuel 750–878 gal.
PERFORMANCE: Speed—Top 118.5 mph at s. l., Landing
    62.5 mph. Service Ceiling 9500′, Climb 5000′/13.8 min.
    Range 1347 miles max., 937 miles as bomber.   USN
(ARC)

HALL XPH-1
Wright GR-1750, 537 hp
DIMENSIONS: Span 72′10″, Lg. 51′, Ht. 17′5″, Wing Area
    1180 sq. ft.
WEIGHT: Empty 6576 lb., Gross 13,228 lb. Fuel 750 gal.
PERFORMANCE: Speed—Top 124 mph, Landing 56 mph.
    Service Ceiling 12,050′, Climb 5000′/9.5 min. Range
    1790 miles.   USN

29, 1927, to build a refined version of the PN series.
The prototype XPH-1 was built in a Buffalo factory
he shared with Consolidated and appeared in December 1929 with an improved all-metal hull,
cowled 537-hp GR-1750D Cyclones, a tall balanced
single rudder, and four open cockpits with twin
Lewis guns on the bow and stern cockpit rings.
Nine production PH-1s ordered June 10, 1930, were
first tested on October 19, 1931, and served with
VP-8 from 1932 to 1937. They had enclosed pilot's
cockpits, R-1820-86 Cyclones, Browning guns fore
and aft, and up to two 1,000-pound bombs.

    These were the last twin-engine biplanes built
for the Navy, since the big Consolidated monoplanes were coming in. But the biplane was not
quite through; since the Coast Guard had need of
a patrol and rescue boat smaller than the PBYs, Hall
got an order for a new version of the old design in
June 1936. Five PH-2s with 750-hp Wright R-1820-
F51 Cyclones were followed in 1939 by seven Hall

HALL PH-1
Wright R-1820-86, 620 hp
DIMENSIONS: Span 72′10″, Lg. 51′10″, Ht. 17′6″, Wing
    Area 1223 sq. ft.
WEIGHT: Empty 8251 lb., Gross 15,479 lb., Max. 16,379
    lb. Fuel 900 gal.
PERFORMANCE: Speed—Top 134.5 mph at s. l., Landing
    60 mph. Service Ceiling 11,200′, Climb 5000′/8.4 min.
    Range 1580 miles normal, 1868 miles max.   ARC

HALL PH-2
Wright R-1820F-51, 750 hp
DIMENSIONS: Span 72′10″, Lg. 51′, Ht. 17′10″, Wing Area
    1170 sq. ft.
WEIGHT: Empty 9150 lb., Gross 15,411 lb., Max. 16,370
    lb. Fuel 750–900 gal.
PERFORMANCE: Speed—Top 151 mph at 2800′, 145 mph
    at s. l., Cruising 126 mph, Landing 60 mph. Service
    Ceiling 21,000′, Climb 1550′/1 min. Range 1830 miles
    normal, 2170 miles max.   WILLIAMS

HALL PH-3
Wright R-1820F-51, 750 hp at 3200'
DIMENSIONS: Span 72'10", Lg. 51', Ht. 19'10", Wing Area
    1170 sq. ft.
WEIGHT: Empty 9614 lb., Gross 16,152 lb., Max. 17,679
    lb. Fuel 750–892 gal.
PERFORMANCE: Speed—Top 159 mph at 3200', 153 mph
    at s. l., Cruising 136 mph, Landing 60 mph. Service
    Ceiling 21,350'. Range 1937 miles normal, 2300 miles
    max.   PMB

PH-3s with improved engine cowls and pilots' enclosure. Built in the old Keystone-Fleetwings factory alongside the Delaware River at Bristol, the
Hall boats were armed during the war for antisubmarine work.

The patrol designation was briefly carried by
Navy versions of the twin-engine Sikorsky S-38
commercial amphibian, which was not really a combat type. One XPS-1 with 220-hp Wright R-790s
and two XPBS-2s (S-38As) with 450-hp Pratt &
Whitney R-1340Bs were acquired with the ten-
place cabins common to these amphibians. Four
PS-3s ordered in October 1928 were completed
with gun positions in the bow and stern of the hulls,
but these were soon covered over when the aircraft
reverted to normal S-38B configuration. Redesignated RS-3, these amphibians served with utility
squadrons, along with ten more assorted RS types
added later.

Sikorsky did build a true patrol biplane, the
three-place XP2S-1, with 450-hp Wasps mounted in
tandem over the hull, two .30-caliber flexible
Brownings, and two 500-pound bombs. Ordered
June 3, 1930, the XP2S-1 was tested in June 1932
but won no production contracts.

By 1932 the Navy had eight patrol squadrons with
twin-engine biplanes developed from the PN series. Four served at Pearl Harbor (VP-1, VP-4, VP-
6, VP-8), two with the aircraft tender USS *Argonne*
(later the *Wright*) at Norfolk (VP-7, VP-9) and two
at Coco Solo in the Canal Zone (VP-2, VP-5), along
with the twin-float torpedo planes of VP-3. The end
of the biplane was in sight, however, when VP-10

SIKORSKY XPS-2   USN

SIKORSKY PS-3
Pratt & Whitney R-1340C, 450 hp at s. l.
DIMENSIONS: Span 71'8", Lg. 40'3", Ht. 13'10", Wing Area
    720 sq. ft.
WEIGHT: Empty 6740 lb., Gross 10,323 lb. Fuel 330 gal.
PERFORMANCE: Speed—Top 123.5 mph at s. l., Cruising
    110 mph, Landing 64 mph. Service Ceiling 15,300',
    Climb 5000'/8 min. Range 594 miles.   MFR

was activated to handle the big new P3M monoplanes. Until monoplanes like the PBY went into
large-scale production in 1937, the biplanes continued to serve, often embellished with refinements
like cockpit enclosures, late-model Cyclone engines, and ring cowls.

SIKORSKY XP2S-1
Pratt & Whitney R-1340-88, 450 hp
DIMENSIONS: Span 56', Lg. 44'2", Ht. 16'4", Wing Area
762 sq. ft.
WEIGHT: Empty 6040 lb., Gross 9745 lb. Fuel 180–350
gal.
PERFORMANCE: Speed—Top 124 mph at s. l., Landing
59.5 mph. Service Ceiling 10,500', Climb 660'/1
min.   ARC

Chapter 8
New Weapons for the Navy, 1918–34

Aircraft bearing the Navy's "Attack" designation have replaced the battleships' heavy guns as the hammer of the fleet's fighting power. Whether attacking enemy vessels with torpedoes or dive-bombing, strafing with cannon and rockets, or striking hundreds of miles inland at surface targets, the carrier-based attack plane has a radius of action and striking speed never equaled by a naval weapon. The use of radar and of atomic weapons adds to its destructive capabilities. Attack planes have made more of a change in naval tactics and strategy than did the armored steamship when it replaced wooden sailing ships.

The weapon was not easily developed, however. It began with frail, short-range seaplanes designed to make torpedo attacks from shore bases. Then the torpedo plane was adapted to the aircraft carrier, making it a part of the fleet. Specialized scouting and dive-bombing types were also developed for the carriers, and shore-based types abandoned. After World War II substituted the carrier for the battleship as the principal arm of the fleet, scouting, bombing, and torpedo functions were successfully combined into a single attack type.

At the outbreak of World War I, however, the Navy had no aircraft suitable for attacking either shipping or land targets, and practical weapons for aircraft use were slow in coming. On October 3, 1912, however, the first test was made of a recoilless gun intended to be fired from aircraft at surface targets. Commander Cleland Davis had designed a two-inch rifle firing a six-pound shell out one end of the barrel and ejecting a counterweight out the other. This weapon was mounted, with a Lewis gun for aiming, on the bow of a Curtiss flying boat and test-fired August 4, 1917.

An aircraft was designed to be a Davis gun carrier, plans were forwarded to the Naval Aircraft Factory on January 24, 1918, and two prototypes were be-

gun.[1] The first Navy aircraft designed and built for the attack role, the NAF N-1, was a two-seat biplane with a Liberty 12 and pusher propeller, giving the gunner a clear field of fire.

The first example was finished on May 22, 1918, but an accidental fire destroyed it before tests began. A second N-1 was rolled into the Delaware River and made its first flight July 25, testing the Davis gun two days later. That weapon, however, had already been tried against submarines by British Handley-Pages, and they had withdrawn the Davis gun from service in February 1918. Clearly, more formidable ordnance would be needed.

Shore-based Torpedo Planes

Rear Admiral Bradley A. Fiske had received a patent in July 1912 for a method of carrying and delivering a torpedo by air, but the first nation to actually use torpedo planes in warfare was Great Britain. In 1915 the British made attacks on Turkish vessels with two-place Short seaplanes handling a small torpedo between the floats. Germany began torpedo attacks on Russian ships in September 1916.

U.S. Navy developments had been hampered by the lack of a lightweight torpedo. Available aircraft could carry no more than 600 pounds of ordnance load, which, according to a Chief of Naval Operations report issued on November 24, 1917, was not enough for a torpedo with enough explosive to damage a large warship. Not until November 22, 1918, was there a successful air launching, when an F-5L dropped a 400-pound dummy torpedo.

While still without a real torpedo plane at the war's end, the Navy did have the Curtiss R-6, an unarmed twin-float biplane with a 200-hp Curtiss V-X-X engine. With the pilot sitting in the rear seat,

[1] This design had been drawn up by the Navy's Bureau of Construction and Repair.

the R-6 was of very limited usefulness. Nevertheless, in January 1918, one squadron became the first to represent American Navy planes overseas when it was sent to the Azores to patrol with two 50-pound bombs against submarines.

The last 40 of 76 planes built were fitted with Liberty engines and designated R-6L. The increased power enabled them to handle a light (1,036-pound) torpedo and successful tests were completed by May 1919. Two torpedo squadrons were then organized at Hampton Roads and San Diego, but the R-6L was not nearly rugged enough for service conditions.

A more practical system was the torpedo-carrying version of Martin's Army MB-1 bomber. First known to the Navy as the MBT and later as the MT-1 (it would subsequently be known as the TM-1 under the system adopted in March 1923 for new aircraft), this biplane had two Liberty engines, pilot, front and rear gunner with four Lewis guns, and a 1,618-pound torpedo between the modified gear. The first of ten ordered September 30, 1919, was flown February 4, 1920; the last was delivered in August 1920. Six went to the Marines at Quantico and four served San Diego's Navy base until they were also transferred to Quantico in April 1923.

N.A.F. N-1
Liberty 12, 360 hp
DIMENSIONS: Span 51', Lg. 31'7", Ht. 15'4", Wing Area 694 sq. ft.
WEIGHT: Empty 4330 lb., Gross 5900 lb.
PERFORMANCE: Speed—Top 94 mph. Climb 3250'/10 min.
USN

CURTISS R-6-L
Liberty 12, 360 hp
DIMENSIONS: Span 57'1", Lg. 33'5", Ht. 14'2", Wing Area 613 sq. ft.
WEIGHT: Empty 3513 lb., Gross 5662 lb. Fuel 112 gal.
PERFORMANCE: Speed—Top 104 mph at s. l., Landing 52.5 mph. Service Ceiling 9900', Climb 5000'/12.3 min. Range 368 miles/1036 lbs. torpedo.
USN

MARTIN MT-1
Liberty 12, 400 hp
DIMENSIONS: Span 71'5", Lg. 45'8", Ht. 15'8", Wing Area 1080 sq. ft.
WEIGHT: Empty 7150 lb., Gross 12,098 lb. Fuel 273 gal.
PERFORMANCE: Speed—Top 105 mph at s. l., 101 mph at 6500'. Service Ceiling 8500', Absolute Ceiling 10,600', Climb 6500'/19.6 min. Endurance 5.5 hrs.   USN

Philadelphia's Naval Aircraft Factory combined the R-6 fuselage, HS-2 wings, and Liberty engine to produce 15 PT-1 and 18 PT-2 two-place torpedo seaplanes from August 1921 to June 1922. Torpedo and Bombing Plane Squadron One conducted the first massive torpedo practice on a live target on September 27, 1922. Eighteen PTs attacked the USS *Arkansas*, running at full speed, and scored eight hits with their MK VII torpedoes.

During the summer of 1922 the Navy tested five prototypes competing for a torpedo-plane contract. Two were twin-engine three-place types venturing a low-wing monoplane layout new for that period. First flown in March 1921, the Curtiss CT-1 had two 300-hp Wright-Hispano engines above twin floats, but in 1922, 350-hp Curtiss D-12s were tried. A short fuselage of wooden construction had pilot and navigator in tandem ahead of a rear gunner, while a biplane tail was suspended behind on tail booms. A 1,446-pound torpedo could be carried, but only one of nine CT-1s ordered was completed.

The Navy's first all-metal low-wing monoplane was the Stout ST torpedo plane, a clean design with two 300-hp Packard V-1237 engines, twin rudders, and wheeled landing gear. Five had been ordered, with the first flown April 25, 1922, but the rest were canceled after the prototype crashed.

N.A.F. PT-1
Liberty 12, 400 hp
DIMENSIONS: Span 74', Lg. 34'5", Ht. 16'7", Wing Area 808.5 sq. ft.
WEIGHT: Empty 4478 lb., Gross 6798 lb. Fuel 110 gal.
PERFORMANCE: Speed—Top 96 mph at s. l., Landing 49 mph. Service Ceiling 8800', Climb 5000'/15.7 min. Endurance 2 hrs. at top speed, 3.5 hrs. cruising.   USN

N.A.F. PT-2
Liberty 12, 400 hp
DIMENSIONS: Span 73'11", Lg. 36'4", Ht. 16'6", Wing Area 808.5 sq. ft.
WEIGHT: Empty 4231 lb., Gross 7075 lb. Fuel 112 gal.
PERFORMANCE: Speed—Top 96 mph at s. l. Service Ceiling 6100', Climb 5000'/20.2 min. Range 286 miles at top speed, 334 miles at cruising speed.   USN

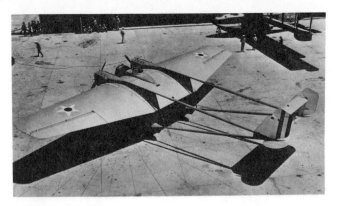

CURTISS CT-1
Curtiss D-12, 350 hp
DIMENSIONS: Span 65′, Lg. 52′, Ht. 15′5″, Wing Area 830 sq. ft.
WEIGHT: Empty 7684 lb., Gross 11,208 lb. Fuel 111 gal.
PERFORMANCE: Speed—Top 107 mph at s. l., Landing 58 mph. Service Ceiling 5200′, Climb 2600′/10 min. Range 350 miles. USN

STOUT ST-1 (Above and Below)
Packard V-1237, 330 hp
DIMENSIONS: Span 60′, Lg. 37′, Ht. 14′, Wing Area 790 sq. ft.
WEIGHT: Empty 6557 lb., Gross 9817 lb. Fuel 195 gal.
PERFORMANCE: Speed—Top 110 mph, Landing 58 mph. Service Ceiling 10,000′. Range 385 miles at top speed. USN

Two foreign-built single-engine designs were also studied. Three twin-float, low, cantilever-wing Fokker FT-1 two-seaters were imported from Holland and were flown in the United States with 400-hp Liberty engines. They were joined by a pair of Blackburn Swifts, biplanes with a 450-hp Napier Lion, wheels "releasable" in emergencies, flotation gear, and folding wings. An interesting point about this British torpedo plane is that it was a single-seater, with the pilot sitting in a humped cockpit.

Donald Douglas had developed a solid-looking two-place biplane from the Cloudster, his first air-

FOKKER FT-1   USN

BLACKBURN SWIFT   USN

DOUGLAS DT-1
Liberty, 400 hp
DIMENSIONS: Span 50′, Lg. 37′8″, Ht. 15′1″, Wing Area
   707 sq. ft.
WEIGHT: Empty 4367 lb., Gross 6895 lb. Fuel 115 gal.
PERFORMANCE: Speed—Top 101 mph, Landing 45 mph.
   Service Ceiling 8700′, Climb 5000′/15.6 min. Range
   232 miles at top speed.   USN

DOUGLAS DT-2 Seaplane
Liberty 12A, 420 hp
DIMENSIONS: Span 50′, Lg. 37′8″, Ht. 15′1″, Wing Area
   707 sq. ft.
WEIGHT: Empty 4528 lb., Gross 7293 lb. Fuel 115 gal.
PERFORMANCE: Speed—Top 99.5 mph at s. l., Landing 51
   mph. Service Ceiling 7400′, Climb 3850′/10 min.
   Range 274 miles/1835 lbs. torpedo.   USN

L.W.F. DT-2 Landplane
Liberty 12A, 420 hp
DIMENSIONS: Span 50′, Lg. 34′2″, Ht. 13′7″, Wing Area
   707 sq. ft.
WEIGHT: Empty 3737 lb., Gross 6502 lb. Fuel 115 gal.
PERFORMANCE: Speed—Top 101 mph at s. l., Landing
   49 mph. Service Ceiling 7800′, Climb 4050′/10 min.
   Range 293 miles/1835 lbs. torpedo.   SI

N.A.F. DT-4 Seaplane (Landplane data)
Wright TA-2, 525 hp
DIMENSIONS: Span 50′, Lg. 37′8″ (34′5″), Ht. 15′1″ (13′5″),
   Wing Area 707 sq. ft.
WEIGHT: Empty 4976 lb. (4224 lb.), Gross 7741 lb. (6989
   lb.). Fuel 115 gal.
PERFORMANCE: Speed—Top 107 mph (108 mph), Landing
   53 mph (51 mph). Service Ceiling 6050′ (11,075′),
   Climb 5000′/23 min. (10 min.). Range 226 miles (240
   miles).   USN

DOUGLAS DT-6   USN

plane since he left the Glenn L. Martin outfit to become an independent producer. Three were ordered on April 14, 1921, and the first was delivered on November 10, 1921, as the single-seat DT-1, but two became two-seat DT-2s, with the radiator moved to the nose. A 1,835-pound torpedo was carried between twin floats that could be replaced by wheels for land-based operations.

After April 1922 tests, the Navy ordered 38 more DT-2s from Douglas, 11 from Dayton-Wright, 20 from LWF, and six from the NAF. Postdelivery modifications of DT-2s included four NAF DT-4s of 1923 with 525-hp Wright T-2s, two becoming DT-5s with a geared T-2B, and the DT-6 flown April 27, 1925, with the first 400-hp Wright P-1 radial. Dayton-Wright modified three LWF ships as SDW-1 long-range scouts. Regular DT-2s first entered service at San Diego with VT-2 in December 1922 and served with other squadrons at Hampton Roads, Cavite, and Pearl Harbor. Douglas also sold a DT-2B to Norway in 1924 and four to Peru; the Norwegians built seven more under license.

Curtiss won a contract to build six examples of a BuAer design for a biplane capable of scouting, torpedo, or bombing missions. The first CS-1 was completed in November 1923 with a 525-hp inline Wright T-2, two cockpits behind the folding wings, a third crewman inside the fuselage, and twin floats interchangeable with wheels. The upper wing had a smaller span than the lower—a reversal of usual biplane practice—and a 1,618-pound torpedo was carried under the fuselage along with a flexible Lewis gun. Two Curtiss CS-2s with a 585-hp Wright T-3 and increased fuel capacity also were delivered, the first appearing in January 1924.

This type was chosen to replace the DT-2s in service and contracts were let in June 1924 after open bidding in which Curtiss, asking $32,000, was underbid by Martin, asking about $20,000. Thirty-five three-place Martin SC-1s with T-2 engines, delivered between February and August 1925, were followed by 40 SC-2s with T-3s, ordered in January and delivered by December 1925. They equipped VS-1, VS-3, VT-1, and VT-2, and carried their Lewis gun on a ring in the center cockpit.

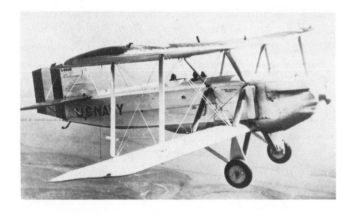

CURTISS CS-1 Seaplane (Landplane data)
Wright T-2, 525 hp
DIMENSIONS: Span 56'6", Lg. 40'3" (38'5"), Ht. 16' (15'2"), Wing Area 856 sq. ft.
WEIGHT: Empty 5390 lb. (4690 lb.), Gross 8670 lb. (7908 lb.). Fuel 214–370 gal.
PERFORMANCE: Speed—Top 100 mph at s. l. (101.5 mph), Landing 53 mph (51 mph). Service Ceiling 6900' (9100'), Climb 5000'/17.5 min. (12.2 min.). Range 430 miles (452 miles).   USN

CURTISS CS-2 Seaplane (Landplane data)
Wright T-3, 585 hp
DIMENSIONS: Span 56'6", Lg. 40'3", Ht. 16', Wing Area 856 sq. ft.
WEIGHT: Empty 6235 lb., Gross 11,333 lb.
PERFORMANCE: Speed—Top 102.5 mph at s. l., Landing 61 mph. Service Ceiling 4020', Climb 1450'/10 min.
MFR

MARTIN SC-1 Seaplane (Landplane data)
Wright T-2, 525 hp
DIMENSIONS: Span 56'6", Lg. 40'3½" (38'5"), Ht. 16' (15'3"), Wing Area 856 sq. ft.
WEIGHT: Empty 5610 lb. (4895 lb.), Gross 9025 lb. (8310 lb.). Fuel 389 gal.
PERFORMANCE: Speed—Top 101 mph at s. l. (100 mph), Landing 55 mph (52.5 mph). Service Ceiling 5850' (7950'), Climb 5000'/20.6 min. (14.7 min.). Range 381 miles/torpedo, 562 miles max. (403–595 miles).   USN

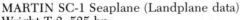

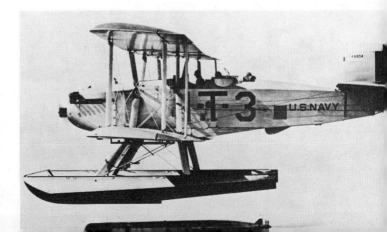

MARTIN SC-2 Seaplane (Landplane data)
Wright T-3, 540 hp
DIMENSIONS: Span 56'6", Lg. 41'9" (37'9"), Ht. 16' (14'8"),
  Wing Area 856 sq. ft.
WEIGHT: Empty 5908 lb. (5007 lb.), Gross 9323 lb. (8422
  lb.). Fuel 389 gal.
PERFORMANCE: Speed—Top 101 mph at s. l. (102 mph),
  Landing 56 mph (53 mph). Service Ceiling 5430'
  (7470'), Climb 5000'/24.2 min. Range 335 miles/tor-
  pedo, 570 miles max. (336–540 miles).   MFR

BOEING TB-1
Packard 1A-2500, 770 hp at s. l.
DIMENSIONS: Span 55', Lg. 42'7", Ht. 15'1", Wing Area
  868 sq. ft.
WEIGHT: Empty 6298 lb., Gross (scout) 10,537 lb., (torpedo) 10,703 lb. Fuel 450 gal.
PERFORMANCE: Speed—Top 106 mph at s. l., Landing
  (scout) 58.5 mph, (torpedo) 59 mph. Service Ceiling
  2600', Climb 1900'/10 min. Range 850 miles.   MFR

Boeing received the next contract to build prototypes to a Navy design centered around the 710-
hp Packard 1A-2500. The pilot and torpedo man sat
side by side ahead of the folding wings, with a
gunner in the rear, and the landing gear was convertible from twin floats to four wheels. Although
three Boeing TB-1 torpedo planes were ordered in
May 1925, the first was not flown until May 4, 1927.

A twin-engine biplane was ordered from the Naval Aircraft Factory in May 1925, and three more
designed to the same BuAer specifications were
assigned to Douglas in July. The first Douglas
XT2D-1 was flown January 27, 1927, and the Navy
XTN-1 was completed in May. Both had two 525-
hp Wright R-1750 Cyclones, folding wings, and a
narrow fuselage with a nose gunner, pilot, and rear
gunner. A 1,618-pound torpedo, or a bomb load,
was carried between twin floats, which could be
exchanged for wheels for land operations. The
Douglas XT2D-1s, which joined VT-2 at San Diego
in May 1927, were the only twin-engine aircraft
tested on the USS Langley.

Nine more T2D-1s ordered from Douglas had a
balanced rudder and four cockpits. Delivered in
1928, they did most of their service at Pearl Harbor.
Eighteen more Douglas twin-engine aircraft were
ordered on June 12, 1930, with R-1820-E Cyclones,
more fuel, and twin rudders. By the time they were
delivered, shore-based torpedo units had been redesignated as patrol squadrons, for land-based attack was held to be an Army mission. Designated
P2D-1, the Douglas ships were completed by June
1932 and served with VP-3 in the Canal Zone until
they were replaced by PBYs in February 1937. Armament comprised two flexible Brownings, a torpedo, or bombs.

Three Men, Two Wings, and a Torpedo

All the torpedo planes described thus far performed
most of their operations while chained to shore
bases, with only occasional practice from the Lang-

N.A.F. XTN-1
Wright R-1750, 525 hp
DIMENSIONS: Span 57', Lg. 44'10", Ht. 15'7", Wing Area
  886 sq. ft.
WEIGHT: Empty 6003 lb., Gross 10,413 lb., Max. 11,926
  lb. Fuel 450 gal.
PERFORMANCE: Speed–Top 121 mph at s. l. with torpedo
  (123 mph as bomber), Landing 58 mph. Service Ceiling
  11,300' (12,600' as bomber), Climb 5000'/8.1 min. (7.1
  min.). Range 375 miles/torpedo, 764 miles max.   USN

DOUGLAS XT2D-1
Wright R-1750, 525 hp
DIMENSIONS: Span 57′, Lg. 42′, Wing Area 886 sq. ft.
WEIGHT: Empty 6011 lb., Gross 9986 lb., Max. 10,840 lb.
Fuel 250 gal.
PERFORMANCE: Speed—Top 124 mph at s. l. Service Ceiling 13,830′, Climb 5000′/5.9 min.   MFR

DOUGLAS T2D-1
Wright R-1750, 525 hp
DIMENSIONS: Span 57′, Lg. 44′4″, Ht. 16′11″, Wing Area 886 sq. ft.
WEIGHT: Empty 6528 lb., Gross 10,503 lb., Max. 11,357 lb. Fuel 250 gal.
PERFORMANCE: Speed—Top 124 mph at s. l. with torpedo (125 mph as bomber), Landing 58 mph. Service Ceiling 11,400′ (12,520′ as bomber), Climb 5000′/6.4 min. Range 384 miles/torpedo, 454 miles max.   USN

DOUGLAS P2D-1
Wright R-1820E, 575 hp at s. l.
DIMENSIONS: Span 57′, Lg. 43′11″, Ht. 17′6″, Wing Area 909 sq. ft.
WEIGHT: Empty 7624 lb., Gross 12,791 lb. Fuel 356–572 gal.
PERFORMANCE: Speed—Top 135 mph as seaplane, 138 mph as landplane, Cruising 108 mph, Landing 62.5 mph. Service Ceiling 11,700′, Climb 885′/1 min., 5000′/7.6 min. Range 1010 miles.   USN

ley. As the new carriers *Saratoga* and *Lexington* neared completion, it was necessary to provide planes designed primarily for flight-deck operation.

Such a type was available in the Martin T3M-1, 24 of which were ordered October 12, 1925, and entered service with VT-1 in September 1926. A development of the SC-2 (T2M), it had the same wings, a 575-hp Wright T-3B, and a welded steel tube fuselage framework, with the pilot and torpedo man seated ahead of the wing and a gunner in the rear. Twin floats or wheels were interchangeable as landing gear. One hundred of the T3M-2s with a 710-hp inline Packard 3A-2500, equal-span wings, and three seats in tandem began appearing by March 1927 and equipped the first squadron (VT-1)

MARTIN T3M-1 Seaplane
Wright T-3B, 575 hp
DIMENSIONS: Span 56'7", Lg. 42'9", Ht. 16', Wing Area
   848 sq. ft.
WEIGHT: Empty 6323 lb., Gross 9855 lb., Fuel 132–80 gal.
PERFORMANCE: Speed—Top 107.5 mph at s. l., Stalling 60
   mph. Service Ceiling 3500'. Range 520 miles at cruis-
   ing speed.   USN

MARTIN T3M-2
Packard 3A-2500, 710 hp at s. l.
DIMENSIONS: Span 56'7", Lg. 41'4", Ht. 15'1", Wing Area
   883 sq. ft.
WEIGHT: Empty 5814 lb., Gross 9503 lb. Fuel 300 gal.
PERFORMANCE: Speed—Top 109 mph at s. l. with torpedo,
   Landing 55 mph. Service Ceiling 7900', Climb 5000'/
   16.8 min. Range 634 miles/torpedo.   MFR

to go aboard the *Lexington* after its commissioning in December. This meant that the Navy carried its aerial punch to sea, but few realized that an actual substitute for battleships had appeared.

These biplanes used water-cooled inline engines, but development of the air-cooled Pratt & Whitney Hornet radial provided a lighter power plant. This engine was tested on the XT3M-3, converted from the first T3M-2, and used on the XT4M-1 (Martin 74), a new prototype introduced in April 1927 with a new metal-wing framework covered by fabric replacing the previous wooden structure. Production T4M-1s first ordered June 30, 1927, had a larger, balanced rudder.

The Navy put 102 T4M-1s into service, beginning in August 1928, with VT-2B on the *Saratoga*. The *Lexington*'s VT-1B also got the T4M-1, while twin-float versions were used by VT-9S (later working in the Atlantic with the tender *Wright*). Other squadrons with torpedo planes in the 1929–30 period were VT-5A with the Asiatic Fleet; VP-2D,[1] VT-3D, and VT-4D at Coco Solo; and VP-1D, VT-6, and VT-7D at Pearl Harbor. All had T3M-2s except for the twin-engine T2D-1s of VP-1D.

Glenn L. Martin decided to move his firm to Baltimore, Maryland, in 1928, and sold his old Cleveland, Ohio, plant to the Great Lakes Corporation, which received a Navy contract June 25, 1929, to continue torpedo-plane production. Eighteen TG-1

biplanes were similar to the T4M-1 except for modified landing gear and an R-1690-28 Hornet. The first TG-1 was tested at Anacostia in April 1930 with twin floats and was armed with a torpedo or 1,000 pounds of bombs, two Lewis flexible guns on the rear cockpit ring, and a fixed .30-caliber Browning in the upper wing, the first forward guns on a single-engine torpedo type. Other TG-1s went to VT-2.

A Wright R-1820-86 Cyclone powered the Great Lakes TG-2, which had two .30-caliber flexible Brownings, one in the rear cockpit and the other in the front cockpit, with guard rails to protect the propeller when the gun moved. The fixed gun was dropped. Thirty-two TG-2s were ordered July 2, 1930, and delivered from June to December 1931, serving on the *Saratoga* with VT-2 until they were replaced by TBD-1 monoplanes late in 1937.

During most of this time, VT-2 was the only torpedo-plane squadron in service, for the shore-based units had become patrol squadrons and VT-1 replaced its T4M-1s with BM-1 dive bombers.

There were two efforts to design a TG-2 replacement, the first being Martin's XT6M-1, ordered June 28, 1929, and completed in December 1930 as an all-metal, long-nosed two-place biplane with a Wright Cyclone, a fixed upper-wing gun, and two Lewis guns. It had no more success than the Douglas XT3D-1, ordered on June 30, 1930, and delivered on September 19, 1931, with a 575-hp Hornet B single-row radial and two flexible Brownings. In May 1932 this aircraft was returned for installation

[1] The D indicated a Naval District shore-based unit.

MARTIN XT3M-3
Pratt & Whitney R-1690, 525 hp
DIMENSIONS: Span 56′7″, Lg. 41′4″, Ht. 15′1″, Wing Area
    883 sq. ft.
WEIGHT: Empty 4600 lb., Gross 8304 lb. Fuel 300 gal.
PERFORMANCE: Speed—Top 102 mph, Landing 52 mph.
    Service Ceiling 3750′, Climb 5000′/15.3 min. Range
    423 miles at top speed.   USN

MARTIN T4M-1 Seaplane
Pratt & Whitney R-1690-24, 525 hp
DIMENSIONS: Span 53′, Lg. 37′8″, Ht. 10′6″, Wing Area
    656 sq. ft.
WEIGHT: Empty 4441 lb., Gross 7387 lb., Fuel 78–132 gal.
PERFORMANCE: Speed—Top 111 mph at s. l., Stalling 59
    mph. Service Ceiling 8400′, Climb 3020′/10 min. USN

MARTIN T4M-1
Pratt & Whitney R-1690-24, 525 hp.
DIMENSIONS: Span 53′, Lg. 35′7″, Ht. 14′9″, Wing Area
    656 sq. ft.
WEIGHT: Empty 3931 lb., Gross 7387 lb., Max. 8071 lb.
    Fuel 200 gal.
PERFORMANCE: Speed—Top 114 mph at s. l. with torpedo,
    113 mph with bombs, Landing 57 mph. Service Ceiling
    10,150′, Climb 5000′/14 min. Range 363 miles/torpedo,
    694 miles max.   USN

GREAT LAKES TG-1 (as seaplane)   USN

GREAT LAKES TG-1
Pratt & Whitney R-1690-28, 525 hp
DIMENSIONS: Span 53′, Lg. 34′8″, Ht. 14′10″, Wing Area
    656 sq. ft.
WEIGHT: Empty 4179 lb., Gross 7652 lb., Max. 7922 lb.
    Fuel 200 gal.
PERFORMANCE: Speed—Top 108 mph at s. l., Landing 58
    mph. Service Ceiling 8000′, Climb 5000′/16 min.
    Range 447 miles/torpedo, 547 miles max.   ARC

GREAT LAKES TG-2
Wright R-1820-86, 620 hp
DIMENSIONS: As TG-1
WEIGHT: Empty 4670 lb., Gross 8463 lb., Max. 9236 lb.
Fuel 220 gal.
PERFORMANCE: Speed—Top 127 mph at s. l., Landing 61
mph. Service Ceiling 11,500', Climb 5000'/11 min.
Range 330 miles/torpedo, 701 miles max.   WL

MARTIN XT6M-1
Wright R-1860, 575 hp
DIMENSIONS: Span 42'3", Lg. 33'8", Ht. 13'10", Wing Area
502 sq. ft.
WEIGHT: Empty 3500 lb., Gross 6841 lb. Fuel 104 gal.
PERFORMANCE: Speed—Top 124 mph at s. l., Landing
61.5 mph. Service Ceiling 11,600', Climb 5000'/8.8
min. Range 323 miles.   USN

DOUGLAS XT3D-1
Pratt & Whitney R-1860B, 575 hp at 8000'
DIMENSIONS: Span 50', Lg. 35'4", Ht. 14'8", Wing Area
636 sq. ft.
WEIGHT: Empty 4319 lb., Gross 7744 lb., Max. 7941 lb.
Fuel 180 gal.
PERFORMANCE: Speed—Top 134 mph at 8000', 120 mph
at s. l., Landing 59 mph. Service Ceiling 17,300', Climb
5000'/7.7 min. Endurance 6.1 hrs. at 75 percent
power.   USN

DOUGLAS XT3D-2
Pratt & Whitney R-1830-54, 800 hp at s. l.
DIMENSIONS: Span 50', Lg. 35'6", Ht. 14', Wing Area 649
sq. ft.
WEIGHT: Empty 4876 lb., Gross 8543 lb. Fuel 225 gal.
PERFORMANCE: Speed—Top 142 mph at s. l., Landing 62
mph. Service Ceiling 13,800', Climb 5000'/8.8 min.
Range 748 miles.   MFR

of an 800-hp twin-row R-1830-54. Redesignated
XT3D-2, it reappeared in February 1933 with a
NACA cowl, wheel pants, and low enclosures for
the three crewmen. "Badly streamlined" was the
official verdict, and no production orders were
placed.

The First Dive Bombers

During expeditions to Haiti (1919) and Nicaragua
(1927) the Marines had developed dive-bombing as
a technique for hitting guerrilla groups with 50-

MARTIN XT5M-1
Pratt & Whitney R-1690-22, 525 hp
DIMENSIONS: Span 41′, Lg. 28′4″, Ht. 12′4″, Wing Area
417 sq. ft.
WEIGHT: Empty 3084 lb., Gross 5693 lb. Fuel 100 gal.
PERFORMANCE: Speed—Top 134 mph at s. l. Service
Ceiling 13,250′, Climb 5000′/7.8 min. Range 442
miles.   USN

N.A.F. XT2N-1
Wright R-1750, 525 hp
DIMENSIONS: Span 41′, Lg. 27′9″, Ht. 12′2″, Wing Area
416 sq. ft.
WEIGHT: Empty 2735 lb., Gross 5333 lb. Fuel 100 gal.
PERFORMANCE: Speed—Top 134.5 mph at s. l., Landing
60 mph. Service Ceiling 14,100′, Climb 5000′/7 min.
Range 408 miles.   ARC

pound bombs dropped by DH-4Bs. The Curtiss
F8C Helldiver, 1928's two-seat fighter, was the first
type built especially for dive-bombing, which, as
the war would amply demonstrate, was far more
accurate against small or moving targets than horizontal bombing. If dive-bombing by fighters was
effective against enemy personnel, it was apparent
that large warships would be threatened by a dive
bomber sturdy enough to attack with a 1,000-pound
bomb. Such designs were first begun under the old
"T" (torpedo) designation and later received a "B"
(bombing) label.

Two very similar two-seat biplanes designed by
BuAer to meet this requirement and ordered June
18, 1929, were the Martin XT5M-1, tested March
1930 with a Pratt & Whitney R-1690-22, and the
Naval Aircraft Factory's XT2N-1, with a Wright R-
1750-D. The first planes capable of pulling out of
a dive while carrying a 1,000-pound bomb, they
had a metal fuselage and a fabric-covered metal
wing structure. Twin Lewis guns were provided for
the observer, and the XT2N-1 had two fixed guns

in the upper wing, while the Martin had a fixed
synchronized gun on the cowl.

Martin received contracts for 12 BM-1s on April
9, 1931, and 16 BM-2s on October 17. These were
to be similar to the XT5M-1 but with R-1690-44s,
ring cowls, and wheel pants, although the latter
streamlining details were omitted after the type
went into service. The first example was received
on September 28, 1931, but the pilot was killed
when it failed to recover from a dive made on its
first flight. Better luck was had with the second
example in January 1932. Four more BM-1s were
added to the contract, with an XBM-1 for special
NACA tests, and production of 33 BMs was completed in January 1933. They went into squadron
service on the *Lexington* in October 1932 with VT-
1B, which became VB-1 in 1934. Along with the
TG-1s of VT-2, the BM squadron constituted the
Navy's carrier-based attack strength from 1932 to
1934. Dive bombers and torpedo planes, unused by
the Navy in World War I, had taken their place as
naval weapons.

MARTIN BM-1
Pratt & Whitney R-1690-44, 625 hp
DIMENSIONS: Span 41′, Lg. 28′9″, Ht. 12′4″, Wing Area
417 sq. ft.
WEIGHT: Empty 3700 lb., Gross 5749 lb., Max. 6259 lb.
Fuel 100–60 gal.
PERFORMANCE: Speed—Top 145 mph at 6000′, Landing
59 mph. Service Ceiling 16,400′, Climb 5000′/5.9 min.
Range 409 miles/1000 lb. bomb, 689 miles max.   USN

MARTIN BM-2
Pratt & Whitney R-1690-44, 625 hp at 6000′
DIMENSIONS: Span 41′, Lg. 28′9″, Ht. 12′4″, Wing Area
436 sq. ft.
WEIGHT: Empty 3662 lb., Gross 5657 lb., Max. 6218 lb.
Fuel 104–64 gal.
PERFORMANCE: Speed—Top 146 mph at 6000′, Landing
59 mph. Service Ceiling 16,800′, Climb 5000′/5.7 min.
Range 413 miles/1000 lb. bomb, 695 miles max.
USN (ARC)

Chapter 9
Navy Observation Aircraft, 1917–31

Every Navy combat flight of World War I was carried out from shore bases and not from ships. But even before the war the Navy had investigated the possibilities of operating seaplanes from its warships, and had begun development of catapults to launch them while the ship was under way.

The armored cruiser *North Carolina* was the first U.S. Navy ship equipped to operate aircraft, using a catapult on the stern to launch a small AB-3 flying boat trainer on July 12, 1916. By the time war came, the cruiser *Huntington* also had a stern catapult, which launched a Curtiss R-6 floatplane in July 1917.

These fixed catapults blocked the after turrets and both launching and recovery of the aircraft by crane required that the ship be stopped, an unattractive prospect. The *Huntington* and its two R-6 floatplanes accompanied just a single convoy to England and returned without using its aircraft. In October 1917 the catapults and all aviation gear were removed from both the *Huntington* and *North Carolina* so that these ships' normal cruiser operations would be unimpeded.

The clumsy R-6 two-seater had shown little promise for shipboard work because the observer sat in the front cockpit, where his view was blocked by the wings. Much better visibility was available in the unusual Gallaudet D-4 biplane, whose observer sat in the nose, followed by the pilot and a 360-hp Liberty within the fuselage, which turned four propeller blades on a ring around the fuselage. A large pontoon under the fuselage and small outboard floats near the tip of the swept-back wings was used.

The first of these prototypes, the Gallaudet D-1 with Duesenberg engines, was flown on July 17, 1916. Despite numerous mechanical difficulties, the Army bought four D-2 versions and the Navy ordered two D-4 models in February 1918. Powered by a Liberty engine, the first D-4 crashed on a July 19, 1918, test, but the second was successfully flown in October 1918. It was accepted by the Navy, but the Gallaudet firm built no more of these interesting seaplanes, and its wartime production centered on HS-2 flying boats.

After the war, the Navy operated observation aircraft from shore bases, but its principal concern was still development of shipboard aircraft, and here the Vought biplanes dominated the postwar decade. Light and simple in construction, they were adaptable to the compressed-air turntable catapult developed in 1921. The first warships to get these catapults were the new *Maryland* class battleships, whose 16-inch guns really needed aircraft spotting. Routine shipboard catapult operation began on May 24, 1922, when the USS *Maryland* launched a Vought VE-7.

These first Navy Voughts had actually been developed in 1918 as an Army trainer, and after the war the Navy had purchased its first twenty VE-7 two-seaters with the 180-hp Wright-Hispano E-2 cooled by a nose radiator. The first Navy VE-7 was delivered May 27, 1920, as a landplane trainer, but other versions followed. The VE-7G was armed with a flexible Lewis gun in the rear cockpit and a fixed Vickers gun on the cowl, and became the VE-7GF when emergency flotation was added. A large central pontoon and wingtip floats were fitted to the VE-7H hydroplane, while the single-seat fighter versions were the VE-7S, VE-7SF, and VE-7SH.

Sixty Navy VE-7s were built by Vought and 69 by the Naval Aircraft Factory. One of the latter became the VE-9 in 1922 when fitted with the Wright-Hispano E-3, and Vought also built 21 Navy VE-9s by July 1923.

The Navy appreciated the advantages of the air-cooled engine and quickly adopted the 200-hp nine-cylinder Lawrance radial, which became the

GALLAUDET D-4
Liberty 12, 360 hp
DIMENSIONS: Span 46'5", Lg. 33'6", Ht. 11'8", Wing Area
620 sq. ft.
WEIGHT: Empty 4228 lb., Gross 5440 lb. Fuel 89 gal.
PERFORMANCE: Speed—Top 119 mph at s. l., Landing 58
mph. Service Ceiling 14,000'. Endurance 2.5 hrs. at top
speed, 3.5 hrs. cruising.   USN

VOUGHT VE-7H
Wright-Hispano E-2, 180 hp
DIMENSIONS: Span 34'1", Lg. 31'1", Ht. 10'2", Wing Area
248.5 sq. ft.
WEIGHT: Gross 2300 lb. Fuel 32 gal.
PERFORMANCE: Speed—Top 110 mph at s. l. Service Ceil-
ing 14,800'. Endurance 2.33 hrs.   MFR

VOUGHT UO-1 (Landplane data)
Wright J4 (R-790), 200 hp
DIMENSIONS: Span 34'3½", Lg. 28'4" (24'5"), Ht. 10' (8'9"),
Wing Area 290 sq. ft.
WEIGHT: Empty 1860 lb. (1544 lb.), Gross 2785 lb. (2469
lb.). Fuel 46 gal.
PERFORMANCE: Speed—Top 122 mph (124 mph) at s. l.,
Stalling 55.5 mph (52.5 mph). Climb 5000'/6.3 (4.9)
min. Range 418 miles (448 miles).   USN

Wright J-3 when Wright bought out the Lawrance Company. Essentially the Vought UO-1 was a VE-7 with the radial engine, new tail fin, and a rounded fuselage with twin fuel tanks on each side of the front cockpit. Either float or wheel landing gear could be used.

Vought built 140 UO-1s between 1922 and 1927, including one converted in 1922 to the UO-2 racer with a water-cooled Aeromarine engine. Two or three served on every U.S. battleship and light cruiser of that period, beginning with the USS Tennessee in June 1924. They had no armament, but 20 UO-3 versions became the FU-1 fighters described in the next chapter, while two more were built for the Coast Guard as the UO-4, and six were sold to Cuba.

Shore-based observation squadrons not handicapped by the weight limits of the early catapults showed armament and more advanced design styles. The first production monoplane for the Navy was the Loening two-seater first developed as an Army fighter.

Loening won a Navy order in June 1919, but his first M-8 was demolished during its delivery flight, September 17, 1919. Nevertheless, work went ahead on ten M-8-O observation monoplanes armed with fixed and flexible guns. These were landplanes, but a similar LS-1 was built with twin floats. Larger wings were used in 1920 on the M-8-1 (M-81) landplanes, of which Loening built six and 36 were finished by the Naval Aircraft Factory by March 1921.

Three AS-1 biplanes were built by Aeromarine. Delivered in 1922, they were redesignated AS-2 when the radiator was moved to the front of the 300-hp Hispano. Charles Willard designed this two-seater with two pairs of N struts, twin floats, and tail fin lowered to give the rear gunner a clear fire field.

Elias delivered seven two-seat biplanes designed as Marine expeditionary types intended to replace the DH-4B then used by Marine observation squadrons. The Elias EM-1 design was convertible from wheels to single-float configuration and had a 300-hp Hispano, but the second (EM-2) appeared in January 1922 with a 400-hp Liberty, the power plant used on the remaining aircraft. For economy's sake, however, the Marine squadrons were filled up with ex-Army DB-4Bs.

The Navy also prepared a requirement for a three-place observation type to use the new Curtiss D-12 engine. Glenn Martin responded with an advanced midwing monoplane with an all-metal structure, designed by a former Junkers engineer. Convertible from wheels to twin floats, 36 MO-1s were built in Cleveland, the first going to VO-2 in February 1923, the last delivery being made in Jan-

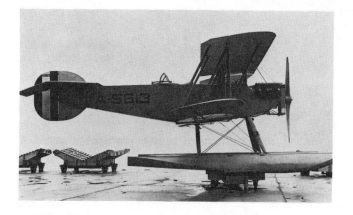

LOENING M-81
Wright-Hispano H, 300 hp
DIMENSIONS: Span 37'10", Lg. 24'2", Ht. 6'10", Wing Area
   260 sq. ft.
WEIGHT: Empty 1600 lb., Gross 2742 lb.
PERFORMANCE: Speed—Top 125 mph at s. l. Service Ceil-
   ing 13,750', Climb 5000'/5.4 min.   ARC

AEROMARINE AS-2
Hispano-Suiza H, 300 hp
DIMENSIONS: Span 37'6", Lg. 30'5½", Ht. 10'8", Wing Area
   3805 sq. ft.
WEIGHT: Empty 2377 lb., Gross 3597 lb. Fuel 98 gal.
PERFORMANCE: Speed—Top 116.5 mph at s. l., Stalling 51
   mph. Service Ceiling 16,000', Climb 5000'/6.4 min.
   Endurance 8 hrs.   ARC

ELIAS EM-1

PETERSON

ELIAS EM-2 (Seaplane data)
Liberty 12, 400 hp
DIMENSIONS: Span 39′8″, Lg. 32′11″, Ht. 13′4″, Wing Area
    482 sq. ft.
WEIGHT: Empty 2933 lb., Gross 4093 lb. Fuel 100 gal.
PERFORMANCE: Speed—Top 111 mph at s. l., Stalling 47
    mph. Service Ceiling 17,600′, Climb 5000′/5 min. En-
    durance 5.4 hrs.   ARC

uary 1924. They proved too heavy and large for
shipboard operation.

A more conservative approach to the three-place
requirement was the biplane designed by the Navy,
which ordered three made at the Naval Aircraft
Factory as the NO-1 and three by Martin as the
M2O-1. They had heavily braced wings, twin floats,
a gun ring on the third cockpit, and differed in
details. Curtiss D-12 engines powered all but the
third NAF aircraft, which became the NO-2 with a
Packard 1A-1500.

Despite these efforts to produce advanced types,
de Havilland's venerable DH-4 received another
lease on life when the last 30 DH-4M-1s from
Boeing in March 1925 were designated O2B-1 and
given to the Marines to supplement the aging DH-
4Bs. At that time the Marines had observation
planes with their First Aviation Group at Quantico,
the Second Aviation Group at San Diego, and Observation Squadron Two in Haiti. In 1927 the O2B-
1 went to Nicaragua and China with VO-7M and
VO-10M. The China tour was quiet, but on July 17,
1927, VO-7M pilots made diving attacks on insur-
gent forces at Ocotal, Nicaragua, that are now remembered as the first use of organized dive-bombing in combat.

Loening Navy Amphibians

The success of Grover Loening's amphibian concept led the Navy to order two examples designated
OL-1. They differed from the Army COA-1 models
by having a Packard 1A-1500, three crew cockpits,
and a hull strengthened for catapult launching. The
first OL-1 flight was on May 1, 1925.

Shortly afterward, the Navy got five OL-2 amphibians, two-seaters identical to the Army's Lib-

MARTIN MO-1 (Landplane data)
Curtiss D-12, 350 hp
DIMENSIONS: Span 53′1″, Lg. 38′1½″, Ht. 12′11″ (12′2½″),
    Wing Area 488 sq. ft.
WEIGHT: Empty 3440 lb. (3137 lb.), Gross 4945 lb. (4642
    lb.). Fuel 112 gal.
PERFORMANCE: Speed—Top 102 mph (104.5 mph) at s. l.,
    Stalling 50 mph (49 mph). Service Ceiling 10,000′
    (10,600′), Climb 5000′/11 (12) min. Range 467 (483)
    miles.   ARC

N.A.F. NO-1
Curtiss D-12, 350 hp
DIMENSIONS: Span 43′6″, Lg. 32′9½″, Ht. 12′6″, Wing Area
    462 sq. ft.
WEIGHT: Empty 3337 lb., Gross 4842 lb. Fuel 112 gal.
PERFORMANCE: Speed—Top 102.8 mph at s. l., Stalling 50
    mph. Service Ceiling 11,200′, Climb 5000′/8.75 min.
    Range 490 miles.   ARC

MARTIN M2O-1
Curtiss D-12, 350 hp
DIMENSIONS: Span 43′6″, Lg. 31′10″, Ht. 12′4″, Wing Area
    462 sq. ft.
WEIGHT: Gross 4173 lb.
PERFORMANCE: Speed—Top 104 mph at s. l. Service Ceil-
    ing 11,750′.   ARC

BOEING O2B-1
Liberty 12, 400 hp
DIMENSIONS: Span 42'5½", Lg. 30'1", Ht. 10'6", Wing Area
440 sq. ft.
WEIGHT: Empty 2647 lb., Gross 4214 lb. Fuel 132 gal.
PERFORMANCE: Speed—Top 122.5 mph at s. l., Stalling
57.6 mph. Service Ceiling 14,000', Climb 5000'/6.8
min. Range 550 miles.   USN

erty-powered COA-1. They had been requisitioned
for Admiral Richard Byrd's naval air unit, which
participated in D. B. MacMillan's Arctic expedition
of 1925, and were then all used by the Marines.

The Packard engine was again chosen for six OL-
3 three-seaters, which were, however, preceded by
four OL-4s fitted with Liberty engines; the latter
were still considered more reliable for the Alaskan
aerial survey planned. The first OL-4s, with three-
bladed propellers and a new balanced rudder, were
delivered in April 1926, and the last OL-3 went to
San Diego in August 1926. The first new aircraft
built for the Coast Guard were three Liberty-powered, unarmed OL-5s delivered in October 1926.

By August 1926 the Navy thought well enough of
amphibians to order 27 OL-6 three-seaters with
475-hp 2A-1500 Packards. They were delivered
from December 1926 to July 1927 and scattered
among various battleships, shore stations, and a
Marine squadron in China. A single Lewis gun was
mounted at the rear cockpit. Grover Loening remembered that these aircraft had been made by a
190-man labor force in his Manhattan factory at a
price of $32,500 per plane, of which nearly $15,000
was profit.

The greatest obstacle to using Loenings on aircraft carriers was that they had too large a wingspan
for the elevator. The Navy redesigned one of the
OL-6 contract aircraft to be the XOL-7, whose single-bay wings had a thicker airfoil and folded backward. Delivered July 6, 1927, it proved too heavy
and was slower than the OL-6.

LOENING OL-1
Packard 1A-1500, 440 hp
DIMENSIONS: Span 45', Lg. 35'4", Ht. 12'8", Wing Area
504.5 sq. ft.
WEIGHT: Empty 3576 lb., Gross 5208 lb. Fuel 148 gal.
PERFORMANCE: Speed—Top 125 mph at s. l., Stalling 59
mph. Service Ceiling 12,750', Climb 5000'/7 min.
Range 415 miles.   ARC

LOENING OL-2
Liberty 12, 400 hp
DIMENSIONS: Span 45', Lg. 33'10", Ht. 12'6", Wing Area
500 sq. ft.
WEIGHT: Empty 3540 lb., Gross 5010 lb. Fuel 140 gal.
PERFORMANCE: Speed—Top 121 mph at s. l., Stalling 57
mph. Service Ceiling 12,100', Climb 5000'/8 min.
Range 405 miles.   ARC

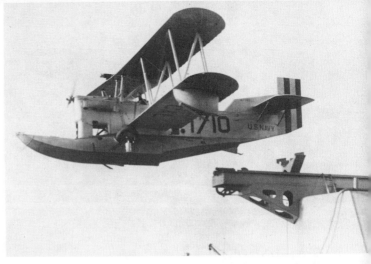

LOENING OL-4
Liberty 12, 400 hp
DIMENSIONS: Span 45′, Lg. 35′, Ht. 12′9″, Wing Area 504 sq. ft.
WEIGHT: Empty 3805 lb., Gross 5448 lb. Fuel 140 gal.
PERFORMANCE: Speed—Top 117 mph at s. l., Stalling 61 mph. Service Ceiling 11,000′, Climb 4500′/10 min. Range 378 miles.   LAWSON

LOENING OL-6
Packard 2A-1500, 475 hp
DIMENSIONS: Span 45′, Lg. 34′11½″, Ht. 12′9″, Wing Area 504 sq. ft.
WEIGHT: Empty 3671 lb., Gross 5350 lb. Fuel 147 gal.
PERFORMANCE: Speed—Top 122 mph at s. l., Stalling 60 mph. Service Ceiling 13,000′, Climb 5000′/9.1 min. Range 423 miles.   SDAM

LOENING XOL-7
Packard 2A-1500, 475 hp
DIMENSIONS: Span 44′4″, Lg. 35′3″, Ht. 12′9″, Wing Area N/A
WEIGHT: Empty 3944 lb., Gross 5623 lb.
PERFORMANCE: Speed—Top 117.5 mph at s. l. Service Ceiling 9750′, Climb 5000′/11.5 min. Range 476 miles.   ARNOLD

LOENING OL-8
Pratt & Whitney R-1340B, 450 hp
DIMENSIONS: Span 45′, Lg. 34′9″, Ht. 13′, Wing Area 502 sq. ft.
WEIGHT: Empty 3429 lb., Gross 4802 lb. Fuel 96 gal.
PERFORMANCE: Speed—Top 121.5 mph at s. l., 112 mph at 10,000′, Cruising 110 mph, Stalling 56.5 mph. Service Ceiling 14,300′, Climb 5000′/7.1 min. Endurance 3.1 hrs.   ARC

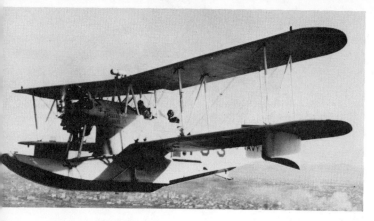

KEYSTONE OL-9
Pratt & Whitney R-1340-4, 450 hp
DIMENSIONS: Same as OL-8
WEIGHT: Empty 3565 lb., Gross 5044 lb.
PERFORMANCE: Speed—Top 121 mph at s. l., 110 mph at
10,000', Cruising 110 mph, Stalling 58 mph. Service
Ceiling 13,400', Climb 5000'/7 min. Endurance 3.1
hrs.   ARC

KEYSTONE-LOENING XO2L-1
Pratt & Whitney R-1340-4, 450 hp
DIMENSIONS: Span 37', Lg. 29'10", Ht. 11'7½", Wing Area
348 sq. ft.
WEIGHT: Empty 2742 lb., Gross 4053 lb. Fuel 112 gal.
PERFORMANCE: Speed—Top 132 mph at s. l., Stalling 59
mph. Service Ceiling 16,200'. Endurance 3.1 hrs. at
110 mph.   ARNOLD

KEYSTONE-LOENING XO2L-2   ARC

The new air-cooled Pratt & Whitney Wasp radial engine gave the same horsepower as the water-cooled power plants but at a lighter weight. One was installed on the last aircraft of the OL-6 contract, which was first flown August 19, 1927, as the XOL-8. Twenty Loening OL-8s with two cockpits ordered in October 1927 were delivered from April to August 1928, followed by 20 similar OL-8As delivered from February to June 1929. Although wing racks for four 116-pound or ten 30-pound bombs had been added, most OL-8s served with utility rather than observation squadrons.

Loening had sold his company to Keystone Aircraft, which moved amphibian production to Bristol, Pennsylvania, where 26 OL-9s were delivered from May 1931 to March 1932. They were similar to the OL-8, but armament now included a .30-caliber fixed Browning with 500 rounds in the upper wing, the flexible Lewis gun with six 97-round drums, and the four 116-pound bombs.

The Navy had received 110 OL amphibians, but Keystone did try a new XO2L-1 with a more streamlined shape. It was tested aboard the *Saratoga* in 1932, and a second prototype, XO2L-2, had a larger rudder, but no production order was given.

The First Corsairs

Corsair is the name given to famous Vought planes spanning three generations. Today's Corsair is the A-7 attack, in World War II it was the F4U-fighter, and for the previous generation it was applied to the most successful Navy observation biplane.

Chance Vought, the vigorous chief of the Long Island City company, realized that his basic VE-7/UO-1 line had exhausted its potential and planned the O2U-1 two-seater around the new Pratt & Whitney Wasp radial. The fuselage and tail were constructed of steel tubing, with fabric covering and aluminum fuel tanks on each side of the front cockpit. The wings were fabric-covered spruce structures with single-bay steel N struts and a 4.75° sweepback on the upper wing.

Armament comprised a 400-round .30-caliber Browning gun in the right upper wing and a Lewis gun and five 97-round drums for the Scarff gun ring on the rear cockpit. A headrest could replace the gun ring when desired. Underwing bomb racks could hold four 116-pound or ten 30-pound bombs.

Two prototypes had been ordered by the Navy, the first flying on November 2, 1926, with a propeller spinner and straight-axle landing gear. It was later fitted with central pontoon gear and set a new world's seaplane record for speed and altitude in April 1927. The second O2U-1 (the X prefix was added to the first aircraft later) dropped the spinner and had the split-axle wheeled gear used on the remaining Corsairs when they were not on pontoons.

An additional 130 O2U-1 two-seaters were built by Vought. Most served as seaplanes aboard every Navy battleship and cruiser, but six of the first O2U-1s went to the Marines' VO-7M as landplanes in December 1927. They replaced the O2B-1s (modernized DH-4s) being used by this squadron in Nicaragua and became involved in the fighting against Sandino's insurgents. They flew observation, bombing, and rescue missions, the latter winning a pilot the Medal of Honor. It introduced Marine aviators to the kind of guerrilla warfare that would make Vietnam a bad memory. Another Marine squadron, VO-9M, used the O2U-1 landplane in Haiti in 1928.

The next version of the Corsair was the O2U-2. Thirty-seven were delivered and used with wheels and arresting gear by VS-1B, VS-2B, and VS-3B aboard the three carriers in 1929 (the B meant the squadrons were assigned to the Battle Fleet) and by the Marine's VS-14M in 1931. The O2U-2's upper wing had an increased span, a larger center-section cutout, and other refinements.

Vought also built 80 O2U-3 Corsairs with refined tail surfaces and 42 O2U-4s by February 1930. Both were also convertible land- or seaplanes that could be used on both catapults and flight decks. Amphibian floats were also developed. The first was Brewster-built, with the wheels outside the pontoon. Then Grumman made eight floats in 1930 with the wheels retracting into the pontoon itself.

Beginning in March 1929, Corsairs were also sold abroad, with 12 O2U-2Ms rushed to put down the last military rebellion in Mexico, where by 1932 32 had been built with engine cowls under license in Mexico City; some served until 1942.

China's Central Government got about 20 O2U-1D Corsairs in 1929, one downing a Junkers W-33 of a rival warlord to win Chiang Kai-shek's first aerial victory. The same year Japan bought a single O2U-1 which Nakajima developed into the Type 90-II seaplane. In February 1932 Chinese Voughts

VOUGHT XO2U-1
Pratt & Whitney R-1340, 450 hp
DIMENSIONS: Span 34'6", Lg. 24'6", Ht. 10'1", Wing Area 320 sq. ft.
WEIGHT: Empty 2342 lb., Gross 3635 lb. Fuel 88 gal.
PERFORMANCE: Speed—Top 149.6 mph at s. l., 142 mph at 10,000', Cruising 110 mph, Stalling 57 mph. Service Ceiling 18,700', Climb 5000'/3.6 min. Range 608 miles.   MFR

VOUGHT O2U-1 (Seaplane data)
Pratt & Whitney R-1340C, 450 hp
DIMENSIONS: Span 34'6", Lg. 28'7", Ht. 11'7", Wing Area 320 sq. ft.
WEIGHT: Empty 2600 lb., Gross 3893 lb. Fuel 88 gal.
PERFORMANCE: Speed—Top 147 mph at s. l., 140 mph at 10,000', Cruising 110 mph, Stalling 59 mph. Service Ceiling 18,700', Climb 10,000'/11.5 min. Range 571 miles.   ARC

VOUGHT O2U-2
Pratt & Whitney R-1340B, 450 hp
DIMENSIONS: Span 36', Lg. 25'4", Ht. 11', Wing Area 318.5 sq. ft.
WEIGHT: Empty 2371 lb., Gross 3830 lb. Fuel 80 gal.
PERFORMANCE: Speed—Top 147 mph at s. l., 141 mph at 10,000', Cruising 110 mph, Stalling 59.5 mph. Service Ceiling 20,100', Climb 10,000'/11 min. Range 725 miles.   LAWSON

VOUGHT O2U-2 in China   TIEN

engaged Japanese Navy aircraft around Shanghai. One Vought and a Junkers K-47 two-seater attacked Type 13 bombers on February 26, sending two down before the Vought's pilot was mortally wounded by one of the escorting Type 3 fighters.[1]

In 1929–30 other Voughts were exported to Argentina (one O2U-1A), Brazil (six O2U-2As), Canada (two O2U-1s), Cuba (26 O2U-3As), Peru (six O2U-1Es and two O2U-3Bs), and the Dominican Republic (two O2U-3SDs). Like the Chinese examples, they had R-1340 engines and usually operated as wheeled aircraft. Seven O2Us were sold to civilian agencies and one became the Army's O-28.

Curtiss Helldivers

With the appearance of the Curtiss Helldiver in 1928, the Marines were finally able to replace the reconditioned DH-4s of their observation squadrons. This type had begun with the XF8C-1 two-seat fighter (described in the next chapter). Four F8C-1s and 21 F8C-3s delivered in March/April 1928 were redesignated OC-1 and OC-2 when they reached VO-8M and VO-10M in San Diego; both were later also used in Nicaragua by VO-7M.

Powered by a 410-hp Pratt & Whitney Wasp, these biplanes were armed with two .30-caliber Browning guns with 800 rounds in the lower wings, two Lewis guns with ten drums in the rear cockpit,

VOUGHT O2U-3 (Landplane data)
Pratt & Whitney R-1340C, 450 hp
DIMENSIONS: Span 36', Lg. 28'10" (25'¾"), Ht. 13'2" (11'6"), Wing Area 318.5 sq. ft.
WEIGHT: Empty 2705 lb. (2490 lb.), Gross 3991 lb. (3967 lb.). Fuel 80 gal.
PERFORMANCE: Speed—Top 136 mph (138 mph) at s. l., 128 mph (130 mph) at 10,000', Cruising 110 mph, Stalling 60.7 mph. Service Ceiling 16,100' (17,100'), Climb 10,000'/12 min. Range 440 (632) miles.   SHIPP

VOUGHT O2U-4 (Seaplane data)
Pratt & Whitney R-1340C, 450 hp
DIMENSIONS: Span 36', Lg. 25' (28'10"), Ht. 11'6", Wing Area 318.5 sq. ft.
WEIGHT: Empty 2518 lb., Gross 3995 lb. (4004 lb.). Fuel 110 gal.
PERFORMANCE: Speed—Top 138 mph (136 mph) at s. l., 130 mph at 10,000', Cruising 110 mph, Stalling 60.7 mph. Service Ceiling 17,900', Climb 10,000'/11.2 min. Range 495 miles.   MFR

[1] This information was provided by Dr. Masahiro Nakayama.

CURTISS OC-2
Pratt & Whitney R-1340, 410 hp
DIMENSIONS: Span 38', Lg. 27'11", Ht. 11'8", Wing Area
  351 sq. ft.
WEIGHT: Empty 2508 lb., Gross 4021 lb. Fuel 110 gal.
PERFORMANCE: Speed—Top 137 mph at s. l., 131 mph at
  10,000', Cruising 110 mph, Stalling 59 mph. Service
  Ceiling 16,850', Climb 10,000'/12.9 min. Range 550
  miles.   ARC

and wing racks for ten 30-pound bombs. A single
XOC-3 was the second XF8C-1, modified to test the
Curtiss H-1640 engine in 1930.

A more advanced version was the Curtiss O2C-1
"Helldiver," which was stressed for dive-bombing
with a 500-pound bomb under the fuselage or four
116-pound bombs under the wings. The two fixed
guns were now in the upper wing, whose span was
reduced to match that of the lower wing. A tail
wheel replaced the skid, and ring cowls were later
added to streamline the 450-hp Wasp.

Ninety-three O2C-1 Helldivers, originally F8C-
5s, were issued to VO-6M, VO-7M, VO-9M, and to
Naval Reserve stations from September 1930 to November 1931. A Wright R-1820 Cyclone was installed in the unarmed XF8C-7, which was purchased in November 1930 as a transport for the
Assistant Secretary of the Navy, and this aircraft was

CURTISS O2C-1 (F8C-5)
Pratt & Whitney R-1340C, 450 hp
DIMENSIONS: Span 32', Lg. 26', Ht. 10'3", Wing Area 308
  sq. ft.
WEIGHT: Empty 2520 lb., Gross 4020 lb. Fuel 120 gal.
PERFORMANCE: Speed—Top 140 mph, Cruising 110 mph,
  Landing 63 mph. Service Ceiling 16,050'. Range 560
  miles.   USN

briefly redesignated XO2C-2 before reverting to the XF8F-7 label.

Three more Cyclone-powered O2C-2 Helldivers were purchased on December 30, 1930, and two appeared in January 1931 with ring cowls, wheel pants, and sliding cockpit canopies. Armed with two Brownings in the upper wing and a third in the rear cockpit, they served on the two big carriers in 1931. The second O2C-2 was tested with a twin-row Wright R-1510 in June 1933. The third aircraft, completed in September 1931, had a new fuselage structure and metal tail. While still marked O2C-2 on its rudder, this aircraft was designated O3C-1 in Navy correspondence. It crashed during a test dive, killing the company pilot, so Curtiss had to build

another two-seater using the same serial number, 8847, to fulfill its contract.

This aircraft became the XS3C-1, reflecting a new designation for carrier or land-based scout planes. The riveted duraluminum tube structure of previous Helldivers was replaced with a welded steel-frame fuselage, and the XS3C-1 had a new panted, single-strut landing gear, balanced elevators, and open cockpits. Armed with the usual three guns, the XS3C-1 may have been known as the XF10C-1 on paper. But it was as the XS3C-1 that this two-seater was first tested at Buffalo on January 29, 1932, flown to Anacostia on February 14, and destroyed on February 25, when it lost its elevators in a dive.

CURTISS O2C-2
Wright R-1820-58, 575 hp
DIMENSIONS: Span 32′, Lg. 25′8″, Ht. 10′10½″, Wing Area 308 sq. ft.
WEIGHT: Empty 2997 lb., Gross 4627 lb. Fuel 120 gal.
PERFORMANCE: Speed—Top 174 mph at s. l., 172 mph at 5000′, Stalling 65.5 mph. Service Ceiling 20,000′, Climb 5000′/3 min. Range 696 miles.   SI

CURTISS O2C-2 Modified (O3C-1)   SI

CURTISS O2C-2 Modified (R-1510)   SI

CURTISS S3C-1
Wright R-1820-E, 620 hp
DIMENSIONS: Same as O2C-2
WEIGHT: Empty 3387 lb., Gross 4959 lb. Fuel 120 gal.
PERFORMANCE: Speed—Top 178 mph at s. l., Stalling 64 mph. Service Ceiling 19,800′, Climb 1680′/1 min., 10,900′/10 min.   SI

VOUGHT O3U-1
Pratt & Whitney R-1340-96, 450 hp
DIMENSIONS: Span 36', Lg. 26'1", Ht. 10'8", Wing Area
325.6 sq. ft.
WEIGHT: Empty 2546 lb., Gross 4057 lb. Fuel 80–110 gal.
PERFORMANCE: Speed—Top 138 mph at s. l., 129 mph at
10,000', Cruising 110 mph, Stalling 59 mph. Service
Ceiling 16,300', Climb 10,000'/16.5 min. Range 506
miles.   USN

Vought O3U-1

Vought retained leadership of the naval-observation
class with the O3U-1, developed from the O2U series, except that the lower wing now had the same
span and sweep as the upper. Powered by a 450-hp
Wasp and convertible from wheels to floats, it had
a .30-caliber Browning with 500 rounds in the upper wing, a Lewis gun and six drums in the rear
cockpit, and bomb racks for the same 300- to 464-
pound load as the Helldivers. In May 1931 the
O3U-1 was tested with an improved Grumman amphibian float and 15 floats were purchased for occasional service use.

The O3U-1 had been ordered January 18, 1930,
and entered service with VO-3B in July 1930, with
87 built by September 1931 to three contracts in
the new Vought plant at East Hartford, Connecticut.
The O3U-1s generally operated as floatplanes from
battleships and cruisers.

Another Navy effort was made to develop a lightweight observation type for the Omaha class cruisers, whose catapults had a 5,450-pound limit. BuAer
Design No. 86 was prepared, and on June 28, 1929,
prototypes were ordered from Keystone (XOK-1)
and Berliner-Joyce (XOJ-1). Using a 400-hp Wright
Whirlwind and a ring cowl, the XOK-1 appeared in
January 1931. By April it had been fitted with arresting gear and a gun on the upper wing and the
rear cockpit, but it was destroyed in a crash that
same month.

The Berliner-Joyce XOJ-1 flew around May 1931,
using a 400-hp Pratt & Whitney R-985A and full-
span Zap flaps on both wings, allowing more lift
with a smaller wing area. Test results were less
than satisfactory, and the flaps were not used when
the Navy got the OJ-2 production version in 1933.

Vought attempted a more advanced structural design in the XO4U-1, with all-metal monocoque fuselage and fabric-covered metal wings, the swept-
back upper one attached to the fuselage. Ordered
May 13, 1930, the XO4U-1 landplane crashed
shortly after its first flight on February 28, 1931.

VOUGHT O3U-1 Seaplane
Pratt & Whitney R-1340-96, 450 hp
DIMENSIONS: Span 36', Lg. 29'11", Ht. 12', Wing Area
325.6 sq. ft.
WEIGHT: Empty 2747 lb., Gross 4057 lb. Fuel 80 gal.
PERFORMANCE: Speed—Top 135 mph at s. l., 126 mph at
10,000', Cruising 110 mph, Stalling 59 mph. Service
Ceiling 15,200', Climb 10,000'/16.5 min. Range 352
miles.   USN

KEYSTONE XOK-1 (Landplane data)
Wright R-975C, 400 hp
DIMENSIONS: Span 34'8", Lg. 28'9½" (24'10"), Ht. 11'4"
(9'9"), Wing Area 293 sq. ft.
WEIGHT: Empty 2219 lb. (2000 lb.), Gross 3395 lb. (3176
lb.). Fuel 60 gal.
PERFORMANCE: Speed—Top 139 mph (143 mph) at s. l.,
133 mph (137 mph) at 10,000', Stalling 57 mph (55
mph). Service Ceiling 19,900' (22,500'). Endurance 2.9
hrs. (3 hrs.).   SI

BERLINER-JOYCE XOJ-1 (Landplane data)
Pratt & Whitney R-985-A, 400 hp
DIMENSIONS: Span 33', Lg. 29'1" (25'8"), Wing Area 284 sq. ft.
WEIGHT: Empty 2215 lb. (1950 lb.), Gross 3376 lb. (3111 lb.). Fuel 60 gal.
PERFORMANCE: Speed—Top 143 mph (146 mph) at s. l., 136 mph (140 mph) at 10,000', Stalling 60.4 mph (58 mph). Service Ceiling 19,700' (22,000'), Climb 10,000'/ 9.2 (8.9) min. Endurance 3 hrs. (3.1 hrs.) at 110 mph.   USN

VOUGHT XO4U-1
Pratt & Whitney R-1340D, 500 hp
DIMENSIONS: Span 37', Lg. 27'9", Ht. 9'7", Wing Area 335 sq. ft.
WEIGHT: Empty 2178 lb., Gross 3696 lb. Fuel 110 lb.
PERFORMANCE: Speed—Top 143 mph at s. l., 137 mph at 10,000', Stalling 55.9 mph. Service Ceiling 21,200', Climb 10,000'/10.6 min. Endurance 4.9 hrs. at 110 mph.   MFR

Chapter 10
Adapting the Fighter to the Flight Deck, 1918–32

A Humble Beginning

The Navy's fighters have had the same basic mission as those of the Air Force: destruction of enemy aircraft. However, since they are based on aircraft carriers, they present a more difficult design problem. The carrier fighter must have a short takeoff and landing run for operations from a limited flight deck. To conserve space, carrier types should have either small wings or some way of folding large ones. An arresting hook is necessary for deck landing, and safety gear should be available for overwater flying.

In World War I the United States had no aircraft carriers, so the first Navy fighter was shore-based. The Curtiss HA single-float seaplane was a short-nosed two-place biplane with a Liberty engine and four-bladed wooden propeller, two .30 caliber Marlin synchronized nose guns, and twin .30-caliber Lewis guns in the rear cockpit.

Called the "Dunkirk fighter" since it was intended for operations in that area, the HA was ordered December 3, 1917, and first flown March 21, 1918, at Port Washington, Long Island. Fire destroyed the seaplane on its second flight and two modified examples were not completed until the war was over.

The second fighter for the Navy was also a four-gun two-seater, but the Curtiss 18-T was a triplane with a Curtiss engine designed by Charles Kirkham. Two examples ordered March 30, 1918, were first flown July 5 with wheeled landing gear; it didn't take long to build a prototype in those days. Performance and flying qualities were good in comparison to the dreadful experiences with the HA type, and the Army also bought two examples.

No Navy fighters were actually used in the war, but David Ingalls became the first Navy ace flying a Sopwith Camel with the RAF. Eight Camels, 12 Nieuport 28s, and two S.E. 5s were transferred from

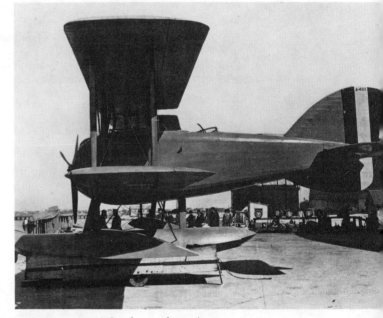

CURTISS HA (Third one shown)
Liberty 12, 400 hp (Later Curtiss K-12, 400 hp)
DIMENSIONS: Span 36', Lg. 30'9", Ht. 10'7", Wing Area 380 sq. ft.
WEIGHT: Empty 2638 lb., Gross 4012 lb.
PERFORMANCE: Speed—Top 132 mph at s. l., Landing 62 mph. Climb 8500'/10 min.   USN

CURTISS 18-T
Curtiss Kirkham K-12, 400 hp
DIMENSIONS: Span 31'11", Lg. 23'3", Ht. 9'10", Wing Area 309 sq. ft.
WEIGHT: Gross 2864 lb., Max. 2902 lb.
PERFORMANCE: Speed—Top 160 mph. Climb 12,000'/10 min.   USN

HARRIOT HD-1
Le Rhône, 110 hp
DIMENSIONS: Span 28′6″, Lg. 19′2″, Ht. 9′8″, Wing Area
   188 sq. ft.
WEIGHT: Empty 904 lb., Gross 1521 lb.
PERFORMANCE: Speed—Top 108 mph. Climb 6560′/6 min.
   Endurance 2.5 hrs.   PMB

VOUGHT VE-7SF
Wright E-2, 180 hp
DIMENSIONS: Span 34′1″, Lg. 24′5″, Ht. 8′7″, Wing Area
   284 sq. ft.
WEIGHT: Empty 1505 lb., Gross 2100 lb. Fuel 30 gal.
PERFORMANCE: Speed—Top 117 mph at s. l., Landing 51
   mph. Service Ceiling 15,000′, Climb 5000′/5.5 min.
   Range 291 miles.   USN

CURTISS TS-1 (Landplane)
Wright J-4, 200 hp
DIMENSIONS: Span 25′, Lg. 22′1″, Ht. 9′, Wing Area 228
   sq. ft.
WEIGHT: Empty 1240 lb., Gross 1920 lb. Fuel 50 gal.
PERFORMANCE: Speed—Top 125 mph, Landing 48 mph.
   Service Ceiling 16,250′, Climb 5000′/5.5 min. Range
   482 miles.   USN

the Army in 1919, along with a Loening M-8 two-seater used as a prototype for the M-80 observation series. Ten French Harriot HD-1 single-seaters were assembled at the Naval Aircraft Factory.

In an effort to take these fighters to sea with the fleet, wooden flying platforms were built on two turrets of eight battleships, and the single-seaters mentioned above had a takeoff run short enough, with luck, to fly off these ships and land at the nearest shore base. The first such flight was made by a Camel from the USS *Texas* on March 9, 1919, but the technique had obvious limitations and was abandoned after 1920. The Marines, however, established a shore-based fighter unit with 11 Thomas-Morse MB-3s acquired in January 1922.

When the first U.S. carrier, the *Langley,* was commissioned, the Navy had two fighter squadrons, but they were equipped only with Vought VE-7SF double-bay biplanes designed as trainers. Powered by a 180-hp Wright E-2 and converted to a single-seater with one Vickers gun, a VE-7SF made the Navy's first carrier takeoff on October 17, 1922. The SF designation stood for single-seat, with flotation-gear modifications. At least 50 Voughts were modified in this way in 1921, with two Marlin fixed guns replacing the Vickers of the first ships. Both VF-1 and VF-2 were based at San Diego at the time.

The first single-seater specially designed for operation from Navy ships was the TS-1, with a 200-hp Lawrence J-1 air-cooled radial (which later became the Wright J-4). It was a single-bay biplane with the lower wing hung below the fuselage and containing the fuel in a droppable center-section fuel tank. Either wheels or twin floats could be used, and twin .30-caliber fixed guns were mounted on the cowl. The structure of the fuselage was welded-steel tubing, and the wings were of wood; both were fabric-covered.

Rex Beisel, at BuAer's design department, was put in charge of the TS (tractor single-seater) project in March 1921, and the contract for production of his design went to Curtiss. The first of 34 Curtiss-built TS-1 fighters was delivered May 9, 1922, and by the end of the year reached the *Langley* for flight-deck trials. Squadron VF-1 at San Diego operated the TS-1 until 1927, both from the *Langley* and with floats from battleships.

The Naval Aircraft Factory also built five TS-1s as a cost-yardstick project and four as racer versions with water-cooled engines and racing wings. The racers were two TS-2s with 240-hp Aeromarine U-873s and two TS-3s with Wright E-2s (later called TR-2s and TR-3s). The last versions of the TS to be built were two aircraft with an all-metal fabric-covered structure designed by Charles W. Hall; they had raised lower wings and two Marlin guns. This

CURTISS TS-1 (Seaplane)
Wright J-4, 200 hp
DIMENSIONS: As TS-1 landplane, except height 9'7".
WEIGHT: Gross 2123 lb. Fuel 50 gal.
PERFORMANCE: Speed—Top 123 mph. Service Ceiling 14,450'. Range 339 miles.   MFR

CURTISS F4C-1
Lawrence-Wright J-4, 200 hp
DIMENSIONS: Span 25', Lg. 18'4", Ht. 8'9", Wing Area 185 sq. ft.
WEIGHT: Empty 1027 lb., Gross 1707 lb. Fuel 50 gal.
PERFORMANCE: Speed—Top 126 mph, Landing 49 mph. Service Ceiling 17,400', Climb 5000'/3.9 min. Range 340 miles at top speed, 525 miles cruising.   MFR

version began flight tests September 4, 1924, as the Curtiss F4C-1.

That designation reflected the system of designating aircraft by their manufacturer, irrespective of design origin, and was affected by the Navy's efforts to explore high-speed flights by building unarmed racers. Curtiss had built the CR, R2C, and R3C racers, and they were considered to have covered the FC, F2C, and F3C designations. There was no F5C fighter in order to avoid confusion with the F-5 flying boats.

Boeing's first naval fighter was the FB-1, based on the Army's PW-9, with tapered single-bay biplane wings and a Curtiss D-12 inline engine with water radiator under the nose. Armament was the arrangement standard on Navy fighters before World War II: two .30-caliber synchronized guns on the cowl, with one replaceable by a .50-caliber weapon.

Fourteen Boeings were ordered in December 1924, and delivery was made in December 1925 on

BOEING FB-1
Curtiss D-12, 400 hp
DIMENSIONS: Span 32′, Lg. 23′6″, Ht. 8′9″, Wing Area 241 sq. ft.
WEIGHT: Empty 2132 lb., Gross 2944 lb. Fuel 112 gal.
PERFORMANCE: Speed—Top 167 mph at s. l., Landing 57.5 mph. Service Ceiling 21,200′, Climb 5000′/2.8 min. Range 509 miles. USN

BOEING FB-5
Packard 2A-1500, 525 hp
DIMENSIONS: Span 32′, Lg. 23′8″, Ht. 9′1″, Wing Area 241 sq. ft.
WEIGHT: Empty 2416 lb., Gross 3196 lb. Fuel 50–100 gal.
PERFORMANCE: Speed—Top 169 mph at s. l., 163 mph at 5000′, Cruising 110 mph, Landing 60 mph. Service Ceiling 20,200′, Climb 5000′/3.2 min. Range 323 miles. USN

BOEING FB-3
Packard 1A-1500, 510 hp
DIMENSIONS: Span 32′, Lg. 22′11″, Ht. 8′9″, Wing Area 241.5 sq. ft.
WEIGHT: Empty 2387 lb., Gross 3204 lb. Fuel 112 gal.
PERFORMANCE: Speed—Top 170 mph, Landing 59 mph. Service Ceiling 23,100′, Climb 5000′/3 min. Range 460 miles. MFR

BOEING FB-6
Pratt & Whitney R-1340, 400 hp
DIMENSIONS: Same as FB-4
WEIGHT: Empty 1904 lb., Gross 2737 lb.
PERFORMANCE: Speed—Top 159 mph at s. l. Service Ceiling 22,800′, Climb 5000′/2.5 min. Range 414 miles USN

BOEING FB-4
Wright P-2, 440 hp
DIMENSIONS: Span 32′, Lg. 22′10″, Ht. 8′9″, Wing Area 241.5 sq. ft.
WEIGHT: Empty 2000 lb., Gross 2817 lb. Fuel 112 gal.
PERFORMANCE: Speed—Top 160 mph, landing 58 mph. Service Ceiling 22,500′, Climb 5000′/3.18 min. Range 428 miles. MFR

ten FB-1s used by the Marine fighter squadron in China and two FB-2s with arresting gear for carrier trials. An FB-3 with a Packard 1A-2500 and twin floats crashed on December 31, 1925, and an FB-4 was delivered with a Wright radial and floats in January 1926. In April 1926, two more FB-3s were built with Packards, and the FB-4 became the FB-6 with a Pratt & Whitney R-1340 Wasp in August 1926.

The production version of this Boeing was the FB-5, with a Packard 2A-1500, convertible wheels or float gear, and a balanced rudder. The first example was tested on October 7, 1926, and all 27 were delivered by barge to the *Langley* in Seattle on January 21, 1927.

Curtiss gave Boeing strong competition in this period with a seagoing version of the Army's P-1 Hawk series. Nine Hawks were ordered in January 1925, and the first F6C-1 was completed in August, with five being delivered in September. Powered by the Curtiss D-12, they had interchangeable wheels or twin-float landing gear, but four F6C-2s delivered in November 1925 had straight-axle wheels and arresting gear for the *Langley*. Tapered wings, N struts, and a tunnel radiator for their D-12 engines were features shared by both the Boeing and Curtiss fighters.

Thirty-five Curtiss F6C-3 Hawks, with deliveries beginning in January 1927, were the last Navy service fighters with water-cooled engines. At that time the Navy's fighter force comprised VF-1, VF-6, and later VF-3 with FB-5s; VF-5 with F6C-3s; and VF-2 testing the first FB-2, F6C-1, and F6C-2 types. The Marines had VF-1M, VF-2M, and VF-3M with F6C-3, F6C-1, and FB-1 fighters.

In addition to their two guns, these fighters could carry two 116-pound bombs, and on October 26, 1926, VF-2 made the first fleet demonstration of dive-bombing. Further success with this method led to the redesignation of VF-5 and VF-6 as VB-1B and VB-2B in July 1928. This meant that the second single-seat squadron on the *Saratoga* and *Lexington* would be listed as a bomber-fighter unit.

CURTISS F6C-1
Curtiss D-12, 412 hp
DIMENSIONS: Span 31′6″, Lg. 22′8″, Ht. 10′, Wing Area 252 sq. ft.
WEIGHT: Empty 2055 lb., Gross 2803 lb. Fuel 50–100 gal.
PERFORMANCE: Speed—Top 163.5 mph at s. l., 139 mph at 15,000′, Cruising 110 mph, Landing 59 mph. Service Ceiling 21,700′, Climb 1600′/1 min. Endurance 3.19 hrs. at 110 mph.   ARC

CURTISS F6C-1 Seaplane   MFR

CURTISS F6C-3
Curtiss D-12, 400 hp
DIMENSIONS: Span 31′6″, Lg. 22′10″, Ht. 10′8″, Wing Area 252 sq. ft.
WEIGHT: Empty 2161 lb., Gross 2963 lb., Max. 3349 lb. Fuel 50–100 gal.
PERFORMANCE: Speed—Top 154 mph at s. l., Landing 59 mph. Service Ceiling 20,300′, Climb 5000′/3.5 min. Range 351 miles normal, 655 miles max.   USN

CURTISS F6C-2
Curtiss D-12, 400 hp
DIMENSIONS: As F6C-1
WEIGHT: Empty 2090 lb., Gross 2838 lb. Fuel 50–100 gal.
PERFORMANCE: Speed—Top 159 mph at s. l., Landing 59 mph. Service Ceiling 22,700′, Climb 5000′. Range 330 miles.   USN

VOUGHT FU-1
Wright R-790, 220 hp
DIMENSIONS: Span 34'4", Lg. 24'5", Ht. 8'10", Wing Area
  290 sq. ft.
WEIGHT: Empty 1715 lb., Gross 2409 lb. (Seaplane 2774
  lb.). Fuel 46 gal.
PERFORMANCE: Speed—Top 147 mph at 13,000', 125 mph
  at s. l., Landing 53 mph. Service Ceiling 27,300', Absolute Ceiling 29,600', Climb 5000'/5.1 min. Range 430
  miles.   USN

WRIGHT XF3W-1 (Seaplane version shown)
Pratt & Whitney R-1340B, 450 hp
DIMENSIONS: Span 27'4", Lg. 22'1", Ht. 8'6", Wing Area
  215 sq. ft.
WEIGHT: Empty 1414 lb., Gross 2128 lb. Fuel 47 gal.
PERFORMANCE: Speed—Top 162 mph at s. l., Landing 54
  mph.   USN

Battleship Fighters

In 1927, VF-2 was deployed among the 12 battleships of the Pacific Battle Fleet, operating as individual floatplanes from their catapults along with
the UO-1 and OL-6 observation aircraft. The type
selected for this role was the Vought FU-1, a single-
seat fighter version of the UO-1, with new double-
bay wings and steel struts.

Armed with two .30-caliber Brownings, the FU-
1 had a 220-hp Wright J-5 with a Rootes integral
supercharger, making it the first Navy fighter faster
at altitude than sea level. It operated with a central
main float from ships and with wheels ashore.
Twenty FU-1s ordered June 30, 1926, were delivered from January to April 1927 and served on the
battleships until September 1928. After that time,
Navy fighter squadrons would be carrier-based, and
the Voughts were converted to FU-2s, with a second
cockpit for utility service.

The Air-cooled Single-seaters

The adoption of the Pratt & Whitney Wasp as the
standard engine for fighters came as the Navy
squadrons prepared to go aboard the new *Lexington*
and *Saratoga*. This engine was first airborne on
May 5, 1926, with the Wright F3W-1 biplane.

This Wright single-seater was the last of several
prototypes (NW and F2W) designed to explore new
engine and design arrangements and had been intended for a Wright P-1 radial until that engine
failed to work out. Never intended as a production
prototype, the F3W-1 was used for research from
1927 to 1930, setting many altitude records.

The first Curtiss Navy fighter with the Wasp was
the XF6C-4,[1] converted in September 1926 from
the first F6C-1. Thirty-one production F6C-4s were
delivered from February to June 1927, most of them
later going to Pensacola as advanced trainers. Further development of this series was seen in the
XF6C-5, which was the XF6C-4 airframe fitted with
the Pratt & Whitney R-1690 Hornet in September
1927. The unarmed XF6C-6 was specially built for
the 1930 air races with lower wing removed, wheel
pants, and a Curtiss Conqueror inline engine. The
latter's fatal crash killed the pilot and ended Navy
competition in the air races. Wind-tunnel experiments and careful engineering were proving a more
efficient method of advancing performance than
trial-and-error racers unsuitable for actual service
work. The last modification of this series appeared
in 1932 as an XF6C-7 with a 450-hp air-cooled inverted inline Ranger.

Designed from the very beginning as a carrier
type by Rex Beisel, the Curtiss XF7C-1 had a R-
1340B neatly mounted behind a large prop skinner,
an upper wing swept back 7° over a straight lower
wing, and a life raft in a tube behind the pilot. The
XF7C-1 was begun December 8, 1926, and first
flew on February 28, 1927. Seventeen production
F7C-1s completed from November 1928 to January
1929 had strengthened landing gear, omitted the
spinner, and served with the Marines of VF-5M at
Quantico.

---

[1] The X designation was not actually applied to Navy prototype
aircraft until 1927, but it is used here for convenience.

CURTISS F6C-4
Pratt & Whitney R-1340, 410 hp
DIMENSIONS: Span 31'6", Lg. 22'6", Ht. 10'11", Wing Area
252 sq. ft.
WEIGHT: Empty 1980 lb., Gross 2785 lb., Max. 3171 lb.
Fuel 50–100 gal.
PERFORMANCE: Speed—Top 155 mph at s. l., Landing 57
mph. Service Ceiling 22,900', Climb 5000'/2.5 min.
Range 361 miles normal, 676 miles max.   USN

CURTISS XF6C-5
Pratt & Whitney R-1690, 525 hp
DIMENSIONS: Span 31'6", Lg. 22'6", Ht. 9'8", Wing Area
252 sq. ft.
WEIGHT: Empty 2109 lb., Gross 2960 lb. Fuel 50–100 gal.
PERFORMANCE: Speed—Top 159 mph, Landing 60 mph.
Service Ceiling 21,900', Climb 5000'/2.5 min. Range
329 miles.   PMB

CURTISS XF7C-1   USN

CURTISS F7C-1
Pratt & Whitney R-1340B, 450 hp
DIMENSIONS: Span 32'8", Lg. 22'2", Ht. 10'4", Wing Area
276 sq. ft.
WEIGHT: Empty 2038 lb., Gross 2782 lb., Max. 3219 lb.
Fuel 80–110 gal.
PERFORMANCE: Speed—Top 151 mph at s. l. Service Ceil-
ing 23,350', Climb 5000'/2.6 min. Range 330 miles nor-
mal, 671 miles max.   USN

HALL XFH-1
Pratt & Whitney R-1340B, 450 hp
DIMENSIONS: Span 32', Lg. 22'6", Ht. 11', Wing Area 255
sq. ft.
WEIGHT: Empty 1773 lb., Gross 2514 lb. Fuel 80 gal.
PERFORMANCE: Speed—Top 153 mph at s. l., Landing 55
mph. Service Ceiling 25,300', Climb 5000'/2.8 min.
Range 275 miles.   USN

EBERHART FG-1
Pratt & Whitney R-1340C, 425 hp
DIMENSIONS: Span 32', Lg. 27'3", Ht. 9'10", Wing Area
241 sq. ft.
WEIGHT: Empty 2145 lb., Gross 2938 lb., Max. 3208 lb.
PERFORMANCE: Speed—Top 154 mph. Service Ceiling
18,700', Climb 5000'/3.7 min.   PMB

More Boeing Fighters

Designed especially for carrier use with the R-1340B Wasp, the Boeing XF2B-1 was first flown November 2, 1926, and was developed from the FB-6 and XP-8 designs. The large nose spinner was omitted from production ships, which added the balanced rudder of the FB-5. Thirty-two F2B-1s ordered March 1927 began entering service in November 1927 and served on the *Saratoga* with VF-1B and VB-2B. They also were used by the Navy's first precision aerobatic team, the "Three Sea Hawks," to perform at air shows. One example each was sold to Brazil and Japan.

The Boeing XF3B-1 first flew March 2, 1927, as a company venture called Model 74, with a 425-hp

Wasp, central-float landing gear, and wings and tail surfaces like those of the F2B-1. Rejected by the Navy, it was returned to the factory to be rebuilt. When flown again on February 3, 1928, it had larger wings with constant chord and sweepback on the upper wing. The tail surfaces and ailerons were made of corrugated aluminum.

This aircraft was accepted and followed by 73 F3B-1 fighters delivered from June to December 1928. Production articles differed from the original by a new vertical fin and deletion of the float provisions, which were no longer required for Navy fighters. Armament comprised two .30-caliber guns and five 25-pound bombs. The F3B-1 served on all three carriers with VF-2, VF-3, VB-1, and VB-2.

BOEING XF2B-1   MFR

BOEING F3B-1
Pratt & Whitney R-1340-80, 450 hp
DIMENSIONS: Span 33', Lg. 24'10", Ht. 10'1", Wing Area 275 sq. ft.
WEIGHT: Empty 2183 lb., Gross 2950 lb., Max. 3340 lb. Fuel 60–110 gal.
PERFORMANCE: Speed—Top 156 mph at s. l., Landing 55 mph. Service Ceiling 20,900', Climb 5000'/3.1 min.
USN (ARC)

BOEING F2B-1
Pratt & Whitney R-1340B, 450 hp
DIMENSIONS: Span 30'1", Lg. 22'11", Ht. 10'1", Wing Area 243 sq. ft.
WEIGHT: Empty 2058 lb., Gross 2874 lb., Max. 3204 lb. Fuel 50–100 gal.
PERFORMANCE: Speed—Top 158 mph at s. l., Landing 58 mph. Service Ceiling 21,500', Climb 5000'/3 min. Range 372 miles normal, 704 miles max.   MFR

Two-seat Fighters

Two-seat fighters emerged from a Marine Corps requirement for aircraft capable of observation, light bombing, and fighting on expeditions made by the Corps to Caribbean trouble spots. Since World War I the Marines had been equipped with DB-4Bs with which they had developed a dive-bombing technique, utilizing small fragmentation bombs, against guerrilla opponents in Haiti and Nicaragua.

First to meet this requirement was the Curtiss F8C-1 (Model 37), a development of the Army A-3 Falcons. Using an air-cooled Wasp instead of the Falcon's inline engine, the F8C series had the upper wing swept back from the center section

CURTISS F8C-1 (OC-1)
Pratt & Whitney R-1340, 432 hp
DIMENSIONS: Span 38′, Lg. 25′11″, Ht. 10′6″, Wing Area
353 sq. ft.
WEIGHT: Empty 2440 lb., Gross 3918 lb., Max. 4367 lb.
Fuel 120 gal.
PERFORMANCE: Speed—Top 137.5 mph at s. l., 129 mph
at 10,000′, Landing 58 mph. Service Ceiling 17,300′.
Range 378 miles.   USN

and a balanced rudder. Two .30-caliber Brownings
mounted in the lower wing fired outside of the
propeller arc, and two Lewis guns were on the
observer's ring.

Two XF8C-1 two-seaters ordered June 30, 1927,
along with the F3B and F7C single-seaters, were
delivered in January 1928 and went to VO-7M in
Nicaragua. Four F8C-1s and 21 F8C-3s delivered
in March/April 1928 also went to Marine observation squadrons VO-8M and VO-10M and so were
soon redesignated OC-1 and OC-2 (discussed in the
previous chapter).

A more advanced version was the XF8C-2, ordered March 15, 1928, and flown in November
1928. The upper wing was reduced to the same
span as the lower and was stressed for dive-bombing, with two 116-pound bombs under each wing,
or a 500-pound bomb below the fuselage. Although
the first prototype crashed, another was flown in
April 1929, sometimes with a cowl around the engine cylinders. The pilot had a telescopic sight for
dive-bombing alongside the ring sight for the two
.30-caliber guns in the upper wing. In June 1929
orders were placed for an XF8C-4 and 36 production aircraft. The XF8C-4 that appeared in April
1930 was much like the XF8C-2. It was followed by
25 F8C-4 "Helldivers," which went into service
with VF-1 aboard the *Saratoga* in August 1930 as
the only two-seaters in the Navy's fighter squadrons. They were followed by 91 aircraft originally
designated F8C-5, which had no arresting gear and
were allotted to Marine observation squadrons.
Shortly after entering service, they were redesignated O2C-1s and served with VO-6M, VO-7M, and
various reserve air stations.

Two more aircraft begun as F8C-4s became F8C-
6s for special trials with slots and flaps, and finished
as O2C-1s. Four Helldivers were accepted with

CURTISS XF8C-2
Pratt & Whitney R-1340-80, 450 hp
DIMENSIONS: Span 32′, Lg. 25′11″, Ht. 10′6″, Wing Area
308 sq. ft.
WEIGHT: Empty 2229 lb., Gross 3347 lb., Max. 3548 lb.
Fuel 86 gal.
PERFORMANCE: Speed—Top 145 mph at s. l., Landing 56
mph. Service Ceiling 20,800′, Climb 5000′/4 min.
Range 333 miles.   MFR

CURTISS F8C-4
Pratt & Whitney R-1340-88, 450 hp at s. l.
DIMENSIONS: Span 32′, Lg. 25′11″, Ht. 10′10″, Wing Area
308 sq. ft.
WEIGHT: Empty 2513 lb., Gross 3783 lb., Max. 4238 lb.
Fuel 86–136 gal.
PERFORMANCE: Speed—Top 137 mph at s. l., Landing 59
mph. Service Ceiling 15,000′, Climb 5000′/6 min.
Range 455 miles normal, 722 miles max.   USN

Wright R-1820 Cyclones. The first was the XF8C-7,
purchased in November 1930 as an unarmed command transport for David Ingalls, Assistant Secretary of the Navy. It had a 575-hp R-1820-65, wheel
pants, and cockpit enclosure. Another, built in December 1930 as a private venture registered N 983V,
had three guns. This aircraft was also labeled F8C-
7 by Curtiss, but seems to have become one of the
three O2C-2s purchased by the Navy on December
30, 1930 (described in the previous chapter). It

crashed before final acceptance, and was replaced by the O3C-1, bearing the same serial number.

Vought also tried to enter the two-seat fighter field with the XF2U-1, delivered June 25, 1929. It introduced the wing shape later used on the O2U-2 but had a cowled R-1340C Wasp, two fixed Brownings in the upper wing, and a Lewis gun in the rear cockpit. Vought's biplane did not, however, dislodge the Helldiver from its place.

Experimental Single-seaters, 1926–32

Several other companies made unsuccessful attempts to capture Navy single-seat fighter contracts from the successful Boeing ships. The earliest of these was the Eberhard FG-1, with a Wasp engine and fabric-covered welded-steel tube fuselage. The wings had a fabric-covered dural structure with a 7° sweepback on the upper wing and a 6° sweep forward on the lower wing. The FG-1 was tested as a landplane in November 1926 and reappeared in January 1928 as a single-float seaplane with modified wings and an XF2G-1 designation.

Another biplane with sweepback on the upper wing and forward sweep on the lower was the Hall XFH-1, whose main feature was an all-metal watertight monocoque fuselage. The landing gear could be dropped for emergency landings. Built of aluminum, the XFH-1 was delivered from Buffalo on June 18, 1929, but crashed February 3, 1930, after generally unsatisfactory performance.

To compare American technique with developments abroad, the Navy imported the British Bristol Bulldog fighter for tests. The first example crashed in November 1929, but a second was purchased in March 1930. Powered by a 515-hp Bristol Jupiter VII, the Bulldog was not considered as rugged as American types but had a good performance record.

Among this period's most interesting types was the Berliner-Joyce XFJ-1, which was distinguished by a gap between the metal fuselage and the lower wing, while the upper wing was joined to the fuselage behind a 450-hp R-1340C Wasp. Ordered May 16, 1929, the XFJ-1 was tested in May 1930 but was damaged in a crash and was returned to the Dundalk, Maryland, factory for modification in November. On May 22, 1931, the prototype, now designated XFJ-2, resumed tests at Anacostia using an R-1340D of 500 hp, wheel pants, ring cowl, prop spinner, and a larger vertical tail. Top speed increased from 177 to 193 mph, but the aircraft was now unstable and no longer satisfactory.

Another biplane with the upper wings joined to an all-metal fuselage was the XFA-1 built by General Aviation, formerly Atlantic-Fokker. A 450-hp R-1340C Wasp was fitted with a two-bladed propeller and a ring cowl. Ordered June 24, 1930, the XFA-1 could be distinguished by a fairing over the land-

CURTISS XF8C-7 (Data for unarmed model)
Wright R-1820-64, 575 hp
DIMENSIONS: Span 32′, Lg. 26′, Ht. 11′, Wing Area 308 sq. ft.
WEIGHT: Empty 2958 lb., Gross 4274 lb. Fuel 120 gal.
PERFORMANCE: Speed—Top 179 mph at s. l., Landing 63 mph. Service Ceiling 20,800′, Climb 5000′/3.2 min.

MFR

CURTISS XF8C-7 (N983V)   MFR

VOUGHT XF2U-1
Pratt & Whitney R-1340C, 450 mph
DIMENSIONS: Span 36′, Lg. 27′, Ht. 10′, Wing Area 318 sq. ft.
WEIGHT: Empty 2539 lb., Gross 3907 lb., Max. 4208 lb. Fuel 110 gal.
PERFORMANCE: Speed—Top 146 mph, Cruising 110 mph, Landing 57.5 mph. Service Ceiling 18,700′, Climb 9100′/10 min. Range 495 miles.   MFR

BRISTOL BULLDOG (Navy test)
Bristol Jupiter VII, 515 hp at 9000'
DIMENSIONS: Span 33'10", Lg. 27'6", Ht. 9'4", Wing Area
    306 sq. ft.
WEIGHT: Empty 2174 lb., Gross 3264 lb. Fuel 70 gal.
PERFORMANCE: Speed—Top 173 mph at 9000', 141 mph
    at s. l., Landing 59 mph. Service Ceiling 27,300', Climb
    5000'/2.7 min.   USN

BERLINER-JOYCE XFJ-1
Pratt & Whitney R-1340C, 450 hp at s. l.
DIMENSIONS: Span 28', Lg. 20'7", Ht. 9'10", Wing Area
    179 sq. ft.
WEIGHT: Empty 2046 lb., Gross 2797 lb. Fuel 91 gal.
PERFORMANCE: Speed—Top 172 mph at s. l., Landing 65
    mph. Service Ceiling 23,800', Climb 5000'/3.9 min.
    Range 404 miles normal, 716 miles max.   MFR

BERLINER-JOYCE XFJ-2
Pratt & Whitney R-1340-92, 500 hp
DIMENSIONS: Span 28', Lg. 20'10", Ht. 9'10", Wing Area
    179 sq. ft.
WEIGHT: Empty 2102 lb., Gross 2847 lb., Max. 3116 lb.
    Fuel 91 gal.
PERFORMANCE: Speed—Top 193 mph at 6000', Landing
    64 mph. Service Ceiling 24,700', Climb 14,300'/10 min.
    Range 520 miles.   USN

FOKKER XFA-1
Pratt & Whitney R-1340C, 450 hp
DIMENSIONS: Span 25'6", Lg. 22'2", Ht. 9'3", Wing Area
    175 sq. ft.
WEIGHT: Empty 1837 lb., Gross 2508 lb. Fuel 60 gal.
PERFORMANCE: Speed—Top 170 mph, Landing 64 mph.
    Service Ceiling 20,200', Climb 5000'/3.4 min. Range
    375 miles normal, 518 miles max.   USN

ing-gear strut and was also seen with a three-bladed propeller. Delivered to the Navy on March 5, 1932, it was built to BuAer Design No. 96, the same small-size fighter specification that produced the Curtiss Sparrowhawk.

The Curtiss XF9C-1 Sparrowhawk was a little biplane with upper wings joined to the metal fuselage behind a Wright R-975C Whirlwind with ring cowl. Ordered on June 30, 1930, the XF9C-1 made its first flight February 12, 1931, the last plane built at the Curtiss Garden City facility. Another prototype, the XF9C-2, was built at Buffalo by September 1931 with a higher upper wing, modified landing gear, and vertical fin.

At that time the Navy's giant airship, the *Akron*, was entering service, and its sister ship, the *Macon*, was under construction. A hangar and trapeze allowed the airship to carry, launch, and recover up to five small aircraft in order to extend its search area.

The Sparrowhawk's small size recommended it for this mission, so the XF9C-1 had a hook-on device erected in front of the cockpit in September and six production F9C-2s were ordered on October 14, 1931. The XF9C-1 successfully hooked on to the dirigible *Los Angeles* on October 23. The first F9C-2 was flown April 14, 1932.

Armed with two .30-caliber guns, the Sparrowhawks sometimes operated from the airships with wheeled gear removed and 30-gallon auxiliary tanks to extend range. During maneuvers, however, the airships seemed unable to avoid destruction by hostile aircraft. After the loss of the *Akron* on April 4, 1933, and the *Macon* on February 12, 1935, both due to storms, no other large dirigibles were built by the Navy.

CURTISS XF9C-1
Wright R-975C, 421 hp
DIMENSIONS: Span 25′6″, Lg. 19′5″, Ht. 7′1″, Wing Area
   173 sq. ft.
WEIGHT: Empty 1836 lb., Gross 2502 lb. Fuel 59 gal.
PERFORMANCE: Speed—Top 176.5 mph at s. l., 160 mph
   at 10,000′, Landing 63 mph. Service Ceiling 22,600′,
   Climb 5000′/2.6 min. Range 396 miles normal, 536
   miles max.   MFR

CURTISS F9C-2
Wright R-975-22, 420 hp at s. l.
DIMENSIONS: Span 25′6″, Lg. 20′1″, Ht. 7′1″, Wing Area
   173 sq. ft.
WEIGHT: Empty 2114 lb., Gross 2776 lb., Max. 2888 lb.
   Fuel 60–90 gal.
PERFORMANCE: Speed—Top 176.5 mph at s. l., Landing
   65 mph. Service Ceiling 19,200′, Climb 5000′/3.5 min.
   Range 366 miles normal, 507 miles max.   USN

Boeing's F4B

To many the height of traditional biplane design in the Navy was the F4B series. Compact and maneuverable, these planes captured public interest in their time and remain a favorite of model builders today.

The first prototype was the Boeing Model 83, powered by a 500-hp Pratt & Whitney Wasp and constructed with fabric-covered, bolted aluminum tube fuselage and wooden wings, with corrugated metal control surfaces. First flown June 25, 1928, and shipped to San Diego for Navy tests, Model 83 had cross-axle landing gear.

A second prototype, Model 89, made its first flight at Anacostia on August 7 with a split-axle landing gear that allowed room for a 500-pound bomb or a 49-gallon belly tank. Both were armed with the usual two fixed guns, had cylinder fairings, and were known as XF4B-1s in Navy documents. Twenty-seven F4B-1s (Model 99) were ordered on November 28, 1928, with supercharged Wasps and split-axle gear. The Army version was the P-12. First flown on May 6, 1929, and delivered in June, the F4B-1 was used by VB-1B and VF-2B.

Another Boeing private venture was the Model 205, which, after demonstration tests at Anacostia in February 1930, was purchased May 10, 1930, as the XF5B-1. Resembling the F4B-1, it was a high-

BOEING XF4B-1 (Model 83)
Pratt & Whitney R-1340B, 500 hp at s. l.
DIMENSIONS: Span 30′, Lg. 20′7″, Ht. 9′3″, Wing Area
227.5 sq. ft.
WEIGHT: Empty 1811 lb., Gross 2557 lb., Max. 3087 lb.
PERFORMANCE: Speed—Top 169 mph at s. l., Landing 56
mph. Service Ceiling 26,900′, Climb 2920′/1 min. MFR

BOEING XF4B-1 (Model 89)   MFR

BOEING F4B-1
Pratt & Whitney R-1340-8, 500 hp at 6000′
DIMENSIONS: Span 30′, Lg. 20′1″, Ht. 9′4″, Wing Area
227.5 sq. ft.
WEIGHT: Empty 1950 lb., Gross 2750 lb., Max. 3169 lb.
Fuel 57–107 gal.
PERFORMANCE: Speed—Top 176 mph at 6000′, Landing
59 mph. Service Ceiling 27,700′, Climb 5000′/2.9 min.
Range 371 miles normal, 771 miles max.   WL

BOEING XF5B-1
Pratt & Whitney R-1340D, 500 hp at 6000′
DIMENSIONS: Span 30′6″, Lg. 21′, Ht. 9′4″, Wing Area 157
sq. ft.
WEIGHT: Empty 2091 lb., Gross 2848 lb. Fuel 50–132 gal.
PERFORMANCE: Speed—Top 183 mph at 6000′, Landing
71 mph. Service Ceiling 27,100′, Climb 5000′/2.7
min.   USN

wing monoplane and, like the XP-15 offered to the
Army at the same time, used a 450-hp R-1340D and
metal-covered fuselage and wings. Trials were
made with a ring cowl, which added 15 mph to the
top speed with bare cylinders. The Navy, however,
was not yet ready for monoplanes aboard carriers,
and instead contracted for 46 F4B-2s in June 1930.
Delivered from January to May 1931, they were
similar to the F4B-1 except for ring cowl, Frise
ailerons, and a spreader-bar axle landing gear with
a tail wheel. Similar to the P-12C, they served VF-
2, VF-5, and VF-6.

In December 1930 Boeing offered Model 218,
with a new all-metal fuselage, to both the Army and
Navy, leading to orders for the P-12E and F4B-3.
Contracts let on April 23 and August 15, 1931,
called for 75 F4B-3s, but 54 of these aircraft were
delivered as F4B-4s. The F4B-3s, powered by R-
1340-10s, were delivered from December 24, 1931,
to January 20, 1932. They replaced the Helldivers
of VF-1, where they served until transferred to the
Marine's VB-4M in 1933.

The most famous of the series was the F4B-4,
similar to the F4B-3 except for an R-1340-16, a
wider fin, and, on the last 45, an enlarged headrest. Armed with two .30-caliber guns under the
cowl, the F4B-4 had wing bomb racks for two 116-
pound bombs, and a 55-gallon drop tank under the
fuselage could double the internal fuel load. A telescopic sight for dive-bombing alongside the gunsight helped distinguish the F4B from its Army P-
12 sister ships.

Another contract brought Boeing's F4B-4 order to
92 planes, delivered from July 1932 to February 28,
1933. Brazil also got 14 F4B-4s, minus Naval gear,

BOEING F4B-2
Pratt & Whitney R-1340-8, 500 hp at 6000'
DIMENSIONS: Span 30', Lg. 20'1", Ht. 9'1", Wing Area
    227.5 sq. ft.
WEIGHT: Empty 2067 lb., Gross 2799 lb., Max. 3260 lb.
    Fuel 55–110 gal.
PERFORMANCE: Speed—Top 186 mph at 6000', 170 mph
    at s. l., Landing 59 mph. Service Ceiling 26,900', Climb
    5000'/2.5 min. Range 403 miles normal, 812 miles
    max.   USN

BOEING F4B-3
Pratt & Whitney R-1340-10, 500 hp
DIMENSIONS: Span 30', Lg. 20'5", Ht. 9'9", Wing Area
    227.5 sq. ft.
WEIGHT: Empty 2242 lb., Gross 2958 lb., Max. 3419 lb.
    Fuel 55–110 gal.
PERFORMANCE: Speed—Top 187 mph at 6000', 167 mph
    at s. l., Cruising 160 mph, Landing 61 mph. Service
    Ceiling 27,500', Climb 5000'/2.9 min. Range 401 miles
    normal, 829 miles max.   USN

in September 1932, and nine modified Boeings in
February 1933. Altogether, Boeing built 586 of this
series, including 188 for the Navy, 32 for export,
and 366 for the Army. In addition, another F4B-4
was assembled by the Marines from spare parts,
and 23 various Army P-12s turned over to the Navy
in 1940 for radio-controlled targets were called
F4B-4As.

Although the F4B series was used by both the
Army and the Navy, it would be two decades before
another fighter type would prove successful in both
roles (North American F-86 and FJ series). The
Army's shift to high-speed monoplanes could not
be followed by the Navy for many years, and when
it was, monoplanes designed for carrier work were
basically different from their land-based counterparts.

Early in 1933 the Navy's fighter force consisted
of five carrier-based and two Marine squadrons, all
using Boeings and all but VF-1 and VF-2 equipped
with F4B-4s. The latter were not replaced in Marine service by F3F-2s until June 1938.

BOEING F4B-4
Pratt & Whitney R-1340-16, 550 hp at 6000'
DIMENSIONS: As F4B-3
WEIGHT: Empty 2354 lb., Gross 3128 lb., Max. 3611 lb.
    Fuel 55–110 gal.
PERFORMANCE: Speed—Top 188 mph at 6000', Landing
    62.5 mph. Service Ceiling 26,900'. Range 370 miles
    normal, 734 miles max.   USN

PART TWO:

Monoplanes and World War II, 1932–45

Chapter 11
Background of World War II Development

To even the most casual observer, World War II aircraft are very different from those of World War I and the biplane period. Streamlined monoplanes with enclosed cockpits, retractable wheels, and all-metal structure replaced the open cockpits, struts, and fabric covering of the first generation of combat planes.

How this change in appearance came about is the subject of this section. A decade before Pearl Harbor, biplanes filled the squadrons of both the Army and Navy, but rather suddenly they were replaced by the new generation of aircraft. A technical revolution in aircraft design was under way. It had appeared on drawing boards in the 1920s and, unencouraged by the military, took the form of commercial aircraft built by Boeing, Consolidated, and Northrop. Meanwhile, Army squadrons continued to operate their old biplanes. The technical revolution had two elements: the use of new discoveries in metallurgy for lightweight all-metal structures of new strength and reliability; and the shaping of these structures into streamlined forms in which dragging struts, undercarriages, and open cockpits were submerged into cantilever wings, retractable landing gear, and Plexiglas enclosures. The availability of monoplanes—due to increased knowledge of internally braced metal wing construction and of the cause and cure of wing flutter and other aberrations—was about to make a radical improvement in the appearance and performance of combat planes.

The relatively slow-paced progress of aviation in the 1920s contrasts sharply with the changes that took place in the air forces during the 1930s. The Depression knocked the bottom from the private-plane market, although U.S. expenditures on military aircraft rose from $25 million in fiscal 1925 to $69 million in fiscal 1931. It also caused an international social crisis that changed governmental leadership around the world.

This Consolidated Y1P-25 being tested in January 1933 already has the shape of World War II fighters; an all-metal low-wing monoplane with enclosed cockpits and retractable landing gear.   MFR

This Boeing XF7B-1's monoplane layout was rejected by the Navy in 1934, but the cockpit canopy and retractable wheels soon became standard.   USN

The most fateful of the changes was the rise of aggressive dictatorships in Japan and Germany. Japan's invasion of Manchuria in September 1931 pinpointed the direction of the next threat to America, creating a market for 600 aircraft in 1932–38, when China became the largest buyer of American aircraft, and stimulated a Soviet industrial drive that included the purchase of 4,990 American aircraft engines in 1932–34.

China was the leading U.S. warplane customer in 1933–38, and the Northrop 2E made the first bombing attacks on Japanese forces on August 14, 1937.   SDAM

Army Air Corps flying in 1938 is remembered for formations like these 1st Pursuit Group P-35s.   AF

In Washington, D.C., a new presidential administration was friendly to social and technical progress, while Nazi rule and rearmament in Germany put Europe on the road to war. The social climate promoted an arms race—with air power being of the greatest concern—in which American airplanes took a leading place.

The year 1935—during which Mussolini attacked Ethiopia, Hitler officially announced the formation of his air force, and Congress passed a legislative program of social reforms—was also a big year in combat aviation. The Baker Board (aviation had become the most investigated service) had recommended an Air Corps of 2,320 planes and a General Headquarters Air Force (GHQAF) for operations not dependent on particular ground armies. Officially begun in March 1935, the GHQAF was structured so that its forces could be concentrated for a blow in any direction.

The GHQAF consisted of all of the attack, bomber, and pursuit units in the United States, excluding only observation squadrons of the corps areas and the five groups in overseas departments. The total Air Corps strength remained at 15 active groups from June 1932 to January 1940. The General Staff saw no need for more and seldom spent the full amount of money allotted each fiscal year by Congress.

Fortunately, technical progress in those years was rapid, and when the time for expansion came, a new generation of advanced aircraft was ready. The results of the Munich crisis made a general war inevitable, and President Roosevelt called a meeting of U.S. government leaders on September 28, 1938, in which he gave air power the first priority in American rearmament. Not only were the Army and Navy air arms to be enlarged, but the aircraft industry should reach a 10,000-planes-per-year production quota, with the manufacturers encouraged by cost-plus-fee contracts whose profits would be a strong incentive for expansion. Roosevelt asserted that Hitler would be impressed by aircraft, not by minor improvements in facilities for ground forces. This view reflected the widespread opinion that fear of the Luftwaffe had promoted the disastrous appeasement policy of Britain.

General Henry A. Arnold, who had become Air Corps Chief that same month, left that meeting "with the feeling that the Air Corps had finally achieved its Magna Carta." Expansion of the Air Corps and of the aircraft industry had begun.

An important factor was the large numbers of aircraft ordered by Britain and France. While their early-delivery requirements often conflicted with the immediate supply of Air Corps and Navy aircraft, these orders expanded plant capacity for future wartime needs. (General Arnold had feared that combat squadrons in action would suffer attrition at a rate of 25 percent of aircraft and personnel per month.) Production of military aircraft in the United States rose from 1,800 in 1938 to 6,086 in 1940, 19,290 in 1941, and 96,369 in 1944.

History's Largest Air Force

The Army and Navy had some 2,400 and 1,700 planes, respectively, when the 1939 expansion program proposed an Army Air Corps of 5,500 planes with 24 groups and a Navy air service with 3,000. This expansion had hardly gotten under way when German successes in Europe led President Roosevelt to call for 50,000 service planes in May 1940.

Navy carrier-based planes in the 1930s had colorful markings, as these Grumman F2F-1 fighters of VF-2.   USN

The figure seemed preposterous, but was authorized: 13,500 for the Navy and 36,500 for the Army, including 54 groups.

In 1941 still another plan calling for 84 groups by mid-1942 hardly seemed realistic in view of lend-lease commitments. Although by December 7, 1941, 70 groups had been activated in the now virtually autonomous Army Air Forces (AAF)—the name replacing the Air Corps on June 20, 1941—the 24 fighter, 13 heavy-bomber, ten medium-bomber, five light-bomber, nine observation, two composite, one photographic mapping, and six

Heavy bombers, like this Fifteenth Air Force B-24L-10 from Ford's Willow Run factory, were the main thrust of the AAF's wartime power.   AF

The Navy's heaviest punch was the dive-bombers, the best-liked being the Douglas SBD.   USN

transport groups had only 3,305 combat planes plus 7,024 other types. Navy aviation had expanded in 1941 from 2,553 planes in January to 5,260 in December.

Foreign countries bought U.S. combat types in large quantities even before the war began in 1939. On March 25, 1940, permission was granted for the sale of Army and Navy service types as soon as a newer model became available, while a year later lend-lease assumed the cost of thousands of planes built for America's allies.

By 1945 the United States had the largest air force ever assembled, including 243 groups[1] and 65 separate squadrons with 72,726 aircraft (41,961 combat) in the Army Air Forces as of January 1, and 41,180 naval aircraft (28,032 combat) as of June 30. Great air armadas were assembled for the major battles of the war. For the cross-Channel invasion of Europe, the AAF alone assembled 10,637 planes (8,351 combat) in 98 groups: 40 heavy-bomber, eight medium-bomber, three light-bomber, 33 fighter, and 14 troop-carrier groups. The Navy assaulted Okinawa with the support of 919 planes on fast carriers and 564 planes on escort carriers. Navy combat planes on hand in mid-1945 included 13,940 fighters, 5,101 scout bombers, 4,937 torpedo bombers, and 4,054 patrol bombers operating from 28 large carriers, 72 escort carriers, and numerous land bases. What these planes did in the war has been described in detail in official histories. Air power, both carrier and land-based, was the largest single factor in Japan's defeat. More controversial is the role of air power against Germany, although it is significant that no Allied victories were won until after Germany's early control of the air was smashed.

Aircraft Design for World War II

From 1931 to 1939 the chief concern of designers had been the rapid improvement of performance through better streamlining and more powerful engines. Flaps were added to supplement the monoplane's limited wing area during takeoff and landing, and controllable-pitch propellers, supercharging, and high-octane fuels added to power plant efficiency.

Both the added useful load of the new plane and the threat of combat compelled designers to improve armament. Two fixed guns had been sufficient firepower for an Army fighter from 1918 to 1938, three flexible guns provided for most bombers, and five guns provided for attack types. Armament of the .30-caliber (7.6-mm) type was custom-

[1] Seventy-one fighter, 72 heavy, 25 very heavy, 20 medium, and 8 light bombardment groups, with 29 troop-carrier, 13 reconnaissance, and 5 composite groups.

Hand-held twin .30-caliber guns in the PBY-5 in December 1942.   ARC

A hand-held .50-caliber gun on an A-25A in November 1943 with Australian markings for lend-lease.   MFR

A completely enclosed, but still manual, turret with a .50-caliber gun on Boeing's XB-15 in 1937.   MFR

ary, except for the occasional use of .50-caliber (12.7-mm) on pursuits; less than 5 percent of the ammunition practice-fired by a typical pursuit group was of .50-caliber.

In Europe firepower increased quickly. Four-gun fighters were becoming common in 1936 when Britain introduced the eight-gun Hurricane and Spitfire. Most multigun fighters mounted their weapons in the wings, where there was more room than in the nose and where synchronization was unnecessary.

Larger-caliber guns have a slower rate of fire but are especially effective against bombers and ground targets. The first really practical aircraft gun with exploding shells was the 20-mm Oerlikon adopted by Germany, but the Allies chose the 20-mm (.78 inch) Hispano gun used by France since 1937, by Britain and the U.S.S.R. in 1940, and adopted in the United States in 1941.

Armor protection in the pilot's cockpit became standard on Soviet fighters in 1937, and by 1940 all of the warring countries had adopted pilot armor and revived the 1918 fuel-tank protection system of an inner self-sealing lining of rubber to make the tank leakproof. Air-launched rockets were another Soviet development, first used in 1939.

In subsequent chapters the reader will see how American aircraft gradually adopted these armament systems. After a transition period in 1939–40, six .50-caliber guns were mounted in the wings of most fighters, while bomber armament increased from the single, hand-held .30-caliber Browning to .50-caliber Brownings paired in power-operated turrets. Power-operated turrets had appeared on British bombers by 1936, but RAF practice favored two or four .30-caliber weapons. Computing sights were introduced on American bombers in 1942 and appeared on fighters in 1944.

Twin .50-caliber guns in a power-operated armored Consolidated turret in the XB-41 in 1942.　　MFR

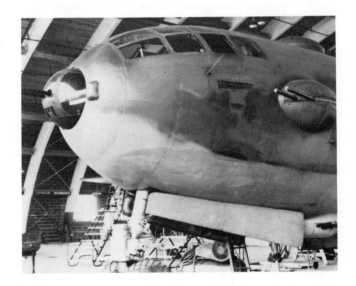

Many power-operated guns were added to the bomber escort conversion of a YB-29 in 1943.　　MFR

Airborne radar came into use in 1942 on this P-70A-2, whose gun muzzles have flash hiders for night work.
MFR

Chapter 12
Observation Monoplanes, 1930–42

The First Observation Monoplanes, 1930–32

When monoplanes replaced biplanes in Air Corps and National Guard observation squadrons, the monoplanes were not of the low-wing type standard in attack and pursuit aviation. Since visibility was the first consideration, observation monoplanes had their wing in a high position, either the gull or "parasol" style.

The higher performance offered by the monoplanes was especially attractive to the long-neglected requirement for a twin-engine, three-place army observation type capable of deep penetrations into enemy territory to get information for GHQ and Air Corps commands. Such aircraft could also be configured as light bombers.

Two such prototypes, the XO-27 and XB-8, were ordered from Fokker Aircraft on June 19, 1929. The XO-27 was tested at Wright on October 20, 1930, with two V-1570-9 Conquerors in the leading edge of the cantilever wing and the first retractable landing gear on an Air Corps observation type. All-wood veneer-covered wing construction was used, along with a steel-tubed, fabric-covered fuselage with three open cockpits.

Later the prototype was modified with a pilot's cabin and the geared V-1570-29 engines, with three-bladed propeller chosen for the YO-27 version. Fokker, which had become General Aviation in 1930, received a service-test contract April 11, 1931, for six aircraft, increased to 12 the next month. The first YO-27 was tested September 10, 1932, and the service trials were made by the 12th Observation Group at Brooks Field, Texas. Longer nacelles, bow windows, and three-bladed propellers distinguished the YO-27s from the prototype, and armament consisted of a Browning gun in the front and rear cockpits.

Douglas also prepared a twin-engine three-place design as the XO-30, which was soon superseded

FOKKER XO-27
Curtiss V-1570-9, 600 hp
DIMENSIONS: Span 64′, Lg. 47′4″, Ht. 11′9″, Wing Area 615 sq. ft.
WEIGHT: Empty 6522 lb., Gross 8918 lb. Fuel 202 gal.
PERFORMANCE: Speed—Top 160 mph at s. l., 152 mph at 10,000′, Cruising 128 mph, Landing 65 mph. Service Ceiling 22,600′, Absolute Ceiling 24,400′, Climb 1350′/1 min., 10,000′/9.5 min.   MFR

FOKKER XO-27A   MFR

by the XO-35. Two prototypes with V-1570-11s were ordered April 14, 1930, as the XO-35 and XO-36, but the latter became the XB-7. The XO-35 was delivered October 24, 1931 as an all-metal, externally braced, gull-wing monoplane. Twelve service-test examples were ordered in August 1931, five as YO-35s and the others as bombers. The YO-35 was quite similar to the prototype except for the smooth, instead of corrugated, covering on the monocoque fuselage. Armament comprised two flexible .30-caliber guns with 1,200 rounds.

Despite promising performance, the twin-engine observation type never went into production because it was decided that missions beyond a 50-mile penetration of enemy territory could be done best by using the same type aircraft as bomber units with more fuel substituted for bombs. Long-range, multiengine observation aircraft would be designated "reconnaissance" aircraft; and several observation squadrons were redesignated reconnaissance squadrons in 1937–38 and equipped with twin-engine B-10 and B-18 bombers.

This left the Army observation squadrons with the conventional single-engine two-seater, which had to be adapted to the all-metal monoplane style coming in. The first was the Douglas XO-31, an all-metal monoplane with corrugated dural fuselage, straight, fabric-covered gull wings braced by wires to a pylon, wheel pants, and the inline Curtiss Conqueror engine.

Two prototypes were ordered January 7, 1930, and the XO-31 was first completed in December 1930 with a blunt nose and chin Prestone cooler, but was revised in February 1931 by moving the radiator back and adding a nose spinner. The second prototype, the YO-31, was completed in April 1931 with a geared Conqueror and numerous refinements. One fixed and one flexible .30-caliber Browning were provided, which was standard armament for all of the Douglas observation monoplanes. The fixed gun was placed in the right wing and had 300 rounds of ammunition.

Six service-test examples were ordered June 23, 1931, and the first four were built as the YO-31A.

FOKKER (General Aviation) YO-27
Curtiss V-1570-29, 600 hp
DIMENSIONS: Span 64', Lg. 47'6", Ht. 14'6", Wing Area 628 sq. ft.
WEIGHT: Empty 8092 lb., Gross 10,639 lb. Fuel 207–409 gal.
PERFORMANCE: Speed—Top 177 mph at s. l., 174 mph at 10,000', Cruising 152 mph, Landing 68 mph. Service Ceiling 20,750', Absolute Ceiling 22,400', Climb 1370'/1 min., 10,000'/9.7 min. Range 840–954 miles.   MFR

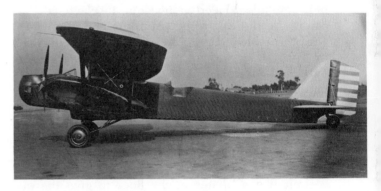

DOUGLAS XO-35
Curtiss V-1570-29, 600 hp
DIMENSIONS: Span 65'8", Lg. 46'6", Ht. 12'6", Wing Area 609 sq. ft.
WEIGHT: Empty 7276 lb., Gross 10,254 lb. Fuel 297 gal.
PERFORMANCE: Speed—Top 178 mph at s. l., 172 mph at 10,000', Cruising 156 mph, Landing 65 mph. Service Ceiling 21,750', Absolute Ceiling 23,300', Climb 1560'/1 min., 10,000'/8.4 min. Range 765 miles.   MFR

DOUGLAS Y1O-35
Curtiss V-1570-53, 600 hp
DIMENSIONS: As XO-35
WEIGHT: Empty 7896 lb., Gross 10,376 lb. Fuel 297 gal.
PERFORMANCE: Speed—Top 179 mph at s. l., Cruising 157 mph. Service Ceiling 21,750'. Range 700 miles.   MFR

DOUGLAS XO-31
Curtiss V-1570-25, 600 hp
DIMENSIONS: Span 45'8", Lg. 33'2", Ht. 12', Wing Area 335 sq. ft.
WEIGHT: Empty 3277 lb., Gross 4428 lb. Fuel 82 gal.
PERFORMANCE: Speed—Top 176 mph at s. l., 168 mph at 10,000', Cruising 152 mph, Landing 62 mph. Service Ceiling 23,000', Absolute Ceiling 24,600', Climb 1620'/1 min., 10,000'/7.9 min. Range 498 miles.   MFR

DOUGLAS YO-31
Curtiss V-1570-7, 600 hp
DIMENSIONS: Span 45′8″, Lg. 33′5″, Ht. 12′, Wing Area
  335 sq. ft.
WEIGHT: Empty 3496 lb., Gross 4654 lb. Fuel 82 gal.
PERFORMANCE: Speed—Top 182 mph at s. l., 174 mph at
  10,000′, Cruising 157, Landing 65 mph. Service Ceiling
  24,300′, Absolute Ceiling 25,800′, Climb 1700′/1 min.,
  10,000′/7.4 min.   MFR

DOUGLAS YO-31A
Curtiss V-1570-53, 600 hp
DIMENSIONS: Span 45′11″, Lg. 33′10″, Ht. 11′9″, Wing
  Area 340 sq. ft.
WEIGHT: Empty 3751 lb., Gross 4865 lb. Fuel 78–127 gal.
PERFORMANCE: Speed—Top 191 mph at s. l., 187 mph at
  10,000′, Cruising 168 mph, Landing 65 mph. Service
  Ceiling 22,700′, Climb 1870′/1 min., 10,000′/6.9 min.
  Range 635 miles.   MFR

Delivered in December 1931, the YO-31A had a new smooth-surfaced monocoque fuselage, cockpit canopy, elliptical wing planform and V-1570-53 with three-bladed propeller. The YO-31B, finished in April 1932, was an unarmed officer's transport with dual-control cockpits completely enclosed and faired back to a high fin. It was delivered to the Militia Bureau, the National Guard command post in Washington, D.C.

Last on the order was the YO-31C of July 1932, which had a high, peaked tail, a new gull-wing joint, and a single-strut landing gear. Under the cockpit was a blister in the floor to give the observer's legs more room. The Douglas O-31s, like the twin-engine O-35, were transferred back and forth around Brooks, Langley, and Mitchel fields to give the biplane-equipped squadrons experience with the high-wing monoplane concept.

Curtiss O-40 Raven

Curtiss tried to follow its Falcon series with the Raven, featuring the Wright Cyclone radial, metal monocoque fuselage, cockpit canopy, and swept-back upper wing. The landing gear in the roots of the narrow lower wing retracted inwards into the fuselage.

A YO-40 prototype ordered October 10, 1931, was completed in January 1932 and forwarded to Wright Field in February. Tests soon demonstrated a useful turn of speed, but the Curtiss crashed on May 20.

The Air Corps had Curtiss rebuild the sesquiplane as the YO-40A, while giving the company a contract on June 30, 1932, for four YO-40Bs, a development in monoplane form. In this version the stubs for landing gear remained, but to make up for

DOUGLAS YO-31C
Curtiss V-1570-53, 600 hp
DIMENSIONS: As YO-31A
WEIGHT: Empty 3852 lb., Gross 4982 lb. Fuel 78–130 gal.
PERFORMANCE: Speed—Top 190 mph at s. l. Service Ceil-
  ing 23,000′.   AF

the lift lost by removing the lower wings, a system of slots and flaps was used.

The first YO-40B monoplane was finished in June 1933, and retained the cockpit canopy of the YO-40, but the rebuilt YO-40A differed from the original in having separate open cockpits. Instead of the original two-bladed propeller, both the YO-40A and YO-40B were tested together at Wright Field in August 1933 with three-bladed propellers. Later YO-40Bs were used at Mitchel Field.

An Officers Board met September 15, 1933, to compare the sesquiplane and monoplane configurations. Both models were credited with very satisfactory flying characteristics. The YO-40B monoplane was rated the fastest, with the best vision and with a lower landing speed due to the slots. The YO-40A exceeded in climb and slightly in maneuverability, but the cockpit arrangement was unsat-

CURTISS YO-40
Wright YR-1820-E, 630 hp
DIMENSIONS: Span 44'1", Lg. 28'6", Ht. 10'7", Wing Area
325 sq. ft.
WEIGHT: Empty 3429 lb., Gross 4565 lb. Fuel 78–130 gal.
PERFORMANCE: Speed—Top 193 mph at s. l., 185 mph at
10,000', Cruising 165 mph, Landing 64 mph. Service
Ceiling 24,000', Absolute Ceiling 25,600', Climb 1685'/
1 min., 10,000'/7.5 min.   AF

CURTISS YO-40A
Wright R-1820-37, 670 hp
DIMENSIONS: Span 44', Lg. 28'10", Ht. 10'7", Wing Area
312 sq. ft.
WEIGHT: Empty 3590 lb., Gross 4744 lb. Fuel 78–126 gal.
PERFORMANCE: Speed—Top 181 mph at s. l., 177 mph at
10,000', Cruising 156 mph, Landing 66 mph. Service
Ceiling 23,900', Absolute Ceiling 25,400', Climb 1740'/
1 min., 10,000'/7.3 min. Range 315 miles.   ARNOLD

CURTISS YO-40B
Wright R-1820-37, 670 hp
DIMENSIONS: Span 41'8", Lg. 28'10", Ht. 10'8", Wing Area
266 sq. ft.
WEIGHT: Empty 3754 lb., Gross 4908 lb. Fuel 78–130 gal.
PERFORMANCE: Speed—Top 188 mph at s. l., 182 mph at
10,000', Cruising 160 mph, Landing 62 mph. Service
Ceiling 23,100', Landing 24,600', Climb 1660'/1 min.,
10,000'/7.7 min. Range 324–650 miles.   MFR

DOUGLAS Y1O-43
Curtiss V-1570-53, 600 hp
DIMENSIONS: Span 45'11", Lg. 33'11", Ht. 12'3", Wing
Area 335 sq. ft.
WEIGHT: Empty 3834 lb., Gross 4982 lb. Fuel 78–130 gal.
PERFORMANCE: Speed—Top 188 mph at s. l., 181 mph at
10,000', Cruising 163 mph, Landing 69 mph. Service
Ceiling 23,200', Absolute Ceiling 24,600', Climb 1800'/
1 min., 10,000'/7.1 min. Range 327–630 miles.   AF

isfactory. Both types were criticized for inadequate
fuel capacity, and neither was considered entirely
satisfactory.

The Parasols

Douglas won the contracts to equip Air Corps observation squadrons with monoplanes by changing
from the O-31's gull wing to the parasol wing of the
O-43, which gave the crew the best downward visibility.

Five Y1O-43 monoplanes ordered August 26,
1931, and delivered from February to April 1933
may be the best-looking observation planes ever
built, with smooth lines from the nose spinner,
through the geared V-1570-53, the small oil and
Prestone radiators, the elliptical wings and cockpit
canopy, to the rounded tail cone and fin. Equipment

included camera, radio, flares, a fixed .30-caliber
gun in the right wing with 200 rounds and a flexible
.30-caliber gun with 500 rounds, but no bomb rack.

One Y1O-43 was modified at Wright with the 675-
hp, high-compression V-1510-59 for 24 O-24As ordered March 2, 1933. The first of these was seen in
May 1934 with the rounded tail of the Y1O-43, but
the tall fin of the O-31C was standardized for the
other O-43As and retrofitted to YO-31As. No nose
spinner was used and exhaust collectors were
added. Another change was the roomier cockpit,
which made the belly bulge unnecessary. The O-43
went into service from July to November 1934 at
Brooks Field with the 12th and 22nd Observation
squadrons; it was later passed on to the Texas National Guard, whose 111th Squadron still had five
planes in November 1941.

The last O-43A was completed in October 1934

DOUGLAS Y1O-43 with V-1570-59   AF

DOUGLAS O-43A
Curtiss V-1570-59, 675 hp
DIMENSIONS: Span 45'8", Lg. 34'4", Ht. 12'11", Wing Area
  335 sq. ft.
WEIGHT: Empty 4151 lb., Gross 5331 lb. Fuel 78–129 gal.
PERFORMANCE: Speed—Top 191 mph at s. l., 183 mph at
  10,000', Cruising 166 mph, Landing 67 mph. Service
  Ceiling 22,400', Absolute Ceiling 23,800', Climb 1690'/
  1 min., 10,000'/7.7 min.   PMB

as the XO-46 with an air-cooled Pratt & Whitney
Twin Wasp, the wing braced by metal struts instead
of wires, and using trailing-edge flaps. Later it was
proposed that this prototype be reworked as an XO-
48 with a Wright R-1670-3, but that project was
canceled.

An O-46A production contract was signed April
29, 1935, and the first plane rolled out of Douglas
about January 29, 1936. The cockpit enclosure was
now faired into the fuselage and was folded back to
expose the gun. The ammunition supply was increased to 250 and 1,000 rounds for the fixed and
flexible guns, respectively; a rack for two 116-
pound bombs could be fitted. Ninety O-46As delivered from May 1936 to April 1937 went into Air
Corps and National Guard squadrons.

By 1936, bombers had replaced observation aircraft in several units. These squadrons were redesignated reconnaissance squadrons, and the 9th Observation became the 9th Bombing Group. Aside
from the school squadrons, only six corps observation squadrons remained in the United States: the
12th and 22nd at Brooks Field, the 15th at Scott,
16th at Fort Riley, 91st at Crissy, and the new 97th
at Mitchel Field, along with the 19 National Guard
units. Nearly all of these squadrons used O-46As at
one time or another, usually along with older types
and the new O-47s.

DOUGLAS O-46A
Pratt & Whitney R-1535-7, 725 hp at 4000'
DIMENSIONS: Span 45'9", Lg. 34'9", Ht. 10'4", Wing Area
  335 sq. ft.
WEIGHT: Empty 4700 lb., Gross 6135 lb. Fuel 88–127 gal.
PERFORMANCE: Speed—Top 200 mph at 4000', Cruising
  171 mph, Landing 58 mph. Service Ceiling 24,150',
  Absolute Ceiling 25,400', Climb 1765'/1 min., 10,000'/
  6.4 min. Range 500 miles.   PMB

DOUGLAS XO-46   AF

The O-47

In December 1934 the Air Corps formulated a requirement for an observation aircraft that could exceed 200 mph and yet not require more than 1,500 feet to take off over a 50-foot obstacle. By November 1935 accommodation for three crewmen was desired.

The only aircraft offered to fill this requirement was the General Aviation GA-15, built by the Dundalk, Maryland, firm led by J. K. Kindelberger, who had been chief engineer at Douglas during the firm's domination of observation contracts. An all-metal midwing monoplane powered by a Wright Cyclone, the GA-15 had a long enclosure over its crew, with the observer sitting between the pilot and gunner while working as co-pilot, or moving down to his observation post in the deep belly. Windows under the wing gave him visibility, and for the first time the observer could concentrate on his camera and map work, leaving to the gunner the task of watching for other aircraft. The wheels and their long struts swung outwards into the wing.

Completed in July 1935, the GA-15 went to Wright late that year and was purchased by the Air Corps as the XO-47 on January 22, 1936. By that time its builders had a new name, North American Aviation, and a new California factory.

The Air Corps hesitated to offer a production contract because, although the new plane's performance and crew accommodation were far superior to the older two-seaters, it did require twice as much room to take off and land—a serious consideration for a plane supposed to work closely with ground troops.

But no valid alternative seemed to be available, and 109 O-47s were ordered on February 19, 1937. It was the largest contract for observation planes since the war, but in October was increased to 164 aircraft. The first O-47A was flown at Inglewood, California, on March 7, 1938, armed with a .30-caliber gun in the right wing with 200 rounds and a flexible gun with 600 rounds, but no bombs. The 109th O-47A was modified to an April 1939 NA-60 specification with more glass in the belly, but this was not used in the O-47B.

Since the O-47A worked well in service, 74 O-47B versions with a 1,060-hp Cyclone were ordered March 18, 1939, and delivery began in August. Unlike fiscal 1931, when the Air Corps had seven types to choose from, there was now only one Army observation aircraft in production. When the last O-47B was delivered in March 1940, enough deep-bellied North Americans were around to be used by nearly all of some 33 Army and National Guard observation squadrons. They joined rather than replaced the O-46A, for both types served together. For example, by the end of 1940 Philadelphia's

NORTH AMERICAN XO-47
Wright R-1820G-11, 800 hp at 4000'
DIMENSIONS: Span 46'4", Lg. 33'6", Ht. 9'11", Wing Area 331 sq. ft.
WEIGHT: Empty 5552 lb., Gross 7319 lb. Fuel 156 gal.
PERFORMANCE: Speed—Top 225 mph at 4000', Cruising 197 mph. Service Ceiling 23,800', Absolute Ceiling 25,000', Climb 10,000'/6.8 min.   MFR

NORTH AMERICAN O-47A
Wright R-1820-49, 975 hp takeoff, 835 hp at 3000'
DIMENSIONS: Span 46'4", Lg. 33'7", Ht. 12'2", Wing Area 350 sq. ft.
WEIGHT: Empty 6028 lb., Gross 7650 lb. Fuel 150 gal.
PERFORMANCE: Speed—Top 223 mph at 4000', Cruising 200 mph, Landing 76 mph. Service Ceiling 23,200', Climb 10,000'/6.8 min. Range 900 miles at 150 mph.
                                                                          AF

NORTH AMERICAN O-47B
Wright R-1820-57, 1060 hp takeoff, 900 hp at 3800'
DIMENSIONS: As O-47A
WEIGHT: Empty 6218 lb., Gross 8045 lb. Fuel 134–200 gal.
PERFORMANCE: Speed—Top 227 mph at 4000', Cruising 200 mph. Service Ceiling 24,100', Climb 15,000'/11.8 min. Range 840 miles.   AF

103rd Observation Squadron (NG) had six O-46As, three O-47As, one O-47B, one O-38B, and a BC-1A trainer, while all 21 National Guard squadrons had 76 O-47A, 44 O-47B, 39 O-46A, 6 O-43A, 11 O-38B and 13 O-38E aircraft.

Tracing observation-plane development from the DH-4 to the O-47 shows a remarkable improvement in capability, just as is seen with bombers and fighters. But the results of this development are quite different. While the end products of the 1918-to-1940 story of bombers went into battle in World War II, no O-47 or any other American armed two- or three-place observation type played a significant role in the new war.

In short, the development had led to a technological dead end; the most widely used aircraft type of 1918 became the least important aircraft of 1940. In Europe the Mureaux, Lysander, Battle, and Henschel observation aircraft proved unable to defend themselves against fighter attack. A single .30-caliber gun was almost useless against fighters with up to eight guns or cannon, and there was no way the heavy observation types could have enough speed to escape 350-mph fighters.

On December 7, 1941, seven sorties were flown by O-47Bs of the 86th Observation Squadron on Oahu in a vain effort to find attacking Japanese. They were fortunate not to encounter fighters, which would have made short work of them. The O-47 flew no other real combat mission in World War II.

The End of the Observation Plane

Since the O-47 lacked the speed to escape enemy fighters, and was also too heavy for the short-field operation and low-altitude maneuverability needed, the Air Corps began looking for a short-range liaison type. Germany's Fiesler Storch, seen in the United States in 1938, suggested that light aircraft could have short-field characteristics nearly matching the autogiros that had been unsuccessfully tested as a replacement for the captive balloons of World War I front-line observation.

A February 1939 design competition specified a two-place, high-wing monoplane capable of taking off over 50-foot obstacles in only 500 feet (the O-47A required 1,300 feet), flying as slow as 40 mph and, of course, too light for armament. Three such liaison planes would be issued to each observation squadron to supplement the armed types.

Stinson won a September 20, 1939, contract for 100 O-49 Vigilantes, while three each of the somewhat heavier Bellanca YO-50 and Ryan YO-51 types were purchased for backup tests. When the first O-49 flew on July 15, 1940, with a 295-hp Lycoming, fabric covering, fixed landing gear, 122-mph speed, and no guns, it was evident that this was no combat

STINSON O-49 (L-1)
Lycoming R-680-9, 295 hp
DIMENSIONS: Span 51', Lg. 33'2", Ht. 9'4", Wing Area 330 sq. ft.
WEIGHT: Empty 2583 lb., Gross 3315 lb. Fuel 52 gal.
PERFORMANCE: Speed—Top 122 mph at s. l., Cruising 109 mph, Landing 31 mph. Service Ceiling 20,000', Climb 15,000'/27.2 min. Range 278 miles, Endurance 2.5 hrs.   AF

plane. They were parceled out to Army and Guard squadrons, with 324 built by March 1942, but a new designation was appropriate and so the Stinsons began the new liaison series as the L-1 and L-1A on April 8, 1942.

The O-49's value lay in its light weight, low cost, and ability, with slots and flaps, to land at 31 mph in 415 feet and take off in less than 400 feet over the standard obstacle height. It became a "flying motorcycle" for communications or an artillery spotter, seldom venturing over enemy lines, but depending for protection on the cover of friendly fighters or a quick landing into the shelter of friendly ground fire.

For an O-46 replacement armed for shallow penetrations of enemy airspace, the Air Corps ordered 203 Curtiss O-52 two-seaters on October 12, 1939. An all-metal high-wing monoplane, the O-52 Owl owed its retractable wheels and cockpit enclosure to the Navy SBC series. Powered by a 600-hp Wasp, it was armed with a fixed .30-caliber gun in the nose and a flexible one in the rear cockpit with 500 rounds. It required over 1,000 feet for takeoff.

Delivered from June 1941 to January 1942, the O-52s were scattered among the Army and National Guard squadrons for the traditional observation role, but never went overseas to fight, except for 30 shipped to the Soviet Union in October 1941 and ten with the 2nd Observation Squadron in the Philippines. Like other traditional two-seaters, the O-

CURTISS O-52
Pratt & Whitney R-1340-51, 600 hp takeoff, 550 hp at 4000'
DIMENSIONS: Span 40'4", Lg. 26'7", Ht. 9'9", Wing Area 213 sq. ft.
WEIGHT: Empty 3960 lb., Gross 5099 lb., Max 5319 lb. Fuel 75–108 gal.
PERFORMANCE: Speed—Top 208 mph at 4100', Cruising 192 mph, Landing 70 mph. Service Ceiling 23,200', Climb 10,000'/8.2 min. Range 432–624 miles.   AF

CURTISS O-52 of National Guard   AF

52 fell between two requirement stools: too slow and light to defend itself but still too heavy for the small-field operations needed for close service to ground forces. It was the last Army plane completed as an armed observation type. All the O-52s were offered to the U.S.S.R. in September 1941, but more were refused after the first batch arrived.

In the fall of 1940 a committee representing various interested Army elements, including the Air Corps, Artillery, and Infantry, decided that two separate types of observation aircraft were needed: a short-range, unarmed, single-engine liaison type and a longer-range twin-engine type armed for penetration of enemy airspace beyond the 50-mile pre-war limit.

Since the Air Corps had already ordered three Douglas A-20 light bombers converted to perform photographic reconnaissance duties, this type was selected as the three-place, twin-engine reconnaissance aircraft. On October 2, 1940, 775 Douglas O-53s were ordered with 1,700-hp supercharged R-2600-7 Cyclones that were expected to confer 395 mph at 25,000 feet, with a 604-mile range and six machine guns. This program had to be canceled in June 1942 when other needs for A-20 type aircraft had priority.

At the other extreme of cost and size were the six YO-54s bought from Stinson in August 1940: standard off-the-shelf Model 105 sports planes with 80 hp. The cost of the YO-54 was $3,989, compared to $24,578 for an O-52, $17,560 for an O-49, or $31,780 for an O-47A. At this point the story of the "O" type separates itself from the combat types, for none of

the remaining aircraft completed as "O" ships were armed.

That 20 years of development of the specialized armed observation types should have been abandoned in wartime in favor of light aircraft designed solely to provide sports pilots with safe fun at the lowest possible price seems remarkable. What actually happened was that procurement of light liaison aircraft intended to give the ground forces the kind of close support they wanted relieved the Air Force of the need to compromise combat-plane performance with short-field and special-vision needs. This, in turn, allowed wartime Air Force reconnaissance to be done by standard fighter and bomber aircraft modified with cameras.

During the Louisiana maneuvers in August 1941, the Army had tested borrowed civilian light planes as observers for division and corps artillery. Success was immediate, and the first dozen Taylorcraft, Aeronca, and Piper (four each) 65-hp lightplanes were purchased September 17, 1941, with the YO-57, YO-58, and YO-59 designations. They were able to work more intimately with artillery than the O-49s, so more were bought in November. These aircraft became the L-2, L-3, and L-4 liaison series in April 1942, the Army's own "grasshoppers" that were an organic part of the ground organizations, with each division getting its own aircraft.

Details of that story, of course, are separate from combat-plane history, and here we confine ourselves to recording the demise of observation aviation as such. For many months the situation in squadron equipment and organization was chaotic, as the Air Force tried to assimilate the new developments. In December 1941 the now-federalized National Guard squadrons had 251 observation aircraft of seven armed and four light types, and the regular Army units included 11 squadrons in the United States and four in the overseas possessions. These Army squadrons had 168 observation aircraft, including 150 O-46s, 53 O-47As, 18 O-47Bs, 32 O-49s, 31 O-52s, and 19 light aircraft scattered through the units. The most important Guard types were 32 O-46s, 61 O-47As, 37 O-47Bs, 51 O-49s and 19 O-52s.

As the uselessness of the conventional armed types in combat was apparent, and the light aircraft were redesignated as liaison aircraft on April 8, 1942, the Air Force tried to fit modified fighter and bomber aircraft into observation units. As late as July 1, 1942, the "standard observation squadron" was to comprise nine liaison, six fighter, and six twin-engine bomber-type aircraft. This unlikely mixture could not be carried out, especially since combat units had first priority in getting the new fighter and bomber types.

Chapter 13
Army Attack Monoplanes, 1931–47

The first branch of American military aviation to completely replace biplanes with monoplanes was the Army attack force. Four Curtiss Falcon squadrons that comprised this branch in 1931 had been replaced by monoplanes in 1936 and had expanded to eight squadrons of Curtiss and Northrop types in 1938.

First came the all-metal Fokker XA-7 and the Curtiss XA-8, two-place, low-wing monoplanes powered by a 600-hp inline liquid-cooled Curtiss Conqueror. Each was armed with four .30-caliber guns firing forward outside of the propeller arc and a fifth Browning for the rear gunner. The XA-7 had a thick cantilever wing, wheel pants, open cockpits, and tunnel radiator. This prototype had been built to a contract approved January 8, 1930, completed in April 1931, and had its nose and landing-gear configuration modified before tests at Wright Field in June 1931.

Its competitor, the Curtiss XA-8 Shrike, had thin wings externally braced by wires and landing gear entirely enclosed in spats. Construction was all-metal, the structure used in all attack or light-bomber aircraft following this machine. Cooling was accomplished by a radiator below and behind the engine, which was neatly streamlined behind the prop spinner. Modern features of the XA-8 were its wing slots and flaps to minimize landing speed, the first to appear on a U.S. combat plane. It also had the first enclosed cockpits, several feet apart, for both crewmen. The prototype was ordered in May 1930 and flown June 1931.

The Curtiss design was judged the better of the pair and was awarded a contract on September 29, 1931, for 13 service-test examples. These went into service July 1932, as the YA-8 (later A-8). Heavier than the original, they also had a pair of forward guns in each wheel spat, with 600 rounds for each of these and the rear gun. The last of these ships, the Y1A-8A, was tested in October 1932 with a

FOKKER XA-7
Curtiss V-1570-27, 600 hp
DIMENSIONS: Span 46'9", Lg. 31', Ht. 9'5", Wing Area 333 sq. ft.
WEIGHT: Empty 3866 lb., Gross 5650 lb. Fuel 102 gal.
PERFORMANCE: Speed—Top 184 mph, Landing 61 mph.
MFR

CURTISS XA-8
Curtiss V-1570-23, 600 hp
DIMENSIONS: Span 44', Lg. 32'6", Ht. 9', Wing Area 285 sq. ft.
WEIGHT: Empty 3673 lb., Gross 5413 lb. Fuel 96–123 gal.
PERFORMANCE: Speed—Top 197 mph at s. l., 191 mph at 5000', Cruising 162.5 mph, Landing 75 mph (65 mph/flaps). Service Ceiling 19,800', Absolute Ceiling 21,450', Climb 1265'/1 min. Range 682 miles. AF

CURTISS YA-8
Curtiss V-1570-31, 600 hp
DIMENSIONS: Span 44'3", Lg. 32'10", Ht. 9', Wing Area
  285 sq. ft.
WEIGHT: Empty 3938 lb., Gross 5706 lb. Fuel 101–53 gal.
PERFORMANCE: Speed—Top 183 mph at s. l., 179.5 mph
  at 5000', Cruising 157.5 mph, Landing 69 mph. Service
  Ceiling 18,100', Absolute Ceiling 19,700', Climb 1325'/
  1 min. 5000'/4.4 min. Range 425 miles/464 lbs. bombs,
  734 miles max.   DEIGAN

CURTISS Y1A-8A (A-8A)
Curtiss V-1570-57, 675 hp
DIMENSIONS: Span 44'3", Lg. 33'7", Ht. 9'2", Wing Area
  285 sq. ft.
WEIGHT: Empty 4330 lb., Gross 6287 lb. Fuel 105–57 gal.
PERFORMANCE: Speed—Top 181 mph at s. l., 176 mph at
  5000', Cruising 156 mph, Landing 75.5 mph. Service
  Ceiling 17,000', Absolute Ceiling 18,600', Climb 1225'/
  1 min. Range 624 miles.   PMB

CURTISS YA-10
Pratt & Whitney R-1690-9, 625 hp at s. l.
DIMENSIONS: Span 44'3", Lg. 32'6", Ht. 9', Wing Area 285
  sq. ft.
WEIGHT: Gross 6135 lb. Fuel 101–53 gal.
PERFORMANCE: Speed—Top 175 mph at s. l.   PMB

geared Conqueror "F" engine, which was less
noisy but heavier than the standard model. The
field trials of the Shrike were successful enough to
merit a 46-plane production order on February 27,
1933.

The first YA-8 was returned to Curtiss for installation of an air-cooled, 625-hp Pratt & Whitney Hornet (renamed YA-10) and came back to Wright Field
on September 8, 1932. Air-cooled radials were less
streamlined than inline engines but offered other
advantages for attack planes: The Army found them
less expensive to operate and with no radiators to
expose to hostile gunfire. The Army then favored
air-cooled engines for future production attack
planes, despite a loss in speed, as a comparison of
the A-12 with the A-8 and A-11 will show.

Curtiss offered a Navy version of the YA-10 as the
XS2C-1 (see pp. 000–00) and completed the 46 production Shrikes not as A-8Bs but as the A-12 with
the air-cooled 670-hp Wright Cyclone. Similar to
the A-8s except for the radial engine and two open
cockpits joined together, the A-12 had the usual five
guns and bombs. Ten 30-pound bombs could be
carried internally, or four 116-pound bombs externally, or a 52-gallon drop tank could replace the
latter. The forward guns in the wheel pants could
be adjusted 2° down, 1° up, or 1° to either side.

The A-12s were delivered from November 1933
to February 1934 and used by the 3rd Attack Group
at Fort Crockett, Texas. In 1935 the A-8s and an A-
12 were passed to the new 37th Attack Squadron at
Langley Field. When the 3rd Attack Group received A-17s in 1936, 15 A-12s went to Kelly Field
as trainers and 20 went to the 26th Attack Squadron
in Hawaii, where they served until 1941.

China purchased 20 Curtiss Shrikes (labeled
Model 60 by the company) powered by Wright SR-
1820-F52 Cyclones rated at 775 hp at 5,800 feet,
improving performance over the Army version. Delivery began in July 1936, and the Shrikes were
used by China's 9th Group.

While attack squadrons were receiving the Curtiss products, work proceeded on some more advanced projects. The first of these was the Lockheed YA-9, projected as an attack version of the
experimental YP-24. This design incorporated the
most modern features then available, including
fully retractable landing gear, flaps, and enclosed
cockpits. Its misfortunes are described more fully
in Chapter 16.

When Lockheed proved unable to fulfill the five-
plane service-test order placed in September 1931,
Consolidated produced a development of the basic
design in January 1933 called the Y1A-11. With
increased power and improved nose, it was similar
to the Y1P-25 but lacked its turbosupercharger, and

CURTISS A-12
Wright R-1820-21, 670 hp at s. l.
DIMENSIONS: Span 44', Lg. 32'3", Ht. 9'4", Wing Area 285
   sq. ft.
WEIGHT: Empty 3898 lb., Gross 5756 lb., Max. 5900 lb.
   Fuel 114–66 gal.
PERFORMANCE: Speed—Top 177 mph at s. l., 173.5 mph
   at 5000', Cruising 150.5 mph, Landing 69.5 mph. Serv-
   ice Ceiling 15,150', Absolute Ceiling 16,600', Climb
   5000'/5.1 min. Range 510 miles/464 lbs. bombs.   AF

despite a crash on January 20, four more A-11s were
ordered on the same day as the A-12s.

Using the 675-hp V-1710-59 Curtiss Conqueror
engine and armed with ten 30-pound bombs, four
fixed-wing guns, and one flexible gun, the A-11 had
a performance far advanced over its contemporaries
when delivery began in August 1934. Apparently
the Army's policy opposing liquid-cooled engines
in attack ships blocked its wider acceptance. However, the pursuit versions of the ship (P-30 and PB-
2A) won larger orders. An XA-11A engine test ship
modified by Bell Aircraft in December 1936 became the first plane to take the 1,000-hp Allison V-
1710 into the air.

Northrop Attack Planes

The most famous attack plane of the 1930s and the
first American monoplane to enter combat was the
low-wing two-seater designed by John K. Northrop.
His company had been formed in 1932 in El Segundo as a Douglas subsidiary to manufacture the
Gamma, a civilian all-metal monoplane with mul-
ticellular wing, stressed-skin fuselage construction,
large wheel pants, a deep engine cowl, and split
trailing-edge flaps.

CURTISS SHRIKE Model 60
Wright SR-1820F-52, 775 hp at 5800'
DIMENSIONS: Span 44', Lg. 31'6", Ht. 9'4", Wing Area 285
   sq. ft.
WEIGHT: Empty 4024 lb., Gross 5925 lb. Fuel 114 gal.
PERFORMANCE: Speed—Top 202 mph at 5800', 182 mph
   at s. l., Cruising 171 mph. Service Ceiling 20,700',
   Range 481 miles.   SI

CONSOLIDATED A-11
Curtiss V-1570-59, 675 hp
DIMENSIONS: Span 43'11", Lg. 29'3", Ht. 9'10", Wing Area
   297 sq. ft.
WEIGHT: Empty 3805 lb., Gross 5490 lb. Fuel 90–180 gal.
PERFORMANCE: Speed—Top 227.5 mph at s. l., Cruising
   193 mph, Landing 84 mph. Service Ceiling 23,300',
   Absolute ceiling 24,900', Climb 5000'/3.4 min. Range
   470 miles/327 lbs. bombs, 950 miles max.   PMB

These features were seen in the first military Northrop, the Gamma 2C, completed in July 1933 with enclosed cockpits, Wright Cyclone, and two-bladed propeller. The Army purchased this aircraft June 28, 1934, as the YA-13, armed with four fixed guns in the wings, a flexible Browning in the rear cockpit, 3,000 .30-caliber rounds, and 600 pounds of bombs.

While waiting for the Air Corps to make up its mind, Northrop had sold 49 light bombers, designated Model 2E, to China. They differed from the YA-13 in having a retractable bomber's window under the rear cockpit, two guns in the wings, a third in the rear cockpit, and external bomb racks for one 1,100-pound, two 600-pound, or ten 100-pound bombs.

Powered by an R-1820-F3 rated at 710 hp at 7,000 feet, the first Chinese 2E appeared in February 1934, and by 1935 Northrops equipped Groups 1 and 2. They were the first planes sent against the Japanese invaders on August 14, 1937. This attack had a tragic result when a 1,100-pound bomb hit among Shanghai civilians. Much of the air fighting that followed involved Northrops.

An example of the 2E was purchased by Britain (K5093) after being used as a demonstrator. Various canopy and tail refinements were used to produce the 775-hp R-1820-F52 Cyclone-powered Northrop 5A of October 1935 and a Wasp-powered Gamma (5B) said to have been exported to Japan and the Soviet Union.

In the meantime Northrop had built another pro-

NORTHROP XA-13
Wright R-1820-37, 712 hp at 3300'
DIMENSIONS: Span 48', Lg. 29'2", Ht. 9'2", Wing Area 362 sq. ft.
WEIGHT: Empty 3600 lb., Gross 6463 lb., Max. 6575 lb. Fuel 245 gal.
PERFORMANCE: Speed—Top 207 mph at 3300', 198 mph at s. l., Cruising 172 mph, Landing 70 mph. Service Ceiling 21,750', Absolute Ceiling 23,600', Climb 1300'/1 min., 5000'/4.3 min. Range 1100 miles.   AF

NORTHROP 5A   MFR

NORTHROP 2E
Wright R-1820-F3, 710 hp at 7000'
DIMENSIONS: Span 48', Lg. 28'10", Ht. 9'1", Wing Area 363 sq. ft.
WEIGHT: Empty 3856 lb., Gross 6400 lb. Fuel 287–352 gal.
PERFORMANCE: Speed—Top 219 mph at 7000', 198 mph at s. l., Cruising 64 mph. Service Ceiling 23,300', Climb 972'/1 min., 10,000'/12.5 min. Range 1430 miles. MFR

totype for the Army, which appeared in October 1934 as Model 2F with a Pratt & Whitney R-1535, three-bladed propeller, new tail, and wheels folding back into bulky fairings. Northrop then won the largest prewar Army attack contract for 110 aircraft, purchased December 19, 1934, for $2,047,774.

It was hoped that a bigger GR-1820 Cyclone or an R-1830-7 Wasp could be installed in the production version, so the YA-13 was returned to Northrop in January 1935 for reworking. It was flown in March with the R-1830-7, but on April 25 the Army was told that either a larger tail or a smaller engine would be necessary. To prevent disruption of production, the Army chose to retain the smaller R-1535 for production ships. The 2F prototype was rebuilt with the 750-hp R-1535-11 Wasp, Jr., new open-sided wheel fairings, perforated flaps, and further changes involving the canopy and tail. The armament was five .30-caliber guns and 20 30-pound fragmentation bombs carried in chutes inside the fuselage. Larger bombs might be carried externally, the maximum bomb load being 654 pounds. Thus redone, the 2F became the first A-17 (35-51) when delivered to Wright Field in July 1935 and accepted in November.

Northrop did persevere with the R-1830 installation, and the YA-13 was redesignated XA-16 and redelivered to the Army in August 1936 with the 850-hp R-1830-9.

A-17 deliveries continued, with the first true production aircraft (35-52) being sent to Wright Field in December 1935, and in February 1936 A-17s began arriving at the 3rd Attack Group's new base at Barksdale Field. When the last was completed in January 1937, Army attack units also included the 17th Attack Group, which had begun conversion from P-26A Pursuits at March Field in June 1936, and 15 A-17s with Langley's 37th Attack Squadron.

NORTHROP 2F   MFR

NORTHROP XA-16
Pratt & Whitney R-1830-9, 950 hp takeoff, 850 hp at 8000'
DIMENSIONS: Span 48', Lg. 29'8", Wing Area 362 sq. ft.
WEIGHT: Gross 6750 lb.
PERFORMANCE: Speed—Top 212 mph.   PMB

NORTHROP A-17
Pratt & Whitney R-1535-11, 750 hp
DIMENSIONS: Span 47'9", Lg. 32', Ht. 12', Wing Area 362 sq. ft.
WEIGHT: Empty 4913 lb., Gross 7337 lb. Fuel 150–287 gal.
PERFORMANCE: Speed—Top 206 mph at s. l., Cruising 170 mph, Landing 67.5 mph. Service Ceiling 20,700', Absolute Ceiling 22,150', Climb 5000'/3.8 min. Range 650 miles/654 lbs. bombs, 1242 miles max.   MFR

NORTHROP A-17A
Pratt & Whitney R-1535-13, 825 hp at 2500'
DIMENSIONS: Span 47'9", Lg. 31'8", Ht. 12', Wing Area
362 sq. ft.
WEIGHT: Empty 5106 lb., Gross 7550 lb. Fuel 151–247
gal.
PERFORMANCE: Speed—Top 220 mph at 2500', Cruising
170 mph, Landing 64 mph. Service Ceiling 19,400',
Absolute Ceiling 20,800', Climb 1350'/1 min., 5000'/
3.9 min. Range 732 miles/654 lbs. bombs, 1195 miles
max.   MFR

Retractable wheels distinguished 100 A-17As ordered January 29, 1936, but they were preceded by
delivery in July 1936 of two A-17As three-place
command planes, powered by 600-hp R-1340-45
Wasps, for the Air Corps Chief and his deputy. General Oscar Westover was killed in his on September
21, 1938, and his deputy, General Henry A. Arnold,
became Air Corps Chief for a term that was to include all of World War II.

The first true A-17A arrived at Wright Field in
January 1937, and 100 were delivered by December
1937, with 29 more added from June to September
1938. They replaced the A-17s in the 3rd and 17th

Groups[1] and the 37th Squadron, so 15 A-17s were
shipped to the new 74th Attack Squadron in the
Canal Zone, and the rest to Kelly Field or to depots
as trainers, although Hawaii's 26th Squadron continued to make do with their A-12s.

Ninety-three of these A-17As were transferred
back to Douglas on June 20, 1940, leaving about 20
in the Army. In exchange, Douglas added 20 planes
to the current A-20A order. Of the 93 A-17As, 32
went to Canada in August 1940 and the remainder
went to England in July, with 47 forwarded to South
Africa as trainers.

Attack Bombers for Export

After Jack Northrop left his company on January 1,
1938, and the factory became the Douglas El Segundo Division, the Northrop design was exported
as the Douglas 8A.

An 8A-1 with fixed gear and the Swedish-built
Bristol 875-hp engine went to Sweden in April 1938
as the prototype for 102 SAAB B-5 light bombers
built under license. Parts for another 8A-1 were
forwarded for assembly in Sweden. Argentina received 30 8A-2s with 840-hp Wright Cyclones from
February to May 1938. These were the last fixed-
gear types, for the remaining models had retractable
wheels.

Ten Cyclone-powered 8A-3Ps were built for Peru
beginning in November 1938. Twin-row Wasps
powered 18 8A-3Ns that went to the Netherlands
from September to November 1939, but they were
destroyed in the German invasion of May 1940.
Cyclone engines were used on 15 similar 8A-4s
shipped to Iraq in June 1940.

Thirty-six Douglas 8A-5 attack planes ordered by
Norway were completed between October 1940
and February 1941 and sent to the Norwegians
training in Toronto, Canada. Similar to the A-17A
except for a 1,200-hp Wright R-1820-87 Cyclone
and a hinged bomber's window, the A-33 had two
.50-caliber and four .30-caliber wing guns, a .30-
caliber flexible gun, and up to 1,800 pounds of
bombs.

Peru was to purchase the surviving planes in August 1941, but the U. S. State Department objected
because the aircraft might be used against Ecuador.
Therefore, the Army took over 31 8A-5s in 1942,
designated them A-33s, and used them for general-
utility service.

Vultee's Bombers

Vultee offered Douglas competition with the V-11,

[1] 3rd Attack Group: 8th, 13th, and 90 squadrons; 17th Attack
Group: 34th, 73rd, and 95 squadrons.

DOUGLAS 8A-1
Bristol Hercules, 875 hp
DIMENSIONS: Span 47′9″, Lg. 31′9″, Ht. 12′11″, Wing Area
    363 sq. ft.
WEIGHT: Empty 4680 lb., Gross 7500 lb. Fuel 290 gal.
PERFORMANCE: Speed—Top 219 mph at 6250′, Cruising
    190 mph, Landing 66 mph. Service Ceiling 22,500′,
    Climb 1430′/1 min. Range 1380 miles max.   MFR

SAAB B-5 In Sweden   SALO

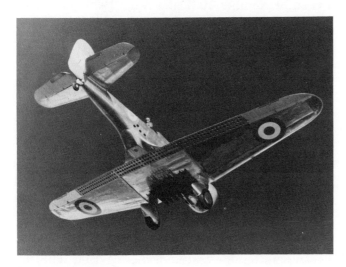

DOUGLAS 8A-2
Wright R-1820G-3, 840 hp
DIMENSIONS: Span 47′9″, Lg. 31′6″, Ht. 12′4″, Wing Area
    363 sq. ft.
WEIGHT: Empty 4899 lb., Gross 7500 lb. Fuel 225 gal.
PERFORMANCE: Speed—Top 223 mph at 8700′, Cruising
    200 mph, Landing 65 mph. Service Ceiling 25,400′,
    Climb 1300′/1 min. Range 1190 miles max.   MFR

NORTHROP 8A-3P
Wright R-1820G-103A, 840 hp
DIMENSIONS: Span 47′9″, Lg. 32′1″, Ht. 9′9″, Wing Area
    363 sq. ft.
WEIGHT: Empty 4820 lb., Gross 7500 lb. Fuel 235 gal.
PERFORMANCE: Speed—Top 238 mph at 8700′, 208 mph
    at s. l., Cruising 208 mph, Landing 66 mph. Service
    Ceiling 24,000′, Climb 1200′/1 min. Range 1180
    miles.   MFR

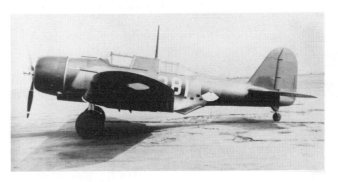

DOUGLAS 8A-3N
Pratt & Whitney R-1830-SC3G, 1050 hp takeoff, 900 hp
    at 12,000′
DIMENSIONS: Span 47′9″, Lg. 32′5″, Ht. 9′9″, Wing Area
    363 sq. ft.
WEIGHT: Empty 5508 lb., Gross 7848 lb., Max. 8948 lb.
    Fuel 250 gal.
PERFORMANCE: Speed—Top 260 mph, Cruising 205 mph,
    Landing 66 mph. Service Ceiling 29,600′, Climb 1430′/
    1 min. Range 910 miles.   MFR

DOUGLAS 8A-5 (A-33)
Wright R-1820-87, 1200 hp takeoff, 1000 hp at 6900′
DIMENSIONS: Span 47′9″, Lg. 32′6″, Ht. 9′4″, Wing Area
    363 sq. ft.
WEIGHT: Empty 5510 lb., Gross 8600 lb., Max. 9200 lb.
    Fuel 173–252 gal.
PERFORMANCE: Speed—Top 248 mph at 15,700′, Landing
    67 mph. Service Ceiling 29,000′.   PMB

VULTEE V-11GB
Wright GR-1820-G2, 850 hp at 5800'
DIMENSIONS: Span 50', Lg. 37'6", Ht. 10', Wing Area 384
sq. ft.
WEIGHT: Empty 6176 lb., Gross 9441 lb., Max. 11,437 lb.
Fuel 250–504 gal.
PERFORMANCE: Speed—Top 229 mph at 5800', 214 mph
at s. l., Cruising 207 mph, Landing 68 mph. Service
Ceiling 23,000', Climb 1285'/1 min. Range 1225 miles/
600 lbs. bombs, 2380 miles max.   MFR

a development of that firm's 1934 V-1A transport.
When single-engine transports were banned from
commercial airlines, Vultee turned to the military
market. The V-11 attack was a low-wing monoplane
with retractable wheels and a long cockpit enclosure over two crewmen. A third crew member was
accommodated in the fuselage behind the gunner
in the V-11GB model. Armament of the V-11 included the four .30-caliber wing guns and flexible
gun used on Army attack planes, but another gun
in the retractable belly mounting was added for the
third man. The V-11 could be operated as an attack
plane, with 600 pounds of bombs in internal racks
and a 1,125-mile range. Alternatively, it was a
bomber carrying 1,100 pounds, with a range of 2,-
380 miles.

On September 18, 1935, the first V-11 rolled out
to begin its flight tests, but the 745-hp SR-1820-F53
failed on takeoff and both fliers were killed in the
crash. A second prototype (NR 14980) was completed October 9, and its successful tests won contracts for 100 aircraft from four foreign countries.

China bought 30 V-11 bombers. The first was
completed in December 1936 with an F-53 Cyclone,-and the rest, V-11Gs, completed, beginning
July 1937, with the 850-hp R-1820-G2. They were

used on raids, beginning in January 1938, by the
14th Squadron, an international unit with American
and French pilots and Chinese gunners.

The Soviet Union bought four three-place V-
11GB attack bombers with the G-2 Cyclones, along
with the license and tools to manufacture them as
replacements for their R-5 biplanes. The first V-
11GB (as 17328) was completed January 31, 1937,
at Downey, California, and the Soviet version entered production as the BSh-1 with an M-62 engine
and armor added. Soviet production stopped after
only 36 aircraft when their air force decided that
maneuverable I-15bis biplanes would make better
interim attack aircraft while awaiting development
of the BSh-2, the prototype for the most famous
World War II attack plane, the Il-2 Shturmovik.

Turkey received 40 V-11GBs, completed between September 1937 and April 1938, for its 2nd
Regiment, and Brazil ordered 26, with delivery beginning in June 1938. Twin floats and a modified
tail were seen on the last Brazilian Vultee, flown
March 7, 1939.

Not until after the V-11 became popular abroad
was it tested by the U.S. Army, which was committed to smaller, more economical Northrops. Seven
service-test examples were ordered June 24, 1938,
as the YA-19. Unlike the export versions, they were
powered by Pratt & Whitney Wasps, the R-1830-17
giving 1,200 hp for takeoff. Six .30-caliber guns and
1,080 pounds of bombs (36 × 30-pound bombs)
constituted the armament.

The first YA-19 was flown January 27, 1939, and
five more were delivered in June/July, but the last
became an engine test-bed, the XA-19A, with the
1,200-hp Lycoming 0-1230-1 inline engine balanced by a lengthened tail, and first flown May 22,
1940. Pratt & Whitney's big new R-2800-1 was also
first flown in the XA-19B, which had been the second YA-19. The remaining YA-19s served at March
Field until they were moved to the Canal Zone,
where they were utilized by military attachés in
neighboring countries.

In an effort to improve the type, Vultee produced
a prototype V-12 (X 18935), which was flown September 13, 1938, with a more streamlined canopy,
a GR-1830-S1C3-G Twin Wasp, and .50-caliber
guns on the inboard wing mounts. China then ordered 26 V-12Cs with Wright R-1820-G105B and 52
V-12Ds with the big R-2600-A5B, deeper fuselage,
and nose guns. One of each was completed and
flown by Vultee in February 1940, but the others
were shipped in parts for assembly in Asia. After
their intended assembly plant at Loiwing, China,
was bombed out in October 1940, the surviving
assemblies were sent to Bangalore, India, where
only three were assembled by Hindustani Aircraft
before that factory became otherwise occupied.

VULTEE YA-19A   CANARY

VULTEE YA-19
Pratt & Whitney R-1830-17, 1200 hp takeoff, 1050 hp at 6500'
DIMENSIONS: Span 50', Lg. 37'10", Ht. 10', Wing Area 384 sq. ft.
WEIGHT: Empty 6452 lb., Gross 10,421 lb. Fuel 311–30 gal.
PERFORMANCE: Speed—Top 230 mph at 6500', Cruising 207 mph, Landing 80 mph. Service Ceiling 20,400', Absolute Ceiling 22,000', Climb 1320'/1 min. Range 1110 miles/1080 lbs. bombs, 1385 miles max.   MFR

VULTEE V-12C
Wright GR-1820-105B, 1050 hp takeoff
DIMENSIONS: Span 50', Lg. 38'2", Ht. 12'11", Wing Area 384 sq. ft.
WEIGHT: Empty 6641 lb., Gross 10,111 lb., Max. 12,078 lb. Fuel 494 gal.
PERFORMANCE: Speed—Top 254 mph at 18,000' as attack (231 mph as bomber), Cruising 226 mph (194 mph), Landing 70 mph. Service Ceiling 25,200' (20,200'), Climb 6560'/5.8 min.   MFR

VULTEE V-12D
Wright GR-2600-A5B, 1600 hp takeoff, 1275 hp at 11,500'
DIMENSIONS: As V-12C
WEIGHT: Empty 7416 lbs., Gross 10,886 lbs., Max. 12,853 lbs. Fuel 350 gal.
PERFORMANCE: Speed—Top 281 mph at 11,000' as attack (270 mph as bomber), Cruising 248 mph (230 mph). Service Ceiling 28,000' (25,400'), Climb 2000'/1 min.
                                              MFR

BELLANCA 28-90
Pratt & Whitney R-1830 Wasp, 900 hp at 6200'
DIMENSIONS: Span 46'2", Lg. 26'6", Ht. 7', Wing Area 279 sq. ft.
WEIGHT: Empty 4450 lb., Gross 6755 lb., Max. 7849 lb. Fuel 150 gal.
PERFORMANCE: Speed—Top 280 mph at 6500', Cruising 250 mph, Landing 68 mph. Service Ceiling 30,500', Climb 2800'/1 min., 15,000'/7.5 min. Range 800 miles.   SI—MFR

The potential market for attack bombers lured commercial aircraft companies to adapt their designs for combat. Bellanca's "Flash," for example, was a two-place monoplane whose fabric-covered construction included a wing braced by external wires running to two steel cabane struts below the fuselage. The prototype had first flown September 1, 1934, as a long-range racer.

When the Spanish Civil War began, this prototype was purchased by the Republicans. By June 1937, 20 more had been built as Model 28-90, alleged to be a high-speed mail plane for Air France.

SPARTAN ZEUS
Pratt & Whitney R-1340-S3H-1, 550 hp
DIMENSIONS: Span 39', Lg. 27'3", Ht. 8'6", Wing Area 256
  sq. ft.
WEIGHT: Empty 3440 lb., Gross 4953 lb. Fuel 112 gal.
PERFORMANCE: Speed—Top 234 mph at 5000', Cruising
  218 mph, Landing 65 mph. Service Ceiling 29,400',
  Climb 2100'/1 min. Range 760 miles.   MFR

NORTH AMERICAN A-27 (NA-69)
Wright R-1820-75, 785 hp takeoff, 745 hp at 9600'
DIMENSIONS: Span 42', Lg. 29', Ht. 12'2", Wing Area 258
  sq. ft.
WEIGHT: Empty 4520 lb., Gross 6006 lb., Max. 6700 lb.
  Fuel 120–70 gal.
PERFORMANCE: Speed—Top 250 mph at 11,500', Cruising
  220 mph, Landing 70 mph. Service Ceiling 28,000'.
  Range 575 miles/400 lbs. bombs, 800 miles max. MFR

CURTISS XA-14
Wright R-1670-5, 775 hp at 10,000'
DIMENSIONS: Span 59'5", Lg. 40'3", Ht. 10'9", Wing Area
  526 sq. ft.
WEIGHT: Empty 8456 lb., Gross 11,738 lb. Fuel 287–617
  gal.
PERFORMANCE: Speed—Top 254 mph at 9750', 249 mph
  at 4550', Cruising 211 mph, Landing 75 mph. Service
  Ceiling 27,125', Absolute Ceiling 28,500', Climb 1685'/
  1 min. Range 816 miles/600 lbs. bombs.   AF

When the State Department blocked their delivery because it appeared they were intended for Spain, 19 were sold to China, and they appeared at Hankow in January 1938 armed as light bombers.

One example had been retained by the company as a "fighter-bomber" demonstrator armed with four .30-caliber fixed guns, one flexible gun, and bomb racks under the wings. Another batch was ordered in December 1937 by a Greek firm, but again it appeared that Spain was the intended destination for the 28-90B (which had flaps) and export permits were refused. In 1939, 21 Bellancas were moved to Vera Cruz, where they were taken over by the Mexican Air Force when the Spanish Republic lost the war. After two fatal crashes, they were withdrawn from service.

The story of the single-engine Army attack plane may be concluded with the lightweight two-seaters built to offer a low-cost aircraft to the Latin American market. The Spartan Executive was a popular cabin low-wing monoplane, and the company built a military version, the Zeus, which had with a crew of two, two guns, and a 250-pound bomb load, powered by a 550-hp Wasp. Completed with Mexican markings in 1938, it may have actually been sold to Spain. A direct light-bomber conversion of the Executive was also offered for sale without success, although a Spartan equipped for photography was used in China in 1937.

North American Aviation had some success with a souped-up attack version of the famous AT-6. A demonstration model, the NA-44, was begun in December 1937, flew in 1938 with five guns and a 775-hp R-1820-F52, and was eventually sold to Canada in 1940. Brazil received 30, designated NA-72, from July to October 1940.

Ten more ordered on November 29, 1939, by Thailand were completed as NA-69s by September 1940 and shipped abroad but were intercepted by the Army for fear they might fall into Japanese hands. Designated the A-27, they were with the Army in the Philippines when the war began. Powered by the Wright R-1820-75, the A-27 carried four 100-pound bombs and three .30-caliber guns, two in the nose and a flexible rear gun.

Twin-engine Attack Bombers

Although the use of two engines would have improved performance and safety, the Army was cautious about adding to the cost and complexity of its attack planes, and it took a decade before twin-engine types replaced the smaller ships used through the 1930s.

In May 1934 an attack version of the Martin YB-10 bomber was projected. Designated XA-15, it was to have two Wright R-1820-25s, weigh 12,356 pounds gross, and do 214 mph at 4,500 feet. This design was dropped in the paper stage in favor of the faster Curtiss XA-14.

The XA-14 was a carefully streamlined all-metal monoplane with retractable wheels, pencil-pointed nose, and a crew of two under a long enclosure. Two 755-hp Wright twin-row R-1670-5 Whirlwinds turned two-bladed propellers. Standard armament was the same as the A-17s (five .30-caliber guns with 20 30-pound or four 116-pound bombs) expect that the four fixed guns were grouped in the nose.

First flown as Curtiss Model 76 on July 17, 1935, the prototype was purchased by the Army on November 29. Although top speed was much higher than other attack or bomber types, the Army hesitated to enter large-scale production, for the cost of the plane was more than three times that of the A-17A. Curtiss wanted to try to break some records with the prototype, but instead it was decided in June 1936 to use the XA-14 to test a new 37-mm gun.

Thirteen examples were ordered July 23, 1936, for service tests with single-row Cyclones and three-bladed propellers. Designated Y1A-18, the first was flown July 3, 1937, and the contract completed in October. Twelve Y1A-18s served the 8th Attack Squadron at Barksdale until transferred to the 15th Attack Squadron at Lawson in 1941.

Standard armament of the XA-14 and YA-18 included four .30-caliber nose guns and another for the rear gunner, plus a 654-pound internal bomb load. An export version, the Curtiss 76-D with the Cyclone G-3 of 840 hp at 10,200 feet, was offered but found no buyers.

Twin-engine attack types meant more than improved performance and safety. Additional power also allowed larger bomb loads, so that American attack planes could match the capabilities of the swift twin-engine light bombers then being acquired by European powers. Prodded by the threatening war, the Army announced a design competition for "attack bombers," a new specification foreshadowed by the A-18's two engines and the A-19's larger bomb load. The minimum requirements included a 1,200-pound bomb load to be carried 1,200 miles at an operating speed of at least 200 mph.

The preliminary designs submitted in July 1938 included one with inline engines, Bell's Model 9. Two Allison V-1710s were expected to yield a top speed of 255 mph at 3,000 feet, with a 19,500-pound gross weight, including two 37-mm guns. Faster speeds, however, were promised by the radial-engine proposals, including the 17,470-pound Stearman X-100 at 269 mph, the 15,800-pound Martin 167F at 275 mph, and the 14,700-pound Douglas Model 7 offering 280 mph. Encouraged by results,

CURTISS XA-14 with 37 mm. gun   AF

CURTISS A-18
Wright R-1820-47, 930 hp takeoff, 850 hp at 2500'
DIMENSIONS: Span 59'6", Lg. 42'4", Ht. 15', Wing Area 526 sq. ft.
WEIGHT: Empty 9410 lb., Gross 12,679 lb., Max. 13,170 lb. Fuel 287–630 gal.
PERFORMANCE: Speed—Top 238.5 mph at 2500', Cruising 211 mph, Landing 73 mph. Service Ceiling 28,650', Absolute Ceiling 30,000', Climb 5000'/2.2 min. Range 1443 miles/654 lbs. bombs, 1700 miles max.   AF

the Army invited the companies to build sample planes and submit bids to be opened March 17, 1939. Bell dropped out, but the other three firms, plus North American, did build prototypes for the competition that determined the World War II attack-bomber pattern.

All four prototypes were three-place all-metal monoplanes with two radial engines, three-bladed propellers, and retractable wheels, reflecting European light bombers like the Bristol Blenheim and Dornier DO-17. All had four .30-caliber fixed guns for ground attack and an internal bay for the bomb load.

Two Pratt & Whitney R-2180-7 Twin Hornets powered the Stearman X-100, which had its wing mounted high on a squared-off fuselage. Appearing first with its bombardier and pilot under an unbroken Plexiglas nose, it was later reworked to have a separate pilot's windshield, the broken nose sacrificing streamlining for visibility. This caused the top speed to drop below early estimates, but the Army bought the prototype as the XA-21. A socket in the nose allowed for a flexible front gun, while the rear gunner had a .30-caliber gun in a turret

STEARMAN X-100   AF

STEARMAN XA-21
Pratt & Whitney R-2180-7, 1400 hp takeoff, 1150 hp at 7000'
DIMENSIONS: Span 65', Lg. 53'1", Ht. 14'2", Wing Area 607 sq. ft.
WEIGHT: Empty 12,760 lb., Gross 18,257 lb. Fuel 450–520 gal.
PERFORMANCE: Speed—Top 257 mph at 5000', Cruising 200 mph, Landing 72 mph. Service Ceiling 20,000'. Range 720 miles/1200 lbs. bombs, 1500 miles max. AF

behind the wing, side guns, and another gun in a belly fixture. Four wing guns and two 600-pound, six 300-pound, or 90 30-pound bombs could be used against ground targets.

Another high-wing design was offered in the North American NA-40B, which had two Wright R-2600-A2 Cyclones, twin rudders, and featured tricycle landing gear. Armament included seven .30-caliber guns (four in the wings, one in the nose ball and socket turret, and the rear gunner's upper and lower flexible guns). The layout was a forerunner of the B-25 bomber. The NA-40 had 1,100-hp Pratt & Whitney R-1830-S6C3-G Wasps when first flown February 10, 1939, but was fitted with Wright GR-2600-A71 Double Cyclones when flown to the Air Corps tests as the NA-40B in March.

During its tests at Wright Field, the NA-40B crashed, eliminating it from the competition. The Douglas 7B prototype had met the same fate while still in the building stage, leaving the Stearman ship and Martin's 167 the only survivors. To these firms' disappointment, no contract was awarded; instead the Army called for new bids in April for design proposals without prototypes. The same firms submitted new bids, in addition to Vincent Burnelli, who offered an Allison-powered job with a radical airfoil fuselage and twin tail booms.

Douglas offered a new version of their plane, with Wright R-2600 engines instead of the R-1830 Wasps used on the 7B prototype. This won an order for 186 attack bombers, while only the prototypes of Stearman and Martin were purchased.

NORTH AMERICAN NA-40B
Wright R-2600-A71, 1500 hp takeoff, 1275 hp at 12,000'
DIMENSIONS: Span 66', Lg. 48'3", Ht. 23', Wing Area 598.5 sq. ft.
WEIGHT: Empty 13,961 lb., Gross 19,741 lb. Fuel 476 gal.
PERFORMANCE: Speed—Top 309 mph at 14,000', Cruising 282 mph. Service Ceiling 25,000'. Range 1200 miles/1200 lbs. bombs. AF

Douglas A-20 Havoc

The most important and famous Army attack bomber of World War II was the Douglas A-20, winner of the 1939 competition. Its design had actually begun in 1936 at El Segundo as the Northrop 7A before that organization became part of the Douglas company. The design was revised as Douglas Model 7B for submission in the July 1938 attack-bomber design contest, and a prototype was constructed to compete for the 1939 production contract.

DOUGLAS 7B (Prototype A-20)
Pratt & Whitney R-1830-S6C3-6, 1100 hp at 5000'
DIMENSIONS: Span 61', Lg. 45'5", Wing Area 464 sq. ft.
WEIGHT: Gross 15,200 lb. Fuel 370 gal.
PERFORMANCE: Speed—Top 304 mph at 5000'. Service Ceiling 27,600'. Range 1350 miles. MFR

As first flown October 26, 1938, the 7B had two 1,100-hp Pratt & Whitney Wasps, a shoulder-high wing, and the first tricycle landing gear on an American combat plane. This nose-wheel gear permitted faster landing speeds and thus made a smaller wing possible, leading, in turn, to the highest speed of any contemporary American bomber. The metal-covered nose could accommodate six guns or be replaced by a bombardier's post with Plexiglas windows. The rear gunner had a retractable "birdcage" turret and a second gun to fire downwards through a floor opening.

The first flights were not announced to the public, but a crash on January 23, 1939, brought the plane widespread controversial attention. It was discovered that a French officer had been aboard, in violation of the Air Corps policy of not releasing information on its aircraft types until they were approaching obsolescence. An investigation revealed that President Roosevelt himself had made the decision to allow France and Britain to buy up-to-date American warplanes.[1]

France did order 100 Douglas DB-7s on February 15, 1939, and the first flew at El Segundo on August 17, 1939, with 900-hp R-1830-SC3G Wasps. The French DB-7 could be distinguished from the prototype by a transparent bombardier's nose, engine nacelles below the wings, intakes on the cowl top, and the rear turret replaced by sliding canopy. Armament included four 7.5-mm nose guns, a 7.5-mm upper rear gun, another for the ventral post, and from 1,764 to 2,080 pounds of bombs.

Five French squadrons received the first 64, but the DB-7 did not get into combat until May 31, 1940, and flew about 61 sorties before France surrendered and the Douglas squadrons were withdrawn to North Africa. Britain took over all French contracts and undelivered aircraft on June 25.

The British named the DB-7 Boston I, using them as trainers introducing nose-wheel gear to RAF pilots. An additional 170 DB-7s had been ordered October 14, 1939, and 1,000-hp R-1830-S3C4-G Wasps were used, beginning with DB-7 No. 131, on the remainder of the 270 DB-7s completed by September 3, 1940, and taken over by Britain as Boston II.

The 131st DB-7 had also been tested July 26, 1940, with a twin-rudder arrangement requested by the French, whose Leo 45 bomber was thought to have a better rear gunner's fire field due to twin tails. This system was not adopted for production, however.

Night operations had become a major RAF con-

DOUGLAS DB-7 (BOSTON I)
Pratt & Whitney R-1830-SC3G, 1050 hp takeoff, 900 hp at 12,000′
DIMENSIONS: Span 61′4″, Lg. 46′11″, Ht. 15′10″, Wing Area 464 sq. ft.
WEIGHT: Empty 11,400 lb., Design Gross 16,000 lb., Max. 17,031 lb. Fuel 325 gal.
PERFORMANCE: Speed—Top 314 mph at 15,000′, Cruising 270 mph, Landing 81 mph. Service Ceiling 28,570′, Climb 2440′/1 min. Range 630 miles.   MFR

DOUGLAS HAVOC I
Pratt & Whitney Wasp SC4-G, 1100 hp at 6200′; 1000 hp at 12,500′
DIMENSIONS: As DB-7
WEIGHT: Empty 11,520 lb., Max. 17,151 lb. Fuel 325 gal.
PERFORMANCE: Speed—Top 322 mph at 15,200′, 293 mph at s. l., Landing 86 mph. Service Ceiling 33,800′. Range 462 miles/2080 lbs. bombs.   IWM

cern, so the Boston IIs went to six Fighter Command squadrons as the Havoc I (Intruder), painted black and fitted with flame-damper exhausts and four .303-caliber fixed guns to supplement the bomb load. As aircraft Intercept (AI) radar became available, the Havoc I (Night Fighter) appeared with the bomber's compartment replaced by four more guns in a solid nose fairing.

Britain also inherited a contract for 100 DB-7As with 1,275-hp Wright R-2600-A5B Cyclones, longer nacelles, armor, and a broader vertical tail. Ordered October 20, 1939, the first DB-7A was flown on July 30, 1940, but crashed before acceptance. The remainder were accepted from November 1940 to February 1941 and were converted in Britain to

DOUGLAS DB-7A
Wright R-2600-A5B, 1500 hp takeoff, 1275 hp at 11,500'
DIMENSIONS: Span 61'4", Lg. 48', Ht. 15'10", Wing Area
  464 sq. ft.
WEIGHT: Empty 13,584 lb., Design Gross 16,700 lb., Max.
  19,322 lb. Fuel 325 gal.
PERFORMANCE: Speed—Top 344 mph at 12,500', 308 mph
  at s. l., Landing 97 mph. Service Ceiling 32,000', Range
  490 miles/2129 lbs. bombs.   MFR

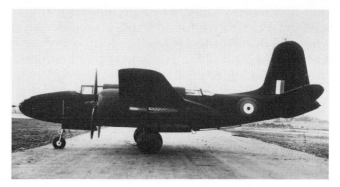

DOUGLAS HAVOC II   IWM

Havoc II night fighters with 12 nose guns and radar
and to Havoc II (Turbinlite).[2]

The first Army version was the A-20A, powered
by Wright R-2600-3 Cyclones with a larger nose
enclosure; more fuel; one 1,100-pound, four 300-
pound, or up to 80 30-pound bombs; and seven
.30-caliber guns (four set low in the nose, two in
the rear cockpit, and one in the belly). Armor and
leakproof fuel tanks were provided.

A May 20, 1939, contract approved on June 30
called for 123 A-20As, and 20 more were added in
exchange for the A-17As Douglas resold to Britain.
The first A-20A flight was September 6, 1940, and
the aircraft was delivered November 30. The fifth
A-20A went to the Navy in December as the BD-1,
with the A-20A contract completed in September
1941.

The 3rd Light Bombardment Group (formerly the
3rd Attack), was equipped with A-20As at its new
Savannah, Georgia, base in 1941. Hawaii and the
Canal Zone got 12 each, while others were parceled
out to the new Light Bombardment units, the 15th
Bomb Squadron (L) at Lawson Field, the 46th
Bomb Group (L) at Bowman Field, and the 48th
Bomb Group (L) at Will Rogers Field.

Sixty-three A-20 light bombers ordered the same
day as the A-20As were to get R-2600-7 Cyclones
turbosupercharged to give 1,500 hp at 20,000 feet.
Delivery was delayed by the engines, however, and
it was realized that high-altitude performance (395
mph at 20,000 feet was anticipated) was of little
value when small bomb loads required accurate,
low-level bombing. Turbosuperchargers were fitted

DOUGLAS HAVOC II (Turbinlite)   IWM

DOUGLAS A-20A
Wright R-2600-3, 1600 hp takeoff, 1275 hp at 12,000'
DIMENSIONS: Span 61'4", Lg. 47'7", Ht. 17'7", Wing Area
  464 sq. ft.
WEIGHT: Empty 15,165 lb., Design Gross 19,750 lb., Max.
  20,711 lb. Fuel 390 gal.
PERFORMANCE: Speed—Top 347 mph at 12,400', Cruising
  295 mph, Landing 85 mph. Service Ceiling 28,175',
  Climb 10,000'/5.1 min. Range 525 miles/2400 lbs.
  bombs, 675 miles/1200 lbs. bombs, 1000 miles max. AF

[2] See Chapter 17 for details concerning Turbinlite.

to the 15th aircraft, which became the only actual pure A-20 tested. Since these engines proved almost impossible to cool, the superchargers were dropped from the program and the A-20 became the XP-70 night-fighter prototype.

Sixty-two A-20 airframes remained empty in the Douglas yard awaiting the equipment to convert three into YF-3 photographic planes, and the rest were assigned to the P-70 program by an October 15, 1941, order.

Previously the "photographic" designation had denoted stock civilian cabin planes modified as the Fairchild F-1 and Beechcraft F-2 types used by the photographic mapping unit, but in 1941 F became the code letter for camera-equipped combat planes intended to penetrate hostile airspace. The YF-3s were delivered in March 1942, modified with R-200-11 Cyclones, fuel tanks enlarged to carry 480 to 600 gallons, and tandem T-3A cameras. Armament consisted of seven .30-caliber guns, with two fixed in the nose, two flexible top and one flexible tunnel weapons, and another fixed gun pointing from the rear of each engine nacelle. This rather impractical defense was also planned for the A-20B series but was not used on production aircraft.

On February 20, 1940, Britain had ordered the DB-7B version, similar in appearance and armament to the A-20A but with R-2600-A5B Cyclones and British .303-caliber guns. The first was flown January 10, 1941, and 541 were delivered from May to December 1941. Boeing also received an order (originally placed by France) for 240 DB-7Bs on May 18, 1940, which were delivered from August 1941 to January 1942.

Known as the Boston III, they replaced Blenheims in five RAF bomber squadrons and first sortied against the enemy in occupied France on February 12, 1942. Three night intruder squadrons received Bostons with four 20-mm guns in a tray under the fuselage, and some Boston IIIs were modified for the Turbinlite units.

Many RAF Bostons were diverted after the Soviet Union and the United States entered the war, with some 151 sent to the U.S.S.R. and 162 Douglas-built and 194 Boeing-built DB-7Bs requisitioned by the USAF. Not until late 1942 did deliveries to the RAF resume with 202 of the lend-lease Boston IIIA (A-20C) models.

On October 2, 1940, the AAF ordered 999 A-20Bs and 775 O-53 reconnaissance versions. The O-53s were canceled in June 1942, but the A-20Bs were delivered at the new Douglas Long Beach plant between December 1941 and January 1943. Eight went to the U.S. Navy as the BD-2 in May 1942, while the U.S.S.R. got 665 on lend-lease. The A-20B had R-2600-11 engines, armor, leakproof tanks, two .50-caliber fixed nose guns, one .50-caliber flex-

DOUGLAS A-20
Wright R-2600-7, 1700 hp at 20,000' (turbosuperchargers)
DIMENSIONS: As A-20A
WEIGHT: Gross 20,329 lb. Fuel 414 gal.
PERFORMANCE: (Estimated) Speed—Top 388 mph at 20,-000', Cruising 218 mph, Landing 93 mph. Service Ceiling 31,500', Climb 10,000'/5 min. Range 767 miles/1200 lbs. bombs, 1100 miles max.   MFR

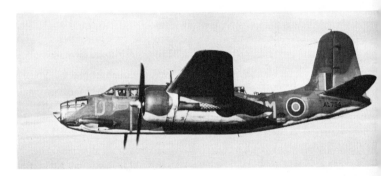

DOUGLAS DB-7B (BOSTON III)
Wright R-2600-A5Bo, 1500 hp takeoff, 1275 hp at 11,500'
DIMENSIONS: Span 61'4", Lg. 47'3", Ht. 18'1", Wing Area 464 sq. ft.
WEIGHT: Empty 15,051 lb., Design Gross 19,750 lb., Max. 21,580 lb. Fuel 390 gal.
PERFORMANCE: Speed—Top 338 mph at 12,500', 311 mph at s. l., Landing 95 mph. Service Ceiling 27,600', Range 525 miles/2000 lbs. bombs.   IWM

DOUGLAS A-20B
Wright R-2600-11, 1600 hp takeoff, 1275 hp at 11,500'
DIMENSIONS: Span 61'4", Lg. 48', Ht. 18'1", Wing Area 464 sq. ft.
WEIGHT: Empty 14,830 lb., Gross 21,000 lb., Max. 23,800 lb. Fuel 394–490 gal.
PERFORMANCE: Speed—Top 350 mph at 12,000', Cruising 278 mph, Landing 95 mph. Service Ceiling 28,600', Climb 10,000'/5 min. Range 825 miles/1000 lbs. bombs, 2300 miles ferry.   AF

DOUGLAS A-20B (gun nose)   MFR

DOUGLAS A-20C
Wright R-2600-23, 1600 hp takeoff, 1275 hp at 11,500'
DIMENSIONS: Span 61'4", Lg. 47'3", Ht. 17'7", Wing Area
    464 sq. ft.
WEIGHT: Empty 15,625 lb., Gross 21,000 lb., Max. 24,500
    lb. Fuel 400–540 gal.
PERFORMANCE: Speed—Top 342 mph at 13,000', 314 mph
    at s. l., Cruising 280 mph, Landing 100 mph. Service
    Ceiling 25,320', Climb 10,000'/6.3 min. Range 745
    miles/1000 lbs. bombs, 1400 miles max.   MFR

ible upper gun, a .30-caliber tunnel gun, and the stepped nose enclosure used on the French DB-7s. Provision was made to increase fuel capacity for transoceanic ferry to 1,094 gallons internal overload, or 1,479 gallons with a belly tank.

The A-20C had the distinction of being the first plane ordered by a "lend-lease" contract, dated April 28, 1941. Similar to the DB-7B except for exhaust stacks, it was named Boston IIIA and had R-2600-23 Cyclones, seven .30-caliber guns, 415 pounds of armor, and 2,076 pounds of bombs or a torpedo. Concurrently with the A-20B, Douglas built 808 at Santa Monica and 140 were made by Boeing early in 1942. The Dutch bought 48 similar DB-7Cs with torpedo gear, but they were not ready until July 1942. Instead, 28 DB-7Bs were rushed to Java, but only six arrived before the Japanese landed, and the rest went to Australia. The DB-7Cs themselves eventually went to Soviet naval air units. During 1942, the A-20Cs were delivered to the AAF, the RAF, and the Soviet Air Force.

There was no A-20D model built, but the A-20Es were 17 A-20As fitted with R-2600-11 engines like the B. The XA-20F was an A-20A with a 37-mm fixed nose gun and two General Electric remote-control turrets installed to test and develop a gunnery system for the projected A-26.

After America entered the war, the A-20 found itself in action all over the world, and the name "Havoc" was given to all Army Air Force A-20s. An A-20A squadron was a victim of the Pearl Harbor attack.

The A-20A did not have enough range to fly to the distant theaters of action, so the first Army crews trained on Havocs were shipped overseas without their aircraft; the 3rd Bomb Group (L) left for Australia in February 1942 and the 15th Bomb Squadron for England in May. Six crews from the 15th used borrowed DB-7Bs to join six RAF crews in a July 4 attack on German airfields in the Netherlands that was publicized (incorrectly) as the first American attack on German forces. Three Havocs were lost and three damaged in what was essentially a propaganda operation to make up for previous American inactivity in Europe. After this, the

squadron moved to North Africa. Air Force Havocs did not strike from England again until March 1944, but British and Soviet pilots used them in great numbers.

When the 3rd Group's 39 A-20As arrived in Australia, they were modified for ground strafing by adding four .50-caliber nose guns, but the 89th Squadron did not go into combat in New Guinea until August 31, 1942, the three other 3rd Group squadrons having previously substituted A-24 and B-25C bombers for attacks on Japanese forces.

The American invasion of North Africa brought the A-20Bs of the 47th Bomb Group into combat on December 14, after using its ferry tanks to cross the Atlantic, joined by the A-20Bs that equipped half of the 68th Observation Group and by the Bostons of the 15th Squadron.

Some of these A-20Bs working in Africa had also been modified with solid "gun noses," and this fixed-gun arrangement was chosen for the A-20G attack bomber ordered June 1, 1942, and first delivered in February 1943 with more firepower, armor, and fuel. Powered by the R-2600-23, it carried four 500-pound bombs in the bay or a 2,000-pound torpedo under the fuselage; and, in model A-20G-20 and subsequent models, four more 500-pound bombs could be added under the wings for short ranges.

The first 250 (A-20G-1) had four 20-mm and two .50-caliber nose guns, while the remaining 2,600 Gs used six .50-caliber bow guns with 350 rounds per gun. A hand-operated .50-caliber gun in the rear seat of the first 750 (to A-20G-15) was replaced by two .50s in a power-operated Martin turret in the A-20G-20 of August 1943. Beginning with this model, the .30-caliber belly gun was replaced by a .50-caliber weapon.

The first A-20J was an A-20G-25 with a transparent bombardier's nose enclosure and two .50-caliber nose guns. Four hundred and fifty were produced concurrently with later A-20G models. Britain received 169 and named them Boston IV. Wright R-2600-20 Cyclones of 1,700 hp were fitted to the A-20H and A-20K. Solid noses with six .50-caliber guns distinguished 412 Hs from the 413 Ks with the bombardier nose. Ninety of the latter became the Boston V of the RAF whose medium-altitude operations had no need for the gun-nose versions.

When Havoc production ended September 20, 1944, 7,098 of these planes had been built by Douglas, 380 under license by Boeing, while AAF inventories were at a peak of over 1,700 A-20s. Havocs then equipped seven USAF groups in action: the 3rd, 312th, and 417th with the Fifth Air Force in the Pacific, the 47th with the Twelfth Air Force in Italy, while the 409th, 410th, and 416th with the Ninth Air Force in Britain bombed ahead of the D-Day invasion at Normandy. While treetop attacks were favored in the Pacific, European missions were at medium altitudes. Those groups usually operated a glass-nosed A-20J or K for every three gun-nose G or H models, the formation releasing

DOUGLAS A-20G-5
Wright R-2600-23, 1600 hp takeoff, 1275 hp at 11,500′
DIMENSIONS: Span 61′4″, Lg. 48′, Ht. 17′7″, Wing Area 464 sq. ft.
WEIGHT: Empty 15,984 lb., Gross 21,971 lb., Max. 27,200 lb. Fuel 540–916 gal.
PERFORMANCE: Speed—Top 339 mph at 12,400′, Cruising 272 mph, Landing 95 mph. Service Ceiling, 25,800′, Climb 10,000′/7.1 min. Range 1090 miles.   AF

DOUGLAS A-20G-20
Wright R-2600-23, 1600 hp
DIMENSIONS: As A-20G-5
WEIGHT: Empty 16,993 lb., Gross 24,127 lb., Max. 27,000 lb. Fuel 725–1105 gal.
PERFORMANCE: Speed—Top 333 mph at 12,300′, Cruising 272 mph, Landing 95 mph. Service Ceiling 23,700′, Climb 10,000′/8.8 min. Range 1000 miles normal, 2100 miles ferry.   AF

DOUGLAS A-20G-40
Wright R-2600-23, 1600 hp
DIMENSIONS: As A-20G-5
WEIGHT: Empty 16,910 lb., Gross 23,967 lb., Max. 26,000 lb. Fuel 725–1105 gal.
PERFORMANCE: Speed—Top 312 mph at 10,000′, 302 mph at s. l. Climb 1300′/1 min., 10,000′/8.8 min., Range 1025 miles/2000 lbs. bombs.   MFR

DOUGLAS A-20H-1 (BOSTON V)
Wright R-2600-29, 1700 hp takeoff
DIMENSIONS: As A-20G-5
WEIGHT: Empty 16,842 lb., Gross 23,987 lb., Max. 27,000 lb. Fuel 725–1105 gal.
PERFORMANCE: Speed—Top 333 mph at 15,600′, Cruising 269 mph, Landing 100 mph. Service Ceiling 25,300′, Climb 10,000′/6.6 min. Range 880 miles normal, 2200 miles ferry.   AF

DOUGLAS A-20J (French)
Wright R-2600-23, 1600 hp takeoff
DIMENSIONS: Span 61'4", Lg. 48'4", Ht. 17'7", Wing Area
    464 sq. ft.
WEIGHT: Empty 17,117 lb., Gross 23,748 lb., Max. 27,000
    lb. Fuel 725–1105 gal.
PERFORMANCE: Speed—Top 317 mph at 10,700', Cruising
    257 mph, Landing 95 mph. Service Ceiling 23,100',
    Climb 10,000'/8.8 min. Range 1000 miles/2000 lbs.
    bombs, 2100 miles max.   MA

DOUGLAS A-20K
Wright R-2600-29, 1700 hp takeoff
DIMENSIONS: As A-20J
WEIGHT: Empty 17,266 lb., Gross 23,953 lb., Max. 27,000
    lb. Fuel 725–1105 gal.
PERFORMANCE: Speed—Top 333 mph at 15,600', Cruising
    269 mph, Landing 100 mph. Service Ceiling 25,100',
    Climb 10,000'/6.6 min. Range 830 miles normal, 2200
    miles ferry.   MFR

their bombs at the leader's signal. Forty-six A-20Js
and Ks became F-3A night reconnaissance planes
with K-19B camera, four flash bombs, and with the
lower vertical gun omitted. The last A-20 mission
by American pilots was a sortie on August 12, 1945,
by the 3rd Group.

Since the Havoc was produced to give close support to ground troops, and since the largest Allied
army was Soviet, the U.S.S.R. was allotted 3,125
Douglas Havocs at a promised rate of 100 a month.
Of these, 2,908 actually arrived, the first being Boston III (DB-7B) and IIIA (A-20C) aircraft originally
scheduled for Britain; this accounted for the designation of B-3 in Soviet service. Torpedo provisions on models A-20C-5 to A-20G-35, not used by
American crews, were used by the Soviet 36th Air
Division, cited for an October 15, 1944, attack on a
German convoy near Norway, and by another naval
air division in the Black Sea.

Australia acquired 78 Havocs from 1942 to 1944,
including nine A-20As, nine A-20Cs, 22 DB-7Bs, 28
A-20Gs, and an A-20J. A Free French squadron (No.
342, "Lorraine") began operations from England on
June 12, 1943, with Boston IIIAs and IVs received
via the RAF. Joined by 13 AAF and RAF squadrons
in support of the 1944 Normandy invasion, these
pilots had come a long way since the first 12 French
DB-7s had sortied in 1940.

Boston bombers were used by two South African
and four RAF squadrons in the Mediterranean theater, and by three more RAF squadrons on operations
over the English Channel.

From Baltimore, Maryland

Martin's Model 167 was a low-wing, tail-down rival
of the A-20, but had less performance than the
Douglas. The prototype had two R-1830-37 Wasps

MARTIN XA-22
Pratt & Whitney R-1830-37, 1200 hp takeoff, 1100 hp at
    5000'
DIMENSIONS: Span 61'4", Lg. 46'8", Ht. 10', Wing Area
    538.5 sq. ft.
WEIGHT: Empty 11,170 lb., Gross 16,000 lb., Max. 17,000
    lb. Fuel 390–530 gal.
PERFORMANCE: Speed—Top 280 mph at 5000', Cruising
    260 mph. Service Ceiling 20,000'. Range 750 miles/
    1800 lbs. bombs, 1200 miles/1200 lbs. bombs, 1900
    miles max.   MFR

MARTIN 167 (MARYLAND I)
Pratt & Whitney R-1830-SC3G, 1050 hp takeoff, 900 hp
    at 12,000'
DIMENSIONS: As XA-22
WEIGHT: Empty 10,586 lb., Gross 15,297 lb., Max. 16,571
    lb. Fuel 255–510 gal.
PERFORMANCE: Speed—Top 304 mph at 13,000', 275 mph
    at s. l., Cruising 248 mph, Landing 71 mph. Service
    Ceiling 29,500', Climb 2000'/1 min. Range 1300
    miles.   MA

and three crewmen in a narrow fuselage, with a retractable rear-gun turret covered by a panel sliding forward when the turret was raised. Armament included four .30-caliber guns in the wings, another in the turret, and another in a deeply cut lower position behind the bay for 60 30-pound or four 300-pound bombs.

Flown from Baltimore to Wright Field on March 14, 1939, Martin's attack bomber was purchased by the Air Corps as the XA-22 on May 20. Glenn L. Martin protested the production contract awarded Douglas on the grounds that the 7B prototype had crashed and was not present for the competition, but he could be consoled by a French contract for 115 aircraft placed January 26, 1939.

French aircraft could carry two 624-pound or eight 116-pound bombs and six 7.5-mm guns, but they had no cover over the turret and used 900-hp Wasps supercharged to 12,000 feet. The first 167F flew by August 1939 and the contract was increased to 215 aircraft, but the Martins did not reach French North Africa until December 25. After the German invasion, four *groupes* flew 418 combat sorties from May 22 to June 24, 1940, losing 18 Martins in action. In the meantime, deliveries on a third contract had begun; 223 Martins had arrived in Casablanca by June 15, but only 182 had been assembled and turned over to the French Air Force.

After the French defeat, Britain took over the last 50 167s, along with 75 built on a direct RAF contract completed in July 1940. Known as the Maryland I, they were powered by 900-hp R-1830-SC3G Wasps. Between December 1940 and April 1941, 150 Maryland IIs were delivered to the RAF with R-1830-S3C4-G Wasps of 1,000 hp at 12,500 feet.

Marylands served with a general reconnaissance unit in Malta in 1940 and in 1941 with one British and three South African light-bomber squadrons in northwest Africa. Those remaining with Vichy French forces were used to attack Allied forces in Syria in June 1941 and American forces near Casablanca in November 1942.

Martin had planned to use Wright R-3350-11 engines in an XA-23 designed for the Army. This project was dropped, but in May 1940 an order had been placed for 400 Martin 187s designed to meet British requirements for increased power and armament. The Lend-Lease Act made available more funds to the British, and 575 more planes were ordered June 17, 1941.

First flown June 14, 1941, the Martin 187B, dubbed the Baltimore, differed from the Maryland by having Wright 1,600-hp R-2600-A5B engines, self-sealing fuel tanks, 211 pounds of armor, and a deeper fuselage for a four-man crew and four 500-pound bombs. Fifty Baltimore I and 100 Baltimore II types had eleven .30-caliber guns; four fixed in

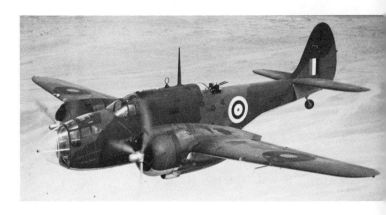

MARTIN BALTIMORE I (187B)
Wright R-2600-19 (A5B), 1600 hp takeoff, 1400 hp at 10,000′
DIMENSIONS: Span 61′4″, Lg. 48′6″, Ht. 11′3″, Wing Area 538.5 sq. ft.
WEIGHT: Empty 15,149 lb., Gross 21,750 lb., Max. 22,958 lb. Fuel 490–980 gal.
PERFORMANCE: Speed—Top 308 mph at 13,000′, 284 mph at s. l., Cruising 230 mph. Service Ceiling 22,300′, Climb 13,130′/7.9 min. Range 1082 miles/1000 lbs. bombs, 2800 miles max.   IWM

the wings, two flexible guns for the upper rear cockpit, another for the ventral spot, and an unusual mounting of four belly guns pointing aft and fixed at an angle 9° down and 1.5° out. Hand-held upper guns were replaced on the 250 Baltimore IIIs by a Boulton Paul power turret with four .30-caliber guns.

By 1941's end, 146 Baltimores had been accepted, but 41 were sunk on torpedoed ships. The original contract for 400 was completed in June 1942, and the first RAF sorties were made on May 23, 1942, in Libya. Messerschmitts downed all four, proving that light bombers still needed fighter escorts.

Known as the A-30 on U.S. records, 281 Baltimore IIIA lend-lease aircraft began appearing in August 1942 with two .50-caliber guns in a Martin power turret replacing the hand-held dorsal guns. They were followed, beginning in January 1943, by 294 Baltimore IVs (A-30A-1/A-30A-5). Six hundred Baltimore Vs (A-30A-10/A-30A-30) with 1,700-hp Wright R-2600-29 Cyclones were ordered September 23, 1942, and delivery began by July 1943. Wing guns were now also of the .50-caliber type.

When production ended in May 1944, 1,575 Baltimores had been built, and all combat missions were flown in the Mediterranean area. Besides the RAF and South African squadrons, Baltimores also served a Greek and a French squadron in 1944, and became the last bomber used by the Italian Air Force when supplied to a unit of the Co-Belligerent Air Force from November 1944 to May 1945.

MARTIN BALTIMORE III   IWM

The Hudsons

Another light bomber built with the attack designation during the war was not intended for ground attack at all but for overwater operations. The twin-engine Hudson had been the Lockheed 14 transport until the British Purchasing Commission came to the United States looking for a twin-engine trainer.

Lockheed quickly put together a military mockup, and offered a specification that was far superior to the current RAF coastal reconnaissance type, so the British ordered 200 on June 23, 1938, and the first Hudson I flew on December 10, 1938. War brought more orders and 351 Hudson Is were built, followed by 20 Hudson IIs, alike except for propellers. The Hudson I (Model 214) had 1,100-hp Wright R-1820-G102A Cyclones and had the tapered wings, twin rudders, and tail-down landing gear of previous Lockheed transports.

Armament of the Hudson I consisted of four 250-pound or ten 100-pound bombs, two fixed .303 Brownings in the nose above the bombardier's windows, and two in the rear Boulton Paul power turret, which was installed after the aircraft reached Britain.

The first Hudsons were shipped to Liverpool by February 1939. Squadron No. 224 was operational in time to become the first RAF pilots to exchange shots with the Luftwaffe on the war's second day. The Hudson's first victory was won against a Do 18 flying boat on November 10, 1939; by April 1940, five Hudson squadrons operated over the North Sea. That month the normal routine of open-sea patrolling was broken by bombing raids against the German invaders of Norway. Hudsons covered the evacuation of Dunkirk in June, even attacking enemy dive bombers. Antisubmarine patrols became the main Hudson mission, but despite installation of the first ASV Mark I radar sets in January 1940, confirmed successes were slow in coming.

Australia had ordered Hudsons with twin-row 1,050-hp Pratt & Whitney SC3G Wasps in December 1938, and delivery began in February 1940. One hundred were shipped to Melbourne and

MARTIN A-30 (BALTIMORE IV)
Wright R-2600-19, 1600 hp takeoff, 1275 hp at 11,500′
DIMENSIONS: Span 61′4″, Lg. 48′6″, Ht. 14′2″, Wing Area 538.5 sq. ft.
WEIGHT: Empty 15,460 lb., Gross 22,600 lb., Max. 27,100 lb. Fuel 490–1440 gal.
PERFORMANCE: Speed—Top 305 mph at 11,500′, Cruising 225 mph, Landing 87 mph. Service Ceiling 23,300′, Climb 10,000′/7 min. Range 800 miles/2000 lbs. bombs, 1100 miles/1000 lbs. bombs, 2800 miles ferry.   AMC

MARTIN A-30A-10
Wright R-2600-29, 1700 hp takeoff, 1450 hp at 12,000′
DIMENSIONS: As A-30
WEIGHT: Empty 15,875 lb., Gross 22,622 lb., Max. 27,850 lb. Fuel 490–1440 gal.
PERFORMANCE: Speed—Top 320 mph at 15,000′, Cruising 224 mph, Landing 87 mph. Service Ceiling 25,000′, Climb 10,000′/4.8 min. Range 920 miles/2000 lbs. bombs, 980 miles/1000 lbs. bombs, 2600 miles ferry.
                    MFR

LOCKHEED HUDSON I
Wright R-1820-G102A, 1100 hp takeoff, 900 hp at 6700′
DIMENSIONS: Span 65′6″, Lg. 44′4″, Ht. 11′10″, Wing Area 551 sq. ft.
WEIGHT: Empty 11,630 lb., Gross 17,500 lb.
PERFORMANCE: Speed—Top 246 mph, Cruising 220 mph, Landing 70 mph. Service Ceiling 25,000′, Absolute Ceiling 26,000′, Climb 2180′/1 min. Range 1960 miles.   SWISHER

listed as Hudson Mark IV by the RAF, which had already ordered the Mark III version. These Australian aircraft faced the Japanese advance in December 1941 and were the first Hudsons heavily engaged in the Pacific.

More powerful Wright G-205A Cyclones, producing 1,200 hp at takeoff, powered the 430 Hudson IIIs that began to appear in August 1940. Labeled Lockheed 414-56s by the company, this model added a retractable ventral gun, provisions for a gun on each side, up to 1,600 pounds of bombs, and extra fuel capacity in the wings. The added tankage enabled the remaining Hudsons for Britain to be delivered by air, beginning with the first transatlantic ferry on November 10, 1940.

With the aid of ASV Mark II radar, antisubmarine patrols became more effective, and on August 27, 1941, an Iceland-based Hudson forced the U-570 to surrender. Fifty-four of the Hudson IIIs went to New Zealand in 1941, and three went to Canada.

Parallel production of Wasp-powered Hudsons for the RAF continued in 1941, along with the Cyclone versions, including 30 Mark IVs (Model 414-08) with the SC3G Wasp and 409 Hudson Vs with 1,200-hp S3C4-G Wasps and the IIIA's armament provisions.

The Lend-Lease Act made American funds available for Allied contracts, which were then given Army aircraft designations. Thus, on May 29, 1941, Defense Aid contract DA 5 ordered 52 A-28 (Mark IVA) Hudsons for Australia with 1,050-hp R-1830-45 Wasps and 417 A-29 (Mark IIIA) Hudsons with 1,200-hp R-1820-87 Cyclones for the RAF. Later contracts added 383 A-29As to the program.

As it happened, the first 20 A-29s went to the U.S. Navy as PBO-1s in October 1942, serving with VP-82 in Newfoundland, the Navy's first landplane patrol squadron. Canada received 133 A-29s, of which 33 began a hazardous trip to China. Army Air Force requisitioned 153 A-29s to fill out its own bomber units for antisubmarine patrols. They were used by the 13th, 30th, and 41st Bomb Groups, as well as by various antisubmarine units. Air Force A-29s usually replaced the power turret with an open pit and a .50-caliber gun. Twenty-four fitted with four cameras for the 1st Mapping Group were redesignated A-29B.

Lend-lease contracts made November 22, 1941, and May 23, 1942, provided 450 A-28A (Hudson VI) models whose 1,200-hp Wasps were designated R-1830-67. Provisions had been made in both the A-28A and A-29A models for conversions to transport work.

Most of these Hudsons went to the RAF, but Australia's Mark IV and IVAs were joined by 106 IIIAs; Canada got three Mark IIIs, 137 IIIAs, 43 Vs, and 36 VIs; and New Zealand got 54 IIIs, 37 IIIAs, and

LOCKHEED HUDSON III
Wright R-1820-G205A, 1200 hp takeoff, 900 hp at 15,200'
DIMENSIONS: As Hudson I
WEIGHT: Empty 12,536 lb., Gross 18,500 lb., Max. 20,000 lb.
PERFORMANCE: Speed—Top 255 mph, Cruising 223 mph. Service Ceiling 24,500'. Range 2160 miles max.   IWM

LOCKHEED HUDSON IV   IWM

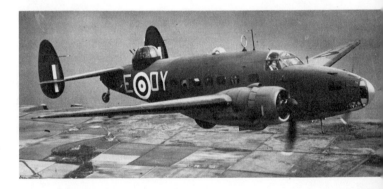

LOCKHEED A-28 (HUDSON V)
Pratt & Whitney R-1830-45, 1050 hp takeoff, 1000 hp at 11,500'
DIMENSIONS: As Hudson I
WEIGHT: Empty 12,810 lb., Gross 18,500 lb., Max. 20,500 lb. Fuel 644 gal.
PERFORMANCE: Speed—Top 260 mph at 12,500', Cruising 206 mph, Landing 68 mph. Service Ceiling 26,000', Climb 10,000'/7.8 min. Range 1500 miles/1400 lbs. bombs, 1800 miles max.   IWM

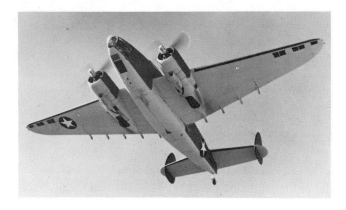

LOCKHEED A-28A (HUDSON VI)
Pratt & Whitney R-1830-67, 1200 hp
DIMENSIONS: Span 65'6", Lg. 44'4", Ht. 11'10", Wing Area
    551 sq. ft.
WEIGHT: Empty 13,195 lb., Gross 18,500 lb., Max. 22,360
    lb. Fuel 644–1028 gal.
PERFORMANCE: Speed—Top 261 mph, Cruising 224 mph,
    Landing 72 mph. Service Ceiling 27,000', Climb 2160'/
    1 min. Range 2160 miles max.   MFR

LOCKHEED A-29 (HUDSON IIIA)
Wright R-1820-87, 1200 hp takeoff, 1000 hp at 14,200'
DIMENSIONS: Span 65'6", Lg. 44'4", Ht. 11'11", Wing Area
    551 sq. ft.
WEIGHT: Empty 12,825 lb., Gross 20,500 lb., Max. 21,300
    lb. Fuel 644–1028 gal.
PERFORMANCE: Speed—Top 253 mph at 15,000', Cruising
    205 mph, Landing 68 mph. Service Ceiling 26,500',
    Climb 10,000'/6.3 min. Range 1550 miles/1400 lbs.
    bombs, 2800 miles max.   MFR

LOCKHEED A-29 with turret   MFR

six Vs. RAF Hudsons joined the 1,000-plane night
raids over Germany in 1942, knocked out three U-
boats near North Africa in November 1942, and
fought over the Bay of Bengal. The Navy's PBO-1
Squadron was responsible for the first two U-boat
sinkings by U.S. forces in March 1942, and an Army
Hudson hit the first U-boat (U-701) destroyed by
the Army Air Forces on July 7, 1942. When the last
A-29A came off the Burbank, California, production
line in May 1943, Lockheed had delivered 2,642
Hudson bombers, plus 300 AT-18 and AT-18A training and target-towing versions, the former with
Martin twin .50-caliber gun turrets.

The Army's Dive Bombers

"Stuka" became a fearful word in 1940, as Junkers
dive bombers smashed ground forces resisting the
Nazi conquest of Europe. American authorities
were startled into the realization that dive attacks
were more accurate than conventional bombing
techniques.

"Can the A-20 bomb from a dive?" asked an official
in June. No, not from angles over 30°, but the Army
might get two-place dive bombers like the Douglas
SBD. Get them, said General Henry H. Arnold, and
in July 1940, 78 were ordered and designated A-24
(SBD-3A).

Delivered from June to October 1941, the A-24s
had a 1,000-hp Wright R-1820-52 and were like the
Navy models except for no deck-landing gear and
a new tailwheel. Armament included 1,200 pounds
of bombs, two .50-caliber nose guns, and twin .30-
caliber flexible guns.

The A-24 two-seaters went to the principal Army
light-bomber station at Savannah, Georgia, where
they equipped three of the four squadrons of the
new 27th Bombardment Group (L) and one squadron of the veteran 3rd Bombardment Group (L).
These groups' other four squadrons had twin-engine A-20A level bombers.

The 27th Group's dive-bomber squadrons were
shipped to the Philippine Islands, but unfortunately the airmen arrived without their aircraft, the
52 A-24s sailing in convoy from Honolulu on November 29, 1941, and then being diverted by the
war to Australia, which they reached December 22.

Some pilots were evacuated to rejoin their aircraft, whose operations were delayed by missing
parts. Eleven A-24s flew up to Java in February
1942 to join a losing fight, and the remainder began
missions from Port Moresby with the 8th Bombardment Squadron on April 1. After five of seven were
lost on the last mission (July 29), these dive bombers were withdrawn from action as too slow, short-
range, and ill-armed. This same type, of course, did
excellent Navy work, but the Air Force was comparing it to land-based twin-engine types.

A new allocation of the Dauntless dive bomber to the Army was made by an April 16, 1942, contract on which deliveries resumed in July 1942 with 90 more A-24s and 170 A-24As (SBD-4A) built by March 1943 at the Douglas El Segundo plant. A 1,200-hp Wright R-1820-60 powered the A-24B (SBD-5), 615 of which were delivered between March and December 1943 from the Douglas factory at Tulsa, Oklahoma.

Thirteen new Army groups were designated as dive-bomber units from July 1942 to August 1943, and ten used A-24s during this period, but the only unit to take them into combat was the 58th Bomb Squadron (Dive) at Wheeler Field, Hawaii. This squadron went to the Gilbert Islands and, redesignated the 531st Fighter-Bomber Squadron, used its A-24Bs to pound Japanese installations in December 1943. Earlier the 407th Bomb Group flew an August 4, 1943, mission against Kiska, but the enemy had already fled that island. Mexico did receive 26 A-24Bs to form a squadron that later turned to P-47s.

The next Navy dive bomber ordered by the Air Force was the Curtiss SB2C-1 (described more fully in Chapter 21). Shortly after the prototype was flown, the Army was allotted 100 as the SB2C-1A (A-25A) on a December 31, 1940, contract. After Pearl Harbor the Navy would need the Curtiss Columbus, Ohio, factory's full output, so a separate production line for the Army was set up in St. Louis. The A-25 specification, dated April 3, 1941, called for a weight of 7,868 pounds empty, 10,982 pounds gross, and 12,175 pounds maximum. So many changes had been made that the weight had increased to 10,363 pounds empty, 15,076 pounds gross, and 17,162 pounds maximum. Expected performance had included a top speed of 313 mph and a service ceiling of 29,000 feet; the A-25A actually

DOUGLAS A-24B (Below)
Wright R-1820-60, 1200 hp takeoff, 900 hp at 14,000'
DIMENSIONS: Span 41'6", Lg. 33', Ht. 12'11", Wing Area 325 sq. ft.
WEIGHT: Empty 6330 lb., Gross 9250 lb., Max. 10,250 (with 1000 lbs. bombs). Fuel 260 gal.
PERFORMANCE: Speed—Top 254 mph at 15,000', Cruising 180 mph, Landing 75 mph. Service Ceiling 27,000', Climb 10,000'/6.1 min. Range 950 miles/1000 lbs. bombs, 1250 miles as scout.   AF

DOUGLAS A-24
Wright R-1820-52, 1000 hp takeoff, 800 hp at 16,000'
DIMENSIONS: Span 41'6", Lg. 32'8", Ht. 12'11", Wing Area 325 sq. ft.
WEIGHT: Empty 6265 lb., Gross 9200 lb., Max. 10,200 lb. Fuel 260 gal.
PERFORMANCE: Speed—Top 250 mph at 17,200', Cruising 173 mph, Landing 75 mph. Service Ceiling 26,000', Climb 10,000'/7 min. Range 950 miles/1000 lbs. bombs, 1300 miles max.   PMB

CURTISS A-25A (SB2C-1A)
Wright R-2600-8, 1700 hp takeoff, 1450 hp at 12,000'
DIMENSIONS: Span 49'9", Lg. 36'8", Ht. 14'9", Wing Area
    422 sq. ft.
WEIGHT: Empty 10,363 lb., Gross 15,076 lb., Max. 17,162
    lb. Fuel 320–566 gal.
PERFORMANCE: Speed—Top 285 mph at 12,400', 269 mph
    at s. l., Cruising 155 mph. Service Ceiling 24,600',
    Climb 1580'/1 min., 10,000'/7.4 min., Range 1130
    miles/1000 lb., 1090 miles/2000 lb., 2020 miles ferry.

AF

had a top speed of 285 mph and a 24,600-foot service ceiling. These figures are presented as an example of what wartime increases in armament, armor, and fuel often cost in performance.

The A-25A was armed with four .50-caliber wing guns, a single .50-caliber flexible rear gun, and one or two 1,000-pound bombs. Underwing racks could carry two 58-gallon drop tanks or 500-pound bombs. Additional protection added under the nose and around the cockpits increased armor weight from 195 pounds on the Navy version to 669 pounds. The Army version had no carrier gear and different wheels than its Navy sisters, and only the first ten had folding wings.

The first A-25A was flown September 29, 1942, but not accepted until December, with the second accepted in January 1943. Before enough for a full Army group were available, the Army decided to replace its two-seat dive bombers with single-seat fighter-bombers, and the A-25As went to second-line duties. Australia was to get 150, but only ten were actually delivered in November 1943. Of 900 built by March 1944, the last 410 went to the Marines and Navy as SB2C-1A operational trainers.

Another dive bomber for the Air Force had originated as a land-based two-seater, the Vultee V-72, ordered for the Royal Air Force in 1940. Contracts were placed for 500 from Vultee and 200 to be built under license by the reorganized Northrop Corporation. Lend-lease contracts on June 28, 1941, added 400 Vultees and 200 more Northrops to these

orders, and gave the V-72 the Army designation A-31. A pre-production prototype was built at Downey, California, first flown March 30, 1941, and christened Vengeance.

The Vengeance used the 1,600-hp Wright R-2600-19 and had odd swept-back wings with lattice dive brakes, armor, and leakproof tanks. Armament included six .30-caliber guns and two 500-pound bombs in an internal bay, with room for two more 250-pound bombs as overload. The four wing guns had 750 rounds each, while 500 rounds were provided for each of the two flexible guns.

Northrop delivered 200 Vengeance I (V-72) and 200 Vengeance IA (A-31-NO) dive bombers to the RAF between January 1942 and April 1943 before that company shifted to P-61 production. Vultee began quantity deliveries from a Nashville, Tennessee, plant in March 1942, and 500 Vengeance IIs (V-72) were followed by 100 Vengeance IIIs (A-31-VN) in 1943. One XA-31A, accepted in June 1942 at Downey without engine or armament for use as an engine test ship for the Pratt & Whitney XR-4360-1, was known as the XA-31B. Five Vultee V-72s modified to test Wright R-3350s with four-bladed propellers for the B-29 program were known as YA-31Cs.

In July 1942, Army pilots recommended that the Vengeance be equipped according to AAF armament standards and given an increased angle of wing incidence. These changes were incorporated in the next 99 ships on the 1941 order, which were designated A-35A and had five .50-caliber guns. The four fixed wing guns had 425 rounds each, and the flexible gun had 400 rounds. Tests on the first

VULTEE V-72 Prototype
Wright GR-2600-A5B-5, 1600 hp takeoff
DIMENSIONS: Span 48', Lg. 39'9", Ht. 15'4", Wing Area
    332 sq. ft.
WEIGHT: Empty 9592 lb., Gross 11,338 lb., Max. 12,939
    lb. Fuel 200–360 gal.
PERFORMANCE: Speed—Top 285 mph at 12,000', 277 mph
    at 3,000', Cruising 237 mph, Landing 82 mph. Service
    Ceiling 25,700'. Climb 8800'/5 min. Range 810 miles/
    1000 lbs. load, 1420 miles max.   MFR

VULTEE VENGEANCE I (V-72-NO)   MFR

VULTEE A-31 (VENGEANCE IA)
Wright R-2600-19, 1600 hp takeoff, 1250 hp at 11,500'
DIMENSIONS: Span 48', Lg. 39'9", Ht. 15'4", Wing Area
    332 sq. ft.
WEIGHT: Empty 9725 lb., Gross 12,940 lb., Max. 14,300
    lb. Fuel 320 gal.
PERFORMANCE: Speed—Top 275 mph at 11,000', Cruising
    235 mph, Landing 80 mph. Service Ceiling 22,500',
    Climb 19,700'/20.4 min. Range 700 miles/1500 lbs.
    bombs, 1400 miles ferry.   MFR

A-35A in September 1942 showed satisfactory
flying traits, and 630 more Vengeances were purchased.

The last model to appear was the A-35B (Vengeance IV) of May 1943, which had a 1,700-hp R-
2600-13, six .50-caliber wing guns, and wing racks
for ferry tanks or two more 500-pound bombs. When
Vengeance production ended on June 6, 1944, 1,931
had been built, including 831 A-35Bs. The RAF
received 1,205 Vengeances but limited their combat
use to the Burma front, where four squadrons began
combat missions on March 19, 1943. They were
joined by two Indian Air Force squadrons, and operations continued until July 16, 1944. Later many
Mark IVs served as target-tow aircraft.

At least 122 Northrop-built V-72s were used by
the United States in 1942 for three of the newly
organized dive-bomber groups, while two more
groups got A-31s and two had A-35 Vengeances to
replace their A-24s. All of the groups trained in the
United States on the Vengeance, but got single-seaters before the end of 1943. Australia received 221
V-72/A-31, 23 A-35A, and 98 A-35B models, and
flew dive-bombing missions against Japanese-held
island bases from June 18, 1943, to March 8, 1944.
Brazil also got 29 A-35Bs, and about 50 were given
to the Free French in September 1943.

The disappearance of two-seat dive bombers from
AAF combat groups can be attributed to the greater
success of single-seat fighter-bombers in the same
mission. Bomb-equipped fighters like the A-36 and
P-47 had much better performance, proved excellent for close support, and could take care of their
own defense after their bombs had been dropped.

VULTEE VENGEANCE II (V-72-VN)   MFR

Officials in the United States did not anticipate the
lack of demand for the Vengeance planes, and their
continued production was criticized as a "shining
example of the waste . . . caused by pressure for
sheer numbers of planes not actually needed at the
front."

Three groups formerly using the Vengeance two-
seaters went into combat with the single-seat North
American A-36A. These were actually P-51 Mustang fighters begun on April 16, 1942, that had been
completed as dive bombers. Five hundred were

VULTEE A-35A-1
Wright R-2600-19, 1600 hp takeoff, 1275 hp at 11,500′
DIMENSIONS: As A-31
WEIGHT: Empty 10,060 lb., Gross 13,500 lb., Max. 15,600
  lb. Fuel 300 gal.
PERFORMANCE: Speed—Top 273 mph at 11,000′, Cruising
  235 mph, Landing 83 mph. Service Ceiling 21,500′,
  Climb 15,000′/12.8 min. Range 600 miles/2000 lbs.
  bombs, 1250 miles ferry.   PMB

VULTEE A-35B
Wright R-2600-13, 1700 hp takeoff, 1350 hp at 13,000′
DIMENSIONS: As A-31
WEIGHT: Empty 10,300 lb., Gross 16,400 lb., Max. 17,100
  lb. Fuel 300–625 gal.
PERFORMANCE: Speed—Top 279 mph at 13,500′, Cruising
  230 mph, Landing 84 mph. Service Ceiling 22,300′,
  Climb 15,000/11.3 min. Range 550 miles/1000 lbs.
  bombs, 2300 miles max.   AF

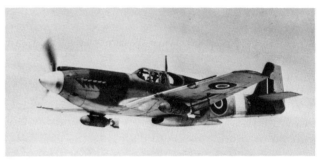

NORTH AMERICAN A-36A as Mustang IA   IWM

NORTH AMERICAN A-36A
Allison V-1710-87, 1325 hp at 3000′, 1500 hp at 5400′ WE
DIMENSIONS: Span 37′, Lg. 32′3″, Ht. 12′2″, Wing Area
  233 sq. ft.
WEIGHT: Empty 6610 lb., Gross 8370 lb., Max. 10,000 lb.
  Fuel 105–80 gal.
PERFORMANCE: Speed—Top 310 mph at 5000′/two 500-lb.
  bombs, 366 mph clean, Cruising 250 mph, Landing 85
  mph. Service Ceiling 25,100′ (bombs), 27,000′. Range
  550 miles/two 500-lb. bombs, 2300 miles ferry.   AF

accepted between October 1942 and March 1943,
with a 1,325-hp Allison V-1710-87, six .50-caliber
guns, wing racks for two 500-pound bombs, and
dive brakes under the wings.

Combat missions against Italy were begun from
Tunisia on June 6, 1943, by the 27th Fighter-
Bomber Group, joined by the A-36As of the 86th
Fighter-Bomber Group in July. They flew 23,373
sorties and dropped over 16,000 bombs before
being replaced by P-47s in 1944. In India the A-
36A was operated by the 311th Fighter-Bomber
Group. They were the only liquid-cooled attack aircraft and the last dive bombers used in the war by
the Army Air Force. Their success demonstrated
the value of single-seat fighter-bombers and led to
widespread use of later P-51 and P-47 models on
close-support missions.

The Douglas Invader

As thousands of Havocs rolled out of the plant,

Douglas, in January 1941, began designing a better and larger light bomber with twice the A-20's bomb load and defensive firepower. The resulting design by E. H. Heinemann was the A-26 Invader, the last propeller-driven twin-engine bomber in production for the Air Force.

Contracts were placed on June 2, 1941, for prototypes and on October 31 for the first 500 production aircraft. The first XA-26 flew July 10, 1942 as a three-place monoplane with two 2,000-hp R-2800-27 Wasps, tricycle gear, and wings with a low-drag laminar-flow airfoil and double-slotted flaps. It had a transparent bombardier's nose, 4,000 pounds of bombs, and six .50-caliber guns. Two guns were fixed in the nose, two in a top turret, and two in a lower rear turret. The turret guns were aimed through periscopic sights and remote controls in the rear cockpit.

Night-fighter equipment was installed on the second prototype, the XA-26A, with radar nose, four 20-mm fixed guns in a belly tray, and a top turret with four .50-caliber guns. The success of Northrop's P-61 made this version superfluous, however. The third prototype was the XA-26B, which had a 75-mm T-7 cannon on the right side of a short, solid nose and four .50-caliber guns paired in turrets.

The large propeller spinners on the prototypes were dropped from the production A-26Bs built at Long Beach. The first of five A-26B-1-DL Invaders appeared in September 1943. Fifteen A-26B-5s that followed had minor changes and eliminated the camouflage formerly customary on bombers. These models both had the 75-mm gun in the nose with two .50-caliber guns on the left side, but a new all-purpose nose was installed on later aircraft, beginning with the A-26B-10 of March 1944.

Several gun arrangements were now possible: two 37-mm and four .50-caliber; one 37-mm and one 75-mm; or one 75-mm and two .50-caliber guns. But the usual arrangement actually installed was six .50-caliber nose guns, with 400 rounds per gun, along with the usual guns paired in the two turrets with 500 rounds each. The bomb bay could accommodate six 500-pound or four 1,000-pound bombs. Beginning with the A-26B-15, fixtures under the wings could accommodate eight more .50-caliber guns or four more 500-pound bombs. Five aircraft from the A-26B-15-DL line were finished as A-26C-DL bombers with transparent nose enclosures and two nose guns.

While the first 500 Invaders (up to A-26B-40-DL) rolled out of Long Beach, a parallel production line was established at Tulsa, Oklahoma, for 500 aircraft ordered March 17, 1943, the first appearing in January 1944. Of these, 205 were delivered as A-26B-5 to A-26B-25-DT models and the rest as A-26C-15 to A-26C-25-DT with glazed noses. On most of

DOUGLAS XA-26
Pratt & Whitney R-2800-27, 2000 hp takeoff, 1600 hp at 13,500'
DIMENSIONS: Span 70', Lg. 51'2", Ht. 18'6", Wing Area 540 sq. ft.
WEIGHT: Empty 21,150 lb., Gross 31,000 lb. Fuel 830–1050 gal.
PERFORMANCE: Speed—Top 370 mph at 17,000', Cruising 212 mph, Landing 100 mph. Service Ceiling 31,300', Climb 20,000'/10.2 min. Range 1800 miles/3000 lbs. bombs, 2500 miles ferry.   AF

DOUGLAS XA-26A
Pratt & Whitney R-2800-27, 2000 hp takeoff
DIMENSIONS: Span 70', Lg. 52'5", Wing Area 540 sq. ft.
WEIGHT: Empty 20,794 lb., Gross 25,300 lb., Max. 28,893 lb. Fuel 440–800 gal.
PERFORMANCE: Speed—Top 365 mph at 17,000', Cruising 264 mph. Service Ceiling 25,900', Climb 20,000'/10.5 min. Range 700 miles normal, 1420 miles max.   MFR

DOUGLAS XA-26B
Pratt & Whitney R-2800-27, 2000 hp takeoff, 1600 hp at 13,500'
DIMENSIONS: Span 70', Lg. 50', Wing Area 540 sq. ft.
WEIGHT: Empty 20,225 lb., Gross 28,855 lb. Fuel 440–800 gal.
PERFORMANCE: Speed—Top 359 mph at 16,000'. Service Ceiling 25,700'. Range 695 miles normal, 1260 miles max.   MFR

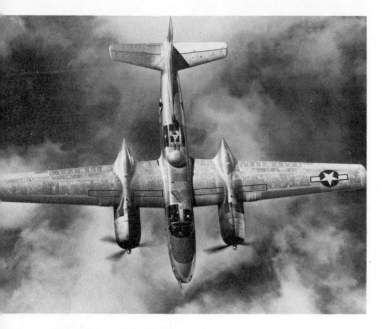

DOUGLAS A-26B-10
Pratt & Whitney R-2800-27 or -71, 2000 hp takeoff, 1600 hp at 13,500'
DIMENSIONS: Span 70', Lg. 50', Ht. 18'6", Wing Area 540 sq. ft.
WEIGHT: Empty 22,370 lb., Gross 35,000 lb. Fuel 925–1600 gal.
PERFORMANCE: Speed—Top 355 mph at 15,000', Cruising 284 mph, Landing 100 mph. Service Ceiling 22,100', Climb 10,000'/8.1 min. Range 1400 miles/4000 lbs. bombs, 3200 miles ferry.   MFR

DOUGLAS B-26B-66
Pratt & Whitney R-2800-79, 2000 hp takeoff, 2360 hp WE
DIMENSIONS: As A-26B-10
WEIGHT: Empty 22,362 lb., Gross 40,015 lb., Combat 31,725 lb. Fuel 1360–2055 lb.
PERFORMANCE: Speed—Top 371 mph at 10,000', 360 mph at s. l., Cruising 230 mph, Landing 113 mph. Service Ceiling 19,200', Combat Ceiling 21,800', Climb 2515'/1 min. Range 966 miles/4000 lb., 3354 miles ferry.   ARNOLD

these the engine model was the R-2800-71, with a new ignition system.

A new production contract for over 5,000 Invaders was approved March 29, 1944, and the first appeared in January 1945 as the A-26B-45-DL, introducing the R-2800-79 water-injection engine yielding 2,350-hp war-emergency power. Beginning with B-26B-50-DL, 14 5-inch rockets could be carried under the wings and six .50-caliber guns were mounted within the wings. Additional range could be attained from two 155-gallon external wing tanks, or a 125-gallon tank could replace the lower gun turret. Parallel changes were made on the A-26C line at Tulsa. The last batch of A-26Bs got eight .50-caliber nose guns, bringing the total to 14 fixed guns.

Invader production ended at Long Beach in September 1945 after 655 B-26B-45/-66-DLs had been built to that contract, and at Tulsa in August after 791 more B-26C-30/-55-DTs had been manufactured. Altogether, Douglas had made 2,451 Invaders, with wartime cancellations eliminating the proposed A-26D and E models.

One XA-26D-DL was completed with R-2800-83 Wasps in 1945. Another A-26B was delivered after the war as the XA-26F, in which an I-16 jet engine and 125 gallons of jet fuel replaced a B-26B's rear gunner and turret. The jet intake was atop the fuselage and the exhaust was in the tail. Two 2,100-hp R-2800-83 Wasps turned four-bladed props, and although no rear guns were carried, eight nose and six wing .50-caliber guns were retained. In June 1946 the XA-26F averaged 413 mph over a 621-mile course. One B-26B was fitted with a 105-mm T7 gun and 30-round automatic feed and ground tested in 1945.

DOUGLAS A-26C-50 (B-26C)
Pratt & Whitney R-2800-79, 2000 hp takeoff, 2360 hp WE
DIMENSIONS: Span 70', Lg. 51'3", Ht. 18'6", Wing Area 540 sq. ft.
WEIGHT: Empty 22,690 lb., Gross 37,740 lb., Combat 29,920 lb. Fuel 1235–1910 gal.
PERFORMANCE: Speed—Top 372 mph at 10,000', 361 mph at s. l., Cruising 226 mph, Stalling 109 mph. Service Ceiling 20,450', Combat Ceiling 23,100', Climb 2745'/1 min. Combat Radius 892 miles/4000 lbs. bombs, 3267 miles ferry.   PMB

DOUGLAS XA-26F   PMB

Combat began for the Invader after it reached the Ninth Air Force in Britain. The 416th Bomb Group flew the first mission November 17, 1944, its B-26Bs led on a medium-altitude bombing strike by glazed-nosed A-20Ks, since A-26Cs had not yet arrived. By January 23, 1945, the 409th Bomb Group joined the effort, making the first low-level attacks by Ninth Air Force bombers in Europe since 1943.

Two more A-26 groups, the 386th and 391st, joined the fighting by April, with the final mission by 124 A-26s and eight B-26s on May 3, 1945. The RAF was also to get 140 Invaders, but Germany's collapse canceled that program after two A-26C-25s were delivered for evaluation. Air Force A-26s flew 11,567 sorties in the European war.

The 47th Bomb Group in Italy also received some A-26s in 1945 but returned to the United States in July for specialized training in night attacks. While it did not go into combat again, its black-painted B-26Cs equipped with radar served the group until they were replaced by B-45s in 1948. In the Pacific the veteran 3rd Bomb Group converted from A-20s to A-26s and they bombed for the Fifth Air Force from July 9 to August 12, 1945, while the 319th Bomb Group used A-26s in the Seventh Air Force.

After the war the 3rd Bomb Group was stationed in Japan with the occupation forces. After 1948 it was the only light-bomber group left in the Air Force. Concentrating on its strategic mission, the USAF had built no light bombers after the war, and had even dropped the A designation for attack bombers in June 1948, changing the Douglas Invaders from A-26s to B-26s. Many were relegated to noncombat duties; for example, 142 A-26Cs became the Navy's JD-1 and JD-1D target-towing and drone control planes, redesignated UB-26J and DB-26J in 1962.

Yet the Douglas had more wars to fight. When the Korean War began, there were 1,054 B-26s in the USAF inventory. All were in reserve units or storage except for 26 B-26Bs in Japan with the 3rd Bombardment Wing (L), and 46 RB-26C night-reconnaissance aircraft serving with Tactical Reconnaissance wings (TRW).

The first American bombing mission into Korea was flown by 12 3rd Bomb Wing B-26Bs on June 28, 1950, against railways supplying enemy forces, and the following day 18 B-26Bs struck the first blow into North Korea itself with a successful attack on the principal enemy air base. This same unit dropped the last American bombs in Korea on July 27, 1953; an RB-26C flew the last combat sortie of the Korean War the same evening. In between those dates 60,096 B-26 and 11,944 RB-26 sorties were made, the majority at night, with 226 aircraft lost, including 56 to enemy action. In 1954 there were four B-26 and two RB-26 active wings in the USAF. By 1956 they were replaced by B-57 and RB-66 jets.

Another war was going on at the same time in Vietnam, and the Douglas was sent there to serve with the French. On January 1, 1951, GB1/19 was formed with 17 B-26B and eight B-26C bombers. It was soon joined by four RB-26C Invaders of a reconnaissance unit. By July 1954, 111 B-26s had been received, but a French defeat at Dien Bien Phu halted the fighting and a cease-fire was signed on July 27.

French B-26s found themselves at war again in Algeria, where by 1960 they were being used by escadrons 91 EB and ER 32 (RB-26). This war went on until 1962, by which time a few B-26s had seen action in Cuba during the Bay of Pigs incident. Saudi Arabia's first combat planes were nine B-26Bs received in 1955, when Peru also acquired eight B-26Cs, while Brazil acquired about 30 B-26s in 1957. Chile received four B-26Bs and 34 B-26Cs beginning in 1957. Other countries getting surplus B-26s included Cuba (18), Colombia (19), and Nicaragua (6).

Four USAF RB-26s joined the "Farm Gate" detachment in Vietnam in December 1961, and in January 1963, ten B-26Bs and two more RB-26s began arriving. They served the 1st Air Commando Squadron on attack missions until February 11, 1964, when all the B-26s were grounded because of in-flight structural failures due to age. Portugal received seven B-26Bs in 1965 for use in Angola, but further deliveries by a private arms dealer were stopped by the U.S. Government.

On Mark Engineering, a firm experienced in modification of B-26s to custom executive transports, had started modification of a YB-26K COIN prototype in October 1962. First flown January 28, 1963, it had completely rebuilt wings and fuselage, 2,500-hp water-injection Pratt & Whitney R-2800-103W engines with reversible propellers, eight wing pylons, and 14 fixed guns, but it omitted turrets.

Forty more conversions were ordered in November 1963, the first B-26K flying May 26, 1964. Sim-

ON MARK YB-26K prototype   MFR

ON MARK B-26K (A-26A)
Pratt & Whitney R-2800-52W, 2500 hp takeoff, 1750 hp at
    15,000′
DIMENSIONS: Span 71′6″, Lg. 51′7″, Ht. 19′, Wing Area
    541 sq. ft.
WEIGHT: Empty 25,130 lb., Gross 38,314 lb., Max. 39,250
    lb., Combat 30,809 lb. Fuel 1230–2365 gal.
PERFORMANCE: Speed—Top 323 mph at 15,000′, 291 mph
    at s. l., Cruising 169 mph, Stalling 114 mph. Service
    Ceiling 28,600′, Combat Ceiling 24,400′. Climb 2050′/
    1 min. Combat Radius 700 miles/3518 lb. Ferry Range
    2700 miles.   MFR

ilar to the YB model except for the elimination of
prop spinners and six wing guns, the B-26K was
armed with eight .50-caliber nose guns and 4,000
pounds of bombs or stores in the bay, plus up to
8,000 pounds on the wing pylons. Besides the fixed-
wing tip tanks, two 230-gallon drop tanks or a 675-
gallon bay tank could be carried.

This version could also be converted into an RB-
26K camera plane by installation of a glazed nose
and removable bomb bay system of four cameras
and flash ejectors. These remodeled aircraft went
to the 1st Air Commando Wing.

In 1967 B-26K aircraft were redesignated A-26A,
supposedly because bombers could not, by treaty,
be stationed in Thailand at that time. The A-26As

had come to Thailand in June 1966 with the 609th
Special Operations Squadron (originally the 606th
Air Commando). Operating with 18 aircraft on night
interdiction missions against trucks on the Ho Chi
Minh Trail, the squadron made the last American
combat sorties with the Douglas on November 9,
1969. Nearly 25 years had passed since the first
major A-26 combat mission, but one A-26K squadron still remained in Zaire's air force.

Attack Prototypes, 1943–44

The Brewster XA-32 was the only plane built by
that company for the Air Force, and was the first
single-seat attack monoplane. A midwing, barrel-
shaped monoplane with wide-track mainwheels retracting into the wings and a fixed tail wheel, the
XA-32 had a 2,100-hp Pratt & Whitney R-2800-37
Wasp and a four-bladed propeller. Heavy armor and
increased speed was expected to conpensate for the
lack of a gunner.

The design was proposed on April 15, 1941, and
two prototypes were ordered on October 31, 1941.
When the mockup was inspected in May 1942, Ma-
teriel Command officers considered the A-32 the
"most desirable" dive-bomber design available and
a possible replacement for the A-25. But in June it
was realized that the prototype would be delayed
long past the September 1942 date scheduled, and
Brewster was, in any case, too tied up by Navy
orders to undertake new production. Immediate requirements for dive bombers were then met by
ordering the P-51 Mustang's attack version, the A-
36A, and the Vultee A-35B.

The Brewster did not begin flight tests until May
22, 1943, and then went to Eglin Field, Florida, for
operational-suitability trials. Armament on the XA-

BREWSTER XA-32
Pratt & Whitney R-2800-37, 2100 hp takeoff, 1600 hp at
    13,500′
DIMENSIONS: Span 45′1″, Lg. 40′7″, Ht. 12′8″, Wing Area
    425 sq. ft.
WEIGHT: Empty 11,820 lb., Gross 15,512 lb., Max. 19,960
    lb. Fuel 200–530 gal.
PERFORMANCE: Speed—Top 311 mph at 13,200′, 279 mph
    at s. l., Cruising 236 mph, Landing 75 mph. Service
    Ceiling 26,000′, Climb 10,000′/5.7 min. Range 500
    miles/3000 lbs. bombs, 1600 miles max.   MFR

32 consisted of four 20-mm guns with 120 rpg in the wings, along with six .50-caliber guns with 400 rpg. Four 37-mm guns were provided on the second prototype, the XA-32A. An internal bomb bay accommodated 1,000 pounds, with another 1,000-pound bomb under each wing.

Tests showed that the Brewster's speed and range fell below expectations, and below the standard A-20's capabilities. While flying qualities were satisfactory and armor protection (650-pounds) good, performance was not suitable for operations and development ended. Brewster was assigned the A-34 designation in May 1942 for lend-lease documentation of the Bermuda dive bombers for the RAF, but these aircraft were not used by the Army. (They are described together with the Navy's SB2A series in Chapter 21.)

Two engines were used on the rather mysterious Hughes XA-37, an aircraft which, as of this writing, has had no published photograph. The project began with a company proposal, on December 5, 1939, for a twin-boom bomber powered by two projected liquid-cooled Wright Tornado engines and built of Duramold, a process involving heat-bonded wood and plastic. Pratt & Whitney R-2800-49 Wasps replaced the Tornado when that engine failed to materialize.

In June 1942 the Hughes D-2A was designated XA-37 by the Air Force and a prototype was built at company expense. Like the all-wood de Havilland Mosquito bomber whose performance it was expected to exceed, the Hughes D-2A had no guns. This two-seater had a 60-feet, 6-inch span, 31,672 pounds of gross weight, and was expected to have a 433-mph top speed and a 1,000-mile range with 2,200 pounds of bombs.

Howard Hughes himself flew the aircraft on June 20, 1943, at an isolated California location, but the aircraft was never tested by the Air Force before it was destroyed in a hangar fire. So successful was the shroud of secrecy imposed by Mr. Hughes that no photographs or descriptions were released to the public, although the design was later developed into the XF-11 reconnaissance plane of 1946. Over 30 years passed before research by Walter Boyne revealed the foregoing information.

The next attack type actually began as a twin-engine two-place fighter designed to destroy bombers with an automatic 75-mm gun. Since another aircraft for that purpose was already under way (the stillborn Curtiss XP-71), the two prototypes of the Beech Model 28 were ordered as XA-38 attack planes on September 23, 1942.

BEECH XA-38
Wright R-3350-53, 2700 hp takeoff to 2800'
DIMENSIONS: Span 67'4", Lg. 51'9", Ht. 13'6", Wing Area 626 sq. ft.
WEIGHT: Empty 22,480 lb., Design Gross 29,900 lb., Max. 32,000 lb. Fuel 825–1425 gal.
PERFORMANCE: Speed—Top 376 mph at 4800', Cruising 344 mph, Landing 103 mph. Service Ceiling 27,800', Climb 10,000'/5 min. Range 1070 miles/2000 lbs. bombs, 1960 miles ferry.   MFR

Flown May 7, 1944, the XA-38 was a two-place low-wing monoplane with two Wright R-3350-43 Cyclones, twin rudders, tail-down landing gear, and external studs for 2,000 pounds of bombs. The rear-gun arrangement was like the A-26s: two pairs of .50-caliber guns in upper and lower remote-control turrets. The nose, however, was as individual as a swordfish's; the long barrel of a 75-mm cannon protruded far beyond the pair of .50s in the bow. Twenty rounds of ammunition were fed to the big gun by automatic loading, and 3,000 rounds were carried for the machine guns.

Delayed by the lack of availability of engines, also needed for the B-29 program, the A-38 never reached production, although it had good flying qualities.

Meanwhile, development proceeded on a trio of heavily armed single-seat, single-engine monoplanes with large internal bomb bays. They were halfway between the single-seat fighter and the two-seat dive bomber, and were close to the bomber-torpedo single-seaters developed for the Navy.

First were the Kaiser-Fleetwings XA-39 and Curtiss XA-40, neither of which got past the mockup stage. The former was to have used a 2,000-hp R-2800-27, and had two 37-mm and four .50-caliber wing guns. A 2,300-hp R-3350-8 was planned for the XA-40, which was a torpedo dive bomber similar to the Navy XSB3C-1. Both designs had room in their internal bays for either a 1,000-pound bomb or a 2,000-pound torpedo, and external wing racks for two 500-pound bombs.

More progress was made on the XA-41, which was begun in September 1942 as the Vultee 90, ordered November 10, 1942, and first flown February 11, 1944. Powered by the big new 3,000-hp XR-4360-9 tested on the XA-31B, the XA-41 had four 37-mm and four .50-caliber guns in the wings, with 50 and 600 rounds per gun, respectively. The internal bomb bay normally carried 3,000 pounds, but the aircraft could accommodate a torpedo, four 1,600-pound bombs, or extra fuel tanks. The wing

had a straight leading edge, tapered trailing edge, and an 8° dihedral.

Flight tests showed much promise, but in 1944 close-support bombing for the Army seemed well provided for by the P-47 Thunderbolt's fighter-bomber operations, with the A-26 coming along for heavier attacks. Only one XA-41 was built, and was the last new Army Air Force type flown with an attack designation.

Although four other designs were allotted attack designations during the war, none were completed in that class. The twin-engine Douglas XA-42 was redesignated XB-42, while the Curtiss jet-propelled XA-43 developed into the XP-87. Convair's strange canard jet XA-44 became the XB-53, while Martin's XA-45 jet was completed as the XA-51.

CONSOLIDATED-VULTEE XA-41
Pratt & Whitney XR-4360-9, 3000 hp takeoff, 2400 hp at 13,500'
DIMENSIONS: Span 54', Lg. 48'8", Ht. 14'6", Wing Area 540 sq. ft.
WEIGHT: Empty 13,400 lb., Gross 18,800 lb., Max. 23,260 lb. Fuel 350–445 gal. (1140 gal. ferry)
PERFORMANCE: Speed—Top 353 mph at 15,500', Cruising 270 mph, Landing 74 mph. Service Ceiling 27,000', Climb 10,000'/4.3 min. Range 950 miles/3000 lbs. bombs.   MFR

Chapter 14
Bomber Monoplanes, 1931–39

An opportunity to improve on the old Keystone biplane bombers appeared when the new, fast twin-engine monoplanes originally designed for long-range Army observation missions were adapted to short-range bombers. The Fokker XO-27 and Douglas XO-35 were the monoplanes projected, and in 1929 it was decided to complete the second prototype of each as a day bomber.

Both aircraft were three-place high-wing monoplanes whose main landing wheels retracted back into the nacelles behind 600-hp Curtiss Conqueror engines, and both were armed with 1,200 pounds of bombs and a flexible .30-caliber Browning in the front and rear cockpits. The first bomber to appear with retractable wheels was the Fokker XB-8, ordered June 19, 1929, and delivered to Wright Field in February 1931 with a straight, all-wood, cantilever wing and fabric-covered steel-tubed fuselage.

The Douglas XB-7, however, had the engines below gulled fabric-covered wings braced by metal struts, and had a corrugated aluminum fuselage. Ordered April 14, 1930, the XB-7 was completed in Santa Monica, California in June 1931. Seven Y1B-7 bombers and five Y1O-35 observation types were ordered for service tests, and the first Y1B-7 was completed in September 1932 with three-bladed propellers on its 675-hp engines, a smooth-skinned monocoque fuselage, and an armament of two .30-caliber flexible guns and two 624-pound bombs. The Douglas monoplanes served the 31st Bomb Squadron at March Field.

Monoplanes built entirely of metal, including the skin, were operating successfully on airlines and suggested themselves as bombers. A bomber version of Ford's famous trimotor was tested by the Army in June 1931. A high-wing monoplane with antidrag rings on three 500-hp R-1340-E radials, the Ford XB-906 was like the "Tin Goose" transport except for bombardier's windows behind the front engine, a bay for 2,000 pounds of bombs, a front

FOKKER XB-8
Curtiss V-1570-23, 600 hp
DIMENSIONS: Span 64′, Lg. 47′, Ht. 11′6″, Wing Area 619 sq. ft.
WEIGHT: Empty 6861 lb., Gross 10,545 lb. Fuel 209.5 gal.
PERFORMANCE: Speed—Top 160 mph.   MFR

DOUGLAS XB-7
Curtiss V-1570-25, 600 hp
DIMENSIONS: Span 65′, Lg. 45′6″, Ht. 11′7″, Wing Area 621 sq. ft.
WEIGHT: Empty 6865 lb., Gross 10,537 lb., Max. 11,287 lb. Fuel 200–300 gal.
PERFORMANCE: Speed—Top 169 mph at s. l., 165.5 mph at 5000′, Cruising 147 mph, Landing 66 mph. Service Ceiling 18,950′, Absolute Ceiling 20,600′, Climb 1220′/ 1 min., 5000′/4.7 min.   MFR

DOUGLAS YB-7
Curtiss V-1570-27, 675 hp at s. l.
DIMENSIONS: Span 65'3", Lg. 46'7", Ht. 12'1", Wing Area
    621 sq. ft.
WEIGHT: Empty 7519 lb., Gross 9953 lb., Max. 11,177 lb.
    Fuel 200–300 gal.
PERFORMANCE: Speed—Top 182 mph at s. l., 177 mph at
    5000', Cruising 158 mph, Landing 78 mph. Service
    Ceiling 20,400', Absolute Ceiling 21,800', Climb 5000'/
    3.7 min. Range 411 miles/1200 lbs. bombs, 632 miles
    max.   AF

FORD XB-906
Pratt & Whitney R-1340E, 500 hp at 7000'
DIMENSIONS: Span 77'11", Lg. 51'6", Ht. 13'8", Wing Area
    835 sq. ft.
WEIGHT: Empty 8345 lb., Gross 14,137 lb. Fuel 325 gal.
PERFORMANCE: Speed—Top 145 mph at s. l., 142 mph at
    5000', Cruising 135 mph, Landing 66 mph. Service
    Ceiling 18,400', Absolute Ceiling 20,000', Climb 775'/
    1 min., 7000'/11.9 min.   AF

gun ring above and behind the pilot, and top and
tunnel rear guns. Wheel pants did not compensate
enough for the landing gear's drag, and performance was far below that of new types with retractable gear. An Army board inspecting the XB-906
reported that the front gun could not be handled in
the propeller slipstream and coverage of the rear
guns was inadequate. On September 19, 1931, the
XB-906 failed to recover from a dive, killing two
company pilots.

Even less progress was made by the Keystone
XB-908, designed as an all-metal low-wing monoplane with retractable wheels and two Curtiss V-
1570 Conquerors. A mockup was inspected in April
1931, but neither the Army nor the company chose
to finance the project further. When production of
older Keystone biplanes ended in 1932, the Bristol,
Pennsylvania, factory closed, and unemployment
hurt the Bucks County community. A senator was
asked to intercede for Army contracts, but new
Boeing and Martin designs eclipsed competition
and the company suffered the penalty of inadequate
technical advances.

Boeing's aggressive design staff had developed in
1930 an all-metal low-wing transport with retractable wheels called the Monomail. The same princi-
ples were next applied to a twin-engine bomber
built as a private venture and labeled XB-901. First
flown on April 13, 1931, the XB-901 had 575-hp
Pratt & Whitney commercial engines and a top
speed of 163 mph at sea level. The crew sat in four
separate open cockpits along the narrow fuselage.

Excellent flying qualities won an Army contract
on August 21, 1931, for the prototype and six ser-

BOEING XB-901 (YB-9)
Pratt & Whitney R-1830-13, 575 hp at s. l. (R-1830-11,
    600 hp at 6000')
DIMENSIONS: Span 76'9", Lg. 51'6", Ht. 12'8", Wing Area
    954 sq. ft.
WEIGHT: Empty 7650 lb. (8362 lb.), Gross 12,663 lb.
    (13,351 lb.). Fuel 250–308 gal.
PERFORMANCE: Speed—Top 163 mph at s. l., 158 mph at
    5000' (188 mph at 6000'), Cruising 137 mph (165 mph),
    Landing 62 mph (63 mph). Service Ceiling 19,400'
    (22,600'), Absolute Ceiling 21,700' (24,400'), Climb
    950'/1 min. (1060'/1 min.), 5000'/6 min. Range (495
    miles/1997 lbs. bombs).   MFR

vice-test models. Refitted with Hornets supercharged to yield 600 hp at 6,000 feet and three-
bladed propellers, the prototype was designated
YB-9 and did 188 mph at that altitude during January 1932 tests. Armament included a ton of bombs
and a .30-caliber gun in the front and rear cockpits.

The second example was flown November 13,
1931, with Curtiss V-1570-29 Conquerors, the last
inline engines to be used on an Army bomber for
over 11 years. The top speed of the Y1B-9 was only

173 mph. The remaining five ships, designated Y1B-9A and completed with R-1860-11 Hornets, did 188 mph clean and 186 mph with an external bomb load of two 1,130-pound bombs. The first Y1B-9A was flown July 14, 1932, and served with its later sisters at Langley Field with the 2nd Bomb Group, getting a modified rudder in 1933.

Boeing's bomber was a tremendous achievement, offering speeds more than 50 percent higher than that of the Keystones built at the same time. With bomber speed now comparable to that of the pursuit ships, defense problems became much greater than in the days of the biplane. Boeing's metal monoplane became the parent of the bombers that fought the next war. But the B-9 itself was not built in quantity, for a new machine even more advanced in scope eclipsed it and became the first American-built bomber to take part in actual warfare.

The Martin Bomber

Between the biplanes of the 1920s and the heavily armed monoplanes of World War II, the most important American bomber was the Martin B-10 series. While retaining the modest armament and range of its elders, it suddenly displayed speeds

faster than the biplane fighters designed to catch it.

The Army saw the bomber's role at that time as one of coastal defense. This had been formalized by the MacArthur-Pratt agreement of January 9, 1931, between the Army's Chief of Staff and the Chief of Naval Operations, which assigned Army air forces to defense of homeland and overseas coasts while naval air forces would be free to move with the fleet on offensive missions. This arrangement continued the old tradition of concentrating Army efforts on coastal fortifications while the Navy would be the first offensive force. Seen from this perspective, the Army bombers were essentially long-range coast guns.

The Martin Aircraft Company's Model 123 was developed in response to Air Corps pressure for a midwing, all-metal monoplane. The monocoque fu-

BOEING Y1B-9
Curtiss V-1570-29, 600 hp at s. l.
DIMENSIONS: As YB-9
WEIGHT: Empty 8618 lb., Gross 13,591 lb. Fuel 263–308 gal.
PERFORMANCE: Speed—Top 173 mph at s. l., 171.5 mph at 5000', Cruising 151 mph, Landing 62 mph. Service Ceiling 19,200', Absolute Ceiling 21,000', Climb 1160'/1 min.   AMC

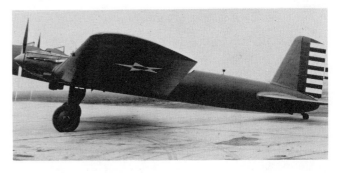

BOEING Y1B-9A (Y1P-26 in background)
Pratt & Whitney R-1860-11, 600 hp at 6000'
DIMENSIONS: Span 76'10", Lg. 52', Ht. 12', Wing Area 954 sq. ft.
WEIGHT: Empty 8941 lb., Gross 13,932 lb., Max. 14,320 lb. Fuel 263–504 gal.
PERFORMANCE: Speed—Top 188 mph at 6000', Cruising 165 mph, Landing 67 mph. Service Ceiling 20,750', Absolute Ceiling 22,500', Climb 900'/1 min., 5000'/7.1 min. Range 540 miles/2260 lbs. bombs, 990 miles max.   MFR

MARTIN XB-907
Wright SR-1820E, 600 hp at 6000'
DIMENSIONS: Span 62'2", Lg. 46'2", Ht. 12'8", Wing Area 551 sq. ft.
WEIGHT: Empty 6978 lb., Gross 10,580 lb. Fuel 200–300 gal.
PERFORMANCE: Speed—Top 197 mph at 6000', 190 mph at s. l., Cruising 171 mph, Landing 91.5 mph. Service Ceiling 20,000', Absolute Ceiling 21,600', Climb 1600'/1 min. Range 650 miles, 980 miles max.   AF

MARTIN XB-10 (XB-907A)
Wright R-1820-19, 675 hp at 6000'
DIMENSIONS: Span 70'7", Lg. 45', Ht. 10'4", Wing Area 640 sq. ft.
WEIGHT: Empty 7294 lb., Gross 12,230 lb., Max. 12,560 lb. Fuel 250 gal.
PERFORMANCE: Speed—Top 207 mph at 6000', 196 mph at s. l., Cruising 169.5 mph, Landing 71 mph. Service Ceiling 21,000', Absolute Ceiling 22,750', Climb 1380'/1 min. Range 600 miles/2260 lbs. bombs.   AF

MARTIN YB-10
Wright R-1820-17, 675 hp at 4500'
DIMENSIONS: Span 70'6", Lg. 45'3", Ht. 11', Wing Area 678 sq. ft.
WEIGHT: Empty 7688 lb., Gross 12,829 lb., Max. 14,192 lb. Fuel 226–452 gal.
PERFORMANCE: Speed—Top 207 mph at 4500', 196.5 mph at s. l., Cruising 178.5 mph, Landing 80 mph. Service Ceiling 21,800', Absolute Ceiling 23,600', Climb 1075'/1 min., 10,000'/10.2 min. Range 523 miles/2260 lbs. bombs, 1360 miles max.   AF

selage had corrugated top and bottom surfaces, with a deep belly and doors for the internal bomb bay. The wheels retracted into nacelles behind two 600-hp Wright SR-1820E Cyclones covered by antidrag rings, and three open cockpits were provided, with room for a fourth crew member within the fuselage.

Known as the XB-907, the first version was flown on February 26, 1932, at Baltimore, Maryland. Numerous difficulties delayed testing by the Army, but a July 1932 Wright Field report announced a 197-mph top speed. The aircraft was returned to the factory for rebuilding with a larger wing and 675-hp R-1820F series Cyclones in full cowlings moved forward ahead of the wings.

The new XB-907A, later designated XB-10, first flew October 4, 1932. The first rotating transparent turret on a U.S. bomber protected the front gunner from the slipstream of a 207-mph speed. Not only were the Keystones now totally obsolete, but the Martin was faster than any pursuit plane then in Army service. The technical revolution accomplished in bomber design by all-metal monoplanes would now be forced on fighter design. Little wonder that the Collier Trophy was awarded in 1932 to Glenn L. Martin for this ship.

The XB-10 prototype was purchased by the Army at the same time that a contract approved January 24, 1933, ordered 48 production Martins at a unit cost of $50,840 each. (Costs had more than doubled in the decade since Martin's last bomber, the NBS-1.) These ships differed from the prototype in having a sliding canopy over the pilot's and rear gunner's cockpit. Three .30-caliber Brownings with 500 rpg were located in the front turret, rear cockpit, and lower tunnel position. The bomb bay could accommodate two 1,130-pound bombs, or five 300-pound bombs, and accuracy was improved by provisions for the very secret Norden Mk XV bomb sights that the Army began receiving via the Navy in April 1933. An external shackle could be fitted under the right wing for a 2,000-pound bomb.

The first Martin off the production line, a YB-10, was delivered to Wright Field in November 1933 with a 665-hp R-1820-25 Cyclone; 14 had been delivered by April 1934. They can be distinguished from their successors by an oil-cooler intake atop the engine cowling. A single YB-10A delivered in June 1934 had experimental turbosupercharged R-1820-31 Cyclones, but the installation was not yet reliable. Pratt & Whitney Hornets of 700 hp were used on seven YB-12 and 25 YB-12A models, the first appearing in February 1934 with the oil-cooler intakes on the nacelle's port side. These intakes were on top, behind the cowl, on the B-12As, first seen in June 1934 and introducing provisions for extra bomb-bay fuel tanks and sealed flotation compartments in the wings. A plan for a dozen YB-13s

MARTIN YB-10A
Wright R-1820-31, 675 hp takeoff
DIMENSIONS: As YB-10
WEIGHT: Empty 8139 lb., Gross 13,212 lb. Fuel 230–456 gal.
PERFORMANCE: Speed—Top 236 mph at 25,000'. Climb 10,000'/7.1 min.   WL

MARTIN B-12A   AF

with R-1860-17 Twin Hornets was canceled, but one XB-14 in May 1934 had 950-hp R-1830-9 Twin Wasps. Proposed XA-15 and XO-45 conversions from the YB-10 were dropped, but a B-12A was fitted with twin floats and set a seaplane speed record on August 24, 1935.

Ten YB-10s demonstrated their serviceability with a survey flight to Alaska in July 1934. Most of the Martins were based at March Field, California, until December 1934, when the Hornet-powered B-12/12A versions went to the new Hamilton Field, near San Francisco, with the 7th Bomb Group. The YB-10s remained at March for the 19th Bomb Group.

The main production version was the B-10B, with 750-hp R-1820-23 Cyclones, intake atop the nacelle, and exhaust pipes moved from the lower nacelle to outlets at the nacelle top behind the air intakes. A June 28, 1934, contract for 81 B-10Bs was later increased to 103, with two more assembled by the Army from spare parts. The first B-10B arrived in July 1935 at Wright, where it remained for type tests, and quantity deliveries to Langley Field began in December 1935 and were completed in August 1936.

Martins reached all Army bomber groups, which in 1936 included the 2nd Bomb Group at Langley and the 9th at Mitchel Field, both with B-10Bs on

MARTIN YB-12
Pratt & Whitney R-1690-11, 700 hp at 6500'
DIMENSIONS: As YB-10
WEIGHT: Empty 7728 lb., Gross 12,824 lb. Fuel 226–456 gal.
PERFORMANCE: Speed—Top 212 mph at 6500', 190 mph at s. l., Cruising 170 mph, Landing 71 mph. Service Ceiling 24,600', Absolute Ceiling 26,600', Climb 1740'/1 min., 10,000'/10.1 min. Range 524 miles normal, 1360 miles max.   AF

MARTIN XB-14
Pratt & Whitney YR-1830-3, 950 hp takeoff, 850 hp at 8000', 800 hp at 10,000'
DIMENSIONS: As YB-10
WEIGHT: Empty 8467 lb., Gross 13,560 lb. Fuel 226–456 gal.
PERFORMANCE: Speed—Top 222.5 mph at 7900', 190 mph at s. l., Cruising 191.5 mph. Climb 1640'/1 min. Range 600 miles/2260 lbs. bombs, 1210 miles/456 gal.   PMB

MARTIN B-10B
Wright R-1820-33, 775 hp takeoff, 750 hp at 5400'
DIMENSIONS: Span 70'6", Lg. 44'9", Ht. 15'5", Wing Area 678 sq. ft.
WEIGHT: Empty 9681 lb., Gross 14,600 lb., Max. 16,400 lb. Fuel 226–452 gal. (702 gal. ferry)
PERFORMANCE: Speed—Top 213 mph at 10,000', 196 mph at s. l., Cruising 193 mph, Landing 65 mph. Service Ceiling 24,200', Climb 5000'/3.4 min. Range 590 miles normal, 1240 miles (overload)/2260 lbs. bombs, 1830 miles ferry.   MFR

the East Coast, and the 7th (with B-10Bs and B-12s) and the 19th (with YB-10s and B-10Bs) in California. Most of the B-12As went to Hawaii's 5th Bomb Group in 1936, and B-10Bs filled out the 6th Bomb Group in the Canal Zone in 1937. The last squadron to get the B-10B was the 28th in the Philippines, where they were used until 1940. By that time most Stateside Martins were relegated to target-towing and utility work.

With such a performance record, export orders would have been easily acquired, but the Army forbade release of their design until its own deliveries had been completed. In the meantime an attempt at export sales was made by builders of less advanced designs.

The Curtiss-Wright BT-32 was a bomber version of the Condor transport armed with five .30-caliber guns and up to 3,968 pounds of bombs. The last large biplane built in the United States, the BT-32 had two R-1820-F2 Cyclones, fabric covering, retractable wheels, pilots in the nose, top gunners before and behind the wings, and guns in side and bottom openings. Completed on February 9, 1934, the demonstration aircraft went to China and was sold to Chiang Kai-shek. Three Condor bombers delivered in June 1934 became the first bombers sold to Colombia, where they usually operated on floats.

CURTISS-WRIGHT BT-32 CONDOR
Wright R-1820F-2, 716 hp (R-1820F-3, 750 hp for takeoff)
DIMENSIONS: Span 82', Lg. 49'6", Ht. 16'4", Wing Area 1276 sq. ft.
WEIGHT: Empty 11,233 lb., Gross 17,500 lb. Fuel 447–750 gal.
PERFORMANCE: Speed—Top 176 mph at 4100' (180 mph at 7000'), Cruising 161 mph, Landing 58 mph. Service Ceiling 22,000' (23,500'), Absolute Ceiling 24,200' (25,300'), Climb 1290'/1 min. (1020'/1 min.). Range 840 miles/2260 lbs. bombs, 1400 miles max.   SI

Bellanca's 77-140 bomber was a bulky, fabric-covered, high-wing monoplane with R-1820-F3 Cyclones, externally braced, squared-off wings, and fixed landing gear at the intersection of stub wings and struts. Armament included 2,200 pounds of

bombs and five .30-caliber guns located in the nose pit and at top, bottom, and side openings in the cabin. The first example had wheels and a nose gunner's turret in 1934, but was destroyed in a hangar fire. Four more with twin floats and open gunner's pit were flown to Colombia in March 1935.

Glenn L. Martin was finally allowed to sell an export version of the B-10, and a demonstrator (NR 15563) was completed in August 1936 as the Model 139W, the W indicating the 750-hp Wright R-1820-F53 Cyclones. This aircraft was shipped to Argentina in September to compete against the Junker Ju 86 and Savoia SM-79B. The Martin won, with Argentina buying 13 bombers for the Navy and an additional 26 for the Army, delivered by April 1938. One of the former, returned to the United States in 1976 to be refurbished for the Air Force Museum, is the oldest bomber on exhibit in the United States.

Six Martin 139WCs powered by 850-hp R-1820-G2 Cyclones went to China in February 1937. Used by China's 10th Group, along with Heinkel He 111s and Savoia SM-72s, they became the first American-designed twin-engine bombers to enter combat when the Japanese invasion began in August 1937. Three more Martins arrived after the war began and were used in February 1938 by American pilots of China's 14th Squadron. Most Martins were lost to enemy raids while on the ground rather than to fighters. Two Martins, perhaps the last survivors, were defiantly flown over Japan by Chinese crews on the night of May 19, 1938. At that range only propaganda leaflets could be dropped on Nagasaki.[1]

Less eventful was the service of some other Martins sold abroad. These included six sold to Siam by April 1937 with R-1820-G3 Cyclones, 20 to Turkey by September with the R-1820-G2, and a single 139WR (X16706) sold to Russia for evaluation. A plan to sell Martins to Spain was blocked by the State Department, so the Republicans used Soviet SB-2 bombers, sometimes incorrectly identified as Martins.

But the largest, first, and last customer for the Martin export bomber was the Netherlands East Indies, whose rich oil fields were threatened by Japanese expansion. The first Dutch order was for 13 139WH-1 bombers, powered by 750-hp R-1820-F53 Cyclones and delivered from September 1936 to February 1937. Twenty-six 139WH-2s, powered by R-1820-G3s giving 840 hp at 8,700 feet, were added from November 1937 to March 1938.

---

[1] According to the official Chinese historian Hu Pu-Yu (Taipai, 1974). Previous American reports giving the month as February seem incorrect, and the report that American-piloted Martins bombed Taiwan is a fabrication; that raid was made by Soviet-flown SB-2s.

BELLANCA 77-140
Wright R-1820F-3, 710 hp at 7000'
DIMENSIONS: Span 76', Lg. 40', Ht. 14', Wing Area 770
  sq. ft.
WEIGHT: Empty 8215 lb., Gross 14,136 lb., Max. 16,333
  lb. Fuel 300–635 gal.
PERFORMANCE: Speed—Top 190 mph at 7000', Cruising
  172 mph, Landing 58 mph. Service Ceiling 23,500',
  Absolute Ceiling 25,000', Climb 1200'/1 min. Range
  710 miles normal, 1500 miles max.   SI

BELLANCA 77-140 Seaplane   SI

The last version of the Martin bomber appeared
in May 1938 as the WH-3, or Model 166, as it was
described in the press. Refined streamlining included a long, unbroken canopy from the pilot's
cockpit to the rear pit, a rounded nose, and 900-hp
R-1820-G102 Cyclones. Performance was consid-
erably improved, although the company specifications cited here may be viewed as optimistic compared to the rigorous measurement of the Air Corps
test results given in this book for Army bombers.
Seventy-eight of these new Martins were built
when the last was delivered on May 5, 1939.

Six Martin squadrons were serving in the Indies
when Japan attacked, and on December 17, 1941,
they began strikes on advancing Japanese ships and
landing forces. Severe losses were suffered to the
fast and heavily armed Zero fighters, whose development made the Martin's speed and protection
inadequate. A surviving Martin 166 fled to Australia
on March 7, 1942, and was taken over by the Americans as a utility aircraft.

MARTIN 139-WC
Wright GR-1820-G2, 850 hp at 5800'
DIMENSIONS: Span 70'10", Lg. 44'9", Ht. 11'5", Wing Area
  682 sq. ft.
WEIGHT: Empty 9411 lb., Gross 14,675 lb., Max. 14,675
  lb. Fuel 226–452 gal.
PERFORMANCE: Speed—Top 229 mph, Cruising 200 mph,
  Landing 65 mph. Service Ceiling 24,200', Climb 1665'/
  1 min. Range 1440 miles (452 gals.).   SDAM

Four-Engine Bombers, 1935–39

Strategic bombing means attacking targets vital to
a nation's war-making capacity. This concept had
been much discussed by leaders like General William Mitchell, but its implementation would require heavy bombers, an air force organization to
use them, and a total war.

That war drew nearer even as aviation began its
conversion to monoplanes. When Japan seized

MARTIN 166 (WH-3)
Wright R-1820G-102, 900 hp at 6700'
DIMENSIONS: Span 70'10", Lg. 44'2", Ht. 11'7", Wing Area
  682 sq. ft.
WEIGHT: Empty 10,322 lb., Gross 15,624 lb. Fuel 762 gal.
  max.
PERFORMANCE: Speed—Top 260 mph, Cruising 205 mph,
  Landing 68 mph. Service Ceiling 25,200', Climb 1680'/
  1 min. Range 2080 miles max.   MFR

Manchuria, the only objection from the United States was in the form of nonrecognition. At the World Disarmament Conference in Geneva in 1932, abolition of the bombing plane was proposed by the United States and supported by a majority of the nations present.

Hitler came to power in January 1933 and Germany withdrew from Geneva, ending hopes for disarmament. Preparations were made in Germany, Italy, and Japan to build or strengthen bomber fleets for aggressive purposes. The ideas of Giulio Douhet, an Italian strategist, about the primacy of bombardment, awakened interest in bombers in many minds, and more attention and money was given to offensive aviation.

The Roosevelt administration was friendly to new ideas, and since William Mitchell had headed the Virginia delegation to the Democratic Convention in Chicago in 1932, which elected Roosevelt the party standard-bearer, it is not surprising that Air Corps expenditures rose from $17.4 million in 1934 to $50.9 million in 1938, and bombardment vied for a serious place in national strategy.

Creation of the General Headquarters Air Force provided a central command for the four bomber groups in the United States that could be concentrated against an enemy, although the geographic situation meant that the enemy's invasion force would be the target, not its vital centers. Design of bombers large enough for the range desired was also under way.

As early as July 1933, Wright Field had studied the problem of maximum range with a one-ton bomb load. When a 5,000-mile range seemed possible, the Air Corps submitted "Project A," a proposal to build such a plane. Approval was given by the Army's General Staff and on April 14, 1934, a request for design proposals was issued. Boeing's Model 294 and Martin's Model 145 were the responses, both projects originally to have four Allison V-1710 inline engines, and on May 12, 1934, the Chief of Staff authorized negotiations with Boeing and Martin for preliminary designs.

The designs prepared by these firms were heroic in size compared with the existing bombers, but developments abroad included such monoplanes as the Soviet Union's 177-foot-span, six-engine TB-4 bomber in July 1933 and the 210-foot span, eight-engine ANT-20 transport flown on June 17, 1934. Boeing's design, which was known for a while as the XBLR-1 (experimental bomber, long range), won a contract on June 28, 1934, for design data, wind tunnel tests, and a mockup. It became the XB-15, was to be a 149-foot-span, four-engine, 35-ton monoplane, while the Martin XB-16 became enlarged to a 173-foot-span monoplane of 52 tons. Six 1,000 Allison V-1710-3 engines were utilized, four

as tractors, two as pushers, with twin rudders behind two tail booms and proposed tricycle landing gear, but the XB-16 was too expensive to build.

On June 29, 1935, a contract was approved for Boeing to build the XB-15, the actual aircraft to be powered by air-cooled radial engines. By this time Boeing had nearly finished the prototype of Model 299, which, as the B-17, would become the first Air Corps strategic bomber in production. The XB-15 itself would take much longer to build, and made its first flight on October 15, 1937.

The largest aircraft then built in America, the XB-15 had passageways in the wings' leading edges to four 1,000-hp Pratt & Whitney R-1830-11 Wasps. Double wheels and two ailerons on each wing testified to the 70,700 pounds of bulk. The crew of ten had "soundproofed, heated, and ventilated" quarters with rest bunks, kitchen, and lavatory, and, for the first time in an airplane, small auxiliary engines operated a 110-volt electrical system.

Armament was the heaviest then found on a bomber, three .30-caliber and three heavy .50-caliber guns. A nose turret like the B-17's, a forward-facing belly turret below the pilot's cabin, a top turret whose .50-caliber gun could rotate 360°, two waist blisters behind the wings, and a rearward-facing belly turret covered every approach to the ship except directly behind the huge tail—a weakness common to all U.S. bombers of the decade.

Strategically, the most important facts about the XB-15 were its 12,000-pound maximum bomb capacity and its 3,400-mile range with 2,511 pounds—not only much greater than any other bomber but enough to fly from Guam to Japan and back, dropping something heavier and noisier than the leaflets sprinkled by Chiang's Martins.

The XB-15 joined the 2nd Bomb Group in August 1938, and in 1942 was converted to the XC-105 cargo carrier, which served until it was dismantled in 1945. Its large wing design was used on the Boeing 314 flying boats, and much of its service experience would contribute to the B-19 and B-29 designs. It was underpowered for its size, but this was expected to be corrected in Boeing's YB-20, planned as an improved B-15 with 1,400-hp engines.

The most important four-engine bomber of the period, however, was Boeing's Flying Fortress, which led the strategic bombing offensive against Germany. For the Air Corps, the B-17 story started with a specification for a "multi-engined four to six place" bomber to replace the B-10 series. Dated July 18, 1934, this specification stated that the desired performance should include a top speed of 250 mph at 10,000 feet, a ten-hour endurance at cruising speed, a 25,000-foot service ceiling, and double the B-10's bomb capacity. Interested aircraft

BOEING XB-15   PMB

BOEING XB-15
Pratt & Whitney R-1830-11, 1000 hp takeoff, 850 hp at
   6000'
DIMENSIONS: Span 149', Lg. 87'7", Ht. 19'5", Wing Area
   2780 sq. ft.
WEIGHT: Empty 37,709 lb., Gross 65,068 lb., Max. 70,700
   lb. Fuel 4190 gal.
PERFORMANCE: Speed—Top 197 mph at 6000', Cruising
   171 mph, Landing 70 mph. Service Ceiling 18,850',
   Absolute Ceiling 20,900', Climb 5000'/7.1 min., 10,-
   000'/14.9 min. Range 3400 miles/2511 lbs. bombs. MFR

of bombs 2,040 miles. Immediately recognized as
the most advanced bomber yet built, the eight-place
Model 299 had five enclosed positions for .30-cali-
ber guns. A nose turret could cover the whole forward hemisphere, while teardrop blisters studded
the top, bottom, and sides of the rear fuselage.

Martin and Douglas also sent prototypes to
Wright Field for the opening of bids and trials in
August 1935. The Martin 146 was an enlarged B-
10, with a wider fuselage to accommodate a larger
bomb load and crew compartment, Fowler flaps on
the wings and two Wright R-1820-G5 Cyclones.
What was done with the Martin after the competition is not known, but Glenn L. Martin wrote the
Secretary of War, complaining that despite the lowest bids and his $350,000 investment in the proto-
type, he had won no contract.

builders were to produce prototypes at their own
expense to compete for the production contract in
August 1935.

When Boeing received this proposal on August
8, 1934, company President Clairmont Egtvedt
made certain that "multi-engined" also permitted
four, as well as two, power plants. A design study
for a four-engine bomber, Model 299, was already
under way, based on experience with the 247 transport and the Project A long-range bomber. Midway
in size between the B-10 and the B-15, Model 299
promised performance far beyond that which any
twin-engine design could achieve. On September
26, the company's directors agreed to take the risk,
which eventually required over $600,000. The proj-
ect engineer was E. G. Emery until 1935, when his
assistant, Edward C. Wells, became project engineer. He was then 24 years old and in charge of the
most important airplane of its time. It has been a
long time since young men have been given such
responsibility in the aviation industry.

First flown on July 28, 1935, a little over four
months after Hitler renounced the Versailles Treaty
and officially announced rearmament, the Boeing
299 had four 750-hp Pratt & Whitney R-1690 Hornets on its low wing and could carry 2,500 pounds

MARTIN 146
Wright R-1820G-5, 800 hp at 10,000'
DIMENSIONS: Span 75', Lg. 50', Wing Area 729 sq. ft.
WEIGHT: Empty 10,943 lb., Gross 16,000 lb., Max. 17,100
   lb. Fuel 404 gal.
PERFORMANCE: Speed—Top 234 mph at 13,500', 204 mph
   at s. l., Cruising 170 mph. Service Ceiling 28,500'.
   Range 1237 miles normal, 1589 miles max.   AF

DOUGLAS DB-1 (B-18 prototype)
Wright R-1820-G12, 850 hp at 9000'
DIMENSIONS: Span 89'7", Lg. 57'3", Ht. 15'4", Wing Area
   959 sq. ft.
WEIGHT: Empty 14,806 lb., Gross 20,159 lb. Fuel 204–802
   gal.
PERFORMANCE: Speed—Top 220 mph at 10,000', Cruising
   173 mph, Landing 62 mph. Service Ceiling 25,000',
   Climb 10,000'/8.8 min. Range 1030 miles/2532 lbs.
   bombs.   AF

The Douglas DB-1 bore a family resemblance to that firm's DC-2 transports, even down to a cabin with bunks on which the six-man crew might rest. Two Wright R-1820-G2 Cyclones powered this mid-wing monoplane, which was armed with three .30-caliber guns. One of these was in the nose turret, a second fired through a trapdoor in the floor at the rear, while the third was in a retractable, fully rotating turret just ahead of the tail. A 2,532-pound bomb load could be carried only about half the distance of the Boeing and with less speed.

Quantity or Quality?

In spite of the prototype's destruction on October 30 in a crash due to pilot error, the Air Corps recommended adoption of the Boeing 299. Although airmen enthusiastically greeted the advanced performance, the General Staff was concerned with economy. Prices quoted per ship (exclusive of engines), in lots of 25 and 220, were as follows: Martin, $85,910 and $48,880 each; Douglas, $99,150 and $58,500; and Boeing, $196,730 and $99,620. Operating under budgetary limitations, the Air Corps recommended purchase of 65 B-17s instead of 185 other authorized aircraft. The General Staff

preferred quantity to quality; and contracts made in 1936 called for only 13 four-engine Boeing YB-17s and 133 twin-engine Douglas B-18s.

The first production versions of Boeing's Flying Fortress were the 13 YB-17s ordered, with a static-test airframe, on January 17, 1936. Wright R-1820-39 Cyclones, rated at 775 hp at 14,000 feet, replaced the prototype's Hornets, and Cyclones remained standard on all future production B-17s. The landing gear and turret structure were simplified, and a long carburetor intake on top of the engine nacelles distinguished these aircraft from later models. Designated YB-17 when ordered, it then became the Y1B-17, and later just plain B-17.

Armament included five .30-caliber guns with 1,000 rpg and room in the bomb bay for eight 600-pound, four 1,100-pound, or two 2,000-pound bombs, or two 396-gallon ferry tanks.[2] Top speed was 256 mph and range was 2,260 miles, with a normal load of 2,511 pounds of bombs and 850 gallons of fuel. The range in an overload condition

[2] The actual bomb weights were 624, 1,130, and 2,030 pounds, respectively, but contemporary documentation used the approximations.

BOEING 299
Pratt & Whitney R-1690E, 750 hp at 7000'
DIMENSIONS: Span 103'9", Lg. 68'9", Ht. 15', Wing Area 1420 sq. ft.
WEIGHT: Empty 22,125 lb., Gross 32,432 lb., Max. 43,000 lb. Fuel 1700 gal.
PERFORMANCE: Speed—Top 236 mph at 10,000', Cruising 204 mph. Service Ceiling 24,620'. Range 2040 miles/2573 lbs. bombs, 3010 miles max.   MFR

BOEING YB-17
Wright R-1820-39, 930 hp takeoff, 775 hp at 14,000'
DIMENSIONS: Span 103'9", Lg. 68'4", Ht. 18'4", Wing Area 1420 sq. ft.
WEIGHT: Empty 24,458 lb., Gross 34,873 lb., Max. 42,600 lb. Fuel 1700–2492 gal.
PERFORMANCE: Speed—Top 256 mph at 14,000', Cruising 217 mph, Landing 70 mph. Service Ceiling 30,600', Climb 10,000'/6.5 min. Range 2260 miles/850 gal. with 2511 lbs. bombs, 1377 miles/10,496 lbs. bombs, 3320 miles max.   MFR

(4,000 pounds of bombs and 1,700 gallons) was 2,400 miles or 3,320 miles with 2,490 gallons and no bombs.

This performance was the best of any heavy bomber in the world, and the Air Corps lost no opportunity to display its new weapon. The first Y1B-17 was flown on December 2, 1936, and by January was at Wright Field, where it remained as the test example, as was customary for the first production aircraft. Langley Field received the other 12 from March 1 to August 4, 1937, and they served alongside the B-10Bs and B-18s of the 2nd Bomb Group. With over three years of vigorous flying without a serious accident, the B-17s proved themselves practical weapons and were transferred to the 19th Bomb Group at March Field in October 1940.

Douglas Bombers, 1936–42

The mostly widely used Air Corps bomber when World War II began was the Douglas B-18. Its acceptance was due to its low cost and reliable airline-type flying qualities rather than its performance. Essentially, Army leadership, represented by the Chief of Staff and the Secretary of War, had rejected the strategic-bombing idea. The B-18's role was seen as one of coastal defense, for which a greater number of twin-engine aircraft seemed more helpful than a smaller number of expensive four-engine B-17s.

While the defensive armament was completely inadequate for wartime conditions, three .30-caliber guns were also what was carried then by foreign bombers like the Heinkel He 111, the Mitsubishi G3M, or the Soviet DB-3. A normal load of 2,200 pounds of bombs and 418 gallons of fuel could take the B-18 1,082 miles with a modest 217-mph top speed. When in overload condition, the bomb bay could contain six 600-pound, four 1,100-pound, or two 2,000-pound bombs, with 802 gallons for a 1,200-mile range or two 184-gallon ferry tanks.

A contract for 82 B-18s, ordered January 28, 1936, was increased to 132 by June. The prototype DB-1 was brought up to production standards and was also purchased by the Air Corps in September 1936. The first true production B-18 arrived at Wright Field February 23, 1937.

In March 1937 tests were begun on the Douglas DB-2 and North American NA-21 to investigate improved armament provisions. The DB-2 was actually a B-18 airframe fitted with a power-driven nose turret and a large bombardier's enclosure designed for the XB-19; it was eventually accepted as the last aircraft on the B-18 contract. Another armament experiment was the installation, in August 1939, of a 75-mm M1897 cannon in the bomb bay of the B-18 prototype.

DOUGLAS B-18
Wright R-1820-45, 930 hp takeoff, 810 hp at 10,200'
DIMENSIONS: Span 89'6", Lg. 56'8", Ht. 15'2", Wing Area 959 sq. ft.
WEIGHT: Empty 15,719 lb., Gross 21,130 lb., Max. 27,087 lb. Fuel 802–1170 gal.
PERFORMANCE: Speed—Top 217 mph at 10,000', Cruising 167 mph, Landing 64 mph. Service Ceiling 24,200', Absolute Ceiling 25,850', Climb 1355'/1 min., 10,000'/ 9.1 min. Range 1082 miles/412 gal. with 2200 lbs. bombs, 1200 miles/4000 lbs. (Max. load), 2225 miles ferry.   AF

DOUGLAS DB-2 (Last B-18, with power turret)   MFR

Begun in January 1936, North American's NA-21 was first flown December 22, 1936, reworked in October 1937, and accepted by the Air Corps as the XB-21, although a plan to build five more for service tests was dropped. Powered by two 1200-hp Pratt & Whitney R-2180-1 Twin Hornets with F-10 superchargers, this six-place midwing monoplane had five .30-caliber guns mounted in power turrets in the nose, on top, and at transparent panels in waist and ventral orifices. Two 1,100-pound bombs could be carried 1,960 miles or eight 1,100-pound bombs for a 660-mile range. Once again price was a factor, for in 1937 North American had bid $122,600 for each plane, to be produced in quantities of 50, while cost savings due to previous production en-

NORTH AMERICAN XB-21
Pratt & Whitney R-2180-1, 1200 hp takeoff
DIMENSIONS: Span 95', Lg. 61'9", Ht. 14'9", Wing Area
1120 sq. ft.
WEIGHT: Empty 19,082 lb., Gross 27,253 lb., Max. 40,000
lb. Fuel 600–2400 gal.
PERFORMANCE: Speed—Top 220 mph at 10,000', Cruising
190 mph. Service Ceiling 25,000', Climb 10,000'/10
min. Range 1960 miles/2200 lbs. bombs, 660 miles/
10,000 lbs. bombs, 3100 miles max.   MFR

DOUGLAS B-18A
Wright R-1820-53, 1000 hp takeoff, 850 hp at 9600'
DIMENSIONS: Span 89'6", Lg. 57'10", Ht. 15'2", Wing Area
965 sq. ft.
WEIGHT: Empty 16,321 lb., Gross 22,123 lb., Max. 27,673
lb. Fuel 802–1170 gal.
PERFORMANCE: Speed—Top 215.5 mph at 10,000', Cruis-
ing 167 mph, Landing 69 mph. Service Ceiling 23,900',
Absolute Ceiling 25,600', Climb 1030'/1 min., 10,000'/
9.9 min. Range 1150 miles/2496 lbs. bombs.   AF

DOUGLAS B-18B   AF

abled Douglas to cut B-18A unit bids to $63,977.

Douglas received a contract for 177 B-18As on
June 10, 1937, and on June 30, 1938, 78 additional
bombers (completed as 40 B-18As and 38 B-23s)
were added. Changes in the neat Douglas nose had
been ordered on October 11, 1937, to give more
visibility and comfort to the bombardier. This resulted in the B-18A's unusual nasal arrangement in
which the bombardier sat above and ahead of the
bow gunner. First appearing in April 1938, 217 B-
18As had R-1820-53 Cyclones and a dome top on
the power-operated rear turret.

The Army's last three B-18As were delivered in
January 1940, and were followed by 20 built by
March 1940 for Canada. Named the Digby by the
RCAF, they served with a squadron based in Newfoundland. Air Corps B-18 and B-18A bombers mingled in all four bomber groups in the United States,
each of which by 1940 had four squadrons, one
designated as reconnaissance. Hawaii's 5th Group
got 40 B-18s in 1938, the Canal Zone's 6th got 33
in 1939, and, finally, the 28th Squadron in the Philippines was given 18 B-18s in 1941.

As expansion multiplied the bomber groups in
1940–41, the Douglas bombers were scattered
about for training purposes and were christened the
Bolo. When the war arrived, they were far too obsolete for combat duty except for one case. An antisubmarine version, the B-18B, had SCR-517 radar[3]
in the nose and magnetic airborne detection gear in
the tail, 76 were converted from B-18As. Their monotonous patrols were occasionally interrupted, in
the Caribbean, by several engagements with surfaced submarines. During one of these the B-18B
was shot down, but on August 22, 1942, another B-
18B sank U-654 near the Panama Canal, and a B-
18B also sank U-512 on October 2, 1942.

Douglas had plans to improve their twin-engine
design, at first as the B-22, a B-18A with new
R-2600-1 Cyclone engines. This project was superseded, in November 1938, by the B-23, which
had 1,600-hp Wright R-2600-3 Cyclones and a new
streamlined fuselage incorporating the latest ideas
in armament. It was thought that the 282-mph top
speed reduced the threat of frontal attacks, so the
bow turret of earlier years was replaced by a simple
plastic nose with a flat bombardier's panel and a
ball-and-socket mount for a .30-caliber gun. Two
other .30s were placed in top and belly positions,
while a .50-caliber gun armed the first Air Corps
tail gunner. Bomb capacity remained the same as
that of the B-18, 4,520 pounds.

There was no B-23 prototype, as they had been
ordered as part of the B-18A contract, so the first B-

---

[3] The first American-built airborne radar was first flown on a B-
18A on March 10, 1941.

23 was flown by Douglas July 27, 1939, and arrived at Wright in October. The remaining 37 were delivered from February to September 1940, replacing A-17As with the 17th Bomb Group at March Field until that group got B-25s. They were then passed on to the 12th Bomb Group (McChord) and 13th Bomb Group (Orlando), but in no case did they see combat. About 19 were converted to UC-67 transports and most B-23s were modified to civilian executive transports after the war.

Strategic Bombers Advance in Performance

Four-engine bombers were what Air Corps leaders really wanted, and GHQ Air Force Commander General Frank Andrews had urged the War Department in June 1937 that future bombers bought should be four-engine, since enough B-18s were on order already. He favored only two bomber types: the heavy bomber for long-range missions and the attack bomber for close support. Bombers were seen as the basic element of air power and as vital to the nation as land or sea power.

Constant improvement of performance was needed if strategic bombing was to become a reality, and the exhaust-driven turbosupercharger, developed over the years, offered the main chance of improving the B-17. The static-test airframe of the first contract was chosen for completion with turbosuperchargers on May 12, 1937.

Designated Y1B-17A, it made its first flight on April 29, 1938, with the turbos installed on top of the nacelles. When this system proved unworkable, they were moved to the bottom and the reworked aircraft flown again on November 20. This time the system worked so well and improved performance so much that turbos became standard on the B-17B and all future B-17 models.

The B-17B also had R-1820-51 Cyclones giving 900 hp up to 25,000 feet, and a new, cleaner nose better accommodating the bombardier and navigator. The nose turret was replaced by a short transparency with the flat bomb-aiming panel, formerly in a fuselage cutout, and a simple socket for a .30-caliber flexible gun. The flaps were enlarged, a

DOUGLAS B-23
Wright R-2600-3, 1600 hp takeoff, 1275 hp at 12,000'
DIMENSIONS: Span 92', Lg. 58'4", Ht. 18'6", Wing Area 993 sq. ft.
WEIGHT: Empty 19,059 lb., Gross 26,500 lb., Max. 30,477 lb. Fuel 870–1290 gal.
PERFORMANCE: Speed—Top 282 mph at 12,000', Cruising 210 mph, Landing 80 mph. Service Ceiling 31,600', Climb 10,000'/6.7 min. Range 1455 miles/4000 lbs. bombs.　　AF

BOEING YB-17A
Wright R-1820-51, 1000 hp takeoff, 800 hp at 25,000'
DIMENSIONS: Span 103'9", Lg. 68'4", Ht. 18'4", Wing Area 1420 sq. ft.
WEIGHT: Empty 26,520 lb., Gross 37,000 lb., Max. 45,650 lb. Fuel 1700–2492 gal.
PERFORMANCE: Speed—Top 295 mph at 25,000', Cruising 230 mph, Landing 78 mph. Service Ceiling 38,000', Climb 10,000'/7.8 min. Range 2400 miles/4000 lbs. bombs, 3600 miles max.　　MFR

BOEING B-17B
Wright R-1820-51, 1000 hp takeoff, 800 hp at 25,000'
DIMENSIONS: Span 103'9", Lg. 67'11", Ht. 15'5", Wing Area 1420 sq. ft.
WEIGHT: Empty 27,650 lb., Gross 37,810 lb., Max. 46,650 lb. Fuel 850–1700 gal. (2492 gal. max.).
PERFORMANCE: Speed—Top 291.5 mph at 25,000', Cruising 231 mph, Landing 80 mph. Service Ceiling 36,000', Climb 1430'/1 min., 10,000'/7.1 min. Range 2400 miles/4000 lbs. bombs, 3600 miles ferry.　　MI

plastic dome added to the cabin roof, and external bomb racks could be added to increase the capacity another 4,000 pounds if needed.

While the first B-17B contract called for ten air-craft on August 3, 1937, by June 30, 1938, the total was increased to 38. Boeing flew the first June 27, 1939, and delivered the last March 30, 1940. They served with the 2nd, 7th, and 19th groups except for the first B-17B, which was retained at Wright. This aircraft was reworked to test the new arma-ment installations planned for the future B-17C ver-sion. Many of the service B-17Bs were modernized in 1940–41 to use such features as the flush-type side openings for .50-caliber guns.

When they were replaced at their original stations by newer models in 1941, the B-17Bs were scat-tered among the several bomb groups. One dropped the first bomb in anger by the Air Force when a B-17B based in Newfoundland with the 41st Recon-naissance Squadron, 2nd Bomb Group, attacked a U-boat on October 27, 1941, without producing vis-ible results. Since the United States was not offi-cially at war, the incident was not reported in the press.

The XB-19

The largest airplane ever built before the cold war, the Douglas XB-19 of 1941 was among the most famous planes of its day. Although only one was built—and it never flew a combat mission—the XB-19 became a symbol of prewar American air power. A 212-foot wingspan and a 162,000-pound gross weight made the big Douglas the largest in the air until the B-36 of 1946.

This design's main purpose was to find out just how far a bomber could be made to fly in the prewar state of the art. This inevitably led to a giant air-plane whose development made possible future air monsters.

In February 1935 the U.S. Army Air Corps began Project D, a long-range bomber idea "investigating the maximum feasible distance into the future," and classified the whole project "Secret." Contracts with Douglas Aircraft and Sikorsky Aviation were prepared to cover preliminary design and wooden mockups, with an option to purchase a completed aircraft if prospects looked good.

Douglas was assigned the designation XBLR-2 (experimental bomber, long-range) on July 9, 1935. Originally it had estimated that the plane could be completed by March 31, 1938, and a design contract was approved on October 31, 1935. The wooden mockups of both Douglas and Sikorsky were in-spected in March 1936, and the former was consid-ered superior as a military weapon. Sikorsky's con-tract was canceled, with a payment of $103,000.

Among the then new features of the Douglas de-sign were retractable tricycle gear, power turrets, and a tail gun position. None of these features had

ever been seen on an American combat type. A Douglas OA-4 Dolphin amphibian was loaned back by the Army in May 1936 to test the tricycle-gear idea, and experiments were so successful that the nose-wheel plan was also adopted for the com-pany's forthcoming DC-4 transport and A-20 attack-bomber series.

The power-operated nose turret was tested on the DB-2, but the tail turret was then considered of "questionable value." Originally 1,600-hp Allison XV-3420-1 liquid-cooled inline engines (actually two V-1710s joined together) were to be used on both the Douglas and Sikorsky designs, but on No-vember 2, 1936, 2,000-hp Wright R-3350-5 air-cooled radials were substituted.

After a staff study examining a Navy contention that long-range flying was a function of that service, authority to proceed with detailed designs and tests on Project D was granted on September 29, 1936. A contract change calling for a prototype to be com-pleted and designated XB-19 instead of XBLR-2 was dated November 19, 1937, but not approved until the following March 8.

At the same time, the Air Force went ahead with plans to follow up the B-15 with a more advanced bomber of the same size. In March 1938 the Boeing Model 316 and Douglas DB-4 were offered as four-engine long-range bomber projects, with tricycle landing gear and R-2180 Twin Hornets of 1,400 hp. The low-wing Douglas ship, based on the DC-4 transport, was to weigh 71,000 pounds gross, have a crew of nine, and house six .50-caliber guns in four power turrets and two waist openings. Esti-mated performance included 260 mph at 15,000 feet, a 4,000-mile range with 4,500 pounds of bombs, and 1,000 miles with 20,000 pounds. Boeing's high-wing project was offered in several forms, and the 80,000-pound gross, seven-gun, ten-place, 152-foot span, pressurized cabin 316D ver-sion was designated Y1B-20 in June 1938.

Prototypes of these designs were considered too expensive, especially in view of an Army and Navy Joint Board (June 29, 1938) that the Air Corps would not require bombers of greater range and carrying capacity than those of the B-17. The Y1B-20 was dropped, and the Douglas DC-4 transport prototype was sold to Japan, where a bomber version, the G5N-1, was built in 1941 for the Japanese Navy.

The XB-19 was endangered when the Douglas Company itself recommended cancellation of the contract on August 30, 1938, arguing that the ex-pensive ship was becoming obsolete, that weight was increasing excessively, and that its personnel was needed on designs more likely to be produced in quantity. The Army insisted that the company proceed with the $1,400,000 contract, which was eventually to cost the company nearly $4 million.

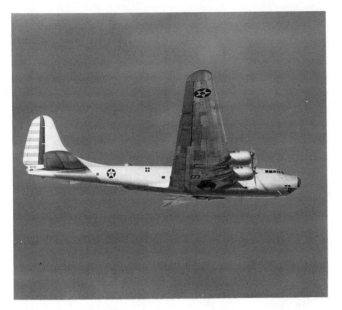

DOUGLAS XB-19
Wright R-3350-5, 2000 hp takeoff, 1500 hp at 15,700'
DIMENSIONS: Span 212', Lg. 132'2", Ht. 42'9", Wing Area
    4285 sq. ft.
WEIGHT: Empty 84,431 lb., Gross 140,000 lb., Max. 162,-
    000 lb. Fuel 10,350–11,174 gal.
PERFORMANCE: Speed—Top 224 mph at 15,700', Cruising
    135 mph, Landing 73 mph. Service Ceiling 23,000',
    Absolute Ceiling 24,500', Climb 545'/1 min. Range
    7300 miles/6000 lbs. bombs, 7900 miles max.   MFR

DOUGLAS XB-19A
Allison V-3420-11, 2600 hp at 25,000'
DIMENSIONS: As XB-19
WEIGHT: Empty 92,400 lb., Gross 140,230 lb. Fuel 6400
    gal.
PERFORMANCE: Speed—Top 265 mph at 20,000', Cruising
    185 mph. Service Ceiling 39,000'. Range 4200 miles/
    2500 lbs. bombs.   AF

Only actual flight tests could establish the data needed for future development of such large aircraft. After many delays, the XB-19 was flown from Santa Monica on June 27, 1941.

Armament of the XB-19 was quite formidable, according to standards of the day. As specified on January 1, 1939, the armament included two 37-mm guns, five .50-caliber guns, and six .30-caliber guns with 50, 200, and 600 rpg, respectively. The big bomb bay could accommodate eight 2,000-pound, 16 1,100-pound, or 30 600-pound bombs, while ten external wing racks accommodating bombs up to 2,000 pounds could be added for short-range missions, for a maximum bomb capacity of 37,100 pounds. No armor plate or leakproof fuel tanks were included, as these features were not specified for Army planes before 1940.

The crew included up to 16 men. The front gunner sat in the power-operated turret with a 37-mm gun below a .30-caliber weapon. Behind and below him were the bombardier and another gunner with .30-caliber machine guns pointing from each side of their compartment. Above them the main cabin accommodated the pilot, co-pilot, plane commander, navigator, engineer, and radio operator, while the main upper gunner handled a power-operated turret with a 37-mm and .30-caliber gun. Behind the bomb bay two waist gunners, an upper rear turret gunner, and a belly gunner each had a single .50-caliber gun. The tail compartment had a .30-caliber gun on each side for a gunner below the stabilizer, and the last crewman operated the .50-caliber tail gun. Above the bomb bay was a crew compartment with six bunks and eight seats for a relief crew or extra flight mechanics. Passages in the low wing gave direct access to the engines.

Despite all the guns, the XB-19 was less of a weapon than a flying laboratory to test such technical problems as stress and weight increases on large aircraft. As such, it encouraged work on the B-29 and B-36 projects. In 1943, 2,600-hp Allison V-3420-11 turbosupercharged engines were installed to improve performance as the XB-19A, and later the aircraft was used as a cargo carrier until it was scrapped in June 1949.

When the XB-19 is compared to the B-9 of a decade earlier, the improvement in range and bombing power is striking. In ten years the technology for a new kind of war had been prepared.

Chapter 15
Bombers for World War II, 1939-45

Turning Point After Munich

Despite progress in the 1930s, the six Army bomber groups active in 1938 could only make much the same kind of raids as those made in 1918. While their equipment of B-18s and a dozen B-17s had the monoplane's new look, the Army's General Staff saw them as coast defense rather than as a strategic force. But warfare in China and Spain had made the public, and younger military leaders in particular, concerned about air power.

The European crisis in September 1938 led to the Munich agreement and dramatized the importance of bombers in power politics, alerting Americans to the need for air power. Some advocates of appeasement had been motivated by Hitler's professed intention to expand only eastward, but much acceptance of Czech dismemberment was due to fear of Germany's well-advertised bombers. Wrote General Henry H. Arnold, who had just been appointed Chief of the Air Corps: "The nation with the greatest navy in the world in . . . alliance with the nation having the most powerful army in the world [France was meant] capitulated without a struggle to Germany's newly created air power."

When President Roosevelt decided to enlarge the Army and Navy air forces, General Arnold prepared expansion plans, and appropriations were requested in the presidential message to Congress in January 1939. By April the Air Corps was authorized to expand from 2,300 planes to 5,500 in 24 groups by June 1941. Bombers, in five heavy, six medium, and two attack (light) bombardment groups, were the big stick of the new force. In the words of its chief, "The No. 1 job of an air force is bombardment. We must have the long-range bombers which can hit the enemy before he hits us; . . . the best defense is attack." No longer was the bomber merely a long-range coast-defense gun.

On August 10, 1939, the Army ordered 461 new bombers of four different models. One contract was for improved Boeing B-17Cs, but others were for B-24, B-25, and B-26 types not even flown yet in prototype form.

When war was declared in Europe in September 1939, Roosevelt appealed to every belligerent government that "under no circumstances" there be any bombing of civilians in unfortified cities, upon the understanding that the same rules be observed by all belligerents. Except for the quick conquest of Poland, the "phony war" phase gave some hope that the air weapon would remain sheathed; no one then realized that the United States itself would demonstrate bombing of cities in its most violent form.

The German invasion of western Europe in May 1940 was accompanied by unrestrained air attacks on civilians, and Britain began her struggle for survival. President Roosevelt called for expansion of Army aviation to 36,500 planes and 54 groups. Basic equipment of the bomber component was to be a pair each of four-engine and twin-engine types: the B-17 and B-24, and the B-25 and B-26.

Before any of the 461 bombers ordered in 1939 had reached Army groups in 1941, 2,753 more of these four types had been added to Army contracts. With this expansion, specific strategic plans for their use were drawn up.

Rainbow No. 5

Since autumn of 1939 the Army had been preparing basic war plans against potential enemies; Rainbow No. 5, code name for the plan finally adopted, contemplated an offensive in Europe while maintaining a strategic defense against Japan. After talks with British officials in February 1941, this strategy was approved on May 14, 1941, by the Joint Board of the Army and Navy.

At the President's request, the now virtually autonomous Army Air Forces prepared AWPD/1 (Air War Plans Division) by August 12, 1941, which defined the Air Force plan to fulfill Rainbow No. 5. AWPD/1 was approved and included in the joint Army-Navy report to Roosevelt on September 11, 1941. This remarkably precise program projected German defeat by the destruction of 154 selected targets in the electric power, petroleum, aluminum, magnesium, aircraft, and transportation industries. Required for this bombardment were 6,834 bombers in 98 groups: 20 heavy (B-17 and 24), 24 very heavy (B-29 and 32), and ten medium groups (B-25 and 26), the latter "included because of availability only." Larger planes would be "far more economical" and it was hoped that by 1944, 44 groups of bombers of 4,000-mile radius would be available. Sixteen pursuit groups were to protect the bombers' bases.

Now that a war plan and the bomber designs to meet its requirements had been prepared, the problem remaining was one of improving the weapons to meet battle conditions and building them in numbers sufficient to execute the plan and still have enough to allot some to allies.

B-17s at War

Boeing's B-17 led the strategic-bombing offensive against Germany, but at first the name Flying Fortress represented journalistic and advertising hyperbole. Before sustained daylight operations could be made, protection against enemy fighters had to be improved. A detailed description of how the airmen fought their battles in the B-17 and other wartime bombers would require another book (See Bibliography, section III). The present discussion is limited to the identification of the major steps in weapons development.

The first Flying Fortress used in air combat was the B-17C, with the 1,200-hp R-1820-65, armor, leakproof tanks, and the four gun blisters replaced by new openings for each .50-caliber gun. Flush panels were provided on the sides, another over the radio compartment, and a bathtublike mount for the bottom gun. A single .30-caliber gun could be fired from any of six sockets in the nose. Bomb bay capacity remained the same (4,996 pounds) as on the YB-17.

Thirty-eight B-17Cs were ordered on August 10, 1939. Poland had been overrun by the Germans before this contract was approved by the Secretary of War on September 20. The first B-17C flew July 21, 1940, and was retained by the company for test purposes, while the last was delivered by November 29. Twenty were sold to Britain as the Fortress I, and the rest were returned to Boeing in January 1941 to be modified to B-17D standards.

Forty-two more had been ordered April 17, 1940, but were redesignated B-17Ds on September 6. Delivered from February to April 1941, they could be distinguished from the Cs by their cowl flaps. Improved protection included a new self-sealing fuel-tank system and paired guns in the belly and top positions, bringing the total up to one .30-caliber and six .50-caliber guns. Twenty-one B-17Ds were flown to Hawaii in May 1941, and the rest joined older models in the 7th and 19th Bomb Groups.

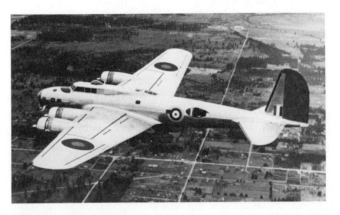

BOEING B-17C
Wright R-1820-65, 1200 hp at 25,000'
DIMENSIONS: As B-17B
WEIGHT: Empty 30,600 lb., Gross 39,320 lb., Max. 49,650 lb. Fuel 1700 gal.
PERFORMANCE: Speed—Top 323 mph at 25,000', Cruising 250 mph, Landing 84 mph. Service Ceiling 37,000', Climb 10,000'/7.5 min. Range 2000 miles/4000 lbs. bombs, 3400 miles max.   MFR

BOEING B-17D   MFR

The RAF Fortresses began arriving in Britain in April 1941 and were assigned to No. 90 Squadron for high-altitude bombing, but results were disappointing. The first 39 sorties, begun July 8, resulted in only two certain bomb hits for a combat and operational loss of eight Boeings. Americans blamed this record on excessively high attack altitudes and on not flying in formation to promote defensive firepower and a good bombing pattern;

but it was evident that something had to be done to counter the speed and firepower added by fighter planes since the original B-17 had been designed.

The war plan, APWD/1, would be useless unless the bombers had adequate protection to penetrate to their targets, an ability not yet demonstrated by U.S. planes. It was hoped that part of the answer could be found in the B-17E, ordered August 30, 1940, and first flown September 5, 1941. Armament included one .30-caliber and eight .50-caliber guns, plus the protective armor and leakproof tanks provided on all subsequent U.S. bombers. The .50-caliber gun at each squared-waist opening was hand-operated, but the rest were paired in turrets: a power-operated dome behind the pilots; a turret in the belly and a tail emplacement; while the .30-caliber gun was fired from sockets in the nose enclosure. The belly turrets on the first 112 B-17Es were operated by remote control from a periscopic sight, but this proved unsatisfactory and was replaced by a Sperry ball turret with the gunner curled up inside.

BOEING B-17E
Wright R-1820-65, 1200 hp at 25,000'
DIMENSIONS: Span 103'9", Lg. 73'10", Ht. 19'2", Wing Area 1420 sq. ft.
WEIGHT: Empty 32,250 lb., Gross 40,260 lb., Max. 53,000 lb. Fuel 1730–2520 gal.
PERFORMANCE: Speed—Top 317 mph at 25,000', Cruising 195–223 mph, Landing 80 mph. Service Ceiling 36,600', Climb 1430'/1 min., 5000'/7 min. Range 2000 miles/4000 lbs. bombs, 3300 miles max.   MFR

Since power plants were the same as on the previous models, the increased weight and drag of protruding turrets made the Fortress slow, although its ability to defend itself was greatly improved. The distinguishing feature of this and succeeding Fortresses was a large dorsal fin. The B-17E arrived just as America entered the war. Forty-two were delivered by November 30, 1941, mostly to the 7th Bomb Group, with 60 more B-17Es in December and the last of 512 by May 28, 1942.

In 1941 there were 13 heavy-bomber groups, but they were far below the 32-plane strength expected. Only some 150 B-17s were on hand on December 1, 1941, including older models, together with some B-18s for training. First priority was given to the groups deployed overseas.

Six B-17Cs and 29 B-17Ds were with the 19th Bomb Group in the Philippines, along with 18 B-18s. They expected to be joined by the 38th Reconnaissance Squadron, which arrived in Hawaii with four B-17Cs and two B-17Es on December 7, in the middle of the Japanese attack. Parked at Hickam Field were 12 B-17Ds of the 5th Bomb Group. Five B-17s were destroyed and eight of the 18 present that morning were damaged.

Near the Canal Zone the 6th Bomb Group had eight B-17Bs and 19 B-18s, and got eight new B-17Es the first week in December. In Newfoundland six B-17Bs and a B-18A served the 41st Reconnaissance Squadron. In the United States the only combat-ready group was the 7th, whose 35 B-17Es left Salt Lake City, Utah, on December 5 for deployment to the Far East. Six arrived in Hawaii just after the attack, but the rest were diverted to Muroc to parry any threat to California. As for the other six heavy-bomber groups, their total scattered equipment included only 12 YB-17s, 22 B-17Bs, five B-17Cs and a few B-18As. Only 19 B-17Bs could be sent to Spokane to join the five B-17Cs of the 39th Bomb Group to help defend the Northwest, and two B-17Bs were stationed in Alaska.

After some gallant sorties from the Philippines, 14 19th Bomb Group Boeings retreated to Australia to carry on. In January they were joined in Java by B-17E and LB-30 bombers of the 7th Bomb Group. That group retreated to India in March, leaving the 19th, now re-equipped with B-17Es, as the only Boeing group in the South Pacific. In Hawaii the Seventh Air Force had the 5th and 11th groups for the Battle of Midway, and the 36th Bombardment Squadron had 12 B-17Es in Alaska at the same time. By August 1942 the 43rd Bomb Group in Australia had become the fifth B-17E group to be deployed against Japan.

Yet by 1943 B-17s had been withdrawn from the Pacific in favor of the longer-range B-24s. The type had not been especially successful in its originally intended role of attacking moving surface ships, a job best done by low-altitude twin-engine bombers. Instead the B-17 flew over 98 percent of its combat sorties in Europe. On July 1, 1942, the first 97th Bomb Group B-17E reached the United Kingdom (the first Air Force tactical aircraft to do so), the group losing four of its 49 aircraft[1] over the North

---

[1] A heavy-bomber group's authorized strength was 48 bombers in four squadrons during most of the war.

Atlantic ferry route. This group flew the first B-17E mission against Nazi-occupied Europe on August 17, 1942. Forty-five B-17Es went to the RAF Coastal Command as the Fortress IIA from March to July 1942.

One B-17E was fitted with 1,425-hp Allison V-1710-89 inline engines and was called XB-38. The

varied with model and modification center, but two guns were usually mounted in the side windows, with one or two more in the nose itself. Another gun was added at the opening on top of the radio compartment on the B-17F-30.

The production history of the B-17F series began with a lend-lease contract signed in June 1941 for

BOEING XB-38
Allison V-1710-89, 1425 hp at 25,000'
DIMENSIONS: Span 103'9", Lg. 74', Ht. 19'2", Wing Area 1420 sq. ft.
WEIGHT: Empty 34,748 lb., Gross 56,000 lb., Max. 64,000 lb. Fuel 1730–2520 gal.
PERFORMANCE: Speed—Top 327 mph at 25,000', Cruising 226 mph. Service Ceiling 29,700'. Range 2400 miles/3000 lbs. bombs, 1900 miles/6000 lbs. bombs, 3600 miles max.   MFR

BOEING B-17F
Wright R-1820-97, 1200 hp at 25,000' (1380 hp WE)
DIMENSIONS: Span 103'9", Lg. 74'9", Ht. 19'1", Wing Area 1420 sq. ft.
WEIGHT: Empty 34,000 lb., Gross 55,000 lb., Max. 65,500 lb. Fuel 1730–2550 gal. (3614 gal. later models).
PERFORMANCE: Speed—Top 299 mph at 25,000' (314 mph WE), Cruising 200 mph, Landing 90 mph. Service Ceiling 37,500', Climb 20,000'/25.7 min. Range 1300 miles/6000 lbs. bombs, 2880 miles max.   AF

first liquid-cooled bomber design in a decade was begun in March 1942, ordered the following July 10, and flown on May 19, 1943.

B-17F and G Models

The B-17F followed the B-17E into production with a new molded plastic nose, more armor, new propellers, and R-1820-97 Cyclones whose standard 1,200 hp could be raised to 1,380 hp ("war emergency" power). The top speed in light (55,000-pound) condition was increased from 299 mph to 314 mph. Extra tankage now accommodated up to 2,810 gallons in the wings and 820 gallons in the bomb bay.

While the normal bomb load remained 4,000 pounds, the bomb bay could accommodate up to 12,500 pounds: six 1,000-pound or 1,600-pound bombs, or two 2,000-pound bombs, and, from B-17F-30 to B-17F-95, two external racks under the wings could hold a 4,000-pound bomb. Armament operated by the ten crewmen was originally the same as that of the E, but protection for the nose increased when the .30-caliber gun was dropped and .50-caliber weapons were installed. Positions

300 Fortress II bombers for the RAF. These aircraft became available for the Army when the British decided to use the Boeings not as bombers but only for coastal patrol. The first B-17F-1-BO was delivered May 30, 1942 to the Army, but after August, 19 B-17Fs did go to Coastal Command as the Fortress II. Later contracts for B-17F-30-BOs to B-17F-130-BOs brought the total to 2,300 built at Boeing by September 2, 1943. Douglas received an order for 600 B-17F-DLs on August 28, 1941, and Lockheed-Vega received one for 500 B-17F-VEs in September. Delivery from their Long Beach and Burbank factories, respectively, began in July 1942.

These were the bombers that launched the American operation POINTBLANK, the Combined Bomber Offensive against Germany. "Precision" bombing in daylight was more effective than the night "area" bombing practiced by the RAF, and it was supposed that bomber firepower in mass formation would frustrate fighter defense. But resistance by German fighters grew more bitter and effective as bomb tonnage delivered mounted, and raids like those on Ploesti and Schweinfurt from August through October 1943 cost such losses that the ability of the bombers to execute their part of the war plan was in doubt.

In August 1942 an Air Force board had suggested that bombers be accompanied by "destroyer escort" planes. Existing fighters being too short-range to protect the bombers, the logical proposal was a specially armed B-17. One XB-40 escort plane was converted from the second B-17F in November 1942 by replacing the bombs with more armor, 11,200 rounds of ammunition, and 14 .50-caliber guns, which were placed in pairs in a new chin turret, in a power-operated mount amidship, in each side window, as well as in the usual top, belly, and tail positions.

Thirteen B-17F-10-VEs went to a modification center in November 1942 for conversion to YB-40 escorts by March 1943. Another 12 modifications were ordered, but only one of these followed the first 13 to the Eighth Air Force, the rest being stripped down as TB-40 trainers after the escort function failed in combat.

Between May 29 and July 4, 1943, nine YB-40 combat missions were flown from England, claiming five kills and two probables for one YB-40 lost, but the experiment failed as a protection system. According to the official history, "Being heavily armored and loaded, they could not climb or keep speed with the standard B-17, a fact which . . . resulted in the disorganization of the formation they were supposed to protect."

The chin turret developed for the B-40 was useful in discouraging frontal attacks and was adopted in the last Fortress production model, the B-17G (British Fortress III), for which deliveries began September 4, 1943.

Armament of the B-17G included 13 .50-caliber guns, 6,380 rounds, and from 6,000 to 9,600 (6 × 1600) pounds of bombs in the bay. Two guns were placed in the chin turret below the nose; above them a pair of hand-operated "cheek" guns. The other gun locations were the same as on the B-17F, although the installations had been improved. Later models dropped the radio operator's gun and introduced an improved tail turret and enclosed waist positions.

Of 8,680 Gs built, 2,395 were by Douglas, 2,250 by Vega, and the rest by Boeing, which completed Fortress production April 13, 1945. With Germany defeated, production closed at the other plants in July.

Eighty-five went to Britain as the Fortress III, where they were used with radar by Coastal Command and by two "pathfinder" radar countermeasures squadrons in 1944–45. About 878 were delivered as TB-17G trainers for replacement training units (RTU).

Total B-17 production was 12,276, and the peak

BOEING XB-40
Wright R-1820-97, 1200 hp at 25,000'
DIMENSIONS: As B-17F
WEIGHT: Empty 36,898 lb., Gross 58,000 lb., Max. 63,295 lb. Fuel 1730–2520 gal.
PERFORMANCE: Speed—Top 292 mph at 25,000', 248 mph at s. l., Cruising 196 mph, Landing 94 mph. Service Ceiling 29,200', Climb 780'/1 min., 10,000'/13.3 min. Range 2260 miles, 2460 miles max.   AMC

BOEING B-17G
Wright R-1820-97, 1200 hp at 25,000' (1380 hp WE)
DIMENSIONS: Span 103'9", Lg. 74'4", Ht. 19'1", Wing Area 1420 sq. ft.
WEIGHT: Empty 36,135 lb., Gross 55,000 lb., Max. 65,500 lb. Fuel 2810–3630 gal.
PERFORMANCE: Speed—Top 287 mph at 25,000' (302 mph with WE), Cruising 182 mph, Landing 90 mph. Service Ceiling 35,600', Climb 20,000'/37 min. Range 2000 miles/6000 lbs. bombs, 3400 miles max.   AF

AAF inventory was 4,574 in August 1944, with 26 combat groups with the Eighth Air Force in England and six groups with the Fifteenth Air Force in Italy. (Their combat record is summarized in Table 7, p. 231.)

How the bomber crews found the courage to overcome violence, pain, and death in order to complete their missions has been dramatized in books and films such as *Twelve O'Clock High*. Until friendly long-range fighters dominated the sky, failure always threatened the bomber offensive. The 91st Bomb Group's experience illustrates this point. Flying 340 missions, averaging 28 group planes on each, from November 7, 1942, to April 25, 1945, the 91st Bomb Group lost 197 B-17s missing in action and claimed to have downed 420 enemy fighters.

Besides the bombing missions, B-17s filled other roles. None was more dramatic than that of the BQ-7, a radio-controlled drone loaded with 18,428 pounds of explosives (torpex). The secret project assigned the code name Aphrodite to the bombers, often named simply Weary Willie by the participants. The first ten were converted from worn B-17Fs at Ridgewell, England, in July 1944. Visual control from a guide plane equipped with a 50-pound control box was used, and later a TV camera in the nose was tried. Wooden guns disguised the aircraft's role and smoke bombs could be used to simulate an aircraft in distress.

The first drones were launched against V-1 flying bomb sites on August 4. Their effect proved to be less than had been expected, for essentially this was a light-case weapon with no penetrating power, limited to a 30° slant descent.

Noncombat conversions of the B-17, which were numerous, fall outside the scope of this book. The most common were the F-9, F-9A, and F-9B camera ships converted from B-17Fs, while modified B-17Gs became the F-9C (and later the RB-17G), serving photographic mapping units until 1950. Late-model B-17Gs completed after bombing in Europe had ended were modified to B-17H (later SB-17) lifeboat-carrying rescue planes, while 17 became PB-1G Coast Guard rescue aircraft and 31 PB-1W Navy radar warning aircraft.

The last B-17s to bomb were three civilian B-17Gs purchased by Israel and armed in Czechoslovakia, where they took off and raided the Cairo area July 14, 1948, on their way to Israel. They flew about 200 sorties in Israel's war of independence and served that country's bomber force for ten years. Brazil operated a B-17G search-rescue squadron for over 20 years. In the United States civilian fire fighters used B-17 chemical bombers into the 1970s to preserve, not destroy, life and property.

The B-24 Liberator

More B-24 Liberators were built than any other American warplane, and more than any bomber type in any other country in the world. Although less famous than the B-17, the B-24 was much more widely used.

The Liberator began in January 1939 as the Consolidated 32, a four-engine design by I. M. Laddon, utilizing the new Davis high wing and the twin tail featured on the Model 31 flying boat. A prototype ordered March 30, 1939, was designated XB-24, and additional orders were placed for seven YB-24s on April 27 and 38 B-24As on August 10.

First flown on December 29, 1939, at San Diego, the seven-place XB-24 had the first tricycle landing gear flown on a large bomber. The nose wheel permitted faster landings and takeoffs, thus allowing for a heavier wing loading on the low-drag Davis airfoil. A bombardier's enclosure began the nose of the deep fuselage, which terminated behind twin rudders with a tail gunner's position. Armament included three .50-caliber guns and four .30-caliber hand-operated guns fired through openings in the fuselage sides, top, and bottom, and in a nose socket, while eight 1,100-pound bombs could be accommodated, twice the capacity of the B-17's bay. Power plants were Pratt & Whitney R-1830-33 Wasps of 1,000-hp at 14,500 feet.

When the prototype's speed was measured at 273 mph instead of the 311 mph estimated by the specification, the Air Corps ordered, on July 26, 1940, that turbosuperchargers and leakproof fuel tanks be installed. Redesignated XB-24B, with R-1830-41 Wasps giving 1,200 hp at 25,000 feet and wing slots deleted, the reworked prototype was flown February 1, 1941.

In the meantime, in April 1940, Consolidated had interested the French in an export version, the LB-30. By the time a contract was made in June 1940, France was near defeat. Britain took over the contract, specifying 165 LB-30s with self-sealing fuel tanks, armor, and power-operated turrets. These features, plus turbosuperchargers, were also specified for the first Air Corps mass-production version, the B-24D, first ordered August 16, 1940.

Delivery on the B-24s ordered in 1939 was deferred by the Air Corps on November 9, 1940, so that the first 26 could go to Britain and be replaced

CONSOLIDATED XB-24
Pratt & Whitney R-1830-33, 1200 hp takeoff, 1000 hp at 14,500'
DIMENSIONS: Span 110', Lg. 63'9", Ht. 18'8", Wing Area 1048 sq. ft.
WEIGHT: Empty 27,500 lb., Gross 38,360 lb., Max. 46,400 lb. Fuel 2400–3000 gal.
PERFORMANCE: Speed—Top 273 mph at 15,000', Cruising 186 mph, Landing 90 mph. Service Ceiling 31,500', Climb 10,000'/6 min. Range 3000 miles/2500 lbs. bombs, 4700 miles max.   MFR

CONSOLIDATED XB-24B   MFR

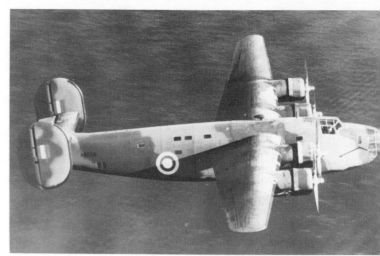

CONSOLIDATED LIBERATOR IA (YB-24)   MFR

CONSOLIDATED B-24A
Pratt & Whitney R-1830-33, 1200 hp takeoff, 1000 hp at
   14,500′
DIMENSIONS: As XB-24
WEIGHT: Empty 30,000 lb., Gross 39,350 lb., Max. 53,600
   lb. Fuel 2150–3100 gal.
PERFORMANCE: Speed—Top 292.5 mph at 15,000′, Cruising 228 mph, Landing 92 mph. Service Ceiling 30,500′,
   Absolute Ceiling 32,000′, Climb 1780′/1 min., 10,000′/
   5.6 min. Range 2200 miles/4000 lbs. bombs, 4000 miles
   max. at 190 mph.   AF

by later Army models with turbosuperchargers and power turrets. The first ships off the production line in December 1940 were six YB-24s, identical to the original XB-24 except for the deletion of wing slots and the addition of de-icers. These six went to the RAF as the LB-30A, used for transatlantic ferry transports, while the seventh YB-24 had armor and self-sealing fuel tanks and was accepted by the Army in May 1941. The first 20 B-24As, whose delivery began March 29, 1941, went to No. 120 Coastal Command Squadron as the Liberator I (LB-30B). Equipment installed in Britain included a complicated radar installation, the ASV Mark II, with both a forward and sideways-looking aerial array. Six to eight 250-pound depth charges could be carried on 16-hour patrols, along with four 20-mm fixed guns in a tray under the fuselage and six .303-caliber guns (British Brownings), two of them in the tail turret.

Nine B-24As accepted by the Army from June 16 to July 10, 1941, had R-1830-33 Wasps like their predecessors. Mounts for six .50- and two .30-caliber guns were provided, but these planes went to the newly organized Army Air Force Ferry Command, which retained only a tail gun and used these planes to pioneer intercontinental routes vital to Allied cooperation. They were the only Army planes with enough range for flights like the Harriman mission to Moscow in September 1941. The first of these aircraft to be lost to enemy action was

a B-24A at Hickam Field on December 7, 1941; it had been fitted with cameras and three guns for a secret mission to photograph Japanese mandated islands in the Pacific.

The Liberator II, built under the LB-30 contract, was the first model with a longer nose and provision for two power-operated gun turrets. Commercial R-1830-S3C4-G engines and Curtiss (instead of the usual Hamilton) propellers were used, along with 14 .303-caliber guns. Four were in the Boulton-Paul top turret, four in the tail turret, two in each waist window, one at the tunnel hatch, and another in the nose. Except for test examples, the armament was

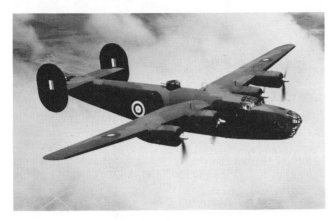

CONSOLIDATED LIBERATOR II (LB-30)
Pratt & Whitney R-1830-S3C4, 1200 hp takeoff, 1000 hp
   at 12,500'
DIMENSIONS: As B-24C
WEIGHT: Gross 46,250 lb.
PERFORMANCE: Speed—Top 263 mph (with turrets). Serv-
   ice Ceiling 24,000'.   MFR

installed in Britain. The first LB-30 crashed on a
test flight made June 2, 1941, but 139 more were
built, with deliveries beginning August 8, 1941.

These aircraft were for RAF bomber squadrons
intended for the Middle East, but when the United
States entered the war 75 LB-30s were taken over
by the Air Force, the last on January 6, 1942. Eight
.50-caliber guns could be fitted, including two
hand-operated tail guns, single guns in the nose,
waist, and tunnel positions, and two in a Martin
power turret installed on top behind the wing; but
the latter item was scarce and not always available.

Twelve of these LB-30s were flown by the 7th
Bomb Group crews to Java, from where the first
three Air Force Liberator combat sorties were flown
January 17, 1942. Seventeen others fitted with ASV
Mark II radar were rushed to the Canal Zone to fill
out the 6th Bomb Group, while six sent to Hawaii
and three sent to Alaska flew a few sorties in June
1942. Others served the AAF as transports, but 23
Army LB-30s were returned to British control in
1942, bringing the RAF LB-30 total to 87.

American power turrets and turbosupercharged
1,200-hp R-1830-41 Wasps were used on nine B-
24Cs, the first delivered December 20, 1941. Seven
.50-caliber guns and 2,900 rounds of ammunition
were carried: one gun in the nose, two in a Martin
turret forward of the wing, one at each waist panel,
and a pair in a Consolidated tail turret. The remaining Liberators on early orders became B-24Ds
and were delivered in 1942.

The first mass-production Liberator was the B-
24D, ordered in August 1940 and first delivered
from Consolidated's San Diego factory January 23,
1942. A production pool of five factories had been
established for the Liberator, including a new Con-

solidated factory in Fort Worth, a Douglas Tulsa
factory, North American near Dallas, and an enormous Ford plant at Willow Run, Michigan, that
produced both complete B-24E aircraft and subassemblies for the Fort Worth and Tulsa factories.

These aircraft were similar in appearance but varied in details. Designations included 2,415 B-24D-
COs from San Diego, 303 B-24D-CFs and 144 B-
24E-CFs at Forth Worth (beginning May 1, 1942),
and 10 B-24D-DTs and 167 B-24E-DTs, which began emerging from Tulsa in August 1942. Willow
Run delivered the first of 490 B-24E-FO Liberators
September 1, 1942, while the first 25 B-24G-NTs
built at Tulsa (beginning March 1943) were also
similar to the B-24D series.

CONSOLIDATED B-24C
Pratt & Whitney R-1830-41, 1200 hp at 25,000'
DIMENSIONS: Span 110', Lg. 66'4", Ht. 18', Wing Area
   1048 sq. ft.
WEIGHT: Empty 32,330 lb., Design Gross 41,000 lb., Max.
   53,700 lb. Fuel 2364–3164 gal.
PERFORMANCE: Speed—Top 313 mph at 25,000', Cruising
   233 mph, Landing 93 mph. Service Ceiling 34,000',
   Climb 10,000'/6.1 min. Range 2100 miles/5000 lbs.
   bombs, 3600 miles max.   AF

CONSOLIDATED B-24D
Pratt & Whitney R-1830-43, 1200 hp at 23,400'
DIMENSIONS: Span 110', Lg. 66'4", Ht. 17'11", Wing Area
   1048 sq. ft.
WEIGHT: Empty 32,605 lb., Gross 55,000 lb., Max. 60,000
   lb. Fuel 2364–3664 gal.
PERFORMANCE: Speed—Top 303 mph at 25,000', Cruising
   200 mph, Landing 95 mph. Service Ceiling 32,000',
   Climb 20,000'/22 min. Range 2300 miles/5000 lbs.
   bombs, 3500 miles max.   MFR

Powered by Pratt & Whitney R-1830-43 Wasps, the first 82 B-24Ds had seven guns, with a top Martin power turret behind the pilots and a Consolidated power turret in the tail, each with two .50-caliber guns. Hand-held single guns were mounted at each waist window, and the nose enclosure, originally provided with one, eventually had three hand-operated .50s at the sides and bottom. Belly protection on 179 B-24Ds was provided by a Bendix power turret with periscopic sights, but this was replaced by a single manual tunnel gun. The last 93 B-24D-CO and all but the first five B-24Gs had a Sperry ball turret like that of the B-17. Armor plate ⅜-inch thick protected gun stations and pilot seats.

With a crew of nine men, the B-24D grossed from 55,000 to 64,000 pounds, depending on the load. The bomb bay accommodated up to eight 1,100-pound bombs, but the B-24D-25-CO, B-24D-10-CF, and later models could accommodate eight 1,600-pound bombs. Underwing racks for two 4,000-pound bombs were available but were seldom used.

The first B-24Ds to go abroad were those of the Halvorsen detachment, originally organized to bomb Japan from China but 'rerouted to Egypt. From there 12 struck at Ploesti on June 12, 1942—the first AAF mission into Europe—and then flew operations with the Ninth Air Force. Britain-based B-24Ds began operations October 9, while the first B-24D squadron in the Pacific attacked Kiska on June 11, 1942, and the 90th Group went to the Southwest Pacific in November 1942, where, because of superior range, Liberators eventually replaced all B-17s. The B-24E, however, was used for replacement training in the United States, and very few went overseas.

CONSOLIDATED LIBERATOR III with radar for anti-submarine search   IWM

Like the Boeings, the Liberator also suffered from enemy fighters, so in August 1942 an escort-fighter counterpart to the B-40 was approved. Converted from a B-24D, the Consolidated XB-41 had 11,135 rounds for 14 .50-caliber guns paired in a Bendix

CONSOLIDATED XB-41
Pratt & Whitney R-1830-43, 1200 hp at 25,000′
DIMENSIONS: As B-24D
WEIGHT: Empty 37,050 lb., Gross 61,500 lb., Max. 63,000 lb. Fuel 2814 gal.
PERFORMANCE: Speed—Top 289 mph at 25,000′, Cruising 200 mph. Service Ceiling 28,500′, Climb 1050′/1 min. Range 3100 miles.   MFR

chin turret, two top turrets, tail turret, ball turret, and at each waist opening. One was delivered January 29, 1943, but was not reproduced. Another B-24D modification was the B-24F testing treated-surface anti-icing equipment in May 1942.

Nose turrets to improve frontal protection had been installed in the field on some Pacific-based B-24Ds and this feature was incorporated on the production lines. An Emerson nose turret and a retractable Sperry ball belly turret were introduced on the B-24H, first delivered June 30, 1943. Ten .50-caliber guns with 4,700 rounds of ammunition were carried, paired in the nose, top, belly, and tail turrets, and at hand-operated waist mounts where panel coverings were provided on later blocks. Total production included 1,780 B-24H-FOs, 738 B-24H-CFs, and 582 B-24H-DTs.

Nose turrets were also fitted, beginning in November, on all but the first 25 of 430 B-24Gs built at Dallas, and on the B-24J, which first appeared August 31, 1943, with a Consolidated nose and a Briggs ball turret. Both the B-24H and the B-24J used the R-1830-65 Wasp, with 2,792 B-24J-COs, 1,558 B-24J-CFs, 1,587 B-24J-FOs, 205 B-24J-DTs and 536 B-24J-NTs produced.

A new hand-held tail-gun mount had been specified for the B-24L, but only 186 of 417 B-24L-CO

CONSOLIDATED B-24G-15   AF

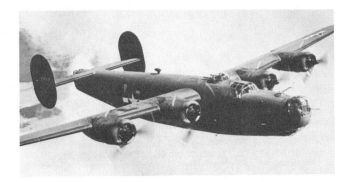

CONSOLIDATED B-24H
Pratt & Whitney R-1830-65, 1200 hp at 26,500' (or 31,800'
  WE)
DIMENSIONS: Span 110', Lg. 67'2", Ht. 18', Wing Area
  1048 sq. ft.
WEIGHT: Empty 36,500 lb., Gross 56,000 lb., Max. 65,000
  lb., Fuel 2364–3614 gal.
PERFORMANCE: Speed—Top 290 mph at 25,000', 300 mph
  at 30,000', Landing 95 mph. Service Ceiling 30,000',
  Climb 20,000'/25 min. Range 2100 miles/5000 lbs.
  bombs, 3300 miles max.   MFR

CONSOLIDATED B-24J
(Data as B-24H)   AF

CONSOLIDATED B-24L   AF

Liberators actually received these installations, the
rest getting standard turrets. Willow Run delivered
1,250 B-24L-FOs beginning in August 1944 and
1,677 B-24M-FOs built with lightweight turrets by
June 1945. Performance of models B-24G through
M was essentially the same.

A high, single tail was tested on the XB-24K, a
modified B-24D first flown September 9, 1943, with
R-1830-75 engines and nose turret. Improvements
in flight handling and field of fire for the rear guns
was so great that on April 26, 1944, the Eglin Field
proving ground recommended that all future B-24s
be ordered with single tails.

An XB-24N-FO with the single tail, R-1830-75
Wasps, and new nose and tail turrets was delivered
in November 1944, but of 5,176 single-tailed Liberators ordered from Ford, only seven YB-24Ns
were delivered in May–June 1945. Other rarely
seen Liberators were the XB-24P, a B-24D modified
in July 1945 to test Sperry fire-control systems, and
the XB-24Q, a B-24L testing the General Electric
radar-controlled tail gun in July 1946.

As with any aircraft built in large numbers, there
were many variations, only the most important of
which can be mentioned here. The C-87 was a
transport version, with 286 delivered from Fort

CONSOLIDATED B-24M   MFR

CONSOLIDATED B-24K   AF

CONSOLIDATED XB-24N
Pratt & Whitney R-1830-75, 1350 hp at 30,000'
DIMENSIONS: Span 110', Lg. 67'2", Ht. 26'9", Wing Area
    1048 sq. ft.
WEIGHT: Empty 38,300 lb., Gross 56,000 lb., Max. 65,000
    lb. Fuel 2814–3614 gal.
PERFORMANCE: Speed—Top 294 mph at 30,000', Cruising
    213 mph, Landing 95 mph. Service Ceiling 28,000',
    Climb 20,000'/29 min. Range 2000 miles/5000 lbs.
    bombs, 3500 miles max.   MFR

Worth beginning September 14, 1942. Two hundred bombers converted to aerial tankers to support China-based B-29s became C-109s, while five AT-22s were built to train flight engineers. A B-24D was converted to an XF-7 photographic aircraft with 11 cameras in January 1943, followed by 213 conversions of later aircraft to F-7, F-7A, and F-7B aircraft for use by Pacific reconnaissance units.

The story of the Navy's use of the Liberator and its subsequent offspring, the Privateer, is discussed in Chapter 18. Total Liberator production was 18,-482, the largest of any American military airplane. The peak AAF B-24 inventory occurred in September 1944, when 6,043 were on hand. Because of their superior range, they were preferred over the B-17 in most areas, but in Britain the Eighth Air Force favored the B-17 because it was easier to fly, had a higher ceiling, and seemed better able to defend itself against enemy gunfire. (See Table 7, p. 231 for comparisons.)

Nineteen Eighth Air Force groups used Liberators, but five of these were re-equipped with B-17Gs by September 1944. Twelve Liberator groups worked with the Fifteenth Air Force in the Mediterranean and 11 groups operated against Japan, plus a single Aleutian-based squadron that made its first attack against the Kurils on July 18, 1943. Eight U-boats were sunk in the Atlantic by USAF antisubmarine squadrons in 1943.

The Lend-Lease Program and other transfers provided Britain with 366 B-24Ds as the Liberator III (and G.R.V for Coastal Command), eight B-24Gs and 22 B-24Hs (Lib. IV), 1,157 B-24Js (Lib. VI), 24 C-87s (Lib. VII), and 355 B-24Ls (Lib. VIII). The Coastal Command used them in antisubmarine service, while they were used as heavy bombers in the Middle and Far East.

Australia received 12 B-24D, 145 B-24J, 83 B-24L, and 47 B-24M Liberators (for a total of 287), while Canada got 19 B-24D, 49 B-24J, 16 B-24L,

and four B-24M bombers. A single B-24D was acquired by the U.S.S.R. in November 1942, and two by France in 1944, while China received 37 B-24Ms in 1945. Most Liberators, of course, were processed for scrap metal after the war. Some survived many transfers, but the last Liberator in service was in an Indian Air Force reconnaissance squadron that flew them until 1966.

Flying alone on antisub patrols or in mass formations deep into enemy territory, Liberators were seen from Alaska to the Indian Ocean, and often their missions were as dangerous and violent as the famous low-level attack on Ploesti on August 1, 1943. Their service has been recorded in many wartime histories, and a club of Liberator enthusiasts still publicized its career a generation after the war.

Medium Bombers in Wartime

Although four-engine heavy bombers flew most of the Air Force's bombing missions, there were many targets for which twin-engine medium bombers were more appropriate. The North American B-25 and Martin B-26 were the types used by the Air Force for attacks over shorter ranges and at lower altitudes than those of their larger companions.

Development of the medium bombers proceeded in parallel, both being designed to a five-place bomber specification issued by the Air Corps on January 25, 1939. Bids were opened July 5 and contracts for 184 B-25 and 201 B-26 aircraft were announced August 10 and finally approved September 20. These production contracts were made without testing a prototype so that deliveries could be made more quickly. Both types did begin arriving at their bases in February 1941, and both entered combat in April 1942.

North American's B-25 design, developed from the earlier NA-40 attack bomber, had a larger fuselage and fuel capacity. Two 1,700-hp Wright R-2600-9 Cyclones had three-bladed Hamilton propellers, and the airframe was designed for easy production in component subassemblies.

The wing originally had an unbroken dihedral from root to tip, but to improve directional stability the outer panels were made horizontal on the tenth and subsequent aircraft. This shape remained on all B-25s, along with the twin rudders and tricycle gear.

The bomb bay could accommodate one 2,000-pound, two 1,100-pound, four 600-pound, or smaller bombs, or an extra 420-gallon tank. Four hand-held flexible guns reflected 1939's modest armament levels. A .30-caliber gun was provided in the bombardier's nose enclosure. Two more .30-caliber guns were mounted to fire through waist windows and panels in the fuselage top and bottom. A .50-caliber gun in the tail was fired by a prone gunner.

The first B-25 was flown August 19, 1940, at Inglewood, California, by Vance Breese. Never delivered to the Army, it was retained by the company as a test aircraft. This policy had replaced the previous custom of delivering the first aircraft of each type to Wright Field. Eventually this aircraft became a company executive transport.

Martin's B-26, designed by Peyton Magruder, was a more expensive and heavily armed medium bomber. Although also a midwing monoplane with tricycle gear, the B-26 was highly streamlined, with a circular fuselage, single rudder, and a smaller wing despite the heavier weight. Two Pratt & Whitney 1,850-hp R-1830-5 Wasps with four-bladed Curtiss propellers—the most powerful power plants then available—were used. A double bomb bay could hold up to two 2,000-pound, four 1,100-pound, or six 600-pound bombs, up to a maximum of 4,800 pounds.

Four .30-caliber guns had been specified for the original armament, but this was increased when Martin developed an electric-power gun turret, the first to go into American production. Two .50-caliber guns were placed in the top turret and another was for the gunner seated in the tail. A .30-caliber gun was provided in the conical nose enclosure and a second could be fired from an opening in the fuselage bottom behind the turret. Self-sealing fuel tanks and 555 pounds of armor were specified for the B-26A version, added by an option to the original contract, and by September 30, 1940, the Army decided to include these features on all B-26s under construction.

On November 25, 1940, the first B-26 was flown at Baltimore by William K. Ebel. By that time the estimated gross weight had increased from 26,625 to over 28,600 pounds, and top speed had dropped from an estimated 323 mph to 315 mph—still 100 mph faster than the B-18As it would replace.

B-25 Development

The improved protection features introduced on the B-26 were soon added to North American's bomber. Twenty-four B-25s accepted from February to May 1941 had no internal protection, but these were followed by 40 B-25As with ⅜-inch armor back of the crew's seats and self-sealing fuel tanks.

Power-operated turrets were provided for the remaining ships on the contract, labeled B-25B. The tail and waist guns and windows were deleted, and two .50-caliber guns with 400 rounds each were in the top Bendix power turret. Two more with 350 rounds each were in a retractable belly turret lowered behind the bomb bay and aimed through a periscopic sight by a kneeling crewman. The bombardier's hand-held .30-caliber gun, with 600 rounds, was retained in the nose.

The first 14 B-25Bs were accepted in August 1941, but the 15th was destroyed before delivery and deleted from the order. North American had delivered 130 bombers on this contract at the time of the Pearl Harbor attack and 171 by the end of 1941. During January 1942, with 119 B-25Bs accepted, deliveries shifted to the new B-25C contract. By that time the bomber had been named the Mitchell, after Brigadier General William Mitchell, the air-power pioneer.

The first Air Force group to use the Mitchell was the 17th Bomb Group at Pendleton, Oregon, which reached its full 52-plane strength in September 1941. At that time the Air Force had ten medium-bomber groups, but except for one with B-26s, the other groups had Douglas B-18 and B-23 aircraft,

NORTH AMERICAN B-25
Wright R-2600-9, 1700 hp takeoff, 1350 hp at 13,000'
DIMENSIONS: Span 67'6", Lg. 54'1", Ht. 14'10", Wing Area
610 sq. ft.
WEIGHT: Empty 16,767 lb., Gross 23,714 lb., Max. 27,310
lb. Fuel 434–916 gal. (1336 gal. max.).
PERFORMANCE: Speed—Top 322 mph at 15,000', Landing
90 mph. Service Ceiling 30,000', Absolute Ceiling
31,200', Climb 2090'/1 min. Range 2000 miles/916 gal.
with 3000 lbs. bombs.   PMB

NORTH AMERICAN B-25C-10
Wright R-2600-13, 1700 hp takeoff, 1450 hp at 12,000'
DIMENSIONS: Span 67'7", Lg. 52'11", Ht. 15'10", Wing
Area 610 sq. ft.
WEIGHT: Empty 20,300 lb., Gross 33,500 lb., Max. 34,000
lb. Fuel 974–1559 gal.
PERFORMANCE: Speed—Top 284 mph at 15,000', Cruising
233 mph, Landing 105 mph. Service Ceiling 21,200',
Climb 15,000'/16.5 min. Range 1500 miles/3000 lbs.
bombs, 2750 miles max.   AF

NORTH AMERICAN B-25A
Wright R-2600-9, 1700 hp takeoff, 1350 hp at 13,000'
DIMENSIONS: Span 67'7", Lg. 54'1", Ht. 15'9", Wing Area
610 sq. ft.
WEIGHT: Empty 17,870 lb., Gross 25,322 lb., Max. 27,100
lb. Fuel 434–670 gal. (1090 gal. max.).
PERFORMANCE: Speed—Top 315 mph at 15,000', Cruising
262 mph, Landing 90 mph. Service Ceiling 27,000',
Climb 15,000'/8.4 min. Range 1350 miles/3000 lbs.
bombs.   MFR

too obsolete for combat. When war came, these
groups were assigned to offshore antisubmarine patrols.

Crewmen from the 17th Bomb Group, however,
were assigned to a unique mission: They were the
only Army bombers ever to fly an attack from an
aircraft carrier. Led by Lieutenant Colonel James
H. Doolittle, 16 B-25Bs were launched from the
U.S.S. *Hornet* on April 18, 1942, each loaded with
2,000 pounds of bombs and 1,141 gallons of fuel,
and they made a low-level attack on Tokyo and
other targets in Japan.

The first mass-production Mitchell was the B-
25C, with 863 ordered from the Inglewood factory
September 28, 1940, and 162 for the Dutch East
Indies on June 24, 1941. A new bomber factory was
also begun in Kansas City in December 1940, and
an initial order for 1,200 B-25D Mitchells was approved June 28, 1941. This model was to be identical to the B-25C, and the first 100 were assembled
from parts made in Inglewood until the Fisher Body
Division of General Motors took over parts supply.

The first B-25C, flown on November 9, 1941, was
identical to the B-25B except for the R-2600-13 engines, with new carburetor, an anti-icing system,
and a new electrical system. Changes were introduced on later production aircraft, such as increased
fuel capacity and a navigator's scanning blister atop
the fuselage on ship 385, and these were included
on parallel B-25D aircraft.

The B-25C-1 (beginning with plane 606) and B-
25D-1 (plane 201) had external wing bomb racks
that could hold eight 250-pound bombs in addition
to the bomb bay's racks for two 1,600-pound, three
1,000-pound, or six 500-pound bombs, up to a maximum of 5,200 pounds. A 2,000-pound torpedo
could be carried externally, although there is no
mention of its use in combat. In October 1942 a .50-

NORTH AMERICAN B-25B (Mitchell I)
Wright R-2600-9, 1700 hp takeoff, 1350 hp at 13,000'
DIMENSIONS: Span 67'7", Lg. 52'11", Ht. 15'9", Wing Area
610 sq. ft.
WEIGHT: Empty 20,000 lb., Gross 26,208 lb., Max. 28,460
lb. Fuel 670–1090 gal.
PERFORMANCE: Speed—Top 300 mph at 15,000', Cruising
262 mph, Landing 93 mph. Service Ceiling 23,500',
Climb 15,000'/8.8 min. Range 1300 miles/3000 lbs.
bombs, 2900 miles ferry.   IWM

NORTH AMERICAN B-25D-15   AF

caliber flexible gun and a .50-caliber fixed gun were mounted in the nose of the B-25C-5 (plane 864), the B-25D-5 (plane 301), and subsequent aircraft, for a total of six .50-caliber guns and 1,350 rounds. The lower turret, however, was ineffective and was often removed in service. Winterization changes[2] were made on the B-25C-10 and B-25D-10, but in January 1943 the B-25C-15 (plane 1,177), and later the B-25D-15 (plane 706), had multiple flame-dampening exhaust stacks. This corrected the bright flame spurts from the older exhaust pipes that could betray the bomber on night raids.

Production of the B-25C was completed in May 1943, with 1,619 built, but deliveries of 2,290 B-25Ds continued at Kansas City from February 1942 until March 1944. The last block of 250 B-25D-35s were modified to use the tail turrets and waist guns standard on the B-25H/J models.

The first of these Mitchells to see combat were 48 early B-25Cs ferried across the Pacific to Australia beginning in March 1942. Although intended for the Dutch East Indies, most were taken over by the 3rd Bomb Group's 13th and 90th squadrons, which flew to the Philippines on April 11, 1942, where they raided Japanese shipping and returned without suffering losses. These two squadrons, and a Dutch squadron (No. 18) operated these Mitchells in the New Guinea area, and were joined by two B-25 squadrons of the 38th Bomb Group in September.

Another B-25 group joined the Fifth Air Force with the arrival of the 345th Group in June 1943, and shortly thereafter the 22nd Group converted to B-25s with the departure of the Martin B-26 Marauder from the Pacific war scene. The B-25's rival was considered more suitable for Europe because the B-26 needed larger airfields and had less range.

The next Air Force to use the Mitchell was the Tenth, in the China-Burma-India Theater. Two squadrons of the 7th Bombardment Group got B-25s, with the 11th Squadron flying into China in June 1942 and the 22nd remaining in India to be-

come the nucleus of the 341st Group activated in September.

The next Mitchell unit in combat was the 12th Bomb Group, which flew 57 B-25Cs across the South Atlantic and Africa to Egypt without a loss. They made their first raid in support of British forces on August 14, 1942.

After the Americans landed in North Africa, three more B-25 groups joined the struggle for the Mediterranean under the direction of the Twelfth Air Force. The Air Force, however, never used the Mitchell on raids from United Kingdom bases, reserving these for the B-26. The B-25 was also used for antisubmarine patrol in 1942–43.

More pressure was put on Japan in 1943 by the arrival of the 41st and 42nd groups in the South Pacific. In Alaska, both medium-bomber squadrons replaced B-26s with B-25s. By the end of 1943, the Fifth Air Force in the Southwest Pacific was operating three Mitchell groups, the 22nd, 38th, and 345th.

The Fifth Air Force added a new modification to the Mitchell line when they modified B-25s for strafing. The bombardier's position and the lower turret were removed, two pairs of guns were added to the nose, and another pair attached in a blister on each side. These eight forward-firing .50s were supplemented by the two in the upper turret. A crew of three operated the strafer, and 60 small fragmentation bombs plus six 100-pound demolition bombs could be carried.

The first example was tested in December 1942, and 175 B-25Cs and Ds had been so converted for low-level strafing by the depot at Townsville, Australia, by September 1943. Deadly work was done by the Mitchells against shipping in the Battle of the Bismarck Sea, and against Japanese airfields in the Rabaul area.

Improving the B-25's Firepower

A remarkable Mitchell modification was to fit a standard 75-mm M-4 cannon to a B-25C-1, which became the XB-25G, tested October 22, 1942. Five B-25C-15s were completed as B-25G-1s, the first flown March 16, 1943, and the last 400 B-25C-25s completed as B-25Gs by August 1943.

The 75-mm gun was mounted in the lower left nose and handloaded with 21 rounds from the loading tray behind the pilot. The shortened solid nose had two fixed .50-caliber nose guns with 400 rounds each, and armor ⅜-inch thick covered the front and left side of the pilot's cockpit. The usual two-gun top turret and its armor bulkhead was retained, but the two-gun lower turret on the first 221 Gs was omitted on later ships. The cannon was accurate, but the aircraft had to be held steady while only about four shells could be fired in a single run.

[2] The XB-25E and XB-25F were B-25Cs reworked to use heated surface and thermo anti-icing equipment.

NORTH AMERICAN B-25G-10
Wright R-2600-13, 1700 hp takeoff, 1450 hp at 12,000′
DIMENSIONS: Span 67′7″, Lg. 51′, Ht. 15′9″, Wing Area
610 sq. ft.
WEIGHT: Empty 19,975 lb., Gross 33,500 lb., Max. 35,000
lb. Fuel 974–1649 gal.
PERFORMANCE: Speed—Top 281 mph at 15,000′, Cruising
248 mph, Landing 105 mph. Service Ceiling 24,300′,
Climb 15,000′/15.5 min. Range 1560 miles/3000 lbs.
bombs, 2450 miles max.   AF

NORTH AMERICAN B-25H-5
Wright R-2600-13, 1700 hp
DIMENSIONS: As B-25G
WEIGHT: Empty 19,975 lb., Gross 33,500 lb., Max. 36,047
lb. Fuel 434–974 gal. (1624 gal. ferry).
PERFORMANCE: Speed—Top 275 mph at 13,000′, Cruising
230 mph. Service Ceiling 23,800′, Climb 15,000′/19
min. Range 1350 miles/974 gal. with 3000 lbs. bombs,
2700 miles ferry.   MFR

Although the Fifth Air Force used them often
against shipping and ground targets, the cannons
were removed from 82 B-25Gs and replaced by two
.50-caliber guns in the cannon tunnel, two more in
the nose, and a pair of .30s in the tail. Beginning
November 1943 these modifications were made in
the Townsville depot.

Heavier armament was introduced on the B-25H
model, which had a 75-mm T13E-1 in the nose,
along with four fixed .50-caliber guns and two more
in blisters on the right side of the fuselage. The
two-gun power turret was moved forward to just
behind the pilot, improving the field of fire. The
unpopular retractable belly turret was replaced in
the waist by a flexible gun firing out of a window
on each side. A tail gunner was seated in a power-
operated Bell two-gun turret. The load included
3,200 pounds of bombs, with provisions on late
models for eight 5-inch rockets under the wings.

One thousand B-25Hs had been ordered on August 21, 1942, and the first B-25H-1 flew July 31,
1943. Twelve .50-caliber guns were carried on the
300 B-25H-1s, but the remaining blocks, beginning
with B-25H-5, carried 14, with twin package guns
on both sides of the nose. Production of the B-25H
ended in July 1944 when North American's Inglewood factory completely changed over to P-51
fighter production.

The most widely used Mitchell was the B-25J,
which followed the B-25D at the Kansas City factory. A six-place model with the B-25D's transparent bombardier's nose enclosure, the B-25J had no
cannon; instead it had a flexible gun in the nose,

NORTH AMERICAN B-25J-5
Wright R-2600-29, 1700 hp takeoff, 1450 hp at 12,000′
DIMENSIONS: Span 67′7″, Lg. 53′6″, Ht. 16′4″, Wing Area
610 sq. ft.
WEIGHT: Empty 19,490 lb., Gross 27,560 lb., Max. 33,400
lb. Fuel 974–1624 gal.
PERFORMANCE: Speed—Top 293 mph at 13,850′, 273 mph
at s. l., Cruising 242 mph, Stalling 112 mph. Service
Ceiling 24,500′, Climb 10,000′/6.3 min. Range 1520
miles/2000 lbs., 3240 miles ferry.   MFR

NORTH AMERICAN B-25J-22   MFR

NORTH AMERICAN PBJ-1J
Wright R-2600-13, -29, 1700 hp takeoff, 1450 hp at 12,000′
DIMENSIONS: Span 67′7″, Lg. 53′7½″, Ht. 16′4″, Wing Area
   610 sq. ft.
WEIGHT: Empty 20,273 lb., Gross 32,516 lb., Max. 34,846
   lb. Fuel 974–1524 gal.
PERFORMANCE: Speed—Top 278 mph at 12,700′, 264 mph
   at s.l., Cruising 159 mph, Landing 112 mph. Service
   Ceiling 24,300′, Climb 1180′/1 min. Range 2010 miles
   patrol/1189 gal., 1940 miles/1200 lbs. bombs, 1520
   miles/4000 lbs. bombs.   MFR

with a fixed gun on the right side of the nose. The
balance of the twelve .50-caliber guns were the
same as those on the B-25H, with four fixed in
packages and six for the three gunners.

Begun by North American in April 1943, 4,318 B-
25Js were manufactured on supplements to the B-
25D contract, and the first B-25J-1 flew December
14, 1943. Later production blocks to B-25J-35 varied
in detail and gradually increased in weight. Power
plants were the R-2600-13 or the similar R-2600-29
Cyclone. Another .50-caliber fixed gun was added
below the fixed gun in the right-hand side of the
nose of the B-25J-20. When in a training configuration, these aircraft were designated AT-24D and,
later, TB-25J.

An attack modification replaced the bombardier's
compartment with eight .50-caliber fixed guns in a
solid nose. Appearing in August 1944, the B-25J-22
had twelve .50-caliber fixed guns as well as the six
flexible guns, for a total of 7,300 rounds of ammunition. This was the most heavily armed aircraft of
its size in service. There were 510 Mitchells completed in this configuration, designated B-25J-22,
-27, -32, and -37, according to their production
block.

All B-25Js had ⅜-inch armor for crew members,
and the bomb bay normally accommodated two
1,600-pound, three 1,000-pound, or six 500-pound
bombs. Other racks could be fitted to hold a 2,000-
pound bomb or eight 500-pound bombs inside, or
a Mark 13 torpedo externally.

By the end of 1944, the Air Force had 11.5 B-25
groups overseas, with each medium-bomber group
normally having 64 aircraft distributed among four
squadrons. The total inventory, including those in
reserve and at training stations, reached a peak of
2,656 in July 1944. Production ended in August
1945 with 9,816 Mitchells accepted, not including
72 B-25J-35s in flyable condition at the war's end
but not accepted contractually.

Marine Corps medium-bomber squadrons were
also activated to use the Mitchell, beginning with
VMB-413, whose first combat mission was against

Rabaul on March 15, 1944. Six more squadrons,
each with 15 aircraft and 30 crews, served in the
Pacific war, and five more squadrons were commissioned too late for combat. In 1943 50 B-25C and
152 B-25D bombers were redesignated PBJ-1C and
PBJ-1D for the Marines, followed by one B-25G,
248 B-25Hs, and 255 B-25Js with PBJ designations
by June 1945.

The Mitchell was the only medium bomber supplied to the Soviet Union under the Lend-Lease
Act. Soviet fliers sent to the United States in August
1941 were given five B-25As for testing, but they
considered them inadequate and also found the B-
26 tested in September unsuitable. Five B-25Bs
were substituted in November and shipped to
northern Russia by sea. Thirty-eight B-25Cs started
from Florida in March 1942 to be delivered by air
through Africa and Iran, and a total of 103 arrived
by the end of 1942. During the war 862 of 870
Mitchells dispatched were delivered for use by Soviet long-range bomber regiments.

The Royal Air Force used the B-25 to attack Ger-
man-occupied Europe from the United Kingdom.
The RAF had received 23 B-25Bs, named them
Mitchell I, and used them for operational training.
The B-25C and B-25D became the Mitchell II,
which was issued to No. 98 and No. 180 squadrons
in September 1942. These squadrons flew their first
combat mission January 22, 1943, and were later
joined by five more squadrons. By that time the
RAF had been allocated 287 B-25Cs, 84 B-25Ds,

two B-25Gs, and 316 B-25Js, 40 of the latter being returned to the USAAF.

Canada received seven B-25B, 74 B-25D, and 83 B-25J models, and the Netherlands was assigned 249 Mitchells, but some of both country's aircraft were transferred from the previous RAF totals. China received 134 B-25s in 1943–44 and 25 went to Brazil in 1945. Australia got 32 B-25Ds and 18 B-25Js in 1944–45.

The war's end also finished the B-25's combat career, and its place in this account, but for many years they were flown around the United States in both civil and military work. In 1950–53, the USAF converted B-25Js to new training configurations: the TB-25K to TB-25N models prolonging the Mitchell's service life until 1960. Thousands of memories were left behind by the B-25, from the Tokyo raid to a spectacular crash into the world's tallest skyscraper, the Empire State Building, July 28, 1945.

Development of the B-26

The Martin Marauder was not built in as large a quantity as the Mitchell because it proved more expensive to produce and maintain and had a higher accident rate. On paper the Martin was the more advanced design, and even before the first flight the original B-26 contract had been increased by orders for 139 B-26As on September 16 and 791 B-26Bs on September 28, 1940. This brought the total to 1,131 aircraft, a large risk on an untested aircraft.

The B-26A differed from the B-26 mainly by provision for an extra 250-gallon ferry tank in the bomb bay. Armament remained three .50-caliber and two .30-caliber guns. Thirty planes still had R-2800-5 Wasps, while the rest had R-2800-39s and were known as B-26A-1s.

When the B-26A acceptances replaced the B-26 in October 1941, only the 22nd Bomb Group had its 52-plane strength. The remaining aircraft waited undelivered because of a lack of power turrets and other mechanical difficulties. As they were made ready, the B-26 and B-26A mingled in service with the 38th and 42nd groups, which were the next units chosen for this equipment.

The day after the Pearl Harbor attack, the 22nd Group, still the only operational B-26 unit, was ordered from Langley Field, Virginia, to Muroc, California. It remained there until January 31, when it was moved by ship to Hawaii, where ferry tanks were fitted and the bombers flown to Australia. On April 5, 1942, this group flew the war's first Air Force medium-bomber mission, attacking Rabaul with nine B-26s.

In a series of attacks on Japanese-held bases, against strong opposition by Zero fighters, the B-

MARTIN B-26
Pratt & Whitney R-2800-5, 1850 hp takeoff, 1500 hp at 14,000'
DIMENSIONS: Span 65', Lg. 56', Ht. 19'10", Wing Area 602 sq. ft.
WEIGHT: Empty 21,375 lb., Gross 27,200 lb., Max. 32,000 lb. Fuel 465–962 gal.
PERFORMANCE: Speed—Top 315 mph at 15,000', Cruising 265 mph, Landing 102 mph. Service Ceiling 25,000', Climb 15,000'/12.5 min. Range 1000 miles/3000 lbs. bombs, 2200 miles max.   MFR

MARTIN B-26A
Pratt & Whitney R-2800-5, 1850 hp takeoff, 1500 hp at 14,000'
DIMENSIONS: Span 65', Lg. 58'3", Ht. 19'10", Wing Area 602 sq. ft.
WEIGHT: Empty 21,741 lb., Gross 28,367 lb., Max. 33,022 lb. Fuel 465–962 gal. (1462 gal. max.).
PERFORMANCE: Speed—Top 313 mph, Cruising 243 mph. Service Ceiling 23,500'. Range 1000 miles/3000 lbs. bombs, 2600 miles max.   AF

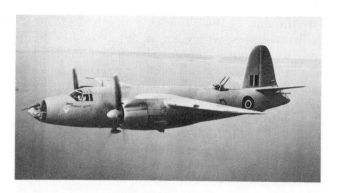

MARTIN B-26A-1 (Marauder 1A)   IWM

26's speed and ruggedness won praise from its crews. Another 24 B-26s, formerly of the 42nd Group, were moved to Alaska for the 28th Group. There, weather proved a greater problem than the enemy when the Japanese attacked on June 3, 1942, and the B-26s had to hunt through fog for the enemy.

The B-26B

A new tail defense distinguished the B-26B, the model used in the greatest quantity. In place of a single hand-held gun with 400 rounds of ammunition, two .50-caliber guns, each supplied with 1,500 rounds, were in a stepped-down tail position. Ammunition was fed from containers in the aft bomb bay on a pair of roller tracks. Slightly longer than earlier models, the B-26B could accommodate 4,000 pounds in the bomb bay, or a 2,000-pound Mark 7 torpedo on an external rack. This latter installation had been tested on earlier models, and made the Marauder the only Army bomber to use torpedos in combat.

The first B-26Bs appeared in May 1942. They re-equipped two 38th Group squadrons, which then made the first B-26 overwater flight to Hawaii. The first two B-26Bs arrived in time for the Battle of Midway, when they and two 22nd Bomb Group B-26s made a gallant but unsuccessful torpedo attack on June 4, 1942.

These two squadrons later moved to Fiji, and then to Guadalcanal, where combat sorties were begun November 15, 1942. In 1943, however, all B-26s in the Pacific were replaced by B-25s, whose longer range and shorter takeoff runs were more suitable for island-hopping than the fast, "hot" Martins.

The first 307 B-26Bs had the R-2800-5, but the 2,000-hp R-2800-41 and block numbers were introduced in August 1942 on 95 B-26B-2 aircraft. One

MARTIN B-26B for R.A.F.   IWM

MARTIN B-26B-2
Pratt & Whitney R-2800-41, 2000 hp takeoff, 1600 hp at 13,500'
DIMENSIONS: As B-26A
WEIGHT: Empty 22,380 lb., Design Gross 27,200 lb., Max. 34,000 lb. Fuel 962–1462 gal.
PERFORMANCE: Speed—Top 317 mph at 14,500', Cruising 260 mph, Landing 103 mph. Service Ceiling 23,500', Climb 15,000'/12 min. Range 1150 miles/3000 lbs. bombs, 2800 miles max.   AF

.50-caliber flexible gun and one fixed gun were provided in the nose cone. The similar R-2800-43 used on the remaining Marauder models was introduced on 28 B-26B-3s. They also had the enlarged air intakes so that filters could be fitted, when necessary, to protect carburetor intakes during desert operations. Then the B-26B-4 appeared about October 1942 with a lengthened nosewheel strut and equip-

MARTIN B-26B-3   AF

MARTIN B-26B-4   AF

The bad domestic reputation of the Marauder contrasts sharply with its success in overseas combat; this can be explained primarily by the pilots involved. Increases in weight were steadily making the B-26's wing loading, and therefore its stalling and landing speeds, higher and higher. The veteran pilots of the overseas units had the experience to deal with such an aircraft; the new pilots at home did not. Many of the new pilots had not flown any twin-engine aircraft at all, and when inexperienced ground crews and overloading of the aircraft were added, the accident rate was understandable.

Air Force inspection boards therefore decided to solve the problems by initiating a new training program and enlarging the aircraft's wing. The new wing increased its span from 65 to 71 feet and its area from 602 to 658 square feet and was introduced on the 642nd B-26B and the new B-26C models. In the meantime, in July and again in October 1942, the AAF considered canceling the B-26, but commendations from the Fifth Air Force kept it in production.

ment changes. Of 211 built, the last 141 replaced the light tunnel gun with a pair of .50-caliber waist guns firing through side hatches at the fuselage bottom—an arrangement previously seen on modified aircraft of combat units. Some aircraft added four more fixed guns in outside packages, bringing the total to 12.

Nine new AAF medium-bomber groups were activated in 1942 as Marauder units, but it was in this period that criticism of the type reached its height. A series of bad accidents while training new pilots had brought upon the B-26 such nicknames as "Widow Maker" and "Flying Prostitute."

In September 1942 the 28th B-26B had been tested with heavier armament, including four fixed package guns and a new Bell tail turret, and these features were to be included on the wide-winged production aircraft as soon as possible.

The first Marauder with the new wing was the B-26C-5-MO, ordered on June 28, 1941, from a new Martin factory in Omaha. The first three were accepted in August 1942, and 86 were accepted by the year's end. The wide wing was introduced on Baltimore's production line after 641 short-winged B-26Bs had been built by the end of 1942. The first

MARTIN B-26C-5
Pratt & Whitney R-2800-43, 1920 hp takeoff, 1490 hp at 14,300'
DIMENSIONS: Span 71', Lg. 58'3", Ht. 21'6", Wing Area 658 sq. ft.
WEIGHT: Empty 24,000 lb., Gross 37,000 lb., Max. 38,200 lb. Fuel 962–1962 gal.
PERFORMANCE: Speed—Top 282 mph at 15,000', 270 mph at s. l., Cruising 214 mph, Landing 135 mph. Service Ceiling 21,700', Climb 15,000'/23 min. Range 1150 miles/3000 lbs. bombs, 2600 miles max.   AF

was the B-26B-10-MA in January 1943, with 150 built under the original B-26B contract.

Except for place of manufacture, the B-26B-10 and the 175 B-26C-15s were alike. Twelve .50-caliber guns with 4,250 rounds were carried. One flexible and one fixed gun in the nose, four fixed package guns on the side, two in the top turret, two in the lower waist, and two in the tail.

A new power-operated Martin-Bell tail turret was introduced in March 1943 on the B-26B-20-MA and B-26C-10-MO. The double bomb bay could accommodate two 2,000-pound, four 1,000-pound, eight 500-pound, or 30 100-pound bombs, or 1,000 gallons of extra fuel. However, on the B-26B-25, the B-26C-30, and later models the external torpedo rack and the rear bays were deleted. While four 1,000-pound bombs could still be carried, there was room now for just six 500-pound or twenty 100-pound bombs, or 500 gallons of added fuel. The nose fixed gun was also deleted from late models.

Production of 1,883 B-26Bs ended at Baltimore in February 1944 with the last B-26B-55-MA. In addition, Martin built 208 AT-23As for the Air Force. First appearing in August 1943, the AT-23A had no armor, guns, or turret, but it had a tow target windlass installed for its gunnery training mission.

Marauder production ended at Omaha in April 1944 after 1,210 B-25C-5 to B-25C-45-MO and 375 AT-23B tow target trainers had been built. Of the tow target planes, the U.S. Navy got 200 in September–October 1943 and the last 25 in 1944. Known as the JM-1, their bright orange-yellow finish was familiar at Navy stations around the country. Air Force AT-23Bs, however, retained their natural metal finish and were redesignated TB-26 in 1944.

By March 1944 the AAF B-26 inventory peaked at 1,931 aircraft, with 11 groups of 64 planes each deployed against Germany. But the first Marauders in action against Germany were those of the RAF, which had been allocated lend-lease B-26Bs with the name Marauder I. Before these became available, 19 B-26As were transferred to the RAF as the Marauder IA. The first three were ferried across the Atlantic shortly before the attack on Pearl Harbor, and the rest were intended for the Middle East.

By August 1942, 52 short-winged B-26Bs[2] had been transferred to the RAF, and their first sortie was made from Egypt on October 28, 1942, by No. 14 Squadron. Two months later a B-26A of this squadron began torpedo reconnaissance flights. Other squadrons flying the Martins in the Mediterranean were South African units with 100 Marauder

<hr>

[2] Figures for RAF B-26A and B-26B deliveries have been reversed in earlier accounts, but photographic evidence indicates those given here are correct.

MARTIN B-26B-25 *Flack Bait* AF

MARTIN B-26B-55 MFR

IIs (B-26C-30s) and six Free French squadrons with the B-26C-45s.

The first Marauder group to cross the Atlantic was the 319th, which moved its short-winged B-26Bs to England in September 1942, and then flew into combat from Algeria on November 28. It was joined by the 17th Group, the pioneer B-25 Mitchell outfit that had converted to B-26B-2s, -3s, and -4s in 1942, flew to North Africa, and made its first combat mission over Tunis on December 30, 1942. The third B-26 group in the Mediterranean area with the Twelfth Air Force was the 320th, which entered combat in April 1943.

The first Marauder group to fly a combat mission from England was the 322nd, which made its first sortie May 14, 1943. On the second mission three days later, all ten B-26B-4s crossing the Channel were downed by the enemy. This defeat showed that the low-level attack for which the B-26 crews had trained was impractical against heavy German antiaircraft.

New medium-altitude tactics were devised and missions resumed on July 17 with wide-winged B-26Cs. The Marauders in Britain were assigned to the Ninth Air Force, which by May 1944 had eight B-26 groups and a pathfinder squadron. On June 6, 1944, 742 B-26 sorties were flown in support of the cross-Channel invasion. A B-26B-25 named "Flak Bait" became the first American bomber to complete 200 missions.

The Last B-26 Models

The lone XB-26D was an early B-26 modified to test heated-surface-type de-icing equipment. A stripped version of the B-26B—with less weight and the upper turret moved forward to the navigator's compartment—was planned as the B-26E but was never actually built.

Three hundred B-26F-MAs ordered September 1942 began appearing in February 1944, with the wing's angle of attack increased 3.5° to reduce the takeoff run and landing speed. All had four fixed and seven flexible .50-caliber guns.

The last variant was the B-26G, which differed only in mechanical details. Production amounted to 893 B-26G-MAs and 57 TB-26Gs, of which 15 TB-26G-15s and the last 32 TB-26G-25s went to the U.S. Navy as the JM-2 in March 1945. Production ceased on March 26, 1945, with the 5,157th Marauder, although a single B-26G-25 modified in May 1945 to try out the bicycle landing gear planned for the B-47 and B-48 jets became the XB-26H.

In 1944 British lend-lease contracts supplied 200 B-26F and 150 B-26G bombers as the Marauder III for RAF and South African units.

The AAF record against the European Axis powers included 129,943 Marauder sorties, a bomb tonnage of 169,382 pounds, with 911 B-26s lost in combat (see Table 7). The last group-sized B-26 attacks in April 1945 were opposed by Me 262 jets, but time was running out for the Nazis. The final B-26 mission on May 3, 1945, was by eight pathfinder squadron planes leading 124 A-26 light bombers against an ammunition plant.

The Ventura

Lighter than AAF twin-engine types, the Lockheed Vega Ventura (Model 37) was a midwing medium bomber with twin rudders and tail-down landing gear that had been designed in May 1940. Developed from the Hudson light bomber, 675 Venturas were ordered by the RAF in 1940, and 200 more were designated B-34 by a lend-lease contract added in August 1941.

The Ventura I was first flown on July 31, 1941, with Pratt & Whitney R-2800-S1A4-C Wasps of 1,850 hp and a crew of four. Armament included 2,500 pounds of bombs, two fixed .50-caliber and two flexible .30-caliber guns in the nose, a pair of .30-

MARTIN B-26F-1
Pratt & Whitney R-2800-43, 1920 hp takeoff
DIMENSIONS: Span 71', Lg. 56'1", Ht. 20'4", Wing Area 658 sq. ft.
WEIGHT: Empty 23,700 lb., Gross 37,000 lb., Max. 38,200 lb. Fuel 465–1502 gal.
PERFORMANCE: Speed—Top 283 mph at 5000', 281 mph at s. l., Landing 122 mph. Service Ceiling 20,000', Climb 10,000'/17 min. Range 1125 miles/4000 lbs., 1875 miles ferry.   AF

MARTIN B-26G-15   AF

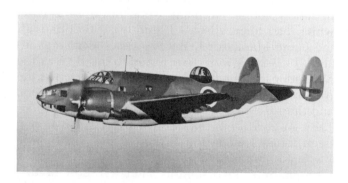

LOCKHEED-VEGA VENTURA I
Pratt & Whitney R-2800-S1A4-G, 1850 hp takeoff
DIMENSIONS: Span 65'6", Lg. 51'5", Ht. 11'11", Wing Area 551 sq. ft.
WEIGHT: Empty 17,233 lb., Gross 22,500 lb., Max. 26,000 lb. Fuel 565 gal.
PERFORMANCE: Speed—Top 312 mph, Cruising 272 mph, Landing 80 mph. Service Ceiling 25,200', Climb 2035'/1 min. Range 1000 miles/2500 lbs. bombs.   MFR

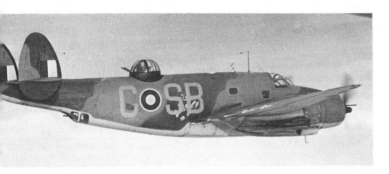

LOCKHEED-VEGA VENTURA II   IWM

LOCKHEED-VEGA B-34A (VENTURA IIA)
Pratt & Whitney R-2800-31, 2000 hp takeoff, 1600 hp at
13,500'
DIMENSIONS: Span 65'6", Lg. 51'5", Ht. 11'11", Wing Area
551 sq. ft.
WEIGHT: Empty 17,275 lb., Gross 25,600 lb., Max. 27,750
lb. Fuel 565–1345 gal.
PERFORMANCE: Speed—Top 315 mph at 15,500', Cruising
230 mph, Landing 80 mph. Service Ceiling 24,000',
Climb 15,000'/8.2 min. Range 950 miles/3000 lbs.
bombs, 2600 miles max.   AAF

caliber guns in a power-operated British top turret,
and another pair at a ventral opening.

Of 188 Ventura Is, the first 30 were finished by
January 1942 and held in Canada, while six others
were transferred to the South African Air Force.
They were followed by 487 Ventura IIs with 2,000-
hp R-2800-31 engines and 200 lend-lease Ventura
IIAs or B-34As, which were completed by November 1942. The USAAF took over 14 Ventura Is, 208
Ventura IIs, and all the B-34s, using them for coastal
patrol and training roles. The former models were
called R-37s in Air Force service. Beginning in May
1943, Australia was sent 20 B-34 and 41 R-37 Venturas from AAF stock, and New Zealand got 23 B-
34s.

On USAAF versions a Martin turret with twin
.50-caliber guns replaced the British turret, and armament could total four .50-caliber and six .30-cal-
iber guns, with up to 3,000 pounds of bombs. Designations for aircraft modified for specific training
missions were B-34A-2 bombardier, B-34A-3 gun-

nery, B-34A-4 tow target, and B-34B-1 navigation
trainers. The last 27 Ventura IIs went as the PV-3
to the U.S. Navy, which was assigned all future
Ventura production.

Three RAF bomber squadrons used the Ventura
for cross-Channel daylight attacks beginning November 3, 1942. Losses tended to be heavy, and the
Ventura was retired from Bomber Command after
July 1943 for service with Coastal Command and
weather units.

The last Ventura model was the B-37, or Ventura
III, which began with an order for 550 O-56 reconnaissance aircraft on August 8, 1941. Powered by
Wright R-2600-13 Cyclones, they were to provide
a twin-engine type suitable for observation groups,
but this role was eliminated and the order was cut
back to 18 aircraft delivered as B-37s from January
to April 1943. Armed with two .50-caliber fixed and
two .50-caliber turret guns, plus twin .30-caliber
tunnel guns, the B-37 could be recognized by round
openings in the lower waist for two additional .30-
caliber guns.

XB-28 and XB-42

The next twin-engine bomber to appear had originally been designed in August 1939 to a specification for high-altitude versions of the B-25 and B-26.
Both the Martin XB-27 (Model 182) and North
American XB-28 (NA-63) were to have turbosupercharged Pratt & Whitney Wasps and pressurized
cabins, but the Martin project was dropped. Two
XB-28s, however, were ordered on February 13,
1940, and the first was flown on April 26, 1942.
Powered by the R-2800-11, the XB-28 had tricycle
landing gear, single rudder, five men in a pressure
cabin, and carried 4,000 pounds of bombs and six
.50-caliber guns with 1,200 rounds. The guns were
paired in upper, lower, and tail turrets, remote-controlled from periscopic stations behind the pilots'
seats. The second prototype was completed as the
XB-28A photo version with R-2800-27s.

Although the high-altitude performance of the
XB-28 far exceeded that of service types, wartime
medium bombing was done at relatively low altitudes, and authorities were unwilling to interrupt
Mitchell production for an untried type.

A fitting end to the story of twin-propellered
bomber design is the Douglas ship proposed on
June 15, 1943. The original design was designated
XA-42 and had two Allison V-1710-93 liquid-cooled
engines in the fuselage. However, when the experimental contract was awarded on June 25, it was
seen as a way of "increasing the heavy long-range
bombing attack with minimum industrial effort."
Redesignated XB-42 in November, it became a
high-speed bomber that could match the B-29's

LOCKHEED-VEGA B-37 (VENTURA III)
Wright R-2600-13, 1700 hp takeoff, 1450 hp at 12,000'
DIMENSIONS: As B-34A
WEIGHT: Empty 18,160 lb., Gross 27,000 lb., Max. 29,500 lb. Fuel 565–1300 gal.
PERFORMANCE: (26,500 lb.) Speed—Top 298 mph at 13,-500', Cruising 198 mph, Landing 77 mph. Service Ceiling 22,400', Climb 10,000'/5.5 min. Range 1300 miles/2000 lbs. bombs, 2700 miles max.   MFR

DOUGLAS XB-42
Allison V-1710-125, 1800 hp WE
DIMENSIONS: Span 70'6", Lg. 53'7", Ht. 20'9", Wing Area 555 sq. ft.
WEIGHT: Empty 20,888 lb., Gross 33,208 lb., Max. 35,702 lb. Fuel 650–1750 gal.
PERFORMANCE: Speed—Top 410 mph at 23,440', 344 mph at s. l. Service Ceiling 29,400'. Range 1840 miles normal, 5400 miles max.   AMC

NORTH AMERICAN XB-28
Pratt & Whitney R-2800-11, 2000 hp takeoff, 1840 hp at 25,000'
DIMENSIONS: Span 72'7", Lg. 56'5", Ht. 14', Wing Area 676 sq. ft.
WEIGHT: Empty 25,575 lb., Gross 35,740 lb., Max. 37,200 lb. Fuel 1170–1508 gal.
PERFORMANCE: Speed—Top 372 mph at 25,000', Cruising 255 mph, Landing 86 mph. Service Ceiling 34,600', Climb 10,000'/9 min. Range 2040 miles/600 lbs. bombs.   AMC

DOUGLAS XB-42A
Allison V-1710-133, 1325 hp takeoff, 1800 hp WE at s. l., and Westinghouse 19B-2, 1600 lbs.
DIMENSIONS: Span 70'7", Lg. 53'10", Ht. 18'10", Wing Area 555 sq. ft.
WEIGHT: Empty 24,775 lb., Gross 39,000 lb., Max. 44,900 lb. Fuel 650–2402 gal. (2570 gal. max.).
PERFORMANCE: Speed—Top 488 mph at 14,000', Cruising 251 mph. Range 4750 miles max.   MFR

striking range at a much lower cost in terms of economic strain, fuel, and crew requirements. First flown on May 6, 1944, the XB-42 minimized drag by burying both inline engines in the fuselage behind the pilots and extending drive shafts (each of five P-39 shafts) to co-axial pusher propellers behind the tail. Radiators in the wings cooled 1,800-hp Allison V-1710-125s.

The usual bombardier sat in the transparent nose, with the pilot and co-pilot seated under individual canopies, the latter facing backward when operating the remote-controlled guns. Two .50-caliber

guns in the trailing edge of each wing had a limited azimuth but were thought adequate enough to meet attacks that, because of the bomber's speed, could come only from the rear. Two fixed forward guns were located in the nose, and a total of 2,400 rounds were provided for all six guns. An alternate attack solid nose with eight guns was anticipated. A range of over 5,000 miles with a one-ton bomb load was expected, but the bomb bay had an 8,000-pound capacity and normal range was 1,800 miles.

A second XB-42 flown on August 1, 1944, was later given a more conventional canopy. It was lost on December 16, 1945, shortly after setting a transcontinental flight record, with the help of tail winds, of 433 mph. When jet engines became available, the design evolved into the XB-43 (see Chapter 26). Douglas did propose the addition of Westinghouse jets of 1,600-pound thrust under each wing on February 23, 1945, and the first prototype was reworked in this manner and flown again as the XB-42A on May 27, 1947. All guns were removed, but fuel capacity was increased.

Although none of the experimental medium bombers designed after 1939 went into production, more than enough of the earlier models were available to win the war. Table 7 summarizes the work of AAF bombers in the air offensive against Germany and her European allies.

Table 7

AAF BOMBERS IN THE EUROPEAN WAR, 1942–45

Type	Number of Sorties	Bomb Tonnage	U. S. Aircraft Lost in Combat	Enemy Aircraft Claimed Destroyed in Air
B-17	291,508	640,036	4,688	6,659
B-24	226,775	452,508	3,626	2,617
B-26	129,943	169,382	911	402
B-25	63,177	84,980	380	193
A-20	39,492	31,856	265	11
A-26	11,567	18,054	67	7
Total	762,462	1,396,816	9,937	9,889

Chapter 16
Fighter Monoplanes, 1932-39

Since World War I dogfighting had left pursuit pilots more conscious of twisting and turning with enemy fighters than of chasing bombers, pilots preferred sturdy, maneuverable biplanes to untried monoplanes—not a bad choice so long as bombers were slow biplanes of the traditional pattern. But new all-metal monoplanes like the Martin XB-10 with retractable wheels sharply reduced interception capabilities of biplane pursuit planes. The XB-10's 207-mph speed was faster than any 1931 Army biplane and pressed fighter designers to use monoplane layouts.

The P-12E and P-6E types on order were simply not fast enough to catch the Martin bomber, and the Army abruptly turned to the monoplane pattern for its fighters. The switch was made sooner than that of the Navy, which persisted with the Grumman biplanes, and was far ahead of most foreign powers, who as late as 1941 were still using in battle biplanes like the British Gladiator, Italian Fiat, and Soviet I-15.

The first low-wing monoplane to begin the new trend in Army fighters was the XP-900, designed by the Lockheed Company, which was then a subsidiary of an ill-fated combine called Detroit Aircraft. This two-seater was developed from the low-wing Sirius, built for Colonel Lindbergh in 1929, whose two cockpits were enclosed by a sliding canopy installed at Anne Lindbergh's suggestion. This design became the Altair when fitted with retractable landing gear, and an example purchased by the Army on June 6, 1931 was the Y1C-23.

The enclosed cockpits, low wooden wing, and inward-retracting landing gear were combined in the XP-900 with a metal fuselage and Curtiss Conqueror engine. Besides the usual two synchronized guns, a .30-caliber gun was provided for the gunner, sitting back to back with the pilot.

After mockup inspection at Detroit in March 1931, the Air Corps considered the type as a P-16

LOCKHEED YP-24 (XP-900)
Curtiss V-1570-23, 600 hp at s. l.
DIMENSIONS: Span 42'9", Lg. 28'9", Ht. 8'6", Wing Area 292 sq. ft.
WEIGHT: Empty 3193 lb., Gross 4360 lb. Fuel 75 gal.
PERFORMANCE: Speed—Top 214.5 mph at s. l., 210.5 mph at 5000', Cruising 186 mph, Landing 73 mph. Service Ceiling 26,400', Absolute Ceiling 28,000', Climb 1800'/ 1 min., 5000'/3.1 min. Range 556 miles.   MFR

replacement, and on September 23, 1931, the prototype and four additional examples were purchased and assigned the designations YP-24 and Y1P-24. Five Y1A-9 attack versions were also planned.

Delivered September 29, 1931, the YP-24 soon proved itself the fastest (214 mph) fighter yet offered to the Air Corps. But on October 19 the landing gear failed to extend—a common occurrence at the time—and the pilot bailed out. On October 27 Detroit Aircraft went out of business and the contract for more aircraft was rescinded.

Fortunately the YP-24's young designer, Robert Wood, had joined Consolidated Aircraft, then located in Buffalo, and was able to plan a new two-seater of similar layout but of all-metal construction. On April 4, 1932, Air Corps funds from the former project were allotted to Consolidated's Y1P-25, Wood's new design.

The Y1P-25 was built with a turbosupercharged V-1570-57 in a streamlined nose, and a second prototype completed without a supercharger was to be redesignated XA-11. Wood also projected, in May 1932, two air-cooled versions with Pratt & Whitney radials: a YP-27 with a 550-hp R-1340-21 and a YP-28 with a 600-hp R-1340-19. Both aircraft were canceled, however.

Delivered to Wright Field December 9, 1932, Consolidated's Y1P-25 got 247 mph at 15,000 feet from its turbosupercharged Conqueror. Although the Y1P-25 crashed January 13, 1933, followed by another fatal accident to the XA-11 a week later, an Army board impressed with its speed recommended purchase of an improved version, which became the A-30. Before the P-30 appeared, the Air Corps purchased a more conservative single-seater.

BOEING Y1P-26 (XP-936)
Pratt & Whitney R-1340-21 (SR-1340G), 525 hp at 6000′
DIMENSIONS: Span 27′5″, Lg. 23′9″, Ht. 7′6″, Wing Area 150 sq. ft.
WEIGHT: Empty 2120 lb., Gross 2789 lb. Fuel 50–106 gal.
PERFORMANCE: Speed—Top 227 mph at 6000′, Cruising 193 mph, Landing 73.5 mph. Service Ceiling 27,800′, Absolute Ceiling 28,900′, Climb 2230′/1 min.   JONES

CONSOLIDATED Y1P-25
Curtiss V-1570-27, 600 hp
DIMENSIONS: Span 43′10″, Lg. 29′4″, Ht. 8′7″, Wing Area 296 sq. ft.
WEIGHT: Empty 3887 lb., Gross 5110 lb. Fuel 90–173 gal.
PERFORMANCE: Speed—Top 247 mph at 15,000′, 205 mph at s. l. Climb 10,000′/6.7 min.   MFR

Boeing's Monoplane Fighters

The first all-metal monoplane in Air Corps pursuit-squadron service, the P-26 was popular with both pilots and the public. It was also the last Army fighter with an open cockpit, fixed landing gear, and external wires to brace the wings.

Boeing began the design as Model 248, and the Army agreed December 5, 1931, to lend the R-1340-21 engines for three privately financed airframes. The first prototype was flown March 20, 1932, as the XP-936, the second was shipped to Wright Field for static tests, the third was delivered April 25, and all three were purchased by the Army on June 15 as Y1P-26s.

A production contract for 111 P-26A pursuits at $9,999 each[1] was approved January 24, 1933, and

BOEING P-26A
Pratt & Whitney R-1340-27, 600 hp at 6000′
DIMENSIONS: Span 27′11½″, Lg. 23′7¼″, Ht. 10′5″, Wing Area 149.5 sq. ft.
WEIGHT: Empty 2271 lb., Gross 3012 lb. Fuel 52–107 gal.
PERFORMANCE: Speed—Top 234 mph at 7500′, 211 mph at s. l., Cruising 199 mph, Landing 82.5 mph (74 mph with flaps). Service Ceiling 27,400′, Absolute Ceiling 28,300′, Climb 2360′/1 min., 6000′/3 min. Range 360 miles normal, 570 miles max.   AF

the first was flown January 10, 1934. Powered by 600-hp R-1340-27 Wasps, they were all delivered by June, but it became necessary to add flaps to reduce the landing speed and to raise the headrest to protect the pilot if the plane overturned. Armament included two .30-caliber guns with 500 rpg at a level with the pilot's knees (with the right gun replaceable by a .50-caliber one if needed) and a

[1] Minus such government-furnished equipment (GFE) as engines and instruments, of course.

rack for two 116-pound or five 30-pound bombs. A radio was standard equipment.

Twenty-five P-26Bs were also ordered, the first two being delivered in June 1935 with R-1340-33 fuel-injection Wasps and flaps. Until sufficient fuel-injection engines became available, 18 of the remaining planes used standard R-1340-27s and were temporarily designated P-26C models. Boeing Model 281 was an export version flown August 2, 1934, and sent to China in September, while another was sold to Spain. Ten more were purchased by China, delivered in January 1936, and used by No. 17 Squadron in defense of Nanking in the fall of 1937.

BOEING 281
Pratt & Whitney R-1340-33, 600 hp
DIMENSIONS: Span 27′11½″, Lg. 23′7¼″, Ht. 7′10½″, Wing Area 149.5 sq. ft.
WEIGHT: Empty 2354 lb., Gross 3039 lb., Max. 3390 lb. Fuel 55–107 gal.
PERFORMANCE: Speed—Top 235 mph at 6000′, 215 mph at s. l., Cruising 210 mph, Landing 68 mph. Service Ceiling 28,200′, Climb 2210′/1 min. Range 386 miles normal, 745 miles max.   MFR

When the Air Corps received its last Boeing fighter on March 7, 1936, they had been issued to the 20th, 17th, and 1st Pursuit groups, in that order. The 17th was soon re-equipped as an A-17 attack outfit, and after replacement by P-35s and P-36s in the fall of 1938, the surviving Boeings went to the three overseas fighter units. In December 1938 these were Hawaii's 18th Group, with 21 P-26A, 12 P-26B, and 24 P-12E pursuits; the Canal Zone's 16th Group, with 25 P-26A, 17 P-12E, and 10 P-12F models; and the 3rd Squadron in the Philippines, with 20 P-26A, three P-12E and three P-12C models.

These Boeings were obsolete before the United States entered the war, but Filipino pilots took nine P-26As, given to their infant air arm, into combat against Japanese bombers in December 1941. Three P-26As went to Panama and six to Guatemala for training in 1942–43, and two of the latter even-

tually returned to the United States for museum display.

Curtiss entered the competition with the XP-934 "Swift," which resembled the A-8 attack and was an all-metal monoplane with wheel pants connected by V struts to the thin wing. Slots, flaps, and enclosed cockpit were featured, along with two fixed guns on each side of the cockpit and a 50-gallon drop tank.

When the mockup was inspected in May 1932, a Curtiss V-1570F engine was planned, but the Air Corps insisted that an alternative air-cooled installation be made available, so the prototype had an SR-1340 when it was completed in July. By August

CURTISS XP-934 (with R-1340 engine)   MFR

CURTISS XP-31 (XP-934)
Curtiss V-1570-53, 600 hp at s. l.
DIMENSIONS: Span 36′, Lg. 26′3″, Ht. 7′9″, Wing Area 203 sq. ft.
WEIGHT: Empty 3334 lb., Gross 4143 lb. Fuel 75–125 gal.
PERFORMANCE: Speed—Top 208 mph at s. l., 202.5 mph at 5000′, Cruising 184 mph, Landing 80.5 mph. Service Ceiling 24,400′, Absolute Ceiling 25,600′, Climb 2130′/ 1 min., 5000′/2.6 min. Range 370 miles.   AF

26 the inline Conqueror had been installed, and after various changes the single-seater was tested at Wright Field in December 1932. It was much too heavy, compared to the P-26, but was accepted as the XP-31 on March 1, 1933.

BOEING XP-940   MFR

BOEING YP-29 (P-29)
Pratt & Whitney R-1340-31 (or -39), 550 hp at 10,000'
DIMENSIONS: Span 29'5", Lg. 25'2", Ht. 7'8", Wing Area
   177 sq. ft.
WEIGHT: Empty 2573 lb., Gross 3572 lb. Fuel 73–110 gal.
PERFORMANCE: Speed—Top 244 mph at 10,000', Cruising
   208 mph, Landing 81 mph. Service Ceiling 24,200',
   Climb 1570'/1 min., 10,000'/6.8 min. Range 520 miles
   normal, 707 miles max.   PMB

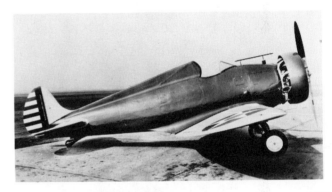

BOEING YP-29A (P-29A)
Pratt & Whitney R-1340-35 (or -27), 570 hp at 7500'
DIMENSIONS: Span 29'5", Lg. 25'1", Ht. 7'8", Wing Area
   177 sq. ft.
WEIGHT: Empty 2502 lb., Gross 3270 lb. (Design 3267
   lb.). Fuel 73–110 gal.
PERFORMANCE: Speed—Top 242 mph at 7500', Cruising
   206 mph, Landing 82 mph. Climb 1840'/1 min.   MFR

BOEING YP-29B (P-29B)   MFR

Boeing made the next step in single-seat fighter design with the cantilever low-wing of the XP-940, whose wheels retracted backwards about halfway into the wings. Based on the Navy's XF7B-1 design, the XP-940 first flew January 20, 1934, and went to Wright in February with a deep-cowled R-1340-31 and enclosed cockpit faired back to the tail. This cockpit arrangement proved unsatisfactory and the aircraft was returned to Boeing.

Three Boeings purchased on June 29, 1934, were designated YP-29, YP-29A, and YP-29B. The YP-29 was delivered by September 4, 1934, with an anti-drag ring around an R-1340-31, a roomy pilot's canopy, 6° dihedral, and oleo tailwheel. The YP-29A—actually the reworked XP-940 prototype—was delivered September 7 with an R-1340-35, open cockpit and long fairing, 7° dihedral, and P-26A tailwheel. Armament was the usual two fixed guns and up to ten 30-pound bombs.

On October 11 the YP-29B arrived with the same engine, open cockpit, and dihedral as the YP-29A, but with a one-piece flap installed. This flap was later added to the earlier aircraft, which became the P-29 and P29A when fitted with an R-1340-39 and R-1340-27, respectively. Boeing also projected another single-seater in 1934 called Model 278, or XP-32, with a 700-hp twin-row R-1535-1 and wheels retracting into the fuselage, but it was not accepted and Boeing went out of the Army fighter business to concentrate on bombers.

Consolidated Two-Seaters

The Consolidated P-30 two-seater was built like the Y1P-25 except for a turbosupercharged V-1710-57, simplified nose gear, and omission of the nose spinner. Four were purchased, along with four A-11 attack versions, under a contract approved March 1, 1933, and delivery began in January 1934. Wright Field pilots complained that the rear gunner became valueless if even the simplest maneuvers were performed. Nevertheless, the Air Corps made

CONSOLIDATED P-30
Curtiss V-1570-57, 675 hp at 15,000'
DIMENSIONS: Span 43'11", Lg. 29'4", Ht. 8'4", Wing Area
  297 sq. ft.
WEIGHT: Empty 3832 lb., Gross 5092 lb. Fuel 90–130 gal.
PERFORMANCE: Speed—Top 239 mph at 15,000', 194 mph
  at s. l., Cruising 201.5 mph, Landing 77 mph. Climb
  10,000'/7.6 min., 15,000'/10.9 min. Range 495 miles.

CONSOLIDATED PB-2A
Curtiss V-1570-61, 700 hp at 15,000'
DIMENSIONS: Span 43'11", Lg. 30', Ht. 8'3", Wing Area
  297 sq. ft.
WEIGHT: Empty 4306 lb., Gross 5643 lb. Fuel 90–180 gal.
PERFORMANCE: Speed—Top 274.5 mph at 25,000', 255.5
  mph at 15,000', 214 mph at s. l., Cruising 215 mph,
  Landing 62 mph. Service Ceiling 28,000', Climb 15,-
  000'/7.78 min. Range 508 miles.   MFR

CONSOLIDATED PB-2A as a single-seater   MFR

a $1,966,700 contract for 50 P-30As on December 6, 1934.

Consolidated moved from Buffalo to San Diego, and these aircraft were the first built in the new plant. First flown on December 17, 1935, the P-30A was redesignated PB-2A (pursuit biplace), while the P-16 and P-30 models became the PB-1 and PB-2. These Consolidated two-seaters were innovations for American production fighters: first low-wing monoplanes with completely retractable gear, first with enclosed cockpits, and first with a constant-speed propeller for the 700-hp V-1570-61 engine. The effect of the General Electric F-2H turbosupercharger on speed was revealed in April 1936 trials when a PB-2A did 214 mph at sea level, 255 mph at 15,000 feet, and 274 mph at 25,000 feet. At that altitude, however, overheating interfered and the actual ceiling was not obtained. Armament included the usual two fixed and one flexible .30-caliber gun, and ten 17-pound fragmentation bombs.

The first PB-2A was lost at Wright in May during tests and the seventh had been completed in March as a single-seater for the pursuit competition won by the P-35. The remainder were delivered by July 1936 and divided between the 1st and 8th Pursuit groups, until all were concentrated in the latter group at Langley Field in 1937. There they served until replaced by P-36As in 1939.

An air-cooled version, the Consolidated P-33, was planned with an 800-hp Pratt & Whitney R-1830-1. This project was canceled and the PB-2A was the only two-place fighter monoplane in American service before World War II. Valuable mainly for experience with turbosupercharging, the PB-2A was the last two-seater in the tradition begun by the Bristol fighter. The rear gun's firepower was insufficient compensation for lost speed and maneuverability, and future two-seaters were built only for special night or long-range missions in which the second crewman's role was that of direction rather than gunnery.

Pursuit Competitions, 1935–36

Up to 1932 it looked as if future fighters would be the same open-cockpit biplanes that had prevailed in World War I, but by 1936 it became evident that the whole layout of fighters had been altered to the pattern that became familar in World War II: all-metal low-wing monoplanes with enclosed cockpits and retractable landing gear.

A series of design competitions, held in an international atmosphere charged with the menace of aggressive fascism, demonstrated what designers had learned about streamlining aircraft. All entries in these contests followed the general form that was fast becoming a worldwide fighter style. All were low-wing monoplanes with retracting wheels, enclosed cockpit, and a three-bladed, controllable-pitch propeller. Armament, however, showed the persistence of 1917 habits, for two synchronized guns mounted on the cowling were considered sufficient. The caliber of both was still .30, unless an alternative installation of one .50 and one .30 was made.

Wedell-Williams, a Louisiana builder of racers, had considered offering a fighter design to the Air Corps. In February 1934 inquiries indicated the Matériel Division would not be interested in anything as light as their famous racer, but on January 15, 1935, the Army invited bids on design competitions for both single-place and two-place pursuits.

No less than 16 bids were received by the May 6 closing date. Wedell-Williams won the XP-34 design-study contract on October 1, 1935, for a 4,250-pound fighter with a Pratt & Whitney R-1535, inwardly retracting wheels, and capable of 286 mph at 10,000 feet. By that time another competition held in August 1935 had required sample aircraft to compete for production contracts, resulting in the Curtiss 75 and Seversky Sev-1 with superior potential. The XP-34 was revised in June 1936 to use a 900-hp R-1830 and do 308 mph. The contractor lost interest in the project, however, and never finished the aircraft.

From its experience with the Navy XFT-1, Northrop had prepared a design known as the XP-948, or Northrop 3A. On July 30, 1935, the prototype completely disappeared on a test flight over the Pacific. Powered by a Pratt & Whitney R-1535-G Twin Wasp, the XP-948 had wheels retracting into the wing roots as on the A-17A.

Chance Vought then purchased the design and built the plane anew as the V-141, with a 750-hp Pratt & Whitney R-1535-A5G. First flown March 29, 1936, the V-141 was the smallest type in the 1936 competition, but suffered from tail vibrations despite an enlarged rudder. Rejected by the Army, it was offered to Argentina without success.

An export version with a longer fuselage and new tail, the V-143, was flown June 18, 1937, with a 750-hp R-1535-SB4G and carried two .30-caliber guns, 1,000 rounds of ammunition, and up to 300 pounds of bombs. The Japanese Army purchased the prototype in July 1937. During the war commentators noticed a resemblance between Mitsubishi's

NORTHROP 3A (XP-948)
Pratt & Whitney SR-1535-6, 830 hp takeoff
DIMENSIONS: Span 33'6", Lg. 21'10", Wing Area 187 sq. ft.
WEIGHT: Gross 1485 lb.
PERFORMANCE: Speed—Top 278 mph at s. l., 266 mph at 10,000', Stalling 67 mph at landing. Service Ceiling 31,600', Climb 10,000'/3.3 min.   AF

VOUGHT V-141
Pratt & Whitney R-1535-A5G, 750 hp at 8000'
DIMENSIONS: Span 33'6", Lg. 22'10", Ht. 9'8", Wing Area 187 sq. ft.
WEIGHT: Empty 3515 lb., Gross 4430 lb. Fuel 75–112 gal.
PERFORMANCE: Speed—Top 274 mph at 10,000', Cruising 249.5 mph, Landing 73 mph. Service Ceiling 28,300', Climb 10,000'/3.86 min. Range 704 miles.   AF

VOUGHT V-143
Pratt & Whitney R-1535-SB4G, 825 hp takeoff, 750 hp at 9000'
DIMENSIONS: Span 33'6", Lg. 26', Ht. 9'4", Wing Area 187 sq. ft.
WEIGHT: Empty 3490 lb., Gross 4370 lb. Fuel 112 gal.
PERFORMANCE: Speed—Top 292 mph at 11,485', 256 mph at s. l. Cruising 221 mph, Landing 65 mph. Service Ceiling 30,600', Climb 10,000'/3.1 min. Range 808 miles.   MFR

"Zero" and the American design. The Japanese plane's designer has stated that the Zero's system of wheel retraction was based on the V-143, but has also pointed out that, apart from the general similarity in appearance of most radial-engine low-wing fighters, each fighter type is built in response to particular needs and experiences.

The Air Corps fighter competition had been held on April 15, 1936. Curtiss was low bidder on the contract: $29,412 each in lots of 25 and $14,150 each in lots of 200. Other bids on these lots were Vought, $34,148–$16,051; Seversky, $34,900–$15,800; and Consolidated, $44,000–$24,260. The Consolidated single-seater was clearly outclassed in price and performance, the Vought was a bit too light and tricky, but a newcomer to combat aviation, Seversky, won the production contract.

Seversky P-35

Alexander P. de Seversky and his chief engineer and fellow Russian immigrant, Alexander Kartveli, developed a carefully streamlined low-wing monoplane. Appearing in June 1933, it was known as the SEV-3 for the three persons that could be carried in the enclosed cockpits.

The first version had a Wright Whirlwind radial engine and twin Edo amphibian floats and attracted attention by setting a world's amphibian speed record. The next year the Seversky was fitted with wheels in deep pants and offered to the Army as a basic trainer. These demonstrations won the company its first contracts: three SEV-3M military amphibians for Colombia and 30 BT-8s, the first Air Corps all-metal monoplane basic trainers. The first SEV-3M, in August 1935, had a 440-hp Wright Whirlwind R-975 and was like the prototype except for fixed and flexible guns and a military canopy.

SEVERSKY SEV-3M-WW
Wright R-975, 440 hp
DIMENSIONS: Span 36', Lg. 28', Ht. 10'2", Wing Area 222 sq. ft.
WEIGHT: Empty 3205 lb., Gross 4600 lb. Fuel 130 gal.
PERFORMANCE: Speed—Top 175 mph, Cruising 152 mph, Landing 65 mph. Service Ceiling 16,200'. Range 900 miles.
                                                                    SHIPP

SEVERSKY SEV-2XP   MFR

Meanwhile, Seversky's second prototype was built in Farmingdale, New York, as the SEV-2XP two-place pursuit with a Wright GR-1670-5 and wheel pants. Damaged on the way to Wright Field, this aircraft did not arrive until June 18, 1935, too late for the competition originally scheduled for May, and was returned to the factory to be rebuilt for the new competition planned for August.

Realizing that the Army was now more interested in single-seaters, Seversky rebuilt his fighter with a new canopy over a single pilot, a large baggage compartment, and wheels retracting backwards into fairings under the wings. Next the twin-row radial was replaced by a single-row Wright XR-1820-G5 rated at 850 hp. The fuel tank was integral with the center section of the one-piece, semielliptical Seversky wing, whose shape remained the same for the whole series.

On August 15, 1935, the Seversky returned to Wright Field as the SEV-1XP, but troubles with the Cyclone limited speed to 289 mph instead of the 300 mph promised. Actually, the Matériel Division was undecided about this Cyclone engine and asked each aircraft builder for alternate performance estimates based on Pratt & Whitney's twin-row R-1830 Wasp, whose smaller diameter promised better visibility and a bit less drag. During the trials the Seversky's R-1820 was replaced by an R-1830 rated at 850 hp. In this case only 277 mph was achieved, for the power plant seemed to yield only 738 hp. Nevertheless, the R-1830 was specified for both Seversky and Curtiss ships when production orders were placed. Wright R-1820 Cyclones, however, were used on B-17, B-18, and A-18 types ordered that same year, because of the Cyclone's lower fuel consumption.

The Army favored giving Seversky the first production contract in November, but Curtiss protested that unfair advantage had been given by allowing Seversky to modify its aircraft and arrive late. A third bid opening was then held April 15, 1936, with the Curtiss 75B, Consolidated single-seater, and Vought V-141 sample aircraft also present for tests. Again the Seversky was considered the best, and 77 P-35s were ordered June 16, 1936.

The original SEV-1 prototype was used as a personal plane and racer by Major Seversky and Frank Sinclair in 1937. A larger contract was to be awarded in 1937, and another Seversky prototype was prepared, the AP-1. This fighter arrived at Wright in March 1937 with a Twin Wasp, bulged windshield, and the retracting wheels fully enclosed in fairings. Although often mistaken for a P-35, the AP-1 was a private venture retained by the company and used as a test ship registered as NR-1390. It was also tested with a large spinner and tight cowl in an effort to reduce the drag of the radial engine.

SEVERSKY SEV-1
Wright R-1820-G-5, 850 hp at 10,000'
DIMENSIONS: Span 36', Lg. 25', Wing Area 220 sq. ft.
WEIGHT: Empty 3706 lb., Gross 5014 lb.
PERFORMANCE: Speed—Top 300 mph at 10,000' (285 mph on test), Cruising 265 mph. Service Ceiling 30,000', Climb 10,000'/3 min. Range 1192 miles.   AF

SEVERSKY SEV-1
(with Pratt & Whitney R-1830-9)   MFR

SEVERSKY AP-1   AF

SEVERSKY AP-1 Revised   MFR

SEVERSKY P-35
Pratt & Whitney R-1830-9, 950 hp takeoff, 850 hp at 8000'
DIMENSIONS: Span 36', Lg. 25'2", Ht. 9'1", Wing Area 220 sq. ft.
WEIGHT: Empty 4315 lb., Gross 5599 lb., Max. 6295 lb. Fuel 110–200 gal.
PERFORMANCE: Speed—Top 281.5 mph at 10,000', Cruising 259.5 mph, Landing 79 mph. Service Ceiling 30,-600', Absolute Ceiling 31,750', Climb 2440'/1 min., 5000'/2.05 min., 15,000'/6.9 min. Range 1150 miles/200 gal. at 259.5 mph, 800 miles/134 gal. at 200 mph.   AF

The first true production P-35 arrived at Wright Field in May 1937 with the standard windshield and enclosed wheels, but the second arrived in July with open wheel fairings and wing dihedral increased to 7°. This became standard for all P-35s, including the first, which remained at Wright Field, as was the custom. The other 75 P-35s were delivered to the 1st Pursuit Group at Selfridge by August 1938. Standard P-35 armament was two fixed guns on the cowl and racks for ten 30-pound bombs. As they were replaced by more advanced types in 1940–41, they were passed on to the 31st, 49th, 52nd, and 53rd groups for training.

Private versions of the P-35 for Frank Fuller and Jacqueline Cochran won the Bendix air race three years in a row (1937–39). Two Cyclone-powered examples were also built, one for James Doolittle and the other for Navy fighter tests (see NF-1 in Chapter 22).

The last aircraft of the P-35 contract was completed in February 1939 as the XP-41. Changes included installation of a 1,200-hp R-1830-19 with a two-stage supercharger, wheels retracting flat into the center section, and the carburetor intake moved to the top.

A two-seat export version known as the "Convoy Fighter," with an R-1820, was developed in 1937 by reworking an advanced trainer demonstrator. The Soviet Union bought one 2PA-A and one 2PA-L two-seater, the former delivered in March 1938 with amphibian floats and extended wings. Manufacturing rights were also acquired by the Soviet Union, although its air force subsequently decided against further two-seater fighter production. Twenty more Convoy Fighters were built in 1938 for the Japanese Navy and (as the A8V1) were the only American planes used operationally by a Japanese squadron. Armament on the 2PA-L included a .30-caliber flexible gun, two fixed guns, and up to 600 pounds of bombs.

Seversky next developed the AP-9 in February 1939, a single-seater with an 825-hp R-1830-S3C5, top carburetor intake, and wheels retracting inwardly. On the EP-1 (export pursuit) appearing at the same time, however, the usual P-35 landing gear was used. A two-seat version, the 2PA-200 Guardsman, was destroyed in a crash on April 1, 1939. The Guardsman had added a flexible gun and racks for up to 1,350 pounds of bombs.

An expected Chinese contract fell through, although both the AP-9 and EP-1 prototypes were later sold to the Dominican Republic. Sweden, however, ordered the EP-1 on June 15, 1939, to replace its Gladiator biplanes, and 60 completed by May 1940 entered service as the J9. Sixty more ordered in January 1940 were completed from July 1940 to January 1941, but were requisitioned Oc-

SEVERSKY 2PA-A
Wright R-1820-G2, 850 hp at 5800'
DIMENSIONS: Span 41', Lg. 30', Ht. 11'3", Wing Area 246 sq. ft.
WEIGHT: Empty 4791 lb., Gross 6687 lb. Fuel 130–200 gal.
PERFORMANCE: Speed—Top 225 mph at 5800', Cruising 200 mph. Service Ceiling 23,000', Climb 1900'/1 min. Range 900 miles/130 gal.   MFR

SEVERSKY 2PA-L
Wright R-1820, 1000 hp takeoff
DIMENSIONS: Span 36', Lg. 25'5", Ht. 9"6", Wing Area 220 sq. ft.
WEIGHT: Empty 4034 lb., Gross 5952 lb. Fuel 200 gal.
PERFORMANCE: Speed—Top 290 mph at 16,500', Cruising 270 mph, Landing 65 mph. Service Ceiling 30,000', Climb 3150'/1 min.   SHIPP

SEVERSKY AP-9   AF

SEVERSKY EP-1 (J9)   MFR

tober 18, 1940, by the U.S. Army as the Republic
P-35A[2]. The Swedes had also ordered the two-
seater Guardsman but received only two, with 50
others taken over by the United States as AT-12
advanced trainers. The Swedes replaced the P-35A
in their plans with a remarkably similar Italian
fighter, the Reggiane 2000.

The P-35A added a .50-caliber gun in each wing
to the two .30-caliber guns on the cowl. It could be
distinguished from P-35s by the top intake for the
R-1830-45 Wasp and the longer oil cooler intake
under the cowl. There were 51 P-35As in the Philippines a week before the Japanese invasion in
December 1941. By that time they were outclassed
by the enemy's Zero fighters, but they fought
through the war's early weeks.

Curtiss P-36

The first American fighter to down German planes
in World War II and the first to pass the 1,000-plane
production total was the Curtiss P-36 Hawk. This
single-seater took a long time to enter mass production, but proved a successful combat type.

Designated Model 75 by Curtiss, the prototype
was begun in October 1934, when the company
hired former Northrop engineer Donovan R. Berlin
to design a fighter for the Air Corps competition
scheduled for May 1935. Using a unique landing
gear whose wheels rotated as they folded back flat
within the wings, the prototype actually experienced four engine changes within a year's testing.
When first flown on May 13, 1935, by Lloyd Childs,
a 700-hp Wright XR-1510 Twin Whirlwind was
used, but this power plant proved unsatisfactory.

[2] After Seversky left the firm, the name was changed to Republic
on October 18, 1939.

REPUBLIC P-35A
Pratt & Whitney R-1830-45, 1050 hp takeoff, 1000 hp at
  11,500', 900 hp at 12,000'
DIMENSIONS: Span 36', Lg. 26'10", Ht. 9'9", Wing Area
  220 sq. ft.
WEIGHT: Empty 4575 lb., Gross 6118 lb., Max. 6723 lb.
  Fuel 130–200 gal.
PERFORMANCE: (6118 lb.) Speed—Top 290 mph at 12,-
  000', Cruising 260 mph, Landing 80 mph. Service Ceiling 31,400', Absolute Ceiling 32,300', Climb 1920'/1
  min. Range 600 miles/130 gal. at 260 mph, 950 miles/
  200 gal. at 220 mph with 350 lbs. bombs.   AF

REPUBLIC GUARDSMAN (AT-12)
Pratt & Whitney R-1830-45, 1050 hp
DIMENSIONS: Span 41', Lg. 27'8", Ht. 9'10", Wing Area
  250 sq. ft.
WEIGHT: Empty 5146 lb., Gross 7480 lb., Max. 8360 lb.
  Fuel 130 gal.
PERFORMANCE: Speed—Top 285 mph at 11,500', Cruising
  250 mph, Landing 86 mph. Service Ceiling 28,000',
  Climb 2050'/1 min. Range 580 miles.   BACHMAN

Since no other company's plane was ready in time, the Army postponed the competition, enabling Curtiss to try again with a Wright XR-1670-5, another twin-row radial rated at 775 hp at altitude. Again the power plant was unsuitable for production, so by August 7, 1935, the Model 75 reappeared with a 750-hp Pratt & Whitney GR-1535. This engine, however, was too small and gave the advantage to Seversky's prototype, which had bigger engines.

Fortunately, Model 75 had been designed from the beginning to accommodate larger engines, and when the Army competition was set back a third time, Curtiss could install an 850-hp single-row Wright XR-1820-39 (G-5). With rearward visibility improved by indentations behind the cockpit, the prototype was flown as Model 75B on April 4, 1936. Top speed was guaranteed as 294 mph with this Wright radial, or 297 mph with a Wasp engine, but

only 285 mph was actually obtained, according to the test report.

Although Seversky had won the first production contract, three Y1P-36 service-test articles with the R-1830-13 Twin Wasp, retractable tailwheel, and improved cockpit were provided by a contract approved August 5, 1936. Curtiss delivered two to Wright Field in March 1937, and the third to Selfridge in April. This time performance was superior to the rival Seversky AP-1 prototype. On July 7, 1937, Curtiss won the largest fighter contract awarded since 1918: 210 planes for $4,113,500.

The first P-36A was flown April 20, 1938, by Mr. Childs, using the same R-1830-13 engine with 92-octane fuel and a new cowl with cooling flaps and blast covers for the two cowl guns. This aircraft can still be seen in the Air Force Museum in Dayton, Ohio.

The fourth P-36A (serial number 38-4) arrived at

CURTISS Design 75 (Prototype P-36)   SALO

CURTISS Design 75 (R-1535)   AF

CURTISS Design 75B
Wright XR-1820-39, 850 hp at 10,000'
DIMENSIONS: Span 37'4", Lg. 28'1", Ht. 9', Wing Area 236 sq. ft.
WEIGHT: Empty 4049 lb., Gross 5075 lb. Fuel 133–151 gal.
PERFORMANCE: Speed—Top 285 mph at 10,000', Cruising 260 mph, Landing 66 mph. Service Ceiling 32,500', Climb 10,000'/3.87 min. Range 730 miles.   MFR

CURTISS YP-36
Pratt & Whitney R-1830-13, 1050 hp takeoff, 900 hp at 12,000'
DIMENSIONS: Span 37'4", Lg. 28'2", Ht. 9', Wing Area 236 sq. ft.
WEIGHT: Empty 4389 lb., Gross 5437 lb., Max. 5960 lb. Fuel 100–151 gal.
PERFORMANCE: Speed—Top 294.5 mph at 10,000', Cruising 256 mph, Landing 65 mph. Service Ceiling 35,100', Absolute Ceiling 36,150', Climb 3145'/1 min., 10,000'/3.44 min. Range 752 miles/150 gal.   AF

CURTISS P-36A
Pratt & Whitney R-1830-17, 1200 hp takeoff, 1050 hp at
  6500'
DIMENSIONS: Span 37'4", Lg. 28'6", Ht. 8'5", Wing Area
  235 sq. ft.
WEIGHT: Empty 4504 lb., Gross 5650 lb., Max. 5840 lb.
  Fuel 105–62 gal.
PERFORMANCE: Speed—Top 313 mph at 10,000', Cruising
  270 mph, Landing 75 mph. Service Ceiling 33,000',
  Absolute Ceiling 34,000', Climb 3900'/1 min., 20,000'/
  7.6 min., 15,000'/4.8 min., 10,000'/2.8 min. Range 800
  miles at 270 mph, 1060 miles at 200 mph.   AF

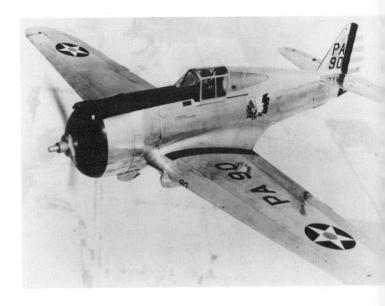

Wright in September with an R-1830-17 using
newly available 100-octane fuel to improve speed
from 299 to 313 mph. These engines were then
standardized, beginning with the fifteenth P-36A,
while 38-4 itself returned to the factory to become
the XP-42. The tenth aircraft on the contract became
the XP-40, the twentieth was temporarily the P-36B
while testing an R-1830-23 in November, and the
eighty-fifth, a P-36C, arrived in December 1938
with an additional .30-caliber gun with 500 rounds
in each wing. These guns, along with underwing
retainer boxes for empty cartridges, were specified
on January 26, 1939, for the last 30 contract aircraft.
No bomb racks were used on any Army P-36s.

The Curtiss fighter was a "much better flying
plane than the P-35," wrote Colonel Charles Lindbergh in 1939, and other pilots usually agreed. After
the last P-36C was delivered in May 1939, Air Corps
pursuit strength consisted of the 1st Group, with
one squadron each of P-35, P-36A, and P-36C fighters (with a large reserve of the first type), and the
8th and 20th groups, with the P-36As. Overseas
squadrons still used older Boeings until the Canal
Zone's 16th Group got P-36As in September 1939.

Unfortunately, the Air Corps had been surpassed
by fighter development abroad. In June 1936, the
same month the Army ordered 77 two-gun, 281-mph
P-35s, the RAF ordered 600 Hurricane and 310
Spitfire fighters with *eight* guns. Hurricanes entered service in December 1937 with a 320-mph
top speed, and the 362-mph Spitfire joined a squadron in August 1938. Rolls-Royce Merlin inline engines in streamlined noses contrasted with the
built-in drag of the American air-cooled radials.

Since America's failure to match such speeds
seemed due to a lack of a high-powered inline engine, development was pushed on the liquid-cooled
power plant built by the Allison division of General
Motors. The first plane designed around the Allison
was the Curtiss XP-37, whose V-1710-11 was cooled
by side radiators and used a General Electric turbosupercharger to get a rating of 1,000 hp at 20,000
feet with 87-octane fuel. The XP-37 was actually
the Model 75B airframe with a new fuselage, the

CURTISS P-36C
Pratt & Whitney R-1830-17, 1200 hp takeoff, 1050 hp at
  10,000'
DIMENSIONS: As P-36A
WEIGHT: Empty 4620 lb., Gross 5800 lb., Max. 6150 lb.
  Fuel 105–62 gal.
PERFORMANCE: Speed—Top 311 mph at 10,000', Cruising
  270 mph, Landing 75 mph. Service Ceiling 33,700',
  Climb 15,000'/4.9 min. Range 820 miles at 200 mph,
  600 miles at 270 mph.   AF

CURTISS XP-36F   AMC

B-1 turbo under the Allison engine, and the cockpit moved to the rear.

Under a contract approved February 16, 1937, the XP-37 was flown to Wright on April 20, 1937, and was damaged in a wheels-up landing. Redelivered on June 16, it quickly proved itself the fastest Army plane yet, exceeding 300 mph. On December 11, 1937, 13 YP-37s were ordered and appeared with a longer, heavier fuselage and V-1710-21 with B-2 supercharger. Two fixed nose guns were standard.

The first YP-37 was flown to Wright Field January 24, 1939, and was accepted, along with the second, in April, with ten more in November and the last in December. Ten served the 8th and, later, the 36th Pursuit Group at Langley. Pilot visibility for landing was poor and performance below guarantees, but experience with the engine and supercharger was valuable preparation for future fighters.

Curtiss also tried a turbosupercharged version of the Wasp radial on the Hawk 75R, a private-venture P-36 modification. Delivered to Wright Field on January 20, 1939, it proved unsatisfactory and was returned to the company for further work.

The fourth P-36A returned to Wright Field on March 5, 1939, modified to the XP-42. Reflecting an attempt to give the radial engine the streamlining associated with inline power plants, the XP-42's R-1830-31 Wasp had an extended propeller shaft enclosed behind a large spinner with a cooling air intake underneath and paired carburetor air intakes on top. Maximum speed was only 315 mph at first, but a large variety of cowl forms were tested, and by August 1941, 343 mph had been achieved with a short-cowled configuration.

Air Corps concern with its inadequate fighter armament was reflected in a September 6, 1939, order that produced three P-36A conversions: an XP-36D with two .50-caliber guns on the cowl and four .30-caliber wing guns at Wright by October along with the XP-36E, which had eight .30-caliber guns in the wings and one .50-caliber cowl gun; and the XP-36F, which appeared in December with an imported Danish 23-mm Madsen attached below each wing, as well as a .50-caliber and a .30-caliber gun on the cowl.

Many of these Curtiss monoplanes were also built for export, beginning with the Hawk 75. This type differed from the P-36 in having a Wright R-1820-G3 Cyclone (giving 840 hp at 8,700 feet) and fixed, panted wheels. Armament included two cowl guns (one .30-caliber with 600 rounds and one .50-caliber with 200 rounds), two .30-caliber wing guns, and racks for ten 30-pound bombs.

The first Hawk demonstrator, H75H, followed the Y1P-36s with its first flight May 18, 1937. Shipped to China and demonstrated there in August, it was purchased for use as a command and reconnais-

CURTISS XP-37
Allison V-1710-11, 1150 hp takeoff, 1000 hp at 20,000'
DIMENSIONS: Span 37'4", Lg. 31', Ht. 9'6", Wing Area 236 sq. ft.
WEIGHT: Empty 5272 lb., Gross 6350 lb., Max. 6643 lb. Fuel 104–48 gal.
PERFORMANCE: Speed—Top 340 mph at 20,000', Cruising 304 mph, Landing 75 mph. Service Ceiling 35,000', Climb 20,000'/7.1 min. Range 485 miles normal, 625 miles max.   AMC

CURTISS YP-37
Allison V-1710-21, 1000 hp takeoff, 880 hp at 25,000'
DIMENSIONS: Span 37'4", Lg. 32'10", Ht. 9'6", Wing Area 236 sq. ft.
WEIGHT: Empty 5723 lb., Gross 6889 lb., Max. 7178 lb. Fuel 108–64 gal.
PERFORMANCE: Speed—Top 331 mph at 20,000', Cruising 305 mph, landing 85 mph. Service Ceiling 34,000', Climb 2920'/1 min., 20,000'/8.5 min. Range 570 miles normal, 870 miles max.   AF

CURTISS 75R
Pratt & Whitney R-1830-SC2-G
DIMENSIONS: As P-36A
WEIGHT: Empty 5074 lb., Gross 6163 lb.
PERFORMANCE: Speed—Top 330 mph at 15,000', Cruising 302 mph, Climb 15,000'/4.75 min. Range 600 miles.
                                                    AF

CURTISS XP-42 (Short-nose version)   NA

CURTISS HAWK 75H   MFR

CURTISS HAWK 75M
Wright GR-1820-G3, 840 hp at 8700'
DIMENSIONS: Span 37'4", Lg. 28'7", Ht. 9'4", Wing Area 236 sq. ft.
WEIGHT: Empty 3975 lb., Gross 5172 lb., Max. 6418 lb. Fuel 107–220 gal.
PERFORMANCE: Speed—Top 280 mph at 10,700', Cruising 240 mph, Landing 68 mph. Service Ceiling 31,800', Climb 2340'/1 min. Range 547 miles normal, 1210 miles max.   MFR

CURTISS XP-42
Pratt & Whitney R-1830-31, 1050 hp takeoff, 1000 hp at 14,500'
DIMENSIONS: Span 37'4", Lg. 30'7", Ht. 12', Wing Area 236 sq. ft.
WEIGHT: Empty 4818 lb., Gross 5919 lb., Max. 6260 lb. Fuel 105–61 gal.
PERFORMANCE: Speed—Top 315 mph at 15,000', Cruising 286 mph. Range 730 miles normal, 1200 miles max.   COPP

sance plane by General Claire Chennault, who was an "advisor" to China during the Japanese invasion. Thirty[3] Hawk H75M fighters were ordered by China in September, first flown June 8, 1938, and completed by August. Serving with the 5th Group, they were not especially successful in combating the light Japanese fighters due to the inexperience of the pilots.

A second demonstrator completed in June 1937 went to Argentina, where it was purchased for their army, along with 29 six-gun H75O models built in November–December 1938, and 20 more built under license in Argentina in 1940. Twelve H75Ns completed for Thailand made a first flight November 1, 1938. They were similar except for the armament: two 7.9-mm nose guns and underwing mounts for two 23-mm Madsen guns to be fitted by the customer. The Thai fighters flew a successful attack against a French air base in Cambodia on January 11, 1941, during a border dispute.

No major country seemed more in need of fighters than France, for that country's industry had failed to produce, in quantity or quality, aircraft equal to the threat presented by Germany's bombers and the Bf 109 fighter. Curtiss Hawks were attractive, but obstacles arose, among them the refusal of the Air Corps to allow the French to examine retractable-wheeled versions and the fact that the price was nearly twice that of contemporary French equipment.

President Roosevelt, however, made the Air Corps allow French pilot Michel Détroyat to secretly test a Y1P-36 on March 20, 1938, and on May 13, 1938, France did buy 100 H75A-1s, along with an option for 100 H75A-2s taken when initial deliveries met expectations. The French version, styled H75-C1 (*chasse*, one-place, according to their system) had a 900-hp R-1830-SC3G with 87-octane fuel, French instrumentation, four 7.5-mm guns, and pilot's back armor. This was the first armor on American production aircraft, although Soviet fighters had used pilot armor since 1937.

The first French Hawk flew November 21, 1938,

---

[3] Different totals given in older publications were based on errors made in a company listing circulated after the war.

CURTISS HAWK 75A-1   MFR

CURTISS H75A-2 (France)   MA

CURTISS H75A-3 (Finland)   SALO

and the first two reached France by sea on December 24, 1938. Beginning with plane 141, six 7.5-mm guns were carried, with four located in the wings. Production of the full order was completed on July 29, 1939, with 99 H75A-1s and 100 H75A-2s reaching France. When the war began, they equipped two *escadres*[4] of 54 planes each, plus reserves. On September 8, 1939, the first French victory of the war was scored when Curtiss Hawks downed two Bf 109Ds without loss to themselves.

French pilots found the H75A more maneuverable than its adversaries, and this superiority even showed up in a comparison with the Spitfire. Of course, the latter had a big edge in firepower and speed, and when the Germans replaced the Messerschmitt Bf 109Ds with Bf 109Es, the Hawk was at a disadvantage.

Hoping for more contracts, Curtiss offered new power-plant installations: one with a fully rated high-octane twin-row Wasp and another with the single-row Cyclone. These would become the H75A-3 and H75A-4, although the French did not feel pressed enough to order them until after war actually began. In the meantime, Curtiss completed a demonstrator with a Cyclone to promote the power plant made by its affiliate in the Curtiss-Wright combine.

Powered by a GR-1820-G105A whose two-speed supercharger offered 900 hp at 8,000 feet and 750 hp at 19,000 feet, the Hawk H75Q was completed in November 1938 and shipped to China, where it was flown again February 11, 1939. Equipment included a 67-pound armor plate behind the pilot, racks for ten 30-pound bombs, one .30-caliber and one .50-caliber nose gun, and two 23-mm Madsen guns under the wings. These cannons arrived from Denmark and were tested March 8, nine months before the same caliber was tested in the United States on the XP-36F. The Chinese decided by June 1939 to order 50 H75A-5 fighters and 100 Madsen

CURTISS H-75Q
Wright GR-1820-G105A, 1100 hp takeoff, 900 hp at 8000',
   750 hp at 19,000'
DIMENSIONS: Span 37'4", Lg. 28'7", Ht. 9'3", Wing Area
   236 sq. ft.
WEIGHT: Empty 4515 lb., Gross 5725 lb., Max. 6940 lb.
   Fuel 105–81 gal. (internal)
PERFORMANCE: Speed—Top 258 mph at s. l., 305 mph at
   20,000', Cruising 282 mph, Landing 68 mph. Service
   Ceiling 32,800', Climb 2800'/1 min., 10,000'/3.4 min.,
   20,000'/9 min. Range 677 miles/105 gal., 1169 miles/
   181 gal., Ferry 1440 miles with 70 gal. drop tank added.
                                    MFR

---

[4] Two *groupes* each, viz. I/4, II/4, I/5, and II/5

guns, with one pattern fighter to be completed at Buffalo and the rest at a Chinese factory at Loiwing, near the Burma border. The H75Q was destroyed in a crash on May 5, but the report that it had been used to attack Japanese bombers remains unsubstantiated.

Norway also ordered Hawks in September 1939, and their 24 H75A-6s began coming off the reopened Hawk assembly line February 5, 1940, with SC3G engines and four guns like the H75A-1. Beginning February 15, deliveries also proceeded on a new French contract placed October 9, 1939, with 135 H75A-3s with six 7.5-mm guns and an R-1830-S1C3G Wasp of 1,050 hp at 7500 feet, increasing speed from 301 to 311 mph.

The remaining Hawks were powered by single-row Wright R-1820-G205 Cyclones of 1,000 hp at 15,000 feet, designated R-1820-95 by the Army. A single H75A-5 pattern aircraft built in March 1940 for China was followed, from April to August 1940, by 285 H75A-4s with six 7.5-mm guns for France. Twenty H75A-7s completed in May/June for the Dutch East Indies had four 12.7-mm Brownings. Norway bought 36 H75A-8 Hawks, delivered between December 16, 1940, and February 4, 1941, with two 12.7-mm nose guns and four 7.7-mm wing guns. The last of the Curtiss Hawks were ten H75A-9s, completed from March 9 to April 8, 1941, for Iran—the first American fighters built for that country. All these types had wing bomb racks and pilot armor.

Most of these Hawks never flew for their original buyers and some fought against the Allies. Norwegian H75A-6s were being assembled there as Germany attacked on April 9, 1940, when four planes were destroyed by bombs and at least 13 were captured by Germany. Another shipload is said to have been diverted to Britain.

With capitulation near, France, on June 17, 1940, turned over to Britain all Hawks that were undelivered on their contracts. Precise numbers are uncertain, but France had taken 316 Hawks, including the first six H75A-4s, on charge. There were 17 more Hawks of this type diverted to Martinique, six to Guadeloupe, and 30 on a freighter sunk at La Rochelle; some of the latter may have been the H75A-4s that fell into German hands.

The Hawks were the most successful of the French fighters, being credited with 230 confirmed victories by June 1940, after which they transferred to North Africa. In November 1942 they were used by Vichy French forces against American Navy planes over Morocco.

Britain designated the H75A-3 and A-4 the Mohawk III and IV, but had little use for the Curtiss fighters at home, where they were not considered equal to the RAF fighters. Instead, South Africa was

CURTISS HAWK 75A-4
Wright R-1820-95, 1200 hp takeoff, 1000 hp at 15,000′
DIMENSIONS: Span 37′4″, Lg. 28′10″, Ht. 9′6″, Wing Area 236 sq. ft.
WEIGHT: Empty 4541 lb., Gross 5750 lb. Fuel 105–63 gal.
PERFORMANCE: Speed—Top 323 mph at 15,100′, Cruising 262 mph, landing 69 mph. Service Ceiling 32,700′, Absolute Ceiling 33,600′. Range 1003 miles max. IWM

sent 72 in 1941 and Portugal 12 in October 1941. Some also went to India, along with the Iranian H75-9s captured—while still in crates—by the British occupation. Altogether, 235 Mohawks received RAF serial numbers.

Mohawks of No. 5 Squadron began combat patrols June 17, 1942, as northern India's only air defense against Japan, until they were joined in November by No. 155 Squadron, whose Mohawks served through 1943. The RAF in India also inherited China's H75A-5 program, including the pattern aircraft. Bombed out of Loiwing October 26, 1940, and with Madsen guns never delivered, the remaining Hawk parts had been turned over to India's first airplane factory, Hindustani Aircraft. Only five H75A-5s were completed at Bangalore, the first not until July 31, 1942. By that time the Mohawk was quite obsolete, so the factory was better used as a repair facility.

Finland arranged to buy captured Hawks from Germany. Seven H75A-4 and 13 H75A-6 types arrived, beginning June 23, 1941, just before Finland joined the war against the Soviet Union. Nine more ex-French Hawks were received from the War Booty Depot by November, and 15 replacement aircraft began arriving in June 1943, including six H75A-1, nine A-2, and nine A-3 types. These 44 Curtiss fighters, flown in combat by Finns from July 14, 1941, to September 4, 1944, were credited with 190 victories for only 24 losses.

Back in the United States, the P-36A was being replaced by the P-40. The 8th Pursuit Group passed its P-36As and YP-37s to the 36th Group in 1940 and to the 56th Group in 1941, while the 20th Group's P-36As went to the 35th at Hamilton Field and then to the 51st at March Field. Overseas deployment sent 20 P-36As to Anchorage, Alaska, with the 18th Pursuit Squadron on February 20, 1941, and 42 P-36As were transferred to Hawaii shortly thereafter. The 27th Squadron's P-36Cs at Selfridge went to the 1st Pursuit Squadron at the Eglin Field Proving Ground. Fifteen P-36As remained in the Canal Zone with the 16th Group and 17 stayed with Puerto Rico's 36th Group on November 30, 1941.

Latin America saw Curtiss Hawks when Brazil received ten P-36As in March 1942 and Peru obtained 30 P-36G Hawks. The latter were survivors of the Norwegian H75A-8s used for training in Canada until purchased by the United States in April 1942 for resale with a lend-lease designation.

Only once did the P-36A fight with U.S. markings: On the morning of December 7, 1941, 14 P-36A and 11 P-40B sorties were flown during the surprise attack on Pearl Harbor. The older Hawks were credited with at least two victories, for one loss to enemy fighters and one to American anti-aircraft fire.

The Airacuda

The most unusual prewar combat type was the only twin-engine pusher fighter ever built in the United States. Intended as a heavily armed, long-range answer to four-engine bombers, the five-place, low-wing Bell XFM-1 (experimental fighter multiplace) was the first twin-engine American plane intended solely for fighting, and was begun in response to an Air Corps request made in September 1935.

Bell Aircraft had Consolidated Aircraft's old Buffalo plant and some personnel, including Robert Wood, the P-30's designer. He prepared a design utilizing two new 37-mm Colts, adapted from an antiaircraft gun, and Allison engines. A rival Lockheed XFM-2 design used the same engines in conventional tractor fashion, with twin rudders, tricycle gear, one cannon in a nose turret, and another turret on top of the fuselage.

The outstanding feature of the Bell Airacuda was the nacelle on each wing, containing a gunner in front and a turbosupercharged Allison V-1710-13 turning a pusher propeller in back. The wing gunners were to have a 37-mm gun with a .30-caliber gun alongside. Behind the pilot and navigator, seated tandem in the nose of the main fuselage, was a rear gunner who fired a .50-caliber gun from a teardrop blister on each side. Bell won the prototype contract on June 4, 1936, and the XFM-1 flew September 1, 1937. Wooden dummy guns were carried since the heavy-caliber Colts were not yet available.

Service-test models ordered May 20, 1938, for $3,168,265 were originally designed to have turbosuperchargers like the prototype and were expected to do 305 mph at 20,000 feet. Altitude-rated Allisons limiting top speed to 270 mph at 12,600

BELL XFM-1
Allison V-1710-13, 1150 hp takeoff, 1000 hp at 20,000'
DIMENSIONS: Span 69′10″, Lg. 44′10″, Ht. 13′7″, Wing Area 684 sq. ft.
WEIGHT: Empty 13,376 lb., Gross 17.333 lb. Fuel 400–800 gal.
PERFORMANCE: Speed—Top 271 mph at 20,000', Cruising 244 mph, Landing 77 mph. Service Ceiling 30,500', Climb 15,000'/10 min. Range 800 miles normal, 2600 miles max.   AF

BELL YFM-1
Allison V-1710-23, 1150 hp takeoff
DIMENSIONS: Span 70′, Lg. 46′, Ht. 12′9″, Wing Area 600 sq. ft.
WEIGHT: Empty 13,630 lb., Gross 18,000 lb., Max. 19,000 lb. Fuel 400–800 gal.
PERFORMANCE: Speed—Top 270 mph at 12,600', Landing 77 mph. Service Ceiling 30,500', Climb 15,000'/10.3 min. Range 940 miles normal, 1800 miles max.   MFR

feet were substituted because of an explosion of the turbo on the YFM-1's first flight on September 28, 1939. Other YFM-1 features were radiator placement in the wings, rather than atop the nacelle, and improvement of the rear defense. Two .50-caliber guns fired from extending side mounts. One .30 rode in a retractable 360° top turret and another was in the 180° belly turret. Twenty 17- or 30-pound bombs could be carried in the fuselage, and ammunition supply comprised 110 37-mm, 1,200 .50-caliber, and 1,000 .30-caliber rounds.

Delivery of the 37-mm T9 guns began in April 1939. They could be aimed through a 25° cone of fire by the gunners, or by the navigator using a Sperry fire-control system whose sight protruded below the fuselage.

Nine YFM-1s were accepted from March to July 1940, and another crashed before delivery. Their landing gear retracted backwards halfway into the nacelles, as on the XFM-1. Three YFM-1As introduced in August 1940 were identical to the YFM-1 except for the addition of a retracting nosewheel for the tricycle gear becoming popular on bombers. On this version the main wheels folded inward to fit flat within the wings. A pair of YFM-1s fitted with V-1710-41s became YFM-1B types.

Although the Airacuda aroused much excitement on its appearance, it proved a disappointment as a bomber interceptor. Comparison of XFM-1 performance with the contemporary XP-37 shows the multiseater far behind in speed, climb, and ceiling, while the single-seater was far less expensive to build and operate. Not only was the Airacuda's speed insufficiently greater than the bombers it had to catch, but the big fighter's lack of maneuverability would have made it easy prey for single-seat escorts attacking from the rear. Nor did the unwieldy arrangement recommend itself for protecting bombers against light interceptors.

Export Fighters

Three single-seaters that appeared just before the war were developed from trainer designs to provide relatively low-cost fighters for the export market. They were the Curtiss-Wright CW-21, the North American NA-50, and the Vultee Vanguard.

The St. Louis branch of the Curtiss-Wright Corporation produced the CW-21 as a fast-climbing interceptor developed from the CW-19 trainer. Powered by a Wright Cyclone, it had a swept-back leading edge and wheels retracting backwards into fairings below the wing. One .30-caliber and one .50-caliber nose gun was carried and ¼-inch armor installed behind the pilot despite the very lightweight construction.

The CW-21 prototype was first flown October 11, 1938, and was later shipped to China, where a competitive test on March 3, 1939, proved the interceptor better in climb and maneuverability than other available fighters. When China bought the Hawk H75A-5 in June 1939, 30 CW-21 Interceptors were also ordered, of which three were made in St. Louis and the rest were to be assembled at Loiwing. This program proved as ill-fated as the H75A-5 plan. While the three pattern aircraft were completed in June 1940 and managed to reach Burma, all were destroyed on a ferry flight to China on December

BELL YFM-1A
Allison V-1710-23, 1150 hp
DIMENSIONS: As YFM-1
WEIGHT: Empty 13,962 lb., Gross 18,431 lb., Max. 19,301 lb. Fuel 400–800 gal.
PERFORMANCE: As YFM-1   MFR

BELL YFM-1B
Allison V-1710-41, 1090 hp at 13,200'
DIMENSIONS: Span 70', Lg. 46', Ht. 12'5", Wing Area 600 sq. ft.
WEIGHT: Empty 13,023 lb., Gross 18,373 lb., Max. 21,150 lb. Fuel 400–800 gal.
PERFORMANCE: Speed—Top 268 mph at 12,600', Cruising 240 mph, Landing 77 mph. Service Ceiling 30,000', Climb 15,000'/10.6 min. Range 650 miles normal, 1675 miles max.   PMB

CURTISS-WRIGHT CW-21
Wright R-1820-G5, 850 hp at 6000', 750 hp at 15,200'
DIMENSIONS: Span 35', Lg. 26'6", Ht. 8'8", Wing Area 174 sq. ft.
WEIGHT: Empty 3050 lb., Gross 4092 lb. normal, Max. 4250 lb. Fuel 96 gal.
PERFORMANCE: Speed—Top 304 mph at 12,200', 261 mph at s. l., Cruising 275 mph, Landing 68 mph. Service Ceiling 35,000'. Climb 4800'/1 min., Range 630 miles.   SDAM

23, 1941, and just before the first examples were to be finished at Loiwing, the factory was burned and abandoned on May 1, 1942, before advancing Japanese troops.

On April 17, 1940, the Netherlands ordered 24 CW-21B interceptors, whose wheels folded inward completely into the wing. Armament provisions were made for two .30-caliber and two .50-caliber guns under the cowl, although only two 7.7-mm guns may have been fitted in service. Completed between October and December 1940, they went to a squadron in Java. The Dutch also acquired the CW-22 trainer (a two-seat, low-powered CW-21), used by the U.S. Navy as the SNC-1, for reconnaissance work, but did not buy the CW-23, a prototype trainer version of the CW-21B.

On February 3, 1942, these fighters, along with H75A-7s, rose against the Japanese invaders, but the Dutch lost ten of the 14 interceptors sortied in that first day's attack; the Zeros were too much for them.

North American Aviation designed a single-seat fighter version of their famous trainer series for Peru. Powered by an 840-hp Wright R-1820-G3 Cyclone, the NA-50 had two .30-caliber cowl guns and wing bomb racks. Seven planes begun on August 1, 1938, and completed between February and May 1939 served Peru in the 1941 border war with Ecuador.

A redesigned version of this single-seater was ordered by Thailand on November 30, 1939, as the NA-68. Armed with four .303 guns (two in the nose and two in the wings) and two 20-mm guns under the wings, with racks for two 110-pound bombs, the NA-68 had a revised cowl and rudder. Six were completed by November 1940 but were taken over by the Air Corps on March 4, 1941, and, instead of being shipped overseas, served at western training bases without armament.

The Air Corps designated the NA-68 as the P-64 since it was a single-seater design. This number was so late in the Army's fighter catalog because intervening numbers had been issued to the many projects already in progress. For the same reason the Vultee fighters acquired that year became the P-66.

Vultee Aircraft, having built 27 transports and 111 attack bombers by 1939, opened new markets with a set of four prototypes designed by Richard Palmer with similar wing and tail configurations. The first was a two-seat advanced trainer with retractable wheels purchased by the Air Corps as the BC-3, and the next two were fixed-gear basic trainers that won acceptance as the standard wartime BT-13/15 trainers.

Vultee's Model 48 Vanguard fighter had a special 1,200-hp Pratt & Whitney Wasp with an extended

CURTISS-WRIGHT CW-21B
Wright R-1820-G5, 1000 hp takeoff, 750 hp at 15,200′
DIMENSIONS: Span 35′, Lg. 27′2″, Ht. 8′11″, Wing Area 174 sq. ft.
WEIGHT: Empty 3382 lb., Gross 4500 lb. Fuel 100 gal.
PERFORMANCE: Speed—Top 314 mph at 12,200′, 277 mph at s. l. Cruising 282 mph, Landing 68 mph. Service Ceiling 34,300′, Absolute Ceiling 35,000′, Climb 4500′/ 1 min., 13,120′/4 min. Range 630 miles.   MFR

NORTH AMERICAN NA-68
(P-64 with original 20-mm. armament and Siamese markings)   MFR

NORTH AMERICAN P-64 (NA-68)
Wright R-1820-77, 840 hp at 8700′
DIMENSIONS: Span 37′3″, Lg. 27′, Ht. 9′, Wing Area 227.5 sq. ft.
WEIGHT: Empty 4660 lb., Gross 5990 lb., Max. 6800 lb. Fuel 120–70 gal.
PERFORMANCE: Speed—Top 270 mph at 8700′, Cruising 235 mph, Landing 70 mph. Service Ceiling 27,500′. Range 630 miles normal, 965 miles max.   PMB

drive shaft enclosed within a pointed cowling like that of the XP-42. An air intake under the nose provided cooling. The Vanguard first flew September 8, 1939, the sixth new American fighter type flown that year, but the cowling arrangement proved unsatisfactory, the extra weight and cooling difficulties overpowering the drag reduction gained.

A conventional cowl on a standard S1C3-G Wasp was more successful on a rebuilt version flown February 11, 1940, and this style was selected by Sweden for a 144-plane contract. Another prototype, Model 48C, was flown September 6, 1940, with an S3C4-G Wasp and six guns.

After Sweden was barred from U.S. aircraft by the State Department, the Vanguards were given RAF serials and allocated to Canada on December 15, 1940. Although British colors were painted on the first two production aircraft, China was given the fighters on June 19, 1941, under a lend-lease contract. The aircraft were now designated P-66.

Armament consisted of two .50-caliber nose guns and four .30-caliber wing guns, and armor was provided the pilot. Delivery of 144 P-66s was made from October 24, 1941, to April 20, 1942, but in December 1941 the Vanguards were requisitioned by the Army and used to fill out the 14th Group's strength at March Field for the defense of southern California. When sufficient P-38s became available to replace that group's P-43A and P-66 fighters, the Vultees, minus U.S. attrition, were shipped to Asia. A depot in Karachi, India, received 129 in the summer of 1942 for the Chinese Air Force, which flew them to Cheng-tu. They replaced Soviet fighters formerly in use, but no reports of their combat service are presently available.

VULTEE VANGUARD (Prototype)
Pratt & Whitney R-1830-S4C4-G, 1200 hp takeoff, 900 hp at 15,400'
DIMENSIONS: Span 36', Lg. 29'2", Ht. 9'5", Wing Area 197 sq. ft.
WEIGHT: Empty 4657 lb., Gross 6029 lb. Fuel 240 gal.
PERFORMANCE: Speed—Top 358 mph at 15,600', Cruising 316 mph, Landing 73 mph. Service Ceiling 34,300', Climb 3300'/1 min. Range 738 miles normal.   MFR

VULTEE VANGUARD (Short-nose modification)   MFR

VULTEE P-66
Pratt & Whitney R-1830-33 (S3C4-G), 1200 hp takeoff, 1050 hp at 13,100'
DIMENSIONS: Span 36', Lg. 28'5", Ht. 9'5", Wing Area 197 sq. ft.
WEIGHT: Empty 5237 lb., Gross 7100 lb., Max. 7384 lb. Fuel 124–85 gal.
PERFORMANCE: Speed—Top 340 mph at 15,100', Cruising 290 mph, Landing 82 mph. Service Ceiling 28,200', Absolute Ceiling 29,750', Climb 2520'/1 min., 19,700'/9.2 min. Range 850 miles normal, 950 miles at 240 mph.   MFR

Chapter 17
World War II Fighters, 1939–45

The Long P-40 Line

Although seven different fighter types were in mass production for the Air Force during World War II, the Curtiss P-40 was the first available in large numbers. From 1940 to 1942 more P-40s were built than all of the other major fighter types together, and so the Warhawk was seen on nearly every front.

The P-40 offered little new in design over the P-36 except for a streamlined nose with an inline engine; in fact, the prototype was the tenth P-36A with an Allison V-1710-19 using a geared supercharger. Since the P-37's high-altitude supercharger was still unreliable, designer Don Berlin advocated a less complex medium-altitude, single-stage blower built into the engine.

His proposal was accepted with an April 26, 1938, modification contract for the XP-40. First flown October 14, 1938, by Ed Elliot, the XP-40 was further modified by February 1939 by moving the radiator from behind the wing to under the nose and installing the usual two guns in blast tubes over the cowl.

The Army's pursuit competition held on January 25, 1939, had called for bids on designs whose top speeds of 310 to 370 mph were to be reached at 15,000 feet, with a two-hour endurance at cruising speed. Higher critical altitudes and speeds were offered by the turbosuperchargers on the Lockheed XP-38 and Bell XP-39 "pursuit-interceptors" designed for "cannon" armament. Turbosuperchargers were also used on the Curtiss YP-37, Hawk 75R, and Seversky AP-4, while medium-altitude radial engines powered the Seversky XP-41 and AP-9. But at that time the Air Corps still preferred to mass-produce a medium-altitude pursuit first, and compared to the air-cooled types, the XP-40 was faster, less expensive, and available for rapid delivery. On April 26, 1939, funds from the new Air Corps Expansion Act were allocated for 524 P-40 pursuits at

CURTISS XP-40
Allison V-1710-19, 1160 hp takeoff, 1000 hp at 10,000'
DIMENSIONS: Span 37'4", Lg. 31'1", Ht. 12'4", Wing Area 236 sq. ft.
WEIGHT: Empty 5417 lb., Gross 6260 lb., Max. 6870 lb. Fuel 100–58 gal.
PERFORMANCE: Speed—Top 342 mph at 12,200', Cruising 299 mph, Landing 72 mph. Range 460 miles normal, 1180 miles at 200 mph with full load.   AMC

$22,929 each, less GFE, and 13 each of the YP-38 and YP-39 pursuit-interceptors were approved the same day.

Curtiss had promised to increase the 342-mph prototype speed to 360 mph on production models, so the XP-40 was sent to NACA for wind-tunnel tests. From these tests emerged such 1940 refinements as a new radiator arrangement under the nose, individual exhaust stacks replacing the one-piece manifold, a carburetor intake between and ahead of the gun muzzles, and improved landing gear.

These features, plus flush riveting, were seen on the first production P-40, flown April 4, 1940. Powered by an Allison C-15 (V-1710-33) offering 1,040

CURTISS XP-40 (Modified)   AMC

CURTISS P-40
Allison V-1710-33, 1040 hp at 15,000'
DIMENSIONS: Span 37'4", Lg. 31'9", Ht. 12'4", Wing Area
  236 sq. ft.
WEIGHT: Empty 5376 lb., Gross 6787 lb., Max. 7215 lb.
  Fuel 120–81 gal.
PERFORMANCE: Speed—Top 357 mph at 15,000', Cruising
  277 mph, Landing 80 mph. Service Ceiling 32,750',
  Absolute Ceiling 33,800', Climb 3080'/1 min., 15,000'/
  5.3 min. Range 650 miles normal, 950 miles at 250
  mph, 1400 miles max. at 188 mph.   AF

hp at 15,000 feet, it was armed with two .50-caliber
guns with 200 rpg on the cowl and provision for a
.30-caliber gun with 500 rpg in each wing, but no
bomb racks were carried. The first three aircraft
were delivered in natural metal, but the remainder
introduced the olive drab paint and gray underbot-
tom of wartime Army planes, while these P-40s
were the last model delivered with traditional tail
stripes.

   Two hundred of the P-40 model reached the
Army, but the remaining 324 were deferred in April
1940 to enable earlier delivery on the Curtiss H81A
ordered by France and taken over by Britain. The
deferred aircraft were to be replaced later by ships
incorporating armor, fuel-tank protection, and more
firepower. Some may have had the P-40A designation not used on production aircraft.

   The first 11 P-40s were accepted in May 1940,
and by October the type equipped the 8th Pursuit
Group, which moved from Langley to Mitchel Field
in November, and the 20th Pursuit Group, which

arrived at Hamilton Field in September. Lastly,
about 30 P-40s were sent to Selfridge Field for the
31st Pursuit Group. Now the Army squadrons had
a type comparable to the Bf 109E although weaker
than the Spitfire in speed and firepower.

   On October 5, 1939, France had ordered 100 Curtiss H81A fighters along with H75As. The first example was flown June 6, 1940, with French equipment, provisions for four 7.5-mm wing guns, and
wavy camouflage paint. After the RAF took over
contracts for the Curtiss fighters from France on
June 17, 1940, they increased these contracts to
1,180 aircraft.

   Delivery of 140 H81A-1s, known as the Tomahawk Mk. I, began on September 18, 1940. Tomahawk Mk. IIA, or H81A-2, whose deliveries began
October 30, had British equipment, two .50-caliber
nose guns and four .303-caliber wing guns, pilot
armor and, for the first time, self-sealing fuel tanks.
By the end of 1940, 558 Tomahawks had been accepted by the RAF.

CURTISS P-40B
Allison V-1710-33, 1040 hp at 15,000'
DIMENSIONS: As P-40
WEIGHT: Empty 5590 lb., Gross 7325 lb., Max. 7600 lb.
  Fuel 120–60 gal.
PERFORMANCE: (6835 lb.) Speed—Top 352 mph at 15,-
  000', Cruising 280 mph, Landing 80 mph. Service Ceil-
  ing 32,400', Climb 15,000'/5.1 min. Range 730 miles
  normal, 940–1230 miles max.   AF

CURTISS P-40C
Allison V-1710-33, 1040 hp at 15,000'
DIMENSIONS: As P-40
WEIGHT: Empty 5812 lb., Gross 7549 lb., Max. 8058 lb.
  Fuel 134–86 gal.
PERFORMANCE: (7327 lb.) Speed—Top 345 mph at 15,-
  000', Cruising 270 mph, Landing 86 mph. Service Ceil-
  ing 29,500', Absolute Ceiling 30,500', Climb 2690'/1
  min.   ARNOLD

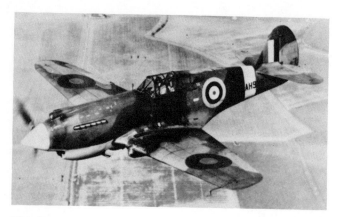

CURTISS TOMAHAWK IIA (R.A.F.)   MFR

CURTISS H-81A-2 (A.V.G.)   AF

The Army's equivalent of the H81A-2 was the P-40B, ordered September 12, 1940, which also had armor, self-sealing tanks, two .50-caliber nose guns with 380 rpg, and four .30-caliber wing guns. Delivery of 131 planes began January 3, 1941, followed by 193 P-40C fighters beginning March 31. This model had a new radio and a new fuel system with internal self-sealing tanks and a 52-gallon drop tank.

Beginning in April 1941, the first P-40Bs and P-40Cs delivered were deployed to Hawaii by Navy carrier, flying off the decks to Army airfields. This would become a common wartime fighter-delivery method. To modernize its older P-40s, 50 sets of H87A-2 wings with four guns and protected tanks were ordered, and the first was installed on the sixty-sixth P-40, which was redesignated P-40G on August 14, 1941. Some 44 such conversions were made, and the P-40G went to Hamilton and Mitchel fields.

Tomahawk IIB, or H87A-3, was the concurrent British P-40C version, first flown April 23, 1941, with deliveries made until August 21, 1941, when the British had accepted 1,180 Tomahawks. They became the first P-40s to fight. Unwanted by Fighter Command, Tomahawks were first used in 1941 to replace the two-place Lysanders of 11 Army Cooperation squadrons, whose Tomahawks were fitted with an oblique camera for tactical reconnaissance. Four more squadrons later got them for training. These squadrons served only in the United Kingdom and fought no air battles before the Tomahawks were replaced in 1942–43 by Mustang Is.

About 300 Tomahawks were sent to the Middle East to replace RAF Hurricanes, and the first P-40 victory was scored June 8, 1941, when an Italian bomber was destroyed near Alexandria by a No. 250 Squadron pilot. No. 3 Squadron (Australian) used Tomahawks in Syria, downing three Ju 88s June 18 and six Vichy French Martin Marylands on June 28. This squadron then joined the Tomahawks

of Nos. 112 and 250 Squadrons in Egypt, along with two South African squadrons.

During the brisk desert fighting, the Tomahawk was reputed to be a heavy but robust aircraft, inferior to the new Bf 109F in speed and climb but better in maneuverability. Superior German pilot experience added to the difficulties, but Australian Clive Caldwell did score 20 victories flying P-40s—probably the most successful ace on the type.

Many Tomahawks remained in reserve, so on January 6, 1941, 100 H81A-2s were sold to China and shipped from New York to Burma for the American Volunteer Group (AVG). Turkey also received at least 15 by November 1941, and 31 others were lost at sea.

After the Soviet Union had been invaded, Churchill promised Stalin 200 surplus Tomahawks on July 25, 1941. The last 49 Tomahawk IIBs built were shipped directly from the United States; 24 IIA and 146 IIB types came from British depots, while the Americans also shipped 21 P-40Gs. The aircraft were convoyed to Arkhangelsk, where between September 10 and 29 two Army pilots qualified the first 120 Soviet pilots on the P-40 with only one loss. The 126th Fighter Air Regiment was the first Soviet P-40 unit, fighting in the Moscow battle, and the 154th Regiment served the Leningrad front.

Improving the P-40

Even before the P-40 entered service, Curtiss engineers planned a replacement. The first possibility was a response to an Army circular proposal dated June 15, 1939, for pursuit designs for 1941 production. An improved 1,150-hp Allison F (V-1710-39) was specified for the Curtiss offer. Although it took third place to the Republic P-44 and Bell P-45, prototype development of the Curtiss XP-46 was authorized September 29, 1939.

The original lightweight conception was replaced by October 19 with provision for two .50-caliber nose guns, four .30-caliber wing guns, 65 pounds of pilot armor, and self-sealing fuel tanks, apparently the first to be required by an Air Corps specification. The armament was the same as that later specified for the P-40B, although the XP-46 was a smaller aircraft, with the wheels retracting inwards instead of backwards and the radiator moved back below the slatted wings.

The contract signed October 31 called for two prototypes, one (the XP-46A) being delivered without armament to expedite tests and insure against accidents like the one that interrupted XP-38 development. The mockup was inspected March 4, 1940, but Curtiss was permitted to delay the project in order to devote itself to improving the P-40, which had more rapid production possibilities in that crucial period. Substitution of a modified P-40 for the P-46 was proposed by the Matériel Division on June 10, 1940. By the time the XP-46A flew on February 15, 1941, it had already lost any production hopes, and the company suffered a financial penalty when performance failed to meet contract guarantees, which had once called for 410 mph.

The P-40 development, which also used the 1,-150-hp V-1710-39, were 560 H87A Kittyhawks, ordered by Britain in May 1940 and by the Army on September 13, for concurrent production as the P-40D. On May 22, 1941, flight tests began on the first Kittyhawk I, which differed from the Tomahawk by a modified fuselage, with radiator and top intakes moved forward on a nose given a new shape by the V-1710-39. About 175 pounds of armor were carried, together with 148 gallons in self-sealing internal fuel tanks, and fittings for a 52-gallon drop tank, a 500-pound bomb under the fuselage, or six 20-pound fragmentation bombs under the wings.

The armament originally planned consisted of four .50-caliber guns in the wings with two 20-mm guns mounted externally below them. But the heavy guns could not be made available in time, so a February 18, 1941, order fixed six .50-caliber guns with 1,686 rounds for the P-40E version. These six wing guns became standard for most American wartime fighters.

The first 20 Kittyhawk Is were delivered, beginning August 27, 1941, with four guns, but the remaining 540 had six guns and were completed by December 16. Most went directly to Egypt, beginning in December 1941, where they replaced the Tomahawk in nine squadrons, but 72 went to Canada beginning in October 1941. At least six were shipped with the P-40E-1s sent to Russia, and 17 were passed from the Middle East to Turkey.

Accepted on the parallel Army contract in July 1941 were 22 P-40Ds with four guns, while 820 P-

CURTISS XP-46
Allison V-1710-39, 1150 hp at 11,800'
DIMENSIONS: Span 34'4", Lg. 30'2", Ht. 12', Wing Area 208 sq. ft.
WEIGHT: Empty 5625 lb., Gross 7322 lb., Max. 7665 lb. Fuel 103–56 gal.
PERFORMANCE: Speed—Top 355 mph at 12,200', Landing 79 mph. Service Ceiling 29,500', Climb 12,300'/5 min. Range 325 miles at 332 mph., max. 717 miles.   PMB

CURTISS H87A-1 (Kittyhawk I)   MFR

CURTISS P-40-D
Allison V-1710-39, 1150 hp at 11,800'
DIMENSIONS: Span 37'4", Lg. 31'2", Ht. 12'4", Wing Area 236 sq. ft.
WEIGHT: Empty 5970 lb., Gross 7740 lb., Max. 8810 lb. Fuel 148–200 gal.
PERFORMANCE: Speed—Top 359 mph at 15,000', Cruising 258 mph, Landing 85 mph. Service Ceiling 30,600', Absolute Ceiling 31,600', Climb 2580'/1 min., 15,000'/6.4 min. Range 800 miles normal, 1150 miles max. at 195 mph.   MFR

CURTISS P-40E
Allison V-1710-39, 1150 hp at 11,800'
DIMENSIONS: As P-40D
WEIGHT: Empty 6350 lb., Gross 8280 lb., Max. 9200 lb.
    Fuel 148–200 gal.
PERFORMANCE: Speed—Top 354 mph at 15,000'. Service
    Ceiling 29,000'. Climb 15,000'/8.3 min. Range 700
    miles normal, 895 miles max.   PMB

CURTISS P-40E-1   MFR

40Es with six guns and a new radio began deliveries August 29. They went first to the 20th Group at Hamilton Field and then to the Philippines and the Panama Canal Zone.

The third lend-lease contract (DA-3), approved May 12, 1941, provided 1,500 P-40E-1 (Kittyhawk IA) models, which replaced the Kittyhawk I on production lines in December 1941. They were produced alongside the Army P-40Es until May 1942, when both contracts were completed. Most Kittyhawk IAs went under that name to the Soviet Union, Commonwealth Air Forces, and the RAF Middle East, but all Army P-40s were renamed Warhawks in January 1942.

Army pursuit strength had increased from five groups plus one separate squadron with 464 fighters in January 1940 to 24 groups plus two squadrons with 1,618 aircraft at the beginning of December 1941. Curtiss fighters were in the majority, with

older models being passed on to the less-experienced units.

Hawaii had been sent 87 P-40B and 13 P-40C fighters for the 15th and 18th pursuit groups. Eleven P-40B sorties were flown during the December 7 attack, when Lieutenant George S. Welch downed four attacking planes, but 42 P-40s were destroyed and 30 damaged that morning.

In the Philippines the 24th Pursuit Group had five squadrons with 51 P-35A, 28 P-40B, and 106 P-40E pursuits. Despite losses during the surprise attack, they fought on until all were lost in April, although Lieutenant Boyd D. Wagner downed eight enemies with his P-40E to become the war's first AAF ace.

Defense forces in the Canal Zone in December included the 16th, 32nd, and 37th pursuit groups, with 17 P-36A, six P-40B, 49 P-40C, 22 P-40D, and 24 P-40E fighters. Puerto Rico's 36th Pursuit Group began December with 15 P-36As, 34 P-39Ds, 17 P-40Cs, and 30 P-40Es scattered on several eastern Caribbean fields.

In the northeast United States the First Air Force had six pursuit groups. The 8th had turned over its old model P-40s to the 33rd at Mitchel and sent one squadron with 30 P-40Cs to Iceland via the *Wasp* in July 1941. Most remaining P-40Cs served at Windsor Locks with the 57th, which had lost nine planes in a cross-country flight begun October 24. Bell P-39Ds had been issued to the rest of the 8th Group, as well as to the 31st and 52nd at Selfridge, with the 1st's P-38s.

The Second Air Force in the Northwest had old model P-40s with the 54th Group and P-43s with the 55th Group. The Third Air Force had five pursuit groups in the Southeast; the 49th, 50th, and 58th pursuit groups had P-40s, while the 53rd and 56th had P-39 and P-36 types. In the Southwest the Fourth Air Force had P-40E and P-40G fighters at Hamilton Field for the 20th and 35th groups (the latter's personnel were in transit to the Philippines), while the 14th and 51st groups at March Field were getting P-43s and P-40Es, respectively.

As the Pacific war got under way, the Warhawk became the most important fighter against the enemy advance. The most famous were the Tomahawks of the "Flying Tigers," the AVG pilots commanded by Claire Chennault, fighting Japanese Army squadrons over Burma and southern China. Beginning on December 20, 1941, with the destruction of a Mitsubishi Ki. 21 bomber squadron near Kunming, the AVG's exploits were highly glamorized by the press.

Their air victories did not change the rapidly deteriorating ground situation, and not until March 1942 did the first of 30 P-40E replacements and the 51st Group's P-40Es begin arriving. In July the remaining AVG aircraft and a few of its pilots became the AAF's 23rd Pursuit Group in China. During its 30 weeks in combat, the AVG was credited with 297 victories for the loss of 80 aircraft: 12 in air combat, ten to ground fire, 13 on the ground, 23 in accidents, and 22 destroyed in evacuations. Much of the P-40's success was due to the tactics developed by Chennault, which avoided dogfighting with the more maneuverable Japanese fighters and utilized superior P-40 speed and firepower to "bounce" the enemy with quick passes and breakaways, fighting in pairs.

As the Japanese advanced southward in the Pacific, 337 P-40Es arrived in Australia between December 23, 1941, and March 18, 1942. Of these, 120 were forwarded to Java with provisional squadrons, but only 36 actually arrived able to join the fight, which ended in a Japanese victory on March 1. The 49th Group used the P-40E to defend Darwin and Port Moresby against frequent Japanese raids beginning on March 14. Australian pilots also received P-40Es and went into combat with No. 75 Squadron on March 21. P-40 pilots in Pacific areas were seldom as successful as the Flying Tigers, for Japanese Navy Zero fighters were tougher opponents, and the American pilots less experienced.

Entirely different weather conditions faced the 50 P-40Es of the 11th and 18th fighter[1] squadrons in the Aleutians when Japan attacked Dutch Harbor on June 3, 1942. They operated against Japanese forces on Attu and Kiska, and were joined to a P-38 squadron to form the 343rd Fighter Group on September 11, 1942.

By that time Japan was surrounded by a ring of Warhawk units: the 343rd Group in Alaska; the 15th and 18th groups in Hawaii (with 134 P-40Bs, Cs and Es in June); the 68th Fighter Squadron with 25 P-40Es on Tongatabu in the South Pacific; the 49th Fighter Group and the Australian squadrons in the southwest Pacific; and the 23rd and 51st groups in Asia. In addition, there were Warhawks serving defense and training units from California to Panama, as well as in the zone of interior (ZI).

Rolls-Royce Warhawks

The Allison engine's poor high-altitude output limited P-40 performance severely below that of the Bf 109F used by the Germans. Better possibilities were offered with the production in America by Packard of the Rolls-Royce Merlin with a two-speed integral supercharger. Packard Merlins were scheduled for 1,000 aircraft in a September 1940 contract, as well as 312 added by a contract approved on May 3.

A prototype was made by installing an imported Merlin 28 on a P-40D airframe. The new XP-40F first flew June 30, 1941, and eliminated the carburetor intake above the nose that had been the Allison-engine P-40's trademark. Beginning in January 1942, Curtiss delivered 1,311 P-40Fs powered by the Packard V-1650-1 Merlin, yielding 1,300 hp at 12,000 feet and 1,120 hp at 18,500 feet. They went down assembly lines side by side with the P-40E-1, for the supply of Merlin engines was insufficient to fill half of the Curtiss fighter's production. These Merlin-powered Hawks were allocated to the five groups sent to the Mediterranean Theater.

The first 699 P-40Fs had the same fuselage as the P-40E, but the P-40F-5 of August 1942 had 20 inches added to the fuselage to improve directional stability. Minor mechanical changes were made on the P-40F-10, F-15, and F-20 series. Armament was the same as the P-40E, but a 170-gallon drop tank could be used.

Seven hundred P-40Ls ordered June 15, 1942, replaced the P-40F-20 on the production line in January 1943 and were similar in appearance with V-1650-1 Merlins. In fact, the first 50 P-40L-1s were identical to the last Fs, but the P-40L-5 was made lighter by the elimination of the two .50-caliber outboard guns and the 37-gallon wing tank.

CURTISS P-40F
Packard V-1650-1, 1300 hp at 12,000', 1120 hp at 18,500'
DIMENSIONS: Span 37'4", Lg. 33'4", Ht. 12'4", Wing Area 236 sq. ft.
WEIGHT: Empty 6590 lb., Gross 8500 lb., Max. 9350 lb. (10,000 lb. ferry). Fuel 157 gal. (327 gal. ferry).
PERFORMANCE: Speed—Top 364 mph at 20,000', Cruising 290 mph, Landing 82 mph. Service Ceiling 34,400', Climb 15,000'/7.6 min. Range 375 miles/500 lbs. bombs. 700 miles normal, 1500 miles max.   PMB

CURTISS YP-40F   MFR

[1] Pursuit Groups were renamed Fighter Groups in May 1942.

Production of Merlin-powered Warhawks ended with the last P-40L-20 on April 28, 1943, as the new P-51B and P-51C Mustangs took the full Packard engine output. Because of the shortage of Packard engines, 300 P-40F and P-40L aircraft used in the United States for training had to be re-engined with Allison V-1710-81s and were redesignated P-40R.

The 57th Fighter Group first took the P-40F into combat in Egypt on August 9, 1942. They had crossed the Atlantic on the *Ranger*. The 72 Warhawks flew off the deck to make a difficult flight across Africa and fought along with the British in the Battle of El Alamein. The *Ranger*'s next trip brought the 79th Group the same way, arriving in Egypt by November. A third P-40F group, the 324th, was added later to what had become the Ninth Air Force.

The Twelfth Air Force, formed to support the American occupation of North Africa, had two Warhawk groups, the 33rd and 325th. The former flew 76 P-40Fs from the *Chenango* on November 8, 1942, and landed near Casablanca, while the latter came with 72 P-40F-10s on the *Ranger* on January 19. On June 2, 1943, they were joined on ground attacks by the 99th Squadron's P-40L-1s. This squadron was unique in that it was the first one entirely flown by black pilots, then barred from regular units by segregation.

The RAF allotted 230 serial numbers to the P-40F as the Kittyhawk II, but only a few reached service with No. 260 Squadron, since most were retained by the AAF. Twenty-five P-40Fs went to a Free French squadron in November 1942, and 49 P-40L-10 replacements were supplied in March 1943.

Warhawks in the Mediterranean were replaced in AAF groups by the P-47, and their last P-40 mission was flown July 18, 1944, by the 324th Group. In 67,054 sorties, the P-40s lost 553, downed 481 enemies, and destroyed 40 on the ground.[2] Their best day was the "Palm Sunday Massacre" of 59 Axis transports and 16 fighters, and the top P-40 ace in that area was Major Levi Chase with ten victories.

While Merlin-powered Warhawks fought in the Mediterranean Theater, the 44th Fighter Squadron of the 18th Fighter Group received P-40Fs in Oahu about October 1942, and went to Guadalcanal in January 1943 to fight many brisk actions.

Later P-40 Models

Development of the P-40 continued with efforts to catch up with the more advanced types' performance. The third P-40F was remodeled with a deep

radiator back under the wing and called the YP-40F. A P-40H, apparently with a more advanced Merlin engine, and a P-40J with a turbosupercharged Allison were projected, but designer Don Berlin left Curtiss in December 1941 when the company showed no interest, and both projects were dropped. The creative impulse at Curtiss seems to have left, too, for no more new fighter projects there met success.

Had the P-40 been replaced by the P-60A, as planned, the last Warhawks would have been 600 P-40K-1s ordered October 28, 1941 for lend-lease to China. Fearing to interrupt production for an unproven type, authorities canceled the P-60A program in January 1942 in favor of the P-47G and more P-40s. A new contract approved June 15, 1942, added 1,400 more P-40K and M types to the schedule.

CURTISS P-40K-1
Allison V-1710-73, 1325 hp takeoff, 1150 hp at 11,800′
DIMENSIONS: As P-40F
WEIGHT: Empty 6400 lb., Gross 8400 lb., Max. 10,000 lb. Fuel 120–57 gal. (327 gal. ferry).
PERFORMANCE: Speed—Top 362 mph at 15,000′, Cruising 290 mph, Landing 82 mph. Service Ceiling 28,000′, Climb 15,000′/7.5 min. Range 350 miles/500 lbs. bombs, 1600 miles max.   PMB

CURTISS P-40L-20
Packard V-1650-1, 1300 hp to 12,000′
DIMENSIONS: Span 37′4″, Lg. 33′4″, Ht. 8′2″, Wing Area 236 sq. ft.
WEIGHT: Empty 6480 lb., Gross 8080 lb., Max. 8900 lb. Fuel 120–270 gal.
PERFORMANCE: Speed—Top 370 mph at 20,000′, Cruising 295 mph, Landing 80 mph. Service Ceiling 36,000′, Climb 3300′/1 min.   MFR

[2] See Table 8, page 285 for data concerning fighter scores.

The first P-40K-1 delivered May 5, 1942, was similar to the P-40E-1 except for an improved V-1710-73 engine. A small dorsal fin was fitted to the P-40K-1, late P-40E-1s, and 200 P-40K-5s to correct a swinging tendency during takeoff, but the lengthened fuselage of parallel late F models was introduced in October 1942 on 500 P-40K-10 and K-15 aircraft. Some were delivered with only four guns and winterization. The P-40Ks replaced the Es in AAF groups battling Japan, while some went to Ninth Air Force and others to lend-lease.

In November 1942 the P-40M replaced the K on the production lines. Ordered under lend-lease agreements, the 600 P-40Ms had six guns and a V-1710-81 with war-emergency power and a cooling grill behind the propeller spinner.

Four thousand P-40N fighters were ordered by a contract approved January 25, 1943, and this type began to replace the P-40M and L models at Curtiss in March 1943. By then the far superior P-38, P-47, and P-51 fighters were scheduled to equip all AAF groups in Europe and most of the Pacific, but increasing P-40 output provided a quick and less expensive way to meet commitments to lend-lease schedules and secondary Pacific sectors.

Four hundred P-40N-1s had a lighter structure, with only four guns and the V-1710-81, and, at 378 mph, were the fastest production Warhawks. Six guns and wing racks for drop tanks or 500-pound bombs greatly increased the ground-attack or ferry capability of the P-40N-5, which also introduced an improved canopy. Allison V-1710-81 engines were also used on 1,100 P-40N-5s, 100 P-40N-10s winterized for Alaska's 343rd Group, and 377 P-40N-15s with more internal fuel.

Warhawk production reached a high point of 463 P-40Ns in August 1943, and the following month the 80th Group in India became the seventh P-40 group in continuous combat against Japan. The other groups (15th, 18th, 23rd, 49th, 51st, and 343rd) also used P-40Ns, along with the 8th Group's 35th Squadron.

Allison V-1710-99s with an automatic engine control unit were used on 3,022 P-40N-20 to N-35 blocks, which differed in minor details. Twenty-five of these were completed as TP-40N two-place trainers. As late as June 30, 1944, another 1,000 were ordered, but the contract was cut back to 220 P-40N-40s with V-1710-115 engines and metal-covered ailerons. These were the last service model, and included five finished as two-seaters.

There was a development effort to advance P-40 performance with the P-40P and P-40Q programs, but the Packard-powered P-40P was canceled and none were built. The latter project included two reworked P-40K-10s and another begun as a P-40N-25, but the best example was the XP-40Q shown

CURTISS P-40M
Allison V-1710-81, 1200 hp takeoff, 1360 hp WE, 1125 hp at 14,600'
DIMENSIONS: As P-40F
WEIGHT: Empty 6464 lb., Gross 8400 lb., Max. 9100 lb. Fuel 120–57 gal. (327 gal. ferry).
PERFORMANCE: Speed—Top 360 mph at 20,000', Cruising 272 mph, Landing 82 mph. Service Ceiling 30,000', Climb 15,000'/7.2 min. Range 350 miles/500 lbs. bombs, 1600 miles max.   PMB

CURTISS P-40N-1
Allison V-1710-81, 1360 hp max. WE
DIMENSIONS: As P-40F
WEIGHT: Empty 6000 lb., Gross 7400 lb., Max. 8850 lb. Fuel 122–292 gal.
PERFORMANCE: Speed—Top 378 mph at 10,500', Cruising 288 mph, Landing 82 mph. Service Ceiling 38,000', Climb 15,000'/6.7 min. Range 240 miles/500 lbs. bombs, 1400 miles ferry.   AF

CURTISS P-40N-5   AF

CURTISS P-40N-20
Allison V-1710-99, 1200 hp takeoff, 1125 hp at 17,300'
DIMENSIONS: As P-40F
WEIGHT: Empty 6200 lb., Gross 8350 lb., Max. 11,400 lb.
PERFORMANCE: Speed—Top 350 mph at 16,400', Cruising
  290 mph, Landing 82 mph. Service Ceiling 31,000',
  Climb 14,000'/7.3 min. Range 340 miles/500 lbs.
  bombs, 3100 miles at 198 mph ferry load.   AF

CURTISS XP-40Q
Allison V-1710-121, 1425 hp takeoff, 1300 hp at 23,200'
DIMENSIONS: Span 35'3", Lg. 35'4".
WEIGHT: Max. 9000 lb.
PERFORMANCE: Speed—Top 422 mph at 20,500'. Service
  Ceiling 39,000', Climb 20,000'/4.8 min.   MFR

here; actually the first P-40K-1 rebuilt in 1944 with
a bubble canopy, V-1710-121 with two-stage supercharger, four-bladed propeller, clipped wing tips,
new radiators, and four wing guns.

When the last P-40N-40 was accepted November
30, 1944, the Curtiss Buffalo factory had delivered
13,738 P-40 fighters since 1940. Peak AAF inventory had been 2,499 in April 1944, and six other air
forces used them under lend-lease. Production had
continued long past the P-40's prime, and the end
of the P-40 also meant the end of quantity fighter
production by Curtiss.

The Kittyhawk became the RAF's most important
fighter in the Mediterranean after it entered combat
January 1, 1942, but it never operated in the United
Kingdom itself. While it won its last air battle on
April 7, 1944, one squadron continued in the

ground-support role until the war's end. Just how
many Kittyhawks were used by the RAF is uncertain, since most of the 1,500 Kittyhawk IAs (P-40E-
1s) and 230 IIAs (P-40Fs) were diverted in 1942 to
other countries. Beginning in September 1942, the
British Middle East received the Kittyhawk III, including 338 P-40Ks and 94 P-40Ms shipped from
the United States, plus a few P-40Ks transferred
from local AAF units. The 456 Kittyhawk IVs received in 1943–44 were P-40Ns.

Australia formed eight squadrons of Kittyhawks,
receiving 811: 163 P-40E and E-1, 42 P-40K-10 and
K-15, 90 P-40M-5 and M-10, and 516 P-40N-1 to
N-40 models. New Zealand equipped its seven
fighter squadrons with 62 P-40E-1, 23 P-40K, one
P-40L, 35 P-40M, and 172 P-40N Kittyhawks. Besides the 72 Kittyhawk Is obtained from the RAF,
Canada lend-leased 12 P-40E-1, 15 P-40M-5 to M-
10, and 35 P-40N-1 to N-20, and nine P-40K-1s were
borrowed but returned in 1943.

The Soviet Union was shipped 2,430 P-40s from
the United States, in addition to the 170 Tomahawks shipped from Britain. Of these, 304 were lost
in transit, with 248 sunk on the dangerous Murmansk route. Models shipped included 70 Tomahawks, 313 P-40Ks (50 via Alaska-Siberia), 220 P-
40Ms, and 980 P-40Ns, with the remainder believed
to be P-40E-1s sent on the northern route in 1942.
The first Soviet unit to get Kittyhawks was the 72nd
Fighter Air Regiment near Murmansk in March
1942. This naval unit produced the most successful
Soviet P-40 pilot, Senior Lieutenant Nicolai Kuy-
netzov, with 15 victories.

Aside from AVG aircraft, China was shipped 14
P-40K, 15 P-40M, and 299 P-40N fighters for the
eight Chinese fighter squadrons in the Chinese-
American Composite Wing. Brazil acquired 32 P-
40K, ten P-40M-5, and 41 P-40N Warhawks to train
a fighter group. Apparently, the last P-40 in combat
was among 59 P-40N-20s received by the Dutch
No. 120 Squadron in Australia from December 1943
to July 1945 and used after the war against Indo-
nesian nationalists.

Lockheed Lightning

The fastest American fighter available when World
War II began, the Lockheed Lightning was the first
twin-engine single-seat fighter ever mass-produced.
Designed by C. L. "Kelly" Johnson as Lockheed
Model 22, it became the XP-38 when the prototype
was ordered June 23, 1937, but took over five years
to enter combat.

There were two engines—the same Allison C-9s
used on the XP-37—but they had their propellers
turned inward to counteract each other's torque.
Designated V-1710-11 and V-1710-15, the Allisons
were rated at 1,150 hp and had General Electric

LOCKHEED XP-38
Allison V-1710-11, -15, 1150 hp takeoff, 1000 hp at 20,000'
DIMENSIONS: Span 52', Lg. 37'10", Ht. 12'10", Wing Area
  327.5 sq. ft.
WEIGHT: Empty 11,507 lb., Gross 13,500 lb., Max. 15,416
  lb. Fuel 230–400 gal.
PERFORMANCE: Speed—Top 413 mph at 20,000', Landing
  80 mph. Service Ceiling 38,000', Climb 20,000'/6.5
  min. Endurance 1 hr. at top speed.   MFR

LOCKHEED YP-38
Allison V-1710-27, -29, 1150 hp takeoff
DIMENSIONS: Span 52', Lg. 37'10", Ht. 9'10", Wing Area
  327.5 sq. ft.
WEIGHT: Empty 11,171 lb., Gross 13,500 lb., Max. 14,348
  lb. Fuel 230–410 gal.
PERFORMANCE: Speed—Top 405 mph at 20,000', 353 mph
  at 5000', Cruising 330 mph, Landing 80 mph. Service
  Ceiling 38,000', Climb 3333'/1 min. 20,000'/6 min.
  Range 650 miles normal, 1150 miles max.   MFR

turbosuperchargers in the twin booms that extended back to twin rudders. A short central nacelle held the pilot and armament of one 23-mm Madsen and four .50-caliber Browning guns, which shot a concentrated stream of bullets from the nose without interruption by synchronization.

The first tricycle gear on a fighter permitted faster landings than had been safe for older types, although an elaborate system of extended flaps was needed to keep stalling speed within reason. Designer Johnson also provided a control wheel, instead of the usual stick, for the metal-covered control surfaces.

Europe already had twin-engine fighters in 1937, with the Messerschmitt Bf 110 and Fokker G-1, the latter even anticipating the Lightning's tail booms, but these ships were long-range two-seaters. Lockheed's XP-38 was a single-seat pursuit-interceptor, far outdoing the comparable Westland Whirlwind built in 1938 by the British. The original XP-38 specification called for a 417-mph top speed at 20,000 feet (which was to be reached in 4.5 minutes), a service ceiling of 39,100 feet, and an endurance of 1.75 hours at 393 mph. This was promised at weights of 7,802 pounds empty and 10,500 pounds gross.

By the time of the XP-38's first flight by Lieutenant Ben Kelsey on January 27, 1939, 3,700 pounds had been added to that weight, and Lockheed had spent $761,000 on a $163,000 contract. It was a good investment, for despite flap trouble on its first flight the XP-38 was clearly the most advanced anti-bomber weapon available in the world.

The secrecy that had surrounded the project was lifted for a transcontinental speed dash on February 11, 1939. Although the flight ended in a crash that destroyed the prototype, 13 YP-38s (Model 122)

were ordered on April 27. Sixty-six Model 222 production aircraft were added by a contract announced August 10 and approved September 16, 1939. These aircraft used Allison F-2s (V-1710-27/29) with outward turning propellers, and their short gearbox and higher thrust line gave a new shape to the engine nacelles.

Britain was allowed by buy 667 export versions (Lockheed 322-61) on June 5, 1940,[3] but they were to be powered by 1,090-hp V-1710-C15s turning both propellers in the same direction. These engines, the same as those used by the P-40, had no turbosupercharger. On paper the threat to the type's performance was not fully realized. Guaranteed YP-38 performance at a design weight of 11,171 pounds empty and 13,500 pounds gross promised 353 mph at 5,000 feet, 405 mph at 20,000 feet, and a climb to 20,000 feet in six minutes; while the 322-61 without turbos was expected to do 361 mph at 5,000 feet, 404 mph at 16,000 feet, and climb to 16,000 feet in 5.6 minutes. The addition of armor and leak-proof tanks, however, was to increase the "Lightning Is" weight to 11,945 pounds empty and 14,467 pounds gross. Moreover, performance with the C-15 engines was very disappointing.

The armament originally considered in 1937 involved a 25-mm weapon projected by Army Ordinance, but when this did not materialize, the prototype was to get one of four Danish 23-mm Madsens the Army imported, although it was never actually fitted. On the YP-38, two .50-caliber with 200 rpg and two .30-caliber guns with 500 rpg were specified just as on the early P-40, but below them was a 37-mm M-4 with only a 15-round magazine. An August 5, 1940, order changed all four machine

---

[3] The contract was originally negotiated with the French.

guns to .50-caliber on later P-38 models and provided armor.

In December 1939 the United States had ordered 33 Hispano 20-mm guns from France, which began arriving February 10, 1940. Since tests were favorable and this gun had been selected by the British for their fighters, the 20-mm M2 was ordered into U.S. production for 607 Army Lightnings contracted for on August 30, 1940. The Army and British models were to be produced concurrently, with similar armament and numerous details simplified for mass production.

Shortly after Spitfires and Hurricanes broke the back of the German bomber offensive in the Battle of Britain, the first YP-38 was flown on September 18, 1940. It is fortunate that this victory could be won without recourse to U.S. fighter production, which that month was limited to one each of the YP-38, YP-39, and YP-43, with 114 P-40s. Only the first ship outperformed the British types.

The first YP-38 was retained by the company for developmental testing, the second went to Wright Field in January 1941, and later examples went to Selfridge Field for service, along with early P-39 and P-43 fighters. In June the last YP-38 was followed by the first of 30 P-38s, similar except for armor and four .50-caliber guns with the 37-mm weapon. One P-38 was held back for completion with the pressurized cockpit planned for the XP-49. That aircraft was tested as the XP-38A in May 1942, but no B or C model ever appeared.

Self-sealing fuel tanks, reducing capacity from 410 to 300 gallons, were introduced on the P-38D, first seen in August 1941 and covering the last 36 aircraft on that contract. By October 31, 1941, when another 1,000 Lockheeds were ordered, 80 had been delivered by the company on the early con-

LOCKHEED P-38D
Allison V-1710-27, -29, 1150 hp
DIMENSIONS: As YP-38
WEIGHT: Empty 11,780 lb., Gross 14,456 lb., Max. 15,500 lb. Fuel 230–300 gal.
PERFORMANCE: Speed—Top 390 mph at 25,000', Cruising 300 mph, Landing 85 mph. Service Ceiling 39,000', Climb 20,000'/8 min. Range 400 miles normal, 975 miles at 200 mph max.   AF

tracts, including the first two British 322-61s. Their medium-altitude engines were scheduled to be replaced, beginning with the 144th plane in April 1942, with turbosupercharged power plants on the Lightning II version.

Standard Lightning armament on the 322, the AAF's P-38E, which appeared in November 1941, and on all later models included one 20-mm gun with 150 rpg and four .50-caliber guns with 500 rpg.

When the United States entered the war, the only group with Lightnings was the 1st, which left its 20-year home at Selfridge Field on December 8, 1941, to fly to San Diego. There this group, representing southern California's defense force, was joined by the 14th Group as P-38s replaced that unit's P-43s and P-66s early in 1942. The British allocation of Lightnings was eliminated, except for three shipped for evaluation, and 140 Lightning Is were taken as "P-322s" by the Army, whose pilots found them nose-heavy, unable to keep in formation with regular P-38s over 12,000 feet, and therefore suitable only for training. The 524 Lightning IIs scheduled were absorbed into AAF P-38F and P-38G contracts, and 120 P-322s had their engines replaced with Air Force F series power plants.

Delivery went ahead with 210 P-38Es and 100 F-4s, which replaced the guns with four K-17 cameras. The first two F-4s were delivered in December 1941, giving the Air Force its first high-speed photo reconnaissance capability, and a pair of 75-gallon drop tanks could be added to increase their range. The first Lightnings deployed to a Theater of War were F-4s, which were shipped to Australia, where they flew their first missions for the Fifth Air Force on April 16, 1942.

As the first fighter fast enough to encounter com-

LOCKHEED P-38
Allison V-1710-27, -29, 1150 hp
DIMENSIONS: As YP-38
WEIGHT: Empty 11,672 lb., Gross 14,178 lb., Max. 15,340 lb. Fuel 230–410 gal.
PERFORMANCE: Speed—Top 390 mph at 20,000', Cruising 310 mph, Landing 80 mph. Climb 3200'/1 min. Range 825 miles normal, 1490 miles max.   PMB

LOCKHEED P-38E
Allison V-1710-27, -29, 1150 hp
DIMENSIONS: As YP-38
WEIGHT: Empty 11,880 lb., Gross 14,424 lb., Max. 15,482
  lb. Fuel 230–310 gal.
PERFORMANCE: Same as P-38D   MFR

LOCKHEED P-38F
Allison V-1710-49, -53, 1325 hp takeoff, 1150 hp at 25,000′
DIMENSIONS: As YP-38
WEIGHT: Empty 12,264 lb., Gross 15,900 lb., Max. 18,000
  lb. Fuel 230–300 gal. (600 gal. max.)
PERFORMANCE: Speed—Top 395 mph at 25,000′, 347 mph
  at 5000′, Cruising 305 mph, Landing 85 mph. Service
  Ceiling 39,000′, Climb 20,000′/8.8 min. Range 350
  miles/230 gal. at 305 mph, 425 miles/300 gal. at 290
  mph, 1925 miles/600 gal. at 195 mph.   AF

LOCKHEED 322-61 (LIGHTNING I)
Allison V-1710-C15, 1040 hp at 15,000′
DIMENSIONS: As YP-38
WEIGHT: Empty 11,945 lb., Gross 14,467 lb.
PERFORMANCE: Speed—Top 357 mph. Service Ceiling
  40,000′, Climb 2850′/1 min.   MFR

LOCKHEED P-38G
Allison V-1710-51, -55, 1325 hp takeoff, 1150 hp at 25,000′
DIMENSIONS: As YP-38
WEIGHT: Empty 12,200 lb., Gross 15,800 lb., Max. 19,800
  lb. Fuel 230–300 gal. (900 gal. max.)
PERFORMANCE: Speed—Top 400 mph at 25,000′, Cruising
  340 mph, Landing 89 mph. Service Ceiling 39,000′,
  Climb 20,000′/8.5 min. Range 275 miles normal, 350
  miles at 310 mph, 2400 miles at 203 mph.   MFR

pressibility, the P-38 suffered buffeting when diving too steeply; the first YP-38 lost its tail while pulling out of a dive. Deployment into combat was delayed until this problem could be alleviated with wing fillets and the range could be extended for offensive missions. The P-38F introduced new Allison F-5s (V-1710-11/-15) with 1,325 hp for takeoff and a pair of 165-gallon[4] drop tanks or 1,000-pound bombs. Delivery of 527 P-38Fs and 20 F-4As began in March 1942. Maneuvering flaps were introduced with the P-38F-15 block. They were followed by 80 P-38G-1 with the Allison F-10 engines and underwing racks for 300-gallon ferry tanks or 1,600-pound bombs. To obtain better performance B-13 turbo-superchargers were used on 1,002 P-38G-3 to G-15 series aircraft.

More power became available with the Allison F-15, yielding 1,425 hp for takeoff, and 1,600 war-emergency hp for short bursts when needed. This

power plant was tested on a preproduction P-38H prototype in September 1942; 225 P-38H-1s began appearing in April 1943, followed by 375 P-38H-5 models, whose B-33 turbos raised critical altitude from 24,900 to 29,000 feet.

The same engines (V-1710-89/-91) were used in the P-38J, which was distinguished from older models by a new chin intake below the engine with core-type intercoolers. A 55-gallon leading-edge fuel tank added in each wing, with two 310-gallon external tanks, increased Lightning ferry range to 2,600 miles at 198 mph. On actual combat missions two 165-gallon drop tanks gave the P-38J a radius of 795 miles for fighter sweeps or medium-bomber escort. Two 1,000-pound bombs instead of tanks could be carried out to a radius of 375 miles. For

[4] They are often listed as 150 gallons, but the actual capacity is that given here.

LOCKHEED P-38H-1
Allison V-1710-89, -91, 1425 hp takeoff, 1240 hp at 27,000'
DIMENSIONS: As YP-38
WEIGHT: Empty 12,380 lb., Gross 16,300 lb., Max. 20,300 lb. Fuel 230–900 gal.
PERFORMANCE: Speed—Top 402 mph at 25,000', Cruising 300 mph, Landing 88 mph. Climb 25,000'/9.7 min. Range 300 miles normal, 2400 miles ferry at 215 mph.   MFR

LOCKHEED F-5A   AF

short-range bombing two 1,600-pound bombs could be carried.

After ten P-38J-1s had been completed in the experimental shops, in August 1943, the assembly line began building 2,960 P-38J-5 to J-25s, with the last model adding dive flaps to allow for steeper dives. One Lightning was completed as the XP-38K, with V-1710-75/-77 Allisons and larger, 12-foot 6-inch propellers.

In June 1944 the P-38L appeared with Allison F-30 engines, and could add fittings under the wing for ten 5-inch rockets. Before the war's end halted Lightning production in August 1945, 3,810 P-38L-LOs had been built at the Burbank factory. Two thousand P-38L-VNs had been ordered June 26, 1944, from Consolidated-Vultee's Nashville plant, but this contract was canceled after 113 were accepted between January and June 1945.

Five cameras replaced guns in the F-5 photo-recon series, the first being a single F-5A-2 converted from an F-4 in April 1942 and fitted with two 165-gallon drop tanks. Twenty F-5A-1s preceded the P-38G-1 off the line in June 1942, using the same engine, followed, in August, by 20 F-5A-3s with B-13 superchargers and by 140 F-5A-10s beginning in November. Two hundred blue-painted F-5B-1s, es-

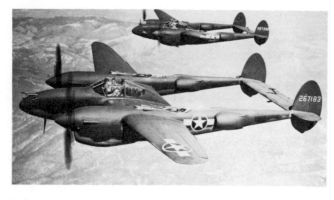

LOCKHEED P-38J
Allison V-1710-89, -91, 1425 hp takeoff, 1600 hp at 27,000'
DIMENSIONS: As YP-38
WEIGHT: Empty 12,780 lb., Gross 17,500 lb., Max. 21,600 lb. Fuel 410–1010 gal.
PERFORMANCE: Speed—Top 414 mph at 25,000', Cruising 290 mph, Landing 105 mph. Service Ceiling 44,000', Climb 20,000'/7 min. Range 450 miles/3200 lbs. bombs, 2600 miles max. at 198 mph.   MFR

LOCKHEED P-38L
Allison V-1710-111, -173, 1475 hp takeoff, 1600 hp WE at 28,700'
DIMENSIONS: As YP-38
WEIGHT: Empty 12,800 lb., Gross 17,500 lb., Max. 21,600 lb. Fuel 410–1010 gal.
PERFORMANCE: Speed—Top 414 mph at 25,000', Landing 105 mph. Service Ceiling 44,000', Climb 20,000'/7 min. Range 450 miles with 3200 lbs. bombs, 2600 miles ferry.   PMB

LOCKHEED F-5G   MFR

LOCKHEED P-38J (with "droop snoot")   MFR

sentially P-38J camera versions, were delivered from September to December 1943.

All later camera versions were converted at Lockheed's Modification Center in Dallas, and included 128 F-5Cs with special cameras, a single two-place XF-5D with a Plexiglas nose and three cameras, 205 F-5Es from P-38Js, and some 500 F-5Fs or F-5Gs from P-38Ls. Two torpedoes were tested from a P-38F-13 in December 1942, and a P-38E tried a high swept-up tail as part of a stillborn project to fit twin floats for transoceanic deliveries. Glass-nosed P-38J "droop-snoots" guided bomber missions begun April 10, 1944, with a bombardier replacing nose armament. The "Pathfinder" P-38L modification had an APS-15 radar in the nose.

The final Lightning model was the P-38M, a black-painted night fighter with an APS-4 radar under the nose and a radar operator seated behind and above the pilot. This model had been preceded by the modification of two P-38J-20 single-seaters in April 1944 with the radar behind the nosewheel, and a third fitted as a two-seater in September 1944, with the radar on the right wing. A P-38L-5 converted to a night fighter at the Dallas Modification Center was flown February 5, 1945, and 75 similar conversions were ordered as P-38Ms. Weighing 17,646 pounds with combat load, the two-seater's top speed was reduced from the P-38L's 414 mph to 391 mph at 27,700 feet for the P-38M. The war ended before the P-38M went overseas, and only four were sent to the 418th NIS on occupation duty in Japan.

By the war's end 9,535 fighter and 500 reconnaissance Lightnings had been completed. The average 1944 cost of a P-38 was $97,147, compared to $44,892 for a P-40.

LOCKHEED P-38M   MFR

The P-38 in Combat

The P-38 was the fastest Army fighter in the earliest stages of the war and the first fighter useful for long-range escort. Its main limitation was the relatively awkward maneuverability inherent in the machine's size, but when proper tactics were devised to take advantage of the P-38's speed and ceiling, the fighter became more successful in combat, and the safety factor of the second engine brought many damaged Lightnings home.

A threat to Alaska brought the first P-38 combat deployment when the 54th Squadron was detached from the 55th Group and sent to Elmendorf Field on May 29, 1942. The squadron's 25 P-38Es had been winterized and fitted with drop tanks, and scored the first Lightning combat victories on August 4, 1942, when two Type 97 four-engine flying boats were shot down near Umnak. The 54th

Squadron joined the 343rd Fighter Group, which was in action until July 1943 in the Aleutians, and remained there until the war's end.

Operation Bolero was the trans-Atlantic movement of aircraft to the Eighth Air Force in the United Kingdom. The 1st and 14th fighter groups were the first to fly single-seat fighters across the Atlantic. Re-equipped with P-38Fs after their service as California's air defense, they moved to Maine and crossed via Greenland and Iceland, led by B-17E guides. During July and August 164 Lockheeds made the flight safely, with a flight of six others forced down in Greenland; all the pilots were rescued. On the way over, a squadron stayed in Iceland long enough for the first P-38 victory against Germany, when an Fw 200 Condor was destroyed on August 15, 1942.

Although over 340 Lightning sorties were flown from Britain, none encountered the enemy, and both P-38 groups were transferred to Operation Torch, the Northwest Africa occupation, beginning their movement November 14, 1942. The first P-38 victory in Africa, over a Bf 109, was scored on November 21. On Christmas Day the 82nd Group's P-38s joined the fighting over Tunisia. These three Lightning groups served in the Mediterranean Theater of Operations (MTO) throughout the war, flying first for the Twelfth and then for the Fifteenth Air Force. Top P-38 ace in the MTO was the 82nd Group's Lieutenant William J. Sloan, with 12 victories.

While the Eighth Air Force had lost all its P-38s to the Twelfth in 1942, it still needed them since neither the P-39 nor P-40 was considered suitable for the cross-Channel offensive. The 20th and 55th groups left their Seattle area-defense stations and flew P-38Hs to Britain by August and September 1943. The 55th Group's first combat mission was on October 15, just after the Schweinfurt attacks had proven that the daylight bombing offensive against Germany could not succeed without fighter escort. At that point "nothing [was] more critical . . . than the early arrival of P-38s and P-51s," urged General Ira C. Eaker, then Eighth Air Force commander.

The Eighth was soon given the 364th and 479th groups, while the Ninth Tactical Air Force got the 367th, 370th, and 374th groups. All seven P-38 groups in Britain were used to cover the D-day landings in Normandy, for their distinctive shape made them less likely to be shot at by Allied gunners. In the following months five of the groups were re-equipped with P-51s, one with P-47s, and only the 374th still used the P-38 until V-E Day.

In the Pacific the Lightnings tended to appear one squadron at a time to upgrade the scattered P-39 and P-40 groups. The first such squadron was the 39th, of the 35th Group, whose P-39s were re-placed by P-38Fs. These Lightnings scored their first kills for the Fifth Air Force on December 27, 1942. Likewise, the 9th and 80th squadrons of the 49th and 8th groups, respectively, got P-38s early in 1943. Not until September 1944 were the remaining squadrons of these groups provided with P-38s. One full P-38 group, the 475th, had already joined the Fifth Air Force in combat on August 13, 1943.

It was here in the Southwest Pacific that Lockheed's fighter had its greatest success as the top AAF aces ran up their scores on P-38s: Major Richard Bong with 40 victories from December 27, 1942, to December 17, 1944; and Thomas McGuire, Jr., with 38 victories from August 18, 1943, to December 26, 1944. These scores, and the 475th Group's wartime score of 545 victories in two years, were the product of very carefully worked out tactics. Another victory in a P-38 was that of a famous civilian pilot flying with the group: Charles Lindbergh, on July 28, 1944. The 49th Group, which had the Air Force's highest score of 678 planes, downed most of them in P-38s.

In addition, the P-38 was used by both Thirteenth Air Force fighter groups (the 8th and 347th) and by one squadron in each of the following groups in other Pacific air forces: the 531st Squadron, 21st Group, Seventh Air Force; the 459th Squadron, 80th Group, Tenth Air Force; the 54th Squadron, 343rd Group, Eleventh Air Force; and the 449th Squadron, 51st Group, Fourteenth Air Force. I have omitted those P-38 units not using the Lightning in combat, nor have I listed the F-5 equipped Photo-Reconnaissance groups or squadrons that served in every wartime theater.

Lend-lease programs seldom involved Lockheed fighters. However, Australia got three used F-4s in August 1942, and two Free French units (GR I and II/33) operated F-5 series aircraft in 1943–45. China received 15 P-38Ls and some F-5Es in 1945. After the war 50 P-38Ls and F-5Es were passed to Italy, and the Honduran Air Force acquired a few P-38Ls.

Bell Airacobra

Placing the engine behind the pilot has become common since jet propulsion, but this arrangement was first introduced to American fighters by Bell's Airacobra. Previously it had been seen abroad in Westland and Koolhoven fighters, but the P-39 was the first such design in mass production.

Several advantages became apparent when the engine was moved back to the center of gravity. A slimmer nose allowed for better streamlining and visibility, and there was room for heavier armament and the retracted nosewheel of a tricycle landing gear. This undercarriage offered better ground handling and permitted higher landing speeds, which in turn led to smaller wings—not an unmixed blessing since the higher wing loadings handicapped climb and maneuverability at high altitudes.

Designer Robert Wood had experience with the new Allison engine in Bell Model 2, the XA-11A modification that first tested that power plant. In response to an Army invitation dated March 13, 1937, to bid on experimental single-engine interceptor pursuits, the Buffalo company offered Bell models 3 and 4, the former with the cockpit behind the engine, but the latter, with the cockpit ahead of the Allison, was chosen by the Army. The XP-39 prototype ordered October 7, 1937, had a turbosupercharged V-1710-17 with 1,000 hp at 20,000 feet and a ten-foot extension drive shaft to the reduction gearbox behind the propeller.

Radiators, which on the XP-39 were behind the engine on each side of the fuselage, were placed within the modified wing roots with intakes at the leading edge. The cockpit enclosure was lowered and the main wheels covered for smoother streamlining. A carburetor air scoop was placed behind the cockpit, the turbosupercharger was removed, and the original engine replaced by a V-1710-37 rated at 1,090 hp at 13,300 feet with a single-stage geared supercharger.

First flown November 25, 1939, the revised prototype was designated XP-39B and proved satisfactory enough for its features to be incorporated into the YP-39s on order. Originally the YP-39 was to have a turbosupercharger like the prototype, was to do 375 mph at 20,000 feet, climb to that altitude in six minutes, and have a 41,300-foot service ceiling,

BELL XP-39
Allison V-1710-17, 1150 hp takeoff, 1000 hp at 20,000'
DIMENSIONS: Span 35'10", Lg. 28'8", Ht. 11', Wing Area 200 sq. ft.
WEIGHT: Empty 3995 lb., Gross 5550 lb., Max. 6204 lb. Fuel 115–200 gal.
PERFORMANCE: Speed—Top 390 mph at 20,000', Landing 80 mph. Service Ceiling 32,000', Climb 20,000'/5 min. Endurance 1 hr. at top speed.   AF

BELL XP-39B
Allison V-1710-37, 1090 hp at 13,300'
DIMENSIONS: Span 34', Lg. 29'9", Ht. 11'10", Wing Area 213 sq. ft.
WEIGHT: Empty 4530 lb., Gross 5834 lb., Max. 6450 lb. Fuel 115–200 gal.
PERFORMANCE: Speed—Top 375 mph at 15,000', Cruising 310 mph, Landing 103 mph. Service Ceiling 36,000', Climb 20,000'/7.5 min. Range 600 miles normal, 1400 miles/200 gal. at 190 mph.   MFR

Specifications called for top speeds of 330 mph at sea level and 400 mph at 20,000 feet, climbing to that altitude in five minutes, but this was at 3,995 pounds empty and 5,550 pounds gross, weights far exceeded by future evolution. Provision was made for two synchronized .50-caliber guns with 400 rounds, above a 25-mm gun with 50 rounds and the barrel pointed through the propeller hub; but that was replaced by a 37-mm T-9 cannon with 20 rounds on December 2, 1938. (Actually, no weapons seem to have been installed on the prototype during flight tests.)

The first test flight was made at Wright Field on April 6, 1939, and on April 27 a service-test contract was approved for 12 YP-39s and one YP-39A. After initial trials, the prototype was studied by NACA and shipped back to the factory for modifications.

while the YP-39A would have no turbo and reach 360 mph at 10,000 feet. But instead of the V-1710-17 and V-1710-19 engines planned, the V-1710-37 without turbosupercharger was chosen in January 1940 for all 13 service-test aircraft.

This decision to omit the turbosupercharger was a crucial one in Airacobra development, for while it made the the type less expensive and handier at low altitudes, high-altitude performance was seriously crippled, a handicap shared by earlier P-40s and the British version of the P-38. Thirteen YP-39s (Bell Model 12) delivered from September to December 1940 had a top speed of 368 mph at 13,600 feet. Like the YP-38, armament consisted of one 37-mm gun with 15 rounds, two .50-caliber guns with 400 rounds, and two .30-caliber guns with 1,000 rounds, all mounted in the nose. The pilot's

cockpit was protected by armor and was entered by an auto-style side door instead of the common sliding canopy.

The first production order approved October 12, 1939, was for 80 fighters, originally designated P-45 by the Army but redesignated P-39C in 1940. Top speed was guaranteed to be 375 mph at 6,662 pounds gross, but this weight would soon rise. An export version, the Bell Model 14, was ordered by France on April 13, 1940, which specified a 20-mm Hispano gun as the central armament. This contract was taken over in June by the RAF, which increased the number from 170 to 675 aircraft. By September 13, 1940, the Army had added 623 Model 15s with wing guns and leakproof tanks, and ordered that these additions be made to the last 60 aircraft on the previous contract. The first 20 were completed from January to March 1941 as P-39Cs with camouflage finish and 1,150-hp V-1710-35 engines. Selfridge Field got them for the 31st Pursuit Group, although three were later shipped to Britain.

The first P-39D was accepted in April 1941 with self-sealing tanks and four .30-caliber wing guns with 1,000 rpg added. Two synchronized .50s with

BELL P-39C
Allison V-1710-35, 1150 hp at 13,800'
DIMENSIONS: As YP-39
WEIGHT: Empty 5070 lb., Gross 7075 lb. Fuel 104–70 gal.
PERFORMANCE: Speed—Top 375 mph at 13,800', Cruising 308 mph, Landing 80 mph. Service Ceiling 33,200', Climb 12,000'/3.9 min. Range 450 miles normal, 730 miles max.

BELL YP-39
Allison V-1710-37, 1090 hp at 13,300'
DIMENSIONS: Span 34', Lg. 30'2", Ht. 11'10", Wing Area 213 sq. ft.
WEIGHT: Empty 5042 lb., Gross 7000 lb., Max. 7235 lb. Fuel 104–70 gal.
PERFORMANCE: Speed—Top 368 mph at 13,600', Cruising 257 mph, Landing 80 mph. Service Ceiling 33,300', Absolute Ceiling 34,500', Climb 20,000'/7.3 min. Range 600 miles normal, 1000 miles max.   MFR

BELL P-39D
Allison V-1710-35, 1150 hp at 13,800'
DIMENSIONS: As YP-39
WEIGHT: Empty 5462 lb., Gross 7500 lb., Max. 8200 lb. Fuel 120–95 gal.
PERFORMANCE: Speed—Top 368 mph at 13,800', Cruising 213 mph, Landing 82 mph. Service Ceiling 32,100', Absolute Ceiling 33,200', Climb 2720'/1 min., 15,000'/5.7 min. Range 800 miles/500 lbs. bombs, 1545 miles ferry at 195 mph.   MFR

400 rounds were in the nose above the 37-mm M-9 gun with 30 rounds. Since tank protection reduced internal fuel capacity from 170 to 120 gallons, the P-39D had provision for a 75-gallon belly drop tank or a 500-pound bomb. All this weight, including 184 pounds of armor and 61 pounds of armor-glass windshield, had a negative effect on climb.

Bell delivered the 429 P-39D models in 1941 faster than the guns or Curtiss Electric propellers became available; a total of only 390 37-mm aircraft guns were completed that year. The aircraft were sometimes flown to a base, where the propeller was removed, shipped back to Bell, and reused to fly another plane. Aeroproducts hydromatic propellers were substituted on 229 P-39Fs, delivered beginning in December 1941, while 25 other ships on this contract with Allison V-1710-59 engines and automatic boost control were designated P-39J. All these aircraft were known as Model 15 on company records and had the same characteristics.

British Model 14s were produced concurrently with Army P-39Ds and had the same V-1710-35

BELL P-39F CAREY

BELL P-39J CAREY

BELL P-400 (Airacobra I)
Allison V-1710-E4, 1150 hp takeoff
DIMENSIONS: As YP-39
WEIGHT: Empty 5462 lb., Gross 7845 lb. Fuel 120 gal.
PERFORMANCE: Speed—Top 355 mph at 13,000', 326 mph at 6000', Cruising 217–327 mph. Service Ceiling 29,-000', Climb 2040'/1 min., 10,000'/5.1 min. Range 760 miles at 217 mph. IWM

engine and armament, except for replacement of the 37-mm gun by the more rapid-firing 20-mm gun with 60 rounds. These planes were called Airacobra I by the RAF and P-400 in U.S. records.

The RAF knew little about the fighter it had inherited except for the company's performance guarantees, which promised a top speed of 383 mph at 14,400 feet, an altitude that should be reached in 5.5 minutes. A company report claimed that 392 mph had been achieved on an April 29, 1941, test; it was actually achieved with the second P-400 in light and highly polished condition, with a smaller rudder. But when the P-39C began tests in England on July 6, with the first P-400 Airacobra arriving on July 30, 1941, their actual top speeds were measured at only 359 and 355 mph, respectively.

This loss of speed could not be explained by the American support group, and it became apparent that the company had greatly exaggerated its product's virtues. Compared to the Spitfire VB, the Airacobra was faster at low levels but decidedly slower in climb and increasingly slower at altitudes over 15,000 feet.

The only Fighter Command squadron to use the Bell flew just nine strafing sorties across the Channel (October 9–11) before compass troubles ended operations. Since Fighter Command no longer

wanted the type, the squadron was re-equipped with Spitfires on March 1942. While the Airacobra could have given good service to Army Cooperation squadrons, these had a goodly number of Mustang Is on the way. New British commitments to the Soviet Union indicated the next direction for the Airacobra. After the United States entered the war, 315 P-400s were requisitioned by the Air Force at the factory or in the United Kingdom. The Soviet Union received some 212, while 54 others were lost at sea.

Lend-lease funds were used for the Model 14A, first ordered June 11, 1941, to follow the Model 14 to England in 1942. The first 336 were designated P-39D-1 and had 20-mm guns. Those not requisi-

BELL P-39D-1
Allison V-1710-63, 1150 hp at 12,000'
DIMENSIONS: As YP-39
WEIGHT: Empty 5700 lb., Gross 7631 lb. Fuel 120–95 gal.
PERFORMANCE: Speed—Top 368 mph at 12,000', 309 mph at s. l., Cruising 250 mph, Stalling 89 mph. Service Ceiling 30,850', Absolute Ceiling 31,800'. Range 780 miles/250 mph combat, 1063 miles ferry.
(Data from P-39D-2 test) AF

tioned by the AAF went to the Soviet Union. The AAF received 158 P-39D-2s with 37-mm guns on V-1710-63 engines. For long-range ferry flights, a flush belly tank could increase fuel capacity to 265 gallons.

A new square-cut, laminar-flow wing was designed for the XP-39E (Bell Model 23), and two prototypes were ordered April 11, 1941, with a replacement added in 1942. Armed with a 37-mm nose gun with 30 rounds, plus two .50-caliber guns in the nose and four in the wings with 300 rpg, the XP-39E was to use a Continental IV-1430-1. This power plant was not ready in time and was replaced by an Allison V-1710-35 when the first prototype was flown February 26, 1942. It spun to a crash March 20, but the second prototype, flown April 2, and the last, flown September 19, had the new V-1710-47 with two-stage superchargers. Each of the three examples tested a different vertical tail surface, and engineering studies made on this project contributed to the development of the Bell P-63 Kingcobra. Four thousand production models, designated P-76, were ordered on February 24, 1942, from the new Bell facility at Marietta, Georgia, but this contract was canceled on May 20 so that this plant would be free for B-29 production and Bell engineers could concentrate on the P-63.

The next Airacobra production batch was externally like the P-39D, and began with a contract approved August 25, 1941, for 1,800 P-39Gs. Changes in engine model led to different designations when deliveries began in July 1942. Using a V-1710-63 of 1,325 hp for takeoff, the first 210 were P-39Ks with an Aeroproducts 10-foot, 4-inch propeller, while 250 P-39Ls built at the same time had Curtiss propellers. In November 1942 the P-39M appeared with a V-1710-67 or -83 of 1,200 hp for takeoff and 1,420 hp (war emergency) at 9,500 feet.

BELL P-39K
Allison V-1710-63, 1325 hp takeoff, 1150 hp at 11,800'
DIMENSIONS: As YP-39
WEIGHT: Empty 5658 lb., Gross 7600 lb., Max. 8400 lb. Fuel 104–295 gal.
PERFORMANCE: Speed—Top 368 mph at 13,800', Cruising 213 mph, Landing 82 mph. Service Ceiling 32,000', Climb 15,000'/5.7 min. Range 750 miles normal, 800 miles/500 lbs. bombs with 120 gal., 1500 miles max.
                                                                    PMB

BELL XP-39E
Allison V-1710-47, 1325 hp takeoff, 1150 hp at 21,300'
DIMENSIONS: Span 35'10", Lg. 31'11", Ht. 11'10", Wing Area 236 sq. ft.
WEIGHT: Empty 6936 lb., Gross 8918 lb. Fuel 100–50 gal.
PERFORMANCE: Speed—Top 386 mph at 21,680', Cruising 205 mph, Landing 88 mph. Service Ceiling 35,200', Climb 20,000'/9.3 min. Range 500 miles normal, 800 miles max.
                                                                    MFR

BELL P-39M
Allison V-1710-83, 1200 hp takeoff, 1420 hp at 9500'
DIMENSIONS: As YP-39
WEIGHT: Empty 5610 lb., Gross 7500 lb., Max. 8400 lb. Fuel 104–295 gal.
PERFORMANCE: Speed—Top 386 mph at 9500', Cruising 200 mph, Landing 84 mph. Service Ceiling 36,000', Climb 15,000'/4.4 min. Range 650 miles/500 lbs. bombs, 1500 miles max.
                                                                    AF

BELL P-39N
Allison V-1710-85, 1200 hp takeoff, 1420 hp at 9700'
DIMENSIONS: Span 34', Lg. 30'2", Ht. 12'5", Wing Area
   213 sq. ft.
WEIGHT: Empty 5657 lb., Gross 7600 lb., Max. 8200 lb.
   Fuel 87–295 gal.
PERFORMANCE: Speed—Top 399 mph at 9700', Landing
   85 mph. Service Ceiling 38,500', Climb 15,000'/3.8
   min. Range 750 miles/500 lbs. bombs with 120 gal.,
   1250 miles max.   PMB

BELL P-39Q-20
DIMENSIONS: As P-39N
WEIGHT: Empty 5645 lb., Gross 7700 lb., Max. 8300 lb.
   Fuel 104–295 gal.
PERFORMANCE: Speed—Top 385 mph at 11,000', Landing
   88 mph. Service Ceiling 35,000', Climb 15,000'/4.5
   min. Range 650 miles/500 lbs. bombs, 1250 miles max.
   ferry   MFR

After 240 P-39Ms had been accepted, Bell rolled
out 2,095 P-39Ns. This Airacobra had internal fuel
capacity reduced to 87 gallons, and a V-1710-85 of
1,420 hp at 9,700 feet for war-emergency power.
Armor weight on the last 695 (block P-39N-5) was
reduced from 231 to 193 pounds. All the aircraft in
these lots, known as Model 26 on company records,
are so alike in appearance that they can be told
apart only by serial numbers.[5]

---

[5] No P-39G, H, or P was ever finished. I and O are not used for
designation letters since they might be confused with numbers.

On September 17, 1942, the Airacobra's wing-gun
installation was ordered changed from four .30-cal-
iber to two .50-caliber guns with 600 rounds, and
these underslung weapons distinguished the 4,905
P-39Qs that began appearing in May 1943 with a V-
1710-85. Internal arrangements varied. The first 150
(P-39Q-1) had 87 gallons of fuel and 231 pounds of
armor, the next group of 950 (Q-5) had 110 gallons
and 193 pounds, and the remainder (Q-10 to Q-30)
had 120 gallons and 227 pounds of armor weight.
Blocks Q-21 to Q-30 could be recognized by a four-
bladed propeller.

In 1943 Bell produced more fighters than any
other manufacturer, with production reaching 511
P-39Ns in April. Peak AAF inventory was 2,150 in
February 1944, but then all P-39 groups were converted to more advanced types by August. When
the last P-39Q-30 was delivered in August 1944,
9,589 Airacobras had been completed, most of them
for lend-lease.

P-39s in Combat

When the United States entered the war, P-39Ds
equipped five pursuit groups: the 8th at Mitchel,
the 31st and 52nd at Selfridge, the 36th in Puerto
Rico, and the 53rd at MacDill Field. On December
8, 1941, the 31st Group was rushed to Seattle and
the 53rd to the Canal Zone for defense purposes.

Neither location suffered attack, and the 31st
transferred its pilots to the reorganizing 35th Group,
while the 53rd returned to the mainland in November, leaving its Airacobras among the three groups
remaining in Panama through the war. The Japanese offensive in the Southwest Pacific presented
the greatest threat, and P-39Ds and pilots were
rushed to Australia along with over 100 P-400s requisitioned from the British contract.

Combat began for the P-39D on April 30, 1942,
with sorties by the 8th Group's 35th and 36th
squadrons, which would be followed in July by P-
39D-1s of the 80th Squadron. Ex-British P-400s
equipped the 35th Group, which entered combat
June 2, although some P-39D-2s arrived later. The
battle for Guadalcanal added the 67th Squadron's
P-400s to front-line combat and they were incorporated into the new 347th Fighter Group along
with the 70th Squadron's P-39s on Fiji.

The threat to Alaska brought the 54th Group up
from West Coast defense in June 1942 with P-39F
and J models. They escorted bombers on raids to
Kiska until December 1942, after which the group
returned to the United States as a replacement
training unit. Two P-39Q-1 squadrons, the 46th and
72nd, sortied from Makin Island from December
18, 1943, to February 12, 1944, but the last Airacobra missions in the Pacific were flown by the
347th Group in New Guinea in August 1944.

The first Airacobra groups scheduled for European operations had been the 31st and 52nd. But their most experienced pilots had been transferred to Pacific-based units, and their P-39Fs lacked the range to safely make the trans-Atlantic flight planned for Operation Bolero. Instead, the 31st pilots sailed for England in June, leaving their planes behind.[6] They were provided with reverse lend-lease—the Spitfire.

Armed with two 20-mm and four .303-caliber guns in the wings, the Spitfires were superior in speed, climb, and ceiling to the Airacobra, but quite short on range. Their characteristics have been included here for comparison. The 31st Group flew its first six sorties July 26, 1942, losing one plane. On August 19, 123 sorties were flown to support the Dieppe raid. An Fw 190 was downed, representing the first USAAF victory in Europe, although eight American Spitfires were lost. Clearly, the American pilots' limited experience would be costly.

SUPERMARINE SPITFIRE VB
Rolls-Royce Merlin 45, 1440 hp
DIMENSIONS: Span 36'10", Lg. 29'11", Wing Area 242 sq. ft.
WEIGHT: Empty 5065 lb., Gross 6650 lb. Fuel 102–210 gal.
PERFORMANCE: Speed—Top 369 mph at 19,500', Cruising 272 mph, Stalling 78 mph. Service Ceiling 35,500', Absolute Ceiling 36,700', Climb 20,000'/7.5 min. Range 470 miles combat, 1135 miles ferry.   AF

Two more Spitfire groups had joined the Eighth Air Force; these included the 52nd, which had also come without its P-39s, and the 4th, made up from the RAF's "Eagle" squadrons of American volunteer pilots. Only the 4th Group remained with the Eighth Air Force, since Torch, the North African invasion, was to be supported by the Lightnings of the 1st and 14th groups, Spitfires of the 31st and 52nd, and the P-39s of the 81st and 350th groups.

[6] Reports that the 31st flew P-39s from England are incorrect.

Airacobras had re-entered the scene in October when the latter two groups were equipped with P-400s that had been waiting in Britain for shipment to the U.S.S.R.

Both the 81st and 350th groups flew from Britain to North Africa by January 1943, losing 15 fighters on the way; these were interned in, and later purchased by, Portugal. The Airacobras served the Twelfth Air Force in the ground-support role, along with P-39s of the 111th and 154th tactical reconnaissance squadrons. In February 1944 the Twelfth Air Force added the 332nd Group, whose black pilots flew P-39Q-20s until June.

This survey does not include the P-39 groups that never reached combat, detached squadrons serving uneventful guard duty on islands like Ascension in the South Atlantic or Canton, Christmas, and the Galapagos in the Pacific. More active were the 33rd Squadron's P-39Ds on Iceland, downing two German bombers in October 1942.

Most P-39s were lend-leased to the Soviet Air Force (VVS), for whom 4,924 were delivered at the factory and 4,746 actually reached the VVS. Not included are those P-400s transferred by the British from their stock in the United Kingdom. Models shipped from the United States included 108 P-39D-1s, 40 P-39Ks, 137 P-39Ls, 157 P-39Ms, 1113 P-39Ns, and 3291 P-39Qs. The first to be sent were the P-400s, of which 93 had arrived over the northern route by June 1942, when the first VVS fighter regiment with Airacobras entered combat near Voronezh.

The most successful Soviet Airacobra unit was the 16th Guards Fighter Air Regiment, which received P-39Ns in Iran and used Airacobras in combat from April 1943 to October 1944, when LA-7s replaced the American type. Alexander Pokryshkin used a P-39 for the last 47 of his 59 victories in 600 sorties, which made him the second greatest Soviet ace and the most successful ace on any American fighter. Another ace in this regiment who scored most of his victories on P-39s was Gregori I. Rechkalov, credited with 58 victories on 526 sorties.

These successes with the P-39 were due to its use on short-range, low-altitude missions—the best for the P-39—in close support of ground troops with the most experienced VVS pilots. Wing guns were often removed to save weight. On July 19, 1943, the VVS asked that P-39s completely replace the P-40 on their lend-lease allocations.

Australia used 22 P-39D, P-39F, and P-400 aircraft from the Fifth Air Force for a squadron at Sydney in May 1942, returning them in November 1943. French squadrons got some 90 P-39N-5s in North Africa, beginning in April 1943, and 75 P-39Q-20s were shipped from the United States in 1944. Italian Co-Belligerent forces also received secondhand

74 P-39Ns and 75 P-39Qs, began using them in September 1944 for ground support in the Balkans until the war's end, and retained these planes until 1951.

The Airacobra was a disappointment to the Army, for it was outclimbed by the Zero and seemed "practically useless over 17,000 feet." The P-40 was thought "much better" because a lower wing loading allowed a faster climb. In North Africa the P-39's internal armor and high sea-level speed made it useful for ground strafing. "Unusually resistant" to enemy flak, it had the lowest rate of losses per sortie of any AAF fighter in the ETO, but downed only 14 enemy aircraft. Flying qualities, including a fast dive and roll, were good, but turns were slow and a flat spin was a dangerous possibility. It is probable that the wing was too small; 213 square feet of area may have been adequate for the prototype's weight, but production models were over a third heavier.

Republic Thunderbolt

Contrasting sharply with the pointed noses of in-line-engine types was the barrel-shaped P-47 Thunderbolt, the largest single-engine fighter used in the war. The last successful air-cooled, radial-powered single-seat type, it represented the only radial fighter series to survive the Army's 1939 selection of liquid-cooled Allisons as the primary power plant for pursuits.

In February 1939 Wright Field received the Seversky XP-41 and private-venture AP-4 prototypes, each with wheels retracting inwards flush into the center section and the usual .30- and .50-caliber guns paired over the engine. Both had Wasp radials of 1,050 hp at critical altitudes, but the former's built-in mechanical supercharger was best at 15,000 feet, while the AP-4's R-1830-SC2-G went higher with a turbosupercharger added in the belly behind the pilot.

Both had conventional close cowls at first, but the AP-4 was also tested with its engine completely enclosed behind a huge spinner. An in-flight fire destroyed this Seversky before the prototype could be sold to the Army, but a service-test contract for the AP-4A was made. This became the Republic YP-43, for the company's new owners had not allowed Major Seversky inside the plant since November 1938.

Thirteen YP-43s ordered May 12, 1939, were powered by a 1,200-hp turbosupercharged R-1830-35, and the company specification guaranteed 351 mph at 6,900 pounds gross. Armament was the same as the early P-40's: two synchronized .50-caliber guns on the cowl and two .30-caliber guns in the wings. The first YP-43 was delivered in September

SEVERSKY XP-41
Pratt & Whitney R-1830-19, 1200 hp takeoff, 1050 hp at 17,500'
DIMENSIONS: Span 36', Lg. 27', Ht. 12'6", Wing Area 220 sq. ft.
WEIGHT: Empty 5390 lb., Gross 6600 lb., Max. 7200 lb. Fuel 150–230 gal.
PERFORMANCE: Speed—Top 323 mph at 15,000', Cruising 292 mph. Range 730 miles normal, 1860 miles max.   AMC

SEVERSKY AP-4   AF

1940, the second in December, and the rest completed by April 10, 1941.

In the meantime Republic engineers tried to improve this type so that the speeds of its liquid-cooled competitors could be surpassed. The company AP-4J proposal used a 1,400-hp Pratt & Whitney R-2180-1 and was estimated to do 386 mph; 80 were ordered October 12, 1939, as the P-44. Another proposal, AP-4L, suggested a big 2,000-hp Pratt & Whitney R-2800-7 to increase P-44 speed to 406 mph. On July 12, 1940, an Air Corps letter of intent promised a contract for 225 of the new aircraft and a September 9, 1940, order scheduled 602 more. Proposed armament was two .50-caliber and four .30-caliber guns.

In contrast to the chunky P-44 design, Republic engineers had also offered on August 1, 1939, the AP-10 with a liquid-cooled 1,150-hp Allison V-

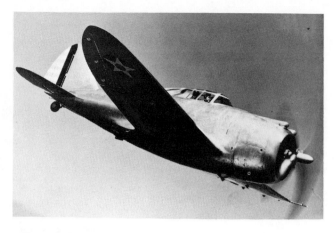

REPUBLIC YP-43   AF

REPUBLIC P-43
Pratt & Whitney R-1830-47, 1200 hp at 25,000'
DIMENSIONS: Span 36', Lg. 28'6", Ht. 14', Wing Area 223
   sq. ft.
WEIGHT: Empty 5654 lb., Gross 7810 lb., Max. 7935 lb.
   Fuel 145–218 gal.
PERFORMANCE: Speed—Top 349 mph at 25,000', Cruising
   280 mph, Landing 78 mph. Service Ceiling 38,000',
   Climb 2850'/1 min., 15,000'/5.5 min. Range 800 miles
   normal, 1300 miles max.   MFR

1710-39, two synchronized guns, and a small (115-square-foot) wing. Weighing only 4,900 pounds, it was supposed to do 415 mph and climb to 15,000 feet, in only 3.5 minutes. A prototype contract was drawn up in November, but Air Corps engineers requested an enlarged 6,150-pound design, increasing armament to two .50-caliber and four .30-caliber guns and reducing speed to 400 mph. Two prototypes, an XP-47 and a stripped-down XP-47A, were approved on January 17, 1940, the same day as the Curtiss XP-46s.

Neither the P-44 nor the XP-47 were ever flown, for war in Europe demonstrated the need for more firepower and internal protection on future fighters. Republic's Russian-born chief engineer, Alexander Kartveli, offered a new specification dated June 12, 1940, calling for an eight-gun, 11,500-pound fighter built around an XR-2800 Double Wasp turbosupercharged to deliver 2,000 hp at 27,800 feet. Top

speed was over 400 mph and a climb to 15,000 feet took five minutes. Evaluation by Wright Field engineers led to abandonment of the earlier projects, in spite of nearly a million dollars' worth of engineering study and a P-44 mockup. On September 6, 1940, the XP-47 prototype contract was changed, now calling for an XP-47B with the Double Wasp, and on September 13, 1940, the P-44 contracts negotiated during the previous two months were replaced by a $56 million contract for 171 P-47Bs and 602 P-47Cs, plus 54 P-43s to fill the delivery gap until the P-47 and Double Wasp were available. The 80 P-44s ordered in 1939 were to be finished as P-43As for the same reason; since the P-43 and P-44 were similar except for engines, the change wasn't too costly.

Fifty-four P-43 Lancers, delivered from May 16 to August 28, 1941, with R-1830-47 engines, were similar to the YP-43. Eighty P-43As with new carburetors on R-1830-49 Wasps began appearing in September. A lend-lease contract approved June 30, 1941, for China assured production continuity at Republic, with 125 P-43A-1 fighters with self-sealing tanks and racks for two 100-pound bombs. Delivered from December 1941 to March 1942, 108 were reported to have reached China.

In the Army Air Force the P-43 went to the 1st Pursuit Group at Selfridge, the 55th at Portland, and then the 14th at March. In each case they were interim equipment until they were replaced by P-38s. A total of 152 were then modified to photo-recon configuration (P-43B, C, D, or E, depending on cameras). Again, they were used to train squadrons until Lockheed F-4s became available. Only a few went to the Southwest Pacific; of these, Australia obtained four P-43A-1s and four P-43Ds. As the first turbosupercharged, air-cooled fighter, the P-43 is remembered as the predecessor of the P-47.

On May 6, 1941, Lowry Brabham piloted the first XP-47B. The largest single-engine fighter then built, it had a four-bladed propeller, pilot armor, leakproof tanks, and a low cockpit entered from the port side by a door. The prototype was destroyed on August 8, 1942, but the XP-47B did achieve 412 mph at 25,800 feet, where 1,960 hp was available. Eight .50-caliber guns in the wings represented the strongest armament of any single-seater ordered into production.

Production aircraft had a sliding canopy, beginning with the first of 169 P-47Bs delivered on December 21, 1941. Five more were accepted in March 1942, but failures of the fabric-covered elevators delayed further acceptances to May, when they were replaced with metal-covered surfaces. These Republic Thunderbolts were issued to the 56th Group to break in, that unit being nearest to the Farmingdale, New York, factory. Tests and op-

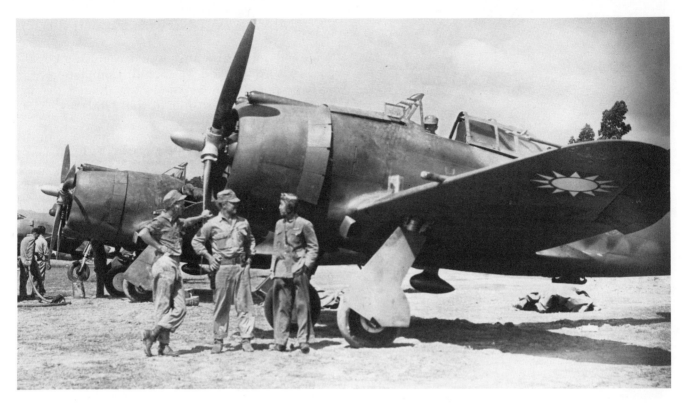

REPUBLIC P-43A-1
Pratt & Whitney R-1830-57, 1200 hp at 25,000'
DIMENSIONS: As YP-43
WEIGHT: Empty 5996 lb., Gross 7435 lb., Max. 8480 lb.
  Fuel 145–268 gal.
PERFORMANCE: Speed—Top 356 mph at 20,000', Cruising
  280 mph, Landing 78 mph. Service Ceiling 36,000',
  Climb 15,000'/6 min. Range 650 miles/200 lbs. bombs,
  1450 miles max.   AF

REPUBLIC P-47B
Pratt & Whitney R-2800-21, 2000 hp at 27,800'
DIMENSIONS: As XP-47B
WEIGHT: Empty 9346 lb., Gross 12,245 lb., Max. 13,360
  lb. Fuel 205–305 gal.
PERFORMANCE: Speed—Top 429 mph at 27,800', 340 mph
  at 5000', Cruising 335 mph, Landing 100 mph. Service
  Ceiling 42,000', Climb 2560'/1 min., 15,000'/6.7 min.
  Range 550 miles normal, 1100 miles ferry.   AF

REPUBLIC XP-47B
Pratt & Whitney XR-2800-21, 2000 hp at 27,800'
DIMENSIONS: Span 40'9", Lg. 35'5", Ht. 12'8", Wing Area
  300 sq. ft.
WEIGHT: Empty 9189 lb., Gross 12,086 lb., Max. 12,700
  lb. Fuel 205–305 gal.
PERFORMANCE: Speed—Top 412 mph at 25,800' on test.
  Service Ceiling 38,000', Climb 15,000'/5 min. Range
  575 miles normal, 1150 miles max.   AF

276

MONOPLANES AND WORLD WAR II, 1932–45

REPUBLIC P-47C
Pratt & Whitney R-2800-21, 2000 hp at 27,800' (2300 hp WE)
DIMENSIONS: Span 40'9", Lg. 36'1", Ht. 14'2", Wing Area 300 sq. ft.
WEIGHT: Empty 9900 lb., Gross 13,500 lb., Max. 14,925 lb. Fuel 305–605 gal.
PERFORMANCE: Speed—Top 420 mph at 30,000', Cruising 350 mph, Landing 100 mph. Service Ceiling 42,000', Climb 20,000'/11 min. Range 325 miles/305 gal., 835 miles max.   MFR

erational training went slowly, accompanied by the loss of 13 pilots and 41 aircraft. Completion of P-47B production in September facilitated the formation shortly thereafter of the 348th and 355th groups.

The first Thunderbolt to go overseas was the P-47C, first delivered September 14, 1942. It had a new radio and vertical mast and introduced an extended engine mount that added eight inches to the length. By February 1943, 602 P-47Cs had been delivered from Farmingdale.

Production expansion had been projected by new contracts adding 850 P-47Ds to Farmingdale's lines

REPUBLIC P-47D-11
Pratt & Whitney R-2800-63, 2000 hp takeoff (2300 hp at 27,500' WE)
DIMENSIONS: As P-47C
WEIGHT: Empty 9957 lb., Gross 13,500 lb., Max. 18,300 lb. Fuel 305–605 gal.
PERFORMANCE: Speed—Top 433 mph at 30,000' (WE), 353 mph at 5000', Cruising 340 mph, Landing 100 mph. Service Ceiling 42,000', Climb 20,000'/11 min. Range 325 miles/305 gal., 835 miles max.   USN

REPUBLIC P-47G-15   LAWSON

on October 14, 1941, and 1,050 P-47Ds ordered January 31, 1942, from a new Republic facility in Evansville, Indiana, as well as 354 P-47Gs to be built by Curtiss in Buffalo along with the P-40s. Evansville flew the first P-47D in September 1942, and the first 114 built there and the first 20 P-47Gs at Curtiss, beginning in October, were similar to the concurrent P-47C.

Additional cowl flaps and mechanical refinements distinguished the P-47D-1-RE of February 1943, as well as the P-47D-2-RA and P-47G-5-CU models, whose suffixes denoted the Republic Farmingdale, Evansville, and the Curtiss plants, respec-

REPUBLIC P-47D-22   AF

tively. Later modifications were indicated by later block numbers introduced on both Republic production lines. Curtiss completed its contract in March 1944, with most P-47Gs used only for training, but production that month from Republic reached 641 Thunderbolts.

All early Thunderbolts used the R-2800-21, but water injection for emergency power was added, beginning with P-47D-3-RA and P-47D-5-RE, and shackles for a belly tank or 500-pound bomb were added to P-47D-4-RA. Drop tanks under the wings were introduced on the P-47D-15-RA and P-47D-16-RE, along with R-2800-63 engines. Pratt & Whitney R-2800-59 power plants were standardized on the P-47D-21 model, with larger propellers on the P-47D-22-RE and P-47D-23-RA. Armament in-

cluded eight .50-caliber guns with 2,136 rounds and underwing racks for two 1,000-pound bombs or 310-gallon tanks.

The Thunderbolts in Combat

First priority for Thunderbolts was given to the Eighth Air Force, whose bombers had the most important role in the air offensive against Germany and badly needed strong fighter support. When P-47Cs arrived in Britain, they were issued to three groups: the veteran 4th, which reluctantly gave up its Spitfires; the 56th, fresh from flying P-47Bs in America; and the 78th, whose previous experience had been with P-38s.

Engine and radio problems caused delays, but on April 15, 1943, the first Thunderbolt kill was made by a 4th Group leader. As compared to the enemy Fw 190, the Thunderbolts were faster over 15,000 feet, had a higher ceiling, and had massive firepower, but their weaknesses were slow climb at low levels and too wide a turn radius. Combat experience soon taught American pilots the tactics needed to maximize the plane's advantages. Another Thunderbolt virtue was its sturdy construction.

The greatest problem was that of increasing the radius of action needed to support the bombers. The 200-gallon flush ferry tank provided for early C and D models was unsuitable for combat, and sufficient 75-gallon drop tanks were not available. The British were able to produce a 108-gallon tank of paper composition: one under the belly extended the P-47D's combat radius to 350 miles; two under the wings permitted a 445-mile radius.

There were ten Thunderbolt groups with the Eighth Air Force by the end of 1943, but since the P-51 promised better range, the P-47 was then directed into the Ninth Air Force, where its firepower could be used for ground attack. By June 1944, 17 P-47D groups were stationed in the United Kingdom.

In the Pacific the Fifth Air Force got three P-47D groups, beginning with the arrival of the 348th at Port Moresby in June 1943. More Thunderbolts replaced the 35th Group's P-39s and the 58th Group arrived in November. The 49th Group operated one squadron each of P-38, P-40, and P-47 fighters in 1944. The 318th Group in Hawaii got P-47Ds, which entered combat in Saipan after being flown off escort carriers in June 1944.

Thunderbolts also re-equipped the 33rd and 81st groups when they were sent to China in 1944, and in India they served the 1st Air Commando Group. In the Mediterranean the P-47 replaced the 57th and 325th groups' P-40s in December 1943, and P-47Ds were flown by five more Twelfth Air Force combat groups in Italy during 1944.

Wartime Developments

New technology proposed for future fighters, like the XP-69, were tested on experimental aircraft begun as P-47Bs. The XP-47E, ordered October 16, 1941, had a pressurized pilot's cabin installed on the 171st P-47B, completed in September 1942 and tested for nearly two years. A laminar-flow wing with straight trailing edges, 42-foot span, and 322-foot area was added to the 44th aircraft, the XP-47F, flown to Wright Field on September 17, 1942.

The only pencil-nosed Thunderbolt was the XP-47H, a flying test-bed for an experimental Chrysler 16-cylinder XI-2220-1 inverted inline engine. Although the project was begun in August 1943, the two P-47D-15 airframes were not converted until 1945. Test flights began July 26, 1945, but speed fell below the 490 mph expected and jet propulsion killed official interest in the Chrysler power plant.

REPUBLIC XP-47H
Chrysler XI-2220-11, 2500 hp takeoff and at 25,000'
DIMENSIONS: Span 40'9", Lg. 38'4", Ht. 13'8", Wing Area 300 sq. ft.
WEIGHT: Empty 11,442 lb., Gross 14,010 lb., Max. 15,135 lb. Fuel 205–95 gal.
PERFORMANCE: Speed—Top 414 mph at 30,000'. Service Ceiling 36,000', Absolute Ceiling 37,700', Climb 2740'/1 min. Range 770 miles normal, 1000 miles max. MFR

REPUBLIC XP-47J
Pratt & Whitney R-2800-57, 2100 hp takeoff, 2800 hp at 30,000'
DIMENSIONS: Span 40'11", Lg. 33'3", Ht. 17'3", Wing Area 300 sq. ft.
WEIGHT: Empty 9663 lb., Gross 12,400 lb., Max. 16,780 lb. Fuel 287 gal.
PERFORMANCE: Speed—Top 507 mph at 34,300', Cruising 400 mph, Landing 92 mph. Service Ceiling 45,000', Climb 15,000'/4.5 min. Range 765 miles/210 gal., 1070 miles max. MFR

By November 1942 an XP-47J project was planned to reduce Thunderbolt weight and explore the speed limits of propeller-driven aircraft. Powered by an R-2800-57 giving 2,800 hp for war emergencies, this type had a fan behind a prop spinner to suck cooling air over the cylinders, exhaust ejection to boost speed, and lightweight wing construction with ordnance reduced to six .50-caliber guns and 1,602 rounds. The contract was approved June 18, 1943, and the XP-47J first flown November 26. On August 5, 1944, the XP-47J did 505 mph, the fastest speed for a propeller-driven aircraft officially announced during the war, although AAF reports credited the J with 507 mph. A proposal to use counterrotating propellers with an R-2800-61 was dropped, and P-72 development replaced the P-47J.

The next Thunderbolt models tested features that were more readily adaptable to production aircraft. A bubble canopy was introduced on the XP-47K, completed July 3, 1943, from the last D-5, and on the XP-47L, which was the last D-20 with internal fuel capacity increased from 305 to 370 gallons.

Visibility with this cockpit cover, copied from the Hawker Tempest, was so improved that in April 1944 production lines in both factories changed over from the old "razorback" shape to the bubble canopy and larger tanks for the P-47-25-RE and P-47-26-RA. The first 2,963 P-47D-1 to P-47D-22-RE produced at Farmingdale had the old-style cockpit, while the last 2,546, with block numbers from P-47D-25 on, had the bubble canopy. At Evansville the first 2,350 P-47D-2 to P-47D-23-RA were old style; the last 3,743 (Blocks 26-40) were new.

REPUBLIC XP-47K   MFR

Characteristics of the P-47D-25 are typical of the line. Fuel load could include up to 370 gallons internally plus 330 in drop tanks, which could extend the radius of action to 690 miles for fighter sweeps. Radius with one 165-gallon drop tank and one 1,000 pound bomb was 518 miles; with two 1,000 pound bombs, 320 miles. In this latter role as a low-altitude fighter-bomber, the heavily armed Thunderbolt was outstanding through the last year of the European war. Additional firepower appeared in the D-30 block, with rails for ten 5-inch rockets, and a dorsal fin was added.

REPUBLIC P-47D-25-RE
Pratt & Whitney R-2800-59, 2300 hp at 31,000'
DIMENSIONS: Span 40'9", Lg. 36'1", Ht. 14'2", Wing Area
300 sq. ft.
WEIGHT: Empty 10,000 lb., Gross 14,500 lb., Max. 19,400
lb. Fuel 370–700 gal.
PERFORMANCE: Speed—Top 428 mph at 30,000', 350 mph
at s. l., Landing 100 mph. Service Ceiling 42,000',
Climb 20,000'/9 min. Range 475 miles/500 lbs. bombs,
1700 miles max. MFR

REPUBLIC P-47D-30-RE AF

REPUBLIC P-47M
Pratt & Whitney R-2800-57, 2800 hp WE at 32,500'
DIMENSIONS: Span 40'9", Lg. 36'4", Ht. 14'9", Wing Area
308 sq. ft.
WEIGHT: Empty 10,423 lb., Gross 13,275 lb., Max. 15,500
lb. Fuel 370–480 gal.
PERFORMANCE: Speed—Top 473 mph at 32,000', Landing
99 mph. Service Ceiling 41,000', Climb 32,000'/13.4
min. Range 530 miles normal. MFR

The new Thunderbolts went to the Ninth Air Force, which had 13 P-47D groups for the D-day landing in France and 14 groups at V-E Day. These Thunderbolts' attacks ahead of the Allied armies advancing into Germany helped cripple enemy resistance in the war's last stage.

Only one Eighth Air Force unit, the 56th Fighter Group, still used P-47s in 1945. This famous outfit won the highest score of any Eighth Air Force group: 674 enemy aircraft destroyed in the air and 311 on the ground. Francis Gabreski and Robert Johnson each won 28 air victories on 153 and 91 combat missions, respectively. In both cases, all victories were against enemy fighters.

When the new R-2800-57 "C" series Wasp, producing 2,800 hp war-emergency power became available, four P-47D-27-RE aircraft to be fitted with the new Wasps were designated YP-47M. This installation was ordered in September for the last 130 P-47D-30-RE aircraft, which were delivered as P-47M-1s in December 1944. They were rushed to England for the 56th Fighter Group, but engine problems delayed their use until April 1945.

One YP-47M had actually been completed as the XP-47N using a new, larger wing designed to accommodate additional fuel. This conversion had been ordered May 19, 1944, as it was realized that the P-47D range, less than that of the P-38L or P-51D, made it less suitable for Pacific warfare.

Confidence in the Republic design, whose wing had already been tried on the XP-47K, was such that 1,900 P-47Ns were approved June 30, 1944, before the XP-47N flew July 22. The first P-47N-1-RE appeared in September, and 24 were delivered by the year's end. Farmingdale completed 1,667 P-

47Ns before the Thunderbolt line closed in December 1945. In Evansville production on the P-47D-30/-40-RA continued until July 1945, followed by 149 P-47N-20-RAs before V-J Day canceled the rest of the contract.

The heaviest single-engine fighter used in action, the P-47N could carry up to 1,156 gallons in internal and drop tanks. A radius of action up to 1,000 miles was possible, provided the pilot's physical condition permitted a solo flight of nine or more hours. Alternately, ten 5-inch rockets or three 1,000 pound bombs could augment the eight .50-caliber guns, with 2,136 rounds, in attacks on surface targets.

The P-47N was first used in the Pacific by the 318th Group, which flew them from Hawaii to Le Shima, off Okinawa. On May 25, this group destroyed 34 Japanese aircraft without loss to themselves. They were joined on Le Shima by the 413th and 507th groups by July 1, while another P-47N group, the 414th, was established on Iwo Jima in July. The last missions were flown in August.

The Thunderbolt production total of 15,683 is the largest in American fighter-plane history, but is not as large as those for the Bf 109, Spitfire, or Yak series fighters abroad. There were 31 AAF P-47 groups in combat areas by the end of 1944, and a peak AAF inventory of 5,595 planes in May 1945.

Lend-lease provided Britain with 240 P-47D-22-RE razorbacks as the Thunderbolt I, while the Thunderbolt II, with the bubble canopy, included 360 P-47D-25/-30-RE and 230 P-47D-30/-40-RA allocations. RAF Thunderbolts were shipped to India and began operations on the Burma front in September 1944, with 12 squadrons equipped by the war's end.

France was sent 446 P-47Ds to serve seven fighter squadrons and three P-47D-10-REs flown to the Soviet Union via Alaska in September 1943 were followed by a shipment of 100 P-47D-22-REs and 100 P-47D-27-REs in 1944.

Brazil received 66 P-47D-25/-30-REs, which served the Brazilian fighter squadron that began operations in Italy in October 1944. Mexico's 201st Fighter Squadron flew ground-support missions in the Philippines, beginning June 5, 1945, using P-47Ds seconded from the Fifth Air Force, and got 25 new P-47D-30-RAs.

After the war's end, Thunderbolts continued to serve Air Force and National Guard units. One group, the 86th, remained in Germany with P-47Ds until it became the only USAF fighter group in Europe when the Berlin blockade began. With the

REPUBLIC XP-47N   MFR

REPUBLIC P-47N-1
Pratt & Whitney R-2800-57, -73, or -77, 2800 hp at 32,500'
DIMENSIONS: Span 42'7", Lg. 36'1", Ht. 14'8", Wing Area 322 sq. ft.
WEIGHT: Empty 11,000 lb., Gross 16,300 lb., Max. 20,700 lb. Fuel 556–1156 gal.
PERFORMANCE: Speed—Top 467 mph at 32,500', Cruising 300 mph, Landing 98 mph. Service Ceiling 43,000', Climb 25,000'/14.2 min. Range 800 miles/2000 lbs. bombs, 2200 miles at 281 mph.   MFR

system of postwar alliances, the P-47D became the standard fighter of Iran (about 160), Portugal (50), Turkey and Yugoslavia (126). China had one P-47D group, and secondhand aircraft were also acquired by Italy and various Latin American countries, but the last time the big Republic fighter fired its guns was during the Guatemalan revolution in June 1954.

North American Mustang

The most effective American fighter of World War II had no radical layout or major departure from conventional patterns. An untrained observer, seeing the Mustang at a distance, might be hard put to tell it from the P-40, Messerschmitt, Spitfire, Yak, or any of the numerous low-wing single-seaters powered by an inline engine. North American's highly successful fighter was good because it represented the highest refinement of a fighter layout which could be seen in America as far back as the old P-24: the long, pointed nose, opposite of the barrel-shaped radial-engine jobs.

The Mustang's story began in April 1940, when British officials asked the North American firm to produce the Curtiss H-87 (P-40D) in quantity for the RAF. Company officials countered with a proposal to design a superior machine around the same 1,150-hp Allison V-1710-39 engine, which was accepted by the British on condition that the prototype be available in 120 days. On May 4, 1940, the Army released the NA-73, as the new design was labeled, for sale to Britain provided that two of the initial lot be transferred to the Air Corps for tests. After 320 NA-73s were ordered May 29, 1940, the fourth and tenth aircraft were allotted the Air Corps designation XP-51 in a contract approved September 20, and the RAF increased its purchase to 620 planes by September 24.

A prototype, the NA-73X, was quickly completed and flown October 26, 1940, by Vance Brese. German-born chief designer Edgar Schmued planned the NA-73 for mass production with a low, square-cut wing, whose laminar-flow airfoil had the lowest

NORTH AMERICAN NA-73X   MFR

NORTH AMERICAN XP-51 (MUSTANG I)
Allison V-1710-39, 1150 hp at 11,800'
DIMENSIONS: Span 37', Lg. 32'3", Ht. 12'2", Wing Area 233 sq. ft.
WEIGHT: Empty 6278 lb., Gross 7965 lb., Max. 8400 lb. Fuel 105–70 gal.
PERFORMANCE: Speed—Top 382 mph at 13,000', Cruising 325 mph, Landing 83 mph. Service Ceiling 30,800', Climb 2200'/1 min., 15,000'/7 min. Range 750 miles normal.   AF

drag of any fighter. A radiator scoop was streamlined into the fuselage's underside behind the pilot.

Although the prototype crashed November 30, 1940, the first Mustang I production NA-73 was flown on April 23, 1941, and retained by the company for necessary testing. The Air Corps' first XP-51 was flown to Wright Field on August 24, while the second aircraft was accepted by RAF representatives in September and began a long journey by ship through the Panama Canal to Liverpool, arriving October 24.

Tests soon showed the Mustang superior to the Kittyhawk, Airacobra, and Spitfire in both speed and maneuverability at low altitudes. Top speed went from 328 mph at 1,000 feet to 382 mph at 13,000 feet. Equipment included armor, leakproof tanks, two .50-caliber guns with 400 rpg placed low in the nose and two more in the wings inboard of four .30-caliber guns with 500 rpg.

RAF Mustangs were issued to Army Cooperation squadrons to replace Tomahawks, and were fitted with a camera behind the pilot. Tactical reconnaissance calls for avoidance of enemy fighters, and so the Mustang's combat virtues were not yet fre-

quently demonstrated. In May 1942 No. 26 Squadron flew its first sorties across the Channel. The Mustang's first air battles were fought on August 19. The Allison-powered Mustang was the first single-seat fighter to penetrate German air space from England. Fifteen squadrons served the RAF in January 1943, with five remaining in June 1944 and two serving in the low-altitude role until the war's end.[7]

A lend-lease contract approved September 25, 1941, added 150 designated P-51s to the schedule. These aircraft were armed with four 20-mm guns in the wings, with 125 rpg. The first 20 P-51s to follow the last Mustang Is off the line in July 1942 were taken by the AAF and fitted with two cameras for tactical reconnaissance duties. This worked so well that they were sent to the 68th Observation Group, whose 154th Squadron flew the first AAF P-51-2-NA mission on April 9, 1943. When this contract was completed in September, the RAF had received

NORTH AMERICAN MUSTANG I   IWM

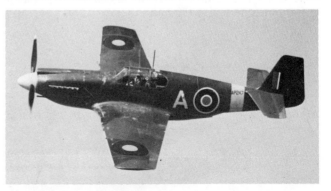

[7] At least 10 Mustangs were forwarded to Russia and used against Finland.

NORTH AMERICAN P-51   MFR

93 planes as the Mustang IA, while the AAF got 55 P-51 photographic types. Two airframes were diverted to the XP-78 project.

From October 1942 to March 1943 North American delivered the 500 dive-bomber Mustangs designated A-36A (see Chapter 13). They differed from the P-51 in their V-1710-87 engines, which were boosted for low-altitude operations, dive brakes, bomb racks, and six-gun armament.

The P-51A used the V-1710-81 with war-emergency boost, and a contract for 1,200 planes was approved by August 24, 1942. Actually, 310 were delivered from March to May 1943, before production shifted to the P-51B. Armament consisted of four .50-caliber wing guns with 1,260 rounds and wing racks for two 500-pound bombs or drop tanks. The first P-51A group was the 54th, which remained in Florida for replacement training, while later P-51As went to Asia for the 23rd, 311th, and 1st Air

NORTH AMERICAN P-51A
Allison V-1710-81, 1200 hp takeoff, 1470 hp WE at 11,800'
DIMENSIONS: Span 37', Lg. 32'3", Ht. 12'2", Wing Area 233 sq. ft.
WEIGHT: Empty 6433 lb., Gross 8600 lb., Max. 9000 lb. Fuel 105–80 gal. (480 gal. max.).
PERFORMANCE: Speed—Top 390 mph at 20,000', 340 mph at 5000', Cruising 307—228 mph, Landing 90 mph. Service Ceiling 31,350', Climb 20,000'/9.1 min. Range 750 miles normal, 2350 miles max.   MFR

Commando groups, and flew their first missions on Thanksgiving Day 1943.

The major weakness of the early Mustang was that performance at high altitudes was limited by the Allison engine, and in the summer of 1942 "crossbreeding" of the airframe with the new Merlin 65 engine was proposed. Rolls-Royce received five Mustang Is for conversion, with the first in the air by October 13, 1942, as the Mustang X. Data on this work was sent to the United States, and North American was issued a contract July 31, 1942, for two XP-78 aircraft to be converted from lend-lease P-51s, with the Packard Merlin V-1650-3 engine and two-stage supercharger rated by the Air Force at 1,295 hp at 28,750 feet, with 1,595 war-emergency hp available to 17,000 feet.

NORTH AMERICAN XP-51B
Packard V-1650-3, 1380 hp takeoff, 1595 hp WE
DIMENSIONS: Span 37', Lg. 32'3", Ht. 13'8", Wing Area 233 sq. ft.
WEIGHT: Empty 7030 lb., Gross 8350 lb., Max. 8880 lb. Fuel 105–80 gal.
PERFORMANCE: Speed—Top 441 mph at 29,800'. Service Ceiling 42,000', Climb 20,000'/5.9 min.   MFR

Redesignated XP-51B in September, the first U.S. Merlin Mustang flew November 30, 1942, with a four-bladed Hamilton propeller and the carburetor intake below, instead of above, the engine. This configuration was selected to replace the P-51A, and the first P-51B-1-NA was flown May 5, 1943. Armament still consisted of four .50-caliber guns, half that of a P-47, but the 440-mph top speed was the fastest among fighters then in combat. Even more important, after another fuel tank was added behind the cockpit, and with two 108- or 150-gallon drop tanks below the wings, the Mustang had the range needed to accompany bombers to any target in Germany.

Mass production of the new Mustang was ordered both at North American's Inglewood, California, factory and at the Dallas, Texas, plant. Inglewood built 1,788 P-51Bs with the V-1650-3 Merlin, except for the improved V-1650-7s on the last 350 P-51B-15-NAs. In August 1943, Dallas began deliveries of

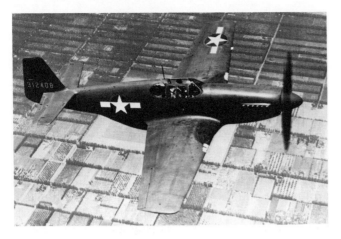

NORTH AMERICAN P-51B
Packard V-1650-3, 1380 hp takeoff, 1595 hp WE at 17,-
000', 1295 hp at 28,750'
DIMENSIONS: As XP-51B
WEIGHT: Empty 6985 lb., Gross 9800 lb., Max. 11,800 lb.
Fuel 105–269 gal. (569 gal. max.).
PERFORMANCE: Speed—Top 440 mph at 30,000', 427 mph
at 20,000', 388 mph at 5000', Cruising 343–244 mph,
Landing 100 mph. Service Ceiling 42,000', Climb
20,000'/7 min. Range 550 miles normal, 2200 miles
max.   MFR

NORTH AMERICAN P-51C
Packard V-1650-7, 1490 hp takeoff, 1720 hp at 6,200',
1505 hp at 19,300'
DIMENSIONS: As XP-51B
WEIGHT: Empty 6985 lb., Gross 9800 lb., Max. 11,800 lb.
Fuel 105–269 gal. (569 gal. max.).
PERFORMANCE: Speed—Top 439 mph at 25,000', 426 mph
at 20,000', 395 mph at 5000', Cruising 362 mph, Land-
ing 100 mph. Service Ceiling 41,900', Climb 20,000'/
6.9 min. Range 950 miles normal, 2440 miles max.
PMB

350 similar P-51C-1-NT Mustangs with the V-1650-
3, but the remaining 1,400 P-51Cs built there had
the V-1650-7.

A plastic canopy with all-around vision, six .50-
caliber wing guns with 1,880 rounds, a V-1650-7,
and a Hamilton propeller appeared on the P-51D,
which replaced the B model at Inglewood in March
1944. This was the most widely used Mustang, with
6,502 P-51D-NAs built in California by July 1945.
A small dorsal fillet was added to most examples.
The Texas factory built 1,454 P-51D-NTs, inter-
spersed with 1,337 P-51Ks (similar except for an

NORTH AMERICAN P-51D-5
Packard V-1650-7, 1490 hp takeoff, 1720 hp at 6200', 1505
hp at 19,300'
DIMENSIONS: As XP-51B
WEIGHT: Empty 7125 lb., Gross 10,100 lb., Max. 11,600
lb. Fuel 269–489 gal.
PERFORMANCE: Speed—Top 437 mph at 25,000', 413 mph
at 15,000', 395 mph at 5000', Cruising 362 mph, Landing 100 mph. Service Ceiling 41,900', Climb 3475'/1
min., 30,000'/13 min. Range 950 miles/269 gal., 2300
miles/489 gal.   MFR

Aeroproducts propeller), 136 F-6D and 163 F-6K
reconnaissance variants, and ten TP-51D two-place
trainers. Ten 5-inch rockets, two 500-pound bombs,
or drop tanks could be carried below the wings.

Allied offensive operations from the United Kingdom had top priority for the new Mustangs, and the
first P-51B group there, the 354th, flew its first cross-
Channel sweep December 1, 1943. American forces
increased steadily until 1945, when 14 P-51 groups
and one P-47 group served the Eighth Air Force,
while 14 P-47 groups, three P-51 groups, and one
P-38 fighter group served the Ninth Air Force.

The top Mustang group was the 357th, with 609
air and 106 ground kills from February 11, 1944, to
April 25, 1945. The 4th Group, which used Spitfires, P-47s, and P-51s (received in February 1944),
had 583 air and 469 ground kills. Top Mustang aces
were George Preddy with 25 victories, John C.
Meyer, 24, and Don Gentile, 23.

In Italy four fighter groups replaced older types
with P-51s (the 31st, 52nd, 325th, and 332nd),
which joined the Fifteenth Air Force's three P-38
groups for the war's last year in Europe.

Merlin-powered Mustangs were used against Japan in 1944 by the 23rd, 51st, and 311th groups in
China, while the Fifth Air Force received P-51Ds
in 1945 for the 3rd Commando, 35th, and 348th
groups. Perhaps the most significant Mustang missions in the Pacific were those flown from Iwo Jima
by the 15th, 21st, and 506th groups to support B-29
attacks against Japan.

When fitted with two cameras behind the cockpit,
the Mustang made an excellent tactical reconnaissance supplement to Lockheed's F-5s, as the 68th

Observation Group's P-51-2s had shown in 1942 for the Twelfth Air Force. The factory-pattern aircraft for this configuration had temporarily been known as an F-6A, and in 1943, 35 P-51A-10s were converted to F-6B form and first sortied across the English Channel by the 107th TRS on December 20, 1943.

Seventy-one Merlin-powered P-51B-1s and 20 P-51C-1s were modified to F-6Cs in 1943, while 136 F-6Ds and 163 F-6Ks were built at Dallas beginning in November 1944. All of these aircraft still carried their wing guns and frequently used them; in fact, the last German fighter destroyed in the war was an Fw 190, downed by an F-6C on May 8, 1945.

An Evaluation

Now that the major fighter types with which the Army Air Forces fought the war have been described, it may be helpful to summarize their role. Table 8 shows what fighters were used by the AAF in the European Theater of Operations from 1942 to 1945. The planes are given in order of number of sorties, as an indication of each type's relative importance, including Spitfires and Beaufighters obtained on reverse lend-lease and P-61 night fighters. Unfortunately, this data is not available for the Pacific theaters.

The first two columns give the number of sorties and show the decisive role in Europe of the Thunderbolt, Mustang, and Lightning. The next column indicates the extent that fighters were used for tactical bombing, and shows the P-47 delivering over two thirds of the bombs dropped by fighters. Columns four and seven list total losses of each type on combat missions and percentage of aircraft loss per sortie. The reader should remember that loss-rate reflects not only the type's vulnerability but also the relative risk taken on its particular missions. With this in mind, Lightnings seem to have suffered the heaviest losses, 1.4 percent, and Airacobras the lowest, with only 0.4 percent per sortie.

The lower losses of the night fighters and fighter-bombers probably indicate that attacking enemy bombers or ground targets is less risky than tackling enemy fighters.

Column five indicates how many enemy aircraft were believed destroyed in the air by each type, while the sixth column shows the number of enemy aircraft destroyed while on the ground. This data gives only a rough index of each fighter design's relative efficiency in the job of destroying enemy aircraft, which is its *raison d'être*. The effect of groundfire and the uneven risks of interception and offensive missions, of course, limits this index's value. Nevertheless, the Mustang accounted for almost half the enemy aircraft destroyed in Europe by U.S. fighters and clearly emerges as the most effective type, especially when we remember that Mustangs did relatively little bombing and almost no interception, but were used for long-distance penetration of enemy-fighter territory. Column six indicates Mustang success at strafing planes at their home fields, this largely in the war's last weeks.

The reader may draw his own conclusions from these figures. Why did Lightnings suffer losses greater than Airacobras when the former had a much better record in destroying the enemy? Possibly because the P-39's low-level maneuverability and extensive armor reduced the effects of hostile fire, while the P-38's speed and ceiling enabled it to close with an enemy that more often wished to avoid combat than to join it; but no doubt the where and when of each type's mission was also important here.

It would be highly interesting to have comparable data for the fighter types of other countries, but until then what we do have is a record of U.S. Air Force success in building fighters. The relative quality of fighter pilots is not constant, so it may not really be possible to make precise comparison of each type's efficiency, but quality of aircraft remains a significant factor, if not always the decisive one.

NORTH AMERICAN F-6D   MFR

Lend-Lease Mustangs

British Mustang Is and IAs continued to serve Army Cooperation Command squadrons throughout the war; they were replenished in June 1943 by 50 Mustang IIs (P-51As) plus a single A-36A for evaluation. Fighter Command did want the new Merlin-powered models but had to wait for the AAF to get them before beginning operations in February 1944.

The RAF was allocated 308 P-51B and 636 P-51C fighters as the Mustang III in 1944, but some were repossessed by the AAF. A British-made "Malcolm Hood" improved cockpit visibility on most of these.

Table 8

AAF FIGHTERS IN THE EUROPEAN WAR, 1942–45

Type	No. of Sorties	Bomb Tonnage	U. S. A/C Lost in Combat	Enemy A/C Claimed Destroyed in Air	Enemy A/C Claimed Destroyed on Ground	Combat Missions Loss Rate Per Sortie
P-47	423,435	113,963	3,077	3,082	3,202	0.7%
P-51	213,873	5,668	2,520	4,950	4,131	1.2%
P-38	129,849	20,139	1,758	1,771	749	1.4%
P-40	67,059	11,014	553	481	40	0.8%
P-39	30,547	121	107	14	18	0.4%
Spitfire	28,981	212	191	256	3	0.7%
A-36	23,373	8,014	177	84	17	0.8%
Beaufighter	6,706	—	63	24	—	0.9%
P-61	3,637	141	25	58	—	0.7%
Total	927,460	159,272	8,471	10,720	8,160	0.9%

NORTH AMERICAN MUSTANG III   IWM

The Mustang IVs, consisting of 282 P-51Ds and about 400 P-51Ks, were allocated in 1945.

Actual totals of lend-lease aircraft often vary, due to reassignments made overseas, but the RAF operated 16 Merlin-powered Mustang squadrons in the United Kingdom and six in Italy at the war's end.

China got P-51C Mustangs to replace the P-40s of the Chinese-American Composite Wing, and after P-51Ds arrived in 1945 there were three Chinese Mustang groups. Australia replaced its P-40s in 1945 with 84 P-51K and 214 P-51D Mustangs from Texas, along with parts for the first 80 Mustang XXs assembled in Australia, the first flown April 29, 1945. Like 40 P-51Ds and ten P-51Ks lend-leased to two Dutch East Indies squadrons, they were too late to enter combat against Japan.

Improved Mustangs

A new, lightweight NA-105 design was offered in January 1943, and a July 20 contract called for five prototypes. By using load factors reduced to British standards and only four guns with 1,000 rounds, their weight was reduced. The first, an XP-51F with Packard V-1650-3 (later V-1650-7), flew February 14, 1944, while the fourth, an XP-51G, flew on August 9 with an imported Rolls-Royce Merlin 145 and a unique five-bladed prop. The third XP-51F

and second XP-51G went to Britain, while two more prototypes were ordered in June. These became the XP-51J, first flown April 23, 1945, with an Allison V-1710-119.

Lessons learned from these projects were incor-

NORTH AMERICAN XP-51F
Packard V-1650-7, 1490 hp takeoff
DIMENSIONS: As XP-51B
WEIGHT: Empty 5635 lb., Gross 7610 lb., Max. 9060 lb. Fuel 105–80 gal. (330 gal. max.).
PERFORMANCE: Speed—Top 466 mph at 29,000', Cruising 379 mph, Landing 100 mph. Service Ceiling 42,500', Climb 19,500'/4.9 min. Range 650 miles normal, 2100 miles max.   MFR

NORTH AMERICAN XP-51G
Rolls-Royce Merlin 145, 1675 hp takeoff, 1910 hp at 15,400', 2080 hp at 20,000'
DIMENSIONS: As XP-51B
WEIGHT: Empty 5750 lb., Gross 7265 lb., Max. 8885 lb. Fuel 105–80 gal. (330 gal. max.).
PERFORMANCE: Speed—Top 472 mph at 20,750', Cruising 315 mph, Landing 100 mph. Service Ceiling 45,700', Climb 20,000'/3.4 min. Range 485 miles normal, 1865 miles max.   MFR

porated into the last production Mustang, the P-51H, with a V-1650-9, refined structure, and new wing and tail design. A thousand were ordered June 30, 1944, from Inglewood, with the first P-51H-1-NA flying February 3, 1945. The war's end limited production to 555, the last being completed November 9, 1945. One example went to the RAF in March 1945 and another to the U.S. Navy, which had tested a P-51D on a carrier in November 1944.

The P-51H was probably the fastest prop-driven plane actually produced in wartime. Top speed was 487 mph at 25,000 feet when used as an interceptor, 450 mph when carrying two 500-pound bombs and added fuel. Range with two 110-gallon drop tanks could be extended to 2,400 miles at 241 mph or 850 miles when carrying two 1,000-pound bombs. Armament was six .50-caliber guns, plus optional external loads comprising the two bombs or ten 5-inch rockets. Ammunition supply included 400 rounds for each inner-wing gun and 270 rounds for each of the others. Armor included 7/16 inch behind the pilot's head, 5/16 inch behind his back, and 1/4 inch at the front fire wall.

Production of the P-51D had ended at Dallas in August 1945, with the last P-51D-30-NT actually completed as the only P-51M with a V-1650-9A engine. None of the 1,700 P-51Ls (V-1650-11) on order were completed. Total Mustangs completed—including attack, photographic, and experimental aircraft—amounted to 15,484, with 5,541 on hand in the AAF when the war ended.

Mustangs After 1946

The postwar Air Force used the Mustang (which was known as the F-51H since 1947) in its regular wings (formerly called groups) until they were replaced by jet fighters. Air National Guard part-time fliers had F-51D and RF-51D models in 15 wings.

When the Korean War began in June 1950, 1,804 Mustangs remained with the Air Guard and in storage, and many were rapidly recalled to active service. Within a year the Air Force had ten F-51 wings, of which three with F-51Ds served in Korea, along with squadrons of South Korean, South African, and Australian pilots, the latter using some of the 200 Mustangs made in Australia. By the end of its Korean combat on January 23, 1953, the F-51 had flown 62,607 sorties and lost 194 planes to enemy action on missions that were primarily for ground support.

After the war the last two F-51 wings gave up their planes for jets, but the Air Guard didn't yield their last F-51D to the Air Force Museum until March 1957.

Sweden had become interested in the Mustang after examining P-51Bs that had run out of gas and landed in that neutral state in May 1944. Requests

NORTH AMERICAN P-51H
Packard V-1650-9, 1380 hp takeoff, 2220 hp at 10,200', 1800 hp WE at 25,000'
DIMENSIONS: Span 37', Lg. 33'4", Ht. 13'8", Wing Area 233 sq. ft.
WEIGHT: Empty 6585 lb., Gross 9500 lb., Max. 11,054 lb. Fuel 255–475 gal.
PERFORMANCE: Speed—Top 487 mph at 25,000', Cruising 380 mph, Landing 96 mph. Service Ceiling 41,600', Climb 30,000'/12.5 min. Range 850 miles/1000 lbs. bombs, 940 miles normal, 2400 miles at 241 mph. MFR

NORTH AMERICAN P-51J
Allison V-1710-119, 1500 hp takeoff, 1720 hp WE at 20,700'
DIMENSIONS: Span 37', Lg. 32'11", Ht. 13'8", Wing Area 233 sq. ft.
WEIGHT: Empty 6030 lb., Gross 7550 lb., Max. 9140 lb. Fuel 105–80 gal. (330 gal. max.).
PERFORMANCE: Speed—Top 491 mph at 27,400', Landing 84 mph. Service Ceiling 43,700', Climb 20,000'/5 min. MFR

NORTH AMERICAN P-51D-30 (ANG)   WL

were made to the U.S. Government for a supply to replace their obsolete Italian-made fighters. The Americans felt confident enough of their aircraft supply to fly 50 P-15Ds to Sweden in March 1945. Wartime internments and more purchases in 1946–48 brought the total of Swedish P-51s to 161, known as J-26s there.

In 1952–53 the Swedes sold 25 to Israel, 42 to Dominica, and 25 to Nicaragua. The former Mustangs once more went to war in October 1956 during Israel's successful Sinai campaign.

Many other secondhand Mustangs were sold or

given to over a dozen different countries. Filipino P-51Ds attacked guerrillas in 1948. Other deliveries included 130 to Canada (beginning in June 1947), 100 to Switzerland, and 48 to Italy. This survey must exclude details of the Mustang's long service in noncombatant roles. Many are still to be seen as civilian sports planes, and examples refurbished by Florida's Cavalier Aircraft in 1967 operated in both military and civilian utility roles.

Crisis-Born Projects

Now that the five types that did the most Air Force fighter work in World War II have been discussed, attention can be given the numerous experimental projects begun by the Matériel Division. In the two years between the outbreak of war in Europe and the attack on Pearl Harbor, an extraordinary variety of designs received pursuit designations XP-46 to XP-72. Nevertheless, only three of over two dozen projects reached production in time to join the P-38, P-39, and P-40 types already on order when Germany's invasion of Poland began the war.

The first flurry of designs were the XP-46 to XP-50 prototypes ordered in October–November 1939. None passed the prototype stage, since the Curtiss XP-46, Republic XP-47, and Lockheed XP-49 were submerged by P-40, P-47B, and P-38 developments. Douglas made its only attempt at a land-based fighter with their XP-48 (Model 312), but it never was built.

The Douglas proposal was for a lightweight single-seater with a 525-hp Ranger SGV-770, tricycle gear, and two guns. Weight was expected to be only 3,400 pounds, requiring only 92 square feet of wing area. The Air Corps rejected this approach and instead ordered prototypes of the top two competitors, the XP-49 and XP-50, in an August 1939 competition for twin-engine fighters.

Lockheed attempted to make a basic improvement on the P-38 by using more advanced engines. This project, known as the XP-49 (Lockheed Model 522), began with a company proposal to the Air Corps in August 1939. Purchase of a prototype was ordered in October and a contract readied by November 30, but it was not finally approved until January 8, 1940.

The first specification called for the proposed Pratt & Whitney X-1800 (H-2600) 24-cylinder engine, and a speed of 473 mph at 20,000 feet was anticipated. When this engine failed to materialize, Continental XIV-1430s were substituted in September 1940, and the new specification estimated top speed to be 458 mph at 25,000 feet, where 1,600 hp per engine was expected, and 372 mph at 5,000 feet.

Flight tests began on November 4, 1942, and continued until the following June—with discouraging results. Top speed was only 361 mph at 5,000 feet

LOCKHEED XP-49
Continental XIV-1430-13-15, 1350 hp takeoff
DIMENSIONS: Span 52', Lg. 40'1", Ht. 9'10", Wing Area 327.5 sq. ft.
WEIGHT: Empty 15,410 lb., Gross 18,750 lb. Fuel 300–600 gal.
PERFORMANCE: (18,500 lb.) Speed—Top 406 mph at 15,-000', 361 mph at 5000', 347 mph at s. l. Climb 3075'/1 min., 20,000'/8.7 min. Range 679 miles.   MFR

and 406 mph at 15,000 feet. Armament included two 20-mm guns with 60 rpg and four .50-caliber guns with 300 rpg, but neither weapons nor a proposed pressurized cabin was installed.

Grumman's only Army fighter, the XP-50, was a twin-engine counterpart of the Navy's XF5F-1, with a short, squared-off wing, stubby fuselage, twin rudders, and tricycle landing gear. Armament included two 20-mm guns with 120 rounds, two .50-caliber guns in the nose, and a rack for two 100-pound bombs under the fuselage.

The XP-50 was ordered November 25, 1939, and since the power plant choice—turbosupercharged Wright Cyclones—was less speculative than that of the rival XP-49, the Grumman was first in the air. A maiden flight was made February 18, 1941, but a landing accident on March 14 delayed the test program. A turbosupercharger explosion on May 14 caused the loss of the $353,828 prototype.

Undaunted, Grumman then proposed its Model 51, with two 1,700-hp Wright R-2600-10 Double Cyclones, and two prototypes designated XP-65 were authorized June 16, 1941. Essentially this design was like the Navy's XF7F-1, prepared at the same time, but the Army wanted turbosupercharging, a pressurized cabin, and two 37-mm guns. The Army came to feel that "commonalities" with Navy

GRUMMAN XP-50
Wright R-1820-67, -69, 1200 hp takeoff, 1000 hp at 25,000'
DIMENSIONS: Span 42', Lg. 31'11", Ht. 12', Wing Area 304 sq. ft.
WEIGHT: Empty 8307 lb., Gross 10,558 lb., Max. 13,060 lb. Fuel 217–450 gal.
PERFORMANCE: Speed—Top 424 mph at 25,000', Cruising 317 mph. Service Ceiling 40,000', Climb 20,000'/5 min. Range 585 miles normal, 1250 miles max.   MFR

design were a handicap, and since Grumman's concentration was on Navy projects, cancellation was recommended December 15 and completed by January 16, 1942.

By June 1940 France was crumbling before the Nazi onslaught, and Congress was providing funds for expansion and development of combat aviation. New designations, from XP-51 to XP-60, were assigned that year by the Matériel Division, exploring new possibilities of advancing fighter performance. Ironically, the most successful was the XP-51, which was not adopted by the Air Force until 1942, after it had been operated by Britain. Republic's XP-47B, which replaced two earlier projects, was the most fruitful Army development that summer. But the Matériel Division also backed the Bell XP-52 and XP-59—which, like the radical XP-54, XP-55, and XP-56, had pusher propellers—as well as the conventional Curtiss XP-53 and XP-60, the lightweight XP-57, and the giant XP-58.

Of 11 new projects begun that year, four were canceled before prototypes were made. The first to drop out was the XP-57, which had been proposed to General Arnold in May 1940 by Tucker Aviation of Detroit. A light (3,400-pound) fighter armed with two .50-caliber and one 20-mm gun, the wooden-winged Tucker was to attain 308 mph from a 720-hp Miller L-510 engine driving its propeller by means of an extended shaft like that on the P-39. By February 1941, however, the little company was in financial difficulties, and since current fighter trends were to heavier and faster aircraft, the contract was allowed to lapse.

Pusher Prototypes

Among the most unusual American fighters was the group designed to explore effects of pusher-propeller arrangements on fighter performance. Single-seaters with rearward-facing propellers and engines behind the pilot had been built abroad as early as 1915, and offered a nose cleared for pilot visibility and heavy armament installations. Numerous complications of structure presented themselves, however, and the layout was untried in the United States until June 1940, when several prototypes were begun to test various approaches to the problem.

Bell Aircraft had used a pusher arrangement on its multiplace Airacuda, and their Model 16 single-seater was the first pusher type to receive an Air Corps pursuit designation. The XP-52 had tricycle landing gear, twin booms to support the tail assembly, and a new inline engine, the 1,250-hp Continental XIV-1430-5, cooled by a nose radiator and turning contrarotating propellers. Specifications called for a 435 mph speed, 8,200 pounds gross, and an armament of two 20-mm and six .50-caliber guns.

Another Bell pusher was the XP-59, which had a 2,000-hp Pratt & Whitney R-2800-23 cooled by air from a nose intake, and an estimated 11,698 pounds gross and 450 mph top. Neither Bell type was built because the XP-59 was replaced by the XP-59A jet project, and the XP-52 was canceled November 25, 1941, to relieve the load on Bell's engineering staff.

Pusher types seemed to offer lower drag, better visibility and more room for armament, and a specification issued November 27, 1939, resulted in a design competition for radical pusher fighters in May 1940. The three winners were designated Vultee XP-54, Curtiss-Wright XP-55, and Northrop XP-56, and preliminary engineering contracts were issued June 22, 1940. All three were to be single-seat pushers powered by the Pratt & Whitney 2,200-hp liquid-cooled 24-cylinder X-1800-A3G (H-2600), but this engine was canceled in October and other power plants were used in the actual prototypes.

First to appear was the XP-54, whose first prototype was approved January 8, 1941, and flown January 15, 1943. The only aircraft ever powered by a Lycoming XH-2470-1, the XP-54 had twin rudders suspended on tail booms extending from the gulled wing. The largest single-seater offered the Air Force, its bullet-shaped fuselage stood so high on tricycle gear that the pilot was raised through the bottom up to the pressurized cockpit by an elevating seat. In emergencies the seat dropped downward on a swinging arm to catapult the pilot clear of the four-bladed propeller. Built of welded magnesium, the XP-54 had excellent pilot's visibility

VULTEE XP-54
Lycoming XH-2470-1, 2300 hp at 25,000'
DIMENSIONS: Span 53'10", Lg. 54'9", Ht. 13', Wing Area 456 sq. ft.
WEIGHT: Empty 15,262 lb., Gross 18,233 lb., Max. 19,335 lb. Fuel 223–395 gal.
PERFORMANCE: Speed—Top 403 mph at 28,500', Cruising 328 mph, Landing 110 mph. Service Ceiling 37,000', Climb 26,000'/17 min. Range 500 miles normal, 850 miles max.   MFR

and two 37-mm guns with 120 rounds mounted in the nose below a pair of .50-caliber guns with 1,000 rounds. Only two prototypes were built.

Flight tests produced only a disappointing 381 mph, far below the 510 mph projected in 1940 and below the 403 mph of the revised specification. Much weight had been added by the high-altitude supercharging and pressurization, as well as by a nose-elevating system added to give more reach to the cannons. A second prototype was flown just once, on May 24, 1944.

Although the Curtiss XP-55 was to have a Continental XIV-1430-3 and do 507 mph, the prototypes were flown with an Allison V-1710-95. After studies on a full-scale wooden flying model flown December 1941 with a 275-hp Menasco, three prototypes were approved July 10, 1942, and the first flown on July 13, 1943.

This prototype was the only one to test a "canard" layout in which the tail assembly was eliminated, the elevators placed at the nose, and the vertical tail surface divided and placed near the tips of a sharply swept-back wing. Like the other pushers, it had tricycle wheels. A dorsal fin above and ventral fin below the engine contained air intakes for the supercharger and radiator, and the three-bladed prop could be jettisoned to make a pilot's bailout safer. Armament consisted of four .50-caliber guns in the nose, and wing racks were provided for two drop tanks or bombs. The XP-55, however, proved 1,000 pounds overweight and disappointing in performance.

The most radical of these pushers was Northrop's XP-56, a tailless interceptor with short fuselage mounted on a swept-back wing. After the prototype was ordered September 26, 1940, the original engine was replaced by an R-2800-29 Wasp cooled by air from wing-root intakes and turning contrarotating propellers behind dorsal and ventral fins. Utilizing welded magnesium construction, the XP-56 had tricycle gear, drooping wingtips with air-operated bellows rudders, and the "elevon" control surfaces used on Northrop flying wings. Armament included two 20-mm guns with 200 rounds and four .50-caliber guns with 1,600 rounds.

A very low-level test hop was made on September 6, 1943, by the prototype, but it was destroyed on October 8. A second XP-56, with larger upper fin, was flown March 23, 1944, but the type was no longer of tactical value.

CURTISS XP-55
Allison V-1710-95, 1275 hp takeoff, 1125 hp at 15,500'
DIMENSIONS: Span 44', Lg. 29'7", Ht. 10'1", Wing Area 235 sq. ft.
WEIGHT: Empty 6354 lb., Gross 7931 lb., Max. 7711 lb. Fuel 110–210 gal.
PERFORMANCE: Speed—Top 277.5 mph at 16,900', Landing 80 mph. Service Ceiling 36,200', Climb 2460'/1 min., 20,000'/7.1 min. Range 635 miles at 296 mph, 1440 miles max.   AF

NORTHROP XP-56
Pratt & Whitney R-2800-29, 2000 hp takeoff, 1800 hp at 19,500'
DIMENSIONS: Span 42'7", Lg. 23'7", Ht. 9'9", Wing Area 306 sq. ft.
WEIGHT: Empty 9879 lb., Gross 12,145 lb. Fuel 320 gal.
PERFORMANCE: Speed—Top 465 mph at 19,500', 417 mph at s. l. Service Ceiling 33,000', Climb 20,700'/7.8 min. Range 445 miles normal, 660 miles max.   MFR

NORTHROP XP-56 (First Prototype)   MFR

Curtiss Developments

Curtiss planned to replace the P-40 with the XP-53, whose specification promised 450 mph with a 1,250-hp Continental XIV-1430-3 and laminar-flow wing. Two prototypes were ordered October 1, 1940, but in January 1941 the Curtiss Model 90 design called for substitution of an imported Merlin V-1650-1 engine, and the aircraft was redesignated XP-60.

On September 18, 1941, the XP-60 was first flown, while the second prototype was used for static tests. A three-bladed propeller headed a neat nose, with the radiator ahead of the low-tapered wing, and the wheels retracted inward of eight .50-caliber wing guns and 2,000 rounds.

An order for 1,950 P-60As powered by Allison V-1710-75s was placed October 31, 1941, but after the United States entered the war, officials had second thoughts about the desirability of interrupting P-40 production at that crucial point. In January 1942 the P-60A program was dropped in favor of more P-40s and some P-47Gs from Curtiss.

For developmental purposes three aircraft labeled XP-60A, XP-60B, and XP-60C were allowed to survive the cut. On November 1, 1942, the XP-60A was flown with a turbosupercharged Allison V-1710-75, a four-bladed propeller, larger radiator, and six .50-caliber wing guns with 1,200 rounds. At first the P-60B was to be similar, with a new supercharger, and the P-60C was to try a Chrysler XIV-2220 like the XP-47H. In September 1942 the P-60C changed to an R-2800-53 radial with contrarotating propellers and four .50-caliber wing guns

CURTISS XP-60
Packard V-1650-1, 1300 hp takeoff, 1120 hp at 19,000'
DIMENSIONS: Span 41'5", Lg. 33'4", Ht. 14'4", Wing Area 275 sq. ft.
WEIGHT: Empty 7010 lb., Gross 9351 lb., Max. 9961 lb. Fuel 135–228 gal.
PERFORMANCE: Speed—Top 380 mph at 20,000', 330 mph at 5150', Landing 85 mph. Service Ceiling 29,000', Climb 20,000'/7.3 min. Range 995 miles/228 gal. MFR

CURTISS XP-60A
Allison V-1710-75, 1425 hp at 25,000'
DIMENSIONS: Span 41'4", Lg. 33'8", Ht. 12'4", Wing Area 275 sq. ft.
WEIGHT: Empty 7806 lb., Gross 9616 lb., Max. 10,160 lb. Fuel 116–200 gal.
PERFORMANCE: Speed—Top 420 mph at 29,000', 324 mph at s. l., Cruising 300 mph. Service Ceiling 35,200', Absolute Ceiling 36,000', Climb 2560'/1 min., 10,000'/4.2 min.
                                                    MFR

CURTISS XP-60C
Pratt & Whitney R-2800-53, 2000 hp at 20,000'
DIMENSIONS: Span 41'4", Lg. 33'11", Ht. 15', Wing Area
  275 sq. ft.
WEIGHT: Empty 8600 lb., Gross 10,525 lb., Max. 10,785
  lb. Fuel 178–225 gal.
PERFORMANCE: Speed—Top 414 mph at 20,350', Landing
  89 mph. Service Ceiling 37,900', Absolute Ceiling
  38,400', Climb 3890'/1 min.   MFR

CURTISS XP-60D   MFR

with 1,000 rounds. This version began flight tests
on January 27, 1943.

In August 1942 the XP-60 was returned to be
rebuilt as the XP-60D, with a V-1650-3, a four-
bladed propeller like the P-51B, and a new vertical
tail, but this aircraft crashed May 6, 1943. Meanwhile, an R-2800-10 with an ordinary four-bladed
propeller was substituted for the P-60B's Allison by
a December 2, 1942, order, and this aircraft was
completed as the XP-60E, first flown on May 26,
1943, with four wing guns.

Another production order for 500 P-60A-1s with
R-2800-10 Wasps was placed in November 1942 but
was cut back in June 1943 when the type proved
inferior to the P-47D and P-51B. Only a single YP-
60E was flown, on July 15, 1944, with an R-2800-
18, six .50-caliber wing guns with 1,602 rounds, an
unbalanced rudder, and a bubble canopy which
made it look much like a P-47D-25.

Another single-seat fighter was developed by
Curtiss during this same period. Designated XP-62
and powered by a turbosupercharged R-3350-17
with contrarotating three-bladed propellers, this big
low-wing monoplane was armed with four to eight
20-mm guns in the wings with 150 rpg. The pressure cabin hatch opened upward instead of sliding

CURTISS XP-60E
Pratt & Whitney R-2800-10, 2000 hp at 20,000'
DIMENSIONS: As XP-60C
WEIGHT: Empty 8574 lb., Gross 10,320 lb., Max. 10,667
  lb. Fuel 178–225 gal.
PERFORMANCE: Speed—Top 410 mph at 20,200', Cruising
  348 mph. Service Ceiling 38,000', Climb 4200'/1 min.,
  10,000'/2.5 min.   MFR

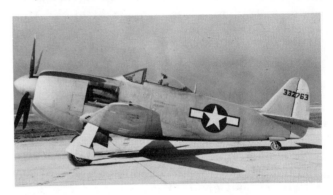

CURTISS YP-60E
Pratt & Whitney R-2800-18, 2100 hp
DIMENSIONS: As XP-60C
WEIGHT: Empty 8285 lb., Gross 10,270 lb., Max. 11,520
  lb. Fuel 178–225 gal.
PERFORMANCE: Speed—Top 405 mph at 24,500'. Service
  Ceiling 34,000', Climb 15,000'/4.8 min.   AF

CURTISS XP-62
Wright R-3350-17, 2300 hp takeoff, 2250 hp at 25,000'
DIMENSIONS: Span 53'8", Lg. 39'6", Ht. 16'3", Wing Area
  420 sq. ft.
WEIGHT: Empty 11,773 lb., Gross 14,660 lb., Max. 16,651
  lb. Fuel 245–384 gal.
PERFORMANCE: Speed—Top 448 mph at 27,000', 358 mph
  at 5000', Cruising 340 mph, Landing 85 mph. Service
  Ceiling 35,700', Climb 15,000'/6.6 min. Range 900
  miles normal, 1500 miles max.   MFR

back, and a long dorsal fin led back to the rudder.

Authority for the purchase of the XP-62 was dated May 16, 1941, a contract was approved June 27, and the mockup was inspected in December. A letter contract dated May 25, 1942, scheduled 100 P-62As, but R-3350 engine production was so involved with supplying B-29 bombers that the P-62 could not supplant the P-40 in production. Without high priorities, the P-62A became just another fighter that never quite made it when the project was canceled July 27, 1942. Only the XP-62 was completed, making its first flight July 21, 1943.

Lockheed XP-58 "Chain Lightning"

The last of 1940s fighter projects to be flown was the Lockheed XP-58, the only two-seater begun that year and the heaviest fighter built during the war. This type began with a Lockheed proposal in May 1940 for a twin-engine, two-place convoy fighter whose tactical role was comparable to the Messerschmitt Bf 110 then active in Europe.

On October 14 two XP-58 prototypes were ordered, scheduled to use Pratt & Whitney X-1800 (H-2600) liquid-cooled engines also planned for the XP-49. In December the 2,350-hp Wright R-2160s were substituted, since the earlier units did not materialize, and two remote-controlled turrets were added. By 1941 the specification called for a long-range fighter for escorting bombers, basically a bigger Lightning with 35,559 pounds gross. Carrying two 20-mm and eight .50-caliber guns, it was expected to do 450 mph.

LOCKHEED XP-58
Allison V-3420-11, -13, 2600 hp takeoff, 3000 hp at 25,000'
DIMENSIONS: Span 70', Lg. 49'5", Ht. 13'7", Wing Area 600 sq. ft.
WEIGHT: Empty 31,624 lb., Gross 39,192 lb., Max. 43,020 lb. Fuel 656–760 gal. (1690 gal. max.).
PERFORMANCE: Speed—Top 436 mph at 25,000', Cruising 274 mph. Service Ceiling 38,400', Absolute Ceiling 39,975', Climb 2660'/1 min., 25,000'/12 min. Range 1150 miles/650 gal., 1250 miles/800 gal., 2650 miles max.   MFR

In September 1942 the XP-58's mission was changed to antishipping instead of convoy work, and in April 1943 Allison V-3420s were substituted for the Wrights. Even so, no production was scheduled, and even the second prototype was canceled, leaving the XP-58, finally flown on June 6, 1944, the sole example of the type.

Looking much like an enlarged P-38 except for four-bladed propellers, double wheels on the tricycle gear, and a gunner at the rear of the center nacelle, the XP-58 had a remote-controlled turret above and below the crew's position. Two .50-caliber guns were in each turret with 300 rpg, while the nose contained four 37-mm fixed guns with 250 rpg. Four 1,000 pound bombs could be carried, or the nose armament replaced by one 75-mm and two .50-caliber guns. Too heavy to maneuver against enemy fighters, the XP-58 might have been useful for attack missions.

The Night-Fighter Problem

In spite of the common division of European offensive aircraft into day- and night-bomber categories, few night attacks were made in the early months of World War II. Far less accurate than daylight bombing, night bombing was unnecessary for the Germans since they had air supremacy, and considered impolitic for the Allies. As more vigorous air operations developed in 1940, heavy losses on daytime sorties led Britain's Bomber Command to concentrate on nocturnal raids. Their enemies began the Battle of Britain in the daytime, but when losses rose past a tolerable figure despite fighter escort, the Luftwaffe turned more and more to night work.

Precision was still lacking, but as unhappy Coventry was to learn, increasing tonnage volume could severely hurt industrial targets. And difficult to find at night as a factory might be, it was much less so than a moving airplane. The speedy interceptors which served London so well in sunshine groped about in darkness as Göring's bombers unloaded, and only occasional searchlight illumination gave opportunity for attack.

The perfection of radio-location equipment light enough to be airborne gave the fighter a better chance, and Britain developed a specialized night fighter large enough to carry the radar and its operator plus armament sufficient to destroy any bomber. While speed and climb could not match that of a single-seater, enough margin over bomber performance was required to insure successful interception. Other requirements included a moderate landing speed for safe operation from small, blacked-out fields, and endurance enough to permit persistence in ambush or pursuit.

Such weight and relatively low-wing loading requirements would limit severely a single-engine aircraft's performance, and therefore the first successful plane for this work was a development of the Blenheim twin-engine bomber. First flown in July 1939, the Bristol Beaufighter first scored against the Germans in November 1940 and became the most important British night fighter. Powered by two Bristol Hercules radial engines, its pilot had good visibility forward, while the radar operator sat within the rear fuselage. Armament included four 20-mm guns firing forward from the lower part of the nose and six .30-caliber guns in the wings.

BRISTOL BEAUFIGHTER (RAF)   MFR

The U.S. Army expressed interest in a Northrop design for a night fighter offered in November 1940, and two XP-61 prototypes were ordered January 30, 1941, followed by 13 YP-61s on March 10. A Radiation Laboratory established at the Massachusetts Institute of Technology undertook the construction of AI (airborne interception) radar.

During the time required for the Northrop design to enter service, another American plane was pressed into night-fighter duty. In 1940 the British were receiving Douglas Boston attack bombers whose admirable agility suggested a type that could function as a night fighter. The Boston's endurance and tricycle gear immediately made it a safer night operator than most, and when the nose enclosure was blocked in and replaced by 12 .30-caliber guns, and exhaust dampers and black paint added, it became the Havoc night fighter.

Other Havocs operated as night "intruders," which attempted to ambush enemy bombers over their home fields. Yet another modification was the "Turbinlight" of 1942; over 70 Havocs were fitted with a 1,400-amp searchlight to be used after the Havoc closed within minimum range of its AI IV radar. A beam of 30° divergence illuminated an area 150 yards wide at one mile range, enabling accompanying conventional fighters to fire at the target. The powerful lamp was fitted behind an armored glass disk three feet in diameter and fed by a ton of batteries in the bomb bay. This system was a waste

of good aircraft, for not a single German bomber was destroyed.

In the United States an early airborne radar set was installed in the first Douglas A-20, which became the XP-70 when delivered October 1, 1941. Sixty of the A-20s were planned as high-altitude attack bombers, but delivery of the supercharged engines had been delayed and low-altitude operations seemed the rule for light bombers. On October 15 the remaining A-20s were ordered converted to P-70 night fighters, with imported AI IV radar whose antennae included the arrowlike transmitter in the nose and receivers on each side and on the port wing. The radar operator sat in the rear cockpit, while four 20-mm guns on a tray below the bomb bay had 60 rpg.

Powered by R-2600-11 Cyclones, the first P-70 was delivered in April 1942, and 58 from June to September. Additional Havocs included 13 P-70A-1s and 26 P-70A-2s converted from A-20Cs and A-20Gs, with six .50-caliber nose guns instead of the 20-mm weapons, SCR-540 radar, and R-2600-23 Cyclones. Another 65 P-70A-2s were converted at modification centers, as well as 105 P-70B trainers converted from A-20G/J aircraft with an SCR-720

DOUGLAS P-70
Wright R-2600-11, 1600 hp takeoff, 1275 hp at 12,000'
DIMENSIONS: Span 61'4", Lg. 47'7", Ht. 17'7", Wing Area 464 sq. ft.
WEIGHT: Empty 16,031 lb., Gross 21,264 lb. Fuel 600 gal.
PERFORMANCE: Speed—Top 329 mph at 14,000', Cruising 270 mph, Landing 97 mph. Service Ceiling 28,250', Climb 12,000'/8 min. Range 1060 miles normal, 1460 miles max.   AF

DOUGLAS P-70A-2   AF

radar in the nose. Six .50-caliber guns were in blisters on each side of the first P-70B-1, while the others could be fitted instead with a gun tray under the fuselage.

Since the Air Force had no night-fighter units when it entered the war, a training organization was established at Orlando, Florida, and the P-70s gathered there for the 12 squadrons formed in 1943. In September 1942, 25 P-70s were deployed to Hawaii for the 6th Night Fighter Squadron, which did have a detachment on Guadalcanal from February to September 1943. While P-70s were flown by three squadrons sent to the Pacific, they were rather unsuccessful in combat (only two kills) due to their poor performance at altitude. Most P-70s remained in the United States, to be passed on to six more squadrons formed in 1944. When four night-fighter squadrons were sent to North Africa in 1943 for the Twelfth Air Force, they used Bristol Beaufort VIF fighters obtained under reverse lend-lease.

Production of the Northrop P-61 began with a 150-plane contract approved September 17, 1941, which was increased to 560 by a new order approved February 26, 1942. The complicated aircraft was slow to appear, for while the first XP-61 was flown May 21, 1942, the first YP-61 was not delivered until August 6, 1943, and the first P-61A-1 was accepted in October.

The first American night fighter designed for this specific purpose, the P-61 was as big as a medium bomber, with two 2,000-hp Pratt & Whitney R-2800-10 Wasps, twin rudders supported by tail booms, and tricycle gear. The central nacelle had radar in the nose, a pilot's cabin with a gunner above and behind him, and a radar operator's enclosure. Retractable ailerons permitted flaps the full length of the wing's trailing edge. An SCR-720 radar transmitter designed for the P-61 had a rotating reflector dish in the Plexiglas (or Fiberglas) nose, permitting location of targets ten miles away, depending on altitude and conditions.

Armament consisted of four 20-mm fixed guns, with 600 rounds, in a bulge below the fuselage and four .50-caliber guns, with 1,600 rounds, in a top remote-controlled turret. The latter guns were usually fired forward, like the cannon, by the pilot, but they could be unlocked and aimed by either gunner as flexible defense for the upper hemisphere. Only the first 37 P-61A-1s had top turrets, for tail-buffeting troubles led to their omission on later ships.

Forty-five P-61A-1s were followed by 35 P-61A-5s with provision for water injection, 100 P-61A-10s with the R-2800-65 and 2,040 war-emergency hp, and 20 P-61A-11s with fixtures for two 310-gallon drop tanks or bombs. Most of these entered service with two crewmen and bore the glossy paint that went with the Black Widow's official name.

NORTHROP XP-61
Pratt & Whitney R-2800-10, 2000 hp
DIMENSIONS: Span 66', Lg. 48'11", Ht. 14'8", Wing Area 663 sq. ft.
WEIGHT: Empty 19,245 lb., Gross 25,150 lb., Max. 28,870 lb. Fuel 540–640 gal.
PERFORMANCE: Speed—Top 370 mph at 20,900', Cruising 200 mph, Landing 95 mph. Service Ceiling 33,100', Climb 2900'/1 min., 20,000'/9 min. Range 1200 miles normal, 1450 miles max.   AF

NORTHROP YP-61
Pratt & Whitney R-2800-10, 2000 hp
DIMENSIONS: As XP-61
WEIGHT: Empty 21,910 lb., Gross 27,950 lb., Max. 28,830 lb. Fuel 540–640 gal.
PERFORMANCE: As XP-61   MFR

Delivery of 450 P-61Bs with several mechanical improvements began by August 1944. The P-61B-10 had underwing fittings for four 1,600-pound bombs, or drop tanks of 165- or 300-gallon size. Turrets were omitted on the first 200 (P-61B-1 to P-61B-10) but were restored on the rest (P-61B-15 to P-61B-20), since the buffeting condition had been eliminated.

Despite its size, the Black Widow was remarkably maneuverable. Its first victories were won by the 6th Night Fighter Squadron, which landed on Saipan with P-61As on June 21, 1944, scored its first victory June 30, and a second July 6. Ten P-61 squadrons were deployed against the Japanese Empire by March 1945, two entered combat from England in July 1944, and four night-fighter squadrons served the Twelfth Air Force. After the war, a dozen P-61Bs were used by the Marines as F2T-1 trainers.

The P-61C appeared in July 1945 with turbosupercharged R-2800-73s offering 2,800 hp for war emergencies. Forty-one were completed before V-

NORTHROP P-61A
Pratt & Whitney R-2800-65, 2000 hp takeoff, 2040 hp WE
DIMENSIONS: As XP-61
WEIGHT: Empty 20,965 lb., Gross 27,600 lb. (29,240 lb. with turret on). Fuel 550–640 gal.
PERFORMANCE: Speed—Top 372 (369) mph at 17,600′, 333 mph at s. l., Stalling 85 mph. Service Ceiling 33,700′ (32,100′), Climb 2925′ (2610′)/1 min., 20,000′/8.5 (9.6) min. Range 1210 miles at 200 mph.   MFR

NORTHROP P-61B-15
Pratt & Whitney R-2800-65, 2000 hp takeoff, 2040 hp WE
DIMENSIONS: Span 66′, Lg. 49′7″, Ht. 14′8″, Wing Area 664 sq. ft.
WEIGHT: Empty 22,000 lb., Gross 29,700 lb., Max. 38,000 lb. Fuel 550–1880 gal.
PERFORMANCE: Speed—Top 366 mph at 20,000′, Landing 93 mph. Service Ceiling 33,100′, Climb 20,000′/12 min. Range 3000 miles max. ferry.   MFR

NORTHROP P-61C
Pratt & Whitney R-2800-73, 2100 hp takeoff, 2800 hp WE
DIMENSIONS: As P-61B
WEIGHT: Empty 24,000 lb., Gross 30,600 lb., Max. 40,300 lb. Fuel 640–1880 gal.
PERFORMANCE: Speed—Top 430 mph at 30,000′, Cruising 307 mph, Landing 87 mph. Service Ceiling 41,000′, Climb 30,000′/14.6 min. Range 330 miles at top speed, 415 miles/4000 lbs. bombs, 1725 miles at 195 mph.
                MFR

NORTHROP XP-61D
Pratt & Whitney R-2800-77, 2100 hp takeoff, 2800 hp at 30,000'
DIMENSIONS: As XP-61
WEIGHT: Empty 23,205 lb., Gross 29,850 lb., Max. 39,715 lb. Fuel 528–1880 gal.
PERFORMANCE: Speed—Top 430 mph at 30,000', Landing 90 mph. Service Ceiling 43,000', Climb 30,000'/13.5 min. Range 1050 miles/528 gal. at 197 mph, 3000 miles max.   MFR

NORTHROP XP-61E
Pratt & Whitney R-2800-65, 2000 hp takeoff
DIMENSIONS: Span 66', Lg. 49'7", Ht. 13'5", Wing Area 664 sq. ft.
WEIGHT: Empty 21,350 lb., Gross 31,425 lb., Max. 40,181 lb. Fuel 1158–2398 gal.
PERFORMANCE: Speed—Top 376 mph at 17,000'. Service Ceiling 30,000', Climb 20,000'/13 min. Range 2250 miles normal, 3750 miles ferry.   MFR

J Day ended production. Two P-61As refitted with R-2800-77 engines and different turbosuperchargers became XP-61Ds in November 1944.

Two XP-61E prototypes were converted by April 1945 from P-61Bs with R-2800-65 Wasps. This was a long-range day fighter with radar and turret removed to enable a smaller, more streamlined fuselage. The two-man crew sat under a bubble canopy ahead of a fuselage fuel tank, while four .50-caliber nose guns supplemented the usual four 20-mm belly guns. This model didn't reach production in wartime, but 36 F-15A reconnaissance versions were built in 1946.

The 706 Black Widows served adequately during the war's last year as the standard AAF night fighter. By then the Axis was on the defensive and no saturation raids were met. Generally, P-61s fought alone on their sorties, ambushing individual enemy raiders.

America's First Jets

While visiting England in April 1941, the U.S. Air Force Commanding General, Henry H. Arnold, saw the Gloster E28/39, which made the first British jet flight on May 15 of that year. He returned to the United States with details of its Whittle engine, and on September 4 asked General Electric, which had learned much from turbosupercharger experience about the heat-resistant alloys necessary for whirling turbine blades, to build copies of the jet engine. The following day Bell Aircraft, because of its proximity to GE's Schenectady plant, was assigned construction of three twin-jet prototypes. For security reasons the first jet airframes were designated XP-59A and the engines the "I" series, in the hope of disguising them as the canceled XP-59 pusher and General Electric superchargers.

The XP-59A contract was approved October 3, 1941, and work went ahead with great secrecy. Muroc Dry Lake, in California, was selected for the initial flights for the purpose of concealment. This site later became Edwards Air Force Base, which has replaced Wright Field as the center of Air Force flight testing. The prototype was secretly shipped across the country from Buffalo by train, and on October 1, 1942, a company pilot made taxi runs that inadvertently became short hops. An Air Force pilot made the first official flight the next day.

America's first jet fighter was a single-seat, mid-wing monoplane sitting low on tricycle landing gear and was powered by a General Electric I-A unit of 1,400-pound thrust under each wing root. Two 37-mm guns with 88 rounds were mounted in the nose. Top speed of 404 mph at 25,000 feet was below expectations, but at least the principle of jet propulsion had been demonstrated.

Thirteen YP-59As had been ordered in March 1942, and the first was delivered in July 1943 with an improved jet unit called the I-16 (later J31). The third YP-59A went to Britain in September in trade for a Gloster Meteor, while the U.S. Navy got the eighth and ninth in December. These aircraft had the same guns as the prototypes, but the last four YP-59As had the installation standard on later Airacomets: one 37-mm with 44 rounds and three .50-caliber guns with 600 rounds.

Limitations in the Airacomet's performance and a tendency toward "snaking" made it a bad gun platform and confined its use to orientation experience with jet flying. On October 30, 1943, the 100-

BELL YP-59A

General Electric I-16 (J31), 1650 lbs.

DIMENSIONS: Span 45′6″, Lg. 38′2″, Ht. 12′, Wing Area 385 sq. ft.

WEIGHT: Empty 7626 lb., Gross 10,532 lb., Max. 12,562 lb. Fuel 290–590 gal.

PERFORMANCE: Speed—Top 409 mph at 35,000′, 350 mph at s. l., Cruising 314 mph, Landing 80 mph. Service Ceiling 43,200′, Climb 2970′/1 min., 36,000′/20.4 min. Range 640 miles normal.   MFR

BELL P-59A

General Electric J31-GE-5, 2000 lbs.

DIMENSIONS: Span 45′6″, Lg. 38′10″, Ht. 12′4″, Wing Area 385 sq. ft.

WEIGHT: Empty 7950 lb., Gross 10,822 lb., Max. 13,000 lb. Fuel 290–590 gal.

PERFORMANCE: Speed—Top 413 mph at 30,000′, 380 mph at 5,000′, Cruising 375 mph. Service Ceiling 46,200′, Climb 10,000′/3.2 min., 30,000′/15.5 min. Range 375 miles at 400 mph, 400 miles at 375 mph, 550 miles at 308 mph.   MFR

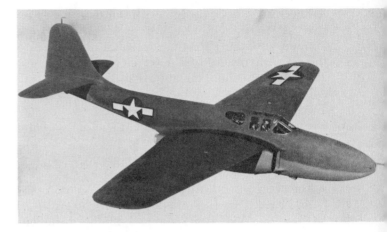

BELL XP-59A

General Electric I-A, 1400 lbs.

DIMENSIONS: Span 45′6″, Lg. 38′2″, Ht. 12′4″, Wing Area 385 sq. ft.

WEIGHT: Empty 7320 lb., Max. 12,562 lb. Fuel 570–850 gal.

PERFORMANCE: Speed—Top 404 mph at 25,000′. Absolute Ceiling 45,756′.   MFR

BELL P-59B

General Electric J31-GE-5, 2000 lbs.

DIMENSIONS: As P-59A

WEIGHT: Empty 8165 lb., Gross 11,040 lb., Max. 13,700 lb. Fuel 356–656 gal.

PERFORMANCE: As P-59A, but range 375 miles at 400 mph, 525 miles at 371 mph, 950 miles at 304 mph.   MFR

plane production order was cut in half. The first 20 P-59As were delivered after August 1944, with jet units now designated J31-GE-3, and 30 P-59Bs were completed by May 1945. The latter model had J31-GE-5s and 66 gallons more of internal fuel.

Although not suitable as a weapon, the Airacomet gave useful training to future P-80 pilots, and it is notable that there were no test losses of XP or YP aircraft in spite of the pioneering nature of these trials. Nevertheless, Air Force leaders would have been more uncomfortable had they known what they learned later—that Germany not only had developed jet planes but had one of combat quality going into mass production.

The world's first jet flight, in fact, had been made on August 27, 1939, by the Heinkel He 178, and the He 280 twin-jet fighter flew on April 5, 1941. Messerschmitt's Me 262 flew with jets on July 27, 1942, and production deliveries of this 540-mph interceptor began in March 1944. Before long it became the first jet fighter to be used in action, and

the United States knew it had fallen behind again in fighter design.

Bell Kingcobra

Although nine new single-seat fighter types were flown in the two years following America's entry into the war, only the P-63, successor to the Bell Airacobra, reached mass production. Built mainly for lend-lease to the Soviet Union, the P-63 Kingcobra did not match the Mustang and Thunderbolt in high-altitude performance, but was considered good at low-level fighting.

The Kingcobra's design evolution began in February 1941 with the XP-39E project, proposing a laminar-flow wing for the Airacobra. Prototypes of the XP-39E ordered in April were flown early in 1942 with the laminar airfoil, square-cut tail, and Allison V-1710-47 engine later used on the XP-63. Two XP-63 prototypes were ordered on June 27, 1941, and the first flew on December 7, 1942. Damage ended tests the next month, and a second prototype flown February 5, 1943, crashed the following May.

Fortunately, a third prototype, the XP-63A, had been ordered in June 1942 and flew on April 26, 1943, with a V-1710-93 giving 1,325 hp for takeoff and 1,150 hp at 22,400 feet. The Kingcobra's general arrangement was similar to the P-39's, with the Allison behind the pilot, tricycle gear, and a nose armament of one 37-mm cannon and two .50-caliber guns, but the larger P-63 could be distinguished by its taller tail, wider wings, and four-bladed propel-

BELL XP-63
Allison V-1710-47, 1325 hp takeoff, 1150 hp at 22,140′
DIMENSIONS: Span 38′4″, Lg. 32′8″, Ht. 11′5″, Wing Area 248 sq. ft.
WEIGHT: Empty 6054 lb., Gross 7525 lb. Fuel 100–211 gal.
PERFORMANCE: Speed—Top 407 mph.   MFR

BELL P-63A-9
Allison V-1710-95, 1325 hp takeoff, 1150 hp at 22,400′
DIMENSIONS: Span 38′4″, Lg. 32′8″, Ht. 12′7″, Wing Area 248 sq. ft.
WEIGHT: Empty 6375 lb., Gross 8800 lb., Max. 10,500 lb. Fuel 126–451 gal.
PERFORMANCE: Speed—Top 408 mph at 24,450′, Cruising 378 mph, Landing 100 mph. Service Ceiling 43,000′, Climb 25,000′/7.3 min. Range 390 miles/100 gal. at 378 mph, 450 miles/500 lbs. bombs, 2575 miles ferry. MFR

ler. The load included 88 pounds of armor, 100 gallons of internal fuel, and provisions for a 500-pound bomb or a 75-gallon drop tank beneath the fuselage.

Deliveries of production aircraft, ordered September 29, 1942, began in October 1943, and blocks P-63A-1 to P-63A-10 introduced successive increases in armor and external loads. Besides the nose cannon and twin .50s, a .50-caliber gun was installed below each wing, with a total of 900 rounds for all four machine guns. The ammunition supply for the 37-mm gun was increased from 30 rounds in early models to 58 in the P-63A-9. A 175-gallon ferry tank fitted flush under the belly could be replaced by a 500-pound bomb or 75-gallon drop tank, while Kingcobras from P-63A-6 on had outboard wing racks for additional drop tanks or two more 500-pound bombs. Armor weight increased to 179 pounds on the A-5, 189 pounds on the A-8, 199 pounds on the A-9, and 266 pounds on the A-10.

After completion of 1,725 P-63As, acceptances began in January 1945 on 1,227 P-63Cs which had a V-1710-117, an extension fin under the tail, internal fuel capacity of 107 gallons, and 201 pounds of armor.

An improved version of the Kingcobra appeared in 1945 with a V-1710-109 and modified wings. The first, a single P-63D, sported a bubble canopy but 13 heavier P-63Es whose tests began in May had the standard cockpit and equipment. A contract for 2,930 more was canceled by the end of lend-lease. A tall tail and the V-1710-135 distinguished the only example of the P-63F.

Noncombat P-63s were reworked for tests of a V-shaped "butterfly" tail, swept-back wings, and a second cockpit for instrument training. Nor should one forget the target versions (RP-63A and RP-63C) built to train gunners in bombers. Combat equipment was removed and a 1,488-pound extra-thick skin applied to shatter frangible bullets fired by student gunners. A red nose light blinked like a pinball machine when hits were felt. Three hundred were built during the war, followed by 32 RP-63Gs in 1945–46.

Bell built 3,303 Kingcobras, including target and experimental types, and 2,421 were lend-leased to the Soviet Union. Except for the three P-63As shipped to northern Russia, all were flown via Alaska to Siberia, resulting in the loss of 21 planes on the way before they were turned over to Soviet pilots at Ladd Field.

Two P-63As went to the RAF, the first in May 1944, and 100 P-63Cs went to France. While the first P-63As went to the AAF, which had 339 on hand by August 1944, they were used only for operational training, except for the RP-63 target aircraft received later.

BELL P-63C
Allison V-1710-117, 1510 hp takeoff, 1100 hp at 27,000'
DIMENSIONS: As P-63A
WEIGHT: Empty 6800 lb., Gross 8800 lb., Max. 10,700 lb. Fuel 107–393 gal.
PERFORMANCE: Speed—Top 410 mph at 25,000', Cruising 356 mph, Landing 115 mph. Service Ceiling 38,600', Climb 25,000'/8.6 min. Range 320 miles/500 lbs. bombs, 2100 miles ferry.   MFR

BELL P-63D
Allison V-1710-109, 1425 hp takeoff, 1100 hp at 28,000'
DIMENSIONS: Span 39'2", Lg. 32'8", Ht. 11'2", Wing Area 255 sq. ft.
WEIGHT: Empty 7076 lb., Gross 8740 lb., Max. 11,000 lb. Fuel 107–393 gal.
PERFORMANCE: Speed—Top 437 mph at 30,000', Cruising 188 mph, Landing 91 mph. Service Ceiling 39,000', Climb 28,000'/11.2 min. Range 700 miles/107 gal., 950 miles/500 lbs. bombs, 2000 miles ferry.   MFR

BELL P-63E
Allison V-1710-109, 1425 hp takeoff, 1100 hp at 28,000'
DIMENSIONS: Span 39'2", Lg. 32'8", Ht. 12'9", Wing Area 255 sq. ft.
WEIGHT: Empty 7300 lb., Gross 9400 lb., Max. 11,200 lb. Fuel 107–421 gal.
PERFORMANCE: Speed—Top 410 mph at 25,000', Cruising 188 mph, Landing 117 mph. Climb 25,000'/7.6 min. Range 725 miles/500 lbs. bombs, 2150 miles max. MFR

BELL P-63F   MFR

Later Wartime Prototypes

Experimental fighters discussed thus far were ordered by the end of fiscal year 1940 (June 30, 1941), the federal fiscal year in which Air Force expansion gathered impetus toward wartime goals. Although fiscal year 1941 added more fighter projects, production programs received higher priorities, and experimental ships lagged. The Pearl Harbor attack put further stress on service-type deliveries and only unusually high priority prototypes like the XP-59A jet and XP-61 night fighter were finished in less than 18 months. Other projects drifted for two or three years, with the longest gestation being the XP-58's 44 months.

An example of this delay is the twin-engine single-seat monoplane that began the career of the now well-known McDonnell Aircraft Corporation of St. Louis. Assigned the XP-67 designation on July 29, 1941, two prototypes were approved October 29, 1941, and the first wasn't flown until January 6, 1944. After a generally unsatisfactory performance, the XP-67 burned on September 6, and the second example was canceled.

An airfoil-shaped fuselage and center section gave the XP-67 a unique appearance. It contained large fuel tanks, a pressurized cockpit, tricycle gear, and six 37-mm M-4 fixed cannons. Power plants were Continental XIV-1430s driving four-bladed propellers and utilizing their exhausts for extra thrust. Unfortunately, these engines delivered only 1,060 of the 1,350 hp expected, and left the XP-67 with an excessive takeoff run. Instead of the anticipated 448 mph top speed, only 405 mph at 25,000 feet was achieved.

The next two single-seat fighter designs were begun in July 1941 around the proposed 2,350-hp Wright R-2160 Tornado, a 42-cylinder, six-row radial with contrarotating propellers. Vultee's XP-68 was similar to its XP-54 pusher, but the Republic XP-69 had the engine behind the pilot, with an extension shaft to the nose. An air intake for cooling was placed under the fuselage, and a pressurized

McDONNELL XP-67
Continental XIV-1430-17, -19, 1350 hp takeoff, 1150 hp
　at 25,000'
DIMENSIONS: Span 55', Lg. 44'9", Ht. 15'9", Wing Area
　414 sq. ft.
WEIGHT: Empty 17,745 lb., Gross 22,114 lb., Max. 25,400
　lb. Fuel 280–735 gal.
PERFORMANCE: Speed—Top 405 mph at 25,000' (on test),
　Cruising 270 mph, Landing 93 mph. Service Ceiling
　37,400', Absolute Ceiling 38,000', Climb 2600'/1 min.,
　25,000'/17 min. Range 2384 miles max.　　　　AMC

REPUBLIC XP-69 (Mockup)
Wright R-2160-3, 2350 hp
DIMENSIONS: Span 51'8", Lg. 51'6", Ht. 17', Wing Area
　505 sq. ft.
WEIGHT: Empty 15,595 lb., Gross 18,655 lb., Max. 26,164
　lb. Fuel 240–700 gal. (1300 gal. ferry)
PERFORMANCE: (Estimated) Speed—Top 450 mph at 35,-
　000', Cruising 260 mph. Service Ceiling 48,900', Climb
　35,000'/20 min. Range 780 miles normal, 3000 miles
　max.　　　　MFR

cockpit and laminar wing were planned. Proposed armament was two 37-mm and four .50-caliber wing guns.

Neither type was completed, as the XP-68 was canceled November 22, 1941, and while the XP-69 reached mockup inspection in June 1942, it was canceled May 11, 1943.

As big as a bomber, the Curtiss XP-71 was to have two turbosupercharged 3,450-hp R-4360-13 Wasp Majors turning contrarotating pusher propellers, a pressurized cockpit for two, and a big 75-mm gun in the nose with two 37-mm weapons. It was canceled August 26, 1943, but a photo of the wind-tunnel model is included to show what the largest American fighter (82-foot span) would have looked like.

Pratt & Whitney's Wasp Major engine made better progress than the other big power plants of the time and had been chosen for the Republic XP-72 interceptor. When this engine seemed ready, two prototypes were ordered June 18, 1943, and were similar in appearance to the P-47 except for enlarged landing gear, an air scoop under the fuselage, and a gear-driven supercharger. An R-4360-13, four-bladed propeller, and six .50-caliber wing guns were fitted to the XP-72, which was flown February 2, 1944, while the second one was flown June 26 with an R-4360-19 and six-bladed contraprop. A plan to build 100 production P-72s was dropped when jet propulsion provided faster interceptors.

In 1942 General Motors engineers planned a fighter to utilize the V-3420-19 of that company's Allison engine division. A proposal sent to the Matériel Division in September by designer Don R. Berlin resulted in a letter contract by October for two prototypes to be built in Detroit. In order to assemble prototypes as fast as possible, spare parts from aircraft already in production were brought to Detroit. Tail surfaces from the Douglas Dauntless, outer wings from the Curtiss P-40, and landing gear

from the Vought Corsair were joined to a fuselage in which the big engine behind the pilot, Airacobra-style, drove two co-axial, three-bladed props in the nose. Since this conglomeration was supposed to win the war, historian James Fahey claimed that P-73 and P-74 were skipped to give the plane "a good symbolic number. French 75 in World War I, P-75 in World War II."

Even before the XP-75-GM began flight tests, plans were approved June 7, 1943, to produce 2,500 P-75As at General Motors Fisher Body plant in Cleveland. These ships had V-3420-23s, and specifications calling for top speeds of 434 mph at 20,000 feet and 389 mph at sea level. Armament included four .50-caliber synchronized nose guns with 300 rpg, up to six .50-caliber wing guns with 235 rpg, and two 1,000-pound bombs. The main order was preceded by six XP-75A-GC preproduction prototypes built at Cleveland, which differed from the XP-75-GM in terms of a modified tail and wing tips, a bubble canopy, and a V-3420-23.

Flight tests started November 17, 1943, showed the XP-75 suffering from instability, low rate of roll, poor spinning characteristics, and trouble with the engine, (actually two V-1710s joined side by side). Redesign of the six Cleveland prototypes improved things somewhat but spoiled the quick-production advantage of the original components.

Needing long-range fighters, the Air Force expected to get the first P-75A-1 in May 1944 and have 586 by the end of October. The first production "Fisher Eagle" was not flown until September 15, proved to be 30 mph below the guaranteed speed, and had a fatal crash October 10. The P-75A program was terminated October 27 after the completion of only six aircraft. Over $50 million had been spent by the government, but fortunately the P-51s were solving the long-range fighter problem.

The last propeller-driven single-seat fighter prototype built for the Air Force, apart from P-47 and P-51 developments, was also the smallest and lightest type flown since the P-29. Inspired by the maneuverability of Japan's Zero fighter and the shortage of strategic metals, Bell's XP-77 was a lightweight single-seater of wooden construction. Designed to beat both the metal shortage and the Zero, the XP-77's procurement was authorized May 16, 1942, and after inspection of the mockup in September, six prototypes were approved October 10, 1942.

The only all-wood American fighter, the XP-77 had a 520-hp air-cooled, inline Ranger XV-770-7 in the nose with a 20-mm gun firing through the propeller shaft. Two .50-caliber synchronized guns and a 325-pound bomb were included in the armament. A sharply tapered low-wing, tricycle landing gear, two-bladed propeller, and plastic canopy also distinguished the little Bell.

CURTISS XP-71 (model)
Pratt & Whitney R-4360-13, 3450 hp takeoff
DIMENSIONS: Span 82'3", Lg. 61'10", Ht. 19', Wing Area 602 sq. ft.
WEIGHT: Empty 31,060 lb., Gross 39,950 lb., Max. 46,950 lb. Fuel 1940 gal.
PERFORMANCE: Speed—Top 428 mph at 25,000', Landing 97 mph. Service Ceiling 40,000', Climb 25,000'/12.5 min. Range 3000 miles.   MFR

REPUBLIC XP-72
Pratt & Whitney R-4360-13, 3450 hp
DIMENSIONS: Span 40'11", Lg. 36'7", Ht. 16', Wing Area 300 sq. ft.
WEIGHT: Empty 11,475 lb., Gross 14,414 lb., Max. 17,492 lb. Fuel 535–755 gal.
PERFORMANCE: Speed—Top 490 mph at 25,000', Cruising 300 mph, Landing 104 mph. Service Ceiling 42,000', Climb 20,000'/5 min. Range 1200 miles normal, 1330 miles max.   MFR

GENERAL MOTORS XP-75-GM
Allison V-3420-19, 2600 hp takeoff
DIMENSIONS: Span 49'1", Lg. 41'6", Ht. 15'6", Wing Area 342 sq. ft.
WEIGHT: Empty 11,495 lb., Gross 13,807 lb., Max. 18,210 lb. Fuel 535–830 gal.
PERFORMANCE: Speed—Top 433 mph at 20,000', Cruising 314 mph, Landing 88 mph. Service Ceiling 36,400', Absolute Ceiling 39,500', Climb 4200'/1 min., 20,000'/5.5 min. Range 2050 miles/535 gal., 3500 miles max.   AMC

Delayed by trouble with wood assembly, the contract was cut back in August 1943 to two aircraft, the first flown on April 1, 1944. The basic concept that a small, maneuverable fighter could be produced of nonstrategic materials at less than average cost and time was not borne out. Performance fell below the 350 mph estimated, and a low-speed fighter that cannot force an enemy to do battle does not suit offensive combat tactics.

BELL XP-77
Ranger XV-70-7, 520 hp takeoff, 670 hp WE
DIMENSIONS: Span 27′6″, Lg. 22′10″, Ht. 8′2″, Wing Area 100 sq. ft.
WEIGHT: Empty 2855 lb., Gross 3583 lb., Max. 3940 lb. Fuel 52–90 gal.
PERFORMANCE: Speed—Top 330 mph at 4000′, 328 mph at 12,600′, Landing 92 mph. Service Ceiling 30,100′, Climb 3600′/1 min., 9000′/3.7 min. Range 284 miles at 305 mph.   MFR

GENERAL MOTORS XP-75A-GC   AF

GENERAL MOTORS P-75A-GC
Allison V-1710-23, 2600 hp takeoff, 2300 hp at 20,000′
DIMENSIONS: Span 49′4″, Lg. 41′4″, Ht. 15′6″, Wing Area 347 sq. ft.
WEIGHT: Empty 11,255 lb., Gross 17,875 lb., Max. 19,420 lb. Fuel 210–638 gal. (858 gal. max.).
PERFORMANCE: Speed—Top 404 mph at 20,000′, Cruising 250 mph, Landing 87 mph. Service Ceiling 38,000′, Climb 20,000′/5.8 min. Range 1150 miles normal, 3150 miles/638 gal., 3850 miles max.   PMB

Chapter 18
Navy Patrol Bombers

The Big Boats

Perfection of patrol types capable of safely flying to overseas bases in Alaska, Hawaii, the Philippines, or the Canal Zone was viewed as the major problem facing American flying-boat designers. Bureau of Aeronautics engineers planned a 100-foot span monoplane that represented a big step toward this capability, and on February 28, 1928, ordered Consolidated Aircraft, then in Buffalo, New York, to build a prototype.

First flown January 10, 1929, the XPY-1 had two 450-hp Pratt & Whitney R-1340-38 Wasps suspended on struts between a fabric-covered, metal-frame wing and an all-metal single-step hull with five open cockpits. Isaac M. Laddon designed the first Navy monoplane patrol type, with outboard pontoons to keep the wing tips out of the water and a twin-rudder tail assembly. At the Navy's request, a third Wasp was installed above the wing in August, an effort to increase speed that Laddon regarded with distaste.

Glenn L. Martin, however, underbid Consolidated for production of the type, starting a patrol-plane rivalry that continued for over two decades. Consolidated did build a successful commercial XPY-1 development known as the Commodore.

Nine examples of Martin's version, ordered June 29, 1929, were designated P3M-1. The first, tested January 26, 1931, was similar to the twin-engine XPY-1, but the P3M-2 appeared in September with 525-hp R-1690-32 Hornets, ring cowls, and enclosed pilots' seats. All nine were delivered by May 1932, the three P3M-1s being modified to P3M-2 standard.

Martin also received a contract June 28, 1929, for a developmental prototype with the same wing lowered and two cowled 575-hp Wright R-1820-64 Cyclones installed on the leading edge. It first ap-

peared in June 1931 as the XP2M-1, with a third Cyclone mounted above the wing, but this engine was dropped when the aircraft was modified to the XP2M-2. This reduction in power lowered overall performance but increased range as a result of reduced fuel consumption.

CONSOLIDATED XPY-1
Pratt & Whitney R-1340-38, 450 hp
DIMENSIONS: Span 100′, Lg. 61′9″, Ht. 17′4″, Wing Area 1110 sq. ft.
WEIGHT: Empty 8369 lb., Gross 13,734 lb., Max. 16,492 lb. Fuel 1021 gal.
PERFORMANCE: Speed—Top 118 mph at s. l., Cruising 110 mph, Landing 56 mph. Service Ceiling 15,300′, Climb 5000′/8.3 min. Range 1716 miles normal, 2620 miles max.   MFR

CONSOLIDATED XPY-1 (3 engines)   ARC

MARTIN P3M-1
Pratt & Whitney R-1340, 450 hp
DIMENSIONS: Span 100′, Lg. 61′9″, Ht. 16′8″, Wing Area
    1115 sq. ft.
WEIGHT: Empty 9988 lb., Gross 15,797 lb. Fuel 850 gal.
PERFORMANCE: Speed—Top 113 mph at s. l., Landing 60
    mph. Service Ceiling 7500′, Climb 4300′/10 min.
    Range 1000 miles, 450 miles with bombs.   MFR

MARTIN P3M-2
Pratt & Whitney R-1690-32, 525 hp
DIMENSIONS: Span 100′, Lg. 61′9″, Ht. 16′8″, Wing Area
    1119 sq. ft.
WEIGHT: Empty 10,032 lb., Gross 15,688 lb., Max. 17,977
    lb. Fuel 844 gal.
PERFORMANCE: Speed—Top 115 mph at s. l., Landing 61
    mph. Service Ceiling 11,900′, Climb 5000′/10.9 min.
    Range 1010 miles normal, 1570 miles max.   USN

MARTIN XP2M-1
Wright R-1820-64, 575 hp
DIMENSIONS: Span 100′, Lg. 61′2″, Ht. 22′8″, Wing Area
    1204 sq. ft.
WEIGHT: Empty 12,467 lb., Gross 19,937 lb., Max. 22,916
    lb. Fuel 1194 gal.
PERFORMANCE: Speed—Top 143 mph at s. l., Landing 68
    mph. Service Ceiling 13,400′, Climb 5000′/5.9 min.
    Range 1257 miles normal, 1855 miles max.   USN

Navy Patrol Bombers

The last patrol biplane built for the Navy, and the
last with inline engines, was the Hall XP2H-1, ordered June 30, 1930, and first flown November 15,
1932. The largest American flying boat since the
NC-4, it had a crew of six and four 600-hp Curtiss

V-1570-54 Conquerors mounted in tandem pairs
and cooled by radiators below the front engines.
Armament included a 2,000-pound bomb load and
five .30-caliber Browning guns at positions in the
nose, rear deck, waist, and tail. The last weapon
was aimed by a prone airman between clamshell
doors, the first tail gun on a Navy plane.

Consolidated offered an improved XPY-1 design
with 575-hp Wright R-1820 Cyclones and a small
lower wing, creating a sesquiplane (1½ wing) layout with room for more fuel tanks and bomb racks.
This design won the next Navy design competition,
with contracts for an XP2Y-1 prototype on May 26,
1931, and 23 similar P2Y-1s on July 7.

The XP2Y-1 was first flown March 26, 1932, with
three engines, but on May 18 tests began with the

HALL XP2H-1
Curtiss V-1570-54, 600 hp
DIMENSIONS: Span 112', Lg. 70'10", Ht. 25'6", Wing Area 2742 sq. ft.
WEIGHT: Empty 20,856 lb., Gross 35,393 lb., Max. 43,193 lb. Fuel 3368 gal.
PERFORMANCE: Speed—Top 139 mph at s.l., Cruising 120 mph, Landing 59 mph. Service Ceiling 10,900', Climb 5000'/8.7 min. Range 2150 miles normal, 3350 miles max. USN

CONSOLIDATED XP2Y-1
Wright R-1820E, 575 hp
DIMENSIONS: Span 100', Lg. 61'9", Ht. 16'8", Wing Area 1430 sq. ft.
WEIGHT: Empty 10,950 lb., Gross 20,047 lb., Max. 21,547 lb. Fuel 1200 gal.
PERFORMANCE: Speed—Top 126 mph at s. l., Landing 61 mph. Service Ceiling 11,000', Climb 5000'/10.7 min. Range 1768 miles normal, 1940 miles max. MFR

two-engine layout chosen for production ships. Three-bladed propellers, ring cowls, and enclosed cockpits were featured on the five-place patrol plane. Armament included up to 2,000 pounds of bombs under the wings, a .30-caliber machine gun in the bow cockpit, and two others beneath the sliding hatch of the twin waist openings.

On February 1, 1933, the first P2Y-1s went to Norfolk for Patrol Squadron Ten (VP-10), which found them far superior in endurance to the old biplane boats. Two then-spectacular demonstrations of their capabilities come to mind: the nonstop flight from Norfolk to Coco Solo, the Canal Zone base, by VP-5 in September 1933, and by six VP-10 boats from San Francisco to Pearl Harbor in January 1934. The latter 2,400-mile formation flight took 24

hours, 35 minutes, and satisfied a Navy ambition frustrated in 1925, when the PN-9 biplane ran out of fuel and had to go the rest of the way by sail!

The last P2Y-1 became the XP2Y-2 in August 1933, with the R-1820-88 Cyclones inserted into the upper wing's leading edge. This layout was adopted for 23 P2Y-3 models ordered December 27, 1933, and delivered from January to May 1935, with 700-hp R-1820-90 Cyclones.

This new engine position was so successful that the P2Y-1s in service were modernized to P2Y-2 configuration with conversion kits made up by Consolidated and shipped to Pearl Harbor and Coco Solo. Consolidated's P2Y-2 and P2Y-3 boats were to continue in squadron service until 1941, after which they were sent to Pensacola as trainers.

CONSOLIDATED P2Y-1
Wright R-1820-E, 575 hp
DIMENSIONS: Span 100′, Lg. 61′9″, Ht. 17′3″, Wing Area 1430 sq. ft.
WEIGHT: Gross 19,852 lb., Empty 10,950 lb., Max. 21,052 lb. Fuel 1200 gal.
PERFORMANCE: Speed—Top 126 mph at s. l., Landing 60.4 mph. Service Ceiling 11,200′, Climb 5000′/10.2 min. Range 1750 miles normal, 2050 miles max.   ARC

CONSOLIDATED XP2Y-2
Wright R-1820-88
DIMENSIONS: Span 100′, Lg. 61′9″, Ht. 17′3″, Wing Area 1430 sq. ft.
WEIGHT: Empty 11,349 lb., Gross 20,251 lb., Max. 24,043 lb. Fuel 1632 gal.
PERFORMANCE: Speed—Top 135 mph (138 mph on test), Landing 61 mph. Service Ceiling 10,800′, Climb 5000′/12.6 min. Range 1890 miles normal, 2900 miles max.   MFR

CONSOLIDATED P2Y-3
Wright R-1820-90, 750 hp takeoff, 700 hp at 4000′
DIMENSIONS: Span 100′, Lg. 61′9″, Ht. 19′1″, Wing Area 1514 sq. ft.
WEIGHT: Empty 12,769 lb., Gross 21,291 lb., Max. 25,266 lb. Fuel 1620 gal.
PERFORMANCE: Speed—Top 139 mph at 4000′, 131 mph at s. l., Cruising 117 mph, Landing 63 mph. Service Ceiling 16,100′, Climb 650′/1 min. Range 1800 miles normal, 1180 miles/2000 lbs. bombs.   ARC

Foreign sales included a P2Y-1C for Colombia and a P2Y-1J for Japan, the latter assembled and flown there by the Kawanishi Company on April 12, 1935, for evaluation by the Japanese Navy. Six P2Y-3 boats were ordered by Argentina in May 1936 and delivered from San Diego between June and August 1937.

A generous quantity of struts had been necessary to support the wings of Navy patrol planes before the perfection of cantilever, internally braced wings made a more streamlined design possible. Douglas received a contract on May 20, 1933, for engineering studies of a twin-engine monoplane, and on February 11, 1934, the Navy exercised its option for construction of an XP3D-1 prototype, first flown on February 6, 1935. Powered by two Pratt & Whitney R-1830-58 Wasps mounted above the cantilever wings, the XP3D-1 had the first enclosed gunner's turret on an American patrol plane. This turret, set back from the bow to allow room for an open mooring hatch, was followed by an enclosed cabin for the pilots and two open gunners' hatches behind

DOUGLAS XP3D-1
Pratt & Whitney R-1830-58, 825 hp at s. l.
DIMENSIONS: Span 95', Lg. 69'10", Ht. 22'5", Wing Area
1295 sq. ft.
WEIGHT: Empty 13,799 lb., Gross 21,346 lb., Max. 26,662
lb. Fuel 1667 gal.
PERFORMANCE: Speed—Top 161 mph at s. l. Service Ceiling 15,000', Climb 5000'/7.1 min. Range 1900 miles
normal, 3530 miles max. ARC

DOUGLAS XP3D-2
Pratt & Whitney R-1830-64, 900 hp takeoff, 850 hp at
8000'
DIMENSIONS: Span 95', Lg. 69'7", Ht. 22'5", Wing Area
1295 sq. ft.
WEIGHT: Empty 15,120 lb., Gross 22,909 lb., Max. 27,946
lb. Fuel 1620 gal.
PERFORMANCE: Speed—Top 183 mph at 8000', Landing
63.5 mph. Service Ceiling 18,900', Climb 5000'/6.1
min. Range 2050 miles normal, 3380 miles max. MFR

DOUGLAS YOA-5
Wright YR-1820-45, 860 hp at 3200'
DIMENSIONS: Span 89'9", Lg. 69'9", Ht. 21', Wing Area
1101 sq. ft.
WEIGHT: Empty 14,038 lb., Gross 20,000 lb. Fuel 700 gal.
PERFORMANCE: Speed—Top 170 mph at 2800', 161 mph
at s. l., Cruising 152 mph, Landing 75 mph. Climb
10,000'/13 min. Service Ceiling 18,900'. RW

type was not ordered by the Navy since the Consolidated PBYs offered similar performance at a lower price, but Russia and Japan bought two each of a transport version called the Douglas DF.

The Catalina

Flying boats are rare on the aviation scene today, but one flying boat is still remembered by every aviation enthusiast. The PBY Catalina is the most widely used flying boat ever built.

Success in building the P2Y patrol series led Consolidated to the design that became the principal Allied patrol plane of World War II. Isaac M. Laddon designed the Consolidated Model 28 as an all-metal monoplane using two new Pratt & Whitney Twin Wasp engines, the 14-cylinder, twin-row, R-1830-58 giving 800 hp at sea level. Careful attention was paid to streamlining—even to having the outboard floats fold upward to become wing tips. The wings, which were metal except for fabric covering aft of the rear spar, contained integral fuel tanks.

An XP3Y-1 prototype ordered October 28, 1933, was built in Buffalo, shipped by rail to Anacostia, and first flown March 21, 1935. Consolidated's offer of a more streamlined boat than the rival XP3D-1 at a lower price ($90,000 each) won the contract for 60 aircraft on June 29, 1935.

the wings. Metal covered the hull and forward part of the wings, while fabric covered the rear wings and movable control surfaces.

This same basic design had been used for the Douglas YOA-5 amphibian, built for the Army with two 930-hp R-1820-45 Cyclones, a crew of five, and three .30-caliber guns. Intended for long-range reconnaissance, this aircraft had been designated YB-11 when ordered on December 7, 1932, became the YO-44 when a mockup was inspected in April 1933, and was delivered as the YOA-5 on February 24, 1935. Since the Army's YOA-5 could be used to land on water and rescue landplane crews forced down at sea, it foreshadowed the OA-10 Catalina rescue amphibians of World War II.

The Navy's prototype was rebuilt as XP3D-2 and reappeared in May 1936. Raised to the fuselage's top, the wing had 850-hp R-1830-64 Wasps on the leading edge, with floats retracting inward. This

CONSOLIDATED XP3Y-1 (XPBY-1)
Pratt & Whitney R-1830-58, 825 hp at s. l. (R-1830-64, 850 hp at 8000')
DIMENSIONS: Span 104', Lg. 63'6", Ht. 18'6", Wing Area 1400 sq. ft.
WEIGHT: Empty 12,512 lb. (13,000 lb.), Gross 19,793 lb. (20,226 lb.), Max. 24,803 lb. (25,236 lb.). Fuel 1750 gal.
PERFORMANCE: Speed—Top 169 mph at s. l. (184 mph at 8000'), Landing 58 mph. Service Ceiling 18,600' (24,000'), Climb 5000'/4.1 min. (4.6 min.). Range 2070 miles normal (2110 miles), 4270 miles max. (4010 miles).   MFR

Consolidated's president, Reuben Fleet, had moved his company to San Diego to escape the Buffalo winter climate, which had often blocked flight testing. In the new factory at Lindbergh Field, the prototype, which had set a new world distance record for seaplanes on its way to California, was modified and redelivered in May 1936 with the new designation XPBY-1. Its configuration now included a rotating nose turret, modified tail, and new Pratt & Whitney R-1830-64 Wasps giving 850 hp at 8000 feet and 900 hp for takeoff. The improvement was needed because Douglas had also modified its prototype into the XP3D-2, with the same engines and retractable floats. But the XPBY-1 was favored, with the Navy ordering 50 PBY-2s on July 25, 1936.

CONSOLIDATED PBY-1
Pratt & Whitney R-1830-64, 900 hp takeoff, 850 hp at 8000'
DIMENSIONS: Span 104', Lg. 65'2", Ht. 18'6", Wing Area 1400 sq. ft.
WEIGHT: Empty 14,576 lb., Gross 22,336 lb., Max. 28,447 lb. Fuel 1750 gal.
PERFORMANCE: Speed—Top 177 mph at 8000', 164 mph at s. l., Cruising 105 mph, Landing 67 mph. Service Ceiling 20,900', Climb 840'/1 min. Range 2115 miles normal, 1210 miles/2000 lbs. bombs, 4042 miles max.
                                                    USN

In October 1936 the first production PBY-1 was delivered. Sixty PBY-1s were followed by 50 PBY-2s completed by February 1938. They were similar except for a modified tail.

On these early models a .30-caliber gun with 1,000 rpg was provided for the front turret, two more were mounted at the two sliding waist hatches, and another gun with 500 rpg was aimed through a tunnel opening in the hull's bottom rear. Alternately, .50-caliber guns and 800 rounds could be mounted in the waist if adapters were used. Underwing racks could accept four 325-pound depth charges, 500-pound bombs, 1,000-pound bombs, or two 1,435-pound Mark XIII torpedoes.

A civilian PBY (Model 28-1) was built for an explorer in June 1937, who sold it to the Soviet Union in August for an Arctic rescue mission; he obtained a second plane (28-3) in December. Known as the *Guba*, it explored New Guinea, was flown around the world, and sold to Britain as a transport in 1940.

The Soviet Union also purchased three Model 28-2 cargo-mail boats, along with a license to build them in Russia. The first was begun March 29, 1937, and delivered in December, together with the parts for the others for assembly in Taganrog. These were the only PBYs using Wright engines, R-1820-G3 Cyclones rated at 840 hp at 8,700 feet. These engines were chosen because they were already in Soviet production. The Consolidated boats were known as GSTs in Soviet civil aviation, while later Taganrog boats were completed as patrol bombers, with the front cargo hatch replaced by a Soviet-designed front turret and M-62 engines in enclosed cold-weather cowls.

Sixty-six PBY-3s with 1,000-hp R-1830-66 Wasps were ordered by the U.S. Navy on November 27, 1936, and the first was accepted a year later, with the remainder delivered from March to August

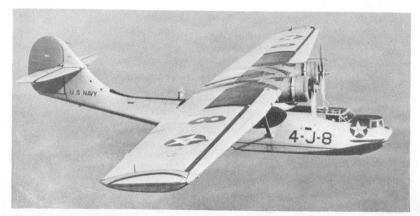

CONSOLIDATED PBY-2

Pratt & Whitney R-1830-64, 900 hp takeoff, 850 hp at 8000'

DIMENSIONS: As PBY-1

WEIGHT: Empty 14,568 lb., Gross 22,490 lb., Max. 28,640 lb. Fuel 1750 gal.

PERFORMANCE: Speed—Top 178 mph at 8000', 165 mph at s. l., Cruising 105 mph, Landing 68 mph. Service Ceiling 21,100', Climb 860'/1 min. Range 2131 miles normal, 1242 miles/2000 lbs. bombs. USN

CONSOLIDATED PBY-3

Pratt & Whitney R-1830-66, 1050 hp takeoff, 900 hp at 10,000'

DIMENSIONS: As PBY-1

WEIGHT: Empty 14,767 lb., Gross 22,713 lb., Max. 28,863 lb. Fuel 1750 gal.

PERFORMANCE: Speed—Top 191 mph at 12,000', 171 mph at s. l., Cruising 114 mph, Landing 67 mph. Service Ceiling 24,400', Climb 930'/1 min. Range 2175 miles normal, 1258 miles/2000 lbs. bombs, 4170 miles max. MFR

CONSOLIDATED PBY-4

Pratt & Whitney R-1830-72, 1050 hp takeoff, 900 hp at 12,000'

DIMENSIONS: As PBY-1

WEIGHT: Empty 16,837 lb., Gross 24,813 lb., Max. 32,011 lb. Fuel 1750 gal.

PERFORMANCE: Speed—Top 197 mph at 12,000', 176 mph at s. l., Cruising 115 mph, Landing 71 mph. Service Ceiling 24,100', Absolute Ceiling 25,700', Climb 870'/1 min. Range 2070 miles normal, 1285 miles/2000 lbs. bombs, 4430 miles max. ARC

1938. By now, squadron delivery flights to overseas stations became routine.

Thirty-three PBY-4s were ordered December 18, 1937, and the first was accepted in May 1938 with R-1830-72 Wasps yielding 1,050 hp for takeoff. From October 1938 to June 1939, 31 PBY-4s were accepted, leaving delivery of the last deferred for special modification. Three were fitted with new enclosures over the waist gunner's positions and a straight-rudder trailing edge.

A single Model 28-5 completed for the RAF in July 1939 with R-1830-S1C3C engines and standard PBY-4 configuration became the first military aircraft delivered by trans-Atlantic flight. A commercial version, the 28-4, was obtained by American Export Airlines in March 1939. The last PBY-4 was converted to an amphibian by a Navy order dated April 7, 1939. Provided with retractable tricycle wheels, it flew November 22, 1939, as the XPBY-5A.

Wartime Expansion

When the war began in September 1939, the Navy had 224 Consolidated PBY and P2Y boats in 19 squadrons deployed in five Patrol Wings. Patrol Wings 1 to 5 were based at San Diego, Pearl Harbor, Coco Solo, Seattle, and Norfolk, respectively.

There was a lull of over a year in PBY deliveries to service squadrons and its days in the front line seemed numbered. New prototypes such as the XPBM-1, the XPB2Y-1, and Consolidated's own Model 31 far surpassed it in performance. But now aircraft were needed by the Navy for its Neutrality Patrol and by the RAF for control of the Atlantic. Early delivery of a reliable patrol plane was now the main consideration.

On December 20, 1939, the Navy ordered 200 Consolidated PBY-5s, the largest single Navy aircraft order since World War I. Contracts with Britain, France, Australia, and Canada were drawn up for 174 similar 28-5Ms in the same period. The French orders were absorbed by Britain, and a new assembly line was begun in San Diego. The first

PBY-5 was accepted September 18, 1940, with 1,-200-hp (at takeoff) R-1830-82 engines, the first to use 100-octane fuel. Armament included two .50-caliber guns in the waist blisters with 840 rounds and a .30-caliber gun in the bow and the tunnel with 1,500 rounds.

The second PBY-5 was delivered to the Coast Guard in October, and November deliveries included three PBY-5s and the first three Model 28-5ME boats for Britain, which were named Catalinas. British Catalina Is had R-1830-S1C3G Wasps, eight crewmen, and six .303-caliber Vickers guns, including two in each blister with 1,200 rounds, 225 pounds of armor for the rear gunners, and 1,176 pounds of self-sealing fuel tank protection. Weight was now up to 17,382 pounds empty, compared to 15,534 pounds on the first PBY-5.

By September 1941, 167 PBY-5s had been accepted by the Navy, and the last 33 aircraft on that contract were delivered October-December 1941 as PBY-5A amphibians.

Deployment first strengthened the Neutrality Patrol in the Atlantic, which was being extended by bases in Bermuda, Newfoundland, and Iceland. First to operate from Bermuda on November 15, 1940, were the PBY-2s of VP-54. On May 18, 1941, PBY-5s of VP-52 arrived at Argentia, Newfoundland, operating from the seaplane tender U.S.S. *Albemarle*.

A severe climate made patrol work hazardous, and on May 24, 1941, the squadron was ordered to look for the *Bismarck*, hiding somewhere in the Atlantic after sinking the H.M.S. *Hood*. Catalinas of the RAF from Northern Ireland were also search-

CONSOLIDATED PBY-5 (early)
Pratt & Whitney R-1830-82, 1200 hp takeoff, 1050 hp at 5700'.
DIMENSIONS: Span 104', Lg. 63'10", Ht. 18'11", Wing Area 1400 sq. ft.
WEIGHT: Empty 17,400 lb., Gross 26,200 lb. Max. 33,389 lb. Fuel 1260–750 gal.
PERFORMANCE: Speed—Top 200 mph at 5700', 189 mph at s. l., Landing 72 mph. Service Ceiling 21,600', Climb 990'/1 min. Range 1945 miles patrol, 1245 miles/2000 lbs. bombs, 1895 miles max.   WES

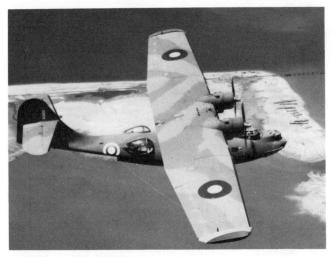

CONSOLIDATED CATALINA I (RAF)   MFR

CONSOLIDATED PBY-5 (late)
Pratt & Whitney R-1830-92, 1050 hp at 7000'
DIMENSIONS: As PBY-5 (early)
WEIGHT: Empty 18,790 lb., Gross 31,813 lb., Max. 34,000
    lb. Fuel 1475 gal.
PERFORMANCE: Speed—Top 195 mph at 7000', Cruising
    110 mph, Landing 75 mph. Service Ceiling 17,700',
    Climb 660'/1 min. Range 2860 miles patrol, 2370 miles/
    four 325 lb. bombs, 2645 miles/2000 lb. bombs.   MFR

CONSOLIDATED PBY-5A
Pratt & Whitney R-1830-92, 1200 hp takeoff, 1050 hp at
    7000'
DIMENSIONS: Span 104', Lg. 63'10", Ht. 20'2", Wing Area
    1400 sq. ft.
WEIGHT: Empty 20,910 lb., Gross 33,975 lb., Max. 35,300
    lb. Fuel 603–1478 gal.
PERFORMANCE: Speed—Top 179 mph at 7000', Cruising
    117 mph, Landing 78 mph. Service Ceiling 14,700',
    Climb 10,000'/19.3 min. Range 2545 miles patrol, 1660
    miles/four 325 lb. bombs, 1820 miles/2000 lbs.
    bombs.   ARC

ing, flying 19 to 22 hours on each trip. On May 26
a Catalina from No. 209 Squadron with an American
officer as co-pilot found the *Bismarck*. Another Catalina took up contact and the battleship was soon
caught and destroyed by the British Navy.

The first Navy plane with airborne search radar
early in 1941 was a PBY-2. By July 18, 1941, British
ASV radar had been installed in one PBY-5 each of
VP-71, 72, and 73, the first Navy squadrons in service with airborne radar. Atlantic patrol units were
reorganized, most of the squadrons becoming part
of Patrol Wing 7 in July. On August 6, 1941, six
PBY-5s of VP-73 and five Martin PBM-1s of VP-74
began operations from Iceland.

By November 1941 Consolidated had completed
99 Catalina Is and seven Catalina IIs on RAF orders, 18 similar Model 28-5AMEs for Australia, 36
28-5NMEs for the Dutch East Indies, and was turning out 50 Catalina IIAs for Canada. These aircraft
were sometimes reassigned among Commonwealth
forces.

After Pearl Harbor

When American entered the war, the Navy had 25
patrol squadrons equipped as follows: 16 with the
PBY-5, three the PBY-3, two the PBY-4, and one
squadron each with the PBY-5A, PBM-1, PB2Y-2,
and PBO-1 types. A hundred older survivors were
located mostly at Gulf naval training stations.

Hawaii had seven squadrons with 54 PBY-5s and
27 PBY-3s, while two squadrons with 28 PBY-4s
were in the Philippines. Seattle had 24 PBY-5s in
four squadrons and San Diego had a transition training squadron (VP-13) with four PB2Y-2s and a few
PBYs. Two squadrons in the Canal Zone had 13
PBY-3s and 11 PBY-5s, while the Atlantic Fleet's
11 squadrons had 81 PBY-5s, ten PBY-5As, 13 PBY-
3s, 13 PBM-1s, and the only landplanes (14 PBO-1
Hudsons).

Most of Hawaii's PBYs were put out of action by
the surprise attack, but a PBY-5 on patrol attacked
a midget submarine just prior to the attack. Patrol
Wing 10, in the Philippines, carried out several
PBY-4 bombing attacks before 11 survivors fled to
the East Indies by December 26. Replacement aircraft were received from Hawaii and from the
Dutch, but of 44 Catalinas used by Patwing 10, 41
were lost by March 3, 1942.

After the Pearl Harbor attack, the San Diego factory went ahead on additional contracts for the Navy
and for Defense Air (lend-lease). These totaled 516
PBY-5s (delivered April 1942 to July 1943), 710
PBY-5A amphibians (December 1941–March 1944),
and 225 PBY-5Bs (Catalina IBs) and 70 Catalina
IVA flying boats (May 1942–July 1943) for British
lend-lease. Another foreign order filled in September 1942 was for 12 PBY-5A amphibians for a Dutch
squadron (No. 321) stationed in Ceylon.

Pressures of war led to many changes in the Catalina. Instead of the unprotected, 1,750-gallon system of earlier models, self-sealing tankage was provided for 600 gallons of a 1,475-gallon total capacity in wing tanks. Pratt & Whitney R-1830-92 Wasps were now rated at 1,050 hp from sea level to 7,000 feet. While the first PBY-5As had one .30-caliber gun in the bow, two-gun turrets became standard by the end of 1942, and radar had been added at the factory since May 1942. There was much variation in weight among PBY-5 models, and the data given here compares characteristics from 1941 and 1945 charts.

Catalinas were involved in every Navy campaign of the Pacific war. A PBY was the first to sight the enemy in the Midway battle, where they also made the Navy's first night torpedo attack, later night bombing at Guadalcanal. In the Atlantic the hunt for U-boats was the primary task, and fourteen submarines were sunk by Navy PBYs in the Atlantic from August 1942 to July 1943.

One PBY-5A squadron, VP-63, became the first to be fitted with Magnetic Airborne Detector (MAD) gear, as well as the first Navy squadron to operate from Great Britain in World War II when it arrived July 23, 1943. Antisubmarine operations over the Bay of Biscay were carried on, though they were interrupted by German fighter attacks. In January 1944, VP-63, now equipped to fire 65-pound rocket bombs back and down at submerged U-boats, went to Morocco. VP-63 set up barrier patrols across the Strait of Gibraltar, where three U-boats were sunk in early 1944 with help from surface ships.

The most popular use of the Catalina, as far as fliers of other types were concerned, was the rescue of fliers down at sea. At first this was done by the regular patrol squadrons. Then special rescue squadrons of Catalinas were organized: Army Emergency-Rescue squadrons with OA-10 amphibians and Navy Air-Sea Rescue squadrons (VH) were first formed in the Pacific on April 15, 1944.

Catalina production at San Diego was completed in March 1944 (its place being taken by the PB4Y-2 Privateer) but continued in four satellite plants. On July 16, 1941, 156 PBN-1 Nomads had been ordered from Philadelphia's Naval Aircraft Factory (NAF). This permitted the adoption of a new hull design without disrupting established production. First accepted in February 1943, these planes introduced a higher rudder, enlarged fuel capacity, and a longer clipper bow and extended afterbody. Armament included a .50-caliber gun in the nose turret and in each side blister, as well as the usual small-caliber tunnel gun. The armor weight was 426 pounds.

Seventeen PBNs were completed for the Navy by September 1943, when the Navy canceled a 124-

N.A.F. PBN-1
Pratt & Whitney R-1830-92, 1200 hp takeoff, 1050 hp at 7000'
DIMENSIONS: Span 104'3", Lg. 64'8", Ht. 21'3", Wing Area 1400 sq. ft.
WEIGHT: Empty 19,288 lb., Gross 36,353 lb., Max. 38,000 lb. Fuel 622–2085 gal.
PERFORMANCE: Speed—Top 186 mph at 6700', 174 mph at s. l., Cruising 111 mph, Landing 78 mph. Service Ceiling 15,100'. Range 2590 miles/four 325 lb. depth charges, 3700 miles max.   ARC

plane follow-up contract. The remaining planes under the 1941 contract, minus one accidentally burned, were allotted to the U.S.S.R. One was lost in the United States, but 137 were dispatched from Elizabeth City, North Carolina, from November 1943 to March 1945, when NAF deliveries ended.

Two Canadian facilities were utilized for PBY production: Boeing at Vancouver and Canadian Vickers (Canadair since December 1944) at Montreal. Boeing began with an order for 55 duplicates of Consolidated's PBY-5A amphibian, the "Canso A." Deliveries to the Royal Canadian Air Force (RCAF) began after the first flight July 27, 1942, and were followed after July 1943 by 240 PB2B-1 (PBY-5 duplicates) flying boats built with lend-lease funds for the RAF. New Zealand received 34 and Australia seven, all called Catalina IVBs.

The PB2B-2 (Catalina VI) version, with a tall PBN tail and revised radar, appeared in September 1944. Of 67 built by March 1945, 47 went to Australia and six operated with U.S. Army markings. Canadian Vickers built 369 amphibians, of which 139 were "Canso As" for the RCAF and the rest for the AAF.

The Army Air Force acquired 54 PBY-5As, designated OA-10, in 1942–43 for use in rescue operations. They were so successful that the AAF was allotted 230 Vickers amphibians. Designated OA-10A, they were accepted from December 1943 to February 1945, and retained the original PBY-5A characteristics: a 1,750-gallon fuel capacity and armament of two .50-caliber and two .30-caliber guns.

The last factory involved in PBY production was the Consolidated Vultee New Orleans facility, originally established to build the advanced P4Y-1, the Navy version of the Model 31. When this type's engine supply was appropriated by the B-29 program, the P4Y-1 was replaced by a PBY contract on

VICKERS OA-10A WL

CONSOLIDATED PBY-6A
Pratt & Whitney R-1830-92, 1200 hp takeoff, 1050 hp at 7000'
DIMENSIONS: Span 104', Lg. 63', Ht. 22'4", Wing Area 1400 sq. ft.
WEIGHT: Empty 21,480 lb., Gross 34,550 lb., Max. 36,400 lb. Fuel 603–1778 gal.
PERFORMANCE: Speed—Top 178 mph at 7000', 167 mph at s. l., Cruising 107 mph, Landing 79 mph. Service Ceiling 16,200', Climb 630'/1 min. Range 2535 miles patrol, 1405 miles/four 325 lb. depth charges, 2195 miles/2000 lbs. bombs. MFR

July 9, 1943. The first aircraft completed in the New Orleans plant was a single PBY-5, accepted in April 1944. They were followed by 59 PBY-5As completed by January 1945.

The last Catalina model was the PBY-6A amphibian, with PBN tail, two .50-caliber guns in the bow turret with 1,000 rounds, and radar over the cockpit. Of 175 built from January to September 1945, 75 went to the Army as the OA-10B and 48 to the U.S.S.R. The war's end closed the New Orleans plant and Catalina production. At that point production included: San Diego, 2,160; New Orleans, 235; Canada, 731; and Philadelphia, 155—a total of 3,281 planes.

The exact distribution of these Catalinas is difficult to establish because aircraft were frequently seconded to other users. As the largest foreign customer, the RAF purchased 99 Mk. I, seven Mk. II, and 36 Mk. IIA Catalinas in 1941; lend-lease funds in 1942 provided 225 Mk. 1B (minus 60 kept by the U.S. Navy) and only 11 Mk. III amphibians seconded from a USN PBY-5A contract. In 1943 the RAF got 77 Mk. IVA flying boats from San Diego, and 193 Mk. IVBs (PB2B-1s), and 14 Mk. VIs (PB2B-2s) from Vancouver in 1943–45. No Mk. V (PBN) was delivered to the RAF.

These 602 Catalinas, minus a few transferred to Canada and others, served 21 RAF squadrons at bases as diverse as Murmansk and Singapore. Australia had its original 18 Catalinas when Japan attacked, adding nine Vickers boats, a refugee PBY-4, plus 40 PBY-5s and 46 PBY-5As from USN contracts. From Vancouver came the seven PB2B-1 and 47 PB2B-2 boats mentioned earlier.

Canada received ten Catalina I, eight IB, and 14 IIA boats and 185 Canadian-built amphibians. The first Canadian squadron, No. 116, was formed around the Catalina Is in 1941. It was followed by ten more, plus two (Nos. 413 and 422) operating RAF Catalinas with Coastal Command. Canadians are credited with destroying seven U-boats, five of them by No. 162 Squadron in 1944.

New Zealand got 14 PBY-5 and eight Catalina IVA boats from April to October 1943, and 34 PB2B-1s in 1944. Of 185 PBN and PBY-6As sent to the U.S.S.R., all were dispatched through Elizabeth City, North Carolina, except for 15 PBY-6As flown

out through Alaska. Thirty PBY-5A amphibians went to the Free French, whose first patrol squadron was commissioned September 15, 1943. Brazil also operated a PBY-5A squadron that year.

The Catalina was to have a long postwar history in at least 15 different air forces. Although the last PBY-6A retired from the U.S. Navy on January 3, 1957—20 years after the war—many still served in a variety of civilian functions, from cargo to firefighting work. The Catalina was a combat type that lasted longer in peaceful tasks than those of war.

Floatplanes for Patrol

During the PBY's long service life, many efforts were made to develop more advanced types for the mission. Unique among Navy types was the Hall XPTBH-1, a twin-engine, twin-float monoplane capable of patrol, torpedo, or bombing missions. This type had its German counterpart in the Heinkel He 115.

Ordered June 30, 1934, as the XPTBH-1 with Wright R-1820 Cyclones, the high-wing monoplane was built in Bristol, Pennsylvania, with XR-1830-60 Wasps, redesignated XPTBH-2, and received by the Navy on January 30, 1937. A pair of large floats was installed under the engines, while the long fuselage contained the crew of four and the bay for a torpedo or bombs. In the nose was a rotating turret with a .30-caliber gun. Behind the wings a hatch slid forward and up to reveal a rear gunner and a .50-caliber Browning, while a floor panel opened to reveal a .30-caliber tunnel gun. Since water-based torpedo planes were not included in Navy procurement plans, no further contracts were awarded for this type.

HALL XPTBH-2
Pratt & Whitney XR-1830-60, 800 hp at 8000'
DIMENSIONS: Span 79'4", Lg. 55'11", Ht. 24'1", Wing Area
828 sq. ft.
WEIGHT: Empty 11,992 lb., Gross 17,983 lb., Max. 21,414
lb. Fuel 830–1180 gal.
PERFORMANCE: Speed—Top 182 mph at 8000', 169 mph
at s. l., Landing 69.5 mph. Service Ceiling 19,200',
Climb 5000'/5.3 min. Range 850 miles/torpedo, 2620
miles max.   USN

However common the twin-float configuration for
patrol planes was abroad, its only other American
application was on the single-engine Northrop N-
3PB, ordered by Norway March 12, 1940, for coastal
patrol. Twenty-four were completed from January
to March 1941, powered by Wright R-1820-G205A
Cyclones giving 1,200 hp for takeoff. They carried
three men, four .50-caliber fixed wing guns, a .30-
caliber flexible gun, another .30-caliber gun aimed
through a trap door in the belly, and up to a ton of
bombs, depth charges, or a torpedo. Exiled Norwegian pilots who had formed No. 330 Squadron,
RAF, took 18 to Iceland and began antisubmarine
patrols June 23, 1941. One of the fastest seaplanes
ever built, the Northrop was agile enough to down
an Fw 200 bomber in 1942.

NORTHROP N-3PB
Wright R-1820G-205A, 1200 hp
DIMENSIONS: Span 48'11", Lg. 38', Ht. 12', Wing Area 377
sq. ft.
WEIGHT: Empty 6560 lb., Gross 10,600 lb. Fuel 320 gal.
PERFORMANCE: Speed—Top 257 mph at 16,400', Cruising
215 mph, Landing 65 mph. Service Ceiling 28,800',
Climb 2540'/1 min. Range 1400 miles max.   IWM

Four-Engine Flying Boats

Another way to advance performance was through
the use of four engines, and Sikorsky contracted to
design such a patrol bomber June 29, 1935.

First flown on August 13, 1937, the Sikorsky
XPBS-1 had R-1830-68 Wasps, fixed outboard floats,
and a single high tail fin. Armament included a .50-
caliber gun in a manual front turret, two .30-caliber
guns at side-by-side waist hatches, and a hand-operated .50-caliber tail gun—the first real one on an
American plane, although Sikorsky had put them
on czarist bombers over 20 years earlier. (One predecessor, however, was the very limited mount on
the XP2H-1.)

Publicized as the "Flying Dreadnaught," Sikorsky's boat soon had a rival in Consolidated's XB2Y-
1, ordered July 23, 1936, with four R-1830-72 Wasps
and similar crew accommodations and racks hold-
ing anywhere from four to 12 1,000-pound bombs.
A cleaner appearance was obtained by retractable
wing tip floats and by carrying eight bombs within
the wings. Single .50-caliber guns were mounted in
the bow turret and tail position, while .30-caliber
guns were provided for the waist hatches and a
tunnel mount.

On December 17, 1937, the same day the hun-
dredth PBY was delivered, the XPB2Y-1 was flown,
but the single fin's area was too small for directional
stability. After three flights it was beached to add a
pair of elliptical fins on the stabilizer. This still was
not satisfactory, and in July 1938 twin rudders were
installed. This proved satisfactory and the aircraft
was turned over to the Navy. It became the first
official "flagplane" to accommodate the Admiral,
Aircraft Scouting Force.

Despite their advanced performance, these giants
did not win generous orders, for admirals looked
askance at their high cost and complexity, and reflected that "a large plane over a given area of sea
is not, necessarily, any more effective as an observation post than is a small plane . . . the small
plane . . . may be at an advantage in that the facilities which made it and maintain it can make and
maintain more units." With so much money already
invested in the PBYs, the Navy bought no patrol
bombers at all in 1938. During the following year
it concentrated funds on twin-engine types that
could be obtained in quantity.

Six Consolidated PB2Y-2s were ordered March
31, 1939, at a unit cost ($300,000) triple that of a
PBY. They had a new hull, R-1830-78 Wasps with
two-stage superchargers, and a crew of nine. Six
.50-caliber guns were distributed among the nose
turret, top blister, circular side windows, tunnel ori-
fice, and tail post. The first was delivered to the
new VP-13 at San Diego on December 31, 1940.
Five were accepted by July 1941, but the last was

SIKORSKY XPBS-1
Pratt & Whitney XR-1830-68, 1050 hp takeoff, 900 hp at 12,000'
DIMENSIONS: Span 124', Lg. 76'2", Ht. 27'7", Wing Area 1670 sq. ft.
WEIGHT: Empty 26,407 lb., Gross 46,617 lb., Max. 48,541 lb. Fuel 1970–3600 gal.
PERFORMANCE: Speed—Top 227 mph at 12,000', 203 mph at s. l., Landing 63 mph. Service Ceiling 23,100', Climb 640'/1 min. Range 3170 miles/4000 lbs. bombs, 4545 miles max.   MFR

CONSOLIDATED XPB2Y-1
Pratt & Whitney XR-1830-72, 1050 hp takeoff, 900 hp at 12,000'
DIMENSIONS: Span 115', Lg. 79'3", Ht. 27'4", Wing Area 1780 sq. ft.
WEIGHT: Empty 26,847 lb., Gross 49,754 lb., Max. 52,994 lb. Fuel 2300–3500 gal.
PERFORMANCE: Speed—Top 230 mph at 12,000', 206 mph at s. l., Landing 65 mph. Service Ceiling 22,000', Climb 830'/1 min. Range 4390 miles normal, 3420 miles/4000 lbs. bombs, 4950 miles max.   USN

delayed until December due to modification to the XPB2Y-3 configuration for the future production model. The fourth PB2Y-2 became the XPB2Y-4 with Wright R-2600 Cyclones.

A heavier production version was ordered November 19, 1940: the PB2Y-3 Coronado with R-1830-88s, self-sealing fuel tanks, 2,000 pounds of armor, eight .50-caliber guns, and 4,840 rounds of ammunition. Power-operated bow, top, and tail turrets had two guns each, and a single hand-held gun was at each side opening. Consolidated delivered 136 PB2Y-3s to the Navy from June 1942 to October 1943, plus 33 set aside for the British. However, only ten Coronados actually reached the RAF and these were used as transports. Some Navy Coronados were reworked with Catalina-type R-1830-92 engines with single-stage superchargers and became PB2Y-5s, with less speed but more range.

CONSOLIDATED PB2Y-2
Pratt & Whitney R-1830-78, 1200 hp takeoff, 1000 hp at 19,000'
DIMENSIONS: Span 115', Lg. 79', Ht. 27'6", Wing Area 1780 sq. ft.
WEIGHT: Empty 34,315 lb., Gross 60,441 lb., Max. 63,700 lb. Fuel 4400 gal.
PERFORMANCE: Speed—Top 255 mph at 19,000', 224 mph at s. l., Cruising 141 mph, Landing 71 mph. Service Ceiling 24,100', Climb 830'/1 min. Range 3705 miles normal, 1330 miles/12,000 lbs. bombs, 4275 miles max.   USN

A transport role for deep-hulled flying boats was foreshadowed when the Sikorsky prototype made an emergency dash across the Pacific with high-priority cargo early in 1942. After Liberators took over patrol-bombing tasks, the Coronado seemed most useful as a transport. The last 41 Coronados on order were completed by Rohr in 1944 as PB2Y-3R transports with R-1830-92 engines, and similar conversions were made on previous Coronados.

CONSOLIDATED PB2Y-3
Pratt & Whitney R-1830-88, 1200 hp takeoff, 1000 hp at 19,500'
DIMENSIONS: Span 115', Lg. 79'3", Ht. 27'6", Wing Area 1780 sq. ft.
WEIGHT: Empty 41,031 lb., Gross 68,000 lb. Fuel 1575–3500 gal.
PERFORMANCE: Speed—Top 224 mph at 19,500', 199 mph at s. l., Cruising 140 mph, Landing 76 mph. Service Ceiling 20,900', Climb 550'/1 min. Range 2310 miles/four 325 lb. depth charges, 1380 miles/8000 lbs. bombs, 3120 miles ferry.   MFR

CONSOLIDATED PB2Y-5

Pratt & Whitney R-1830-92, 1200 hp at s. l., 1050 hp at 7000'

DIMENSIONS: Span 115', Lg. 79'5", Ht. 27'6", Wing Area 1780 sq. ft.

WEIGHT: Empty 41,180 lb., Gross 68,000 lb. Fuel 3017–796 gal.

PERFORMANCE: Speed—Top 211 mph at 7000', 198 mph at s. l., Cruising 154 mph, Landing 76 mph. Service Ceiling 13,100', Climb 490'/1 min. Range 2570 miles/four 325 lb. depth charges, 1640 miles/8000 lbs. bombs. MFR

Martin Mariners

During 1937 Martin engineers designed a new twin-engine patrol bomber and tested its air and sea behavior on a ⅜-scale two-passenger flying model. An XPBM-1 prototype was ordered June 30, 1937, together with 20 PBM-1s on December 28. The XPBM-1 was completed in February 1939 with Wright R-2600-6 Cyclones mounted high on gulled wings to keep the three-bladed propellers clear of the water. Outboard floats retracted into the wings and twin rudders were perched behind the all-metal hull.

Twenty PBM-1s accepted between September 1940 and March 1941 could be distinguished from the prototype by the dihedral on the stabilizers.

MARTIN XPBM-1

Wright R-2600-6, 1600 hp takeoff, 1275 hp at 12,000'

DIMENSIONS: Span 118', Lg. 77'2", Ht. 24'6", Wing Area 1405 sq. ft.

WEIGHT: Empty 24,006 lb., Gross 40,814 lb. Fuel 2700 gal.

PERFORMANCE: Speed—Top 213 mph at 12,000', Landing 64 mph. Service Ceiling 20,600', Climb 840'/1 min. Range 3450 miles/1000 lbs. bombs. USN

The crew of seven operated five .50-caliber and one .30-caliber gun mounted in a power-operated nose turret, a power top turret, circular waist fixtures, and prone tail position. Two tons of bombs or depth charges could be carried within the engine nacelles. An XPBM-2 ordered the same day, with fuel capacity increased from 2,700 to 4,815 gallons, was accepted in April 1941. The PBMs served in the Atlantic with VP-74, sinking U-158 on June 30, 1942. Nine more U-boats would be sunk in 1943 by PBM-3s.

Contracts made November 1, 1940, and August 20, 1941, were to provide 379 PBM-3 and 180 PBM-4 Mariners, as the Martin boat was named, but wartime changes led to the abandonment of these types' original form. First accepted in April 1942, the new Mariners had 1,700-hp R-2600-12 Cyclones and larger nonretractable floats. The first 50 were completed without armament as PBM-3R transports. A total of 272 PBM-3Cs began appearing in October with internal protection, power-operated two-gun bow and top turrets, and hand-operated .50-caliber guns at waist openings and a tail position.

Search radar installed behind the pilot's cabin in the Mariner had become the means to catch surfaced submarines at night or in bad weather. A special antisubmarine version, the PBM-3S, had a longer range and omitted power turrets, limiting protection to two hand-held .50-caliber nose guns, a third in the waist, and a fourth in the tail, with 800 rounds and 261 pounds of armor.

After 95 PBM-3S Mariners had been delivered from July to October 1943, 262 PBM-3Ds were delivered with R-2600-22 Cyclones, four-bladed propellers, power turrets, eight .50-caliber guns, 4,840 rounds, 1,058 pounds of armor, self-sealing tanks, up to eight 325-pound depth charges or 1,000-pound bombs and radar equipment. During 1943, 54 Mariners were allocated to Britain, but they were used only by one RAF coastal squadron, with most of these Martins retained by the U.S. Navy. Twelve PBM-3S Mariners went to Australia.

When the PBM-3Ds were completed in June 1944, production continued with the PBM-5, using the 2,100-hp R-2800-34 Wasps first introduced on two XPBM-5s converted from PBM-3Ds. With eight .50-caliber guns and 1,067 pounds of armor, 592 PBM-5s were completed by the end of 1945.

MARTIN PBM-1
Wright R-2600-6, 1600 hp takeoff, 1275 hp at 12,000'
DIMENSIONS: As XPBM-1
WEIGHT: Empty 24,143 lb., Gross 41,139 lb. Fuel 2700 gal.
PERFORMANCE: Speed—Top 214 mph at 12,000', 197 mph at s. l., Cruising 128 mph, Landing 65 mph. Service Ceiling 22,400', Climb 640'/1 min. Range 3434 miles/ 1000 lbs. bombs, 2590 miles/4000 lbs. bombs.   USN

MARTIN PBM-3S
Wright R-2600-12, 1700 hp takeoff, 1350 hp at 13,000'
DIMENSIONS: Span 118', Lg. 79'10", Ht. 27'6", Wing Area 1408 sq. ft.
WEIGHT: Empty 29,915 lb., Gross 51,860 lb., Max. 54,525 lb. Fuel 2350–3138 gal.
PERFORMANCE: Speed—Top 209 mph at 13,000', 194 mph at s. l., Cruising 134 mph, Landing 76 mph. Service Ceiling 17,600', Climb 550'/1 min. Range 2725 miles/ four 650 lb. bombs, 3530 miles max., 3130 miles/four 325 lb. depth charges.   USN

MARTIN PBM-3D
Wright R-2600-22, 1900 hp takeoff, 1350 hp at 15,400'
DIMENSIONS: Span 118', Lg. 79'10", Ht. 27'6", Wing Area 1408 sq. ft.
WEIGHT: Empty 32,848 lb., Gross 51,608 lb., Max. 58,000 lb. Fuel 1950–2744 gal.
PERFORMANCE: Speed—Top 202 mph at 15,900', 192 mph at s. l., Cruising 135 mph, Landing 76 mph. Service Ceiling 20,800', Climb 740'/1 min. Range 2260 miles normal, 2580 miles/four 325 lb. depth charges, 3000 miles max.   USN

MARTIN PBM-3C
Wright R-2600-12, 1700 hp takeoff
DIMENSIONS: Span 118', Lg. 80', Ht. 27'6", Wing Area 1408 sq. ft.
WEIGHT: Empty 32,378 lb., Gross 52,665 lb., Max. 58,000 lb. Fuel 1750–2536 gal.
PERFORMANCE: Speed—Top 198 mph at 13,000'. Service Ceiling 16,900', Climb 410'/1 min. Range 2137 miles/ eight 325 lb. depth charges, 3074 miles patrol.   USN

MARTIN PBM-5
Pratt & Whitney R-2800-34, 2100 hp takeoff, 1700 hp at 9400'
DIMENSIONS: Span 118', Lg. 79'10", Ht. 27'6", Wing Area 1408 sq. ft.
WEIGHT: Empty 32,803 lb., Gross 56,000 lb., Max. 60,000 lb. Fuel 2671 gal.
PERFORMANCE: Speed—Top 215 mph at 19,200', 198 mph at s. l., Cruising 115 mph, Landing 82 mph. Service Ceiling 20,200', Climb 588'/1 min. Range 2700 miles/ four 325 lb. depth charges, 2480 miles/4000 lbs. bombs.   MFR

Production and service continued in the postwar period, with 629 PBM-5s completed by June 1947, some modified to PBM-5E (APS-15 radar) and PBM-5G (APS-31, for Coast Guard). Thirty-six PBM-5A amphibious models with retractable tricycle gear were added from April 1948 to March 1949, bringing the Mariner production total to 1,366. Some served the Navy until July 1956.

Experimental Boats

The twin-engine P4Y-1 project grew out of the Consolidated Model 31, an advanced private venture begun by the company in July 1938 as the world's fastest flying boat. First flown May 5, 1939, Model 31 had the new Davis wing and twin rudders later adopted for the B-24, and was the first aircraft to fly with Wright's 18-cylinder, 2,000-hp R-3350s. The deep double-deck hull had room for retractable tricycle beaching gear and the outboard floats retracted inwards instead of to the wing tips.

CONSOLIDATED XP4Y-1
Wright R-3350-8, 2300 hp takeoff, 1800 hp at 13,600'
DIMENSIONS: Span 110', Lg. 74'1", Ht. 25'2", Wing Area 1048 sq. ft.
WEIGHT: Empty 29,334 lb., Gross 46,000 lb., Max. 48,000 lb. Fuel 1545–3000 gal.
PERFORMANCE: Speed—Top 247 mph at 13,600', 231 mph at s. l., Cruising 136 mph, Landing 89 mph. Service Ceiling 21,400', Climb 1230'/1 min. Range 2300 miles/eight 325 lb. depth charges, 1745 miles/two torpedos, 2695 miles/1845 gal., 3280 miles max.   MFR

Tests were carried out with secrecy, but the Navy seemed uninterested, even when the prototype was reworked and reappeared with dummy turrets and a higher tail in April 1941. Another modification was made, and the prototype was purchased April 13, 1942, as the XP4Y-1 Corregidor, with two R-3350-8 Cyclones, radar, a 37-mm gun in the bow, four .50-caliber guns in dorsal and tail turrets, and up to 4,000 pounds of bombs. Production was to begin at a new factory in New Orleans, but the program was canceled because B-29 production required the entire R-3350 engine supply, so the plant was instead given a contract for 450 Catalinas in July 1943.

Two wartime flying boats of unusual size should be mentioned. The largest of all patrol planes was the Martin XPB2M-1 Mars, ordered August 23, 1938, and powered by four 2,200-hp Wright R-3350-18s. The size of the aircraft inspired publicity men to arrange formal ceremonies at the launching on November 5, 1941, but an accidental fire delayed the first flight until July 3, 1942.

The spacious hull contained two decks and all the room the 11-man crew needed; rumor has it that there was a shower and two mess rooms—one for officers and one for men! The Mars had been designed too early to include internal protection and other combat features, but power turrets were placed in the bow, on top amidships, and behind the twin rudders. They were removed when the Mars was ordered converted to transport configuration on February 27, 1943. As a patrol bomber, the Mars was far less practical than the much larger

MARTIN XPB2M-1
Wright R-3350-18, 2200 hp takeoff, 2000 hp at 4000'
DIMENSIONS: Span 200', Lg. 117'3", Ht. 38'5", Wing Area 3683 sq. ft.
WEIGHT: Empty 75,573 lb., Gross 144,000 lb. Fuel 10,410 gal.
PERFORMANCE: Speed—Top 221 mph at 4500', Landing 83.5 mph. Service Ceiling 14,600', Climb 440'/1 min. Range 4945 miles max.   ARC

MARTIN XPB2M-1 as transport   USN

number of conventional aircraft that could be manufactured with the same productive effort. The remodeled Mars was delivered to a transport squadron November 27, 1943. Twenty cargo versions (JRM) were ordered in June 1944, and six would enter service after the war.

Consolidated designed a flying boat almost as large, the XPB3Y-1, ordered April 2, 1942. This design was to have four Pratt & Whitney R-2800-18s, a 169-foot wingspan, 121,500-pound gross weight, two 20-mm and ten .50-caliber guns, and carry ten tons of bombs at a top speed of 241 mph at 22,500 feet; but on November 4 the project was canceled to expedite production of standard types.

The largest twin-engine flying boat was the Boeing XPBB-1 Sea Ranger, ordered June 29, 1940, and first flown July 5, 1942. Powered by two R-3350-8 Cyclones, it had the wing later used on B-29s, large, fixed floats, a high single rudder, and a crew of ten. Eight .50-caliber guns were provided in two-gun power-operated bow, top, and tail turrets, and a tear-shaped blister on each side with one .50-caliber gun. Up to 20,000 pounds of bombs or 6,890 gallons of fuel could be carried. Five hundred were to be built in the new Boeing plant at Renton, Washington, but this program was dropped so the plant and engines could be used for the B-29, leaving the prototype the Lone Ranger.

BOEING XPBB-1
Wright R-3350-8, 2300 hp takeoff, 1800 hp at 13,600'
DIMENSIONS: Span 139'8", Lg. 94'9", Ht. 34'2", Wing Area 1826 sq. ft.
WEIGHT: Empty 41,531 lb., Gross 62,000 lb., Max. 101,130 lb. Fuel 2490–6890 gal.
PERFORMANCE: Speed—Top 228 mph at 14,200', 214 mph at s. l., Cruising 127 mph. Service Ceiling 22,400', Climb 980'/1 min. Range 2320 miles/1000 lbs. bombs, 6300 miles max.   ARC

Borrowed Bombers

The Navy's exclusive reliance on flying boats for patrol missions was rooted in national policy giving naval aircraft responsibility for fleet support and overseas scouting and Army aircraft responsibility for coastal defense and cooperation with land forces. Land-based aircraft were employed by the Army, and the Navy was limited to water-based and ship-based aircraft. This had the unfortunate result that the superior performance of landplanes for long-distance reconnaissance was not utilized by the Navy.

Acquisition of bases in Iceland and Newfoundland for the Neutrality Patrol, however, created a requirement for patrol craft capable of land takeoffs, for water-based operations in these areas were subject to interference from winter ice conditions. This requirement was eventually met by procurement of amphibian Catalinas, but in the meantime the Lockheed Hudson being built for the RAF's Coastal Command was an available and proven antisubmarine patrol type. The long-standing flying-boat tradition was broken by 20 Hudsons requisitioned in October 1941 by the Navy and labeled PBO-1. Powered by two R-1820-40 Cyclones, they were similar to the A-29s described in Chapter 13 and were armed with four 325-pound depth charges, two fixed and three flexible .30-caliber guns.

Unlike Catalinas, they were fast enough to catch surface submarines before they crash-dived, so against competition of four flying-boat squadrons and many surface ships, PBO-1s of squadron VP-82 at Argentia, Newfoundland, sank on March 1 and March 15, 1942, the first two U-boats killed by American forces.

Early in the war, as flying boats suffered grievous losses at the hands of the Zero, the disadvantages of the big boats as patrol bombers became painfully apparent. Since the hull's performance handicap was all too often proving fatal, a feeling arose that the ability to land on water might not be an essential requirement for patrol planes. The theory that the flying boats' blind spot, due to the hull, could be covered by flying close to the water seldom worked out; a forced dive to low altitude was often too late or was more damaging than gunfire, while

LOCKHEED PBO-1 HUDSON
Wright R-1820-40, 1200 hp takeoff, 900 hp at 14,000'
DIMENSIONS: Span 65'6", Lg. 44'4", Ht. 16'10", Wing Area 551 sq. ft.
WEIGHT: Empty 12,680 lb., Gross 18,837 lb., Max. 20,203 lb. Fuel 644 gal.
PERFORMANCE: Speed—Top 262 mph at 15,300', 237 mph at s. l., Cruising 129 mph. Service Ceiling 26,200', Climb 1450'/1 min. Range 1750 miles/four 325 lb. depth charges, 1890 miles max.   USN

enemy fighters firing at long range could correct their aim by using the water splashes of their bullets.

Seldom did the flying boats' much-vaunted ability to operate without prepared landing fields have great importance in the war. Instead, it was apparent that landplanes could be better armed and had higher speeds, enabling them to attack and escape more quickly. The Navy was now eager to acquire land-based patrol planes and requested in February 1942 a reallocation of bomber production, especially of the long-range B-24 Liberators already being used by the British for patrol work. The Army wanted every bomber it could get, so it required much negotiation before Chief of Staff George C. Marshall agreed to a Navy share on July 7, 1942.

Consolidated B-24Ds were scheduled for Navy use on July 11, 1942, redesignated PB4Y-1s, and began to arrive in August. Liberator deliveries began slowly but gathered volume. They were joined in 1943 by the entire Lockheed Ventura production, so that the majority of Navy patrol planes during the latter part of the war were landplanes. Most of the 1,174 PB4Y-1 Liberators assigned to the Navy had front turrets like later B-24s, but Erco power turrets were used. Eight .50-caliber guns with 3,770 rounds, 1,318 pounds of armor, 2,110 pounds of fuel tank protection, and up to 8,000 pounds of bombs were carried. Cameras were provided on those planes supplied to four photographic squadrons.

The last Navy Liberators, B-24Ms, arrived in January 1945, and 20 Navy bomber squadrons used PB4Y-1s in the Pacific and the Atlantic. Liberator squadrons operated against U-boats from Britain, Iceland, the Azores and Ascension Islands, Morocco, and are credited with about 11 sinkings. Several PB4Y-1s in Britain had been converted to radio-controlled drones carrying 21,248 pounds of explosives. They were to attack German V-1 sites, but only two sorties were made. The first, on August 12, 1944, exploded with the pilot, Joseph P. Kennedy, Jr., still aboard.

It is notable that the patrol-bomber appellation was replaced by a simple patrol label on Lockheed PV-1 Venturas, denoting overwater patrol rather than medium bombing. A good short-range supplement to long-range Liberators, the Ventura was allocated to the Navy July 24, 1942, and 1,600 PV-1s were delivered from December 1942 to May 1944, including 380 lend-leased to the RAF as Ventura G.R.5s. The first Venturas actually accepted by the Navy were 27 PV-3s (AAF B-34s) requisitioned from the British Ventura II contract in September 1942, but the Navy's PV-1s were specially equipped for patrol missions. Powered by two Pratt & Whitney R-2800-31s, they carried two .50-caliber fixed guns in the nose, two in a top power turret, and two .30-caliber guns in a ventral mount near the twin

CONSOLIDATED PB4Y-1
Pratt & Whitney R-1830-65, 1200 hp at 25,000'
DIMENSIONS: Span 110', Lg. 67'3", Ht. 17'11", Wing Area 1048 sq. ft.
WEIGHT: Empty 37,160 lb., Gross 60,000 lb., Max. 63,000 lb. Fuel 2814–3614 gal.
PERFORMANCE: Speed—Top 287 mph at 26,700', 231 mph at s. l., Cruising 149 mph, Landing 95 mph. Service Ceiling 32,600', Climb 990'/1 min. Range 2065 miles/8000 lbs. bombs, 3090 miles patrol.   USN

tails. Six 325-pound depth charges, six 500-pound bombs, or a single torpedo could be carried in the fuselage, and a pair of drop tanks might be added below the wings.

Other PV-1 features included 762 pounds of armor, ASD-1 search radar, which could be added in the nose, and three additional .50-caliber fixed guns that were often added under the nose. The first Venturas replaced the Hudsons of VP-82 on Newfoundland, other Venturas served in Iceland, and five squadrons were stationed in Brazil. Atlantic patrols sank four U-boats in 1943.

The Ventura appeared in the Pacific with Fleet Air Wing Four, whose four squadrons started operations from the Aleutians in May 1943 and began attacks on the Kuriles from Attu in November. Marine aviation's first night-fighter squadron, VMF(N)-531, received radar-equipped Venturas with six nose guns in March 1943 and attempted its first interceptions in November. Australia got 14 PV-1s and New Zealand received 116 PV-1s and four PV-2s.

Five hundred Lockheed PV-2 Harpoons were ordered on June 30, 1943. A larger and longer-range development of the PV-1, the Harpoon had greater span, larger fins, 714 pounds of armor, five .50-caliber fixed nose guns, two more in the power turret, and eight 5-inch rockets. Delivered from March 1944 to December 1945, the PV-2 went to 14 Navy squadrons, the first striking from Attu against the

LOCKHEED-VEGA PV-1
Pratt & Whitney R-2800-31, 2000 hp takeoff, 1600 hp at 11,900'
DIMENSIONS: Span 65'6", Lg. 51'9", Ht. 13'2", Wing Area 551 sq. ft.
WEIGHT: Empty 20,197 lb., Gross 26,500 lb., Max. 31,077 lb. Fuel 981–1771 gal.
PERFORMANCE: Speed—Top 312 mph at 13,800', 296 mph at s. l., Cruising 164 mph, Landing 91 mph. Service Ceiling 26,300', Climb 2230'/1 min. Range 1660 miles/six 325 lb. depth charges, 1360 miles/torpedo.　MFR

LOCKHEED-VEGA PV-2
Pratt & Whitney R-2800-31, 2000 hp takeoff, 1600 hp at 11,900'
DIMENSIONS: Span 75', Lg. 52'1", Ht. 13'3", Wing Area 686 sq. ft.
WEIGHT: Empty 21,028 lb., Gross 33,668 lb., Max. 36,000 lb. Fuel 1149–863 gal.
PERFORMANCE: Speed—Top 282 mph at 13,700', 271 mph at s. l., Cruising 171 mph, Landing 83 mph. Service Ceiling 23,900', Climb 1630'/1 min. Range 1790 miles/six 325 lb. depth charges, 2930 miles ferry.　MFR

Kuriles with bombs and rockets in April 1945, while two other squadrons fought in the central Pacific.

The last Harpoons built were 35 PV-2Ds built from July to December 1945, the remaining 379 aircraft on this order being canceled. This model had eight fixed .50-caliber guns grouped around the nose radar, as well as the eight rockets and 3,000-pound bomb load of the previous models. Lockheed's PV-2 Harpoons remained in Navy service until 1948.

Five hundred North American Mitchells allotted to the Navy on January 14, 1943, were designated PBJ-1, although they actually were used by the Marine Corps for medium bombing rather than patrol missions. (Since they were identical to Army Mitchells, the reader should consult the B-25 description in Chapter 10.)

Meanwhile, experience with Liberators indicated that a superior patrol plane could be obtained by redesigning the Consolidated planes specifically for naval tasks. In May 1943 three XPB4Y-2 prototypes were ordered converted from PB4Y-1s. The wings and tricycle landing gear were those of the B-24, but more fuel, guns, and radar were added, the fuselage was lengthened, and a high single tail replaced the earlier twin rudders. Since patrol planes work at low altitudes, the turbosuperchargers were omitted, giving the Privateer a higher sea-level speed, with a consequent loss in high-altitude performance.

The first XPB4Y-2 Privateer was flown September 20, 1943, and on October 15, 660 PB4Y-2s were ordered. Delivery began in March 1944, and 710 more Privateers were ordered on October 19. Cancellations, however, ended PB4Y-2 production in October 1945 after 740 were completed.

Using four R-1830-94 Wasps, the Privateer was operated by a crew of 11, including two electronics operators for the war's most elaborate airborne radar. Twelve .50-caliber guns were disposed in six power turrets: Erco nose and Convair tail, two Martin top domes, and tear-shaped Erco side blisters. Up to 8,000 pounds of bombs and 1,171 pounds of armor were carried in the fuselage. Three squadrons had special PB4Y-2Bs with a Bat antishipping missile below each wing; these were glide bombs with a 12-foot wing, 1,000-pound warhead, and radar homing. On April 23 they became the first and only automatic homing missiles used in war.

Privateers remained in squadron service for several years after the war, and in 1951 they were redesignated P4Y-2, P4Y-2B, and P4Y-2S, the latter an antisub version.

Landplanes like these reduced flying boats to a minority of the patrol force. On December 31, 1941, the Navy had 466 patrol bombers, including 423 Catalina and 20 Mariner twin-engine flying boats, five four-engine boats, and only 18 twin-engine landplanes. Of 4,054 Navy patrol planes on hand as of June 30, 1945, there were 1,629 twin-engine and 55 four-engine flying boats, and 1,374 twin-engine and 996 four-engine landplanes.

CONSOLIDATED PB4Y-2
Pratt & Whitney R-1830-94, 1350 hp
DIMENSIONS: Span 110', Lg. 74'7", Ht. 29'2", Wing Area 1048 sq. ft.
WEIGHT: Empty 37,405 lb., Gross 64,000 lb. Fuel 2364–3964 gal.
PERFORMANCE: Speed—Top 247 mph at 14,000', 238 mph at s. l., Cruising 158 mph, Landing 96 mph. Service Ceiling 19,500', Climb 990'/1 min. Range 2630 miles/4000 lbs. bombs, 2900 miles patrol.　MFR

Chapter 19
Navy Scout and Observation, 1932-36

Vought SU Corsairs

Putting monoplanes on Navy ships was a good deal more difficult than putting them on Army airfields, for shipboard aircraft had strict size and weight limitations. This is why each carrier's scouting squadron still used Vought biplanes with fixed landing gear until 1938, and why biplanes remained aboard some warships until the war's end.

In 1931 the three scouting squadrons on Navy carriers were using the same Vought Corsair design as the seaplane units aboard battleships and cruisers. To improve their performance by means of more engine power, they would have to transcend the limits of catapult launching weights and the modest R-1340 Wasp engines. Such new types would be classified VS for Scouting in June 1932.

The answer for the carrier-based squadrons was the Vought SU-1, sporting a new look with its 600-hp Pratt & Whitney R-1690 Hornet in a ring cowl, a tail wheel, and straight-axle landing gear. While the wing bomb racks and fixed .30-caliber gun in the upper wing remained, the observer now had a .30-caliber Browning on a new post mount instead of the Lewis gun and Scarff ring used since World War I. A tail hook was provided for deck landings and metal covers on the fuselage sides indicated emergency flotation gear.

Despite these changes from the first O3U type, the SU-1 had been ordered in March 1931 and was delivered from October 1931 to April 1932 with an O3U-2 designation, and the similar O3U-4 was first flown May 12, 1932. They became the SU-1 and SU-2 in June 1932, while the camera-equipped SU-3 began flying as such on August 31, 1932.

Twenty-nine SU-1s were built, serving on the *Lexington* in 1932 with VS-2B and a Marine detachment, VS-14M, and on the *Langley* in 1933 with VS-1B. When 44 SU-2 and 20 SU-3 Corsairs arrived, these Voughts could also be used by VS-3B and VS-

15M on the *Saratoga*, VO-8M at San Diego, and VO-9M in Haiti until it returned to Quantico. These Corsairs were also popular with admirals as brightly painted "command" ships.

The XO3U-5 was the second aircraft of the O2U-4/SU-2 contract. Flown in April 1932 with Pratt & Whitney's new 625-hp Twin Wasp, Jr., in an enclosed cowling, it was otherwise similar to the SU-2.

A seaplane Corsair light enough for the catapults was still needed, however, so the O3U-3 reverted to the R-1340-12 Wasp and pontoons, introducing a new, rounded, longer rudder. Seventy-six were built, with the first example flown as a landplane on May 20 and with pontoons on July 1, 1932. Easily convertible from floats to wheels, it did most of its flying from warship catapults.

The Corsair story can be confusing because of the shifts in designations and missions. For example, the XO4U-2 was apparently fitted for the scout mission and has nothing in common with the XO4U-1 of 1931 except the serial number. This number was retained when this aircraft replaced the first prototype, which was destroyed in a crash. The XO4U-2 was first flown June 5, 1932, with the Pratt & Whitney twin-row Twin Wasp, Jr. under a neat cowling, the O3U-3's rounded rudder, and a metal wing structure. When a supercharger and a controllable-pitch propeller were fitted to the 700-hp R-1535-64, this became the fastest Corsair to date.

One SU-2 was modified and grandly provided with a cowled R-1690D Hornet, enclosed cockpits, a longer rudder, and wheel pants. Flown on May 1, 1933, this XSU-4 remained at Anacostia station without the wheel pants. Vought did build 20 SU-4s for VS-1 in 1933, but they seemed identical to the open-cockpit SU-1/-3 series except for the longer rudder.

The last of the Navy's biplane Corsairs was the

VOUGHT SU-1
Pratt & Whitney R-1690-40, 600 hp
DIMENSIONS: Span 36′, Lg. 26′3″, Ht. 11′6″, Wing Area 325.6 sq. ft.
WEIGHT: Empty 2949 lb., Gross 4467 lb., Max. 4587 lb. Fuel 110 gal.
PERFORMANCE: Speed—Top 170 mph at s. l., 168 mph at 5000′, Stalling 60.5 mph. Service Ceiling 19,900′, Climb 5000′/4 min. Range 654 miles normal, 770 miles max. MFR

VOUGHT SU-2
Pratt & Whitney R-1690-40, 600 hp
DIMENSIONS: Same as SU-1
WEIGHT: Empty 2966 lb., Gross 4481 lb., Max. 4601 lb. Fuel 110 gal.
PERFORMANCE: Speed—Top 171 mph at s. l., 168 mph at 5000′, Stalling 60 mph. Service Ceiling 19,500′, Climb 5000′/3.9 min. Range 674–788 miles. ARC

VOUGHT SU-3
Pratt & Whitney R-1690-40, 600 hp
DIMENSIONS: Same as SU-1
WEIGHT: Empty 2978 lb., Gross 4522 lb., Max. 4642 lb. Fuel 110 gal.
PERFORMANCE: Speed—Top 171 mph at s. l., 168 mph at 5000', Stalling 60.4 mph. Service Ceiling 19,900', Climb 5000'/3.9 min. Range 694–814 miles.   USN

VOUGHT O3U-3
Pratt & Whitney R-1340-12, 550 hp
DIMENSIONS: Span 36', Lg. 31', Ht. 13'2", Wing Area 325 sq. ft.
WEIGHT: Empty 3100 lb., Gross 4585 lb. Fuel 110 gal.
PERFORMANCE: Speed—Top 156 mph at s. l., 153 mph at 5000', Stalling 61.6 mph. Service Ceiling 16,600', Climb 5000'/4.9 min. Endurance 4.58 hr.   ARC

VOUGHT XO4U-2
Pratt & Whitney R-1535-64, 700 hp at 8900'
DIMENSIONS: Span 36', Lg. 27'2½", Ht. 11'6", Wing Area 325.6 sq. ft.
WEIGHT: Empty 3155 lb., Gross 4669 lb., Max. 4984 lb. Fuel 110 gal.
PERFORMANCE: Speed—Top 196 mph at 8900', Stalling 60.6 mph. Service Ceiling 27,100', Climb 5000'/4.2 min. Range 646–916 miles.   MFR

VOUGHT SU-4
Pratt & Whitney R-1690-42, 600 hp
DIMENSIONS: Span 36', Lg. 27'11", Ht. 11'5", Wing Area 337 sq. ft.
WEIGHT: Empty 3307 lb., Gross 4773 lb., Max. 4913 lb. Fuel 110 gal.
PERFORMANCE: Speed—Top 167.5 mph at s. l., Stalling 62 mph. Service Ceiling 18,600', Climb 5000'/3.5 min. Range 611 miles.   USN

VOUGHT O3U-6
Pratt & Whitney R-1340-18, 550 hp
DIMENSIONS: Span 36′, Lg. 27′3″, Ht. 11′5″, Wing Area 342 sq. ft.
WEIGHT: Empty 3300 lb., Gross 4743 lb., Max. 4875 lb. Fuel 110 gal.
PERFORMANCE: Speed—Top 164 mph at s. l., 160 mph at 5000′, Stalling 53 mph. Service Ceiling 17,800′, Climb 5000′/4.8 min. Range 688–806 miles.   USN

VOUGHT V-66E
Pratt & Whitney R-1340 Wasp, 500 hp at 7500′
DIMENSIONS: Span 36′, Lg. 26′2″, Ht. 10′8″, Wing Area 326 sq. ft.
WEIGHT: Empty 2742 lb., Gross 4204 lb.
PERFORMANCE: Speed—Top 165 mph at s. l., Cruising 99 mph, Stalling 59 mph. Service Ceiling 22,900′, Climb 1310′/1 min.   SI

O3U-6 series, which began when the last aircraft on the O3U-3 contract was modified as an XO3U-6 with a deep cowl and enclosed cockpits, and flown June 13, 1934. A production contract was made October 23, 1934, and the first O3U-6 flew February 27, 1935. Thirty-two were delivered by July, replacing the Curtiss O2C-1s of the Marine's VO-7M and VO-8M squadrons at Quantico and San Diego.

Standard O3U-6 armament consisted of Browning guns with 1,100 .30-caliber rounds and wing racks for four 116-pound bombs. The last example was returned to the factory to be rebuilt with flaps on both wings and flown as the XOSU-1 on October 20, 1936. Afterwards the aircraft returned to normal O3U-6 configuration.

Corsairs for Export

Vought had much success selling these Corsairs to foreign countries as land-based military types. Beginning in September 1932, Brazil's Army received 37 Hornet-powered V-65B two-seaters, and her Navy received eight Wasp-powered V-66Bs, which were convertible to seaplanes. These aircraft were similar to the SU-1 in most respects, except for Scarff rings in the rear cockpits.

The 500-hp R-1340D Wasp was used on the V-66E, first flown November 17, 1932, for evaluation by the British Navy, and on the single V-66F for Argentina. The Vought V-70A was an attack version of the SU-1, with a 600-hp R-1690D Hornet, wheel pants, four fixed guns (two in the upper wing and two under the cowl), and a flexible observer's gun and bomb racks for 464 pounds. First flown February 8, 1933, it was offered to the U.S. Army and for export but found no buyers. Four-gun fixed armament and bomb racks were also provided on the

VOUGHT V-70A
Pratt & Whitney R-1690C, 600 hp
DIMENSIONS: Span 36′, Lg. 26′2″, Ht. 10′8″, Wing Area 326 sq. ft.
WEIGHT: Empty 3156 lb., Gross 5300 lb., Max. 5600 lb. Fuel 130–80 gal.
PERFORMANCE: Speed—Top 193 mph at s. l., Cruising 157 mph, Landing 63 mph. Service Ceiling 19,000′, Absolute Ceiling 20,500′, Climb 1425′/1 min. Range 610 miles normal, 840 miles max.   MFR

V-80P single-seat fighter, with a Hornet engine and cockpit canopy. The first of three for Peru was flown May 19, 1933.

China got 42 V-65C two-seaters, which had the R-1690 Hornet with split-axle gear, round rudder, and a cockpit canopy. They also had a fixed gun and bomb racks that were often used in China's civil warfare. First flown by Vought on July 11, 1933, they went into action with the bombing of the Fukien rebels in January 1934 and of the Communists on the famous Long March. One V-65C pilot defected to Yen-an, and his aircraft became the first aircraft flown by Red Chinese airmen until it was downed on October 5, 1936.

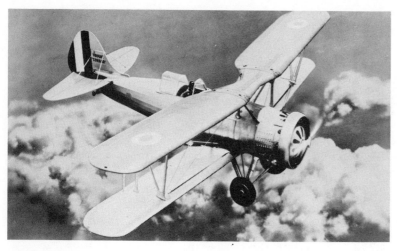

VOUGHT V-80P
Pratt & Whitney Model SD Hornet, 675 hp at s. l.
DIMENSIONS: Span 36′, Lg. 27′7″, Ht. 10′6″, Wing Area
337 sq. ft.
WEIGHT: Empty 3287 lb., Gross 4373 lb.
PERFORMANCE: Speed—Top 197 mph at 6000′, 178 mph
at s. l., Cruising 163 mph, Stalling 61 mph. Service
Ceiling 27,800′, Absolute Ceiling 29,200′, Climb 1850′/
1 min. Range 760 miles.   MFR

VOUGHT V-65C for China   MFR

Next came 12 V-65F Corsairs for Argentina,
which were similar to the SU-4 except for the addition of a sliding cockpit enclosure and an auxiliary
fuel tank; they were armed with one fixed and one
flexible 7.65-mm gun. The first V-65F was flown
October 18, 1933, followed by a single Argentine
V-80F single-seat fighter flown April 10, 1934, with
an extended cockpit enclosure and deep cowl. Six
V-85G "Kurier" single-seaters for Germany were
intended for a ship-to-shore mail project, not military operations.

China received 21 V-92C two-seaters in 1934,
which were like the SU-4/V-65F types, with Hornet
and ring cowl, and armed with a .30-caliber Browning in the upper wing, another in the rear cockpit,
and racks for four 116-pound bombs. They fought
in civil warfare and against Japan in 1937. Thailand
(then Siam) adopted the Corsair as its principal
army type, buying 12 V-93S two-seaters in 1934,

VOUGHT V-65F for Argentina   MFR

with 625-hp Hornets and two Vickers guns, and building a reported 72 in Bangkok.

The last of these two-seaters to be exported were ten V-99Ms for Mexico in December 1937, with supercharged 550-hp T1H-1 Wasp. Company statements report that Vought built 769 Corsair biplanes, including 185 for export and civilian customers.

The Vought seaplanes were joined in service by the lightweight Berliner-Joyce OJ-2. Powered by a 400-hp Pratt & Whitney Wasp, Jr., it was similar to the XOJ-1 of 1931 but had plain biplane wings without flaps and was armed with the usual two .30-caliber guns.

Thirty-nine OJ-2s went aboard light cruisers with VS-5B and VS-6B beginning March 1933 and later served Naval Reserve stations. A June 1934 order had one example rebuilt by October as an XOJ-3, with new cowl, cockpit canopy, and wing flaps, but it crashed in March 1935.

VOUGHT V-80F   SI

Navy Scouts in Transition

The Navy found the task of replacing the Corsairs of the scouting squadrons complicated by uncertainty as to the role future scouts would play. Scouting was a designation applied equally to carrier-based reconnaissance, shore-based Marine observation, and cruiser-based seaplane squadrons. While the Corsairs of 1931 had filled all three roles, advanced-performance requirements made continued commonality impossible.

There had been a hope that an amphibian would be compatible with these combat requirements, and the Loening XS2L-1, Great Lakes SG-1, and Sikorsky XSS-1 prototypes were ordered June 30, 1931, as two-seat scout amphibians of catapult weight with folding wings.

Loening's project was his second with a scout designation; the SL-1 had been a small flying boat intended to operate from a submarine. Ordered June 7, 1930, the SL-1 began tests in February 1931. With only 110 hp, this single-seat monoplane could be folded into an eight-foot tube on the deck of the submarine S-1. Like the little Cox-Klemin XS-1 and Martin-Klemin MS-1 single-seat biplanes of 1923, the unarmed SL-1 was by no means a combat type, but it is included here to complete the "S" category.

In May 1933 the Loening became the XSL-2 when it was fitted with a Menasco B-6, but no more attempts to manufacture submarine-based aircraft were made by the United States. The Japanese Navy, however, often used submarine-based aircraft in World War II.

VOUGHT V-92C in China
Pratt & Whitney R-1690SD, 675 hp
DIMENSIONS: Span 36′, Lg. 27′3″, Ht. 10′5″, Wing Area 337 sq. ft.
WEIGHT: Empty 3090 lb., Gross 4490 lb. Fuel 115 gal.
PERFORMANCE: Speed—Top 184 mph at 6000′, 169 mph at s. l. Climb 13,000′/10 min. Range 709 miles.   TIEN

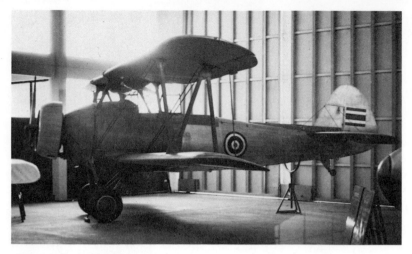

VOUGHT V-93S for Siam
Pratt & Whitney R-1690SD
DIMENSIONS: Span 36′, Lg. 27′, Ht. 11′1″, Wing Area 337
    sq. ft.
WEIGHT: Gross 4561 lb. Fuel 115 gal.
PERFORMANCE: Speed—Top 191 mph at 6000′, 176 mph
    at s. l., Cruising 158 mph, Landing 60.2 mph. Service
    Ceiling 24,300′, Absolute Ceiling 25,500′, Climb 1670′/
    1 min., 14,000′/10 min. Range 736 miles.   BOYNE

BERLINER-JOYCE OJ-2 Seaplane
Pratt & Whitney R-985-38, 400 hp at s. l.
DIMENSIONS: Span 33′8″, Lg. 29′1″, Ht. 12′7″, Wing Area
    284 sq. ft.
WEIGHT: Empty 2520 lb., Gross 3851 lb. Fuel 90 gal.
PERFORMANCE: Speed—Top 149 mph at s. l., 147 mph at
    5000′, Stalling 61.4 mph. Service Ceiling 13,500′,
    Climb 5000′/6.1 min. Endurance 5.09 hr. at 149
    mph.   USN

VOUGHT V-99M
Pratt & Whitney R-1340, 550 hp at 8000′
DIMENSIONS: Span 36′, Lg. 27′6″, Ht. 9′10½″, Wing Area
    342 sq. ft.
WEIGHT: Empty 3245 lb., Gross 4645 lb. Fuel 115 gal.
PERFORMANCE: Speed—Top 176 mph at 8000′, Landing
    61 mph. Service Ceiling 23,900′. Range 803 miles.
                                                      MFR

BERLINER-JOYCE OJ-2

Pratt & Whitney R-985-38, 400 hp at s. l.
DIMENSIONS: Span 33′8″, Lg. 25′8″, Ht. 10′9½″, Wing Area
284 sq. ft.
WEIGHT: Empty 2367 lb., Gross 3726 lb. Fuel 90 gal.
PERFORMANCE: Speed—Top 150 mph at s. l., 149 mph at
5000′, Stalling 60.2 mph. Service Ceiling 15,300′,
Climb 5000′/4.7 min. Endurance 5.09 hr. at 150
mph. USN

BERLINER-JOYCE XOJ-3

Pratt & Whitney R-985-38, 400 hp
DIMENSIONS: Span 33′8″, Lg. 29′5″, Ht. 12′6″, Wing Area
295.8 sq. ft.
WEIGHT: Empty 2932 lb., Gross 4531 lb. Fuel 130 gal.
PERFORMANCE: Speed—Top 149 mph at s. l., 144 mph at
5000′, Stalling 61 mph. Service Ceiling 14,100′, Climb
5000′/6.3 min. Range 856 miles. USN

LOENING XSL-1

Warner Scarab, 110 hp at s. l.
DIMENSIONS: Span 31′, Lg. 27′2″, Ht. 8′11″, Wing Area
148 sq. ft.
WEIGHT: Empty 1114 lb., Gross 1512 lb.
PERFORMANCE: Speed—Top 101 mph at s. l., Stalling 54.8
mph. Service Ceiling 13,000′. ARC

The Loening XS2L-1 amphibian biplane appeared in February 1933 with a 400-hp Pratt & Whitney R-985-38 mounted ahead of the upper wing and above the enclosed cabin for pilot and observer. Another amphibian was the Great Lakes XSG-1, using the same engine but with the observer's enclosure behind and below the pilot's open cockpit. Delivered to Anacostia on November 27, 1932, the XSG-1 was judged very unsatisfactory, underpowered, and below specified performance.

Most unusual among amphibians produced in 1933 was the Sikorsky XSS-1, a monoplane flying boat with a 550-hp R-1340-12 and its two crewmen in the hull behind the wings. None of these amphibians won Navy approval, for tests made it apparent that catapult-launched, amphibian-hulled aircraft were then unable to increase performance levels.

GREAT LAKES XSG-1
Pratt & Whitney R-985A, 400 hp
DIMENSIONS: Span 35', Lg. 32'6½", Ht. 13', Wing Area 347 sq. ft.
WEIGHT: Empty 2707 lb., Gross 4218 lb., Max. 4536 lb. Fuel 120 gal.
PERFORMANCE: Speed—Top 124 mph at s. l., Stalling 70 mph. Service Ceiling 8400'. Climb 4800'/10 min. Range 695–963 miles.   AAHS

LOENING XS2L-1
Pratt & Whitney R-985-38, 400 hp
DIMENSIONS: Span 34'6", Lg. 30'7", Ht. 14'7", Wing Area 355 sq. ft.
WEIGHT: Empty 2833 lb., Gross 4053 lb., Max. 4317 lb. Fuel 80 gal.
PERFORMANCE: Speed—Top 130 mph at s. l., 126 mph at 5000', Stalling 59.7 mph. Service Ceiling 12,400', Climb 5000'/7.1 min. Range 432–633 miles.   ARNOLD

SIKORSKY XSS-2
Pratt & Whitney R-1340-12, 550 hp
DIMENSIONS: Span 42', Lg. 33'1½", Ht. 14'7½", Wing Area 285 sq. ft.
WEIGHT: Empty 3274 lb., Gross 4526 lb., Max. 4790 lb. Fuel 80 gal.
PERFORMANCE: Speed—Top 154 mph at s. l., 149 mph at 5000', Stalling 63 mph. Service Ceiling 14,800', Climb 5000'/5.8 min. Range 417–618 miles.   ARC

One amphibian that year would be very successful, the Grumman XFJ-1, first flown April 24, 1933. Although there was provision for a flexible gun, the XFJ-1 was intended to be a utility type with no provision for catapulting, so a 700-hp R-1830 Twin Wasp could be used. Nicely streamlined, it was built in large numbers from 1934 to 1945.

The long story of the Grumman "Duck" utility amphibians falls outside this history of combat planes, but it should be mentioned that some were armed with depth charges and flexible guns during the war, beginning with nine Cyclone-powered J2F-2As used by the Marines' VMS-3 in the Virgin Islands in 1939.

Other experimental aircraft tested as scouts included the big Bellanca XSE-1 monoplane. Based on that firm's civilian transport designs, it had an enclosed cabin for the crew below the high wing, which was supported by thick fairings from stub wings and wheel pants. Ordered October 19, 1931, it appeared in December 1932 with a Wright R-1820 Cyclone and a fuel capacity for long-range reconnaissance. After a crash, the Bellanca was rebuilt by April 1934 as the XSE-2 with a Wright R-1510 Twin Whirlwind and larger tail, but tests

GRUMMAN J2F-2A
Wright R-1820-30, 790 hp
DIMENSIONS: Span 39′, Lg. 34′, Ht. 12′4″, Wing Area 409 sq. ft.
WEIGHT: Empty 4300 lb., Gross 6180 lb. Fuel 190 gal.
PERFORMANCE: Speed—Top 179 mph, Cruising 150 mph, Stalling 64 mph. Service Ceiling 21,600′, Climb 1500′/1 min. Range 780 miles.   ARNOLD

BELLANCA XSE-1
Wright R-1820-F, 650 hp at s. l.
DIMENSIONS: Span 49′9″, Lg. 29′11″, Wing Area 373 sq. ft.
WEIGHT: Empty 3054 lb., Gross 5526 lb. Fuel 250 gal.
PERFORMANCE: Speed—Top 171.7 mph at s. l., Stalling 60.8 mph. Service Ceiling 21,200′. Range 1392 miles.   ARC

BELLANCA XSE-2
Wright R-1510-92, 650 hp
DIMENSIONS: Span 49′9″, Lg. 29′8″, Ht. 12′2½″, Wing Area 411 sq. ft.
WEIGHT: Empty 2313 lb., Gross 6042 lb. Fuel 250 gal.
PERFORMANCE: Speed—Top 173 mph at s. l., 170 mph at 5000′, Stalling 63.9 mph. Service Ceiling 18,800′, Climb 5000′/4.9 min. Range 1455 miles.   NASA

CURTISS XS2C-1
Wright R-1510-28, 625 hp
DIMENSIONS: Span 44′, Lg. 31′3″, Ht. 12′2″, Wing Area 285 sq. ft.
WEIGHT: Empty 3677 lb., Gross 4822 lb., Max. 5180 lb. Fuel 104–56 gal.
PERFORMANCE: Speed—Top 186 mph at s. l., Landing 71 mph. Service Ceiling 18,900′, Climb 5000′/4.4 min. Range 640 miles/488 lbs. bombs, 912 miles max.   MFR

proved that the aircraft could not be accepted as a Navy type and the contract was terminated.

Curtiss also offered a monoplane to the Navy, which, on December 13, 1932, purchased the XS2C-1 with a Wright R-1510, wire-braced wings and wheel pants. Essentially similar to the Army's YA-10 attack, it probably was bought as an opportunity to test its slots and flaps rather than for tactical purposes. The wings seem too wide for that period's carrier technique. Curtiss also received the XS3C-1 designation in 1932 for a two-seat biplane previously ordered as an O2C-2 (see Chapter 9).

Of all the scouting prototypes tested in this period, the only successful one was developed from a two-seat fighter. Grumman's XFF-1 had demonstrated the value of retractable wheels, and so a second prototype fitted as an XSF-1 scout was ordered June 9, 1931, and first flew August 19, 1932. The XSF-1 had a 750-hp R-1820-78, and the two synchronized cowl guns of the XFF-1 were removed to provide for a larger fuel tank. The pilot was given a fixed gun in the upper wing and another .30-caliber gun was handled by the observer.

The production SF-1 had an R-1820-84, larger cowl, and controllable-pitch propeller. Ordered December 4, 1933, SF-1s were delivered from February to July 1934, and served with VS-3B, replacing Vought Corsairs. Armament was two .30-caliber guns and, when needed, two 116-pound bombs.

The 34th and last Grumman on this contract was completed with a twin-row R-1535 Wasp in a full cowl and a fixed gun mounted on the right side behind the engine. The XSF-2 was first flown November 26, 1934.

The Grumman two-seater got a taste of war when the Canadian Car and Foundry Company decided to open an aircraft factory at Fort William in 1936 by producing 40 aircraft for the Spanish Republic. Direct sales to Spain by Americans were forbidden

GRUMMAN SF-1
Wright R-1820-84, 725 hp
DIMENSIONS: Span 34'6", Lg. 24'11", Ht. 11'1", Wing Area
    310 sq. ft.
WEIGHT: Empty 3259 lb., Gross 5072 lb. Fuel 165 gal.
PERFORMANCE: Speed—Top 206 mph at 4000'. Service
    Ceiling 22,500', Climb 1650'/1 min. Range 800 miles.
                                                        USN

GRUMMAN XSF-2
Pratt & Whitney R-1535-72, 650 hp at 7500'
DIMENSIONS: Span 34'6", Lg. 24'8½", Ht. 10'11", Wing
    Area 310 sq. ft.
WEIGHT: Empty 3259 lb., Gross 4783 lb. Fuel 120 gal.
PERFORMANCE: Speed—Top 215 mph at 8900', Stalling
    62.6 mph. Service Ceiling 24,100', Climb 5000'/3.2
    min. Range 934 miles.   ARC

by the U.S. Government, but Grumman supplied a prototype (CG-1, registered NR12V) in November 1936, as well as 51 fuselages.

Known as the G-23 and powered by an R-1820F-52 of 775 hp at 5800 feet, the first Canadian example was flown in February 1938 and sold to Nicaragua. Thirty-four did arrive in Spain in May 1938 to be used by Grupo No. 28 for attack and reconnaissance. After the Spanish Civil War, nine served the Nationalist Grupo 5W in Morocco as the R6 Delphin. Shipment to Spain of 16 more planes was blocked by the Canadian Government, which had learned that their true destination was not Turkey, as had been claimed. They remained in crates until 15 were acquired in September 1940 by the Royal Canadian Air Force. The Canadians also utilized the landing gear and some of the structural design for a single-seat fighter prototype flown in December 1938.

The Scout Bombers

As the first in the new scout-bomber class and the last fixed landing gear biplanes used in squadron strength on the Navy's carriers, the Vought SBU-1 symbolizes the change from the biplane scout period to the dive-bomber monoplanes of World War II.

This two-seater first flew in May 1933 as the XF3U-1, but the Navy had decided against further two-seat fighter development and was projecting the combination of scout plane and dive bomber. Vought received a contract February 23, 1934, to

rebuild the XF3U-1 prototype to the XSBU-1 scout bomber. First flown May 29, 1934, the XSBU-1 had a 700-hp R-1535-80 in a new cowling with adjustable gills, more wing area and fuel, and could handle a 500-pound bomb.

Eighty-four production SBU-1s were ordered January 3, 1935—enough for all three carrier scouting squadrons. The cowling on the SBU-1 was so efficient that it became the model for all new Navy planes with twin-row radials. Armament included

VOUGHT XSBU-1
Pratt & Whitney R-1535-80, 700 hp at 8900'
DIMENSIONS: Span 33'3", Lg. 27'10", Ht. 12', Wing Area
    327 sq. ft.
WEIGHT: Empty 3558 lb., Gross 5297 lb., Max. 5520 lb.
    Fuel 145 gal.
PERFORMANCE: Speed—Top 208 mph at 8900', 201 mph/
    500 lb. bombs, Landing 65 mph. Service Ceiling
    25,300', Climb 5000'/3.7 min. Range 561 miles/bomber,
    902 miles as scout.   MFR

VOUGHT SBU-2   MFR

VOUGHT SBU-1
Pratt & Whitney R-1535-82, 750 hp takeoff, 700 hp at 8900'
DIMENSIONS: Span 33'3", Lg. 27'9", Ht. 12', Wing Area 327 sq. ft.
WEIGHT: Empty 3645 lb., Gross 5394 lb., Max. 5618 lb. Fuel 145 gal.
PERFORMANCE: Speed—Top 205 mph at 8900', 180 mph at s. l., 198 and 174 mph/500 lb. bombs, Cruising 122 mph, Landing 66 mph. Service Ceiling 24,400', Climb 1180'/1 min. Range 548 miles/500 lb. bombs, 862 miles as scout.   ARC

the usual fixed and flexible guns, plus a 500-pound bomb under the fuselage or two smaller bombs under the wings. Top speed was 205 mph as a scout or 198 mph when the bomb was carried.

The first SBU-1 was flown August 9, 1935, and the others were delivered from November 1935 to May 1936 to serve with VS-1B, -2B, and -3B. Fourteen were also built for Argentina as the V-142A,

the first being flown on December 1, 1936. Forty SBU-2s ordered in November 1936, similar except for a R-1535-98 of equal power, were delivered from April to August 1937 to Naval Reserve stations. The last carrier to use SBU-1s was the *Ranger*, which moved to the Atlantic in 1939 with VS-41 and VS-42, flying the Neutrality Patrol until most SBU-1s were retired in 1940 to Pensacola as trainers.

Chapter 20
Floatplanes of World War II

Scout-Observation, 1935–45: Curtiss Seagull

While World War II was dominated by monoplanes, as far as Americans were concerned, the most widely used Navy type in 1940 was the Curtiss SOC Seagull biplane, which, despite the rapid obsolescence of its contemporaries, still operated in 1944, even replacing the type that was supposed to replace it!

The prototype was the XO3C-1, designed to a Navy specification for a two-place biplane with folding wings, a large central float with retracting wheels, and a catapult-launch weight limit that confined the power plant to a 550-hp R-1340 Wasp and 140-gallon fuel capacity.

Ordered June 19, 1933, the XO3C-1 was first flown by H. L. Childs at Buffalo on March 5, 1934. Cockpits of the prototype were open, and the upper wing had full-length flaps and leading-edge automatic slots. When the wings were folded for storage in cruiser hangars, the width was only 14 feet, 6 inches—an important advantage over the old Corsairs.

Two rival prototypes were built to the same specification: the Douglas XO2D-1 and Vought XO5U-1. The Douglas ship also appeared in March 1934, and its cockpit canopy gave it a bit more modern look than the Curtiss. Vought's XO5U-1 was first flown May 8, 1934, with a cockpit canopy and a swept-back upper wing, its most distinctive feature.

The Navy relented on the amphibian aspect of its requirements, for the wheel-retraction weight penalty was undesirable. All these types were converted to a straight pontoon configuration, and it was planned that production aircraft would have an alternate wheeled undercarriage. The winner in the prototype rivalry became apparent when Curtiss received the largest contract in many years—on March 23, 1935, for 135 SOC-1 aircraft.

In that period floatplanes on battleships were or-

CURTISS XO3C-1
Pratt & Whitney R-1340-12, 550 hp
DIMENSIONS: Span 36', Lg. 30'2½", Ht. 15'7¾", Wing Area 347.8 sq. ft.
WEIGHT: Empty 3582 lb., Gross 5236 lb. Fuel 140 gal.
PERFORMANCE: Speed—Top 159 mph at s. l., 155 mph at 5000', Stalling 62 mph. Service Ceiling 16,100', Climb 5000'/5.6 min. Range 770 miles. MFR

DOUGLAS XO2D-1
Pratt & Whitney R-1340-12, 550 hp
DIMENSIONS: Span 36', Lg. 32', Ht. 16'4", Wing Area 302.8 sq. ft.
WEIGHT: Empty 3460 lb., Gross 5109 lb. Fuel 140 gal.
PERFORMANCE: Speed—Top 162 mph at s. l., 158 mph at 5000', Stalling 58.6 mph. Service Ceiling 14,300', Climb 5000'/6 min. Range 798 miles. USN

VOUGHT XO5U-1
Pratt & Whitney R-1340-12, 550 hp
DIMENSIONS: Span 36′, Lg. 32′6″, Ht. 15′6½″, Wing Area
    337 sq. ft.
WEIGHT: Empty 3563 lb., Gross 5213 lb. Fuel 138 gal.
PERFORMANCE: Speed—Top 157 mph at s. l., 153 mph at
    5000′, Stalling 56.5 mph. Service Ceiling 16,300′,
    Climb 5000′/5.6 min. Range 751 miles.   MFR

CURTISS SOC-1
Pratt & Whitney R-1340-18, 550 hp at s. l.
DIMENSIONS: Span 36′, Lg. 27′5″, Ht. 13′1″, Wing Area
    342 sq. ft.
WEIGHT: Empty 3442 lb., Gross 5130 lb. Fuel 140 gal.
PERFORMANCE: Speed—Top 162 mph at s. l., 158 mph at
    5000′, Stalling 54.6 mph. Service Ceiling 14,600′,
    Climb 1055′/1 min. Range 878 miles.   USN

ganized in observation squadrons whose primary
duty was spotting for the big guns, while cruiser
floatplanes were flown by scouting squadrons for
more distant reconnaissance. Combining the scout-
observation designation indicated that the same aircraft could fit both roles.

The prototype itself had been returned to the
factory and redesignated XSOC-1 when the production contract was drawn up. Modified to production configuration with enclosed cockpits, the
XSOC-1 was flown again April 5, 1935, with the

CURTISS SOC-1 (Seaplane)
Pratt & Whitney R-1340-18, 550 hp
DIMENSIONS: Span 36′, Lg. 32′3″, Ht. 14′10″, Wing Area
    342 sq. ft.
WEIGHT: Empty 3648 lb., Gross 5302 lb. Fuel 140–70 gal.
PERFORMANCE: Speed—Top 159 mph at s. l., 154 mph at
    5000′, Stalling 55.5 mph. Service Ceiling 14,200′,
    Climb 960′/1 min. Range 840–1003 miles.   USN

neatly faired wheeled landing gear. The first production SOC-1, fully convertible from floats to wheels, was flown August 8, 1935.

Armament was the usual for Navy seaplanes: a fixed gun on the cowl and a flexible gun in the rear cockpit, with 500 and 600 .30-caliber rounds, respectively. A rack under each wing could accommodate a 116-pound bomb or, with reduced fuel load, a 325-pound depth charge. A radio and life raft were standard equipment.

Fleet service began on November 12, 1935, when two SOC-1s replaced the OJ-2s on the U.S.S. *Marblehead,* the first cruiser to use the type. By June 1936 the SOC-1 contract was filled, and in October 1936 delivery began on 40 more aircraft redesignated SOC-2 on November 9, 1936, though nearly identical to the SOC-1.

Meanwhile, two experimental VSO projects of this period passed almost unnoticed. The Bellanca XSOE-1 had a 725-hp R-1820-84, folding wings, enclosed pilot's cockpit ahead of the gulled upper wing, and a deep fairing between fuselage and pontoon. When considered in May 1934, this design had attracted Navy approval because of its large float, which afforded protection to the propeller and tail, rugged, built-up structure between float and fuselage, excellent pilot's visibility, and low landing speed.

The XSOE-1 was ordered October 11, 1934, but by the time the prototype was completed on March

28, 1936, the empty weight had increased from the estimated 3,821 pounds to over 4,500 pounds. This threatened landing and catapult launch speeds, so much so that the Navy inspector called the XSOE-1 a "decidedly bad airplane." When the insurance was canceled, both company and Navy lost interest in flight tests. The aircraft taxied up the Delaware River from the Wilmington factory to its delivery point at the Philadelphia NAS on July 13, 1936. Accepted as is, without ever having been flown, it was stripped of equipment, stored, and forgotten.

Even less progress was made by another proposal made at the same time. The Fairchild XSOK-1 was based on a civil monoplane flying boat and powered by a Pratt & Whitney R-1510 over the wing. It was ordered September 27, 1934, but the contract was canceled August 16, 1935, with only the mockup in evidence.

On January 24, 1937, Curtiss first flew the XSO2C-1, which was an SOC with a longer fuselage and flaps added to the lower wings. The standard

CURTISS XSO2C-1
Pratt & Whitney R-1340-36, 550 hp
DIMENSIONS: Span 36', Lg. 31'11", Ht. 14'8", Wing Area 342 sq. ft.
WEIGHT: Gross 5479 lb.
PERFORMANCE: Speed—Top 165.7 mph. Service Ceiling 13,900'.
                                                                            USN

BELLANCA XSOE-1
Wright R-1820-84, 725 hp at 3000'
DIMENSIONS: Span 41', Lg. 34'7", Ht. 14'1", Wing Area 398 sq. ft.
WEIGHT: Empty 4508 lb., Gross 6031 lb., Max. 6552 lb. Fuel 150–226 gal.
PERFORMANCE: Speed—Top 176 mph at 3000', 168 mph at s. l., Landing 51 mph. Service Ceiling 21,400', Climb 5000'/3.6 min. Range 752–1104 miles.   USN

configuration, however, was preferred for 83 SOC-3s ordered May 18, 1937. Powered by the R-1340-22 and delivered from December 1937 to May 1938, this was the first model to go aboard battleships, replacing the O3U-3 Corsair. Three similar SOC-4s without weapons went to the Coast Guard.

The last Seagulls were built by the Naval Aircraft Factory because Curtiss had become too busy with other projects. Ordered on June 10, 1937, as the SON-1 (but identical to the SOC-3), the first of 44 SON-1s was completed in November 1938 and the rest from March to August 1939. A total of 307 Seagulls was built, making it the most widely used U.S. Navy aircraft when World War II began.

Three were usually carried on each of the 15 battleships, which were organized into five divisions, each consisting of three ships. Each division had an observation squadron bearing its division number (VO-1 to VO-5). Two were carried by each of the ten older Omaha class light cruisers and four by each of the 27 larger cruisers. Most operated in Cruiser Divisions of four or five ships, each with a Cruiser Scouting Squadron numbered accordingly VCS-3 to VCS-9. A few unattached cruisers and smaller ships also carried SOCs. The Marines' VS-3M at San Diego also had 12 SOC-3 landplanes, and others served on every carrier and shore station.

When the first escort carrier, the U.S.S. *Long Island,* was commissioned in June 1941, its complement comprised VS-201 (later VSG-1) with 12 SOC-3A and seven F2A-3 aircraft, the Seagulls being former battleship aircraft modified for carrier use. Similar Escort Scouting squadrons were organized in 1942 as more escort carriers joined the fleets. Although all the battleships' SOCs had been replaced with Vought monoplanes by December 1941, all cruisers still used Seagulls through 1942, and 27 cruisers still used them in August 1943.

The program to replace the SOCs with SO3Cs was a failure, and when that monoplane was with-

CURTISS SOC-3
Pratt & Whitney R-1340-22, 550 hp
DIMENSIONS: Same as SOC-1
WEIGHT: Empty 3633 lb., Gross 5306 lb. Fuel 140–70 gal.
PERFORMANCE: Speed—Top 164 mph at 800', 162 mph at s. l., Cruising 127 mph, Stalling 57.4 mph. Service Ceiling 14,400', Climb 880'/1 min. Range 859–1027 miles at 121–97 mph.   ARC

CURTISS SOC-3A
Pratt & Whitney R-1340-22, 550 hp
DIMENSIONS: Same as SOC-1
WEIGHT: Empty 3510 lb., Gross 4977 lb., Max. 5600 lb. with two 325 lb. bombs. Fuel 110 gal.
PERFORMANCE: Speed—Top 171 mph at 800', 167 mph at s. l., Cruising 125 mph, Stalling 55.6 mph. Service Ceiling 15,900', Climb 1080'/1 min. Range 512–620 miles, 468–530 with two 325-lb. bombs.   ARC

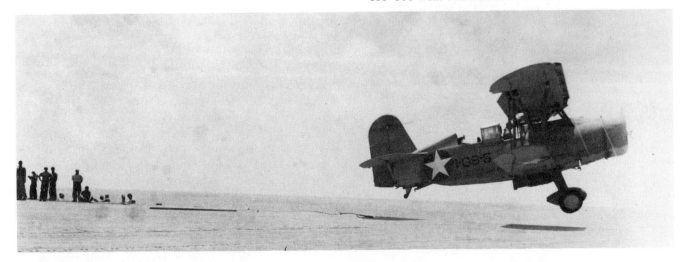

drawn from service in 1944, SOCs were returned to their ships. This may be the only case in which an aircraft replaced the newer aircraft intended to replace it. Not until sufficient SC-1s became available in 1945 did the SOC retire!

Vought Kingfisher

The observation-scout specification was developed in 1937 to provide a two-seat aircraft small enough to operate from battleships without the use of folding wings, while easily convertible to wheeled operations.

The first such prototype was the XOSN-1, ordered from the Naval Aircraft Factory on May 11, 1936, and tested at Anacostia in May 1938. Powered by an R-1340-36 giving 550 hp at 6,000 feet, it had automatic slots and I struts between the wings. The same engine and 36-foot wingspan common to the O3U and SOC aircraft were also used on the Stearman XOSS-1, ordered May 6, 1937, and tested in September 1938. Its most distinctive feature was full-length flaps on the upper wing, but it was less attractive to the Navy than the new Vought monoplane being developed.

Vought had had a little experience with the OS requirement with the XOSU-1, which was the O3U-6 modified with special flaps in October 1936. In 1937 designer Rex Biesel boldly proposed a Navy observation plane designed as an all-metal monoplane. Full-span flaps and spoiler lateral control would be utilized, along with spot welding of the metal structure. Staying within the 36-foot wingspan and catapult weight limitations meant step-

STEARMAN XOSS-1
Pratt & Whitney R-1340-36, 600 hp takeoff, 550 hp at 6000'
DIMENSIONS: Span 36', Lg. 29'10½", Ht. 12'7", Wing Area 377.6 sq. ft.
WEIGHT: Empty 3440 lb., Gross 5026 lb. Fuel 133–70 gal.
PERFORMANCE: Speed—Top 164 mph at 6000', 150 mph at s. l., Stalling 55.4 mph. Service Ceiling 17,200', Climb 800'/1 min. Range 832 miles.   USN

STEARMAN XOSS-1 Seaplane
Pratt & Whitney R-1340-36, 600 hp takeoff, 550 hp at 6000'
DIMENSIONS: Span 36', Lg. 34'6½", Ht. 14'6½", Wing Area 377.6 sq. ft.
WEIGHT: Empty 3826 lb., Gross 5612 lb. Fuel 133–70 gal.
PERFORMANCE: Speed—Top 162 mph at 6000', 148 mph at s. l., Stalling 56.7 mph. Service Ceiling 16,600', Climb 698'/1 min. Range 986 miles.   ARC

N.A.F. XOSN-1
Pratt & Whitney R-1340-36, 550 hp at 6000'
DIMENSIONS: Span 36', Lg. 34' (28'2"), Ht. 15'5½" (14'2"), Wing Area 378 sq. ft.
WEIGHT: Empty 3771 lb. (3475 lb.), Gross 5516 lb. (5250 lb.). Fuel 173 gal.
PERFORMANCE: Speed—Top 160 mph (162 mph) at 6000', 147 mph (149 mph) at s. l., Cruising 103 mph (101 mph), Stalling 54 mph (53 mph). Service Ceiling 14,900' (15,900'). Range 925 (978) miles. (Data for landplane)   USN

ping down to a smaller engine size, the 450-hp Pratt & Whitney R-985-4.

The XOS2U-1 prototype was ordered March 19, 1937, and made its first flight on March 1, 1938, as a landplane and on May 19 as a seaplane. Paul S. Baker was the test pilot, as he had been for the other Vought types since 1932.

When the new Vought proved to be perfectly practical for catapult work, 54 OS2U-1s were ordered May 22, 1939, and delivered from May to November 1940, beginning operations from the battleship *Colorado* in August. Armament was the two .30-caliber guns and two 116-pound bombs traditionally on Navy observation planes, but a radio direction loop had been added to the equipment.

VOUGHT XOS2U-1

Pratt & Whitney R-985-4, 450 hp takeoff, 400 hp at 5500'
DIMENSIONS: Span 36', Lg. 33'10" (30'1"), Ht. 15'3½"
(12'11"), Wing Area 262 sq. ft.
WEIGHT: Empty 3213 lb. (2950 lb.), Gross 4711 lb. (4611
lb.), Max. 4862 lb. Fuel 144 gal.
PERFORMANCE: Speed—Top 175 mph (177 mph) at 5000',
167 mph (169 mph) at s. l., Cruising 114 mph (112
mph), Stalling 55.6 mph (54 mph). Service Ceiling
19,900' (20,300'), Climb 970' (1020')/1 min. Range 1015
(1270) miles. (Data for landplane)   ARC

VOUGHT OS2U-1

Pratt & Whitney R-985-48, 450 hp takeoff, 400 hp to 5000'
DIMENSIONS: Span 35'11", Lg. 30'1", Ht. 12'11", Wing
Area 262 sq. ft.
WEIGHT: Empty 3105 lb., Gross 4780 lb. Fuel 144 gal.
PERFORMANCE: Speed—Top 177 mph at 5500', 169 mph
at s. l., Cruising 114 mph, Stalling 55 mph. Service
Ceiling 19,600', Climb 950'/1 min. Range 1233
miles.   USN

While the small engine kept performance quite modest, the sturdy seaplanes, soon to be named Kingfishers, proved to be reliable types.

The OS2U-2 model added leakproof fuel tanks, armor protection, and used the R-985-50. Of 158 OS2U-2s ordered December 4, 1939, 45 were delivered as seaplanes, beginning in November 1940, while the rest were delivered as landplanes with 70 extra Edo float sets. Most of these aircraft went to shore stations for the Navy's new Inshore Patrol squadrons, the first of which was organized in September 1940. In the antisubmarine role, 325-pound depth charges were carried. Two Kingfishers helped sink U-576 on July 15, 1942.

The mass-production version, OS2U-3, was identical to its predecessor, with the engine redesignated R-985-AN2. The first production contract was made October 31, 1940, and the first OS2U-3 flew May 17, 1941. It replaced the OS2U-2 on the production line in July 1941, with 1,006 completed by September 1942 (175 as seaplanes and 831 as landplanes with 157 extra float sets). To enable Vought to change over to F4U-1 fighters sooner, the Naval Aircraft Factory built 300 identical OS2N-1 Kingfishers from April to October 1942.

Lend-lease allocated 100 of the Voughts to the British Navy. They were delivered from March to July 1942 for use aboard armed merchant cruisers and light cruisers. Australia got 18 originally intended for the Dutch East Indies, while six went to Mexico in March 1942, 15 to Chile, three to the Dominican Republic, and six to Uruguay in April 1942.

The United States Navy had these Voughts

VOUGHT OS2U-1 Seaplane
Pratt & Whitney R-985-48, 450 hp takeoff, 400 hp to 5500'
DIMENSIONS: Span 35'11", Lg. 33'7", Ht. 15'½", Wing Area
262 sq. ft.
WEIGHT: Empty 3432 lb., Gross 4926 lb., Max. 5077 lb.
Fuel 144 gal.
PERFORMANCE: Speed—Top 175 mph at 5500', 167 mph
at s. l., Cruising 116 mph, Stalling 55.9 mph. Serv-
ice Ceiling 19,000', Climb 890'/1 min. Range 982
miles   USN

VOUGHT OS2U-2
Pratt & Whitney R-985-50, 450 hp to 5000'
DIMENSIONS: As OS2U-1
WEIGHT: Empty 3925 lb. (3549 lb.), Gross 5229 lb. (4883
lb.), Max. 6108 lb. Fuel 240 gal.
PERFORMANCE: Speed—Top 170 mph (177 mph) at 5500',
161 mph (168 mph) at s. l., Cruising 116 mph (117
mph), Stalling 58 mph (56 mph). Service Ceiling 16,-
000' (17,100'), Climb 760' (910')/1 min. Range 745 (825)
miles. (Data for landplane)   MFR

VOUGHT OS2U-3   ARC

aboard all its battleships in December 1941, as well
as on many aircraft tenders and carriers as utility
types. Thirty Inshore Patrol squadrons had Kingfishers in 1942, and 53 worked with the Coast
Guard. Five destroyers were commissioned with
catapults for OS2Us in 1942–43. The Voughts had
not been intended for cruiser hangars (battleship

floatplanes were carried in the open) because of
their rigid wings, but some were pressed into
cruiser service in 1943 when the SO3C program
failed.

During the war the Kingfishers were to be seen
on every ocean. Prewar squadron organizations
were abandoned, with the aircraft functioning as

part of each ship or shore station's company. Spotting for big guns became a job for ship's radar, and the floatplanes had other duties, such as antisubmarine warfare. One OS2U was even credited with downing a Zero fighter with its forward gun at Iwo Jima on February 16, 1945.

Yet of all the missions flown by the 1,519 Kingfishers, those best remembered by fliers are the rescue missions in which the seaplanes landed in rough waters and, working under enemy fire, saved downed airmen. On a single day an OS2U-3 from the *North Carolina,* stationed near the Truk Islands, flown by Lieutenant John A. Burns, rescued ten downed airmen, carrying seven at one time while taxiing to a waiting submarine.

Curtiss Scouts

To replace the SOC biplane aboard cruisers, the Navy proposed a specification for a "high speed scout," BuAir Design No. 403, an all-metal, mid-wing monoplane with interchangeable wheels and pontoons. The power plant for the two-seater would be the new 12-cylinder, inverted-V, air-cooled Ranger XV-770-4 developed for the Navy.

While battleship-based aircraft were classed as VOS, the cruiser scouts would be rated as VSO. Besides the limits on catapult weight and landing speed (no more than 6,350 pounds gross, or 56 mph), the VSO had to have a wingspan no greater

VOUGHT XSO2U-1
Ranger XV-770-4, 500 hp takeoff, 450 hp at 9000'
DIMENSIONS: Span 38'2", Lg. 36'1", Ht. 15'11", Wing Area 299.8 sq. ft.
WEIGHT: Empty 4016 lb. (3713 lb.), Gross 5459 lb. (5186 lb.), Max. 5634 lb. Fuel 128 gal.
PERFORMANCE: Speed—Top 190 mph (201 mph) at 9000', 175 mph (185 mph) at s. l., Cruising 127 mph (129 mph), Stalling 54.7 mph (53 mph). Service Ceiling 24,000' (22,200'), Climb 890' (1010')/1 min. Range 778 (872) miles, Max. 984 miles. (Data for landplane) MFR

CURTISS XSO3C-1
Ranger XV-770-4, 500 hp takeoff, 450 hp to 9000'
DIMENSIONS: Span 38', Lg. 37' (34'3"), Ht. 15'3" (14'), Wing Area 290 sq. ft.
WEIGHT: Empty 4250 lb. (4049 lb.), Gross 5660 lb. (5489 lb.), Max. 5855 lb. Fuel 96–126 gal.
PERFORMANCE: Speed—Top 189 mph (198 mph) at 9000', 173 mph (182 mph) at s. l., Stalling 55 mph (54.4 mph). Service Ceiling 17,800' (18,200'), Climb 810' (890')/1 min. Range 722 (782) miles, Max. 933 miles. (Data for landplane)   USN

than 38 feet (folding to 15 feet for cruiser hangars), had to carry more radio gear, be strengthened to 7.5 Gs for dive-bombing, and hopefully have better speed and pilot visibility than the SOCs.

Contracts were made on May 9, 1938, for the Curtiss XSO3C-1 and June 21 for the Vought XSO2U-1 prototypes. Vought finished their prototype with wheels in July 1939 and with floats in December 1939. The Curtiss prototype flew October 6, 1939, with wheels and demonstrated its seaplane capability in December. In both types the pilot sat ahead of the wing and the observer sat near the tail.

The prototypes were longer and more streamlined than the OS2U-1s and seemed to mark a step forward. Although the Vought XSO2U-1 had slightly better performance, that company was

preoccupied with the OS2U and F4U programs. Curtiss received a contract for production of 300 in a new Columbus, Ohio, factory on September 10, 1940, and a lend-lease program for the Royal Navy was added October 21, 1941.

The first Curtiss SO3C-1 delivered in April 1942 had lost the prototype's lightweight and streamlined appearance. Armor and larger leakproof tanks had been added, severe stability problems had been treated with blunt, upturned wing tips and enlarged dorsal fin, and cooling problems had broken the cowl lines. The wings had leading-edge slots and folded backwards for storage. All the aircraft were delivered with panted wheel gear, convertible to Edo center floats on pedestals when needed. Armament included the usual two .30-caliber guns plus two 325-pound depth bombs, and 144 pounds of armor was fitted.

CURTISS SO3C-1
Ranger V-770-6, 530 hp takeoff, 450 hp at 11,800'
DIMENSIONS: Span 38', Lg. 33'9", Ht. 11'4", Wing Area 293 sq. ft.
WEIGHT: Empty 4995 lb., Gross 6600 lb., Max. 7000 lb. Fuel 120–320 gal.
PERFORMANCE: Speed—Top 167 mph at 11,800', 150 mph at s. l., Cruising 117 mph, Stalling 56 mph. Service Ceiling 16,500', Climb 380'/1 min. Combat Radius 115 miles as scout, Range 640 miles as scout, 980 miles ferry. (Seaplane data)   ARC

The SO3Cs went aboard the new *Cleveland*—the first cruiser of its class—on July 15, 1942, but operational difficulties indicated that the aircraft was too heavy for its power plant. When the *Cleveland* sailed for North Africa in November 1942, OS2Us had replaced the unlucky Curtiss monoplanes.

Other models followed the SO3C-1. The SO3C-2, which appeared in October 1942, was equipped for escort-carrier operations and could carry a 500-pound bomb under the fuselage with the wheeled configuration, while the SO3C-2C appeared in December 1942 with the slightly more powerful V-770-8, new radio, and 24-volt system.

CURTISS SO3C-2
Ranger V-770-6, 530 hp takeoff, 450 hp at 11,800'
DIMENSIONS: Span 38', Lg. 34'8", Ht. 14'2", Wing Area 293 sq. ft.
WEIGHT: Empty 4785 lb., Gross 6350 lb., Max. 7000 lb. Fuel 120–360 gal.
PERFORMANCE: Speed—Top 182 mph at 11,800', 164 mph at s. l., Cruising 121 mph, Stalling 53 mph. Service Ceiling 18,200', Climb 520'/1 min. Combat Radius 167 miles as scout, Range 630 miles as scout, 1600 miles ferry. (Data for landplane)   LAWSON

The SO3C-3 of June 1943 had the V-770-8 but no carrier gear. Contracts were cut back by 200 on September 21, 1943, and the following month work began on converting 125 aircraft to radio-controlled target drones.

The British began receiving 250 SO3C-2C Seamews, as they called them, in December 1942, but used them only for training and drone work. The U.S. Navy name for the Seamew was the Seagull (the same as the SOC). A December 1941 bid to have this type built by Ryan as the SOR-1 was canceled when it was realized that the SO3C's power plant was inadequate and the aircraft could not fulfill its mission.

Curtiss built 800 of these two-seaters: 141 SO3C-1s, 150 SO3C-2s, 309 SO3C-2Cs, and 200 SO3C-3s, the last 43 being delivered in January 1944. By that time the Navy had already begun withdrawing the type from operating units, and the last to report an SO3C-3 on hand was VS-42 on March 31, 1944. SOC biplanes were reinstated in service, together with OS2Us, until the new SC-1s became available.

Curtiss Seahawk

The last float plane in service on Navy warships was the Curtiss SC-1 Seahawk, developed to meet the need for a more powerful shipboard scout. German warships, for example, had the Arado 196, with twice the Kingfisher's horsepower. In June 1942 the Navy requested proposals for a single-seat monoplane convertible from wheels to floats.

Curtiss submitted the most attractive proposal and received a letter of intent for XSC-1 and SC-1[1]

[1] The SC-1 designation duplicated that of the torpedo biplane of 1925.

CURTISS SO3C-3
Ranger V-770-8, 550 hp takeoff, 500 hp at 8100'
DIMENSIONS: As SO3C-2 landplane
WEIGHT: Empty 4800 lb., Gross 6370 lb., Max. 7000 lb.
 Fuel 120–320 gal.
PERFORMANCE: Speed—Top 183 mph at 8100', 171 mph
 at s. l., Cruising 121 mph, Landing 53 mph. Service
 Ceiling 17,400', Climb 860'/1 min. Combat radius 167
 miles as scout, Range 630 miles as scout, 1200 miles
 ferry. LAWSON

aircraft dated October 30, 1942, and contracts were approved for two prototypes on March 31 and for 500 aircraft on June 30, 1943. The power plant specified was the Wright R-1820-62, with 1,350 hp for takeoff and turbosupercharged to give 1,300 hp up to 26,800 feet. The anticipated top speed of the wheeled version would rise from 254 mph at sea level to 334 mph at 28,700 feet, making the Seahawk the equal of the F4F-4 Wildcat.

The prototype first flew at Columbus, Ohio, on February 16, 1944, and four XSC-1s were accepted in April 1944, with another deferred to 1945 for developmental testing. Curtiss delivered the first 119 SC-1s from July to December 1944. All appeared with wheeled gear, the Navy adding the Edo float and pedestal as needed, with conversion taking about six hours. The first ship to get Seahawks was the new 12-inch-gun large cruiser *Guam* on October 22, 1944.

Weapons included two .50-caliber guns, with up to 800 rounds. The pilot had 110 pounds of back armor, armor-glass windshield, and a bubble canopy with all-around vision. The wings had slots and folded backwards, with racks that could accommodate an APS-4 radar under the right wing and a 325-pound depth charge under the left. The central pontoon was originally designed with a bomb bay in the center, but this feature was replaced by an extra 95-gallon fuel tank.

Seahawk production continued to September 1945, with 568 delivered and 384 canceled by V-J Day. One SC-1 had been modified to the XSC-1A with the more economical R-1830-76 without turbo. In 1946 this aircraft was reaccepted as the XSC-2.

The R-1820-76 and refinements like a one-piece

CURTISS XSC-1
Wright R-1820-62, 1300 hp s. l. to 26,800'
DIMENSIONS: Span 41', Lg. 30'10", Ht. 14'2", Wing Area
 280 sq. ft.
WEIGHT: Empty 5970 lb., Gross 7590 lb., Max. 8090 lb.
 with two 325 lb. depth charges. Fuel 120 gal.
PERFORMANCE: Speed—Top 334 mph at 28,700', 254 mph
 at s. l., Cruising 136 mph, Stalling 60 mph. Service
 Ceiling 38,200', Combat Ceiling 35,500' with maximum load, Climb 2,650'/1 min., 10,000'/3.8 min. Combat radius 172 miles, Range 710 miles as scout, 760
 miles ferry. USN

CURTISS SC-1
Wright R-1820-62, 1350 hp takeoff, 1300 hp at 26,800'
DIMENSIONS: Span 41', Lg. 36'4½", Ht. 15'4", Wing Area 282 sq. ft.
WEIGHT: Empty 6320 lb., Gross 7936 lb., Max. 8612 lb. Fuel 120–215 gal.
PERFORMANCE: Speed—Top 313 mph at 28,600', 238 mph at s. l., Cruising 125 mph, Stalling 61 mph. Service Ceiling 37,300', Climb 2500'/1 min. Range 625–1090 miles.   USN

canopy were incorporated in 240 SC-2s ordered May 16, 1945. Cancellations reduced this number to nine, delivered from August to October 1946. A tenth SC-2 was accepted in March 1948 as scout-rescue aircraft, with a jump seat in the fuselage behind the pilot. Wing racks could accommodate a choice of two depth bombs, rescue cells, four rockets, or radar; the landplane version could handle a 100-gallon external ferry tank. Rescue equipment was also fitted to postwar SC-1s.

Edo, the company that had built most of the Navy's floats, also designed a seaplane of its own. The idea was to build a light single-seater with the SO3C-3's dimensions and Ranger engine. The Edo XOSE-1[2] prototypes were ordered January 11, 1944, and the first flew on December 28, 1945.

Folding wings, 135 pounds of armor, self-sealing tanks, two .50-caliber guns, and two depth charges were provided, along with a central float that could be replaced by wheels for ferry flights. A two-seat version with just one gun was flown as the XOSE-2 on July 24, 1947, but both versions showed serious flying problems.

The development program was cut back and acceptances were limited to six XOSE-1 single-seaters in April and two XOSE-2 two-seaters in August 1948, along with two unarmed dual-control TE-1 trainers.

CURTISS SC-2
Wright R-1820-76, 1425 hp at 1000', 1100 hp at 11,600'
DIMENSIONS: Same as SC-1
WEIGHT: Empty 6442 lb., Gross 8000 lb., Max. 8770 lb. Fuel 116–216 gal.
PERFORMANCE: Speed—Top 241 mph at 12,700', 235 mph at s. l., Cruising 137 mph, Stalling 75 mph. Service Ceiling 28,800', Climb 2480'/1 min. Range 515–925 miles.   MFR

[2] Originally XSO2E-1, following Bellanca's XSOE-1 of 1936, but then changed to XOSE-1.

After the war, the warships were gradually de-mobilized or had their catapult gear replaced by utility helicopter provisions. The last shipboard seaplane squadrons were disbanded in June 1949, and the shore-based SC-1s were last reported with a utility unit, HU-2, in October 1949. The age of the Navy floatplane was over; the catapult launches, and often hectic recovery operations, were at an end.

EDO XOSE-1
Ranger V-770-8, 550 hp takeoff, 500 hp at 8000'
DIMENSIONS: Span 37'11½", Lg. 31'1", Ht. 14'11", Wing Area 237 sq. ft.
WEIGHT: Empty 3973 lb., Gross 5316 lb., Max. 6064 lb. Fuel 120–78 gal.
PERFORMANCE: Speed—Top 198 mph at 8800', 188 mph at s. l., Cruising 111 mph, Stalling 61 mph. Service Ceiling 22,300', Climb 1350'/1 min. Range 900 miles.   MFR

Chapter 21
Navy Attack Planes, 1932-45

The U.S. Navy and Marines had 20 dive-bomber or torpedo plane squadrons when World War II began in 1939. Seven years earlier its carrier-based attack force had consisted of only two squadrons of open-cockpit biplanes, one of Martin dive bombers and the other of Great Lakes torpedo planes. The story of this tenfold expansion opens in 1932, when development of the next attack-plane generation began.

Navy Bombers, 1932–39

The first all-metal monoplane bomber obtained by the Navy bore little resemblance to the types it would use in World War II. In fact, the Consolidated XBY-1 was based on the commercial Fleetster cabin plane, with a high cantilever wing and wheel pants. The first metal monocoque fuselage on an American production plane contained the passenger cabin with the pilot's enclosure streamlined into the leading edge of the wing on top of the fuselage.

In the XBY-1 this cabin was replaced by a bomb bay with "orange peel" doors and a sliding panel in the roof behind the wing for the gunner's .30-caliber flexible gun. Integral fuel tanks—another first for the Navy—were in the wing's leading edges. Ordered April 9, 1931, the XBY-1 was flown to Anacostia on September 26, 1932, with a 575-hp R-1820-70, but a 600-hp R-1820-78 replaced it in January 1933. Flight tests went well until a crash landing November 24, 1933. The XBY-1 was thought to be too big for carrier stowage and was limited to horizontal bombing instead of the dive-bombing the Navy wanted now.

Returning to a conventional biplane layout, the Navy ordered prototypes from two companies on June 22, 1932. Based on BuAer Design No. 110 for a two-place dive bomber carrying a 1,000-pound bomb beneath its belly, the Consolidated XB2Y-1 and Great Lakes XBG-1 were powered by Pratt & Whitney R-1535-64 Wasps, with neat cowls, metal fuselage, and N struts. One .30-caliber fixed and one flexible gun were carried, with a bomb-dis-

CONSOLIDATED XBY-1
Wright R-1820-78, 600 hp at 8000'
DIMENSIONS: Span 50', Lg. 33'8", Ht. 10'6", Wing Area 361 sq. ft.
WEIGHT: Empty 3879 lb., Gross 6635 lb. Fuel 130 gal.
PERFORMANCE: Speed—Top 170 mph at 8000', 154 mph at s. l., Landing 64 mph. Service Ceiling 20,500', Climb 7600'/10 min.   MFR

placement device to eject the bomb clear of the propeller when diving.

Both the XBG-1 and XB2Y-1 were completed in June 1933, but the Great Lakes model won the contract. A November 22, 1933, order for 27 BG-1s was later expanded to 60, delivered from October 1934 to November 1935 with a sliding canopy over the two cockpits. They went to VB-3, organized for the new carrier *Ranger,* and both Marine dive-bomber squadrons, serving the Marines until they were replaced by SBDs in 1940.

On June 30, 1934, the Navy ordered an improvement of this type, the XB2G-1. Armed with a .50-caliber fixed gun ahead of the pilot and a .30-caliber flexible gun for the gunner, the XB2G-1 was similar to the BG-1 except for a deep belly containing an internal bay for the 1,000-pound bomb and wells for retracting wheels. Completed in November 1935, the XB2G-1 eventually became a Marine Command plane, but it lost production contracts to more modern dive bombers, and the Cleveland firm went out of business in 1936.

CONSOLIDATED XB2Y-1
Pratt & Whitney R-1535-64, 700 hp at 8900′
DIMENSIONS: Span 36′6″, Lg. 27′10″, Ht. 10′10″, Wing Area 362 sq. ft.
WEIGHT: Empty 3538 lb., Gross 6010 lb. Fuel 153–214 gal.
PERFORMANCE: Speed—Top 182 mph at 8900′, Landing 66 mph. Service Ceiling 21,000′, Climb 5000′/4.5 min. Range 487 miles.   MFR

GREAT LAKES BG-1
Pratt & Whitney R-1535-82, 750 hp takeoff, 700 hp at 8900′
DIMENSIONS: Span 36′, Lg. 28′9″, Ht. 11′, Wing Area 384 sq. ft.
WEIGHT: Empty 3903 lb., Gross 6123 lb., Max. 6347 lb. Fuel 165–225 gal.
PERFORMANCE: Speed—Top 188 mph at 8900′ as scout, 187 mph as bomber, Landing 66 mph. Service Ceiling 20,100′, Climb 5000′/5.5 min. Range 549 miles/1000 lb. bomb, 1245 miles as scout.   USN

GREAT LAKES XBG-1
Pratt & Whitney R-1535-64, 700 hp at 8900′
DIMENSIONS: Span 36′, Lg. 28′9″, Ht. 11′10″, Wing Area 380 sq. ft.
WEIGHT: Empty 3474 lb., Gross 5892 lb. Fuel 165–225 gal.
PERFORMANCE: Speed—Top 185 mph at 8900′, Landing 64 mph. Service Ceiling 22,300′, Climb 5000′/4.2 min.   ARC

GREAT LAKES XB2G-1
Pratt & Whitney R-1535-82, 700 hp at 8900'
DIMENSIONS: Span 36', Lg. 28'9", Ht. 11'1", Wing Area
  384 sq. ft.
WEIGHT: Empty 4248 lb., Gross 6394 lb., Max. 6802 lb.
  Fuel 130–90 gal.
PERFORMANCE: Speed—Top 198 mph at 8900', Landing
  61 mph. Service Ceiling 19,500', Climb 5000'/6.5 min.
  Range 582 miles/1000 lb. bomb, 1115 miles max. USN

GREAT LAKES XTBG-1
Pratt & Whitney XR-1830-60, 800 hp at 7000'
DIMENSIONS: Span 42', Lg. 35'1", Ht. 15'1", Wing Area
  547 sq. ft.
WEIGHT: Empty 5323 lb., Gross 8924 lb., 9275 lb./torpedo.
  Fuel 220 gal.
PERFORMANCE: Speed—Top 185 mph at 7000'/bomber,
  171 mph at s. l./torpedo, Landing 60 mph. Service Ceil-
  ing 16,400', Climb 5000'/6.2 min. Range 586 miles/tor-
  pedo, 998 miles/1000 lb. bomb.   ARC

The Torpedo Comes Back on One Wing

While the Navy operated only one torpedo-plane
squadron (VT-2 with TG-2s) from 1932 to 1937,
development of this attack style wasn't forgotten.
Three different prototypes ordered June 30, 1934,
got the new torpedo bomber (TB) designation and
the 800-hp Pratt & Whitney XR-1830-60 Twin
Wasp: the carrier-based XTBG-1 and TBD-1, as
well as the water-based XPTBH-1 (see Chapter 18).

The Great Lakes XTBG-1 was the last torpedo
biplane and was received from the builder on August 20, 1935. Wheels retracted into the all-metal
fuselage ahead of fabric-covered, tapered wings. A
torpedoman sat behind the Twin Wasp under a low
canopy with a bomb-aiming window between the
wheel wells. Pilot and gunner's seats behind the

wings were covered by a sliding enclosure. A torpedo or 1,000-pound bomb and two .30-caliber guns
were carried, but the flight characteristics were
unstable and the performance inferior to the
XTBD-1.

The Douglas XTBD-1 was an all-metal, low-wing
monoplane with the crew of three under a long
enclosure, and wheels retracting backward into the
wing, the left partially protruding for emergency
landings. In order that the big plane could be stored
aboard carriers, the 50-foot wings folded upwards,
reducing their span to 25 feet, 8 inches. The torpedo
officer sat between the pilot and gunner when act-
ing as navigator, but in battle he lay prone to sight
through a window behind the engine. A Norden
sight facilitated the horizontal aiming of a 1,000-

DOUGLAS XTBD-1
Pratt & Whitney XR-1830-60, 800 hp at 7000'
DIMENSIONS: Span 50', Lg. 35', Ht. 14'2", Wing Area 420
   sq. ft.
WEIGHT: Empty 5046 lb., Gross 8385 lb., Max. 8773 lb.
   Fuel 180 gal.
PERFORMANCE: Speed—Top 205 mph at 8000', 188 mph
   at s. l., 201 mph at 8000'/torpedo, Landing 63 mph.
   Service Ceiling 20,800', Climb 5000'/4.8 min. Range
   449 miles/torpedo, 907 miles/1000 lb. bomb.   USN

pound bomb, or a 15-foot Mk XIII torpedo could be
carried instead, with about four feet of its warhead
exposed.

The prototype was first flown at Santa Monica on
April 15, 1935, and reached the Anacostia test station on April 24. This Douglas became the first
monoplane ordered for carrier service (February 3,
1936) when 114 TBD-1s were ordered. The first
was delivered June 25, 1937, with an R-1830-64,
higher pilot's canopy, and the oil cooler moved under the starboard wing root. A .30-caliber fixed gun
was on the cowl's right side, and a .30-caliber flexible gun was provided at the rear cockpit.

As was customary, the first TBD-1 remained at
Anacostia for type testing. In August 1939 it became
the TBD-1A when twin floats were fitted and the
aircraft became a torpedo test aircraft for the Naval

Torpedo Station at Newport News, Virginia. The
remaining TBD-1s were delivered from September
1937 to June 1938, began to replace the *Saratoga*'s
TG-2s on October 5, 1937, and equipped all four
Pacific Fleet torpedo squadrons. Another 15 were
delivered from June to November 1939, and some
TBD-1s were stationed at Norfolk, where they were
issued to VT-8 in October 1941, with a few to the
Ranger and *Wasp*.

The world's best torpedo plane when introduced,
the TBD-1 had the misfortune to be the only torpedo type on hand at the start of 1942, when 100
remaining planes were named Devastators.

February 1 marked the beginning of a series of
raids on enemy islands by TBDs and SBDs, and on
May 7 the types worked together—TBDs with torpedoes at low level and SBDs dive-bombing from
above—and hit *Shoho*, the first Japanese carrier

DOUGLAS TBD-1
Pratt & Whitney R-1830-64, 900 hp takeoff, 850 hp at
   8000'
DIMENSIONS: Span 50', Lg. 35', Ht. 15'1", Wing Area 422
   sq. ft.
WEIGHT: Empty 6182 lb., Gross 9862 lb., Max. 10,194 lb.
   Fuel 180 gal.
PERFORMANCE: Speed—Top 206 mph at 8000', 192 mph
   at s. l., Cruising 128 mph, Landing 68.5 mph. Service
   Ceiling 19,700', Climb 720'/1 min. Range 435 miles/
   torpedo, 716 miles/1000 lb. bomb.   MFR

DOUGLAS TBD-1A

sunk in the war. The next day's torpedo attack on a larger enemy carrier failed and pointed out the TBD's weakness. The unsatisfactory torpedo then available required that runs be made at 80-foot altitudes at no more than 80 knots (92 mph), with release no more than 1,000 yards from the target, and even then the torpedo often failed to work properly. Enemy fighters and antiaircraft soon made such attacks nearly suicidal, and at the Midway battle only five of 41 Devastators launched returned.

The End of the Biplane

The launching of the aircraft carriers *Enterprise* and *Yorktown* in 1936 increased Navy aircraft requirements, and procurement officials selected scout-bomber types to fill the new squadrons and replace the Voughts on the older carriers. Six companies offered two-seat prototypes that year: the Great Lakes XB2G-1, Grumman XSBF-1, and Curtiss XSBC-3 biplanes, and the Northrop XBT-1, Vought XSB2U-1, and Brewster XSBA-1 monoplanes.

In order of appearance, the Great Lakes XB2G-1, described earlier, came first, followed by the smaller Grumman XSBF-1 among the biplanes. Ordered March 26, 1935, first flown December 24, and delivered for tests February 12, 1936, the XSBF-1 was a stubby development of the SF-2 two-seat biplane, with an R-1535-72, wheels retracting into the fuselage, enclosed cockpits, two .30-caliber guns, and provisions for a 500-pound bomb. The smaller bomb, compared to the 1,000 pounders on

GRUMMAN XSBF-1
Pratt & Whitney R-1535-72, 700 hp takeoff, 650 hp at 7000'
DIMENSIONS: Span 31'6", Lg. 25'9", Ht. 11'3", Wing Area 310 sq. ft.
WEIGHT: Empty 3395 lb., Gross 5002 lb., Max. 5442 lb. Fuel 130 gal.
PERFORMANCE: Speed—Top 215 mph at 15,000', 209 mph/ 500 lb. bomb, Landing 65 mph. Service Ceiling 26,-000', Climb 5000'/3.2 min. Range 688 miles/500 lb. bomb, 987 miles as scout.   PMB

the BG series, was specified for the scout-bomber (SB) types, a distinction that would soon disappear with heavier aircraft.

Grumman lost out to Curtiss for the scout-bomber contract. The last combat biplanes built in the United States, the SBC series was actually the culmination of a 1932 contract made for the XF12C-1 two-seat, high-wing monoplane. In December 1933 this type was redesignated XS4C-1 and a Wright R-1820-80 was to be installed. The following month the aircraft was labeled XSBC-1, but it crashed June 14, 1934. It was repaired, but the high wing proved unsafe for diving and another crash in September destroyed the prototype. It now seemed wiser to replace the 41-foot-span folding wing with a strong 34-foot biplane structure, and the prototype was reordered in April 1935 as the XSBC-2, with an XR-1510-12, new cockpit canopy, and new tail. The XSBC-2 version was tested by the Navy on December 9, 1935, and in April 1936 it reappeared once more as XSBC-3 with an R-1535-82.

CURTISS XSBC-1   MFR

This long development was rewarded on August 29, 1936, with a contract for 83 SBC-3s powered by R-1535-94 Wasps. First delivered June 1937, the SBC-3 was similar to its prototype, with wheels retracting into an all-metal fuselage and sliding canopy for pilot and observer. Fabric-covered wings were connected by I struts, the swept-back upper wing having ailerons and the straight lower wing utilizing flaps for landing and as dive brakes. As on most of this period's scout bombers, armament included a .30-caliber gun under the cowl and another in the rear cockpit, while a 500-pound bomb or a drop tank could be carried beneath the fuselage. Delivered by December 1937, they served three scouting squadrons.

One aircraft on this contract was completed in March 1938 as the XSBC-4, with a Wright R-1820-22 Cyclone, and these single-row engines had been

CURTISS XSBC-2
Wright R-1510-12, 700 hp at 7000'
DIMENSIONS: Span 34', Lg. 28'4", Ht. 12'7", Wing Area
317 sq. ft.
WEIGHT: Empty 3769 lb., Gross 5453 lb., Max. 5790 lb.
Fuel 140 gal.
PERFORMANCE: Speed—Top 217 mph at 7000' as scout,
210 mph as bomber, Landing 63 mph. Service Ceiling
24,900', Climb 5000'/3.5 min. Range 612 miles/500 lb.
bomb, 944 miles as scout.   MFR

CURTISS SBC-3   CURTISS XSBC-3   MFR
Pratt & Whitney R-1535-94, 825 hp takeoff, 750 hp at
9500'
DIMENSIONS: Span 34', Lg. 28'1", Ht. 13'2", Wing Area
317 sq. ft.
WEIGHT: Empty 4324 lb., Gross 6023 lb., Max. 6904 lb.
Fuel 135–80 gal.
PERFORMANCE: Speed—Top 220 mph at 9500', 203 mph
at s. l., Landing 67 mph. Service Ceiling 23,800', Climb
1340'/1 min. Range 635 miles/500 lb. bomb, 940 miles
as scout, 1190 miles max.   PMB

chosen for the SBC-4 type first ordered January 5, 1938. Delivery began in March 1939, the SBC-4s being distinguished from the earlier models by their wider-diameter engines and their capacity to handle a 1,000-pound bomb if needed. Additional orders brought the total to 124 completed by April 1940, these planes going to one scouting squadron and several Naval Reserve bases.

On June 6, 1940, 50 SBC-4s were returned to the company for transfer to France. They were repainted and flown to Halifax, with one lost on the way, 44 loaded on the carrier *Bearn,* and five on the British *Furious.*

The *Bearn*'s cargo reached Martinique, while the others got to Britain as the Curtiss Cleveland. In neither case did they do any flying, for the French aircraft were interned for the rest of the war, while the Clevelands were used for mechanics' practice. Fifty more SBC-4s, built between February and May 1941 to replace those sent abroad, went to Naval Reserve units. Except for a 126-gallon self-sealing tank replacing the unprotected 135-gallon fuselage tank, they were similar to their predecessors. Two squadrons served on the new *Hornet* in December 1941, but they were fortunately replaced by SBDs when that carrier reached the West Coast in March 1942, so that the Navy did not have to take these biplanes into battle. A Marine observation squadron, VMO-151, had them on Samoa in 1942.

Vought Vindicator

The dispute between biplanes and monoplanes for carrier service can be illustrated by two Wasp-powered scout bombers offered by Vought to the Navy. The XSB2U-1, ordered October 11, 1934, was a low-wing monoplane with an R-1535-72, while the XSB3U-1, ordered February 7, 1935, was a biplane similar to the SBU-1 except for wheels retracting backwards into the wing roots. The XSB2U-1 was first flown January 4, 1936, and the XSB3U-1 on March 13, and Navy tests held in April demonstrated the monoplane's superior performance. The shipboard stowage problem was solved by folding the wings upwards, as on the TBD.

An all-metal construction was used on the XSB2U-1, except for fabric-covering on the rear fuselage, control surfaces, and part of the wings. A long enclosure covered both crewmen, who had a .30-caliber fixed gun with 500 rounds and a .30-caliber flexible gun with 600 rounds. Gear beneath the fuselage could handle a 500- or 1,000-pound bomb, or droppable fuel tank. Wheels retracted backwards, rotating to fit flat within the wing.

Fifty-four SB2U-1s[1] were ordered October 26, 1936. The first flew May 21, 1937, and they joined VB-3 on the *Saratoga* in December to become the second carrier-based monoplane in service. Using R-1535-96 Wasps with reversible Hamilton propellers to limit diving speeds, they were similar to the prototype, and were followed by 58 SB2U-2s ordered January 27, 1938. With modified retracting gear, the SB2U-2s first flew August 11, 1938, and were completed by July 1939. The last SB2U-1, fitted with twin pontoons and ventral fin, became the XSB2U-3, tested in May 1939. These trials demonstrated a top speed reduction from 251 mph with retractable wheels to 210 mph with pontoons.

After Vought sent a V-156 demonstrator to Europe in November 1938, the French Navy ordered 40 V-156Fs on February 22, 1939, similar to the SB2U-2s except for wing dive flaps, pilot armor, and armament. Two 7.5-mm guns were located in the wings, a third in the rear pit, while racks accom-

[1] They provided two 18-plane squadrons with 50 percent reserves; this size order was common in the prewar period.

CURTISS SBC-4
Wright R-1820-34, 950 hp takeoff, 750 hp at 15,000'
DIMENSIONS: Span 34', Lg. 27'6", Ht. 13'2", Wing Area 317 sq. ft.
WEIGHT: Empty 4552 lb., Gross 6260 lb., Max. 7141 lb. Fuel 135–80 gal.
PERFORMANCE: Speed—Top 237 mph at 15,200', 218 mph at s. l., Cruising 127 mph, Landing 68 mph. Service Ceiling 27,300', Climb 1860'/1 min. Range 555 miles/1000 lb. bomb, 590 miles/500 lb. bomb, 1090 miles max., 876 miles as scout.   MFR

VOUGHT XSB2U-1

Pratt & Whitney R-1535-78, 700 hp at 8900'

DIMENSIONS: Span 42', Lg. 33'2", Ht. 15'10", Wing Area 305 sq. ft.

WEIGHT: Empty 4315 lb., Gross 5916 lb., Max. 6191 lb. Fuel 130 gal.

PERFORMANCE: Speed—Top 230 mph at 8900', 222 mph/ bomb, Landing 66 mph. Service Ceiling 26,600', Climb 5000'/3.7 min. Range 532 miles/1000 lb. bomb, 564 miles/500 lb. bomb, 892 miles max.　　　　MFR

VOUGHT XSB3U-1

Pratt & Whitney R-1535-82, 750 hp takeoff, 700 hp at 8900'

DIMENSIONS: Span 33'3", Lg. 28'2", Ht. 11', Wing Area 327 sq. ft.

WEIGHT: Empty 3876 lb., Gross 5627 lb., Max. 5837 lb. Fuel 145 gal.

PERFORMANCE: Speed—Top 214.5 mph at 8900', 209 mph/ 500 lb. bomb, Landing 66.5 mph. Service Ceiling 26,- 500', Climb 5000'/4.2 min. Range 590 miles/500 lb. bomb, 926 miles as scout.　　　　NASA

VOUGHT SB2U-1

Pratt & Whitney R-1535-96, 825 hp takeoff, 750 hp at 9000'

DIMENSIONS: Span 42', Lg. 34', Ht. 10'3", Wing Area 305 sq. ft.

WEIGHT: Empty 4676 lb., Gross 6323 lb., Max. 7278 lb. Fuel 115–80 gal.　　　　MFR

PERFORMANCE: Speed—Top 250 mph at 9500', 241 mph/ 500 lb. bomb, 231 mph at s. l., Cruising 143 mph, Landing 66 mph. Service Ceiling 27,400', Climb 1500'/ 1 min. Range 635 miles/1000 lb. bomb, 699 miles/500 lb. bomb, 1004 miles as scout.　　　　USN

VOUGHT SB2U-2
Pratt & Whitney R-1535-96, 825 hp takeoff
DIMENSIONS: As SB2U-1
WEIGHT: Empty 4713 lb., Gross 6379 lb., Max. 7332 lb.
  Fuel 115–80 gal.
PERFORMANCE: Speed—Top 251 mph at 9500', 232 mph
  at s. l., Landing 66 mph. Service Ceiling 27,500', Climb
  1340'/1 min. Range 630 miles/1000 lb. bomb, 1002
  miles as scout.   SHERTZER

VOUGHT SB2U-3
Pratt & Whitney R-1535-02, 750 hp at 9500'
DIMENSIONS: As SB2U-1
WEIGHT: Empty 5634 lb., Gross 7474 lb., Max. 9421 lb.
  Fuel 118–420 gal.
PERFORMANCE: Speed—Top 243 mph at 9500', Cruising
  152 mph, Landing 71 mph. Service Ceiling 23,600',
  Climb 1070'/1 min. Range 1120 miles/1000 lb. bomb,
  2450 miles ferry.   USN

modated three 150-kg (330-pound) bombs. The first
V-156F appeared in April 1939, and was shipped to
France in July, where the Voughts equipped two
squadrons on the Channel coast. Most were lost in
the bitter fighting in May 1940.

Fifty-seven SB2U-3 Vindicators with standard retractable gear had been ordered by the Navy on
September 25, 1939, and 50 more ordered by
France on March 28, 1940, were transferred to Britain as the V-156B Chesapeake. The first SB2U-3
flew January 10, 1941, and the first V-156B on February 26, with deliveries on both contracts made
from March to July 1941. SB2U-3s had additional
fuel capacity in self-sealing tanks, plus two .50-cal-
iber wing guns. British Voughts had four .303-cali-
ber wing guns, three 500-pound bombs, more armor, and no dive brakes, but never saw combat.

When America entered the war, the Marines had
two SB2U-3 squadrons, and older Vindicators

served the four scout squadrons on the *Ranger* and
Wasp in the Atlantic. The Marines' VMS-B231 was
hit on December 7 at Ewa but later flew to Midway
Island, where it became the only Vindicator involved in a major battle.

Northrop BT-1

The third carrier-based monoplane in Navy service
was the Northrop XBT-1, ordered November 18,
1934, the predecessor of the famous SBD series.
First flown August 19, 1935, and delivered December 16, the XBT-1 was an all-metal low-wing monoplane resembling the A-17 attack types but with
shorter wings to facilitate stowage aboard carriers.
Another feature was retraction of the wheels back
into fairings under the wings, which had perforated
split flaps at the trailing edge. These flaps were
opened during dives to prevent buffeting at high
speeds from spoiling the aim or making pullouts
dangerous.

Armament included a .50-caliber fixed gun for the
pilot and an observer's .30-caliber flexible gun, as
well as a 1,000-pound bomb carried below the fuselage. The original power plant was a 700-hp R-
1535-66, replaced in April 1936 by the R-1535-94
used on 54 BT-1s ordered September 16, 1936. The
first BT-1 was completed in November 1937, but a
strike at the factory delayed the next acceptances
until March 1938, and they joined VB-5 on the *Yorktown* in April.

The last BT-1 was completed in October 1938
with fixed tricycle gear to test that configuration,[2]
while the thirty-eighth aircraft was completed as
the XBT-2 with a 1,000-hp Wright R-1820-32 Cy-

NORTHROP XBT-1
Pratt & Whitney R-1535-66, 700 hp at 8900'
DIMENSIONS: Span 41'6", Lg. 31'10", Ht. 12'6", Wing Area
  315 sq. ft.
WEIGHT: Empty 4183 lb., Gross 6156 lb., Max. 6718 lb.
  Fuel 183 gal.
PERFORMANCE: Speed—Top 222.5 mph at 8900', 212 mph/
  1000 lb. bomb, Landing 62 mph. Service Ceiling 25,-
  800', Climb 5000'/4.1 min. Range 564 miles/1000 lb.
  bomb, 1063 miles max.   ARC

[2] Dr. Rene Francillon has revealed that this aircraft was later
sold back to Douglas, restored to the BT-1 standard, and sold to
the Japanese Navy as the DB-19 attack plane.

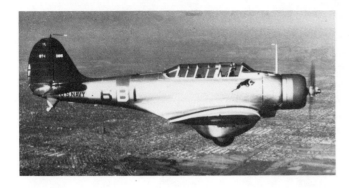

NORTHROP BT-1

Pratt & Whitney R-1535-94, 825 hp takeoff, 750 hp at 9500′

DIMENSIONS: Span 41′6″, Lg. 31′8″, Ht. 9′11″, Wing Area 319 sq. ft.

WEIGHT: Empty 4606 lb., Gross 6650 lb., Max. 7197 lb. Fuel 180 gal.

PERFORMANCE: Speed—Top 222 mph at 9500′, 212 mph/1000 lb. bomb, Cruising 192 mph, Landing 66 mph. Service Ceiling 25,300′, Climb 1270′/1 min. Range 550 miles/1000 lb. bomb, 1150 miles as scout.   USN

NORTHROP XBT-2

(Shown before change to SBD configuration)

Wright XR-1820-32, 1000 hp takeoff, 800 hp at 16,000′

DIMENSIONS: Span 41′6″, Lg. 31′9″, Ht. 12′10″, Wing Area 320 sq. ft.

WEIGHT: Empty 5093 lb., Gross 7231 lb., Max. 7593 lb. Fuel 210 gal.

PERFORMANCE: Speed—Top 265 mph at 16,000′, 252 mph/1000 lb. bomb, 243 mph at s. l., Cruising 155 mph, Landing 67 mph. Service Ceiling 30,600′, Climb 1450′/1 min. Range 604 miles/1000 lb. bomb, 1458 miles as scout.   USN

clone and wheels retracting into the wing roots. By this time the original Northrop firm had become the Douglas El Segundo division, and the XBT-2 first tested by the Navy in August 1938 was modified by its designer, Ed Heinemann, until it acquired the tail configuration of the SBD series.

Douglas Dauntless

When World War II began in September 1939, there were 385 dive bombers for 16 Navy and Marine squadrons, not including the Reserves. This force was comparable to the 366 land-based Stukas with which Germany began the war.

Seven types were included: three squadrons each of BG-1, SBU-1, and SBC-3 biplanes; two squad-

rons each of BT-1, SB2U-1, and SB2U-2 monoplanes; and one with the Cyclone-powered SBC-4. All these aircraft would be replaced within three years by a Douglas design.

On April 8, 1939, Douglas received a contract for 57 SBD-1s and 87 SBD-2s, developed from the XBT-2 with a high tapered fin and later named the Dauntless. The SBD-1 was first flown on May 1, 1940 and replaced the BG-1 in two Marine squadrons, while the SBD-2 appeared in November with more fuel and went aboard carriers. Both had two .30-caliber nose guns and a .30-caliber gun for the observer. Besides the 500-, 1,000-, or 1,600-pound bomb on the center rack, wing racks could accommodate two 100-pound bombs or two 325-pound depth charges.

On September 27, 1940, 174 SBD-3s were ordered and deliveries began March 1941, along with

DOUGLAS SBD-1

Wright R-1820-32, 1000 hp takeoff, 800 hp at 16,000′

DIMENSIONS: Span 41′6″, Lg. 32′2″, Ht. 13′7″, Wing Area 325 sq. ft.

WEIGHT: Empty 5903 lb., Gross 8138 lb., Max. 9790 lb. Fuel 180–210 gal.

PERFORMANCE: Speed—Top 253 mph at 16,000′, 232 mph at s. l., Cruising 142 mph, Landing 70.5 mph. Service Ceiling 29,600′, Climb 1730′/1 min. Range 860 miles/1000 lb. bomb, 985 miles as scout, 1165 miles ferry.   USN

DOUGLAS SBD-2

Wright R-1820-32, 1000 hp takeoff

DIMENSIONS: As SBD-1

WEIGHT: Empty 6293 lb., Gross 9061 lb., Max. 10,360 lb. Fuel 260–310 gal.

PERFORMANCE: Speed—Top 252 mph at 16,000′, Cruising 148 mph, Landing 75.5 mph. Service Ceiling 26,000′, Climb 1080′/1 min. Range 1225 miles/1000 lb. bomb, 1370 miles as scout.   MFR

DOUGLAS SBD-3

Wright R-1820-52, 1000 hp takeoff, 800 hp at 16,000'

DIMENSIONS: Span 41'6", Lg. 32'8", Ht. 13'7", Wing Area 325 sq. ft.

WEIGHT: Empty 6345 lb., Gross 9407 lb., Max. 10,400 lb. Fuel 260–310 gal.

PERFORMANCE: Speed—Top 250 mph at 16,000', 231 mph at s. l., as scout, 241 mph/1000 lb. bomb, Landing 78 mph. Service Ceiling 27,100', Climb 1190'/1 min., 10,000'/9 min. Range 1205 miles/1000 lb. bomb at 152 mph, 1415 miles as scout. USN

78 similar SBD-3As (A-24s) for the Army. This version introduced the R-1820-52, self-sealing fuel tanks, armor plate, and an armament of two .50-caliber fixed and two .30-caliber flexible guns.

Dauntless production might have ended when the last aircraft on this contract was completed in January 1942 had not the Pearl Harbor attack created a sudden demand for all the planes that could be built. New contracts were let, and in March 1942 Douglas resumed deliveries on 500 more SBD-3s. Ninety became A-24s. In October acceptances began on 780 SBD-4s and 170 Army SBD-4As (A-

DOUGLAS SBD-5

Wright R-1820-60, 1200 hp takeoff, 1000 hp at 13,800'

DIMENSIONS: Span 41'6", Lg. 33', Ht. 12'11", Wing Area 325 sq. ft.

WEIGHT: Empty 6533 lb., Gross 9352 lb., Max. 10,700 lb. Fuel 254–370 gal.

PERFORMANCE: Speed—Top 252 mph at 13,800', 238 mph at s. l., Cruising 139 mph, Landing 80 mph. Service Ceiling 24,300', Climb 1700'/1 min. Range 1115 miles/1000 lb. bomb, 1565 miles as scout. USN

24As), similar to the SBD-3 except for a new electrical system.

In February 1943 delivery began on 3,025 SBD-5s, first ordered December 10, 1942, and powered by a 1,200-hp R-1820-60 engine. Nine went to Britain for evaluation. The final version of the Dauntless comprised 450 SBD-6s, with more fuel and a 1,350-hp R-1820-66. When the last Dauntless was completed in July 1944, 5,936 had been built, including those for the Army.

In December 1941 the three Navy carriers in the Pacific had 111 SBDs aboard for their six scout and bomber squadrons, and the Marines had two SBD squadrons at Ewa. The carriers were fortunate enough not to be at Pearl Harbor, and on December 10 an *Enterprise* SBD sank a Japanese submarine (I-70), the first enemy warship sunk by the Navy in the war. (Pilot Clarence E. Dickinson had been one of seven SBD pilots shot down when they flew unawares into the December 7 attack; another 17 Marine SBD-1s were destroyed on the ground.)

Joined by the *Yorktown*'s air group in February 1942, the Dauntless dive bombers, Devastator torpedo planes, and Wildcat fighters struck repeatedly at the Japanese. At the Battle of Midway 110 SBDs from three carriers destroyed all four enemy carriers and turned the tide of the Pacific war. By that time two SBD squadrons were embarked on each U.S. carrier and fought in every carrier action of the next two years.

Although the Dauntless was phased out of attack carrier operations in July 1944, it continued operating in land-based Marine dive-bomber squadrons until the war's end. New Zealand operated 68 planes between July 1943 and May 1944 (18 SBD-3s, 27 SBD-4s, and 23 SBD-5s), and two French Navy *escadrilles* received 32 SBD-5s in November 1944.

During its successful career, the Douglas was credited with sinking 18 warships (including six carriers and a battleship in 1942), often with torpedo-bomber help. Rather surprising is the fact that the downing of 138 Japanese planes was also credited to SBD pilots and gunners in the brisk fights that often followed the bomb drops.

DOUGLAS SBD-6   USN

Brewster's Bombers

The difficulties an apparently good design may encounter in the hands of management inexperienced in aircraft production are illustrated in the story of the Brewster dive bombers. This firm's first airplane was the XSBA-1, ordered by the Navy October 15, 1934. On April 15, 1936, it appeared for tests as a midwing two-seat monoplane with an internal bomb bay, Wright R-1820-4, and two-bladed propeller.

In its original form the XSBA-1 did 242 mph with a gross weight of 3,695 pounds, but was returned to the company for installation of an XR-1820-22. The revised aircraft reappeared in January 1937 with a new cowl and three-bladed propeller. The fastest dive bomber in the air (263 mph), it was very clean, with wheels retracting into the fuselage ahead of the doors covering the 500-pound bomb. Perforated wing flaps acted as dive brakes. The pilot was separated from the observer by a long fairing between their canopies.

Although Brewster itself did not receive a pro-

BREWSTER XSBA-1 (original form)   ARC

BREWSTER XSBA-1
Wright XR-1820-22, 950 hp takeoff, 750 hp at 15,200'
DIMENSIONS: Span 39', Lg. 28'3", Ht. 11'1", Wing Area 259 sq. ft.
WEIGHT: Empty 4080 lb., Gross 5736 lb., Max. 5972 lb. Fuel 136 gal.
PERFORMANCE: Speed—Top 263 mph at 15,200', Landing 69 mph. Service Ceiling 28,500', Climb 1970'/1 min. Range 573 miles/500 lb. bomb, 890 miles as scout.
                                                    USN

duction contract for this type, 30 were ordered on September 29, 1938, from the Naval Aircraft Factory and designated SBN-1. They took uncommonly long to build; the first was not delivered until November 1940, the next 22 were not ready until June and July 1941, and the contract was not completed until March 1942. Powered by an R-1820-38 Cyclone, the SBN-1 carried a .50-caliber fixed gun, a .30-caliber flexible gun, and a 500-pound bomb.

In the meantime Brewster had designed the larger XSB2A-1, ordered April 4, 1939. Except for wheels retracting into the wing and a dummy power-operated turret for the gunner, the XSB2A-1 was rather similar to its smaller predecessor. Known as the Brewster 340 on company records, it was powered by a 1,700-hp Wright R-2600 Cyclone and a three-bladed propeller in a large spinner and carried a 1,000-pound bomb internally.

Even before the prototype's first flight on June 17, 1941, production contracts had been placed by Britain, the Dutch East Indies, and the United States Navy (the day before Christmas 1940). Production models had armor, self-sealing fuel tanks, and a long transparent enclosure, but did not pro-

N.A.F. SBN-1
Wright R-1820-38, 950 hp takeoff, 750 hp at 15,200′
DIMENSIONS: Span 39′, Lg. 27′8″, Ht. 12′5″, Wing Area 259 sq. ft.
WEIGHT: Empty 4503 lb., Gross 6245 lb., Max. 6759 lb. Fuel 136 gal.
PERFORMANCE: Speed—Top 254 mph at 15,200′, 231 mph at s. l., Cruising 117 mph, Landing 68 mph. Service Ceiling 28,300′, Climb 1970′/1 min. Range 1015 miles/500 lb. bomb, 1110 miles as scout.   USN

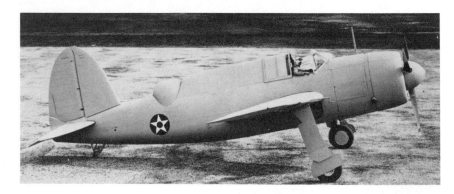

BREWSTER XSB2A-1
Wright R-2600-8, 1700 hp takeoff, 1350 hp at 13,000′
DIMENSIONS: Span 47′, Lg. 38′, Ht. 16′1″, Wing Area 379 sq. ft.
WEIGHT: Empty 6935 lb., Gross 10,168 lb., Max. 10,982 lb. Fuel 304–95 gal.
PERFORMANCE: Speed—Top 311 mph at 15,000′, Cruising 157 mph, Landing 70 mph. Service Ceiling 27,000′, Climb 2310′/1 min. Range 980 miles/1000 lb. bomb, 1570 miles as scout.   MFR

BREWSTER BERMUDA I   MFR

BREWSTER SB2A-2
Wright R-2600-8, 1700 hp takeoff, 1450 hp at 12,000'
DIMENSIONS: Span 47', Lg. 39'2", Ht. 15'5", Wing Area
  379 sq. ft.
WEIGHT: Empty 9924 lb., Gross 13,068 lb., Max. 14,289
  lb. Fuel 174–421 gal.
PERFORMANCE: Speed—Top 274 mph at 12,000', 259 mph
  at s. l., Cruising 161 mph, Landing 87 mph. Service
  Ceiling 24,900', Climb 2080'/1 min. Range 720 miles/
  500 lb. bomb, 1675 miles as scout.   USN

BREWSTER SB2A-4
Wright R-2600-8A, 1700 hp takeoff, 1450 hp at 12,000'
DIMENSIONS: As SB2A-2
WEIGHT: Empty 9785 lb., Gross 12,663 lb., Max. 13,811
  lb. Fuel 174–421 gal.
PERFORMANCE: Speed—Top 275 mph at 12,000', Cruising
  155 mph, Landing 86 mph. Service Ceiling 25,400',
  Climb 2190'/1 min. Range 750 miles/500 lb. bomb,
  1750 miles as scout.   USN

vide the turret planned for the prototype. Those
built for Britain were named Bermudas, while Navy
versions were called Buccaneers. The first Bermudas began appearing in July 1942 and were similar
to 162 planes built for the East Indies, which the
Navy took over beginning October 1942, under the
designation SB2A-4. With instrument panels still
inscribed in Dutch, they were used by Marines for
training. Armament included eight .30-caliber guns:
two in the nose, four in the wings, and two in the
rear cockpit, as well as a 1,000-pound bomb.

Similar in appearance were 80 SB2A-2 Buccaneers, delivered beginning in February 1943 on the

Navy contract and armed with two .50-caliber nose
guns, two .30-caliber wing guns, and two .30-caliber
flexible guns. The last model built comprised 60
SB2A-3s which had folding wings and arresting
gear for carrier operation.

There were numerous production delays before
the last of 770 dive bombers was completed in May
1944 at a Johnsville facility in Bucks County, Pennsylvania. Neither 468 Bermudas for Britain nor the
Navy Buccaneers ever fired a shot in action as far
as can be determined. Some Bermudas were used
for target towing until the entire lot was "reduced
to produce" in April 1945.

Helldivers at War

The most widely used American dive bomber was
first ordered May 15, 1939, and flown as a prototype
on December 18, 1940. A chunky, all-metal, midwing monoplane, the Curtiss XSB2C-1 two-seater
inherited the name Helldiver from earlier Curtiss
dive bombers.

Production models ordered November 19, 1940,
incorporated over 800 changes, including a larger
tail, self-sealing fuel tanks of increased capacity,
and the addition of 195 pounds of armor. Instead of
two .50-caliber fixed guns on the prototype's cowl,
four were placed in the wings of the first 200 SB2C-
1s. Later Helldivers (SB2C-1C) had two 20-mm
wing guns instead. The observer operated two .30-
caliber flexible guns concealed beneath the folding
fairing at the rear of the cockpit enclosure. A 1,700-
hp Wright R-2600-8 Cyclone turned a three-bladed

CURTISS XSB2C-1
Wright R-2600-8, 1700 hp takeoff, 1450 hp at 12,000'
DIMENSIONS: Span 49'9", Lg. 35'4" Ht. 15'5", Wing Area
  422 sq. ft.
WEIGHT: Empty 7122 lb., Gross 10,261 lb., Max. 10,859
  lb. Fuel 270–400 gal.
PERFORMANCE: Speed—Top 322 mph at 14,600', 290 mph
  at s. l., Cruising 155 mph, Landing 69 mph. Service
  Ceiling 29,975', Climb 2380'/1 min. Range 996 miles/
  1000 lb. bomb, 1620 miles as scout, 2260 miles
  ferry.   MFR

CURTISS SB2C-1   AMC

propeller, and wings folded upwards for carrier
stowage. A 1,000-pound bomb in an internal bay
could be dropped from a dive braked by perforated
wing flaps. Wing racks could accommodate a 325-
pound depth charge or a 58-gallon drop tank.

The prototype crashed February 9, 1941, was rebuilt, and completely destroyed in a December 21
dive test. On June 30, 1942, the first SB2C-1 began
flight tests six months behind schedule, but when
Helldivers were issued in December to squadrons
on the first new *Essex* class carrier, too many faults
were found to allow them to begin operations. Truman's congressional investigation found the program "hopelessly behind schedule" and that Curtiss, in April 1943, "had not succeeded in producing
a single SB2C . . . usable as a combat airplane" despite expensive self-praise in advertising.

CURTISS SB2C-1C
Wright R-2600-8, 1700 hp takeoff, 1450 hp at 12,000'
DIMENSIONS: Span 49'9", Lg. 36'8", Ht. 13'2", Wing Area
422 sq. ft.
WEIGHT: Empty 10,114 lb., Gross 14,720 lb., Max. 16,607
lb. Fuel 320–566 gal.
PERFORMANCE: Speed—Top 281 mph at 12,400', 265 mph
at s. l., Cruising 158 mph, Landing 79 mph. Service
Ceiling 24,700', Climb 1750'/1 min. Range 1110 miles/
1000 lb. bomb, 1895 miles max.   USN

Not until November 11, 1943, did an SB2C-1
squadron (*Bunker Hill*'s VB-17) attack the enemy,
and it soon appeared that the numerous modifications had succeeded, for by the fall of 1944 every
large carrier in the U.S. Fleet had a Helldiver
bombing squadron with upwards of 25 or more aircraft.

By March 1944, 978 SB2A-1/-1Cs had been built
at Columbus. The fifth example had become the
XSB2C-2, tested March 1943 with twin floats for
the Marines. A production program was canceled
when it was realized that the Marines need use
land-based aircraft only, and the SB2C-1A was substituted; the latter actually consisted of 410 surplus
Army A-25As with more armor and without folding
wings. None of these entered combat, however, but
were used solely for operational training.

A 1,900-hp R-2600-20 Cyclone with a four-bladed
propeller powered 1,112 SB2C-3s, whose delivery
began by January 1944. They were followed, beginning in June, by 2,045 SB2C-4s, which added
wing fittings for eight 5-inch rockets or 1,000
pounds of additional bombs, perforated flaps, and
radar. The 970 SB2C-5s, which began appearing
in February 1945, had APS-4 radar and a larger
fuel capacity. A 2,100-hp R-2600-22 powered two
XSB2C-6s converted from earlier aircraft.

When Helldiver production ended in October
1945, 5,105 planes had been finished at Columbus,
Ohio, and 900 fixed-wing A-25As had been built for

CURTISS XSB2C-2   MFR

CURTISS SB2C-3
Wright R-2600-20, 1900 hp takeoff, 1450 hp at 15,000′
DIMENSIONS: As SB2C-1
WEIGHT: Empty 10,400 lb., Gross 14,042 lb., Max. 16,471 lb. Fuel 320–566 gal.
PERFORMANCE: Speed—Top 294 mph at 16,700′, 269 mph at s. l., Cruising 158 mph, Landing 79.5 mph. Service Ceiling 29,300′, Climb 1830′/1 min. Range 1165 miles/ 1000 lb. bomb, 1925 miles max.   USN

CURTISS SB2C-4
Wright R-2600-20, 1900 hp takeoff, 1450 hp at 15,000′
DIMENSIONS: As SB2C-1
WEIGHT: Empty 10,547 lb., Gross 14,189 lb., Max. 16,616 lb. Fuel 320–566 gal.
PERFORMANCE: Speed—Top 295 mph at 16,700′, 270 mph at s. l., Cruising 158 mph, Landing 84 mph. Service Ceiling 29,100′, Climb 1800′/1 min. Range 1165 miles/ 1000 lb. bomb, 1235 miles normal as scout.   MFR

CURTISS SB2C-5
Wright R-2600-20, 1900 hp takeoff, 1450 hp at 15,000′
DIMENSIONS: As SB2C-1
WEIGHT: Empty 10,589 lb., Gross 14,415 lb., Max. 16,287 lb. Fuel 355–655 gal.
PERFORMANCE: Speed—Top 290 mph at 16,500′, 267 mph at s. l., Cruising 161 mph, Landing 92 mph. Service Ceiling 27,600′, Climb 1850′/1 min. Range 1324 miles.
          MFR

the Air Force at St. Louis. In addition, two Canadian factories had produced Helldivers beginning in September 1943: 300 from Fairchild, designated SBF, and 834 from the Canadian Car and Foundry plant, designated SBW. The first 26 of the latter went to Britain's Fleet Air Arm but were not used operationally.

Helldivers were the standard Navy dive bombers in every battle during the war's last year, and the last squadron was not retired from service until June 1949. Fifty were given to Greece for use in the civil war in 1948. Some were used by Italy from 1950 to 1959.

The Avengers

The standard torpedo bomber through all but the first six months of the war, Grumman's Avenger was designed as a TBD-1 replacement. Two XTBF-1 prototypes were ordered April 8, 1940, and 286 production TBF-1s on December 23, for the need for a better torpedo bomber could not await the prototype's first flight on August 7, 1941.

Although the first XTBF-1 was destroyed November 28, the second flew December 20, just as post–Pearl Harbor emergency production decisions were being made. Even though Grumman received big new orders, it could not make enough, so the automobile industry's resources were brought in when General Motors contracted to build Avengers on March 23, 1942. Designated TBM-1, they were built at the Eastern Aircraft Division in Trenton, New Jersey.

A fat-bodied midwing monoplane with a 1,700-hp R-2600-8, the TBF-1 had a crew of three, internal bays for a torpedo or a 2,000-pound bomb, and a power-operated turret. The landing gear retracted into the wings, which folded back for carrier stowage. The Avenger's pilot released the torpedo and fired a .30-caliber fixed gun on the cowl's right side, and the gunner's turret was provided with a .50-caliber gun. Between them sat a bombardier who could climb down to a compartment behind the bomb bay to set the torpedo, operate the bombsight, or fire the .30-caliber ventral gun. Four 500-pound

GRUMMAN XTBF-1   MFR

GENERAL MOTORS TBM-1D   USMC

GRUMMAN TBF-1
Wright R-2600-8, 1700 hp takeoff, 1450 hp at 12,000'
DIMENSIONS: Span 54'2", Lg. 40', Ht. 16'5", Wing Area
    490 sq. ft.
WEIGHT: Empty 10,080 lb., Gross 13,667 lb., Max. 15,905
    lb. Fuel 335–95 gal.
PERFORMANCE: Speed—Top 271 mph at 12,000', 269 mph/
    torpedo, 251 mph at s. l., Cruising 145 mph, Landing
    76 mph. Service Ceiling 22,400', Climb 1430'/1 min.
    Range 1215 miles/torpedo, 1450 miles as scout.   USN

GENERAL MOTORS TBM-3
Wright R-2600-20, 1900 hp takeoff, 1450 hp at 15,000'
DIMENSIONS: As TBF-1
WEIGHT: Empty 10,843 lb., Gross 16,761 lb., Max. 18,250
    lb. Fuel 335–810 gal.
PERFORMANCE: Speed—Top 267 mph at 15,000', Cruising
    151 mph, Landing 78 mph. Service Ceiling 23,400',
    Climb 1170'/1 min. Range 1130 miles/torpedo, 1565
    miles/drop tanks, 2530 miles max.   PMB

bombs, four 325-pound depth charges, or added
fuel were alternative loads.

Grumman delivered the first TBF-1 in January
1942 and completed 1,525 TBF-1 and 764 TBF-1C
Avengers by December 1943, after which all
Avenger production was at Trenton so that Grumman could concentrate on fighters. The TBF-1C,
introduced in July 1943, had two .50-caliber wing
guns for forward firepower, and bulletproof glass in
the turret was added to the Grumman's 331 pounds
of armor. One TBF-1 became the XTBF-2, flown
May 1, 1942, with an XR-2600-10 Cyclone, and two
XTBF-3s, first completed in July 1943, were distinguished by R-2600-20 engines with multiple cowl
flaps.

Trenton-built Avengers simply paralleled the
models just described, beginning with the first
TBM-1 accepted in November 1942 and proceeding
through 550 TBM-1s, 2,332 TBM-1Cs and, finally,
4,661 TBM-3s manufactured between April 1944
and September 1945. Some of these became TBM-

GENERAL MOTORS TBM-1C
Wright R-2600-8, 1700 hp takeoff, 1450 hp at 12,000'
DIMENSIONS: As TBF-1
WEIGHT: Empty 10,555 lb., Gross 16,412 lb., Max. 17,364
    lb. Fuel 335–726 gal.
PERFORMANCE: Speed—Top 257 mph at 12,000', Cruising
    153 mph, Landing 77 mph. Service Ceiling 21,400',
    Climb 10,000'/13 min. Range 1105 miles/torpedo, 2335
    miles max.   USN

GENERAL MOTORS TBM-3E
Wright R-2600-20, 1900 hp takeoff, 1450 hp at 15,000'
DIMENSIONS: Span 54'2", Lg. 40'11½", Wing Area 490 sq.
    ft.
WEIGHT: Empty 10,545 lb., Gross 14,160 lb., Max. 17,895
    lb. Fuel 335–810 gal.
PERFORMANCE: Speed—Top 276 mph at 16,500', 251 mph
    at s. l., Cruising 147 mph, Landing 81 mph. Service
    Ceiling 30,100', Climb 2060'/1 min. Range 1010 miles/
    torpedo, 1145 miles normal, 1920 miles as scout.   USN

1Ds and TBM-3Ds when fitted with APS-6 radar ahead of the starboard wing. TBM-3Es had APS-4 radar below the wing and three XTBM-4s were added with revised wing structures.

The Avenger's first combat deployment was the VT-8 detachment sent to Hawaii with 21 TBF-1s. Six of these sortied from Midway on June 4, 1942, but only one returned. More successful were the squadrons aboard the three carriers that began the Guadalcanal operation on August 7. Avengers helped sink the carrier *Ryujo*, battleship *Hiei*, and cruiser *Kinugasu*.

Every new fast carrier that joined the Pacific Fleet from 1943 to the war's end had its Avenger squadron, and they participated in every major battle. Teamed with dive bombers, they destroyed both of the world's largest battleships, the *Musashi* and the *Yamato*. In the Atlantic Avengers served on escort carriers, first in support of the North African invasion and then with the antisubmarine groups being formed. They made their first kill, U-569, on May 22, 1943, and soon became the most important force to defeat U-boats in the mid-Atlantic. Avengers on ten escort carriers shared in the 49 U-boat kills by the hunter carrier/destroyer groups.

Radar (ASB-3) was first installed on TBF-1s in October 1942, and in January 1944 the first carrier-based night-bombing attacks were made by radar-equipped Avengers in the Pacific. The first American plane to be fitted with forward-firing rockets (the 5-inch HVAR), the Avenger first used them in combat against a U-boat on January 11, 1944. The Marine Corps began land-based operations with Avengers at Guadalcanal in November 1942, and eight Marine squadrons operated them in combat in the Pacific or on escort carriers by 1945.

Britain's Royal Navy received 402 TBF-1s (Avenger I), 334 TBM-1Cs (Avenger II), and 212 TBM-3s (Avenger III) beginning in January 1943, and they served 15 squadrons. New Zealand received six TBF-1s and 42 TBF-1Cs in 1943.

Altogether, there were 9,839 Avengers built, 2,-293 by Grumman and the rest by General Motors' Eastern Aircraft Division. After the war the Avenger remained in Navy service until June 1954. A large APS-20 had been fitted underneath a TBM-3W in December 1945, and by June 1948 the first AEW (airborne early-warning) squadron, VC-2, was formed with TBM-3Ws. For the antisubmarine role, the TMB-3S modification deleted the turret, while the TBM-3Q tested radar countermeasures.

When the Mutual Defense program was established, secondhand TBM-3s of various modifications were sent to Allied powers from 1953 to 1955, including 115 to Canada, 100 to the United Kingdom (as A.S. Mk 4), 50 to the Netherlands, some to France, and 20 to the Japanese Navy (now the Mar-

GENERAL MOTORS TBM-3S (1950)   USN

VOUGHT XTBU-1
Pratt & Whitney R-2800-20, 2000 hp takeoff, 1600 hp at 13,500'
DIMENSIONS: Span 57'2", Lg. 39', Ht. 18'7", Wing Area 439 sq. ft.
WEIGHT: Empty 10,504 lb., Gross 16,247 lb. Fuel 317–587 gal.
PERFORMANCE: Speed—Top 311 mph at 14,700', 295 mph at s. l., Cruising 165 mph, Landing 77 mph. Service Ceiling 27,900', Climb 1820'/1 min. Range 1400 miles/ torpedo.   MFR

itime Self-Defense Force). Ironically, the latter were the last TBMs in active service until their retirement in 1962, but they remained in civilian service in their homeland, dousing forest fires for many years afterwards.

Shortly after Grumman's XTBF had been ordered, a second torpedo-bomber design was chosen as a backup. Vought's XTBU-1 had a Pratt & Whitney XR-2800-6 (later R-2800-20) Wasp, and a single prototype was ordered April 22, 1940. First flown December 22, 1941, it was rather similar to the Avenger's layout, but had a high fin and rounded wing tips. Armament included a .50-caliber fixed cowl gun, another .50-caliber gun in the power-operated rear turret, and a .30-caliber ventral gun, as well as the torpedo or bomb load.

The XTBU's high speed made it an attractive alternate to the Avenger, but Vought was too occupied with fighters to undertake its production. On September 6, 1943, Consolidated contracted to build 1,100 of this type, now designated TBY-2 Sea Wolf, in a new Allentown, Pennsylvania, plant. The first TBY was delivered in November 1944, but only 180 were completed before the contract was canceled due to the slowness in getting the type into production. Similar in appearance to its prototype, the

CONSOLIDATED TBY-2
Pratt & Whitney R-2800-22, 2100 hp takeoff, 1600 hp at 16,400'
DIMENSIONS: Span 56'11", Lg. 39'2", Ht. 15'6", Wing Area 440 sq. ft.
WEIGHT: Empty 11,336 lb., Gross 17,491 lb., Max. 18,940 lb.
PERFORMANCE: Speed—Top 292 mph at s. l., 312 mph at 17,700', Cruising 156 mph, Landing 80 mph. Service Ceiling 29,400', Climb 1770'/1 min., Range 1025 miles/1 torpedo, 1615 miles max. as scout.   MFR

TBY-2 had three .50-caliber fixed guns, one .50-caliber gun in the power turret, a .30-caliber ventral gun, 380 pounds of armor, and radar on the starboard wing. None were ever used in combat.

At the very outset of the war, the combined attack of dive bombers and torpedo planes demonstrated a striking power and reach far beyond that of the traditional warship battle line. No Allied capital ship was ever lost to the guns of a Japanese battleship, but in the very first week of the war Japanese planes destroyed four U.S. and British battleships and disabled six others. The great naval battles of the war became, in the main, contests between opposing fleets of aircraft. As American aircraft grew in numbers and efficiency, carrier-type attack planes sank six of ten Japanese battleships sunk during the war, as well as 11 of 15 carriers and ten of 14 heavy cruisers lost. Of the 12 remaining large Japanese ships, eight were sunk by submarines and four by surface ships. Horizontal bombing by Army aircraft caused no losses of heavy ships.

Achieving these results required a remarkable increase in the number of naval attack aircraft, from 709 scout bombers and 100 torpedo planes in December 1941 to a total of 5,101 scout bombers and 4,937 torpedo bombers on June 30, 1945. These air weapons destroyed the Japanese Navy, virtually ended the era of the battleship, and established U.S. naval superiority over the rest of the world.

Douglas Destroyer

Douglas planned to replace the SBD series with the XSB2D-1 two-seat scout bomber, which had a Wright R-3350-14 and the first retractable tricycle landing gear designed for a carrier aircraft.

Armament included a 20-mm fixed gun at the bend of a gull wing, a .50-caliber gun in both an upper and a lower remote-controlled rear turret, and bombs within an internal bay. Two prototypes

were ordered June 30, 1941, and the first flew April 8, 1943.

The Navy now wanted to combine the dive-bombing and torpedo-attack roles in one single-seat aircraft. This was now possible both because the single-seater's increased power could accommodate either bombs or a torpedo, and because the weight handicap of a gunner and his weapons seemed to have been made unnecessary by American fighter superiority in the air.

Responding to the Navy's new specification, Douglas redesigned the XSB2D-1 by removing the rear gunner and his turrets and enlarging the bomb bay to accommodate a torpedo, two 1,600-pound bombs, or added fuel tankage. A pair of 20-mm guns in the gull wings was retained, along with the R-3350-14, the prop spinner, and tricycle gear. Dive brakes were installed on the fuselage sides. The

DOUGLAS XSB2D-1
Wright R-3350-14, 2300 hp takeoff, 1900 hp at 14,000'
DIMENSIONS: Span 45', Lg. 38'7", Ht. 16'11", Wing Area 375 sq. ft.
WEIGHT: Empty 12,458 lb., Gross 16,273 lb., Max. 19,140 lb. Fuel 350–550 gal.
PERFORMANCE: Speed—Top 346 mph at 16,100', Cruising 180 mph, Landing 88 mph. Service Ceiling 24,400', Climb 1710'/1 min. Range 1480 miles/1000 lb. bomb.   MFR

DOUGLAS BTD-1
Wright R-3350-14, 2300 hp takeoff, 1900 hp at 14,000'
DIMENSIONS: Span 45', Lg. 38'7", Ht. 13'7", Wing Area 373 sq. ft.
WEIGHT: Empty 12,900 lb., Gross 18,140 lb., Max. 19,000 lb. Fuel 460–640 gal.
PERFORMANCE: Speed—Top 344 mph at 16,100', 340 mph/torpedo, 319 mph at s. l., Cruising 188 mph, Landing 91.5 mph. Service Ceiling 23,600', Climb 1650'/1 min. Range 1480 miles/torpedo, 2140 miles max.   MFR

original April 9, 1942, contract was increased on August 31, 1943, to 358 Douglas BTD-1 Destroyers, and the first BTD-1 was flown March 5, 1944. Because of cancellations, only 28 were completed by October 1945.

The next Douglas torpedo bomber was the large three-place XTB2D-1, ordered October 31, 1943, powered by a Pratt & Whitney XR-4360-8 turning eight-bladed counterrotating propellers. Intended for the big *Midway*-class carriers or for shore-based operations, the two XTB2D-1 prototypes had tricycle landing gear and a low wing with a flat center section and dihedral on the outer panels. Not completed until March 1945, the heavy Douglas carried four .50-caliber fixed guns in the wings, two .50-caliber guns in an upper remote-controlled rear turret, another in the lower turret, 527 pounds of armor, and up to 4,000 pounds of bombs.

Even larger would have been Grumman's XTB2F-1, the only twin-engine design in this class. Two R-2800-22 Wasps were mounted on a 75-foot-high wing that folded for stowage, and tricycle gear was provided. Armament included up to four 2,000-pound bombs or two torpedoes, while the nose had

a 75-mm cannon on the right side and two .50-caliber guns on the left, with four more fixed guns in the wing roots. Two .50-caliber guns were in a top rear turret and another pair were located in a retractable ball turret. The mockup was ready by June 1944, but it was realized that since few such aircraft could be operated from even the largest carrier, more bombs could be delivered by a greater number of smaller aircraft. Too heavy for the carriers of that time, the XTB2F-1 project was canceled.

Single-seat Bombers

Using one man and one aircraft to do work previously assigned to two different types of planes, each with two or three crewmen, had obvious advantages for carrier operations despite increased strain put on the pilot. Elimination of defensive guns seemed justified by the superiority of Navy fighters and the limited success of rear gunners in action. During 1944, four single-seat bomber-torpedo designs were begun, all of them low-wing monoplanes with conventional tail-down landing gear and bomb load carried externally. Internal racks like those of the BTD permitted higher cruising speeds to the target,

DOUGLAS XTB2D-1
Pratt & Whitney XR-4360-8, 3000 hp takeoff, 2400 hp at 13,500'
DIMENSIONS: Span 70', Lg. 46', Ht. 22'7", Wing Area 605 sq. ft.
WEIGHT: Empty 18,405 lb., Gross 28,545 lb., Max. 34,760 lb. Fuel 774–1374 gal.
PERFORMANCE: Speed—Top 340 mph at 15,600', 312 mph/torpedo, 292 mph at s. l., Cruising 162 mph, Landing 75 mph. Service Ceiling 24,500', Climb 1390'/1 min. Range 1250 miles/torpedo, 2880 miles max.   MFR

GRUMMAN XTB2F-1 (mockup)
Pratt & Whitney R-2800-22, 2100 hp takeoff, 1600 hp at 16,000'
DIMENSIONS: Span 74', Lg. 52', Ht. 21'2"
WEIGHT: Empty 23,650 lb., Max. 45,000 lb. Fuel 960–1560 gal.
PERFORMANCE: Speed—Top 335 mph at 21,000 ft. Service Ceiling 29,000'. Range 2280 miles as scout. Range 3700 miles ferry.   MFR

but external racks presented fewer design problems and could accommodate a greater variety of weapons shapes. In the order contracts were let, the new single-seaters were the Curtiss BTC, Kaiser-Fleetwings BTK, Martin BTM, and Douglas BT2D.

Using the Pratt & Whitney 3,000-hp Wasp Major, the Curtiss design began with an XBTC-1 contract on December 31, 1943, became the XBTC-2 with a change in engine model, and was not accepted until July 1946. Armed with four 20-mm wing guns and powered by an R-4360-14 with contrarotating six-bladed propellers, the XBTC-2 had the sturdy appearance typical of the low-wing attack types.

Lightest of the new bomber-torpedo single-seaters was the Kaiser-Fleetwings XBTK-1, ordered March 31, 1944, and flown early in April 1945. Four were completed, and a fifth used for static tests at the Bristol, Pennsylvania, plant. A Pratt & Whitney R-2800-34W was the first engine installation cooled by using exhaust gases to pump air through the nose cowl and exhausting it in stainless-steel ducts at the fuselage sides. The wings had picket-type trailing-edge dive brakes and folded vertically to reduce stowage span to 20 feet. Two 20-mm wing guns, 230 pounds of armor, and a self-sealing fuel tank behind the pilot were installed, along with external racks for up to 5,000 pounds of bombs, rockets, torpedoes, radar, or drop tanks for scouting.

Martin's XBTM-1 had a 3,000-hp Pratt & Whitney R-4360-4 and four-bladed propeller, four 20-mm guns in the wings, 297 pounds of armor, and picket-type dive brakes. Two XBTM-1 prototypes were ordered May 31, 1944, and 750 production BTMs were purchased January 15, 1945. The first XBTM-1 flight was August 26, 1944, but the second prototype was not ready until the following May.

CURTISS XBTC-2
Pratt & Whitney R-4360-14, 3000 hp takeoff, 2400 hp at 13,500'
DIMENSIONS: Span 50', Lg. 38'7", Ht. 16'8", Wing Area 406 sq. ft.
WEIGHT: Empty 13,947 lb., Gross 17,910 lb., Max. 20,944 lb. Fuel 360–690 gal.
PERFORMANCE: Speed—Top 386 mph at 16,200', 322 mph/ torpedo, Cruising 180 mph, Landing 85 mph. Service Ceiling 28,000', Climb 2610'/1 min. Range 1245 miles/ torpedo with 460 gal.   PMB

KAISER XBTK-1
Pratt & Whitney R-2800-34W, 2100 hp takeoff, 1850 hp at 16,000'
DIMENSIONS: Span 48'8", Lg. 38'11", Ht. 15'8", Wing Area 380 sq. ft.
WEIGHT: Empty 9959 lb., Gross 12,728 lb., Max. 15,782 lb. Fuel 275–375 gal.
PERFORMANCE: Speed—Top 373 mph at 18,000', 342 mph at s. l., Cruising 158 mph, Landing 80 mph. Service Ceiling 33,400', Climb 3550'/1 min. Range 1250 miles/ torpedo, 1370 miles/1000 lb. bomb.   USN

The war's end cut back the production contract to 149 planes, redesignated AM-1 in the postwar Attack series. Delivery of the Martin AM-1 Mauler was under way in July 1947, but they did not enter service with VA-17A of the Atlantic Fleet until March 1948. Numerous structural modifications delayed carrier operations, although the Martins could easily carry the heaviest attack load yet. In service they proved to be remarkable weightlifters, on one occasion lifting a 14,179-pound useful load, including 10,689 pounds of ordnance (three torpedoes, twelve 250-pound bombs, guns, and ammunition). Gross weight on that flight was 29,332 pounds.

The last AM-1 was delivered in October 1949, including 18 as two-place AM-1Q radar countermeasures versions. They remained in fleet service until 1950, for the Navy decided to standardize on the Douglas BT2D/AD series. (See Chapter 29 for details on postwar Attack planes.)

The second Curtiss bomber-torpedo type, using the same R-3350-24 as the BT2D, was also eclipsed

MARTIN XBTM-1
Pratt & Whitney XR-4360-4, 3000 hp takeoff, 2400 hp at
13,500'
DIMENSIONS: Span 50', Lg. 41'2", Ht. 16'10", Wing Area
496 sq. ft.
WEIGHT: Empty 14,296 lb., Gross 19,000 lb., Max. 23,000
lb. Fuel 500–800 gal.
PERFORMANCE: Speed—Top 367 mph at 16,000', 341 mph
at s. l., Cruising 178 mph, Landing 88 mph. Service
Ceiling 26,800', Climb 2480'/1 min. Range 1200 miles/
torpedo, 2350 miles max.   WL

MARTIN AM-1
Pratt & Whitney R-4360-4, 3000 hp takeoff, 2400 hp at
16,200'
DIMENSIONS: As XBTM-1
WEIGHT: Empty 15,257 lb., Gross 21,141 lb. (scout), 22,-
323 lb. (bomber), Max. 25,737 lb. Fuel 510–810 gal.
PERFORMANCE: Speed—Top 334 mph at 15,400' as scout
(323 mph as bomber), 310 mph at s. l. as scout (304
mph as bomber), Cruising 189 mph, Stalling 108 mph.
Service Ceiling 27,000'. Range 1800 miles/2000 lb.
bomb, max. full.   USN

CURTISS XBT2C-1
Wright R-3350-24, 2500 hp takeoff, 1900 hp at 14,800'
DIMENSIONS: Span 47'7", Lg. 38'8", Ht. 16'5", Wing Area
416 sq. ft.
WEIGHT: Empty 12,268 lb., Gross 15,975 lb., Max. 19,022
lb. Fuel 410–710 gal.
PERFORMANCE: Speed—Top 349 mph at 17,000', 313 mph/
torpedo, Cruising 175 mph, Landing 90 mph. Service
Ceiling 28,100', Climb 2590'/1 min. Range 1435 miles/
torpedo.   MFR

by that type's success. Ten Curtiss XBT2C-1s were
ordered March 27, 1945. First appearing in January
1946, they resembled the XBTC-2, with two 20-mm
wing guns, up to 4,000 pounds of bombs or torpedoes, 182 pounds of armor, and APS-4 radar. The
pilot sat under a bubble canopy; a second crewman
could be accommodated behind him within the fuselage. Only nine of the Navy's last Curtiss type
were actually delivered by October 1946.

Chapter 22
Navy Fighters, 1931-39

Two-seaters

Until 1931 naval aircraft used the open cockpits and fixed landing gear traditional on combat planes since World War I. Gradually, however, metal began to replace fabric as an airframe covering, and efforts to decrease drag led to retractable landing gear and enclosed cockpits.

Retractable landing gear was used for the first time by a Navy fighter on Grumman's first aircraft, the XFF-1, ordered March 28, 1931. The wheels folded into a bulge in the deep metal fuselage behind a Wright Cyclone, ahead of fully enclosed cockpits. Although a two-seater, the XFF-1 was faster than any single-seater carrier-based type then available. When first flown by William McAvoy on December 21, 1931, and officially announced December 29, it did 195 mph with a 616-hp R-1820E. In October 1932 the Grumman reappeared with a

GRUMMAN XFF-1
Wright R-1820E, 616 hp (modified with R-1820F, 675 hp)
DIMENSIONS: Span 34'6", Lg. 24'6", Ht. 9'8", Wing Area 310 sq. ft.
WEIGHT: Empty 2667 lb., Gross 3933 lb. (4565 lb.). Fuel 120 gal.
PERFORMANCE: Speed—Top 195 mph at s. l. (201 mph with R-1820F), Landing 60 mph (63 mph). Service Ceiling 23,600' (20,700'), Climb 5000'/4.3 min. Range 818 miles.   USN

700-hp R-1820F, which raised its speed to 201 mph. A second prototype equipped for scouting missions was the Grumman XSF-1 (see Chapter 10).

Twenty-seven FF-1s ordered December 19, 1932, were delivered from April to November 1933 and served on the *Lexington* with VF-5B and the SF-1s delivered to VS-3B in 1934. After the FF-1's retirement from fleet service, 23 were modified to FF-2s, in 1936, with dual controls for the Reserves.

The next two-seat fighter biplane was the Berliner-Joyce XF2J-1, which had the upper wing gulled into the fuselage behind a 625-hp Wright R-1510-92. Ordered June 30, 1931, the XF2J-1 was not delivered until May 1933, when its fixed landing gear held performance below standards set by the fast Grumman ships. Visibility from the cockpits—originally open but later enclosed—was considered poor.

Three more two-seat fighters were ordered on June 30, 1932. The Douglas XFD-1 and Vought XF3U-1 were both developed from BuAer Design No. 113, with a conventional biplane layout, fixed gear, enclosed cockpits, and a 700-hp Pratt & Whitney R-1535-64 Wasp. Armament consisted of the usual two synchronized guns under the cowling and the observer's .30-caliber flexible Browning, plus two 116-pound bombs. The Douglas plane,

GRUMMAN FF-1
Wright R-1820-78, 700 hp at 4000'
DIMENSIONS: Span 34'6", Lg. 24'6", Ht. 11'1", Wing Area 310 sq. ft.
WEIGHT: Empty 3098 lb., Gross 4677 lb., Max. 4888 lb. Fuel 120–40 gal.
PERFORMANCE: Speed—Top 207 mph at 4000', Landing 64 mph. Service Ceiling 22,100', Climb 5000'/2.9 min. Range 685 miles normal, 800 miles max.   USN

BERLINER-JOYCE XF2J-1
Wright R-1510-92, 625 hp at 6000'
DIMENSIONS: Span 36', Lg. 28'10", Wing Area 303.5 sq. ft.
WEIGHT: Empty 3211 lb., Gross 4539 lb., Max. 4851 lb. Fuel 80–160 gal.
PERFORMANCE: Speed—Top 193 mph at 6000', Landing 66 mph. Service Ceiling 21,500', Climb 5000'/3.1 min. Range 522 miles normal, 1015 miles max.   ARC

DOUGLAS XFD-1
Pratt & Whitney R-1535-64, 700 hp at 8900'
DIMENSIONS: Span 31'6", Lg. 25'4", Ht. 11'1", Wing Area 295 sq. ft.
WEIGHT: Empty 3227 lb., Gross 4745 lb., Max. 5000 lb. Fuel 110 gal.
PERFORMANCE: Speed—Top 204 mph at 8900', Landing 64 mph. Service Ceiling 23,700', Climb 5000'/3.3 min. Range 576 miles.   USN

VOUGHT XF3U-1
Pratt & Whitney R-1535-64, 700 hp at 8900'
DIMENSIONS: Span 31'6", Lg. 26'6", Ht. 10'11", Wing Area 295 sq. ft.
WEIGHT: Empty 3078 lb., Gross 4616 lb. Fuel 110 gal.
PERFORMANCE: Speed—Top 214 mph, Landing 64 mph. Service Ceiling 24,600'. Range 570 miles.   MFR

CURTISS XF12C-1
Wright R-1510-92, 625 hp at 6000'
DIMENSIONS: Span 41'6", Lg. 29'1", Ht. 12'11", Wing Area 272 sq. ft.
WEIGHT: Empty 3884 lb., Gross 5461 lb., Max. 5840 lb. Fuel 110–70 gal.
PERFORMANCE: Speed—Top 217 mph at 6000', Landing 64 mph. Service Ceiling 22,500'. Range 738 miles normal, 1074 miles max.   MFR

delivered to the Navy on June 18, 1933, differed from the Vought, which arrived four days later, in that it had a spreader bar between the wheels.

Vought's XF3U-1 first flew May 3, 1933, as a fighter, but was returned to the factory for rebuilding. It was redesignated XSBU-1 in February 1934, flew again May 29, 1934, and won a scout-bomber contract.

Although ordered the same day, the Curtiss XF12C-1 offered a bolder approach. This all-metal high-wing monoplane had slots and flaps on a swept-back wing braced by V main struts; the wing folded backwards for shipboard stowage. Like the Grumman, the XF12C-1 had wheels retracting into the fuselage behind the engine, plus a 626-hp Wright R-1510-92 Twin Whirlwind. It was the last two-seat fighter of the period, for that aircraft class vanished into the new scout-bomber category. First built as a fighter in July 1933, the XF12C-1 got an SR-1820-80 Cyclone in October, became the S4C-1 in December, and was redesignated SBC-1 in January 1934. A long and often painful development still remained ahead (see Chapter 21).

The Bomber-Fighter Idea

The success of dive-bombing had led the Navy to include this capability on single-seat fighters and two-seat scouts. One of the carrier fighter squadrons on each carrier was to be redesignated a bomber unit, and so the next Boeing and Curtiss fighter types were redesignated BF (bomber-fighter) types in March 1934.

Boeing's last effort to develop a biplane fighter was the XF6B-1, which had a twin-row 625-hp R-1535-44, equal-span biplane wings with metal structure and ailerons only on the lower wing, and

BOEING XF6B-1 (XBFB-1)
Pratt & Whitney R-1535-44, 625 hp at 6000'
DIMENSIONS: Span 28'6", Lg. 22'2", Ht. 10'6", Wing Area 252 sq. ft.
WEIGHT: Empty 2823 lb., Gross 3705 lb., Max. 4007 lb. Fuel 64–109 gal.
PERFORMANCE: Speed—Top 195 mph at 6000', Landing 64 mph. Service Ceiling 20,700', Climb 5000'/4.2 min. Range 437 miles normal, 737 miles max.   ARC

CURTISS XF11C-1
Wright R-1510-98, 600 hp at 6000'
DIMENSIONS: Span 31'6", Lg. 23'1", Ht. 10', Wing Area 262 sq. ft.
WEIGHT: Empty 3290 lb., Gross 4368 lb. Fuel 94 gal.
PERFORMANCE: Speed—Top 203 mph, Landing 67 mph. Service Ceiling 23,800', Climb 5000'/8.2 min. Range 530 miles.   MFR

faired wheel struts. Armament comprised two .30-caliber guns under the cowl and a 500-pound bomb (actual weight was 474 pounds) under the fuselage, or two 116-pound bombs under the wings.

Ordered June 30, 1931, the XF6B-1 first flew February 1, 1933, was delivered to the Navy in April, and was redesignated as XBFB-1 (bomber-fighter) on March 21, 1934. By then traditional open-cockpit biplanes were outmoded.

More successful was the Curtiss Goshawk, whose basic airframe was similar to that of the Army P-6Es except for a radial engine. Two prototypes were purchased by the Navy on April 16, 1932. One had been flying since March 25; it was built as a private demonstrator with a single-row Wright SR-1820-78 Cyclone and two-bladed propeller. This aircraft was delivered to Anacostia on May 2 as the XF11C-2, while the XF11C-1 was built to Navy specifications by September with a twin-row R-1510-98 Whirlwind, three-bladed propeller and larger spat at the end of the streamlined strut.

Cyclones were chosen for 28 F11C-2s ordered October 18, 1932, and first delivered March 11, 1933. One was delivered May 27 as the XF11C-3, with landing gear retracting into the fuselage.

Twenty-seven production models ordered February 26, 1934, had 700-hp R-1820-04s and enclosed

CURTISS XF11C-2
Wright R-1820-78, 700 hp at 8000'
DIMENSIONS: Span 31'6", Lg. 25', Ht. 10'7", Wing Area
262 sq. ft.
WEIGHT: Empty 3000 lb., Gross 4132 lb., Max. 4601 lb.
Fuel 94 gal.
PERFORMANCE: Speed—Top 202 mph at 8000', Landing
65 mph. Service Ceiling 25,100', Climb 10,400'/10 min.
Range 303 miles at top speed.   SI

CURTISS BFC-2 (F11C-2)
Wright R-1820-78, 700 hp
DIMENSIONS: Span 31'6", Lg. 25', Ht. 10'7", Wing Area
262 sq. ft.
WEIGHT: Empty 3037 lb., Gross 4120 lb., Max. 4638 lb.
Fuel 94–146 gal.
PERFORMANCE: Speed—Top 205 mph as fighter, 198 mph
as bomber, Landing 65 mph. Service Ceiling 24,300',
Climb 5000'/2.6 min. Range 560 miles normal, 628
miles max.   PMB

CURTISS BF2C-1 (F11C-3)
Wright R-1820-04, 700 hp at 8000'
DIMENSIONS: Span 31'6", Lg. 23', Ht. 10'10", Wing Area
262 sq. ft.
WEIGHT: Empty 3329 lb., Gross 4555 lb., Max. 5086 lb.
Fuel 110–60 gal.
PERFORMANCE: Speed—Top 225 mph at 8000' (210 mph/
474 lb. bomb), Landing 69 mph. Service Ceiling 27,-
000', Climb 5000'/2.6 min. Range 797 miles normal,
1054 miles max.   ARC

CURTISS XF11C-3 (XBF2C-1)
Wright R-1820-80, 700 hp at 8000'
DIMENSIONS: Span 31'6", Lg. 23', Ht. 10'7", Wing Area 262 sq. ft.
WEIGHT: Empty 3230 lb., Gross 4495 lb., Max. 5020 lb. Fuel 98–150 gal.
PERFORMANCE: Speed—Top 229 mph at 8000', Landing 69 mph. Service Ceiling 26,000', Climb 11,600'/10 min.   USN

cockpits. Like their predecessors, they carried two .30-caliber synchronized Brownings, four 116-pound bombs under wing racks, or one 474-pound bomb or streamlined 50-gallon drop tank beneath the fuselage. In recognition of the type's dive-bombing capabilities, F11C-2s then serving aboard the *Saratoga* were redesignated BFC-2, and the F11C-3s on order became BF2C-1s on March 21, 1934. First delivered on October 7, 1934, the BF2C-1 was the first single-seater assigned to the new light carrier *Ranger*.

Unfortunately, the BF2C-1 dropped the spruce wing framework usual on the Curtiss Hawks for a metal framework, whose periodic vibration coincided with the engine vibrations of the Cyclone. These aircraft had to be withdrawn from service by February 1936, although the wooden-winged BFC-1s remained until 1938.

Curtiss also sold 127 Hawk IIs, an export version of the F11C-2 with the R-1820F-3 and fixed gear. A

CURTISS HAWK II
Wright R-1820F-3, 710 hp at 7000'
DIMENSIONS: Span 31'6", Lg. 22'4", Ht. 9'9", Wing Area 252 sq. ft.
WEIGHT: Empty 2903 lb., Gross 3876 lb. Fuel 94–144 gal.
PERFORMANCE: Speed—Top 208 mph at 6900', 187 mph at s. l., Cruising 179 mph, Landing 63 mph. Service Ceiling 26,400', Absolute Ceiling 27,400'. Range 414 miles normal, 635 miles max.

Hawk III demonstrator with an SR-1820-F53, retractable wheels, and cockpit cover appeared in October 1934, and 137 were quickly sold abroad. Turkey was the first customer, getting 19 Hawk IIs in August-September 1932 and a single Hawk III in April 1935. Colombia acquired 26 Hawk II twin-float seaplanes, delivered beginning in October 1932, and Bolivia got six Hawk II landplanes and three seaplanes beginning in December 1932; these Hawks fought in the Gran Chaco War against Paraguay. Cuba got four Hawk IIs in January 1933, and two were sold to Germany in October 1933 for Ernst Udet; the first modern fighters to fall into Nazi hands, they influenced German dive-bombing development. Norway also acquired a Hawk II in July 1934, and Chile acquired four as seaplanes in January 1935.

China was the best American aircraft customer in that period, receiving 50 Hawk IIs from March to September 1933 for its first fighter squadrons and

CURTISS HAWK II Seaplane
Wright R-1820F-3, 710 hp at 7000'
DIMENSIONS: Span 31'6", Lg. 25'7", Ht. 12'6", Wing Area 252 sq. ft.
WEIGHT: Empty 3293 lb., Gross 4266 lb. Fuel 94 gal.
PERFORMANCE: Speed—Top 192 mph at 6900', 173 mph at s. l., Cruising 163 mph, Stalling 66 mph. Service Ceiling 24,900'. Range 377 miles.   MFR

CURTISS HAWK III (China)
Wright R-1820F-53, 750 hp at 7600'
DIMENSIONS: Span 31'6", Lg. 23'6", Ht. 9'11", Wing Area
　262 sq. ft.
WEIGHT: Empty 3213 lb., Gross 4317 lb. Fuel 110–60 gal.
PERFORMANCE: Speed—Top 240 mph at 11,500', 202 mph
　at s. l., Cruising 203 mph, Landing 68 mph. Service
　Ceiling 25,800', Climb 2280'/1 min. Range 575
　miles.　　　　　　　　　　　　　　　　　　MFR

CURTISS HAWK IV
Wright R-1820F-56, 745 hp at 12,000'
DIMENSIONS: Span 31'6", Lg. 23'6", Ht. 10'10", Wing Area
　262 sq. ft.
WEIGHT: Empty 3404 lb., Gross 4598 lb. Fuel 110 gal.
PERFORMANCE: Speed—Top 248 mph at 12,500', Cruising
　211 mph, Landing 69 mph. Service Ceiling 29,700',
　Absolute Ceiling 30,300'. Range 577 miles.　　MFR

72 Hawk IIIs shipped from March to August 1936. When Japan's invasion began anew in 1937, China had three fighter groups, two with Hawk IIIs and a third with mixed Hawk IIs, Boeing 281s, and Fiats. The 4th Fighter Group began the fight on August 14 by successfully intercepting an attack on Hangchow by Navy G3M bombers. In general, the Hawks did well against Japanese bombers but were badly outclassed by the A5M fighters. Thirty Hawk III replacements were shipped from April to June 1938.

Siam (now Thailand) acquired 12 Hawk IIs in August-September 1934 and 24 Hawk IIIs beginning in August 1935, while Argentina received ten Hawk IIIs beginning in May 1936 and a single Hawk IV with a modified canopy and supercharger in July.

Streamlined Biplanes

The last biplane fighter with old-fashioned fixed landing gear was the Berliner-Joyce XF3J-1, ordered June 30, 1932. First flown January 23, 1934, and tested in April by the Navy, it was a handsome aircraft, with elliptical wings tapered at the tips and roots and a turtleback running from the enclosed cockpit to the rounded rudder. Powered by an SR-1510-26, the XF3J-1 had two .30-caliber cowl guns and could carry two 116-pound bombs under the wings. During its lengthy construction, it was surpassed by more advanced types. As a result of the plane's failure to win a production contract, the Berliner-Joyce firm retired from business, its assets being acquired by North American Aviation.

BERLINER-JOYCE XF3J-1
Wright R-1510-26, 625 hp at 6000'
DIMENSIONS: Span 29', Lg. 22'11", Ht. 10'9", Wing Area
　240 sq. ft.
WEIGHT: Empty 2717 lb., Gross 4016 lb., Max. 4264 lb.
　Fuel 120 gal.
PERFORMANCE: Speed—Top 209 mph at 6000', Landing
　66 mph. Service Ceiling 24,500', Climb 5000'/2.7 min.
　Range 719 miles/232 lb. bombs.　　　　　　MFR

Although the aviation business has resulted in many such failures, it has also produced such successes as Grumman, whose chunky little XF2F-1 biplane—ordered November 2, 1932, and first flown on October 18, 1933—won quick recognition. Fabric covered the wings, and metal covered a teardrop-shaped fuselage with an enclosed cockpit. Wheels retracted into a bulge behind a Pratt & Whitney R-1535-44, and armament included two synchronized guns but no bombs.

Fifty-four F2F-1s with R-1535-72 Wasps were ordered May 17, 1934, and another was added after deliveries began January 19, 1935. These Grumman biplanes began a long series of single-seaters by this company, which has had fighter types under contract for the Navy ever since. The F2F-1s first joined Lexington's VF-2 in February and served that squadron until September 1940.

Premature Monoplanes

Although monoplanes were in production for all classes of Army Air Corps aircraft by 1933, the Navy

GRUMMAN F2F-1
Pratt & Whitney R-1535-72, 700 hp takeoff, 650 hp at
  7500'
DIMENSIONS: Span 28'6", Lg. 21'5", Ht. 9'1", Wing Area
  230 sq. ft.
WEIGHT: Empty 2691 lb., Gross 3847 lb. Fuel 110 gal.
PERFORMANCE: Speed—Top 231 mph at 7500', 203 mph
  at s.l., Landing 66 mph. Service Ceiling 27,100', Climb
  2050'/1 min., 5000'/2.1 min. Range 985 miles max. USN

GRUMMAN XF2F-1
Pratt & Whitney XR-1535-44, 625 hp at 8,400'
DIMENSIONS: Span 28'6", Lg. 21'1", Ht. 8'6", Wing Area
  230 sq. ft.
WEIGHT: Empty 2525 lb., Gross 3490 lb., Max. 3690 lb.
  Fuel 80–110 gal.
PERFORMANCE: Speed—Top 229 mph at 8400', Cruising
  198 mph, Landing 64 mph. Service Ceiling 29,800',
  Climb 3080'/1 min. Range 543 miles normal, 750 miles
  max.   MFR

had hesitated to adopt the more streamlined aircraft
for carrier operation. Only the high-wing XF5B-1
and XF12C-1 had attempted to utilize the speed
offered by monoplane configurations, but problems
of shipboard stowage, structural strength, and relatively high landing speed had precluded the adoption of those types.

Boeing's XF7B-1, ordered March 20, 1933, and
powered by a 550-hp Pratt & Whitney R-1340-30,
was the first low-wing monoplane fighter ever
tested by the Navy. Of all-metal construction, the

Boeing had wheels folding back partially into a
cantilever wing and a long turtleback running from
the enclosed cockpit to the tail. The first flight was
September 14, 1933, and the XF7B-1 was delivered
to the Navy on Armistice Day.

Despite the fastest speed of any Navy fighter to
date, the plane was criticized for its excessively
long takeoff runs, high landing speed, poor maneuverability, and general instability. Visibility from
the enclosed cockpit was especially bad during
landings. The aircraft was sent back to the factory
in April 1935, underwent modification with an open
cockpit and landing flaps, and was returned to Anacostia on March 15, 1935. Weight was increased to
3,868 pounds, top speed reduced to 231 mph and
landing speed to 66 mph, but during a March 9 dive
the plane was so overstressed that repair was impractical.

Curtiss developed the XF13C-1, ordered November 23, 1932, with a Wright R-1510-94, wheels retracting into a clean metal fuselage, a pilot's cabin,
and a remarkable configuration. The Curtiss could
be a high-wing monoplane or use a spare set of

BOEING XF7B-1
Pratt & Whitney R-1340-30, 550 hp at 10,000'
DIMENSIONS: Span 31'11", Lg. 27'7", Ht. 10', Wing Area
  213 sq. ft.
WEIGHT: Empty 2697 lb., Gross 3579 lb. Fuel 112 gal.
PERFORMANCE: Speed—Top 239 mph at 10,000', 214 mph
  at s. l., Landing 78 mph. Service Ceiling 26,900', Climb
  12,600'/10 min. Range 824 miles.   MFR

CURTISS XF13C-1
Wright XR-1510-94, 600 hp at 10,000'
DIMENSIONS: Span 35', Lg. 25'8", Ht. 12'9", Wing Area 205 sq. ft.
WEIGHT: Empty 3238 lb., Gross 4400 lb. Fuel 110 gal.
PERFORMANCE: Speed—Top 236 mph at 10,000', Landing 67 mph. Service Ceiling 23,800', Climb 5000'/3.5 min. Range 864 miles.   MFR

CURTISS XF13C-3
Wright XR-1510-12, 700 hp at 7000'
DIMENSIONS: Span 35', Lg. 26'3", Ht. 12', Wing Area 205 sq. ft.
WEIGHT: Empty 3499 lb., Gross 4721 lb. Fuel 110 gal.
PERFORMANCE: Speed—Top 232 mph at 7000', Landing 70 mph. Service Ceiling 24,100', Climb 5000'/2.5 min. Range 726 miles.   MFR

NORTHROP XFT-1
Wright R-1510-26, 625 hp at 6000'
DIMENSIONS: Span 32', Lg. 21'1", Ht. 9'5", Wing Area 177 sq. ft.
WEIGHT: Empty 2469 lb., Gross 3756 lb., Max. 4003 lb. Fuel 120 gal.
PERFORMANCE: Speed—Top 235 mph at 6000', Landing 63 mph. Service Ceiling 26,500', Climb 6000'/2.6 min. Range 976 miles normal, 902 miles/232 lbs. bombs.
                    MFR

biplane wings. The 35-foot-high wing had slots and flaps to reduce the landing speed, but the alternate arrangement had narrower chord wings without the lift devices, utilizing instead the added area of a 24-foot lower wing. As a biplane the type was known as XF13C-2, although the original type number was retained on the tail fin.

The XF13C-1 was first flown January 7, 1934, and delivered to the Navy on February 10 as a monoplane. Comparative tests showed the monoplane faster, but the biplane had quicker takeoffs and slower landings. In May 1935 the aircraft appeared with a new vertical fin and an XR-1510-12, and it was redesignated XF13C-3.

The Northrop XFT-1 was ordered May 8, 1933, first flown January 16, 1934, and delivered to Anacostia in March 1934. Powered by a 625-hp Wright R-1510-26, it was an all-metal low-wing monoplane with a long turtleback from the enclosed cockpit to the tail, and with deep wheel pants characteristic of early Northrops. Two synchronized cowl guns, two 116-pound bombs, and 120 gallons of fuel were carried.

CURTISS XF13C-2
Wright XR-1510-94, 600 hp at 10,000'
DIMENSIONS: Span 35', Lg. 25'8", Ht. 12'9", Wing Area 282 sq. ft.
WEIGHT: Empty 3183 lb., Gross 4343 lb. Fuel 110 gal.
PERFORMANCE: Speed—Top 218 mph, Landing 68 mph. Service Ceiling 23,900', Climb 5000'/3.6 min. Range 863 miles.   MFR

In August 1935 the Navy ordered the aircraft reworked as the XFT-2, with a 650-hp Pratt & Whitney R-1535-72. Delivered in March 1936, the XFT-2 had modified landing gear, only 80 gallons of fuel, and a new cowling.

The failure of these monoplanes to win Navy contracts has been attributed to their high landing speed and stowage difficulties, although all had wing flaps and were relatively small. In any case,

NORTHROP XFT-2
Pratt & Whitney R-1535-72, 650 hp at 7500'
DIMENSIONS: As XFT-1
WEIGHT: Empty 2730 lb., Gross 3770 lb., Max. 4017 lb.
   Fuel 80 gal.
PERFORMANCE: Speed—Top 240 mph at 7500', Landing
   67 mph. Service Ceiling 27,500', Climb 5000'/2.2 min.
                                                      MFR

the Navy chose to stick to biplanes even though the
Army was now concentrating on faster monoplanes.
Discouraged by their unsuccessful efforts, neither
Boeing, Curtiss, nor Northrop was to offer a Navy
fighter for many years.

Grumman F3F Biplanes

Grumman's first single-seater, the F2F-1, had been
successful, but Navy engineers desired more maneuverability and better directional stability. The
XF3F-1, which had an R-1535-72, larger wings, and
longer fuselage, was ordered October 15, 1934, but
Grumman had to build three aircraft before the contract was completed. The first flew March 20, 1935,
but crashed in a terminal velocity dive two days
later. A replacement flown May 9 was destroyed in
a spin on May 17. A third prototype delivered June

20 was accepted and won the production contract
on August 24. Powered by a 650-hp R-1535-84, 54
F3F-1s were accepted from March through September 1936.

   Instead of the twin-row Wasps and two-bladed
propellers of earlier models, the XF3F-2 had a single-row 750-hp Wright XR-1820-22 Cyclone and
three-bladed propeller. This aircraft was delivered
to Anacostia July 27, 1936, and it could be distin-

GRUMMAN XF3F-1
Pratt & Whitney R-1535-72, 700 hp takeoff, 650 hp at
7500'
DIMENSIONS: Span 32', Lg. 23', Ht. 10'6", Wing Area 261
   sq. ft.
WEIGHT: Empty 2868 lb., Gross 4094 lb., Max. 4327 lb.
   Fuel 110 gal.
PERFORMANCE: Speed—Top 226 mph at 7500', Landing
   64.5 mph. Service Ceiling 29,500', Climb 5000'/2.5
   min. Range 910 miles.   MFR

GRUMMAN F3F-1
Pratt & Whitney R-1535-84, 700 hp takeoff, 650 hp at
7500'
DIMENSIONS: Span 32', Lg. 23'3", Ht. 9'4", Wing Area 261
   sq. ft.
WEIGHT: Empty 2952 lb., Gross 4170 lb., Max. 4403 lb.
   Fuel 110 gal.
PERFORMANCE: Speed—Top 231 mph at 7500', 215 mph
   at s. l., Landing 66 mph. Service Ceiling 28,500', Climb
   1900'/1 min. Range 882 miles normal, 1000 miles
   max.   ARC

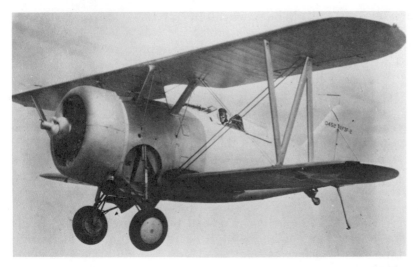

GRUMMAN XF3F-2   MFR

GRUMMAN F3F-2
Wright R-1820-22, 950 hp takeoff, 750 hp at 15,200'
DIMENSIONS: Span 32', Lg. 23'2", Ht. 9'4", Wing Area 260
  sq. ft.
WEIGHT: Empty 3254 lb., Gross 4498 lb., Max. 4750 lb.
  Fuel 130 gal.
PERFORMANCE: Speed—Top 260 mph at 17,250', 234 mph
  at s. l., Landing 69 mph. Service Ceiling 32,300', Climb
  2800'/1 min. Range 975 miles at 123 mph, 1130 miles
  max.   USN

GRUMMAN F3F-3
Wright R-1820-22, 950 hp takeoff, 750 hp at 15,200'
DIMENSIONS: As F3F-2
WEIGHT: Empty 3285 lb., Gross 4543 lb., Max. 4795 lb.
  Fuel 130 gal.
PERFORMANCE: Speed—Top 264 mph at 15,200', 239 mph
  at s. l., Landing 68 mph. Service Ceiling 33,200', Climb
  2750'/1 min. Range 980 miles normal, 1150 miles max.
                                                      MFR

guished from the F3F-1 by the wider-diameter engine and modified rudder.

Eighty-one production F3F-2s were ordered March 23, 1937, and accepted from November 1937 to April 1938, followed by 27 refined F3F-3s ordered June 21, 1938, and delivered from December 16, 1938, to May 10, 1939. These were the last biplane fighters built in the United States, and all F3Fs were armed with one .30-caliber and one .50-caliber gun under the cowl and two 116-pound bombs under the wings.

Grumman biplanes then equipped all six Navy and both Marine fighter squadrons, but the drag of their strut-braced wings prevented performance comparable to the Army's monoplanes. The F3Fs remained on carriers until June 1941, and the Marines did not turn in their last Grumman biplanes until October 11, 1941.

The Navy tried the monoplanes then on order for the Army in order to see if carrier-based adaptations would be practical. In July 1936 Curtiss Design No. 75, the P-36's prototype, was tested at Anacostia. Powered by an 840-hp Wright R-1820G-5, it did 277 mph at 5,265 pounds gross, which was better than the Grumman biplane. A naval version of the Seversky P-35, called the NF-1 (Naval Fighter One) by the company, never received a Navy designation or contract. Powered by a Wright R-1820-22 instead of the Wasps on the Army versions, it had the AP-1's enclosed wheels and large windshield. Completed about June 3, 1937, it was flown to Anacostia on September 24.

The Navy did not consider either of these aircraft suitable for carrier use, but it knew it had to develop monoplane fighters of its own to match the performance of land-based types. Landing speeds thought too dangerous in the 1930s were to become commonplace during the war years. Moreover, ingenious methods of wing folding would solve the stowage problem.

SEVERSKY NF-1
Wright R-1820-22, 950 hp takeoff, 750 hp at 15,200'
DIMENSIONS: Span 36', Lg. 25'2", Ht. 9'1", Wing Area 220 sq. ft.
WEIGHT: Empty 4020 lb., Gross 5231 lb. Fuel 90–200 gal.
PERFORMANCE: Speed—Top 267 mph at 15,000', Landing 69 mph. Service Ceiling 30,700', Climb 2760'/1 min.

                                            USN/WL

Chapter 23
Navy Fighters Against Japan, 1940-45

Brewster Buffalo

The first monoplane fighter actually used by Navy squadrons was the barrel-shaped Brewster Buffalo. A midwing all-metal single-seater with wheels retracting into the fuselage and a Wright R-1820-22, the XF2A-1 prototype was ordered June 22, 1936, and began tests in December 1937.

Fifty-four F2A-1s ordered June 11, 1938, had an R-1820-34, enlarged fin, and provision for two .50-caliber guns in the wings to supplement the two in the nose. Delivery began in June 1939, and by December, 11 of these planes had been accepted and served with the *Saratoga*'s VF-3. The remaining aircraft were released to Finland and completed by February 1940 with commercial R-1820-G5 engines.

On March 22, 1939, the Navy had ordered the original prototype modified to an XF2A-2, with a more powerful R-1820-40 and modified fin. This version was tested in July 1939 and its improve-

BREWSTER F2A-1
Wright R-1820-34, 940 hp takeoff, 750 hp at 17,000'
DIMENSIONS: Span 35', Lg. 26', Ht. 11'8", Wing Area 209 sq. ft.
WEIGHT: Empty 3785 lb., Gross 5055 lb., Max. 5370 lb. Fuel 160 gal.
PERFORMANCE: Speed—Top 301 mph at 17,000', 271 mph at s. l. Service Ceiling 32,500', Climb 3060'/1 min. Range 1095 miles normal, 1545 miles max.   USN

BREWSTER XF2A-1
Wright XR-1820-22, 950 hp takeoff, 750 hp at 15,200'
DIMENSIONS: Span 35', Lg. 25'6", Ht. 11'9", Wing Area 209 sq. ft.
WEIGHT: Empty 3711 lb., Gross 5017 lb. Fuel 164 gal.
PERFORMANCE: Speed—Top 277.5 mph at 15,200', Landing 67 mph. Service Ceiling 30,900', Climb 2750'/1 min.   ARC

BREWSTER B-239 (Finland)
Wright R-1820-G5, 950 hp takeoff, 750 hp at 15,200'
DIMENSIONS: As F2A-1
WEIGHT: Empty 3900 lb., Gross 5820 lb. Fuel 160 gal.
PERFORMANCE: Speed—Top 297 mph at 15,580', Cruising 236 mph. Climb 9840'/4.2 min. Service Ceiling 32,480'.   SALO

BREWSTER XF2A-2
Wright R-1820-40, 1200 hp takeoff, 900 hp at 14,000′
DIMENSIONS: Span 35′, Lg. 25′7″, Ht. 12′1″, Wing Area
209 sq. ft.
WEIGHT: Empty 4131 lb., Gross 5409 lb., Max. 5643 lb.
Fuel 164 gal.
PERFORMANCE: Speed—Top 325 mph at 16,100′, 290 mph
at s. l., Cruising 144 mph, Landing 70 mph. Service
Ceiling 35,000′, Climb 3100′/1 min. Range 1015
miles.   USN

BREWSTER F2A-2
Wright R-1820-40, 1200 hp takeoff, 900 hp at 14,000′
DIMENSIONS: Span 35′, Lg. 25′7″, Ht. 12′, Wing Area 209
sq. ft.
WEIGHT: Empty 4576 lb., Gross 5942 lb., Max. 6890 lb.
Fuel 240 gal.
PERFORMANCE: Speed—Top 323 mph at 16,500′, 285 mph
at s. l., Cruising 157 mph, Landing 78 mph. Service
Ceiling 34,000′, Climb 2500′/1 min. Range 1015 miles
normal, 1670 miles max.   PMB

BREWSTER BUFFALO I
Wright GR-1820-G105A, 1200 hp takeoff
DIMENSIONS: Span 35′, Lg. 26′, Ht. 12′1″, Wing Area 209
sq. ft.
WEIGHT: Empty 4479 lb., Max. 6840 lb. Fuel 240 gal.
PERFORMANCE: Speed—Top 324 mph at 21,000′, 313 mph
at 13,000′, Cruising 256 mph. Service Ceiling 30,675′,
Climb 3070′/1 min., 15,000′/6.3 min.   IWM

ments included on 43 F2A-2s delivered to the Navy,
beginning in September 1940, to replace the Finnish lot. With an R-1820-40, four .50-caliber guns,
and wing racks for two 100-pound bombs, they went
to VF-2 and VF-3.

Forty more Brewsters (Model 339B) had been
completed from April to July 1940 for Belgium; the
first reached France but fell into German hands, six
were diverted to Martinique, and the rest became
British property. The RAF had ordered 170 B339Es
of its own, but tests indicated that this type would
be too slow to fight Germans, so the Brewsters were
allocated to the Far East.

Known as the Buffalo I, these fighters had R-1820-
G105A Cyclones, and their British rating of 294

BREWSTER B339D   MFR

BREWSTER F2A-3
Wright R-1820-40, 1200 hp takeoff, 900 hp at 14,000′
DIMENSIONS: Span 35′, Lg. 26′4″, Ht. 12′, Wing Area 209
sq. ft.
WEIGHT: Empty 4732 lb., Gross 6321 lb., Max. 7159 lb.
Fuel 110–240 gal.
PERFORMANCE: Speed—Top 321 mph at 16,500′, 284 mph
at s. l., Cruising 161 mph, Landing 81 mph. Service
Ceiling 33,200′, Climb 2290′/1 min. Range 965 miles
normal, 1680 miles max.   USN

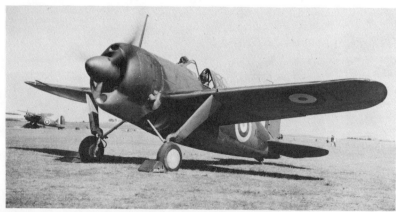

mph at 18,700 feet was far below the level claimed by U.S. figures. Completed from December 1940 to May 1941, most Buffalos went to Singapore, except for 32 sent to Rangoon. Seventy-two similar Buffalos (339D) for the Dutch East Indies were completed from March to June 1941. The Navy ordered 108 F2A-3s delivered from July to December 1941. Total Buffalo production reached 508 by March 1942, with 20 more built for the Dutch, but the latter were shipped to Australia, where 17 were taken on hand by the RAAF.

In December 1941 there were Brewster fighters with VF-2, VF-3, and seven F2A-3s on the first escort carrier, the *Long Island*. Only the Marines of VMF-221—stationed at San Diego on December 7 with F2A-3s and brought to Midway on Christmas Day—used them in combat. On June 4, 16 of 19 Buffalos sent up were downed by attacking Japanese.

This was the last fight by Allied Brewsters, which had been badly beaten in nearly every encounter with the enemy since December over Malaya, Burma, and the East Indies. The addition of armor plate and additional fuel capacity in self-sealing tanks in later models had increased weight so much that climb and maneuverability had been badly affected.

In contrast, the 44 Brewsters operated by Finland from June 30, 1941, to August 1944, in their war with Russia were remarkably successful. Captain Hans Wind was credited with 38 of the 477 victories claimed by the type's Finnish pilots in that period. This original, lighter model was operated by very experienced pilots fighting against an inadequately trained enemy—the reverse of the situation prevailing in the Far East.

Wildcats at War

Grumman's first monoplane fighter actually began as a biplane, the XF4F-1, ordered March 2, 1936. After the Brewster XF2A-1 monoplane and more powerful engines became available, the XF4F-1 was replaced by the XF4F-2 monoplane design on July 28, 1936.

Powered by a Pratt & Whitney R-1830-66 with a single-stage supercharger, the XF4F-2 first flew September 2, 1937, and was delivered December 23. The wheels folded into the fuselage below the wing with rounded tips. Two guns protruded from the cowling top.

Although the XF4F-2 in its original form lost a production contract to Brewster, in October 1938 the aircraft was ordered modified to the XF4F-3, with a larger, square-tipped wing, an XR-1830-76 with two-speed supercharger, and the intake on the cowl's front. Flown on February 12, 1939, the

GRUMMAN XF4F-2
Pratt & Whitney R-1830-66, 1050 hp takeoff, 900 hp at 10,000'
DIMENSIONS: Span 34', Lg. 26'5", Ht. 11', Wing Area 232 sq. ft.
WEIGHT: Empty 4036 lb., Gross 5535 lb. Fuel 130 gal.
PERFORMANCE: Speed—Top 288 mph at 10,000'. Service Ceiling 29,450'. Range 740 miles.   USN

GRUMMAN XF4F-3
Pratt & Whitney XR-1830-76, 1200 hp takeoff, 1000 hp at 19,000'
DIMENSIONS: Span 38', Lg. 28'10", Ht. 12'5", Wing Area 260 sq. ft.
WEIGHT: Empty 4907 lb., Gross 6103 lb., Max. 6404 lb. Fuel 160 gal.
PERFORMANCE: Speed—Top 335 mph at 21,300', 284 mph at s. l., Cruising 145 mph, Landing 68 mph. Service Ceiling 33,500', Climb 3100'/1 min. Range 890 miles normal, 1270 miles max.   USN

XF4F-3's improved speed won a contract August 8 for 54 (later 78) F4F-3s.

The first F4F-3 appeared in February 1940 with a raised stabilizer, and the second tried a nose spinner. Both were armed with two .30-caliber nose and two .50-caliber wing guns. An order issued in April had the third and fourth aircraft finished in June as XF4F-5s with Wright R-1820-40 Cyclones.

Cyclone engines and six 7.5-mm guns had been specified for the G-36A model ordered by the French Navy. The first was flown May 11, 1940, but Britain took the aircraft as the Martlet I, using four .50-caliber wing guns. From July to October, 81 were sent to the RAF, scoring their first German bomber kill on Christmas Day.

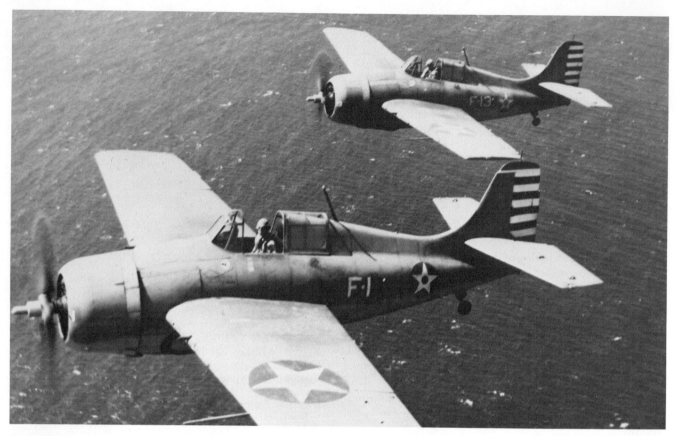

GRUMMAN F4F-3
Pratt & Whitney R-1830-76, 1200 hp takeoff, 1000 hp at 19,000'
DIMENSIONS: Span 38', Lg. 28'9", Ht. 11'10", Wing Area 260 sq. ft.
WEIGHT: Empty 5342 lb., Gross 7002 lb., Max. 8152 lb. Fuel 147–231 gal.
PERFORMANCE: Speed—Top 330 mph at 21,100', 281 mph at s. l., Cruising 147 mph, Landing 76 mph. Service Ceiling 37,500', Climb 2265'/1 min. Range 845 miles normal, 1690 miles max.   USN

GRUMMAN G-36A (Martlet I)   IWM

GRUMMAN XF4F-5
Wright R-1820-40, 1200 hp takeoff, 900 hp at 14,000'
DIMENSIONS: Span 38', Lg. 28'10", Ht. 11'10", Wing Area 260 sq. ft.
WEIGHT: Empty 4887 lb., Gross 6063 lb.
PERFORMANCE: Speed—Top 306 mph at 15,000'. Service Ceiling 35,500', Climb 2350'/1 min.   MFR

Deliveries then resumed on the F4F-3, now standardized with four .50-caliber wing guns and pilot armor. A Ranger squadron, VF-4, was the first using the type in December 1940, and all 78 were completed by the next February.

Mass production had been ordered August 8, 1940, but sufficient two-stage supercharged engines were lacking. A substitute was found in the single-stage R-1830-90 Wasp on the single XF4F-6 obtained in November. Despite a sacrifice of high-altitude performance, this engine was used in the new contract's first 95 aircraft, designated F4F-3A and 100 G-36B (Martlet II ordered for Britain October 1). The F4F-3As were delivered from March to May 1941 and were followed by 107 more F4F-3s with the two-stage R-1830-76. Named the Wild-

GRUMMAN F3F-3A
Pratt & Whitney R-1830-90, 1200 hp takeoff, 1000 hp at
    12,500'
DIMENSIONS: As F4F-3
WEIGHT: Empty 5216 lb., Gross 6876 lb., Max. 8026 lb.
    Fuel 147 gal.
PERFORMANCE: Speed—Top 312 mph at 16,000', 282 mph
    at s. l., Cruising 156 mph, Landing 75 mph. Service
    Ceiling 34,300', Climb 2430'/1 min. Range 825 miles
    normal, 1585 miles max.   IWM

GRUMMAN G-36B (Martlet II)   IWM

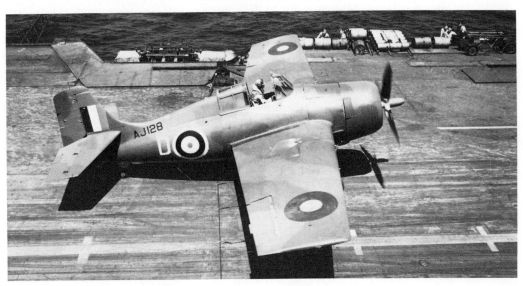

GRUMMAN F4F-4
Wright R-1820-40, 1200 hp takeoff, 900 hp at 14,000'
DIMENSIONS: As F4F-3
WEIGHT: Empty 4942 lb., Gross 6134 lb., Max. 6711 lb.
    Fuel 160 gal.
PERFORMANCE: Speed—Top 312 mph at 15,250', 279 mph
    at s. l., Cruising 148 mph, Landing 68 mph. Service
    Ceiling 34,000', Climb 2240'/1 min. Range 910 miles
    normal, 1250 miles max.   USN

cat, they equipped 10 of the 13 Navy and Marine
fighter squadrons in December 1941.

The first ten Martlet IIs delivered to Britain in
March 1941 had four .50-caliber wing guns, as did
the first 30 F4F-3As shipped to Greece in April
1941 but taken over at Gibraltar by the British as
the Martlet III. From August 1941 to April 1942, 90
more Martlet IIs were delivered with six .50-caliber
guns in folding wings. Six embarked on the H.M.S.
Audacity, the first British escort carrier, and destroyed five Fw 200C bombers from September 20
to December 21, 1941.

Folding wings for carrier stowage were first
planned for a Wildcat in March 1940, and an F4F-
3 on order was finished as the XF4F-4, flown April
14, 1941. By the end of November, delivery began

GRUMMAN F4F-3S (Seaplane)
Pratt & Whitney R-1830-76, 1200 hp
DIMENSIONS: Span 38′, Lg. 39′1″, Ht. 11′10″, Wing Area
  260 sq. ft.
WEIGHT: Empty 5804 lb., Gross 7506 lb.
PERFORMANCE: Speed—Top 266 mph at 20,300′, Cruising
  132 mph. Service Ceiling 33,500′, Climb 10,000′/4.5
  min. Range 600 miles.   PMB

GENERAL MOTORS FM-1 (WILDCAT V)
Pratt & Whitney R-1830-86, 1200 hp takeoff, 1040 hp at
  18,400′
DIMENSIONS: As F4F-3
WEIGHT: Empty 5895 lb., Gross 7975 lb., Max. 8762 lb.
  Fuel 144–260 gal.
PERFORMANCE: Speed—Top 320 mph at 18,800′, 284 mph
  at s. l., Cruising 161 mph, Landing 81 mph. Service
  Ceiling 34,000′, Climb 10,000′/5.6 min. Range 830
  miles normal, 1275 miles max.   MFR

on the F4F-4, with an R-1830-86, folding wings, self-sealing fuel tank, 164 pounds of armor, and six .50-caliber wing guns with 1,440 rounds. These first fought in the Battle of Midway, and 1,169 were completed by the end of 1942. Britain received 220 F4F-4Bs (Martlet IVs), but these had R-1820-40 Cyclones.

Twenty-one F4F-7s delivered in 1942 replaced the guns with unprotected internal wing tanks, increasing fuel capacity to 685 gallons and range to 3,700 miles, while cameras for reconnaissance were installed in the belly. Another modification was the XF4F-8, flown November 8, 1942, with an R-1820-56 and four .50s. The last of 1,977 Grumman Wildcats were 100 ordered as F4F-7s, but completed from January to May 1943 as F4F-3s for training. One was flown February 28 as the F4F-3S seaplane, but speed was reduced to 266 mph and a seaplane fighter wasn't needed after new carriers appeared.

The growing escort carrier fleet led to Wildcat production by General Motors' Eastern Aircraft Division. An April 18, 1942, contract provided the FM-1, identical to the F4F-4 except for having four .50-caliber guns with 1,720 rounds. First flown August 30, the 1,150 FM-1s included 311 lend-leased to Britain as the Wildcat V (formerly Martlet V) by December 1943.

Hellcats replaced the Wildcats at Grumman, but the older type was still wanted for the escort carrier's small decks. Efforts to improve Wildcat performance included fitting the first XF4F-5 with a turbosupercharged R-1820-54 and achieving 340 mph at 26,500 feet by February 1943. More practical was the R-1820-56 on the XF4F-8, first flown November 8, 1942; a second example had a larger vertical fin.

The production version of the XF4F-8 was the FM-2, which became the most widely used Wildcat, with an R-1820-56, high fin, 142 pounds of armor,

GENERAL MOTORS FM-2
Wright R-1820-56, 1350 hp takeoff, 1000 hp at 14,700′
DIMENSIONS: Span 38′, Lg. 28′11″, Ht. 11′5″, Wing Area
  260 sq. ft.
WEIGHT: Empty 5448 lb., Gross 7487 lb., Max. 8271 lb.
  Fuel 126–242 gal.
PERFORMANCE: Speed—Top 332 mph at 20,800′, 306 mph
  at s. l., Cruising 164 mph, Landing 76 mph. Service
  Ceiling 34,700′, Climb 3650′/1 min. Range 900 miles
  normal, 1310 miles max.   USN

and fittings for two 250-pound bombs or six 5-inch rockets. From September 1943 thru August 1945, 4,777 FM-2s were built, including 340 Wildcat VIs for Britain. An XF2M-1 project with a Wright R-1820-70W was canceled.

The first U.S. Wildcats to fight were Marine F4F-3s, lost when Wake Island was captured. By 1942 Wildcats equipped all carrier fighter squadrons and remained our sole carrier fighter in action for the first half of the war, fighting in all the major naval battles. Of all of the U.S. wartime fighters, they were the slowest, even among carrier-based types, yet the Wildcat was fairly successful, for the generous wing's low loading permitted a better climb and maneuverability than some of its faster contemporaries. Inferior to the Mitsubishi Zero in performance but possessing internal protection and more firepower, the Wildcat's victories were really due to the superior tactics and training of U.S. fighter pilots. Utilizing their own strong points against the enemy's weaknesses, American pilots used a two-plane element to dive, fire, and dive away, avoiding any attempt to turn and twist with the lighter Zeros. These tactics had been developed by pilots of the American Volunteer Group in China, commanded by General Claire L. Chennault.

A top Wildcat ace was Marine Major Joseph J. Foss, whose F4F-4 scored 26 victories near Guadalcanal from October 13, 1942, to January 15, 1943. At the war's end Navy figures claimed Wildcats destroyed 1,327 enemy aircraft for a loss of 191 Wildcats in combat, a ratio of almost seven to one.

Vought Corsairs

Three new fighter projects were launched in 1938 in an effort to bring carrier-based performance up to the level of land-based contemporaries. The Grumman XF5F-1 and Vought XF4U-1 were ordered June 30, 1938, and the Bell XFL-1 was ordered November 8.

The first twin-engine single-seater built for the Navy, the XF5F-1, was first flown on April 1, 1940, with Wright R-1820-40 Cyclones slung ahead and below the leading edge of stubby square-cut wings. The short fuselage began behind the wing's leading edge and extended back to twin rudders. Known as the G-34 Skyrocket on company records, it was originally armed with four Madsen cannons, but four

GRUMMAN XF5F-1 (mod.)   MFR

.50-caliber guns were installed instead ahead of the pilot's cockpit. Main wheels folded back into the engine nacelles, while the tailwheel was fixed and the wings folded for carrier stowage.

Delayed by cooling troubles, the prototype did not complete tests until February 1941, and from March to July was returned to the factory for reworking with an extended nose and prop spinners added. After 211 flights the project was abandoned in favor of the XF7F-1, and the XP-50 Army version had no greater success.

First flown May 13, 1940, the Bell XFL-1 was a carrier version of the P-39 Airacobra, with an Allison V-1710-6 placed behind the pilot and turning the propeller by a driveshaft extended to the nose. Instead of tricycle wheels, however, the XFL-1 had conventional tail-down landing gear, with an arrester hook added for carrier landings. Radiators below the wing cooled the only inline engine in post-1927 Navy fighters, and provisions were made for a 37-mm cannon and two .50-caliber guns in the nose.

Both of these experiments were surpassed by the Vought XF4U-1 Corsair, first Navy plane built around the Pratt & Whitney 1850 hp XR-2800-4 Double Wasp, with a 13-foot-4-inch diameter three-

GRUMMAN XF5F-1
Wright R-1820-40, 1200 hp takeoff, 900 hp at 14,000'
DIMENSIONS: Span 42', Lg. 28'11", Ht. 12', Wing Area 303 sq. ft.
WEIGHT: Empty 7990 lb., Gross 10,021 lb., Max. 10,892 lb. Fuel 178–277 gal.
PERFORMANCE: Speed—Top 358 mph at 17,300', 312 mph at s. l., Landing 72 mph. Service Ceiling 34,500', Climb 10,000'/4.2 min. Range 780 miles normal, 1170 miles max.   MFR

BELL XFL-1
Allison V-1710-6, 1150 hp takeoff, 1000 hp at 10,000'
DIMENSIONS: Span 35', Lg. 29'9", Ht. 11'5", Wing Area 232 sq. ft.
WEIGHT: Empty 5161 lb., Gross 6651 lb., Max. 7212 lb. Fuel 126–200 gal.
PERFORMANCE: Speed—Top 338 mph at 11,000', 306 mph at s. l., Cruising 172 mph, Landing 72 mph. Service Ceiling 30,900', Climb 2630'/1 min. Range 965 miles normal, 1475 miles max.   MFR

VOUGHT XF4U-1
Pratt & Whitney XR-2800-4, 1850 hp takeoff, 1460 hp at 21,500'
DIMENSIONS: Span 41', Lg. 31'11", Ht. 15'7", Wing Area 314 sq. ft.
WEIGHT: Empty 7505 lb., Gross 9357 lb., Max. 10,074 lb. Fuel 273 gal.
PERFORMANCE: Speed—Top 405 mph, Landing 73 mph. Service Ceiling 35,200', Climb 2660'/1 min. Range 1070 miles.   MFR

VOUGHT F4U-1
Pratt & Whitney R-2800-8, 2000 hp takeoff, 1650 hp at 21,000'
DIMENSIONS: Span 41', Lg. 33'4", Ht. 16'1", Wing Area 314 sq. ft.
WEIGHT: Empty 8982 lb., Gross 12,039 lb., Max. 14,000 lb. Fuel 237–537 gal.
PERFORMANCE: Speed—Top 417 mph at 19,900', 359 mph at s. l., Cruising 182 mph, Landing 87 mph. Service Ceiling 36,900', Climb 2890'/1 min. Range 1015 miles normal, 2220 miles ferry.   USN

bladed propeller. In order to give the big propeller sufficient ground clearance without making the landing gear too stilted and heavy, the wing was gulled downwards, a technique that also promised reduced drag at the juncture of wing and body. The wheels retracted backwards and swiveled 90° flat into the wing, which folded upwards for stowage. Finished with a smooth spot-welded skin, the XF4U-1 made its first flight on May 29, 1940.

Two .30-caliber guns were mounted above the engine and two .50-caliber guns in the wings, the latter replaceable by 23-mm Madsens, if available. Both the XF4U-1 and XF5F-1 had cells in their wings for a new attack system: forty 5-pound bombs to be dropped on bomber formations from above. A window for aiming was provided in the Vought's cockpit bottom, but these bombs were not included on any production aircraft.

Rex Beisel's design was the first American fighter to surpass 400 mph, except perhaps for the XP-38. On November 28, 1940, the Navy requested a production configuration with increased firepower and fuel capacity.

An initial production contract for 584 F4U-1s was placed June 30, 1941, but the war expanded requirements and the VGB program was set up to pool the resources of Vought, Goodyear, and Brewster to produce Corsair fighters. On June 25, 1942, the first production F4U-1 was flown with a 2,000-hp R-2800-8, lengthened fuselage, and cockpit moved back to make room for an additional self-sealing fuel tank. Six .50-caliber guns in the wings with 2,350 rounds of ammunition and 155 pounds of pilot armor were installed.

In September 1942 the Corsair was tested on an aircraft carrier, but it landed rather fast, displayed poor downward visibility, and had a severe bounce.

In any case, the Corsair was satisfactory for land-based operations and was therefore issued to Marine squadrons first. On February 12, 1943, VMF-124 arrived on Guadalcanal with F4U-1s, nearly 100 mph faster than the F4F-4s they replaced, and soon established a definite superiority over enemy fighters. By the following August, all eight Marine fighter squadrons in the Pacific used Corsairs. The first Navy Corsair squadron in action, VF-17, began a successful tour in the South Pacific in September 1943 with a new cockpit design.

Goodyear began delivery on the FG-1 in April 1943, and Brewster's F3A-1 Corsairs began appearing in June 1943. By May 1943 the Royal Navy was getting Corsairs, some with wing tips clipped so that they could fold inside the smaller hangars on British carriers. A new cockpit canopy and a pilot's seat raised seven inches to improve vision was introduced on Corsair No. 950 on August 9, 1943; these were styled F4U-1A on unofficial reports. Beginning with F4U-1 No. 1302 on October 5, a center-line rack for a 178-gallon drop tank or 1,000-

VOUGHT F4U-1A   USN

VOUGHT F4U-1D   USN

GOODYEAR FG-1D
Pratt & Whitney R-2800-8W, 2250 hp takeoff
DIMENSIONS: As F4U-1
WEIGHT: Empty 8695 lb., Gross 12,039 lb., Max. 13,120 lb. Fuel N/A
PERFORMANCE: Speed—Top 425 mph at 20,000', 328 mph at s. l., Climb 3120'/1 min. Range 500 miles/2000 lbs.   USN

pound bomb was installed; previously only two 116-pound bombs could be carried on wing racks.

The R-2800-8W, with water injection for emergency power, appeared with the 1,551st aircraft on November 25, 1943. These modifications were standardized on the F4U-1D and FG-1D, which had twin pylons under the gull wings for two 1,000-pound bombs or 154-gallon drop tanks. The internal wing tanks were eliminated, and the last 600 added eight 5-inch rockets. The first F4U-1D was accepted in April 1944 for the British, and the last of 1,685 F4U-1Ds was delivered February 2, 1945. Beginning in July 1944, Vought concurrently built 200 F4U-1Cs armed with four 20-mm guns and 220 rpg instead of the usual .50-caliber guns. Altogether,

Vought built 4,699 F4U-1 series Corsairs, including 95 Corsair Is (old cockpit) and 510 Corsair IIs (new canopy) for the British Navy and 370 Corsair IIs for New Zealand.[1] The Navy had closed the badly managed Brewster factory in July 1944 after 735 F3A-1s were finished, including 430 British Corsair IIIs. Goodyear continued production until the war's end, completing 4,006 FG-1 series, with 929 going to Britain and 60 to New Zealand as the Corsair IV.

A night-fighter version had been proposed as early as November 8, 1941, and the Naval Aircraft Factory converted 32 F4U-1s to F4U-2s, with a radome on the starboard wing tip and an outboard gun deleted. These aircraft, delivered from January to September, 1943, were issued to three night-fighter squadrons. Up to this point night fighters had always carried a radar operator to assist the pilot, so the Corsair was the first to attempt the mission with the pilot using his own three-inch radarscope. On the night of October 31, 1943, an F4U-2 made the first kill by a radar-equipped Navy fighter.

Three high-altitude XF4U-3s with a turbosupercharged R-2800-16 fed by a belly intake were ordered in March 1942 as F4U-1 conversions, with the first flown April 22, 1944, but the adaptation proved unsuitable. Vought began the conversion of two F4U-1s to an F4U-4X configuration on May 20, 1943, and five fresh XF4U-4 prototypes and 1,414 F4U-4s were ordered January 25, 1944. Powered by an R-2800-18W and four-bladed propeller, and recognizable by the air intake added under the cowl, the first F4U-4X flew May 19, 1944, the first XF4U-4 on September 20, and the first three F4U-4s were accepted in December. Six .50-caliber guns, 197 pounds of armor, and two 1,000-pound bombs or eight 5-inch rockets were carried. Fighter and dive-bomber operations by Marine squadrons increased in number during 1944 Pacific offensives.

Operations from U.S. aircraft carriers were finally begun January 3, 1945, by Marine squadrons, with successes that made prior reluctance to operate Corsairs from flight decks overly cautious. Navy bomber-fighter squadrons (VBF) joined the battle from the big carriers, while land-based Marine squadrons continued the ground-support role, introducing napalm bombs on April 18 over Okinawa.

Nineteen Fleet Air Arm squadrons were organized around Corsairs at U.S. Navy bases from June 1943 to April 1945 and fought from Norway to Japan. New Zealand's 13 fighter squadrons replaced their Kittyhawks with 424 Corsairs in 1944–45.

At the war's end Corsairs had flown 64,051 action sorties and had shot down 2,140 Japanese aircraft at a loss of 768 F4Us, including only 189 to air

[1] New Zealand actually received 238 F4U-1As and 126 F4U-1Ds from this allocation.

VOUGHT F4U-2

Pratt & Whitney R-2800-8, 2000 hp takeoff, 1650 hp at
21,000'

DIMENSIONS: As F4U-1

WEIGHT: Empty 9170 lb., Gross 11,446 lb., Max. 13,112
lb. Fuel 178–363 gal.

PERFORMANCE: Speed—Top 381 mph at 23,500', 325 mph
at s. l., Cruising 187 mph, Landing 82 mph. Service
Ceiling 33,900', Climb 2970'/1 min. Range 955 miles
normal, 1790 miles max.   USN

VOUGHT XF4U-3

Pratt & Whitney XR-2800-16, 2000 hp at 30,000'

DIMENSIONS: As F4U-1

WEIGHT: Empty 9039 lb., Gross 11,623 lb., Max. 13,143
lb.

PERFORMANCE: Speed—Top 412 mph at 30,000', 314 mph
at s. l., Cruising 180 mph, Landing 83 mph. Service
Ceiling 38,400', Climb 2990'/1 min. Range 780 miles
normal, 1430 miles max.   MFR

VOUGHT F4U-4

Pratt & Whitney R-2800-18W, 2100 hp takeoff, 1950 hp at
23,300'

DIMENSIONS: Span 41', Lg. 33'8", Ht. 14'9", Wing Area
314 sq. ft.

WEIGHT: Empty 9205 lb., Gross 12,420 lb., Max. 14,670
lb. Fuel 234–534 gal.

PERFORMANCE: Speed—Top 446 mph at 26,200', 381 mph
at s. l., Cruising 215 mph, Landing 89 mph. Service
Ceiling 41,500', Climb 3870'/1 min. Range 1005 miles
normal, 1560 miles max.   USN

combat, 349 to antiaircraft, and 230 to operational difficulties. Its most successful pilots were Marines: Gregory Boyington flew Corsairs for 22 of his 28 victories; Robert M. Hanson with 25 victories; and Kenneth A. Walsh with 21 victories.

By the end of August 1945, 1,859 F4U-4s had been accepted, but victory cancellations reduced contracts from 3,149 to 2,056 delivered by April 1946. They were followed by 287 F4U-4Bs with four 20-mm guns and 11 F4U-4P photo ships completed by August 1947.

Goodyear's contracts for 2,500 FG-4s were also canceled, but it had designed the F2G-1 with the big 3,000-hp Wasp Majors. Eight FG-1s were di-

GOODYEAR F2G-1 (Data for F2G-2)
Pratt & Whitney R-4360-4, 3000 hp takeoff, 2400 hp at 13,500′
DIMENSIONS: Span 41′, Lg. 33′10″, Ht. 16′1″, Wing Area 314 sq. ft.
WEIGHT: Empty 10,249 lb., Gross 13,346 lb., Max. 15,422 lb. Fuel 309–609 gal.
PERFORMANCE: Speed—Top 431 mph at 16,400′, 399 mph at s. l., Cruising 190 mph, Landing 92 mph. Service Ceiling 38,800′, Climb 4400′/1 min. Range 1190 miles normal, 1955 miles max. USN

verted to the XF2G-1 program, the first flying May 31, 1944. A March 22, 1944, contract called for 418 F2G-1s and ten F2G-2s with carrier gear and higher tail, but only five of each were actually delivered; the first in June 1945, the rest from August 1945 to February 1946. Faster at low altitudes than the standard Corsair, they had a bubble canopy and an intake above the engine. Four .50-caliber guns with 1,200 rounds were carried in the wings, together with fittings for two 1,600-pound bombs. All F2Gs were eventually sold as surplus and some were used as private racers.

Corsair production continued into the jet age and the Korean War, for early jet types did not meet close-support and night-fighter requirements. Two XF4U-5s had been converted from F4U-4s by installation of the two-stage R-1830-32W Wasp, and they first flew April 4, 1946.

Production F4U-5s had four 20-mm guns and twin cheek inlet ducts, and delivery of 223 ordered July 19, 1946, began in November 1947. In May 1948 delivery began on 75 radar-equipped F4U-5N and 30 camera-fitted F4U-5P Corsairs. Production

VOUGHT F4U-5
Pratt & Whitney R-2800-32W, 2300 hp at 26,200′
DIMENSIONS: Span 41′, Lg. 33′6″, Ht. 14′9″, Wing Area 314 sq. ft.
WEIGHT: Empty 9583 lb., Gross 12,902 lb., Max. 15,079 lb. Fuel 234–534 gal.
PERFORMANCE: Speed—Top 462 mph at 31,400′, 403 mph at s. l., Cruising 190 mph, Landing 91 mph. Service Ceiling 44,100′, Climb 4230′/1 min. Range 1036 miles normal, 1532 miles max. USN

VOUGHT F5U-5N
Pratt & Whitney R-2800-32W, 2300 hp at 26,200′
DIMENSIONS: Span 41′, Lg. 34′6″, Ht. 14′9″, Wing Area 314 sq. ft.
WEIGHT: Empty 9683 lb., Gross 12,901 lb., Max. 14,106 lb. Fuel 234–534 gal.
PERFORMANCE: Speed—Top 470 mph at 26,800′, 379 mph at s. l., Cruising 227 mph, Service Ceiling 41,400′, Climb 3780′/1 min. Range 1120 miles. MFR

then shifted from Hartford, Connecticut, to Dallas, Texas, where deliveries on 240 F4U-5N Corsairs began May 1949 and were finished September 1951.

The last 101 Corsair night fighters were delivered as winterized F4U-5NLs for the Korean War, with the APS-19 scanner on the starboard wing. Four 20-mm guns with 924 rounds were carried in the wings, and either two 1,000-pound bombs, eight 5-inch rockets, or two 150-gallon drop tanks could be attached externally.

When the Korean War began, F4U-4Bs on the *Valley Forge* began attacks on July 3, 1950, and two

Marine squadrons arrived in August to provide close air support. An F4U-5N squadron performed interdiction missions. Navy fighters arrived in June 1953 to interrupt enemy night intruders, when Lieutenant Guy Bordelon became the only Navy night-fighter ace.

A new requirement for a close-support Corsair version was created by the Korean War, and the XF4U-6, later designated AU-1, was designed for this purpose. First flown December 29, 1951, it had a narrow cowl, with the oil coolers moved back into

VOUGHT AU-1
Pratt & Whitney R-2800-83W, 2300 hp takeoff, 2800 hp WE
DIMENSIONS: Span 41', Lg. 34'1", Ht. 14'10", Wing Area 314 sq. ft.
WEIGHT: Empty 9835 lb., Gross 18,979 lb., Max. 19,398 lb. Fuel 234–534 gal.
PERFORMANCE: Speed—Top 238 mph at 9500', Cruising 184 mph, Landing 83 mph. Service Ceiling 19,500', Climb 920'/1 min. Range 484 miles.   MFR

the wing roots for protection. An R-2800-83W with a single-stage supercharger provided low-altitude power, and additional armor was placed under the cockpit, fuel tank, and engine accessory compartment. The fuel load and 20-mm armament was the same as that of the F4U-5, but external racks could handle up to 4,000 pounds of bombs or ten rockets. Marine squadrons received 111 AU-1s by October 10, 1952.

At the end of the Korean War in 1953, there were three Marine attack squadrons and four Navy fighter squadrons using Corsairs. These squadrons retired their aircraft by 1954, but Corsairs remained with the Reserves until 1957.

The final Corsair model was the F4U-7, built for the French Navy with R-2800-18W two-stage supercharged engines and a scoop on the cowl's bottom. Ninety-four were built, the first flying July 2, 1952. They were used aboard the carrier *Lafayette* and in Indochina, where they were joined by 25 secondhand AU-1s in April 1954. After France left Vietnam, French Corsairs served in the Mediterranean and Algeria until 1962, and were decommissioned in 1964.

When the last F4U-7 rolled off the line on Christmas Eve 1952, production of the last propeller-

VOUGHT F4U-7   MFR

driven fighter built in the United States had reached a total of 12,571 planes. In terms of production time, the Corsair surpassed any propeller-driven fighter in America.

Hellcats

Since the Corsair was not accepted for carrier operations earlier in the war, it is fortunate that another type more suitable for flight-deck work was available. The Grumman Hellcat also had a 2,000-hp Pratt & Whitney Wasp and six wing guns, but sacrificed speed for better maneuverability, climb, and visibility.

Wright R-2600-16 Cyclones of 1,600 hp were specified for two XF6F-1 prototypes ordered June 30, 1941, and for the large F6F-1 production contract made January 7, 1942. By April 29 a turbosupercharged R-2600-10 was selected for an XF6F-2 version, but Grumman was also studying the 2,000-hp Pratt & Whitney Double Wasp for an XF6F-3 model. The turbosupercharged XF6F-2, expected to do 419 mph at 30,000 feet, was never accepted in that form, but was delivered as an F6F-3.

On June 3, 1942, the Navy decided to complete the second prototype with the Double Wasp, so the

GRUMMAN XF6F-1   MFR

GRUMMAN XF6F-3   MFR

XF6F-1 (s/n 02982) flown June 26 was the only Cyclone-powered Hellcat completed. It had a Curtiss propeller in a large spinner and bulky landing gear. The XF6F-3 (02981)[2] was completed with an R-2800-10 and flown July 8.

After a cylinder failure ended the XF6F-3's third flight with landing damage, the XF6F-1's engine was quickly changed to an R-2800-10 to expedite tests, while the other aircraft was repaired as an XF6F-4. Meanwhile, the production contract, finally approved May 23, had been changed to the F6F-3 model, the first flying October 3 with an R-2800-10, Hamilton propeller without spinner, and simplified landing gear. By November prototype 02981 was back in the air as the XF6F-4, with a two-speed R-2800-27 rated at 1,600 hp at 13,500 feet but offering no real advantage.

Ten F6F-3s were delivered by the end of 1942 and production accelerated rapidly, the 2,545 Hellcats delivered in 1943 being enough to equip every fighter squadron on the fast carriers. There was lit-

GRUMMAN F6F-3
Pratt & Whitney R-2800-10W, 2000 hp takeoff, 1975 hp at 16,900'
DIMENSIONS: Span 42'10", Lg. 33'7", Ht. 13'1", Wing Area 334 sq. ft.
WEIGHT: Empty 9101 lb., Gross 12,441 lb., Max. 15,487 lb. Fuel 250–400 gal.
PERFORMANCE: Speed—Top 375 mph at 17,300', 335 mph at s. l., Cruising 160 mph, Landing 84 mph. Service Ceiling 37,300', Climb 3500'/1 min. Range 1090 miles normal, 1590 miles max.   USN

[2] The serial numbers are given because their appearance in reverse order has confused several accounts.

tle change in the basic configuration, although water injection for emergency power was standardized by 1944.

Powered by an R-2800-10W with a Hamilton three-bladed propeller, the Hellcat had the largest wing area of any U.S. single-engine service fighter in order to keep wing loading low. The wheels folded backwards flat into the wings, which folded backwards aboard ship. Seating the pilot high on top of the fuel tanks gave him fine visibility. A downward angle given the engine thrust line enhanced his view, and keeping the tail down in relation to the thrust line made climb the aircraft's natural tendency.

Installations on the F6F-3 included six .50-caliber guns with 2,400 rounds in the wings, 212 pounds of armor, and the self-sealing fuel tanks standard on wartime Navy types. In September 1943 acceptances began on F6F-3N night fighters with APS-6 radar on the starboard wing, while the F6F-3E was delivered in January 1944 with the lighter APS-4 radar. A total of 4,156 F6F-3, 229 F6F-3N, and 18 F6F-3E Hellcats were completed by April 1944.

First flown April 4, 1944, the F6F-5 had a modified cowl and windshield, armor was increased to 242 pounds, and 20-mm guns could be substituted for the two inner-wing weapons. Fittings for six rockets under the wings or two 1,000-pound bombs under the fuselage were provided. Contracts for 6,436 F6F-5s and 1,432 F6F-5Ns were completed, bringing Hellcat totals to 12,275 when production ended November 1945. The British Royal Navy received 332 F6F-3s as the Hellcat I, 850 F6F-5s as the Hellcat II, and 80 F6F-5Ns. Two XF6F-6s with the 2,100-hp R-2800-18W and four-bladed propeller were first flown July 6, 1944, but this advanced model wasn't produced.

Hellcats joined the Navy at the same time as the new carriers begun in 1941. The *Essex*, name-ship

GRUMMAN HELLCAT I   IWM

GRUMMAN F6F-3N
Pratt & Whitney R-2800-10W, 2000 hp takeoff, 1975 hp at
  16,900′
DIMENSIONS: As F6F-3
WEIGHT: Empty 9331 lb., Gross 13,015 lb., Max. 14,074
  lb. Fuel 250–400 gal.
PERFORMANCE: Speed—Top 360 mph at 18,000′, 305 mph
  at s. l., Cruising 161 mph. Service Ceiling 38,100′,
  Climb 3090′/1 min. Range 865 miles normal, 1235
  miles max.   MFR

GRUMMAN F6F-5
Pratt & Whitney R-2800-10W, 2000 hp takeoff, 1975 hp at
  16,900′
DIMENSIONS: As F6F-3
WEIGHT: Empty 9238 lb., Gross 12,740 lb., Max. 15,413
  lb. Fuel 250–408 gal.
PERFORMANCE: Speed—Top 380 mph at 23,400′, 315 mph
  at s. l., Cruising 168 mph, Landing 88 mph. Service
  Ceiling 37,300′, Climb 2980′/1 min. Range 945 miles
  normal, 1355 miles max.   USN

GRUMMAN F6F-5N
Pratt & Whitney R-2800-10W, 2000 hp takeoff, 1975 hp at
  16,900′
DIMENSIONS: As F6F-3
WEIGHT: Empty 9421 lb., Gross 13,190 lb., Max. 14,250
  lb. Fuel 250–400 gal.
PERFORMANCE: Speed—Top 366 mph at 23,200′, Cruising
  166 mph, Landing 89 mph. Service Ceiling 36,700′,
  Climb 2840′/1 min. Range 880 miles normal, 1260
  miles max.   USN

GRUMMAN HELLCAT II   IWM

GRUMMAN XF6F-6
Pratt & Whitney R-2800-18W, 2100 hp takeoff, 1800 hp at
  21,900′
DIMENSIONS: As F6F-3
WEIGHT: Empty 9526 lb., Gross 12,768 lb., Max. 13,823
  lb. Fuel 250–400 gal.
PERFORMANCE: Speed—Top 417 mph at 21,900′, Cruising
  171 mph, Landing 85 mph. Service Ceiling 39,000′,
  Climb 3070′/1 min. Range 1170 miles normal, 1730
  miles max.   MFR

of the class, got the first F6F-3 squadron, VF-9, in January 1943. The new ship and fighter went into action together—along with its sister ship, the new *Yorktown*, and the *Independence*, first of the new light carriers—with an attack on Marcus Island on August 31, 1943. This was only 14 months after the prototype's first flight. (The corresponding time on the Corsair was over 32 months.) The highmark of the Hellcats' success was the June 1944 Battle of the Philippine Sea, when the Grummans smashed the Japanese attack, with very small losses to themselves, in the famous "Turkey Shoot." At the outset each Essex-class carrier transported 36 Hellcats, 36 dive bombers, and 18 torpedo bombers, but the fighter numbers increased at the expense of the bombers as the war progressed. Night fighters operated as detachments with regular carriers, as a squadron on special night carriers, or as land-based Marine squadrons.

By the war's end, Hellcats were credited with 5,156 out of a total of 9,282 enemy aircraft destroyed in aerial combat by Navy and Marine planes, although only 270 Hellcats were lost to enemy aircraft in combat. The leading Hellcat ace, and the top Navy ace, was Captain David McCampbell, with 34 victories, including nine confirmed on one mission from the *Essex*. The Navy's second-ranking ace, Commander Cecil E. Harris, scored 24 victories in his Hellcat, and Commander Eugene Valencia got 23.

Royal Navy Hellcats began delivery in May 1943, and 12 squadrons formed from July 1943 to June 1945 served aboard British carriers from the North Sea to the Pacific. After the war 48 Hellcats went to a French Navy squadron in Indochina in 1950, but its last combat action was in Korea, when F6F-5K drones of a guided-missile unit attacked bridges beginning August 26, 1952.

Too Late for the War

On the same day, June 30, 1941, the Navy ordered the Hellcat prototypes, it ordered two prototypes each of the Curtiss XF14C-1 and the Grumman XF7F-1. The first Curtiss Navy fighter since 1935, the XF14C-1 was to be powered by a 2,200-hp Lycoming H-2470-4, and the second prototype was redesigned to take a 2,300-hp Wright R-3350-16 Cyclone. When the inline Lycoming proved unsatisfactory, the XF14C-1 was canceled in December 1943, but the second prototype was accepted as the XF14C-2 in July 1944. Co-axial contrarotating propellers were provided for the big Cyclone, along with an intake under the cowl for the turbosupercharger. The wheels folded inwards into the roots of the low wing, which could fold upwards for stowage. Four 20-mm guns protruded from the wing leading edge.

CURTISS XF14C-2
Wright XR-3350-16, 2300 hp takeoff, 2250 hp at 32,000'
DIMENSIONS: Span 46', Lg. 37'9", Ht. 17', Wing Area 375 sq. ft.
WEIGHT: Empty 10,582 lb., Gross 13,405 lb., Max. 14,582 lb. Fuel 230–380 gal.
PERFORMANCE*: Speed–Top 424 mph at 32,000', 317 mph at s. l., Cruising 172 mph. Service Ceiling 39,500', Climb 2700'/1 min. Range 950 miles normal, 1355 miles max.
*Design estimates.   MFR

The Curtiss design was as unsuccessful as the parallel XP-62 for the Air Force. The actual speed in tests is reported at only 398 mph, instead of the 424 mph promised, and the type was inferior to the F4U-4 already in production.

Grumman's twin-engine XF7F-1 Tigercat first flew November 2, 1943, with tricycle landing gear appearing for the first time on a naval fighter; it had the heaviest armament to date. Like the Hellcat, the big Tigercat design began with Wright XR-2600-14 Cyclones and shifted to Pratt & Whitney engines. Short, shoulder-high, square-tip wings folded upwards outboard of two R-2800-22W Wasps. The pilot sat ahead of the wings, with four .50-caliber guns with 1,200 rounds mounted low in the pointed nose. Four 20-mm guns with 800 rounds were mounted in the wing roots and 377 pounds of armor were installed. External fittings could carry two 1,000-pound bombs, drop tanks, a rocket, or a standard torpedo—the first time this weapon could be handled by a service fighter.

Five hundred Tigercats had been ordered for Marine Corps squadrons, with delivery beginning

GRUMMAN XF7F-1   USN

GRUMMAN F7F-1
Pratt & Whitney R-2800-22W, 2100 hp takeoff, 1600 hp at
  16,000'
DIMENSIONS: Span 51'6", Lg. 45'4½", Ht. 15'2", Wing Area
  455 sq. ft.
WEIGHT: Empty 15,943 lb., Gross 21,425 lb., Max. 22,560
  lb. Fuel 426–576 gal.
PERFORMANCE: Speed—Top 427 mph at 19,200', 394 mph
  at s. l., Cruising 177 mph, Landing 89 mph. Service
  Ceiling 36,200', Climb 4360'/1 min. Range 1170 miles
  normal, 1485 miles max.   USN

GRUMMAN F7F-2N
Pratt & Whitney R-2800-22W, 2100 hp takeoff, 1850 hp at
  14,000'
DIMENSIONS: As F7F-1
WEIGHT: Empty 16,321 lb., Gross 21,857 lb., Max. 26,194
  lb. Fuel 375–975 gal.
PERFORMANCE: Speed—Top 421 mph at 20,600', 362 mph
  at s. l., Cruising 183 mph, Landing 84 mph. Service
  Ceiling 39,800', Climb 4540'/1 min. Range 960 miles
  normal, 1250 miles/525 gal.   MFR

on April 29, 1944. Thirty-four were F7F-1 single-
seaters, but in July 1944 the third Tigercat was
accepted as an XF7F-2N two-seater. This version,
which had a radar operator seated behind the pilot,
omitted some fuel and the nose guns.

Sixty-five F7F-2Ns, whose delivery began October 31, 1944, were followed, on March 14, 1945, by
the first F7F-3, a single-place version with R-2800-
34Ws, more fuel and armor, the F7F-1's armament,
and a higher fin. Cancellations limited deliveries to
189 F7F-3s by January 1946 and 60 F7F-3Ns by
June 20. The latter were two-seaters with SCR-720
radar in the nose. Most of the former models were

GRUMMAN F7F-3
Pratt & Whitney R-2800-34W, 2100 hp takeoff, 1850 hp at
  15,500'
DIMENSIONS: Span 51'6", Lg. 45'4", Ht. 16'7", Wing Area
  455 sq. ft.
WEIGHT: Empty 16,270 lb., Gross 21,720 lb., Max. 25,720
  lb. Fuel 455–755 gal.
PERFORMANCE: Speed—Top 435 mph at 22,200', 367 mph
  at s. l., Cruising 222 mph, Landing 91 mph. Service
  Ceiling 40,700', Climb 4530'/1 min. Range 1200 miles
  normal, 1572 miles max.   MFR

modified to the -3N or -3P camera configurations.
Armament included four 20-mm guns, eight rockets,
and 2,000 pounds of bombs.

Production of 364 Tigercats ended November 7,
1946, with the last 13 being F7F-4N two-seaters,
the only model actually equipped for carrier operations. The first Marine Tigercat squadron arrived
at Okinawa the day before Japan's surrender, but
the type remained in squadron service until the
Korean War. Two Marine squadrons used F3F-3Ns
on ground-support and night missions from September 1951 to November 1952, after which F3D-
2 jets replaced them.

The Grumman Bearcat was designed as a replacement for the Hellcat. It would have better climb
and maneuverability and be able to operate from
even the smallest carriers. Two XF8F-1 prototypes
ordered November 27, 1943, had a Pratt & Whitney
R-2800-22W with a four-bladed propeller, a bubble
canopy, and low, square-tipped wings that could be
folded upwards. First flown August 31, 1944, the
XF8F-1 lacked the fin fillet of production jobs.

Small and strictly limited in weight, the Bearcat
was armed with four .50-caliber guns and 1,200
rounds in the wings, had 169 pounds of armor, and
external fittings for two 1,000-pound bombs, drop
tanks, or four rockets. Contracts for 2,023 Bearcats
were approved October 6, 1944, and General Motors received a February 5, 1945, order for 1,876
Bearcats, to be designated F3M-1.

The first production F8F-1, with the R-2800-34W
and more fuel, was delivered December 31, 1944,
and accepted in February 1945. In May VF-19 became the first Bearcat squadron and was embarked
on the light carrier Langley, but the war ended
before combat deployment, cutting back Grum-

GRUMMAN F7F-3N
Pratt & Whitney R-2800-34W, 2100 hp takeoff, 1850 hp at 15,500'
DIMENSIONS: As F7F-3
WEIGHT: Empty 16,400 lb., Gross 21,476 lb., Max. 25,846 lb. Fuel 375–675 gal.
PERFORMANCE: Speed—Top 423 mph at 21,900', Cruising 170 mph, Landing 91 mph. Service Ceiling 40,800', Climb 4580'/1 min. Range 960 miles/525 gal., 1595 miles max. MFR

GRUMMAN F7F-4N
Pratt & Whitney R-2800-34W, 2100 hp takeoff, 1850 hp at 14,000'
DIMENSIONS: Span 51'6", Lg. 46'10", Ht. 16'7", Wing Area 455 sq. ft.
WEIGHT: Empty 16,954 lb., Gross 21,960 lb., Max. 26,167 lb. Fuel 375–675 gal.
PERFORMANCE: Speed—Top 430 mph at 21,900', 360 mph at s. l., Cruising 235 mph, Landing 92 mph. Service Ceiling 40,450', Climb 4385'/1 min. Range 810 miles normal, 1360 miles max. MFR

GRUMMAN XF8F-1
Pratt & Whitney R-2800-22W, 2100 hp takeoff, 1600 hp at 16,000'
DIMENSIONS: Span 35'6", Lg. 28'8", Ht. 13'8", Wing Area 244 sq. ft.
WEIGHT: Empty 6733 lb., Gross 8788 lb., Max. 9537 lb. Fuel 150–250 gal.
PERFORMANCE: Speed—Top 424 mph at 17,300', 393 mph at s. l., Cruising 170 mph. Service Ceiling 33,700', Climb 4800'/1 min. Range 955 miles normal, 1450 miles max. ARC

GRUMMAN F8F-1
Pratt & Whitney R-2800-34W, 2100 hp takeoff, 1850 hp at 15,500'
DIMENSIONS: Span 35'10", Lg. 28'3", Ht. 13'10", Wing Area 244 sq. ft.
WEIGHT: Empty 7070 lb., Gross 9386 lb., Max. 12,947 lb. Fuel 183–333 gal.
PERFORMANCE: Speed—Top 421 mph at 19,700', 382 mph at s. l., Cruising 163 mph, Landing 92 mph. Service Ceiling 38,700', Climb 4570'/1 min. Range 1105 miles normal, 1965 miles ferry. USN

man's contracts and eliminating the F3M program. Grumman had furnished 151 by the end of August 1945 and completed 658 F8F-1s by August 1947. Four 20-mm cannons were provided on 226 F8F-1B Bearcats, accepted from February 1946 to January 1948, and APS-19 radar was provided on 12 F8F-1N night fighters accepted from August to November 1946.

An XF8F-2 accepted in February 1947 tested the modified fin and cowl that distinguished the F8F-2, ordered June 28, 1946, and first flown October 11, 1947, with an R-2800-30W. By May 1949 Grumman delivered 1,263 Bearcats, including 293 F8F-2s and a dozen F8F-2Ns. Four 20-mm guns, 800 rounds, and 173 pounds of armor were carried. Sixty F8F-2P photo jobs had cameras and two 20-mm guns. Two G-58A civilian models are not included in the total.

Many Navy pilots considered Bearcats the best of the propeller-driven fighters, but no opportunity to prove this occurred. After serving up to 28 Navy squadrons from 1945 to 1949, the Grumman missed the Korean War because it lacked the Corsair's load and the jet's speed. Conflict in Southeast Asia did bring the F8F some action when Bearcats were used by the French in Indochina from 1951 to 1954, after which a squadron was passed to the new Republic of Vietnam. Its role in that war was strictly one of ground attack, for there were no enemy aircraft. In 1953 Thailand was supplied 100 F8F-1s and 29 F8F-1Bs for its air force.

A few Bearcats were used for private racing, and one F8F-2, highly modified by Darryl Greenamyer, broke the world speed record for propeller-driven aircraft. Previously held for over 30 years by a Messerschmitt Bf 209, the new record of 483 mph was made on August 16, 1969.[3]

Boeing interrupted its retirement from fighter design with the XF8B-1. A large low-wing monoplane built around a 3,000-hp Pratt & Whitney R-4360-10 with contrarotating propellers, the Boeing's wheels rotated 90° to retract backwards into the wing. Armament included six .50-caliber wing guns, two 1,600-pound bombs in an internal bay, and two more on external racks, which could also be used for 2,000-pound bombs, torpedoes, or drop tanks. Recognition features included the large scoop below the engine and a bubble canopy.

Three long-range fighter-bomber prototypes contracted April 10, 1943, were built, the first being flown on November 27, 1944, and delivered to the Navy on March 10, 1945. The second XF8B-1, which flew a year later, was tested by the Air Force,

[3] The Greenamyer record still remained on the official list of world records in 1980; the 545 mph mark set by a Soviet Tu-114 turboprop transport in April 1960 did not get official international recognition.

GRUMMAN F8F-2
Pratt & Whitney R-2800-34W, 2300 hp takeoff, 1600 hp at 22,000'
DIMENSIONS: Span 35'6", Lg. 27'8", Ht. 12'2", Wing Area 244 sq. ft.
WEIGHT: Empty 7690 lb., Gross 10,426 lb., Max. 13,494 lb. Fuel 185–335 gal.
PERFORMANCE: Speed—Top 447 mph at 28,000', 387 mph at s. l., Cruising 182 mph, Landing 105 mph. Service Ceiling 40,700', Climb 4420'/1 min. Range 865 miles normal, 1435 miles max.   USN

BOEING XF8B-1
Pratt & Whitney XR-4360-10, 3000 hp takeoff, 2540 hp at 22,000'
DIMENSIONS: Span 54', Lg. 43'3", Ht. 16'3", Wing Area 489 sq. ft.
WEIGHT: Empty 14,190 lb., Gross 20,508 lb., Max. 22,960 lb. Fuel 384–954 gal.
PERFORMANCE: (At 19,523 lb. combat) Speed—Top 432 mph at 26,500', Cruising 225 mph, Stalling 82 mph. Service Ceiling 37,500', Climb 3660'/1 min. Range 2300 miles.   MFR

since the Navy had lost interest in the type after the war.

The last propeller-driven fighter Vought offered the Navy was also the oddest. The XF5U-1 was based on a proposal by C. H. Zimmerman for a circular flying wing aircraft designed to be capable of hovering by standing on its tail and using its propeller as helicopter rotors. A full-scale wood and fabric flying model with panted fixed landing gear, the V-173 was flown November 23, 1942, and construction began on a single-place fighter development known as XF5U-1. This was powered by two 1,600-hp turbosupercharged Pratt & Whitney R-2000-2 radials buried within the thick circular wing on each side of the cockpit and driving two large four-bladed propellers located at the wing tips. Twin rudders were mounted at the wing's trailing edge, and horizontal controls extended outboard of the weird saucer-shaped airframe. Dual main wheels and a tailwheel retracted backwards.

Armed with six .50-caliber guns, the aircraft had a span of 23 feet, 4 inches at the wing tips and 36 feet, 5 inches at the propeller tips. While a vertical takeoff was beyond the power capacity of the plane, a short takeoff combined with a high top speed seemed possible. On September 17, 1942, a letter of intent was issued for the XF5U-1, a mockup inspected in June 1943, and the contract dated July 15, 1944. The prototype was completed by August 20, 1945, with 1,350-hp R-2000-7 engines, since the planned XR-2000-2 units and special propellers were not ready.

With the temporary power plant, expected top speed was 388 mph at 15,000 feet and a 14,500 pound gross weight. (Characteristics of the XR-2000-2 version are provided in the accompanying photo caption.) Initial flight tests required transportation by sea to the Muroc test base in California, an expense the postwar Navy was unwilling to meet. On March 17, 1947, the XF5U-1 contract was terminated and the aircraft was demolished for scrap without ever being flown.

VOUGHT XF5U-1
Pratt & Whitney R-2000-2, 1600 hp at 23,000′
DIMENSIONS: Span 23′4″, Lg. 28′1½″, Ht. 16′8″, Wing Area 475 sq. ft.
WEIGHT: Empty 13,107 lb., Gross 16,722 lb., Max. 18,772 lb. Fuel 300–450 gal.
PERFORMANCE: (Estimated) Speed—Top 476 mph at 28,-000′, 366 mph at s. l., Cruising 202 mph. Service Ceiling 34,500′, Climb 3590′/1 min. Range 710 miles normal, 910 miles max.   MFR

VOUGHT XF5U-1   MFR

Chapter 24
The Magic Weapon, 1942–46

Superfortress over Japan

Had the war ended on V-E Day there could have remained doubt as to the decisive effects of strategic bombardment. Postwar study revealed that German production actually increased during 1944, and had the Nazi jet fighter program not foundered, defeat of Hitler might have depended entirely on Allied ground forces.

But war against Japan demonstrated air power's full weight. Japan, whose armed forces suffered 780,000 combat casualties in the entire war, sustained in nine months 806,000 civilian casualties, including 330,000 dead. All were victims of the Boeing B-29 Superfortress, which had proved itself a weapon of war without equal in the history of mankind.

The bomber which accomplished this feat, making the Kaiser's Gothas, Hitler's Heinkels, and our own B-17s seem rather primitive, was the first Very Heavy Bomber (VHB)-class aircraft. Boeing's B-29, based on B-15, B-17, and B-19 developments, added a pressurized crew cabin so attacks could be made above the effective reach of antiaircraft fire. Manual turrets seemed incompatible with pressurization, so a remote-control firing system was provided.

On November 10, 1939, General Arnold asked the War Department for permission to initiate development of a four-engine bomber of 2,000-mile radius "superior in all respects to the B-17B and the B-24." Permission was granted, and on January 29, 1940, Request for Data R-40B was issued to leading aircraft builders.

When R-40B, which called for a range of 5,333 miles with a ton of bombs, reached Boeing, the Seattle engineers completed a design already under way as Model 341. Sent to Wright Field by March 5, 1940, the 341 had a design gross weight of 76,000 pounds, a span of 124 feet 7 inches, speed of 405 mph, capacity for 4,120 gallons of fuel or five tons

of bombs, and six hand-operated .50-caliber guns. A few weeks later Wright Field requested the design be revised to incorporate leakproof tanks and heavier armament. Boeing replied on May 11, 1940, with Model 345, with a design gross of 97,700 pounds, a span of 141 feet 2 inches, speed of 382 mph, capacity for 5,440 gallons of fuel or eight tons of bombs, and ten .50-caliber and one 20-mm gun in remote-controlled turrets.

Other entries in the design competition also used the new 2,200-hp Wright R-3350-13. "An evaluation board appraised the designs and rated the competitors in this order of preference: Boeing, Lockheed, Douglas, Consolidated. Contracts for preliminary engineering data were issued to the firms on June 27 and their planes were designated, repectively, the XB-29, XB-30, XB-31, XB-32."

On the strength of the engineering data then offered, Boeing won a $3,615,095 contract for two XB-29 prototypes on September 6, 1940. A similar contract went to the XB-32 at the same time, while a third prototype machine was added to each in November. The Douglas and Lockheed designs were withdrawn, although the latter finally appeared in transport form as the Constellation. The Douglas design was developed to be the largest, with four R-4360 engines, 207 feet span, and a large single tail fin, but was canceled late in 1941.

Even before flight testing began, the pressures of war led the Air Force to program 1,644 production aircraft in a $3 billion effort that finally produced 3,960 B-29s from four different factories.

So that the B-17 program would not be obstructed, a new plant was built at Wichita, Kansas, utilizing midwestern labor reserves. An order for 14 YB-29s, approved on June 6, 1941, was followed on September 6 by a contract for 250 B-29s, and 500 more were added on January 31, 1942. Later Bell Aircraft was enlisted to build others at a Marietta, Georgia, facility, the first aircraft plant in the

Old South. A Renton, Washington, plant built for Boeing flying boats was released by the Navy for B-29A production in exchange for Mitchell medium bombers. Finally, Martin's Omaha factory, then building B-26Cs, was also, after a short reservation for 400 stillborn B-33As, assigned to B-29s.

Three XB-29s were built at Seattle, using four Wright R-3350-13 Cyclones, each with double turbosuperchargers and 2,200 hp at 25,000 feet. The first, flown September 21, 1942, by Edmund T. Allen, had three-bladed propellers, an astrodome behind the pilot's cockpit, and teardrop blisters for the periscopic sights of a Sperry fire-control system. These were replaced in the third prototype by hemispheric covers for the General Electric fire-control system adopted for production aircraft.

Problems with the big new engines were the main threat to B-29 tests: 16 engine changes were made in the XB-29's first 27 test hours. An engine fire interrupted the second XB-29's maiden flight December 30, 1942, and another caused a crash that killed everyone aboard on February 18, 1943. Flight tests were halted and the big gamble involving industrial resources placed on an untested aircraft and power plant was in doubt, but after hasty engine improvements the third prototype was airborne June 6.

The first YB-29-BW flew in Kansas on June 26, 1943, with the R-3350-21 and full armament system. This aircraft later became the XB-39 when Allison V-3420-11 inline engines were fitted and this model was delivered in March 1944.

Wichita delivered its first production B-29-1-BW in September 1943 and completed 1,620 by October

BOEING XB-29

Wright R-3350-13, 2200 hp at 25,000'
DIMENSIONS: Span 141'3", Lg. 98'2", Ht. 27'9", Wing Area 1739 sq. ft.
WEIGHT: Empty 66,120 lb., Gross 105,000 lb., Max. 120,-000 lb. Fuel 5155–7494 gal.
PERFORMANCE: Speed—Top 368 mph at 25,000', Cruising 247 mph, Landing 105 mph. Service Ceiling 32,100', Climb 25,000'/27 min. Range 4100 miles/16,000 lbs. bombs (120,000 lbs. gross), 5850 miles max.   MFR

1945. The first 240 (blocks 1 to 20) had R-3350-23 engines, four-bladed propellers, ten .50-caliber guns with 5,000 rounds, and 100 rounds for a 20-mm gun. Later blocks (40 to 100) had more fuel, twelve .50-caliber guns with 11,500 rounds, APQ-13 radar, and newer Cyclone models (R-3350-41 or -57). The Renton plant began B-29A deliveries in January 1944, with a new wing center section structure, and production of 1,119 planes wasn't completed until May 28, 1946. Martin delivered 536 B-29-MOs and Bell alternated between 357 B-29-BA and 311 B-29B-BA models by September 1945. The latter was a night bomber with APQ-7 bombing radar, no turrets, and APG-15 radar for the two or three .50-caliber tail guns.

All Superfortresses were similar in appearance, with an unbroken nose, a crew of 11 in pressurized compartments connected by a tunnel through double bomb bays, and double wheels for the retractable tricycle gear. The distinguishing armament feature was an elaborate General Electric fire-control system, with computing sights in the nose and in rear top and side blisters directing four remote-controlled turrets with 360° arcs. Each had two .50-caliber guns, but the upper front turret soon got four. On night raids late in the war, range and speed were improved by dispensing with all four turrets. A tail gunner remained, whose two .50-caliber guns and one 20-mm gun turned 30° around center. The heavy gun was later omitted and was sometimes replaced by a third .50-caliber gun. Up to forty 500-pound or sixteen 1,000-pound bombs could be carried.

The bombardier sat in the nose with his bombsight and gunsight, with panels of armor and bulletproof glass behind him protecting pilot and copilot. Behind them was more armor, then the flight engineer, radio operator, and navigator, then armor, and the bomb bays. The rear compartment contained three gunners and the radar man, all protected by an armor bulkhead. The radar protruded below between the bomb doors, while the tail gunners' compartment was also protected and, like the

BOEING YB-29   AF

BOEING YB-29 as escort fighter   AF

BOEING B-29
Wright R-3350-23, 2200 hp takeoff, 2430 hp WE
DIMENSIONS: Span 141'3", Lg. 99', Ht. 29'7", Wing Area
  1736 sq. ft.
WEIGHT: Empty 70,140 lb., Gross 134,000 lb., Combat
  110,000 lb. Fuel 5638–8198 gal.
PERFORMANCE: Speed—Top 358 mph at 25,000', 295 mph
  at 5000', Cruising 230 mph, Landing 105 mph. Service
  Ceiling 31,850', Climb 20,000'/38 min. Range 3150
  miles/20,000 lbs. bombs, 4700 miles max.
Data for blocks B-29-1 to B-29-20-BW, at military
  power.   AF

BOEING B-29-90-BW
Wright R-3350-41, 2200 hp takeoff, 2430 hp WE
DIMENSIONS: Span 141'3", Lg. 99', Ht. 29'7", Wing Area
  1736 sq. ft.
WEIGHT: Empty 71,360 lb., Gross 137,500 lb., Max. 141,-
  000 lb. Fuel 6988–9548 gal.
PERFORMANCE: (At 110,000 lb.) Speed—Top 361 mph at
  25,000', 302 mph at 5000' (WE), Cruising 230 mph,
  Stalling 105 mph, Service Ceiling 31,850', Climb 20,-
  000'/38 min. Range 3800 miles/16,000 lb. bombs, 5500
  miles ferry.
Data for blocks B-29-25 to B-29-90-BW.   MFR

BOEING B-29A-25-BN
Wright R-3350-57, 2200 hp takeoff, 2500 hp WE
DIMENSIONS: As B-29
WEIGHT: Empty 72,208 lb., Gross 140,000 lb. Fuel 7748–9150 gal.
PERFORMANCE: (At 101,480 lbs., combat weight) Speed— Top 399 mph at 30,000', 381 mph at 25,000', Cruising 253 mph, Stalling 119 mph. Service Ceiling 23,950', Combat Ceiling 36,150', Climb 1620'/1 min. Combat Radius 1931 miles, 5418 miles ferry range.
Data for 1952 configuration.   MFR

BOEING B-29B-60-BA (Bell)
Wright R-3350-23, 2200 hp takeoff
DIMENSIONS: As B-29
WEIGHT: Empty 69,000 lb., Gross 110,000 lb., Max. 137,-500 lb. Fuel 6988–9548 gal.
PERFORMANCE: Speed—Top 364 mph at 25,000', 367 mph WE, Cruising 228 mph, Landing 105 mph. Service Ceiling 32,000', Climb 20,000'/38 min. Range 3875 miles/18,000 lbs. bombs, 5725 miles ferry.   PMB

BOEING XB-39
Allison V-3420-11, 3000 hp takeoff, 2600 hp at 25,000'
DIMENSIONS: Span 141'3", Lg. 98'2", Ht. 27'9", Wing Area 1739 sq. ft.
WEIGHT: Empty 75,037 lb., Gross 105,000 lb., Max. 135,-000 lb. Fuel 3333 gal.
PERFORMANCE: Speed—Top 405 mph at 25,000', 312 mph at s. l., Cruising 282 mph. Service Ceiling 35,000', Climb 1300'/1 min., 30,000'/29.3 min. Range 2840 miles/4000 lbs. bombs, 6290 miles max.   PMB

main cabins, was pressurized to maintain an internal altitude of 8,000 feet up to an actual altitude of 30,000 feet.

Extra armament was fitted to the fourth YB-29 to test it as an escort fighter, like the B-40. Two .50s were mounted in a nose turret and each of four side blisters. The top and bottom turrets were retained with a 20-mm gun added to the lower turret and a 37-mm gun in the tail, for a total of 22 guns. One experimental B-29-25-BW replaced the remote-controlled turrets with conventional dome top and belly "ball" turrets, plus two chin barbettes. Production aircraft, however, usually kept the 12-gun configuration.

The B-29 in Service

Although the first Superfortress to go overseas was a YB-29 flown to England on March 8, 1944, this was just a feint to obscure the concentration of bombers against Japan. Four groups began moving to India on March 26, and on June 5, 77 planes raided Bangkok, the longest (2,261-mile) bombing mission to date. The first attack on Japan itself was staged through China on June 15. These and all future B-29 missions were made by the Twentieth Air Force, created solely to use the big Boeings. The longest American air raid of the war was a 4,030-mile, 19-hour mission from Ceylon to Sumatra on August 10, 1944.

When Chinese bases proved too difficult to supply and defend, the B-29s shifted to the newly captured Mariana Islands. From there they began the 177,000-ton bombing of the main Japanese islands in November 1944, which eventually inflicted the casualties mentioned before. Japanese weather frustrated the precision bombing technique used in Europe, and General Curtis E. LeMay shifted his method to night incendiary attacks on Japanese cities. The worst of these on Tokyo, March 9, 1945, caused more casualties than either of the atomic bombs. On March 27 the B-29s added Operation Starvation to their effort, eventually dropping 12,-035 mines in coastal waters to destroy Japanese shipping. Even without the atomic bomb, these fire bomb and mining attacks crippled Japan.

In his letter to President Roosevelt on August 2, 1939, suggesting creation of the atomic bomb, Albert Einstein had feared that "such bombs might very well prove too heavy for transport by air." However, the weapon, completed at Los Alamos, was well within the capacity of the B-29, which in September 1943 was selected as its carrier. Minor modifications were made to the bomb bay, but "the atom bomb was tailored to fit the plane rather than the reverse." A specially trained squadron received its modified B-29s (15 had been ordered) in May 1945 and flew to Tinian, in the Marianas, in June. There it awaited both the test-firing of the first bomb on July 16 in New Mexico and the rush of the next two bombs to Tinian by cruiser in time for the August 6 strike on Hiroshima.

The 9,700-pound uranium bomb was dropped from the *Enola Gay,* an Omaha-built B-29-45-MO flying 328 mph at 31,600 feet. On August 9 a B-29-35-MO, also equipped with only two .50-caliber tail guns, dropped a 10,000-pound Mk. II plutonium weapon on Nagasaki. The largest single-day B-29 effort with conventional bombs had been the 836 planes dispatched on August 1, while 809 made their last attack of the war on August 14, 1945.

BOEING B-29-45-MO (Martin) *Enola Gay*   AF

Mk. I "Little Boy" used at Hiroshima
    Length 126″, Diameter 29″, Weight 9700 lb.   AF

By the war's end there were about 2,865 B-29s on hand, and 40 VHB groups, of which 21 had been deployed in the Pacific. Six cameras had been fitted to 118 photo-recon conversions known as F-13s during the war and redesignated RB-29 in 1947. Retaining standard B-29 armament, they played a vital role in target location and damage evaluation.

So many modifications were made during a long service life that variations in weight and performance makes selection of "typical" characteristics difficult. The accompanying data is for early wartime models. Early sets of engines were eventually replaced with modernized R-3350-79s or -81s, and cruise-control experience improved range capabilities.

Postwar performances were calculated on a different basis, measuring speed at a "combat weight" defined as fuel load remaining over the target area. In 1945 the B-29 was credited with a top speed of 358 mph at 25,000 feet with military power, or 361 mph with war-emergency power. This was based upon 110,000 pounds, but in 1952 the B-29, with new engines and a 101,082-pound combat weight, could be credited with 381 mph at 25,000 feet and 399 mph at 30,000 feet.

As a result of postwar reductions, six B-29 bomb groups (45 a/c each) remained for Strategic Air

Command in 1947, with only the 509th Group configured for nuclear bombs. But many Boeings remained in storage and some tested postdelivery modifications. Most, like the SB-29 rescue version with lifeboat and the WB-29 weather version, were not combat configurations. An Air Refueling Squadron was formed for each B-29 group to extend range. The first was activated in June 1948 with KB-29M tankers using the British method with trailing hoses. Boeing's flying-boom system, however, won SAC's lasting approval and went into service with the KB-29P in September 1949.

When the Korean War began, the USAF inventory included 1,787 B-29 bombers and 162 RB-29 reconnaissance aircraft in storage or service with eight Bomb groups and one Strategic Reconnaissance group. Three groups flew their first combat mission on July 13, 1950, against Wŏnsan. By September five groups had accomplished the destruction of all scheduled strategic targets, but two groups and a reconnaissance squadron were retained in combat for attacks against transportation and for tactical support. During the war 21,328 effective combat sorties were flown, 167,100 tons of bombs were dropped, and 24 B-29s were lost to enemy action.

Although 417 B-29s served 14 bomber groups in December 1952, and 179 KB-29Ps served ten refueling squadrons, the bombers were replaced with B-47s by 1954, and the tankers were replaced with KC-97s by 1957. The last USAF Superfortresses in service were those used by a Radar Evaluation squadron until June 1960.

Beginning in March 1950, 88 B-29s were loaned to the Royal Air Force as the Boeing Washington and served Bomber Command until the jet V-bombers became available. Boeing's design also became the U.S.S.R.'s first very long-range strategic bomber. Three B-29s had force-landed in Siberia in 1944, and were copied and produced at Kazan as the Tu-4. The first three Tu-4s appeared at an airshow in August 1947, and it is reported that about 1,200 were built, some going to China. This program provided an interim strategic bomber without expensive development costs, so that the Russian effort could be concentrated on advanced jet types.

The B-32

The success of the Superfortress made the parallel heavy-bomber development by Convair superfluous. The first XB-32 had the same engines and pressurization of the B-29, with the high wing and twin tails of its B-24 ancestors. The first prototype, ordered September 9, 1940, and flown September 7, 1942, crashed after 30 flights; the second flew July 2, 1943; and the single high tail of the production ships was introduced on the third XB-32, flown No-

BOEING KB-29P   AF

vember 9. Proposed armament included 20,000 pounds of bombs, fourteen .50-caliber guns, and two 20-mm guns. Four guns were placed in a retractable turret on top of the fuselage behind the wing, with another such turret underneath. Three guns were installed in the rear of each outboard engine nacelle, remote-controlled from aiming stations in the tail and in fuselage blisters.

Pacific war tacticians, now thinking of attacks from lower altitudes, eliminated weighty pressurization and remote-controlled turrets from production models ordered in March 1943. Ten .50-caliber guns were paired in power-operated turrets like those in the B-24s: one in the nose, two on top, and one in the tail; and a retractable belly turret.

When delivery began in September 1944 on B-32 Dominators, official opinion was that B-32s were no longer needed as "insurance against failure of the B-29," and that they were overweight and had poor bombardier's vision. By the following summer it was decided to cut back orders and equip only one

CONVAIR XB-32
Wright R-3350-13, 2200 hp at 25,000'
DIMENSIONS: Span 135', Lg. 83', Ht. 20'10", Wing Area 1422 sq. ft.
WEIGHT: Empty 64,960 lb., Gross 101,662 lb., Max. 113,500 lb. Fuel 5226 gal.
PERFORMANCE: Speed—Top 376 mph at 25,000', Landing 96 mph. Service Ceiling 30,700', Climb 25,000'/22.6 min. Range 4450 miles/2000 lbs. bombs.   MFR

CONVAIR XB-32 (Second prototype)   MFR

CONVAIR B-32
Wright R-3350-23, 2200 hp at 25,000'
DIMENSIONS: Span 135', Lg. 82'1", Ht. 33', Wing Area 1422 sq. ft.
WEIGHT: Empty 60,278 lb., Gross 100,000 lb., Max. 121,-000 lb. Fuel 5460–6960 gal.
PERFORMANCE: Speed—Top 357 mph at 30,000', 281 mph at 5000', Landing 96 mph. Service Ceiling 30,700', Climb 25,000'/38 min. Range 2400 miles/20,000 lbs. bombs, 3800 miles max.   MFR

combat group. When the war's end halted production, only 114 of 1,213 ordered had been finished at Fort Worth, and just one of 500 more ordered from Convair's San Diego plant was ready. The last 40 were completed as TB-32 trainers without turrets.

Dominators (later renamed Terminators for political reasons) were sent to the 312th Bomb Group on Luzon, where two flew a ground-support mission May 29, 1945. Enemy fighters were not encountered until a photographic sweep near Tokyo on August 17, after surrender had been announced. The following day a B-32 got the last Japanese fighter to be downed by American aircraft. By the

month's end all B-32 training had been halted and the aircraft scheduled for scrapping.

Another bomber design of this period never reached the flying stage. Martin's XB-33 project, submitted in March 1941 with two R-3350s, was redesigned by May 8, 1941, with four 1,800-hp R-2600-15 Wrights and twin tails. Two prototypes were projected, but an order for 402 B-33As approved January 17, 1942, was canceled on November 25 to make way for the B-29. The high-wing Super Marauder was to have had a 134-foot span and be able to carry seven men, eight .50-caliber guns, and up to a 12,000-pound bomb load, but the prototypes were not completed.

PART THREE:

Air Power
Since 1945

Chapter 25
Air Weapons for the Cold War

The A-Bomb and the Cold War

While American occupation troops thoughtfully examined the burned-out heart of Tokyo and the flattened wasteland at Hiroshima, United States policy makers considered the postwar military establishment. Adherence to the United Nations implied a global security system in which armed forces might be dispatched anywhere. Continental defense, the center of prewar plans, became secondary to offensive capabilities of global range.

As the United States had the world's only atomic weapons and, in its B-29 fleet, by far the world's best agency to deliver them, it appeared that the nation was well able to fill the role of world policeman with little aid from other nations or even from its own land armies. Long-range nuclear bombing was seen by many as a magic weapon which had ended the war with Japan, could deter any future aggression, and established American leadership in world affairs.

In the years following World War II, the world polarized into two camps as hostility and tension increased between the United States and Russia, and U.S. bombardment capacity was a major weight in the balance of power between them. Air power had achieved equal status with the Army and Navy through creation of the National Military Establishment on September 18, 1947, with Secretaries of Air, Army, and Navy under a Secretary of Defense. On July 18, 1947, President Truman appointed an Air Policy Commission, headed by Thomas K. Finletter, to formulate "an integrated national aviation policy."

The commission's report, submitted on December 30, 1947, called for an Air Force consisting of 70 groups: 20 strategic bomber; five light bomber; 22 day fighter; three all-weather fighter; four tacti-

cal and six strategic reconnaissance; and ten troop carrier.

Resistance to the program arose as the Navy demanded renewed recognition for carrier and anti-sub aviation. The Army pointed to neglect of tactical air, and development of Soviet atomic weapons raised concern over continental defense. The sky-rocketing cost of air weapons limited procurement. Thus, on January 1, 1950, the Air Force had 48 groups with some 17,000 aircraft (8,000 combat), about half of which were World War II types held in storage. Naval Air had 4,900 planes attached to the fleet, plus 1,900 in the Reserves and 550 in storage.

The Finletter report was made at a time when "no possible enemy could make a [sustained] assault" on the American mainland. It suggested January 1, 1953, as a target date for the Air Force to be capable of dealing with a possible atomic attack on the United States. The only possible attacker was not named in the report.

At the start of 1946 the Soviet Union lacked the main elements visible in American air power, having no atomic bombs, heavy bombers, aircraft carriers, or jet fighters. Its air force, while substantial in size, was entirely equipped to support the large land army and for coastal defense. Soviet wartime losses, including twenty million people, and its naval weakness, made an attack by the U.S.S.R. on the United States very unlikely for many years to come.

Just as American war plans like Rainbow No. 5 had been prepared for attack on Germany, so plans were made for the new adversary. Only 51 days after Japan surrendered, the vulnerability of Russian cities to a "limited air attack" with atomic bombs had been analyzed by a Joint Intelligence Staff study. By 1948 cold war tension produced an

Air Force strategic power in 1950–55 is represented by this RB-36D escorted by Marine F9F-5P Panthers. The turrets may safely be retracted, for these Marines carry cameras, not guns! GANN

After 1956, strategic bombing power meant the Boeing B-52, first to drop a live H-bomb. MFR

American war plan called Charioteer. Strategic Air Command had the leading role, to drop 133 atomic bombs on 70 Soviet vital centers in 30 days, including eight on Moscow and seven on Leningrad.[1]

But the Soviet Army was strong enough to occupy western Europe, probably within 20 days, and could threaten the bases in Britain and the Middle East necessary for B-29/B-50 attacks. Soviet technical progress gradually began to reduce the substantial gap between American long-range weapons and its own. By the end of 1949 atomic bombs, long-range bombers, and jet fighters were in the Soviet inventory. While the capability for a sustained attack on the United States did not yet exist, the capability was there to overrun all of continental Europe and the Near East, which would be an "unacceptable threat" to United States security.

A new global war plan, Dropshot, was developed in 1949 by the Joint Chiefs of Staff on the basic assumption that war would be "forced upon the United States by an act of aggression of the U.S.S.R. and/or her satellites," on or about January 1, 1957, the date selected for planning purposes. The USAF would be built up to the level needed to sustain a strategic air offensive, ward off attack on the Western Hemisphere, support allies (like NATO and CENTO) overseas, and begin a counteroffensive.

These war plans, however, were for big, relatively short nuclear wars, but the future actually brought small, long, nonnuclear struggles. The outbreak of war in Korea did make funds available for a new rearmament, which increased the Air Force to 134 Wings (replacing the old group organization) with 24,949 aircraft by December 31, 1956. Along

with expansion came an enormous increase in performance and firepower, fruits of vigorous development since 1945. Table 9 details Air Force expansion in this period.

War in Korea did show that tactical air power, long neglected in favor of strategic air power, had to be revitalized. After 1957 the number of aircraft declined, especially when ballistic missiles began replacing bombers, thus reducing the need for defensive fighters. An Air Force built for massive retaliation had to adapt itself to limited warfare.

Tactical ground support was the most important aspect of Air Force activity in Vietnam. It began on a small scale when the "Farm Gate" detachment began arriving November 4, 1961, its aircraft bearing Vietnamese markings. As Air Force activity increased, careful "rules of engagement" were developed to avoid provoking the direct Chinese intervention that made Korea so costly. But after the first direct clash between American and North Vietnamese forces in the Tonkin Gulf, on August 2, 1964, American involvement escalated into the longest war in that nation's history.

In 1968, 840,117 combat sorties in support of ground forces were made by the Air Force, which had 737 aircraft in Vietnam on June 1 and about 600 in Thailand. Combat operations continued in Vietnam, until January 23, 1973, and in Cambodia until August 15. Air operations became the responsibility of the Vietnam National Air Force (VNAF), which had increased from 362 American-built aircraft in 1968 to 2,075 on January 27, 1973. Although it represented the world's fourth largest air force at the time, it was unable to reverse the situation on the ground, and the battle ended after April 22, 1975, when the VNAF still had 1,492 a/c, of which 132 were evacuated to Thailand.

During the cold war period, Navy aviation's greatest constraint was the competition with the Air Force and Army for defense funds. The huge surface fleet inherited from World War II seemed sufficient for its time, and Air Force needs in the 1950s had greater priority. In the 1960s the struggle in Vietnam diverted funds to the Army and to allied forces.

[1] Anthony C. Brown, *Dropshot: The American Plan for World War III* (New York, 1978) includes details of U.S. war plans during this period.

Table 9 409

USAF COMBAT WINGS, 1951–57

Type	10 July 1951	30 June 1952	30 June 1953	30 June 1954	30 June 1955	30 June 1956	30 June 1957
F-47N	2	2	—	—	—	—	—
F-51	10	8	2	—	—	—	—
F-80	6	2	2	—	—	—	—
F-82	1	—	—	—	—	—	—
F-84	9	11	14	9	12	11	5
F-86A, E, F	5	7	13	19	13	7	3
F-86D	—	—	3	13	19	20	15
F-86H	—	—	—	—	3	3	1
F-89	—	—	1	3	6	7	7
F-94	3	4	7	6	3	3	1
F-100	—	—	—	—	1	6	16
F-102	—	—	—	—	—	—	4
TOTAL FIGHTERS	36	34	42	50	57	57	52
B-26	3	3	3	4	4	—	—
B-29	9	14	10	3	—	—	—
B-36	2	3	5	6	6	9[1]	5
B-45	1	1	1	1	1	1	1
B-47	—	1	4	13	21	27	28
B-50	4	5	5	2	—	—	—
B-52	—	—	—	—	—	1	3
B-57	—	—	—	—	1	4	4
B-66	—	—	—	—	—	—	1
TOTAL BOMBERS	19	27	28	29	33	42	42
RECONNAISSANCE	8	9	10	12[2]	14[3]	11[4]	9[5]
TROOP CARRIER, ETC.	24	25	26	24	17	21	20
TOTAL WINGS	87	95	106	115	121	131	123

[1] Includes 3 RB-36 wings, previously carried as reconnaissance wings
[2] 4 RB-47s, 4 RB-36s, 2 RB-26s, and 2 RF-80s
[3] 5 RB-47s, 4 RB-36s, 2 RB-26s, 2 RF-80s, and 1 RF-84
[4] 5 RB-47s, 1 RB-26, 1 RB-66, and 4 RF-84s
[5] 5 RB-47s, 2 RB-66s, and 2 RF-84s

Tactical fighter-bombers, like this F-4E over Laos in January 1969, had the most important role in the Southeast Asian war.   LAWSON

Nevertheless, Navy aircraft also increased in performance and efficiency and their inventory went from 14,036 (9,422 combat) on July 1, 1950, to 16,-440 (8,884 combat) on July 1, 1955. This inventory declined to 10,101 (5,127 combat) in 1965. The major cost factor was the replacement of the World War II carriers with the giants of postwar design. Eight conventionally powered carriers were commissioned, from the *Forrestal* in October 1955 to the *John F. Kennedy* in September 1968, and the first nuclear carrier, the *Enterprise,* joined the fleet in November 1961. Three more were scheduled, beginning with the *Nimitz* in May 1975. Their air

When the Korean War began, the Navy still relied mainly on propeller-driven aircraft, like the F4U-4, operating from World War II *Essex*-class carriers. MADDON

First of the super-carriers, the *USS Forrestal*, commissioned in July 1955, could handle the most advanced jet aircraft. CV-59 carried over three times the aircraft fuel of earlier types, and its broad decks and new equipment cut the accident rate in half. Overhead are an RF-8A and two F-8D Crusaders. USN

groups, known as Carrier Air Wings since December 1963, carried a mixture of attack, fighter, antisubmarine, reconnaissance, and early-warning aircraft.

The average age of Navy aircraft increased from four to ten years from 1957 to 1977, while yearly procurement dropped from 2,000 to less than 200 aircraft, and the force supply leveled off at about 6,000 aircraft. During the war in Vietnam Navy aircraft steadily attacked enemy targets from carriers stationed off the coast. Attacks on the enemy mainland, along with operations against enemy submarines, had replaced attacks against surface vessels as the main role of naval aviation.

On the way to Vietnam, November 1970; *Kitty Hawk* with A-5, A-6, A-7, F-4 and EKA-3 aircraft.   LAWSON

Commissioned in May 1975, the nuclear-propelled *Nimitz* and its sister ships are the world's largest warships, had no fear of running out of fuel, and had missiles instead of guns.   USN

Cold War Aircraft and Weapons Development

Since 1946 combat planes have evolved into the shape of contemporary aircraft, with gas-turbine power plants, wings swept back for high speeds, and extensive electronics. These aircraft became much heavier and expensive than their ancestors, consumed enormous amounts of fuel, but they did have a much longer service life.

Wartime research indicated that propeller-driven aircraft could not be expected to achieve speeds much beyond 500 mph. When information was received in 1941 on the British Whittle jet engine, General Electric began developing this centrifugal-flow gas turbine into the J31 and J33 units. Meanwhile, in 1943 Westinghouse developed an axial-flow turbine, the J34. Axial-flow units are smaller in diameter but longer than the centrifugal-flow types. Their development led, in 1953, to the Pratt & Whitney J57 used in the B-52 and the F-100, the world's first supersonic fighter. By 1973 the same company was producing the F-100 turbofan power plant for Air Force fighters.

When long endurance was required, such as the Navy's patrol and early-warning types, propellers retained their place, now powered by turbojet engines with the propeller driven from the turbine shaft. The Allison T56 used on the P-3 is an example of these turboprop engines.

Weapons

The most prominent weapons of the new generation were, of course, the atomic bombs. First tested at Alamogordo on July 16, 1945, with a yield of 19 kilotons, was the "Fat Man," actually the 10,000-pound Mk II plutonium bomb used at Nagasaki and Bikini.

By April 1948 improved models exploded at Eniwetok realized yields up to 49 kilotons. A family of nuclear weapons developed in two directions, one to increase blast and the other to provide smaller packages for smaller aircraft: thus, the first lightweight bomb, the 3,175-pound Mk 5; and the powerful 8,500-pound Mk 6, mass-produced for the heavy bombers.

The next step was a smaller bomb shaped to be carried beneath fast fighters, the 1,680-pound Mk 7 of 1952. To attack underground facilities, the Navy developed the 3,250-pound Mk 8 with delayed action detonation, instead of the air bursts of the earlier weapons. The compact Mk 12 weighed only 1,050 pounds.

A thermonuclear device yielding over ten megatons was exploded October 31, 1952, and led to the first 15-megaton "H-bomb," detonated February 28, 1954. Carried within the B-36, the huge Mk 17 weighed 41,400 pounds. Miniaturized H-bombs soon followed, leading to several versions of the Mk 28 series or larger weapons like the Mk 39 or Mk 53.

The shape of the cold war Air Force in 1951: the swept wings and J47 turbojet-powered B-47A and F-86A. AF

Navy single-seaters of 1961 show four different wing styles; clockwise from the top: FJ-4B, A4D-2, F8U-1, and F4D-1. USN

EARLY NUCLEAR WEAPONS

Mk II "Fat Man" Length 10′8″, Diameter 5″, Weight 10,000 lb. AF

Mk 6 Length 8′11″, Diameter 5′1″, Weight 8500 lb. AF

Mk 5 Length 10′8½″, Diameter 3′8″, Weight 3175 lb. AF

Mk 7 Length 15′5″, Diameter 2′6½″, Weight 1680 lb. (Shown below A-4A) USN

Mk 17 Length 24'8", Diameter 5'1", Weight 41,400 lb.
(thermonuclear)   AF

Mk 8 Length 9'7", Diameter 1'2", Weight 3250 lb.   AF

Radar directed the fire of two 20-mm. M-24 guns on early
RB-52B   BULINSKI

Such weapons on bombers made it all the more necessary to arm fighters with weapons most likely to destroy the bomber on the first pass.

Fifty-caliber guns were soon replaced by the fast-firing 20-mm M-39 and then the M-61 Vulcan. Six rotating barrels gave the Vulcan a rate of fire equal to four of the earlier weapons (see Table 3). For bomber interception the favorite weapon soon became the air-to-air missile. First came salvos of rockets, then radar-directed Falcons and Sparrows, heat-seeking Sidewinders, the nuclear Genie, and the long-range Phoenix.

Another series of missiles was developed for ground attack: the short-range Bulldog, the antira-dar Shrike, and long-range Harpoon. Use of both air-to-air and air-to-surface missiles added more importance to an aircraft's electronics, with radar and miniaturized computers becoming essential for both target search and weapons launching as well as for navigation at high speeds and altitudes.

The contemporary warplane's electronic and weapons systems are far more sophisticated than the eyeball- and brain-directed aircraft that were used at the start of World War II, and the cost of these aircraft has risen accordingly. The high initial costs have been balanced by a long production and service life, as witnessed by the A-4, B-52, and F-4 series.

Six-barreled 20-mm. M-61 Vulcan on B-52H had the firepower of four earlier guns.   MFR

Salvo of 2.75″ rockets is fired from Convair F-102A in this
picture sequence. Twenty-four rockets from 12 tubes
in four missile bay doors are fired in less than half a
second, leaving in 12 rapid pulses, two at a time. MFR

Sparrow I missiles, shown on F3H-2M, were the Navy's
first air-to-air missiles riding the aircraft's radar beam
to its target.   PMB

Air-to-air Falcon missiles. From left to right, the Hughes
GAR-11, GAR-1D, GAR-2A, GAR-4A, and GAR-3A. MFR

For details see Table 10

Table 10

AIR-TO-AIR GUIDED MISSILES

Popular Name	Maker	Former Designation	Current Designation	Approximate Weight	Length	Type
Falcon	Hughes	GAR-1D	AIM-4A	120 lb.	6.5′	homing
Falcon	Hughes	GAR-2A	AIM-4C	120 lb.	6.5′	infrared
Falcon	Hughes	GAR-3A	AIM-4E	150 lb.	7.2′	homing
Falcon	Hughes	GAR-4A	AIM-4F	145 lb.	6.7′	infrared
Falcon	Hughes	GAR-11	AIM-26A	200 lb.	7′	nuclear
Falcon	Hughes	GAR-9	AIM-47A	800 lb.	12.5′	nuclear
Genie	Douglas	MB-1	AIR-2A	835 lb.	9′	unguided
Sidewinder 1A	Philco	GAR-8	AIM-9B	155 lb.	9.4′	infrared
Sparrow 1	Sperry	AAM-N-2	AIM-7A	300 lb.	12.5′	beam rider
Sparrow 3	Raytheon	AAM-N-6	AIM-7C	350 lb.	12′	homing radar
Sparrow 3	Raytheon	AAM-N-6B	AIM-7E	400 lb.	12′	homing radar

Cost was more important than performance in halting the XB-1A in 1977.   MFR

Chapter 26
Bombers Since 1945

The new Strategic Air Command (SAC) inherited a wide program of bomber development from the World War II period, with a trio of Boeing, Northrop, and Consolidated projects built around the Pratt & Whitney R-4360 Wasp Major. These 3,000-hp radials were installed on a B-29A, which became the XB-44. Ordered in July 1944, the XB-44 began tests in May 1945 with redesigned engine nacelles.

This became the prototype for the next Boeing series, originally designated B-29D but relabeled B-50. First flown June 25, 1947, these planes had 3,500-hp R-4360-35s, thirteen .50-caliber guns, and could be distinguished from B-29s by their engine nacelles and tall tail, which folded for hangar storage. Beginning on January 14, 1949, 79 B-50As were followed by 45 B-50Bs with drop tanks on strengthened wings. All but the first B-50B were modified with cameras to RB-50Bs and issued to a strategic reconnaissance group. In February 1948 B-50As entered service with the 43rd Bomb Wing, which flew one B-50A nonstop around the world, arriving at its

BOEING B-50A
Pratt & Whitney R-4360-35, 3500 hp
DIMENSIONS: Span 141′3″, Lg. 99′, Ht. 32′8″, Wing Area 1720 sq. ft.
WEIGHT: Empty 81,050 lb., Max. 168,480 lb. Fuel 7195–10,772 gal.
PERFORMANCE: (At 120,500 lbs., combat weight) Speed—Top 391 mph at 30,000′, Cruising 244 mph, Stalling 136 mph. Combat Ceiling 36,000′, Climb 2260′/1 min. Combat Radius 2193 miles/10,000 lbs. bombs, 5230 miles max. range. PMB

destination on March 2, 1949, thus demonstrating in-flight refueling from KB-29M tanker planes.

A B-50C was proposed with Pratt & Whitney R-4360-51 compound VDT engines, but this change required complete redesign of the airframe. Forty-three were ordered in May 1948 as the Boeing B-54A, but on April 5, 1949, they were canceled in favor of the B-36. Production continued on R-3350-35-powered B-50Ds with modified nose, more fuel, and underwing fixtures for a pair of 700-gallon drop tanks, or 4,000 pounds of bombs.

ASB-23 bombing radar and a receptacle for an in-flight refueling boom greatly increased the B-50's potential over the B-29. Between May 1949 and December 1950, 222 B-50Ds were built for five SAC wings. Twenty-four TB-50H trainers were added from April 1952 to February 1953.

As B-50s began their retirement from bomber service in 1954, many early models were converted into TB-50D trainers; RB-50E, RB-50F, and RB-50G reconnaissance types; WB-50D and WB-50E

BOEING XB-44
Pratt & Whitney R-4360-33, 3000 hp takeoff, 2500 hp at 25,000′
DIMENSIONS: Span 141′3″, Lg. 99′, Ht. 29′7″, Wing Area 1728 sq. ft.
WEIGHT: Empty 75,035 lb., Gross 105,000 lb., Max. 140,-000 lb.
PERFORMANCE: Speed—Top 392 mph at 25,400′, Cruising 282 mph. Range 2400 miles normal. AF

BOEING B-50D
Pratt & Whitney R-4360-35, 3500 hp takeoff
DIMENSIONS: As B-50A
WEIGHT: Empty 80,609 lb., Max. 173,000 lb. Fuel 11,685
    gal.
PERFORMANCE: (At 121,850 lbs., weight) Speed—Top 395
    mph at 30,800', Cruising 244 mph, Stalling 137 mph.
    Combat Ceiling 36,650', Climb 2200'/1 min. Combat
    Radius 2396 miles/10,000 lbs. bombs, 5762 miles max.
    range.   MFR

NORTHROP XB-35
Pratt & Whitney R-3350-17 and -21, 3000 hp
DIMENSIONS: Span 172', Lg. 53'1", Ht. 20'1", Wing Area
    4000 sq. ft.
WEIGHT: (Estimated) Empty 89,560 lb., Gross 180,000 lb.,
    Max. 209,000 lb. Fuel 10,000–18,000 gal.
PERFORMANCE: (Estimated) Speed—Top 391 mph at 35,-
    000', Cruising 183 mph, Service Ceiling 39,700', Climb
    35,600'/57 min. Range 8150 miles at 183 mph with
    16,000 lbs. bombs, 720 miles at 240 mph with 51,070
    lbs. bombs.   MFR

weather reconnaissance; and KB-50J and KB-50K tankers. The latter were delivered in 1958 with 7,550 gallons of transferable fuel and jet pods under the wings so they could keep pace with the Tactical Air Command (TAC) fighters they refueled.

The most unconventional bomber of this era was the XB-35 flying wing, designed by John K. Northrop. His experimental twin-engine N-1M, flown July 1940, had demonstrated the possibilities of aircraft carrying all loads and controls within the wing and dispensing with fuselage and tail sections. The larger the aircraft, the greater the savings in weight and drag reduction, so an Air Force request on April 11, 1941, for bomber designs that could carry a 10,000-pound load halfway across a 10,000-mile range gave Northrop a chance for a bold step. In September 1941 his company proposed a four-engine design, and a prototype contract was approved November 22, 1941.

Two XB-35 prototypes were built at Hawthorne, California, to be followed by 13 service-test aircraft ordered December 17, 1942. A wartime plan to build another 200 at Martin's Omaha plant was dropped when the B-29 seemed adequate to win the war, but the radical design's potential continued to spark Air Force interest. Four ⅓-scale flying models (N-9M) were built to test the configuration's characteristics before prototype construction began. The first XB-35 flew June 25, 1946, and the second June 26, 1947.

Power plants consisted of Pratt & Whitney Wasp Majors (two R-4360-17s and two R-4360-21s) with double turbosuperchargers and co-axial counterrotating four-bladed pusher propellers. These dual propellers proved unsatisfactory, and after 11 flights by the first prototype and four by the second the big Northrops were grounded in August 1947 to replace the dual-rotation system with single-rotation propellers. Seven more flights were made by the first XB-35 from February 12 to April 1, 1948, but it wasn't flown again until its return to the factory on October 7, and was scrapped in 1949 after less than 24 flight hours. All test flights had been made from Muroc by company pilots.

Single-rotation propellers were also fitted to the second XB-35 and to the first YB-35, flown May 15, 1948, which was the only flying wing actually fitted with turrets. The crew consisted of nine persons in the pressurized center section (two pilots, a bombardier, an engineer, a navigator, a radioman, and three gunners), plus accommodations for six relief men. The bomb bays held from ten to thirty-two 1,600-pound bombs, and twenty .50-caliber guns were provided for. Seven remote-controlled turrets were aimed from central sighting stations behind the pilot and on top of a cone protruding from the trailing edge. Four-gun turrets were spotted above

NORTHROP YB-35   AF

NORTHROP YB-49
Allison J35-A-15, 3750 lbs.
DIMENSIONS: Span 172', Lg. 53'1", Ht. 15'2", Wing Area
    4000 sq. ft.
WEIGHT: Empty 88,442 lb., Gross 193,938 lb., Combat
    133,559 lb. Fuel 12,752–14,542 gal.
PERFORMANCE: Speed—Top 493 mph at 20,800', 464 mph
    at 35,000', Cruising 420 mph, Stalling 90 mph. Service
    Ceiling 45,700', Combat Ceiling 40,700', Climb 3785'/
    1 min. Combat Radius 1615 miles/10,000 lbs. bombs,
    3575 miles ferry range.   AF

and below the center section, two-gun turrets were visible outboard of the engines, one pair on top, another below, and four guns could be placed in the cone.

Jet propulsion had rendered the original concept obsolete, but interest in the flying-wing principle had continued. A June 1, 1945, contract had the next aircraft completed with Allison J35-A-15 jets. First flown October 21, 1947, the six-place YB-49 fed eight 3,750-pound thrust engines through leading-edge intakes, added four wing fences and vertical stabilizing fins, and eliminated turrets and guns. Sixteen 1,000-pound bombs could be carried less than half the range of the B-35, but the jets added 100 mph to the speed. A second YB-49 was flown January 13, 1948, but crashed mysteriously on June 5. Edwards Air Force Base was renamed after the dead pilot, Glen W. Edwards. Nevertheless, contracts were placed for 30 RB-49s and con-

version of the remaining ten B-35 airframes to RB-35B strategic reconnaissance types.

Many deficiencies turned up in the second phase of YB-49 tests. The test report complained that the aircraft was extremely unstable and difficult to fly and was unsuitable as a bombing platform. Cancellations ended the RB-49 program in April 1949 in favor of the B-36, and the RB-35B program was scrapped by November. Only one more flying wing was completed, the YRB-49A flown May 4, 1950. Four 5,000-pound thrust Allison J35-A-19 engines were in the wing, two more in pods below it, and photographic equipment was installed in a bulge

NORTHROP YRB-49A   MFR

below the center section. The first YB-49 had been demolished in an accident in March 1950, and when the YRB-49 was retired in 1951 the dream of the giant all-wing aircraft was over.

The Intercontinental Bomber

The B-36, which symbolized American bombers during the cold war and became the most controversial native combat type since the DH-4, began its career before the attack on Pearl Harbor. The world's largest bomber owed its size to the desire to achieve intercontinental range, for in 1941 the United States faced the possibility that Nazi Germany would control all of Europe, and that only bases in America would be available for strikes at enemy strategic targets.

A design competition for a bomber that could carry a 10,000-pound load halfway across a 10,000-mile range was opened on April 11, 1941. By October 6 Consolidated Aircraft had submitted a design with six pusher engines, and two XB-36 prototypes were ordered November 15, 1941.

The project was moved from San Diego to Fort Worth, Texas, in August 1942, but progress was slow due to the company's concentration on B-24 production and B-32 development. General Arnold saw that the B-36 might be needed for attacking Japan if bases near enough for B-29 strikes were not secured. The company's president complained that it was difficult to get subcontractors for a two-plane order; however, they would be interested if large-scale production was promised. A letter of intent for 100 B-36 bombers was issued July 23, 1943, at which time company officials planned to fly the XB-36 in September 1944 and begin production deliveries in March 1945, with 29 delivered by the end of August.

By the time a firm contract was approved on August 19, 1944, capture of the Mariana Islands, from which B-29s could bomb Japan, had made the B-36 unnecessary for that war. Again the B-36 program was neglected in favor of the B-32, but Japan's surrender, and the new importance the atomic bomb gave strategic bombing, once again revived the giant bomber program. An airstaff conference on August 9, 1945, recommended that four B-36 groups be included in the postwar Air Force.

Delayed by manpower shortages, late engine delivery, and engineering changes like the shift from twin tails to a stronger single fin, the XB-36 made its first flight nearly five years after it had been ordered—instead of the 30 months originally planned. Powered by six 3,000-hp R-4360-25 radials with pusher propellers, it took off on August 8, 1946. Weighing 100 tons, it was the heaviest and largest plane ever to fly up to that time.

Production aircraft differed from the XB-36 in their pilots' canopy, landing gear, and armament provisions. The new canopy, raised over the top deck, was installed on the second prototype, the YB-36 flown with better superchargers December 4, 1947. The prototype's single 110-inch wheels on each side required special runways, but subsequent models had four 56-inch wheels on each side, along with the dual nosewheels. This gear was introduced on the first B-36A, which had been flown from Fort Worth to Wright Field in unfinished condition on August 30, 1947, to be demolished in static tests.

Twenty-one more B-36As were delivered to the Air Force from June to November 1948, and were used to train the 7th Bomb Group, whose base at Carswell, Texas, adjoined the Fort Worth factory. Combat radius (⅜ of range) was 3,880 miles with a 10,000-pound bomb load, or 2,100 miles with 72 1,000-pound bombs.

Two pressurized compartments contained the crew: two pilots, radar-bombardier, navigator, flight engineer (a second was added on the B-36H), two radiomen, and three gunners forward were separated from five gunners in the rear compartment by an 85-foot bomb bay. Four rest bunks were provided for reliefs, and personnel shifted between compartments by rolling on a little dolly in a tunnel through the bomb cells.

Defensive armament designed for the XB-36 had included five 37-mm and ten .50-caliber guns in four retractable turrets and a radar-directed tail turret. This system was to be replaced in production aircraft by the most formidable armament of any warplane, sixteen 20-mm guns, with 9,200 rounds, paired in eight General Electric remote-controlled turrets. Computing sights at blisters in the nose and six side spots aimed the front turret and six retractable turrets, which disappeared behind sliding panels, and radar aimed the tail guns.

No turrets had been installed in the prototypes and B-36As, so the first armed model was the B-36B, first flown July 8, 1948, and delivered November 25. Power plants were the 3,500-hp R-4360-41 Wasp Majors, and ANQ-24 bomb-navigation radar was provided, and the bomb bay could handle two 43,000-pound bombs if needed. Combat radius with a 10,000-pound bomb load was up to 4,300 miles, and total mission time was 42.43 hours. Takeoff distance needed at full load was 8,520 feet.

As early as December 1946, SAC Commander General George C. Kenney had suggested cancellation of B-36 production in favor of the faster and smaller B-50. In that case, strategic bombing would require advanced bases or aerial refueling. Increased B-36 over-the-target speed was needed, so in March 1947 Convair proposed the installation of Pratt & Whitney's new experimental VDT engines

CONVAIR XB-36
Pratt & Whitney R-4360-25, 3000 hp
DIMENSIONS: Span 230', Lg. 163', Ht. 46'10", Wing Area
    4772 sq. ft.
WEIGHT: (Estimated) Empty 131,740 lb., Gross 276,506
    lb. Fuel 19,976 gal.
PERFORMANCE: (Estimated) Speed—Top 346 mph at 35,-
    000', Cruising 216 mph. Service Ceiling 36,000', Ab-
    solute Ceiling 38,000', Climb 25,000'/42 min. Range
    9500 miles/10,000 lbs. bombs, 3850 miles/77,784 lbs.
    bombs.   MFR

CONVAIR B-36A
Pratt & Whitney R-4360-25, 3250 hp takeoff, 3000 hp at
    40,000'
DIMENSIONS: Span 230', Lg. 162'¼", Ht. 46'10", Wing
    Area 4772 sq. ft.
WEIGHT: Empty 135,020 lb., Gross 310,380 lb., Combat
    212,800 lb. Fuel 21,010–26,745 gal.
PERFORMANCE: Speed—Top 345 mph at 31,600', Cruising
    218 mph, Stalling 113 mph. Service Ceiling 39,100',
    Combat Ceiling 35,800'. Climb 20,000'/53 min., Com-
    bat Radius 3880 miles/10,000 lb., 9136 miles ferry
    range.   MFR

CONVAIR B-36B
Pratt & Whitney R-4360-41, 3500 hp
DIMENSIONS: As B-36A
WEIGHT: Empty 140,640 lb., Max. 328,000 lb. Fuel 21,-
    020–26,217 gal.
PERFORMANCE: (At 227,700 lbs., combat weight) Speed—
    Top 381 mph at 34,500', 354 mph at 25,000', Cruising
    203 mph, Landing 115 mph. Service Ceiling 42,500',
    Combat Ceiling 38,800', Climb 1510'/1 min. Combat
    Radius 4300 miles/10,000 lbs. bombs. Ferry Range
    8820 miles.   AF

with tractor propellers. This project, designated B-36C, was approved December 4, 1947. The last 34 bombers on order were to get the VDT engines. Top speed might be increased to 410 mph, and increased costs were met by reduction of the total program from 100 to 95 planes. These engines, however, did not reach anticipated levels of development, so the B-36C was abandoned on May 21, 1948.

On June 24, 1948, all traffic into Berlin was stopped by the Soviet blockade, and the same day the Air Force decided to go ahead with all 95 B-36s in the original contract. But if the B-36s were to be a believable strategic deterrent, more speed and altitude was still needed to improve survival over enemy territory. On October 5, 1948, Convair proposed adding a pair of turbojet engines under each wing, using the engines and nacelles, or "pods," already available on the Boeing B-47.

Conversion of a B-36B was authorized January 4, 1949, and the modified aircraft flew with J35 jets on March 26. The improved performance led the Air Force to contract for more bombers as B-36Ds and to plan future modifications of all B-36A and B-36B models to jet pod configuration. The jets gave short bursts of speed over the target at a moderate cost of range. Money for the program was obtained by canceling contracts for smaller planes, including the RB-49 flying wing.

As a strategic deterrent, the B-36 could threaten any industrial center in the world with nuclear attack. The key to any estimate of the big bomber's value was its ability to escape destruction by hostile fighters. Supporters of the B-36 argued that current jet fighters could not climb to high altitudes in time to intercept the bomber. Once in position, the fighter's limited speed advantage might permit only slow tail cone passes in the face of heavy defensive gunfire.

Others challenged the B-36's ability to penetrate an effective defense system. Critics insisted that radar would detect the big ship soon after it began its approach, and that the latest jet fighters could indeed reach high altitudes quickly enough to stop it. A British engineer attacking "piston-engined giantism" wrote that jet fighters would find the B-36 "practically a sitting duck."

On May Day in 1949 the Russians first displayed formations of a jet interceptor eventually known as the MiG-15. Large numbers were built, and its capabilities would make daylight flying over Russia dangerous for hostile bombers. Climbing in 6.4 minutes to 40,000 feet, where top speed was 620 mph, the MiG-15 had a 51,000-foot service ceiling. Its guns may have been less of a threat than the propensity of zealous Soviet pilots to ram.

Official controversy suddenly exploded into the open with a congressional investigation of charges that political favoritism had influenced procurement of a costly sitting duck. Secretary of Defense Louis A. Johnson (a former Convair director) was blamed. More serious were the technical issues raised by the Navy, which resented Johnson's cancellation, on April 23, 1949, of the big carrier ordered by his predecessor, James V. Forrestal. That ship had been seen as a way of giving the Navy a strategic bombing capability, but the Air Force leaders insisted that strategic bombing was an Air Force function. Before the Korean War available defense funds could provide new strategic bombers or a new carrier force, but not both.

The B-36 was expensive, for the prototypes had cost over $39 million, the first 95 $6,248,686 each, and the next 75 $4,732,939 per airplane. The investigation held in June 1949, however, found the Air Force defending its bomber's capabilities against both political and Navy critics. The B-36 program survived the investigation, and the Korean War made funds available for both strategic bombers and big carriers.

Penetration capabilities of the new B-36 versions were increased by the added boost of jet pods and provision for elaborate 1,700-pound K-1 bombing-navigation systems used to find targets in the worst weather conditions. SAC's 28th Strategic Reconnaissance Group received its first RB-36D on June 3, 1950, and the first B-36D bomber was delivered August 19, 1950. By June 1951, 26 B-36Ds and 24 RB-36Ds had been finished at Fort Worth.

Fifty-nine of the 62 B-36Bs accepted earlier were returned to the company for conversion to B-36Ds, and were redelivered with jets by February 1952. Twenty-one B-36As and the YB-36 were also converted to RB-36E jets, the last being delivered in July 1951. The RB-36D and RB-36E reconnaissance versions increased the crew from 15 to 18, had 14 cameras, 80 flash bombs, additional electronic countermeasure (ECM) equipment, and retained the 16 guns.

On November 18, 1950, the first B-36F was flown with the 3,800-hp R-4360-53 engines and K-3A radar. From May to November 1951, 34 B-36Fs and 24 RB-36Fs were accepted. The B-36H, first flown April 5, 1952, had an APG-41A twin-radar tail defense and provision for 1,400 pounds of chaff to jam enemy radar. By July 1953, 83 B-36Hs and 73 RB-36Hs had been delivered.

Last was the 33 B-36Js, first flown September 3, 1953, with an additional 2,770 gallons of fuel. Project Featherweight was a program to reduce airframe weight to balance this extra fuel. Class II Featherweights kept their guns, but the B-36J (III) delivered in February 1954 had all but the tail turret removed, just 13 crewmen, and flush windows in-

CONVAIR B-36D

Pratt & Whitney R-4360-41, 3500 hp, and J47-GE-19, 5200 lbs.

DIMENSIONS: As B-36A

WEIGHT: Empty 161,371 lb., Gross 370,000 lb., Combat 250,300 lb. Fuel 29,995 gal.

PERFORMANCE: Speed—Top 406 mph at 36,200′, Cruising 222 mph, Stalling 123 mph. Service Ceiling 43,800′, Combat Ceiling 40,700′, Climb 2210′/1 min. Combat Radius 3528 miles/10,000 lbs. bombs (29,995 gal.), 8807 miles (30,716 gal.) ferry range.　　　　　MFR

CONVAIR B-36F

Pratt & Whitney R-4360-53, 3800 hp, and J47-GE-19, 5200 lbs.

DIMENSIONS: As B-36A

WEIGHT: Empty 167,646 lb., Gross 370,000 lb., Combat 264,300 lb. Fuel 29,017–33,626 gal.

PERFORMANCE: Speed—Top 417 mph at 37,100′, 414 mph at 40,200′, Cruising 235 mph, Stalling 123 mph. Service Ceiling 44,000′, Combat Ceiling 40,900′, Climb 2060′/ 1 min. Combat Radius 3230 miles/10,000 lbs. bombs, 7743 miles (30,630 gal.) ferry range.　　　　　AF

CONVAIR RB-36E　　　　　AF

CONVAIR B-36H

Pratt & Whitney R-4360-53, 3800 hp, and J47-GE-19, 5200 lbs.

DIMENSIONS: As B-36A

WEIGHT: Empty 168,487 lb., Gross 370,000 lb., Combat 253,900 lb. Fuel 28,688–33,626 gal.

PERFORMANCE: Speed—Top 416 mph at 36,700′, Cruising 234 mph, Stalling 123 mph. Service Ceiling 44,000′, Combat Ceiling 40,800′, Climb 2060′/1 min. Combat Radius 3113 miles/10,000 lbs. bombs and 1408 lbs. chaff, 7691 miles ferry range.　　　　　PMB

CONVAIR B-36J (III)

Pratt & Whitney R-4360-53, 3800 hp, J47-GE-19, 5200 lbs.

DIMENSIONS: As B-36A

WEIGHT: Empty 166,165 lb., Gross 410,000 lb., Combat 262,500 lb. Fuel 36,396 gal.

PERFORMANCE: Speed—Top 418 mph at 37,500′, Cruising 227 mph, Stalling 129 mph. Service Ceiling 43,600′, Combat Ceiling 39,500′. Combat Radius 3990 miles/ 10,000 lb., Ferry Range 9440 miles.　　　　　GANN

CONVAIR GRB-36F   AF

stead of blisters. The last 14 B-36Js were finished in this configuration, which was then done to some previous B-36F, B-36H, and B-36J aircraft.

Delivery of the final B-36J (III) on August 14, 1954, brought the Convair total to 382, not including two B-36Gs redesignated YB-60 or the unarmed NB-36H, flown September 17, 1955, with the world's first airborne nuclear reactor. Ten SAC Wings used B-36s from 1953 to 1955, until replacement by B-52s was finally completed with the retirement of the last B-36J from SAC on February 12, 1959. Serving as a strategic deterrent, the B-36 never saw combat.

FICON (FIghter-CONveyor) was a plan intended to carry a fighter aircraft on the B-36. The first such project was the XF-85 (see Chapter 27). All of its tests were made from a B-29B. On January 19, 1951, Convair was ordered to modify an RB-36F to carry and recover an F-84E, and redesignated GRB-36F, it began its first retrieval and launch tests January 9, 1952. Next May a swept-wing YF-84F modified to fit the cradle below the GRB was successfully tested. Ten GRB-36Ds (III) with cradles for RF-84K reconnaissance jets were delivered to SAC in February/March 1955. They could carry the RF-84K out to a 2,810-mile radius, launching the 29,500-pound parasite at 25,000 feet for its dash over the target area. The partnership lasted less than a year's service with the 93rd Strategic Reconnaissance Wing.

Another range-extension program was Project Tom-Tom, which attempted to have the jets attach themselves to each wing tip. In 1953 the same GRB-36F previously mentioned was fitted with wing tip mechanisms to mate with two RB-84Fs. But a similar system tried with a B-29A and two F-84Bs resulted in the fatal crash of all three aircraft on April 24, 1953, and dangerous test experiments with the GRB-36F soon led to the program's termination.

Three B-36Hs became DB-36H models when modified to carry the Bell GAM-63 "Rascal," a 32-foot, 18,200-pound air-to-ground missile launched at a target up to 75 miles away. These conversions

were begun in March 1953, but the system was deleted from B-36 plans by the time the last was completed in July 1955.

Jet Bombers

Adapting jet propulsion to bombers was no easy task. The first gas turbine units made in America were centrifugal-flow units with wide diameter and a fuel consumption too great to guarantee the endurance needed for bomber missions.

By April 1944, however, General Electric's J35 (then called TG-180) had made its bench run, providing an axial-flow turbojet engine whose narrow diameter and smaller fuel needs recommended it for bomber use. The first American bomber to use jet engines then became the Douglas XB-43, a development of the pusher-propeller XB-42, ordered on March 31, 1944.

First flown on May 17, 1946, the XB-43 replaced the Allisons of its predecessor with two J35s fed by air intakes behind the pilots and delivering 4,000 pounds thrust each from jet exhausts in the tail. Like the XB-42, it was a three-place, high-wing monoplane with an 8,000-pound bomb capacity, but no guns were installed on either XB-43 prototype.

Early in the study of bomber jet propulsion, it became apparent that more than two engines would be required for the capabilities needed. As early as January 1944 Boeing offered its model 413 photo-reconnaissance design to the Air Force. Basically a B-29 powered by four turbojets paired in nacelles slung under the wings, the 413 was not accepted. Shortly after the J35 engine was satisfactorily tested

DOUGLAS XB-43
General Electric J35-GE-3, 4000 lbs.
DIMENSIONS: Span 71'2", Lg. 51'5", Ht. 24'3", Wing Area 563 sq. ft.
WEIGHT: Empty 22,890 lb., Gross 40,000 lb. Fuel 1209–2309 gal.
PERFORMANCE: Speed—Top 515 mph at s. l. Service Ceiling 38,200', Absolute Ceiling 41,800', Climb 2470'/1 min. Range 1100 miles, 1765 gals., with 8000 lbs.   AF

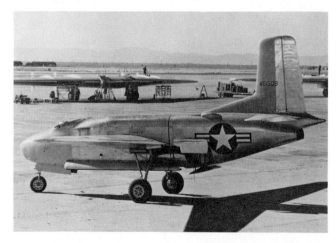

in April, the Air Force invited bids on a jet-powered bomber capable of a speed of 500 mph, a service ceiling of 40,000 feet, and a 1,000-mile tactical radius. By December 1944, four manufacturers responded with proposals, all of which were accepted and ordered as design studies.

All types then ordered were three-place high-wing monoplanes powered by the 4,000-pound thrust J35 engine, which was transferred from General Electric to Allison in September 1946. The North American XB-45, ordered September 17, 1944, and the Consolidated XB-46, ordered January 17, 1945, had four J35s, while the Boeing XB-47 and Martin XB-48 had six. (By June 1945 Northrop was given the designation YB-49 for two flying wings fitted with eight jets.) Since it was necessary to minimize drag by suppressing protrusions, and since it was believed that the bomber's high speed would permit enemy fighters to make only tailcone passes, planned armament was limited to a pair of .50-caliber tail guns trained by radar and fired by the co-pilot. With gunners unnecessary and endurance short, the crew was kept small and weight was saved for fuel. The normal bomb load was 8,000 pounds (16 × 500 pounds), but a single 22,000-pound bomb (the largest pre-atomic size) could be carried by all types.

All of these prototypes first flew in 1947: the XB-45 on St. Patrick's Day, XB-46 on April 2, XB-48 on June 22, YB-49 on October 21, and XB-47 on December 17. The first two had a pair of J35s in a nacelle under each wing and landed on tricycle gear. Three XB-45s and one example of Convair's larger XB-46 were built. The more graceful XB-46

NORTH AMERICAN XB-45
Allison J35-A-7, 4000 lbs.
DIMENSIONS: Span 89'6", Lg. 74', Ht. 25'2", Wing Area 1175 sq. ft.
WEIGHT: Empty 41,876 lb., Gross 66,820 lb., Max. 82,600 lb. Fuel 3400–4477 gal. (5684 gal. max.).
PERFORMANCE: (At 67,235 lbs.) Speed—Top 516 mph at 14,000', 494 mph at s. l., 483 mph at 30,000'. Service Ceiling 37,600', Climb 2070'/1 min., 30,000'/19 min. Range 2236 miles/8350 lbs. bombs, 1700 miles/14,000 lbs. bombs, 2921 miles max.   AF

carried more fuel but was slower than the smaller North American design, which became the first U.S. jet bomber to go into production.

Ninety-six B-45A Tornados were ordered January 20, 1947, and delivered beginning February 1948, the first 22 (B-45A-1) with J35s and the rest with new J47 engines (B-45A-5). Since the radar gun direction originally planned was not yet perfected, a tail gunner's cockpit was provided with twin .50-caliber guns and 1,200 rounds, with an APS-23 radar-bombing system. No B-45B was built, but a

NORTH AMERICAN B-45A
General Electric J47-GE-7, -9, 5200 lbs.
DIMENSIONS: Span 89', Lg. 75'4", Ht. 25'2", Wing Area 1175 sq. ft.
WEIGHT: Empty 45,694 lb., Gross 81,418 lb., Combat 58,548 lb. Fuel 5746 gal.
PERFORMANCE: Speed—Top 571 mph at 3500', 503 mph at 37,000', Cruising 470 mph, Stalling 125 mph. Combat Ceiling 42,800', Climb 5950'/1 min. Combat Radius 533 miles/10,000 lbs. bombs.   PMB

1,200-gallon wing tip drop tank and water injection was added to ten B-45Cs and 33 RB-45Cs, with 12 cameras, ordered November 11, 1947, first flown May 3, 1949 (RB-45C), and completed April 1950.

The first USAF jet bomber group, the 47th, got B-45As in November 1948, and in May 1952 flew to Britain, where it remained until 1958. In January 1951 RB-45Cs of the 91st TRW began missions over North Korea.

Martin's XB-48, the third to appear, had six J35s in individual nacelles under the wings. As on the previous ships, the crew consisted of a bombardier

NORTH AMERICAN B-45C
General Electric J47-GE-13, -15, 5200 lbs., 5820 lbs. WE
DIMENSIONS: As B-45A
WEIGHT: Empty 48,969 lb., Gross 110,050 lb., Combat
73,715 lb. Fuel 6933–8133 gal.
PERFORMANCE: Speed—Top 573 mph at s. l., 509 mph at
32,500′, Cruising 466 mph, Stalling 153 mph. Combat
Ceiling 37,550′, Climb 4550′/1 min. Combat Radius
1008 miles/10,000 lbs. bombs, 2426 miles (7974 gal.)
ferry range.   MFR

NORTH AMERICAN RB-45C   AF

CONSOLIDATED-VULTEE XB-46
General Electric J35-GE-3
DIMENSIONS: Span 113′, Lg. 105′9″, Ht. 27′11″, Wing Area
1285 sq. ft.
WEIGHT: Empty 48,018 lb., Gross 91,000 lb., Max. 95,600
lb. Fuel 4280–6682 gal.
PERFORMANCE: Speed—Top 491 mph at s. l., Cruising 439
mph at 35,000′. Service Ceiling 40,000′, Climb 35,000′/
19 min. Range 2870 miles/8000 lbs. bombs.   MFR

MARTIN XB-48
Allison J35-A-7, 4000 lbs.
DIMENSIONS: Span 108′4″, Lg. 85′9″, Ht. 26′6″, Wing Area
1330 sq. ft.
WEIGHT: Empty 72,226 lb., Design Gross 102,600 lb. Fuel
4150–968 gal.
PERFORMANCE: Speed—Top 516 mph at 20,000′, 479 mph
at 35,000′, 486 mph at s. l., Cruising 453 mph. Service
Ceiling 39,200′, Climb 2660′/1 min., 30,000′/21.5 min.
Estimated Range 2400 miles/8000 lbs. bombs.   AF

in the nose enclosure, followed by pilot and co-
pilot seated in tandem under a canopy. Fourteen
1,000-pound or one 22,000-pound bomb could be
accommodated. The most unusual feature was the
retractable landing gear: a pair of large wheels forward, another pair aft, and a smaller outrigger
wheel under each wing. This tandem gear had been
tested two years before on a converted Marauder
called the XB-26H. Only two XB-48 prototypes
were built, for the design was over 50 mph below
guaranteed speed and was outclassed by the XB-47.

Boeing's XB-47 Stratojet also had six J35 engines
and the tandem landing gear, but its construction
had been delayed so that captured German research
data on the high-speed advantages of swept-back
wings could be verified and incorporated in the
layout. The December 1944 proposal was Boeing's
Model 432, with a straight wing and power units
buried within the fuselage. In September 1945
Model 448, with a swept-back wing, was substituted, but the enclosed engines were unsatisfactory.

Model 450 replaced this project in October, with four engines paired in pods below and forward of the wing, where interference with airflow over the wing would be minimized. The other two engines were in individual pods at the wing tips.

By November 1945 Model 450 was finalized with a sweepback of 35°, an aspect ratio of 9.6, and outboard engines mounted below the wings. The mockup was approved in April 1946, and contruction of two XB-47 prototypes began in June, costing $8 million in addition to $2 million already spent on engineering. A bombardier-navigator in the

BOEING XB-47
General Electric J35-GE-7
DIMENSIONS: Span 116′, Lg. 107′6″, Ht. 27′8″, Wing Area 1427 sq. ft.
WEIGHT: Empty 74,623 lb., Gross 121,080 lb., Max. 162,500 lb. Fuel 6051–11,550 gal.
PERFORMANCE: (At 115,000 lb.) Speed—Top 580 mph at 15,000′, 545 mph at 35,000′, 568 mph at s. l., Cruising 466 mph, Stalling 129 mph. Service Ceiling 41,000′. Range 2650 miles/10,000 lb.   MFR

BOEING B-47A   MFR

nose had a radar bombing system whose antenna bulged below in a plastic fairing, and the pilot and co-pilot sat in tandem under a bubble canopy. Up to 16 1,000-pound or one 22,000-pound bomb could be accommodated, and two .50s mounted in the tail cone were aimed by an Emerson radar system. Flight tests on the XB-47 began on December 17, 1947, and a 580-mph top speed, 74 mph greater than the XB-48, was demonstrated at Muroc next summer. When J47-GE-3 power plants became available, they were fitted to both XB-47s, the second flying with the new engines July 21, 1948, and raising top speed past the 600-mph level.

Cautiously the USAF put the Stratojet into production at Wichita, Kansas, while reserving its main funds for the B-36. Ten B-47As were ordered October 28, 1948, and the first 88 B-47B aircraft were added to the contract November 14, 1949. First flown June 25, 1950, the B-47A had 5,200-pound-thrust J47-GE-11s, it increased takeoff weight from 121,080 to 151,324 pounds, and was used for service tests and training.

The Korean War opened the national purse, the North Atlantic Treaty provided bases abroad (encircling the potential enemy), and the B-47B model Stratojet had extended range. To carry out the largest bomber-production program since World War II, Stratojet production by Boeing-Wichita was joined in December 1952 by B-47s from the factories in Tulsa and Marietta reopened under the management of Douglas and Lockheed.

The B-47B, first flown April 26, 1951, had J47-GE-23s, a pair of 1,780-gallon drop tanks, a receptacle for flying boom in-flight refueling, and a modified nose with periscopic sight for a K-4A bombing

BOEING B-47B
General Electric J47-GE-23, 5970 lbs.
DIMENSIONS: Span 116′, Lg. 106′10″, Ht. 27′11″, Wing
  Area 1428 sq. ft.
WEIGHT: Empty 78,102 lb., Gross 184,908 lb., Combat
  122,650 lb. Fuel 13,900–15,213 gal.
PERFORMANCE: Speed—Top 608 mph at 16,300′, 565 mph
  at 35,000′, Cruising 498 mph, Stalling 177 mph. Service
  Ceiling 33,900′, Combat Ceiling 40,800′, Climb 4775′/
  1 min. Combat Radius 1961 miles/10,000 lbs. bombs,
  4444 miles (15,213 gal.) ferry range.   MFR

system. A shorter bomb bay accommodated 18,000
pounds of nuclear or conventional bombs, and two
radar-aimed .50-caliber guns with 1,200 rounds provided for rear defense.

Strategic Air Command received its first B-47B
on October 23, 1951, and deployed them in 45-
plane medium-bomber wings, each accompanied
by an air-refueling squadron with 20 KC-97 tanker-
transports. Since SAC's first jet bombers had much
longer takeoff and landing runs than the B-29s they
replaced, they had JATO rockets to accelerate takeoffs and drag chutes to decelerate landings. Of 398
B-47Bs delivered by June 1953, eight were assembled by Lockheed and ten by Douglas. Many B-
47Bs were later modified to B-47E standards (as the

BOEING B-47E
General Electric J47-GE-25, 5970 lbs., 7200 lbs. WE
DIMENSIONS: Span 116′, Lg. 107′1″, Ht. 28′, Wing Area
  1428 sq. ft.
WEIGHT: Empty 80,756 lb., Gross 198,180 lb., Combat
  124,875 lb. Fuel 14,610–18,000 gal.
PERFORMANCE: Speed—Top 607 mph at 16,300′, 557 mph
  at 38,550′, Cruising 498 mph, Stalling 175 mph. Service
  Ceiling 33,100′, Combat Ceiling 40,500′, Climb 4660′/
  1 min. Combat Radius 2013 miles/10,845 lbs. bombs,
  4035 miles (16,318 gal.) ferry range.   MFR

B-47B-II), 66 became TB-47B trainers, and 24 became RB-47Bs with camera pods.

The 88th B-47B was first redesignated XB-56 and
then YB-47C, with a January 1950 design substituting four Allison J71s for the original six power
plants. This aircraft was canceled in April 1951 before its completion.

Two XB-47Ds were actually B-47Bs completed
as test-beds for a pair of 9,710-hp Curtiss-Wright
YT-49-W-1 turboprops in the inboard engine pods,
which first flew August 26, 1955, and were reported
to have a 597-mph top speed.

The principal Stratojet model was the B-47E,
which replaced the twin .50s of the B with two 20-
mm M-24As and 700 rounds in a General Electric
radar tail turret; it also had engine water injection
for takeoff. First flown January 30, 1953, the E could
carry a nuclear bomb or eighteen 1,000-pound
bombs, plus 845 pounds of chaff. Beginning with
the 862nd ship in February 1955, an MA-7A radar-
bombing system replaced the K-4A, and this model
became the B-47E-IV. Heavier landing gear permitted an increase in fuel and raised takeoff weight
from 99 to 113 tons, giving a 2,360-mile combat
radius.

Production included 691 B-47E-BWs, 386 B-47E-
LOs, 264 B-47E-DTs, and 240 RB-47E-BWs with
elongated noses and 11 cameras. The YB-47F receiver and KB-47G tanker, however, were B-47Bs
modified to test the probe-drogue in-flight refueling
system. One YDB-47B and two YDB-47Es were
modified to carry a radio-controlled Bell Rascal
(GAM-63) air-to-surface missile on the fuselage
starboard side. The first successful launching was
made February 17, 1958, but the Rascal was canceled November 29 in favor of the Hound Dog
program.

Beginning in June 1955, 35 RB-47H models were
completed as electronic reconnaissance aircraft.
These aircraft carried an additional three men in
the bomb bay, with equipment to locate and analyze
enemy radar. A single YB-47J was modified to test
an MA-2 radar system and 15 RB-47Ks with new
equipment were added to the RB-47E line. The
EB-47Ls were "post-attack communication relay
stations" converted from 36 B-47Es in 1962–63.

BOEING RB-47H   LAWSON

When SAC received its last production-line Stratojet, a B-47E, on February 18, 1957, it had 28 Medium Bomb and five Medium Strategic Reconnaissance wings, with about 1,306 B-47 and 254 RB-47 aircraft. A total of 2,041 Stratojets were built, the largest number of any bomber never involved in a war. SAC retired its last B-47E in February 1966 and its last RB-47H in December 1967, although a few remained in noncombat roles elsewhere.

MARTIN XB-51 (2nd model)　　　　　　MFR

Light Bombers Revived

When the Korean War ended in 1953, the 28 USAF bomber wings included ten with B-29 and five with B-50 medium bombers, five with intercontinental B-36s, one B-45 jet unit, and four with the new B-47. For short-range light bombing, the three wings with Douglas B-26 Invaders had the only type available. Tactical Air Command (TAC) had no jet bombers for direct support.

Two such projects had been started under the old "Attack" category: Convair's XA-44 and Martin's XA-45. Redesignated XB-53 in 1948, the former, an odd canard design with three J35 jets and a swept-forward wing, was canceled before completion. Martin's XA-45 had been proposed on April 1, 1946, as a straight-winged, six-place bomber with two TG-110 turboprop and two I-40 turbojets, but by February 1947 that design had been replaced by a smaller swept-wing, two-place design with three jet engines. This became the XB-51, whose mockup was inspected in February 1948 by the Air Force, which directed Martin to go ahead with two prototypes on April 23, 1948.

The XB-51 had two J47-GE-13s attached below the fuselage, with a third in the tail. Wings were swept back 35°, had a 6° cathedral (droop), in-

MARTIN XB-51
General Electric J47-GE-13, 5200 lbs.
DIMENSIONS: Span 53'1", Lg. 85'1", Ht. 17'4", Wing Area 548 sq. ft.
WEIGHT: Empty 29,584 lb., Gross 55,923 lb., Max. 62,457 lb. Fuel 2835–3535 gal.
PERFORMANCE: (At 41,457 lbs., combat weight) Speed— Top 645 mph at s. l., Cruising 532 mph. Landing 153 mph. Service Ceiling 40,500', Climb 6980'/1 min. Range 1075 miles normal, 1613 miles max.　　MFR

creased their incidence for takeoff and landing, and had spoilers instead of ailerons, with leading-edge slots and full-span flaps. Tandem dual main wheels, like those on the B-47, were used, along with a high T-tail. The pilot sat under a bubble canopy and the navigator was placed behind him within the fuselage. Eight 20-mm nose guns with 160 rpg and up to 10,400 pounds of bombs could be carried, with the basic mission the delivery of 4,000 pounds over a 475-mile radius. Flight tests began October 28, 1949, with the second, slightly modified example flown the following April 17.

Another two-seat jet bomber of very different design philosophy, the English Electric Canberra, had been flown in Britain on May 13, 1949, and put into production for the Royal Air Force. Although not as fast or well armed as the XB-51, it had advantages in endurance, range, and maneuverability, and two Canberras were obtained for the USAF, the first flying across the Atlantic on February 22, 1951. The Korean War created the need for a B-26 replacement for night intruder operations, and tests of the XB-51, B-45, and the Navy's AJ-1 indicated that they were less suitable than the British aircraft for these missions.

To the surprise of the American industry, Martin received a letter contract March 23, 1951, for the first 250 Canberras. On July 20, 1953, Martin's first B-57A Canberra was flown, powered by two J65 Sapphires, a British engine built under license first by Buick and then by Wright. The short, wide wings had an aspect ratio of only 4.27, the pilot had a clear bubble canopy, and the second crew member sat

MARTIN B-57A   MFR

behind him within the fuselage. Added to the original design were the rotary bomb door Martin introduced on the XB-51, wing-tip 320-gallon drop tanks, underwing pylons, and provisions for eight .50-caliber guns with 300 rpg in the wings.

Eight B-57As for test work and 67 RB-57As were completed from January to October 1954, first serving the 363rd Tactical Reconnaissance Wing. A new double-canopy distinguished the B-57B, first flown June 24, 1954, and the eight .50-caliber guns in the first 90 were replaced by four 20-mm M-39s with 200 rpg. By September 1956, 202 B-57Bs and 38 B-57Cs with dual controls had been built to replace the B-26s of four TAC bomb wings, the 345th and 463rd in the United States, the 3rd in Japan, and the 38th in France.

Sixty-eight B-57E target tugs were similar to the B-57B and were adaptable to combat configurations, but 20 RB-57Ds for high-altitude reconnaissance had J57 engines and a 106-foot wingspan. First flown in November 1955, the unarmed RB-57D single-seater was intended for SAC's new Light Strategic Reconnaissance Wing, which began receiving the B-57C and RB-57D in May 1956 and the Lockheed U-2 in June 1957. Another noncombat modification was the WB-57F weather aircraft, rebuilt from older models by General Dynamics at Fort Worth, with two TF-33 turbofans, and two J60 auxiliary jets on a new 122-foot wing. The first was originally designated RB-57F when first flown on June 23, 1963, and 21 of these two-seaters were delivered by March 1967. They were used on many very secret intelligence missions before retirement from Air Force service in June 1964.

Martin completed 403 Canberras by March 1957 with the last RB-57D and B-57E aircraft. The Canberra TAC bomb wings' mission changed in 1957 from night intrusion to nuclear bombing, so the black paint was scraped off and a LABS (Low-altitude Bombing System) was installed. SAC retired its Canberras in April 1960. The Canberra began retirement from TAC bomber service in 1958. Twenty-two B-57Bs transferred to Pakistan in June 1959 did fight in the September 1965 conflict in Kashmir.

MARTIN RB-57A
Wright J65-W-5, 7220 lbs.
DIMENSIONS: Span 64', Lg. 65'6", Ht. 14'10", Wing Area 960 sq. ft.
WEIGHT: Empty 24,751 lb., Gross 48,847 lb., Combat 34,917 lb. Fuel 2252–892 gal.
PERFORMANCE: Speed—Top 609 mph at 4500', 534 mph at 45,700', Stalling 119 mph. Combat Ceiling 48,350', Climb 7180'/1 min. Combat Radius 1267 miles/3618 lbs. bombs at 495 mph, 2568 miles ferry range.   MFR

MARTIN B-57B
Wright J65-W-5, 7220 lbs.
DIMENSIONS: As B-57A
WEIGHT: Empty 27,091 lb., Gross 53,721 lb., Combat 38,689 lb. Fuel 2892–3440 gal.
PERFORMANCE: Speed—Top 598 mph at 2500', 575 mph at s. l., Cruising 476 mph, Stalling 124 mph. Combat Ceiling 45,100', Climb 6180'/1 min. Combat Radius 948 miles/5240 lbs. bombs, 2722 miles ferry range.
                                                                        MFR

MARTIN RB-57D
Pratt & Whitney J57-P-27, 10,500 lb.
DIMENSIONS: Span 106', Lg. 65'6", Ht. 15'7", Wing Area 1505 sq. ft.
WEIGHT: Empty 27,275 lb., Gross 45,085 lb., Max. 54,072 lb. Fuel 2740 gal.
PERFORMANCE: Combat Radius 1560 miles at 475 mph, Altitude over Target 59,700'.   MFR

Only two Canberra squadrons of the 3rd Bomb Wing remained active when war in Vietnam revived the need for light bombers. Two converted RB-47Es were sent first and made the first sortie May 7, 1963, and 36 B-57Bs were sent in August 4, 1964. Only tentative use seems to have been made of them, but a November 1 mortar attack destroyed five and damaged 15. On February 19, 1965, 24 made the first heavy attack on the Viet Cong, joining the Rolling Thunder bombing campaign against North Vietnam in March, and four B-57s were provided to the Vietnam Air Force in August 1965. The Canberras shifted to their original planned role of night intrusion, but target location proved quite difficult. To solve this problem, 16 aircraft were returned to Martin for conversion to the B-57G. The nose was reshaped to house APQ-139 radar, an infrared detection system, a low-level light television, and laser range finder. Eleven B-57Gs arrived in Thailand with the 13th Bomb Squadron in September 1970. They operated against trucks on the Ho Chi Minh Trail until 1972, when the aircraft returned to the United States for a Kansas ANG squadron, retiring in 1974.

Despite withdrawal from combat units, the Canberra continued in many utility roles, especially in weather investigations. Two Defense System Evaluation squadrons (DSES) were established, using modified EB-57s to simulate enemy attempts to penetrate our airspace.

The next tactical bomber began as the Navy's carrier-based Douglas A3D Skywarrior, but in February 1952 the Air Force decided to purchase a development called the B-66. Contracts were approved for five test RB-66As on January 26, 1953, and for the first B-66Bs on August 24. A three-place high-wing monoplane with two Allison YF-71-A-9s under 35° swept-back wings, the RB-66A-DL first flew June 28, 1954, at Long Beach, California. These were followed by 72 similar B-66B-DLs, first flown January 4, 1955, and 145 RB-66B-DLs, with J71-A-13s, for night reconnaissance, which entered service in 1956 as the Destroyer. The Douglas Tulsa factory added 30 RB-66B-DTs and six RB-66C-DTs, a seven-seat, radar-reconnaissance version flown October 29, 1955, with radomes at the wing tips and below the ECM compartment, which had replaced the bomb bay. Finally, Tulsa delivered 36 WB-66D weather-reconnaissance models from June 1957 to June 1958, bringing the B-66 total to 294.

The B-66B, used by the 17th Bomb Wing in Florida and, after 1958, the 47th Bomb Wing in Britain, carried up to 15,000 pounds of bombs aimed by a K-5 radar system in the nose, with no forward guns; MD-1A fire control aimed two M-24A guns, with 1,000 rounds, in a General Electric tail turret.

Since this turret is similar to those used in the B-

DOUGLAS RB-66A   MFR

DOUGLAS B-66B
Allison J71-A-13, 10,200 lbs.
DIMENSIONS: Span 72′6″, Lg. 75′2″, Ht. 23′7″, Wing Area 780 sq. ft.
WEIGHT: Empty 42,549 lb., Gross 83,000 lb., Combat 57,800 lb. Fuel 4309–5383 gal.
PERFORMANCE: Speed—Top 631 mph at 6000′, 577 mph at 35,000′, Cruising 528 mph, Stalling 153 mph. Combat Ceiling 39,400′, Climb 5000′/1 min. Combat Radius 902 miles/10,000 lbs. bombs, 2468 miles ferry range.   PMB

DOUGLAS RB-66C
Allison J71-A-11, 9700–10,200 hp
DIMENSIONS: As B-66B
WEIGHT: Empty 44,771 lb., Combat 65,360 lb., Max. 83,000 lb. Fuel 5285 gal.
PERFORMANCE: Speed—Top 613 mph at 8000′, 544 mph at 35,500′, Cruising 502 mph, Landing 153 mph. Combat Ceiling 35,500′, Climb 4320′/1 min., Combat Radius 1090 miles. 2228 miles ferry range.   MFR

DOUGLAS EB-66B   J. SULLIVAN

47 and B-36, a description of its function by the General Electric Company is of interest. Things have changed since the days when the bomber gunner used brute strength to swing Lewis guns against the slipstream, and guessed at leading his target, or peered through the night for the glow of enemy exhaust pipes. Today, the gunner sits comfortably within the fuselage, aiming power-operated guns with electronics. When the bomber enters a danger area ". . . the gunner switches the radar to 'search' and adjusts the system control panel to provide the computer with air temperature, altitude and air speed information.

"When the radar picks up an attacking plane, a bright spot shows on the screen. By means of a control handle, the gunner easily moves the radar antenna until it is centered on the target. Once the target is 'acquired' and the radar is 'locked on,' the target is tracked automatically.

"Radar then supplies the computer with the position and range of the attacking plane. Necessary gun deflections and corrections are computed automatically. When the hostile aircraft enters gun range, the gunner presses a trigger which fires the guns electrically."

The RB-66B, used by two tactical-reconnaissance wings, replaced the bombs with four K-47 cameras and 8,044 pounds of photoflash bombs. But when the Douglas Destroyer did go to war from 1965 to 1972, it went to war as an electronic countermeasure (ECM) aid to the bomber offensive against North Vietnam. Modified B-66Bs and RB-66Bs became the EB-66B and EB-66E, respectively, with bomb bay radar pallets, dispensers for 2,492 pounds of chaff, and an ECM fairing to replace the tail gun turret.

The B-52

"The most formidable expression of air power in the history of military aviation" was how Air Force Secretary Donald A. Quarles described the B-52. "Its range, which can be augmented by refueling techniques, its bomb load, its highly skilled crews, coupled with electronic equipment which makes it possible to find and hit any target anywhere in the world in any weather, constitute a weapons system which no other nation can match."

This 1955 estimate was made of the plane which would carry America's new H-bombs, and the first thermonuclear weapon to be dropped from a U.S. plane was released from a B-52B on May 20, 1956, at Bikini Island. Boeing's Stratofortress was to serve in front-line squadrons longer than any other USAF type, although its combat experience was to be very different than expected.

When the Air Force issued a specification in Jan-

uary 1946 for an intercontinental bomber, Boeing answered with a 180-ton project, Model 462, incorporating six 5,500-hp Wright XT35 turboprops on a straight wing. A design contract was awarded in June 1946, and engineers began another struggle to combine long range with speed. Two XB-52 prototypes were ordered in July 1948, with the turboprops and 20° sweepback, but in September Pratt & Whitney's XJ57 engine seemed to offer a new chance at higher speeds. The actual B-52 configuration, Model 464-49, with eight J57s suspended on pods below a wing swept back 35°, was accepted October 27, 1948. After mockup approval in April 1949, contruction of the prototypes proceeded at a cost that finally reached $53 million.

Meanwhile, Boeing offered Model 474 to the USAF in 1949. Powered by four 5,643-hp Allison T40-A-2 turboprops slung below a slightly swept high wing and designated XB-55, the 153,000-pound design had twelve 20-mm guns in three turrets. Since only 490 mph was expected from the six-bladed contraprop propulsion, the XB-55 was abandoned in favor of the faster pure-jet Model 464 (B-52) layout.

The first of these prototypes to fly, on April 15, 1952, was actually the YB-52, since new installations delayed the XB-52's flight until October 2. Both aircraft had a narrow canopy over tandem pilots' seats, eight main wheels retracting into the fuselage, small outrigger wheels at the wing tips, and a tall fin. Eight J57-P-3s were paired below the 36.5° swept wings, with a Sperry K-1A bombing system in the nose and two .50-caliber guns for the tail gunner.

Production aircraft first planned in February 1951 and ordered December 16, 1952, introduced side-by-side pilots' seats, provisions for two 1,000-gallon drop tanks and air refueling, and the J57-P-1W. The first three were B-52As, whose tests began August 5, 1954, and one became a carrier plane for the X-15 research program. Twenty-seven RB-52Bs, first flown January 25, 1955, had a bomb bay fitted for an interchangeable pressurized capsule with cameras for reconnaissance and room for two additional crewmen.

Then came 23 B-52Bs ordered June 17, 1953, the first 11 with J57-P-1Ws, the rest with J57-P-19W or 29W engines. The crew included two pilots, two bombardier-navigators and an ECM operator in the pressurized nose, and a lonely gunner in the tail. Armament included four .50-caliber M-3 guns with 2,400 rounds or a pair of 20-mm M24A1 guns, with both optical and radar fire control. Electronics included a Sperry K-3A bombing system, plus five transmitters and two receivers for radar countermeasures. Bomb load could include twenty-seven 1,000-pound bombs or a thermonuclear weapon of

BOEING XB-52
Pratt & Whitney J57-P-3, 8700 lbs.

DIMENSIONS: Span 185′, Lg. 152′8″, Ht. 48′3″, Wing Area 4000 sq. ft.

WEIGHT: Empty 155,200 lb., Gross 390,000 lb., Combat 256,800 lb. Fuel 38,270 gal.

PERFORMANCE: Speed—Top 611 mph at 20,000′, 594 mph at 35,000′, Cruising 519 mph, Stalling 146 mph. Combat Ceiling 46,500′, Climb 4550′/1 min. Combat Radius 3535 miles/10,000 lbs. bombs, 7015 miles ferry range.   MFR

BOEING B-52C
Pratt & Whitney J57-P-19W, -29WA, 12,100 lbs.

DIMENSIONS: As B-52B

WEIGHT: Empty 164,486 lb., Gross 450,000 lb., Combat 283,100 lb. Fuel 41,098–550 gal.

PERFORMANCE: Speed—Top 634 mph at 20,200′, 570 mph at 45,000′, Cruising 521 mph, Stalling 169 mph. Combat Ceiling 46,350′, Climb 5310′/1 min. Combat Radius 3800 miles/10,000 lbs. bombs, 7856 miles ferry range.   MFR

BOEING B-52B
Pratt & Whitney J57-P-19W, -29W, 12,100 lbs.

DIMENSIONS: Span 185′, Lg. 156′7″, Ht. 48′4″, Wing Area 4000 sq. ft.

WEIGHT: Empty 164,081 lb., Gross 420,000 lb., Combat 272,000 lb. Fuel 37,550 gal.

PERFORMANCE: Speed—Top 634 mph at 20,300′, 598.5 mph at 35,000′, 571 mph at 45,750′, Cruising 521 mph, Stalling 162 mph. Combat Ceiling 47,100′, Climb 5500′/1 min. Combat Radius 3534 miles/10,000 lbs. bombs, 7343 miles ferry range.   MFR

BOEING B-52D (Data as B-52C)   MFR

BOEING B-52E
Pratt & Whitney J57-P-19W, -29WA, 12,100 lbs.
DIMENSIONS: As B-52B
WEIGHT: Empty 163,752 lb., Gross 450,000 lb., Combat 282,600 lb. Fuel 41,217 gal.
PERFORMANCE: Speed—Top 634 mph at 20,200′, 570 mph at 45,050′, Cruising 521 mph, Stalling 169 mph. Combat Ceiling 46,350′, Climb 5310′/1 min. Combat Radius 3820 miles/10,000 lbs. bombs, 7875 miles ferry range.   MFR

BOEING B-52F
Pratt & Whitney J57-P-43WA, 13,750 lbs.
DIMENSIONS: Span 185′, Lg. 156′6″, Ht. 48′4″, Wing Area 4000 sq. ft.
WEIGHT: Empty 162,685 lb., Gross 450,000 lb., Combat 283,600 lb. Fuel 41,098 gal.
PERFORMANCE: Speed—Top 636.5 mph at 20,500′, 570 mph at 45,650′, Cruising 523 mph, Stalling 169 mph. Combat Ceiling 46,600′, Climb 5680′/1 min., 33,450′/19.8 min. Combat Radius 3850 miles/10,000 lbs. bombs, 7976 miles ferry range.   AF

BOEING B-52G
Pratt & Whitney J57-P-43WB, 13,750 lbs.
DIMENSIONS: Span 185′, Lg. 157′7″, Ht. 40′8″, Wing Area 4000 sq. ft.
WEIGHT: Empty 158,590 lb., Gross 450,000 lb., Combat 294,650 lb. Fuel 42,345–47,975 gal.
PERFORMANCE: Speed—Top 636.5 mph at 20,500′, 570 mph at 46,000′, Cruising 523 mph, Stalling 169 mph. Service Ceiling 38,400′, Combat Ceiling 47,100′, Climb 5850′/1 min., 33,400′/19 min. Combat Radius 3980 miles/10,000 lbs. bombs, 8900 miles ferry range.   MFR

up to 43,000 pounds. Over half the Stratofortress takeoff weight consisted of fuel carried in the fuselage and wings, mostly in self-sealing tanks.

Larger 3,000-gallon drop tanks and an MA-6A bombing system by International Business Machines Corporation was provided on the B-52C, flown March 9, 1956. Thirty-five B-52Cs were built at Seattle. Boeing's Wichita factory was added to the Stratofortress program by a December 1954 contract, and the first of B-52Ds was flown there on June 4, 1956, with MD-9 fire control and omission of the recon capsule capability. There were 69 B-52D-BWs from Wichita and 101 B-52D-BOs from Seattle.

An even more advanced ASB-4 bombing-navigation system was used on the B-52E flown at Seattle on October 3, 1957. There were 42 B-52E-BOs and 58 B-52E-BWs. New J57-P-43As were used on 44 B-52F-BOs, first flown May 6, 1958, and completed when production in Seattle ceased in November 1958. Concurrently Wichita built 45 B-52F-BWs.

Even the most advanced bomber is threatened by missiles from enemy surface batteries and interceptors, so development proceeded on the "stand-off bomb," an air-to-surface missile launched from the bomber at a safer distance from the target. Structural provisions had been made on some B-52s for the Bell GAM-63 Rascal tested on the YDB-47s, but this missile was canceled in favor of the North American AGM-28 (formerly GAM-77) Hound Dog carried under each B-52G wing. The 42-foot, 10,000-pound, air-breathing jet missile used a nuclear warhead. Two could be released to knock out enemy defenses up to 600 miles away, so the bomber could deliver its main weapons.

Other B-52G innovations included a shortened fin, enlarged integral wing tanks, and fixed 700-gal-

lon external tanks. The tail gunner was moved to the forward fuselage cabin, with ASG-15 remote fire control. An ASB-9 bombing system was provided, and enemy radar could be confused by 14 ECM transmitters, 400 pounds of chaff, and up to four McDonnell ADM-20A (formerly GAM-72) Quail decoy missiles carried along with four nuclear bombs. The 13-foot, 1,200-pound Quail reflected a radar image resembling a B-52.

The first of 193 B-52Gs flew October 26, 1958, and a prototype Hound Dog was successfully launched April 23, 1959. Quails became operational with a B-52G squadron on February 1, 1961, and production Hound Dogs reached B-52G bases in August 1961.

The last Stratofortress model was the B-52H, first flown March 6, 1961, with TF33-P-3 turbofans of reduced fuel consumption, 960 pounds of chaff, and a 20-mm M-61 multibarrel Vulcan tail gun with 1,-242 rounds and ASG-21 fire control. There was a plan to carry four Douglas GAM-87 Skybolt missiles below the wings, but this two-stage ballistic missile was canceled December 21, 1962, and Hound Dogs were substituted.

BOEING B-52H
Pratt & Whitney TF33-P-3, 17,000 lbs. takeoff
DIMENSIONS: Span 185′, Lg. 156′, Ht. 40′8″, Wing Area 4000 sq. ft.
WEIGHT: Empty 169,822 lb., Gross 450,000 lb., Combat 289,000 lb. Fuel 41,321–48,030 gal.
PERFORMANCE: Speed—Top 639 mph at 20,700′, 603 mph at 35,000′, 560 mph at 46,650′, Cruising 525 mph, Stalling 169 mph. Combat Ceiling 47,200′, Climb 6990′/1 min. Combat Radius 4480 miles/10,000 lbs. bombs, 10,145 miles.   MFR

Boeing's Stratofortress had entered SAC service in June 1955, and production of the manned bomber came to a halt in the United States when the 102nd B-52H, last of 744 Stratofortresses, was delivered October 26, 1962. Aircraft cost had increased from $5,948,000 for the B-52E to $8,965,000 for the B-52H.

At first B-52s were concentrated in three-squadron 45-plane bomb wings on a single base, along with a KC-135 Heavy Tanker squadron, but they were gradually dispersed in 15-plane wings among many bases for greater safety. At the end of 1962, SAC had 639 B-52s, along with 547 Hound Dog, 436 Quail missiles, and 515 KC-135 tankers.

During the Cuban missile crisis in October 1962, SAC launched an airborne alert with some B-52s in the air on 24-hour missions designed to keep them within reach of potential targets, and others were on 15-minute ground alert. The nuclear holocaust didn't happen, however, and only two B-52s were ever used for live tests of nuclear weapons. Instead, combat operations with conventional weapons were the norm during the war in Southeast Asia. On June 18, 1965, 27 B-52Fs flew from Guam to attack an enemy base north of Saigon. Each bomber carried 27 750-pound bombs in the bay and 24 others under the wings.

As these operations continued, all B-52Ds in service were modified to carry 42 750-pound or 84 500-pound bombs in the bay, plus 24 of either size under the wings, and these aircraft replaced the B-52F on operations in August 1967. These missions in support of ground operations were unopposed, but the war's most important attack, Linebaker II, would be challenged by stronger means. From December 18 to 29, 1972, 700 sorties were flown at night against the Hanoi-Haiphong area, whose principal defense against the high-altitude attacks was surface-to-air missiles. The SAMs downed 15 B-52Ds; but the few enemy fighters were ineffective, and two MiG-21s were downed by B-52D tail gunners. Between June 1965 and August 15, 1973, SAC launched 126,615 B-52 sorties against Vietnam, Laos, and Cambodia, losing 29 aircraft—only 17 to hostile action.

Development of the B-52's primary strategic mission, however, continued during the war. Overhaul programs were utilized to strengthen the aircraft for low-level, beneath-radar penetrations of hostile territory. Another modification, made to 281 late-model aircraft, was the addition of SRAM (Short-range Attack Missile) capability. These 14-foot, 2,247-pound rockets were first flight-tested from a B-52H on July 29, 1969, with production models reaching SAC in March 1972. Eight SRAMS (AGM-69As) were carried on a rotary launcher in the rear bomb bay, behind the usual nuclear weapons, and up to 12 others could be carried on wing pylons. An Electro-optical Viewing System (ASQ-151 EVS) was added under the nose of all B-52G/H types in 1973.

While SAC had 639 active B-52s by the end of 1962, attrition and the retirement of the last B-52B in September 1965 and the last B-52C in September 1971 had reduced the force to 450 by 1972. After 1975 a force level of about 350 remained active.

Convair Bombers

Convair's Fort Worth factory, which became part of General Dynamics in 1953, was Boeing's competitor in jet-bomber development. Convair proposed a B-36G using 72 percent of the older type's parts, but with a swept wing and tail, eight XJ57-P-3 jets, and more fuel. While the 72,000-pound bomb capacity remained, the crew could be reduced from nine to five men and all the turrets could be omitted except for the twin 20-mm guns in the tail. No ordnance was actually installed on the prototypes.

On March 5, 1951, the Air Force ordered two prototypes be modified from production aircraft and redesignated YB-60, and the first was flown April 18, 1952. Since the YB-60 was much slower than the B-52, it did not replace the B-36 at Fort Worth. Instead, Convair concentrated on the design of the world's first supersonic bomber.

Air Force bomber design studies resulted in a three-place delta-wing design submitted by Convair on December 11, 1951. Further development led to Convair's MX-1964 and Boeing's MX-1965, which became the XB-58 and XB-59. Boeing used four General Electric J73s and a swept wing, but when both detail designs were presented October 9, 1952, Convair's was chosen. A mockup was inspected in August 1953, and after the J79 engine was chosen, the design was finalized and 13 test aircraft were ordered October 13, 1954.

CONVAIR YB-60
Pratt & Whitney J57-P-3, 8700 lbs.
DIMENSIONS: Span 206′5″, Lg. 175′2″, Ht. 60′5″, Wing Area 5239 sq. ft.
WEIGHT: Empty 153,016 lb., Gross 410,000 lb., Combat 260,250 lb. Fuel 36,965–41,462 gal.
PERFORMANCE: Speed—Top 508 mph at 39,250′, 502 mph at 43,400′, Cruising 467 mph, Stalling 140 mph. Service Ceiling 36,650′, Combat Ceiling 44,650′, Climb 3555′/1 min. Combat Radius 2920 miles/10,000 lbs. bombs, 6192 miles (38,590 gal.) ferry range.   MFR

Known as the Convair Hustler, the first XB-58 was flown November 11, 1956, with four General Electric J79-GE-1 turbojets with afterburners in pods below the conical-cambered delta wing. A pressurized crew compartment was provided, and honeycombed skin panels resisted the high temperatures of supersonic air friction. The stilted 18-wheel landing gear held the narrow area-ruled fuselage high enough to clear an MB-1C pod containing a W39Y1-1 nuclear warhead and over 4,000 gallons of fuel.

CONVAIR B-58A
General Electric J79-GE-5B, 10,300 lbs. (15,500 lbs. AB)
DIMENSIONS: Span 56′10″, Lg. 96′9″, Ht. 31′5″, Wing Area 1542 sq. ft.
WEIGHT: Empty 55,560 lb., Gross 163,000 lb., Combat 81,750 lb. Fuel 14,850 gal. (ground); 15,499 gal. (in flight).
PERFORMANCE: Speed—Top 1321 mph at 63,150′, 700 mph at s. l., Cruising 610 mph. Combat Ceiling 64,800′, Climb 17,830′/1 min. Combat Radius 1750 miles/MB-1C, 5028 miles ferry range.   MFR

The pod, slung beneath the fuselage, was carried at Mach .91 cruising and released on a Mach 2 dash over the target at 55,000 feet. Air refueling could increase combat radius from 1,750 to 5,577 miles. A dual pod, the BLU-2B, flown May 12, 1960, had a 54-foot lower fuel section released before the 35-foot upper section with a BA53-Y1 warhead. This configuration provided a Mach .91 sea-level attack capability, and by March 1962 pylons for four small weapons were added.

Navigation and bombing at Mach 2 presented unusual problems, which on the B-58 were solved by a Sperry (AN/ASQ-42) system which used active radar navigation during a mission's approach phase, with inertial and star-tracking methods employed over enemy territory. Weighing 1,948 pounds, the system had an analog computer receiving data from search radar in the nose, an astro-star-tracker amidship, a doppler radar in the tail, inertial sensors, and radio altimeter. Sitting at his console behind the pilot, the bombardier-navigator was provided with continuous and precise information on aircraft position, heading, ground speed, altitude, steering data, and distance to target, as well as ballistic computations for weapons release.

The third crewman was the defense systems operator, seated behind the navigator, who manned the controls for the 20-mm M-61 Vulcan, with 1,120 rounds, in the tail and a choice of electronic countermeasures for enemy radar.

The first 30 Hustlers were built as test ships, but ten were modified to the B-58A tactical configuration and eight to dual-control TB-58A trainers. Eighty-six more standard B-58As with J79-GE-5As were delivered from September 1959 to October 26, 1962. The B-58A joined SAC's 43rd Bomb Wing in March 1960 and the 305th Bomb Wing the following year—the only two wings to get the type.

Considering the high performance and sophisticated equipment of the B-58, it was surprising that its service life was curtailed. By January 16, 1970, the last Hustlers were retired from SAC. Part of the reason was the B-58A's high accident rate, resulting in the loss of nine of the first 30 aircraft, but the major factor was the intercontinental ballistic missiles (ICBM), whose entrance into SAC paralleled B-58 service.

The first SAC Atlas ICBM squadron was declared operational September 2, 1960, and by 1969 enough more advanced weapons were on hand for an operational force stabilized at 1,000 Minuteman and 54 Titan missiles, while the Navy had 656 submarine-launched missiles.

In 1951 bomber designations had been assigned to five guided missiles then at various stages of development: the Martin B-61 Matador tactical cruise missile; the Northrop B-62 Snark strategic cruise missile; the Bell B-63 Rascal air-launched missile; the North American B-64 Navaho strategic supersonic cruise missile; and the Convair B-65 Atlas, the first American ICBM. All of these projects were redesignated according to a standardized missile nomenclature system and consequently fall outside the scope of this book.

The B-66 tactical bomber has already been described in an earlier section of this chapter. The B-67 designation was used briefly by the Radioplane Crossbow (GAM-67) decoy missile, and the XB-68 was Martin's last jet-bomber design. RB-69A was the designation allotted to seven Lockheed P2V-7U Neptunes ordered from the Navy in May 1954 for special Electronics Intelligence missions.

Martin's XB-68 was ordered in September 1956 as a two-place tactical bomber powered by two Pratt & Whitney 27,500-pound thrust J75s mounted on each side of the long (109-foot) fuselage. Like the company's earlier XB-51, it had a high T-tail and rotary bomb door, but the 53-foot wings were straight and short like those on an F-104. Armament included a radar-aimed 20-mm T-171, like the one on the B-58, and a 3,500-pound nuclear bomb that was to be carried over a 588-mile combat radius. Estimated top speed was 1,589 mph at 54,700 feet, a velocity requiring evaporation cooling and a structure primarily of steel.

Although two prototypes and a static-test article had been planned, the XB-68 was canceled in 1957, leaving the XB-70 as the only manned strategic-bomber prototype under way. Subsequent numbers were assigned to the SR-71 reconnaissance design and to several missile projects, but the XB-70 was to be the last bomber in the series that began with a Keystone biplane in 1927.

The XB-70

The North American XB-70 Valkyrie was designed as a B-52 replacement, cruising at Mach 3 over 75,000 feet.

Such a tremendous advance in performance required both an entirely new aircraft configuration and a radical change in construction. Since the temperatures of up to 600°F encountered on these flights were too much for the usual aluminum alloys, about 69.5 percent of the airframe weight was of welded steel honeycomb sandwich and 9.5 percent was titanium for the forward structure. Prominent features were the canard foreplane near the long nose, delta wing with tip folding down for stability in supersonic flight, and twin rudders. Six General Electric YJ93-GE-3s with continuous afterburning and two intakes with controlled air induction were mounted under the center section.

In September 1955 both Boeing and North American initiated engineering studies for a WS-110 strategic piloted weapons system. The resulting proposals seemed impractical until the appearance of the "compression-lift" theory, which stated that the aircraft shock waves would provide additional lift in supersonic flight. A design contract was awarded to North American on December 23, 1957, for the XB-70, which used boron fuel. The latter feature was canceled in 1959.

Continuous review of future manned-aircraft requirements for the USAF caused many disturbances in the program. On the one hand, SAC wanted a manned bomber; on the other, Defense Department officials said that expensive bomber programs had been made unnecessary by the growing force of intercontinental missiles, while bomber-penetration prospects had been reduced by progress in the field of surface-to-air missiles.

The conflict among the Defense Department, Air Force, and Congress swung back and forth. The first cancellation on December 3, 1959, cut back the program to one prototype so that the next fiscal year's budget could be balanced, but Congress restored funding in October 1960. However, on March 28, 1961, the new President, John F. Kennedy, also recommended that the program be limited to research prototypes and considered development as a weapons system unnecessary and economically unjustifiable. Three XB-70 prototypes authorized October 4, 1961, were to have no weapons provisions and only two—not four—crewmen in the pressurized nose.

An RS-70 (reconnaissance-strike) version was offered to introduce a capability not available in missiles, but an Air Force request for 60 RS-70s to be operational in 1969 was rejected, and the third prototype canceled in March 1963. Nearly two years

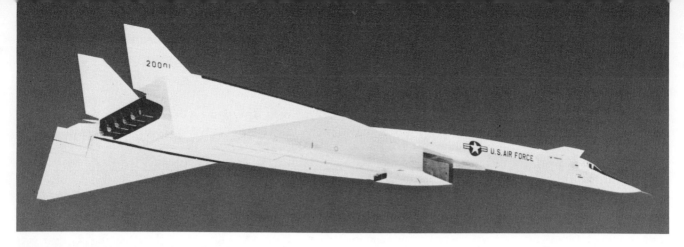

NORTH AMERICAN XB-70A Valkyrie
Six General Electric YJ-93-GE-3, 28,000 lb. max.
DIMENSIONS: Span 105', Lg. 185', Ht. 30'8", Wing Area
6297 sq. ft.
WEIGHT: Empty 231,215 lb., Gross 521,056 lb., Max.
534,792 lb., Combat 341,096 lb. Fuel 43,646 gal. (orig-
inally 47,101 gal.)
PERFORMANCE: Speed—Top 1982 mph at 75,550', 1254
mph at 35,000', Cruising 1982 mph, Touchdown 184
mph. Service Ceiling 75,500', Combat Ceiling 75,250',
Climb 27,450'/1 min. Combat Range 3419 miles. Max.
Range 4290 miles.   MFR

behind the 1960 schedule, the first XB-70A was
flown from Palmdale, California, on September 21,
1964, and the refined second plane flew July 17,
1965.

By then there was no plan to use the Valkyrie as
a bomber, so the prototypes were just air vehicles
to "demonstrate air-worthiness in a sustained Mach
3 high altitude environment." The second aircraft
was destroyed in a midair collision June 8, 1966,
and the first made its 83rd, and last, flight February
4, 1969, to the Air Force Museum at Wright-Pater-
son AFB, Ohio. Over $2 billion had been expended
on the B-70 program.

The FB-111

In April 1964 the number of intercontinental missiles on alert surpassed the number of intercontinental bombers on alert, and the destruction of all
possible enemy strategic fixed targets seemed assured. No strategic bombers were being produced
in the United States. While strategic heavy- and
medium-bomber squadrons decreased from 78 in
June 1964 to 40 in June 1968 and 24 in September
1977, Air Force leaders continued to press development of new manned bomber designs.

The next bomber to enter SAC service was the
General Dynamics FB-111A, which was developed
from the F-111A tactical fighter-bomber. Powered
by two Pratt & Whitney TF-30-P-7s, its outstanding
feature was variable-sweep wings that could be
swept back 72.5° for high speed attack. Terrain-following radar permitted a low-altitude attack approach that avoided the dangers of a high-altitude

approach: early detection by enemy radar and interception by SAMs.

Two crewmen sat side by side and depended on
speed and electronics for protection rather than
guns. On the basic mission two 2,247-pound
SRAMs (AGM-69As) were carried in the weapons
bay and two more under the wings, along with four
600-gallon drop tanks over a 6,150-mile range,
which could be extended another 3,300 miles with
air refueling. Alternatively, underwing pylons
could hold six drop tanks for ferry flights or 24 750-
pound bombs. Six gravity nuclear bombs could be
carried, as well as the B77 nuclear bomb, whose
yield is adjustable during flight and whose gas gen-
erator, with lifting and retardant parachute, enables
release at altitudes as low as 150 feet.

The FB-111A program was first announced December 10, 1965, a contract approved a year later,
and a prototype converted from an F-111A flew July
30, 1967. The first production aircraft flew at Fort
Worth on July 13, 1968, but on March 19, 1969, a
new Defense Secretary, Melvin Laird, cut the program from 263 to 76 aircraft. SAC formally accepted
its first FB-111A on October 8, 1969, and the first
successful FB-111A SRAM launch was made March
27, 1970. After the last FB-111A was received June

GENERAL DYNAMICS FB-111A
Pratt & Whitney TF30-P-7, 20,350 lb. (A/B)
DIMENSIONS: Span 70', Lg. 75'64", Ht. 17', Wing Area 550
sq. ft.
WEIGHT: Empty 47,481 lb., Gross 110,646 lb., Max. 114,-
277 lb., Combat 70,380 lb. Fuel 5010–9223 gal.
PERFORMANCE: Speed—Top 1453 mph at 50,000', 838
mph at s. l., Cruising 511 mph, Stalling 183 mph. Service Ceiling 50,263', Combat Ceiling 49,993', Climb
23,418'/1 min. Combat Range 6150 miles/8988 lb. (with
refueling), Ferry Range 4786 mph (no refueling) six
600 gal. tanks.   AF

30, 1971, they were operated by the 380th and 509th Bomb Wings.

The B-1A

Only one new American bomber, the Rockwell B-1A, appeared during the seventies. It was intended to replace the B-52 for the SAC mission of penetrating enemy defenses to deliver nuclear or conventional weapons on strategic targets.

After several years of Air Force mission-requirement studies, a Request for Proposal was issued in November 1969. North American Rockwell won the B-1 contract award on June 5, 1970, for three prototypes, the Air Force program being on a "fly-before-buy" basis, the pre-1939 system of requiring satisfactory flight-test performance before launching production.

Powered by four General Electric F101 engines in the "30,000 lb. thrust class," the B-1A was two-thirds the size of the B-52 but carried triple the weapons load over a greater range at over twice the high-altitude speed. Low-level attacks, guided by terrain-following radar, could be made at "nearly" sonic speed (760 mph at sea level), and Mach 2 could be exceeded at high altitudes.

Survival in a surprise missile attack was a prime concern. The B-1A could therefore be dispersed to smaller air bases that could not easily accommodate B-52s and was expected to be able to take off from and clear a threatened base within four minutes.

Combining high speed with short takeoff required a swing-wing configuration enabling the wing to fold back, like the F-111, 67.5° during high-speed flight. Four crewmen sat in a self-contained capsule that could be detached for emergency escapes, and a pair of horizontal vanes near the nose were part of a Low-Altitude Ride Control system to reduce the effects of air turbulence.

Each of the three internal weapons bays could accommodate a rotary launcher for eight 2,247-pound AGM-69 missiles, which could be directed at targets within 100 miles of the aircraft. No guns were carried, but extensive ECM equipment was provided. Materials used in the airframe were 41.3 percent aluminum, 6.6 percent steel, and 21 percent titanium, the later percentage limited by cost considerations.

Accompanied by an extensive publicity campaign, the first B-1A rolled out of the Palmdale, California, factory October 26, 1974, and began its flight tests December 23, 1974. It was joined by a second plane on April 1, 1976, and a third June 14, 1976. By November 1977 the prototypes had made 144 flights, had attained Mach 2.1 (1,350 mph) at 50,000 feet, and been up over ten hours on a single flight. From a performance viewpoint, the B-1A

ROCKWELL B-1A
General Electric F-101, 30,000 lb.
DIMENSIONS: Span 137' (78' swept), Lg. 151'2", Ht. 33'7".
WEIGHT: Gross 389,800 lb.
PERFORMANCE: Classified.   MFR

ROCKWELL B-1A   MFR

seemed entirely successful and far more capable than the B-52.

Air Force leaders such as Chief of Staff General George Brown advocated the B-1 as necessary to the TRIAD concept, in which land-based and submarine-launched missiles are combined with manned bombers to be a deterrent against hostile attack or threats. Manned bombers offer a flexibility of response impossible for missiles, and the B-1 was seen as "the most efficient and effective manned penetrating weapons system ever conceived."

The chief obstacle to a production program was the high cost of the 244 aircraft desired by 1986, quoted at $22.9 billion in 1976 for the total program in "then-year" dollars, or more than $84 million per unit, including development and inflation costs. Questions of cost effectiveness arose, comparing this cost with that of the missiles required to destroy the same targets. The nation, which had just expended some $150 billion on the war in Vietnam—enough to pay for several B-1 programs—no longer seemed willing to accept the inflationary costs of a possibly redundant system.

On June 30, 1977, as President Carter faced the beginning of his first fiscal year, he canceled the B-1A production program as unnecessary and too expensive, allowing completion of the flight tests and the fourth prototype. Instead, the emphasis was shifted to cruise missiles like the AGM-109 Tomahawk, which in its air-launched form weighed about 2,650 pounds, was 18.2 feet long, and could carry a 1,000-pound nuclear warhead 1,500 miles. Eight could be carried inside a modified B-52, which could now attack targets without penetrating enemy defense areas itself.

The fourth B-1A, flown on February 14, 1979, was the only one with an integrated defensive avionic system. Performance of this new electronic countermeasures suite against simulations of hostile detection and missile systems could indicate the future of the manned bomber. Another approach to bomber survivability was the exploration of radar-absorbing materials for aircraft. This caused some excitement in August 1980, when Defense Secretary Harold Brown mentioned a "Stealth" strategic bomber project using such new technology.

In 1980 cruise missiles were the center of efforts to improve the manned bomber. After the Boeing AGM-86B won the Air Force air-launched cruise missile (ALCM) competition, plans were made to modify 173 B-52Gs to strategic missile launchers. Eight AGM-86Bs were to be carried on a rotary launcher in the internal weapons bay, and wing pylons could be mounted under the wings for another 12 missiles.

Rockwell International proposed a missile launcher version of the B-1, carrying 16 ALCMs internally and 14 externally. To reduce aircraft costs, this B-1 version would lose its supersonic capability. The variable-sweep wings would be replaced by fixed wings set at 25° sweep, and the aircraft structure could be simplified and lightened.

Since cost in 1980 dollars was reduced from $68.5 million to $43.3 million each (on an order for 100), and the aircraft could be also used for conventional bombing, it was hoped this B-1 design could find a place in the 1981 budget.

Without American bomber production, the seventies saw a shift in the strategic-force balance. At the end of 1969 the United States had about 3,950 strategic nuclear warheads for 1,710 ICBM and SLBM missiles and 549 SAC bombers. The U.S.S.R. was credited with 1,659 warheads for 1,514 missiles and bombers. By 1979 the United States had added 5,250 more strategic warheads, for a total of 9,200, while the U.S.S.R. added 3,590, for a total of 5,100 warheads. When delivery vehicles were counted, however, the U.S.S.R. had increased its force to over 2,500 vehicles, while the United States had kept the same number of missiles and actually decreased its bomber force to 330.

The most important changes on the U.S. side had been to replace the single-warhead Minuteman II by the Minuteman III, with three independently targetable (MIRV) warheads and improved accuracy, upgrade Minuteman silo protection, and provide the bomber force with better electronics and some 1,250 SRAMs to batter their way through enemy defenses. Submarine-launched missiles were also MIRVed. Whether these improvements would provide a deterrent position adequate for the remaining decades of the century remained a highly controversial question.

Chapter 27
Air Force Fighters, 1945-61

The end of World War II also ended the era of propeller-driven fighters. Development of jet propulsion had obsoleted most existing fighters, and the postwar period saw production of new jet types to re-equip the world's fighter units.

Invention of the atomic bomb, and strategic elements of the growing cold war between America and Russia tended to center Air Force attention on bombers rather than fighters, and not until the unexpected appearance of Soviet atomic weapons in 1949 did jet fighter production reach really large numbers. The terrible destructive capability of bombardment now lent a new urgency to development of defensive weapons. Only the ability to clear skies of enemy intruders seemed to offer any shield against annihilation.

Although the United States had no jets ready in time for combat during the big war, wartime development had begun projects from the XP-79 to the XP-86, and had gotten the P-80 Shooting Star into successful production. At the opening of the Korean War, Air Force fighters in actual service consisted almost entirely of types begun before the end of World War II.

The first of these wartime projects started in December 1942 as a tailless flying-wing interceptor designed by Northrop to be operated by a pilot lying prone in the cockpit. It was hoped that this prone position would reduce strain on the pilot during violent maneuvers and sudden pullouts, and present a minimum silhouette to enemy gunners. Three XP-79 prototypes designed for 2,000-pound thrust Aerojet rockets were ordered in January 1943, to be built under Northrop subcontract by Avion, Inc. Availability of jet engines led to a decision in March to utilize two Westinghouse 19-B axial-flow jets in the third ship, designated XP-79B.

The radical layout required tryouts in the form of towed gliders with fixed tricycle gear. One, the MX-324, was towed into the air by a P-38 on July 5, 1944, and became the first rocket-powered U.S. aircraft to fly. Aerojet was unable, however, to perfect a rocket motor suitable for the XP-79, so both prototypes were canceled.

This left only the XP-79B, which arrived at Muroc for testing in June 1945. Sitting low on the ground, it had four retractable wheels and twin vertical fins atop the jet exhaust. The welded magnesium flying wing had air bellows-operated split-flap wing-tip rudders outboard of elevons, as on the XP-56, and was armed with four .50-caliber guns. The wing itself was constructed of a heavy gauge to provide some protection for the fuel tanks and prevent a dangerous mix of the two rocket fuels originally planned. On its first test flight, delayed until September 12, 1945, the XP-79B crashed, test pilot Harry Crosby was killed, and the project ended.

Shooting Stars

The most successful jet fighter to come out of the war began when Lockheed was asked, on May 17, 1943, to build a single-seater around a De Havilland Goblin engine imported from England. By June 21, a letter contract was issued, and 23 engineers and 105 mechanics finished in 143 days the neat prototype that made its first flight on January 8, 1944. Although the engine developed only a 2,460-pound thrust instead of the 3,000-pound thrust expected, the Lockheed XP-80 did 502 mph and became the first American plane in that speed class.

General Electric had prepared a larger jet engine, now known as the J33 (originally I-40), and two more prototypes were ordered. Designated XP-80A and first flown June 1, 1944, they introduced the design followed on production models.

The first of 13 YP-80As flew on September 13, 1944, and as the fastest wartime AAF fighter, the Shooting Star won orders for 5,000 P-80A copies. One thousand were to be built at North American's

NORTHROP XP-79B
Westinghouse 19B, 1365 lbs. max. thrust
DIMENSIONS: Span 38′, Lg. 14′, Ht. 7′6″, Wing Area 278
 sq. ft.
WEIGHT: Empty 5840 lb., Gross 8670 lb. Fuel 300 gal.
PERFORMANCE: Speed—Top 547 mph at s. l., 508 mph at
 25,000′, Cruising 480 mph. Climb 25,000′/4.7 min.
 Range 993 miles, cruising on one engine.   AF

LOCKHEED XP-80A
General Electric J33, 4000 lbs.
DIMENSIONS: Span 39′, Lg. 34′6″, Ht. 11′4″, Wing Area
 238 sq. ft.
WEIGHT: Empty 7225 lb., Gross 9600 lb., Max. 13,750 lb.
 Fuel 485–815 gal.
PERFORMANCE: Speed—Top 553 mph at 5700′, Cruising
 410 mph, Landing 95 mph. Service Ceiling 48,500′,
 Climb 20,000′/4.6 min. Range 560 miles normal, 1200
 miles max.   MFR

LOCKHEED XP-80
De Havilland Goblin H-1b, 2460 lbs. actual thrust
DIMENSIONS: Span 37′, Lg. 32′10″, Ht. 10′3″, Wing Area
 240 sq. ft.
WEIGHT: Empty 6287 lb., Gross 8916 lb. Fuel 200–85 gal.
PERFORMANCE: Speed—Top 502 mph at 20,480′. Service
 Ceiling 41,000′, Absolute Ceiling 41,800′, Climb 3000′/
 1 min., 10,000′/3.7 min.   MFR

LOCKHEED P-80A
Allison J33-A-11, 4000 lbs.
DIMENSIONS: Span 39′11″, Lg. 34′6″, Ht. 11′4″, Wing Area
 238 sq. ft.
WEIGHT: Empty 7920 lb., Gross 11,700 lb., Max. 14,500
 lb. Fuel 470–800 gal.
PERFORMANCE: Speed—Top 558 mph at s. l., 508 mph at
 30,000′, Cruising 410 mph. Service Ceiling 45,000′,
 Climb 4580′/1 min. Range 540 miles normal, 1440
 miles max.   MFR

Dallas plant, the remainder by Lockheed, which began P-80A deliveries in April 1945. At last the United States had a fighter equal to the Messerschmitt Me 262, but the Shooting Star didn't see action. With the war won, Lockheed's contracts were reduced to 1,217 and the Dallas order dropped, leaving the P-80A the only Air Force single-seater in production after V-J Day.

Powered by a 4,000-pound-thrust Allison J33-A-11[1] behind the pilot, with intakes ahead of the wing roots and jet exhaust in the tail, the P-80A sat low on tricycle gear. There was a clear plastic canopy of common practice, six .50-caliber guns with 1,800 rounds in the nose, a 165-gallon drop tank below each wing tip, and a fuselage dive brake.

Wanting a photo-recon jet with the P-80's speed, the Air Force had, on September 23, 1944, ordered the second YP-80A completed as the XF-14, with three cameras replacing the guns in a longer nose. First flown October 15, 1944, the aircraft was destroyed as a result of a collision December 6, but the concept was proven and an interchangeable camera nose was substituted on production FP-80As (later RF-80As) in 1946.

Lockheed delivered 825 P-80A and 152 FP-80A jets, followed, after March 1947, by 240 P-80Bs with an ejector seat for the pilot, underwing rocket launchers, new M-3 .50-caliber guns (firing 1,200 rpm instead of the 800 rpm of the wartime M-2) and a water-alcohol injection system giving the engine bursts of emergency power. Most of the P-80As on hand were retroactively brought up to B standards, using several models of the J33 engine (A-9B, -11B, -17A, or -21).

On March 1, 1948, the first P-80C was flown, with 670 delivered between October 1948 and June 1950. Since the F (fighter) designation replaced the old P (pursuit) designation in June 1948, these planes became known as F-80Cs. They had an Allison J33-A-23 rated at 4,600-pound thrust. Besides the two 165-gallon drop tanks (often increased to 260 in Korea), wing racks could handle ten rockets or two 1,000-pound bombs.

On June 27, 1950, the F-80C entered combat in Korea, serving the 8th, 35th, and 49th Fighter-Bomber groups. In this war, the F-80Cs flew 98,515 sorties, with 143 losses to enemy action (mostly antiaircraft), compared with 62,607 sorties and 194 losses for the F-51 Mustangs. On November 8, 1950, an F-80C destroyed a MiG-15 in air history's first all-jet air battle. Six MiGs and 31 prop aircraft were downed in air-to-air combat during the war, resulting in a loss of 14 F-80s.

The most widely used Shooting Star version was the two-place T-33 trainer, originally seen in 1948

[1] Allison produced the General Electric-designed J33 engine after 1945.

LOCKHEED P-80B
Allison J33-A-21, 4500 lbs. WE
DIMENSIONS: As P-80A
WEIGHT: Empty 8176 lb., Gross 11,975 lb., Max. 16,000 lb. Fuel 425–755 gal.
PERFORMANCE: Speed—Top 577 mph at 6000', 497 mph at 35,000', Cruising 386 mph, Landing 122 mph. Service Ceiling 36,800', Climb 6475'/1 min. Range 1210 miles.   MFR

LOCKHEED P-80C
Allison J33-A-23, 4600 lbs., 5400 lbs. WE
DIMENSIONS: As P-80A
WEIGHT: Empty 8240 lb., Gross 15,336 lb., Max. 16,856 lb. Fuel 425–755 gal.
PERFORMANCE: (12,330 lbs., combat weight) Speed—Top 580 mph at 7000', Cruising 439 mph, Landing 122 mph. Service Ceiling 42,750', Climb 6870'/1 min. Range 1380 miles.   AF

as the TF-80C. Lockheed built 5,871 for the USAF, the Navy, and allied nations by August 1959. The Navy began testing three P-80As on June 29, 1945, and acquired 50 F-80C and 699 T-33 jets for training as the TO-1 and TO-2 (later TV-1 and TV-2). Other modifications included the XP-80R, a P-80A with modified wings, canopy, and J33-A-23 engine, which did 624 mph in June 1947, and another P-80A tested in 1947, with an automatic rocket launcher protruding from the nose. Numerous F-80s became drones for missile targets (QF-80), and the DT-33A was a drone director, while the RT-33A was a recon version, and the AT-33A was a light-attack version.

Twin-engine Types

Their short range was the most obvious limitation

of early jet types, and three twin-engine fighters with longer endurance were begun early in 1944 to meet this problem. The first was the XP-81 single-seater proposed in January by Consolidated's Vultee division, a combination of jet propulsion for high speeds with propeller-driven power for cruising. Two prototypes ordered February 11 were powered by a J33-GE-5 installed behind the pilot, while in the nose the first turboprop engine used in America, a General Electric XT-31 (formerly TG-100), turned a four-bladed propeller.

When first flown on February 11, 1945, a Packard V-1650 Merlin was installed in the XP-81's nose, but on December 21, 1945, flight tests with the XT-

CONSOLIDATED-VULTEE XP-81
General Electric XT-31-GE-1, 2300 hp; J33-GE-5, 3750 lbs.
DIMENSIONS: Span 50′6″, Lg. 44′10″, Ht. 14′, Wing Area 425 sq. ft.
WEIGHT: Empty 12,755 lb., Gross 19,500 lb., Max. 24,650 lb. Fuel 811–1511 gal.
PERFORMANCE: Speed—Top 507 mph at 20,000′. Service Ceiling 35,500′, Climb 30,000′/7 min. Range 2500 miles.   MFR

NORTH AMERICAN XP-82
Packard V-1650-23, -25, 1380 hp takeoff, 1830 hp at 18,-500′
DIMENSIONS: Span 51′3″, Lg. 39′, Ht. 13′6″, Wing Area 408 sq. ft.
WEIGHT: Empty 13,402 lb., Gross 19,100 lb., Max. 22,000 lb. Fuel 600–1045 gal.
PERFORMANCE: Speed—Top 468 mph at 22,800′, Landing 130 mph. Service Ceiling 40,000′, Climb 4900′/1 min., 25,000′/6.4 min. Range 1390 miles normal, 2600 miles max.   MFR

31 began. Six .50-caliber guns with 1,800 rounds were mounted in the low, squared-off wing, while 3,200 pounds of bombs or drop tanks could be carried. Since the XP-81 was a pioneer effort in the turboprop field, mechanical difficulties plagued its power plant, and plans to build 13 YP-81 service test examples were dropped.

The last propeller-driven fighter purchased by the Air Force was the North American XP-82, begun in January 1944 to provide a twin-engine long-range fighter with accommodations for a relief pilot to aid navigation. Essentially, two P-51H fuselages joined together on a single wing and stabilizer, the XP-82 Twin Mustang had the pilot on the left side and the co-pilot on the other, with a retractable main wheel underneath each fuselage and twin tailwheels—the last on Air Force aircraft, since later ships all have nosewheels. Armament included six .50-caliber fixed guns with 400 rpg in the wing center section. Wing racks handled four drop tanks, up to 6,000 pounds of bombs or 25 rockets, or a center pod containing eight more guns.

Powered by Packard Merlins with opposite-rotating propellers, the XP-82 (NA-120) was first flown July 6, 1945.[2] A second flew in August, and one XP-82A with Allison V-1710-119s was accepted in October. Five hundred P-82Bs ordered in June 1944 were cut back to 20 after V-J Day. First flown October 19, 1945, and delivered by March 1946, they were similar to the XP-82, except for two examples equipped as night fighters. The P-82C was flown March 27, 1946, with SCR-720 radar, and the P-82D was flown two days later with an APS-4 radar in a pod under the center section. One P-82B was flown 5,000 miles nonstop from Hawaii to New York City on February 28, 1947, setting a distance record for fighters, and another began tests with a camera pod for reconnaissance on November 15, 1948.

On October 10, 1946, a contract for 250 more Twin Mustangs with Allison V-1710-143 and -145 engines was approved. The first flew February 17, 1947, but engine difficulties soon showed that switching from the Merlins had been a mistake. By the year's end, only four had been accepted as F-82As, while empty airframes awaited satisfactory power plants. Allison did get engine production under way, so that from January to July 1948, 96 F-82Es were accepted for the only USAF escort-fighter group. As engines and radar became available for all-weather versions, an F-82F flew March 11, 1948, with APG-28 radar. The USAF accepted 91 F-82Fs, 45 F-82Gs with older SCR-720 radar, and 14 F-82Hs winterized for Alaskan duty. Twin Mustang production ended in March 1949 as the type replaced the P-61.

[2] This is the date according to the Air Force, but company reports say June 16.

NORTH AMERICAN P-82B   OLMSTEAD

NORTH AMERICAN P-82D   MFR

NORTH AMERICAN F-82E
Allison V-1710-143, -145, 1600 hp
DIMENSIONS: Span 51'3", Lg. 39'1", Ht. 13'10", Wing Area
    408 sq. ft.
WEIGHT: Empty 14,914 lb., Gross 24,813 lb., Max. 24,864
    lb. Fuel 576–1176 gal.
PERFORMANCE: (20,741 lbs., combat weight) Speed—Top
    465 mph at 21,000', Cruising 304 mph, Landing 124
    mph. Service Ceiling 40,000', Climb 4020'/1 min.
    Range 2504 miles normal, 2708 miles ferry.   MFR

NORTH AMERICAN F-82F
Allison V-1710-143, -145, 1600 hp, 1700 hp WE at 21,200'
DIMENSIONS: Span 51'7", Lg. 42'2", Ht. 13'10", Wing Area
    418 sq. ft.
WEIGHT: Empty 16,309 lb., Gross 26,208 lb. Fuel 576–
    1196 gal.
PERFORMANCE: (22,116 lbs., combat weight) Speed—Top
    460 mph at 21,000', Cruising 288 mph, Landing 128
    mph. Service Ceiling 38,500', Climb 3690'/1 min.
    Range 2200 miles, 2400 miles ferry.   AF

NORTH AMERICAN F-82G
Allison V-1710-143, -145, 1600 hp
DIMENSIONS: Span 51'7", Lg. 42'5", Ht. 13'10", Wing Area
    418 sq. ft.
WEIGHT: Empty 15,997 lb., Gross 25,891 lb. Fuel 576–
    1196 gal.
PERFORMANCE: (21,810 lbs., combat weight) Speed—Top
    461 mph at 21,000', Cruising 286 mph, Landing 127
    mph. Service Ceiling 38,900', Climb 3770'/1 min.
    Range 2240 miles, 2495 miles ferry.   OLMSTEAD

SAC's 27th Fighter-Escort Group used the F-82E until August 1950. Beginning in September 1948, the all-weather versions went to the 52nd Fighter Group at Mitchel Field to protect the northeastern states, the 325th FG at McChord AFB to protect the northwest, and the 347th FG in Japan. The latter group's F-82Gs became the first American planes to down North Korean aircraft on June 27, 1950. These Twin Mustangs flew 1,868 sorties in the Korean War, including fighter-patrol, close-support, and night-intrusion missions. The last USAAF squadron to use the type was the 449th, whose P-82Hs operated in Alaska until 1952.

When Bell offered its Model 40 in March 1943, it was an interceptor, but the design was redone in April as a long-range escort fighter, and a letter contract for XP-83 prototypes issued March 29, 1944, was approved July 31. An enlarged Airacomet with a J33-GE-5 and bubble canopy, the XP-83 had large fuselage fuel tanks, supplemented by two 150-gallon drop tanks or two 1,000-pound bombs. Six .50-caliber guns with 1,800 rounds armed the first XP-83, flown February 27, 1945, but on October 19 the second flew with six .60-caliber T17E3 guns. The XP-83 seems to have lacked the speed necessary to survive the tight postwar budgets.

BELL XP-83
General Electric J33-GE-5, 3750 lbs.
DIMENSIONS: Span 53', Lg. 44'10", Ht. 15'4", Wing Area 431 sq. ft.
WEIGHT: Empty 14,105 lb., Gross 24,090 lb., Max. 27,500 lb. Fuel 1450–750 gal.
PERFORMANCE: (At 21,950 lbs.) Speed—Top 522 mph at 15,660', Cruising 441 mph. Service Ceiling 42,300', Climb 3750'/1 min., 30,000'/11.9 min. Range 1750 miles/1450 gal.   MFR

Thunderjet

The first new fighter of the postwar period was Republic's XP-84, begun in November 1944 to obtain the best speed and range obtainable from jet propulsion. General Electric's J35 axial-flow engine permitted a long, narrow fuselage whose streamlining contributed to the expected 600-mph speed and 1,300-mile range.

First flown on February 28, 1946, at Muroc (now Edwards AFB), the midwing single-seater had the tricycle landing gear customary on jet aircraft. Fuel was carried within the fuselage, wings, and disposable wing-tip tanks. The second of three XP-84 pro-

REPUBLIC XP-84
General Electric J35-GE-7, 3750 lbs.
DIMENSIONS: Span 36'5", Lg. 37'2", Wing Area 260 sq. ft.
WEIGHT: Empty 9080 lb., Gross 13,400 lb., Max. 16,200 lb.
PERFORMANCE: Speed—Top 592 mph at s. l., Cruising 425 mph. Climb 35,000'/13 min. Range 1300 miles normal.   AF

REPUBLIC YP-84A   MFR

REPUBLIC F-84B
Allison J35-A-15, 3750 lbs.
DIMENSIONS: Span 36'5", Lg. 37'7", Ht. 12'8", Wing Area 260 sq. ft.
WEIGHT: Empty 9538 lb., Gross 16,475 lb., Max. 19,689 lb. Fuel 416–786 gal.
PERFORMANCE: (13,465 lbs., combat weight) Speed—Top 587 mph at 4000', Cruising 436 mph, Landing 132 mph. Service Ceiling 40,750', Climb 4210'/1 min. Range 1282 miles.   PMB

totypes set a U.S. speed record of 611 mph in September 1946, but this could not be matched under service conditions.

One hundred aircraft ordered January 15, 1946, began with 15 YP-84As delivered by April 1947. These planes were similar to the prototypes, but the J35-A-15 engine was now made by Allison. Four .50-caliber M-2 guns were mounted above the nose air intake and two more were in the wing roots. Successful tests resulted in the addition of another 486 planes to the contract by October 1947, and the 14th Fighter Group was chosen to be the first to use the P-84.

Production Thunderjets began appearing in June

REPUBLIC F-84C
Allison J35-A-13, 3750 lbs.
DIMENSIONS: As F-84B
WEIGHT: Empty 9662 lb., Gross 16,584 lb., Max. 19,798 lb. Fuel 416–786 gal.
PERFORMANCE: (13,574 lbs., combat weight) Speed—Top 587 mph at 4000', Cruising 436 mph, Landing 132 mph. Service Ceiling 40,600', Climb 4180'/1 min. Range 1274 miles. ARNOLD

REPUBLIC F-84D
Allison J35-A-13, 3750 lbs.
DIMENSIONS: As F-84B
WEIGHT: Empty 9860 lb., Gross 16,862 lb., Max. 20,076 lb. Fuel 416–786 gal.
PERFORMANCE: (13,894 lbs., combat weight) Speed—Top 587 mph at 4000', Cruising 441 mph, Landing 133 mph. Service Ceiling 39,300', Climb 4060'/1 min. Range 1198 miles. ARNOLD

1947 and standardized the faster-firing M-3 guns, with 300 rpg, underwing rocket racks, and ejector seat used on service types. The first 226 were F-84Bs with J35-A-15s, followed after April 1948 by 191 F-84Cs, and in November by 154 F-84Ds. (By this time P-84 became F-84.) The C and D were similar to the Bs in appearance but used J35-A-13s which were found more serviceable than the A-15 engine. Only internal mechanical changes distinguished the D from the C.

The F-84E, ordered December 29, 1948, and flown May 18, 1949, improved performance with a 4,900-pound-thrust J35-A-17 and increased fuel capacity in a longer fuselage. Two 230-gallon drop tanks could be carried on inboard pylons under the wings, with two more on the wing tip to extend range. For ground-attack missions two 1,000-pound bombs or two 11.75-inch rockets could replace the inner drop tanks. A Sperry APG-30 radar-ranging gunsight was standard. Republic delivered 843 F-84Es by June 1951, the last (after F-84E-25) with a new tailpipe ejector that increased top speed to 619 mph at sea level and 543 mph at 35,000 feet.

REPUBLIC F-84E
Allison J35-A-17, 4900 lbs.
DIMENSIONS: Span 36'5", Lg. 38'6", Ht. 12'10", Wing Area 260 sq. ft.
WEIGHT: Empty 10,205 lb., Max. 22,463 lb. Fuel 452–1372 gal.
PERFORMANCE: (14,724 lbs., combat weight) Speed—Top 613 mph at s. l., Cruising 481 mph, Landing 142 mph. Service Ceiling 43,220', Climb 6061'/1 min. Range 1485 miles/two 230 gal. drop tanks, 1950 miles max. AF

REPUBLIC F-84G
Allison J35-A-29, 5600 lbs.
DIMENSIONS: Span 36'5", Lg. 38'1", Ht. 12'7", Wing Area 260 sq. ft.
WEIGHT: Empty 11,095 lb., Gross 18,645 lb., Max. 23,525 lb. Fuel 1362 gal. max.
PERFORMANCE: Speed—Top 622 mph at s. l., Cruising 483 mph, Landing 142 mph. Service Ceiling 40,500', Absolute Ceiling 42,100', Climb 35,000'/9.4 min. with tanks (7.9 min. without tanks). Range 2000 miles at 21,700 lbs. BESECKER

REPUBLIC YF-84F (YF-96A)
Allison XJ35-A-25, 5200 lbs.
DIMENSIONS: Span 33'7", Lg. 43'1", Ht. 15'2", Wing Area 325 sq. ft.
WEIGHT: Empty 12,150 lb., Max. 23,230 lb. Fuel 1505 gal. max.
PERFORMANCE: Speed—Top 693 mph at s. l., Cruising 514 mph, Landing 140 mph. Service Ceiling 38,300', Climb 35,000'/14.8 min. Range 1716 miles. MFR

The F-84E's increased power brought the Thunderjet close to the airframe's speed limit (Mach 82), and Republic began an YF-84F swept-wing version in November 1949. Known for a while as YF-96A, it made its first flight on June 3, 1950, with a 5,200-pound-thrust J35-A-25 and 40° sweep on wings and tail. Alarm over the Korean War led in July to a large order for production models powered by 7,200-pound-thrust Wright J65s, an American-built version of the British Sapphire engine. On September 8 the prototype regained the YF-84F designation.

Production of the F-84F was delayed by complexities of the new wing structure and the engine, and an interim type, the F-84G, appeared in June 1951 with the straight wing, a 5,600-pound-thrust J35-A-29, and reinforced canopy. Essentially an F-84E fitted for long-range flying, the F-84G had an automatic pilot and a receptacle on the left wing for air refueling by means of a flying boom of a Boeing KC-97 or KB-29 tanker instead of the probe-drogue technique tested earlier on modified F-84Es. The value of air refueling was demonstrated in 1952 by nonstop deployment of the 31st Fighter-Escort Wing from Turner AFB, located in Albany, Georgia, to Japan. Jet squadrons could now fly to any point in the world, refueling from flying tankers at prearranged rendezvous. The F-84G was also the first USAF jet fighter to handle a tactical atomic weapon, released by a low-altitude bombing system (LABS). The 20th Fighter-Bomber Group received such F-84Gs in November 1951. In August 1953 the LABS-equipped 20th Fighter-Bomber Wing flew 4,485 miles to Britain, the longest nonstop mass movement in history.

The first Thunderjets to enter combat belonged to the 27th Fighter-Escort Wing, whose F-82Es were replaced by F-84Es in the summer of 1950. The wing began its Korean missions on December 6, scoring its first MiG kill on January 21, 1951. The 49th, 58th, 116th, and 474th wings also used Thunderjets when they replaced F-80s in the fighter-bomber role. As an air-to-air fighter, the F-84 downed nine enemy aircraft for a loss of 18; it was too slow to do well against swept-wing MiGs. Most of the 86,400 F-84E and F-84G sorties were used to deliver 55,987 tons of bombs, resulting in the loss of 122 planes to antiaircraft fire.

Due to delays in getting the swept-wing F-84F into production, deliveries of the F-84G continued until July 27, 1953, the last day of the Korean War. Of 3,025 F-84Gs built, 2,236 went overseas, preceded by 100 F-84Es, to Allied nations joined in the Mutual Defense Assistance Program (MDAP, later MAP). Straight-wing Thunderjets were being used in 1953 by 14 USAF wings (about 75 a/c each) and 21 NATO wings. Belgium had one F-84E and two F-84G wings; Denmark, Norway, and the Netherlands each had two F-84G wings; France had four; Italy and Greece each had three; Turkey had four; and Portugal had two squadrons. Three more wings were formed on Taiwan, while 169 F-84Gs sent to Yugoslavia, 75 to Iran, and 30 to Thailand, were the first jet fighters owned by these countries.

The first aircraft completed on the swept-wing program was a pre-production YF-84F flown February 14, 1951, with an imported Sapphire engine. The fuselage was deepened for the new power plant, but the sliding canopy and belly speed brake of previous models were retained. A second version with the Sapphire engine, in December 1951, had wing-root intakes and a solid cover on the nose, which resulted in thrust losses but left room for cameras in the later reconnaissance version. A definitive production contract was made April 9, 1951.

Nose intakes were retained on production F-84F Thunderstreaks, which used six M-3 guns and 1,800 rounds, 6,000 pounds of bombs, two perforated fuselage speed brakes, and the J65-W-3. The F-84F-25 introduced the all-movable horizontal tail, and the F-84F-50 introduced the J65-W-7 in March 1955. Although the first F-84F-1-RE was flown November 22, 1952, deliveries mounted slowly, and not until January 1954 did the 506th Fighter Wing get its aircraft. By August 1957, 2,711 Thunderstreaks were built, including 599 F-84F-GKs from the Kansas City plant managed by General Motors. These swept-wing fighters were so different from the straight-wing versions that it's regrettable that the F-96 designation was not used. The cockpit canopy now swung upwards; leading-edge slats, an air-refueling receptacle in the port wing, and an automatic pilot were provided. A low-altitude bombing system (LABS) was provided for aiming a nuclear bomb, the F-84F racing in only 50 feet over the ground to the target, making a half loop up, releasing the bomb, and escaping with a turn. Less impressive was the nickname "Hog," given the F-84F for its excessively long takeoff runs.

The F-84Fs went to six SAC escort-fighter wings and six TAC fighter-bomber wings, but by July 1957 all the SAC wings were also transferred to TAC. After being replaced in front-line service by F-100s, the F-84F was given to Air National Guard squadrons, but four F-84F Tactical Fighter wings were reactivated in 1961 and served until they were replaced by F-4Cs by July 1964.

NATO received 1,301 F-84F fighter-bombers to replace the F-84Gs, with Belgium, Greece, and Turkey getting two wings each, Italy three, and France five *escadres* (of 50 a/c each). The French Thunderstreaks were the only ones to enter combat, during the Suez Crisis. *Escadres* based in Cyprus and Israel successfully attacked the Egyptian Air

REPUBLIC F-84F
Wright J65-W-3, 7200 lbs. (or W-7, 7800 lbs.)
DIMENSIONS: Span 33'7", Lg. 43'4", Ht. 14'4½", Wing Area
325 sq. ft.
WEIGHT: Empty 13,645 lb., Gross 25,226 lb., Ferry 27,000
lb., Combat 18,700 lb. Fuel 1479–758 gal.
PERFORMANCE: Speed—Top 685 mph at s. l., 608 (612)
mph at 35,000', Cruising 539 mph, Stalling 151 mph.
Service Ceiling 36,150' (37,500'), Combat Ceiling 42,-
250' (44,850'), Combat Radius 860 (856) miles, 2314
(2343) miles ferry range.   MFR

REPUBLIC RF-84F
Wright J65-W-7, 7800 lbs.
DIMENSIONS: Span 33'7", Lg. 47'6", Ht. 15', Wing Area
325 sq. ft.
WEIGHT: Empty 14,014 lb., Gross 25,390 lb., Combat
20,091 lb. Fuel 1475 gal.
PERFORMANCE: Speed—Top 629 mph at 5000', 582 mph
at 35,000', Cruising 542 mph, Stalling 166 mph. Service
Ceiling 36,300', Climb 5820'/1 min., 35,000'/11.6 min.
Range 840 miles, 1800 miles ferry.   MFR

Force on the ground on November 1, 1956. Republic Thunderjets served NATO until Belgium retired the last of its 197 F-84Fs in May 1972.

The Thunderstreak was the first combat type to go to the revived German Air Force, which, beginning in November 1956, received 450 F-84Fs and 108 of the RF-84F Thunderflash reconnaissance versions. The RF-84F had six cameras in an elongated nose, four .50-caliber wing guns, wing-root inlets, dual fences on each wing, and two 450-gallon drop tanks.

Ordered June 12, 1951, a YRF-84F prototype completed in February 1952 had the old sliding canopy, but standard hinged covers were used on production RF-84Fs. The first RF-84F flew September ber 9, 1953, but squadron service was delayed until March 1954, and further production was halted until November 1955. Four USAF reconnaissance wings used the RF-84F. Of 715 Thunderflashes built by Republic by January 1958, 327 were exported for the Mutual Security Program. Squadrons were used by Belgium, Denmark, France, Germany, Greece, Italy, the Netherlands, Norway, Turkey, and Nationalist China.

The FICON (FIghter-CONveyor) project was an effort to extend the range of fighter and reconnaissance jets by teaming F-84s with the giant B-36s. The 1952 tests of an F-84E and the YF-84F with the GRB-36F have already been mentioned (see Chapter 26). These resulted in the completion of

25 RF-84F-17s, redesignated RF-84K, with a retractable hook ahead of the cockpit and downturned horizontal tail fins. Equipping the 91st Strategic Reconnaissance Squadron in 1955, they operated with SAC's GRB-36s until May 1957.

Designed to explore the possibilities of a turbo-prop strike fighter, the XF-84H had an Allison XT-40-A-1 with 5,332 hp for its three-bladed propeller, plus added jet thrust, an anti-torque fin behind the cockpit, and a high T-tail. Design armament included a single .60-caliber T-45 gun with 1,200 rounds and 4,000 pounds of bombs.

REPUBLIC RF-84K   MFR

REPUBLIC XF-84H
Allison XT40-A-1, 5332 hp takeoff, and 1296 lbs.
DIMENSIONS: Span 33'6", Lg. 55'4", Ht. 15'4", Wing Area 325 sq. ft.
WEIGHT: Empty 17,389 lb., Gross 29,700 lb., Combat 23,000 lb. Fuel 1700 gal.
PERFORMANCE: Speed—Top 670 mph at 10,000', 639 mph at 30,000', Cruising 456 mph, Stalling 165 mph. Service Ceiling 25,250', Combat Ceiling 39,800', Climb 5230'/1 min., 35,000'/12 min. Combat Radius 1027 miles, 2356 miles ferry range.   AF

REPUBLIC YF-84J   MFR

The mockup inspection was held in May 1952 and a contract for two prototypes was approved December 18, 1952. Only eight flights with the first prototype and four flights with the second were made by company test pilots from July 22, 1955, to October 9, 1956, all but one flight ending in emergency landings. The project was a failure, and this plane was never flown by an Air Force pilot. One of the noisiest aircraft ever heard, it never flew more than 520 mph of the 670-mph design speed. Originally the Navy had been interested in the project, but development of steam catapults, angled deck, and air refueling made propeller-driven substitutes for jets unnecessary. As the Navy lost interest and mechanical difficulties persisted, the project was abandoned.

Two F-84F-25s were completed with the 8,920-pound General Electric YJ73-GE-7 in a deeper fuselage and designated YF-84J. First flown May 7, 1954, the type wasn't accepted for production. The YF-84J reached Mach 1.09, but the Air Force rejected it, based on the expense involved in changing engines on the production line and canceled the second example in June and the whole F-84J program on August 31.

Sabre Jets

Shortly after Hitler's defeat, captured German scientific data indicating the advantages of swept-back wings arrived in the United States. At that time aircraft speeds were becoming limited less by power than by compressibility effects; as sonic speeds were approached, shock waves built up over airframe projections caused buffeting and other phenomena. Sweeping wing and tail surfaces back towards their tips delays the onset of compressibility troubles and permits higher speeds.

The first American aircraft to take advantage of this knowledge was North American's NA-140, ordered as the XP-86 on May 18, 1945. Similar to the Navy's XFJ-1, this single-seater's mockup had been approved in June with conventional straight wings, but on November 1 the Air Force accepted a proposal to sweep back wings and tail 35°. First flown on October 1, 1947, at Muroc, California (now Edwards AFB), the low-wing XP-86 had a 3,750-pound-thrust Chevrolet-built J35-C-3, nose air scoop, fuselage dive brakes, and leading-edge slots to reduce the swept wing's stalling point.

Thirty-three production aircraft had been ordered on December 20, 1946, designated P-86A (F-86A-1 Sabre after June 1948), and 188 P-86Bs (F-86A-5s) were later added. After the first F-86A-1 flew on May 20, 1948, 333 more Sabres were purchased in June. Power plants comprised the General Electric J47-GE-1, GE-3, and GE-7 until sufficient GE-13s were available. The 5,200-pound thrust enabled the

NORTH AMERICAN XP-86
General Electric J35-C-3 or J35-A-5, 4000 lbs.
DIMENSIONS: Span 37′1″, Lg. 37′6″, Ht. 14′9″, Wing Area 288 sq. ft.
WEIGHT: Empty 9730 lb., Gross 13,790 lb., Max. 16,438 lb. Fuel 435–848 gal.
PERFORMANCE: Speed—Top 618 mph at 14,000′, 599 mph at s. l., 575 mph at 35,000′. Service Ceiling 41,300′, Climb 4000′/1 min., 30,000′/12.1 min.   MFR

NORTH AMERICAN F-86A-5
General Electric J47-GE-13, 5200 lbs.
DIMENSIONS: Span 37′1″, Lg. 37′6″, Ht. 14′9″, Wing Area 288 sq. ft.
WEIGHT: Empty 10,093 lb., Gross 15,876 lb., Combat 13,791 lb. Fuel 435–675 gal.
PERFORMANCE: Speed—Top 679 mph at s. l., 601 mph at 35,000′, Cruising 533 mph, Stalling 121 mph. Service Ceiling 48,000′, Climb 7470′/1 min., 40,000′/10.4 min. Combat Radius 330 miles, 1052 miles ferry range. MFR

third F-86A-1 to set a world's speed record of 670.98 mph on September 1, 1948. Six .50-caliber M-3s with 267 rpg at the sides of the nose intake were aimed by using range-finding radar in the intake's upper lip. External racks handled two 120-gallon drop tanks, 1,000-pound bombs, or up to sixteen 5-inch rockets.

The first swept-wing fighters were extensively tested before replacing the F-80s of the First Fighter Group at March AFB, which received 83 F-86As from February to May 1949. Next came the 4th Fighter Group at Langley AFB and the 81st at Kirtland AFB. When the swept-wing MiG-15 appeared over Korea on November 1, 1950, the 4th FG was ordered to make ready to move to Korea. The 81st Fighter Group became the first USAF unit

stationed in Britain since 1945 when it arrived to support NATO in August 1951.

Production of 554 F-86As ended in December 1950, and on December 17 the Sabres flew their first Korean combat mission and won their first victory. When MiGs had operated against straight-wing Americans, they were fairly successful, downing 42 F-51s, -80s, and -84s for a loss of 15 MiGs—as well as 23 B-26 and B-29 bombers—against 16 to bomber gunners. Although the F-86 was inferior to the lighter Soviet type in climb and ceiling, it proved superior in air-to-air combat. In 87,177 sorties, Sabres were credited with downing 792 MiGs and 13 older aircraft, losing 78 F-86s to the MiGs, 19 to ground fire and 127 to unknown, operational, or nonoperational causes. Much of this success was due to the superior experience and skill of American pilots, as well as to the improvements made on the F-86F. The story of how the Sabres defeated the MiG-15 and thus won the air war in Korea has been discussed elsewhere.[3]

Work on improved versions proceeded. The F-86C became the YF-93 penetration fighter (described in a later section), while the F-86D designation was given the night-fighter project known as F-95 until July 24, 1950. This aircraft—with its radar, air-to-air rockets, and afterburner—is so different in operation from day-fighting Sabres that one regrets that the more distinctive F-95 designation was abandoned. For convenience sake, this night-fighter Sabre is considered in the next section on all-weather fighters.

The next Sabre version in production was the F-86E, which introduced the power-operated movable horizontal tail surface but was otherwise identical to late F-86As with J47-GE-13s. Between February 1951 and April 1952 the USAF accepted 336 F-86Es plus 60 F-86E-6s from Canadair by July.

NORTH AMERICAN F-86E
General Electric J47-GE-13, 5200 lbs.
DIMENSIONS: As F-86A
WEIGHT: Empty 10,555 lb., Gross 16,346 lb., Combat 14,255 lb. Fuel 435–675 gal.
PERFORMANCE: Speed—Top 679 mph at s. l., 601 mph at 35,000′, Cruising 537 mph, Stalling 123 mph. Service Ceiling 47,200′, Climb 7250′/1 min., 30,000′/6.3 min. Combat Radius 321 miles, 1022 miles ferry range. AF

[3] See Ray Wagner, *North American Sabre* (Garden City, N.Y.: Doubleday, 1963).

NORTH AMERICAN F-86F-5
General Electric J47-GE-27, 5910 lbs.
DIMENSIONS: As F-86A
WEIGHT: Empty 10,815 lb., Gross 17,772 lb., Combat
14,857 lb. Fuel 435–835 gal.
PERFORMANCE: Speed—Top 688 mph at s. l., 604 mph at
35,000', Cruising 513 mph, Stalling 128 mph. Service
Ceiling 48,000', Climb 9300'/1 min. Combat Radius
463 miles, 1317 miles ferry range. MFR

NORTH AMERICAN F-86F-30
General Electric J47-GE-27, 5910 lbs.
DIMENSIONS: Span 37'1", Lg. 37'6", Ht. 14'9", Wing Area
302 sq. ft.
WEIGHT: Empty 10,890 lb., Gross 17,921 lb., Max. 20,357
lb., Combat 13,076 lb. Fuel 437–1077 gal.
PERFORMANCE: Speed—Top 695 mph at s. l., 608 mph at
35,000', Cruising 486 mph, Stalling 144 mph. Service
Ceiling 48,000', Climb 9300'/1 min. Combat Radius
458 miles, 1615 miles ferry range. AF

NORTH AMERICAN F-86F-40
General Electric J47-GE-27
DIMENSIONS: Span 39'1", Lg. 37'7", Ht. 14'9", Wing Area
313 sq. ft.
WEIGHT: Empty 11,125 lb., Gross 18,152 lb., Max. 20,611
lb., Combat 15,352 lb. Fuel 437–837 gal.
PERFORMANCE: Speed—Top 678 mph at s. l., 599 mph at
35,000', Cruising 529 mph, Stalling 124 mph. Service
Ceiling 47,000', Climb 30,000'/5.2 min. Combat Radius
463 miles, 1525 miles ferry range. MFR

A 5,910-pound-thrust J47-GE-27 was used by the
F-86F, first flown March 19, 1952. The first 135
planes (F-86F-1 to F-86F-15) had two drop tanks,
but in October the F-86F-30 introduced fittings for
four drop tanks, or two tanks and two 1,000-pound
bombs. The first version with adequate range for
bombing, the F-86F-30 also was the first to replace
the slatted wing with an extended leading edge,
thereby improving speed and maneuverability.

Previous models were built in Los Angeles, but
North American had leased a Columbus, Ohio,
plant in September 1950 and began delivery of 100
F-86F-20s (2 tanks) and 600 F-86F-25s (4 tanks) in
May 1952. They were followed by the Sabre's Navy
version, the FJ-2 Fury. In Los Angeles 859 F-86F-
30s were followed, from January to June 1954, by
264 F-86F-35s, the first models fitted to carry a
1,200-pound tactical nuclear bomb under the port
wing, released by a low altitude bombing system.

By June 1954 the USAF had 14 F-86F wings in
service, including the four (1st, 8th, 18th, and 51st)
of Korean combat experience. The top aces of that
war included Captain Joseph McConnell, Jr., with
16 victories; Major James Jabara (15); Captain Man-
uel J. Fernandez (14.5); and Major George A. Davis,
Jr. (14). Wartime modifications included a few RF-
86A and RF-86F camera planes and ten F-86F-2s
armed with four 20-mm T-60 guns. Two F-86Fs
were completed in December 1953 and August
1954 as two-place TF-86F trainers.

The first Sabre actually designed as a fighter-
bomber was the F-86H, ordered March 16, 1951,
which used a larger intake and fuel capacity for a
J73 engine. Its mockup was inspected in July 1951,
and the first of two F-86Hs built at Los Angeles
flew May 9, 1953. The Columbus, Ohio, plant flew

its first F-86F-1 on September 4 and delivered 113
F-86H-1s, armed with six .50-caliber guns with 300
rpg, a LABS for a nuclear weapon or conventional
stores. Extended wing tips and leading edges were
added beginning with the fifteenth aircraft.

Four 20-mm M-39s with 150 rpg armed 360 F-
86H-5s and H-10s delivered from January 1955 to
March 1956. The F-86H entered operational service
with the 312th FBW in October 1954 and was used
by three wings until it was passed along to the Air
National Guard in June 1958. Despite the increase
in power, airframe limits prevented much increase
in speed over the F-86F, but acceleration and climb
were better.

No less than 26 foreign nations used the Sabre,
beginning with those made near Montreal by Can-

NORTH AMERICAN F-86H-10
General Electric J73-GE-30, 8920 lbs.
DIMENSIONS: Span 39'1", Lg. 38'10", Ht. 15', Wing Area
    313 sq. ft.
WEIGHT: Empty 13,836 lb., Gross 21,852 lb., Max. 24,296
    lb., Combat 18,683 lb. Fuel 562–1202 gal.
PERFORMANCE: Speed—Top 692 mph at s. l., 617 mph at
    35,000', Cruising 552 mph, Stalling 138 mph. Service
    Ceiling 50,800', Climb 12,900'/1 min. Combat Radius
    519 miles, 400 miles/2000 lbs. bombs, 1810 miles ferry
    range.   MFR

CANADAIR SABRE Mk, 6   MFR

adair. The first Canadair Sabre was a single Mark 1, assembled from U.S. F-86A parts and flown August 9, 1950, a year after the contract. Then 350 Mk 2s (F-86E-6s) and 438 similar Mk 4s followed by 1953. Twelve RCAF squadrons were flown across the ocean to back NATO. The first swept-wing fighters with the RAF were 430 Canadair Sabres for 12 squadrons, first delivered in October 1956.

Canadian Avro Orenda engines used on the remaining Canadair Sabres were tested first on a U.S. F-86J (modified F-86A) in October 1950 and a single Canadair Sabre Mk 3. Beginning in July 1953, 370 Mk 5s (6,355-pound-thrust Orenda 10) and 655 Mk 6s (7,275-pound-thrust Orenda 14) were built by October 9, 1958, with a total of 1,815 Canadair Sabres. Most went to the RCAF, but West Germany got 75 Mk 5s and the last 225 Mk 6 Sabres, while six Mk 6s went to Colombia and 34 to South Africa.

When replaced by newer models, Mk 2 and Mk 4 Sabres were passed on to Italy (180), Greece (104), Turkey (105), and Yugoslavia (121). Other European allies got secondhand USAF F-86Fs beginning in April 1956, with 244 for Spain. Norway got 115 F-86F-35s in 1957, with Belgium (5) and Por-

tugal (50) also using Sabres. South American countries getting F-86Fs were Peru (14) and Venezuela (22) in 1955 and Argentina (28) in 1960.

Australia's Commonwealth Aircraft was chosen in April 1951 to build its own Sabre version, with a 7,500-pound-thrust Rolls-Royce Avon and two 30-mm Aden guns. A prototype built of U.S. components was flown August 3, 1953, and 111 production CA-27 Sabres followed after July 1954.

Chinese Nationalists on Taiwan got 320 F-86F and seven RF-86F Sabres beginning on November 29, 1954, and these secondhand USAF jets engaged MiGs again in the 1958 fight over the offshore islands. Sidewinder infrared homing missiles were first used in combat by the Sabres on September 24, 1958, destroying ten enemy jets and ending the seven-week battle.

South Korea got 112 F-86Fs and ten RF-86As beginning in June 1955, and the Philippine Air Force got 36 F-86Fs in 1957–58. Japan used the Sabres in the greatest numbers. An agreement made July 13, 1954, provided for joint production of a new model, F-86F-40, by North American and Mitsubishi, maker of the wartime Zero fighter. With both new extended wing tips and leading-edge slats, the new model, flown in October 1955, had greatly improved handling qualities and lower stalling speeds than earlier models, which were often modified to the new standards.

North American delivered the last of 280 F-86F-40s on December 28, 1956, with 6,210 Sabres built in the United States and 300 sets of parts forwarded to Mitsubishi in Japan. Japan received 28 secondhand F-86Fs and 180 F-86F-40s by June 1957, but returned 45 of the latter to the United States. Mitsubishi's first F-86F-40 was flown August 9, 1956, but a 1959 typhoon delayed the contract's completion until February 1961.

Saudi Arabia received ten F-86F Sabres in 1957 and eight more in 1969, Iraq five F-86Fs in 1958, Thailand 40 by April 1962, Tunisia 12 in 1969, and Ethiopia 14. The Sabre next saw combat with Pakistan, which received 120 F-86F-40s in 1956–57. These served seven of the ten Pakistani Air Force squadrons (the rest had B-57Bs and F-104As) during the September 1965 war with India. Again, Sidewinders were used successfully, this time against Hawker Hunters. This conflict halted U.S. supplies to Pakistan, which nevertheless managed to obtain 90 ex-German Canadair Mk 6 Sabres in 1966.

All-weather Fighters

Jet-propelled day fighters had made quick progress, but night fighters, which needed room for radar and an electronics operator, posed a more difficult design problem. Shortly after the war's end in 1945, the Air Force issued a specification for a jet plane

CURTISS XF-87
Westinghouse XJ34-WE-7, 3000 lbs.
DIMENSIONS: Span 60', Lg. 62', Ht. 20'6", Wing Area 600 sq. ft.
WEIGHT: Empty 27,935 lb., Gross 39,875 lb. Fuel 1380–3100 gal.
PERFORMANCE: Speed—Top 582 mph at s. l. Service Ceiling 45,500', Climb 5500'/1 min. Ferry Range 2175 miles.   MFR

capable of operating in darkness or fog—a true "all-weather fighter."

The first type built for this purpose was the Curtiss XF-87 Blackhawk, which had four Westinghouse J34s paired under the wings, double wheels for the tricycle gear, and side-by-side seats for the pilot and radar operator. Armament was to include four 20-mm nose guns and two .50-caliber guns in a remote-controlled tail turret. The forward guns were to be located in a Martin conical nose turret, which could swing the barrels in a 60° arc around the nose and was aimed by a periscopic sight or by APG-3 radar.

Curtiss received authorization on November 21, 1945, to go ahead with its night-fighter design by using the funds remaining from the aborted XA-43 contract. The mockup was officially inspected July 16, 1946, but when it was realized that the Martin turret would not be available until 1949, the prototype was completed without any guns at the Columbus, Ohio, factory in October 1947. Shipment by road to the test base at Muroc met with accidents and flight tests were delayed until March 1, 1948.

Although the overweight XP-87 (soon redesignated XF-87) did not reach the 600-mph speed promised, a contract for 58 F-87As and 30 RF-87Cs was authorized June 10, 1948. They were to use the two 6,000-pound-thrust J47 engines planned for the uncompleted second prototype, but on October 18, 1948, the contract was canceled to free funds for other projects, and the famous Curtiss name was never again used on a new combat plane.

The postwar period's most successful long-range all-weather fighter was Northrop's Scorpion. This type began with a proposal to the Air Force in December 1945 and received a developmental contract in May 1946. After mockup inspection in September, the contract for two prototypes was finalized on December 18.

The first prototype, XF-89, flew on August 16, 1948, and the second, YF-89A, on November 15, 1949. They had two Allison J35 jets tucked against the fuselage under the thin wing, with split-edge full-span flaps lining the trailing edge out to wing-tip fuel tanks. The outer panels of these flaps acted as both ailerons and speed brakes.

Pilot and radarman sat in tandem ejection seats. The XF-89 had a rounded nose, 4,000-pound-thrust J35-A-9s, and a black finish, while the YF-89A had a pointed nose, 5,200-pound-thrust J35-A-21s with afterburners added, and dispensed with the solid black coat of paint that was formerly the night owl's uniform.

Forty-eight F-89As were ordered on a contract approved July 14, 1949, and deliveries began in

NORTHROP XF-89
Allison J35-A-15, 4000 lbs.
DIMENSIONS: Span 52', Lg. 50'6", Ht. 17'8", Wing Area 606 sq. ft.
WEIGHT: Empty 25,864 lb., Gross 43,910 lb. Fuel 2360 gal. max.
PERFORMANCE: Speed—Top 603 mph at 2500', Cruising 497 mph, Landing 127 mph. Service Ceiling 35,500', Climb 35,000'/21 min. Range 1750 miles.   MFR

NORTHROP YF-89A   MFR

September 1950. When a new autopilot and instrument landing system (ILS) was installed beginning with the twelfth aircraft, they became F-89Bs. Like the YF-89A, these Northrops were powered by J35-A-21 engines and had APG-33 radar in the nose with six 20-mm guns and 200 rpg, and underwing fittings could accommodate two 1,600-pound bombs or 16 5-inch rockets. Northrop Scorpions first went into service with the 78th Fighter-Interceptor Group at Hamilton AFB in June 1951, but the high-performance fighters were so complex that they required a long time to become fully operational.

A refined version, the F-89C, ordered June 20, 1950, and first flown September 18, 1951, replaced the external elevator mass-balances with internal ones. Of 163 F-89Cs, the first 64 were delivered with J35-A-21A engines, the next 45 (beginning February 1952) with J35-A-33s, and the rest completed with J35-A-35s by November 1952. The F-89C entered service in January 1952, but since several aircraft were lost as a result of fatigue failure of wing fittings due to aeroelasticity, all Scorpions were grounded September 22, 1952, until the wing structure could be changed. In 1953 all the planes had to be returned to the factory to be rebuilt.

The first all-weather jet fighter actually in Air Force service was the Lockheed Starfire, a less sophisticated single-engine type that could be delivered more quickly since 75 percent of its parts were included in F-80Cs then in production. Lockheed was told to go ahead on the F-94 on October 12, 1948. A YF-94 prototype, rebuilt from the first TF-80C two-seat trainer, made its first flight July 1, 1949, and 110 similar F-94As were ordered August 26.

Starfire wings, tail, and landing gear were those of the F-80; only the fuselage was new. There were

NORTHROP F-89C
Allison J35-A-33, 5600 lbs. (7400 lbs. AB)
DIMENSIONS: Span 56', Lg. 53'6", Ht. 17'6", Wing Area 606 sq. ft.
WEIGHT: Empty 24,570 lb., Gross 37,348 lb., Combat 33,100 lb. Fuel 1559 gal.
PERFORMANCE: Speed—Top 650 mph at s. l., 562 mph at 40,000', 531 mph at 47,800', Cruising 489 mph, Stalling 122 mph. Service Ceiling 50,500', Combat Ceiling 47,800', Climb 12,300'/1 min., 50,000'/24.5 min. Combat Radius 389 miles, 905 miles ferry range.   MFR

LOCKHEED F-94A
Allison J33-A-33, 4600 lbs. (6000 lbs. AB)
DIMENSIONS: Span 38'11", Lg. 40'1", Ht. 12'8", Wing Area 238 sq. ft.
WEIGHT: Empty 9557 lb., Gross 12,919 lb., Max. 15,330 lb. Fuel 318–648 gal.
PERFORMANCE: Speed—Top 606 mph at s. l., 546 mph at 35,000', Cruising 443 mph, Landing 122 mph. Service Ceiling 49,750', Climb 11,274'/1 min. Range 1079 miles.   MFR

NORTHROP F-89B
Allison J35-A-21, 5200 lbs. (6800 lbs. AB)
DIMENSIONS: Span 56', Lg. 53'5", Ht. 17'8", Wing Area 606 sq. ft.
WEIGHT: Empty 23,645 lb., Gross 36,400 lb., Combat 31,680 lb. Fuel 1616 gal.
PERFORMANCE: Speed—Top 642 mph at s. l., 570 mph at 35,000', Cruising 497 mph, Stalling 113 mph. Service Ceiling 37,400', Combat Ceiling 50,200', Climb 10,800'/1 min. Combat Radius 425 miles, 1300 miles ferry range.   ARNOLD

LOCKHEED F-94B   BESECKER

940 pounds of radar in the nose above four .50-caliber guns, and a radar operator sat behind the pilot. Behind them there was a 4,600-pound dry-thrust Allison J33-A-33. An afterburner could boost this to a 6,000-pound thrust for brief moments of climb and dash, but it consumed fuel so fast that it could be used only sparingly. The F-94A was the first production job with an afterburner; they have since become standard on fighters in which short bursts of power are more important than range.

One F-94A was modified to the YF-94B configuration in December 1950. First ordered March 3, 1950, 356 F-94Bs were delivered from April to January 1952, and appeared with center-mounted 230-gallon tanks on each wing tip instead of the 165-gallon tanks on the F-94A. A Sperry Zero Reader was added to aid blind landings.

Lockheed Starfires entered USAF service in May 1950 with the 325th Fighter-Interceptor Group at McChord AFB, and then with the 52nd Group at McGuire AFB in New Jersey. The former group's 319th Squadron was transferred to Korea in March 1952. At first its missions were limited to local defense—so the radar equipment would not be captured—but more aggressive tactics were allowed in 1953. An F-94B made the first Starfire kill (reported as a prop-driven LA-9) January 30, 1953, and the squadron downed two more aircraft in the spring, while a fourth enemy collided with an F-94B on June 12, destroying both aircraft.

Rocket-firing Interceptors

The detonation of the first Soviet atomic bomb on August 29, 1949, spurred American interceptor development. The Air Defense Command (ADC) was directed to prepare a defense against the probability that the long-planned Strategic Air Command (SAC) attack against the adversary would be matched by a counterstroke from enemy long-range bombers.

There were 293 U.S. facilities defined by a May 1949 JCS study as *vital*, that is, those whose "loss would mean the elimination of our ability to retaliate with strategic air power . . . and would delay for serveral years the development of our war potential to fight offensively in enemy-held territories." War plan Dropshot projected a Soviet long-range force by 1957 of 1,800 bombers directed against the United Kingdom and the United States. The ADC had to anticipate that enemy radar development by then would enable all attacks to be made at night, and therefore all U.S. interceptors should have all-weather capability.

Atomic weapons place exceptional demands on defense systems. No longer will prospects of heavy losses discourage an attacker when his surviving bombers may inflict fatal injuries on an enemy. Fighters may fail to stop an attack if their guns are poorly aimed or if enemy bombers withstand damage long enough to reach their targets. Defense now requires weapons systems capable of guaranteeing the destruction of bombers at first contact.

One answer to this problem is a new weapons system, largely replacing guns on ADC fighters, consisting of 2.75-inch air-to-air rockets aimed and fired in salvo by a radar-directed automatic computer. With this system an interceptor takes off and is vectored by directions from ground radar to a lead-collision course at right angles to the bomber's path instead of approaching from the rear in the pursuit-curve attack of the past. After the target is picked up by the fighter's radar, the pilot directs his plane so as to center the target on his scope. When a certain range is closed, the Hughes electronic computer takes over flight control through an autopilot and at the proper moment automatically fires a salvo of rockets. The pilot only monitors the actual attack, resuming control to return to his base.

The system has several advantages. Exposure of the fighter to bomber defense guns is brief, accuracy is greater in all kinds of weather, and only one of the rockets must strike the target to destroy it. The four-foot, 18-pound FFAR (Folding Fin Aircraft Rocket) was called Mighty Mouse. Firing a salvo of mice at an invisible aircraft presumes one too large and steady to evade the missiles; one pilot shot down by mistake the B-17 guide plane instead of his radio-controlled target.

The first plane designed for the new weapon was the swept-wing North American YF-95A, later designated YF-86D. This plane was begun March 28, 1949, as an all-weather interceptor version of the F-86, with radar and afterburner added, and became the first single-seat all-weather jet fighter of any country. A letter contract for two YF-86Ds and 122 F-86Ds was prepared by October 7, 1949, and the first prototype was flown December 22 without armament provisions.

In February 1950 a firm choice of rocket armament was made and Hughes fire-control systems specified, and a formal production contract for 153 aircraft approved June 2, 1950. These aircraft (NA-165) were known as F-95As until July 24, 1950, when the designation reverted to F-86D. The second prototype went to Hughes Aircraft in October 1950 to prove out the E-3 fire-control system. The initial YF-86D became the first American fighter to fire air-to-air (not air-to-surface) rockets in February 1951.

Twenty-four 2.75-inch rockets were carried in a retractable tray that popped out of the belly just long enough to launch them at targets about 500 yards away. The Sabre Dog's effectiveness, how-

NORTH AMERICAN YF-86D (firing first air-to-air rockets)   MFR

NORTH AMERICAN F-86D-1
General Electric J47-GE-17, 5425 lbs. (7500 lbs. AB)
DIMENSIONS: Span 37'1", Lg. 40'3", Ht. 15', Wing Area 288 sq. ft.
WEIGHT: Empty 13,518 lb., Gross 18,183 lb., Max. 19,975 lb., Combat 16,068 lb. Fuel 608–848 gal.
PERFORMANCE: Speed—Top 692 mph at s. l., 612 mph at 40,000', Cruising 550 mph, Stalling 130 mph. Service Ceiling 49,750', Climb 12,150'/1 min., 40,000'/7.2 min. Combat Radius 277 miles, 769 miles ferry range. MFR

ever, depended on its fire-control system, and this development fell behind schedule. The first 37 F-86D-1s, were to have simplified E-3 systems, but these were not finished when delivery began in March 1951, and all 37 could not be accepted until October 1952, three years after the original letter contract.

As for the more complex E-4 system needed for a lead-collision attack course, the one installed in the first F-86D-5, delivered in July 1952, still required improvement. By 1953 more than 320 F-86Ds were parked at the factory waiting for various electronic items to appear. Yet the Air Defense Command depended on the F-86D, which entered squadron service in April 1953 despite unsolved problems.

New contracts had been approved in April 1951 for 188 more F-86Ds and 638 in July; the latter were briefly known as F-86Gs but were returned to the F-86D series. By June 1953 production orders reached 2,504 aircraft, and three ADC wings flew them, along with seven Starfire wings and a Scor-

pion wing. General Electric J47-GE-17 engines were replaced by -17B engines on 1,517 F-86D-1 to D-40s and improved J47-GE-33s powered the last 987, beginning with F-86D-45.

When the last F-86D-60 was completed in September 1955, the ADC could fill twenty 75-plane wings, along with six F-89 wings and three with F-94Cs. In 1957–58 the Air National Guard received 25 F-86Ds for each of nine squadrons. Fifty-six F-86Ds were transferred to Denmark beginning June 26, 1958; 114 went to Japan in 1957–60; 40 to South Korea; and 130 were sold to Yugoslavia in 1961.

A less complicated weapons system was installed in the F-86K all-weather interceptor for export to NATO nations. In May 1953 two YF-86Ks were ordered and a license agreement with Fiat was made for production in Italy. Four 20-mm M-24A-1 guns with 132 rpg and MG-4 fire control (lead-pursuit instead of lead-collision course) distinguished the K from the D model. The YF-86K flew July 15, 1954, with both YF-86Ks being shipped to join 221 F-86Ks assembled by Fiat for the Italian, French, and German air forces. North American itself made 120 planes for Norway and the Netherlands from March to December 1955.

Beginning in May 1956 the F-86L versions were converted from 981 Ds by extending the wing tips

NORTH AMERICAN F-86D-60
General Electric J47-GE-33, 5550 lbs. (7650 lbs. AB)
DIMENSIONS: As F-86D-1
WEIGHT: Empty 13,498 lb., Gross 18,160 lb., Max. 19,952 lb., Combat 15,956 lb. Fuel 610–850 gal.
PERFORMANCE: Speed—Top 693 mph at s. l., 616 mph at 40,000', Cruising 550 mph, Stalling 129 mph. Service Ceiling 49,750', Climb 12,000'/1 min., 40,000'/6.9 min. Combat Radius 270 miles, 769 miles ferry range. MFR

NORTH AMERICAN F-86K
General Electric J47-GE-17B, 5425 lbs. (7950 lbs. AB)
DIMENSIONS: Span 37'1", Lg. 40'11", Ht. 15', Wing Area
288 sq. ft.
WEIGHT: Empty 13,811 lb., Gross 18,379 lb., Max. 20,171
lb., Combat 16,252 lb. Fuel 610–850 gal.
PERFORMANCE: Speed—Top 692 mph at s. l., 612 mph at
40,000', Cruising 550 mph, Stalling 130 mph. Service
Ceiling 49,600', Combat Ceiling 47,700', Climb 12,-
000'/1 min., 40,000'/7.3 min. Combat Radius 272 miles,
744 miles ferry range.   MFR

NORTH AMERICAN F-86L
General Electric J47-GE-33, 5550 lbs.
DIMENSIONS: Span 39'1", Lg. 40'3", Ht. 15', Wing Area
313 sq. ft.
WEIGHT: Empty 13,822 lb., Gross 18,484 lb., Combat
16,252 lb. Fuel 610–850 gal.
PERFORMANCE: Speed—Top 693 mph at s. l., 616 mph at
40,000', Cruising 550 mph, Stalling 130 mph. Service
Ceiling 49,600', Combat Ceiling 48,250', Climb 12,-
200'/1 min., 40,000'/7 min., Combat Radius 260 miles,
750 miles ferry range.   WL

and leading edge, adding engine cooling ducts, and
a "Data Link" receiver. Although performance was
little changed, the interceptor was now fitted into
the Semiautomatic Ground Environment (SAGE)
system operated by computers. Entering ADC service in October 1956, this improvement extended
the Sabre Dog's life until it was replaced by the
supersonic delta-wing F-102. The F-86Ls were
transferred to 24 Air National Guard squadrons in
1959–60, where they served until they were retired
in 1965.

The Lockheed F-94C Starfire was the second
"nearly automatic" night fighter using Mighty
Mouse rockets to be purchased by the ADC. Essentially similar to the earlier F-94 two-seaters, it replaced the J33 with a Pratt & Whitney J48-P-5 with
afterburner, had increased dihedral, and used a

thinner wing and swept horizontal tail to increase
the critical Mach number.

The most important innovation was the armament
of twenty-four 2.75-inch rockets ringed around the
nose radar in launching tubes concealed by snap
doors. Each wing carried drop tanks at the tips and
a pod for 12 more rockets on the leading edge. An
E-5 fire-control system was in the F-94C's nose,
whose original rounded plastic radar cover was replaced by a bullet-shaped bow.

A modified F-94B, flown January 18, 1950, with
the new features, had been designated YF-97 until
September 12, when the YF-94C label was restored.
Production F-94Cs were ordered July 21, 1950,
with 387 delivered from May 1952 to May 1954.
The 112 single-place F-94D ground-support versions ordered in May 1951 were canceled.

Although nine F-94Cs were completed by June
1952, they did not enter ADC service with the 437th
FIS until March 7, 1953. Reliability problems with
missiles and engines had put the F-94C nearly two
years behind schedule; on early tests the engine
flamed out when the nose rockets were salvoed
over 25,000 feet. While the problems were solved,
the contract was cut back from 617 to 387, for the
interceptor could handle no bomber more advanced
than a Tu-4 (Soviet B-29). Seven ADC wings used
F-94B/C Starfires in June 1953, but only three F-
94C wings served through 1955–56, with the last
unit remaining until February 1959.

The third USAF fighter type with Mighty Mouse
rockets was the Northrop F-89D, ordered in April
1951 and preceded by a YF-89D first flown October
23, 1951. In June 1952 delivery began on F-89D
Scorpions, providing the ADC with a fighter car-

LOCKHEED F-94C
Pratt & Whitney J48-P-5, 6350 lbs. normal (8750 lbs. AB)
DIMENSIONS: Span 37'4", Lg. 44'6", Ht. 14'11", Wing Area
233 sq. ft.
WEIGHT: Empty 12,708 lb., Gross 20,824 lb., Combat
16,689 lb. Fuel 866–1326 gal.
PERFORMANCE: Speed—Top 640 mph at s. l., 578 mph at
40,000', Cruising 493 mph, Stalling 152 mph. Service
Ceiling 51,400', Combat Ceiling 49,700', Climb 10,-
800'/1 min., 49,700'/19 min. Radius 239 miles area intercept, 1275 miles ferry range.   MFR

rying 104 2.75-inch rockets. No guns were carried, but wing-tip pods each contained 52 rockets and fuel, with additional fuel in the fuselage; the nose was enlarged for APG-40 radar, E-6 fire control, and an E-11 autopilot. There were 682 F-89Ds built, most with J35-A-35s.

Again ADC hopes for early deployment of rocket-firing fighters were disappointed when the entire F-89 force was grounded on September 22, 1952, just as F-89D deliveries were getting under way. Full production did not resume until November 1953 and was completed in March 1956. The F-89D entered operational service with the 18th FIS in January 1954.

A pair of Allison YJ71-A-3s were tested on a lone YF-89E accepted in August 1954, a converted F-89C. No F-89F or G model was produced, but the F-89H was the first USAF plane to enter service with the Hughes Falcon (GAR-1, later AIM-4A), a semiactive radar-guided missile that had a five-mile range. Ordered February 24, 1955, and first accepted in September 1955, the 156 F-89Hs had redesigned tip pods, each with three Falcons, and 21 2.75-inch rockets. It became operational in March 1956.

When Scorpion production ended in August 1956, 1,052 planes had been delivered and seven ADC wings had used them. Though slower than the F-86D single-seaters, they provided more range and firepower and were posted at the outer edges of the continental defenses, in Alaska and Greenland.

The first air-to-air rocket with a nuclear warhead, the Douglas MB-1 (AIR-2) Genie, an unguided 820-pound rocket, was first fired live from a modified F-

NORTHROP F-89H   MFR

89D on July 19, 1957. Northrop later modified 350 F-89Ds to the F-89J configuration, with J35-A-35 engines, MG-12 fire control, underwing racks for two Genies and four GAR-2 infrared homing Falcons and wing-tip pods that were interchangeable with a 600-gallon tank or rocket pods. The remodeled aircraft were delivered from November 1956 to February 1958, entering service in January 1957.

When the Northrops were replaced by supersonic F-101Bs, they were passed to the ANG, which retired the last squadrons in 1969. From 1950 to 1956, 4,412 all-weather jet interceptors of the first generation had been produced for the USAF, but except for the few F-94B skirmishes in Korea, none were used in combat. The Soviet bombers were never built in the numbers feared. When ADC strength peaked, the anticipated war situation had changed. A new generation of supersonic interceptors rapidly retired these subsonic jets to obsolescence and scrap metal.

Penetration Fighters

While some engineers wrestled with the problem of stopping the bombers, others tried to build fighters to protect bombers from enemy interception. Heavy losses of bombers on daytime sorties had made escort missions penetrating deep into enemy territory the main concern of wartime Air Force fighters, and postwar designers did not forget the problem.

The most specialized of all postwar designs was the McDonnell XF-85, ordered October 1945 as a parasite fighter to be carried inside a B-36. When big bombers on a mission were menaced, certain ones might open their bomb bay, lower parasites on a trapeze, launch them, and at the end of the engagement recover any survivors. Thus the XF-85 Goblin would have to be small enough to fit inside bomb bays yet be equal to enemy interceptors in performance.

McDonnell's answer to the unique problem was short enough to fit a 16-foot-long bay, and its swept wings folded to only 5 feet, 5 inches in width and 10 feet, 3 inches in height. The pilot straddled a 3,000-pound-thrust Westinghouse J34-WE-22 with

NORTHROP F-89D
Allison J35-A-35, 5440 lbs. (7200 lbs. AB)
DIMENSIONS: Span 59′8″, Lg. 53′10″, Ht. 17′6″, Wing Area 606 sq. ft.
WEIGHT: Empty 25,194 lb., Gross 42,241 lb., Combat 37,190 lb. Fuel 1772–2372 gal.
PERFORMANCE: Speed—Top 635 mph at 10,600′, 558 mph at 40,000′, Cruising 467 mph, Stalling 136 mph. Service Ceiling 49,200′, Combat Ceiling 46,500′, Climb 8360′/1 min., 46,500′/18.1 min. Combat Radius 382 miles, 1367 miles ferry range.   MFR

McDONNELL XF-85
Westinghouse J34-WE-22, 3000 lbs.
DIMENSIONS: Span 21'1", Lg. 14'10", Ht. 8'4", Wing Area
    100.5 sq. ft.
WEIGHT: Empty 3984 lb., Gross 5600 lb., Combat 5600 lb.
    Fuel 115–201 gal.
PERFORMANCE: Speed—Top 648 mph at s. l., 581 mph at
    35,000', Service Ceiling 48,000', Combat Ceiling 46,-
    750', Climb 12,500'/1 min., 35,000'/5.1 min. Combat
    Endurance 20 min. full power, 32 min. cruising. MFR

McDONNELL XF-85 (launch from B-29)   AF

about 30 minutes of fuel, and preliminary estimates
promised a top speed of 664 mph. Four .50-caliber
guns were grouped about the nose intake. Instead
of landing wheels there was a retractable hook for
the trapeze of the carrier plane. Tail span was reduced by dividing the tail into six odd-shaped surfaces. As the Goblin descended on its trapeze from
the mother plane, it looked like a fat little bug.

A mockup of the parasite fighter and the B-36 bay
and trapeze was inspected at St. Louis in June 1946,
and a June 18 contract approved February 5, 1947,
called for two prototypes. Since a B-36 would not
be available on time, a B-29B was modified as a
carrier plane.

On August 23, 1948, the Goblin flew for the first
time, but when the XF-85 attempted to return to
the mother plane, the trapeze smashed the canopy
and the pilot was forced to make an emergency
landing on a belly skid. Another attempt in October
succeeded, but the difficulty of recovering the parasites had been demonstrated. After seven flights
the test program was terminated and a service-test
contract was forgotten. The parasite-fighter concept,
first seen in the Navy's Sparrowhawks, would be
tried again with the RF-84F FICON system, but it
had not earned the Air Force's confidence.

A more conventional approach to the escort
fighter were the two twin jets, the XF-88 and XF-
90, begun in June 1946. Both had two Westinghouse
J34s buried within the fuselage, with large fuel
tanks, 35° swept wings, and six 20-mm guns.

McDonnell's XF-88 contract was approved February 14, 1947, and the first flew October 20, 1948,
with 3,000-pound-thrust XJ34-WE-13s. A second
prototype, XF-88A, had 3,600-pound-thrust XJ34-
WE-22s, with afterburners to boost speed. After 265
test flights, both aircraft were retired in August
1950, but the XF-88 was later reworked as a test-
bed for the Allison XT38 turboprop engine. Known
as the XF-88B, it was flown in this three-engine
configuration April 14, 1953.

Lockheed's XF-90, flown June 6, 1949, was distinguished by a needle nose, jet exhausts running
back to the tail, and wings flush with the fuselage
bottom. The guns were mounted under the air intakes, and a 220-gallon drop tank could be carried
on each wing tip. Westinghouse J34-WE-11s used
on early flights were replaced on both prototypes
by the XJ34-WE-15.

McDONNELL XF-88
Westinghouse J34-WE-13 (also -22)
DIMENSIONS: Span 39'8", Lg. 54'2", Ht. 17'3", Wing Area
    350 sq. ft.
WEIGHT: Empty 12,140 lb., Gross 18,500 lb., Max. 23,100
    lb. Fuel 734–1434 gal.
PERFORMANCE: Speed—Top 641 mph at s. l., Cruising 527
    mph, Landing 140 mph. Service Ceiling 36,000', Climb
    35,000'/14.5 min. Range 1737 miles.   AF

McDONNELL XF-88A   MFR

LOCKHEED XF-90
Westinghouse XJ34-WE-11 (later WE-15, 4000 lbs. AB)
DIMENSIONS: Span 40', Lg. 56'2", Ht. 15'9", Wing Area
   345 sq. ft.
WEIGHT: Empty 18,520 lb., Gross 27,200 lb., Max. 31,060
   lb. Fuel 1665 gal. max.
PERFORMANCE: Speed—Top 667 mph at 1000', Cruising
   473 mph, Landing 145 mph. Service Ceiling 39,000',
   Climb 25,000'/4.5 min. Range 1050 miles normal. MFR

A third penetration fighter was begun by North
American on December 17, 1947, as the NA-157.
As a Sabre development, it was designated F-86C,
but two were ordered by the Air Force as the YF-
93A, although an additional 118 ordered in June
1948 were canceled in January 1949 to provide
more funds for bombers.

First flown January 25, 1950, the YF-93A was
larger than the Sabres and had a long, solid nose,
flush side intakes, wider fuselage for the centrifugal-flow J48 with afterburner, and double main
wheels. Automatic wing slots were provided, with
an armament of six 20-mm guns and two 1,000-
pound bombs if desired. After Air Force tests were
completed, both prototypes went to NACA for a
study of various intake arrangements.

A shortage of funds and improvement of the F-84
series blocked procurement of a single penetration
fighter—even the XF-88, which was considered the
best in comparative tests. SAC had six F-84G Strategic Fighter wings attached by 1953, but they were
reequipped with swept-wing F-84Fs (ex F-96s).

Towards the Supersonic Fighter

Fighter designers have always wanted to make their
products faster, and American engineers were the

NORTH AMERICAN YF-93A
Pratt & Whitney J48-P-1, 6000 lbs. (8000 lbs. AB)
DIMENSIONS: Span 38'11", Lg. 44'1", Ht. 15'8", Wing Area
   306 sq. ft.
WEIGHT: Empty 14,035 lb., Gross 21,610 lb., Max. 26,516
   lb., Combat 21,610 lb. Fuel 1581 gal.
PERFORMANCE: Speed—Top 708 mph at s. l., 622 mph at
   35,000', Cruising 534 mph, Landing 150 mph. Service
   Ceiling 46,800', Combat Ceiling 45,500', Climb 11,-
   960'/1 min. Range 1967 miles.   MFR

first to produce a generation of supersonic fighters.
This was possible because the nation's financial
and industrial resources could be called upon for a
costly effort beyond the reach of most countries.

An aerodynamic research program costing over
$360 million had produced a series of research air-
craft, beginning with the rocket-powered Bell X-1,
which was launched from a B-29 and achieved the
world's first manned supersonic flight on October
14, 1947. Another program developed advanced
propulsion systems, and even more money went
into the development of new machines for shaping
light-alloy metal, including enormous stretch
presses, heavy presses to squeeze out large forg-
ings, and automatic precision machinery for cutting,
drilling, and riveting.

The first fighter designed for supersonic speeds
was the Republic XF-91 interceptor, whose J47 jet
could be supplemented by a 90-second blast from

REPUBLIC XF-91
General Electric J47-GE-9, 5000 lbs., and four Curtiss-
   Wright XLR-27-CW-1, 1000 lbs. each
DIMENSIONS: Span 31'3", Lg. 43'3", Ht. 18'1", Wing Area
   320 sq. ft.
WEIGHT: Empty 14,140 lb., Gross 28,300 lb., Combat
   18,600 lb. Fuel 1568 gal.
PERFORMANCE: Speed—Top 984 mph at 47,500' (with 2
   rockets), 918 mph at 35,000', Stalling 138 mph. Service
   Ceiling 48,700', Climb 47,500'/2.5 min., Cruise 15 min.
   at 560 mph, 3 min. of combat, 5 min. for descent. Total
   mission time—25.5 min.   MFR

four rocket units in the tail. It was designed for a 25.5-minute mission: climb to 47,500 feet in 2.5 minutes; 15-minute cruise; 3-minute combat; and 5 minutes for descent. The proposed armament of four .20-mm guns was never fitted to the two prototypes.

To avoid tip stalls at low speeds, the XF-91 had unique inverse tapered wings that were wider at the tips than at the roots. Swept back 35°, they had variable incidence to provide a low angle of attack for flight and a higher angle for extra lift on takeoffs and landings. A pair of tandem main wheels was kept small enough to fit into the thin wings, which also had fittings for two 230-gallon drop tanks. A General Electric J47-GE-3 was used for the first flight on May 9, 1949.

An afterburner and rockets made by Reaction Motors, totaling 6,000 pounds of thrust, became available in 1952 to replace the original Curtiss-Wright units, and Republic announced the "first supersonic rocket-powered flight by a U.S. combat-type plane" in December 1952. An XF-91A version with a 5,200-pound-thrust J47-GE-22 and four 1,-500-pound XLR-11-RM-9 rockets was expected to reach 1,126 mph at 50,000 feet, but this configuration was not actually tested.

Convair was more successful in approaching supersonic flight via the delta-wing configuration. This shape had been promoted in Germany by Dr. Alexander Lippisch, designer of World War II's fastest fighter, the Me 163 rocket-powered interceptor. Next Dr. Lippisch designed a tailless delta-wing fighter, which was preceded by a delta glider for test work. The glider, preliminary design, and the engineer himself were brought to the United States after the war.

As early as September 1945 the Air Force announced a design competition for a supersonic interceptor capable of climbing to 50,000 feet in four minutes and reaching 700 mph. Consolidated-Vultee won the contest in May 1946 with a design including a 45° swept-back wing, V-tail, and a power plant composed of a ramjet, four rocket motors for acceleration and a turbojet for cruising. In July 1946, after wind-tunnel tests and meetings with German engineers, a delta-shaped wing with a 60° sweepback on the leading edge was chosen. Other novelties of the XP-92, as the design was now known, were a high triangular fin, a pressurized cockpit within the ramjet intake duct at the front of the barrel-shaped fuselage, and a takeoff trolley. Armament was to be four 20-mm guns, and projected top speed was 1,165 mph at 50,000 feet.

To test the actual flight characteristics of the delta wing, the Air Force authorized construction of a full-scale flying model in November 1946. After the XP-92 itself was canceled in June 1948 because of

CONVAIR XF-92A
Allison J33-A-29, 5900 lbs. (7500 lbs. AB)
DIMENSIONS: Span 31′4″, Lg. 42′6″, Ht. 17′9″, Wing Area 425 sq. ft.
WEIGHT: Empty 9078 lb., Gross 14,608 lb., Combat 13,000 lb. Fuel 300 gal.
PERFORMANCE: Speed—Top 718 mph at s. l., 655 mph at 35,000′. Combat Ceiling 50,750′, Climb 35,000′/4.3 min.   MFR

the undeveloped nature of the power plant as well as other features, the flying model became known as the XF-92A. Using some parts from other aircraft and an Allison J33-A-21, the plane arrived at Muroc Dry Lake on April 9, 1948. During a taxi test, June 9, test pilot E. D. Shannon lifted it a few feet off the ground for a short run, but he made the first official flight of an American delta-wing aircraft September 18, 1948, after a 4,250-pound-thrust J33-A-23 had been fitted.

After 47 flights by company pilots proved the XF-92A's practical qualities, Major Charles Yeager, who had made the X-1's first supersonic flight, began Air Force tests. There wasn't enough power for supersonic speeds except in very steep dives, so the XF-92A returned to San Diego in 1950 to get a J33-A-29 with afterburner. Tests resumed July 20, 1951, but the aircraft remained subsonic, although 118 research flights did validate the wing design and clear the way for the successful F-102 and B-58 designs.

The F-100

The first supersonic aircraft in production anywhere in the world was the F-100 Super Sabre. North American began the design on January 19, 1951, as the NA-180, using a new Pratt & Whitney J57 with afterburner, a 45° swept low wing, and movable "slab" horizontal tail surfaces combining stabilizer and elevator functions. A speed brake was located in the fuselage bottom and a tail drag chute reduced the landing run.

Two prototypes were ordered November 1, 1951, along with a production commitment. The YF-100A designation was finalized on the tenth anniversary of the Pearl Harbor attack, beginning the "Century" series of supersonic Air Force fighters. The F-100, or "Hundred," eventually became the "Hun" in Air Force slang. Preceding fighter designations were soon forgotten: the F-95, F-96, and F-97 having reverted to F-86D, F-84F, and F-94C, respectively, while the Hughes F-98 became the Falcon air-to-air missile and the Boeing F-99 became the Bomarc "pilotless interceptor," a surface-to-air missile.

A sense of urgency impelled the F-100 program ahead of the usual time schedule: the fear that the fast MiGs would soon have a supersonic successor; the desire of fighter pilots for more speed and altitude; and an awareness at the highest levels of command that 1957—the year of danger in war plan Dropshot (see Chapter 25)—was drawing near. A letter contract for the first 23 F-100As (NA-192s) was awarded February 11, 1952, on a contract for 273 planes that was approved by August 1952.

Pearl Harbor veteran George Welch exceeded sonic speed on the YF-100A's first flight on May 25, 1953, at Edwards AFB. He also flew the second YF-100A on October 14 and the first F-100A-1—which also used the J57-P-7 but had a shorter tail fin—on October 29. On the same day the YF-100A set a 755-mph world speed record by Lieutenant Colonel F. K. Everest; this was the last time the rules required that this record be set at less than a 100-foot altitude.

Pilots of TAC's 479th Fighter Day Wing enthusiastically received the fast fighters in September

NORTH AMERICAN YF-100A
Pratt & Whitney XJ57-P-5, 8450 lb.
DIMENSIONS: Span 36'9", Lg. 46'2", Ht. 14'5", Wing Area 376 sq. ft.
WEIGHT: Empty 18,279 lb., Gross 28,965 lb., Combat 24,789 lb. Fuel 1307 gal.
PERFORMANCE: Speed—Top 660 mph at 43,350', Cruising 600 mph, Landing 160 mph. Combat Ceiling 52,600', Climb 12,500'/1 min. Combat Radius 422 miles, 1410 miles ferry range.   MFR

NORTH AMERICAN F-100A
Pratt & Whitney J57-P-7 or -39, 9700 lbs. (14,800 lbs. AB)
DIMENSIONS: Span 38'10", Lg. 47'10", Ht. 15'6", Wing Area 385 sq. ft.
WEIGHT: Empty 18,185 lb., Gross 28,899 lb., Combat 24,996 lb. Fuel 744–1294 gal.
PERFORMANCE: Speed—Top 852 mph at 35,000', 760 mph at s. l., Cruising 589 mph, Stalling 159 mph. Service Ceiling 44,900', Combat Ceiling 51,000', Climb 23,800'/1 min. Combat Radius 358 miles, 1294 miles ferry range.   MFR

1954, but the program suffered a severe setback. Four aircraft had been lost to in-flight structural failure after the pilot lost control. On October 12, 1954, George Welch was killed when the ninth F-100A-1 disintegrated in a high-speed test dive. The Air Force grounded its entire F-100 inventory while waiting for the company to determine what was wrong.

The problem was one of directional stability. Fortunately the fix was relatively easy: an enlarged fin, extended wing tips, and modified controls. The changes were made to all Super Sabres either in the works or already delivered, and by February 1955 they were back in the air. By April 1955, 203 F-100As were completed, although they were operational only with the 479th Wing. The remaining Air Force day-fighter strength at the time consisted of 12 F-84F, 13 F-86F, and 3 F-86H wings. (The 28 all-weather interceptor wings' equipment has already been described in an earlier section.)

Super Sabre armament consisted of four new 20-mm M-39 guns with 200 rpg, while two 1,000-pound bombs could replace the 275-gallon drop tanks, and in 1956 two Sidewinder missiles were added. Four planes were converted to RF-100A camera versions in 1954 and went to Taiwan in 1961. The Air Force soon found that in addition to higher performance the F-100 created problems of cost and maintenance. Titanium, a rare, heat-resistant metal combining strength and light weight, was used in the structure and helped raise the F-100A price past $1,014,000 per aircraft. A shortage of skilled maintenance men kept many aircraft on the ground in 1955. An F-100B project was diverted into the later YF-107 design, but on December 30, 1953, the F-100C fighter-bomber configuration had been selected for future Super Sabre production.

NORTH AMERICAN F-100C
Pratt & Whitney J57-P-21, 10,200 lbs. (16,000 lbs. AB)
DIMENSIONS: As F-100A
WEIGHT: Empty 19,270 lb., Gross 32,615 lb., Combat 27,587 lb. Fuel 1702–2139 gal.
PERFORMANCE: Speed—Top 924 mph at 35,000′, 904 mph at 39,500′, Cruising 593 mph, Stalling 168 mph. Service Ceiling 38,700′, Combat Ceiling 49,100′, Climb 21,-600′/1 min., 35,000′/2.3 min. Combat Radius 572 miles, 1954 miles ferry at 35,696 lb. gross.   MFR

The F-100C had a J57-P-21 (beginning with the 101st a/c), more fuel, an air-refueling probe on the right wing, and wings strengthened to handle six 750-pound bombs, an Mk 7 nuclear weapon released by an MA-2 LABS, or two pods with 42 2.75-inch air-to-air rockets.

North American flew its first F-100C-1-NA from Los Angeles on January 17, 1955, and built 451 F-100Cs by April 1956. They entered service with TAC in July 1955. A second production source was begun at Columbus, Ohio, where delivery of 25 F-100C-10-NHs began in September 1955.

Added wing and tail area and an autopilot distinguished the F-100D, ordered October 1954 and first flown January 24, 1956. Alternate underwing loads included either six 750-pound bombs or four 1,000-pound bombs, two GAM-83A Bullpup missiles, a 1,680-pound Mk 7 nuclear store, two 450-gallon air-refuelable buddy tanks, or four GAR-8 Sidewinder air-to-air missiles. Production amounted to 940 F-100D-NAs and 334 F-100D-NHs by August 1959, to which 339 two-seat F-100F trainers added by October 1959 brought Super Sabre production totals to 2,294.

Deliveries of F-100Ds to TAC began in September 1956. By June 1957, 16 TAC wings used Super Sabres, and as more F-100Ds arrived, F-100A and F-100C models were passed to ANG squadrons, beginning in February 1958. Exports of 203 F-100Ds and 45 F-100Fs began in May 1958, when France began receiving 68 Ds and seven Fs for two *escadres de chasse,* serving with them until 1967. Denmark got 48 F-100Ds and 24 F-100Fs, beginning in June 1959, and Turkey received 87 F-100Ds in the same period. Eighty modernized F-100As went to Taiwan in 1959–60, plus 38 later transfers and a few F-100Fs.

In 1962, TAC began replacing its F-100s with F-4s, but ten wings remained in 1964, when war in Indochina called them into action. None of these actions involved fighting enemy aircraft, however, since they were all attacks on surface targets. Individual F-100D squadrons of four TAC wings, beginning in August 1964 with the 3rd TFW, rotated through the area on tours of about six months, flying more sorties than all the P-51s in World War II. Seven F-100F two-seaters, modified to the "Wild Weasel I" ECM versions, began operations to detect and attack enemy radar sites on December 3, 1965.

The last F-100Ds in Vietnam, belonging to the 35th TFW, left in July 1971. The last "Hun" left Air Force service when the 27th TFW retired its F-100Ds in June 1972, but out of 28 ANG F-100 squadrons ten still continued to use F-100Ds in 1978. On November 10, 1979, the last operational flight by an ANG F-100D ended the first supersonic fighter's long service.

The F-101

McDonnell's F-101A Voodoo was a long-range fighter based on the earlier XF-88. Powered by two J57-P-13 turbojets with afterburners, the Voodoo had a 35° sweep, one-piece horizontal stabilizer set high on its fin, and mid-span ailerons on the thin wing. Armament included four 20-mm M-39 guns with 200 rpg in the nose, with attachments below the fuselage for drop tanks or a nuclear bomb released by a LABS.

A letter contract for 29 F-101As was placed on January 3, 1952, the mockup inspected in July, and the first flew September 29, 1954. After that, orders were increased to include 77 F-101A (completed October 1957) and 47 F-101C (completed May 1958) Voodoos, the C being identical except for wings strengthened for low-altitude tactical bombing. For reconnaissance two YRF-101As (first flown May 10, 1955), 35 RF-101As (flown June 1956), plus 166 RF-101Cs, completed from July 1957 to March 1959, were delivered.

The first 1,000-mph fighter in production, the F-101As had been intended for SAC's fighter-escort units, but these were transferred to TAC, which wanted a low-altitude fighter-bomber that could deliver Mk 7 nuclear bombs. Serious problems re-

NORTH AMERICAN F-100D
Pratt & Whitney J57-P-21 or -21A, 10,200 lbs. (16,000 lbs. AB)
DIMENSIONS: Span 38'10", Lg. 49'4", Ht. 16'2", Wing Area 400 sq. ft.
WEIGHT: Empty 20,638 lb., Gross 34,050 lb., Combat 28,847 lb. Fuel 1739–2139 gal.
PERFORMANCE: Speed—Top 910 mph at 35,000', 728 mph at 47,500', Cruising 590 mph, Stalling 169 mph. Service Ceiling 36,100', Combat Ceiling 47,700', Climb 19,-000'/1 min., 35,000'/2.2 min. Combat Radius 534 miles, 1995 miles ferry at 37,124 lb. gross.   AF

McDONNELL F-101A
Pratt & Whitney J57-P-13, 10,200–15,000 lbs.
DIMENSIONS: Span 39'8", Lg. 67'5", Ht. 18', Wing Area 368 sq. ft.
WEIGHT: Empty 25,374 lb., Gross 48,001 lb., Combat 39,495 lb. Fuel 2250–3150 gal.
PERFORMANCE: Speed—Top 1005 mph at 35,000', Cruising 550 mph, Stalling 198 mph. Service Ceiling 38,900', Combat Ceiling 49,450', Climb 33,750'/1 min. Combat Radius 677 miles, 2186 miles ferry range.   MFR

McDONNELL RF-101A
Pratt & Whitney J57-P-13, 10,200 lbs. (15,000 lbs. AB)
DIMENSIONS: Span 39'8", Lg. 69'3", Ht. 18', Wing Area 368 sq. ft.
WEIGHT: Empty 25,335 lb., Combat 35,751 lb., Max. take-off 47,331 lb. Fuel 3150 gal.
PERFORMANCE: Speed—Top 1008 mph at 35,000', 884 mph at 44,400', Cruising 550 mph, Stalling 198 mph. Service Ceiling 39,200', Combat 51,450', Climb 8480'/1 min. Combat Radius 1046 miles, 2435 miles ferry range.   MFR

vealed through testing led the Air Force to suspend production from May 23 to November 26, 1956, after which the program resumed on new versions. The Voodoo fighters joined TAC in May 1957, serving until January 1966, when the last F-101C left the 81st TFW, stationed in Britain, as the F-4C arrived. On December 12, 1957, an F-101A modified with 16,900-pound-thrust J57-P-55s and no armament set a 1,207-mph speed record.

The reconnaissance version had a longer history, although it also entered TAC service in May 1957, replacing the RF-84Fs. Four RF-101Cs were transferred to the Chinese on Taiwan in November 1959. Four RF-101As arrived at Tan Son Nhut on October 18, 1961, becoming the first Air Force unit to operate from Vietnam. Rotating RF-101 units continued to fly there until November 1970. Sorties over North Vietnam were the most dangerous, and the first RF-101 loss was on April 3, 1965. Seven more were lost to antiaircraft fire in 1966. The Voodoos had no trouble evading MiG-17s, but after a MiG-21 downed one in September 1967, RF-4Cs replaced the RF-101s on missions over North Vietnam, the older type confining itself to Laos and the south. By October 1971 all RF-101s had been relegated to the ANG.

A two-place long-range interceptor Voodoo ordered by letter contract in March 1955 was temporarily called the F-109,[4] but 480 were completed as the F-101B. The F-101B had two J57-P-55s with afterburners, MG-13 radar-fire control, two MB-1 Genie nuclear air-to-air missiles carried externally, three Falcon GAR-1D radar or GAR-2A infrared guided missiles inside, and two 450-gallon drop tanks.

First flown March 27, 1957, the F-101B was issued to 17 ADC Fighter-Interceptor squadrons between January 1959 and March 1961, when Voodoo production ended after 807 aircraft. TF-101Bs were 72 fitted with dual controls, and 153 F-101Bs with infrared sensors were redesignated F-101F in 1962. Sixty-six went to Canada, beginning in July 1961, where they were known as CF-101Bs. In 1970 they were exchanged for 66 replacements with a new fire-control system. After Air Force F-101A/Cs were transferred to the ANG in 1966, they were rebuilt as RF-101G and R-101H aircraft. The interceptor versions served the ANG after December 1969, and three F-101B squadrons remained in service in 1980.

Delta-wing Interceptors

Convair developed the next century series interceptor as part of a "weapons system" (WS201A) consisting of air-to-air guided missiles, all-weather

[4] The F-109 was incorrectly identified as a Ryan VTOL project by some contemporary sources.

McDONNELL F-101B
Pratt & Whitney J57-P-55, 10,700–16,900 lbs.
DIMENSIONS: Span 39'8", Lg. 71'1", Ht. 18', Wing Area 368 sq. ft.
WEIGHT: Empty 28,492 lb., Gross 45,461 lb., Max. 51,724 lb., Combat 40,853 lb. Fuel 2084–984 gal.
PERFORMANCE: Speed—Top 1094 mph at 35,000', 610 mph at 51,000', Cruising 546 mph, Stalling 212 mph. Service Ceiling 52,100', Combat Ceiling 51,000', Climb 50,000'/5.6 min. Combat Radius 829 miles intercept, 1755 miles ferry range.   MFR

McDONNELL CF-101B   LAWSON

radar search and fire control, and supersonic single-seat fighters. The electronics came first, with the selection of Hughes Aircraft in May 1950 as developer of the Falcon homing missile and fire control. Before it became the GAR-1, the Falcon was known as the F-98.

Proposals for the aircraft itself were requested by the Air Force on June 18, 1950, and Convair, Lockheed, and Republic named the winners July 2, 1951. On August 31, 1951, Convair got a design and mockup letter contract for an enlarged development of the delta-wing XF-92A, and two YF-102 prototypes were added December 19, 1951. The original design had a Wright J67 engine, Hughes MA-1 fire control, and Falcon missiles. When it was realized that the J67 and MA-1 could not be completed in time, a J57-P-11 and MG-3 system was substituted for the interim YF-102 and F-102A, with the more sophisticated systems planned for the ultimate F-102B. Preliminary engineering on ten YF-102s began in April 1952, and the first 32 F-102A production aircraft were ordered December 17, 1952, under a contract approved the following June 12.

Carrying 1,194 pounds of armament, 1,050 gallons of fuel, and nearly a ton of electronics, the F-102 was half again as heavy as the F-86D at combat weight. The promised 870 mph at 35,000 feet proved to be far above the actual speed. Even before the YF-102's first flight on October 24, 1953, wind-tunnel tests warned that the drag hump at sonic speed was above the airplane's capability. The first prototype encountered severe buffeting at Mach 0.9 and crashed on its seventh takeoff. The second YF-102 flew January 11, 1954, but was limited to Mach .99 on the level; dives over this speed resulted in severe yaw oscillations.

The whole F-102 program—and with it ADC's principal weapon for the 1955–60 period—faced sudden termination at a time when American leadership was alarmed by Soviet weapons progress. A Soviet H-bomb had been tested on August 12, 1953, and on May 1, 1954, the prototype of the Myasishchev Mya-4 "Bison" jet bomber was displayed over Moscow. By 1957–58, it was assumed, the U.S.S.R. would possess a large fleet of intercontinental bombers with enough thermonuclear weapons to devastate U.S. targets. This assumption would prove to be false, but it was the basis of U.S. planning for that period.

What saved Convair's delta wing was the application of the area rule, a system of drag reduction developed by NACA scientist Richard Whitcomb. The F-102's fuselage was redesigned, and the ten YF-102s were followed by four longer YF-102As built with the J57-P-23, cambered leading edges for the thin wings, modified canopy, and an area-ruled fuselage incorporating lengthened nose and tail fairings. Supersonic speeds were achieved on December 21, 1954, the day after the first YF-102A flight. Two thirds of the 30,000 tools prepared for the original configuration had to be discarded in favor of the new shape.

The first F-102A flew June 24, 1955, but the production plan provided very slow deliveries until testing and modifications were complete. Many airframe changes were made, including a three-foot addition to the tail fin, tested in December 1955 and standardized on all F-102As built after the twenty-fifth plane. A TF-102A trainer with two side-by-side seats and full armament was ordered July 19, 1954, and first flown November 8, 1955.

Armament on the Delta Dagger, carried in a fuselage bay, consisted of six Falcon GAR-1D radar or GAR-2A infrared homing missiles and 24 2.75-inch FFARs. The smaller rockets were carried in the bay doors, which snapped open when the Falcons were extended into the airstream for launching. Three missiles of each type of guidance system were usually carried, to be used against targets up to six miles away, but the short-range rockets were omitted in service. Two 230-gallon tanks could be attached for ferry missions. In October 1957 a new wing configuration improved performance.

CONVAIR YF-102
Pratt & Whitney J57-P-11, 9200–14,800 lbs.
DIMENSIONS: Span 37', Lg. 52'6", Ht. 18', Wing Area 661 sq. ft.
WEIGHT: Empty 17,954 lb., Gross 26,404 lb., Combat 23,989 lb. Fuel 1050 gal.
PERFORMANCE: Speed—Top 870 mph at 35,000', Cruising 596 mph, Landing 145 mph, Service Ceiling 55,900', Combat 54,400', Climb 25,000'/1 min., 50,000'/7 min., Radius 575 miles. Ferry Range 1550 miles.
(pretest estimates)   MFR

CONVAIR YF-102A   MFR

CONVAIR F-102A
Pratt & Whitney J57-P-23, 10,200 lbs. (16,000 lbs. AB)
DIMENSIONS: Span 38'2", Lg. 68'2", Ht. 21'2", Wing Area 695 sq. ft.
WEIGHT: Empty 19,350 lb., Gross 28,150 lb., Combat 24,494 lb. Fuel 1085–515 gal.
PERFORMANCE: Speed—Top 780 mph at 35,000', 637 mph at 51,800', Cruising 605 mph, Stalling 154 mph. Service Ceiling 53,400', Combat Ceiling 51,800', Climb 18,-700'/1 min., 51,800'/9.9 min. Combat Radius 386 miles area intercept, 1492 miles ferry at 31,276 lbs.   MFR

The first F-102A delivery to an operational ADC unit, the 327th FIS, was made on May 1, 1956—almost three years behind the original program date—and the Air Force at last had a fighter in which guided missiles replaced guns or unguided rockets. Convair's San Diego factory completed 875 F-102As and 63 TF-102As by September 1958, serving 25 ADC squadrons. About 450 F-102As were modified by 1963 with MG-10 fire control, GAR-11 (later called AIM-26A) nuclear Falcon missiles, and infrared search system. The aircraft cost $1.2 million each but enjoyed a good safety record in service.

In 1960, Delta Darts began transfering to ANG squadrons, but there were still 20 ADC squadrons in 1964, and F-102As were rotated to Vietnam, although no enemy bombers were ever intercepted. The last Air Force squadron with F-102As, from 1962 to 1973, was the 57th FIS in Iceland. Turkey got 40 and Greece 20 in 1969, and 68 were converted by the USAF to PQM-102 target drones.

Republic also designed an interceptor with delta wings, but the XF-103 design study ordered in September 1951 had a radical shape, with a dual-cycle power plant combining a 12,950-pound-thrust Wright XJ67 and a ramjet for a maximum 22,350-pound thrust. Mach 3 speeds, listed in January 1954 estimates as 1,985 mph at 50,000 feet, would create so much heat that titanium was chosen as the main structural element. The long fuselage had the pilot's cockpit flush behind the radar nose, with an escape capsule and a periscope. Short delta wings and separate tail surfaces were used, and fuselage bays contained six Falcon missiles and a pack of thirty-six 2.75-inch rockets.

REPUBLIC XF-103
Wright XJ67-W-3/XRJ55-W-1, 22,350 lbs.
DIMENSIONS: Span 34′5″, Lg. 76′9½″, Ht. 16′7″, Wing Area 401 sq. ft.
WEIGHT: Empty 24,949 lb., Gross 38,505 lb., Combat 31,219 lb., Max. 42,864 lb. Fuel 2440 gal.
PERFORMANCE: Speed—Top 1985 mph at 50,000′, Cruising 678 mph, Stalling 180 mph. Service Ceiling 69,-600′, Absolute Ceiling 69,200′, Climb 50,000′/7.1 min., Radius 245 miles, 1545 miles ferry range.   AF

Although the prototype, ordered in July 1954, was supposed to fly in February 1957, the power plant did not materialize. Republic proposed a larger research version, but the airframe was never completed and the contract was canceled August 21, 1957, after a six-year expenditure of $104 million.

The F-104 Starfighter

The first Air Force fighter with Mach 2 speed was designed by C. L. "Kelly" Johnson to meet the demands of Korean War pilots for the highest possible speed and ceiling obtainable. This could be achieved with the new J79 engine, keeping the airframe light and avoiding heavy electronics, and, to the surprise of many, without the swept-back wings of most contemporary types.

The smallest and thinnest wings used on an American jet distinguished the Starfighter, whose design began in November 1952 as the Lockheed Model 83. Two XF-104 prototypes were ordered March 11, 1953, with Wright 11,500-pound-thrust XJ65-W-6 engines, and the first flew February 7, 1954. A Mach 1.79 speed was achieved, but the General Electric J79-GE-3—with afterburners and air-inlet shock-control ramps—used on the next 17 Starfighters (ordered October 1954) achieved Mach 2 speeds with the afterburner.

The first YF-104A, flown February 17, 1956, was 5.5 feet longer and 1,000 pounds heavier empty than the prototypes, but it did reach Mach 2 on April 27, 1956. Production contracts added 153 more F-104A and 26 F-104B Starfighters, completed by December 1958. The latter, an unarmed two-seat trainer, was flown February 7, 1957. Not until January 26, 1958, did the F-104A join the 83rd FIS, the first of the four ADC squadrons to use the type.

An F-104A became the first plane to set world records for both speed and altitude: 1,404 mph and 91,249-foot zoom in May 1958. Armament consisted of a six-barrel Vulcan 20-mm M-61 (ex-T-171) with 750 rounds, which could be fired in about 7.5 seconds, while two GAR-8 Sidewinder infrared mis-

LOCKHEED XF-104   MFR

LOCKHEED F-104A
General Electric J79-GE-3A, 9600 lbs. (14,800 lbs. AB)
DIMENSIONS: Span 21'11", Lg. 54'9", Ht. 13'6", Wing Area
   196 sq. ft.
WEIGHT: Empty 12,782 lb., Gross 22,614 lb., Combat
   17,768 lb. Fuel 1292–632 gal.
PERFORMANCE: Speed—Top 1324 mph at 35,000', 1232
   mph at 50,000', Cruising 599 mph, Stalling 198 mph.
   Combat Ceiling 55,200', Climb 35,000'/2 min. Combat
   Radius 403 miles/2 GAR-8, 1585 miles ferry range at
   24,804 lbs.   AF

siles could replace the 170-gallon tanks at the tips
of the short, anhedraled wing.

A fighter-bomber version was the F-104C, with
a J79-GE-7A, ASG-14 fire control, M-61 gun, and
provisions for flight refueling, two 195-gallon and
two 170-gallon tanks or two 1,000-pound bombs, a
Mk 28 nuclear store, or four GAR-8 missiles. First
flown in July 1958, there were 77 F-104Cs and 21
F-104D two-seat trainers built, and they replaced
the 479th Tactical Fighter Wing's F-100s by June
1959.

The 296 Starfighters supplied the Air Force by
September 1959 had the highest accident rate of
any service type: 49 aircraft and 18 pilots lost in the
first 100,000 hours. Lacking all-weather radar, the
F-104As were retired from the ADC to the ANG by
1960, and 25 were sent to the Chinese on Taiwan,
12 to Pakistan, and 18 to Jordan in 1967. Twenty-
four became QF-104 target drones and three were
converted, beginning September 1962, to rocket-
powered NF-104As to train astronauts. But during
the Cuban crisis of 1962, two F-104A squadrons
were called back into ADC service and stationed in
Florida and Texas. All the F-104Bs were sent
abroad: 22 to Taiwan and two each to Pakistan and
Jordan.

Though TAC F-104Cs had a longer service life—
a few even visited Thailand in 1966–67—the war in
Vietnam had small use for their limited endurance
and weapons load. After July 1967 they were passed

on to the ANG, whose 198th TFS was the last
American squadron to use them, retiring the final
F-104C on July 31, 1975. The only air-to-air combat
by F-104s in this period was by Pakistani F-104As
in December 1971. Ten of these planes had been
loaned by Jordan.

Lockheed was undiscouraged by its USAF recep-
tion and made a very successful drive to sell its
fighter abroad,[5] beginning with Germany's search
for a supersonic multipurpose type to do all-
weather tactical bombing, interception, and even
reconnaissance. A new version, the F-104G,
crammed with new electronic navigation and weapons-delivery systems, was chosen by Germany over
a dozen rival designs. Contracts signed February 5
and March 18, 1959, resulted in Lockheed furnish-
ing Germany 96 F-104Gs and 114 TF-104Gs, and
launched a European consortium that would produce over 1,250 planes in German, Dutch, Belgian
and—by a March 1961 addition—Italian factories.
Canada signed up for its own production plan September 17, 1959, and Lockheed got the first contract
for 84 F-104Gs and 29 two-seat TF-104Gs for the
Military Aid Program (MAP) in February 1961.

Lockheed flew the first F-104G on October 5,
1960, at Palmdale, California, and built 30 unarmed
TF-104F two-seaters for the German pilots' school
established at Luke AFB in Arizona. Canada's first
Montreal-built CF-104 flew May 26, 1961, and the
first German-built F-104G flew August 14, 1961.

The F-104G was similar to the F-104C except for
a J79-GE-11A, enlarged fin, F-15A fire control, LN-
3 navigation system, and strengthening for one
2,000-pound and two 1,000-pound bombs. Four
Sidewinder missiles could be carried along with
the 20-mm M-61 gun, the latter removable for re-

---

[5] The large sales commissions paid, including $1 million to the
Netherlands' Prince Bernard, resulted in a great scandal. A company report in August 1975 stated that it had paid foreign officials
$22 million.

LOCKHEED F-104C
General Electric J79-GE-7, 10,000–15,800 lbs.
DIMENSIONS: As F-104A
WEIGHT: Empty 12,760 lb., Gross 22,410 lb., Combat 19,470 lb. Fuel 1237–627 gal.
PERFORMANCE: Speed—Top 1324 mph at 35,000' to 50,-000', Cruising 584 mph, Stalling 196 mph. Service Ceiling 36,900', Combat Ceiling 58,000', Climb 35,-000'/1.6 min. Combat Radius 352 miles, 1727 miles ferry at 25,015 lb. MFR

LOCKHEED F-104G
General Electric J79-GE-11A, 10,000 lbs. (15,800 lbs. AB)
DIMENSIONS: As F-104A
WEIGHT: Empty 13,996 lb., Gross 27,300–29,038 lb., Combat 20,002 lb. Fuel 1748 gal.
PERFORMANCE: Speed—Top 1328 mph at 35,000', 1320 mph at 46,100', 860 mph at s. l., Cruising 586 mph, Stalling 215 mph. Combat Ceiling 46,300', Climb 35,-000'/2.9 min. Combat Radius 736 miles intercept, 620 miles/2000 lb. bomb, 1875 miles ferry range. MFR

connaissance missions. All-weather capability was the principal difference from preceding models.

Japan signed a licensed production contract January 29, 1960, for 180 similar F-104Js and 20 two-seat F-104DJs. Three of the F-104Js and the F-104DJs were completed by Lockheed, the first being flown June 30, 1961. The rest, to be assembled by Mitsubishi, were similar to the G model but armed solely as interceptors. The first of seven Japanese squadrons became operational in October 1964, and another 30 F-104Js were added before Mitsubishi finished in 1967.

Italy wanted a new edition with a Sparrow missile capability. Lockheed responded with the F-104S, whose prototype, the CL-901 Super Starfighter, appeared in November 1966 with a new 17,900-pound-thrust J79-GE-19. Fiat received contracts for 205 aircraft for the Italian Air Force and 40 for Turkey. Armament could include the gun or two Sparrows and up to four Sidewinders. The first Fiat F-104S flew December 30, 1968, and when the last was delivered in December 1978, Starfighter production had ended.

Many shifts had been made in the original program, but 57 F-104G, 24 RF-104G, and 158 TF-104G exports had reportedly raised California-built aircraft to 740. Canada got 38 CF-104D two-seaters from Lockheed, built 200 CF-104Gs for the RCAF, and exported 140 more for the U.S. Military Aid Program. Belgium built 198, Germany 283, Italy 417, Japan 207, and the Netherlands 354, for a world total reported at 2,539. Because of the involved transfers among the countries and many sales of used aircraft, an accurate list is unavailable, but it appears that the major recipients of F-104G series aircraft were Germany (917), Italy (354), Canada (238), Japan (230), the Netherlands (138), and Belgium (112) from foreign and consortium sales, while the U.S./Canadian MAP aircraft were divided among Denmark (29), Norway (32)—plus 22 secondhand CF-104Gs—Spain (21), Greece (36), Turkey (55), Taiwan (95), and three for NASA.

Although 15 air forces operated the Lockheeds, the fighters saw very little combat. It is primarily remembered as a very fast, but very unforgiving, aircraft with terribly high crash rates in Germany and Italy. Yet pilots in some smaller countries, like Norway, had no such high accident rate, and the Japanese lost only 10 percent (23) of their aircraft in ten years of operation.

The F-105 Thunderchief

Republic's F-105 was the first type designed from the start as a TAC fighter-bomber, with Mach 2 speed, a nuclear bomb in an internal bay, electronic navigation and target computing, and a structure stressed for low-level strikes.

The design was offered to the Air Force in April 1952 as the Republic AP-63, a letter contract for engineering design was made in September, and 37 F-105As with J57s were ordered in March 1953. A mockup was inspected in October, but the contract was cut back to 15 in February 1954, and in August 1954 the J75 engine was selected for the F-105B. Only the first two aircraft were completed with the J57-P-25, with the YF-105A first flown October 22, 1955, by Russell Roth.

Meanwhile, Alexander Kartveli's design had been improved with a J75-P-3, area-ruled fuselage, higher fin, and new intakes, and the first F-105B-1 flew May 26, 1956. Three aircraft on this contract originally planned as RF-105s were completed as JF-105B test aircraft. A second contract for 65 F-105B-10/-20 fighters had been approved by June 28, 1957, the first 27 using the J75-P-5 and the rest J75-P-19. Ten F-105B test aircraft were followed by the 65 service types from May 1958 to December 1959.

The outstanding Thunderchief feature was the internal bomb bay—the first to be used on a fighter—containing a 2,000-pound Mk 28 nuclear bomb or a 390-gallon tank. A YF-105A made the first supersonic bomb drops.

The long fuselage also contained all the internal fuel, and petal-type dive brakes were located be-

REPUBLIC YF-105A
Pratt & Whitney J57-P-25, 10,200 lbs.
DIMENSIONS: Span 34'11", Lg. 61'5", Ht. 17'6", Wing Area 385 sq. ft.
WEIGHT: Empty 21,010 lb., Gross 40,561 lb., Combat 28,966 lb. Fuel 2500–850 gal.
PERFORMANCE: Speed—Top 857 mph at 33,000', 778 mph at s. l., Cruising 560 mph, Stalling 185 mph, Combat Ceiling 49,950', Climb 30,000'/17.6 min., Radius 1010 miles/Mk 7, 2720 miles ferry range.   AF

REPUBLIC F-105B
Pratt & Whitney J75-P-19, 16,100 lbs. (24,500 lbs. AB)
DIMENSIONS: Span 34'11", Lg. 63'1", Ht. 19'8", Wing Area 385 sq. ft.
WEIGHT: Empty 25,855 lb., Gross 46,998 lb., Combat 34,870 lb. Fuel 2510–900 gal.
PERFORMANCE: Speed—Top 1376 mph at 36,089', 864 mph at s. l., Cruising 585 mph, Stalling 204 mph. Service Ceiling 32,750', Combat Ceiling 48,100', Climb 35,000'/1.7 min. Combat Radius 744 miles/MK-28, 2228 miles ferry range.   MFR

hind the afterburner. The small wings were swept back from root intakes with raked-forward lips. A 20-mm M-61 with 1,080 rounds and MA-8 fire control was fitted, as well as external fittings for drop tanks or bombs, or 114 2.75-inch rockets in six pods, four Sidewinders, or any combination of six tons total weight.

The most widely used variant was the F-105D, an all-weather model with nose lengthened for the R-14A radar, ASG-19 fire control, and APN-131 doppler navigation radar. The F-105D was first flown on June 9, 1959, by Lin Hendrix. Other improvements included a water-injected J75-P-19W and a toss-bomb computer. As the emphasis was shifting from nuclear warfare to conventional bombs, provision was made to close the internal bomb bay and install a center-line pylon with a multiple ejector rack. Utilizing the four underwing pylons, sixteen 750-pound bombs could be carried for a short distance, although the more usual wartime load was

REPUBLIC F-105D
Pratt & Whitney J75-P-19W, 16,100 lbs. (24,500 lbs. AB)
DIMENSIONS: Span 34'11", Lg. 64'5", Ht. 19'8", Wing Area
385 sq. ft.
WEIGHT: Empty 26,855 lb., Gross 48,976 lb., Max. 52,546
lb., Combat 35,637 lb. Fuel 2710–3100 gal.
PERFORMANCE: Speed—Top 1372 mph at 36,089', 836
mph at s. l., Cruising 778 mph, Stalling 208 mph. Service Ceiling 32,100', Combat Ceiling 48,500', Climb
35,000'/1.75 min. Combat Radius 778 miles/MK-28,
2208 miles ferry at 49,371 lbs.   AF

REPUBLIC F-105F   AF

eight. Alternate loads were two 3,000-pound
bombs, three 450-gallon tanks, four Bullpup or
Sidewinder missiles, or six rocket pods. This adaptation, introduced on the F-105D-25, was
retrofitted to earlier B and D models.

The 610 F-105Ds completed by January 1964
were followed by 143 F-105F two-seaters, first
flown June 11, 1963, which were 5 feet, 4 inches
longer and fitted with the gun and full external
stores points, bringing the production total to 833
accepted by December 1964. No F-105C (a two-
seat trainer) or F-105F (proposed as an all-weather
fighter) were ever built.

Operational use of the Thunderchief began with
the 4th TFW, which received a single F-105B-6
from the first order May 26, 1958, but a complete
squadron wasn't operational until a year later. In
April 1964 the F-105Bs in this wing were replaced
by Ds and were passed on to the ANG, where they
had a long service record. Seven TAC wings used
F-105Ds, experiencing accidents and operational
problems that led to ten groundings and earned the
heavy fighter the nickname "Thud" and a questionable reputation.

With twice the F-100D's bomb load and half
again as much speed, the F-105D was chosen to
deliver over three quarters of the bomb tonnage of
Rolling Thunder, the air offensive against North
Vietnam. Flying from Korat, Thailand, 25 F-105s
launched the attack March 2, 1965, losing two aircraft to antiaircraft artillery (AAA). On April 3, 46
F-105Ds, supported by 21 F-100Ds from South
Vietnam, struck at the Thanh Hoa Bridge, and 48
F-105Ds returned the next day. Four MiG-17s
flying the North Vietnamese Air Force's (NVAF)
first successful interception mission downed two F-
105Ds and AAA a third. As for the bridge, it survived the Bullpup missiles and 750-pound bombs
and remained in operation until 1972.

Antiaircraft guns and, later, missiles caused the
loss of most of the 60 F-105s lost in 1965, since
MiGs were few in number and seldom got past the
F-4 fighter cover. In 1966 more frequent interceptions often forced the F-105s to jettison their bombs,
but F-105Ds from the 355th and 388th TFWs did
destroy 27 MiG-17s from June 29, 1966, to October
27, 1967. They were victims of the 20-mm Vulcan
gun's 6,000 rpm, although two were downed by
Sidewinders.

Wild Weasel, a weapons system with a pilot, electronic warfare officer (EWO), and ECM equipment,
was used to locate and destroy radar-directed AAA
and SAM installations. The work was begun in November 1965 by F-100F two-seaters, which also
introduced the AGM-45 Shrike antiradiation missile against a SAM site on April 18, 1966. In May
1966 the F-100Fs were replaced by an F-105F
squadron, for 86 two-seat F-105Fs had been
equipped with Wild Weasel equipment. Besides
many attacks with rockets and Shrikes, Wild Wea-
sels also downed two MiGs.

Most F-105Ds were withdrawn from SEA, as the
F-4 took over fighter-bomber work, but the F-105Fs
remained until the war's end. Sixty were to be modified to F-105G configuration. These were first
tested in September 1968 with new QRC-380 jam-
mer blisters under the fuselage and heavier AGM-
78 missiles. Although the F-105Ds were withdrawn
from SEA by October 1970, F-105Gs remained until
the war's end. The ANG began getting F-105Ds in
January 1971. A single F-105B and four F-105D
ANG squadrons remained in 1979, while two F-
105G squadrons served TAC's 35th TFW until they
were replaced by F-4Gs in 1980.

The F-106

Convair's F-106A Delta Dart, a development of the
F-102B design, utilized a Pratt & Whitney J75-P-
17, had air intakes moved back behind the cockpit,
a squared-off fin, and dual nosewheels. Seventeen
test examples ordered on an April 28, 1955, con-

REPUBLIC F-105G   MFR

CONVAIR F-106A
Pratt & Whitney J75-P-17, 16,100 lbs. (24,500 lbs. AB)
DIMENSIONS: Span 38'2", Lg. 70'9", Ht. 20'3", Wing Area 698 sq. ft.
WEIGHT: Empty 24,038 lb., Gross 34,510 lb., Combat 30,357 lb. Fuel 1304–968 gal.
PERFORMANCE: Speed—Top 1328 mph at 35,000', 1308 mph at 50,000', Cruising 594 mph, Landing 173 mph. Service Ceiling 52,700', Combat Ceiling 51,800', Climb 51,800'/6.9 min. Combat Range 364 miles area intercept, 1809 miles ferry at 37,772 lbs.   MFR

tract, approved the following April 18, had a delta wing and a new fuselage utilizing the hard-won F-102 experience so well that the shape remained unchanged during F-106 production. The most remarkable feature was the Hughes MA-1 fire-control system.

This electronic system was linked with SAGE ground control and enabled the all-weather interceptor to be "flown automatically from wheels-up following takeoff to flare-out before touchdown." The pilot monitored the mission on a map display projected on a cockpit screen and could take over the controls anytime he desired. When radar had selected the correct target range, the F-106A could fire an AIR-2A Genie missile with nuclear warhead (which will destroy any aircraft within 1,000 feet of its detonation) and four Falcon AIM-4E radar-homing or AIM-4F[6] infrared heat-seeking missiles.

First flown December 26, 1956, by Richard L.

[6] Before 1962 these missiles were the MB-1, GAR-3A, and GAR-4A.

Johnson, the F-106A had a J75-P-9 substituting for the P-17 installed later and lacked the MA-1 system until 1958. Costing $4.7 million apiece, the F-106A joined the ADC in May 1959 and became the first Air Force fighter to last over 20 years in front-line service. (Imagine a 1919 Thomas-Morse in 1939 or a 1939 P-37 in 1959!) Even the 1,525-mph world single-engine speed record set by an F-106 on December 15, 1959, remained unbroken in that period.

San Diego built 277 F-106As and 63 two-place F-106Bs, delivering the last to ADC on July 20, 1961, completing the Air Force's equipment with supersonic fighters. During their long service, many improvements were made to their electronic systems without changing the aircraft's appearance. Larger drop tanks were fitted, and an M-61 20-mm Vulcan gun could be installed in the weapons bay. Two planes tested a YF-106C configuration with new radar and engine.

ADC's fighter strength would be reduced from 30 wings in 1956 to 51 squadrons in 1964, and to 34 squadrons in 1968. By 1976 ADC had only six 18-plane F-106A squadrons, supported by six more squadrons in the ANG. Two Canadian CF-101B squadrons and three ANG F-101B squadrons also covered the approaches to North America, and several F-4 ANG and TAC squadrons were available for continental defense.

The reduction in the interceptor force reflected a change in the type of threat. Intercontinental ballistic missiles (ICBMs), not bombers, comprised the principal menace to the continent. The much-publicized Bison bomber had inadequate range for its mission—only some 150 to 180 had been made—while its partner, the turboprop Bear, was too slow. The Soviet Union converted its long-range bombers into reconnaissance aircraft and came to rely on the Strategic Rocket Force created as a separate branch May 7, 1960. By the time the first Strategic Arms Limitation Treaty (SALT) agreement was made in 1972, over 1,500 Soviet strategic missiles were in place.

North American's Last Fighter Designs

North American Aviation ended 20 years of fighter production—from the NA-50 to the F-100F—in 1959, but its last two fighter designs represented a strong effort to stay in the business. Trying to compete with the F-105 for the fighter-bomber mission, the NA-212 project began in October 1953 as the F-100B, but the letter contract in August 1954 labeled nine prototypes YF-107A.

Designed for Mach 2 speed, the YF-107A had a J75-P-3 with an overhead intake behind the cockpit, a variable area inlet, and one-piece vertical and horizontal tail surfaces. Instead of an internal bomb bay, a nuclear store, including 250 gallons of fuel,

NORTH AMERICAN F-108A
General Electric J93-GE-3AR, 20,900 lbs. (29,300 lbs. AB)
DIMENSIONS: Span 57′5″, Lg. 89′2″, Ht. 22′1″, Wing Area 1865 sq. ft.
WEIGHT: Empty 50,907 lb., Gross 102,533 lb., Combat 76,118 lb. Fuel 7109 gal.
PERFORMANCE: Speed—Top 1980 mph at 76,550′, Stalling 107 mph. Service Ceiling 80,100′, Combat Ceiling 76,550′, Climb 50,000′/5.4 min., Combat Radius 1020 miles/three GAR-9, 2488 miles ferry range.   CARTER

NORTH AMERICAN F-107A
Pratt & Whitney J75-P-9, 15,500 lbs. (23,500 lbs. AB)
DIMENSIONS: Span 36′7″, Lg. 61′8″, Ht. 19′6″, Wing Area 376 sq. ft.
WEIGHT: Empty 22,696 lb., Gross 39,755 lb., Max. 41,537 lb., Combat 30,272 lb. Fuel 2000–650 gal.
PERFORMANCE: Speed—Top 1295 mph at 36,000′, 890 mph at s. l., Cruising 598 mph, Stalling 186 mph. Service Ceiling 53,200′, Combat Ceiling 47,300′, Climb 39,900′/1 min. Combat Radius 788 miles, 2428 miles ferry range.   MFR

was semirecessed underneath the fuselage. Radar fire control and four 20-mm M-39 guns were carried, along with four underwing points for drop tanks, bombs, or rocket pods. For the basic nuclear mission the ventral store and two 275-gallon drop tanks were carried, or a 500-gallon ventral tank and two 1,000-pound bombs could be used.

Only three prototypes were completed, the first flying September 10, 1956, but the design was not able to equal the F-105's success and was abandoned in February 1957.

North American began the F-108A long-range interceptor project June 6, 1957, as the NA-157. Designed for a speed of 1,980 mph at 76,550 feet and armed with three advanced GAR-9 missiles, the big two-seater delta wing had two 29,300-pound-thrust J93-GE-3 engines behind variable inlets under the wing roots. Gross weight was 51 tons, including 7,100 gallons of fuel, enough for a 1,020-mile combat radius.

A mockup was inspected in January 1959 and the first flight planned for March 1961, but the project was canceled September 23, 1959; by the time the F-108A could have been in service, ballistic missiles would have already replaced strategic bombers as the primary threat.

Chapter 28
Navy Patrol Planes Since 1945

The Neptune

By war's end, patrol-plane performance had greatly advanced beyond prewar standards, mainly through the substitution of landplanes for flying boats. These landplanes, however, were basically adaptations of Army bombers, and not until 1945 did a landplane designed from its inception as a patrol type become available.

Developed for the primary mission of antisubmarine and antisurface-vessel patrol work, the Lockheed Model 26 Neptune was a twin-engine high-wing monoplane with tricycle landing gear and a high single fin. Secondary missions were rocket and night torpedo attack, mine laying, bombing, and reconnaissance, although these capabilities were limited to those available after providing the best possible facilities for the primary mission. Long range, the ability to operate from small fields, and high speed were listed as the desired characteristics.

Lockheed received a letter of intent for prototypes on February 19, 1943, two XP2V-1s and 15 P2V-1s were approved April 4, 1944, and 151 more Neptunes added December 16. The prototype was flown May 17, 1945, with 2,300-hp Wright R-3350-8 Cyclones. The P2V-1s began to appear in September 1946 and became operational with VP-2 in March 1947. A crew of seven operated radar and six .50-caliber guns with 466 rounds each: two in a hand-operated bow emplacement, two in the rear-deck power turret, and two for the tail gunner.

The Neptune's bomb bay could accommodate twelve 325-pound depth charges or two 2,000-pound torpedoes for night attacks, or as much as four tons for short-distance horizontal bombing or 1,000 gallons of additional fuel. For rocket attacks sixteen 5-inch or four 11.75-inch rockets could be carried on underwing studs. The third P2V-1 was specially modified by stripping off all armament,

building a new, streamlined nose, and adding fuel tanks in the fuselage and on the wing tips. On September 29, 1946, it took off from Australia with 8,396 gallons of gasoline and 85,500 pounds of gross weight. When the *Truculent Turtle* landed in Ohio 55 hours later, it had established a world nonstop, nonrefueling flight record of 11,236 miles (great circle distance).

The *Truculent Turtle*'s longer nose was incorporated into an XP2V-2 and 81 P2V-2 production models were accepted beginning in June 1947. Nose armament consisted of six 20-mm fixed guns, and additional speed was provided by R-3350-24W engines of 2,800 hp with water-injection. Other additions included de-icers and sonobuoy launchers for underwater submarine detection. The latter are buoys dropped in a pattern to send out a sonar

LOCKHEED XP2V-1
Wright R-3350-8, 2300 hp takeoff, 1900 hp at 14,000'
DIMENSIONS: Span 100', Lg. 75'4", Ht. 28'6", Wing Area 1000 sq. ft.
WEIGHT: Empty 32,651 lb., Gross 54,527 lb., Max. 58,000 lb. Fuel 2350–3350 gal.
PERFORMANCE: Speed—Top 289 mph at 15,600', 231 mph at s. l., Cruising 163 mph, Landing 93 mph. Service Ceiling 23,200', Climb 1120'/1 min. Range 2879 miles/ eight 325 lb. depth charges, 4210 miles max.   MFR

LOCKHEED P2V-1
Wright R-3350-8A, 2300 hp
DIMENSIONS: As XP2V-1
WEIGHT: Empty 33,720 lb., Gross 60,731 lb., Max. 61,153 lb. Fuel 2350–3350 gal.
PERFORMANCE: (At 47,115 lbs., combat weight) Speed—Top 303 mph at 15,300', Cruising 176 mph. Service Ceiling 27,000'. Range 4130 miles max.　　　PMB

LOCKHEED P2V-2
Wright R-3350-24W, 2100 hp normal, 2800 hp WE
DIMENSIONS: Span 100', Lg. 77'10", Ht. 28'1", Wing Area 1000 sq. ft.
WEIGHT: Empty 33,962 lb., Max. 63,078 lb. Fuel 2350–3350 gal.
PERFORMANCE: (At 49,040 lbs., combat weight) Speed—Top 320 mph at 13,500', Cruising 178 mph, Landing 77 mph. Service Ceiling 26,000', Climb 810'/1 min. Range 3985 miles.　　　LAWSON

LOCKHEED P2V-3
Wright R-3350-26W, 3200 hp WE
DIMENSIONS: As P2V-2
WEIGHT: Empty 34,875 lb., Gross 50,062 lb., Max. 64,100 lb. Fuel 2350–3350 gal.
PERFORMANCE: Speed—Top 338 mph at 13,000', Cruising 180 mph, Landing 77 mph. Service Ceiling 28,000', Climb 1060'/1 min. Range 3935 miles.　　　USN

LOCKHEED P2V-4
Wright R-3350-30W, 2650 hp normal, 3250 hp WE
DIMENSIONS: As P2V-2
WEIGHT: Empty 42,021 lb., Gross 67,500 lb., Max. 74,129 lb. Fuel 4210 gal.
PERFORMANCE: Speed—Top 352 mph at 9500', 312 mph at s. l., Landing 109 mph. Service Ceiling 31,000'. Range 4200 miles.　　　USN

signal that rebounds from a submarine hull and is automatically transmitted by the buoy to the search plane. Several must be dropped if the submarine's area is to be enclosed and the vessel's position determined.

All but the first eight P2V-2s had a new tail turret with a pair of 20-mm guns. These were standard on the P2V-3, which appeared in July 1948 with 3,200-hp R-3350-26 Cyclones and four-bladed propellers. Two of 53 ordered were converted to armored special transports (P2V-3Z) and 11 others became P2V-3Cs modified for carrier takeoff and used by VC-5, the first Navy squadron trained to deliver nuclear bombs. On March 7, 1949, a P2V-3C took off from the *Coral Sea*—it weighed 74,000 pounds, including a 10,000-pound dummy atomic weapon—flew 2,000 miles to a target, and 2,000 more to its landing site. An early-warning Neptune was the P2V-3W, 30 of which were delivered beginning in August 1949, with a bulging APS-20 radar in the forward bomb bay operated by two radarmen who sat with the bomber-navigator and radio operator in the cabin between the pilots and the deck turret.

The P2V-4 model had increased fuel capacity, including wing-tip tanks, new radar, and, after some delay, Wright R-3350-30W Turbo-Compound Cyclones of 3,250 hp. Fifty-two were built, the first delivered in September 1949, the rest beginning in January 1950.

The next model was P2V-5, appearing in April 1951 with fixed guns removed and an Emerson ball turret with two 20-mm guns in the nose, providing a lookout and bombing station. Other armament included two 20-mm tail guns, two .50-caliber guns in the deck turret, and two 1,200-pound Mk 41 homing torpedoes. Later aircraft replaced the tail turret with a magnetic anomaly detector (MAD) in the 17-foot plastic "stinger." A searchlight in the nose of

LOCKHEED P2V-5 (RAF)
Wright R-3350-30WA, 3250 hp at 3400', 2550 hp at 15,400'
DIMENSIONS: Span 104', Lg. 91'2", Ht. 28'1", Wing Area
    1000 sq. ft.
WEIGHT: Empty 43,000 lb., Gross 71,400 lb., Max. 80,000
    lb., Combat 61,320 lb. Fuel 2800–3900 gal.
PERFORMANCE: Speed—Top 323 mph at 17,400', 306 mph
    at 1500', Cruising 207 mph, Landing 109 mph. Service
    Ceiling 23,200', Climb 1820'/1 min. Range 3194 miles/
    2400 lbs., 3885 miles ferry   MFR

the starboard tip tank was controlled by movement
of the bow turret, which had been first tested in
1948. The crew of nine included pilots under a
raised canopy, radarmen, gunners, navigator, and
radioman.

The first P2V-5 flight was on December 29, 1950,
and 422 were accepted between April 1951 and
September 1954. Fifty-two went to Britain, first arriving on January 13, 1952, and served four Coastal
Command squadrons until 1956. Eight of these
were passed on to Argentina in June 1958. Twenty
new P2V-5s went to Australia in 1952 and 12 to the
Netherlands in 1954, with the latter 12 seconded to
Portugal in 1960, and Brazil got 14 secondhand from
the United States.

The mine-laying P2V-6 had four 20-mm guns
with 1,600 rounds in front and tail turrets, two .50-
caliber guns in the deck turret, and eight 1,000-
pound mines, 12,000 pounds of bombs, or 16 rockets. An APS-33B radar and 1,092 pounds of armor
protection were provided. The first P2V-6 flew October 16, 1952, and 83 delivered by November 1953
included 26 for France and 16 P2V-6Bs (P2V-6Ms)
equipped with Fairchild Petrel antisub missiles.

In 1953 a Westinghouse J34 jet was mounted
under each wing of a P2V-5, shortening the takeoff
run and increasing dash speed. Beginning in October 1954, all Navy P2V-5s were rotated back to
Lockheed for modification to the P2V-5F with J34
jets, and all turrets, unnecessary for antisub warfare,
were removed. Jets were also added to the P2V-6F,
and under the new designation system these Neptunes became the P-2E (P2V-5F), DP-5E (P-2E for
aerial target launching), SP-2E (P-2E with Julie/Jez-
ebel sub detection gear), P-2F (P2V-6) and P-2G
(P2V-6F).

The final Neptune version was the P2V-7 (Model

726), now known as the P-2H. Strictly an antisubmarine warfare (ASW) aircraft, dispensing with all
guns but the twin .50s in the deck turret, the P-2H
had a clear nose enclosure, raised pilot's canopy,
MAD gear in the tail, two R-3350-32W Cyclones,
and two J34-WE-36 jets. The first flight of the P-2H
was on April 26, 1954. A total of 212 went to the
Navy, seven to the USAF in 1954 for special ECM
work as the RB-69A, and 76 to MAP, including Canada (25), the Netherlands (15), France (12), Australia (12), and Brazil (8), while other Neptunes
were direct foreign sales, including 16 to Japan, ten
to Argentina, and four to Chile.

The last P2H was delivered by Lockheed on September 11, 1962, bringing the Navy total to 1,036,

LOCKHEED P-2E (P2V-5F)
Wright R-3350-32W, 3750 hp, and Westinghouse J34-WE-
    34, 3250 lbs.
DIMENSIONS: Span 101'4", Lg. 89'4", Ht. 28'1", Wing Area
    1000 sq. ft.
WEIGHT: Empty 48,500 lb., Gross 75,700 lb., Max. 80,000
    lb., Combat 68,020 lb. Fuel 2800–3900 gal.
PERFORMANCE: Speed—Top 398 mph at 14,000', 374 mph
    at 1500', Cruising 185 mph, Landing 110 mph. Service
    Ceiling 23,000', Climb 2850'/1 min. Range 2850
    miles.   WL

LOCKHEED P-2F (P2V-6)
Wright R-3350-30WA, 3500 hp takeoff, 3250 hp at 3500',
    2550 hp at 15,400'
DIMENSIONS: Span 102', Lg. 84'10", Ht. 28'1", Wing Area
    1000 sq. ft.
WEIGHT: Empty 44,383 lb., Max. 80,000 lb., Combat 64,-
    477 lb. Fuel 2800–4200 gal.
PERFORMANCE: Speed—Top 318 mph at 16,500', 303 mph
    at 1500', Cruising 201 mph, Landing 114 mph. Service
    Ceiling 20,200', Climb 1650'/1 min. Range 2660 miles
    as minelayers, 4126 miles ferry.   MFR

LOCKHEED P-2H (P2V-7)
Wright R-3350-32W, 3700 hp takeoff, 3400 hp at 2500',
  2400 hp at 18,000', and Westinghouse J34-WE-36
DIMENSIONS: Span 101'4", Lg. 91'8", Ht. 29'4", Wing Area
  1000 sq. ft.
WEIGHT: Empty 44,460 lb., Gross 73,139 lb., Max. 80,000
  lb., Combat 65,027 lb.
PERFORMANCE: (piston only) Speed—Top 312 mph at
  18,400', 300 mph at 1500', Cruising 188 mph, Landing
  109 mph. Service Ceiling 22,400', Climb 1760'/1 min.
  Range 3505 miles, 4293 miles ferry (no pods).
With jets boost, Top Speed 402 mph, Service Ceiling
29,700'.   MFR

of which 186 went abroad under MAP. In Japan,
Kawasaki built 42 P-2H Neptunes by 1965, followed by 83 improved P-2Js built in Japan by February 1979.

Neptunes equipped 20 Navy patrol squadrons.
The last SP-2H retired from a first-line squadron,
VP-23, in February 1970, but they remained in Naval Reserve squadrons and in utility units until July
1980.

The war in Southeast Asia inspired two special
modifications, the OP-2E tactical observation aircraft and the AP-2H night-attack version, provided
with gun pods under the wings, tail turret, infrared
sensors, and exhaust shrouds. From November 1967
to June 1968 12 OP-2Es of VO-67 dropped acous-
tical devices in Vietnam to detect enemy night
movements on the Ho Chi Minh Trail, while VAH-
21 used the AP-2H during the same time period to
hit enemy traffic.

Although Lockheed has dominated the patrol
field since 1947, Martin offered three competing
types, the first being the XP4M-1 Mercator. This
Baltimore-built monoplane resembled an enlarged
Neptune, but behind each of the two Pratt & Whitney R-4360-4 Wasp Majors was a J33 jet for extra
bursts of power. Armament on the Mercator included six tons of bombs, depth charges or mines,
pairs of .50-caliber guns in nose and rear-deck
power turrets, two .50-caliber waist guns, and two
20-mm guns in the tail turret.

Two prototypes ordered July 6, 1944, were first

LOCKHEED SP-2H   LAWSON

LOCKHEED OP-2E   OLSEN

LOCKHEED AP-2H   MILLER

MARTIN XP4M-1
Pratt & Whitney R-4360-4, 2975 hp takeoff, 2400 hp at
  16,200', and Allison J33-A-17, 3825 lbs.
DIMENSIONS: Span 114', Lg. 82'7", Ht. 26'1", Wing Area
  1300 sq. ft.
WEIGHT: Empty 45,739 lb., Gross 77,729 lb., Max. 79,657
  lb. Fuel 2800–4200 gal.
PERFORMANCE: Speed—Top (4 engines) 395 mph at 19,-
  100', 363 mph at s. l., (prop.) 289 mph at 17,800', 273
  mph at s. l., Cruising 170 mph, Landing 99 mph. Service Ceiling 32,800', Climb 2380'/1 min. Range 4230
  miles max., 3167 miles/two torpedos.   USN

MARTIN P4M-1
Pratt & Whitney R-4360-20, 2250 hp takeoff, 2500 hp at
  16,800', and Allison J33-A-23, 4600 lbs.
DIMENSIONS: Span 114', Lg. 84', Ht. 26'1", Wing Area
  1300 sq. ft.
WEIGHT: Empty 48,536 lb., Gross 81,463 lb., Max. 83,378
  lb. Fuel 2800–4200 gal.
PERFORMANCE: Speed—Top (4 engines) 415 mph at 20,-
  100', 379 mph at s. l., (prop.) 296 mph at 18,700', 282
  mph at s. l., Cruising 168 mph, Landing 88 mph. Service Ceiling 34,600', Climb 2730'/1 min. Range 3800
  miles max., 2840 miles/two torpedos.   LAWSON

MARTIN XP5M-1
Wright R-3350-26, 2700 hp
DIMENSIONS: Span 118', Lg. 88', Ht. 37'11", Wing Area
  1406 sq. ft.
WEIGHT: Empty 39,000 lb., Gross 60,000 lb. Fuel 1330–
  2763 gal.
PERFORMANCE: Speed—Top 249 mph at 15,700', 234 mph
  at s. l., Cruising 140 mph, Landing 76 mph. Service
  Ceiling 24,000'. Range 1036 miles/four 325 lb. depth
  charges, 1360 miles/1330 gal.   MFR

flown September 20, 1946, followed, from December 1949 to September 1950, by 19 P4M-1s with
improved engines and 20-mm guns in the bow turret, which served with VP-21. Some were later assigned to Electronic Countermeasures Squadron
VQ-1, commissioned in June 1955 with P4M-1Q
Mercators.

The Last Flying Boats

After World War II, water-based aircraft had only a
small place in Navy programs. During the five years
after the war, the only armed hull types accepted
for service were the 36 PBM-5A amphibians built
for rescue work. Before the Korean War of 1950, the
Navy's patrol force consisted of eight squadrons of
Neptunes, six of Privateer landplanes, and six with
PBM-5 flying boats. Of the Reserve air wings,
eleven used Harpoons and nine amphibian Catalinas.

The flying boat, however, got a new lease on life
through the development of new hulls, featuring a
high ratio of length to beam and greater streamlining. These hulls reduced the performance differ-
ential between water- and land-based craft and renewed interest in the virtues of water landing,
namely, added safety and a less destructible base.

The first to demonstrate the new look in hulls
was Martin's XP5M-1, ordered June 26, 1946, which
made its first flight May 30, 1948, powered by two
2,700-hp Wright R-3350-26 Cyclones. Although utilizing wings intended for the last aircraft on wartime PBM-5 contracts, the XP5M-1 introduced the
new longer, narrower hull, with a single step and
planing bottom all the way back to a high, single
tail. Hydroflaps were provided for quick turns on

the water, radar was placed above the flight deck,
and gun turrets were mounted at the nose, rear
deck, and tail.

The new hull proved successful and four P5M-1s
were ordered in December 1949. Named the Marlin, the first of these flew June 22, 1951, and all four
were accepted in December. Two 3,200-hp R-3350-
30W Cyclones and new fixed floats were used, with
two 20-mm guns and 600 rounds in the tail turret.
Its antisubmarine warfare mission required 2,500
pounds of APS-44A radar in a bulbous nose and
homing torpedoes or depth charges in the engine
nacelles. Korean War contracts added 110 P5M-1s,
completed by April 1954, plus seven P5M-1Gs for
the Coast Guard.

A new T-tail, with the horizontal surface atop
the vertical fin, was introduced on the P5M-2, first
flown in production form April 29, 1954. Other
changes included a modified bow, 3,400-hp R-
3350-32Ws, more fuel, a 130-million-candlepower
searchlight under the starboard wing tip, and magnetic detection gear high on the tail. When the last
of 117 P5M-2s was delivered in December 1960,
American flying-boat production had ended, leaving the Navy with ten squadrons of Marlin flying
boats and 20 of Neptune landplanes. France got ten
P5M-2s in 1959 and the Coast Guard four P5M-2Gs.

By 1962 the Marlins were redesignated and modified to SP-5A and SP-5B configuration, with 12
crewmen and an elaborate range of electronics, including APS-80 search radar, ECM receivers and
direction finder, ASQ-8 MAD, sonobuoy (Julie/Jez-
ebel) receivers, echo-sounding, and an integrated
display system. Weapons bays contained two Mk 43
torpedoes or four 2,025-pound Mk 39 mines, and
eight 5-inch rockets could be carried under the

MARTIN P5M-1
Wright R-3350-30W, 3250 hp WE
DIMENSIONS: Span 118', Lg. 90'8", Ht. 37'3", Wing Area
    1406 sq. ft.
WEIGHT: Empty 36,800 lb., Gross 72,837 lb. Fuel 2815
    gal.
PERFORMANCE: Speed—Top 262 mph. Service Ceiling
    22,400'. Range 3600 miles.   LAWSON

MARTIN P5M-2   MFR

MARTIN SP-5B (P5M-2S)
Wright R-3350-32WA, 3700 hp takeoff, 3420 hp/2400'
DIMENSIONS: Span 118'2", Lg. 100'2", Ht. 30'11", Wing
    Area 1406 sq. ft.
WEIGHT: Empty 49,218 lb., Gross 76,595 lb., Max. 78,000
    lb., Combat 65,986 lb. Fuel 2843–3993 gal.
PERFORMANCE: Speed—Top 266 mph at 17,400', 251 mph
    at s. l., Cruising 159 mph, Stalling 112 mph, Service
    Ceiling 20,600', Combat Ceiling 18,200', Climb 1470'/
    1 min., Combat Range 2471 miles. Ferry Range 3060
    miles.   LAWSON

wings. Tail guns were omitted, although 7.6-mm M-60 guns were installed at the four side hatches in the hull on surveillance missions off the Vietnamese coast. By then (1965–66) only three Navy flying-boat squadrons remained, based at San Diego's North Island and rotating aircraft to the Philippines.

The Navy ended 56 years of seaplane flying on November 6, 1967, with the last operational flight by an SP-5B (formerly P5M-2S) Marlin flying boat of VP-40. Appropriately, this squadron's base in San Diego was the site of the first American seaplane's flight, by Glenn Curtiss, January 26, 1911.

During the Marlin and Neptune's service, attempts were made to develop more advanced patrol planes utilizing gas-turbine engines. The first such effort was the Convair XP5Y-1, with four Allison T-40-A-4 units yielding 5,100 hp to six-bladed propellers, and 830 pounds of residual exhaust thrust. These power plants were to present serious mechanical difficulties. The hull was long, narrow, and streamlined, but wing-tip floats were fixed; retractable floats like those of the PBYs were inappropriate to the thin, low-drag wing.

As early as December 27, 1945, the Navy invited proposals for a turboprop flying boat using the new hull shapes under development, and Convair received a letter contract for two XP5Y-1 prototypes June 19, 1946. After many engine delays, Convair's last flying boat, last patrol type, and the only Navy turboprop boat took off from San Diego Bay on April 18, 1950.

A radar scanner was located in the nose, armor protected the flight deck, nacelles, and turrets, 8,000 pounds of bombs could be carried, and five

CONVAIR XP5Y-1
Allison XT-40-A-4, 5100 hp and 830 lbs.
DIMENSIONS: Span 146'10", Lg. 127'11", Ht. 46'2", Wing
    Area 2102 sq. ft.
WEIGHT: Empty 71,824 lb., Gross 123,500 lb., Max. 140,-
    374 lb. Fuel 6768–8762 gal.
PERFORMANCE: Speed—Top 388 mph at 30,000', 372 mph
    at s. l., Cruising 225 mph, Landing 99 mph. Service
    Ceiling 39,700', Climb 3310'/1 min. Range 2785 miles/
    eight 325 lb. depth charges, 3450 miles max.   MFR

pairs of 20-mm guns could be mounted on remote-controlled turrets. Four turrets were on the hull's sides—two ahead of the cockpit, and two behind the single rudder—although no weapons were ever fitted. The power-plant problems were never overcome, the second prototype was not flown, and the original aircraft crashed July 15, 1953. Eleven R3Y transport versions were built, but they were retired in 1958 due to engine troubles.

In October 1952 Convair entered a Navy design competition for a jet-propelled mine-laying seaplane, but its design was bested by the Martin Seamaster, designed for the same purpose. Flown on July 14, 1955, the XP6M-1 had a long, narrow hull, high T-tail, and swept wing with plastic floats at the tips for balance in the water. Four Allison J71 turbojets were paired in nacelles atop the wings, and equipment included radar in the nose, two 20-mm guns with 1,000 rounds in the tail, 30,000 pounds of mines or other stores, and 1,079 pounds of armor. The mines were carried in a hull bay with a watertight rotary door and a hatch for loading at sea. Pressurized compartments were provided for the crew of five.

Both XP6M-1 prototypes were destroyed in tests, but the similar YP6M-1, flown January 20, 1958, was followed by five sister ships. Next was the P6M-2, flown March 3, 1959, with 15,000-pound-thrust Pratt & Whitney J75-P-2s, but four were scarcely finished on a contract originally calling for 24 when the Navy suddenly terminated the Seamaster program in August. With the last of Martin's Model 275, the Navy halted American flying-boat development, and Martin left the airplane business to concentrate on missiles.

MARTIN P6M-2
Allison J75-P-2, 15,800 lbs.
DIMENSIONS: Span 100', Lg. 134', Ht. 31', Wing Area 1900 sq. ft.
WEIGHT: Gross 160,000 lb.
PERFORMANCE: Speed—Top 686 mph at s. l. Service Ceiling 43,900', Range 868 miles/30,000 lb. mines.   USN

The Orion

Lockheed Aircraft Corporation was very successful in developing transport aircraft designs into patrol configurations. Roomy passenger cabins could accommodate electronic systems and weapons and provided the crew with the comfort needed for antisub operations. Specialization in ASW had eliminated the gun turrets formerly carried to deal with enemy aircraft and surface vessels.

The famous four-engine Constellation received a patrol designation when it was flown June 9, 1949, as the PO-1W, with huge radar installations, including an eight-foot dome atop the fuselage for target altitude measurements and a round search radome under the belly. Since its sole mission was to provide early over-the-horizon warning of strategic bombers, and not any combat mission of patrol types, the designation was changed to the WV-2 Warning Star in production models.

The smaller Electra transport, with four turboprop engines, however, was developed into a true combat plane, the Navy's standard land-based ASW type, the P-3 Orion. Using an existing transport saved the Navy much time and money, as was hoped would be the case when Lockheed won the design competition in April 1958 for a Neptune replacement. Since the winning design had the Electra airliner's wing, tail, and engines, the third Electra was used in August to test the aerodynamic qualities of the new fuselage.

A YP3V-1 prototype ordered February 2, 1959, was flown by November 25. The first seven P3V-1s were ordered October 25, 1960, and first flown March 30, 1961—a rapid development for a contemporary type. Redesignated P-3A in 1962, the Orion had four Allison T56-A-10W turboprops and a spa-

MARTIN YP6M-1
Allison J71-A-6, 9500 lbs. normal, 13,000 lbs. AB
DIMENSIONS: Span 102'7", Lg. 134'4", Ht. 33'9", Wing Area 1900 sq. ft.
WEIGHT: Empty 84,685 lb., Gross 167,011 lb., Max. 190,000 lb., Combat 147,609 lb. Fuel 11,020 gal.
PERFORMANCE: Speed—Top 646 mph at 5000', Cruising 540 mph, Landing 145 mph. Service Ceiling 35,000', Climb 3550'/1 min. Range 1595 miles as minelayer, 2745 miles high altitude reconnaissance.   MFR

LOCKHEED P-3A (P3V-1)
Allison T56A-10W, 4500 hp for takeoff
DIMENSIONS: Span 99'8", Lg. 116'10", Ht. 33'8", Wing Area 1300 sq. ft.
WEIGHT: Empty 59,201 lb., Gross 127,500 lb., Combat 103,280 lb. Fuel 9200 gal.
PERFORMANCE: Speed—Top 455 mph at 14,000', 421 mph at s. l., Cruising 357 mph, Stalling 136 mph. Combat Ceiling 27,700', Climb 10,000'/6.8 min., Combat Radius 1612 miles, 5570 miles ferry range.   USN

LOCKHEED P-3B
Allison T56-A-14, 4910 hp at takeoff
DIMENSIONS: As P-3A
WEIGHT: Empty 61,491 lb., Gross 132,990 lb., Max. 140,337 lb., Combat 107,966 lb. Fuel 9200 gal.
PERFORMANCE: Speed—Top 474 mph at 14,600', 430 mph at s. l., Cruising 331 mph, Stalling 138. Combat Ceiling 29,000', Climb 10,000'/5.8 min., Combat Radius 1670 miles, 5620 miles ferry range.   NAGAKUBO

cious pressurized cabin containing ten crewmen. A tactical coordinator and his sensor operators searched for subs with APS-80A radar, ASQ-10 MAD gear, active and passive sonobuoys, and ECM equipment. For attack, the P-3A weapons bay contained eight Mk 44 torpedoes or four torpedoes and one or two Mk 101 Lulu nuclear depth charges, and ten underwing pylons could carry more torpedoes or four 5-inch rocket pods.

The P-3A entered service with VP-8 in August 1962, and 157 were completed by December 1965. More powerful T56-A-14 engines were used on the P-3B, first flown September 24, 1962. Armament

provisions now included eight Mk 46 homing torpedoes, four Mk 101 depth bombs, up to eleven Mk 36 mines, or four rocket pods or AGM-12B Bullpup missiles for attacking cargo ships. Lockheed delivered 152 P-3Bs, including five for New Zealand in 1966, ten for Australia in 1968, and five for Norway in 1969.

Although similar in appearance and armament to earlier versions, the P-3C represented a major improvement in search capability. An ASQ-114 digital computer integrated and stored information from the new APS-115 radar, ASQ-81 MAD, ECM systems, and various acoustic sensors for which 84 sonobuoys were carried. A surveillance camera was mounted in the nose, and the searchlight under the wing was replaced by a low-level-light television system.

A YP-3C was converted on the P-3B assembly line and first flown September 18, 1968, and production P-3Cs were first deployed overseas to Iceland in 1970. The Navy decided to replace the earlier models with P-3Cs by buying 257 aircraft during fiscal 1970–82. There were 24 first-line and two training patrol squadrons during the 1970s, including eight P-3C squadrons at NAS Moffet, California, five at Barber's Point, Hawaii, seven at Jacksonville, Florida, and six at Brunswick, Maine. Except for three P-3As sent to Spain and three modified to other configurations, the P-3As were transferred to the Naval Reserve's 19 patrol squadrons, along with P-3Bs, as they were replaced in first-line units.

Navy P-3Cs had their capabilities improved through update programs in which aircraft were rotated through the shops to be fitted with the latest in equipment. Update I aircraft introduced in 1975 had a sevenfold increase in the computer's memory storage and an Omega worldwide navigation system. Update II, first delivered in August 1977, introduced an infrared detector under the nose, a sonobuoy reference system, and Harpoon antiship-

LOCKHEED P-3C
Allison T56-A-14
DIMENSIONS: As P-3A
WEIGHT: Empty 66,211 lb., Gross 135,000 lb., Max. 142,-
000 lb., Combat 111,252 lb. Fuel 9200 gal.
PERFORMANCE: Speed—Top 455 mph at 12,300', 412 mph
at s. l., Cruising 325 mph, Stalling 140 mph. Combat
Ceiling 27,200'. Climb 10,000'/6.3 min., Combat Ra-
dius 1455 miles/six Mk 46 torpedoes, 5200 miles ferry
range.   LAWSON

LOCKHEED EP-3E   NAGAKUBO

LOCKHEED P-3F (Iran)   MFR

LOCKHEED P-3C Update II   MFR

ping-missile provisions. Although the Orion was
the only propeller-driven aircraft still in first-line
American service, its electronics and weapons capability and its 12-hour mission endurance seemed
likely to keep it in service for a third decade.

Special Orion conversions included RP-3As for

research, an RP-3D magnetic surveyor, WP-3D
weather research, and 12 EP-3E aircraft for VQ-1
and VQ-2, the electronic surveillance squadrons.
Orion exports began with six P-3Fs for Iran in 1974,
while Australia got the first of ten P-3Cs in February
1978. Canada ordered 18 designated CP-140 Au-
rora, with different electronic provisions, on July
21, 1976, and the first flew in March 1979. Japan
signed a contract June 9, 1978, for 45 Orions, three
to be completed by Lockheed and four to be
shipped in parts for assembly by Kawasaki, which
would build the remainder in Japan. The Netherlands decided in December 1978 to purchase 13
P-3Cs.

Chapter 29
Navy Attack Planes of the Cold War

The A-1 Skyraider

On March 11, 1946, the Navy replaced the VB and VT designations (for dive and torpedo bombers, respectively) with VA, for attack aircraft whose primary mission was attacking surface targets. Subsequently the BT2D and BTM aircraft on order were redesignated AD and AM attack planes. As described in Chapter 22, Martin's AM-1 served four postwar squadrons, but was soon replaced by the Douglas Skyraider series, which became the A-1 in the current designation system.

Douglas Aircraft's chief engineer, Ed Heinemann, wanted to overcome the troubles that crippled the BTD Destroyer. In June 1944 he proposed a more simple, light design that used a straight high-lift wing for quicker takeoffs with heavy loads instead of the BTD's low-drag gull wing. In place of tricycle gear and internal bomb bay the tail-down gear and external weapons pylons of contemporary BTC, BTK, and BTM types was chosen.

Twenty-five XBT2D-1 preproduction prototypes were ordered July 21, 1944, and the first was flown March 18, 1945. An R-3350-8 used on the first four was replaced by the 2,500-hp R-3350-24W on later models. Two 20-mm wing guns with 400 rpg were carried, and three external hard points could handle two tons of bombs, torpedoes, rockets, drop tanks, or an APS-4 radar pod. The pilot had good visibility under a bubble canopy, and 208 pounds of armor. The wheels turned through 90° as they retracted backwards into the wings, which folded upwards for stowage, and dive brakes were placed at the fuselage sides and bottom. The remaining BT2D-1s, completed in 1946–47, included two XB2D-2N night-attack planes, an XBT2D-1P photo, and an XB2D-1Q radar countermeasures conversion.

On April 18, 1945, an order was placed for 548 production Skyraiders, reduced to 277 after V-J Day and redesignated AD-1 under the new designation system. Delivery began in November 1946 on 242 AD-1s and 35 AD-1Qs. The latter was a radar countermeasures version with a technician in the fuselage behind the pilot operating devices to identify and jam hostile radar. An XAD-1W early-warning prototype, converted from a BT2D-1, had a huge belly radome, two radarmen in the fuselage, and no dive brakes or guns. The AD-1 began service with VA-19A in December 1946. It equipped eight carrier attack squadrons by 1948, but hard landings on carriers revealed structural weaknesses, which were corrected on the AD-2.

The first AD-2, converted from an AD-1 had strengthened wings, more internal fuel, two additional wing racks, and a 2,700-hp R-3350-26W. Deliveries of AD-2s began in April 1948, enabling some AD-1s to be passed to Reserve bases. A total of 156 AD-2s and 22 AD-2Qs were purchased, followed by the AD-3, which differed only in a

DOUGLAS XBT2D-1
Wright R-3350-24W, 2500 hp takeoff, 2200 hp at 11,000'
DIMENSIONS: Span 50', Lg. 39'5", Ht. 9', Wing Area 400 sq. ft.
WEIGHT: Empty 10,093 lb., Gross 13,500 lb., Max. 17,500 lb. Fuel 365–665 gal.
PERFORMANCE: Speed—Top 375 mph at 13,600', 357 mph at s. l. clean, Cruising 164 mph, Landing 83 mph. Service Ceiling 33,200', Climb 3680'/1 min. Range 1427 miles/torpedo with 515 gal. MFR

DOUGLAS AD-1
Wright R-3350-24W, 2500 hp takeoff, 2200 hp at 11,500'
DIMENSIONS: Span 50', Lg. 39'5", Ht. 9', Wing Area 400 sq. ft.
WEIGHT: Empty 10,508 lb., Gross 13,924 lb., Max. 18,030 lb. Fuel 365–665 gal.
PERFORMANCE: Speed—Top 366 mph at 13,500', 348 mph at s. l., Cruising 185 mph, Landing 84 mph. Service Ceiling 33,000', Climb 3590'/1 min. Range 1935 miles/ 2000 lbs. bombs.   WL

DOUGLAS AD-1Q   USN

DOUGLAS AD-2
Wright R-3350-26W, 2700 hp takeoff
DIMENSIONS: Span 50', Lg. 38'2", Ht. 15'5", Wing Area 400 sq. ft.
WEIGHT: Empty 10,546 lb., Gross 16,268 lb., Max. 18,263 lb. Fuel 380 gal.
PERFORMANCE: Speed—Top 321 mph at 18,300', Cruising 198 mph, Landing 83 mph. Service Ceiling 32,700', Climb 2800'/1 min. Range 915 miles.   WL

strengthened internal structure. A total of 125 AD-3, 23 AD-3Q, 31 AD-3W, and 15 AD-3N aircraft were purchased.

The Skyraider used throughout the Korean War was the AD-4, which appeared in June 1949 with

an automatic pilot, APS-19 radar, 156 pounds of armor, and two 20-mm guns, but armament was increased to four 20-mm guns with 200 rounds in December 1950 for all 372 AD-4s built. Three 2,000-pound bombs, torpedoes, or drop tanks could be carried on the main pylons, while outer-wing stations were used for 500-pound bombs or rockets, with a maximum capacity of up to 9,900 pounds (shore) or 6,500 pounds (ship).

Other versions included 39 AD-4Qs appearing in November 1949, 307 AD-4Ns beginning in February 1950, 152 AD-4Ws appearing in March, and 165 AD-4Bs first flown in August 1952. The AD-4B was the first with a low-altitude bombing system (LABS) for a tactical nuclear weapon, the fuselage rack accommodating the 1,680-pound Mk 7 or 3,250-pound Mk 8 stores.

One AD-4 was converted to the AD-5 prototype, first flown August 17, 1951, with a larger tail, four wing guns, and an expanded fuselage serving as a universal chassis on which several different conversions could be made from prepared kits. The two-man flight crew sat side by side under the canopy, and up to eight passengers or four litter patients could be squeezed into the fuselage. Day- or night-attack, early-warning, antisubmarine-warfare, ambulance, cargo, or personnel-transport conversions were possible. After the last AD-4B was delivered in June 1953, the El Segundo plant concurrently turned out three AD-5 versions and the standard AD-6 ground-support single-seater. Deliveries of 212 AD-5, 239 AD-5N (of which 54 became AD-5Q), one AD-5S, 218 AD-5W, 713 AD-6 and, finally, 72 single-seat AD-7 (R-3350-26WB) Skyraiders (the last on February 18, 1957) brought the total to 3,180 from El Segundo. Of these, the British Navy received the last 20 new AD-4Ws from Douglas and about 31 from Navy stocks from November 1951 to April 1953.

DOUGLAS AD-3 (also AD-3N data)
Wright R-3350-26W, 2700 hp takeoff
DIMENSIONS: As AD-2
WEIGHT: Empty 10,812 (11,483) lb., Gross 16,520 (18,044) lb., Max. 18,515 (19,664) lb. Fuel 380 gal.
PERFORMANCE: Speed—Top 321 (296) mph at 18,300', Cruising 200 (197) mph, Landing 84 (87) mph. Service Ceiling 32,300' (28,800'), Climb 2760'/1 min. (2260'/1 min.). Range 900 miles (1175 miles).   WL

DOUGLAS AD-4

Wright R-3350-26WA, 2700 hp takeoff, 2100 hp at 14,500'
DIMENSIONS: Span 50', Lg. 39'3", Ht. 15'8", Wing Area
400 sq. ft.
WEIGHT: Empty 11,712 lb., Gross 21,483 lb., Max. 25,000
lb., Combat 17,818 lb. Fuel 380–830 gal.
PERFORMANCE: Speed—Top 349 mph at 20,000', 316 mph
at s. l., Cruising 227 mph, Stalling 81 mph. Service
Ceiling 23,500', Combat Ceiling 25,300', Climb 2880'/
1 min., 10,000'/7.5 min. Combat Range 1347 miles/2000
lbs. bombs and 12 HVAR, 2/150 gal. tanks.   USN

DOUGLAS AD-4B

Wright R-3350-26WA, 2700 hp takeoff, 2100 hp at 14,500',
(3150 hp combat at s. l.)
DIMENSIONS: As AD-4
WEIGHT: Empty 11,783 lb., Gross 18,669 lb., Max. 24,221
lb., Combat 17,757 lb. Fuel 380–980 gal.
PERFORMANCE: Speed—Top 320 mph at 15,000', 303 mph
at s. l., Cruising 196 mph, Stalling 85 mph. Service
Ceiling 26,000', Combat Ceiling 23,800', Climb 2980'/
1 min., 10,000'/5.3 min. Combat Range 900 miles/
MK-7, 2061 miles/MK-8 and 2/300 gal. tanks.   USN

DOUGLAS AD-4N   MFR

DOUGLAS AD-5   USN

DOUGLAS A-1E (AD-5 for USAF)

Wright R-3350-26WD, 2700 hp takeoff, 2100 hp at 14,500'
DIMENSIONS: Span 50', Lg. 40', Ht. 15'10", Wing Area
400.3 sq. ft.
WEIGHT: Empty 12,293 lb., Gross 24,179 lb., Max. 24,872
lb., Combat 17,354 lb. Fuel 378–988 gal.
PERFORMANCE: Speed—Top 329 mph at 15,200', 310 mph
at s. l., Cruising 201 mph, Stalling 114 mph, Combat
Ceiling 26,200', Climb 2860'/1 min., Combat Range
524 miles/4500 lbs. bombs, 3028 miles ferry.   USAF

DOUGLAS A-1G (AD-5N)
Wright R-3350-26WA, 2700 hp
DIMENSIONS: Span 50′, Lg. 40′, Ht. 13′11″, Wing Area 400 sq. ft.
WEIGHT: Empty 12,112 lb., Gross 20,517 lb., Max. 25,000 lb., Combat 18,505 lb. Fuel 380–980 gal.
PERFORMANCE: Speed—Top 322 mph at 15,100′, 303 mph at s. l., Cruising 190 mph, Stalling 82.5 mph. Service Ceiling 24,500′, Climb 2580′/1 min. Combat Range 662 miles/1100 lbs. bombs, 547 miles/2700 lbs. bombs.
USN

DOUGLAS EA-1E (AD-5W)　　　　　USN

DOUGLAS EA-1F (AD-5Q) dispensing chaff　　USN

DOUGLAS A-1H (AD-6)
Wright R-3350-26WB, 2700 hp takeoff, 2100 hp at 14,000′
DIMENSIONS: As AD-4
WEIGHT: Empty 12,072 lb., Gross 18,398 lb. (2000 lb. bomb load), Max. 24,091 lb., Combat 15,486 lb. (clean), 17,486 lb. (2000 lb. bomb). Fuel 380–1280 gal.
PERFORMANCE: Speed—Top 342 mph at 15,400′ (333 mph/2000 lbs. bombs), 319 (312) mph at s. l., Cruising 180 mph, Stalling 92 mph, Combat Ceiling 29,400′, Climb 10,000′/4.5 min., Combat Radius 275 miles/2000 lbs. bombs, 3240 miles ferry.
USAF

DOUGLAS A-1J (AD-7)
Wright R-3350-26WB, 2700 hp
DIMENSIONS: As AD-4
WEIGHT: Empty 12,094 lb., Gross 22,795 lb., Max. 25,000 lb., Combat 16,199 lb. Fuel 380–980 gal.
PERFORMANCE: Speed—Top 343 mph at 20,000′, 316 mph at s. l., Cruising 195 mph, Stalling 77 mph. Service Ceiling 30,650′, Climb 3230′/1 min. Combat Range 1300 miles/2000 lbs. bombs, 12 HVAR, and 2/150 gal. tanks.
MFR

Skyraiders in Service

When the Korean War began there were 12 Navy AD attack squadrons, plus two AD-4N night-attack and two AD-3W early-warning squadrons. Two radar operators were carried within the fuselage of the N and W types, necessitating the omission of dive brakes, but the N had a radar pod and searchlight under the wings, while the W had the big APS-20 under the fuselage for over-the-horizon detection. The *Valley Forge*'s VA-55 sent its AD-4s out on July 3, 1953, for the first attack in the three-year, carrier-based bombing campaign against North Korea. The first Marine Skyraider squadron, VMA-121, brought AD-3s to Korea in October 1951, flying from land bases throughout the war. The AD's usefulness in Korea was due to its bomb-carrying ability, endurance over target areas, and precision bombing; the AD-4 carried a one-ton bomb and 12 rockets on a six-hour mission over a 620-mile combat radius.

When the war ended in July 1953, there were 24 Navy and eight Marine Skyraider squadrons, and the "Able Dog" had been so successful that AD-5 and AD-6 aircraft replaced older models and filled out 29 Navy and 13 Marine squadrons by September 1955. Replacement of each carrier's second AD squadron by A4D jet aircraft began a year later, and in 1963 the A-6A all-weather jets started replacing the remaining squadrons. In 1962 the Skyraiders had been designated A-1E (AD-5), EA-1E (AD-5W), EA-1F (AD-5Q), A-1G (AD-5N), and the similar A-1H (AD-6) and A-1J (AD-7) single-seaters.

Although most retired Skyraiders wound up in storage in Arizona, many would again be called into combat before long. France obtained 93 AD-4Ns in 1959 for her war in Algeria, and a few of these were passed on to former colonies like Cambodia and Chad. The Republic of Vietnam got 25 AD-6s for the small VNAF in September 1960 to replace the grounded F8F Bearcats left by the French.

American involvement in Southeast Asia found the Air Force without a proper attack plane of its own, so 50 A-1E (formerly AD-5) Skyraiders were removed from storage, refurbished, and delivered, beginning in April 1963, to the Air Force Special Warfare Center at Eglin AFB. Another batch was delivered by December 1965. These A-1Es had dual controls for a second (side-by-side) crewman, four 20-mm M3 guns with 200 rpg, and 15 external stations for 6,500 pounds of bombs, rocket pods, or drop tanks.

In February 1964 Defense Secretary Robert McNamara decided to send 25 of these A-1Es to Vietnam to replace the 1st Air Commando Squadron's T-28s and B-26s and to provide 25 A-1H (AD-6) single-seaters from Navy stocks for the VNAF. American pilots trained Vietnamese flyers and flew A-1E combat missions with Vietnamese observers. A second Air Commando A-1E squadron was authorized in May 1964, with enough A-1Hs for four VNAF squadrons.

By April 1965 there were 89 VNAF A-1Hs and 54 Air Commando A-1Es in Vietnam. In January 1966 the VNAF had about 100 A-1Hs and 20 A-1Gs piloted by men trained on A-1Es at Eglin. Of these aircraft, 72 remained in March 1972, and heavy losses that year were partially replaced by the remaining USAF A-1Es. At the war's end, 11 were evacuated to Thailand in 1975 and 26 A-1E/Gs were captured.

Navy Skyraiders entered the war on August 5, 1964, when the North Vietnamese coast was hit by 12 A-1Hs from VA-52 and VA-145, two of the 12 Navy A-1 squadrons still remaining. Strikes from the carriers continued throughout the war, and two "Spads" (as their pilots now called the A-1) even shot down attacking MiG-17s. The last Navy squadron with the rugged Douglas was the carrier *Coral Sea*'s VA-25, which flew its final combat sortie February 20, 1968, and retired its aircraft on April 10.

Douglas made an attempt at a radical improvement in performance with the XA2D-1 Skyshark, powered by an Allison XT40-A-6 turboprop engine delivering 5,035 hp to contrarotating six-bladed propellers plus 1,225-pound exhaust thrust. The wing plan was that of the AD, but a thinner airfoil was used. The pilot sat high above the engine and ahead of the fuel tank, which required a larger capacity than that of the AD because of higher fuel consumption. Four 20-mm guns were mounted in the wings and 8,000 pounds of bombs or 450 gallons of fuel could be carried externally.

DOUGLAS XA2D-1
Allison XT40-A-6 (orig. A-2), 5035 hp and 1225 lbs. at 14,300'
DIMENSIONS: Span 50', Lg. 41'4", Ht. 16'11", Wing Area 400 sq. ft.
WEIGHT: Empty 14,139 lb., Max. 22,966 lb., Combat 18,-720 lb. Fuel 500–950 gal.
PERFORMANCE: Speed—Top 501 mph at 25,000', 467 mph at s. l., Cruising 286 mph, Stalling 115 mph, Combat Ceiling 40,600', Climb 7290'/1 min., Combat Range 1470 miles.   MFR

The Navy desired a turboprop power plant in an attack type, and had been encouraging Douglas to prepare such a design since 1945. It ordered two XA2D-1 prototypes September 25, 1947. The first flight was delayed by the XT40-A-2 engine until May 26, 1950, but the Korean War led the Navy to order ten A2D-1s on June 30 and 331 production aircraft soon afterwards. Power plant and propeller gear troubles were continuous, however, destroying the first prototype on December 19, and the second (with an XT40-A-6) could not be flown until April 3, 1952. By then contract terminations had begun, being made final in September 1953, with only five A2D-1s accepted between April 1953 and January 1954. The designers, however, learned from the failure and went on to produce the very successful A-4.

The Big Punch

Versatile as the Navy's single-engine bombers were, they compared poorly with the strategic striking power of the Air Force's bigger weapons. This was inherent in the limitations imposed by flight-deck operations: A carrier bomber can only be so big and so heavy; it must have arresting gear, a folding wing, and specialized shipboard equipment, and thus can't have the tremendous power and armament of its heavier competitors.

A larger carrier-based type was needed to enable the Navy to contribute an atomic punch to a strategic-bombing offensive. New Heavy Attack squadrons were formed for strategic-bombing missions and their first plane type used was the North American Savage. A high-wing monoplane with a crew of three in a pressurized cockpit, nose radar, and an internal bomb bay, the AJ-1 had two Pratt & Whitney R-2800-44W Wasps under the wings and an Allison J33-A-10 jet in the fuselage to boost speeds over short distances. The wings folded up and the fin folded down to facilitate stowage aboard carriers. No guns were carried, the AJs depending on speed for protection, while up to six tons of bombs could be carried, such as a 7,600-pound Mk 15 nuclear store, or six 1,600-pound conventional bombs, along with two 300-gallon tip tanks.

The first of three XAJ-1 prototypes ordered June 24, 1946, was flown on July 3, 1948. Fifty-five AJ-1 Savages, begun in June 1947, were first flown May 10, 1949. Similar to the prototypes except for reinforced canopies, they were accepted from the Los Angeles plant from August 1949 to January 1952. North American leased the former Helldiver factory in Columbus, Ohio, for the second series of 30 AJ-2P reconnaissance models, first flown March 30, 1952, and for 55 standard AJ-2s, first flown February 18, 1953. The AJ-2P could be distinguished by its bulbous camera nose, while the bombers could be

NORTH AMERICAN A-2A (AJ-1)
Pratt & Whitney R-2800-44W, 2300 hp at 30,000', and Allison J33-A-10, 4600 lbs.
DIMENSIONS: Span 71'5", Lg. 63'1", Ht. 21'5", Wing Area 836 sq. ft.
WEIGHT: Empty 30,776 lb., Gross 50,963 lb., Max. 54,000 lb., Combat 46,352 lb. Fuel 1217-2457 gal.
PERFORMANCE: Speed—Top 449 mph at 34,000', 357 mph at s. l., Cruising 270 mph, Landing 120 mph. Combat Ceiling 40,800', Climb 2900'/1 min. Range 1732 miles/7600 lb. bomb, MK-15, 2/300 gal. tanks, 2993 miles ferry.   MFR

NORTH AMERICAN A-2B (AJ-2)
Pratt & Whitney R-2800-44W, 2300 hp at 30,000', and Allison J33-A-10, 4600 lbs.
DIMENSIONS: As AJ-1
WEIGHT: Empty 30,776 lb., Gross 50,580 lb., Max. 54,000 lb., Combat 46,990 lb. Fuel 1217-2517 gal.
PERFORMANCE: Speed—Top 449 mph at 34,000', 357 mph at s. l., Cruising 260 mph, Landing 119 mph. Combat Ceiling 41,500', Climb 3050'/1 min. Range 2475 miles/3200 lb. bomb, and 2/300 gal. tanks, 3056 miles ferry.   MFR

fitted as flying tankers to refuel other aircraft in flight by a probe-drogue system.

Allison T40-A-6 turboprop engines with six-bladed contrarotating propellers were used on the XA2J-1, designed by North American as an AJ replacement. Other changes included a swept-back tail fin, dual nosewheel, and two radar-aimed 20-mm guns. Two prototypes were begun October 1, 1948 (NA-163) and the first flew January 4, 1952,

NORTH AMERICAN XA2J-1
Allison T40-A-6, 5035 hp and 1225 lbs. at 14,300′
DIMENSIONS: Span 71′6″, Lg. 70′, Ht. 22′6″, Wing Area
836 sq. ft.
WEIGHT: Empty 32,164 lb., Gross 43,712 lb., Max. 58,000
lb. Fuel 1802–2620 gal.
PERFORMANCE: (Design estimated) Speed—Top 451 mph
at 24,000′, Cruising 400 mph, Stalling 100 mph. Service Ceiling 37,500′. Range 2180 miles/8000 lbs.
bombs.   MFR

but the same T40 difficulties that plagued other
turboprop designs of the time halted this type.

Production of the North American Savage continued until June 1954, and survivors were redesignated A-2A/B in 1962. They entered service in September 1949 with VC-5, which made the first AJ-1
takeoff from the *Coral Sea* on April 21, 1950, and
was joined by seven more heavy-attack and two
photographic squadrons. They were stationed at
shore bases, rotating detachments to the fleet's 17
(as of 1953) attack carriers, but their large size limited their use. They did provide the Navy with a
carrier-based strategic punch, carrying the Mk 6
nuclear bomb in 1950 and the more compact Mk 15
at a later date.

The A-3 Skywarrior

Real progress towards the creation of a Navy strategic bomber required full jet power, with all the
fuel and weight that this implied. The obvious answer was an aircraft carrier large enough to handle
bigger bombers, but funds for this were hard to get.
Hadn't the Navy a surplus of carriers already, including three of the *Midway* and 24 of the *Essex*
class—several times more than the rest of the
world's carrier fleets put together? Besides, the Air
Force felt itself perfectly capable of doing all the
strategic bombing necessary and wanted any available funds invested in its own big bombers.

A huge 65,000-ton carrier was ordered August 10,
1948, by pro-Navy Defense Secretary James V. Forrestal, but it was canceled April 23, 1949—just 5
days after the keel was laid—by Louis A. Johnson,
his successor in the Cabinet post. Another chance
came for the Navy with the Korean War, and funds

became available for the first 60,000-ton super-car-
rier, ordered July 12, 1951, and named *Forrestal*
after the late Secretary of Defense. New flight decks
for big jet bombers were on their way, and the
replacement of the World War II fleet had begun.

Douglas engineers, led by Ed Heinemann, designed a heavy attack type for the new super-carriers before the Korean War that could also operate
from the older *Essex*- and *Midway*-class carriers that
had been rebuilt with stronger, angled decks and
new catapults. The A3D-1 Skywarrior would weigh
35 tons at takeoff, compared to the eight-ton TBMs,
which were the heaviest carrier attack planes in
1945. An Mk 15 nuclear bomb, six 1,600-pound
bombs, or six Mk 36 mines could be delivered on
a target 1,150 miles away at 621-mph top speed—
which was faster than the Air Force's big Boeings.

The A3D-1's high wing was swept back 36°, fitted
with slots, and folded for stowage. The fuselage
contained wells for the retractable tricycle landing
gear, a radar-bombing system in the nose, a three-
place pressurized cabin, internal bomb bay and fuel
tanks, and a remote-controlled radar-aimed tail turret with two 20-mm guns and 1,000 rounds.

Two XA3D-1 prototypes were ordered March 31,
1949, and the first flew October 22, 1952, with two
7,500-pound-thrust Westinghouse XJ40-WE-3 jets
in pods below the wings. Pratt & Whitney J57-P-6
jets were used on 50 A3D-1s, first flown September
16, 1953, but not until March 31, 1956, did deliveries begin to a service squadron (VAH-1). Beginning in June 1956, the Navy received the A3D-2
model, redesignated A-3B in 1962, which had J57-
P-10 engines and provision in the bomb bay for an
auxiliary fuel tank and two Mk 28 nuclear weapons.
Douglas delivered 164 A3D-2s, 30 A3D-2Ps (RA-
3Bs) with 12 cameras first appearing in July 1958,
25 A3D-2Qs (EA-3Bs) of December 1958 with four
electronic-countermeasures operators, one A3D-2W
early-warning model, and 12 A3D-2Ts (TA-3Bs) for
training ECM operators. The last 21 A-3B bombers
were delivered from April 1960 to January 1961,
with a new cambered-wing leading edge, flight-refueling capability, a new ASB-7 bombing system,
and the tail turret replaced by new ECM devices.
These changes were made to most earlier aircraft,
which equipped 12 heavy-attack, two training, two
ECM, and two photographic squadrons.

The 284 big Douglas aircraft served the Navy
well, and the B-66 version served the Air Force.
After retirement as a strategic bomber, their useful
life was extended in 1966–67 by their conversion
to KA-3A aerial tankers (50 aircraft) and EKA-3B
aircraft (39) combining ECM and tanker capability.
These aircraft proved very useful in the Vietnam
War, and EKA-3Bs still served squadrons VQ-1 and
VQ-2 in 1979.

DOUGLAS XA3D-1   MFR

DOUGLAS A3D-1 (A-3A)
Pratt & Whitney J57-P-6, 10,000 lbs.
DIMENSIONS: Span 72'6", Lg. 74'5", Ht. 22'10", Wing Area
   779 sq. ft.
WEIGHT: Empty 35,899 lb., Gross 70,000 lb., Combat
   60,250 lb. Fuel 4506 gal.
PERFORMANCE: Speed—Top 621 mph at 1000', 585 mph
   at 35,000', Cruising 529 mph, Stalling 149 mph. Com-
   bat Ceiling 40,500', Climb 20,000'/5.6 min., Combat
   Radius 1150 miles/7600 lb. Mk 15.   USN

DOUGLAS A3D-2 (A-3B)
Pratt & Whitney J57-P-10, 10,500 lbs.
DIMENSIONS: Span 72'6" (49'2" folded), Lg. 75'8", Ht.
   22'9", Wing Area 779 sq. ft.
WEIGHT: Empty 37,077 lb., Gross 73,000 lb., Max. 78,000
   lb., Combat 62,089 lb. Fuel 4338–5086 gal.
PERFORMANCE: Speed—Top 643 mph at s. l., 590 mph at
   35,000', Cruising 528 mph. Combat Ceiling 41,500',
   Climb 20,000'/4.9 min., Combat Radius 1380 miles/
   4100 lb. (2 Mk 28).   USN

DOUGLAS A-3B (1960 modification)
Pratt & Whitney J57-P-10, 10,500 lbs.
DIMENSIONS: Span 76'6", Lg. 74'9", Ht. 22'9", Wing Area
   812 sq. ft.
WEIGHT: Empty 39,620 lb., Gross 73,000 lb., Max. 78,000
   lb. Fuel 4338–6310 gal.
PERFORMANCE: Speed—Top 640 mph at 2500', 585 mph
   at 35,000', Cruising 502 mph, Stalling 143 mph. Com-
   bat Ceiling 42,300', Climb 20,000'/4.7 min. Combat
   Radius 1325 miles/4100 lb.   USN

DOUGLAS EKA-3B   USN

A-4 Skyhawks

One of the most successful attack aircraft in Navy
service was the light, simple design called Heinemann's Hot Rod, after the Douglas chief engineer
who insisted on reversing the trend towards con-
stantly increasing weight and cost. Designed to deliver a tactical nuclear weapon, the single-place A-
4 had a low delta wing small enough not to require
folding on carrier decks. Armed with two 20-mm
guns in the wing roots with 100 rpg, the Skyhawk
had LABS provisions for a Mk 7 or Mk 8 nuclear
store under the fuselage and wing racks for 300-
gallon drop tanks or conventional bombs; a total of
5,975 pounds of bombs could be carried on the first
model.

Twenty developmental aircraft had been ordered
June 13, 1952, and the first flew as the XA4D-1 on
June 22, 1954, with a Wright 7,200-pound-thrust
J65-W-2, but a 7,700-pound-thrust J65-W-4 was
used on 165 A4D-1s accepted beginning in August
1954. A new rudder, flight-refueling probe, and a
J65-W-16 were on 542 A4D-2s, the first flown March
26, 1956, with the order completed on August 19,
1959. The wing racks on this model could be used
for two Bullpup missiles or a dozen 300-pound Mk

DOUGLAS A-4A (A4D-1)
Wright J65-W-4, 7700 lbs.
DIMENSIONS: Span 27′6″, Lg. 39′4″, Ht. 15′2″, Wing Area
260 sq. ft.
WEIGHT: Empty 8391 lb., Gross 15,093 lb., Max. 19,910
lb., Combat 11,963 lb. Fuel 800–1400 gal.
PERFORMANCE: Speed—Top 677 mph at s. l., 609 mph at
35,000′, Cruising 506 mph, Stalling 124 mph. Combat
Ceiling 46,600′, Climb 11,600′/1 min., Combat Range
1489 miles/Mk 7.

DOUGLAS A-4B (A4D-2)
Wright J65-W-16, 7700 lbs.
DIMENSIONS: As A-4A
WEIGHT: Empty 9146 lb., Gross 17,535 lb., Max. 22,500
lb., Combat 15,359 lb. Fuel 800–1700 gal.
PERFORMANCE: Speed—Top 649 mph at 4000′, 593 mph
at s. l., Cruising 496 mph, Stalling 137 mph. Combat
Ceiling 41,800′, Climb 7950′/1 min., Combat Range
1000 miles/2025 lb. Mk 28, 1650 miles/Mk 28/two 300
gal. tanks.   USN

DOUGLAS A-4C (A4D-2N)
Wright J65-W-16, 7700 lbs.
DIMENSIONS: Span 27′6″, Lg. 40′1″, Ht. 15′, Wing Area
260 sq. ft.
WEIGHT: Empty 9827 lb., Gross 18,443 lb., Max. 22,500
lb., Combat 16,267 lb. Fuel 800–1700 gal.
PERFORMANCE: Speed—Top 657 mph at 4000′ (clean), 633
mph at 10,000′/Mk 28, Cruising 496 mph, Stalling 140
mph. Combat Ceiling 44,000′ clean, 40,100′/Mk 28,
Climb 7100′/1 min., 20,000′/4.5 min (Mk 28), Combat
Range 1140 miles clean, Combat Radius 535 miles
clean, 558 miles/2040 lb. Mk 28, 2/300 gal., 1860 miles
ferry.   USN

DOUGLAS A-4E
Pratt & Whitney J52-P-6A, 8500 lbs.
DIMENSIONS: Span 27′6″, Lg. 41′4″, Ht. 15′, Wing Area
260 sq. ft.
WEIGHT: Empty 9624 lb., Gross 18,311 lb., Max. 22,950
lb., Combat 16,135 lb. with Mk 28. Fuel 800–1700 gal.
PERFORMANCE: Speed—Top 673 mph at s. l. (clean), 636
mph at s. l. (with Mk 28), Cruising 498 mph, Stalling
139 mph. Combat Ceiling 40,050′, Climb 20,000′/4
min., Combat Radius 230 miles/Mk 28 (680 with 2/300-
gal. tanks), 2130 miles ferry.   JANSSON

81 conventional bombs on multiple-ejector racks.
The center pylon could carry a 2,025-pound Mk 28
or 3,500-pound Mk 91 nuclear bomb.

A limited all-weather capability was provided on
the F4D-2N, ordered September 9, 1957, with APG-
53A radar and ASQ-17 fire-control package. The
first example flew August 21, 1958, and production
got under way the following year, with 638 delivered by 1963. The A4D-1, A4D-2, and A4D-2N became the A-4A, A-4B, and A-4C, respectively, under
the current designation system.

No A-4D model reached flight status, but on July
30, 1959, the Navy ordered two A4D-5 aircraft complete with Pratt & Whitney J52 engines. The first

flew July 12, 1961, and 498 production models, now
designated A-4E, were delivered from May 1962 to
April 1966. They had two more underwing pylons,
accommodating three Bullpup missiles or up to
9,155 pounds of rockets on multiple racks.

As the Skyhawk entered service, it was usually
issued to jet-fighter squadrons redesignated as attack outfits, and served alongside the prop-driven
Skyraider squadron on each carrier. The first squadron to receive them was VA-72, which got A4D-1s
on September 27, 1956, and VMA-224 became the
first Marine Skyhawk squadron in January 1957.
The Marines got the first A-4Bs, which joined VMA-
211 in September 1957, and the first A-4Cs in March

1960. The A-4E joined the fleet in December 1962.

At the start of 1958, when carrier air power was still at its peak, the Navy attack force included 12 A4D, 10 F9F-8B, and 10 FJ-4B 14-plane squadrons with jets and 25 with piston-engine ADs. The Marines had six A4D jets and six AD attack squadrons with 20 planes each.

During the sixties the Navy usually operated 15 attack carriers. Each Carrier Air Wing (CAW) had three attack squadrons, two thirds with A-4s, and 12 Marine squadrons had A-4s when direct intervention in the Vietnam War began in 1964. On August 5, 1964, the Navy's first strike at North Vietnam was made by 64 aircraft, including 15 A-4Es from the *Constellation* and 16 A-4Cs from the *Ticonderoga*.[1] Continuous carrier air strikes began in February 1965, and in June 1965, Marine A-4 squadrons began rotating to Vietnam for close-support missions that continued until June 28, 1973.

Douglas[2] production continued, with final assembly at Palmdale having replaced the El Segundo plant used for the first 342 Skyhawks. A two-place trainer version first flew June 30, 1965, retaining most of the armament capabilities, and 238 were accepted as the TA-4F; some becoming EA-4F aircraft trainers in 1970. In 1969 delivery began on 293 TA-4J two-seat trainers.

The last new Navy version was the A-4F, first flown August 31, 1966, with a new engine, ejection seat, and wing landing spoilers. An avionics pod with ECM gear was soon added atop the fuselage, and this hump was retrofitted on all A-4Es then in service. The original A-4F was followed by 146 production examples, beginning in June 1967.

The first export Skyhawks, 25 A-4Bs refurbished for the Argentine Air Force, were delivered beginning in October 1966. These aircraft, plus an additional 25 in 1969, and 25 more in 1975, were redesignated A-4P in 1972, and 16 more for the Argentine Navy became A-4Qs. Beginning in July 1967, Australia bought eight new A-4G and two TA-4G trainers and got ten refurbished A-4Es in 1971.

Forty-eight A-4H single-seaters were the first American planes officially sold to Israel. Appearing in October 1967, they had a drag chute added and 30-mm DEFA guns with 150 rpg replacing the usual 20-mm guns. Additional orders brought the Israeli total to 90 A-4Hs and ten TA-4Hs, to which 28 refurbished A-4Es were added during the "War of Attrition" beginning in 1969. Israel also bought 117 A-4Ns, whose first flight June 12, 1972, revealed

DOUGLAS A-4F
Pratt & Whitney J52-P-8A, 9300 lbs.
DIMENSIONS: As F-4E
WEIGHT: Empty 10,169 lb., Gross 19,356 lb., Max. 23,999 lb., Combat 17,180 lb. with Mk 28. Fuel 800–1700 gal.
PERFORMANCE: Speed—Top 679 mph at 3500' (clean), 647 mph at 8000' (Mk 28), Cruising 472 mph, Stalling 144 mph. Combat Ceiling 38,600', Climb 20,000'/3.6 min., Combat Radius 620 miles/Mk 28/2/300 gal. tanks, 2000 miles ferry.   USN

DOUGLAS A-4H   GANN

them to be a counterpart of the Marines' A-4M, with 30-mm DEFA guns.

New Zealand bought ten A-4K single-seaters and four TA-4K two-seaters for her Navy, with delivery beginning in January 1970. In November 1974 Kuwait ordered 30 A-4KU and 6 TA-4KU aircraft for 1977 delivery. The last Skyhawks sent abroad from Douglas were 40 A-4S and three TA-4S aircraft with 30-mm Aden guns, refurbished from old A-4Bs in 1975 for Singapore.

Conversion of 100 A-4Cs to the A-4L configuration for Navy and Marine Reserve squadrons assured a long life at shore stations. Delivery began in March 1969, with updated engines and electronics. The Marines got its own model, the A-4M, authorized in May 1969 and first flown April 10, 1970, with updated engine, enlarged canopy, drag chute, and double ammunition load. Delivery to five Marine attack squadrons began in April 1971 and 158 were built. A heads-up computer display was added in 1976. Twenty-three two-seat OA-4M tactical con-

---

[1] One was downed by AAA. The unfortunate pilot was subjected to the longest POW experience ever endured by an American.

[2] McDonnell Douglas as of April 28, 1967, but Douglas is used here for aircraft built in California, while McDonnell is used for the St. Louis series.

DOUGLAS A-4K   GANN

DOUGLAS A-4L
Wright J65-W-20, 8400 lbs.
DIMENSIONS: As A-4C
WEIGHT: Empty 9861 lb., Gross 18,501 lb., Max. 22,500
   lb., Combat 16,325 lb. with Mk 28. Fuel 800–1700 gal.
PERFORMANCE: Speed—Top 676 mph at s. l. (clean), 648
   mph at 2500′ (Mk 28), Cruising 495 mph, Stalling 140
   mph. Combat Ceiling 41,300′, Climb 20,000′/3.9 min.,
   Combat Radius 489 miles/Mk 28/2/300-gal. tanks, 1770
   miles ferry.   LAWSON

DOUGLAS A-4N   GANN

DOUGLAS A-4M
Pratt & Whitney J52-P-408, 11,187 lbs.
DIMENSIONS: As A-4E
WEIGHT: Empty 10,418 lb., Gross 19,833 lb., Max. 24,472
   lb., Combat 17,657 lb. with Mk 28. Fuel 800–1700 gal.

PERFORMANCE: Speed—Top 687 mph at 5000′ (clean), 666
   mph at 12,000′ (Mk 28), Cruising 483 mph, Stalling 145
   mph. Combat Ceiling 40,600′, Climb 20,000′/2.7 min.,
   Combat Radius 524 miles/Mk 28 and two 300 gal. tanks,
   1860 miles ferry.   GANN

trol aircraft were converted from TA-4Fs from 1978 to 1980.

When the last A-4M was accepted February 27, 1979, 2,960 Skyhawks, including 555 trainers, had been completed in nearly 25 years of production. The last three A-4F squadrons in the fleet were retired when the *Hancock* was decommissioned in 1976, but Skyhawks continued in reserve, training, and utility units.

A-5 Vigilante

The fastest—and so far the only—supersonic bomber flying from any carrier deck was the A-5 Vigilante. This two-place Mach 2 strategic bomber was begun in July 1955 as the North American NA-233, or A3J-1, the first bomber design to take full advantage of the giant carrier's capabilities.

A 3,020-pound Mk 27 nuclear store, or an 1,885-pound configuration of the Mk 28, was ejected rearwards from an internal linear bay, and an ASB-12 Bombing-Navigation system permitted all-weather attacks on enemy seaports. Two pylons under the wings carried 400-gallon drop tanks, bombs, or air-refueling stores. Ejection seats and pressurization were provided for the tandem cockpits. The 37.5° swept wings had droopable landing edges, boundary flaps, and folded for stowage, as did the all-movable swept-back tail.

In June 1956 a letter of intent began A3J-1 engineering with two flight articles ordered August 29, 1956, and first flown on August 31, 1958, powered by two General Electric J79-GE-2s of 16,150-

NORTH AMERICAN A-5B   MFR

pound thrust. The first production contract followed in January 1959, and the A3J-1 entered squadron service in June 1961. The J79-GE-8s with afterburners was used on most of the 59 A-5As (A3J-1s) made by March 1963.

Additional fuel was added to six A-5Bs (A3J-2s), first flown April 29, 1962, by using a faired hump behind the bombardier-navigator's cockpit and another pair of drop tanks under the wings. This type was just a transition to the RA-5C, which had a reconnaissance pod in the bomb bay enclosing a multisensor system that included six cameras, passive ECM and side-scanning radar in a fairing below the fuselage. If desired, the pod or any of the four drop tanks could be replaced by Mk 28 weapons. The RA-5C first flew June 30, 1962, and deliveries of 91 from the Columbus, Ohio, factory began in December 1963. The last of 156 Vigilantes was delivered November 5, 1970.

The Vigilante's first full squadron deployment was with VAH-7 on the nuclear carrier *Enterprise*'s first cruise in August 1962. Ironically, the Navy had hardly received the full strategic bombing capability it had been striving for since 1946 when the Navy's strategic mission was placed entirely with the Polaris missiles on nuclear submarines. All the heavy-attack squadrons were redesignated RVAH for reconnaissance missions in 1964, and all remaining A-5As were returned to the factory for con-

NORTH AMERICAN A-5A (A3J-1)
General Electric J79-GE-8, 17,000 lbs.
DIMENSIONS: Span 53', Lg. 76'6", Ht. 19'5", Wing Area 700 sq. ft.
WEIGHT: Empty 32,714 lb., Gross 56,293 lb., Max. 62,953 lb., Combat 48,663 lb. with Mk 27. Fuel 2215–3015 gal.
PERFORMANCE: Speed—Top 1320 mph at 40,000', 805 mph at s. l., Cruising 560 mph, Stalling 156 mph, Combat Ceiling 43,800', Climb 30,000'/6.3 min., Combat Radius 985 miles/Mk 27, 1295 miles/Mk 27 and two 400 gal. tanks.   MFR

NORTH AMERICAN RA-5C
General Electric J79-GE-8, 1700 lbs.
DIMENSIONS: As A-5A
WEIGHT: Empty 37,498 lb., Gross 65,589 lb., Max. 79,189
  lb., Combat 55,617 lb. Fuel 2715–4315 gal.
PERFORMANCE: Speed—Top 1290 mph at 40,000', 783
  mph at s. l., Cruising 567 mph, Stalling 154 mph. Combat Ceiling 48,400', Climb 30,000'/7.7 min., Combat Radius 547 miles or 944 miles/four 400 gal.
  tanks.   LAWSON

version to RA-5C configurations, as had been done
to all A-5Bs. Ten RVAH squadrons used the RA-5C,
the last becoming operational in June 1964, but all
were to be decommissioned by September 1979.
Eighteen RA-5Cs were confirmed combat losses in
Vietnam.

A-6 Intruder

Grumman's Intruder was the first jet-attack type
designed for both limited and nuclear warfare, and
its accuracy and weapons capacity enabled it to
replace the last prop-driven A-1 in Navy service.
Originally designated A2F-1, the A-6A was designed for short takeoffs and landings, long-range,
all-weather location of targets, and low-level attack
with conventional or nuclear bombs, rockets, or
missiles.

Two Pratt & Whitney J52-P-6 jets were mounted
below the wing roots of wings swept back 25° with
full-span leading-edge slots, slotted flaps, and flap-
erons (spoilers serving as ailerons). The two crewmen sat side by side, with the bombardier-navigator
operating a digital integrated attack navigation system (DIANE) that included search and track radar,
a computer, and two screens for presenting both the
ground and the airspace ahead of the aircraft. They
could attack without any outside visibility at all,
but no guns were provided. The wings folded upwards and a flight-refueling boom was placed above
the radar nose.

Five store stations were provided beneath the A-
6A, offering several weapons choices. A Mk 28 or
2,080-pound Mk 43 nuclear bomb on the center line
and four 300-gallon tanks represented one choice;
another possibility was five 1,030-pound Mk 83
conventional bombs or five multiple racks for up to
30 Mk 81 Snakeye bombs; or a 15,939-pound load
that could be carried on a 2.9-hour mission with
internal fuel or 5.8 hours with refueling from an A-

6A Buddy Tanker. Four Bullpup or Shrike missiles
or rocket pods could also be handled.

Of eight companies submitting designs for a May
1957 competition, Grumman was chosen in December, and a contract for the first four aircraft was
approved March 26, 1959. The first A2F-1 was
flown April 19, 1960, with four aircraft accepted that
year, four more in 1961, and monthly production
deliveries began in April 1962.

In February 1963 Intruders joined fleet-replace-
ment squadron VA-42. The first operational unit,
VA-75, began sorties against North Vietnam on July
1, 1965. Marine A-6A deployment to Vietnam began
in December 1967. By 1968 A-6A medium-attack
squadrons had replaced all A-1s on carriers.

Grumman completed 482 A-6As by December
1970, many of which were modified to later configurations. The second one became an EA-6A ECM
type, first flown April 26, 1963. It was followed by
five more EA-6A conversions. Six EA-6As were converted from the production line in 1965, and 15
more new EA-6As delivered in 1969. All went to
the Marines' VMAQ-2. Nineteen A-6Bs were As
modified to use AGM-78 antiradiation missiles

GRUMMAN A-6A
Pratt & Whitney J52-P-6A, 8500 lbs.
DIMENSIONS: Span 53', Lg. 54'9", Ht. 16'2", Wing Area
  529 sq. ft.
WEIGHT: Empty 25,298 lb., Gross 48,051 lb. (close support), Max. 53,699 lb. (Mk 43 store), Combat 41,675 lb./
  5 Mk 83, 44,831 lb./Mk 43. Fuel 2344–3821 gal.
PERFORMANCE: At 44,831 lb.: Speed—Top 646 mph at
  s. l., 555 mph at 35,900', Cruising 481 mph, Stalling
  133 mph. Combat Ceiling 40,250', Combat Radius 1585
  miles/Mk 43, 673 miles/six Mk 83.   LAWSON

GRUMMAN EA-6A   LAWSON

against hostile radar sites, and a dozen became A-6C night-attack models with infrared and low-light television in a ventral fairing. The first KA-6D tanker conversion was flown in May 1966, but 54 more were modified by Grumman in 1970–72, providing the Navy with a carrier-based air refueler that could transfer 3,000 gallons of its 3,844-gallon load via hose and reel.

The EA-6B Prowler was an ECM version with J52-P-408 jets. Like the EA-6, it had a large fairing atop the tail fin, with receivers to pick up enemy radar, but the enlarged front fuselage contained the pilot and three ECM operators for the jamming systems contained in five pods. The first EA-6B was converted from an A-6A and flown May 25, 1968. It was followed by two more conversions, with 48 new aircraft beginning service in January 1971. Two Navy squadrons were deployed in 1972 to support strike operations against North Vietnam. Improved electronics were introduced in 1975, and the production program increased to 77 EA-6Bs to serve 12 squadrons operating as four-plane units on each carrier.

The first A-6E, converted from an A-6A and flown on February 27, 1970, was identical in appearance to the A, with the J52-P-8A engines used on the last 223 aircraft, but it had an entirely new electronics suit, including new radar, computer, and weapons-delivery system. Later additions included provision for target-finding multisensors, laser-guided weapons, and new Condor missiles. The A-6E entered service in December 1971 with a program scheduling 94 new aircraft and 228 conversions from earlier aircraft. In the late seventies, the Navy had 15 squadrons of A-6E medium-attack squadrons and ten EA-6B tactical electronics warfare squadrons, as well as one Marine EA-6A and five A-6E squadrons.

When World War II ended, Navy attack planes existed mainly to bomb or torpedo enemy warships. Two decades later the attack plane was concerned almost entirely with land targets. By 1968, the piston-engine A-1s and A-2s had been replaced with an all-jet force of A-4 Skyhawks primarily for clear-weather work, RA-5C Vigilantes for reconnaissance, and A-6 mediums for all-weather operations. All three types were getting operational experience in Vietnam.

GRUMMAN EA-6B   LAWSON

GRUMMAN A-6E
Pratt & Whitney J52-P-8A, 9300 lbs.
DIMENSIONS: As A-6E
WEIGHT: Empty 25,980 lb., Gross 54,393 lb., Max. 58,807 lb., Combat 45,525 lb./Mk 43. Fuel 2344–3821 gal.
PERFORMANCE: Speed—Top 635 mph at s. l. (653 mph clean), Cruising 390 mph, Stalling 142 mph, Combat Radius 890 miles/Mk 43 and four 300 gal. tanks, 450 miles/10,296 lbs. and two 300 gal. tanks, 3300 miles ferry.   LAWSON

Chapter 30
Search and Attack: ASW

In three decades carrier antisubmarine-warfare squadrons have had three aircraft types built for ASW operations: the Grumman AF-2/3 Guardian, the Grumman S-2 Tracker, and the Lockheed S-3 Viking. None carried guns, for they were equipped to find and destroy an underwater enemy.

The Guardian began in August 1944 as the Grumman G-70, designed to replace the TBM Avenger, and three prototypes were ordered February 19, 1945. The XTB3F-1 had a 2,100-hp R-2800-34W, with the pilot and observer sitting side by side over an internal weapons bay that accommodated two torpedoes or 4,000 pounds of bombs. The wings had provision for two 20-mm guns, wells for the outward-retracting main wheels, and folded backwards in typical Grumman fashion. Instead of a rear gunner the prototype had a Westinghouse 19XB jet producing a 1,600-pound thrust through a tail nozzle, providing an estimated top speed of 356 mph for short bursts. This jet unit, however, was never tested. Just six days after the XTB3F-1's first flight on December 19, 1945, the company received a stop-work order; the Navy saw little need for a torpedo bomber in the postwar environment.

While hostle surface fleets did not present a substantial threat, submarines certainly did, and the most successful force against them, outside the range of land-based patrol planes, had been the Avengers based on escort carriers. Adaptation of the XTB3F to ASW configuration was proposed, using R-2800-46W engines and without the jet's high fuel consumption. A mockup was ready by April 28,

1947, and the remaining two prototypes were completed as ASW aircraft. An XTB3F-1S with an APS-20 radar but no armament was completed in November 1948, and the armed XTB3F-2S flew January 12, 1949. The first production order was placed May 3, 1948, for 30 aircraft designated as Attack types.

First flown November 17, 1949, production Guardians used the 2,400-hp R-2800-48W and came in two versions: AF-2W and AF-2S. They worked in pairs. A four-place AF-2W with the big belly radome for the APS-20 flew at low altitudes, searching the surface for a submarine periscope or snorkel. When the AF-2W located a target, an accompanying AF-2S pinpointed it with an APS-31 radar under the starboard wing. If it surfaced at night, the target could be illuminated with the searchlight under the port wing; if submerged, the target was located with 16 sonobuoys. The three-place AF-2S could attack with a 1,167-pound Mk 34 torpedo from the weapons bay, or with up to four depth charges carried under the wings. Up to six rockets could be

GRUMMAN AF-2S
Pratt & Whitney R-2800-48, 2300 hp takeoff and at 3500'
DIMENSIONS: Span 60', Lg. 43'5", Ht. 16'7", Wing Area 549 sq. ft.
WEIGHT: Empty 14,658 lb., Gross 20,298 lb. normal, Max. 22,565 lb., Combat 18,123 lb. Fuel 420–720 gal.
PERFORMANCE: Speed—Top 275 mph at 4000', 265 mph at s. l., Cruising 166 mph, Stalling 80 mph. Service Ceiling 22,900', Combat Ceiling 21,600', Climb 2300'/1 min., 10,000'/7.3 min. Combat Range 915 miles normal, 1140 miles max. USN

GRUMMAN XTB3F-1   MARTIN

carried under the wings instead of the depth charges or drop tanks.

The Guardians entered service in October 1950 with VS-25 at San Diego, the headquarters of the Pacific Fleet ASW forces. Grumman delivered 193 AF-2S, 153 AF-2W, and 40 AF-3S Guardians by April 1953, the last model having MAD gear added. The largest single-engine aircraft operated from carriers, they replaced the TBMs used on the light carrier *Wright* and escort carriers operating as ASW forces. The last Guardians were withdrawn from squadron service in August 1955 and were replaced by the Grumman S-2 Tracker.

S-2 Tracker

The Grumman S-2 (S2F) Tracker was the first aircraft designed from the beginning for the Navy's antisubmarine warfare carriers, whose mission was the destruction of submarines in high-priority areas, especially those outside easy reach of shore-based patrol planes. Rather than speed, this mission requires the endurance and detection equipment formerly common only on large patrol bombers. The uneconomical two-plane search and attack partnership of the Grumman AF-2 Guardians was combined into a single aircraft in the Grumman G-89 Tracker.

Powered by two Wright R-1820-82 Cyclones, this high-wing monoplane had retractable wheels and long-span flaps to reduce stalling speed for deck landings and for hovering when tracking submarines. Both pilots enjoyed fine visibility from the nose, and two electronics operators behind them had ALD-3 equipment for detecting enemy radar transmissions and APS-38 radar in a retractable radome for surface search. Underwater detection was handled by an ASQ-10 MAD in the tail and sonobuoys dropped from the engine nacelles' rear. A searchlight was under the starboard wing, six rocket racks were installed, and a 1,575-pound homing torpedo was accommodated in the weapons bay.

Two XS2F-1 prototypes and the first 15 production S2F-1s were ordered June 30, 1950, and the

GRUMMAN S-2A (S2F-1)
Wright R-1820-82, 1525 hp max., 1275 hp normal
DIMENSIONS: Span 69'8" (27'4" folded), Lg. 42', Ht. 16'4", Wing Area 485 sq. ft.
WEIGHT: Empty 17,357 lb., Gross 23,470 lb., Max. 24,408 lb., Combat 22,222 lb. Fuel 520 gal.
PERFORMANCE: Speed—Top 272 mph at 3100', 264 mph at s. l., Cruising 150 mph, Stalling 86 mph. Service Ceiling 22,800', Climb 2330'/1 min., 10,000'/6.7 min. Combat Range 968 miles.   MFR

GRUMMAN S-2C (S2F-2)
Wright R-1820-82, 1525 hp
DIMENSIONS: Span 69'8" (27'4" folded), Lg. 42'3", Ht. 16'4", Wing Area 485 sq. ft.
WEIGHT: Empty 17,640 lb., Gross 25,145 lb., Max. 25,985 lb., Combat 23,897 lb. Fuel 520 gal.
PERFORMANCE: Speed—Top 263 mph at 3100', 255 mph at s. l., Cruising 150 mph, Stalling 89 mph. Service Ceiling 21,100', Climb 2040'/1 min., 10,000'/7.5 min. Combat Range 858 miles.   USN

XS2F-1 flew December 4, 1952, its success leading to a large production order and abandonment of two rival Vought XS2U-1 prototypes under construction. Monthly deliveries began in September 1953, with VS-26 becoming the first squadron to convert to the Tracker in February 1954. By 1958, two 20-plane VS squadrons operated, along with a helicopter squadron, from each *Essex*-class carrier (CVS) modified for ASW operations; these ships were far superior in speed and accommodations to the escort carriers previously used.

Grumman built 755 S2F-1s, along with 60 S2F-2s with an enlarged weapons bay for a nuclear depth charge or two torpedoes delivered from July 1954 to January 1955. Navy acceptances of the original model continued until December 1959, with later aircraft produced for export. Japan purchased 60 S2F-1s, minus carrier gear and folding wings, in 1958–59, followed by 24 for Italy, 26 for the Netherlands, and 13 for Brazil. These were new aircraft, but secondhand Navy aircraft were also passed along to Argentina (6), Taiwan (9), Thailand (6), and Uruguay (3). Canada built 100 C2F-1s for her own Navy.

When the current designation system was adopted, the S2F-1 became the S-2A (or the S-2B when the Julie/Jezebel systems were added) and the S2F-2 became the S-2C. After their retirement from first-line squadrons, the Trackers were modified for a variety of roles, including US-2A target tugs, US-2B utility aircraft, and RS-2C photo air-

GRUMMAN S-2D/S-2E (S2F-3/S2F-3S)
Wright R-1820-82A, 1525 hp takeoff, 1425 hp at 2400'
DIMENSIONS: Span 72'7", Lg. 43'6", Ht. 16'7", Wing Area 496 sq. ft.
WEIGHT: Empty 18,726/18,820 lb., Gross 26,664 lb., Max. 29,764 lb., Combat 24,917 lb. Fuel 728 gal.
PERFORMANCE: Speed—Top 251 mph at 4000', 242 mph at s. l., Cruising 150 mph at 1500', Stalling 93 mph, Service Ceiling 20,100', Combat Ceiling 18,300', Climb 1830'/1 min., Combat Range 1150 miles/MK-101, 900 miles/six MK-46, 1300 miles ferry.
Data for S-2E. S-2D similar but 94 lb. lighter.   USN

GRUMMAN S-2E   LAWSON

craft. Very valuable noncombat spinoffs of this type were the C-1A Trader and E-1A Tracer, transport and early-warning types respectively.

A second generation of Trackers—with more fuel, equipment, and sonobuoy capacity increased from 16 to 32—began with a December 17, 1957, order for the first seven S2F-3s, which were first flown on May 21, 1959. Production aircraft entered service in May 1961 and became the S-2D in 1962.

The enlarged S-2D had provisions for the Lulu nuclear depth charge, Julie active echo ranging, Jezebel passive long-range acoustic search, a "sniffer" for snorkel exhaust fumes, and a stronger searchlight and underwing fittings for rockets or torpedoes. An ASN-30 computerized tactical navigational system was tested in a modified S2F-3S, which became the production S-2E. A 2,016-pound Mk 101 nuclear depth bomb or two Mk 46 torpedoes could be carried internally by the S-2D/E Trackers, while four more torpedoes could be carried on wing racks. Grumman delivered 100[1] S-2Ds by June 1962, and the first S-2Es reached the fleet on August 31, 1962, with 228 completed for the Navy by December 1967 and 14 more for Australia by July 1968. Later modifications to Navy planes in service produced the S-2F, actually an S-2B with updated electronics, and the S-2G, which was a former S-2E that reappeared in service in December 1972 with new data-processing equipment. The last S-2Gs in service were retired August 30, 1976, after VS-37 received S-3A Vikings. This squadron's last deployment had been on the *Kitty Hawk,* since all the antisubmarine carriers (CVS) had also been retired.

S-3 Viking

Lockheed's S-3A Viking was the first carrier-based aircraft to combine jet speed with the specialized characteristics of antisubmarine-warfare planes. Two new General Electric TF34 turbofans in pods under the 15° swept wings had a low-altitude fuel consumption much less than that of conventional jet engines, and permitted a loiter endurance of up to 7.5 hours.

[1] Nineteen aircraft counted as S-2Ds elsewhere were delivered in late 1962 as S-2Es.

GRUMMAN S-2G   LAWSON

LOCKHEED S-3A
General Electric TF-34-GE-2, 9275 lbs.
DIMENSIONS: Span 68'8" (29'6" folded), Lg. 53'4", Ht. 22'9", Wing Area 598 sq. ft.
WEIGHT: Empty 26,554 lb., Gross 43,491 lb., Max. 52,539 lb. Fuel 1900–2500 gal.
PERFORMANCE: Speed—Top 514 mph at s. l., Cruising 426 mph, Stalling 67 mph. Service Ceiling 40,000', Climb 4200'/1 min. Combat Radius 530 miles, Range 3040 miles.   MFR

Four crewmen—a pilot, co-pilot, tactical coordinator, and sensor operator—sat in an air-conditioned cabin to protect the delicate electronics, which included a Univac 1832 general-purpose digital computer to integrate and store sensor data that could be displayed at all crew stations. Sensors included the APS-116 high-resolution radar in the nose, a retractable infrared unit, the MAD boom in the tail, wing-tip ECM antenna, and an acoustic system with 60 passive and active sonobuoys. Automatic pilot and carrier-landing systems were provided, along with a computerized inertial navigation system and a 1,000-watt transceiver.

The weapons bay contained racks for four Mk 46 torpedoes, depth charges, 500-pound bombs, or mines. A pylon under each wing could carry a 300-gallon drop tank or weapons, such as three 500-pound bombs on triple ejector racks.

The Viking design was a response to a Navy weapons system requirement dated December 13, 1965, and Lockheed became the contractor on August 1, 1969. Eight S-3A test aircraft were built at Burbank, with the first rolled out in November 1971 and first flown January 21, 1972 at Palmdale. On April 28, 1972, the Navy ordered the first 13 production S-3As, and 187 Vikings were built by August 1978. They entered squadron service in February 1974 with VS-41 at NAS North Island, San Diego, where six squadrons were stationed by 1978, along with six more at Cecil Field, Florida. Vikings were deployed as ten-plane units with each of the big carriers.

LOCKHEED S-3A   MFR

Chapter 31
Navy Fighters of the Cold War

The Navy's First Jets

Wartime gas-turbine development greatly interested the Navy, but actual adoption of jets for carrier service presented many difficulties. Jet aircraft required great quantities of fuel and tricycle landing gear, which was not used on flight decks at that time. The long takeoff run required by jet types made catapult launching desirable, and their high landing speed required an improved arresting technique.

Faced with such difficulties, it is not surprising that the first approach should be via composite aircraft using a normal engine and propeller for cruising and a jet unit only for high speed and quick climb. Such a machine was first proposed in December 1942. Three Ryan XFR-1 prototypes were ordered by a letter contract February 11, 1943, and 100 FR-1s were added December 2. The Model 28 Fireball, as it was called by the company, first flew June 25, 1944, powered by a Wright R-1820-56, and at first glance resembled the usual single-seat low-wing monoplane. Behind the pilot, however, was a General Electric I-16 jet giving 1,600-pound thrust through a tail nozzle, fed by wing root intakes. Landing gear was of the tricycle type, and the wings could fold upwards.

Production FR-1 delivery began January 1945, with an R-1820-72W Cyclone and the I-16 jet. Four .50-caliber wing guns, 189 pounds of armor, and external fittings for two 1,000-pound bombs, two 100-gallon drop tanks, or four 5-inch rockets were carried. Top speed was 295 mph with the propeller only, but increased to 404 mph when the jet unit was turned on.

By January 1945, 1,200 more Fireballs were ordered, but were canceled by the war's end. Sixty-six Fireballs were delivered by November 1945. VF-66 had been selected to introduce the FR-1 to the fleet, making the first deck takeoffs from the training carrier *Ranger* in May 1945. Several fatal accidents marred the Fireball's postwar operations from escort carriers, and the FR-1 was withdrawn from service for safety reasons in July 1947.

Proposed XFR-2 and XFR-3 modifications with new engines were not made, but one FR-1 became an XFR-4 with an R-1820-74W and new fuselage intakes for a 4,200-pound-thrust Westinghouse J34. The Navy's first turboprop aircraft was an FR-1 modified to an XF2R-1. It was flown in November 1946 with a General Electric XT31 giving 1,700 hp to a four-bladed propeller and producing a 550-pound residual thrust, together with a General Electric I-16 in the tail.

Another composite fighter was the XF15C-1, also a low-wing monoplane with tricycle landing gear.

RYAN FR-1
Wright R-1820-72W, 1425 hp takeoff, 1000 hp at 14,800', and General Electric I-16, 1600 lbs.
DIMENSIONS: Span 40', Lg. 32'4", Ht. 13'11", Wing Area 275 sq. ft.
WEIGHT: Empty 7689 lb., Gross 9958 lb., Max. 11,652 lb. Fuel 180–380 gal.
PERFORMANCE: Speed—Top (both engines) 404 mph at 17,800', (prop. only) 295 mph at 16,500', Cruising 152 mph, Landing 91 mph. Service Ceiling 43,100'. Range 1620 miles max.   MFR

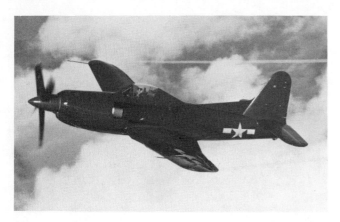

RYAN XF2R-1
General Electric XT31-GE-2, 1700 hp + 550 lbs., and
J31-GE-3, 1600 lbs.
DIMENSIONS: Span 42', Lg. 36', Ht. 14', Wing Area 305
sq. ft.
WEIGHT: Gross 11,000 lb.
PERFORMANCE: (Approx.) Speed—Top 500 mph at s. l.
Service Ceiling 39,100', Climb 10,000'/2 min.   MFR

CURTISS XF15C-1
Pratt & Whitney R-2800-34W, 2100 hp takeoff, and De
Havilland Halford, 2700 lbs.
DIMENSIONS: Span 48', Lg. 44', Ht. 15'3", Wing Area 400
sq. ft.
WEIGHT: Empty 12,648 lb., Gross 16,630 lb., Max. 18,698
lb. Fuel 376–526 gal.
PERFORMANCE: Speed—Top (both engines) 469 mph at
25,300', 432 mph at s. l., (prop. only) 373 mph at 25,-
300', 322 mph at s. l., Cruising 163 mph. Service Ceiling 41,800', Climb 5020'/1 min. Range 1385 miles
max.   MFR

This Curtiss design of December 1943 had a Pratt
& Whitney R-2800-34W turning a four-bladed propeller in the nose and a De Havilland Halford jet of
2,700-pound thrust fitted under the fuselage. Three
prototypes ordered April 7, 1944, were to be armed
with four 20-mm guns in the wings, and two 1,000-
pound bombs or drop tanks could be attached.

The first XF15C-1 flew February 28, 1945, at Buffalo, New York, with only an R-2800-22W installed.
The imported jet unit wasn't flown until May 3, but
tests were interrupted by a crash on May 8. Tests
resumed July 9 on the second prototype, which had
the R-2800-34W and an H-1B jet unit (U.S. copy of
Halford), while the third XF15C-1 was flown March
13, 1946, with a new T-tail. The horizontal tail service was raised to the vertical fin's top, a change
also made on the second prototype by August. Development of pure jet types, however, led the Navy
to discard its last Curtiss fighters.

The Navy's first two all-jet prototypes were ordered January 7, 1943. As the major aircraft pro-
ducers were then tied up by mass-production problems, responsibility for airframe development was
given the young McDonnell firm in St. Louis, while
Westinghouse undertook development of axial-flow
turbojets. Six small engines were originally planned
for each prototype but, fortunately, development of
the 1,600-pound thrust Westinghouse 19XB-2B reduced requirements to two. Each 19-inch diameter
engine was buried in the wing roots on each side
of the smoothly streamlined fuselage. When first
flown on January 26, 1945, the type was known as
the McDonnell XFD-1, but the designation was
later changed to XFH-1 to avoid confusion with
Douglas types, and the engine became known as
the J30.

CURTISS XF15C-1 (with T tail)   MFR

McDONNELL XFD-1 (XFH-1)
Westinghouse WE-19-XB-2B, 1600 lbs. military, 1300 lbs.
normal
DIMENSIONS: Span 40'9", Lg. 37'3", Ht. 14'2", Wing Area
276 sq. ft.
WEIGHT: Empty 6156 lb., Gross 8626 lb., Max. 9531 lb.
Fuel 260–400 gal.
PERFORMANCE: Speed—Top 487 mph at s. l., 483 mph at
20,000', Cruising 250 mph, Landing 80 mph. Service
Ceiling 43,700', Climb 4960'/1 min. Range 540 miles
normal, 750 miles max.   MFR

On March 7, 1945, the first Navy jet production contract was placed; it originally called for 100 planes but was cut back to 60 after the war. Production FH-1s delivered from January 1947 to May 1948 had J30-WE-20s, and were similar to the prototype except for additional fuel and modified tail fin. Four .50-caliber guns were mounted in the upper side of the nose and a 295-gallon drop tank could be fitted flush with the belly.

On July 21, 1946, a prototype became the first jet to fly from a U.S. carrier, the *Franklin D. Roosevelt.* The first navy squadron to get FH-1s was VF-17A, in July 1947, this unit becoming the Navy's first carrier-qualified fighter squadron on the *Saipan* in May 1948. Other Phantoms—as McDonnell had named the jet—were used by the Marines' VMF-122 until July 1950.

The next step in jet fighters began with a September 5, 1944, Navy request for a carrier-based fighter. Grumman responded but was left, for the time being, to develop its F7F and F8F prop design. Three other respondents got prototype contracts: Vought to use a J34 engine, North American a J35, and McDonnell two J34s.

Vought's first jet type was the XF6U-1 Pirate, ordered December 29, 1944, and first flown October 2, 1946. A 3,000-pound-thrust Westinghouse J34-WE-22 behind the pilot was fed by intakes in the wing roots. Four 20-mm cannons were grouped in the rounded nose, and drop tanks were attached to each wing tip. Like the Phantom and most subsequent Navy jet fighters, the three XF6U-1s utilized retractable tricycle landing gear. Construction was of Metalite—two thin sheets of aluminum alloy bonded to a balsa-wood core.

McDONNELL FH-1
Westinghouse J30-WE-20, 1600 lbs.
DIMENSIONS: Span 40'9″, Lg. 38'9″, Ht. 14'2″, Wing Area 276 sq. ft.
WEIGHT: Empty 6683 lb., Gross 10,035 lb., Max. 12,035 lb. Fuel 375–670 gal.
PERFORMANCE: Speed—Top 479 mph at s. l., Cruising 248 mph, Landing 87 mph. Service Ceiling 41,100', Climb 4230'/1 min. Range 695 miles normal, 980 miles max. MFR

VOUGHT XF6U-1
Westinghouse J34-WE-22, 3000 lbs.
DIMENSIONS: Span 32'10″, Lg. 32'10″, Ht. 11'9″, Wing Area 203.5 sq. ft.
WEIGHT: Empty 5876 lb., Gross 9306 lb., Max. 11,125 lb. Fuel 370–650 gal.
PERFORMANCE: Speed—Top 535 mph at s. l., 530 mph at 20,000', Cruising 370 mph, Landing 98 mph. Service Ceiling 40,900', Climb 4560'/1 min. Range 783 miles normal, 1285 miles max. MFR

Thirty F6U-1s ordered February 5, 1947, were to get power plants augmented with the first American afterburners. The third prototype was flown March 5, 1948, with a J34-WE-30A, whose normal thrust was increased to 4,100 pounds for short periods when using the Solar afterburner, hopefully raising the top speed from 535 to 600 mph. But the tail had to be redesigned, numerous engine and stability problems arose, and the prototype was destroyed in November 1948. The first production F6U-1 flew June 29, 1949, and problems persisted even after the last was accepted in February 1950. On October 13 the Pirate was pronounced so submarginal in performance that combat utilization was not feasible, and the planes were never issued to an operational squadron or flown from a carrier.

North American's XFJ-1 Fury featured a nose intake for the General Electric J35 in the fat fuselage behind the pilot. Three prototypes were ordered January 1, 1945, and 100 FJ-1s were ordered on May 18, but the production contract was cut to 30. The XFJ-1 first flew September 11, 1946, and the FJ-1 on July 8, 1947, with an Allison-built J35-A-2. In November 1947 the Fury went to VF-5A, which became VF-51. It made its first carrier trials aboard the *Boxer* in March 1948 and used the FJ-1 until October 1949. The FJ-1 was the fastest plane yet used on carriers, but it required catapult takeoff, engine overhaul every ten flight hours, and lacked the ejection seat now so necessary for safety.

Six .50-caliber guns were mounted at the sides of the nose scoop; these were the last of this caliber on Navy fighters, for the 20-mm cannon has been standard since that time. The Air Force continued using the .50-caliber M-3 gun, however, until the

VOUGHT F6U-1
Westinghouse J34-WE-30A, 3150 lbs. (4100 lbs./AB)
DIMENSIONS: Span 32'10", Lg. 37'8", Ht. 12'11", Wing Area 203 sq. ft.
WEIGHT: Empty 7320 lb., Gross 12,900 lb., Combat 11,060 lb. Fuel 420–700 gal.
PERFORMANCE: Speed—Top 596 mph at s. l., 550 mph at 31,000', Cruising 340 mph, Service Ceiling 46,300', Climb 8060'/1 min. Combat Range 730 miles, 1150 miles ferry. USN

NORTH AMERICAN XFJ-1
General Electric J35, 3820 lbs.
DIMENSIONS: Span 38'1", Lg. 33'5", Ht. 14'1", Wing Area 221 sq. ft.
WEIGHT: Empty 8182 lb., Gross 12,135 lb., Max. 14,386 lb. Fuel 465–805 gal.
PERFORMANCE: Speed—Top 542 mph at 16,000', 533 mph at s. l., Cruising 340 mph, Landing 98 mph. Service Ceiling 47,400', Climb 4690'/1 min. Range 858 miles normal, 1393 miles max. MFR

faster-firing M-39 20-mm gun became available in 1953.

The Phantoms, Pirates, and early Furys were a transitional phase between props and jets. They demonstrated that jet types could operate from carriers and paved the way for complete replacement of propeller-driven fighters by more advanced jet types.

NORTH AMERICAN FJ-1
Allison J35-A-2, 4000 lbs. takeoff and military
DIMENSIONS: Span 38'2", Lg. 34'5", Ht. 14'10", Wing Area 221 sq. ft.
WEIGHT: Empty 8843 lb., Gross 15,115 lb., Max. 15,600 lb. Fuel 805 gal. max.
PERFORMANCE: Speed—Top 547 mph at 9000', Cruising 432 mph, Landing 121 mph. Service Ceiling 32,000', Climb 3300'/1 min. Range 1500 miles. MFR

Jet Planes Go to War

During 1947 and 1948, four new fighter types appeared and were ordered into production. They became known to the public as the Banshee, Panther, Skyknight, and Cutlass, and the outbreak of the Korean War found them to be the available Navy jet fighters.

First was the McDonnell XF2H-1 Banshee, a twin-engine enlargement of the Phantom, powered by 3,000-pound-thrust Westinghouse J34-WE-22s. Three prototypes ordered March 2, 1945, were first flown January 11, 1947. Fifty-six F2H-1s, ordered April 22, 1947, and delivered from August 1948 to July 1949, were identical to the prototype except for the elimination of a stabilizer dihedral. Four 20-mm guns were mounted low in the nose, and the wings folded upwards for stowage.

In June 1948 a contract was made for the F2H-2, which had 3,150-pound-thrust J34-WE-34s, more internal fuel, and a 200-gallon drop tank on each wing tip. In addition to the usual four 20-mm guns, two 500-pound bombs could be carried. From November 1949 to April 1952, 334 F2H-2s were accepted, plus 14 F2H-2Ns with APS-6 radar added in the nose for night fighting. Eighty-eight F2H-2P reconnaissance types had no guns but mounted six cameras in an elongated nose. The F2H-2Bs were 25 F2H-2s modified to carry a Mk 7 or Mk 8 nuclear bomb under the port wing.

The F2H-3 was an all-weather fighter with APQ-41 radar in the nose, more internal fuel, droppable tip tanks, four 20-mm guns with 600 rounds, two pylons for 500-pound bombs, and eight for 250-pound bombs or rockets; the F2H-4 was similar except for APG-37 radar. Acceptances began in June

McDONNELL F2H-1

Westinghouse J34-WE-22, 3000 lbs.
DIMENSIONS: Span 41'6", Lg. 39', Ht. 14'5", Wing Area 294 sq. ft.
WEIGHT: Empty 9794 lb., Gross 14,234 lb., Max. 18,940 lb. Fuel 526 gal.
PERFORMANCE: Speed—Top 587 mph at s. l., 563 mph at 20,000', Cruising 351 mph, Landing 101 mph. Service Ceiling 48,500', Climb 7380'/1 min. Range 1278 miles. MFR

McDONNELL F2H-2

Westinghouse J34-WE-34, 3250 lbs.
DIMENSIONS: Span 44'10", Lg. 40'2", Ht. 14'6", Wing Area 294 sq. ft.
WEIGHT: Empty 11,146 lb., Gross 17,742 lb., Max. 22,312 lb., Combat 15,640 lb. Fuel 877–1277 gal.
PERFORMANCE: Speed—Top 582 mph at s. l., 532 mph at 35,000', Cruising 495 mph, Stalling 121 mph. Service Ceiling 49,100', Combat Ceiling 49,500', Climb 7300'/1 min., 30,000'/6.7 min., Combat Radius 620 miles/drop tanks, 305 miles/1580 lb. load. Combat Range 1475 miles/two 200 gal. tanks. MFR

McDONNELL F2H-2B

DIMENSIONS: As F2H-2, with Mk 8
WEIGHT: Empty 11,268 lb., Gross 23,693 lb., Combat 18,113 lb. Fuel 1216 gal.
PERFORMANCE: Speed—Top 579 mph at s. l., 565 mph at 10,000', Cruising 465 mph, Stalling 136 mph. Service Ceiling 36,500', Combat Ceiling 40,500', Climb 5400'/1 min., Range 1163 miles/3250 lb. Mk 8. USN

McDONNELL F2H-2N USN

1952 for 250 F2H-3s and 150 F2H-4s, with the last delivered October 30, 1953. Banshee production totaled 895. VF-171 began F2H-1 squadron use in March 1949, and VF-172's F2H-2s from the *Essex* joined combat in Korea on August 23, 1951. The Banshees retired from Navy fighter squadrons after September 1959, and 39 F2H-3s served the Canadian Navy from November 1955 to September 1962.

The Grumman Panther was a single-engine single-seater, but the design began with an April 22, 1946, contract for a two-seat XF9F-1 with four 1,500-pound-thrust Westinghouse J30s. Searching for a more efficient way of getting the power required, Grumman decided to import from Britain the 5,000-pound-thrust Rolls-Royce Nene (the engine also sold to Russia for the MiG-15 prototype), and in August 1946 the Grumman G-79 design was submitted to the Navy. The original configuration was canceled in October and the new XF9F-2 ordered December 16, 1946. The Nene power plant arrived in time for the first XF9F-2 to fly November 24, 1947.

The third prototype was flown August 16, 1948, as the XF9F-3, with an Allison J33-A-8 of 4,600-pound normal thrust. This engine, similar in size to the Nene, was planned as a second-source power plant in case the program to produce Nenes by Pratt & Whitney (as the J42) proved unsuccessful. The first production contract for the Panther called for 47 F9F-2s with the Pratt & Whitney J42-P-6 and 54 F9F-3s with Allison J33-A-8s. The first example flown was an F9F-3 on January 17, 1949, while the F9F-2 was not available for tests until August 17. Since the engines were interchangeable, all the F9F-3s were later converted to F9F-2s after their completion in October 1949. One F9F-3 was flown with an experimental four-gun turret (see photograph).

By August 1951, 520 more F9F-2s were built. Like the prototype, they were armed with four 20-mm nose guns, six 5-inch rockets or two 500-pound bombs. Permanent wing-tip tanks carried auxiliary fuel, which could be jettisoned from outlets in the rear in emergencies. Fuselage brakes under the

McDONNELL F2H-3
Westinghouse J34-WE-34, 3250 lbs. takeoff and military
DIMENSIONS: Span 41'9" (44'11" with tanks), Lg. 48'2", Ht.
 14'6", Wing Area 294 sq. ft.
WEIGHT: Empty 13,183 lb., Gross 21,013 lb., Max. 25,214
 lb., Combat 18,367 lb. Fuel 1102–442 gal.
PERFORMANCE: Speed—Top 580 mph at s. l., 524 mph at
 35,000', Cruising 461 mph, Landing 114 mph. Service
 Ceiling 47,000', Combat Ceiling 46,600', Climb 6000'/
 1 min. Range 1170 miles normal, 1716 miles max. USN

GRUMMAN F9F-2
Pratt & Whitney J42-P-8, 5750 lbs. WE takeoff, 5000 lbs.
 military
DIMENSIONS: Span 38', Lg. 37'3", Ht. 11'4", Wing Area
 250 sq. ft.
WEIGHT: Empty 9303 lb., Gross 16,450 lb., Max. 19,494
 lb., Combat 14,235 lb. Fuel 923 gal.
PERFORMANCE: Speed—Top 575 mph at s. l., 529 mph at
 35,000', Cruising 487 mph, Landing 105 mph. Service
 Ceiling 44,600', Climb 6000'/1 min. Range 1353
 miles.   MFR

McDONNELL F2H-4   USN

GRUMMAN XF9F-2
Rolls-Royce Nene, 5000 lbs. normal, 5700 lbs. military
DIMENSIONS: Span 35'3", Lg. 37'8", Ht. 11'3", Wing Area
 250 sq. ft.
WEIGHT: Empty 7107 lb., Gross 10,840 lb., Max. 12,442
 lb. Fuel 358–597 gal.
PERFORMANCE: Speed—Top 594 mph at s. l., 573 mph at
 20,000', Cruising 350 mph, Landing 100 mph, Climb
 7700'/1 min., Range 1100 miles max.   MFR

GRUMMAN F9F-3   MFR

GRUMMAN F9F-4
Allison J33-A-16, 6900 lbs. max.
DIMENSIONS: Span 38', Lg. 38'10", Ht. 12'3", Wing Area
  250 sq. ft.
WEIGHT: Empty 10,042 lb., Gross 17,671 lb., Max. 21,250
  lb., Combat 15,264 lb. Fuel 1003 gal.
PERFORMANCE: Speed—Top 593 mph at s. l., 547 mph at
  35,000', Cruising 495 mph, Stalling 131 mph. Service
  Ceiling 43,300', Climb 5600'/1 min. Range 1324 miles
  normal, 904 miles/eight 5" rockets.   MFR

GRUMMAN F9F-5
Pratt & Whitney J48-P-6, 7000 lbs. WE takeoff, 6250 lbs.
  military
DIMENSIONS: As F9F-4
WEIGHT: Empty 10,147 lb., Gross 17,766 lb., Max. 18,721
  lb., Combat 15,359 lb. Fuel 1003 gal.
PERFORMANCE: Speed—Top 604 mph at s. l., 543 mph at
  35,000', Cruising 481 mph, Stalling 131 mph. Service
  Ceiling 42,800', Climb 6000'/1 min. Combat Range
  1300 miles, 886 miles/six 5" rockets.   WL

nose reduced speed in descent, and wings folded
upwards for stowage.

The Allison A33-A-16 used on the F9F-4 was
replaced by a Pratt & Whitney J48-P-2 (based on
the Rolls-Royce Tay) used in the F9F-5. Distinguished from the earlier models by higher pointed
tails, an XF9F-5 flew December 21, 1949, preceding the XF9F-4 flown July 5, 1950. Both were converted from F9F-2s. They were produced in parallel after March 1951 on contracts inflated by the
Korean War, with 109 F9F-4s accepted by April
1952 and 619 F9F-5s and 36 F9F-5P photo Panthers
by December 1952.

When F9F-3s replaced VF-51's FJ-1s in May
1949, that unit became the first Panther squadron,

making its first operations from the *Boxer* in September. The F9F-2 scored the Navy's first jet combat victories July 3, 1950, when 30 on the *Valley
Forge* provided top cover for the carrier's AD-4 and
F4U-4B piston-engine attack missions. When fitted
with four additional racks for up to 2,800 pounds of
bombs after December 1950, the Panther became
the F9F-2B, which made the Navy's first bombing
attack by a jet April 2, 1951; it also did Marine
ground-support work with VMF-115.

The Navy accepted 1,388 Panthers, which were
715 of the 826 Navy and Marine Corps jets deployed to Korea, and flew about 78,000 combat sorties. On November 9, 1950, an F9F-2 became the
first Navy jet to down an enemy jet, the swept-wing
MiG-15, which used the same Rolls-Royce engine
design.

The Navy's first jet-propelled night fighter was
the two-place Douglas XF3D-1 Skyknight. Over
1,000 pounds of radar were carried within the
plane, including a scanner under the plastic nose
and a warning device in the plastic tail cone. The
radar operator and pilot sat side by side in a pressurized cockpit from which they could escape, even
at high speeds, by bailing out through a tunnel to
the fuselage's bottom. A high-wing monoplane, the
XF3D-1 had a pair of Westinghouse 3,000-pound-
thrust J34-WE-22 jets low on the fuselage sides and
the now usual four 20-mm guns behind and below
the nose scanner. Fittings beneath the wing could
accommodate two 300-gallon drop tanks or two
1,000-pound bombs.

Three prototypes ordered April 3, 1946, first flew
March 23, 1948, and 28 F3D-1s purchased in June
first flew February 13, 1950. They had J34-WE-34
jets, but larger 4,600-pound-thrust Westinghouse
J46s were specified for F3D-2s ordered in August
1949. Since these engines were unavailable when
the first F3D-2 flew February 14, 1951, the J34-WE-
36 was substituted. The 237 F3D-2 Skyknights built
by October 1953 included 16 F3D-2Ms with four
Sparrow I radar beam-riding missiles and 30 F3D-
2Qs for radar countermeasures.

DOUGLAS XF3D-1   USN

DOUGLAS F3D-1
Westinghouse J34-WE-34, 3250 lbs. takeoff
DIMENSIONS: Span 50′, Lg. 45′5″, Ht. 16′1″, Wing Area 400 sq. ft.
WEIGHT: Empty 14,890 lb., Gross 24,485 lb., Max. 27,362 lb., Combat 21,245 lb. Fuel 1350–650 gal.
PERFORMANCE: Speed—Top 478 mph at 33,000′, 443 mph at 14,000′, Cruising 428 mph, Stalling 117 mph. Service Ceiling 34,000′, Climb 3040′/1 min. Range 1068 miles normal, 1318 miles max.   BODIE

DOUGLAS F3D-2
Westinghouse J34-WE-36, 3400 lbs. takeoff
DIMENSIONS: As F3D-1
WEIGHT: Empty 14,989 lb., Gross 24,614 lb., Max. 26,731 lb., Combat 21,374 lb. Fuel 1350–650 gal.
PERFORMANCE: Speed—Top 493 mph at 35,000′, Cruising 455 mph, Landing 116 mph. Service Ceiling 36,700′, Climb 3570′/1 min. Range 1145 miles normal, 1375 miles ferry.   ARNOLD

While the faster single-seat Banshee was used on carriers, the Skyknight served the Marines except for tests and training work. One Korean-based squadron, VMF(N)-513, got F3D-2s to replace the F7F-3N, and downed six enemy aircraft beginning November 3, 1952—the best night-fighter record of the war, although this was credited more to the APQ-35 radar's 20-mile range than to the F3D's modest agility. The last Skyknight retired from a Marine ECM unit in June 1970.

This period's most radical design was the Vought XF7U-1 Cutlass, a tailless single-seater with two Westinghouse J34-WE-32 units and twin rudders midway out on the 38° swept-back wing. Pressurized cockpit, ejection seat, and ailevators (combined ailerons and elevators) were used. The short, stubby wings had an aspect ratio of 3:1 and leading-edge slots. At rest the Cutlass had a nose-high at-

titude due to the long strut for the nosewheel, a feature designed to maintain a high angle of attack for the wing during takeoff and landing. The Cutlass was also the first Navy fighter designed from the beginning for engine afterburners, and the first swept-wing, tailless carrier plane. Its performance was phenomenal for its design era, but it would take too many years to become operational.

Vought engineers began their design in June 1945, choosing the swept-wing, tailless shape to avoid compressibility problems, and their chief aerodynamicist has stated that this decision was made before German research on the type was available. Six companies responded to a Navy day-fighter design competition announced January 25, 1946, but the Vought V-346A design submitted April 15, 1946, won a contract on June 25 for three XF7U-1 prototypes, first flown September 29, 1948, powered by two 3,000-pound-thrust J34-WE-22 engines and armed with four 20-mm guns below the cockpit.

An F7U-1 contract had been awarded July 28, 1948, but the first flight was delayed until March 1, 1950, because of Vought's move from Stratford to Dallas. Four of 14 F7U-1s were completed that year, but two crashed—as had all three prototypes— killing three Vought test pilots. A September 1949 order for 88 F7U-2s was canceled and serious problems discouraged the Navy from attempting any squadron use of the F7U-1.

The Korean War led the Navy to persist in developing a high-performance potential, and on August 21, 1950, the F7U-3, powered by J46-WE-8A engines with afterburners, was ordered. A heavier aircraft, with more fuel, strengthened landing gear with extended front strut, dual nosewheels, and two wing pylons for 1,000-pound bombs or 250-gallon drop tanks, the F7U-3 could add a belly pack for thirty-two 2.75-inch rockets. APQ-30 radar in the nose aimed the four Mk 12 20-mm guns, with 720 rounds, which had been moved to upper lips of the engine air intakes.

Since the Westinghouse engine deliveries were delayed, the first 16 F7U-3s were provided with Allison J35-A-29s without afterburners. The first example flew December 20, 1951, but the J46s were not available until 1953. Accidents and mechanical problems delayed fleet introduction until February

VOUGHT XF7U-1   MFR

VOUGHT F7U-3M
Westinghouse J46-WE-8, 5725 lbs.
DIMENSIONS: As F7U-3
WEIGHT: Empty 19,488 lb., Gross 32,975 lb., Max. 37,000
    lb., Combat 26,968 lb. Fuel 1570–2090 gal.
PERFORMANCE: (with four Sparrows) Speed—Top 678
    mph at s. l., 615 mph at 35,000', Cruising 449 mph,
    Stalling 139 mph. Service Ceiling 45,400', Climb 10,-
    500'/1 min., 30,000'/17.4 min., Combat Range 650
    miles/four Sparrows.   PMB

VOUGHT F7U-1
Westinghouse J34-WE-32, 3370–4900 lbs.
DIMENSIONS: Span 38'8", Lg. 39'7", Ht. 11'10", Wing Area
    496 sq. ft.
WEIGHT: Empty 12,837 lb., Gross 20,038 lb., Max. 24,000
    lb., Combat 17,707 lb. Fuel 971–1471 gal.
PERFORMANCE: Speed—Top 693 mph at s. l., 626 mph at
    35,000', Cruising 460 mph, Stalling 112 mph. Service
    Ceiling 50,000', Climb 15,100'/1 min. Range 1125
    miles normal, 1634 miles max.   MFR

VOUGHT F7U-3P   MFR

VOUGHT F7U-3
Westinghouse J46-WE-8, 3960–5800 lbs. AB
DIMENSIONS: Span 39'9", Lg. 44'3", Ht. 14'7", Wing Area
    535 sq. ft.
WEIGHT: Empty 18,262 lb., Gross 28,173 lb., Max. 35,000
    lb., Combat 24,741 lb. Fuel 1220–726 gal.
PERFORMANCE: Speed—Top 696 mph at s. l., 608 mph at
    35,000', Cruising 518 mph, Landing 137 mph. Service
    Ceiling 46,500', Climb 11,150'/1 min., 30,000'/13.9
    min. Range 696 miles normal, 817 miles max.   MFR

2, 1954, when F7U-3s reached NAS Miramar on the
West Coast. Deliveries of 180 F7U-3s ended March
9, 1955.

Four Sparrow I beam-riding missiles, or four
1,000 pound bombs, could be carried by the F7U-
3M, which had APQ-51 radar and additional fuel.
Two converted from F7U-3s first flew July 12, 1954.
Vought delivered the last of 98 new F7U-3Ms August 12, 1955, and VA-83 made the first overseas
deployment (to the Mediterranean) of a Navy missile squadron in March 1956, when 11 Cutlass
squadrons were operating.

Twelve unarmed F7U-3P photo planes never became operational, but are included in the Cutlass
total of 307. Some Navy fighter squadrons had been
redesigned attack (VA) units in anticipation of
fighter-bomber equipment. An order for 146 A2U-1
attack versions of the Cutlass, however, was canceled in November 1954, and standard fighter
models were issued to three such squadrons.

Bedeviled with a high accident rate, the big
Vought fighters were withdrawn from squadron
service after November 1957, but they did serve to

introduce the fleet to the new, complex breed of airplanes that the future would bring to carrier service.

Swept Wings for the Carriers

Since the Korean War, the outstanding feature of contemporary fighter aircraft has been the use of swept wings to delay the effects of compressibility encountered at sonic or near-sonic speeds. Several swept-wing fighters went into production to equip the expanding Naval air force.

The first new prototype to appear after the outbreak of war in Korea was the XF4D-1 Skyray, a single-engine, single-place delta-wing interceptor ordered December 16, 1948, and first flown January 23, 1951. A 5,000-pound-thrust Allison J35-A-17 powered both prototypes temporarily until the first Westinghouse J40s became available. A J40-WE-8 of 11,600 pounds thrust with afterburner enabled the second prototype to establish a 753-mph record in October 1953—the first time the world speed record was held by an aircraft designed for carriers.

Because of production difficulties suffered by the Westinghouse power plant, the Navy in June 1953 decided to install Pratt & Whitney J57s in production Skyrays. The first F4D-1 with a J57-P-2 (later J57-P-8) flew on June 5, 1954. Armament included four 20-mm guns in the wings or 76 2.75-inch rockets in four pods. A clean F4D-1 set a climb record of 39,370 feet in 111 seconds and 49,212 feet in 156 seconds.

Production of 419 Skyrays was completed at El Segundo in December 1958. Douglas Skyrays were first delivered to an operational squadron, VC-3 (later redesignated VF [AW]-3) on April 16, 1956; when VF(AW)-3 was stationed at San Diego, it was

DOUGLAS F4D-1
Pratt & Whitney J57-P-8, or -8B, 10,200–16,000 lbs.
DIMENSIONS: Span 33′6″, Lg. 45′8″, Ht. 13′, Wing Area 557 sq. ft.
WEIGHT: Empty 15,150 lb., Max. 26,000 lb., Combat 19,-100 lb. Fuel 640–1240 gal.
PERFORMANCE: Speed—Top 723 mph at s. l., 634 mph at 50,000′, Cruising 587 mph, Landing 134 mph. Service Ceiling 55,000′, Climb 29,000′/1 min. Range 593 miles normal, 1220 miles max.   MFR

the only Navy squadron attached to the ADC. On practice intercepts, its F4D-1s carried an electronics store on the central pylon, a pair of 12 2.75-inch rocket packs, two 300-gallon drop tanks, and two Sidewinder missiles on the outer pylons.

The next unit to get F4D-1s was VMF(AW)-115, which flew them longer than any other unit. This Marine squadron's experience included crisis deployments to Taiwan (1958) and Guantánamo Bay (1962), as well as the usual carrier service of most Navy Skyray squadrons. Their last F4D-1s (called F-6As since 1962), retired February 29, 1964, leaving behind a reputation for fast climb, high ceiling, speed, and a good APQ-50A radar, but also as a difficult plane to fly.

The F4D-2 had the same German-inspired Lippisch wing plan but was designed for supersonic speeds, with a thinner wing, longer fuselage, and more fuel. Eleven ordered were redesignated F5D-1 Skylancers when flown April 21, 1956, with a J57-P-8 and provisions for a new radar fire control and all-missile armament: two Douglas Sparrow IIs (AAM-N-3s) and 72 two-inch rockets. Production versions with General Electric J79 engines were expected to reach a supersonic 1,098 mph, but the program was canceled after only four F5D-1s had been completed.

Another interceptor type appearing in 1951 was the McDonnell XF3H-1 Demon, a single-seater with a 7,200-pound-thrust Westinghouse XJ40-WE-6 and swept-back wings and tail. Two prototypes had been ordered September 30, 1949, and a program was planned as early as March 1951 for 150 Demons. Production aircraft, known as F3H-1Ns, were to have more fuel and the increased radar required for all-weather capabilities. Gross weight increased from 22,000 to 29,000 pounds, but a more powerful J40-WE-24 turbojet was expected to compensate for the increase.

The XF3H-1 prototype flew August 7, 1951, and the production program was increased to 528 aircraft, with an additional quantity to be built by Temco. In April 1952 McDonnell recommended utilization of the Allison J71-A-2 instead of the J40, which was suffering various difficulties, and in November the Navy decided that, beginning with the sixty-first Demon, the J-71 turbojet would be used. In September 1953 it became apparent that the J40-WE-24 would not materialize, and that the F3H-1N would have to be content with the 7,200-pound-thrust J40-WE-22.

The first of 56 F3H-1Ns was first flown on January 24, 1954, and the handicap of the additional weight soon became apparent. In November the contract was reduced to 280, and in July 1955, after the fourth pilot was killed in a series of 11 accidents that had destroyed six F3H-1Ns during tests, the

DOUGLAS F5D-1
Pratt & Whitney J57-P-8, 10,200–16,000 lbs.
DIMENSIONS: Span 33'6", Lg. 53'10", Ht. 14'10", Wing
   Area 557 sq. ft.
WEIGHT: Empty 17,444 lb., Gross 29,122 lb., Combat
   25,495 lb. Fuel 1333 gal.
PERFORMANCE: Speed—Top 791 mph at 35,000', 748 mph
   at s. l., Stalling 155 mph. Range 1226 miles.   MFR

McDONNELL F3H-2N   PMB

McDONNELL XF3H-1   USN

McDONNELL F3H-1N
Westinghouse J40-WE-22, 6500–10,900 lbs.
DIMENSIONS: Span 35'4", Lg. 59', Ht. 14'7", Wing Area
   442 sq. ft.
WEIGHT: Empty 18,691 lb., Gross 29,998 lb., Combat
   26,085 lb. Fuel 1506 gal.
PERFORMANCE: Speed—Top 628 mph at 10,000', 616 mph
   at s. l., Cruising 553 mph, Landing 129 mph. Service
   Ceiling 44,000', Climb 10,900'/1 min. Range 1130
   miles.   USN

type was permanently grounded. The engine's
power was judged insufficient for the airframe's
weight. All of these aircraft could be used only for
mechanics' ground training except for two converted by installation of Allison J-71s into F3H-2
standards. The failure of the F3H-1N program cost
the Navy some $200 million, most of which was
expended on the unsuccessful J-40 engine.

The first F3H-2N, accepted in December 1954,
had an Allison J71-A-2 giving a 14,400-pound thrust
with afterburner and widened the wing chord at
the roots to increase the area. A radar scanner was
fitted in the nose with intakes for the turbojet on
each side, and armament consisted of four 20-mm
guns with 600 rounds under the cockpit and four
infrared Sidewinders under wing pylons.

Entering squadron service in March 1956, the
142 F3H-2Ns were first deployed with VF-14 when
this unit sailed on the giant *Forrestal*'s first overseas deployment. Next came the F3H-2M, which
teamed four Sperry Sparrow I (AAM-N-2) beam-riding missiles with APG-51 radar. After 80 F3H-2Ms,
the remaining Demons delivered after July 1957
were of the definitive F3H-2 configuration, which
introduced four Raytheon Sparrow III radar-homing missiles (AAM-N-6) for distant targets and used
the four guns for close work. Two heat-seeking
Sidewinders (AAM-N-7) could replace the Sparrows if the climb advantages of a lightweight condition were desired.

McDONNELL F3H-2M (with Sparrow I)   USN

McDONNELL F-3B (F3H-2)
Allison J71-A-2B, 14,400 lbs.
DIMENSIONS: Span 35'4", Lg. 59', Ht. 14'7", Wing Area
    519 sq. ft.
WEIGHT: Empty 21,287 lb., Gross 33,424 lb./2 Side-
    winders (38,997 lb./4 Sparrows), Combat 29,020 (31,-
    839) lb. Fuel 1506–788 gal.
PERFORMANCE: Speed—Top 716 (693) mph at s. l., 643
    (624) mph at 35,000', Stalling 112 (114) mph. Service
    Ceiling 35,050' (27,150'), Climb 14,350'/1 min. (12,-
    410'/1 min.). Combat Range 1180 (1239) miles.   USN

McDonnell delivered the last of 519 Demons on
November 17, 1959, and they remained in service
until they were retired in September 1964. The
F3H-2, F3H-2M, and F3H-2N were redesignated
F-3B, MF-3B, and F-3C, respectively.

The first swept-wing fighter actually in carrier
service was the Grumman G-93 Cougar, whose
three XF9F-6 prototypes were ordered converted
from F9F-5s on March 2, 1951, and first flown September 20. Swept-back wings and tail were added
to the standard Panther fuselage. The first production F9F-6, delivered December 28, 1951, and accepted in February 1952, was followed by 645 more
Cougar fighters, delivered by July 1954, and 60
F9F-6P reconnaissance models. Four 20-mm guns
with 190 rpg and 180 pounds of pilot armor were
provided, and the power plant was a J48-P-8, although an Allison J33-A-16 of equal power was used
on 168 F9F-7s also delivered by July 1954. A pair
of drop tanks or 1,000-pound bombs could be carried under the wings. Cougars joined operational
squadrons on November 1952, but only 18 were
deployed to Korea with the Marines before the war
ended.

Grumman's G-99 design became the F9F-8, first
flown December 18, 1953, with a J48-P-8A, an air-
refueling probe in the nose of a longer fuselage,
more internal fuel, an all-movable stabilizer, and
cambered leading-edge extensions instead of the
slats of the previous models. Four Sidewinder missiles supplemented the four 20-mm guns; they were
first deployed overseas with the F9F-8s of VA-46 in
July 1956.

Grumman delivered 601 F9F-8s from February
1954 to March 1957, most of them becoming the
F9F-8B for attack squadrons, with a LABS for a
1,125-pound nuclear bomb, or six rocket pods. The
last Cougars were 110 seven-camera F9F-8Ps,
which served photographic squadrons until February 1960, and 400 F9F-8T two-place trainers
whose completion brought Cougar production to an
end in February 1960 with 1,985 delivered. The
trainer version, later the TF-9J, remained in service
until 1974.

In the hasty search for a quickly available swept-
back wing fighter that occurred after the appearance
of the MIG-15s in Korea, the Navy determined in
February 1951 to procure a Navy version of the
North American F-86 Sabrejet. Three prototypes
were built as modified F-86Es: an XFJ-2B Fury
flown December 27, 1951, with four 20-mm guns,
and two unarmed XFJ-2s, first flown February 19,
1952, with carrier landing gear. Production FJ-2s
were built at Columbus, Ohio, and were similar to
the F-86F except for folding wings, carrier gear, and
four 20-mm guns with 600 rounds. Two hundred

GRUMMAN F9F-6
Pratt & Whitney J48-P-8, 6250 lbs.
DIMENSIONS: Span 34'6", Lg. 40'11", Ht. 12'4", Wing Area
    300 sq. ft.
WEIGHT: Empty 11,255 lb., Gross 18,450 lb., Max. 21,000
    lb., Combat 16,244 lb. Fuel 919–1219 gal.
PERFORMANCE: Speed—Top 654 mph at s. l., 590 mph at
    35,000', Cruising 541 mph, Stalling 128 mph. Service
    Ceiling 44,600', Climb 6750'/1 min., Combat Range
    932 miles.   USN

GRUMMAN F9F-7
Allison J33-A-19, 6250 lbs.
DIMENSIONS: As F9F-6
WEIGHT: Empty 11,255 lb., Gross 18,905 lb., Combat
16,577 lb. Fuel 919–1219 gal.
PERFORMANCE: Speed—Top 628 mph at s. l., 559 mph at
35,000', Cruising 509 mph, Stalling 130 mph, Service
Ceiling 40,200', Climb 5100'/1 min., 30,000'/11.6 min.,
Range 1157 miles.   USN

GRUMMAN F9F-8P   ARNOLD

completed from November 1952 to September 1954
served Marine squadrons, the only common use of
an Air Force fighter since the P-12/F4B series.

Wright J65 engines replaced the J47 on the FJ-3
Fury ordered April 18, 1952. A modified FJ-2 flew
with the J65 on July 3, 1953, and the production
FJ-3 flew on December 11. During 1955 the wing
slats of earlier FJ-3s were replaced by an extended
leading edge with more fuel, although no designation change was made. The addition of launching
pylons for two Sidewinder (GAR-8) missiles or
bombs in February 1956 was noted by the FJ-3M
label. By August 1956, 538 FJ-3/3Ms had been built
for Navy and Marine squadrons.

A complete redesign of the Fury, the FJ-4 had a
thinner wing and larger fuel capacity. An October
1953 contract provided two prototypes (NA-208)
first flown October 28, 1954, with the J65-W-4, and
150 FJ-4s (NA-209) appearing in February 1955 with
the J65-W-16A. Four 20-mm guns and four pylons
for Sidewinders, bombs, or drop tanks were used.

The FJ-4B was an attack version with a LABS for
delivering an Mk 7 nuclear weapon and an extra
pair of speed brakes beneath the tail. Six underwing
stations could be used for 4,000 pounds of bombs,
rocket pods, or up to five Bullpup air-to-surface
missiles, first deployed to the fleets overseas in
April 1959. This Fury model first flew December 4,
1956, with 222 built for Pacific Fleet attack squadrons by May 1958 when production of 1,112 Navy
Furies at the Columbus, Ohio, plant ended.

Since the FJ-2 Fury was less suitable for carrier
operations than the lighter F9F-6s in service, the
FJ-2s went to six Marine VMF squadrons beginning
in January 1954. With improved takeoff, climb, and
altitude performance, the FJ-3 joined VF-173 in
September 1954 and served 18 carrier fighter
squadrons by 1956. Marine FJ-2s were replaced by
three FJ-3 and three FJ-4 squadrons in 1956–57,
while nine Navy and three Marine attack squadrons
got the FJ-4B in 1957–58, serving until September
1962.

Navy fighter strength reached a peak at the end

GRUMMAN F9F-8
Pratt & Whitney J48-P-8A, 7250 lbs.
DIMENSIONS: Span 34'6", Lg. 41'9", Ht. 12'3", Wing Area
337 sq. ft.
WEIGHT: Empty 11,866 lb., Gross 20,098 lb., Max. 24,763
lb., Combat 17,328 lb. Fuel 1063–363 gal.
PERFORMANCE: Speed—Top 647 mph at 2000', 593 mph
at 35,000', Cruising 516 mph, Stalling 132 mph. Service
Ceiling 42,000', Combat Ceiling 42,500', Climb 5750'/
1 min. Range 1208 miles normal, 1312 miles ferry.
MFR

GRUMMAN F9F-8B
Pratt & Whitney J48-P-8A, 7250 lbs.
DIMENSIONS: As F9F-8
WEIGHT: Empty 11,866 lb., Gross 22,575 lb., Max. 24,763
lb., Combat 18,035 lb. Fuel 1063–663 gal.
PERFORMANCE: Speed—Top 638 mph at s. l., 640 mph at
5000', Cruising 475 mph, Stalling 142 mph. Service
Ceiling 41,700', Climb 5410'/1 min. Range 1053 miles
normal, 1295 miles/1125 lb. store and one 150 gal.
tank.   USN

NORTH AMERICAN XFJ-2B   MFR

NORTH AMERICAN FJ-2
General Electric J47-GE-2, 6000 lbs.
DIMENSIONS: Span 37'1", Lg. 37'7", Ht. 13', Wing Area
  288 sq. ft.
WEIGHT: Empty 11,802 lb., Gross 18,791 lb., Combat
  15,813 lb. Fuel 435–835 gal.
PERFORMANCE: Speed—Top 676 mph at s. l., 602 mph at
  35,000', Cruising 518 mph, Stalling 132 mph. Service
  Ceiling 39,100', Combat Ceiling 41,700', Climb 7230'/
  1 min. Combat Range 990 miles.   USN

NORTH AMERICAN FJ-3
Wright J65-W-4, 7650 lbs.
DIMENSIONS: Span 37'1", Lg. 37'7", Ht. 13'8", Wing Area
  302 sq. ft.
WEIGHT: Empty 12,205 lb., Gross 17,189 lb., Max. 21,876
  lb., Combat 15,669 lb. Fuel 559–959 gal.
PERFORMANCE: Speed—Top 681 mph at s. l. (670 mph/2
  GAR-8), 623 mph at 35,000', Cruising 526 mph, Stalling
  133 mph. Service Ceiling 49,000', Combat Ceiling
  49,000', Climb 8430'/1 min. Combat Range 990 miles,
  1784 miles ferry.   USN

NORTH AMERICAN FJ-4
Wright J65-W-16A, 7700 lbs.
DIMENSIONS: Span 39'1", Lg. 36'4", Ht. 13'11", Wing Area
  339 sq. ft.
WEIGHT: Empty 13,210 lb., Gross 20,130 lb., Max. 23,700
  lb., Combat 17,845 lb. Fuel 840–1240 gal.
PERFORMANCE: Speed—Top 680 mph at s. l., 631 mph at
  35,000', Cruising 534 mph, Stalling 139 mph. Service
  Ceiling 46,200', Combat Ceiling 46,800', Climb 7660'/
  1 min. Range 1485 miles normal, 2020 miles/2 GAR-8
  and two 200 gal. tanks.   USN

NORTH AMERICAN FJ-4B
Wright J65-W-16A, 7700 lbs.
DIMENSIONS: As FJ-4
WEIGHT: Empty 13,778 lb., Gross 26,893 lb./two 1000 lb.
  bombs (25,093 lb./4 GAR-8), Combat 23,187 (21,937)
  lb. Fuel 840–1240 gal.
PERFORMANCE: Speed—Top 636 mph at 10,000', 630 (654)
  mph at s. l., Cruising 514 (521) mph, Stalling 125 mph.
  Service Ceiling 36,900' (40,200'), Climb 5100' (5850')/
  1 min. Combat Range 1940 miles.   USN

of 1956, with 79 Navy and Marine squadrons protecting the U.S. Fleet and its bases. Only one stray
fighter squadron still used the straight-wing F9F-5,
although most F9F-6s had already been relegated
to the Reserves, replaced by seven F9F-8, 16 F9F-
8B, five F7U-3, three F7U-3M, three FJ-2, eight FJ-
3, 12 FJ-3M, and one FJ-4 squadron. On December
31, 1956, all-weather fighter squadrons still in-

cluded nine F2H-3 and five F2H-4 straight-wing Banshee squadrons, while two F3H-2M, four F3H-2N, and four F4D-1 squadrons had current production types. Altogether, 13 different types were represented in this extravagant variety, which would be replaced by just two supersonic types in eight years.

Experimental Fighters

While it may have seemed that the Navy was buying every fighter type offered during the fifties, there were prototypes too radical for production but reflecting unique approaches to fighter development. Grumman stepped out first with the XF10F-1, the first American fighter with variable-sweep wings.

When its wings were extended for takeoff and landing, they had a 50-foot, 7-inch span and 13.5° sweep, but in high-speed flight they moved back to a 36-foot, 8-inch span and 52.5° sweep. This feature was a means of giving fast swept-wing aircraft the low-speed stability necessary for carrier operations. The fighter's equipment included four 20-mm guns under a cockpit protected by 348 pounds of armor, APQ-41 radar, and wing points for two 2,000-pound bombs or two 300-gallon drop tanks.

When two XF10F-1 prototypes were ordered April 7, 1948, they were to have delta wings and a J42 engine, but by 1950 the J40 engine and variable-sweep wing were included when 112 were scheduled for the Korean War program. The first flight was made May 19, 1952, with a J40-WE-6, since the WE-8 specified was not yet available. The high T-tail proved unsatisfactory and had to be replaced after 17 flights. The production contract was terminated on April 1, 1953, because the F3H-1 seemed to offer a less complicated solution for the all-weather mission, and the second prototype was never completed. Grumman, however, had found that variable sweep worked and used such wings on its successful F-14 nearly 20 years later. The $30 million spent on the XF10F-1 project was therefore not entirely without result.

Alternatives to carrier-based fighters were explored by the vertical takeoff (VTO) Convair XFY-1 and Lockheed XFV-1, and the water-based Convair XF2Y-1. The only Navy single-seat fighters built by these firms, they were a radical departure from previous concepts.

A VTO fighter could operate from cargo ship deck to beach, providing defense and close support when carriers were unavailable. Powered by an Allison T40-A-14 turning 16-foot-diameter, six-bladed contraprops, the delta-wing XFY-1 Pogo took off vertically from four small wheels at the wing and tips, swung into horizontal flight, and hung on its props to back down to a vertical landing. Design arma-

GRUMMAN XF10F-1
Westinghouse J40-WE-8, 7400-10,900 lbs. (WE-6 used on tests)
DIMENSIONS: Span 50'7"–36'8", Lg. 54'5", Ht. 16'3", Wing Area 467–450 sq. ft.
WEIGHT: Empty 20,426 lb., Gross 31,255 lb., Max. 35,450 lb., Combat 27,451 lb. Fuel 1585–2185 gal.
PERFORMANCE: Speed—Top 710 mph at s. l., 632 mph at 35,000', Cruising 478 mph, Stalling 112 mph. Combat Ceiling 45,800', Climb 13,350'/1 min., 35,000'/4.5 min. Combat Range 1670 miles, 2090 miles max.   USN

ment, not actually installed, was four 20-mm guns in wing-tip pods.

Two prototypes ordered March 31, 1951, were test vehicles for a fighter version planned with a more powerful T54 engine and a design speed of 610 mph. Actually, only the first XFY-1 flew. T. F. Coleman piloted the first free flight August 1, 1954, and on November 2 Coleman made the first successful transition from vertical to horizontal flight, returning to the vertical position to back down to a landing.

The powerful plant, however, was inadequate to lift a useful payload, and backing into the ground was never an attractive prospect. Fearing engine failure, Convair itself suggested project termination after some 65 flights.

Built at the same time for the same purpose and with the same engine, Lockheed's XFV-1 had short, straight wings with gun pods at the tips, with the intended landing wheels at the tips of a four-fin tail. The XFV-1, however, never made a vertical takeoff or landing, but was tested on an ungainly temporary landing gear by H. R. Salmon, who began taxi trials in December 1953 and flew from a horizontal posture on June 16, 1954. Every succeeding test was made the same way, the engine never being trusted enough to remove the auxiliary gear and try the taildown attitude. Performance data accompanying the photograph is that expected for the fighter version with a 6,825-hp XT40-A-16, but only the XT40-A-14 was actually available.

The only water-based jet fighter ever built in America, the XF2Y-1 Sea Dart could operate from coastal waters, bays, and fields. It floated on a watertight belly until enough speed was built up to rise on its retractable twin skis. Two prototypes had been ordered in January 1951, a mockup was inspected in August 1952 when an initial production

CONVAIR XFY-1
Allison XT40-A-14, 5332 hp
DIMENSIONS: Span 27'8", Lg. 32'3", Tail Span 21'8", Wing Area 355 sq. ft.
WEIGHT: Empty 11,139 lb., Gross 14,250 lb., Combat 13,250 lb. Fuel 576 gal.
PERFORMANCE: Speed—Top 489 mph at 24,000', 474 mph at s. l., Service Ceiling 37,500', Climb 9980'/1 min., 20,000'/3.4 min.   MFR

order for 12 (later 22) was received, and the XF2Y-1 was flown April 9, 1953, by E. D. Shannon.

The contract was cut back to five aircraft in March 1954, and the second Sea Dart was destroyed on November 4, 1954. The third, an YF2Y-1, flew March 4, 1955, but the last two were not tested. A Mach .99 aircraft on the level, the Sea Dart had replaced the original Westinghouse J34-WE-42 engines with the J46-WE-12 and exceeded Mach 1 in a shallow dive—the only supersonic seaplane ever flown. The program was abandoned because the Navy never approved an operational requirement for a seaplane fighter, and the Sea Darts were completed as unarmed research aircraft.

LOCKHEED XFV-1
Allison XT40-A-14, 5332 hp
DIMENSIONS: Span 27'5", Lg. 37'6", Wing Area 246 sq. ft.
WEIGHT: Empty 11,599 lb., Gross 16,221 lb., Combat 15,000 lb. Fuel 508 gal.
PERFORMANCE: (Est.) Speed—Top 580 mph at 15,000'. Service Ceiling 43,300', Climb 10,820'/1 min., 30,000'/5 min. Loiter time 1.17 hrs. at 35,000'.   MFR

CONVAIR XF2Y-1
Westinghouse J46-WE-12B, 5725 lbs.
DIMENSIONS: Span 33'8", Lg. 52'7", Ht. 20'9", Wing Area 563 sq. ft.
WEIGHT: Gross 21,500 lb. Fuel 630 gal.
PERFORMANCE: Speed—Top 724 mph at s. l., 648 mph at 35,000', Stalling 132 mph. Service Ceiling 42,500', Climb 17,100'/1 min.   MFR

CONVAIR YF2Y-1   MFR

Supersonic Carrier Fighters

The Navy's first supersonic fighter was the Grumman G-93 Tiger, which had the first application of area-rule design, with an indented fuselage to reduce drag, small, thin swept-back wings, and a Wright J65-W-18 with afterburner. Armament consisted of four 20-mm guns, set low in the nose, with 500 rounds, and provisions for four Sidewinders were added later.

Begun in January 1953 and first ordered April 27, the first Tiger flew July 30, 1954. Three aircraft were delivered in 1954 as F9F-9s, but 41 remaining on the contract were redesignated F11F-1 in April 1955. The last two were completed with the YJ79-GE-3, designated F11F-1F, and first flown May 25, 1956. This engine seemed too heavy for the airframe and had double the fuel consumption of the J65. Instead of the J79 or the J65-WE-6 originally planned, the Wright J65-W-18 was used on 157 more F11F-1s made with a longer nose. By the time the Tigercat entered squadron service in March 1957, Vought's F8U-1 Crusader had surpassed it in performance, and when the final F11F-1 was delivered January 23, 1959, Grumman had no Navy fighter in production for the first time in its history. The Tigercats served seven squadrons, beginning with VA-156 (still designated attack, although no bombs were carried), and were retired from first-

GRUMMAN F11F-1 (F-11A)
Wright J65-W-18, 7400 lbs. (10,500/AB)
DIMENSIONS: Span 31'7½", Lg. 46'11", Ht. 13'2", Wing Area 250 sq. ft.
WEIGHT: Empty 14,330 lb., Gross 21,280 lb., Max. 22,160 lb. Fuel 1049–249 gal.
PERFORMANCE: Speed—Top 753 mph at s. l., 727 mph at 35,000', Cruising 578 mph, Landing 150 mph. Service Ceiling 41,900', Climb 5130'/1 min., Combat Range 1275 miles/clean, 900 miles/four Sidewinders.   USN

GRUMMAN F-11A of "Blue Angels"   ARNOLD

GRUMMAN F11F-1F
General Electric YJ79-GE-3, 9600-15,000 lbs.
DIMENSIONS: Span 31'8", Lg. 48', Ht. 13'10", Wing Area
  250 sq. ft.
WEIGHT: Empty 16,457 lb., Gross 26,086 lb. Fuel 914–
  1214 gal.
PERFORMANCE: Speed—Top 1325 mph at 35,000'. Service
  Ceiling 50,300', Climb 8950'/1 min., Combat Range
  1136 miles.   MFR

line service in April 1961. However, the Blue Angels aerobatic team continued to display the Grumman's maneuverability until 1969.

F-8 Crusader

The first operational carrier-based fighter in the world to exceed 1,000 mph was the Vought F-8 Crusader. This velocity was combined with the low speed limits for flight-deck operation by using shoulder-mounted, thin, swept wings with two-position incidence, pivoting on the rear spar so that their angle of attack could be increased to get more lift for takeoff or landing.

A Navy requirement for a supersonic single-seat day fighter issued to eight manufacturers in September 1952 resulted in a June 29, 1953, contract for two XF8U-1 prototypes. John Konrad piloted the first, passing Mach 1 on the first flight at Edwards AFB on March 25, 1955. A Pratt & Whitney J57-P-11 of 14,800-pound thrust with a titanium-shrouded afterburner—the power plant used for the first generation of supersonic Air Force fighters—gave the Crusader a much easier life than its troublesome F6U and F7U ancestors.

Production F8U-1s were first flown on September 20, 1955, and entered squadron service with VF-32 in March 1957. A 16,000-pound-thrust J57-P-12, or P-4, was used, and an in-flight refueling probe (required on all Navy fighters since September 1955) retracted into the port side. Four 20-mm Mk 12 guns of 500 rounds were mounted behind and below the pilot, together with 32 2.75-inch rockets in a retractable launching pack. Unfortunately, the

fighter pitched upwards when the pack was lowered, thereby spoiling accuracy, so in March 1958 the company recommended the elimination of the rocket packs, which were finally deactivated in June 1960. In the meantime, racks for two Sidewinder missiles were added to the fuselage sides.

The 318 F8U-1s built in Dallas had APG-30 gun-ranging radar, which was replaced by an APS-67 search scanner in the F8U-1E, flown September 3, 1958, and 130 were accepted by June 1959. Cameras replaced armament in the F8U-1P, first flown December 17, 1956, with 144 accepted by March 1960. Major John Glenn flew one from Los Angeles to New York in 3 hours, 22 minutes on July 16, 1957—the first supersonic transcontinental flight. One F8U-1 was converted to the F8U-1T two-place trainer in 1962.

A J57-P-16, airscoops for the afterburner, and twin narrow fins under the fuselage for stability distinguished the F8U-2, first flown as an F8U-1 conversion in December 1957. Vought flew the first production F8U-2 on August 20, 1958, and 187 delivered by September 1960 could carry four Sidewinders on the side racks.

An entirely new development was the larger F8U-3, designed as an all-weather, all-missile Mach 2 interceptor. The fuselage was enlarged to accommodate the Pratt & Whitney J75, the chin intake was raked forwards, and boundary-layer air control on the variable-incidence wings was obtained by blown flaps. Three Sparrow III missiles were semi-submerged in the fuselage, an APQ-50 radar was provided, retractable ventral fins aided stability, and push buttons engaged an automatic flight-control system.

VOUGHT F-8A (F8U-1)
Pratt & Whitney J57-P-44, 10,200 lbs. military (16,000
  lbs. AB)
DIMENSIONS: Span 35'8", Lg. 54'3", Ht. 13'4", Wing Area
  375 sq. ft.
WEIGHT: Empty 15,513 lb., Gross 26,969 lb., Max. 27,468
  lb., Combat 23,659 lb. Fuel 1273 gal.
PERFORMANCE: Speed—Top 1013 mph at 35,000', 733
  mph at s. l., Cruising 570 mph, Stalling 155 mph. Service Ceiling 42,300' (full load), Combat Ceiling 51,-
  500', Climb 20,000'/1 min., Combat Radius 398 miles,
  Combat Range 1474 miles.   MFR

VOUGHT RF-8A (F8U-1P)   USN

VOUGHT F-8C (F8U-2)
Pratt & Whitney J57-P-16, 10,700 lbs. military, 16,900 lbs. (AB)
DIMENSIONS: As F-8A
WEIGHT: Empty 16,483 lb., Gross 27,810 lb., Max. 27,938 lb., Combat 24,347 lb. Fuel 1273 gal.
PERFORMANCE: Speed—Top 1105 mph at 35,000', 1062 mph/two Sidewinders, 736 mph at s. l., Cruising 570 mph, Stalling 157 mph. Service Ceiling 41,700', Combat Ceiling 52,000', Climb 21,700'/1 min., Combat Radius 368 miles/Sidewinders, Combat Range 1490 miles (1375/Sidewinders).   MFR

VOUGHT F8U-3
Pratt & Whitney J75-P-5A, 16,500 lbs. (29,000 lbs. AB)
DIMENSIONS: Span 39'11", Lg. 58'11", Ht. 16'5", Wing Area 450 sq. ft.
WEIGHT: Empty 21,862 lb., Gross 37,856 lb., Combat 32,318 lb. Fuel 2036 gal.
PERFORMANCE: Speed—Top 1457 mph at 50,000', 800 mph at s. l., Cruising 575 mph, Stalling 154 mph. Combat Ceiling 51,500', Climb 35,000'/1.6 min., Combat Radius 645 miles, Range 2044 miles.   MFR

Two prototypes were ordered in May 1957, plus 16 F8U-3s in January 1958, and the first prototype flew June 2, 1958—just six days after McDonnell's rival Phantom. A modified J75-P-6 credited with 29,000-pound thrust powered the first F8U-3. The next was flown September 27 with a 24,500-pound-thrust J75-P-5, and a J57-P-8 was scheduled for production aircraft. An auxiliary rocket to be mounted at the tail fin's base was proposed, and such a device was tested on two FJ-4F Fury conversions but was canceled before the F8U-3 was flown.

During flight tests a speed of Mach 2.39 (1,600 mph) was obtained, and only the windshield's heat limitation prevented higher speeds. Complete performance data is not available, but test pilots reported the F8U-3 to be a highly maneuverable, superior fighter. By December 1958, however, the Navy had chosen the more versatile F4H-1 for the mission, the Vought contract was canceled, and only the third F8U-3 was flown before termination.

Although the McDonnell Phantom became the Navy's first choice for later procurement, the Crusader remained in production since the twin-engine Phantom was built for the giant carriers, while the older *Essex*-class carriers still in use required the smaller Voughts.

Under the current designation system, the F8U-1, F8U-1E, and F8U-2 became the F-8A, F-8B, and F-8C Crusaders, respectively. The F-8D was first flown February 16, 1960, as the F8U-2N. It introduced an APQ-83 radar and AAS-15 infrared scanner for limited all-weather capability, a Vought-developed autopilot, and a J57-P-20. More internal fuel replaced the rocket pack, and the four guns and four Sidewinders were retained on 152 F-8Ds accepted from June 1960 to December 1961.

The last new Crusader for the Navy was the F-

VOUGHT F-8D (F8U-2N)
Pratt & Whitney J57-P-20, 10,700 lbs. military, 18,000 lbs.
   (AB)
DIMENSIONS: As F8U-1
WEIGHT: Empty 17,541 lb., Gross 28,765 lb., Max. 29,000
   lb., Combat 25,098 lb. Fuel 1348 gal.
PERFORMANCE: Speed—Top 1228 mph at 35,000', 764
   mph at s. l., Cruising 570 mph, Stalling 162 mph. Ser-
   vice Ceiling 42,900', Combat Ceiling 53,400', Climb
   31,950'/1 min., Combat Radius 453 miles/missiles,
   Combat Range 1737 miles (guns only).   MFR

VOUGHT F-8E   MFR

8E, first flown at Dallas on June 30, 1961, as the
F8U-2NE, with new APQ-94 radar. The main addition to the previous model made on 286 F-8Es,
delivered from October 1961 to September 3, 1964,
was a pylon under each wing that could handle a
2,000-pound bomb, six 250-pound bombs, or a Bullpup missile, and when eight Zuni rockets were
attached to the fuselage side stations, up to 5,000
pounds of ground-support weapons could be carried.

The French Navy ordered 42 F-8E (FN) Crusaders especially fitted with boundary-layer air control,
double-droop leading edge, and enlarged horizontal tail surfaces to improve landings on the two
smaller French carriers. Provided with the J57-P-
20A engines and provision for French Matia missiles, the first F-8E (FN) flew June 26, 1964, and
completion of 42 by January 1965 brought the Crusader total to 1,261.

About 25 Navy and 12 Marine fighter squadrons
had received Crusaders when the United States

joined the war in Vietnam. The first to sortie over
Vietnam were RF-8A (formerly F8U-1P) Crusader
detachments of Light Photographic Squadron VFP-
63. Operating continuously from 1964 to 1972, the
squadron lost 20 planes and 12 pilots to enemy
action. RF-8As were rotated back to Vought for
modernization to the RF-8G configuration. They
reentered service in October 1965 with an 18,000-
pound-thrust (with afterburner) J57-P-22, ventral
fins, improved navigation and electronics equipment, drop tanks, and four cameras. Despite a
weight increase, the top speed was increased from
985 to 1,000 mph.

Marine F-8Es operated from Da Nang on close-
support missions, but the carrier-based Navy units
flew escorts for attack planes. Their first victory was
a MiG-17 downed with a Sidewinder from a VF-
211 F-8E on June 12, 1966, and 18 more victories
were claimed by VF-211, VF-162, VF-24 (F-8C),
VF-51 (F-8H), VF-53, and VF-111 by September
19, 1968.

During the war Vought remanufactured 448 Crusaders to update their equipment and extend their
service life; 73 RF-8Gs were followed by 89 F-8H
fighters rebuilt from F-8Ds, provided with the J57-
P-20A engine, and flown July 17, 1967. More extensive work was done on 136 F-8Js, which were actually F-8Es with P-20As and modified controls
used on the French version, as well as provisions
for two 300-gallon drop tanks or bombs. Less extensive modernization was made on 87 F-8K and 63
F-8L models, converted from F-8B and C aircraft
for Reserve stations.

The last Marine F-8 squadron retired its Voughts
in December 1975, and first-line Navy fighter-
squadron service ended March 2, 1976, with the
return of the Oriskany's Crusaders from the last
Essex-class carrier's final deployment, but VFP-63's
photo Crusaders remained active at Miramar NAS,
California. The Philippines became the second for-

VOUGHT F-8H
Pratt & Whitney J57-P-20A, 10,700 lbs. military, 18,000
   lbs. (AB)
DIMENSIONS: As F-8D
WEIGHT: Empty 18,700 lb., Gross 29,200 lb.
PERFORMANCE: Speed—Top 1020 mph at 35,000'. Combat
   Radius 396 miles.   MFR

VOUGHT F-8J
Pratt & Whitney J57-P-20A, 18,000 lbs.
DIMENSIONS: Span 35'8", Lg. 54'6", Ht. 15'9", Wing Area 450 sq. ft.
WEIGHT: Empty 19,751 lb., Gross 31,318 lb., Max. 36,587 lb., Combat 30,352 lb. (4 AIM-9D), Fuel 1348–948 gal.
PERFORMANCE: Speed—Top 1086 mph at 35,000', 750 mph at s. l., Cruising 551 mph, Stalling 178 mph. Combat Ceiling 47,800', Climb 21,900'/1 min., Combat Range 1576 miles/four AIM-9D, Combat Range 838 miles/six Mk 82 bombs.   LAWSON

eign country to get Crusaders with the arrival of 35 reconditioned F-8s in 1979.

Promulgation of the current aircraft designation system on September 18, 1962, is a convenient topic to end this chapter on the Navy fighter types entering service since 1945. The new system assigned numbers to Air Force and Navy fighters in the same series and had no manufacturer's symbol. Most of the first 11 numbers alloted were to Navy fighters already retiring from first-line service. The most notable exception was the F-4 in production for both Air Force and Navy (see Chapter 32). New designations of fighter aircraft available in 1962 follow.

New	Old	New	Old
F-1C	FJ-3	RF-8A	F8U-1D
MF-1C	FJ-3M	TF-8A	F8U-1T
DF-1D	FJ-3D	F-8B	F8U-1E
F-1E	FJ-4	F-8C	F8U-2
AF-1E	FJ-4B	F-8D	F8U-2N
F-2C	F2H-3	F-8E	F8U-2NE
F-2D	F2H-4	F-9F	F9F-6
F-3B	F3H-2	QF-9G	F9F-6K2
MF-3B	F3H-2M	F-9H	F9F-7
F-3C	F3H-2N	F-9J	F9F-8
F-4A	F4H-1F	AF-9J	F9F-8B
F-4B	F4H-1	TF-9J	F9F-8T
RF-4B	F4H-1P	RF-9J	F9F-8P
F-5A	N-156	F-10A	F3D-1
F-6A	F4D-1	F-10B	F3D-2
YF-7A	YF2Y-1	EF-10B	F3D-2Q
F-8A	F8U-1	F-11A	F11F-1

Chapter 32
Attack Planes Since 1963

When the war began in Vietnam, the Air Force had no ground-attack planes in current production, for strategic bombing had been its first priority. The first aircraft sent to Saigon's VNAF had been surplus Navy AD-6s (see Chapter 29), and when the Farm Gate Detachment was sent to train and support the VNAF in November 1961, the Air Force provided very old A-26 light bombers and an armed trainer type, the T-28D.

The North American T-28 Trojan had been built as a two-place Air Force and Navy trainer from 1949 to 1957, when it was replaced by T-37 jets after a propeller-driven trainer was no longer relevant. The French wanted a low-cost, light ground-attack type for their war in Algeria, and North American responded with the T-28D Nomad, converted from a T-28 through the installation of a 1,300-hp R-1820-56S, with underwing racks for two 12.5-mm guns, two 500-pound bombs, and two rocket pods.

The first such conversion was sent in July 1959 to France, where Sud Aviation converted 245 surplus T-28s to the armed configuration. Known as the *Fennec*, this type served until the Algerian War was lost, after which some were given to the former French North African colonies. From 1961 to 1969 North American's Columbus factory converted 321 T-28s from the stored surplus to T-28Ds for MAP. The first 31 arrived in Saigon in November 1961 for the second VNAF "fighter" squadron, which was trained by the American Farm Gate Detachment.

The 1st Air Commando Squadron flew the T-28D against the Viet Cong using American pilots and Vietnamese crewmen. Its combat role was terminated in April 1964 after two American pilots were killed when their T-28D wings failed. The Air Commandos were given A-1Es instead, although distribution of T-28Ds to allies continued. Another 72 T-28Ds from the trainer stockpile were modified by Fairchild. Cambodia and Laos each received 60 T-28Ds, and allocations were also made to Thailand, Argentina, Bolivia, the Congo (Zaire), Ecuador, Ethiopia, Haiti, the Philippines, South Korea, and Taiwan.

An improved version, the YAT-28E, with a 2,445-hp Lycoming YT55-L-9 turboprop and taller tail fin, was flown on February 15, 1963. The original aircraft, with two .50-caliber guns and six stores pylons, was destroyed in a crash. Two more built in 1964 could carry up to 4,000 pounds of stores, but no production was ordered.

The twin-jet Cessna T-37 trainer was chosen as an interim attack type for the Air Force until the more advanced A-7D became available. Cessna first proposed an AT-37D attack version in May 1963. and two T-37Bs became YAT-37Ds, with 2,400-pound-thrust J85-GE-5 engines and weapons installations. First flown October 22, 1963, they were prototypes for the similar A-37A. The Air Force did not order the attack Cessna into production until August 1966. Thirty-nine new A-37As were built on the T-37B production line, with delivery beginning in July 1967. The 604th Special Operations Squadron received 25 planes and began operations in Vietnam on August 15, 1967.

With two crewmen placed side by side and two J85-GE-17A jets derated to 2,400-pound thrust, the A-37A had armor, a 7.62-mm minigun with 6,000 rounds in the nose, 90-gallon tip tanks, and eight underwing pylons; the four inner ones could handle 870-pound bombs or 100-gallon drop tanks, while the others could accommodate up to 500 pounds of bombs, dispensers or rockets, or up to 4,130 pounds of stores. Reliability and weapons delivery were rated as superior during the A-37A's combat tour at Bien-hoa.

The strengthened A-37B Dragonfly was similar except for an in-flight refueling probe in the nose and full-rated engines. First ordered January 23,

NORTH AMERICAN T-28D
Wright R-1820-56S, 1300 hp.
DIMENSIONS: Span 40'7", Lg. 32'10", Ht. 12'8", Wing Area
   271 sq. ft.
WEIGHT: Empty 6251 lb., Gross 8118 lb., Max. 8495 lb.
   Fuel 177 gal.
PERFORMANCE: Speed—Top 352 mph at 18,000', 298 mph
   at s. l., Cruising 203 mph, Climb 3780'/1 min., Range
   1184 miles.   GANN

CESSNA A-37A
General Electric J85-GE-17A, 2400 lbs.
DIMENSIONS: Span 38'5", Lg. 29'4", Ht. 9'6", Wing Area
   183.9 sq. ft.
WEIGHT: Empty 5603 lb., Gross 12,000 lb. Fuel 470–870
   gal.
PERFORMANCE: Speed—Top 479 mph at 15,000', 473 mph
   at s. l., Cruising 317 mph, Stalling 113 mph, Service
   Ceiling 42,600', Combat Ceiling 41,000', Climb 9800'/
   1 min. Combat Radius 336 miles/two 550 lb. bombs
   and 16 rockets, 1355 miles ferry range.   AF

NORTH AMERICAN YAT-28E
Lycoming YT-55-L-9, 2445 hp.
DIMENSIONS: Span 40'7", Lg. 36', Ht. 14'4", Wing Area
   271 sq. ft.
WEIGHT: Empty 7750 lb.; Gross 15,600 lb. Fuel 250–1275
   gal.
PERFORMANCE: Speed—Top 360 mph, Cruising 276 mph,
   Climb 5130'/1 min., Ferry Range 2760 miles.   MFR

1967, the A-37B appeared in May 1968. Cessna delivered 577 A-37A/B attack planes by 1977, including 302 for MAP, some for foreign sales, and 134
served ANG and USAF Reserve stations at the end
of 1975. The VNAF got 54 A-37Bs from November
1968 to May 1969 and 140 more from 1970 to 1972.
At the war's end in 1975, 169 remained in service,
of which 27 escaped to Thailand. Other countries

receiving Dragonflys were Cambodia (24), Chile
(34), Ecuador (12), Guatemala (12), Iran (12), Peru
(36), Thailand (16), and Uruguay (8).

Counter-insurgency (COIN) aircraft were intended as low-cost, light planes to strike against
guerrilla bands. This concept assumed an enemy
without sophisticated air defenses and the sort of
aerial police work assigned to the "general pur-

pose" biplanes of the late British Empire. Since the Marines were the American armed force with such experience—beginning with the DH-4s that hit the original Nicaraguan Sandinistas—they were given responsibility for the operational requirement, with input from the other services.

A specification for a Light Armed Reconnaissance Aircraft was finalized in September 1963. The requirements called for a two-place, twin-engine aircraft of minimum size and cost capable of flying from the smallest runways, open fields, roads, or carriers. Four 500-pound bombs and four M60 guns were required for the close-support configuration, although armed reconnaissance was the primary role.

Nine companies submitted designs for evaluation by June 1964, but construction of Convair Model 48 had begun in March as a private venture. Named the Charger, it flew on November 25, with two Pratt & Whitney T74 turboprops, twin booms, a high slab tailplane, and a short, rectangular wing with full-span slotted flaps. Two 7.62-mm M60 guns were mounted on each side of the fuselage and five external store stations were provided. With a normal load—1,200-pound payload and two hours' loiter-time fuel—takeoff over a 50-foot obstacle could be made in 485 feet using the deflected slipstream principle. In heavy condition the Charger could carry cargo, six paratroops, or enough fuel to fly from California to Hawaii.

The Charger proved to be the last airplane of the San Diego factory's 29 years of production since the first PB-2A pursuit. Shortly before the Charger's first flight test, North American won the design competition with the NA-300, which was also a twin-boomed two-seater. On October 15, 1964, seven prototypes were ordered from the Columbus factory for Marine tests as the YOV-10A, the designation being part of the V series of vertical and short-takeoff aircraft, mostly experimental in nature.

First flown July 16, 1965, the YOV-10A had two Garret AiResearch 660-hp T76-G-6/8 turboprops, and sponsons attached to the fuselage carried four 7.62-mm M60 guns with 500 rpg and hardpoints for bombs or rockets. The seventh YOV-10A was flown October 7, 1966, with Pratt & Whitney T74 engines for comparison tests.

A production contract was made October 15, 1966, but the original configuration was too light, and additional stores and protection increased weight so much that the wing had to be enlarged and more powerful engines used. A YOV-10A rebuilt to the new standard was flown in March 1967, and the first OV-10A was flown August 6, 1967. A 150-gallon drop tank or 1,200-pound stores could be carried on the center station, while the four sponson hardpoints could each carry up to 600

CESSNA A-37B
General Electric J85-GE-17A, 2850 lbs.
DIMENSIONS: As A-37A
WEIGHT: Empty 6008 lb., Gross 14,000 lb., Combat 8422 lb. Fuel 457–846 gal.
PERFORMANCE: Speed—Top 502 mph at 12,000', 478 mph at s. l., Cruising 304 mph, Stalling 122 mph, Service Ceiling 47,400', Combat Ceiling 45,100', Climb 12,-120'/1 min., Combat Radius 246 miles/1878 lb., 132 miles/3120 lb., 1182 miles ferry.   AF

CONVAIR MODEL 48
Pratt & Whitney T74-CP-8, 650 hp
DIMENSIONS: Span 27'6", Lg. 34'10", Ht. 13'7", Wing Area 192 sq. ft.
WEIGHT: Empty 4457 lb., Gross 7100 lb., Max. 10,460 lb. Fuel 208–808 gal.
PERFORMANCE: Speed—Top 319 mph at s. l. Range 1990 miles.   MFR

NORTH AMERICAN YOV-10A
Garrett T76-G-6, 660 hp at takeoff
DIMENSIONS: Span 30'3", Lg. 40', Ht. 15'1", Wing Area 218 sq. ft.
WEIGHT: Empty 4850 lb., Gross 8000 lb., Max. 10,550 lb. Fuel 210–360 gal.
PERFORMANCE: (at 8000 lb.) Speed—Top 305 mph at s. l. Service Ceiling 27,000'. 1380 miles ferry.   MFR

pounds of bombs, rockets, or antipersonnel weapons.

North American built 157 OV-10As for the USAF and 114 for the Marines by April 1969. The first examples were delivered to each service on the same day, February 10, 1968. Of five Marine OV-10A squadrons, VMO-2 first took the Bronco to Vietnam, flying the first mission from Da Nang on July 6, 1968. Air Force Tactical Air Support OV-10As arrived soon afterwards and were used for forward air control (FAC) missions, locating targets and directing attacks by jet fighter-bombers. There were 96 OV-10As on FAC duty by June 1969. One Navy light-attack squadron, VAL-4, was commissioned January 3, 1969, with 18 OV-10As from the Marines. They protected river traffic in the Mekong delta.

Eighteen OV-10Bs built for Germany in 1970 were unarmed target tugs, and 38 armed OV-10Cs went to Thailand. Two YOV-10D night-observation aircraft were Marine OV-10As modified in 1971 by addition of an infrared sensor under the nose, with a three-barrel 20-mm gun in a ventral turret slaved to the sensor and underwing pylons for drop tanks. Ventral turrets were not included on 17 OV-10Ds modified from As for the Marines at the Columbus factory in 1979, but new 1,040-hp T76-G-420/1 and a laser target ranger and designator were fitted. The Air Force night-observation conversion program for

NORTH AMERICAN OV-10A
AIResearch T76-G-10/12, 715 hp
DIMENSIONS: Span 40', Lg. 41'7", Ht. 15'1", Wing Area 291 sq. ft.
WEIGHT: Empty 8127 lb., Gross 10,518 lb., Combat 8659 lb. Fuel 252–402 gal.
PERFORMANCE: Speed—Top 284 mph at 5000 ft., Cruising 207 mph, Stalling 86 mph, Service Ceiling 25,900', Combat Ceiling 26,400', Climb 3240'/1 min., Combat Radius 58 miles/16 rockets, plus 2.5 hour loiter, 1427 miles ferry.   MFR

NORTH AMERICAN OV-10A (Marines)   LAWSON

NORTH AMERICAN YOV-10D   LAWSON

13 aircraft was known as Pave Nail. After Venezuela got 16 OV-10Es in 1973, production was halted until it was reinstated by an order from Indonesia for 12 OV-10Fs, with delivery beginning in August 1976, and 24 OV-10Gs were begun for South Korea.

Gunships

An unusual variation in attack planes was the gunship program improvised for the Vietnam War. The idea was to fit guns into available conventional transport planes that had the necessary endurance for night patrols.

Gunship I was the oldest plane in the USAF, the Douglas C-47 Skytrain, with two Pratt & Whitney R-1830-92D Wasps. One was tested in 1965 as the AC-47D, with three 7.62-mm GAU-2B/A guns installed in the open-port cargo door and the two nearest windows, plus 21,000 rounds and 45 flares. Three crewmen loaded—but did not aim—the guns; aiming was done by the pilot, who made the left pylon turn around the target. Slant range, which varied with angle, was about 6,000 feet in a 20° bank.

The AC-47D would cruise about 138 mph from a 2,000- to 3,000-foot altitude above a threatened friendly outpost, illuminating the enemy with flares and banking left to fire its three 6,000-rpm weapons. Arriving in Vietnam on November 23, 1965, the 9th Air Commando Squadron flew 22,752 combat sorties in its first year of operations. As fighting intensified, AC-47D strength was increased early in 1967 from 22 to 33 aircraft. When newer AC-130 and AC-

DOUGLAS AC-47D   GANN

119 types arrived, the old Douglas ships were transferred to the VNAF in 1969.

Gunship II conversions were of the Lockheed C-130 Hercules, powered by four Allison T56-A-9 turboprops. Four 20-mm Vulcan and four 7.62-mm guns were lined up on the port side. The spacious cabin had room for an infrared sensor, searchlight, and image-intensification sights. An AC-130A was converted from a C-130A in 1967, followed by eight more in 1968. Ten more, utilizing improved fire controls and replacing two of the 20-mm guns with 40-mm weapons, were begun in 1969.

Heavier armor and more ammunition were carried by eight AC-130E Hercules. The big Lockheed gunships all served in Vietnam with some success, although AC-130s were downed by hostile fire in 1972, and it became evident that they could not survive sophisticated defenses or fighter opposition. In 1973 the AC-130Es returned home for conversion to AC-130H models, with T56-A-15s and added equipment, and were stationed at Hurlburt Field for TAC's 1st Special Operations Wing.

Gunship III conversions were of the Fairchild Hiller C-119 Flying Boxcars, with two Wright R-3350-89 engines. Twenty-six AC-119Gs were delivered, beginning May 19, 1968, with four six-barrel 7.62-mm GAU-2 guns pointed out the port sides, 27,000 rounds, flares, and an AVQ-8 illuminator light set and night-observation system. They were followed by 26 AC-119K gunships, which added a pair of J85 jets under the wings to boost takeoff power, two 20-mm M61A1 guns, infrared sensor, and new radar.

The AC-119s were introduced into combat by the 17th and 18th Special Operations Squadrons in 1969, the former squadron turning its AC-119Gs to the VNAF in September 1971. The AC-119Ks were left when the USAF departed in 1973. In April 1975, 37 Fairchild gunships were abandoned to the victorious enemy and three others reached Thailand.

LOCKHEED AC-130A Closeup of night sights and guns   AF

LOCKHEED AC-130E   AF

FAIRCHILD HILLER AC-119G   AF

FAIRCHILD HILLER AC-119K
Wright R-3350-89B, 3500 hp, General Electric J85-GE-17, 2850 lbs.
DIMENSIONS: Span 109′3½″, Lg. 86′6″, Ht. 26′5″, Wing Area 1447 sq. ft.
WEIGHT: Empty 60,277 lb., Gross 77,000 lb., Combat 70,102 lb. Fuel 2488 gal.
PERFORMANCE: Speed—Top 290 mph at 5000′, Cruising 170 mph, Stalling 112 mph, Service Ceiling 26,800′, Combat Ceiling 22,950′, Climb 1772′/1 min., Combat Range 692 miles, 1155 miles ferry.   AF

A-7 Corsair II

The Vought A-7 Corsair II was designed to meet a Navy requirement issued in May 1963 for a light single-seat attack plane to replace the A-4. Bomb load and combat radius were to be doubled without any loss of speed. To keep costs as low as possible, and to expedite operational service, speed was to be limited to subsonic levels.

Vought's design, utilizing F-8 experience, was declared the design-competition winner in February 1964, and a March 19, 1964, contract provided for seven test and the first 35 production aircraft, with severe penalty clauses to guarantee prompt delivery and performance standards. These goals were met when the first A-7A began flight tests September 27, 1965, with a high 35° swept wing.

Powered by a Pratt & Whitney TF30-P-6, the A-7A had two 20-mm Mk 12 guns with 500 rounds, two fuselage side racks for Sidewinders or rockets, refueling probe, APQ-116 radar, and electronic bombing and radar systems. Six underwing stations provided a wide variety of weapons stores. For the nuclear strike mission a 2,000-pound Mk 28 and three 300-gallon drop tanks were carried, but for the more common close-support and interdiction roles the A-7A could carry six to 24 250-pound Mk 81 bombs, or 12 500-pound Mk 82 plus six 250-pound bombs. Missile or rocket pods could be substituted as needed.

Vought delivered 199 A-7As and 196 A-7Bs; the latter were similar except for a TF30-P-8 and improved flaps. The Corsair II reached VA-174, a training squadron based at Cecil Field, in October

VOUGHT A-7A
Pratt & Whitney TF30-P-6, 11,350 lbs.
DIMENSIONS: Span 38′9″, Lg. 46′1″, Ht. 16′, Wing Area 375 sq. ft.
WEIGHT: Empty 15,497 lb., Gross 31,936 lb., Max. 34,500 lb., Combat 27,856 lb./3600 lb. bombs. Fuel 1500–2400 gal.
PERFORMANCE: Speed—Top 685 mph at s. l., 585 mph at 13,000′, Cruising 478 mph, Stalling 155 mph. Combat Ceiling 41,500′, Climb 5000′/1 min., Combat Radius 655 miles/3600 lbs.   LAWSON

VOUGHT A-7B
Pratt & Whitney TF30-P-8, 12,200 lbs.
DIMENSIONS: As A-7A
WEIGHT: Empty 16,133 lb., Gross 29,812 lb., Max. 37,027 lb., Combat 25,732 lb./1800 lb. bombs, 32,432 lb./7500 lb. bombs. Fuel 1500–2700 gal.
PERFORMANCE: Speed—Top 683 mph at s. l. (clean), 625 mph at 11,500′, Cruising 459 mph, Stalling 147 mph. Combat Ceiling 43,900′ (clean), Climb 7290′/1 min., Combat Radius 1393 miles/Mk 28/three 300 gal. tanks, or 799 miles/six 300 lb. bombs, or 448 miles/7500 lb. bombs, 3190 miles ferry.   MFR

1966, and was first deployed operationally in November 1967 on the *Ranger* with VA-147. This squadron made the first A-7A attack into North Vietnam on December 3, 1967. First flown February 6, 1968, the A-7B entered combat March 4, 1969, and the last was delivered in May 1969.

There was still no Air Force jet attack type when the A-7A appeared; since World War II all funds had been used for strategic offensive and continental defense capabilities. While close support of Army forces was accepted as part of the Air Force mission, it was considered a secondary role for tactical fighters. First control of the air had to be won; only then could the fighter-bombers turn to surface targets.

The concept of limited war in general, and the Indochinese war in particular, caused the Army to pressure the Air Force for close support by specialized aircraft, not the multipurpose supersonic fighters favored by the Air Force. The Vought attack plane seemed to be a relatively low-cost and quick way to get this capability. On November 5, 1965, the new Secretary of the Air Force, Harold Brown, and USAF Chief of Staff General John P. McDonnell decided to buy A-7s for Tactical Air Command.

Although the original intention was to save money by retaining most of the original configuration, the Air Force insisted on more power, and in October 1966 it contracted with Allison to produce the TF41-A-1, an American version of the Rolls-Royce Spey, for its Corsair version. A M61A1 Vulcan with 1,000 20-mm rounds replaced the two Navy guns, plus a computerized navigation/weapons delivery system with APQ-126 radar and a Head-Up Display (HUD) reflecting all steering and attack displays between the pilot's eyes and the windshield. Two Falcon, Sidewinder, or Maverick missiles could be attached to the fuselage sides, but the basic mission load was eight 800-pound M-117A bombs and two 300-gallon tanks, or any of a variety of attack stores.

The first A-7D flew at Dallas on April 5, 1968, with a TF-30 since the first production TF-41 was not ready for flight tests until September 26. After engine production got under way, deliveries to a TAC training unit began in September 1969, and the 354th Tactical Fighter Wing got its first operational A-7Ds in September 1970.

Vought delivered 459 A-7Ds by December 1976 to serve three TAC wings and two ANG squadrons. In October 1972 the 354th TFW A-7Ds arrived at Korat, Thailand, and began missions into Cambodia, Laos, and North Vietnam. The A-7Ds flew 12,928 sorties, with only four losses. The last U.S. air strike in Cambodia was made by an A-7D on August 15, 1973, ending the nation's longest war.

VOUGHT A-7D
Allison TF41-A-1, 14,250 lbs.
DIMENSIONS: Span 38'9", Lg. 46'1½", Ht. 16'1", Wing Area 375 sq. ft.
WEIGHT: Empty 19,733 lb., Gross 38,008 lb., Max. 42,000 lb., Combat 28,851 lb. Fuel 1425–2625 gal.
PERFORMANCE: Speed—Top 663 mph at 7000', 654 mph at s. l., Cruising 507 mph, Stalling 174 mph. Service Ceiling 38,800', Combat Ceiling 36,700', Climb 10,-900'/1 min., Combat Radius 556 miles (6560 lb.) and two/300 gal. tanks, Combat Range 1330 miles, 3045 miles ferry.   MFR

The Navy took advantage of the electronics, power plant, and armament improvements in the A-7E, first flown November 25, 1968. Powered by a TF41-A-2 and armed with an M61 gun and racks for two Sidewinders, the A-7E had advanced electronic provisions, including the HUD display and ECM devices used on the A-7D. It could handle a 2,140-pound Mk 43 nuclear store plus drop tanks, but the primary mission was delivery of from six to 18 bombs or other stores in close support.

Delays in Allison production also hampered deliveries, so the first 67 aircraft were delivered with TF30-P-8s and designated A-7Cs. The TA-7C designation was applied to a two-seat trainer remanufactured in 1974 utilizing 50 retired A-7A/B aircraft.

The first delivery of the A-7E to a fleet squadron, VA-122, was made in July 1969, and this model's first combat action was on May 23, 1970, flying from the *America*. By 1977 the A-7Es served twenty-seven 14-plane Navy light-attack squadrons, usually operating two squadrons per carrier, while older models had been retired, beginning in April 1971, to Navy Air Reserve squadrons.

An A-7G version was offered to Switzerland in 1972, but the first successful foreign sale was 60 A-7H Corsairs for Greece. Essentially similar to the A-7D, the first A-7H was flown May 6, 1975. The Greeks also bought five TA-7H two-place trainers. Another two-place version was the YA-7K, converted from an A-7D, which was to be followed by 12 new A-7Ks for the Air National Guard in 1981. Production of the A-7E continued, with 570 delivered of 597 (including the 67 delivered as A-7Cs) on order by September 1979.

VOUGHT A-7E
Allison TF41-A-2, 15,000 lbs.
DIMENSIONS: As A-7D
WEIGHT: Empty 18,546 lb., Gross 32,745 lb., Max. 40,449
lb., Combat 28,731 lb. (1800 lb. bombs). Fuel 1476–
2676 gal.
PERFORMANCE: Speed—Top 693 mph at s. l., 653 mph at
6000'/six Mk 81, Cruising 470 mph, Stalling 157 mph.
Combat Ceiling 37,910', Climb 8630'/1 min., Combat
Radius 1054 miles/Mk 43, three 300 gal. tanks, 562
miles/six Mk 81, 295 miles/7500 lbs., 2860 miles/2676
gal. ferry.   LAWSON

VOUGHT A-7H   MFR

AV-8

An entirely new direction in ground-attack aircraft
was introduced to the Marines in the AV-8A. The
first VSTOL combat type was not an American
plane at all but Britain's Hawker Siddeley Harrier.
This single-seater used vectored thrust through four
rotatable nozzles, two located on each side of the
fuselage.

When the Harrier was in light condition, the
thrust from the Rolls-Royce Pegasus was enough to
lift the plane upwards in a vertical takeoff and landing (VTOL); a short takeoff and landing (STOL) of
1000 feet was possible with more weight. A full
load would require a lengthier run, but after stores
were dropped, only a short landing space was
needed. The tactical opportunities for short-deck or
unprepared field operations were apparent to the
Marines.

Another bonus was the possibility for evasive
maneuvers, which can be appreciated by anyone

who has watched the Harrier stop in midair, fly
backwards—and even sideways—like a helicopter.
The two 30-mm guns whose pods could be attached
to the fuselage, or the Sidewinder missiles that
could be carried, might become very deadly to an
attacker. Four underwing pylons could accommodate 1,000-pound bombs, rocket pods, or whatever
stores the mission required and takeoff conditions
allowed.

Hawker first flew its VTOL concept in 1960, and
a series of Kestrel development aircraft tested the
system in the field, including six tested in the
United States as the XV-6A. The Harrier combat
version was already in RAF service when the first
Marine order for 12 AV-8s was announced December 23, 1969.

The first AV-8A was delivered at the Kingston-
upon-Thames factory January 6, 1971, shipped to
the United States, and began service trials with
VMA-513 on April 16, 1971. An additional 90 AV-
8A single-seaters and eight TAV-8A two-seaters
were ordered and equipped VMA-513, 542, and 231
by 1974. While they demonstrated successful weapons delivery from both land bases and amphibious
assault ships, they were troubled by a high accident
rate, with 21 aircraft destroyed by the end of 1977.

A more advanced version, the AV-8B, was built
under license in the United States by McDonnell
Douglas. A new, larger wing of composite materials
and improved engine inlets would enable the AV-
8B to double either the payload or radius of action,
and a new canopy improved pilot vision. Updated
electronics, with HUD and ECM defense would be
included. It was claimed that six 500-pound bombs
could be carried over a 610-mile radius after a
1,200-foot STOL.

Two prototypes, to be converted by McDonnell
Douglas from existing AV-8A airframes, were ordered July 27, 1976, and the first YAV-8B flew at St.

HAWKER SIDDELEY AV-8A
Rolls-Royce Pegasus F402-RR-401, 21,500 lbs.
DIMENSIONS: Span 25'3", Lg. 45'6", Ht. 11'3", Wing Area
201 sq. ft.
WEIGHT: Empty 12,200 lb., Gross 17,050 lb./VTOL, 22,-
300 lb./STOL, Max. 24,600 lb. Fuel 794–1394 gal.
PERFORMANCE: Speed—Top 662 mph at s. l., Service Ceiling 51,000', Combat Radius 275 miles, 1550 miles
ferry.   USN

McDONNELL YAV-8B
Rolls-Royce F402-RR-402, 21,500 lbs.
DIMENSIONS: Span 30'3½", Lg. 42'10", Ht. 11'3½", Wing
Area 230 sq. ft.
WEIGHT: Empty 12,400 lb., Gross 18,450 lb. (VTOL), Max.
29,550 lb.
PERFORMANCE: Classified.   MFR

Louis on November 9, 1978. While Marine Corps
leaders desired to equip all eight of its light-attack
squadrons with AV-8Bs, the A-18 Hornet rivaled the
Harrier for funds as fiscal 1980 began. Meanwhile,
AV-8As on hand were processed with new electronics and became AV-8Cs.

A-10

The A-10 was the first Air Force jet plane in service
specifically designed for a close air-support mission. Low-altitude daylight attack, with a heavy
load of conventional weapons, was its role, and no
compromises in favor of high speed or nuclear delivery were made.

Preliminary design-study contracts for specialized close air-support aircraft had been awarded to
General Dynamics, Grumman, Northrop, and
McDonnell on May 2, 1967. The preliminary data
received was used to prepare new requirements,
and a request for proposals was issued May 7, 1970,
for competitive prototype development. Six companies responded by August 10, and on December
18 the Republic Aviation Division of Fairchild Industries, Farmingdale, New York, and the Northrop
Corporation, Hawthorne, California, were selected
to build two competing prototypes each. The plan
was "fly-before-buy," as had been done before
World War II.

The designations A-9 and A-10 were given the
California and New York contenders on March 1,
1971. Both were to be single-seaters, with two turbofan power plants chosen for fuel economy, not
speed, and straight wings to ease into short field
landings. A new 30-mm Gatling-type gun was carried, along with ten hardpoints under the wing for
up to 16,000 pounds of mixed ordnance. Low cost
was favored over performance beyond stated requirements, and high survivability against enemy
ground fire was important.

Fairchild Republic's A-10 flew at Edwards AFB
on May 10, 1972, and Northrop's A-9 on May 30—
both ahead of schedule. An intensive competitive
flyoff of the four prototypes, involving 635 flying
hours, was completed by December 9. In many
respects they were similar, but the lighter Northrop
had two Lycoming engines under the roots of a high
wing and had a single tail. The A-10 had two General Electric turbofans in pods above and behind
the low wings and had twin tail fins.

Fairchild was proclaimed the winner January 18,
1973, and on March 1 a $159 million cost-plus in-
centive fee contract for ten preproduction aircraft
was made, while General Electric won the engine
and gun-system contracts. Comparing the prototypes, then designated YA-10A, to the A-7D led to
release of funds for 52 production aircraft July 31,
1974. The first preproduction aircraft flew February

NORTHROP A-9A
Lycoming YF102-LD-100, 7500 lbs.
DIMENSIONS: Span 58', Lg. 53'6", Ht. 16'11", Wing Area
580 sq. ft.
WEIGHT: Gross 26,000 lb. (clean), Max. 42,000 lb.
PERFORMANCE: Speed—Top 449 mph at s. l., Cruising 322
mph. Service Ceiling 40,000', Combat Radius 288
miles/9540 lbs., 3622 miles ferry.   LAWSON

FAIRCHILD REPUBLIC A-10A
General Electric TF34-GE-100, 9065 lbs.
DIMENSIONS: Span 57'6", Lg. 53'3½", Ht. 14'8½", Wing
Area 506 sq. ft.
WEIGHT: Empty 19,856 lb., Gross 40,269 lb., Max. 46,786
lb., Combat 34,532 lb./4240 lbs. bombs, 38,136 lb./9540
lbs. bombs. Fuel 1638–3438 gal.
PERFORMANCE: Speed—Top 460 mph at 10,000', 448 mph
at s. l./4240 lb. bombs (448–433 mph/9540 lb. bombs),
Cruising 329 mph, Stalling 120 mph, Service Ceiling
37,800', Combat Ceiling 20,700', Climb 6200'/1 min.,
Combat Radius 288 miles/9540 lbs., 3510 miles
ferry.   MFR

15, 1975, and the first production aircraft, October 21, 1975.

Antitank operations were touted as the major A-10 mission. The seven-barrel 30-mm GAU-8/A cannon and its 1,350 rounds of armor-piercing explosive ammunition, combined with six AGM-65A Maverick missiles, demonstrated a lethal effect on hostile armor. Six 550-pound bombs were carried on escort missions and 18 on close air-support missions, with a 250-nautical-mile (288-statute-mile) radius and two-hour loiter time. Twenty-eight such bombs could be carried with reduced fuel load, or three 600-gallon ferry tanks, as well as many other stores options. Survivability was promised by high maneuverability at low speeds, redundant structural and control elements, foam-protected fuel cells, a titanium armorplate "bathtub" to protect the cockpit, and ECM devices.

The 354th TFW was the first to replace its A-7Ds with A-10s, with one 24-plane squadron fully operational by October 15, 1977, and all 72 planes a year later. Next came the 81st TFW, stationed in Britain, with three more TAC wings and ANG units scheduled for a 733-plane program, of which 483 had been ordered by May 1, 1979, and 220 delivered at a rate of 12 monthly. A two-place all-weather version with radar was converted from a preproduction aircraft and flown May 4, 1979.

FAIRCHILD REPUBLIC A-10A   LAWSON

The A-10's gun is this seven-barrel GAU-8/A, which fires either 2100 or 4200 30 mm. rounds per minute, and weighs 1975 lbs. empty and 4041 lbs. with the 1950 round magazine.   MFR

Chapter 33
Fighters for the Missile Era

F-4

McDonnell's Phantom II successfully opened the era of the Mach 2 missile-launching fighter and became the most widely used American supersonic fighter, despite its design as a specialized carrier aircraft.

Two prototypes had, in fact, been ordered in an October 18, 1954, letter contract as twin-engine AH-1 attack aircraft, but on May 26, 1955, they were redesignated F4H-1 all-weather fighters, and a second crewman, the radar intercept officer (RIO), was added. The first F4H-1 (X prefixes were no longer used on prototypes intended for production) flew May 27, 1958, with two General Electric J79-GE-3A engines using variable-area intakes with flat ramps to shear away the boundary layer from the forward fuselage. The 45° swept wing had a 12° dihedral on the folding outer panel; a 23° anhedral on the one-piece stabilator aided stability.

Competitive tests with the single-place F8U-3 resulted in the Navy choice, in December 1958, of the Phantom II, and the St. Louis factory completed a developmental contract. Sixteen aircraft delivered by November 1959, with 16,500-pound-thrust J79-GE-2 engines and APQ-50 radar with a 24-inch dish in the nose, were followed by 29 accepted from May 1960 to June 1961, whose APQ-72 radar had a 32-inch dish. All of these aircraft became F-4A models under the current designation system and were used for tests and training, joining VF-121 in December 1960. A series of record-breaking flights, including a 1,606-mph (Mach 2.57) world speed record, a climb to 49,212 feet in 114 seconds, and a zoom climb to 98,556 feet, were used to advertise the Phantom's performance, the speed marks being set by the modified second prototype on November 22, 1961.

The first operational version was the F-4B, first flown March 27, 1961, and 637 were delivered from June 1961 to January 27, 1967. A photo-reconnaissance version for the Marines, the RF-4B, flew March 12, 1965, and 46 were delivered by December 1970. Marine F-4B all-weather fighter VFMF(AW) squadrons were redesignated Fighter Attack (VMFA) squadrons in August 1964. Two 14-plane Navy F-4B squadrons served each of the large carriers, while the five *Essex*-class carriers still in service in 1965 retained F-8s.

Powered by J79-GE-8s, the F-4B had a slightly raised canopy, APQ-72 radar with an infrared detector underneath the nose, and leading- and trailing-edge flaps for boundary-layer control. Four Sparrow III (AIM-7) missiles recessed under the fuselage had a ten-mile range, while four heat-homing AIM-9B Sidewinders (two-mile range), or two more Sparrows, could be carried under the outboard wing pylons. Inboard pylons could carry two 370-gallon drop tanks, and a center-line pylon carried a 600-gallon tank or a 2,040-pound Mk 28 nuclear bomb. From 12 to 24 500-pound bombs or other stores could be carried on attack missions.

Air Force intentions to obtain Phantoms were announced January 17, 1962, and 29 F-4Bs were borrowed from the Navy to train instructor pilots.

McDONNELL F-4A (F4H-1)   USN

McDONNELL F-4B
General Electric J79-GE-8, 17,000 lbs. (AB)
DIMENSIONS: Span 38′5″, Lg. 58′3″, Ht. 16′4″, Wing Area 530 sq. ft.
WEIGHT: Empty 27,897 lb., Gross 43,907 lb., Max. 55,948 lb., Combat 38,505 lb./4 Sparrow. Fuel 1986–3326 gal.
PERFORMANCE: Speed—Top 1490 mph at 40,000 ft., 845 mph at s. l., Cruising 580 mph, Stalling 95 mph. Combat Ceiling 56,850′, Climb 40,800′/1 min., Combat Radius 885 miles/Mk 28, 530 miles/twelve 500 lb. bombs, Combat Range 1297 miles/1986 gal., 2076 miles max.   USN

Designated F-110As, the first two arrived at Langley AFB for TAC on January 24. In March the first production contract was placed for 310 F-4C and 26 RF-4C aircraft, and their first examples were flown on May 27 and August 20, 1963, respectively. Essentially the F-4C was similar to its Navy counterpart except for J79-GE-15 engines, APQ-100 radar, flight controls in the second cockpit, Air Force boom flight-refueling provisions, and larger wheels.

McDonnell delivered 583 F-4Cs from November 20, 1963, to May 4, 1966, to serve 23 TAC squadrons. The 505 RF-4Cs delivered from June 1964 to January 1974 substituted cameras and more radar for armament but retained the nuclear bomb provision. They entered operational service in September 1964, the 16th Tactical Reconnaissance Squadron becoming the first to be combat ready in August 1965, and served 12 TAC and three ANG squadrons throughout the seventies.

The F-4D, ordered in March 1964, was first flown December 8, 1965, with a new bomb-aiming system, the Sidewinders replaced by four AIM-4D heat-homing Falcons, and APQ-109A radar. TAC received 793 F-4Ds by February 1968, and they first reached an operational wing, the 33rd TFW, by June 1966.

Phantoms at War

When F-4Bs escorted the first Navy strike on August 5, 1965, the North Vietnamese had no fighters, but two days later MiG-17 fighters and MiG-15U trainers appeared near Hanoi, and by the year's end 34 MiGs of the 179 aircraft imported from China during the war had appeared. This fighter force was increased to 70 in June 1965, and in December 1965 supersonic MiG-21s from the Soviet Union appeared.

McDONNELL F-4C
General Electric J79-GE-15, 10,900–17,000 lbs.
DIMENSIONS: Span 38′5″, Lg. 58′3″, Ht. 16′6″, Wing Area 530 sq. ft.
WEIGHT: Empty 28,496 lb., Gross 51,441 lb., Max. 59,064 lb., Combat 38,328 lb., Fuel 1972–3312 gal.
PERFORMANCE: Speed—Top 1433 mph at 40,000′, 826 mph at s. l., Cruising 587 mph, Stalling 165 mph. Service Ceiling 56,100′, Combat Ceiling 55,600′, Climb 40,550′/1 min., Combat Radius 538 miles/Mk 28, 323 miles/eleven 750 lb. bombs. 1926 miles ferry.   MFR

McDONNELL RF-4C
General Electric J79-GE-15, 10,900–17,000 lbs.
DIMENSIONS: Span 38′5″, Lg. 62′11″, Ht. 16′6″, Wing Area 530 sq. ft.
WEIGHT: Empty 28,104 lb., Gross 52,346 lb., Max. 52,450 lb., Combat 39,788 lb. Fuel 1889–3229 gal.
PERFORMANCE: Speed—Top 1460 mph at 40,000′, 834 mph at s. l., Cruising 587 mph, Stalling 167 mph, Service Ceiling 56,220′, Combat Ceiling 55,790′, Climb 38,950′/1 min., Combat Radius 838 miles, 506 miles/Mk 28, 1750 miles ferry.   LP

McDONNELL F-4D
General Electric J79-GE-15, 10,900–17,000 lbs.
DIMENSIONS: As F-4C
WEIGHT: Empty 28,958 lb., Gross 51,577 lb., Max. 59,380 lb., Combat 38,781 lb. Fuel 1889–3229 gal.
PERFORMANCE: Speed—Top 1432 mph at 40,000′, 826 at s. l., Cruising 587 mph, Stalling 165 mph, Service Ceiling 55,400′, Combat Ceiling 55,850′, Climb 40,100′/1 min. Combat Radius 502 miles/Mk 28, 1844 miles ferry.   USAF

By April 1965 the Vietnamese pilots had enough confidence to challenge the Americans, and on June 17, 1965, F-4Bs of VF-21 scored their first two MiG-17 kills. Navy Phantoms were credited with 32 victories by 1973, including 19 MiG-17, 10 MiG-21, two MiG-19 and two AN-2 aircraft. Marine F-4Bs in Vietnam were usually confined to ground-support missions.

An Air Force F-4C squadron arrived in Southeast Asia early in 1965, but two MiG-17s downed with Sidewinders on July 10 were its only success that year. Ten F-4C squadrons were in SEA by April 1966, and six victories that month included a MiG-21.

The Phantom's missiles, designed with bomber interception in mind, could be evaded with a sharp turn by an alert target. A gun was desired for close-range work, and the 20-mm M61 SUU-16 external gun pod was introduced in May 1967, but it downgraded performance. The F-4Cs downed 42 MiGs: 22 with Sidewinders, 14 with Sparrows, four with gun pods, and two with "maneuvering tactics." Most of the 54 F-4Cs lost in 1965–66 were lost to ground fire. The vital reconnaissance mission of the RF-4C, deployed from October 1965 to the war's end, should not be forgotten.

During 1967, F-4Ds replaced the F-4C in SEA squadrons. Beginning on June 5, 1967, they were credited with 44 victories: 26 with Sparrows, six with gun pods, five each with Falcons and Sidewinders, and two with maneuvers. The F-4D also introduced new ground-attack methods with laser-guided bombs and various rockets and missiles. The widespread enemy use of SAMs also led to the addition of various ECM devices.

On July 22, 1966, the Secretary of Defense authorized procurement of the F-4E, which had the built-in 20-mm M61A1 cannon desired by pilots, J79-GE-17s, APQ-120 radar and new electronics, with the infrared scanner dropped. The first F-4E flew June 30, 1967, but numerous difficulties delayed its deployment overseas. There were 18 in SEA by January 1969 and 72 in June 1971. Since the bombing pause suspended attacks on North Vietnam, their work consisted of close support with a wide variety of weapons. Phantom losses had amounted to 362 by January 1, 1972, mostly to ground fire.

The enemy's 1972 spring offensive escalated the war, and, on May 8, President Nixon suspended peace talks and authorized renewal of air strikes throughout North Vietnam. Using new electronic technology and guided bombs, the Air Force hit missile sites and transportation targets; one example was the F-4Ds with laser-guided 3,000-pound bombs that finally dropped the notorious Thanh Hoa bridge. Another four F-4E squadrons had joined the seven F-4D and F-4E squadrons in SEA for this campaign.

McDONNELL F-4E
General Electric J79-GE-17, 11,870–17,900 lbs.
DIMENSIONS: Span 38'5", Lg. 63', Ht. 16'6", Wing Area 530 sq. ft.
WEIGHT: Empty 29,535 lb., Gross 53,848 lb., Max. 61,651 lb., Combat 38,019 lb./four Sparrows. Fuel 1984–3324 gal.
PERFORMANCE: Speed—Top 1464 mph at 40,000'/4 Sparrows, 1485 mph clean, 914 mph at s. l., Cruising 586 mph, Stalling 158 mph. Service Ceiling 59,200', Combat Ceiling 59,600', Climb 54,200'/1 min., Combat Radius 533 miles/Mk 28, 1885 miles ferry.   USAF

On May 23, 1972, the F-4E scored its first victory over a Chinese-built MiG-19. Of 21 F-4E victories in 1972, ten fell to Sparrows, six to gunfire, four to Sidewinders, and one to maneuvering. The last American victory in North Vietnam was a MiG-21 destroyed by an F-4D's Sparrow on January 8, 1973. Of 137 enemy aircraft downed by the USAF over Vietnam, Phantoms were credited with 107½: 33½ MiG-17s, 8 MiG-19s, and 66 MiG-21s.

After the war ended, the Phantom was the most widely used combat aircraft in the USAF, with six F-4C, 19 F-4D, and 22 F-4E squadrons. A new slatted wing to improve turning qualities appeared on the F-4E in January 1972 and was retrofitted to earlier aircraft. Production continued at St. Louis until the USAF had received 831 by December 1976.

The F-4G designation had first been applied to 12 Navy aircraft, delivered in 1963 with an ASW-21 data-link system, to be tested by VF-213, but these aircraft were later reconfigured to F-4Bs. In 1975 F-4G was applied to F-4Es being equipped as Wild Weasel ECM aircraft. ECM modifications had first been completed on 34 F-4Cs in October 1968, and an F-4D had flown November 27, 1972, with the APR-38 advanced ECM system. The F-4G program called for 116 converted F-4Es to be delivered with APR-38 but no guns.

Similar in armament to the F-4B, the Navy's F-4J had new fire-control, navigation, and bombing systems, including APQ-59 radar, refined engines, landing flaps, and slotted stabilators. The first F-4J flew May 27, 1966, and 522 were delivered by January 7, 1972. They entered service with VF-101 in December 1966, and in 1972, Lieutenant Randy Cunningham and RIO Willie Driscoll became the first American ace team in the Vietnam War.

Britain had ordered the Phantom, announcing production of the F-4K for the Royal Navy on February 27, 1964, and the F-4M for the RAF on February 2, 1965. Both were to use British-made Rolls-Royce Spey engines rated at 20,515-pound thrust, with almost half the cost in British-supplied equipment and parts. The first of two YF-4Ks was flown June 27, 1966, with 50 F-4Ks (Phantom FG Mk 7s) arriving in Britain beginning in April 1968.

Increased power improved the F-4K's takeoff and acceleration, although airframe limitations prevented an increase in top speed. They served aboard Britain's last large aircraft carrier, the *Ark Royal*, from 1970 until its final cruise ended December 4, 1978. In order to fit this carrier's elevators, the radome could be folded back, and the nose landing-gear extension was increased to increase the angle of attack at takeoff.

The RAF's YF-4M flew February 17, 1967, and the production F-4M on December 26. From July 1968 to August 1969 the RAF received 118 Ms, which they designated Phantom FGR Mk 2, and 28 of the Ks. Eight squadrons still flew Phantoms in 1978.

Iran was the next to order Phantoms, on September 30, 1966. It got 32 F-4Ds, which first reached Teheran in September 1968, as well as 177 F-4Es and 16 RF-4Es, delivered from April 1971 to August 1977.

Israel ordered its first 50 F-4Es on December 27, 1968, and they began arriving in September 1969. Later orders increased the total to 204 F-4Es, with 12 RF-4E Phantoms delivered by May 1977. These fighter-bombers supported Israeli operations against Egypt in 1970 and in the October 1973 war, with 33 lost in the latter struggle.

The Republic of Korea is the only Phantom user that got its first aircraft as a gift. Eighteen F-4Ds delivered in 1969 were paid for by MAP, another 18 arrived in 1975, 19 RF-4Es were purchased in 1977, and 18 F-4Es arrived in 1979. Australia leased 24 F-4Es from September 1970 to June 1973 to fill in for deferred F-111Cs.

West Germany's Luftwaffe purchased 88 RF-4E Phantoms, which arrived in 1971, and ordered 175

McDONNELL F-4F   MFR

McDONNELL F-4J
General Electric J79-GE-10, 17,859 lbs.
DIMENSIONS: Span 38'5", Lg. 58'3½", Ht. 15'10", Wing
　Area 530 sq. ft.
WEIGHT: Empty 30,770 lb., Gross 46,833 lb., Max. 55,896
　lb., Combat 41,399 lb. Fuel 1998–3338 gal.
PERFORMANCE: Speed—Top 1416 mph at 36,089', 875
　mph at s. l., Combat Ceiling 54,700', Climb 41,250'/1
　min., Combat Radius 596 miles/4 Sidewinders/600 gal.
　tank, 1956 miles ferry.　　　　　　　　　　USN

McDONNELL YF-4K　　　　　　　　　　MFR

F-4F fighters. First flown May 18, 1973, the F-4F
was lighter than the F-4E, using four Sidewinders
(but deleting the Sparrows) plus leading-edge slots.
Delivered by February 1976, they were followed
by ten F-4Es for crew training in the United States.

Spain was the next user, with 36 ex-USAF F-4Cs
transferred from October 1971 to September 1972.
Japan, however, was unique in building its own
Phantoms under license. The first of two F-4E(J)
pattern aircraft flew at St. Louis on January 14, 1971,
and both flew to Japan in July. Mitsubishi began
the production of 138 F-4EJ fighters, while 14 RF-
4EJs were sent from McDonnell.

Greece received 56 F-4Es beginning in March
1974, and Turkey got 72 F-4Es beginning in August
1974. Each country also ordered eight RF-4Es,
which were the last Phantoms off the production
line. With their completion in 1979, 5,057 Phantoms
had been built at St. Louis. Egypt became a Phantom user when 35 ex-USAF F-4Es began arriving
in October 1979.

The Navy had accepted 1,264 F-4s, extending the
latter's service life by updating their equipment.
North Island NAS (San Diego) modified 228 F-4Bs
to the F-4N configuration, which was first flown
June 4, 1972, with new electronic and fire-control
systems. The same facility modified F-4Js to the F-
4S configuration, which involved updating the elec-

tric systems. Beginning with the forty-seventh of
260 aircraft to be reworked, leading-edge wing slats
would be installed. The first F-4S was delivered
July 22, 1977.

Air Force Phantom deliveries amounted to 2,640.
On December 31, 1975, there remained in the tactical fighter inventory 275 F-4C, 484 F-4D, and 599
F-4E aircraft, along with 380 F-111, 47 F-105G, 29
F-5E, and the first 42 F-15A fighters. ANG and
Reserve bases had another 19 F-4Cs, along with
420 F-100s and 177 F-105s. Tactical reconnaissance
aircraft included 273 TAC RF-4Cs, plus 98 RF-4Cs
and 56 RF-101s in the ANG. These figures indicate
that the Phantoms would remain in U.S. service for
a long time, even as the F-4s were being transferred
to ANG and Reserve status.

McDONNELL F-4N　　　　　　　　　　LAWSON

McDONNELL F-4S LAWSON

F-5

The first Air Force fighter designed primarily for smaller allied nations, the Northrop F-5A was the opposite of the F-4C in weight and cost. From its inception in 1955, the Northrop was designed to have supersonic performance with costs less than any jet type since the F-80. After the successful parallel development of the T-38 trainer, Northrop went ahead with construction of the N156F single-seater as a private venture until a Defense Department contract for three prototypes was received in May 1958.

Although the prototype was flown on July 30, 1959, with two General Electric YJ85-GE-1s of 2,100-pound thrust each, the various official agencies involved could not agree on whether the limitations of performance were balanced by the much lower costs, compared with other potential standard day fighters for MAP. Not until April 23, 1962, was a decision made, by which time the F-104G had cornered much of the potential market.

Nevertheless, a production contract was drawn up October 22, 1962, and increased August 23, 1963, to 142 F-5A single-seat fighters and 27 F-5B two-seat unarmed trainers. The third N156F was completed in May 1963 in F-5A configuration. The first production F-5A flew in October 1963, and the first F-5B, February 24, 1964.

Powered by two J85-GE-13s with afterburners, the F-5A was armed with two 20-mm M-39 guns with 280 rpg and two AIM-9B Sidewinders at the wing tips. Two 50-gallon wing-tip tanks and three 150-gallon drop tanks could be used on ferry flights, or five external stores stations could accommodate three 1,000-pound and two 750-pound bombs; but only 1,500 pounds were carried for a normal ground-support mission. Four cameras replaced guns on the RF-5A version, which appeared in 1968.

The first Northrops went to the training school at Williams AFB, Arizona, where, beginning in September 1964, foreign pilots were introduced to the MAP's new weapon. Iran got the first of 91 F-5A,

NORTHROP N156F MFR

13 RF-5A, and 23 F-5B models in January 1965, and South Korea got 87 F-5As and 35 F-5Bs beginning in April 1965. The Philippines got 19 F-5As and 3 F-5Bs, while Taiwan received 92 F-5A and 23 F-5B aircraft.

The USAF had 17 F-5As and 15 F-5Bs. Twelve of the F-5As arrived in Vietnam on October 23, 1965, to test the type in combat. The provisional squadron's operations resulted in the recommendations that led to the F-5E version, and by June 1967 its aircraft had been transferred to Vietnamese pilots. The VNAF got 46 single-seat and eight two-seat Northrops from the United States and hurriedly leased 80 more F-5As from Taiwan, South Korea, and Iran in 1973.

NATO members getting Northrops from the United States included Norway, with 78 F-5As, 16 RF-5As, and 14 F-5Bs; Greece, with 61 single-seaters and nine two-seaters; and Turkey, with 95 single-seaters and 13 two-seaters. Libya bought eight F-5As and two F-5Bs in 1968 but later transferred them to Pakistan, which passed them on to Greece, thereby illustrating the difficulty the United States experienced in controlling the final disposition of the aircraft. Morocco got 18 F-5As, two RF-5As, and four F-5Bs from MAP in 1966. Thailand received 18 F-5A and two F-5B aircraft that same year.

Northrop delivered the last of 621 F-5As in March 1972 at a flyaway cost of $756,000 each, compared to $2.4 million for the F-4E Phantoms. Eighty-nine RF-5As were delivered by June 1972, while production continued on 160 F-5B trainers. Foreign-

NORTHROP F-5A

General Electric J85-GE-13, 2720–4080 lbs.

DIMENSIONS: Span 25'10", Lg. 47'2", Ht. 13'2", Wing Area 170 sq. ft.

WEIGHT: Empty 8085 lb., Gross 13,433 lb., Max. 19,728 lb., Combat 11,477 lb. Fuel 583–1129 gal.

PERFORMANCE: Speed—Top 925 mph at 36,089', 650 mph at 50,000', 731 mph at s. l., Cruising 587 mph, Stalling 164 mph. Combat Ceiling 50,600', Climb 28,700'/1 min., Combat Radius 270 miles/2 AIM-9B, 420 miles/2 750 lb. bombs, 1318 miles ferry   MFR

NORTHROP F-5E

General Electric J85-GE-21, 5000 lbs.

DIMENSIONS: Span 28', Lg. 48'2", Ht. 13'5", Wing Area 186 sq. ft.

WEIGHT: Empty 9588 lb., Gross 15,745 lb., Max. 20,486 lb., Combat 13,188 lb./2 AIM-9J. Fuel 671–946 gal.

PERFORMANCE: Speed—Top 997 mph at 36,089', 720 mph at 50,000', 753 mph at s. l., Cruising 548 mph, Stalling 160 mph. Service Ceiling 53,800', Combat Ceiling 53,000', Climb 28,536'/1 min./2 AIM-9J, Combat Radius 351 miles/275 gal. drop, 1350 miles ferry.   MFR

license production included 36 SF-5A and 34 SF-5B aircraft by CASA in Spain, beginning in May 1968, with Canadair building 89 CF-5As and 42 CF-5Bs for the RCAF, as well as 75 NF-5As and 30 NF-5Bs for the Netherlands. Venezuela got 18 ex-RCAF fighters in 1977.

The F-5E had more power from J85-GE-21 engines, more internal fuel, leading-edge extensions, maneuvering flaps, and an arresting hook. Two 20-mm M-39 guns and two AIM-9J Sidewinders were carried. Stores stations were provided for a 275-gallon drop tank or 2,000-pound bomb under the fuselage and four 750-pound bombs or rocket pods under the wings. A two-place F-5F trainer version with one gun was first flown September 25, 1974.

Northrop had introduced the new features on a modified F-5B in March 1969, but the Air Force waited until February 26, 1970, to solicit proposals for a new MAP fighter. Northrop's design won over competition from a Lockheed F-104 variant, a stripped McDonnell F-4, and a Vought F-8 variant, and the first contract for 325 F-5Es was made December 8, 1970.

While the first F-5E flew August 11, 1972, engine malfunctions delayed operational service until April 1973. The first 26 (called Tiger IIs) went to the USAF for testing and to the training squadron for foreign pilots at Williams AFB. Late in 1973 Vietnam began getting 151 to replace F-5As. When the war ended in April 1975, 22 F-5Es, three F-5As, one RF-5A, and an F-5B were flown out to Thailand, abandoning 27 F-5Es and about 60 older models.

TAC inherited some 101 F-5Es from the VNAF schedule and used them to form Fighter Weapons Squadrons specializing in simulation of Soviet combat tactics. These "aggressor" units flew against the larger aircraft of other TAC units to train them to duel dissimilar aircraft, such as the smaller MiGs. In 1978, TAC had 36 F-5Es at Nellis AFB, 18 at Alconbury, England, and 12 at Clark in the Philippines, as well as a training squadron for MAP pilots. The U.S. Navy also acquired 17 F-5Es and six F-5Fs for similar units at the Miramar and Oceana fighter bases.

The Republic of Korea got 126 F-5Es and six F-5Fs through MAP, and Thailand acquired 17 F-5Es and three F-5Fs in 1976 to join 20 of the older models. Taiwan purchased 144 F-5Es and 18 F-5Fs partially manufactured for final assembly in Taichung. Saudi Arabia bought 70 F-5E fighters with an inertial navigation system supplementing the usual austere electronics, along with 20 F-5B trainers and 24 F-5F two-seaters delivered from 1972 to 1978.

Iran purchased 141 F-5Es and 28 F-5Fs and sold its older models to Greece, Vietnam, and Jordan. Thirty of the latter's secondhand F-5As and four F-5Fs were joined by 44 F-5Es and two F-5Fs supplied by MAP. Brazil ordered six F-5B trainers and 36 F-5E fighters in October 1974 for 1975 delivery, and Chile got 15 F-5Es and three F-5Fs beginning in June 1976. Switzerland purchased her first American combat planes in the form of 66 F-5Es and six F-5Fs, the first completed in November 1977, while the last 53 were to be assembled by the Swiss themselves.

All F-5 sales were on a government-to-government basis through the FMS/MAP programs. Ethiopia got 13 F-5As and two F-5Bs in 1975. It ordered 14 F-5Es and two F-5Fs, but only eight F-5Es had been delivered when the Ethiopians expelled the American mission in April 1977, thus ending the program. Other recipients were Kenya (10 F-5Es, 2 F-5Fs), Malaysia (14 F-5Es), Singapore (18 F-5Es, 3 F-5Fs), Indonesia (12 F-5Es, 4 F-5Fs), and 12 F-4Es for the Yemen Arab Republic (North). A single RF-5E demonstrator was flown January 29, 1979, with one gun and cameras.

Northrop had delivered 1,000 aircraft by September 1979 on orders for 952 F-5E and 140 F-5F Tigers, including 48 additional planes for Taiwan and six more for Jordan. Egypt was negotiating the funding of another 50 aircraft. Taiwan's orders then totaled 226 F-5E and 30 F-5F Tigers for delivery by mid-1980.

NORTHROP F-5F   MFR

YF-12A

No modern military aircraft have been concealed with as much secrecy over the years as the Lockheed series represented here by the YF-12A fighter prototypes. Their advanced design and high performance excelled all other aircraft for many years, and their SR-71 successors were the only Mach 3 aircraft in USAF service.

Clarence L. Johnson had organized a special design team at the Burbank company's engineering department called the "skunk works" because of the secretive and unorthodox work done there. This team had produced the U-2, first flown August 1, 1955. No combat plane, it was more like a powered glider, but its high-altitude photographic surveillance of the U.S.S.R. for the CIA had an enormous impact on the cold war, including the discovery that the Soviets had foregone mass production of bombers in favor of intercontinental missiles. By the time the last of 53 U-2s had been completed, Lockheed was studying the very different aircraft known as the A-11 by the company.

The interceptor configuration originated in November 1959, and was first flown in July 1962. Three YF-12A prototypes were fitted for Hughes ASG-18 fire-control radar and four GAR-9 (AIM-47A) semiactive radar-homing missiles, weighing about 800 pounds, which were originally developed for the XF-108 Rapier. Everything else about this long two-seater, however, had to be entirely new, for the performance standards included a Mach 3 cruise up to a 1,380-mile combat radius. Such speeds create skin temperatures so high that 93 percent of the airframe had to be made of expensive titanium alloy.

The advanced technology used included two Pratt & Whitney J58 bleed-bypass turbojets designed to run continuously with afterburning, with spiked inlets and ejector nozzles. The long, blended body had area ruling and forebody lift,

LOCKHEED YF-12A
Pratt & Whitney J58, 32,500 lbs.
DIMENSIONS: Span 55'7", Lg. 107'6", Ht. 18'6", Wing Area
  1800 sq. ft.
WEIGHT: Empty 60,000 lb., Gross 136,000 lb. Fuel 12,220
  gal.
PERFORMANCE: (estimated): Speed—Top over 2000 mph.
  Service Ceiling 80,000', Combat Radius 1380 miles/
  four AIM-47A.   MFR

LOCKHEED SR-71   USAF

with chines running back to the delta wing, with
60° leading-edge sweep. Twin all-movable vertical
tails were mounted on the back of each nacelle, and
an automatic flight-control system provided opti-
mum handling. Flying faster than a rifle bullet, the
two crewmen always wore pressure suits in the air.

The public first learned of the YF-12 through a
presidential announcement in February 1964, and
on December 22, 1964, the fourth prototype (YF-
12C) introduced the SR-71 reconnaissance configuration, with chines extending to the tip of the nose.
On May 1, 1965, YF-12A prototypes set world records of 2,070-mph straight-course speed, 1,688.89

mph over a 1,000-km closed course, and 80,257-foot
sustained altitude—although the aircraft used less
than full potential power!

In January 1966 the first of 21 production SR-71
aircraft arrived at Beale AFB for the 9th Strategic
Reconnaissance Wing, joining a U-2 squadron operating with SAC since June 1957. Some of the
original YF-12A records were beaten by a Soviet
MiG-25 in 1967, but on July 27, 1976, the 9th SRW
pilots set new absolute world records: 2,194 mph
over a straight course, 2,092 mph over 1,000 km,
and 85,089-foot altitude in sustained flights.

Despite its high performance, the YF-12A interceptor program was discontinued November 27,
1967, because there was no present bomber threat
that required the expensive Lockheed's performance.

F-111

The General Dynamics F-111 was the most controversial Air Force fighter, and only after years of
service was it possible to understand the aircraft's
place in history. The most conspicuous feature was
the variable-sweep wings, which enabled the big
twin-engine two-seater to operate from smaller air
bases while achieving Mach 1.2 at sea level and 2.2
at altitude. From a 16° sweep and 63-foot span at
takeoff they could be gradually swept back to 72.5°
and a 32-foot span. The two crewmen sat side by
side in a pressurized compartment contained in an
escape module that could be ejected at any speed
and altitude.

While armament provisions included a 20-mm
M61A1 with 2,000 rounds or two AIM-9B Sidewinders, the F-111A never engaged enemy fighters,
but was a tactical bomber. Its basic mission was the
delivery of a nuclear bomb (Mk 43, 57, or 61) in the
weapons bay, or four 2,000-pound or 12 to 24 750-
pound bombs on four wing pylons. These pylons
could also be used for 600-gallon ferry tanks or a
variety of bombs or dispensers. Four more outboard
pylons for smaller stores were seldom used. The F-
111's greatest virtue was the accuracy with which
bombs could be delivered at night by means of the
computerized APQ-113 attack radar and AJQ-20 inertial bombing-navigational system, whose APQ-
110 terrain-following radar enabled the aircraft to
actually fly itself close to the ground, below the
level of radar observation. It should be noted that
the data accompanying the photographs indicates
only the outlines of the flight envelope, which en-
closes a wide range of altitude and load options.

Development of the F-111 series was initially
based on a July 1960 operational requirement for
an all-weather fighter-bomber to replace the F-105
series, utilizing turbofan power plants and a vari-

able-sweep wing. This concept, described as the TFX tactical fighter, was changed in February 1961 when Robert S. McNamara, the new Secretary of Defense, requested that the Air Force try to join with the Navy to produce a common design. Such commonality would work with the F-4 and was an attractive way to control costs.

The Navy had planned a two-place straight-winged fighter with two Pratt & Whitney TF-30 turbofans, designated the Douglas F6D-1 Missileer. Ordered July 21, 1960, it would carry six large Eagle (AAM-N-10) long-range missiles under its wings. The relatively slow aircraft would loiter for up to ten hours until its radar spotted targets for the missiles' own radar-homing system. This program was canceled April 25, 1961.

Instead, Secretary of Defense McNamara insisted on a common fighter design with the Air Force, proposing on September 1, 1961, a twin-engine, supersonic two-seater with accommodations for either 10,000 pounds of bombs or six large air-to-air missiles, with weights and dimensions limited by Navy carrier requirements. The Air Force also insisted on transatlantic ferry capability, with the ability to operate from unprepared fields as part of its NATO support role. On September 29 new requests for proposals were sent to manufacturers, nine of which responded by December. The designation F-111, the last of the old fighter series, was assigned to the program.

Boeing and General Dynamics each received design-data contracts in February 1962 and submitted second, third, and fourth proposals that year. Boeing's design used a General Electric engine design (as yet untested) with intakes above the fuselage, while General Dynamics chose Pratt & Whitney TF-30 turbofans with intakes under the wings. The Air Force Selection Board preferred the Boeing design, which held out the promise of better performance at a lower price, but the Secretary of Defense ordered the TFX contract given to General Dynamics because of the higher degree of identical structure for the Air Force and Navy versions and the belief that Boeing's cost estimate was unrealistic.

Senator John L. McClellan directed a widely publicized critical probe of the situation, but F-111 procurement went ahead anyway. Twenty-three developmental aircraft were ordered from General Dynamics on December 21, 1962, with Grumman as the subcontractor for the Navy's F-111B version.

The first F-111A flew at Fort Worth on December 21, 1964, and on April 12, 1965, a letter contract for 431 aircraft was announced. The first 30 aircraft had no gun provisions and TF30-P-1 engines that suffered numerous compressor stalls, so TF30-P-3s were used on the remainder of 158 F-111s deliv-

ered, beginning in September 1967, at a cost of $8.2 million per production aircraft. They began operational service with the 474th TF Wing in October 1967, and on March 17, 1968, six F-111As arrived in Thailand to attack targets in North Vietnam. When three aircraft had been lost by April 22, operations were halted after 55 missions and the detachment returned to the United States.

F-111A losses amounted to 15 by December 1969, and serious doubts about the plane's structure caused the entire force to be grounded until July 31, 1970. All aircraft were returned to the factory for proof-testing and modification. Despite all the criticism, the F-111A had the lowest accident rate by far of all supersonic Air Force planes.

Another opportunity to prove itself came with the deployment of two squadrons to Thailand on September 27, 1972. Flying over 3,000 missions against strong enemy defenses, they operated at night, proving their ability to deliver five times the F-4's bomb load with great accuracy. Of 52 F-111As deployed, seven were lost before the cease-fire in February 1973. Although the F-111A was much heavier and more expensive than planned, it was considered successful in interdiction missions.

The Navy's F-111B carried two Phoenix (AIM-54A) missiles in the weapons bay and four more under the wings, with a Hughes AWG-9 fire control whose radome nose folded upwards for stowage. A pair of 450-gallon tanks or other weapons stores could be carried on the six underwing pylons, and the wing tips were lengthened for improved range and loiter performance.

Ordered with the F-111A on December 21, 1962, the Grumman-built F-111B flew May 18, 1965, with TF30-P-1 engines. The production contract, signed May 10, 1967, included 24 F-111Bs and TF30-P-12

GENERAL DYNAMICS F-111A
2 Pratt & Whitney TF30-P-3, 18,500 lbs. (A/B)
DIMENSIONS: Span 63' (32' swept), Lg. 73'6", Ht. 17', Wing Area 525 sq. ft.
WEIGHT: Empty 46,172 lb., Gross 82,819 lb., Max. 98,850 lb., Combat 63,051 lb. Fuel 5043–7443 gal.
PERFORMANCE: Speed—Top 1453 mph at 53,450', 914 mph at s. l., Cruising 1194 mph, Stalling 152 mph. Service Ceiling 35,900', Combat Ceiling 56,650', Climb 25,550'/1 min., Combat Radius 1330 miles/2000 lb. bombs, two AIM-9B, 784 miles/12,306 lbs., 3634 miles ferry.   MFR

GENERAL DYNAMICS F-111B
Pratt & Whitney J57-P-1A, 18,500 lbs.
DIMENSIONS: Span 70′ (33′11″ swept), Lg. 66′9½″, Ht. 16′8″, Wing Area 550 sq. ft.
WEIGHT: Empty 46,000 lb., Gross 72,421 lb., Max. 77,566 lb., Combat 68,365 lb./6 AIM-54A. Fuel 3383–4283 gal.
PERFORMANCE: Speed—Top 1450 mph at 40,000′, 780 mph at s. l., Cruising 483 mph, Stalling 131 mph. Combat Ceiling 44,900′, Climb 21,300′/1 min., Combat Radius 546 miles/6 AIM-54A, 3178 miles ferry.   MFR

engines, but this plan was to be frustrated. The weight had increased from 38,804 pounds empty and 62,788 pounds gross on the 1962 contract to 46,000 pounds empty and 77,566 pounds gross in 1965, thereby downgrading performance. Range was greatly reduced and engine stalls were a persistent problem. Desperate measures to reduce weight on succeeding prototypes brought little improvement, and Grumman itself advocated switching to a new, strictly Navy fighter design, the future F-14.

A stop-work order was issued July 10, 1968, and formal contract termination agreed upon on December 10. The seventh and last F-111B was delivered February 28, 1969. Over $377 million had failed to produce a carrier fighter, although the swing wing and missile system would be carried over to the successful F-14.[1]

On October 24, 1963, Australia had contracted for 24 F-111Cs to replace their Canberra bombers, and the first, which had the F-111B's longer wings, was formally accepted in September 1968. The entire order was then stored, pending the results of USAF F-111A testing. The planes were not rebuilt and delivered until June–December 1973, after becoming a scandal in Australian politics. These were the only F-111s sold abroad, for a 50-plane contract for a RAF F-111K version announced February 1, 1967, was canceled in January 1968. The first two were almost complete and were, in fact, redesignated YF-111A for special test programs.

[1] Readers wishing a detailed analysis of the failure of the F-111 commonality concept should consult Robert F. Coulam's book entitled *Illusions of Choice: The F-111 and the Problem of Weapons Acquisition Reform* (Princeton, N.J.: Princeton University Press, 1977).

The F-111D, ordered May 10, 1967, had an improved Mark II avionics system and engines, but delayed development led to an F-111E interim model using the F-111A's engine and radar, with new engine inlets to improve engine operation at high altitudes. They replaced the F-111A on the delivery line in August 1969. The Fort Worth factory delivered 94 F-111Es by May 28, 1971, and 79 served the 20th TFW in England, where they were first received in September 1971.

The first F-111D was flown May 15, 1970, with 19,600-pound-thrust TF30-P-9s, but the remaining 95 had to wait for their advanced electronics so delivery was delayed until July 1971 and not completed until February 28, 1973. They served the 27th TFW at Cannon AFB. The last new production model, the F-111F, was ordered July 1, 1970, but the new P-100 engines were delayed, so that the first entered service with the 347th TFW in September 1971 with TF30-P-9 engines and APQ-144 radar. The P-100 engines became available in 1972 and 106 F-111Fs were completed. Including SAC's FB-111As, 563 F-111-series aircraft were built by November 1976.

Two F-111As were converted to EF-111A ECM aircraft by Grumman, which used its EA-6B experience to fit complete tactical radar-jamming gear in a canoe-shaped belly radome, and they had a large fin-tip pod for the ECM receivers. After tests of a fully modified prototype began May 17, 1977, the Air Force planned to have 40 F-111A aircraft converted to the EF-111A configuration in 1980.

The proposed FB-111H was a bomber design offered in 1977 as a substitute for the high-cost B-1A

GENERAL DYNAMICS F-111E   LAWSON

GENERAL DYNAMICS F-111F
Pratt & Whitney JF30-P-100, 25,100 lbs.
DIMENSIONS: As F-111A
WEIGHT: Empty 47,450 lb., Gross 95,333 lb., Combat 62,350 lb. Fuel 5035–7435 gal.
PERFORMANCE: Speed—Top 1453 mph at 40,000', 914 mph at s. l., Cruising 498 mph, Combat Ceiling 57,900', Climb 43,050/1 min., Combat Radius 920 miles/2000 lb. bomb (Lo-Lo-Hi mission), 3378 miles ferry.

LAWSON

program. Using the same General Electric F101 engines and radar systems, it was purported to provide most of the same capabilities, on the basis of air refueling, as the B-1A at less than half the cost. At this writing, however, the Defense Department was committed to the cruise-missile concept for future strategic deterrence.

F-14

The first new Navy carrier fighter in squadron service in 12 years, Grumman's two-seat F-14A Tomcat benefited from the F-111B program's development of the Phoenix missile, radar fire control, variable-sweep wing, and Pratt & Whitney TF30 turbofans.

Hostile aircraft could be detected 132 miles away across a 170-mile front (2½ times the F-4J's radar range), by the Hughes AWG-9 control system, comprising 1,321 pounds of radar, infrared sensor, computer, and displays. Up to 24 targets could be tracked at once, and all six 13-foot, 989-pound Phoenix missiles could attack separate targets simultaneously. Successful test hits were scored against drone targets as far as 126 miles away, as high as 82,000 feet, at supersonic speeds, and at low altitudes. These AIM-54A missiles were claimed to be immune to ECM, to have launch and leave capability, and proximity fusing. Semiactive homing shifts to active radar homing during the terminal phase.

Sparrow (AIM-7E/F) missiles could replace the Phoenix if the mission was local air superiority instead of long-range fleet defense, while two to four heat-seeking Sidewinders could be carried for short-distance attacks. A 20-mm M61 Vulcan with 675 rounds was mounted on the nose's port side for close-in dogfights. The tandem-cockpit canopy design provided better visibility than on the F-4, and the F-14A was designed to have the maneuverability necessary for dogfighting.

Two TF30-P-412 engines gave the Tomcat a rapid acceleration to Mach 2.34 speed, and the wing sweep varied from 20° at takeoff to 68° in high-speed flight, and back to 75° for shipboard parking. Compared to the F-4 Phantom, the F-14 had 80 percent more combat radius on internal fuel, 20 percent better rate of climb, 21 percent better acceleration, and 40 percent better turn radius. Titanium was used for 24.4 percent of the structure, compared to 9 percent of the F-4, while aluminum totaled 40 percent and steel 18 percent.

The F-14A was begun as a company proposal (Design No. 303-60) for a new airframe to replace the failing F-111B. An impressed Navy Fighter study group issued a Request For Proposals on June 18, 1968, and by October 1, two-seat, twin-engine fighter proposals were made by Grumman, General Dynamics, McDonnell Douglas, North American, and Vought. Grumman got the contract, signed February 3, 1969, for the first six aircraft, later increased to 11 developmental examples.

The first F-14A flew at Calverton, New York, on December 21, 1970, but crashed on its second flight, delaying tests until the second aircraft was ready on May 24, 1971. Eleven test aircraft had been completed by March 1972, and in October 1972 the first training squadrons, VF-1 and VF-2, were commissioned at Miramar NAS. One aircraft modified to F-14B configuration, with Pratt & Whitney F401-PW-400 advanced engines, was flown September 12, 1973, but this power plant was not ready for production.

The F-14A production program proceeded with annual increments, resulting in a serious argument between the company and the Navy about the price, but the first Navy carrier squadrons were successfully deployed in 1974 on the *Enterprise*. Iran ordered 80 F-14As, lacking only some ECM gear, on January 7, 1974, and the first flew December 5, 1975. All had been delivered by August 1978, but

GRUMMAN F-14A
Pratt & Whitney TF30-P-412, 20,900 lbs.
DIMENSIONS: Span 64'1½" (38'2½" swept), Lg. 62', Ht. 16', Wing Area 565 sq. ft.
WEIGHT: Empty 40,070 lb., Gross 66,200 lb., Max. 72,000 lb., Combat 57,000 lb. Fuel 2530–3070 gal.
PERFORMANCE: Classified.

MFR

the Shah's overthrow in 1979 raised doubts about their fate, with their highly sensitive fire-control.

By 1978 the Navy had 14 12-plane fighter squadrons, with Tomcats replacing their F-4s, and the F-14A program had been extended to 521 aircraft for 18 of the 24 carrier-fighter squadrons; the remainder were expecting lightweight F-18s. A camera/radar pod was designed to add a reconnaissance capability for a future RF-14 version.

GRUMMAN F-14A   MFR

GRUMMAN F-14A for Iran   MFR

GRUMMAN F-14A with Phoenix missiles   MFR

F-15

The McDonnell Douglas[2] F-15A Eagle was the first Air Force fighter in many years to be designed purely for the air-superiority role—destroying enemy fighters in combat. Climb and maneuverability were the prime qualities desired.

Air Force concern about Soviet fighter progress was reflected in the request for design proposals sent to seven companies on August 11, 1967. The appearance of the variable-sweep MiG-23 and the very fast MiG-25 threatened the F-4 Phantom's superiority, indicating that the traditional Soviet point interceptor would be replaced by more versatile types.

The Air Force awarded Concept Formulation Study contracts in December 1967 to General Dynamics and McDonnell Douglas, and in September 1968 it began the Contract Definition phase with another Request For Proposals. This document specified one-man operation with 360° cockpit visibility and HUD, a Mach 2.5 maximum capability with a wing optimized for Mach .9 buffet-free performance and maneuverability at 30,000 feet, a high thrust-to-weight ratio, long-range Pulse Doppler radar with look-down capability, low development risk components and systems, and a gross weight in the 40,000-pound class.

Contracts for this phase were awarded in December to Fairchild Hiller (Republic), North American, and McDonnell Douglas, and these companies worked to produce the winning concept until July 1969, when the Air Force began its evaluation of the rival designs, announcing McDonnell the winner on December 23, 1969, and the contract for the

first seven developmental aircraft was signed on December 31. This account reflects the lengthy process involved before the St. Louis factory could build the first F-15A and ship it to Edwards AFB for the July 17, 1972, maiden flight.

Comparison with the Navy's F-14 Tomcat is natural, the most apparent difference being that the F-15A Eagle was a single-place, 45° sweep fixed-wing fighter without the Phoenix missile system, and therefore a much lighter and less expensive aircraft. When the Navy asked for an F-15N version for carrier landings in 1971, the weight estimate was increased by 2,300 pounds, downgrading design performance and increasing costs to an unacceptable level.

Armament of the F-15A was essentially the same as that of the F-4E Phantom: four Sparrow and four Sidewinder missiles and a 20-mm M61 gun. An APQ-63 radar provided long-range search up to 115 miles and semiactive homing for the 510-pound AIM-7F Sparrows carried below the engine nacelles. The 199-pound AIM-9L heat-seeking Sidewinders were below the wings, and the gun, with 940 rounds, was in the starboard wing root, opposite the in-flight refueling receptacle on the port side. Pylons provided for three 600-gallon drop tanks could also accommodate a variety of bombs and stores, although ground attack was not part of the required mission.

Powered by two Pratt & Whitney F100-PW-100 turbofans, the F-15A's structure included 37.3 percent aluminum, 25.8 percent titanium, and 5.5 percent steel. Twin vertical fins were tipped with ECM antenna. A second seat was accommodated in the TF-15A two-place trainer version.

Production go-ahead, on a fly-before-buy basis, was approved in February 1973 for the first 18 F-15A fighters, two TF-15A trainer development aircraft, and 23 F-15A and seven TF-15A production aircraft. The first two-seater flew July 7, 1973, and all of the trainer series were redesignated F-15B. Deliveries to TAC's training wing at Luke AFB began in November 1974, and in January 1975 the nineteenth aircraft was stripped down for world-record attempts. There was no chance of matching the YF-12's speed, of course, but the F-15A climbed faster than the speed of sound at one level—to 12,000 meters (39,372 feet) in 59 seconds; the previous record, set by an F-4, was 77 seconds. A MiG-25 had set a 30,000-meter (98,430-foot) record in 243.5 seconds; the F-15A did it in 207 seconds, although the Soviet aircraft recaptured the latter record shortly thereafter. Annual increments to the production program followed regularly thereafter, with 524 on order by fiscal 1978.

McDONNELL DOUGLAS F-15A
Pratt & Whitney F100-PW-100, 23,820 lbs.
DIMENSIONS: Span 42′10″, Lg. 63′9″, Ht. 18′5″, Wing Area 608 sq. ft.
WEIGHT: Gross 41,500 lb., Max. 56,000 lb., Combat 35,040 lb. Fuel 1714–3514 gal.
PERFORMANCE: Classified.   MFR

In January 1976 the first delivery to an operational unit was made to the 1st TFW at Langley AFB, which formed three 24-plane squadrons during the year. Next came the 36th TFW, which was deployed to Germany in April 1972, and the 49th TFW at Holloman AFB, New Mexico. At that point TAC's other operational fighter wings included 14 F-4 and five F-111 wings, and gradual replacement of the Phantoms by F-15 and F-16 fighters was projected for a 749-plane F-15 program by 1983. A good safety record encouraged this prospect.

Israel was the F-15's first foreign customer, buying 25, the first four being refurbished preproduction aircraft delivered in December 1976.[3] Japan ordered 88 F-15C single-seaters and 12 F-15D two-seaters, and received the first F-15C in July 1980, along with seven other aircraft assembled in the United States, eight in the form of knocked-down assemblies and the rest to be manufactured in Japan. Saudi Arabia ordered 45 F-15C and 15 F-15D Eagles and Israel negotiated for a larger number. At this writing it appears that a long production and service life awaits the Eagle.

The F-15C, first flown February 26, 1979, had 20 percent more internal fuel and fittings for external fuel pallets shaped to fit the aircraft. These "conformal" doubled the original fuel capacity, even without adding the conventional drop tanks.

F-16

In several respects the General Dynamics F-16A represents the complete opposite of the F-111s previously built at the Fort Worth factory. One man, one engine, and a gun in a compact airframe, the F-16A represented another effort to reverse the trend towards greater cost and complexity.

The Air Force, on February 18, 1972, issued a Request For Proposals for a lightweight, low-cost, highly maneuverable fighter with Mach 2 speed capability and about 20,000-pound normal gross weight. Costs per unit should be about $3 million

[2] In April 1967 McDonnell added Douglas to its name when it purchased control of the California firm.

[3] The F-15's first combat came on June 27, 1979, when five Syrian MiG-21s were downed by Israeli F-15 missiles.

McDONNELL DOUGLAS F-15A for Israel   MFR

in then-dollars, because the big disadvantage of the F-14/15 types was that they were too expensive to fill out all the squadrons needed for defense commitments.

Of the five companies responding, General Dynamics and Northrop were awarded contracts in April 1972 for two YF-16 and two YF-17 prototypes. The first YF-16 was flown inside a C-5A transport from Fort Worth to Edwards AFB, where the first planned flight was made February 4, 1974, and the second prototype's tests began May 9. During 330 flights that year in competition with the YF-17, the YF-16 demonstrated a top speed over Mach 2 (1,320 mph at 40,000 feet), a climb to 62,000 feet, and a 2-hour, 55-minute flight without refueling.

On January 13, 1975, the Air Force announced that the F-16 had been chosen for a 650-plane production program to be completed by 1983, beginning with 11 F-16A single-seaters and four F-16B two-seaters. Both competing types, said Air Force Secretary John L. Lucas, performed well, but the YF-16 had lower drag and excelled in agility, turn rate, and endurance.

One advantage of the preproduction F-16A, first flown December 8, 1976, was that it had the same F100-PW-100 engine used in the F-15. The simplicity of one pilot, one gun, and one engine was attractive in terms of easier maintenance and reduced final costs per mission to half those of twin-engine rivals.

Armament included a M61A1 in the left side of the fuselage behind the cockpit, with 500 20-mm rounds, and two AIM-9L Sidewinders on the wing tips. Westinghouse radar fire control weighed only 290 pounds (less than ¼ the weight of an F-14's

GENERAL DYNAMICS YF-16   MFR

GENERAL DYNAMICS F-16A
Pratt & Whitney F100-PW-100, 23,820 lbs.
DIMENSIONS: Span 32′10″, Lg. 47′8″, Ht. 16′5″, Wing Area 300 sq. ft.
WEIGHT: Empty 15,137 lb., Gross 23,357 lb., Max. 35,400 lb. Fuel 1072–812 gal.
PERFORMANCE: Classified.   MFR

radar), but it provided all-weather target detection and tracking, and a radar threat-warning antenna was placed on the single tail fin. Air-to-ground fire control was provided, so seven more external stores stations for two 370-gallon drop tanks and four more Sidewinders could be used to accommodate thirteen 500-pound Mk 82 bombs, four 2,000-pound Mk 84 bombs, or up to 15,200 pounds of other attack stores.

The two-place F-16B, first flown August 9, 1977, had a smaller fuel capacity but retained the weapons capabilities of the single-seater. While the F-16A could not reach the F-4's (or the MiG-21's) speed, it did claim to have three times the combat radius, better acceleration and turn rates, and instantaneous maneuverability. Wing-body blending, variable-wing camber, and a 30° inclined seat for increased pilot "G" tolerance were among the design features, while the structure included 78.3 percent aluminum, 10.5 percent steel, and only 1.6 percent of the more expensive titanium.

Average flyaway costs were projected in 1975 as less than $5 million then-dollars, or less than half

GENERAL DYNAMICS F-16B   MFR

that of its twin-engine rivals. These hopes led the Air Force to announce plans, in January 1977, to increase its F-16 program to 1,388 aircraft, so TAC could have ten active wings, plus Air Force Reserve squadrons and attrition replacements. Production aircraft followed the preproduction series off the line in August 1978, and were introduced to TAC service in January 1979 at Hill AFB, Utah, by the 388th TFW. Their F-4s were replaced by 102 F-16As in 1979, including a fourth squadron for training.

Foreign sales began with the June 1975 announcement of a four-nation European consortium to produce F-16s for NATO powers. Contracts signed in May 1977 called for Fokker and SABCA to divide final assembly of 348 F-16s between the Netherlands and Belgium. This would provide 116 for Belgium, 102 for the Netherlands, 72 for Norway, and 58 for Denmark. To offset costs, European manufacturers would supply about 40 percent of the value of the NATO aircraft and 10 percent of the USAF aircraft. The first Belgian aircraft flew December 11, 1978, while the first Dutch F-16B flew on May 3, 1979.

Israel ordered 75 F-16s in August 1978, but a 1976 Iranian contract for 160 was canceled in 1979. Denmark and Norway received their first F-16Bs in January 1980.

On July 21, 1980, the F-16 was officially named the "Fighting Falcon." By that time, 200 had been delivered, including 128 for the USAF. The rest were in service abroad, including the first F-16As that arrived in Israel in July.

The F-17/-18

Northrop received an Air Force contract on April 13, 1972, for two YF-17 prototypes to compete against the General Dynamics YF-16 for the lightweight fighter contract. Developed from an earlier design study called the P-530 Cobra, Northrop's project differed from the YF-16 in having two engines and twin vertical fins.

Powered by new General Electric YJ101 turbojets, the YF-17 was also armed with an M61 and Sidewinders and had five stores pylons besides the wing-tip missile stations. The first example flew June 9, 1974, and claimed to be the first U.S. aircraft to fly supersonically in level flight without afterburner, while the second YF-17 flew August 21, 1974.

When Northrop learned it had lost the Air Force contract, it then focused on the Navy's need for a lightweight fighter to supplement the F-14. Since Northrop lacked experience with carrier-based aircraft, they joined with McDonnell Douglas on October 7, 1974, to jointly prepare a Navy fighter. The St. Louis factory would build the Navy version and Northrop would work out a land-based variant for NATO. The second YF-17 was turned over to the Navy for thorough testing.

The Navy did not really want to follow the Air Force's F-16 lead, preferring a twin-engine configuration. Adapting the YF-17 to Navy requirements involved increases in fuel load and weapons provisions that added over 10,000 pounds to the weight and required more wing area. Despite the added weight, speed was to remain about Mach 1.8 and combat radius 460 miles. On May 2, 1975, the Navy announced its selection of the design as the F-14's low-cost counterpart, and a January 22, 1976, letter contract provided for 11 developmental aircraft, including two two-seaters.

The first F-18A Hornet flew November 18, 1978, at St. Louis, and armament included a 20-mm M61 with 540 rounds in the nose, two AIM-9L Sidewinders on wing-tip rails, and a pair of AIM-7F Sparrows under the engine nacelles. Hughes APG-65 radar was provided, along with five other stations for 12 500-pound bombs, rocket pods, missiles, or three 300-gallon drop tanks. Up to 13,700 pounds of stores could be carried.

Since the high cost of Grumman's F-14 limited that two-seater's program to 18 of the Navy's carrier fighter squadrons, the remaining six Navy fighter squadrons and all 12 Marine squadrons planned to get F-18 single-seaters to replace their F-4 Phantoms. Provisions for these 18 squadrons, plus six reserve squadrons and an annual attrition of 4.5 percent, would require 455 Hornets. An attack version, the A-18, was announced in June 1976 to replace the A-7 Corsairs in the Navy's 24 attack squadrons, which, with reserves, may bring the Hornet Navy program to 811 aircraft.

The A-18 naval strike-fighter design had nine

NORTHROP YF-17
General Electric YF101-GE-100, 14,800 lbs.
DIMENSIONS: Span 35', Lg. 55'6", Ht. 14'6", Wing Area 350 sq. ft.
WEIGHT: Gross 23,000 lb., Max. 30,630 lb.
PERFORMANCE: Classified.   MFR

weapons stations and modified avionics. In November 1976 an F-18L designation was promulgated for a lighter land-based version offered for export.

As the seventies ended, five fighter and two attack types were in production, while bombardment and interceptor planes vanished from the assembly lines. The F-5, F-16, and F-18 programs, in contrast to the F-14 and F-15 fighters, showed that costs had become as important as superior performance in selecting the American combat planes of the next decade.

This book has traced the American combat plane's growth in effectiveness from the modest aircraft of 1917 to today's very expensive machines.

Fighter development has been most fertile, with new types appearing at a rapid rate during each stage of their evolution. Successful adaptation to ground-attack and reconnaissance missions has strengthened the fighter's role in every air force.

Though the missile era has sharply curtailed the bomber's role, it seems to have actually enhanced the power of the fighter, whose own missiles now strike air and surface targets from beyond the range of gunfire. The fighter's future, like that of the other combat types, will continue to depend on the kinds of missions demanded by international power politics.

NORTHROP YF-17 (Navy)   MFR

McDONNELL DOUGLAS F-18A
General Electric F404-GE-400, 16,000 lbs.
DIMENSIONS: Span 40'8", Lg. 56', Ht. 15'4", Wing Area 400 sq. ft.
WEIGHT: Empty 21,500 lb., Gross 33,580 lb., Max. 45,300 lb. Fuel 1670–2570 gal.
PERFORMANCE: Classified.   MFR

Notes on Sources

Perhaps the most controversial element in a description of military airplanes is the data describing each type's performance. Since the actual data on most military aircraft is kept secret for some time, there is opportunity for unofficial and often inaccurate estimates of each type's capability to be published. Conflicting sets of data have appeared on many of the aircraft described in this book, making it necessary to specify the sources from which the data here presented was selected.

Every effort has been made to select data based on an actual flight test of a typical example of the type described or, when test flights are not available, to give the specifications guaranteed by the manufacturer in his contract with the government. Such data, of course, cannot necessarily be true of every article of that type produced, for there has been much variation from the brand-new aircraft tested by modification and service wear and tear. Pilots usually regard official figures as being decidedly optimistic.

In this book, data on aircraft built for United States air services is taken from the official characteristics charts prepared by each service for the use of the officers in charge. These charts were usually issued annually from 1920 to 1942 and included aircraft on hand or on order at time of issue. Since 1942, charts have been issued individually for each aircraft. The Technical Data Branch, Matériel Division, at Wright Field prepared the "Characteristics and Performance of U.S. Army Airplanes" charts, and these were examined at the Central Air Force Museum at the Wright-Patterson Air Force Base. Data on World War II aircraft was combined in "Army Airplane Characteristics" (#TSEST-A-2) April 1, 1946, prepared by William Englehardt of the Air Matériel Command's Design Branch, Characteristics Section.

Serial Technical Reports of Official Airplane Performance Tests made at Wright Field from 1918 to 1938 are the source for most Army plane data of that period. Official Standard Aircraft Characteristics charts issued since 1947 were available, except for certain current aircraft still classified at this writing. Characteristics charts for Navy aircraft were made available by the Office of Technical Information of the Bureau of Aeronautics, U.S. Navy, which also had official flight-test reports made at Anacostia Naval Air Station prior to World War II. This office became part of the Naval Air Systems Command, whose historian, Lee M. Pearson, continually provided data for this book.

Data on aircraft built for export is drawn from specifications issued by the manufacturers and published in annual surveys of the aircraft industry made by *Jane's All the World's Aircraft*, the *Aircraft Yearbook*, and *Aero Digest* and *Aviation Week* magazines.

The Historical Division of the Air Matériel Command prepared a number of case-history monographs of AAF wartime types. Some of these are restricted to official use only, but others are available at the Air Force Museum, and the author's queries to the Division have been helpfully answered. The Modern Army Section of the National Archives in Washington, D.C., has been another useful source, with Record Group 18 containing the Army Air Forces Central Files, 1919–45, including valuable correspondence, memoranda, and reports filed under 452.1 Aircraft. The Documentary Collection of the Air Corps Library in the same record group contains, under D52.1, many of the old Technical Reports from McCook Field (1918–27) and historical material on early Air Service types.

The Department of Air Commerce published a list of *U.S. Military Aircraft Acceptances, 1940–1945* (Washington: U.S. Government Printing Office, 1946). Bureau of Aeronautics lists of Naval Aircraft, Record of Acceptances, and U.S. Army publications on Aircraft Model Designations were used to establish the numbers of aircraft delivered to each service. Articles in the American and British aeronautical press provided much data on the production of aircraft for export.

The hearings before the Morrow Board in 1925, and official reports of the Truman Committee of the Senate, Admiral Ernest J. King of the Navy, and General Henry H. Arnold of the Air Force have also provided useful information.

Many individuals, most of them members of the American Aviation Historical Society, have contributed information and photographs for this new edition; I have listed them as correspondents. Several of these contributors are personal friends whose help has ranged from modest but very illuminating items to the more than 500 photos Peter Bowers provided for the first edition, and the many Navy photos supplied by Robert Lawson.

On occasion the author was able to fill in between the lines of official documents with insights gained in conversations with men like Ed Heinemann, popularly known as "Mr. Attack Aviation." Access to Convair and North American company records was allowed, and the National Air and Space Museum's library also contained information on company efforts. The names of those who helped in this manner are also included in the list of correspondents. Many companies supplied information and photographs through helpful public relations offices.

Books

The following list is limited to those books that were most useful and complete in providing information on the aircraft themselves and their historical background. I have omitted many accounts of operations, theoretical studies, and some secondary sources that have since become outdated.

I. GENERAL STUDIES

A. AIR FORCE AND ARMY

Arnold, Henry H. *Global Mission.* New York: Harper & Brothers, 1949

———. *Winged Warfare.* New York: Harper & Brothers, 1941

Collier, Basil. *A History of Air Power.* New York: Macmillan, 1974

Fahey, James C. *U.S. Army Aircraft, 1908–1946.* New York: Ships & Aircraft, 1946

———. *USAF Aircraft, 1947–1956.* Falls Church, Va.: Ships & Aircraft, 1956

Futrell, Robert F. *Command of Observation Aviation: A Study in Control of Tactical Air Power.* Maxwell AFB, Alabama, USAF Historical Study, no. 24 (1956)

Goldberg, Alfred, ed. *A History of the United States Air Force, 1907–1957.* Princeton, N.J.: Van Nostrand, 1957

Hinton, Harold B. *Air Victory.* New York: Harper & Brothers, 1948

Index of AF Serial Numbers Assigned to Aircraft 1958 and Prior. Wright-Patterson AFB, Ohio: USAF Procurement Division, Reports Section, April 1961

LeMay, Curtis E., and MacKinlay Kantor. *Mission with LeMay: My Story.* Garden City, N.Y.: Doubleday, 1965

Lindbergh, Charles A. *The Wartime Journals of Charles A. Lindbergh.* New York: Harcourt Brace Jovanovich, 1970

U.S. Army Air Forces, Historical Office. *The Official Pictorial History of the AAF.* New York: Duell, Sloane & Pearce, 1947

B. NAVY AND MARINE

Fahey, James C. *Ships and Aircraft of the U.S. Fleet.* Washington, D.C.: Ships & Aircraft, Eight Editions, 1939–1965

Larkins, William T. *U.S. Marine Corps Aircraft, 1914–1959.* Concord, Calif.: Aviation History Publications, 1959

———. *U.S. Navy Aircraft, 1921–1941.* Concord, Calif.: Aviation History Publications, 1961

Pearson, Lee M., and Adrian O. Van Wyen. *United States Naval Aviation, 1910–1970.* Department of the Navy, Washington, D.C.: Government Printing Office, 1970

Pawlowski, Gareth L. *Flat-tops and Fledglings: A History of American Aircraft Carriers.* New York: Castle Books, 1971

Polmar, Norman. *Aircraft Carriers.* Garden City, N.Y.: Doubleday, 1969

———. *The Ships and Aircraft of the U.S. Fleet,* 11th ed. Annapolis, Md.: Naval Institute Press, 1978

Price, Alfred. *Aircraft Versus Submarines.* Annapolis, Md.: Naval Institute Press, 1974

Turnbull, Archibald D., and C. L. Lord. *History of United States Naval Aviation.* New Haven: Yale University Press, 1949

C. AIRCRAFT AND AIRCRAFT INDUSTRY

Aircraft Yearbook. Washington, D.C.: Lincoln Press (annually 1919–1959. *Aerospace Yearbook* since 1960)

Allen, Richard S. *Revolution in the Sky: Those Fabulous Lockheeds.* Brattleboro, Vt.: Stephen Greene Press, 1964

Anderson, Fred. *Northrop—An Aeronautical History.* Los Angeles, Calif.: Northrop Corporation, 1976

Bowers, Peter M. *Boeing Aircraft Since 1916,* 2nd ed. New York: Funk, 1968

————. *Curtiss Aircraft: 1907–1947*. London: Putnam, 1979

Brown, K. S., and Bruce Robertson. *United States Army and Air Force Fighters, 1916–1961*. Letchworth, England: Harleyford Publications, 1961

Bruchiss, Louis. *Aircraft Armament*. New York: Aerosphere, 1945

Cain, Charles W., ed. *Aircraft in Profile*. 14 vols. Garden City, N.Y.: Doubleday, 1974 (a series of 262 monographs on aircraft types, originally published in Britain)

Francillon, René J. *McDonnell Douglas Aircraft Since 1920*. London: Putnam, 1979

Grey, Charles G. *History of Combat Airplanes*. Northfield, Vt.: Norwich University, 1941

Gunston, Bill. *Night Fighters—A Developmental History*. New York: Scribner, 1976

Jane's All the World's Aircraft. New York: McGraw-Hill, 1909 to date

Jones, Lloyd S. *U.S. Bombers: 1928–1980*. Fallbrook, Calif.: Aero, 1980

————. *U.S. Fighters*. Fallbrook, Calif.: Aero, 1975

————. *U.S. Naval Fighters*. Fallbrook, Calif.: Aero, 1977

Matt, Paul. *Historical Aviation Album*. Temple City, Calif.: 15 vols. to 1977

Matt, Paul R., comp. *United States Navy and Marine Corps Fighters, 1918–1962*, ed. Bruce Robertson. Letchworth, England: Harleyford Publications, 1962

Mayborn, Mitch. *Grumman Guidebook*, vol. 1. Dallas, Texas: Flying Enterprises, 1976

Maynard, Crosby. *Flight Plan for Tomorrow: The Douglas Story*. Santa Monica, Calif.: Douglas Aircraft, 1962

Moran, Gerald P. *Aeroplanes Vought, 1917–1977*. Temple City, Calif.: Historical Aviation Album, 1978

Olmstead, Mearle. *Aircraft Armament*. New York: Sports Car, 1970

Pedigree of Champions: Boeing since 1916. Seattle, Wash.: The Boeing Company, 1963

Rubenstein, Murray, and Richard M. Goldman. *To Join with the Eagles: Curtiss-Wright Aircraft, 1903–1965*. Garden City, N.Y.: Doubleday, 1974

Schoeni, Arthur. *Vought—Six Decades of Aviation History*. Plano, Texas: Aviation Quarterly Publishers, 1978

Sikorsky, Igor. *Story of the Winged-S*. New York: Dodd, Mead, 1943

Swanborough, Gordon. *North American—An Aircraft Album*. New York: Arco, 1973

Swanborough, Frederick G., and Peter M. Bowers. *United States Military Aircraft Since 1909*. London and New York: Putnam, 1971

————. *United States Navy Aircraft Since 1911*. London: Putnam, 1976

Thetford, Owen. *Aircraft of the Royal Air Force, Since 1918*, 4th ed. New York: Funk & Wagnalls, 1968

————. *British Naval Aircraft, 1912–1958*. London: Putnam, 1958

Thruelsen, Richard. *The Grumman Story*. New York: Praeger, 1977

Wagner, William. *Reuben Fleet and the Story of Consolidated Aircraft*. Fallbrook, Calif.: Aero, 1976

Welty, Howard O. *History of Convair, 1908–1956*. San Diego, Calif.: Convair Division, 1966

II. World War I and the Biplane Era

Bruce, J. M. *British Aeroplanes. 1914–1918*. New York: Funk & Wagnalls, 1957

Casari, Robert B. *Encyclopedia of U.S. Military Aircraft. Part 1: 1908–1917* (4 vols.). *Part 2: World War I Production Program* (3 vols.). Chillicothe, Ohio, Casari, 1970–75

Collier, Benedict. *America's Munitions*. Washington, D.C.: Government Printing Office, 1919

Gorrell, E. S. *The Measure of America's World War Aeronautical Effort*. Northfield, Vt.: Norwich University, 1940

Holley, I. B., Jr. *Ideas and Weapons*. New Haven: Yale University Press, 1953

Hudson, James J. *Hostile Skies: A Combat History of the American Air Service*. Syracuse: Syracuse University Press, 1968

Hurley, Alfred F. *Billy Mitchell*. Bloomington: Indiana University Press, 1974

Jones, H. A. *The War in the Air*, vol. 4. Oxford, England: Oxford University Press, 1934

Lamberton, W. M., and E. F. Cheesman. *Fighter Aircraft of the 1914–1918 War*. Letchworth, England: Harleyford Publications, 1960

————. *Reconnaissance and Bomber Aircraft of the 1914–1918 War*. Letchworth, England: Harleyford Publications, 1962

Loening, Grover. *Amphibian: The Story of the Loening Biplane*. Greenwich, Conn.: New York Graphic Society, 1973

————. *Our Wings Grow Faster*. New York: Doubleday, Doran & Co., Inc., 1935

Mixter, George W., and Harold H. Eammons. *United States Army Aircraft Production Facts*. Washington: Government Printing Office, 1919

Smart, Lawrence C. *The Hawks that Guided the Guns* (privately printed, 1968)

Van Wyen, Adrian O. *Naval Aviation in World War I*. Washington, D.C.: Government Printing Office, 1969

Warlick, William W., and V. F. Grant. *Naval Aviation*. Annapolis, Md.: Naval Institute, 1929

III. WORLD WAR II PERIOD

Abrams, Richard. *F4U Corsair at War.* New York: Scribner, 1977

Birdsall, Steve. *Log of the Liberators.* Garden City, N.Y.: Doubleday, 1973

Blue, Allen G. *The B-24 Liberator.* New York: Scribner, 1974

Bowers, Peter M. *Fortress in the Sky.* Granada Hills, Calif.: Sentry, 1976

Buchanan, Peter M. *The Navy's Air War.* New York: Harper, n.d.

Chennault, Claire L. *Way of a Fighter.* New York: Putnam, 1949

Collison, Thomas F. *The Superfortress Is Born.* New York: Duell, Sloan & Pearce, 1945

DuBuque, Jean H., and Robert F. Gleckner. *The Development of the Heavy Bomber, 1918–1944.* USAF Historical Study, no. 6 (1951)

Freeman, Roger A. *The Mighty Eighth: Units, Men, and Machines.* Garden City, N.Y.: Doubleday, 1970

———. *Mustang at War.* Garden City, N.Y.: Doubleday, 1975

———. *B-26 Marauder at War.* New York, N.Y.: Scribner, 1978

———. *Thunderbolt: A History of the P-47.* New York, N.Y.: Scribner, 1978

Garfield, Brian W. *The Thousand-Mile War: World War II in Alaska and the Aleutians.* Garden City, N.Y.: Doubleday, 1969

Glines, Carroll V. *Doolittle's Tokyo Raiders.* Princeton, N.J.: Van Nostrand, 1964

Gruenhagen, Robert W. *Mustang: The Story of the P-51 Fighter.* New York: Genesis, 1969

Gurney, Gene. *Journey of the Giants.* New York: Coward, 1961

Hess, William N. *Fighting Mustang: The Chronicle of the P-51.* Garden City, N.Y.: Doubleday, 1970

———. *Pacific Sweep: The 5th and 13th Fighter Commands in World War II.* Garden City, N.Y.: Doubleday, 1974

Holley, Irving. *Buying Aircraft: Material Procurement for the Army Air Forces, U.S. Army in World War II Series.* Washington, D.C.: Government Printing Office, 1964

Jablonski, Edward. *Flying Fortress: The Illustrated Biography of the B-17s and the Men Who Flew Them.* Garden City, N.Y.: Doubleday, 1965

Jackson, B. R., and Thomas E. Doll. *Douglas TBD-1 Devastator.* Fallbrook, Calif.: Aero, 1973

———. *Grumman TBF/TBM Avenger.* Fallbrook, Calif.: Aero, 1970

Morison, Samuel. *History of the United States Naval Operations in World War II.* 11 vols. Boston: Little, Brown, 1947–60

Operations in World War II. 11 vols. Boston: Little, Brown, 1947–60

Musiano, Walter A. *Saga of the Bent-Wing Birds.* New York: Aerophile, n.d.

Office of Naval Operations, *U.S. Naval Aviation in the Pacific.* Washington, D.C.: Government Printing Office, 1947

Robertson, Bruce. *British Military Aircraft Serials, 1912–1969.* London: Ian Allan, 1969

Rust, Kenn C. *Fifth Air Force Story in World War II.* Temple City, Calif.: Historical Aviation, 1975

———. *The 9th Air Force in World War II.* Fallbrook, Calif.: Aero, 1967

———. *Twelfth Air Force Story in World War II.* Temple City, Calif.: Historical Aviation, 1975

———. *Fifteenth Air Force Story in World War II.* Temple City, Calif.: Historical Aviation, 1976

Sherrod, Robert. *History of Marine Corps Aviation in World War II.* Washington, D.C.: Combat Forces Press, 1952

Tillman, Barrett. *The Dauntless Dive Bomber of World War Two.* Annapolis, Md.: Naval Institute Press, 1976

U.S. Air Force, Historical Division. *Air Force Combat Units of World War II,* ed. Wesley F. Craven and James L. Cate. Chicago: University of Chicago Press, 1948–1958

———. Historical Division. *Combat Squadrons of the Air Force, World War II,* ed. Maurer Maurer. Washington, D.C.: Government Printing Office, 1969

———. Office of Air Force History. *The Army Air Forces in World War II: Combat Chronology,* comp. by Kit C. Carter and Robert Mueller. Washington, D.C.: Government Printing Office, 1973

———. *The Army Air Forces in World War II,* ed. J. L. Cate and W. F. Craven. 7 vols. Chicago: University of Chicago Press, 1947–58

IV. SINCE 1945

Archer, Robert D. *Republic F-105.* Fallbrook, Calif.: Aero, 1969

Berger, Carl et al. *The United States Air Force in Southeast Asia, 1961–1973: An Illustrated Account.* Washington, D.C.: Office of Air Force History, 1977

Bohn, John T. *Development of Strategic Command.* Offut AFB, Nebr.: SAC Headquarters, 1975

Brown, Anthony C. *Dropshot: The American Plan for World War III.* New York: Dial Press/Wade, 1978

Coulam, Robert F. *Illusions of Choice: The F-111 and the Problem of Weapons Acquisition Reform.* Princeton, N.J.: Princeton University Press, 1977

Drendel, John T. *And Kill MIGS: Air-to-Air Combat in the Vietnam War.* Warren, Mich.: Squadron/Signal, 1974

———. *Aircraft of the Vietnam War*. New York: Arco, 1971

———. *Phantom II*. Warren, Mich.: Squadron/Signal, 1977

———. *TAC— A Pictorial History, 1970–1977*. Warren, Mich.: Squadron/Signal 1978

Field, James A. *History of United States Naval Operations, Korea*. Washington, D.C: Government Printing Office, 1962

Futrell, Robert F. *The United States Air Force in Korea, 1950–1953*. New York: Duell, Sloan & Pearce, 1961

Gunston, Bill. *Bombers of the West*. London: I. Allan, 1973

———. *Early Supersonic Fighters of the West*. New York: Scribner, 1976

———. *F-4 Phantom*. New York: Scribner, 1977

———. *F-111*. New York: Scribner, 1978

Holder, William G. *Boeing B-52*. Fallbrook, Calif.: Aero, 1975

———. *General Dynamics F-16*. Fallbrook, Calif.: Aero, 1976

———. *Convair F-106*. Fallbrook, Calif.: Aero, 1977

Jackson, B. R. *Douglas Skyraiders*. Fallbrook, Calif.: Aero, 1975

Knaack, Marcelle S. *Encyclopedia of USAF Aircraft and Missile Systems. Vol. I: Post-World War II Fighters, 1945–1973*. Washington D.C.: Government Printing Office, 1978

Morrison, Wilbur H. *Point of No Return—The Story of the Twentieth Air Force*. New York: Times Books, 1979

Office of Air Force History. *Aces and Aerial Victories—The USAF in Southeast Asia, 1965–1977*. Washington, D.C.: Government Printing Office, 1976

———. *USAF Southeast Asia Monograph Series. Vol. I: Tale of Two Bridges, and Battle for the Skies Over North Vietnam. Vol. 3: The Vietnamese Air Force, 1951–1975*. Washington D.C.: Government Printing Office, 1975

Office of the Historian. *Strategic Air Command: Missile Chronology, 1939–1973*. Offut AFB, Nebr.: SAC Headquarters, 1975

Stevenson, James P. *Grumman F-14*. Fallbrook, Calif.: Aero, 1975

———. *McDonnell Douglas F-15A Eagle*. Fallbrook, Calif.: Aero, 1978

U.S. Congress, Senate Committee on Government Operations. *TFX Contract Investigation: Report to 91st Congress, 2nd Session*. Washington, D.C.: Government Printing Office, 1970

Wagner, Ray. *North American Sabre*. New York: Hanover House, 1963

Periodicals

Hundreds of articles that appeared in aviation periodicals from 1918 to 1960 were consulted in preparing the first edition of this book. Since then there has been enormous growth of periodical literature in aviation history, enabling the expansion or correction of many points in this edition. Complete citation of these articles would require too much space. The most prolific authors have been included in the "Books" section of the Bibliography, as well as among the list of correspondents.

Aero Digest Washington, D.C. Monthly, 1921 to 1959

Aerospace Historian Kansas State University. Quarterly since 1954; formerly *Air Power Historian*

Air Classics Canoga Park, Calif. Monthly since 1965

Air Combat Canoga Park, Calif. Bi-monthly since 1974

Air Enthusiast London. Monthly since June 1971, then quarterly since 1976

Air Force Magazine Washington, D.C. Monthly published by Air Force Association since 1946

Air International London. Monthly; began as *Air Enthusiast* in June 1971, then became *Air International* in July 1974

Air Pictorial London. Monthly since 1938

Airpower/Wings Granada Hills, Calif. Monthly, with alternate titles, since September 1971

American Aviation Historical Society Journal Santa Ana, Calif. Quarterly since 1956

Aviation Week New York. Weekly since 1947; formerly *Aviation*. Monthly since 1922

Flying New York. Monthly since 1927; formerly *Popular Aviation*

Flying Review London. Monthly from 1929 to 1970

The Hook Bonita, Calif. Quarterly published by the Tailhook Association since 1973

Naval Aviation News Washington, D.C. Monthly since 1919

Correspondents and Informants

The author gratefully thanks the following people who have contributed to *American Combat Planes* over the last 25 years. Not everyone's name can be mentioned, but those individuals listed below helped to make this book a reality:

John S. Alcorn	Peter M. Bowers
Robert J. Archer	Walter J. Boyne
Henry G. Arnold	General Mark E. Bradley
Gerald Balzer	Richard Bueschel
Gerry Beauchamp	Ron Bulinski
Dana Bell	Colonel Edwin Carey
Roger F. Besecker	Dustin W. Carter
Beatrice Blackler	Royal D. Frey
Warren M. Bodie	Carl F. Friend

Harry S. Gann
Charles Hansen
Lynn Hendrix
Edward Heinemann
Meyers K. Jacobson
Lloyd S. Jones
William T. Larkins
Robert L. Lawson
Edward A. Leiser
Robert E. McGuire
Dr. Hideo Nakayama
Stan Norris
Merle C. Olmstead
Lee M. Pearson
Dominick Pesano

Larry Peterson
Brewster C. Reynolds
Alfred G. Ruhmel
Santiago Flores Ruiz
Mauno A. Salo
William E. Scarborough
Arthur L. Schoeni
Warren D. Shipp
Richard K. Smith
James P. Stevenson
James F. Sunderman
C. S. Tien
John Underwood
Nick Waters

Glossary of Military Terms

AA	Antiaircraft
AAF	Army Air Force
ADC	Air Defense Command
AEF	American Expeditionary Force
AEW	Airborne Early-warning
AFB	Air Force Base
AGM	Air Surface Attack Missile
AI	Airborne Interception (radar)
AIM	Air Intercept Missile
ANG	Air National Guard
ASR	Airborne Search Radar
ASW	Antisubmarine Warfare
AVG	American Volunteer Group
BG	Bomb Group
BuAer	Bureau of Aeronautics
BW	Bomb Wing
CAW	Carrier Air Wing
CIA	Central Intelligence Agency
CO	Commanding Officer
COIN	Counter-insurgency
CV	Carrier, Aircraft
DMZ	Demilitarized Zone
ECM	Electronic Countermeasures
ETO	European Theater of Operations
EWO	Electronic Warfare Officer
FAC	Forward Air Controller
FBW	Fighter-Bomber Wing
FFAR	Folding Fin Aircraft Rocket
FG	Fighter Group (also FTR GP)
FIS	Fighter Interceptor Squadron
FMS	Foreign Military Sales
FW	Fighter Wing
GFE	Government-furnished equipment
GHQ	General Headquarters
HUD	Head-up Display
ICBM	Intercontinental Ballistic Missile
ILS	Instrument Landing System
JATO	Jet-assisted Takeoff
JCS	Joint Chiefs of Staff (U.S.)
LABS	Low Altitude Bombing System
MAD	Magnetic Airborne Detector
MAP	Military Aid Program (Military Assistance Program after 1954)
Mk	Mark (model)
MSP	Mutual Security Program
MTO	Mediterranean Theater of Operations
NACA	National Advisory Committee for Aeronautics
NAF	Naval Aircraft Factory
NAS	Naval Air Station
NASA	National Aeronautics and Space Administration
NATO	North Atlantic Treaty Organization
NG	National Guard
NIS	Night Interceptor Squadron
NVAF	North Vietnamese Air Force
Photo	Photographic
RAAF	Royal Australian Air Force
RAF	Royal Air Force
RCAF	Royal Canadian Air Force
Recon	Reconnaissance
RIO	Radar Intercept Officer
RPG	Rounds per Gun
RTU	Replacement Training Units
SAC	Strategic Air Command
SAGE	Semi-Automatic Ground Environment
SALT	Strategic Arms Limitation Talks
SAM	Surface-to-Air Missiles
SEA	Southeast Asia
SLBM	Submarine Launched Ballistics Missiles
Sq	Squadron
SRAM	Short-range Attack Missile
SRW	Strategic Reconnaissance Wing
SWPA	Southwest Pacific Area
TAC	Tactical Air Command
TFS	Tactical Fighter Squadron
TFW	Tactical Fighter Wing
TRS	Tactical Reconnaissance Squadron
TRW	Tactical Reconnaissance Wing
USAF	United States Air Force
USN	United States Navy
USSR	Union of Soviet Socialist Republics
V-E	Victory in Europe
V-J	Victory in Japan
VSO	Scout-observation aircraft (Navy)
VTO	Vertical Takeoff
VTOL	Vertical Takeoff and Landing
VVS	Soviet Air Force
ZI	Zone of the Interior

Index